D0288782

Eastern Caribbean

Kevin Anglin
Neal Bedford
Myra Ingmanson
Rowan McKinnon
Daniel Schechter

LONELY PLANET PUBLICATIONS
Melbourne • Oakland • London • Paris

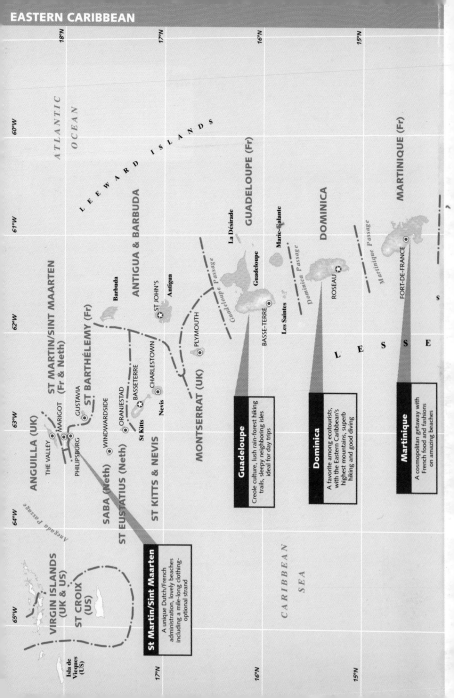

EASTERN CARIBBEAN

St Martin/Sint Maarten

A unique Dutch/French administration, lovely beaches including a mile-long clothing-optional strand

Guadeloupe

Creole culture, lush rain-forest hiking trails, sleepy neighboring isles ideal for day trips

Dominica

A favorite among ecotourists, with the Eastern Caribbean's highest mountains, superb hiking and good diving

Martinique

A cosmopolitan getaway with French food and fashions on amazing beaches

ATLANTIC OCEAN

LEEWARD ISLANDS

CARIBBEAN SEA

L E S S E R

VIRGIN ISLANDS (UK & US)

ST CROIX (US)

Isla de Vieques (US)

Anegada Passage

ANGUILLA (UK)

THE VALLEY

MARIGOT

PHILIPSBURG

ST MARTIN/SINT MAARTEN (Fr & Neth)

GUSTAVIA

ST BARTHÉLEMY (Fr)

SABA (Neth)

WINDWARDSIDE

ST EUSTATIUS (Neth)

ORANJESTAD

BASSETERRE

St Kitts

ST KITTS & NEVIS

CHARLESTOWN

Nevis

Barbuda

ANTIGUA & BARBUDA

ST JOHN'S

Antigua

MONTSERRAT (UK)

PLYMOUTH

GUADELOUPE (Fr)

La Désirade

Guadeloupe

BASSE-TERRE

Les Saintes

Marie-Galante

Guadeloupe Passage

DOMINICA

ROSEAU

Dominica Passage

MARTINIQUE (Fr)

FORT-DE-FRANCE

Martinique Passage

18°N

17°N

16°N

15°N

60°W

61°W

62°W

63°W

64°W

65°W

17°N

16°N

15°N

2 Contents

Eastern Caribbean
3rd edition – September 2001
First published – October 1994

Published by
Lonely Planet Publications Pty Ltd ABN 36 005 607 983
90 Maribyrnong St, Footscray, Victoria 3011, Australia

Lonely Planet Offices
Australia Locked Bag 1, Footscray, Victoria 3011
USA 150 Linden St, Oakland, CA 94607
UK 10a Spring Place, London NW5 3BH
France 1 rue du Dahomey, 75011 Paris

Photographs
Many of the images in this guide are available for licensing from
Lonely Planet Images.
W www.lonelyplanetimages.com

Front cover photograph
Rasta hats on display, Roseau, Dominica (Jean-Bernard Carillet)

ISBN 1 86450 305 X

text & maps © Lonely Planet Publications Pty Ltd 2001
photos © photographers as indicated 2001

Printed through Colorcraft Ltd, Hong Kong
Printed in China

Although the authors
and Lonely Planet try
to make the informa-
tion as accurate as
possible, we accept
no responsibility for
any loss, injury or
inconvenience sus-
tained by anyone
using this book.

Contents

INTRODUCTION — 15

FACTS ABOUT THE EASTERN CARIBBEAN — 17

MUSIC OF THE EASTERN CARIBBEAN — 39

REGIONAL FACTS FOR THE VISITOR — 4

GETTING THERE & AWAY

GETTING AROUND THE REGION

ANGUILLA

GUADELOUPE

MARTINIQUE

MONTSERRAT

SABA

ST BARTHÉLEMY (ST BARTS)

TRINIDAD & TOBAGO 520

LANGUAGE 568

GLOSSARY 574

FOOD & DRINK GLOSSARY 575

THANKS 577

INDEX 583

MAP INDEX

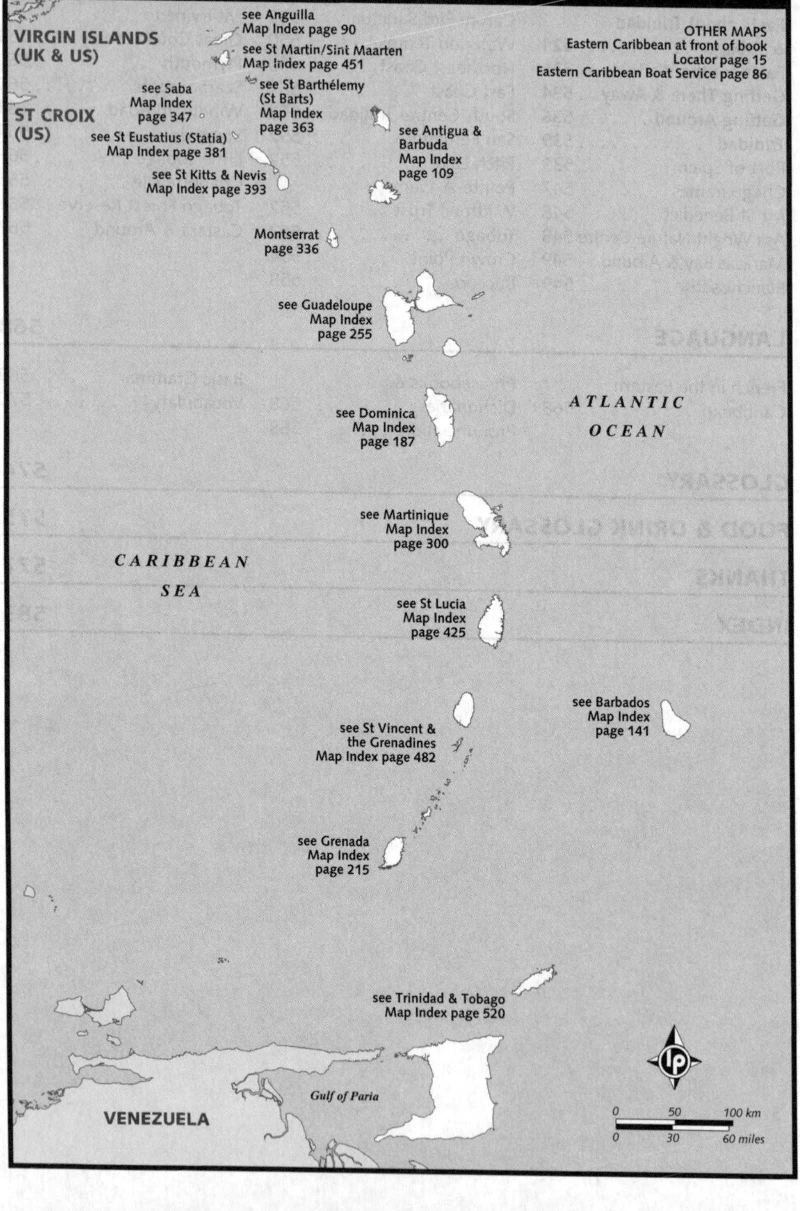

VIRGIN ISLANDS
(UK & US)

see Anguilla
Map Index page 90

see St Martin/Sint Maarten
Map Index page 451

see Saba
Map Index
page 347

see St Barthélemy
(St Barts)
Map Index
page 363

ST CROIX
(US)

see St Eustatius (Statia)
Map Index page 381

see Antigua &
Barbuda
Map Index
page 109

see St Kitts & Nevis
Map Index page 393

OTHER MAPS
Eastern Caribbean at front of book
Locator page 15
Eastern Caribbean Boat Service page 86

Montserrat
page 336

see Guadeloupe
Map Index
page 255

see Dominica
Map Index
page 187

ATLANTIC
OCEAN

see Martinique
Map Index
page 300

CARIBBEAN

SEA

see St Lucia
Map Index
page 425

see St Vincent &
the Grenadines
Map Index page 482

see Barbados
Map Index
page 141

see Grenada
Map Index
page 215

see Trinidad & Tobago
Map Index page 520

Gulf of Paria

VENEZUELA

| 0 | 50 | 100 km |
| 0 | 30 | 60 miles |

The Authors

Kevin Anglin

Kevin began a life of travel with a trip to the Caribbean when he was less than a year old, and he has returned several times since. Despite spending much of his youth vagabonding around the US, he managed to emerge from Middlebury College with a degree in Anthropology, which he shrewdly parlayed into a job baking organic bread in Taos, New Mexico. After a two-year stint as a Peace Corps volunteer in Gabon, Central Africa, he set out on a trip through Africa, Europe and Asia, which led him to Lonely Planet's Oakland office, where he works as an editor. He currently lives in sunny Berkeley, California.

Neal Bedford

Born in Papakura, New Zealand, Neal gave up an exciting career in accounting after university to experience the mundane life of a traveler. Feeding his urge to move, travel led him through a number of countries and jobs, ranging from an au pair in Vienna, lifeguard in the USA, fruit picker in Israel and lettuce washer at rock concerts. Deciding to give his life some direction, he well and truly got his foot stuck in the door by landing the lucrative job of packing books in Lonely Planet's London office. One thing led to another, and he managed to cross over to the mystic world of authoring.

Neal currently resides in Dublin, but the need to move will probably soon kick in and force him to try his luck somewhere else. He has worked on *Spain, Britain, England, Texas* and *Vienna* for Lonely Planet.

Myra Ingmanson

Myra started traveling when she was two months old and has never stopped. The daughter of an itinerant archaeologist, she had already visited 35 US states by the time she was eight. Myra's traveling spirit has continued into adulthood. After a quick burnout in copy-shop management, she took up teaching English in China and Korea, then headed for Puerto Rico to pursue graduate studies in second-language education. It was on a side trip during this period that she first became enchanted with Trinidad. She currently develops cultural study programs and tours for a university in Mexico City.

Myra enjoys learning about a culture through its food and usually heads straight for the market. She speaks workplace Spanish, train-ticket Chinese and menu Korean.

Myra and her husband Daniel recently established a new home in Bellingham, Washington after six years in Mexico City.

Rowan McKinnon

Born in country Victoria, Australia, Rowan spent some early years on Nauru, a tiny mid-Pacific island, and then grew up in Melbourne. He worked as a kitchen hand, poster plasterer, taxi driver, packer, warehouse keeper and carpenter while studying philosophy at university and playing bass in an arty rock band. Despite 10 years of touring and recording, in Australia and overseas, Rowan's band, the perennial 'next big thing,' never quite made it, and, much to the relief of his mother, he got a 'real job' with Lonely Planet as an editor.

Rowan has contributed to Lonely Planet's *Papua New Guinea* and *South Pacific* guidebooks. He has three children, lives in Melbourne and these days plays his arty rock in his garage, coming full circle. Rowan wrote the Grenada and St Vincent & the Grenadines chapters.

Daniel C Schechter

A native New Yorker and movie devotee, Daniel graduated from NYU's film school, the training ground for such motion picture luminaries as Woody Allen, Martin Scorsese and Spike Lee. Daniel's movie career never got off the ground, though, and by 1984 he found himself in front of a classroom of 30 Colombians all expecting to learn English. Thus began a career in language teaching that took him from Bogotá to Lisbon to Barcelona to Washington, DC. In 1992, Daniel decided to get serious about his default profession, devoting the next two years to pursuing an MA in teaching English as a second language in a remote corner of Puerto Rico. This experience, combined with brief visits to the Dominican Republic and Trinidad & Tobago, kindled a far-reaching interest in the Caribbean, a region he had previously thought of as merely a holiday destination.

Attracted by a position at the Monterrey Technological Institute, Daniel moved to Mexico, then promptly left teaching for a minimum-wage job as copy editor at *The News*, Mexico City's English-language daily. Daniel worked his way up to Assistant Managing Editor, but had to leave due to a run-in with a tyrannical editor-in-chief over anachronistic editorial policies. Subsequently, he became executive editor of *Business Mexico*, where he had the luxury of approving the publication of his own stories on travel, culture and food. After close to a decade in Latin America, Daniel and wife Myra have transplanted themselves to the moist earth of the US Pacific Northwest.

FROM THE AUTHORS

Kevin Anglin First and foremost, thanks to Glenda Bendure and Ned Friary, whose hard work on the first two editions paved the way for this book. Thanks also to Claude Albert, Julien Fouin, Isabelle Muller, Jean-Bernard Carillet and Michel Mac Leod, authors of Lonely Planet's French guides to Martinique and Guadeloupe.

In the islands, thanks to the helpful people at the Guadeloupe Tourist Office, Michael and Luke at the Cornerhouse, Hagan Dorival, Jeanette Lindell, and all the friendly folks who gave me rides, information and advice when the buses were on strike.

At Lonely Planet my biggest thanks to Rebecca Northen and Vivek Waglé for all their thoughtful efforts on this book. Thanks also to Molly Green and her crack team of cartographers, to Wendy Smith for all her advice and support, and to senior editors Robert 'Rock Star' Reid and Wade 'Wade Fox' Fox.

Neal Bedford Special thanks goes to Christina for putting up with my dragging her around resort after resort when all she wanted to do was sit on a beach. And I could not have made it without her words of support, Web skills and cups of peppermint tea!

Thanks goes to all the tourist offices that made my life easier on the road, to El Momo Cottages and Shirley and Lou for making me feel like I never wanted to leave.

Rowan McKinnon At LP, thank you to Robert Reid, Rebecca Northern, Vivek Waglé, Molly Green, Monica Lepe and Leonie Mugaven.

Mostly, thanks to the people I left at home – Jane and my kids Lewis, Eadie and Lauren.

Daniel C Schechter & Myra Ingmanson Daniel and Myra would like to thank, in Barbados, the helpful staff at the Barbados Tourism Authority, Pauline Cato and Lora Machula; in Trinidad and Tobago, Mr Dexter Trim and the rest of the staff at Tidco, Gunda Harewood, Dirk and Shani Bache, Anthony Ferguson, and Jim and Sabena Knowles.

This Book

FROM THE PUBLISHER

The triumphant third edition of *Eastern Caribbean* was edited in Lonely Planet's own sun-drenched paradise of Oakland, California. The tropical triumvirate of Rebecca Northen, Vivek Waglé and Kanani Kauka edited the book, with guidance and frothy rum cocktails provided by Robert Reid and Wade Fox. Benevolent overseer 'Carib' Kate Hoffman supervised the editing. The book was proofed by Gabi Knight, Kanani and Vivek. Coordinating author Kevin Anglin provided invaluable assistance during editing. Molly Green led the formidable flotilla of cartographers, eventually passing the captain's hat to Don Patterson, who along with Sherry Veverka sailed the project to completion. Along the way, a number of capable crewpeople pitched in to keep the book floating merrily along; they included Andrew Rebold, Justin Colgan, Patrick Phelan, Patrick Huerta, Rachel Driver, Brad Lodge, Herman So, Eric Thomsen, Tessa Rottiers and Kat Smith. Admirable Admirals Monica Lepe and Sean Brandt kept everything on course, with Alex Guilbert supervising.

The book was impeccably laid out in the sunshine by Margaret Livingston, Josh Schefers and Gerilyn Attebery. Lora Santiago designed the cover and the color sections, for which Vivek wrote the captions. Margaret and Susan Rimerman provided supervision and guidance during the layout process.

Illustrations coordinator Beca Lafore field-marshaled a team of artists that included Mark Butler, Hugh D'Andrade, Hayden Foell, Beca, Justin Marler, Henia Miedzinski, Hannah Reineck and Wendy Yanagihara. Ken DellaPenta indexed the book in style.

Thanks to Glenda Bendure and Ned Friary, who wrote the first two editions of *Eastern Caribbean*.

Special thanks to our authors – Kevin, Neal, Rowan, Myra and Dan – for their insight, hard work, helpfulness and great attitude. This is your book.

Foreword

ABOUT LONELY PLANET GUIDEBOOKS

The story begins with a classic travel adventure: Tony and Maureen Wheeler's 1972 journey across Europe and Asia to Australia. Useful information about the overland trail did not exist at that time, so Tony and Maureen published the first Lonely Planet guidebook to meet a growing need.

From a kitchen table, then from a tiny office in Melbourne (Australia), Lonely Planet has become the largest independent travel publisher in the world, an international company with offices in Melbourne, Oakland (USA), London (UK) and Paris (France).

Today Lonely Planet guidebooks cover the globe. There is an ever-growing list of books, and there's information in a variety of forms and media. Some things haven't changed. The main aim is still to help make it possible for adventurous travelers to get out there – to explore and better understand the world.

At Lonely Planet we believe travelers can make a positive contribution to the countries they visit – if they respect their host communities and spend their money wisely. Since 1986 a percentage of the income from each book has been donated to aid projects and human-rights campaigns.

Updates Lonely Planet thoroughly updates each guidebook as often as possible. This usually means there are around two years between editions, although for more unusual or more stable destinations the gap can be longer. Check the imprint page (usually following the color map at the beginning of the book) for publication dates.

Between editions up-to-date information is available in two free newsletters – the paper *Planet Talk* and email *Comet* (to subscribe, contact any Lonely Planet office) – and on our Web site at www.lonelyplanet.com. The *Upgrades* section of the Web site covers a number of important and volatile destinations and is regularly updated by Lonely Planet authors. *Scoop* covers news and current affairs relevant to travelers. And, lastly, the *Thorn Tree* bulletin board and *Postcards* section of the site carry unverified, but fascinating, reports from travelers.

Correspondence The process of creating new editions begins with the letters, postcards and emails received from travelers. This correspondence often includes suggestions, criticisms and comments about the current editions. Interesting excerpts are immediately passed on via newsletters and the Web site, and everything goes to our authors to be verified when they're researching on the road. We're keen to get more feedback from organizations or individuals who represent communities visited by travelers.

> Lonely Planet gathers information for everyone who's curious about the planet – and especially for those who explore it first-hand. Through guidebooks, phrasebooks, activity guides, maps, literature, newsletters, image library, TV series and Web site we act as an information exchange for a worldwide community of travelers.

Research Authors aim to gather sufficient practical information to enable travelers to make informed choices and to make the mechanics of a journey run smoothly. They also research historical and cultural background to help enrich the travel experience and allow travelers to understand and respond appropriately to cultural and environmental issues.

Authors don't stay in every hotel because that would mean spending a couple of months in each medium-size city and, no, they don't eat at every restaurant because that would mean stretching belts beyond capacity. They do visit hotels and restaurants to check standards and prices, but feedback based on readers' direct experiences can be very helpful.

Many of our authors work undercover; others aren't so secretive. None of them accept freebies in exchange for positive write-ups. And none of our guidebooks contain any advertising.

Production Authors submit their raw manuscripts and maps to offices in Australia, the USA, UK or France. Editors and cartographers – all experienced travelers themselves – then begin the process of assembling the pieces. When the book finally hits the shops, some things are already out of date, we start getting feedback from readers and the process begins again...

WARNING & REQUEST

Things change – prices go up, schedules change, good places go bad and bad places go bankrupt – nothing stays the same. So, if you find things better or worse, recently opened or long since closed, please tell us and help make the next edition even more accurate and useful. We genuinely value all the feedback we receive. A well-traveled team reads and acknowledges every letter, postcard and email and ensures that every morsel of information finds its way to the appropriate authors, editors and cartographers for verification.

Everyone who writes to us will find their name in the next edition of the appropriate guidebook. They will also receive the latest issue of *Planet Talk*, our quarterly printed newsletter, or *Comet*, our monthly email newsletter. Subscriptions to both newsletters are free. The very best contributions will be rewarded with a free guidebook.

Excerpts from your correspondence may appear in new editions of Lonely Planet guidebooks, the Lonely Planet Web site, *Planet Talk* or *Comet*, so please let us know if you *don't* want your letter published or your name acknowledged.

Send all correspondence to the Lonely Planet office closest to you:

Australia: Locked Bag 1, Footscray, Victoria 3011
USA: 150 Linden St, Oakland, CA 94607
UK: 10a Spring Place, London NW5 3BH
France: 1 rue du Dahomey, 75011 Paris

Or email us at: talk2us@lonelyplanet.com.au

For news, views and updates, see our Web site: www.lonelyplanet.com

---

HOW TO USE A LONELY PLANET GUIDEBOOK

The best way to use a Lonely Planet guidebook is any way you choose. At Lonely Planet, we believe the most memorable travel experiences are often those that are unexpected, and the finest discoveries are those you make yourself. Guidebooks are not intended to be used as if they provided a detailed set of infallible instructions!

Contents All Lonely Planet guidebooks follow roughly the same format. The Facts about the Destination chapters or sections give background information ranging from history to weather. Facts for the Visitor gives practical information on issues like visas and health. Getting There & Away gives a brief starting point for researching travel to and from the destination. Getting Around gives an overview of the transport options when you arrive.

The peculiar demands of each destination determine how subsequent chapters are broken up, but some things remain constant. We always start with background, then proceed to sights, places to stay, places to eat, entertainment, getting there and away, and getting around information – in that order.

Heading Hierarchy Lonely Planet headings are used in a strict hierarchical structure that can be visualized as a set of Russian dolls. Each heading (and its following text) is encompassed by any preceding heading that is higher on the hierarchical ladder.

Entry Points We do not assume guidebooks will be read from beginning to end, but that people will dip into them. The traditional entry points are the list of contents and the index. In addition, however, some books have a complete list of maps and an index map illustrating map coverage.

There may also be a color map that shows highlights. These highlights are dealt with in greater detail in the Facts for the Visitor chapter, along with planning questions and suggested itineraries. Each chapter covering a geographical region usually begins with a locator map and another list of highlights. Once you find something of interest in a list of highlights, turn to the index.

Maps Maps play a crucial role in Lonely Planet guidebooks and include a huge amount of information. A legend is printed on the back page. We seek to have complete consistency between maps and text and to have every important place in the text captured on a map. Map key numbers usually start in the top left corner.

Although inclusion in a guidebook usually implies a recommendation, we cannot list every good place. Exclusion does not necessarily imply criticism. In fact there are a number of reasons why we might exclude a place – sometimes it is simply inappropriate to encourage an influx of travelers.

Introduction

Mention the islands of the Eastern Caribbean and people instantly think of relaxing vacations filled with white sand and crystal blue waters. And that's just what thousands of visitors find every year. Honeymooners and families laze on the beach, divers and snorkelers explore the underwater attractions and cruise ships with all the comforts of home (and then some) hop from island to island.

But anyone who takes the time to dig a little deeper will find a lot more than a vacationer's paradise. The Eastern Caribbean is also home to thriving, vibrant cities and towns where people live, work and play (a lot). Shaped by centuries of history, the islands are the birthplace of distinct cultures, languages and music.

Taken individually, the islands vary widely. Some are picture-perfect coral islands, nearly flat and fringed with palm-lined beaches, while other islands are high and mountainous with terrain dominated by waterfalls and steaming volcanoes.

Culturally, the islands are a hybrid – largely of African, English and French heritage, but with a measure of Dutch and East Indian influences as well. Politically, the islands make up eight independent nations, two British colonies, two French *départements* and an affiliated state of the Netherlands.

From Anguilla in the north to Trinidad in the south, these islands make a 600-mile-long sweep that forms the eastern boundary of the Caribbean. Although it's certainly possible – with an open schedule and a fair bit of time – to island-hop from one end of the Eastern Caribbean to the other, most visitors opt for a smaller slice.

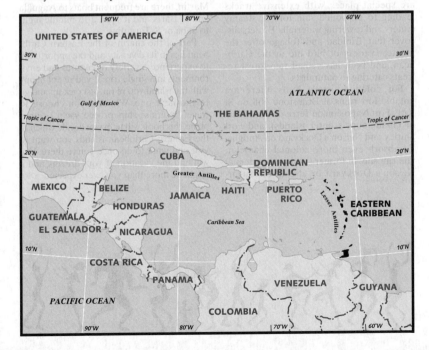

Certainly if you're looking for specific activities or ambience, you'll need to select destinations accordingly. In Martinique you can have croissants and espresso at a sidewalk café and shop for French fashions in trendy boutiques. In Trinidad, though, don't expect to find croissants – the bakeries sell Indian-curry rotis and English meat pies – and instead of boutiques you can pass an afternoon visiting backstreet *mas* camps (workshops), where artisans design and sell elaborate Carnival costumes.

Divers can find a good variety of underwater attractions off most islands, including lesser-known spots such as St Lucia, Dominica and Tobago, which offer pristine dive sites with abundant marine life.

Many of the islands have splendid beaches, but particularly notable as beach destinations are St Martin, Anguilla, St Barts, Antigua, Barbados and some of the smaller Grenadine islands.

For hikers, Dominica and Guadeloupe are special places, with extensive tracks leading to unspoiled rain forests, steamy craters and towering waterfalls. Birders discover that Trinidad and Tobago offer the greatest variety of bird life in the Caribbean, and both have small rain-forest retreats catering to naturalists.

For colonial-history buffs, there are notable fort ruins at Brimstone Hill on St Kitts, Fort Napoléon on Terre-de-Haut (one of Guadeloupe's outer islands), and Fort Shirley and Nelson's Dockyard on Antigua. To absorb even more colonial character, you can stay in former soldiers' quarters at Nelson's Dockyard or else in old sugar-plantation estate houses that have been converted into country inns on St Kitts, Nevis and Martinique.

For a look at the unhurried Caribbean with a rural West Indian character, there's Scottish-influenced Carriacou, the Dutch island of St Eustatius and the sleepy French island of Marie-Galante. On Saba you can easily imagine yourself to be in an Alpine village, while St Barts has much the feel of a Mediterranean isle. Other off-the-beaten-path charmers include Tobago, Bequia and Terre-de-Bas.

If you don't want to budget much money for traveling around, but want to see a number of islands, a few destinations can become a multi-island combination without much effort or cost. From Guadeloupe, high-speed ferries run day-trippers to the nearby islands of Terre-de-Haut, Marie-Galante and La Désirade, and from both St Vincent and Grenada there are mail boats to the nearby Grenadine islands. From St Martin, there are frequent boats to Anguilla and St Barts, and it's just a 15-minute flight to Saba or St Eustatius.

Part of the charm of the Eastern Caribbean lies in its diversity and the opportunity to experience a variety of cultures and environments in a single trip: If you're not happy with the island you're on, just pick up and go to the next one. Whether you choose to travel by cruise ship, private yacht or prop plane, this book will help you decide which of the Eastern Caribbean islands you want to visit and what to do once you're there. You will find the vacation of your dreams, and it might be more than you ever expected.

Facts about the Eastern Caribbean

HISTORY

The Caribbean islands were originally inhabited by Amerindians who migrated from the American mainland. For the most part, early European explorers were intent on ridding the islands of their native inhabitants and in the end enslaved, killed or exiled the majority of Amerindians in the Caribbean.

The Europeans recorded precious little about these societies, and the native islanders had no written languages of their own. Much of what is now known about their cultures comes from archaeological explorations; the discovery of stone tools, shellwork, pottery shards and petroglyphs is the main means for piecing together the history of the pre-Columbian period.

Not all islands in the Eastern Caribbean were populated by the same peoples at the same time. Archaeological research is still ongoing in the region; dates of migration are debated and occasionally revised by new discoveries.

Ciboneys

The first people to arrive in the Eastern Caribbean were wandering Stone Age hunters and gatherers from the Archaic (pre-pottery) Period. Usually called Ciboneys, or Siboneys, they may have been present on some islands as early as 4000 BC. Their existence is mainly known through carbon dating of midden piles, crude stone axes and scraping tools.

Arawaks

The Arawak Period in the Eastern Caribbean is generally thought to have begun about 2000 years ago, near the beginning of the Christian era.

The Arawaks were not a single tribe, but rather a group of South American tribes that all spoke the Arawak language and shared cultural similarities. They were a gentle, peaceful people who fished, hunted and farmed. Among their crops were tobacco, cotton, corn, sweet potatoes and pineapples. Their main crop was cassava, also called manioc or yuca, from whose tuberous roots comes *cassareep*, a bitter juice used as a preservative, and tapioca, a nutritious starch the Arawaks used to make cassava bread, their main food staple.

The Arawaks were very artistic. Women made pottery of red clay that was often engraved, painted with white designs or decorated with figurines called *adornos*.

The society was well organized. Villages consisted of a grouping of round dwellings, each of which housed several families. Like the native people of the American mainland, the Arawaks had bronze-colored skin and straight black hair. They wore little or no clothing.

In the Arawak religion, Yocahu, or Jocahu, was the God of Creation, also known as 'The Giver of Cassava.' The Arawaks carved anthropomorphic objects of stone or shell, called *zemis*, which they kept near places of worship.

It is believed that there were no Arawaks remaining in the Eastern Caribbean at the end of the 15th century, when Europeans first appeared on the scene. There were, however, Arawak-speaking people living in the northern Caribbean in regions the Caribs had not yet conquered. One tribe of Arawaks, the Taino, were the people whom Columbus first encountered and documented. It is from the Taino that much of the early knowledge of the Arawak culture was obtained.

Caribs

Sometime around AD 1200 the Caribs, a group of warring tribes from South America, invaded the Eastern Caribbean and migrated in a northerly direction through the islands. They drove off or killed all of the Arawak men, reputedly eating the flesh of some of their victims (the English word 'cannibal' is derived from 'caribal,' or 'Carib'). Some of the Arawak women were spared to be slaves for Carib men, and for a while these women kept some remnants of the Arawak culture alive.

The Caribs did not farm much, but instead obtained most of their food from hunting and gathering. They were not as sophisticated or artistic as the Arawaks, and their pottery was of an inferior quality. They were, however, ferocious defenders of their land and on many islands managed to keep the Europeans at bay for more than a century.

Spanish Arrival

The first European to explore the Caribbean was Christopher Columbus, who reached the islands in 1492 while looking for a westward route to Asia. Over the course of a decade, Columbus made four voyages to the New World, opening the region to exploitation and colonization. In his first voyage, which took him to the Caribbean's northerly islands, he left a party of soldiers on Hispaniola, establishing Spain's first settlement in the Americas.

On September 25, 1493, just six months after returning to Spain from his initial voyage, Columbus set sail with a flotilla of 17 ships. He took a more southerly course

'I am Columbus. This is India. OK?'

this time, hoping to find new territory on his way back to Hispaniola. It was during this second voyage that he 'discovered' most of the islands of the Eastern Caribbean. The first island was sighted on November 3, a Sunday, and was thus christened 'Dominica.' From Dominica, Columbus sailed north, landing at Marie-Galante, an island he named after his ship, the 'gallant' *Santa Maria*. He next touched land on Guadeloupe's Basse-Terre and then sailed northwest up the chain, sighting and naming the islands of Montserrat, Antigua, Redonda, Nevis, St Kitts, St Eustatius and Saba, before heading to the Virgin Islands and points west.

On Columbus' third voyage, in 1498, he sailed farther south still, making his first landfall at Trinidad. From there he sailed west along the coast of Venezuela and sighted Tobago and Grenada before heading north once again to Hispaniola.

Despite the significance of his journeys, Columbus never fully realized that what he had discovered was indeed a New World and not islands off the coast of east Asia. It is as a consequence of his geographic disorientation that the native peoples of the Americas are still known as 'Indians.'

European Colonialism

The Spanish explorers, in pursuit of gold, concentrated their attention on the larger islands of the northern Caribbean and on the American mainland, paying scant notice to the smaller islands that comprise the Eastern Caribbean. They did, however, settle on Trinidad, conveniently just off the coast of mineral-rich Venezuela.

A flurry of colonial activity was set off in 1623, when the English became the first Europeans to establish a permanent settlement in the Eastern Caribbean (with the exception of Trinidad), founding a colony on the island of St Kitts. In 1625, Captain John Powell landed a party of settlers on Barbados, and other British colonies were soon established on Nevis, Antigua and Montserrat. In the 1630s the French settled Martinique and Guadeloupe, and the Dutch settled Saba, St Eustatius and St Martin.

The Dutch, French and English all laid claims and counterclaims throughout the Eastern Caribbean. In some instances, such as on St Martin and St Kitts, different colonial powers established settlements on opposite sides of the same island. Sometimes the European powers coexisted peacefully, especially when jointly battling the native Caribs, but more often than not they were involved in a tug-of-war, each of them trying to gain control of the other's colonies. Over the next two centuries most islands of the Eastern Caribbean changed hands so many times that they developed societies with an almost hybrid culture, most commonly a British-French mix.

Sugarcane Plantations

The Dutch were largely concerned with establishing military and trade stations on the islands that they held. The French and British, on the other hand, saw the primary value of their Caribbean possessions in terms of agricultural production and quickly went about clearing the forests and planting crops. The original fields were largely of tobacco, cotton and indigo, but by the mid-1600s sugar had proven the most profitable crop, and larger islands like Barbados and Martinique were heavily planted with sugarcane.

Unlike tobacco, which was cultivated in small plots, sugar production was large-scale and labor-intensive. Sugarcane must be crushed almost immediately after cutting or it will spoil, and as the mills that crushed the cane were expensive to build and operate, the plantations needed to be large enough to justify the expense.

To meet the increased demand for labor, the planters began to import great numbers of slaves from Africa. By the end of the 17th century the islands had a firmly established plantation society comprised of a minority of free whites and a majority of black slaves.

On the British islands many of the plantations were owned by absentee planters who returned to England, leaving the plantation operation in the hands of managers. The absentee owners were among the wealthiest members of British society and had a powerful influence in enacting protectionist legislation that guaranteed British markets for their sugar. There were similar parallels in the French West Indies.

By the early 1800s, sugar's heyday had passed. Merchants who were tired of the interruption of supplies during the military skirmishes between the British and the French began to replace Caribbean cane with European-grown beet sugar. As the market for Caribbean sugar waned, so too did the influence of the planters. At the same time, the abolitionist movement was gaining momentum.

In 1807, British legislation abolished the slave trade, although planters were allowed to keep the slaves they already had until 1833. On the French islands emancipation was enacted in 1848.

Even after its decline, sugarcane continued to be grown on most islands and played a formative role in shaping island society. As blacks left the plantations, indentured servants, mostly from India, were brought in to replace them. Sizable Indian minorities were established on Trinidad, Martinique and Guadeloupe, and their culture has become an integral part of these islands' identities.

The 20th Century

During the world depression of the 1930s most of the Caribbean was torn by high unemployment, labor unrest and civil strife. On many islands a concerted labor movement developed, with demands for both economic and political independence. The British responded by enacting the first meaningful measures of internal self-government, the

Slavery in the Caribbean

The Atlantic slave trade stands as one of the most abhorrent social injustices in history, with a scale so overwhelming that it virtually depopulated vast tracts of western Africa. From the slave-trade origins, starting with Portuguese and Spanish colonists in the 1500s, to the final outlawing of New World slavery on Cuba in 1886, an estimated 10 million enslaved African people were brought to the Americas. In addition, countless millions died in the process of being captured or during the long transatlantic crossing.

The Caribbean islands accounted for more than a third of all slave importations – nearly four million people in all. The British and French West Indies each imported an estimated 1.6 million enslaved blacks, while the Dutch-held islands accounted for about 500,000. In contrast, the USA imported an estimated 400,000 slaves.

Snatched from their homelands, these captive people were brought to the New World for one reason only – to provide a cheap labor source – and they were treated as property by those who purchased them.

So much money was involved in the trafficking of captive African people that entire nations laid claim to the slave trade itself. The Treaty of Utrecht, signed in 1713, for example, gave England the sole right to provide slaves to the Spanish colonies. When the Spanish tried to rescind the treaty in 1739, England declared war on Spain to defend its dominance in the West Indies slave trade.

For the British it was a lucrative triangular route. Ships set sail from English ports with trinkets and muskets to barter for slaves in Africa. Once the slaves were delivered to the New World, the ships were loaded with sugar, molasses and rum for the journey back to England.

Slavery was a brutally inhumane institution. West Africans, who were captured from their villages in sweeping raids by rival tribes, were marched like cattle to the coast, where they were sold to European slave traders. The slaves were then crowded shoulder to shoulder into the sweltering holds of cargo ships – some perished from dehydration and suffocation, others from their first contact with Western diseases. It took about two months to complete the wretched middle passage from West Africa to the Caribbean. If at least 90% of the 'cargo' made it alive, it was considered a good crossing, although much higher mortality rates were commonplace.

Upon arrival in the Caribbean the slaves were marched to an auction block, exhibited and sold to the highest bidder. On the British and Dutch islands, families were deliberately broken up and slaves were denied any rights under the law. On the French islands, the *Code Noire,* rather feebly enacted in 1685, forbade the separation of families and gave slaves legal protection from hideous abuses like mutilation and murder, although this same code also prescribed floggings and other degrading penalties for slaves who did not obey their masters.

Despite the dehumanizing conditions of plantation society, Africans uprooted from their homelands managed to maintain elements of their native culture. On the French islands, where the slaves were readily converted to Christianity, they held onto traditional African beliefs as well, and over time merged the Christian and African religions into their own unique spiritual practices. Voodoo, for example, uses the names of both African deities and Catholic saints in its ceremonies.

Slaves were forced to learn the language of the plantation owners, but they blended their own use of it into a hybrid Creole language that was liberally spiced with African terms. To this day, islanders throughout the Eastern Caribbean still slip into Creole when chatting among themselves. Much of West Indian music takes its roots from a spirit of rebellion that prevailed during the slavery period – most prominent is calypso, a sharp, raplike music that was developed by slaves poking fun at their unsuspecting masters.

French by incorporating the islands more thoroughly with mainland France, and the Dutch by allowing heightened domestic rule under association with the Netherlands.

The British Islands In the post-WWII period, Britain moved to divest itself of its Caribbean colonies by attempting to create a single federated state that would incorporate all of the British-held Caribbean. One advantage of the federation was that it was expected to provide a mechanism for decolonizing smaller islands that the British felt would otherwise be too small to stand as separate entities.

After a decade of negotiation, Britain convinced its Caribbean colonies – Jamaica, Barbados, Trinidad and the British Windward and Leeward Islands – to join together as the West Indies Federation. The new association came into effect in 1958, with the intent that the federation work out the intricacies of self-government during a four-year probationary period before the islands emerged as a single new independent nation in 1962.

Although the West Indies Federation represented dozens of islands scattered across some 2000 miles of ocean, the British established Trinidad, at the southernmost end of the chain, to be the governing 'center' of the federation.

For centuries the islanders had related to each other via their British administrators, and the political and economic intercourse between the islands had been quite limited. In the end, the lack of a united identity among the islands, coupled with each island's desire for autonomy, proved much stronger than any perceived advantage in union.

Jamaica was the first to develop a rift with the new association and opted to leave the federation in 1961. Trinidad itself soon followed suit. Both islands felt they were large enough, and rich enough in resources, to stand on their own. They were also wary of getting stuck having to subsidize the federation's smaller islands, which had a history of being heavily dependent upon British aid. Thus in 1962, Jamaica and

Trinidad became independent nations. The concept of a smaller federation limped along for a few more years, but after Barbados broke rank and became an independent nation in 1966, the British were forced to go back to the drawing board.

The remaining islands continued to splinter. Dominica and St Lucia gained independence as single-island nations. Antigua, St Vincent, Grenada and St Kitts were each linked with smaller neighboring islands to form new nations.

Anguilla, which was connected with St Kitts and Nevis, rebelled three months after the new state's inauguration in 1967 and negotiated with the British to be reinstated as a Crown Colony. Montserrat also refused to be dispensed with so readily by the British and was allowed to continue as a Crown Colony.

During the same period, Barbuda made a bid to secede from its union with Antigua, but with barely 1000 inhabitants, its independence movement failed.

The islands linked to St Vincent and to Grenada also initially grumbled, but they have managed to work out their differences well enough to maintain their unions.

The federation of St Kitts & Nevis, which already forms the smallest nation in the Western Hemisphere, narrowly avoided splitting into even smaller parts in August 1998, when a secession referendum on the island of Nevis failed to gain the necessary two-thirds vote.

The French Islands In the French West Indies the policy has been one of assimilation rather than independence. Since 1946, Martinique and Guadeloupe (whose administration includes the islands of La Dèsirade, Marie-Galante and Les Saintes as well as St Barts and the French side of St Martin) have been separate, if somewhat hesitant, departments of France, with representation in the Senate and National Assembly in Paris.

Separatist sentiments have long existed in the French islands, particularly Martinique, although reliance upon French economic aid has tempered the movement. Still, many islanders think it's but a matter of time before the islands achieve some measure of greater internal autonomy.

The Dutch Islands The Dutch, like the British, also hoped to create a single federation of all their Caribbean possessions – Curaçao, Aruba, Bonaire, Sint Maarten, St Eustatius and Saba – collectively known as the Netherlands Antilles. In 1954 a charter was enacted that made these six islands an autonomous part of the Netherlands, with its central administration in the southerly island of Curaçao. Under the charter, island affairs were largely administered by elected officials, although the Dutch continued to hold the purse strings and maintain other controls. The islands were expected to develop the mechanisms for self-rule and move gradually, as a unit, toward full independence from the Netherlands.

The islands, however, have not looked favorably upon the concept of union as a single nation. In the late 1970s, Aruba moved to secede from the federation and in 1986 became a single island state. The remaining five islands have also grown weary of the concept of independence as a single federation; Sint Maarten politics have centered as much upon independence from its union with Curaçao as independence from the Netherlands.

GEOGRAPHY & GEOLOGY
Geographically, the islands in this book make up the easternmost slice of the Caribbean, or West Indies. Included are all of the Leeward Islands (from Anguilla to Dominica) and the Windward Islands (from Martinique to Grenada), plus Barbados, Trinidad and Tobago. All the islands except for Trinidad and Tobago are part of the Lesser Antilles.

Geologically, most of the Eastern Caribbean is part of a double arc of islands running north to south. The islands on the inner arc, which extends from Saba to Grenada, are volcanic in origin. While most of the volcanic activity has long since ceased, there are still steaming craters, bubbling hot-water springs and pungent sulfur

vents on some of the higher islands, and during the past century there have been major eruptions from Mt Pelée (1902) on Martinique and the Soufrière volcano (1979) on St Vincent.

In 1995 the Soufrière Hills volcano on Montserrat awoke from a 400-year sleep and blasted through its dome, beginning an ongoing eruption that has buried the capital of the island and left much of the island uninhabitable.

The outer arc of islands, which extend from Anguilla to Barbados, are not volcanic, but rather of marine origin, comprised of uplifted coral limestone built upon a base of rock.

Trinidad and Tobago are geologically unique, having broken off from the South American continent. Trinidad's southern plains were created by deposits from Venezuela's Orinoco River, and its Northern Range is an extension of the Andes.

CLIMATE
The entire Eastern Caribbean lies in the tropics. Consequently, the islands have near-equable temperatures year-round and only slight seasonable variations in the number of hours of daylight. In the northern islands like Anguilla, year-round highs average around 81°F (27°C), while lows get to around 72°F (22°C). On Trinidad, the southernmost island in the Eastern Caribbean, high temperatures average around 88°F (31°C), with lows around 72°F (22°C). In general, expect muggy days, tempered by sea breezes near the coast and seasonal rains.

Although it's hot and humid most of the time, trade winds blowing from the northeast temper the humidity; they are prevalent most of the year, but are strongest from January to April.

The rainiest time of the year is generally May through November. On low-lying islands rainfall is relatively light. On the high, mountainous islands the precipitation varies greatly with location: rainfall is much heavier on the windward (northeast) sides of the islands and in the interiors, and lighter on the leeward sides.

Hurricanes

The hurricane season in the Caribbean, like that of the eastern USA, is from June to November, with most activity occurring in August and September. Hurricanes can also appear outside the official season but are much less frequent then. While the annual average is only about five hurricanes per year, the frequency can vary greatly from year to year.

Even more important is the intensity. 'Big Ones' – hurricanes that wallop head-on with winds of more than 125mph – have torn into a number of Eastern Caribbean islands in past decades. The most recent example was Hurricane Georges, which hit Antigua, Barbuda and St Kitts in September 1998 before tearing through Puerto Rico and Hispaniola. In late November 1999, Hurricane Lenny broke all the rules by slowly backing in from the Caribbean Sea, causing extensive damage to the usually protected west coasts of islands from Anguilla to Dominica.

Hurricanes are defined as storms that originate in the tropics and have winds in excess of 74mph. Those that hit the Caribbean usually form off the coast of Africa and whip in a westerly direction across the Atlantic. The winds of these hurricanes revolve in a counterclockwise direction around a center of lower barometric pressure, picking up energy and moisture from warm waters as they approach the Caribbean. When wind speeds are under 40mph it's called a 'tropical depression,' and when winds are between 40mph and 74mph it's a 'tropical storm.'

If you are caught by an approaching hurricane, stay calm and follow local warnings. Hotels are typically of concrete-and-steel construction capable of withstanding strong winds with minimal damage. However, in low-lying areas, ocean swells can also pose a hazard – if you have an oceanfront room it's a wise precaution to relocate to a unit farther inland. Most hurricane injuries are the result of flying debris, and most deaths occur due to drowning when people are caught in areas subject to storm surge or inland flooding. Don't be tempted to venture outside in the midst of a storm.

ECOLOGY & ENVIRONMENT

When Columbus first set eyes on the islands of the Eastern Caribbean, they were thickly covered with forest. European colonizers, however, quickly set about uprooting the trees, replacing them with crops such as indigo, coffee and sugar.

While the early colonists concentrated on the more arable lowland areas, a second wave of deforestation occurred in the 20th century. Once modern advances in shipping made bananas a viable export crop, the interior rain forest began to be carved away to make room for banana plantations.

Some islands, such as St Martin and Antigua, have only token tracts of woodlands remaining, while other islands, like Guadeloupe, Martinique and Dominica, have set aside sizable portions of the interior rain forest as national reserves.

For many island governments it's a constant struggle between trying to preserve what remains and resisting influences from overseas developers. On St Lucia, for example, an exclusive resort was built smack between the Pitons, the two coastal mountains that have long stood as the very symbol of that island's unspoiled natural character.

The development crushed a move by islanders to have the land preserved as a new national park. At the same time, however, three large inland tracts of rain forest were set aside as forest reserves, thus giving those areas protection from encroaching development and creeping banana plantations.

In many ways the St Lucia situation represents the potential positive and negative effects of tourism. Upscale resort projects often vie for some of the more environmentally sensitive niches and in the process debase the 'unspoiled nature' that they are attempting to market. On the other hand, the rise in ecotourism and the recognition that nature reserves attract hikers, bird watchers and other visitors sensitive to the environment have all helped contribute to preservation efforts. Indeed, some places, such as Dominica and Saba, primarily target ecotourists, emphasizing hiking and diving in forest and marine preserves.

Travelers can make a positive contribution by exhibiting a healthy respect for the environment, treading lightly and supporting environmentally friendly businesses. When hiking, stick to established paths. When shopping, avoid buying products containing coral, bird feathers or turtle shells. Give thought to the impact businesses have on the native environment and culture, and do what you can to help local communities benefit from the money you spend. Consider staying in locally managed hotels and guest houses, hiring hiking guides from nearby villages, buying island-made handicrafts and patronizing family-owned restaurants.

For more on ecotourism, see Organized Tours in the Getting There & Away chapter.

Lost Species

Dramatic changes to the ecology of the Eastern Caribbean occurred with the arrival of European settlers, who introduced exotic creatures to the islands, some by accident, others by design. Rats, nesting in crevices in ships' holds, sailed to the islands with the first colonists. Plantation managers, irritated by the damage the rats caused to their sugar crops, introduced the Burmese mongoose in an attempt to control the rats. But the mongooses, which do their hunting during the day, turned out to be ill suited for the task of preying on the nocturnal rats. Instead, they developed an appetite for lizards, eggs and the chicks of native ground-nesting birds.

Having evolved with limited competition and few native predators, the islands' indigenous species have generally fared poorly against more aggressive introduced fauna. Uncounted species have become extinct since the colonial era. Parrots, for example, which were once common to rain forests throughout the Eastern Caribbean, now survive on only five islands, and all of the remaining species are endangered, some with populations of just a few hundred birds.

The foraging animals introduced by colonists, particularly goats, which continue to roam freely on many islands, have had a similarly devastating effect on native flora. Their grazing has undermined fragile native ecosystems and spelled extinction for many island plants. Erosion, deforestation and competition from thousands of introduced plants have taken a tremendous toll. In all, an estimated half of the native flora on the islands of the Eastern Caribbean has become extinct or endangered.

Fortunately, conservation efforts ranging from recent attempts at controlling the goat populations in the Grenadines to concentrated efforts to bring the remaining Eastern Caribbean parrots back from the brink of extinction are showing promise.

FLORA & FAUNA

The flora and fauna of the Eastern Caribbean vary with each island's topography and rainfall.

The low islands tend to support largely scrub vegetation and are pocketed with salt ponds that provide habitat for shorebirds and seabirds. The mountainous islands have far more diverse ecosystems that include lush interior rain forests of tall trees, ferns, climbing vines and a variety of colorful forest birds.

Additionally, location is a major determining factor in the types and variations of native flora and fauna. As a general rule, the more isolated an island is from its nearest neighbor and the farther it is from a continental land mass, the more restrictive its plant and animal life.

On isolated Barbados, for instance, indigenous mammals are largely limited to a handful of bat species, while on Trinidad, which lies just a few miles off the coast of Venezuela, there are a hundred types of mammals, replicating those found on the nearby South American mainland.

Correspondingly, Trinidad and Tobago have the greatest diversity of bird life among the Eastern Caribbean islands. More than 400 species of bird are found on these two islands, which is greater than the total found on all the other Eastern Caribbean islands combined. Among the many varieties of colorful

Environmental Groups

Following are some of the groups that are attempting to bring local and international focus on environmental issues in the Caribbean.

Caribbean Alliance for Sustainable Tourism (CAST; ☎ 787-725-9139, fax 787-725-9108, cast@chahotels.com, www.cha-cast.com), 1000 Ponce de Leon, 5th floor, San Juan, Puerto Rico 00907. In an attempt to conserve natural resources, CAST offers travelers a list of member hotels, grouped by island, that have been judged environmentally sound.

Caribbean Conservation Corporation (CCC; ☎ 352-373-6441, ccc@cccturtle.org), 4424 NW 13th St, Suite No A1, Gainesville, FL, USA. In addition to providing general conservation information and advice, the CCC works to protect sea turtles.

RARE Center for Tropical Conservation (☎ 703 522-5070, fax 703 522-5027, rare@rarecenter .org, www.rarecenter.org), 1840 Wilson Blvd Suite 402, Arlington, VA 22201, USA. The RARE center works to preserve threatened habitats and ecosystems throughout the tropics. In the Caribbean they've been active in protecting endangered species and habitats, from the Dominican Republic south to Grenada.

Specially Protected Areas & Wildlife (SPAW; www.cep.unep.org/programmes/spaw/ spaw.html), Caribbean Environment Programme, Regional Co-ordinating Unit, 14–20 Port Royal St, Kingston, Jamaica, West Indies. SPAW supports activities for the protection and management of sensitive and highly valuable natural marine resources in the wider Caribbean region. This subprogram of the Caribbean Environment Program is responsible for initiatives such as the Convention on Biological Diversity (CBD), the International Coral Reef Initiative (ICRI) and the Global Coral Reef Monitoring Network (GCRMN).

World Wildlife Fund (WWF; ☎ 202-778-9744, fax 202-296-5348, www.panda.org), 1250 24th St NW, Washington, DC 20037, USA. WWF sponsors programs throughout the Caribbean as diverse as aiding in the development of the Saba Marine Park to funding brochures that educate people about the illegal trade in wildlife products.

Coral reefs and oceans are facing unprecedented environmental pressures. Groups actively involved in promoting responsible diving, publicizing environmental marine threats, and lobbying for better policies include the **Coral Reef Alliance** (☎ 510-848-0110, www.coralreefalliance.org), the **Cousteau Society** (☎ 757-523-9335, www.cousteausociety.org), **Project AWARE Foundation** (☎ 714-540-0251, www.projectaware.org) in addition to **Ocean Futures** (☎ 805-899-8899, www.oceanfutures.com). All are based in the US.

birds nesting on Trinidad and Tobago are scarlet ibis, blue-crowned motmots, chestnut woodpeckers, palm tanagers, channel-billed toucans and white-bearded manakins.

For comparison, only 28 bird species nest on Barbados, and they tend to be more common birds such as doves, blackbirds, cattle egrets, herons and finches.

Plant life also reaches its greatest diversity on Trinidad and Tobago, which provide a habitat for more than 700 orchid species and 1600 other types of flowering plants. As you continue north up the Eastern Caribbean chain, and away from the South American continent, the diversity of plants markedly decreases.

More information on flora and fauna can be found under the individual island chapters.

Plants

Because the Eastern Caribbean's climate ranges from dry desert conditions to lush tropical rain forests, you'll find it embraces a wide variety of vegetation. There are wetlands with mangrove swamps, dry scrubland areas with Turk's-head and prickly pear cacti, and rain forests with bamboo groves and thick-trunked *gommier* (gum) trees.

Some trees are common to coastal areas throughout the Eastern Caribbean. The ubiquitous coconut palm thrives in coral sands and produces about 75 coconuts a year. Another easily identifiable coastal tree is the pandanus, or screw pine, which has spiny leaves, fruit that resembles pineapples and a trunk that's anchored with multiple prop roots. The sea grape, which grows in sand, is also distinctive, with fruit that hangs in grapelike bunches and round, green leaves.

Three of the most common flowering trees found throughout the region are the umbrella-shaped flamboyant, or poinciana tree, which has gorgeous scarlet blossoms from late May through the summer; the frangipani, or plumeria, which boasts fragrant waxy pink or white flowers in winter and spring; and the African tulip tree, which has large orange blossoms that flower year-round but are most abundant in spring.

A common coastal plant is the beach morning glory, which has pink flowers and is found on the sand just above the wrack line. The flower of the beach morning glory blooms for only a day, as do the colorful blossoms of thousands of varieties of hibiscus that are planted in gardens throughout the Eastern Caribbean.

Other bright tropical Caribbean flowers include blood-red anthuriums, brilliant orange birds of paradise, colorful bougainvilleas, red ginger, torch ginger and various heliconias with bright orange and red bracts. There are also hundreds of varieties of orchids.

On dry islands, where goats are a particular problem, oleander bushes, which have pink or white flowers, are often the main vegetation, as their leaves are toxic to foraging animals.

Birds

The Eastern Caribbean hosts a variety of both resident and migrant birds. Although the diversity of bird life varies greatly among islands, some species are spotted throughout the Eastern Caribbean. These include the brown pelican, which can readily be seen feeding along the shoreline from St Kitts to Tobago; the magnificent frigate bird, an aerial pirate that nests on a limited number of islands but hunts throughout the chain; the cattle egret, a stark white bird common in open fields; and the bananaquit, a friendly little yellow-bellied nectar feeder nicknamed the 'sugar bird.' Other widely dispersed birds include the brown booby, spotted sandpiper, royal tern, Zenaida dove, Antillean crested hummingbird, tropical mockingbird and Lesser Antillean bullfinch.

Native parrots make their home in the mountainous rain forests of Dominica, St Lucia, St Vincent, Trinidad and Tobago.

In terms of bird watching, Trinidad and Tobago are the Caribbean's premier sites, offering splendid birding that includes huge flocks of roosting scarlet ibis, bands of squawking parrots and hundreds of other colorful tropical birds. The country has a number of bird sanctuaries, including the

Asa Wright Centre, a frequent destination of Audubon Society tours.

Mammals

With the exception of Trinidad, the variety of mammals in the Eastern Caribbean is quite limited and consists predominantly of introduced species. The main native mammals found on the more remote islands are bat species.

Early Amerindian settlers are thought to have introduced agoutis (small rabbitlike rodents) and opossums, which are known in the Caribbean as *manicous*. Europeans introduced half a dozen species of rat; the ferretlike mongoose, which on many islands is now the most commonly sighted nondomesticated animal; and the green monkey, which was brought from Africa in the 17th century. The monkeys occupy remote areas on the islands of Barbados, Grenada, St Kitts and Nevis; they tend to be shy, but sightings of them, particularly on St Kitts' southwest peninsula, are not uncommon.

Marine mammals found in the waters of the Eastern Caribbean include numerous species of whale and dolphin. Most plentiful among the whales are pilot whales, which grow to 23 feet, travel in large pods and have an overall black appearance; because of their color and the fact that they are still hunted for meat, they are called 'black fish' by islanders.

Also relatively common are sperm whales. This species can grow as long as 69 feet, has a head that comprises nearly one-third of its body and feeds on squid. Less frequent but spotted seasonally are humpback whales, which reach lengths of 45 feet, have distinctive long white flippers and are renowned for enthralling whale watchers with their arching dives, lobtailing and breaching.

Among the dolphins are spinner dolphins, a slender-beaked, slim and grayish dolphin that grows to 7 feet, swims in large herds and is seen year-round; and bottlenose dolphins, which reach 12 feet, have dark gray backs and a reputation for coming within touching distance of divers.

Amphibians & Reptiles

A variety of frogs and toads exists in the Eastern Caribbean. Visitors are likely to take notice of one of the smallest, the tree frog, which is common throughout the region and creates a symphony that can be almost deafening at night. At the other end of the scale is the *crapaud,* a large forest frog that is found in Dominica and Montserrat; it's also called the 'mountain chicken' for the taste of its legs, considered a delicacy.

Lizards, such as the Jamaican anole, which puffs out a showy orange throat sac as a territorial warning to encroachers, are common throughout the islands. In all, there are more than two dozen species of lizard, from the common gecko that hangs around the windows of houses snatching pesky mosquitoes to colorful ground lizards that are specific to just one island. The iguana, a large arboreal lizard with stout legs, is indigenous to the Caribbean but is now prevalent on only a handful of islands. Despite the fierce-looking crest of spines that runs from its neck to tail, the iguana has a strictly herbivorous diet.

There are several snakes in the islands. Most, such as the Barbadian grass snake *Liophis perfuscus* and the St Lucian *kouwes* snake, have a limited range and are harmless. Boa constrictors, found on Trinidad and St Lucia, are nonvenomous and pose no threat to people. The fer-de-lance, however, which is found in brushy areas on St Lucia, Martinique and Trinidad, is a highly venomous snake whose bite can be fatal. (For information on snakebites see Health in the Regional Facts for the Visitor chapter.)

Sea Turtles Sea turtles are large air-breathing reptiles that inhabit tropical seas but must come ashore to lay eggs. Found in the Caribbean are hawksbill turtles, loggerhead turtles, green turtles, and mighty leatherbacks that can weigh up to a half-ton. All are endangered. Depending on the species, sea turtles take 15 to 50 years to reach their reproductive age. The females dig a shallow pit and lay their eggs in sand just above the high-tide line; they nest only once every two to four years, laying about

Islands at a Glance

This chart presents an overview of basic island information. In the farthest left column, we list the major language spoken in the region, followed by the area's political status and currency of exchange. In the middle column are statistics on population, land area and population density. Finally, in the right column, we outline the region's geographical features.

ANGUILLA
English
UK Dependency
Eastern Caribbean Dollar

pop 11,800
35 sq miles
337 per sq mile

relatively flat, dry, sandy

ANTIGUA & BARBUDA
English
independent
Eastern Caribbean Dollar

pop 66,500
170 sq miles
391 per sq mile

both islands largely dry and scrubby

BARBADOS
English
independent
Barbados Dollar

pop 275,000
166 sq miles
1657 per sq mile

low hills in the interior, white-sand beaches along the coast

DOMINICA
English
independent
Eastern Caribbean Dollar

pop 71,500
290 sq miles
247 per sq mile

ruggedly mountainous with rain forests and waterfalls

GRENADA
English
independent
Eastern Caribbean Dollar

pop 89,000
131 sq miles
679 per sq mile

high mountainous islands with deeply indented coastlines

GUADELOUPE
French
overseas French department
French Franc

pop 386,000
629 sq miles
614 per sq mile

two main adjoining islands and several offshore islands; largely mountainous

MARTINIQUE
French
overseas French department
French Franc

pop 414,500
424 sq miles
978 per sq mile

mountainous interior topped by 4524-foot Mount Pelée

MONTSERRAT
English
UK Dependency
Eastern Caribbean Dollar

pop 6,500
38 sq miles
171 per sq mile

central mountains, with a volcano that's been erupting since 1995

SABA
English/Dutch
part of the Netherlands
Netherlands Antilles Guilder

pop 1200
5 sq miles
240 per sq mile

small but disproportionately high and mountainous

Islands at a Glance

ST BARTS

French	pop 6500	hilly terrain with deeply
part of Guadeloupe	8 sq miles	indented bays
French Franc	813 per sq mile	

ST EUSTATIUS

English/Dutch	pop 2600	largely dry island dominated by
part of the Netherlands	8 sq miles	an extinct crater
Netherlands Antilles Guilder	325 per sq mile	

ST KITTS & NEVIS

English	pop 38,800	both islands high with central
independent	100 sq miles	volcanic peaks
Eastern Caribbean Dollar	388 per sq mile	

ST LUCIA

English	pop 156,000	mountainous rain-forested in-
independent	239 sq miles	terior, bubbling sulfur springs
Eastern Caribbean Dollar	653 per sq mile	

ST MARTIN/SINT MAARTEN

French/English	pop 70,000	hilly interior; shoreline dotted
north side part	34 sq miles	with bays, coves and salt ponds
of Guadeloupe;	2059 per sq mile	
south side part		
of Netherlands		
French Franc/		
Netherlands Antilles Guilder		

ST VINCENT & THE GRENADINES

English	pop 115,900	St Vincent: mountainous;
independent	150 sq miles	the Grenadines: a mix of hilly
Eastern Caribbean Dollar	773 per sq mile	islands and sandy cays

TRINIDAD & TOBAGO

English	pop 1,175,500	mountain ranges, rain forests
independent	1980 sq miles	and lowlands
Trinidad & Tobago Dollar	594 per sq mile	

100 Ping-Pong-ball-size eggs. The hatchlings emerge from their nests, usually at night, about 60 days later.

Predators such as birds take a heavy toll on the hatchlings, but the greatest threat to sea turtles comes from human beings. Shoreline development disturbs their nesting sites; artificial lights lure inland the hatchlings that would otherwise make a beeline to the sea; and improperly discarded trash, such as floating plastic bags that are confused for jellyfish and swallowed, present life-threatening hazards. Despite international bans prohibiting the trade of sea turtles, they are still occasionally hunted in the Caribbean.

National Parks

National parks are an emerging trend in the Eastern Caribbean, and not only for the tourist dollars they bring. As the effects of overfishing, overfarming and population expansion become apparent, local governments have gotten increasingly involved in conservation efforts.

Larger, mountainous islands like Dominica and Guadeloupe have set aside significant tracts of interior rain forest as national parks, and Trinidad and Tobago have a growing number of nature reserves, some accessible only by boat. Smaller islands, including Saba, have established marine preserves with regulations on fishing and boating. Anguilla has two national parks protecting Native American petroglyphs, while Antigua and Barbados preserve colonial history at Nelson's Dockyard and Farley Hill.

GOVERNMENT & POLITICS

Most of those Eastern Caribbean islands that were formerly administered by the British are now independent democracies with a parliamentary form of government and a Commonwealth affiliation. Two of the islands, Montserrat and Anguilla, continue by their own request as British colonies.

The French islands have been incorporated into the fold as overseas departments of France, with a status on par with that of the 96 departments that make up mainland France (a situation similar to that of the US state of Hawaii).

Saba, St Eustatius and Dutch Sint Maarten are part of the Netherlands Antilles, a union that also includes the southern Caribbean islands of Curaçao and Bonaire. The Netherlands Antilles is a parliamentary democracy that's linked to the Netherlands and administered by a governor who is appointed by the queen.

For more information, see the end of the earlier History section as well as individual island chapters.

ECONOMY

The economies of many Eastern Caribbean islands are still heavily dependent upon other countries, either for direct financial assistance or to provide favorable markets for island products.

On many islands agriculture remains the most important sector of the economy. Much of the arable land on some islands, such as Barbados and St Kitts, is still planted in sugarcane, while bananas are the major export crop on high, rainy islands like Dominica, St Vincent and St Lucia.

Because of historic European ties to the Caribbean, the European Union (EU) has maintained a trade policy favoring the import of Caribbean-grown bananas over cheaper Central American ones. That situation is now in jeopardy. Although the USA is not a banana exporter, in 1997 the Clinton administration filed suit with the World Trade Organization (WTO) to force the EU to abandon trade policies that give the edge to Caribbean bananas. The WTO's preliminary ruling was in agreement with the US position.

While this news was given scant attention in the US press, the European media blasted it as a payoff to the agribusiness giant Chiquita Brands, a dominant player in the Central American banana trade and a major donor to US political campaigns. While the court battles continue, the WTO ruling delivered a heavy blow to the economies of the Caribbean's banana-producing islands, which have responded with government subsidies to banana farms and attempts to retrain farmers and diversify their income bases.

In part because of depressed world markets for the Caribbean's agricultural products, and in part because of the strong US dollar and increase in traveling by US citizens, tourism has become an increasingly important industry for most of the islands.

Trinidad, the most resource-rich island in the Eastern Caribbean, has oil, asphalt and other petroleum-based industries. Elsewhere in the region, with the exception of rum distilleries and a few small garment and electronics-assembly factories, there's very little industry. What industry exists doesn't pay well. For example, the prevailing wage on St Lucia for manufacturing laborers is around US$3.50 per hour for men, US$1.80 for women. In the French Caribbean wages are significantly higher, but the per-capita GNP is only about half of what prevails on the French mainland, and unemployment hovers around 25%.

Most trade is with the USA and Europe. In part due to their lengthy colonial history, the Eastern Caribbean islands do not trade extensively among themselves, and customs barriers between islands have thus far frustrated the development of strong regional markets. Although they are outside the North Atlantic Free Trade Agreement (Nafta), the Caribbean nations have been, without success, petitioning for the same duty-free commercial relationship with the US that Mexico and Canada have under the Nafta provision.

POPULATION & PEOPLE

The population of the Eastern Caribbean is nearly three million, of which Trinidad accounts for more than a third.

Population densities vary greatly. One of the world's most densely populated countries is Barbados, which has 275,000 people and a population density of 1650 people per sq mile. Some of the smaller islands, including Saba and Statia, have only around 2000 to 2500 inhabitants.

With some islands, like Grenada, there are more native islanders living abroad than at home. Most overseas West Indians live in the UK, USA or France.

While the vast majority of Eastern Caribbean islanders are of African ancestry, descendants of slaves brought to work in the sugar plantations, the proportion varies widely from island to island. There are also sizable numbers of people of European and South Asian ancestry, as well as many of mixed ethnicities and smaller numbers from the Middle East, Asia and the Americas. Those of South Asian (including present-day India, Pakistan and Bangladesh) ancestry are most commonly referred to as 'East Indian' in the Caribbean, to avoid confusion with West Indian and Native Indian. This is the convention followed in this book.

Although the native Caribs were almost completely wiped out by early colonists, about 3000 Caribs still live on the east side of Dominica, and there are smaller Carib populations on St Vincent and Trinidad.

EDUCATION

All the islands of the Eastern Caribbean have compulsory education for children, though the number of years varies. Most educational systems are modeled on the French, British or Dutch systems.

The University of the West Indies, the largest university in the English Caribbean, has campuses in Trinidad and Barbados. On the French islands, the Université des Antilles-Guyane has campuses in Guadeloupe and Martinique.

Barbados has a literacy rate of close to 99%, the same as Australia and the USA. Literacy rates on other islands range from about 78% in St Lucia to 96% in Trinidad & Tobago.

ARTS
Literature

The Eastern Caribbean has produced a number of notable literary figures. The most widely acclaimed contemporary writer is St Lucia–born poet and playwright Derek Walcott, who won the 1992 Nobel Prize in literature after publishing his epic poem, *Omeros* (1990), which explores themes of exile and spiritual travel.

Another widely recognized regional author is VS Naipaul of Trinidad, who projects a sense of the Caribbean's multi-ethnic culture through the eyes of individuals struggling to make sense of their existence. His classic work, *A House for Mr Biswas* (1961), creates a vivid portrait of life as an East Indian in Trinidad. For more on Naipaul, see the Trinidad & Tobago chapter.

Derek Walcott, St Lucian poet and playwright

Similar sensibilities surface in *The Castle of My Skin* (1954), by acclaimed Barbadian author George Lamming, who presents a vivid image of coming of age as a black person in colonial Barbados.

Dominica's most celebrated author, Jean Rhys, was born in Roseau in 1890. Although she moved to England at age 16, much of her work draws upon her childhood experiences in the West Indies. Rhys touched upon her life in Dominica in *Voyage in the Dark* (1934) and in her autobiography *Smile Please* (1979). Her most famous work, *Wide Sargasso Sea,* a novel set mostly in Jamaica, was made into a film in 1993.

Jamaica Kincaid, another widely read Caribbean author, has penned numerous novels and essays, including *A Small Place* (1988), which gives a scathing account of the negative effects of tourism on Antigua. Other internationally recognized works include her novel *Annie John* (1983), which recounts growing up in Antigua, and *At the Bottom of the River* (1985), a collection of short stories. Her best-selling 1996 novel *The Autobiography of My Mother* deals with racial identity and sexual politics from the point of view of a part-Carib Dominican woman.

The leading contemporary novelist in the French West Indies is Guadeloupe native Maryse Condé. Two of her best-selling novels have been translated into English. The epic *Tree of Life* (1992) centers on the life of a Guadeloupean family, their roots and the identity of Guadeloupean society itself. Condé's 1995 novel *Crossing the Mangrove* is an enjoyable tale that reveals nuances of rural Guadeloupean relationships as it unravels the life, and untimely death, of a controversial villager.

The most renowned poet of the French West Indies was Guadeloupe's Saint-John Perse, who won the Nobel Prize for literature in 1960 for the evocative imagery of his poetry. One of his classic works, *Anabase* (1925), was translated into English by TS Eliot.

Martinique has produced two notable contemporary poets, Aimé Césaire and Édouard Glissant, both of whom write about the struggles of blacks seeking their cultural identity under the burden of colonial influences. Césaire, a poet and political figure, was a force behind the Black Pride phenomenon known as *négritude* that emerged as a philosophical and literary movement in the 1930s. His works have been translated into English under the title *The Collected Poetry of Aimé Césaire* (1983). Édouard Glissant's *Le Quatrième Siècle* (1962) and *Malemort* (1975) examine contemporary West Indian life against the backdrop of slavery.

Green Cane and Juicy Flotsam: Short Stories by Caribbean Women, edited by Carmen Esteves and Lizabeth Paravisini-Gebert, pulls together short works by Caribbean women writers, including stories by Maryse Condé and Jeanne Hyvrad about the French Caribbean and by Jean Rhys and Jamaica Kincaid about the English Caribbean.

Lookin' over at Little Tobago and Goat Island from Speyside, Tobago

Rose de porcelaine, Guadeloupe

Orchids, Martinique

Blooming hibiscus, Barbados

Poison to the touch: manchineel trees, Guadeloupe

Hangin' out with heliconia, St Lucia

Rufous-tailed jacamar, Tobago

Dominica's a great place to spot a spotted dolphin…

…and while you're there, see if you can see a sea turtle.

For iguanas, it's always Monday morning.

Why *do* they call them 'green monkeys'?

The manta ray prowls the depths around Tobago.

The Heinemann Book of Caribbean Poetry, edited by Ian McDonald and Stewart Brown, is a collection of works by English-speaking Caribbean poets, including Derek Walcott, Olive Senior, Edward Kamau Brathwaite and others.

The Traveller's Tree, by Patrick Leigh Fermor, originally published in 1950, is a classic among Caribbean travel journals. This intriguing account of Fermor's jaunt through the Lesser Antilles, Haiti, Jamaica and Cuba gives vivid descriptions of the people and places visited.

Visual Arts

The most celebrated artist to have worked in the Eastern Caribbean was Paul Gauguin, who lived on Martinique for five months in 1887.

While the modern-day Eastern Caribbean has not produced world-renowned artists, numerous native artists and expatriates paint, draw and sculpt, displaying and selling their works in island gift shops and galleries. Most Caribbean art draws upon the island environment for influence – for example, watercolors of rain-forest scenes, tropical flowers and schoolchildren are common themes.

Also ubiquitous are the distinctive folk-art paintings made in Haiti and sold throughout the Eastern Caribbean; among the items are carved and brightly painted images of tropical fish and crowded buses.

Niches of the Eastern Caribbean have their own specialized crafts. On the island of Bequia in St Vincent, boat building, both full-scale and models, has long been a regional art form. Although the hand-hewn lumber vessels that were once built along the Bequian shore have fallen victim to competition from steel-hulled boats, Bequia's shipbuilding heritage lives on through local artisans who now make a living building wooden scale models of traditional schooners and Bequian whaling boats. The model boats are crafted to exact proportions, painted in traditional colors and outfitted with sails and rigging. Popular with collectors, the finest can cost several thousand dollars.

On the island of Saba, the craft most closely identified with island life is Spanish work, or Saba lace, a drawn-thread work first introduced from South America in the 19th century. The lacelike embroidery work is high-quality, but unlike the Bequian ship models, the market for the lace is so limited that the craft is a dying art practiced only by an aging group of craftswomen.

The Caribs of Dominica still maintain their traditional crafts, including the making of dugout canoes and the weaving of quality baskets, for which they use native fibers and traditional Carib designs. The baskets are made for both domestic use and for sale to visitors. In adapting to new markets the weavers also use traditional fibers to make woven place mats, hats and pocketbooks.

Architecture

West Indian architecture is a blending of European tradition and tropical design. When European settlers moved to the islands, they tended to build cities in grid patterns, with houses in orderly rows. Many in-town buildings are substantial two-story structures of stone and wood. Houses are often painted in bright colors such as turquoise, lime, pink and yellow. Peaked corrugated iron roofs that turn a rusty red add a distinctive element, as does frilly architecture such as gingerbread trim, veranda latticework and wooden shutters.

SOCIETY & CONDUCT
Traditional Culture

Because the Eastern Caribbean is so diverse, there are many variations in local customs and lifestyles. The French West Indies are essentially provincial outposts of France, with French language, customs and cuisine predominating. Some of these islands, like St Barts and Terre-de-Haut (off Guadeloupe), retain a character that approximates that of rural France, while others, such as Guadeloupe and Martinique, have a more dominant French Creole culture that strongly reflects African influences.

On the islands with a British past, cultural influences largely represent a mix of African and British heritage. The latter

Caribbean Arts & Crafts

Art and culture along the Eastern Caribbean chain have many influences: African, English, French, Dutch, Spanish, Indian and American. Add the unusual architecture, gorgeous scenery, flora and fauna, and there is no end to inspiration for creativity. Many recognized talents had humble beginnings on their native islands, gained international recognition and continue to create at home.

Craft markets, cruise-pier stalls and beach vendors often sell the same merchandise. They're nice mementos, but the Caribbean harbors so much talent that it's worth a deeper look. So pass by those 'made in Taiwan' items and woven palm hats (which turn brown back home). We'll lead you to more lasting souvenirs indigenous to each island.

Anguilla Female artists are making a splash on the burgeoning art scene. Several taxi drivers do gallery tours, where often the building itself (quaint cottage to historic home) represents an art form. Sculptures by local icons Courtney Devonish and Cheddie Richardson are in demand.

Antigua Since several varieties of clay make up Antiguan soil, potters rule. At many locations, visitors observe the molding of bird feeders, wind chimes and unique lamps. Wood carvings appear as busts of heroes and celebrities. Explore Harmony Hall's gallery and gift shop for gaily painted mobiles and batik cards. Maybe you'll spot an original Annette Platts candelabra, created from disparate objects collected on the beach.

Barbados Excellent road signage leads to several potteries, where visitors follow dinner plates, vases and bowls through each stage of creation. Quaint shopping 'villages' display sophisticated carvings, sculptures, batik and tie-dyed clothes, plus straw craft by top local designer Ireka, including mats, boxes and elaborate baskets. Chattel houses, uniquely Bajan, are copied in wall plaques, light-switch plates or miniatures.

Dominica The most popular craft souvenirs on Dominica are woven baskets, mats and hats from the Carib territory. You'll find them at all the waterfront souvenir stands in Roseau, and at roadside shacks in the territory on the east coast of the island. Dominica is also a good place to pick up brightly colored Creole clothing.

Grenada The isle of Grenada is known as the Spice Island for good reason. As the scent of nutmeg permeates the air, you'll be drawn to perky packages containing spices in raw form, candied, or as jams. Many are attractively arranged in woven baskets, complete with tiny graters. Spice necklaces (US$2 to US$5) make great sachets. The open market is headquarters, but they're sold everywhere.

Guadeloupe The elaborate Fête des Cuisinières in August honors this island's fabulous female cooks, who parade in Creole costume. Feast on their rich dishes, dance and party. Artwork – in sand, clay, plastic and wood – reflects these colorful people. Buy a French Creole doll clad in bright island madras, or jewelry made from calabash and bamboo.

Martinique This island is French-speaking, but true-blue to its own history. Start with its museums to really appreciate artisans' creativity. In one, seashell art depicts sugarcane harvesters, red Carnival devils, gum-tree canoes and similar lifestyle scenes. Another features artist Will

Caribbean Arts & Crafts

Fenton's dolls, wearing authentic dress made entirely out of local plants. Arawak-style pottery, and wickerwork using ancient Carib techniques, are other choices.

Saba Hardy women settlers on this rock are accomplished lace makers, a talent they perfected when their men were away at sea. Whatever can be made in delicate lace, they've made it. If something you want is not there, just ask, and more than likely your very own souvenir will fly from their spools in quick order. Saban spices are also popular.

St Bart's On this sophisticated island, most gift items and wares come from someplace else, featuring everything French, of course. The women of Corrosol still uphold the tradition of straw weaving.

St Kitts & Nevis Caribelle Batik is not the only clothing game in town, although it's a worthy one. John Warden's designer clothes in dashing prints are hot items. Add a gorgeous silk scarf or tie by Kate Spencer, plus a Dale Isaac creative hat, and your outfit is totally Kittitian. Stylish Nevis pottery reflects methods handed down from both Arawaks and Caribs. Easy travelers include island cookbooks and local brown sugar packed in special bags.

St Lucia The top carver is Endovic, and Bagshaw's is the leader in silk-screened clothes. Caribbean markets are a melange of unfamiliar roots and fruits, but Castries Market is a cut above, mixing food, crafts and essentials. Crafters from the onetime Peace Corps school in Choiseul sell primitive but creative pieces. Miniature coal pots (for incense), lacquered boxes and shell picture frames – it's browsing at its best.

St Martin Works in Dutch-side galleries are mainly by French-side artists, a prolific group. Examine the one-of-a-kind cocoa-pod masks with African/Asian influence, flowing sarongs (called 'surrounds') and vases painted so beautifully, you'd never guess they are calabash gourds. Internationally renowned Roland Richardson's gallery is in the St. Martin home where he was born. He's often seen at his easel in the garden.

St Vincent & the Grenadines These islands (especially Bequia) have become a haven for expatriate artists, but local talent persists. Vincentian Dinks Johnson paints homeland scenes with authority. Unusual jewelry is fashioned from rocks gathered at St. Vincent's volcano. The Arts & Crafts Center features handwoven straw goods in colorful patterns. And Bequia's boat builders create miniature models sporting that oddly shaped sail.

Trinidad & Tobago These two islands constitute the birthplace of the famous steel pan, or steel drum, which is now heard around the world. Steel drums come in all sizes – remember that, while the possibilities are endless, your luggage space probably isn't! Don't forget CDs, pod jewelry from tropical trees, Indian chutneys and other food souvenirs emanating from Trinidad's astounding ethnic mix. On tiny Tobago, Cotton House sells batik cloth and demonstrates the art. Mokatika resembles Kahlua but costs less. Stock up on Forro's jellies, jams and hot sauces made in Eileen Forester's kitchen. Life-size cutouts depicting African heritage are great visuals, but alas, they're too big for the suitcase.

– Eleanor M Wilson

predominates in institutional ways, including the form of government, education and the legal framework of the islands. African influences remain strong in music, dance and family life.

Throughout the Caribbean, there tend to be clear divisions of labor along gender lines: Most of the hundreds of vendors in the marketplace are women, most of the taxi and minibus drivers are men.

Cricket is the region's most popular sport, and a number of world-class cricket players have hailed from the Eastern Caribbean. (The West Indies squad has unfortunately fallen on hard times lately, but hope springs eternal among their many fans.) Soccer is also very popular, especially on the French islands.

Most islanders dress neatly. Women's clothing is conservative and rather old-fashioned on some islands, smartly chic on others. Many women vendors in the marketplaces wear matronly dresses and tie up their hair in kerchiefs, while women who work in offices are apt to wear high heels, frosted lipsticks and the latest fashions. Generally, the smaller and more rural the island, the more casual the dress.

Dos & Don'ts

Keep in mind that the tropical climate slows things down and most islanders take life at an easygoing pace, so don't expect things to run like clockwork. Whether you're changing money, having a meal or catching a flight at the airport, always allow plenty of time.

Throughout the Caribbean, neatness in dress and politeness in attitude goes a long way. As a rule, bathing suits, very short shorts and other skimpy clothing should not be worn in town or other nonbeach areas – this holds true even on the French islands, where topless bathing is de rigueur on the beach.

Always start with 'Good day' or 'Bonjour' before launching into a conversation or abruptly asking questions; you'll find that a smile and a courteous attitude go a long way. Many people, especially vendors in the marketplaces, do not like to be photographed; ask first, and respect the wishes of those who refuse.

RELIGION

Roman Catholicism is the dominant religion in the French islands, Protestantism on most of the English and Dutch islands.

There are also Afro-Christian religions. Rastafarianism, which developed in Jamaica in the 1920s and has spread throughout the Eastern Caribbean and around the world, is based on an unorthodox interpretation of the Old Testament which holds that the lineage of Biblical prophets descends from Ham, the African son of Noah, to Haile Selassie, the deposed emperor of Ethiopia (whose precoronation name, Ras Tafari, gives the new belief its name). Influenced by Marcus Garvey's back-to-Africa movement, Rastafarians believe that after centuries of bondage in a foreign land their destiny is exodus and repatriation.

In addition to following strict dietary regimens, Rastafarians usually grow their hair into long, ropey dreadlocks, sport red, gold

Common Colloquialisms

Here are some popular colloquialisms heard in the Eastern Caribbean:

boy, girl – terms commonly used by islanders when casually addressing adults as well as children
fire a grog, fire one – to drink rum
go so, swing so – terms used in giving directions (be sure to watch the hand movements!)
limin' (also 'lime,' 'lime about') – lazing about, hang with friends and pass the time with small talk
natty – dreadlocks, also called *natty dread*
no problem – all-purpose response to any request
one time – immediately, right away
roots – communal experience, or coming from the people
study – to take time to consider, think about
wine – sensuous dance movement winding the hips, essential to Carnival dancing
workin' up – dancing in general

and green clothing and smoke ganja (marijuana) as a sacrament.

Rastafarianism has played an important role in the development of ska and reggae music, whose rhythm is influenced by the Rastafarian *akete* drum.

Some islanders believe in *obeah,* which is not a religion per se but rather embodies a type of black magic used to cast spells on one's enemy. Similar to Haitian voodoo practices, obeah uses conjurations, sorcery and magical rituals to align supernatural forces. Despite centuries of repression by Christian forces, the practice of obeah continues to some extent on most Eastern Caribbean islands, although often in secret.

Hinduism or Islam are the faiths of about 30% of the population of Trinidad; these religions also have followings on other islands (such as Guadeloupe), where there are sizable minorities of East Indians.

LANGUAGE

English is the main language spoken on all the islands in the Eastern Caribbean except for the French West Indies (Guadeloupe, Martinique, St Barts and the French side of St Martin), where French is the primary language.

English-speakers can travel throughout the Eastern Caribbean without major problems. The difficulty of getting around the French West Indies for those travelers who do not speak French is generally exaggerated. Although many people outside the hotel and tourism industry don't speak English, as long as you have an English-French dictionary and phrasebook, a measure of patience and a sense of humor you should be able to get by.

Dutch is spoken on Saba, St Eustatius and Dutch Sint Maarten (the south side of St Martin), and is the official language of government on those islands. However, for most practical purposes Dutch is a secondary language after English.

On many Eastern Caribbean islands the local language is Creole, a complex patois of French, English, and West African languages with remnants of Carib. In addition, Hindi is spoken among family members on islands with sizable Indian populations, most notably on Trinidad.

MUSIC OF THE EASTERN CARIBBEAN

Although much of the artistic output of the Caribbean remains a well-kept secret, many of the region's musical exports have become familiar sounds. Cuban and Puerto Rican salsa and rumba are enjoying comebacks, though they've never really been away, and Jamaican reggae is heard around the world. From Harry Belafonte's 'Banana Boat Song' to the Baha Men singing 'Who Let the Dogs Out?' Caribbean music has regularly made the international charts.

The islands of the Eastern Caribbean are home to a variety of musical forms, some instantly recognizable to the visitor, others little-known outside their home islands. Steel pan and calypso, zouk and cadence – the names may not be familiar, but the music is everywhere. Nightclubs pack in locals and visitors until the wee hours, and in many towns street parties roll all night long. Minibuses blast the radio or favorite reggae tapes, while the passengers sing along. Groups of old men sit in front of stores and rum shops playing the hits of years past, smilingly asking for a little change. And every fancy hotel bar features some kind of combo working their version of 'No Woman, No Cry.'

While styles and trends vary from island to island, some things are true of music throughout the Caribbean.

All Caribbean music, from steel pan to samba to dub, is percussion-based, heavily influenced by the rhythmic traditions rooted in West Africa. Typically, African slaves were not allowed to openly use the language and customs of their homelands, but were permitted or even encouraged to keep their music and dances. As a result, music became a repository of African language and oral history, even as European and African music blended into new styles. To this day, Caribbean music retains West African words, melodies and beats.

Lyrically, the music has encompassed a wide range of topics, but, through the years and across all the islands, two main themes prevail: social commentary and sex.

A lot of Caribbean music is deeply political, covering everything from the evils of colonialism and social inequality to the specific pros and cons of local candidates. Throughout the Caribbean popular artists have been censored for singing hit songs ridiculing unpopular governments. Reggae and calypso are particularly well known for being protest music (albeit protest music with a catchy beat).

Then there's sex. Caribbean music is often described as 'sensual' or 'sultry,' and is usually meant for couples to dance to. Many songs are straightforwardly all about it, with lyrics ranging from the clever risqué innuendo and double entendres of calypso and soca to the explicit boasting of modern dancehall.

Each island has its own vocabulary for the musical styles currently in fashion. Ask around and people will gladly tell you more about Caribbean music; it's a favorite topic of conversation. The following are some of the major styles of music commonly heard in the Eastern Caribbean.

Beguine The beguine arose in the mid-1850s in Saint-Pierre, then the capital of Martinique, a bustling French town known as the 'Paris of the Antilles.' As groups of slaves performed European dance music like the quadrille and the mazurka, they infused it with African rhythms and percussion instruments, creating a uniquely Caribbean music style and dance, which became first a scandal and then a sensation among French plantation society.

MICHAEL LAWRENCE

After the volcanic destruction of Saint-Pierre in 1902, many musicians headed north, where beguine met another Afro-European hybrid, the emerging jazz music of New Orleans. A jazz-influenced beguine enjoyed another wave of popularity in France and the French Caribbean in the 1930s and '40s. Though still performed by big bands and dance orchestras, beguine today is more of an historical artifact than a living dance form, though its influence on current music, particularly zouk, is evident.

Zouk The music of Guadeloupe and Martinique today is zouk, a snappy dance rhythm influenced equally by the African-derived *gwo-ka* and the colonial beguine. The words are often in Creole and usually focus on love, lost loves and the timeless question of who to dance with, with some social commentary on the side. A style of zouk called 'le slow' or 'zouk-love' is an opportunity for some dirty dancing, ranging from the politely suggestive to the full bump-and-grind affair.

Above: Carnival in Domininca

You're not likely to hear zouk on your local radio station, and even in the Caribbean it hasn't really caught on outside the French islands, but it has become a nightclub sensation in mainland France. It's even made its way back to West and Central Africa, where the zouk, and the zouk-love, are dance-floor favorites.

Easily the biggest name in zouk is the band Kassav', currently based in Paris, although they still make occasional tours of the Caribbean. Their recorded music often strikes newcomers as slick and over-produced, but their live shows are powerful spectacles of song, dance and Creole heritage, and are not to be missed.

Calypso Trinidad and Tobago's biggest gift to the world of music, calypso is inseparably linked to Carnival, the islands' annual pre-Lent bash.(For more about Carnival, see the Trinidad & Tobago chapter.)

Originally sung in French Creole (to keep the meaning of the words secret from the British plantation owners), calypso has become an exercise in rhetoric and creativity with the English language, replete with nonsense words and vexacious rhymes. Lyrically, calypso pushes the boundaries of polite Caribbean society, with songs about sexual misbehavior and political shenanigans. (Any opportunity to combine the two is gleefully taken; you'd be amazed how many words rhyme with 'Lewinsky.')

Calypso has also evolved into an annual Carnival competition, as judges score the live performances of calypsonians, based on their originality, topicality and success at working the crowd. Each year's Carnival has its own specific theme, which must be incorporated into the contenders for that year's top songs. Polite but brutal put-downs of the other competitors is always part of the game. To be king or queen of Carnival is one of the highest honors in Trinidad.

Some of calypso's biggest artists have stayed in the spotlight for decades, from the breakout years of the '30s and '40s to the present. The Mighty Sparrow continues to put out the big hits, as he has since the '50s. Sadly, one of calypso's most enduring and beloved singers, Lord Kitchener, passed away in February 2001 after several decades at the top.

Calypso is continuously evolving and incorporating new sounds. Soca has been popular for years; more recent innovations include rapso, a mix of rap and calypso, and chutney, with Hindi songs set to a calypso beat, a contribution from Trinidad and Tobago's Indian population.

Soca A mix of soul and calypso, soca is dance music, less lyric-oriented and political than standard calypso. It's all about *winin'*, the popular Caribbean bump-and-grind dance. The big names in soca are Arrow and Ras Shorty, who is generally credited with inventing soca in the late '70s.

Steel Drum The steel drum, or pan, is a perfect example of Caribbean ingenuity and syncretism. While British authorities in Trinidad and Tobago tried to stifle Carnival by banning African drums, islanders kept the beat on whatever was available, including the plentiful empty oil drums. Eventually, amateur inventors were heating, bending and crimping the concave tops of the drums to create as many as 20 distinct notes from what had previously been a piece of garbage.

Today, steel-drum bands are a staple of Caribbean music, from cheesy hotel bands doing Jimmy Buffet covers to gangs of schoolkids practicing in deserted lots.

Reggae Born in Jamaica, reggae emerged in the early 1960s from West African rhythms combined with ska and mento, as well as a big dose of soul from the US. Reggae music came from the poorest quarters of the island, and addressed previously taboo topics of race, class and colonialism. As the influence of Rastafarianism grew, lyrics focused more on apocalyptic Biblical themes, the back-to-Africa movement of Marcus Garvey, and the legalization of ganja (marijuana).

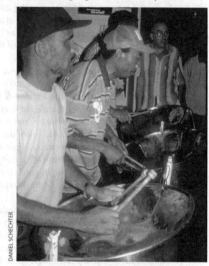

DANIEL SCHECHTER

While numerous artists were making reggae big in Jamaica, the Wailers took reggae international. The original Wailers – Bob Marley, Peter Tosh and Bunny Livingston – started singing together as teenagers and went on to become world famous. After Tosh and Livingston dropped out, the reconfigured Bob Marley and the Wailers toured extensively, introducing millions of people to their Caribbean sounds. Bob Marley died of cancer in 1981, but remains the biggest name in reggae. His music is still heard all over the Caribbean, and much of the world.

Except in the French islands, where zouk holds sway, and Trinidad and Tobago, land of calypso, reggae – although less popular among the young than dancehall – is the music of choice in the Eastern Caribbean, heard in buses, bars, nightclubs, markets and anywhere there's a tape deck.

Ska A Jamaican precursor to reggae, ska first hit the scene in the 1950s, and has come back in popularity in several successive waves. Ska is known for its choppy, insistent beat, and often features horn sections.

Dub Another Jamaican import, dub music was originally another Caribbean effort to make more out of less. Record producers remix the rhythm tracks of every hit reggae single over and over, adding whatever effects they could produce in their studios.

Above: A steel-pan band on Trinidad

Singers, sometimes the producers themselves, chant new words over the tracks, boasting (or *toasting* themselves) in competitions. Some dub artists focus on stoney effects, while others like Mutabaruka, add socially conscious meditations to create dub poetry.

Dancehall Originally a product of Jamaican dub and raggamuffin (a lyric-heavy style popular with Jamaican street youth), much of what is now called 'dancehall' is deeply influenced by American rap and R&B. The beats are heavy and mechanical, and the singing can be tongue-twistingly fast. Dancehall has a reputation for lyrics that glorify violence and other bad behavior, but there's a lot of harmless fun as well.

Regional Facts for the Visitor

HIGHLIGHTS

So many islands, so little time! While all of the Eastern Caribbean can provide the fantasy getaway to paradise, complete with frothy drinks on the beach, snorkeling by day and dancing at night, there's a wide variety in terms of historic attractions, scenic parks, local flavor and degree of luxury. Dig in to the individual chapters for details, but start with this handy and subjective list of bests.

Beaches

Anguilla's Shoal Bay East – one of the Caribbean's finest

Grenada's Grand Anse Beach – vast stretches of white sands

Les Salines on Martinique – the spot where *tout le monde* comes to see and be seen

St Martin's Orient Beach – the place to nude up and go!

Nightlife

St Lucia – Friday night jump-ups in the streets, for locals and visitors alike

Trinidad – Carnival, the Caribbean's biggest party

Seclusion

Bequia (and most of the other Grenadines, for that matter) – the place for solitary bliss

Guadeloupe's outer islands – the spot where you're on your own after the day-trippers leave

St Barts – the island tailor-made for getting away from it all

Diving & Snorkeling

Dominica – wild and woolly paradise, with new sites being explored

Saba – an extensive marine park

Wildlife

Trinidad & Tobago – the unmatched Eastern Caribbean destination for bird and animal viewing

Hiking

Dominica – a lush interior of rain forest, waterfalls and a boiling lake

Montserrat – a smoldering volcano

Sports

Barbados – the cricket-mad island, and proud of it!

History

Antigua – Nelson's Dockyard, an 18th-century naval base that's still a working harbor

Martinique – the ruins of Saint-Pierre, destroyed by a volcano in 1902

Statia – colonial houses and historic forts

St Kitts & Nevis – restored plantation estates and sugar mills

Local flavor

Saba – a low-key, friendly and untouristed destination

Guadeloupe – authentic Creole culture with distinct language and music

Living it up

Mustique – the place where if you have to ask, you can't afford it

St Barts – playground of the French and famous

SUGGESTED ITINERARIES

Since the Eastern Caribbean encompasses a wide variety of destinations, whatever itinerary you plan will depend on your specific interests and the time you have available.

Someone looking at a weeklong vacation may well opt to spend their time on just one island or select a destination, such as Guadeloupe or St Martin, that allow easy access for day trips to nearby islands. With a couple of weeks or more, travelers can begin to do some serious island hopping. LIAT, the main interisland air carrier, offers a tempting 21-day air pass that allows unlimited travel throughout the region, letting you select from all the major islands and a number of the smaller ones as well.

Yachters likewise have a wide variety of islands to choose from. Some of the most popular sailing is found in the Grenadines, where there are protected waters and a plethora of idyllic little isles and cays. Charter operations from Antigua to Grenada make it easy to arrange your own bareboat cruise, and you can even rent the boat just one-way, picking up the yacht at one end of the chain and dropping it off at the other. See the Yacht section in the Getting Around the Region chapter for more information.

PLANNING
When to Go

The busiest time for travel in the Eastern Caribbean is mid-December to mid-April. Although this period does have drier and slightly cooler weather, the principal variable in making it the high season is the weather *elsewhere,* as the bulk of Caribbean tourists are 'snowbirds' escaping colder weather in North America and Europe.

You can enjoy dramatically discounted 'summer' hotel prices by visiting the islands in the low season, mid-April to mid-December. In addition, most airfares to the Caribbean are cheaper during this period, the beaches are less crowded, tourist areas have a more relaxed pace and last-minute bookings for cars, flights and hotels are seldom a problem.

On the minus side, the trade winds aren't as prevalent in summer, so the chance of encountering oppressively muggy weather is higher. Summer is also the hurricane season, though the odds of encountering a hurricane on any particular island aren't much higher than they would be along the southern portion of the US east coast.

November and early December can be a pleasant time to visit. Many hotels take a late-summer break to spruce up, so their rooms are at their preseason finest, the crowds are just beginning to show and the prices are still low.

Maps

Island tourist offices typically provide free tourist maps that will suffice for most visitor needs. Travelers who intend to explore an island thoroughly may want something more detailed.

On the former British islands, British Ordnance Survey maps are generally the best maps available. They show topography and the location of colonial ruins and the like, although they're not always up-to-date. On the French islands, the Institut Géographique National (IGN) maps are very detailed and updated frequently. Both types of maps can be bought at bookstores in the Eastern Caribbean.

In addition, Ordnance Survey and IGN maps can be obtained via the Internet or by mail-order from any of the following establishments:

France
Espace IGN (☎ 0143-98 80 00, www.ign.fr) 107 Rue La Boétie, 75008 Paris

UK
Ordnance Survey International (☎ 023-8079 2912, fax 023-8079 2615, www.ordsvy.gov.uk) Romsey Rd, Southampton S016 4GU
Stanfords (☎ 020-7836 1321, fax 020-7836 0189, www.stanfords.co.uk) 12–14 Long Acre, London WC2E 9LP

USA
Map Link (☎ 805-692-6777, 800-962-1394, fax 800-627-7768, www.maplink.com) 30 S La Patera Lane, Suite 5, Goleta, CA 93117

For information on marine charts, see the Yacht section in the Getting Around the Region chapter.

What to Bring

Traveling light, a good policy anywhere, is easy in the tropics as heavy jackets and bulky clothing are totally unnecessary.

Ideal clothes are made of cotton (which breathes best in hot, humid weather), are loose-fitting and don't need to be tucked in, and can be hand washed in a sink and hung up to dry without wrinkling.

Dress in the Eastern Caribbean is casual. Sportswear, including shorts and neat T-shirts, is fine during the day in most places. For dinner at nice restaurants, a cotton dress for women and lightweight slacks for men are usually sufficient. Only a few top-end restaurants expect men to wear a jacket and tie. Casinos usually have dress codes, but as long as you're presentable this usually boils down to no T-shirts, bathing suits or sneakers. One long-sleeved shirt, lightweight cotton jacket or windbreaker might be useful against indoor air-con and outdoor insects. You'll probably spend most of your time in sandals, but bring footwear with good traction if you're planning on hiking.

A flashlight is good to have on hand for the occasional power blackout and to walk in certain areas at night. Bird watchers should bring along binoculars. A Swiss Army knife is always worth its weight in gold. If you plan to do a lot of snorkeling, you'll save money by bringing your own snorkeling gear, though rentals are readily available in resort areas. You might want to consider a passport pouch or money belt to wear around your neck or waist.

Resealable plastic sandwich bags in a couple of sizes are indispensable for keeping things dry. You can use them to protect your film and camera equipment, seal up airline tickets and passports, and keep wet bathing suits away from the rest of your luggage.

A one-cup immersion heater, usually available for a few dollars from hardware or department stores, and a durable lightweight cup can come in handy. Not only can you boil water and make coffee and tea in your room, but you can also use them to make up a quick meal if you carry a few packets of instant oatmeal, soup, noodles or the like.

Medical supplies and toiletries are available in most places, though on the smaller islands the selection may be limited. See the Health section, later in this chapter, for some suggestions on medical-related items to bring.

Those who don't speak French and are planning to visit Guadeloupe, Martinique, St Barts or St Martin should refer to the Language section at the back of this guide. You may also consider taking along an English-French dictionary and phrasebook.

RESPONSIBLE TOURISM

Visitors to the Caribbean can minimize their impact on the local culture and environment by booking tours with local agencies, which are often regulated by the national tourist bureaus or park departments.

Souvenirs made of coral, seashell and even turtle shell are still sold on some of the islands, but visitors should steer clear of them because of the effect on the environment and the potential fines for attempting to import them back home. The removal of coral, in particular, poses a real threat to the underwater ecosystem. For more information, see 'Things Not to Buy,' later in this chapter.

VISAS & DOCUMENTS

Passport and visa requirements vary from island to island; specific information is given in the individual island chapters.

Note that upon arrival at many islands, the immigration officer will ask how long you're staying and stamp that exact number of days in your passport or on your entry card. Give yourself plenty of leeway, so that if you stay longer than originally planned you won't need to make a special trip to the immigration office or the police station for an extension. Another question commonly asked by the immigration officer is where you will be staying; always have the name of a hotel in mind, even if you don't end up staying there.

One more thing to keep in mind as you travel throughout the region is that many islands require visitors to be in possession of either an onward or roundtrip ticket. As part of this policy, LIAT and other regional airlines often won't allow you to board a flight to

---

Onward & Upward?

While some islands may be lax about enforcing the onward-ticket requirement for entry, we've had reports of travelers enduring substantial frustration over this matter, ranging from fines to threats of imprisonment. It's best to make sure that you have proof of onward passage (or sufficient funds to pay for an onward ticket on the spot) before entering any of the islands.

an island unless you're in possession of an onward ticket off of that island. The same is true, in principle, for interisland ferry services.

Travel Insurance

A travel insurance policy to cover theft, loss and medical problems is a wise idea. There are a wide variety of policies, and your travel agent will have recommendations. Check the fine print, as some policies exclude 'dangerous activities' such as scuba diving, motorcycling and even trekking.

Give serious consideration to a policy that covers emergency flights. Many islands in the Eastern Caribbean are not prepared to handle complicated medical problems, so for something serious a flight home may be the best option. In addition, some of the smaller islands have very limited or no medical facilities, and medevac (medical evacuation) to a larger island (or Miami) is commonplace.

Driver's License & Permits

You'll need your driver's license in order to rent a car. On most of the former British islands, you'll need to purchase a local license when you rent a car, but that's done simply by showing your home license and dishing out the appropriate fee. If you're going to St Lucia, having an International Driving Permit (IDP) will save you the price of a local license there, but on the other islands there's no benefit to having an IDP in addition to your home license.

Other Documents

Divers should bring their certification cards. Those who are members of a National Trust in one of the Commonwealth countries should bring their membership card to gain free or discounted entry to Barbados' National Trust sites. If you have a student or youth card, bring it along, though discounts in the Caribbean are very limited.

An International Health Certificate is required only if you're coming from a country where yellow fever is a problem.

Copies

All important documents (passport data page and visa page, credit cards, travel insurance policy, air tickets, driver's license etc) should be photocopied before you leave home. Leave one copy with someone at home and keep another with you, separate from the originals.

It's also a good idea to store details of your vital travel documents in Lonely Planet's free online Travel Vault in case you lose the photocopies or can't be bothered with them. Your password-protected Travel Vault is accessible online anywhere in the world – create it at www.ekno.lonelyplanet.com.

EMBASSIES & CONSULATES

It's important to realize what your own embassy – the embassy of the country of which you are a citizen – can and can't do to help you if you get into trouble. Generally speaking, it won't be much help in emergencies if the trouble you're in is remotely your own fault. Remember that you are bound by the laws of the country you are in. Your embassy will not be sympathetic if you end up in jail after committing a crime locally, even if such actions are legal in your own country.

In genuine emergencies you might get some assistance, but only if other channels have been exhausted. For example, if you need to get home urgently, a free ticket is exceedingly unlikely – the embassy would expect you to have insurance. If you have all your money and documents stolen, it might assist with getting a new passport, but a loan for onward travel is out of the question.

Some embassies used to keep letters for travelers or have a small reading room with home newspapers, but these days, the mail-holding service has usually been stopped, and even newspapers tend to be out-of-date.

Not all of the Eastern Caribbean nations have diplomatic representation. For the French islands of Guadeloupe, Martinique, St Barts and French St Martin contact the French embassy in your country for visas and information. See the individual island chapters for more information.

CUSTOMS

All islands in the Eastern Caribbean allow tourists to bring in a reasonable amount of personal items duty-free, as well as an allowance of liquor and tobacco. For more details, see the individual island chapters.

Spearguns are prohibited in the waters around many islands; divers interested in spearfishing should make advance inquiries. Most non-French islands prohibit firearms; yachters who have guns on board should declare them on entry. Some islands are free of rabies and have strict rules on the importation of animals; this is mainly of interest to sailors, who might not be allowed to bring their pets onto land.

MONEY
Currencies & Exchange Rates
There are five official currencies in the Eastern Caribbean, which can make things a bit confusing if you're jumping back and forth between islands. Fortunately, the US dollar (US$) can also be used outright on virtually all the islands and is by far the handiest currency to carry. Indeed, many Eastern Caribbean islands quote hotel prices and car rentals in US dollars. However, for most transactions you'll be better off exchanging your money into the local currency. British sterling (UK£) and Canadian dollars (C$) can also be readily exchanged at banks but are not commonly accepted by businesses.

Eastern Caribbean Dollar The Eastern Caribbean dollar (EC$) is the official currency of Anguilla, Antigua & Barbuda, Dominica, Grenada, Montserrat, St Kitts & Nevis, St Lucia and St Vincent & the Grenadines. One dollar is worth 100 cents. Coins are in denominations of 1, 2, 5, 10 and 25 cents and EC$1. Bank notes are in 5-, 10-, 20-, 50- and 100-dollar denominations.

The EC$ is pegged to the US$ at a rate of US$1=EC$2.70. The exchange rate given by banks (on islands where the EC$ is the official currency) is US$1=EC$2.6882 for traveler's checks and US$1=EC$2.67 for cash. If you have leftover EC dollars, you can sell them back at the rate of EC$2.7169=US$1.

When exchanging UK£ or C$ against EC$ there's a greater variation between buying and selling rates than there is for the

US$. The margin between buying and selling is about 2% for sterling and nearly 5% for Canadian dollars. Other foreign currencies are generally treated as an oddity and exchanged at below-market rates or slapped with hefty surcharges.

Major currencies fluctuate against the EC$ in accordance with their value against the US$ on world markets. As we go to print, the current rates of exchange for the EC$ are as follows:

country	units		EC dollars
Australia	A$1	=	EC$1.40
Canada	C$1	=	EC$1.74
Euro	€1	=	EC$2.31
Japan	¥100	=	EC$2.25
Mexico	10 pesos	=	EC$2.98
New Zealand	NZ$1	=	EC$1.13
United Kingdom	UK£1	=	EC$3.83
United States	US$1	=	EC$2.70

French Franc The French franc (F) is the official currency of Guadeloupe, Martinique, St Barts and the French side of St Martin. One franc is worth 100 centimes. French coins come in denominations of 5, 10, 20 and 50 centimes and 1, 2, 5 and 10

A Toss of the Coin

Theoretically, by the end of February 2002 the French franc and Dutch guilder will be withdrawn from use and the transition to the euro – at least in Europe – will be complete. What this means for the islands of the Eastern Caribbean is not entirely clear, but it's possible that the French West Indies and the Netherlands Antilles will not follow their distant relations quite so promptly, and that the multiplicity of currencies (including the French franc and Netherlands Antilles guilder) will continue to circulate.

The euro is pegged at a standard exchange rate:

€1=6.56F
€1=Fls 1.6

francs. Bank notes are issued in denominations of 20, 50, 100, 200 and 500 francs.

In early 2002, the French franc is scheduled to be eliminated as a currency and replaced with the euro. Please see 'A Toss of the Coin' for details.

The French franc fluctuates daily with other currencies according to world markets. As we go to print, the current rates of exchange are as follows:

country	units		francs
Australia	A$1	=	3.96F
Canada	C$1	=	4.94F
Euro	€1	=	6.56F
Japan	¥100	=	6.39F
Mexico	10 pesos	=	8.45F
New Zealand	NZ$1	=	3.22F
United Kingdom	UK£1	=	10.86F
United States	US$1	=	7.66F

Netherlands Antilles Guilder The Netherlands Antilles guilder or florin (commonly written 'NAf' at banks and 'Fls' in stores) is the official currency of Saba, St Eustatius and Sint Maarten (the Dutch side of St Martin).

The Netherlands Antilles guilder, which differs from the guilder used in the Netherlands, has coins in denominations of 1, 5, 10, 25 and 50 cents as well as 1 and 2½ guilders; bank notes are in 5, 10, 25, 50, 100, 250 and 500 Fls. 'Fls 10.50' is spoken '10 guilders 50.'

On the Dutch islands, locals commonly carry both guilders and US dollars; businesses accept and give change in either. As there's no advantage to paying in guilders (and there's a small loss when exchanging money), most visitors simply use US dollars.

In early 2002, the Dutch guilder is scheduled to be replaced by the euro. What this means for the Netherlands Antilles guilder is unclear. Please see 'A Toss of the Coin' for details.

The Netherlands Antilles guilder is pegged to the US dollar. The exchange rate for cash is US$1=Fls 1.77; for traveler's checks it's US$1=Fls 1.79.

Other major currencies fluctuate in accordance with their value with the US dollar in world markets. As we go to print, the current rates of exchange are as follows:

country	units		guilders
Australia	A$1	=	Fls 0.92
Canada	C$1	=	Fls 1.15
Euro	€1	=	Fls 1.52
Japan	¥100	=	Fls 1.48
Mexico	10 pesos	=	Fls 1.96
New Zealand	NZ$1	=	Fls 0.75
United Kingdom	UK£1	=	Fls 2.53
United States	US$1	=	Fls 1.78

Barbados Dollar The Barbados dollar (B$) is the official currency of Barbados. For details, see in the Barbados chapter.

Trinidad & Tobago Dollar The Trinidad & Tobago dollar (TT$) is the official currency of that two-island nation. For details, see the Trinidad & Tobago chapter.

ATMs
Automatic teller machines (ATMs) can be found on most islands throughout the region. For those who want to withdraw money from a bank account back home, ATM cards from the two main networks – Cirrus and Plus – are accepted at many ATMs, including all of those operated by the Royal Bank of Canada.

Credit Cards
Major credit cards are widely, though not universally, accepted throughout the Eastern Caribbean. The most commonly accepted cards are Visa and MasterCard, followed by American Express. Note that on some islands, hotels may add a surcharge if you're using a credit card, so you might want to inquire in advance.

Costs
Overall, the Eastern Caribbean is a fairly expensive region and you'll need a tidy sum to explore it thoroughly. Still, costs can vary greatly depending upon which islands you

visit, the type of accommodations you choose and how you travel.

Accommodations will generally be the heftiest part of your budget. On islands such as Barbados, which has a good range of low- and mid-priced accommodations, expenses for a conventional hotel room or apartment can be quite reasonable, whereas on pricier islands like Antigua it could easily cost twice as much for a comparable room. Of course the type of accommodations will also dictate cost – daily rates can vary from US$25 or less at a cheap guest house to US$1000 at an exclusive resort.

Food is relatively expensive, in part because much of it is imported – prices are generally a good 50% higher than in the USA or Canada.

Transportation costs vary greatly. Car rentals generally cost between US$30 and US$70 a day depending upon the island. On the more developed islands there are public buses that provide a very cheap alternative for getting around.

For interisland travel, there are some reasonably priced ferries, mostly in the Grenadines and around the French islands. Air travel between islands can be expensive, but there are numerous deals floating around, including air passes with LIAT (the main regional airline) that can take you to a few islands for as little as US$262. See the Getting Around the Region chapter for details.

There are also some little nagging costs that can add up quickly, particularly if you're island hopping. On most of the English-speaking islands, car renters are required to buy a temporary local driver's license, which ranges from US$10 to US$15; most islands have airport – and sometimes boat – departure taxes, commonly from US$10 to US$40; and many add tax and service charges (up to 25%) on top of quoted hotel rates and sometimes onto restaurant bills as well.

If you're buying air tickets in the Caribbean, try to buy them on a tax-free island, such as St Martin, as many Eastern Caribbean islands add 5% to 20% sales or value-added tax (VAT) to ticket sales.

Tipping & Bargaining

The tipping situation varies. On some islands it's automatically added to your restaurant bill as a service charge, while on other islands you're expected to add a tip of about 10% to the bill.

Expect to do a bit of gentle bargaining in marketplaces when purchasing produce and souvenirs, though in some situations the asking price will be the final price. When shopping in stores, prices are generally fixed. However, if you are doing any specialized shopping, such as for duty-free electronics on St Martin – you may be able to negotiate a better deal by letting the salesperson know you've seen the same product at a lower price in a nearby shop.

POST & COMMUNICATIONS
Post

Delivery time for airmail sent from the Eastern Caribbean varies greatly. From the French islands it generally takes about a week to European destinations and 10 days to North America, while from some of the smaller independent nations, like St Vincent & the Grenadines, overseas mail can easily take two to three weeks from the postmark date.

Hotels and other businesses on the smaller islands often have no street address or post-office box; when no address is given in this book, you can address correspondence by simply following the hotel name with the town, country and 'West Indies.'

You can receive mail by having it sent care of poste restante or general delivery to the general post office (GPO) on each island you're visiting.

Specific information on island post offices, including hours and postage rates, is given in the individual island chapters.

Telephone

Overall, the telephone systems work relatively well throughout the Eastern Caribbean. You can make both local and long-distance calls from virtually all public phones. Most islands have two types of public telephones: coin phones that accept local currency and card phones for which you can use prepaid phone cards.

eKno Communication Service Lonely Planet's eKno global communication service provides low-cost international calls – for local calls, you're usually better off with a local phone card or coins. eKno also offers free messaging services, email, travel information and an online travel vault where you can securely store all your important documents. You can join online at www.ekno.lonelyplanet.com, where you will find the local access numbers for the 24-hour customer-service center. Once you have joined, check the eKno Web site for the latest access numbers for each country and for updates on new features.

The following islands currently have access for calling. Of course, you can get your email, voice mail and faxes anywhere there is an Internet connection available. Listed below are the registration numbers, which also serve as the access numbers once you have joined:

Netherland Antilles – 0018-886-467-702
St Vincent – 1-888-717-4381
Trinidad & Tobago – 1-888-717-4384

Phone Cards Public card phones are very popular in the Eastern Caribbean. They operate on plastic phone cards the size of a credit card, which are inserted into the phone. Each phone card has an original value, and the cost of each call is deducted automatically as you talk. You can use your phone card for multiple calls, until the initial value of the card runs out.

The card phones are convenient if you make long-distance calls or a lot of local calls, as you don't have to keep pumping in coins. However, on those few islands (mainly the French West Indies) where coin phones have been virtually eliminated, the card phone concept can be a real pain when you want to make just one quick call but are forced to find a phone card vendor and pay for a card you won't fully utilize.

There's little advantage in buying phone cards in the larger denominations, as the per-unit cost is virtually the same on all cards. In addition, phone cards occasionally fail before their value expires.

Calling Cards Foreign calling cards can be used in the Eastern Caribbean. Overseas visitors can make collect (reverse-charge) calls through AT&T's USA Direct, MCI World Phone and Sprint's Global One. On most islands you can reach AT&T by dialing 1-800-872-2881 and MCI by dialing 1-800-888-8000. Sprint has different access numbers for each island. On the Dutch islands prefix the 800 numbers with 011 instead of the initial 1.

In general, calling-card calls to the US cost an initial US$5 plus about US1.50 per minute, depending on which island you're calling from. Rates are the same regardless of the hour or day of the week.

English Islands The English-speaking islands of Anguilla, Antigua & Barbuda, Barbados, Dominica, Grenada, Montserrat, St Kitts & Nevis, St Lucia, St Vincent & the Grenadines and Trinidad & Tobago have a similar telephone system, which on most islands is under the umbrella of the Cable & Wireless Company.

When direct dialing to these islands from North America, dial 1 + area code + the seven-digit local number. When calling these islands from outside North America, dial the access code of the country you're calling from + area code + the seven-digit local number.

Rates for long-distance calls from these islands are similar but not identical. The typical cost for one minute's phone time varies from EC$1.20 to EC$2 to nearby islands and from EC$2.50 to EC$3.75 to more far-flung Caribbean islands, while calls to the Americas average EC$5 a minute, to Europe EC$7, to the rest of the world EC$9. These rates are during the daytime period. In general, rates average about 25% cheaper from 6 pm until 6 am and all day Sunday and public holidays.

Caribbean Phonecards, which can be used on all these islands (as well as the British Virgin Islands, the Cayman Islands and the Turks & Caicos Islands), are sold in amounts of EC$10, EC$20 and EC$40. You can use multiple phone cards on the same phone call. Shortly before a phone card's time runs out, a buzzer goes off; if you then push the star button, on the bottom left side, the old card comes out and you can insert a second card without losing your connection.

French Islands When calling from one French West Indies island to another, or from France to the French West Indies, it's a long-distance domestic call and you need to dial the island code (0596 for Martinique or 0590 for the other French West Indies) + the six-digit local number.

When calling to the French West Indies from other countries, dial the access code of the country you're calling from + the island code + the six-digit local number.

French phone cards, called *télécartes,* are sold in 50- and 120-unit measures, which cost 37F and 89F, respectively. One unit is valid for a few minutes on a local call; seven seconds to nearby non-French Caribbean islands; 3.6 seconds to distant non-French Caribbean islands, the USA or Canada; three seconds to most European countries; and two seconds to Australia. Calls between any two French West Indies islands are substantially cheaper than calls to non-French Caribbean islands.

Dutch Islands The Netherlands Antilles islands of Saba, St Eustatius and the Dutch side of St Martin have a country code of 599. To call these islands from overseas, dial the access code of the country you're calling from + 599 + 3 for St Eustatius, 4 for Saba or 5 for Dutch St Martin + the five-digit local number.

Antelecom, the Dutch telephone company, sells Netherlands Antilles phone cards for US$9.85 (17.35 Fls) for 60 units and US$16.75 (Fls 29.60) for 120 units.

Fax
You can send faxes from the telephone company offices listed in the individual island chapters. In addition, most hotels will provide fax service for customers, though

you may want to inquire about the fee in advance as it can vary from nominal to exorbitant.

Email & Internet Services
Internet services are rapidly expanding in the Eastern Caribbean. On some islands service is available at the phone company's central office, while on others, notably the Dutch islands, public libraries often have access. Internet cafés are now becoming common in heavily touristed areas.

For those traveling with a laptop, a few of the more modern and expensive hotels have separate lines for modem hookup, but this is still relatively rare; if you'll need a modem hookup always inquire before booking.

INTERNET RESOURCES
The World Wide Web is a rich resource for travelers. You can research your trip, hunt down bargain airfares, book hotels, check on weather conditions and chat with locals and other travelers about the best places to visit (or avoid!).

There's no better place to start your Web explorations than the Lonely Planet Web site (www.lonelyplanet.com). Here you'll find succinct summaries on traveling to most places on earth, postcards from other travelers and the Thorn Tree bulletin board, where you can ask questions before you go or dispense advice when you get back. You can also find travel news and updates, and the subWWWay section links you to the most useful travel resources elsewhere on the Web.

Caribseek (www.caribseek.com) is a search directory with links to resources throughout the Caribbean. You can search individual islands or regionwide topics. Other good sites for information and pretrip planning include www.cpscaribnet.com, www.caribbean-on-line.com and also www .caribbeansupersite.com.

BOOKS
Most books are published in different editions by different publishers in different countries. As a result, a book might be a hardcover rarity in one country while it's

readily available in paperback in another. Bookstores and libraries can do a search by title or author, and they are the best places to go for advice on the availability of the following recommendations.

Information on bookstores and books specific to individual islands are found in those island chapters. The following are books that relate to more than one island.

Lonely Planet

If you plan to island hop outside the Eastern Caribbean, then Lonely Planet has a few other Caribbean-island guidebooks – *Jamaica*, *Cuba* and *Puerto Rico* – jammed full of all the nitty-gritty details you'll need to explore those destinations. If Miami is your gateway to the Caribbean and you're considering a stopover, Lonely Planet's *Miami* city guide and *Florida* guide are also invaluable resources. For those visiting the French West Indies, Lonely Planet has a handy French-language phrasebook full of useful things to say.

Lonely Planet's Pisces books cover the best diving and snorkeling with loads of color photos and detailed descriptions of the top sites and operators. Pisces guides to the Eastern Caribbean include *Diving and Snorkeling Dominica* and *Diving and Snorkeling Trinidad & Tobago*. Other Pisces books that can enrich a vacation to the Eastern Caribbean include *Snorkeling…Here's How*, by Bob French, and the detailed *Caribbean Reef Ecology*, by William Alevizon.

Field Guides

The Nature of the Islands: Plants & Animals of the Eastern Caribbean, by Virginia Barlow, is the best overall guide to the region's flora and fauna. This well-written book is easy to use, with descriptions of plants and animals accompanied by numerous color photos and drawings.

A Field Guide to Birds of the West Indies, by James Bond et al, is a new paperback revision of *Birds of the West Indies*, the classic guide to the region's bird life. This comprehensive book has detailed descriptions of each bird, including information on habitat, voice and range, all accompanied by illustrations.

A Guide to the Birds of the West Indies, by Herbert A Raffaele, is a substantial hardcover guide to all birds found in the region, with many illustrations.

Good references for divers and snorkelers include *A Field Guide to Coral Reefs: Caribbean and Florida*, by Eugene H Kaplan, and the *National Audubon Society Field Guide to Tropical Marine Fishes*, by C Lavett Smith. Both have detailed information on marine ecosystems and individual species.

Cruising Guides

There are a number of cruising guides to the Eastern Caribbean for yachters. The most widely used are those published by Cruising Guide Publications (in the USA ☎ 727-733-5322, 800-330-9542, fax 727-734-8179, www.cruisingguides.com), including *Sailors Guide to the Windward Islands* and *Cruising Guide to the Leeward Islands*, both written by Chris Doyle. Updated every couple of years, these books are thoroughly researched and packed with information on navigational approaches and entry regulations to where to pick up provisions and marine supplies.

Those new to sailing might want to read *Deck with a View: Vacation Sailing in the Caribbean*, by Dale Ward and Dustine Davidson. It suggests sailing itineraries, details various yachting options, lists charter-rental companies and even covers basic topics such as determining whether you have the personality to sail with a group.

History & Culture

From Columbus to Castro, by Eric Williams, is an authoritative history book of the West Indies written by the late prime minister of Trinidad & Tobago. It covers the period from the first European contact to the late 1960s and gives a good grasp of the dynamics of colonialism that shaped this region.

A Short History of the West Indies, by JH Parry and Philip Sherlock, provides a historical overview of the West Indies, from colonial times through the post-independence struggles experienced by the islands in the mid-1980s.

Seeds of Change, edited by Herman J Viola and Carolyn Margolis, is one of many books that appeared around the time of the Columbus Quincentennial. Like most of the others, it chronicles Columbus' four journeys and their impact on Caribbean history.

NEWSPAPERS & MAGAZINES

Most Eastern Caribbean islands have their own newspapers – some published daily, others weekly – and these are well worth reading to gain insights into local politics and culture. Foreign newspapers, such as the *International Herald Tribune* and *USA Today,* are usually available as well and can be found at newspaper stands, bookstores and top-end hotels.

Caribbean Week, Leffert's Place, River Rd, St Michael, Barbados, West Indies, is the most substantial weekly newspaper in the English-speaking Caribbean. It covers island news, politics, business, sports and cultural activities for the entire Caribbean region. Written in Barbados and printed in Florida, the newspaper is as widely circulated to islanders living abroad as it is to islanders within the Caribbean. Subscriptions cost US$30 for one year. You can check them out online at cweek.com.

Caribbean Travel & Life, PO Box 420732, Palm Coast, FL 32142, USA, is a four-color monthly magazine covering travel in the Caribbean region. It has feature articles on specific destinations and regular columns on new resorts, food, shopping etc.

RADIO & TV

Most islands have their own radio stations, which is a great way to tune in to the latest calypso, reggae, soca and steelband music. Local radio stations are also a good source of regional news and occasionally offer up interesting glimpses of island life – such as the somber reading of obituaries accompanied by appropriately maudlin music.

There's some kind of TV on almost every island, often relayed by satellite or cable. Not all hotels (not even all top-end hotels) offer TVs in the rooms.

PHOTOGRAPHY & VIDEO
Film & Equipment

Print film is available on the main islands, but it's often hard to find slide film. There are same-day photo processing centers on the French islands and in heavily touristed areas on other large islands, but they can be quite expensive.

In terms of camera and video equipment and videotapes, it's wise to bring everything you'll need from home. The availability of camera gear varies from island to island. Although on the larger French islands you can generally find a fair range of cameras and accessories, on most other islands camera shops are few in number and poorly stocked. In virtually all cases, expect to pay more than you would at home for both film and gear.

Technical Tips

The high air temperatures in the tropics, coupled with high humidity, greatly accelerate the deterioration of film, so the sooner you have exposed film developed, the better the results. If you're in the Caribbean just for a week or two it's no problem to wait until you get home, but if you're traveling for a longer period of time consider making other arrangements. One way to avoid carting film around is to bring prepaid processing mailers with you to send off along the way.

Don't leave your camera in direct sunshine any longer than necessary. A locked car can heat up like an oven in just a few minutes, damaging the film.

Sand and water are intense reflectors, and in bright light they'll often leave foreground subjects shadowy. You can try compensating by adjusting your f-stop or attaching a polarizing filter, or both, but the most effective technique is to take photos in the gentler light of early morning and late afternoon.

Photographing People

It's common courtesy to ask permission before taking photos of people. Occasionally those who have their pictures taken without permission will become quite upset and may demand money. As a general rule, children like to pose, but adults are much more reluctant to have their pictures taken, unless there's been some social interaction. You should always respect people's wishes.

TIME

All islands in the Eastern Caribbean are on Atlantic Time, four hours behind Greenwich Mean Time. Daylight saving time is not observed.

Thus, when it is noon in the Eastern Caribbean (and not daylight saving time elsewhere) it is 11 am in Jamaica, New York and Montreal; 8 am in Los Angeles and Vancouver; 4 pm in London; 5 pm in Paris; 2 am in Sydney; and 4 am in Auckland.

In summer, when North America and Europe go on daylight saving time, it is the same time in New York and Montreal as it is in the Eastern Caribbean; Britain is five hours ahead, rather than four; France is six hours ahead, rather than five.

ELECTRICITY

The electric current varies in the Eastern Caribbean.

On the French islands the current is 220V, 50/60 cycles, and a rounded two-pronged plug is used, the same type as in mainland France.

On the Dutch islands the current is 110V, 60 cycles, and a flat two-pronged plug is used, the same type as in the USA.

The former British West Indies are a mixed lot – a few use 110V, but most use 220V.

Whatever the current, you can still bring along small appliances as long as you have an adapter. Most hotel bathrooms have a dual-voltage outlet for electric shavers, and some hotels can provide adapters for other items.

WEIGHTS & MEASURES

Some Eastern Caribbean islands use the metric system, while others use the imperial system.

On islands that use the metric system, such as those of the French West Indies, distances and elevations are posted in meters and kilometers, while on the former British islands they're posted in feet and miles.

Each of the island chapters throughout this book uses the system of measurement

that is prevalent on that particular island. That makes it easier to use this book in conjunction with local road signs, directions and maps. As roads and sights on many islands are often poorly marked (or not marked at all), this will also make it possible for those exploring by car or motorcycle to follow directions given in this book using their vehicle odometer, which will read in miles on islands using the imperial system and in kilometers on islands using the metric system.

Should you need a conversion table, there's a handy one on the back inside cover of this book.

LAUNDRY

Some of the islands have coin laundries; others have drop-off services for nearly the same price. On a few of the smaller islands, however, the only option is to send out laundry at a hotel. For convenience and to control your budget, it's a good idea to bring a little laundry soap and plan on doing some washing by hand.

TOILETS

The concept of public toilets is not one that has widely taken root in the Eastern Caribbean, and toilet facilities are the exception rather than the rule at beaches and most other public places, though this situation is improving.

HEALTH

In general, the Eastern Caribbean is a fairly healthy place to visit. Still, infections, sunburn, diarrhea and intestinal parasites all warrant precautions.

If you're coming from a cold, dry climate to the heat and humidity of the Caribbean you may find yourself easily fatigued and more susceptible to minor ailments. Acclimatize yourself by slowing down your pace for the first few days.

Predeparture Preparations

Make sure that you have adequate health insurance. See Travel Insurance, under Visas & Documents in the Regional Facts for the Visitor chapter.

Medical Kit Checklist

The following is a list of items you should consider including in your medical kit – consult your pharmacist for brands available in your country.

❑ **Aspirin or paracetamol** (acetaminophen in the USA) – for pain or fever

❑ **Antihistamine** – for allergies, (eg, hay fever); to ease the itch from insect bites or stings; and to prevent motion sickness

❑ **Cold and flu tablets, throat lozenges and nasal decongestant**

❑ **Multivitamins** – consider for long trips, when dietary vitamin intake may not be adequate

❑ **Antibiotics** – consider including these if you're traveling well off the beaten track; see your doctor, as they must be prescribed, and carry the prescription with you

❑ **Loperamide or diphenoxylate** –'blockers' for diarrhea

❑ **Prochlorperazine or metaclopramide** – for nausea and vomiting

❑ **Rehydration mixture** – to prevent dehydration, which may occur, for example, during bouts of diarrhea; particularly important when traveling with children

❑ **Insect repellent, sunscreen, lip balm and eye drops**

❑ **Calamine lotion, sting relief spray or aloe vera** – to ease irritation from sunburn and insect bites or stings

❑ **Antifungal cream or powder** – for fungal skin infections and thrush

❑ **Antiseptic (such as povidone-iodine)** – for cuts and grazes

❑ **Bandages, Band-Aids (plasters) and other wound dressings**

❑ **Water purification tablets or iodine**

❑ **Scissors, tweezers and a thermometer** – note that mercury thermometers are prohibited by airlines

Bring adequate supplies of any prescription medicine or contraceptive pills you are already taking.

Immunizations No immunizations are required to enter any of the islands in the Eastern Caribbean, with one exception: Travelers who have been in any country in the past six months where yellow fever is endemic are required to have a vaccination certificate showing immunization against yellow fever. The disease in endemic in many South American and African countries between 15° north and 15° south of the equator. All vaccinations should be recorded on an International Health Certificate, which is available from your physician or government health department.

Basic Rules

Care in what you eat and drink is the most important health rule; stomach upsets are the most likely travel health problem, but the majority of these upsets will be relatively minor. Don't become paranoid, as trying the local food is part of the experience of travel after all.

Water Water quality varies from island to island. It's safe to drink from the tap in most places, but if you don't know that for certain, always assume the worst.

In general the islands at higher altitudes, which have abundant supplies of freshwater from the interior rain forests, have excellent drinking water. Some of the more developed islands at lower altitudes, such as St Martin, have desalination plants that provide potable, but not necessarily tasty, drinking water. The less developed lower-altitude islands almost invariably get their water from rain catchment, and as a rule their waters should be treated before drinking, as the water can vary greatly in bacteria count and purity.

The simplest way of purifying water is to boil it thoroughly. Technically, this means boiling for 10 minutes, something that happens very rarely! Simple filtering will not remove all dangerous organisms, so if you cannot boil water it should be treated chemically. Chlorine tablets will kill many but not all pathogens. Iodine is very effective in purifying water and is available in tablet form, but follow the directions carefully and remember that too much iodine can be harmful. Stores that specialize in camping gear sell both kinds of tablets.

If you can't find tablets, tincture of iodine (2%) can be used. Four drops of tincture of iodine per liter or quart of clear water is the recommended dosage; the treated water should be left to stand for 30 minutes before drinking. Iodine loses its effectiveness if exposed to air or dampness, so keep it in a tightly sealed container. Flavored powder will disguise the taste of treated water and is a good idea if you are traveling with children.

Bottled water is available just about everywhere; coconut water, soft drinks and beer are other alternatives. Tea or coffee should also be OK, since the water should have been boiled.

Food Food in the Eastern Caribbean is usually sanitarily prepared. Thoroughly cooked food is safest, but not if it has been left to cool or if it has been reheated. Take great care with fish and shellfish (including that in fancy buffets) and avoid undercooked meat. If a place looks clean and well run and if the vendor also looks clean and healthy, then the food is probably safe. In general, places that are packed with travelers or locals will be fine, while empty restaurants are questionable.

Nutrition Make sure your diet is well balanced and you get enough protein. Eat plenty of fruit; there's always some fruit that's plentiful and inexpensive – bananas, papayas and coconuts are good common sources of vitamins.

Because the Caribbean has a hot climate, make sure you drink enough – don't rely on feeling thirsty to indicate when you should drink. Not needing to urinate or very dark yellow urine is a danger sign. Always carry a water bottle with you on long trips or if you're doing any hiking. Excessive sweating can lead to loss of salt and therefore muscle cramping. Salt tablets are not a good idea as

a preventative, but in places where salt is not used much adding salt to food can help.

Medical Care

Hospital locations and emergency numbers are given in each island chapter, and certainly if you have a major ailment you shouldn't hesitate to use them. For less serious ailments, the front desk of your hotel or guest house can usually recommend a doctor, as can many tourist offices.

Environmental Hazards

Sunburn Sunburn is a definite concern in the Eastern Caribbean because the islands are in the tropics, where fewer of the sun's rays are blocked by the atmosphere. Don't be fooled by what appears to be a hazy, overcast day, as the rays still get through. The most severe sun is between 10 am and 2 pm. Fair-skinned people can get first- and second-degree burns in the hot Caribbean sun, so in the first few days particularly meter out your time in the sun carefully.

Sunscreen with a sun protection factor (SPF) of at least 15 is recommended if you're

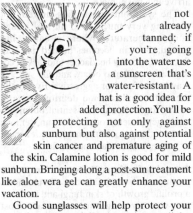

not already tanned; if you're going into the water use a sunscreen that's water-resistant. A hat is a good idea for added protection. You'll be protecting not only against sunburn but also against potential skin cancer and premature aging of the skin. Calamine lotion is good for mild sunburn. Bringing along a post-sun treatment like aloe vera gel can greatly enhance your vacation.

Good sunglasses will help protect your eyes from potentially damaging sunlight. Make sure they're treated to absorb ultraviolet radiation – if not, they'll actually do more harm than good by dilating your pupils and making it easier for ultraviolet light to damage the retina.

Prickly Heat Prickly heat is an itchy rash caused by excessive perspiration trapped under the skin. It usually strikes people who have just arrived in a hot climate and whose pores have not yet opened sufficiently to cope with greater sweating. Keeping cool by bathing often or resorting to air-con may help until you acclimatize.

Heat Exhaustion Dehydration or salt deficiency can cause heat exhaustion. Take time to acclimatize to high temperatures and make sure you get sufficient liquids. Salt deficiency is characterized by fatigue, lethargy, headaches, giddiness and muscle cramps, and in this case salt tablets may help. Vomiting or diarrhea can deplete your liquid and salt levels.

Heat Stroke This serious, sometimes fatal condition can occur if the body's heat-regulating mechanism breaks down and the body temperature rises to dangerous levels. Long, continuous periods of exposure to high temperatures can leave you vulnerable to heat stroke. You should avoid excessive alcohol or strenuous activity when you first arrive in a hot climate.

The symptoms are feeling unwell, not sweating very much or at all and a high body temperature. Where sweating has ceased, the skin becomes flushed and red. Severe, throbbing headaches and lack of co-ordination will also occur, and the sufferer may be confused or aggressive. Eventually the victim will become delirious or convulse. Hospitalization is essential, but meanwhile get patients out of the sun, remove their clothing, cover them with a wet sheet or towel and then fan continually.

Fungal Infections The same climate that produces lush tropical forests also promotes a prolific growth of skin fungi and bacteria. Hot-weather fungal infections are most likely to occur on the scalp, between the toes (athlete's foot), in the groin (jock itch) and on the body (ringworm).

To prevent fungal infections, it's essential to keep your skin cool and allow air to circulate. Choose cotton clothing rather than artificial fibers, and sandals rather than shoes.

If you do get an infection, wash the infected area daily with a disinfectant or medicated soap and water, and rinse and dry well. Apply an antifungal powder like Tinaderm. Try to expose the infected area to air or sunlight as much as possible, and wash all towels and underwear in hot water as well as changing them often.

Motion Sickness Eating lightly before and during a trip will reduce the chances of motion sickness. If you are prone to motion sickness try to find a place that minimizes disturbance – near the wing on aircraft, close to midships on boats, near the center on buses. Fresh air usually helps; reading and cigarette smoke do not. Commercial anti-motion-sickness preparations, which can cause drowsiness, have to be taken before the trip commences; when you're feeling sick it's too late. Ginger is a natural preventative and is available in capsule form.

Infectious Diseases

Diarrhea A change of water, food or climate can all cause the runs; diarrhea caused by contaminated food or water is more serious. Despite all your precautions you may still have a bout of mild travelers' diarrhea, but a few rushed toilet trips with no other symptoms is not indicative of a serious problem.

Dehydration is the main danger with any diarrhea, particularly for children, so fluid replenishment is the number one treatment. Weak black tea or bottled water are good choices. Coconuts, which are readily available on many islands, are not only a good source of uncontaminated water but also an excellent rehydration drink, full of vitamins and minerals.

With severe diarrhea a rehydrating solution is necessary to replace minerals and salts. You should stick to a bland diet as you recover.

Lomotil or Imodium can be used to bring relief from the symptoms, although they do not cure the problem. Only use these drugs if absolutely necessary – for example, if you *must* travel. For children Imodium is preferable. Do not use these drugs if the patient has a high fever or is severely dehydrated.

Dysentery This serious illness is caused by contaminated food or water and is characterized by severe diarrhea, often with blood or mucus in the stool. There are two kinds of dysentery. Bacillary dysentery is characterized by a high fever and rapid onset; headache, vomiting and stomach pains are also symptoms. It generally does not last longer than a week, but it is highly contagious.

Amoebic dysentery is often more gradual in the onset of symptoms, with cramping abdominal pain and vomiting less likely; fever may not be present. It is not a self-limiting disease: It will persist until treated and can recur and cause long-term health problems.

A stool test is necessary to diagnose which kind of dysentery you have, so you should seek medical help immediately.

Hepatitis Hepatitis A is the more common form of this disease and is spread by contaminated food or water. Protection is through the vaccine Havrix or the short-lasting antibody gammaglobulin.

The symptoms are fever, chills, headache, fatigue, feelings of weakness and aches and pains, followed by loss of appetite, nausea, vomiting, abdominal pain, dark urine, light-colored feces and jaundiced skin; the whites of the eyes may also turn yellow. In some cases there may just be a feeling of being unwell or tired, accompanied by loss of appetite, aches and pains, and the jaundiced effect.

You should seek medical advice, but in general there is not much you can do apart from resting, drinking lots of fluids, eating lightly and avoiding fatty foods. People who have had hepatitis must forgo alcohol for six months after the illness, as hepatitis attacks the liver, which needs time to recover.

Bilharzia Also called schistosomiasis, bilharzia is endemic in Guadeloupe, Martinique and St Lucia and may occur sporadically on other islands, such as Antigua.

Bilharzia is carried in water by minute worms. The larvae infect certain varieties of freshwater snails found in rivers, streams and lakes. The worms multiply and are eventually discharged into the water surrounding the snails.

The worms attach themselves to your intestines or bladder, where they produce large numbers of eggs. The worm enters through the skin, and the first symptom may be a tingling and sometimes a light rash around the area where it entered. Weeks later, when the worm is busy producing eggs, a high fever may develop. A general feeling of being unwell may be the first symptom; once the disease is established abdominal pain and blood in the urine are other signs.

The main method of preventing the disease is to avoid swimming or bathing in freshwater where bilharzia is present. If you do get wet, dry off quickly and dry your clothes as well. Seek medical attention if you have been exposed to the disease and tell the doctor of your suspicions, as bilharzia in the early stages can be confused with malaria or typhoid.

Leptospirosis Visitors should be aware of leptospirosis, a bacterial disease found in some freshwater streams and ponds. The disease is transmitted from animals such as rats and mongooses.

Humans most often pick up the disease by swimming or wading in freshwater contaminated by animal urine. Leptospirosos enters the body through the nose, eyes, mouth or cuts in the skin. Symptoms, which resemble the flu, can occur within two to 20 days after exposure and may include fever, chills, sweating, headaches, muscle pains, vomiting and diarrhea. More severe symptoms include blood in the urine and jaundice. Symptoms may last from a few days to several weeks and in rare cases can result in death.

As a precaution, avoid swimming and wading in freshwater, especially if you have open cuts.

HIV/AIDS HIV (Human Immunodeficiency Virus) may develop into AIDS (Acquired Immune Deficiency Syndrome). Any exposure to blood, blood products or bodily fluids may put the individual at risk. Apart from sexual abstinence, the most effective preventative is to always practice safe sex using condoms. It is impossible to detect the HIV-positive status of an otherwise healthy-looking person without a blood test.

HIV/AIDS can also be spread through transfusions of infected blood or by sharing needles – vaccinations, acupuncture, tattooing and ear-piercing can potentially be as dangerous as intravenous drug use if the equipment is not clean.

Insect-Borne Diseases

Dengue Fever There is no malaria in the Eastern Caribbean, but mosquito-spread dengue fever is endemic to most of the region.

There is no prophylactic available for this disease; the main preventative measure is to avoid mosquito bites. Consider using mosquito repellents on exposed areas, burning mosquito coils or using a mosquito net.

A sudden onset of fever, headaches and severe joint and muscle pains are the first signs before a rash starts on the trunk of the body and spreads to the limbs and face. After a few more days, the fever will subside and recovery will begin. Serious complications are not common.

Cuts, Bites & Stings

Cuts & Scratches Skin punctures can easily become infected in hot climates and may be difficult to heal. Treat any cut with an antiseptic solution. Where possible, avoid bandages and Band-Aids, which can keep wounds wet. Coral cuts are notoriously slow to heal, as the coral injects a weak venom into the wound; avoid any contact with coral.

Snakes The poisonous fer-de-lance snake is present in Martinique, St Lucia and Trinidad. It's a very deadly snake as it has an anticoagulating agent in its venom. However, bites are not that common.

To minimize your chances of being bitten, wear boots, socks and long trousers when walking through undergrowth where snakes may be present and don't put your hands into holes and crevices.

Snake bites do not cause instantaneous death and antivenins are usually available, but it's important to get the victim to the hospital as quickly as possible. Keep the victim calm and still, wrap the bitten limb tightly, as you would for a sprained ankle, and then attach a splint to immobilize it. Tourniquets and sucking out the poison are now comprehensively discredited. If the snake has been killed bring it along for identification; if it's still

If you see this snake, run: It's a fer-de-lance.

alive, do not approach it if there is even a remote possibility of being bitten again.

Jellyfish These sea creatures make only periodic appearances in most places that they're found, and local advice is the best way of avoiding contact with them and their stinging tentacles. Stings from most jellyfish are painful. Dousing in vinegar will deactivate any stingers that have not 'fired.' Calamine lotion, antihistamines and analgesics may reduce the reaction and relieve the pain.

Women's Health

Poor diet, sweating, lowered resistance through the use of antibiotics and even contraceptive pills can lead to vaginal infections when traveling in hot climates. Wearing skirts or loose-fitting trousers and cotton underwear will help to prevent infections.

Yeast infections, characterized by a rash, itch and discharge, can be treated with a vinegar or even lemon-juice douche or with yogurt. Nystatin miconazole or clotrimazole pessaries or vaginal cream are the usual treatment.

Sexually transmitted diseases are a major cause of vaginal problems. Symptoms include a smelly discharge, painful intercourse and sometimes a burning sensation when urinating. Sexual partners must also be treated. Medical attention should be sought, and remember in addition to these diseases HIV or hepatitis B may also be acquired during exposure. Besides abstinence, the best thing is to practice safe sex using condoms.

If you're pregnant, take note that most miscarriages occur during the first three months of pregnancy, so this is the most risky time to travel. The last three months should also be spent within reasonable distance of good medical care.

Women travelers often find that their periods become irregular or even cease while they're on the road. Remember that a missed period in these circumstances does not necessarily indicate pregnancy. There are health or family-planning clinics on most islands where you can seek advice and have a urine test to determine whether you are pregnant or not.

WOMEN TRAVELERS

Although the situation varies between islands, women traveling alone should take safety precautions. As a general rule, single women travelers will be more comfortable on the Dutch and French islands than on the former British islands. On some islands, such as Antigua and Grenada, men can be quite aggressive toward unaccompanied women; catcalls and very forward comeons are not uncommon. Avoid walking alone after dark, heading off into the wilderness on your own, hitching or picking up male hitchhikers. Dress as modestly as possible and try not to get into any situations where you're isolated and vulnerable. *Travel Alone & Love It,* by Sharon

Wingler, is filled with advice and handy tips for women travelers.

GAY & LESBIAN TRAVELERS

Taken as a whole, the Eastern Caribbean is not a particularly gay-friendly destination, and on many of the islands an element of homophobia and machismo is prevalent.

In the late 1990s several Caribbean governments made news by refusing gay cruise ships the right to land on their islands. Under the threat of boycotts by several cruise lines, the governments relented publicly, while continuing to campaign at home against outside influences of 'immorality.'

Still, there are some niches for gay travelers. Saba is a gay-friendly little island – albeit there's not a lot happening. Barbados has a gay guest house and is more gay-tolerant than other former British islands. The French islands are reasonably tolerant as well.

The situation for gay men and lesbians is a low-profile one on all the islands, and public hand-holding, kissing and other outward signs of affection are not commonplace. Discretion is advised.

Resources & Organizations

A couple of good Web sites with information on gay and lesbian travel as well as links to tour operators are www.damron.com and www.outandabout.com.

The following organizations can recommend travel agents, tour companies and cruises that book gay-friendly travel:

International Gay & Lesbian Travel Association
(in the USA ☎ 954-776-2626, 800-448-8550, fax 954-776-3303, iglta@iglta.com, www.iglta.org) 52 W Oakland Park Blvd, Suite 237, Wilton Manors, FL 33311, USA

Gay and Lesbian Tourism Australia
(in Australia ☎ 08-8379 7498, www.galta.com.au)

Ferrari International Publishing (in the USA ☎ 602-863-2408, fax 602-439-3952, www.ferrariguides.com), PO Box 37887, Phoenix, AZ 85069, USA, has several travel guides for gay men and lesbians. Another resource is *Odysseus: The International Gay Travel Planner* (in the USA ☎ 516-944-5330, fax 516-944-7540), PO Box 1548, Port Washington, New York, NY 11050 USA.

For more information on companies offering gay-friendly cruises to the Eastern Caribbean, see Cruises in the Getting There & Away chapter.

DISABLED TRAVELERS

Travel in the Eastern Caribbean is not particularly easy for those with physical disabilities. Overall, there is little or no consciousness of the need for curb cuts, jetways or other easy access onto planes, wheelchair lifts on buses, or rental vehicles for the disabled.

Visitors with special needs should inquire directly to prospective hotels for information on their facilities. The larger, more modern resorts are most apt to have the greatest accessibility, with elevators, wider doorways and the like.

While land travel presents obstacles, cruises are often a good option for the disabled in the Caribbean. Many cruise lines can coordinate shore-based excursions in wheelchair-accessible tour buses. For more information, see Cruises in the Getting There & Away chapter.

Resources & Organizations

Travelers might want to get in touch with national support organizations in their home country. These groups commonly have general information and tips on travel and are able to supply a list of travel agents specializing in tours for the disabled. Here are some resources:

Access-Able Travel Source
(in the USA ☎ 303-232-2979, fax 303-239-8486, www.access-able.com) PO Box 1796, Wheat Ridge, CO 80034, USA. This organization has an excellent Web site with links to international disability sites, travel newsletters, guidebooks, travel tips and information on cruise operators.

Royal Association for Disability & Rehabilitation
(in the UK ☎ 020-7250 3222, fax 020-7250 0212, www.radar.org.uk) 12 City Forum, 250 City Rd, London EC1V 8AF, UK. This organization provides general information on overseas travel.

Society for Accessible Travel and Hospitality
(in the USA ☎ 212-447-7284, fax 212-725-8253) 347 Fifth Ave, No 610, New York, NY 10016, USA. This resource publishes a quarterly magazine for US$13 annually and has various free information sheets on travel for the disabled.

The Wheelchair Traveler
(in the USA ☎ 603-673-4539) 123 Ball Hill Rd, Milford, NH 03055, USA. This guide provides information on accessible hotel and motel accommodations.

Some Web sites specializing in accessible travel are Access Travel (www.access-travel .co.uk), Global Access (www.geocities.com/ Paris/1502) and AdventureQuest (www .adventurequest.com).

SENIOR TRAVELERS

The Eastern Caribbean makes a good destination for senior travelers, but the slew of 'senior discounts' that are prevalent in North America and Europe are rare in the Caribbean.

Still, some organizations in your home country may offer discounted tour packages, car rentals and the like to seniors. In the USA, the nonprofit American Association of Retired Persons (AARP) is a good source for travel bargains. For information on joining this advocacy group for Americans 50 years and older, contact AARP (☎ 800-424-3410), 601 E St NW, Washington, DC 20049, USA or visit the organization's Web site (www.aarp.org).

For information on Elderhostel study vacations, see the Organized Tours section in the Getting There & Away chapter.

TRAVEL WITH CHILDREN

The Eastern Caribbean can make a good destination for families with children. Some of the more popular family destinations are Barbados, St Martin and Guadeloupe.

Successful travel with young children requires planning and effort. Try not to overdo things; even for adults, packing too much into the time available can cause problems. Include children in the trip planning; if they've helped to work out where you will be going, they will be much more interested when they get there.

Most major cruise lines now offer special services and activities for children, some extensive enough to keep their parents free (and children happy) for much of the trip. Premier Cruise Lines (in the USA ☎ 407-783-5061, 800-992-4299) actually specializes in family cruises.

For those vacationing with children, Lonely Planet's *Travel with Children,* by Maureen Wheeler, has lots of valuable tips and interesting anecdotes. Another experienced mother and world traveler, Claire Tristram provides great all-around survival strategies for getaways with the younger set, focusing on infants and young children, in her book *Have Kid, Will Travel.*

DANGERS & ANNOYANCES
Pesky Creatures
You can expect to find mosquitoes and sand flies throughout the region, both of which can be quite voracious, so consider bringing insect repellent. In addition, a few of the islands have chiggers and centipedes. For information on poisonous snakes, which are found on Martinique, St Lucia and Trinidad, see the Health section, earlier in this chapter.

Manchineel Trees
All visitors should learn to identify manchineel trees, which grow on beaches throughout the Eastern Caribbean. The fruit of the manchineel, which looks like a small green apple, is very poisonous, and the milky sap given off by the fruit and leaves can cause severe skin blisters, similar to the reaction caused by poison oak. If the sap gets in your eyes, it can result in temporary blindness. Never take shelter under the trees during a rainstorm, as the sap can be washed off the tree and onto anyone sitting below.

Manchineel trees can be quite sizable, growing as high as 40 feet with branches that spread widely. The leaves are green, shiny and elliptical in shape. On some of the more visited beaches, trees will be marked with warning signs or bands of red paint. Manchineel is called *mancenillier* on the French islands and *anjenelle* on Trinidad and Tobago.

Crime
In terms of individual safety and crime, the situation is quite varied in the Eastern Caribbean. For instance, it's hard to imagine a more tranquil area than Saba, where most people don't even have locks on their doors, whereas walking the streets of Port of Spain (Trinidad) or Fort-de-France (Martinique) after dark can certainly be a risky venture. Consequently the precautions you should take depend on which island you're visiting. For a better grasp of the situation, see the individual island chapters.

LEGAL MATTERS
Laws and legal procedures differ under the various islands' governments. On the French and Dutch islands laws are generally the same as in the European home countries, while most of the former British colonies have legal systems based on British law.

BUSINESS HOURS
On most islands, business offices are open 8 or 9 am to 4 or 5 pm weekdays. Shops and stores are typically open from around 9 am to 5 or 6 pm weekdays, till noon Saturday. However, there is variation between islands. For specifics on business hours, see the individual island chapters.

Keep in mind that banks on many islands are open only to noon on the day preceding a public holiday.

Never on Sunday

On our first trip to the Caribbean, we asked a shopkeeper in Grenada about her hours of business. 'We're open daily,' she told us. 'Every day?' we asked. '*Every* day of the week,' she emphasized. 'Even on Sundays?' we asked. 'Oh no – never on *Sundays!*' she answered.

And so we came to realize that in most of the Eastern Caribbean the word 'daily' – whether spoken, written in ads or posted on storefront signs – quite often means 'every day but Sunday.'

– Glenda Bendure & Ned Friary

PUBLIC HOLIDAYS & SPECIAL EVENTS

Specific information on public holidays and special events, which vary throughout the region, is found in the Facts for the Visitor sections of the individual island chapters.

One event, Carnival, stands unique as the major festival throughout the Eastern Caribbean. As elsewhere, it has traditionally been a pre-Lenten celebration – a period of merriment before the abstinence and fasting that many Christians, particularly Catholics, observe during Lent.

On Trinidad and on all of the French-influenced islands, Carnival remains a strictly pre-Lenten celebration, while on many of the British-influenced islands, Carnival celebrations are held at other times of the year.

The changing of Carnival dates has been largely the result of practical considerations – smaller islands simply couldn't compete with larger islands, particularly Trinidad, which attract the finest performers and the lion's share of visitors. As a result, visitors to the Eastern Caribbean can now find Carnival celebrations on one island or another throughout the year.

Carnival festivities usually include contests and performances by calypso singers and steel bands; the election of a Carnival 'king' and 'queen'; street dancing, called 'jump-ups'; costume and dance competitions; and a parade with floats, music and masquerading revelers.

For more information on Carnival celebrations, see the individual island chapters.

ACTIVITIES

For those who get bored just hanging out on the beach, there are a slew of activities available throughout the Eastern Caribbean. Diving and sailing are two of the most popular, but there are also plenty of opportunities for snorkeling, windsurfing, hiking, horseback riding, golf and tennis.

Diving

There's good year-round diving throughout the Eastern Caribbean. As a general rule, the calmer leeward shores of the islands have the best diving conditions.

Most of the Eastern Caribbean has good visibility, with average water temperatures ranging from 75°F (24°C) to 85°F (29°C).

The marine life around the islands is superb. Hundreds of colorful fish species live in Caribbean waters, including common tropicals like the reef-chomping parrot fish. In addition, divers will often encounter stingrays, octopuses, lobsters, moray eels, sea turtles, spinner dolphins and large schools of barracuda.

Caribbean waters also harbor all sorts of colorful sponges and both soft and hard coral, including wavering gorgonian fans and gemlike black coral. One creature common to the Caribbean that warrants caution is the brownish yellow fire coral, which is actually an encrusting hydroid colony that can provide a nasty sting to those who brush against it.

Underwater scenery in the Eastern Caribbean includes sea caves, canyons, pinnacles and vertical walls. Having a long maritime history, the Caribbean also has its share of sunken ships.

Most of the islands of the Eastern Caribbean offer good diving opportunities and numerous dive shops. Complete gear can be rented and prices are quite competitive between shops.

If you want to experience diving for the first time, some of the dive operations offer a short beginner course for nondivers; com-

KEVIN ANGLIN

'Yes, the engine is definitely still there!'

VERONICA BARBUTT

Just another day packing mace, Grenada

LEE FOSTER

Still waiting for a snow day, Grenada

MICHAEL LAWRENCE

Hauling in the day's catch, Dominica

MICHAEL LAWRENCE

Your physical-education class was never this cool.

Guadeloupe gets going during Carnival.

Celebrating Creole Day on Dominica

When you've invited all your friends over for lobster, there's some serious trapping to be done.

Beach fun at Maracas Bay, Trinidad

monly dubbed a 'resort course,' it includes brief instructions, followed by a shallow beach or boat dive (or a dip in the pool at dive shops at the nicer hotels). The cost generally ranges from US$75 to US$100, depending upon the operation and whether a boat is used.

For those who want to jump into the sport wholeheartedly, a number of dive shops also offer full open-water certification courses. The cost generally hovers around US$400, equipment included, and the entire course usually takes the better part of a week.

Generally, no two divers agree on the best sites for diving, but among the places in vogue these days in the Eastern Caribbean are St Lucia, Dominica, Tobago and St Vincent & the Grenadines. More information on diving, including lists of dive operators, can be found in the individual island chapters. For possible trips, see Dive Tours in the Getting There & Away chapter, and for information on diving and snorkeling guides to the region, see the Lonely Planet section under Books, earlier in this chapter.

Snorkeling

Donning a mask and snorkel allows you to turn the beach into an underwater aquarium. There are numerous sites throughout the Eastern Caribbean that offer splendid coral gardens and varied and abundant reef fish. The nearshore waters harbor lots of colorful tropical fish, including many varieties of wrasses, damselfish, sergeant majors, goatfish, butterfly fish, large rainbow-colored parrot fish, angelfish, odd-shaped filefish, ballooning puffers, octopus and moray eels, to list just a few.

Some travelers cart along their own mask, snorkel and fins, but if you prefer to travel light they can be rented for reasonable prices at many dive shops. Snorkel sets can also be rented from water-sports huts on some of the busier beaches, though rates tend to be higher. More information on snorkeling can be found in the individual island chapters; see also Diving, earlier.

Windsurfing

The popularity of windsurfing, or sailboarding, varies widely in the Eastern Caribbean. The main venues, and the most readily available rentals, are found largely on the French islands. However, there are favorable trade winds and good water conditions throughout the region, so if by chance you travel with your own equipment, the range of possibilities is greater. Generally, winds are most constant during the summer months.

Windsurfing gear can easily be rented at the main windsurfing beaches in Guadeloupe, St Barts, Martinique, St Martin and Barbados, and on some of these islands there are also hotels that cater to windsurfers. In addition, many standard 1st-class hotels on Guadeloupe and Martinique have water-sports huts that provide free use of windsurfing gear to their guests – a situation that can make for a reasonably economical windsurfing vacation.

Although the sport is not as widely popular in most of the English-speaking Caribbean, Antigua and the Grenadine island of Bequia each have a windsurfing school and gear rentals. Windsurfing is also catching on in Tobago and the southern tip of St Lucia, and there are a couple of places on those islands where gear can now be rented.

More information on windsurfing can be found in the individual island chapters.

Surfing

The Eastern Caribbean is not a particularly hot spot for surfers. The exception is isolated Barbados, which is situated farther out into the open Atlantic than other Eastern Caribbean islands and is thus exposed to unimpeded Atlantic swells.

In late summer, swells generated by tropical storms off the African coast begin to race toward Barbados, producing the Caribbean's highest waves and finest surfing conditions. The most reliable time for catching good, high, surfable waves is September, October and November. Bathsheba, on Barbados' east coast, is the center of activity, attracting wave action from the north, south and east.

Surfing is also possible at times in Guadeloupe, Tobago and St Martin. For more information see the relevant island chapters and the Surfing Tours section in the Getting There & Away chapter.

Fishing

There's reasonably good deep-sea fishing in the Eastern Caribbean, with marlin, tuna, wahoo and barracuda among the prime catches. Charter fishing-boat rentals are available on a number of islands, but rates tend to be high. Expect a half day of fishing for four people to run about US$350. Charter boats are usually individually owned and consequently the list of available skippers tends to fluctuate; local tourist offices and activity desks can provide the latest information on availability.

Sailing

The Eastern Caribbean is a first-rate sailing destination. If you just want to spend a few hours out on the water, water-sports huts at resort hotels rent Sunfish or other small sailboats that can be used for nearshore exploring. Should you want to take an island-hopping day excursion by sailboat, or join a sunset sail, there are cruises available on most islands. For information on getting about by skippering your own bareboat yacht (or hiring a yacht with a skipper) see the Yacht section in the Getting Around the Region chapter.

Hiking

The hiking situation in the Eastern Caribbean varies significantly between islands. On many of the smaller low-lying islands there are few, if any, established trails, but as cars are also few in number the dirt roads that connect villages can make for good walking.

If you want to get off into the woods, the higher rain-forested islands offer the best opportunities. On lofty Dominica you can hike to a variety of waterfalls, take an easy rain-forest loop trail through a parrot sanctuary or hire a guide for an arduous trek to an eerie volcanic valley with a boiling lake. On Guadeloupe and Martinique there are also established rain-forest hikes that take

in scenic waterfalls and smoldering volcanoes. St Lucia has trails into several nature preserves, so rain-forest hiking is a viable option on that island as well.

Small but steep Saba has some good easy-access hiking, including a trail through a cloud forest to the island's highest point, and a lightly trodden network of footpaths that served to connect Saba's villages before the introduction of paved roads and cars just a few decades ago.

For more detailed information on hiking see the individual island chapters.

Hiking Precautions Some rain-forest hiking trails take you into steep, narrow valleys with gullies that require stream crossings. The capital rule here is that if the water begins to rise it's not safe to cross, as a flash flood may be imminent. Instead, head for higher ground and wait it out.

Another potential danger on trails is falling rocks. Be wary of swimming directly under high waterfalls, as rocks can be dislodged from the top. Often a waterfall will have a second pool farther downstream that's safer.

Island trails are not a good place to be caught unprepared in the dark. It's wise to carry a flashlight when you're hiking, just in case. And of course if you're heading out into the wilderness you should always have a compass and plenty of water.

Long pants will protect your legs from sharp saw grass on overgrown sections of trails. Sturdy footwear with good traction is advisable on most hikes.

Horseback Riding

Horseback riding can be a fun way to explore a place. On about half of the larger Eastern Caribbean islands there are guided horseback rides. Some of the rides head out across quiet valleys, others go along remote beaches, and a few combine both in a single outing. Specific information on horseback riding can be found in the individual island chapters.

Golf & Tennis

While golf is not nearly as popular in the Eastern Caribbean as it is on more northerly locales such as Bermuda and Jamaica, most of the heavily touristed islands of the Eastern Caribbean have at least one golf course. The top-rated golf course in the region is the 18-hole championship course designed by Robert Trent Jones II at the Four Seasons Resort on Nevis. Tennis courts are available at many of the larger resorts throughout the Eastern Caribbean. For more information see the individual island chapters.

WORK

The Eastern Caribbean has high unemployment rates and low wages, as well as strict immigration policies aimed at preventing foreign visitors from taking up work.

Generally the best bet for working is to crew with a boat. As boat hands aren't usually working on any one island in particular, the work situation is more flexible and it's easier to avoid hassles with immigration. Marinas are a good place to look for jobs on yachts; check the bulletin board notices, strike up conversations with skippers or ask around at the nearest bar – most marinas have a watering hole where sailors hang out.

ACCOMMODATIONS

There are a wide range of accommodations available in the Eastern Caribbean, from inexpensive guest houses and good-value efficiency apartments to luxury villa resorts. However, not all islands have rooms in all price categories – and a few have no budget accommodations at all. Accommodation options are detailed in each island chapter.

In this book the phrase 'in summer' refers to the low season and 'in winter' to the high season. At the vast majority of hotels, summer rates are in effect from April 15 to December 14, winter rates from December 15 to April 14. Perhaps 10% of the hotels in the Eastern Caribbean make some minor deviations from these dates, usually with the addition of a mid-range rate in spring and autumn and/or with higher rates for a few weeks at the end of December and the beginning of January.

Many hotels close for a month or so in late summer, usually around September. If business doesn't look promising, some of the smaller hotels and guest houses might even close down for the entire summer.

'Private bath' in this book means that the room has its own toilet and shower – it does not necessarily mean that it has a bathtub, and in most cases it will not.

When you're looking for a hotel keep in mind that new hotels, especially 1st-class hotels, often have enticing rates for the first couple of years until they build up a clientele. Conversely, some of the busier older hotels are not good values but have simply built up name recognition over the years.

Camping is limited in the Eastern Caribbean, and on some islands freelance camping is either illegal or discouraged. This is certainly not the rule everywhere, however, and it's best to check with the local tourist office for rules and regulations.

There are a number of camping possibilities on Trinidad and Tobago, and there is established camping at a handful of small, private campgrounds on Guadeloupe and Martinique. At the Grand Etang National Park in Grenada, and on St Eustatius and St Kitts & Nevis, camping is officially allowed but there are no facilities. Montserrat's National Trust has plans to create a campground in the Centre Hills, so check with that organization for an update.

Reservation Systems

Reservations at some hotels and guest houses can be made through overseas booking agencies. Those that operate on a single island are listed under that island. The following reservation services book many places on multiple islands – as it may be easier and cheaper to inquire about many hotels in a single call, you might want to try them first.

Accor
Accor (in the USA and Canada ☎ 800-221-4542, in France ☎ 0160-77 27 27, in the UK ☎ 020-8283 4530, in Germany ☎ 06196-48 38 00, in Australia ☎ 030-065 65 65, www.accorhotels.com) books all Marine, Mercure, Novotel and Sofitel hotel chains, which together account for nearly a third of the hotel rooms on Martinique and Guadeloupe, as well as a few places on St Martin, St Barts and St Lucia.

International Travel & Resorts
ITR (in the USA ☎ 212-476-9444, in the USA, Canada, Puerto Rico and the US Virgin Islands ☎ 800-365-8484, www.itrhotels.com) books numerous hotels in the moderate and upper ranges. ITR will send out individual hotel brochures on request, as well as an annual directory of all of its members.

West Indies Management Company
Wimco (in the USA ☎ 401-849-8012, 800-449-1553, fax 401-847-6290, in the UK ☎ 0800-89 8318, in France ☎ 0800-90 16 20, in Germany ☎ 0130-81 57 30, www.wimcovillas.com), PO Box 1461, Newport, RI 02840, USA, specializes in renting exclusive villa properties. Its extensive listings include villas on Mustique, St Martin, St Barts, Nevis and Barbados.

FOOD

Foods in the Eastern Caribbean reflect the mix of cultures. Throughout the region you'll find West Indian food – predominantly local root crops, vegetables, fresh seafood and goat – prepared with African and Western influences. Also prevalent on most islands is Creole food, a spicy mix of French and West Indian flavors. On the French islands, pâtisseries, crêpe shops and sidewalk cafés are nearly as prevalent as they would be in a Paris suburb.

East Indian, British, North American and Continental foods can be found in varying degrees throughout the region. Barbados has plenty of places selling English-style fish & chips, on St Eustatius you can enjoy a Dutch smorgasbord breakfast of deli meats and cheeses, while moderately priced pizza and Italian food can be found in most places.

A few chain restaurants like KFC are common on the bigger islands, but the quintessential fast food in the region remains a West Indian creation – the roti. It's made up of a curried filling, most commonly with potatoes and chicken, that's placed inside a tortilla-like wrapping and eaten much like a burrito. It's cheap and as filling as a good-sized sandwich.

Public markets are the place to go for fresh local fruit and vegetables – that's where it's at its freshest, and you're contributing 100% of your money to the local economy by buying it direct from the farmer. On larger islands, capital cities have produce markets that open every day but Sunday. On other islands public markets are commonly held only a couple of days a week. Saturday is invariably the biggest and liveliest market day everywhere.

To figure out what you're about to eat, see the Food & Drink Glossary at the end of this book.

DRINKS

Nonalcoholic Drinks

An island favorite among nonalcoholic drinks is coconut water, which is a nice change from sugar-laden soft drinks and can be purchased inexpensively from street vendors in many places. Another nutritious local drink is sorrel, a lightly tart, bright red drink rich in vitamin C that's made from the flowers of the sorrel plant. Delicious fresh-fruit juices are available in most restaurants; the selection depends on the season.

Bottled water is available at stores throughout the Eastern Caribbean. Water is

---

Things Not to Buy

Sea-turtle shells make beautiful jewelry – too beautiful, in fact, for the welfare of the turtles, which are endangered worldwide. Buying any turtle products increases the demand for hunting the turtles. Turtle-shell jewelry, as well as sea-turtle taxidermy and food products, are prohibited entry into the USA, Canada, Australia and most other countries.

Travelers should also avoid products that contain tropical feathers as many of the most colorful Caribbean birds, such as parrots and the scarlet ibis, are endangered – even people who unwittingly bring home feathers from protected species are subject to steep fines.

The importation of black coral is likewise banned in more than 100 countries. The purchase of other corals, which are often taken live from their fragile reef ecosystems and sold in chunks or made into jewelry, should also give pause to the environmentally conscious.

safe to drink from the tap on many but not all islands; see the individual island chapters for details.

Alcoholic Drinks

With the islands' histories so tightly tied to sugarcane, it's only natural that rum remains the most common alcoholic beverage throughout the Eastern Caribbean. Most larger islands produce their own rum. Some, such as Martinique and Guadeloupe, use freshly harvested sugarcane, while others, such as Grenada, import molasses to produce their rum. There are scores of labels, from internationally recognized favorites like the Barbadian-produced Mount Gay to small obscure distilleries producing products solely for local consumption. Rum is invariably cheap throughout the islands.

Though bars throughout the islands will whip up the frothy, fruity rum cocktails that tourists expect, locals favor the simpler approach of adding a little water and sugar to a small glass of rum (while keeping the bottle close by for the next round).

Certainly the most popular beer in the Eastern Caribbean is Carib, a refreshing light beer first brewed in Trinidad in 1951 and now brewed in St Kitts and Grenada as well. In and around the Dutch islands, Heineken is the beer of choice.

ENTERTAINMENT

Whether you'd prefer to club-hop on Barbados or soak up the steel-pan rhythm at Trinidadian mas camps, the Eastern Caribbean has enough musical and cultural offerings to ensure that you won't be at a loss for things to do after the sun goes down. More information is given in the individual island chapters.

SPECTATOR SPORTS

On the English-speaking islands, cricket is by far the leading spectator sport. During cricket season, those who aren't at the match are generally glued to the radio broadcast. On some islands, the main cricket season is April through September, but on others, such as Barbados, cricket is played year-round.

Second in popularity is soccer (called football in the Eastern Caribbean), which is played throughout the Caribbean, with the main season in winter.

Horse racing is a popular spectator sport on a couple of the larger islands.

SHOPPING

St Martin is the most popular island for duty-free shopping, but virtually any island that has large cruise-ship facilities will have at least a few generic duty-free shops selling liquor, perfumes, jewelry and some designer clothing.

You'll find lots of wood carvings from Bali, colorfully painted ceramic buses and market scenes made in Colombia and folk paintings from Haiti – some quite nice, but not made in the Eastern Caribbean.

Quality crafts that *are* made in the Eastern Caribbean include dolls in native Creole costumes, natural-fiber basketwork and stylish cotton clothing. Caribelle Batik makes good quality batik clothing, as well as wall hangings with Caribbean scenes, which are for sale on several islands. Locally grown spices make nice lightweight souvenirs, and of course there's always rum.

Getting There & Away

This section contains an overview of the transportation options for getting to the Eastern Caribbean from countries outside the region. More specific information, including airfares, can be found in the Getting There & Away section of each island chapter.

Information on LIAT and other regional airlines flying within the Eastern Caribbean, and information on boat services between Eastern Caribbean islands, is in the Getting Around chapter.

The phone numbers listed in this section are the reservation numbers from the countries indicated.

AIR
Airlines
The following are the major international airlines that serve the region, along with their reservations numbers in the USA and Canada:

Air Canada	☎ 800-247-2262
Air France	☎ 800-237-2747
British Airways	☎ 800-247-9297
American Airlines	☎ 800-433-7300
AOM	☎ 800-892-9136
Continental Airlines	☎ 800-525-0280
Delta	☎ 800-354-9822
Qantas	☎ 800-227-4500
KLM	☎ 800-374-7747
TWA	☎ 800-221-2000
United Airlines	☎ 800-538-2929

The following are major domestic airlines that serve the region:

Air Jamaica	☎ 800-523-5585
LIAT	☎ 800-468-0482
BWIA	☎ 800-538-2942

Buying Tickets
Rather than just walking into the nearest travel agent or airline office, it pays to do a bit of research and shop around. If you're buying tickets within the US, the *New York Times, Los Angeles Times, Chicago Tribune, San Francisco Examiner* and other major newspapers all produce weekly travel sections with numerous travel agents' ads. Both Council Travel (☎ 800-226-8624, www.counciltravel.com) and STA (☎ 800-777-0112, www.sta.com) have offices in major cities nationwide. The magazine *Travel Unlimited*, PO Box 1058, Allston, MA 02134, publishes details of the cheapest airfares and courier possibilities.

Those coming from outside the US might start by perusing travel sections of magazines like *Time Out* and *TNT* in the UK, or the Saturday editions of newspapers like the *Sydney Morning Herald* and *The Age* in Australia. Ads in these publications offer cheap fares, but don't be surprised if they happen to be sold out when you contact the agents: They're usually low-season fares on obscure airlines with conditions attached.

The plane ticket will probably be the single most expensive item in your budget, and buying it can be intimidating. It is always worth putting aside a few hours to research the current state of the market. Start shopping for a ticket early – some of the cheapest tickets must be bought months in advance, and some popular flights sell out early. Talk to other recent travelers – they may be able to stop you from making some of the same old mistakes. Look at the ads in newspapers and magazines, consult reference books and watch for special offers.

Phone travel agents for bargains (airlines can supply information on routes and timetables; however, except during fare wars they do not supply the cheapest tickets). Airlines often have competitive low-season, student and senior-citizen fares. Find out the fare, the route, the duration of the journey and any restrictions on the ticket.

Cheap tickets are available in two distinct categories: official and unofficial. The official ones have a variety of names, including advance-purchase fares, budget fares, APEX and super-APEX. Unofficial tickets are simply discounted tickets that the airlines release through selected travel agents (not through airline offices). The cheapest tickets are often nonrefundable and require an extra fee for changing your flight. Many insurance policies will cover this loss if you have to change your flight for emergency reasons.

Roundtrip tickets usually work out cheaper than two one-way fares – often *much* cheaper.

Use the fares quoted in this book as a guide only. They are approximate and based on the rates advertised by travel agents and airlines at press time. Quoted airfares do not necessarily constitute a recommendation for the carrier.

If traveling from the UK, you will probably find that the cheapest flights are being advertised by obscure bucket shops whose names haven't yet reached the telephone directory. Many such firms are honest and solvent, but there are a few rogues who will take your money and disappear, to reopen elsewhere a month or two later under a new name. If you feel suspicious about a firm, don't give them all the money at once – leave a deposit of 20% or so and pay the balance on receiving the ticket. If they insist on cash in advance, go elsewhere. And once you have the ticket, call the airline to confirm that you are booked on the flight.

You may decide to pay more than the rock-bottom fare by opting for the safety of a better-known travel agent. Established firms like STA Travel, which has offices worldwide, Council Travel in the USA or Travel CUTS in Canada are valid alternatives, and they offer good prices to most destinations.

Once you have your ticket, write down its number, together with the flight number and other details, and keep the information somewhere separate. If the ticket is lost or stolen, this will help you get a replacement.

Charters Charter flights from the USA, Canada, the UK and Europe offer another option for getting to the islands. Fares are often cheaper than on regularly scheduled commercial airlines, but you usually have to go and come back on a specific flight, commonly with a weeklong stay, and you'll probably have no flexibility in extending your stay.

In the high season, charters often operate with such frequency that they carry more passengers to some islands than the scheduled airlines.

Although charter companies do most of their business booking package tours that include both accommodations and airfare, they commonly find themselves with a few empty seats on planes that they've chartered. Some companies will then sell these empty seats for bargain prices a week or two prior to departure.

In the USA you can sometimes find these seats advertised in the travel pages of larger Sunday newspapers, such as the *New York*

Warning

The information in this chapter is particularly vulnerable to change: prices for international travel are volatile, routes are introduced and canceled, schedules change, special deals come and go, and rules and visa requirements are amended. Governments and airlines seem to take a perverse pleasure in making price structures and regulations as complicated as possible. You should check directly with the airline or a travel agent to make sure you understand how a fare (and any ticket you may buy) works. In addition, the travel industry is highly competitive, and there are many lurks and perks.

The upshot of this is that you should get opinions, quotes and advice from as many airlines and travel agents as possible before you part with your hard-earned cash. The details given in this chapter should be regarded as pointers and are not a substitute for your own careful, up-to-date research.

Air Travel Glossary

Cancellation Penalties If you have to cancel or change a discounted ticket, there are often heavy penalties involved; insurance can sometimes be taken out against these penalties. Some airlines impose penalties on regular tickets as well, particularly against 'no-show' passengers.

Courier Fares Businesses will often need to send urgent documents or freight securely and quickly. Courier companies hire people to accompany the package through customs and, in return, offer a discount ticket which is sometimes a phenomenal bargain. However, you may have to surrender all your baggage allowance and take only carry-on luggage.

Full Fares Airlines traditionally offer 1st class (coded F), business class (coded J) and economy class (coded Y) tickets. These days, so many promotional and discounted fares are available that few passengers pay full economy fare.

Lost Tickets If you lose your airline ticket, an airline will usually treat it like a traveler's check and, after inquiries, issue you with another one. Legally, however, an airline is entitled to treat it like cash: If you lose it, it's gone forever. Take good care of your tickets.

Onward Tickets An entry requirement for many countries is a ticket out of the country. If you're unsure of your next move, the easiest solution is to buy the cheapest onward ticket to a neighboring country or a ticket from a reliable airline that can later be refunded if you do not use it.

Open-Jaw Tickets These are return tickets that permit you to fly into one place but return from another. If available, these tickets can save you backtracking to your arrival point.

Overbooking Because almost every flight has some passengers that fail to show up, airlines often book more passengers than they have seats. Usually excess passengers make up for the no-shows, but occasionally somebody gets 'bumped' onto the next available flight. Guess who it is most likely to be? The passengers who check in late.

Promotional Fares These are officially discounted fares, available from travel agencies or direct from the airline.

Reconfirmation If you don't reconfirm your flight at least 72 hours prior to departure, the airline may delete your name from the passenger list. Call to find out if your airline requires reconfirmation.

Restrictions Discounted tickets often have various restrictions – for example, they may need to be paid for in advance, or altering them may incur a penalty. Other restrictions include minimum and maximum periods you must be away.

Round-the-World Tickets RTW tickets give you a limited period (usually a year) in which to circumnavigate the globe. You can go anywhere the carrying airlines go as long as you don't backtrack. The number of stopovers or total number of separate flights is decided before you set off, and these tickets usually cost a bit more than a basic return flight.

Transferred Tickets Airline tickets cannot be transferred from one person to another. Travelers sometimes try to sell the return half of a ticket, but officials can ask you to prove that you are the person named on the ticket. On an international flight, tickets are compared with passports.

Travel Periods Ticket prices vary with the time of year. There is a low (off-peak) season and a high (peak) season, and often a low-shoulder season and a high-shoulder season as well. Usually the fare depends on your outward flight – if you depart in the high season and return in the low season, you pay the high-season fare.

Times and the *Boston Globe*. Travel agents who specialize in discount travel can also be helpful.

The USA

There are more flights from the USA to the Eastern Caribbean than from any other part of the world.

American Airlines (☎ 800-433-7300) is the main US carrier into the region. American has direct flights from the US to a few of the larger Eastern Caribbean islands, although to most destinations travelers must first fly to San Juan, Puerto Rico, and then change planes, continuing on American's interisland carrier American Eagle. Overall, American's interisland schedule coordinates closely with its flights between the US mainland and San Juan, making for convenient connections. Low-season roundtrip fares start at around US$550 to US$700, depending on which island you're flying to.

Continental Airlines (☎ 800-525-0280), the only other US carrier offering flights to the Eastern Caribbean, operates flights from New York City to St Martin and Antigua.

The Trinidad-based BWIA (☎ 800-538-2942) has a fairly extensive schedule from both Miami and New York to the larger non-French islands of the Eastern Caribbean.

Air France (☎ 800-237-2747) has a twice-weekly flight from Miami to Guadeloupe and Martinique; low-season fares start at around US$550.

Canada

Air Canada (☎ 800-247-2262) has direct flights from Toronto to Barbados, Antigua, St Lucia and Trinidad, as well as from Montreal to Martinique. Low-season fares start at around C$925.

From Toronto the carrier BWIA (☎ 800-538-2942) also flies to Barbados, Antigua and Trinidad.

Australia

The cheapest fares from Australia to the Eastern Caribbean are all via the USA.

Qantas' roundtrip fare from Melbourne or Sydney to Los Angeles ranges from A$1667 in the low season to A$2800 in the high season. Roundtrip excursion fares from Los Angeles to Barbados start at about A$1000, and to Martinique, A$1200.

The UK

British Airways (☎ 084-5773 3377) operates flights from London to Antigua, St Lucia, Barbados, Grenada and Tobago; low-season fares start at around £450.

BWIA (☎ 020-7745 1100) has flights from London to Antigua, Barbados, St Lucia and Trinidad starting at around £500.

Continental Europe

Paris is the main European gateway to the Eastern Caribbean. Air France (☎ 082-08 20 820) flies from Paris to Martinique, Guadeloupe, St Martin and Antigua. Fares from Paris to Martinique start just under 3000F in low season.

Air Liberté (☎ 080-30 90 909) and Nouvelles Frontières (☎ 082-50 00 825) fly from Paris to Martinique and Guadeloupe.

KLM (☎ 20-47 47 747) operates twice-weekly flights from Amsterdam to St Martin.

South America

There are connections between South America and the Eastern Caribbean with LIAT, Aeropostal (☎ 888-802-8466), Air France and Air Guadeloupe.

SEA
Freighters

While passenger-carrying freighters have become a thing of the past in much of the world, there are still a couple of interesting freighter options for getting to the Caribbean. One is the M/V *Amazing Grace*, a 257-foot 'workhorse' ship that once carried supplies to English lighthouse keepers and now sails the length of the Caribbean servicing Windjammers' fleet of tall ships. The other is CGM, which operates modern cargo ships that carry goods from France to the French West Indies, returning home with bananas from Martinique and Guadeloupe.

Amazing Grace The Windjammers' supply ship, the *Amazing Grace*, departs from West Palm Beach, Florida, once a month. Because it's not allowed to pick up passengers at US ports, southbound passengers board at Freeport, The Bahamas. Northbound passengers can embark at the turnaround point of Port of Spain, Trinidad. In all, the ship makes about 20 stops over the 26-day roundtrip voyage, making it an excellent way to see a wide swath of Caribbean islands. Ports of call can include Antigua, Bequia, Dominica, Grenada, Les Saintes, Palm Island, Statia, St Barts, St Kitts, Nevis, St Lucia, St Martin and Tobago.

To take the voyage one-way – a 13-day trip – fares range from US$1375 for a berth with a washbasin to US$1575 for a top-deck berth with private bath. All meals are included, as is wine with dinner. Roundtrip fares are double. A US$100 premium is charged from November through May, and there's a 20% discount in the hurricane-prone months of August and September. Singles can either share a cabin or pay 175% of the per-person double rate for their own cabin. Although the ship carries 94 passengers, services are streamlined; there's a bar and TV room, but no pool, laundry room or doctor on board. Optional shore excursions are reasonably priced, from US$10 to US$25. Reservations can be made through Windjammer Barefoot Cruises (☎ 305-672-6453, 800-327-2601), PO Box 120, Miami Beach, FL 33119, USA.

CGM The Compagnie Générale Maritime (CGM) sails nearly weekly between mainland France and the French West Indies, stopping in both Guadeloupe and Martinique. The CGM vessels, which are modern cargo ships that carry bananas and limes to France, have a dozen comfortable passenger cabins, a TV room and a swimming pool. French meals with wine are included in the rate, which is approximately 5000F in summer, 5500F in winter (one-way) for the 10-day voyage, with reduced fares offered to travelers age 26 and under. As cabin space is very limited, the boat commonly books up far in advance.

Passage can be booked in Guadeloupe through Transat Antilles Voyages (☎ 0590-83 04 43), Quai Lefevre, Pointe-à-Pitre; in Martinique through CGM (☎ 0596-71 34 23), 8 Boulevard du Général-de-Gaulle, Fort-de-France; or in Paris through either CGM (☎ 014-62 57 000) or Sotramat Voyages (☎ 014-92 42 473), 12 Rue Godot-de-Moroy, 75009 Paris, France.

Cruises

More than two million cruise-ship passengers sail the Caribbean annually, making the Caribbean the world's largest cruise-ship destination. The ships average four to five ports of call each, adding up to a whopping 10 million 'passenger visits' throughout the region.

The most visited ports in the Eastern Caribbean are St Martin, with 500,000 passenger arrivals, Barbados and Martinique, each with 400,000 passenger arrivals, followed by Antigua, Guadeloupe, Grenada, St Lucia, Dominica, St Kitts, St Vincent & the Grenadines and Trinidad & Tobago.

The typical cruise-ship holiday is the ultimate package tour. Other than the effort involved in selecting a cruise, it requires minimal planning – just pay and show up – and for many people this is a large part of the appeal.

Some cruise lines put more emphasis on the thrill of cruising around the seas on a floating resort than they do on visiting any actual destination. If 'being there' is more important than 'getting there,' travelers will need to choose a cruise accordingly.

For the most part, the smaller 'unconventional' ships put greater emphasis on the local aspects of their cruises, both in terms of the time spent on land and the degree of interaction with islanders and their environment. While the majority of mainstream cruises take in fine scenery along the way, the time spent on the islands is generally quite limited, and the opportunities to experience a sense of island life are more restricted.

Still, the fact that most cruise ships call on many islands in a short time can be useful in providing an overview for those who plan to come back to the region later but haven't decided which islands to visit.

Because travel in the Eastern Caribbean can be expensive and because cruises cover rooms, meals, entertainment and transportation in one all-inclusive price, cruises can also be comparatively economical. All cruises will cost more than budget-end independent travel, but the least expensive cruises will not necessarily cost more than a conventional air/hotel package tour or a privately booked vacation at a resort hotel.

Cost Cruise lines do not divide passengers into class categories, but rather provide the same meals and amenities for all passengers on each ship.

Virtually all cruises are offered at a range of rates, however, depending mainly on the size, type and location of the cabin. Budget cabins might well be uncomfortably cramped and poorly located, while top-end cabins are often spacious, luxurious suites. Price also depends on the season and dates of the cruise, the number of people in each cabin, transportation options between your home and the departure point and, of course, which cruise you choose. In addition, discounts off the brochure rates are commonplace.

Standard rates are quoted per person, based on double occupancy. A third and fourth person in the same cabin are usually given a heavily discounted rate.

Provisions vary widely for single travelers who occupy a double cabin; a few cruise lines allow this at no extra charge, while most charge from 110% to 200% of the standard per-person rate. Some cruise lines offer single cabins, and some have a singles share program in which they attempt to match up compatible (same-sex) cabin mates to share the double cabins.

Some cruise lines provide free or discounted airfare to and from the port of embarkation in their quoted rates (or will provide a rebate if you make your own transportation arrangements), while others do not.

Most cruises to the Eastern Caribbean end up costing around US\$125 to US\$350

per person per day, including airfare from a major US gateway city.

Meals, which are typically frequent and elaborate, are included in the cruise price. Alcoholic drinks are usually not included and are comparable in price to those in bars back home.

Guided land tours are almost always offered at each port of call, generally for about US\$35 to US\$100 each. If you opt to see the sights yourself, you'll need to budget for taxis, admission fees, etc.

Entertainment shows and most onboard activities are included in the cruise price, but personal services such as hairstyling and laundry usually cost extra, as do most shoreside activities such as diving or windsurfing.

Some cruise lines include tipping in the quoted price. Most do not, however, and usually suggest that each passenger tip, per day, US\$3 to the cabin steward, US\$3 to the dining-room waiter and US\$1.50 to the table attendant, all given in a lump sum on the last night of the cruise. For cocktail waiters, a 15% tip is sometimes included in the drink price and if not is generally given on the spot.

Port charges and government taxes typically add on about US\$100 per cruise. Be sure to check the fine print about deposits, cancellation and refund policies and travel insurance.

Discounts When all is said and done, very few cruises are sold at the brochure rates.

The general rule is the earlier the booking, the greater the discount (and, of course, the better the cabin selection). Some cruise lines offer an across-the-board discount of around 25% to those who book at least 90 days in advance, while others discount up to 40% for even earlier bookings and then lower the discount rate as the sailing date gets closer.

Still, cruise lines want to sail full, so if there are leftover seats at the end, there will be discounts available.

And then there are promotions: Some cruise lines offer a 50% discount for the second person on designated sailings, offer free cabin upgrades if certain qualifications

Choosing a Cruise

In addition to finding a cruise that fits your budget, here are some other things to consider:

Schedule Most cruises last between one and two weeks. Caribbean cruises are most popular and thus most expensive during the Northern Hemisphere's midwinter (with the peak time being the Christmas/New Year holidays) and least crowded in autumn, with spring and summer in between.

Departure Point Most cruises that take in destinations in the Eastern Caribbean depart from Miami or Fort Lauderdale, Florida; San Juan, Puerto Rico; St Thomas, US Virgin Islands; or from within the Eastern Caribbean itself. Consider the cost and ease of getting to the departure point. Also important is your interest in the port and nearby islands if you plan to extend your holiday.

Itinerary The largest cruise ships generally stop only at islands with substantial port facilities, such as St Martin, Antigua, Guadeloupe, Martinique, Dominica, St Lucia and Grenada, while some of the smaller 'unconventional' ships are able to take in less visited islands like Saba, St Barts and the Grenadines.

Ship Type & Facilities The conventional cruise ship is a floating resort, some holding a good 2500 passengers, with multiple swimming pools, Las Vegas–type entertainment, casinos and nightclubs.

Smaller ships, which might have between 50 and 250 passengers, will have less lavish entertainment but are more personal and can pull into smaller ports, marinas and snorkeling coves.

There is a huge variety in style. Some cruise lines appeal to active vacationers who enjoy water sports, hiking and exploration. Some lines feature luxury boats with a sophisticated ambience and prices to match. Some don't accept young children. Others are more middle-class-oriented, welcoming young families, retired seniors, singles and couples alike, with activities for all ages and interests. Likewise, dress codes, meal quality and types of shore excursions vary.

Some ships can accommodate special diets with advance notice. Many are disabled-accessible, although details such as the measurement of bathroom clearance for wheelchairs should be checked carefully, as problems with cabins for the disabled are not uncommon. In general, the newer ships are more accessible, with fewer barriers, larger cabins situated near elevators, and wider doorways and halls.

Cabin Outside cabins are best and least claustrophobic, as you get a view. The higher decks are preferable, as are of course the largest and fanciest cabins, and prices will correspond accordingly. Although modern cruise ships have stabilizers to prevent roll, if you're prone to motion sickness you might want to get a cabin in the center of the ship, which is more stable and rocks less in bad weather.

The inside cabins (with no portholes) on the lowest decks are the least desirable, but also the cheapest. Bottom-end cabins sometimes have bunk-style beds and minuscule bathrooms, and they can be uncomfortably cramped. Avoid the cabins nearest the engine room, as they may be noisy.

Sanitation All cruise ships that arrive in US ports – which includes the majority that sail the Caribbean – are subject to unannounced US sanitation inspections. The inspectors rate ships in four categories: potable water supply; food preparation and holding; potential contamination of food; and general cleanliness, storage and repair.

The Centers for Disease Control has a description of the inspection program and a database of ships' ratings at www.cdc.gov/nceh/vsp. A summary sheet that lists ships, the latest date of inspection and their ratings may be obtained free by writing to the following address: Chief, Vessel Sanitation Program, National Center for Environmental Health, 1015 North American Way, Room 107, Miami, FL 33132, USA.

Environmental Considerations Not all cruise ships have equally clean environmental records. When you book a cruise ship, consider asking the travel agent whether the company has been cited for violating marine pollution laws.

While on your cruise, be inquisitive about the ship's recycling program and how waste is being handled and disposed – it will help raise the level of environmental consciousness. If you do sight any violations, report them to the Center for Marine Conservation (CMC), a nonprofit organization dedicated to the conservation of marine wildlife, and to your travel agent back home, so the information can be used by travelers who come after you.

The US Coast Guard is responsible for tracking down ships that illegally dump wastes at sea within the USA's 200-mile Exclusive Economic Zone. Efforts are concentrated on cruise ships, which tend to carry more garbage than other vessels.

The CMC has become the unofficial repository of information on cruise-line-dumping cases. It compiles information on violators but as it doesn't have the capacity to have staff on board cruise ships, it relies almost solely upon cruise passengers to report pollution violations.

The center will send anyone planning to go on a cruise (or who is otherwise interested) a packet that includes information about the problem, a list of cruise lines that have been implicated in illegal dumping and a form for reporting unlawful dumpings.

In addition, the US government provides a monetary incentive for passengers to assist with enforcement. If a citizen provides information leading to fines, the court may award that person up to half of the fine, which can be as much as US$250,000!

The information packets are available by writing to the Center for Marine Conservation (☎ 202-429-5609), 1725 DeSales St NW, Suite 600, Washington, DC 20036, USA. Include US$5 for postage and handling.

Other Considerations Cruise-ship passengers who show interest in the local culture and put money directly into the hands of small merchants are more appreciated by islanders than those who stay wrapped in the cocoon of organized land tours or see nothing beyond the duty-free shops.

While the cruise line's optional land tours are conveniently packaged to take in many of the island's sightseeing highlights, they also move quickly and tend to shield visitors from interaction with the local people. In addition, a fair percentage of the money paid for these tours stays with the organizers rather than going into the local economy.

On some islands you might want to take a closer look at a smaller area rather than trying to breeze around the whole island on a tour. It can be a fun alternative to wander the streets of the main town, poke into little shops, eat at local restaurants and buy souvenirs from street vendors and small businesses where you can chat with the owners. Buy local rums in small shops instead of on board – you might even save money in the process.

are met, run two-for-one specials in selected markets, offer discounts to senior citizens etc.

Booking a Cruise A good travel agent should be able to work through the maze, providing comparisons on cruise lines, itineraries, facilities, rates and discounts. Be aware that the industry has also attracted the occasional fly-by-night company that advertises heavily, then takes the money and runs, so be sure you're dealing with a reputable agent.

Those travel agents most knowledgeable about cruises are apt to belong to Cruise Lines International Association (CLIA), an organization of cruise lines that works in affiliation with about 20,000 North American travel agencies. You might also want to find a travel agent who subscribes to the *Official Cruise Guide,* which is a good source of information on cruise lines, listing schedules and facilities for virtually all ships.

Your local travel agent may be able to provide all the help you need. If not, there are numerous travel agents who specialize in cruises and are therefore generally up to speed on the latest promotional deals and other discounts. In the USA, a few of those that book widely in the Eastern Caribbean are the following:

Cruise Outlet (☎ 203-288-1884, 800-775-1884, www.thecruiseoutlet.com) 1890 Dixwell Ave, Hamden, CT 06514

Cruises Inc (☎ 315-463-9695, 800-854-0500), 5000 Campuswood Dr, East Syracuse, NY 13057

Cruise Time (☎ 703-352-1261, 800-627-6131, www.cruisetimebargains.com), 9864 Main St, Fairfax, VA 22031

White Travel Service (☎ 860-233-2648, 800-547-4790), 127 Park Rd, West Hartford, CT 06119

World Wide Cruises (☎ 954-720-9000, 800-882-9000, www.wwcruises.com), 8059 W McNab Rd, Fort Lauderdale, FL 33321

For travelers with physical limitations, Flying Wheels Travel (☎ 507-451-5005, 800-535-6790, www.flyingwheelstravel.com), 143 W Bridge St, Owatonna, MN 55060, USA, specializes in booking disabled-accessible Caribbean cruises.

Conventional Cruises Most travel agents have stacks of cruise-ship brochures available for the taking. Brochures can also be obtained by contacting the cruise lines directly.

The following cruise lines sail to one or more of the islands of the Eastern Caribbean. In some cases, not all ports of call listed are visited on a single cruise. While only Eastern Caribbean ports of call are listed, other parts of the Caribbean might also be visited during the same cruise.

The 800 phone numbers are toll-free from the USA and sometimes from Canada.

Contact details and ports of call of conventional cruise lines are as follows:

American Canadian Caribbean Line (☎ 401-247-0955, 800-556-7450) PO Box 368, Warren, RI 02885, USA
Ships sail from San Juan and Trinidad. Ports of call are mostly at the northern and southern extremities of the chain.

Carnival Cruise Lines (☎ 305-599-2600, 800-327-2058) Carnival Place, 3655 NW 87th Ave, Miami, FL 33178, USA
Ships depart from Miami and San Juan. Ports of call include St Martin, Dominica, Grenada, Barbados, Martinique and St Lucia.

Celebrity Cruises (☎ 305-262-6677, 800-892-6019, www.celebrity-cruises.com) 5201 Blue Lagoon Dr, Miami, FL 33126, USA
Ships depart from San Juan and Fort Lauderdale, FL. Ports of call include Grenada, St Lucia, St Martin, Antigua, Barbados and Martinique. It's now officially Royal Caribbean Celebrity Cruises.

Cunard Line (☎ 305-463-3000, 800-728-6273, www.cunardline.com) 6100 Blue Lagoon Dr, Miami FL 33126, USA
This line operates mainly in Europe but has some sailings from Miami that call upon Grenada, Barbados, St Lucia and Dominica.

Holland America Line (☎ 877-724-5425, www.hollandamerica.com) 300 Elliott Ave West, Seattle, WA 98119, USA
Ships depart from Fort Lauderdale and Tampa, FL. Ports of call include Barbados, Trinidad, Dominica, Martinique, St Kitts, St Lucia and St Martin.

Norwegian Cruise Line (☎ 305-436-4000, 800-343-0098, www.ncl.com) 7665 Corporate Center Dr, Miami, FL 33126, USA
Ships depart from Miami and San Juan. Ports of

call include Antigua, St Kitts, Barbados, Dominica, St Lucia and St Martin.

Princess Cruises (☎ 310-553-1770, 800-568-3262) 10100 Santa Monica Blvd, Los Angeles, CA 90067, USA

Ships depart from Fort Lauderdale and San Juan. Ports of call include Barbados, Dominica, Guadeloupe, Martinique and St Martin.

Royal Caribbean Cruise Line (☎ 305-539-6000, 800-398-9819, www.royalcaribbean.com) 1050 Caribbean Way, Miami, FL 33132, USA

Ships depart from Miami and San Juan. Ports of call include St Martin, Barbados, Antigua and Martinique.

Royal Olympic Cruises (☎ 212-397-6400, in the USA ☎ 800-872-6400, in Canada ☎ 800-368-3888) 1 Rockefeller Plaza, New York, NY 10020, USA

Ships depart from Fort Lauderdale, FL, and Galveston, Texas. Ports of call include Antigua, Barbados, Bequia, St Vincent, Grenada, Tobago and Trinidad, the latter island in conjunction with an Amazon River cruise.

Seabourn Cruise Line (☎ 305-463-3000, 800-929-9391, www.seabourn.com) 6001 Blue Lagoon Dr, Miami, FL 33126, USA

Ships depart from Fort Lauderdale and St Thomas, Virgin Islands. Ports of call include St Martin, Antigua and St Barts.

Unconventional Cruises In addition to the cruises listed here, see the Yacht section in the Getting Around the Region chapter for information on cruising the Caribbean by yacht, and Dive Tours in the Organized Tours section later in this chapter for information on live-aboard dive boats.

Clipper Cruise Line (☎ 314-727-2929, 800-325-0010, www.clippercruise.com) 7711 Bonhomme Ave, St Louis, MO 63105, USA

While it's a conventional cruise ship, the *Yorktown Clipper* carries only 138 passengers and has a shallow draft, enabling it to navigate secluded waterways. One tour departs from Grenada and visits Anguilla, Antigua, Bequia, Dominica, Les Saintes, Saba, Statia, St Kitts, St Lucia and Union Island. Another departs from Curaçao and includes Tobago and Trinidad en route to a tour of Venezuela's Río Orinoco.

Club Med (☎ 800-258-2633) 40 West 57th St, New York, NY 10019, USA

The 617-foot *Club Med I* has computerized sails and a high-tech design, holds 386 passengers and operates much like any other all-inclusive Club Med resort, except that it's at sea. The equally luxurious *Club Med II* is one of the largest sailing ships in the world. Itineraries vary, but ports of call include Marie-Galante, St Kitts, Nevis, St Martin, Dominica, Les Saintes, St Barts and Antigua.

Marpol Annex V

Marine pollution is a serious issue in the Caribbean, and cruise ships dumping rubbish overboard have traditionally been a major part of the problem. Annex V of Marpol 73/78, an international treaty resulting from the 1973 International Convention for the Prevention of Pollution from Ships, makes it illegal to dump plastics anywhere at sea and also places nearshore restrictions on the disposal of other solid waste. Some garbage can still be dumped, as long as it's disposed of at least 3 miles offshore; bottles and cans cannot be dumped within 12 miles of land.

Despite the rules of the treaty, which went into effect in 1988, most countries have paid little heed to enforcing the regulations. Indeed, only a handful of Caribbean countries have ratified the treaty, and thus some cruise ships have continued to randomly dump garbage in Caribbean waters.

On the other hand, the USA, from whose waters most Caribbean cruise ships depart, has cracked down hard on violators within its 200-mile Exclusive Economic Zone.

In 1993 the cruise-ship industry got a wake-up call when the *Regal Princess* of Princess Cruises received the maximum fine of US$500,000 for dumping 20 plastic bags full of garbage off the Florida Keys. The successful prosecution was the consequence of a cruise passenger's videotaping of the dumping.

Princess Cruises, incidentally, has since initiated stringent environmental guidelines. In 1996, it received the American Society of Travel Agents/Smithsonian Magazine Environmental Award for its proactive stance on pollution prevention, becoming the first cruise line to win the award.

The *Sea Cloud* (☎ 201-227-9404, 888-732-2568)
32–40 N Dean St, Englewood, NJ 07631, USA
This four-mast, 360-foot-long ship has luxury accommodations and departs from Antigua. Ports of call include Bequia, Palm Island, Grenada, Carriacou, St Kitts, Nevis, St Lucia, Martinique, Dominica, Barbuda, St Barts, Anguilla and St Martin.

Star Clippers (☎ 305-442-0550, 800-442-0551) 4101 Salzedo Ave, Coral Gables, FL 33146, USA
These modern four-masted clipper ships have tall-ship designs and carry 180 passengers. They depart from Antigua and Barbados. Ports of call include St Martin, Dominica, Les Saintes, Martinique, St Barts, St Kitts, St Lucia, St Vincent, Bequia, Union Island and the Tobago Cays.

Windjammer Barefoot Cruises (☎ 305-672-6453, 800-327-2601, www.windjammer.com) PO Box 120, Miami Beach, FL 33119, USA
The fleet consists of a restored four-mast, 282-foot stay-sail rigged schooner and other tall sailing ships, carrying from 65 to 128 passengers. They tend to attract a younger, more active and budget-minded crowd. Some cruises are geared for singles only. Boats depart from Freeport, Antigua, Grenada and St Martin. Ports of call include Anguilla, Dominica, Les Saintes, Saba, St Barts, St Eustatius, St Kitts, Nevis, St Lucia, Bequia, Canouan, Mayreau, Union Island, Palm Island, the Tobago Cays, Carriacou, Trinidad and Tobago.

Windstar Cruises (☎ 206-281-3535, 800-258-7245, www.windstarcruises.com) 300 Elliott Ave West, Seattle, WA 98119, USA
These luxury four-mast, 440-foot boats have high-tech, computer-operated sails and take 148 passengers. They depart from Barbados. Ports of call include Nevis, St Martin, St Barts, Guadeloupe, Bequia, Tobago, Grenada, the Tobago Cays, Martinique and St Lucia.

Gay & Lesbian Cruises The following US-based companies offer gay-friendly cruises to the Eastern Caribbean:

Cruisemax Cruises (☎ 425-646-9444, 800-229-1165, fax 206-965-2747, www.cruisemaxinc.com)

Journeys By Sea, Inc (☎ 954-522-5865, 800-825-3632, www.journeysbysea.com) PO Box 7500, Fort Lauderdale, FL 33338

Olivia Travel (☎ 510-655-0364, 800-631-6277, fax 510-655-4334, www.oliviatravel.com) 4400 Market St, Oakland, CA 94608

Pied Piper Travel (☎ 212-239-2412, 800-874-7312, fax 212-239-2275, http://home.att.net/~pied-piper-travel/00itino.html) 330 West 42nd St, Suite 1804, New York, NY 10036

ORGANIZED TOURS

There are scores of conventional package tours to the Eastern Caribbean available from the USA, Canada and Europe. Most are a week in duration, though they sometimes can be extended. If you are going to the Caribbean for just a short vacation, package tours can be quite economical, as the cost to book the same flight and hotel separately on your own is typically much higher.

Particularly in the USA package tours are highly competitive, with weeklong tours that include hotel and airfare from the US east coast for as little as US$600. The ads found in the travel sections of big-city Sunday newspapers are a good source of information. Package tours represent a substantial part of the bookings for most travel agents, who can usually pile you high with tour brochures.

Bargain hunters can sometimes find some good last-minute deals, as consolidators that book out a block of hotel rooms and airplane seats often have to pay for them whether they're full or not – it's to their advantage to let them go cheaply (even below cost) a week or two prior to the flight. If you're flexible enough to book a discounted package on relatively short notice, let your travel agent know so he or she can keep you posted.

Ecotourism

An elevated concern for the environment and a healthy desire to minimize the adverse affects of tourism has spurred the growth of tour organizers who promote themselves as environmentally friendly. 'Ecotourism' and 'green tourism' are now becoming trendy terms in the Eastern Caribbean. Some of those using the terms, such as groups affiliated with nonprofit nature and conservation societies, are genuinely promoting travel that contributes to environmental and cultural preservation. On the other hand, some tour operators in the more traditional tourism industry appear to be using ecotourism buzzwords primarily as a marketing opportunity.

Tourism can indeed have a positive impact on host communities. Diving fees in Saba, for instance, help support the Saba Marine Park and are used to install floating buoys that eliminate the need for boats to drop anchor on fragile reefs. On islands such as Dominica, Guadeloupe, Martinique and St Lucia, recognition that the remaining rain forests are a positive asset for both islanders and visitors has contributed to the setting aside of sizable parks and preserves.

In addition to the tours that follow in this section, you'll find information on nature-preserve and bird-sanctuary outings, rain-forest accommodations and ecologically minded tour guides in individual island chapters throughout this book.

Birding & Natural-History Tours

The National Audubon Society (☎ 212-979-3066, fax 212-353-0190, www.audubon.com), 700 Broadway, New York, NY 10003, USA, offers Nature Odyssey tours with a natural-history orientation, led by Audubon staff members. Most of the society's Caribbean tours are aboard regularly scheduled cruises, such as a 12-day bird watcher's trip to Trinidad, Tobago and Venezuela (from US$3140) aboard Clipper Cruise Line's 138-passenger *Yorktown Clipper*. Prices do not include airfares.

Caligo Ventures (☎ 914-273-6333, 800-426-7781, www.caligo.com), 156 Bedford Rd, Armonk, NY 10504, USA, runs frequent birding tours to Trinidad and Tobago, with stays at the Asa Wright Nature Centre in Trinidad and Blue Waters Inn on Tobago. One-week tours of Tobago cost US$1175 in the low season, based on double occupancy and including airfare from Miami; add US$50 for flights from New York. Eleven-day tours that combine Trinidad and Tobago cost US$1875 in the low season, including airfare from either Miami or New York.

Natural History Travel of the Massachusetts Audubon Society (☎ 800-289-9504, fax 617-259-1040, nhtravel@massaudubon.org), 208 S Great Rd, Lincoln, MA 01773, USA, offers an ornithologist-led 10-day bird-watching tour to Trinidad and Tobago each winter. Accommodations are at the Asa Wright Nature Centre in Trinidad and the Blue Waters Inn on Tobago. The cost of US$3100 includes outings, meals and ac-

commodations based on double occupancy and airfare from Miami.

The Smithsonian Institution (☎ 202-357-4700, fax 202-633-9250), 1100 Jefferson Drive SW, Washington, DC 20560, USA, leads natural-history tours and cruises that sometimes include islands at the southern end of the Eastern Caribbean. Costs vary depending upon the type and length of the outing.

Volunteer & Educational Programs

Caribbean Volunteer Expeditions (☎ 607-962-7846, www.cvexp.org), PO Box 388, Corning, NY 14830, USA, sends volunteers to work at historic sites in conjunction with local national trusts, historical societies and other preservation groups. Recent projects have included St Kitts and Anguilla, as well as Puerto Rico and the US Virgin Islands. Fees typically range from US$300 to US$800 per week, including accommodations, food and land transportation, but not airfare.

Elderhostel (☎ 877-426-8056), Avenue de Lafayette, Boston, MA 02111-1746, USA, is a nonprofit organization offering educational programs for those aged 55 or older. The organization has its origins in the youth hostels of Europe and the folk schools of Scandinavia. It has a few courses in the Caribbean, including Anguilla, Dominica, Nevis, St Vincent and Trinidad and Tobago. The cost for weeklong trips starts around US$1000, including accommodations, meals and classes but excluding airfare.

Earthwatch (☎ 978-461-0081, 800-776-0188), 3 Clock Tower Plaza, Suite 100, Maynard, MA 01754, USA, sends volunteers to work on scientific and conservation projects worldwide, sometimes including the Eastern Caribbean. Rates for two-week courses generally hover around US$1700, including meals and accommodations but not airfare.

Dive Tours

PADI Travel Network (☎ 949-858-7234, 800-729-7234, www.padi.com), 30151 Tomas St, Rancho Santa Margarita, CA 92688-2125, USA, has dive package tours at a number of Eastern Caribbean destinations including

Dominica, Saba, Bequia and Anse Chastanet in St Lucia. Rates per person based on double occupancy for a weeklong hotel/dive package start in the high season at US$997 in Dominica, US$789 in Saba and US$1869 in St Lucia. Airfare is not included. Arrangements can be made through any PADI dive center worldwide.

Explorer Ventures (☎ 903-887-8521, 800-322-3577), PO Box 488, Mabank, TX 75147-0488, USA, books the M/V *Caribbean Explorer*, a 16-passenger live-aboard dive boat. One-week tours depart from St Martin on Saturday, and take in two days of diving on St Kitts and four days of diving on Saba before returning to St Martin. The cost of US$1295 per person, based on double occupancy, includes onboard accommodations, meals, five dives daily and the use of tanks, weights and belts. Airfare is not included.

World Dive Adventures (☎ 800-433-3483, fax 954-434-4282, www.worlddive.com) has dive tours to Dominica for around US$900 that include seven nights' accommodations, two dives a day, breakfasts and dinners. This company also arranges tours to Saba, St Eustatius, St Vincent and Tobago and can book the aforementioned M/V *Caribbean Explorer*.

Both Scuba Voyages (☎ 909-371-1831, 800-544-7631, fax 909-279-0478, www.scubavoyages.com), 595 Fairbanks St, Corona, CA 91719, USA, and Landfall Productions (☎ 916-563-0164, 800-525-3833, www.landfallproductions.com), 855 Howe Ave, Suite 6, Sacramento, CA 95825, USA, also book room/dive packages at multiple locations in the Eastern Caribbean.

In addition, most dive shops listed in this book can arrange package tours that include accommodations and diving fees, so if you're interested in a specific island consider contacting the dive shops directly.

Surfing Tours

Surfing package tours to Barbados are offered by Surf Express (☎ 321-779-2124, www.surfex.com), 568 Hwy A1A, Satellite Beach, FL 32937, USA. The summer per-person cost for a one-week tour, including airfare from Miami, starts at US$654 based on triple occupancy in a small efficiency cottage or US$707 based on double occupancy at the Edgewater Inn. From New York, add US$50 in low season, US$75 in high. Reasonably priced two-week packages are also available.

Clothing-Optional Tours

A handful of US tour companies cater to those looking for a holiday au naturel. The most common destinations are Orient Beach on St Martin and Hawksbill Beach Resort on Antigua. There are also clothing-optional cruises on Windjammer and Star Clipper tall ships.

Bare Necessities (☎ 512-499-0405, 800-743-0405, fax 512-469-0179, www.bare-necessities.com) 904 W 29th St, Austin, TX 78705, USA

Go Classy Tours (☎ 727-781-1405, 800-725-2779, fax 813-784-4284, www.goclassy.com) 2676 W Lake Rd, Palm Harbor, FL 34684, USA

Travel Au Naturel (☎ 813-948-2007, 800-728-0185, fax 813-948-2832) 35246 US 19 N, Suite 112, Palm Harbor, FL 34684, USA

Getting Around the Region

AIR

LIAT (formerly Leeward Islands Air Transport) is the Caribbean's main interisland carrier, connecting a total of 18 destinations from Puerto Rico to Caracas, most of which fall within the Eastern Caribbean. The airline has nearly 150 flights each day, which accounts for roughly half of all interisland flights in the region.

BWIA, the Trinidad-based airline, flies between some of the larger islands of the Eastern Caribbean, but it's predominantly an international carrier and has a far more limited interisland schedule than LIAT.

Other airlines cover only a segment of the Eastern Caribbean. Winair services the islands around St Martin, from Anguilla to St Kitts. SVG operates a puddle jumper connecting the Grenadine islands between St Vincent and Grenada. In the French West Indies, Air Guadeloupe and Air Martinique are the main carriers, but there are also a handful of small commuter airlines – like Air St Martin and Air St Barts – that fly between a couple of islands on scheduled flights.

Specific airfare and schedule information is in each individual island chapter. Like everything else, these are subject to change, and it's certainly a wise idea to pick up the latest printed schedules from airline counters as soon as you arrive in the islands.

LIAT

LIAT was once notorious for unreliable service and labor problems, but it has recently been privatized and reorganized. It remains the main interisland carrier in the Eastern Caribbean.

In addition to straightforward one-way and excursion tickets, LIAT offers a varied but confusing array of discounted fares and passes. As any extensive travel in the Caribbean is almost certain to involve flights on LIAT, you can save yourself a great deal of money by figuring out the various options in advance and deciding which one best suits your itinerary.

LIAT offers a range of roundtrip excursion fares, including the standard type valid for either 21 or 30 days that allows one or two en-route stopovers and costs an average of 50% more than a one-way ticket. These excursion tickets are available on most LIAT routes and can be purchased either before or after you arrive in the Caribbean – they generally have no advance-purchase requirements and are fully refundable.

In addition, LIAT offers some deeply discounted one- and seven-day excursion tickets on selected routes; these tickets are often cheaper than the price of a one-way ticket. Some one- and seven-day tickets can be purchased only on the island where they originate, and getting information on these tickets outside the islands is difficult. Essentially, short-stay tickets are marketed to local residents as an affordable opportunity to go to a neighboring island for a shopping spree or brief vacation. However, you don't need to be a Caribbean resident to buy them.

LIAT also has senior-citizen fares and youth fares that normally cut as much as 50% off the regular fares; air passes are not discounted.

LIAT's reservation numbers in the USA are ☎ 800-468-0482 or 268-480-5600, fax 268-480-5625. In France LIAT can be booked through Air France, and in Germany, through Lufthansa.

Unlimited One-Way Fares Many of LIAT's long-distance one-way fares allow unlimited en route stopovers and have virtually no restrictions. They are valid for a year, and you can change your flight dates or have the ticket rewritten to delete or add islands without additional fees. These tickets can be a bargain if you're traveling to and from the Caribbean on an open-jaw ticket – such as flying into Trinidad and out of St Martin. As an example, LIAT's one-way fare between Trinidad and St Martin costs

US$306 and allows en route stopovers on Tobago, Grenada, Carriacou, St Vincent, St Lucia, Martinique, Dominica, Guadeloupe, Antigua, Nevis and St Kitts.

Air Passes The following LIAT air passes can be an excellent deal for anyone interested in doing some serious island-hopping.

The king of the air passes is the LIAT Caribbean Super Explorer, which costs US$475 and is valid for 30 days of travel to any or all of the 18 destinations served by LIAT. You can visit each destination only once, although you can go through an airport any number of times as required for onward connections.

There's no advance-purchase requirement. Passes can be purchased at home before your trip or after you arrive in the Caribbean. You must decide your itinerary at the time of purchase, and any subsequent changes are subject to a US$35 surcharge. Tickets must be purchased at least seven days in advance or within 48 hours of making reservations, whichever comes first. Once you start to use the pass, the remainder of the pass coupons cannot be refunded or used as payment toward another ticket.

The LIAT Explorer is a good air pass if you want to visit just a few islands, especially if they're far-flung. This pass allows you to visit any three islands in LIAT's network, costs US$262 and is valid for 21 days. The ticket must be purchased before you arrive in the Caribbean and must begin and end on the same island. Once ticketed, no changes are allowed.

The LIAT Air Pass is sold only in Europe and in the UK in conjunction with a transatlantic ticket. Coupons for a minimum of three destinations and a maximum of six destinations can be purchased for travel throughout LIAT's Caribbean network, with the exception of Venezuela. Coupons cost US$85 per destination, and the air pass is valid for 21 days from the start of the first flight. Once ticketed, no changes are allowed.

BWIA

BWIA has the Caribbean Air Pass for US$499 that's valid for 30 days and allows travelers to visit all of its Caribbean destinations. All travel is on wide-body aircraft, as each intra-Caribbean flight is a leg of an international flight. Consequently, BWIA features a much more limited Caribbean network than LIAT. Currently, BWIA serves Barbados, Antigua, Grenada, St Lucia, St Martin, Trinidad, Jamaica, Caracas and Guyana only. On this 30-day pass, the itinerary must be set in advance, and there's a US$20 charge to make changes. Each destination can be visited only once, other than for connecting flights.

BWIA's reservation number in the USA and Canada is ☎ 800-538-2942, in the UK ☎ 020-8577 1100.

BUS

There's inexpensive bus service on most islands, although the word 'bus' has different meanings in different places. Some islands have full-size buses, while on others a 'bus' is simply a pickup truck with wooden benches in the back.

Perhaps the most common type of bus is the Toyota minivan, the sort that accommodates a family of six elsewhere. However, in the Eastern Caribbean these minivans have four or five rows of seats, as well as jump seats in the aisle that fold down as the rows fill. As more and more people get on, the bus becomes an uninterrupted mass of humanity – children move onto their parents' laps, schoolkids share seats, people squeeze together, and everyone generally accepts the crowding with good nature. Whenever someone gets off the back of a crowded minivan, it takes on the element of a human Rubik's Cube, with the jump seats folding up and down and everyone shuffling places; on some buses there's actually a conductor to direct the seating.

Buses are often the primary means of commuting to work or school and thus are most frequent in the early mornings and from mid- to late afternoon. There's generally good bus service on Saturday morning as well, as it's the big market day. On Saturday afternoon and also all day Sunday, bus service on many islands is all but nonexistent; plan ahead or you'll find yourself stuck.

CAR & MOTORCYCLE
Road Rules

On islands that were formerly British, driving is on the left-hand side of the road, and on the French and Dutch islands it is on the right-hand side.

On the French islands, note that there's a rather confusing *priorité à droite* rule in which any car approaching an intersection from a road to your right has the right-of-way; you must slow down or stop to let them pass.

Rental

Car rentals are available on all islands, with the exception of a few very small ones. On most islands there are affiliates of one or more of the international chains, such as Hertz, Avis, Budget and National/Europcar.

You can often get a better deal by booking a car before you go. Even on islands such as Martinique and Guadeloupe, where the advance-booking price is often the same as the walk-in price, reservations are a good idea. Without one, you may arrive at the airport and find the cheaper cars all sold out – a situation that's not uncommon in winter.

Island car-rental agents frequently affiliate and disaffiliate with international chains, particularly on the smaller islands, so even if there's not an affiliate listed in the island's car rental section it's worth checking the latest status with the international firms mentioned above.

On many islands you need to be 25 years old to rent a car, and some car rental companies will not rent to drivers over 70.

TAXI

Taxis are available on virtually all of the populated islands, with the exception of a few that don't have roads! Details are in the individual island chapters.

BICYCLE

Although the popularity of cycling in the Eastern Caribbean is limited, some of the islands have bicycles for rent; details on renting bicycles are noted in those island chapters. The quality of rental bikes varies; most have hard seats and soft brakes, not really suited for Caribbean roads. If you want to do any serious riding, consider bringing your own bike. Cyclists should ride on the same side of the road as car traffic.

HITCHHIKING

Hitchhiking is common among islanders on several islands, though the practice among foreign visitors, particularly outside the French islands, is not very common.

Hitchhiking is never an entirely safe practice in any country in the world, and Lonely Planet does not recommend it. Travelers who decide to hitchhike should understand that they are taking a potentially serious risk. People who do choose to hitchhike will be safer if they travel in pairs and let a friend or acquaintance know where they are planning to go.

BOAT
Ferry

There are daily, or near-daily, ferry services between the following pairs of islands: St Martin and Anguilla, St Kitts and Nevis, St Vincent and Bequia, Grenada and Carriacou, and Trinidad and Tobago, as well as from the main part of Guadeloupe to the outlying islands of Terre-de-Haut, Marie-Galante and La Désirade.

In the Grenadines, a ferry connects St Vincent and Bequia with Mayreau, Canouan and Union Island three times a week. There's a catamaran service between St Martin and Saba several days a week that's geared for day tours from St Martin.

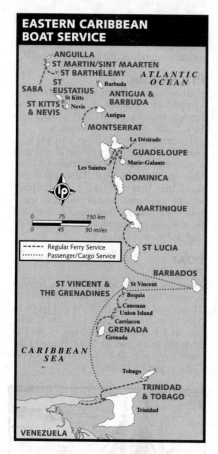

EASTERN CARIBBEAN
BOAT SERVICE

ANGUILLA
ST MARTIN/SINT MAARTEN
ST BARTHÉLEMY   ATLANTIC
ST   OCEAN
SABA EUSTATIUS   Barbuda
        St Kitts   ANTIGUA &
ST KITTS Nevis   BARBUDA
& NEVIS   Antigua
        MONTSERRAT
            La Désirade
              GUADELOUPE
Les Saintes   Marie-Galante
              DOMINICA

              MARTINIQUE

0   75   150 km
0   45   90 miles

----- Regular Ferry Service
..... Passenger/Cargo Service

              ST LUCIA

                    BARBADOS
ST VINCENT &   St Vincent
THE GRENADINES   Bequia
              Canouan
              Union Island
              Carriacou
              GRENADA
CARIBBEAN   Grenada
SEA

        Tobago
              TRINIDAD
              & TOBAGO
              Trinidad

VENEZUELA

Catamarans also sail between St Martin and St Barts for day trips.

High-speed catamaran ferries connect the islands of Guadeloupe, Dominica, Martinique and St Lucia several days a week.

Details on all these boats are in the relevant individual island chapters.

Windward Lines Limited

Windward Lines Limited operates the 180-foot passenger/cargo boat M/V *Windward* between St Lucia (Castries), Barbados (Bridgetown), St Vincent (Kingstown), Trinidad (Port of Spain) and Venezuela

(Guiria one week, Isla de Margarita the next). As it's primarily a cargo boat, it lays over at each port for several hours to unload, giving passengers time to do a little onshore exploring. The boat usually alternates its southbound itinerary every other week, and it occasionally runs an odd week with an altered schedule adjusted to holidays or heavier cargo pickups.

On alternate weeks, arrival and departure times are as follows:

departs	time	arrives	time
St Lucia	9 am Sun	Barbados	7 pm Sun
Barbados	10 pm Sun	St Vincent	7 am Mon
St Vincent	4 pm Mon	Trinidad	8 am Tue
Trinidad	6 pm Tue	Margarita (Ven)	6:30 am Wed

Every other week, the ferry generally abides by the following section:

departs	time	arrives	time
St Lucia	7 pm Sun	Barbados	6 am Mon
Barbados	8:30 am Mon	St Vincent	4 pm Mon
St Vincent	8 pm Mon	Trinidad	10 am Tue
Trinidad	5 pm Tue	Margarita (Ven)	9:30 am Wed

On the northbound schedule, sailing times are as follows:

departs	time	arrives	time
Margarita/ Guiria (Ven)	6/11pm Wed	Trinidad	7 am Thur
Trinidad	5 pm Thur	St Vincent	7:30 am Fri
St Vincent	10 am Fri	Barbados	7 pm Fri
Barbados	10:30 pm Fri	St Lucia	8 am Sat

One-way/roundtrip fares from Trinidad are US$62/95 to St Lucia, US$60/90 to Barbados or St Vincent, US$40/60 to Guiria and US$50/70 to Margarita. Other windward fares are US$39/60 between St Lucia and Barbados, US$46/71 between St Vincent and Barbados, US$106/148 between Venezuela and Barbados, and US$114/158 between Venezuela and St Lucia.

Cabins are available from US$10 per berth per night, based on double occupancy, though it's wise to book them ahead of time.

There's a restaurant and a duty-free shop on board. Check-in is one hour before the scheduled departure time.

Those planning to take the boat should contact one of the following booking agents and request copies of the latest schedule, which is printed in calendar form a couple of months in advance.

St Lucia
Toucan Travel (☎ 758-452-9963, fax 758-452-9806) Rodney Bay Marina, PO Box 1114, Castries

St Vincent
Perry's Customs & Shipping Agency (☎ 784-457-2920, fax 784-456-2619) Sharpe St, PO Box 247, Kingstown

Trinidad
Global Steamship Agencies (☎ 868-624-2279, fax 868-627-5091) Mariners Club, Wrightson Rd, Port of Spain

Venezuela
Acosta Asociados (☎ 294-816 79, fax 294-811 12) Calle Bolívar 31, Guiria

Yacht

The Caribbean is one of the world's prime yachting locales, offering diversity, warm weather and fine scenery. The many small islands grouped closely together are not only fun to explore but also form a barrier against the raging Atlantic Ocean, providing relatively calm sailing waters in the Caribbean Sea.

In the Eastern Caribbean, the major yachting bases are in St Martin, Antigua, Guadeloupe, Martinique, St Lucia, St Vincent and Grenada.

It's easiest to sail down-island, from north to south, as on the reverse trip boats must beat back into the wind. Because of this, several yacht charter companies allow sailors to take the boats in just one direction, later arranging for its own crew to bring the boats back to home base.

Information on ports and marinas can be found in the individual island chapters.

Yacht Charters You can choose from basic types of yacht charters: bareboat and crewed.

In addition, some yacht charter companies offer live-aboard sailing courses, land/sail tours, flotilla sails (consisting of a group of bareboats accompanied by a lead boat with an experienced crew) and other variations.

With a bareboat charter you rent just the boat. You are the captain and you sail where you want, when you want, on your own (more or less, anyway – you must stay within designated geographical areas, and night sailing may be prohibited). You must be an experienced sailor to charter the boat. Although in most cases you won't need proof of having completed a sailing course, any certification or the like, you will need to fill out a written sailing résumé which persuades the charter company that you can handle the boat. You should have experience sailing a similar-sized boat, anchoring and reading charts. Some companies will give you a trial check-out at the dock before allowing you to sail away.

Bareboat yachts generally come stocked with linen, kitchen supplies, fuel, water, a dinghy, an outboard, charts, cruising guides, a cellular phone and other gear. Provisioning (stocking the boat with food) is not included; sometimes it is provided for an additional fee. The charter company can provide a licensed skipper (generally costing from US$125 to US$150 a day) or a cook (about US$100 a day) if you don't want to do all the work yourself (this is sometimes called a semi-bareboat charter), but you still maintain responsibility for the boat. You'll have to pay a security deposit and should check the fine print in regards to refunds, insurance and cancellation penalties.

With a crewed charter, the yacht comes with a captain, crew, cook and provisions. You don't have to know how to sail, or anything else about boats. You can either make your own detailed itinerary or provide a vague idea of the kind of places you'd like to visit and let the captain decide where to anchor.

Cost Rates vary greatly. The better established companies generally charge more than small, little-known operators, and large ritzy yachts of course cost more than smaller, less luxurious boats. These days, many yachts are equipped with amenities such as TV, video, CD player, ice-maker, snorkeling equipment etc, on board – more toys add to the cost.

Although a whole book could be written just comparing prices, the following gives a sense of mid-range costs. The Moorings, which is one of the larger companies, has a fleet containing a dozen different types of yachts that vary in size, amenities and price. At the low end a bareboat charter rate starts at US$320 in spring, US$255 in summer, US$210 in fall and US$375 in winter. The boat holds four passengers comfortably, five in a squeeze. Nearer the top end, a boat that holds eight or nine passengers costs approximately double that rate. Discounts are available for rentals of two weeks or more.

With the Moorings, fully crewed yacht charters can be arranged at a *per-person* rate that in low season begins at around US$1575 per week and in winter begins at around US$2275 per week, based on four passengers on a 50-foot sloop.

Yacht Charter Companies The following charter companies offer both bareboat and crewed yacht charters in the Eastern Caribbean. Listings begin with the yacht charter company's US or European office, followed by the island addresses where the charter boats are based.

Catamaran Charters (☎ 800-262-0308) 4005 N Federal Hwy, Ft Lauderdale, FL 33308, USA
(☎ 0590-87 02 82, fax 87 01 55) Marigot, St Martin
(☎ 0590-90 71 89, fax 90 72 93) Marina Bas du Fort, Guadeloupe

The Moorings (☎ 727-535-1446, 888-952-8420, yacht@moorings.com, www.moorings.com), 19345 US Hwy 19 N, 4th floor, Clearwater, FL 34624, USA
(☎ 0596-74 75 39) Port de Plaisance du Marin, Martinique
(☎ 758-453-4357) Marigot Bay, St Lucia
(☎ 473-444-4924) Secret Harbour, St George's, Grenada
(☎ 0590-90 81 81) Marina Bas du Fort, Guadeloupe
(☎ 0590-87 32 55) Captain Oliver's Marina, Oyster Pond, St Martin

Nautor's Swan Charters (☎ 401-848-7181, 800-356-7926, fax 401-845-2666) 15 Goodwin St, Newport, RI 02840, USA
(☎ 023-8045 4880, fax 023-8045 5547) Port Hamble Marina, Satchell Lane, Hamble, Southampton SO31 4QD, UK
(☎ 0590-87 35 48, fax 87 35 50) BP 5253, Grand Case, 97150 St Martin

Star Voyage (☎ 56 15 62, fax 56 00 17) 42 Rue de Berri, Paris 8e, France
(☎ 0596-74 70 92) Marina du Marin, Martinique
(☎ 0590-90 81 81) Marina Bas du Fort, Guadeloupe

Sun Yacht/Stardust Charters (☎ 207-236-9611, 800-772-3500, fax 207-236-3972, sunyacht@midcoast.com) PO Box 737, Camden, ME 04838, USA
(☎ 0590 87 30 49) Captain Oliver's Marina, Oyster Pond, St Martin
(☎ 268-460-2615, fax 460-2616) English Harbour, Antigua
(☎ 0590-90 92 02, fax 90 97 99) Blue Lagoon, Gosier, Guadeloupe
(☎ 0596-74 98 17) Pointe du Plaisance, Marina du Marin, Martinique
(☎/fax 784-458-8581) Clifton, Union Island, St Vincent & the Grenadines

Sunsail Annapolis Landing Marina (☎ 410-280-2553, 800-327-2276, fax 410-280-2406, www.sunsail.com) 980 Awald Rd, Suite 302, Annapolis, MD 21403, USA
The Port House (☎ 023-9222 2222, fax 023-9221 9827) Port Solent, Portsmouth, Hampshire PO6 4TH, UK
(☎ 0590-90 82 80) Marina Bas du Fort, Guadeloupe
(☎ 0590-87 83 41) Marigot, St Martin
(☎ 758-452-8648) Rodney Bay Marina, St Lucia
(☎ 0596-74 77 61) Marina du Marin, Martinique

Trade Wind (☎ 804-694-0881, 800-825-7245; fax 804-693-7245, www.tradewindyachts.com) PO Box 1186, Court Circle, Gloucester, VA 23061, USA
(☎ 0590 90 76 77) Marina Bas du Fort, Guadeloupe
(☎ 784-456-9736, fax 456-9737) Box 2158, Blue Lagoon, St Vincent

Charter Brokers For those who don't want to be bothered shopping around, charter yacht brokers can help. Brokers work on commission, like travel agents, with no charge to the customer – you tell them your budget and requirements and they help make a match.

A few of the better-known charter yacht brokers in the USA are:

Ed Hamilton & Co (☎ 207-549-7855, 800-621-7855, fax 207-549-7822, www.ed-hamilton.com) 28 Nielson Lane, N Whitefield, ME 04353

Lynn Jachney Charters (☎ 800-223-2050, fax 781-639-0787, www.lynnjachneycharters.com) PO Box 302, Marblehead, MA 01945

Nicholson Yacht Charters (☎ 617-661-0555, 800-662-6066, fax 617-661-0554) 29 Sherman St No 1, Cambridge, MA 02138

Russell Yacht Charters (☎ 203-255-2783, 800-635-8895, fax 203-255-3426) 404 Hulls Hwy, Suite 108, Southport, CT 06490

Other Yacht Options Another option is to book a tour package aboard a yacht, much the same as you would book a traditional cruise. The schedule, itinerary and price will already be fixed, and you will sail with a few other passengers who have booked the same yacht. A number of yacht charter companies provide this service.

If you just want to work in a couple of days of sailing after you arrive in the Caribbean, you may be able to find something on the spot. On many islands, small one-boat operators advertise trips to neighboring islands; look for flyers, ask at local tour companies or check with the island's tourist offices.

For sails on tall ships, windjammers and the like, see Unconventional Cruises in the Cruises section of the Getting There & Away chapter.

Hitching a Ride on a Yacht In major yachting centers such as St Lucia, Antigua and Bequia, it's sometimes possible to hitch a ride between islands with yachters. With luck you might find someone just looking for company; however, most yachters will expect you to either help share expenses or provide crew work in exchange for a ride. Marinas have general

bulletin boards, and these sometimes have a posting or two by yachters looking for crew or passengers. If you don't find anything promising on the boards, you can add a notice of your own. It should include where you want to go; what you're willing to do in exchange for passage, such as cooking and cleaning; the date; and where you can be contacted.

In addition to the boards, there's always a bar or restaurant, usually at or near the marinas, that's a favorite haunt for sailors and thus a ready place to make contacts.

Links to crew placement agencies can be found at www.floydshostel.com.

Resources Cruising guides to the Eastern Caribbean are listed under Books in the Facts for the Visitor chapter.

To navigate through the islands of the Eastern Caribbean, yachters will need either Imray yachting charts, US Defense Mapping Agency charts or British Admiralty charts. They are available throughout the islands, especially at boating supply shops at marinas and in some bookstores. They can also be ordered in advance from Bluewater Books & Charts (☎ 954-763-6533, 800-942-2583, fax 954-522-2278, www.bluewaterweb.com), 1481 SE 17th St Causeway, Fort Lauderdale, FL 33316, USA.

There are various sailing magazines published worldwide. The following US publications have articles and tips for sailors, ads for yacht charter companies and charter brokers, and sometimes a few classified ads for crew positions:

Cruising World (☎ 515-247-7569, 800-727-8473, www.sailingworld.com) PO Box 3045, Harlan, Iowa 51537

Sail (☎ 617-720-8600, 800-745-7245, www.sailmag .com) PO Box 56397, Boulder, CO 80322

Yachting (☎ 212-779-5000, 800-999-0869) 2 Park Ave, New York, NY 10016

Anguilla

Anguilla's main appeal to visitors is its beautiful beaches – long, uncrowded stretches of powdery white-coral sand and clear aquamarine water.

Although it's just a few miles across the channel from bustling St Martin, Anguilla retains the laid-back character of a sleepy backwater, another drawing card for travelers. The island is small and lightly populated, the islanders friendly and easygoing.

HIGHLIGHTS

- Lazing on Shoal Bay East, one of the finest beaches in the Eastern Caribbean

- Hanging out in Sandy Ground, with its casual beach bar and old saltworks

- Snorkeling and having a picnic on Prickly Pear Cays

OTHER MAPS
Anguilla page 91

Central & West Anguilla
page 101

The Valley
page 99

Sandy Ground/Road Bay
page 102

CARIBBEAN
SEA

0   3   6 km
0   2   4 miles

Anguilla, which had almost no visitor facilities until relatively recently, made a decision in the 1980s to develop tourism with a slant toward luxury hotels and villas. It has since become one of the trendier top-end destinations in the Eastern Caribbean.

Although attention goes to the exclusive resorts that are scattered along some of the island's finest beaches, there are also a number of small and locally owned guest houses and apartments that make Anguilla accessible to vacationers on a more moderate budget.

The interior of Anguilla is flat, dry and scrubby, pockmarked with salt ponds and devoid of dramatic scenery. It is so flat compared to other Eastern Caribbean islands that it could be mistaken for a coral reef breaking the surface at a distance. Anguilla's main attraction certainly lies in its fringing beaches, but there are also some offshore coral-encrusted islets that offer good opportunities for swimming, snorkeling and diving.

Inexpensive ferries shuttle between Anguilla and St Martin, making Anguilla easy to visit as a day trip.

Facts about Anguilla

HISTORY

The first Amerindians settled on Anguilla about 3500 years ago. Archaeological finds indicate that the island was a regional center for the Arawak Indians, who had sizable villages at Sandy Ground, Meads Bay, Rendezvous Bay and Island Harbour.

The Carib Indians, who eventually overpowered the Arawaks, called the island Malliouhana. Early Spanish explorers named the island Anguilla, which means 'eel,' apparently because of its elongated shape.

The British established the first permanent European colony on Anguilla in 1650 and despite a few invasion attempts by the

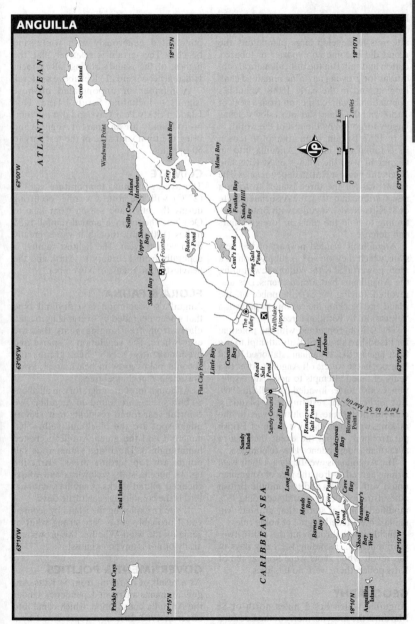

ANGUILLA

French it has remained a Crown Colony ever since. While arid conditions thwarted attempts to develop large plantations, the island did become an exporter of tobacco, cotton and salt. But the difficult natural conditions for growing anything remained challenging, and in the early 1800s Anguilla's population began to taper off from a peak of 10,500 and the island slid into a slow decline, largely forgotten by the rest of the world.

In 1967, Britain, in an attempt to loosen its colonial ties, lumped Anguilla into an alignment with the islands of St Kitts and Nevis, the nearest British dependencies. The intent was for the three islands to form a new Caribbean nation, the Associated State of St Kitts-Nevis-Anguilla, with Britain continuing to hold the reins on foreign affairs and defense.

Anguillians wanted no part of the new state, which they viewed as subjugation to a more powerful St Kitts. Within a few months, the Anguillians had armed themselves and revolted, forcing the St Kitts police off the island and blocking the runway to prevent a 'reinvasion' by Kittitian forces.

The British, concerned with the potential for bloodshed should St Kitts attempt to use force against the Anguillians, stationed Royal Marines in the waters off Anguilla. After two years of failed attempts to negotiate a solution, British forces invaded Anguilla in 1969. But rather than resisting, the islanders, content that some resolution was in the making, welcomed the first wave of British paratroopers, giving the event the bizarre aura of an Independence Day celebration.

The Anguillians eventually got their way: Britain agreed to drop the idea of Anguillian union with St Kitts and to continue British administration of the island according to a modified colonial status that granted Anguilla a heightened degree of home rule.

Incidentally, throughout the entire two-year rebellion, including the early days of the revolt when shots were fired at the St Kitts police, there were no fatalities.

GEOGRAPHY

Anguilla, which lies 5 miles north of St Martin, is the most northerly of the Leeward Islands. The island is about 16 miles long and 3 miles wide and has an indented shoreline punctuated generously with white-sand beaches. The terrain is relatively flat; the highest of the island's rolling hills, Crocus Hill, reaches a mere 213 feet above sea level.

A number of unpopulated offshore islands – including Scrub Island, Dog Island, Prickly Pear Cays and distant Sombrero Island – are also part of Anguilla and bring the total land area of the territory to 60 sq miles.

CLIMATE

The average annual temperature is 81°F (27°C), with the hottest weather occurring during the hurricane season from June to October. The average annual rainfall is 35 inches (890 mm), though it varies greatly from year to year. The lightest rainfall is generally from February to April, and the heaviest from August to November.

FLORA & FAUNA

Anguilla's vegetation is a dryland type that's been degraded by overgrazing, particularly from free-ranging goats that are everywhere. The vegetation is sparse and predominantly scrub. Sea grape and coconut palms grow in beach areas, as do poisonous manchineel trees.

Although most are migratory, in all about 80 bird species are found on Anguilla. Two colorful year-round residents that visitors might spot are the black-and-yellow bananaquit and the green Antillean crested hummingbird. The island's numerous salt ponds are top birding areas, attracting egrets, herons, stilts, yellowlegs and white-cheeked pintail ducks. Anguilla's national bird is the commonly seen turtle dove.

If you're exploring the island by scooter, you'll probably get a very strong whiff of ganja on the wind. Whether this grows naturally or not is anyone's guess!

GOVERNMENT & POLITICS

As a result of its revolt from St Kitts, Anguilla remains a British dependency. Under the Anguilla constitution, which came into effect in 1982, Britain is represented by a governor appointed by the queen. The governor presides over an appointed Executive Council and an elected House of Assembly.

ECONOMY
Many Anguillians still make a living from catching lobsters and fish, though since the 1980s there has been a dramatic shift in the economy toward the tourism industry. Anguilla gets about 120,000 tourists annually of which 80,000 are day visitors.

POPULATION & PEOPLE
The population is approximately 12,800. The majority of islanders are of African descent, though there's a bit of an admixture of Irish blood, particularly among people on the eastern end of the island.

SOCIETY & CONDUCT
Anguilla has a typical West Indian culture with a blend of British and African influences. Because of the dry and barren nature of the island, the small population on Anguilla has traditionally struggled to make ends meet and has looked toward the sea, in the form of fishing and boatbuilding, for its livelihood. One consequence of this seafaring heritage is that they're completely balmy about boat racing. Sunday is the day of practice, and you'll see plenty of small boats out cutting up the ocean.

Dos & Don'ts
Dress is casual and simple cotton clothing is suitable attire for any occasion. In the more upscale restaurants, men will want to wear long pants, but ties and jackets are not necessary. To avoid offense, swimwear should be restricted to the beach.

RELIGION
There are Anglican, Methodist, Roman Catholic, Seventh Day Adventist, Baptist, Jehovah's Witness and Church of God churches on Anguilla.

LANGUAGE
English is the official language, spoken with a distinctive lilt.

Facts for the Visitor

ORIENTATION
The airport is in The Valley, the capital of Anguilla, which is right in the center of the island. The ferry terminal is 4 miles southwest of The Valley in the small village of Blowing Point.

From The Valley a single road leads to the west end of the island and two main roads head to the east end. All other island roads, including the spur roads that lead to the beaches, branch off from these central arteries.

Maps
Two handy maps to the island are *Road Map Anguilla* and *Anguilla*, both free and distributed by the tourist office and island businesses.

TOURIST OFFICES
Local Tourist Offices
The main tourist office (☎ 497-2759, fax 497-2710, atbtour@anguillanet.com), in the Factory Plaza on Wallblake Rd in The Valley, is open 8 am to 5 pm Monday to Friday. There's also a year-round tourist information booth at the Blowing Point ferry terminal.

When requesting information by mail, write to: Anguilla Tourist Board, PO Box 1388, The Valley, Anguilla, British West Indies.

Tourist Offices Abroad
Tourist information can be obtained from these overseas agencies:

Germany
Anguilla Tourist Board (☎ 6257 962920, fax 6257 962919) c/o Sergat Deutschland, IMM Guldenen Wingert 8-C, D-64342 Seeheim

Puerto Rico
R.S.V.P. Travel Services (☎ 787-725-1308, fax 787-725-0882) P.O. Box 16328, San Juan 00908

UK
Anguilla Tourist Board (☎ 020-8876 9025, fax 020-8876 2980, windotel@btinternet.com) c/o Windotel, 7 Westwood Rd, London SW13 0LA

USA

Anguilla Public Relations & Marketing Representative (☎ 516-425-0900, fax 516-425-0903) Wescott Group, 39 Monaton Dr, Huntington Station, NY 11746

VISAS & DOCUMENTS

US citizens can enter Anguilla with proof of citizenship in the form of a birth certificate with a raised seal accompanied by an official photo ID such as a driver's license. Citizens of most other nations require passports, but no visa is necessary.

CUSTOMS

A carton of cigarettes and a bottle of liquor may be brought in duty free.

MONEY

The Eastern Caribbean dollar (EC$) is the official currency. Generally hotels, car rental agents and restaurants list prices in US dollars, while grocers and local shops mark prices in EC dollars, but you can readily use either currency and most places give a fair rate of exchange, between EC$2.65 and EC$2.70 per US$1.

Barclays Bank and Scotiabank, in The Valley, are open 8 am to 2 pm (Scotiabank to 3 pm) Monday to Thursday, 8 am to 5 pm Friday.

Visa, MasterCard and American Express cards are accepted at many (but not all) hotels on Anguilla, as well as at moderate to high-end restaurants.

A 15% service charge is added to most restaurant bills and no further tipping is necessary.

POST & COMMUNICATIONS
Post

Anguilla's post office is in The Valley and is open 8 am to 3:30 pm Monday to Friday.

If you want to send mail to Anguilla, simply follow the business name with the post office box or the village/beach and 'Anguilla, British West Indies.'

The cost to mail a postcard is EC$0.50 to North, South and Central America, and EC$0.90 to Europe; letters (per half-ounce)

cost EC$1.00 to the Americas, EC$1.90 to Europe.

Telephone

Both coin and card phones are common around the island. You can also make calls, as well as send faxes and telegrams, at the Cable & Wireless office in The Valley. It's open 8 am to 5 pm weekdays, 9 am to 1 pm Saturday.

Phone cards are sold at the Cable & Wireless office, the airport and numerous shops. They can be used only on the island. When calling Anguilla from overseas, dial the area code 264 before the seven-digit local number.

Email & Internet Access

Internet access is available at the public library in The Valley for US$2 per half-hour. The library is open 9 am to 6:30 pm Monday to Friday, 9 am to 3 pm Saturday. Body and Soul (☎ 497-8364), in Sandy Ground, runs a small café and provides Internet access at the more expensive price of US$3.75 plus US$0.25 per minute, but is handy if you're staying in Sandy Ground. It's open 8 am to 8 pm daily.

INTERNET RESOURCES

Two good Web sites for information online are www.anguilla-vacation.com, and Bob Green's www.news.ai, which is full of local happenings and current events.

NEWSPAPERS & MAGAZINES

The island's little weekly newspaper, *The Light*, comes out on Monday and covers local news and events.

The tourism guide called *What We Do in Anguilla* has visitor information, restaurant listings, the current entertainment schedule and lots of ads. *Tropical Anguilla*, a large glossy magazine, has similar information in English, Spanish and French. *Anguilla Life* magazine, published three times a year, features articles on everything from archaeology to cultural events and island happenings. All three are free and can be picked up at the tourist office and some hotels.

ANGUILLA

RADIO & TV
The local government-run radio station is Radio Anguilla at 1505 AM and 95.5 FM. Anguilla has cable TV, with local programming on Channel 3.

ELECTRICITY
Electricity is 110V, 60 cycles, and a plug with two flat prongs is used, the same as in the USA.

WEIGHTS & MEASURES
Anguilla uses the imperial system. Speed limit signs are in miles as are most car odometers.

HEALTH
The island's 36-bed hospital (☎ 497-2551) is in The Valley. See the Regional Facts for the Visitor chapter for information on travel health.

DANGERS & ANNOYANCES
Anguilla has very little crime, and no unusual safety precautions are necessary.

EMERGENCIES
For police, fire or ambulance emergencies call ☎ 911.

BUSINESS HOURS
Business hours are generally 8 am to noon and 1 to 5 pm weekdays.

PUBLIC HOLIDAYS & SPECIAL EVENTS
Public holidays observed in Anguilla are the following:

New Year's Day	January 1
Good Friday	late March/early April
Easter Monday	late March/early April
Labour Day	May 1
Whit Monday	eighth Monday after Easter
Anguilla Day	May 30
Queen's Birthday	June 11
August Monday (Emancipation Day)	first Monday in August
August Thursday	first Thursday in August
Constitution Day	August 6
Separation Day	December 19
Christmas Day	December 25
Boxing Day	December 26

Note that holidays falling on the weekend are often taken on the following Monday.

Anguilla's main festival is its Carnival, which starts on the weekend preceding August Monday and continues until the following weekend. Events include boat races, costumed parades, a beauty pageant, calypso competitions, music and dancing. Watch out for the boat races, especially on the last leg to the finishing line. In Anguilla, only the skipper need be onboard when the vessel crosses the finishing line, so don't be surprised to see sand bags emptied, or even crew thrown overboard in order to reach it first!

ACTIVITIES
Beaches & Swimming
Anguilla has lots of picture-postcard white-sand beaches and you never have to go far to find one. Don't be at all surprised to turn up at a stunning beach and find it completely deserted. Sandy Ground has calm turquoise waters, as do the glorious sweeps at Shoal Bay East (one of the best in the Caribbean) and Rendezvous Bay. Other top beaches worth a visit include Meads Bay and Shoal Bay West. Top honors in The Valley area go to Crocus Bay, a quiet beach with good swimming and snorkeling.

Diving & Snorkeling
Anguilla has clear water and good reef formations. In addition, since the mid-1980s a number of ships have been deliberately sunk to create new dive sites; they lie on sandy bottoms in depths of 35 to 75 feet and attract numerous fish.

Offshore islands popular for diving include Prickly Pear Cays, which has caverns, ledges, barracudas and nurse sharks; Dog Island, a drift dive along a rock face with good marine life; and Sandy Island, which has soft corals and sea fans.

Dive Shops Anguillian Divers (☎ 497-4750, fax 497-4632, axadiver@anguillanet.com), at Meads Bay, is the main diving outfit on Anguilla. A single-tank boat dive costs US$50, double-tank dives cost US$70 and night dives US$40. There are a number of packages and PADI certifications available; resort courses are US$75, referrals cost US$225 and open-water certification courses are US$375. Snorkeling trips, accompanied by a diver, are US$15. US$1 per tank dive, included in the price, goes to the marine park.

The Dive Shop (☎ 497-2020), in Sandy Ground, is currently closed but there's a lot of speculation that it will reopen sometime in the future. Check with the tourist office or call before making a special trip to Sandy Ground to see if they're open.

Shoal Bay East, Sandy Island, Little Bay and Prickly Pear Cays are popular snorkeling spots. For more information see Organized Tours in the Getting Around section, later in this chapter.

Horseback Riding
El Rancho Del Blues (☎ 497-6164), next to Anguilla Gases on the road to Blowing Point, offers beach and trail rides for US$25/45 for one/two hours. Beach rides depart at 9 am and 2 pm, and trail rides at 11 am and 4 pm.

ACCOMMODATIONS
Anguilla has a reputation for being an expensive destination and for the most part it's true. But, although visiting Anguilla can be a challenge for budget travelers, there are a few places on the island with simple rooms for around US$20 to US$50. The middle range varies widely, beginning with apartments for US$75 and moving up to small beachside hotels with US$200 rooms. At the top end there are fine luxury hotels, with prices generally beginning around US$400.

In summer, many top-end and mid-range hotels drop prices substantially, while some places close down entirely if bookings are slack. An 8% government tax is added to the prices quoted, and expect an additional 10% service charge to be added as well.

Despite their high prices, even many mid-range hotels lack TV and air-con. The latter is especially noteworthy for summer travelers, as many spots on the island (Sandy Ground is one place in particular) have periods of dead air when nights can be unbearably muggy.

Anguilla is a very rural and laid-back island, and many locals still use nature as an alarm clock, which equates to the rooster. So if you don't want to be woken at 5 am in the morning by an eager rooster, bring a gun or very good earplugs!

FOOD
Lobster (common spiny lobster) and crayfish (spotted spiny lobster) are two locally caught Anguillian specialties. Crayfish, while smaller than lobsters, are reasonably sized creatures that have sweet, moist meat and are commonly served three to an order.

Although a few traditional staples, such as corn and pigeon peas, are still grown on

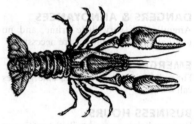

Crayfish – Learn to suck out the brains.

Anguilla, most food is imported, and prices are higher here than on neighboring islands.

DRINKS
Tap water comes from rainwater catchment systems and thus should be boiled before drinking. Bottled water is readily available in grocery stores.

Getting There & Away

AIR
Airports & Airlines
Anguilla's Wallblake Airport (☎ 497-2514) is small and modern. There are counters for LIAT, Winair, American Eagle, Air An-

guilla (a local charter airline) and Tyden Air. During high season there's sometimes a staffed tourist information booth; you can find pay phones near the arrivals exit.

There are no car rental booths at the airport, but two companies, Triple K and Island Car Rentals, are within a five-minute walk north of the airport.

Departure Tax
Departure tax is US$15.

Within the Caribbean
American Eagle (☎ 497-3131) has at least one flight a day to Anguilla from San Juan. A roundtrip excursion fare that allows a stay of up to 30 days is US$187 with a seven-day advance purchase. The one-way fare is US$165.

Winair (☎ 497-2238) has a few flights daily between St Martin and Anguilla. The fare is US$32 one-way, US$64 roundtrip.

LIAT (☎ 497-5000) has direct daily flights to Anguilla from St Thomas, St Kitts and Antigua, and flights on Friday and Sunday from St Martin. The St Martin–Anguilla fare is US$30 one-way, US$56 roundtrip; St Thomas–Anguilla is US$94 one-way, US$152 roundtrip; St Kitts–Anguilla is US$69 one-way, US$116 roundtrip; and Antigua-Anguilla is US$89 one-way, US$169 roundtrip.

Tyden Air (☎ 497-2719, in the USA ☎ 800-842-0261, tydenair@anguillanet.com) flies to Anguilla from St Martin where it connects with flights on American and Continental airlines. The cost is US$40 one-way, US$85 roundtrip. Tyden has a day trip to St Barts on Monday, Wednesday and Friday, leaving Anguilla in the morning and returning in the late afternoon. The cost for a same-day roundtrip ticket (US$125) is the same price as the regular one-way fare.

The USA
There are no direct transatlantic flights to Anguilla. However, it's possible to make same-day international connections to get to Anguilla via St Martin or San Juan, Puerto Rico.

American Airlines' New York–Anguilla (via San Juan) 30-day excursion ticket is about US$670, although discounted fares between the US mainland and San Juan can sometimes make it cheaper to buy separate New York–San Juan and San Juan–Anguilla tickets.

SEA
Departure Tax
Ferry departure tax is US$2.

Ferry
Ferries make the 25-minute run from Marigot Bay in St Martin to Blowing Point in Anguilla an average of once every 30 minutes from 8 am to 7 pm (from 7:30 am to 6:15 pm from Anguilla to St Martin). If you're planning on catching the last ferry, reconfirm that sailing once you arrive on the island as adjustments in schedules aren't uncommon.

The one-way fare is US$10 (US$12 on the last boat of the day). Sign the passenger registration list and pay the US$2 departure tax as soon as you arrive at the dock. The fare for the passage is paid onboard the boat.

Yacht
The main port of entry is at Sandy Ground in Road Bay. The immigration and customs office is open daily 8:30 am to noon and 1 to 4 pm (closed Saturday morning), and can be contacted on VHF channel 16.

Getting Around

There's no bus service on the island and travelers will find it difficult to get around Anguilla without renting either a car or a scooter.

CAR & MOTORCYCLE
Road Rules
In Anguilla, you drive on the left-hand side of the road. The steering wheels on virtually all rental cars, however, are also on the left-hand side. This situation can be quite disorienting!

Visitors must buy a temporary Anguillian driver's license for US$6, which is issued on the spot by the car rental companies.

The roads are generally in bad shape and driving can be a game of pothole evasion. The southwestern end of the island is an exception to the rule. There you'll find many roads well tar-sealed. Be cautious of stray goats that occasionally bolt onto the road.

There are gas stations in The Valley, in Island Harbour, on the west end of the island near the turnoff to Sonesta Beach Resort and in Blowing Point. The tourist office map has the majority of gas stations marked on it.

Rental

Compact air-conditioned cars rent for about US$40 a day with free unlimited mileage in winter, and usually US$5 cheaper in summer. Jeeps cost just a few dollars more.

Triple K Car Rental (☎ 497-2934, fax 497-2503, hertztriplek@anguilla.net), Anguilla's Hertz agent, is on Airport Rd in The Valley. The other major rental agencies are TDC (☎ 497-2656), in The Valley, Island Car Rentals (☎ 497-2723, fax 497-3723, islandcar@anguillanet.com), on Airport Rd in The Valley, and Connor's Car Rental (☎ 497-6433, in the USA and Canada ☎ 800-223-9815), at the intersection at the north end of Blowing Point Rd.

A&S Motor Scooter Rentals (☎ 497-8803), on the road to Shoal Bay West near the turnoff to Anguilla Great House, rents scooters for US$25 a day. They provide free pick-up, but not necessarily free drop-off afterward.

TAXI

Taxis are readily available at the airport and the ferry terminal. The minimum charge is US$6. Rates from the airport are US$12 to Sandy Ground or Shoal Bay East and

US$16 to Meads Bay. From Blowing Point, it costs US$12 to Sandy Ground or The Valley, US$16 to Shoal Bay East. These rates are for one or two people; each additional person is charged US$4.

BICYCLE

Innovation Center (☎ 497-5810), on the main road half a mile west of the airport rotary, rents mountain bikes for US$10 a day.

ORGANIZED TOURS

Taxi drivers provide tours of the island for US$40 for one or two people, US$5 for each additional person.

Among the offshore islands, one of the most popular destinations is Prickly Pear Cays, which has excellent snorkeling conditions. Tour boats leave Sandy Ground for Prickly Pear at around 10 am, returning around 4 pm; the cost averages US$80, including lunch, drinks and snorkeling gear. If you want to pack your own lunch, you can also arrange to simply be picked up and dropped off; Garfield's Sea Tours (☎ 497-2956) charges US$40 per person with a minimum of three passengers.

Also popular are sails to secluded Little Bay, on Anguilla's west coast, which is a lovely cliff-backed cove north of The Valley with a little white-sand beach and fine snorkeling. The best deal is with Calvin (☎ 497-3939), who hangs out at Roy's Place in Crocus Bay and offers a boat shuttle from there to Little Bay for around US$10 per person roundtrip.

Chocolat (☎ 497-3394), a 35-foot catamaran, offers sails to Prickly Pear, sunset cruises and private charters.

For information on boats to Sandy Island see the Sandy Ground/Road Bay section, later in this chapter.

Rerouting

Most roads in Anguilla are not marked with names or numbers, although hotel and restaurant signs point the way to many beaches. Beware of the occasional renegade restaurant sign that appears to point to someplace nearby but is actually an attempt to reroute you halfway across the island.

The Valley

The Valley, the island's only real town, is the geographic, commercial and political center of Anguilla. Although it's not a very large town, it's rather spread out and rambling. In part because the British moved the administration of the island to St Kitts back in 1825,

ANGUILLA

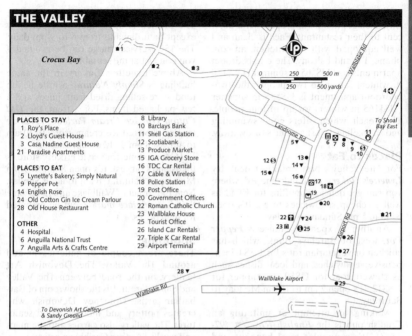

THE VALLEY

Crocus Bay

0   250   500 m
0   250   500 yards

To Shoal
Bay East

To Devonish Art Gallery
& Sandy Ground

Wallblake Rd

Wallblake Airport

Landsome Rd

Airport Rd

PLACES TO STAY
1 Roy's Place
2 Lloyd's Guest House
3 Casa Nadine Guest House
21 Paradise Apartments

PLACES TO EAT
5 Lynette's Bakery; Simply Natural
9 Pepper Pot
14 English Rose
24 Old Cotton Gin Ice Cream Parlour
28 Old House Restaurant

OTHER
4 Hospital
6 Anguilla National Trust
7 Anguilla Arts & Crafts Centre

8 Library
10 Barclays Bank
11 Shell Gas Station
12 Scotiabank
13 Produce Market
15 IGA Grocery Store
16 TDC Car Rental
17 Cable & Wireless
18 Police Station
19 Post Office
20 Government Offices
22 Roman Catholic Church
23 Wallblake House
25 Tourist Office
26 Island Car Rentals
27 Triple K Car Rental
29 Airport Terminal

there are no quaint colonial government buildings or even a central square. Most edifices are the functional type, taking on the appearance of small shopping centers. The Valley has the cheapest accommodations on the island and a decent enough beach close by, but if you want a relaxing beach holiday away from it all it's best to be based elsewhere.

The **Anguilla National Trust**, in the center of town between Wallblake and Airport Rds, displays changing exhibits of Anguilla's history and natural environment; it's usually open 10 am to 5 pm Tuesday to Saturday; admission is free.

The Valley's most interesting building is the **Wallblake House**, which was built in 1787 and is one of the oldest structures on the island. The house can be viewed only from the exterior as it's the rectory for the Roman Catholic church. You can, however, view the interior of the adjacent **church**, which has a unique design incorporating a decorative stone front, open-air side walls and a ceiling shaped like the hull of a ship.

Places to Stay

Friendly *Casa Nadine Guest House* (☎ 497-2358) is a local boarding house with 11 extremely basic rooms, each with a private shower and toilet. Singles/doubles cost US$20/25 – cheap for Anguilla, but you get what you pay for.

Lloyd's Guest House (☎ 497-2351, fax 497-3028) is an old-fashioned guest house with a dozen basic rooms. All are very straightforward, but they do have private baths. The summer rate is US$60/80 for singles/doubles including breakfast, US$70/90 in winter.

Paradise Apartments (☎ 497-2168) is opposite the Central Baptist Church in the Rey Hill area, not far from the airport. The two-story building has four modern apartments, each with a large bedroom, bathroom, separate kitchen, ceiling fans and a view of The Valley. Rates are US$65 year-round.

Roy's Place (☎ 497-2470), on Crocus Bay, manages four inviting apartments adjacent to their restaurant. Each is clean and well equipped with full kitchen, air-con, phone, TV and balcony. The one-bedroom apartments cost US$65 in summer (US$110 in winter) for up to two people; the two-bedroom apartment is US$85 in summer (US$165 in winter) for up to four people. The beach, which offers good swimming and snorkeling, is just a stone's throw away.

Places to Eat

For The Valley's best breakfast deal, try *Lynette's Bakery*, on Landsome Rd, where you can get delicious muffins for EC$1 as well as cheap sandwiches to go. It's open 6 am to 5 pm Sunday to Friday.

Another inexpensive choice is *Pepper Pot*, west of Barclays Bank, which has chicken or vegetarian rotis for US$4, inexpensive sandwiches, and local dishes such as stewed goat for US$9 or snapper for US$12. It's open 7 am to 10 pm Monday to Saturday.

Making an attempt at imitating an English pub is the *English Rose* (☎ 497-5353). It's a popular local hangout, and serves decent food at reasonable prices. Sandwiches and burgers range from US$4 to US$5, and more substantial meals such as seafood, pasta and meat dishes are generally around the US$12 mark.

The *Old House Restaurant* (☎ 497-2228), a local favorite on the Sandy Ground road at the south side of town, has a varied menu at moderate prices. Breakfasts and lunchtime sandwiches start around US$7, while dinners begin at US$18, including the house specialty of Anguillian-style potfish served with peas and rice for US$19. It's open 6:30 am to 10 pm daily.

Roy's Place, a pub-style restaurant and bar on Crocus Bay, has good food and a great beachfront location. The lunch menu includes sandwiches starting at US$5 and flying fish & chips for US$9, while at dinner, seafood dishes range from English-style fish & chips for US$17 to crayfish for US$35. It's busiest on Friday from 5 to 7 pm, when there's a happy hour featuring half-price

beer and a choice of two meals for US$10. The kitchen is open noon to 2 pm daily except Saturday and from 6 to 9 pm daily. The 15% service charge can be avoided if you don't sit at the set tables.

Above Lynette's Bakery in the same building is *Simply Natural*, a little health food store selling dried fruit, juices and a few packaged items. For a treat, the *Old Cotton Gin Ice Cream Parlour* serves up tropical-flavored ice cream from 10:30 am to at least 8 pm daily, except Tuesday.

IGA, an American-style grocery store, is the island's biggest. It's open 8 am to 9 pm Monday to Saturday, 8 am to noon Sunday. Near the corner of Wallblake and Landsome there's a *produce market*, but be prepared for high prices.

Shopping

There are a couple of galleries in and around The Valley. The Devonish Art Gallery, on the road between The Valley and Sandy Ground, is the showroom of Barbadian artist Courtney Devonish who creates pottery and modern wood sculptures. The gallery also carries antique maps and works by other Caribbean artists.

The Anguilla Arts & Crafts Centre sells locally made silk-screened clothing, T-shirts, pottery and baskets, and has a good collection of books about Anguilla.

Central & West Anguilla

SANDY GROUND/ROAD BAY

Sandy Ground, a small village fronting Road Bay, is the closest thing Anguilla has to a travelers' haunt. It has a nice white-sand beach lined with restaurants, a couple of decent bars and a few low-key places to stay. The fishhook-shaped bay is one of the most protected on the island and the main port of entry for yachts.

Sandy Ground is backed by a large salt pond that was commercially harvested until the late 1970s, when the cost of shipping the salt began to exceed its value. The former

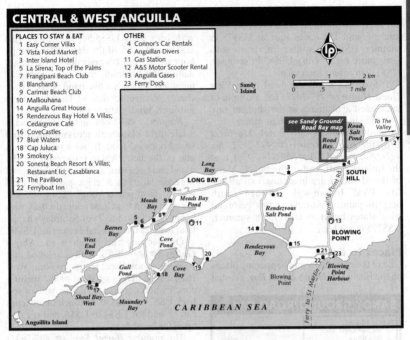

CENTRAL & WEST ANGUILLA

PLACES TO STAY & EAT
1 Easy Corner Villas
2 Vista Food Market
3 Inter Island Hotel
5 La Sirena; Top of the Palms
7 Frangipani Beach Club
8 Blanchard's
9 Carimar Beach Club
10 Malliouhana
14 Anguilla Great House
15 Rendezvous Bay Hotel & Villas;
    Cedargrove Café
16 CoveCastles
17 Blue Waters
18 Cap Juluca
19 Smokey's
20 Sonesta Beach Resort & Villas;
    Restaurant Ici; Casablanca
21 The Pavillion
22 Ferryboat Inn

OTHER
4 Connor's Car Rentals
6 Anguillan Divers
11 Gas Station
12 A&S Motor Scooter Rental
13 Anguilla Gases
23 Ferry Dock

saltworks, which sat idle at the north end of the village, were converted into a bar (The Pumphouse) and visitors are free to go in and take a look at the old salt-processing machinery.

If you enjoy birding, the quieter north end of the salt pond attracts egrets, stilts, herons and other wading birds.

Sandy Island

Sandy Island, lying a mile off Sandy Ground, is a small islet with gleaming white sands and a couple of coconut palms – you can walk around the whole thing in just 10 minutes. The island is surrounded by shallow reefs that offer reasonable snorkeling, with waving finger corals, sea fans and small tropical fish.

Boats leave from the pier in front of the immigration office, making the five-minute jaunt to the island on demand between 10 am and 3 pm. Buy tickets (US$8 roundtrip) at the booth next to Johnno's Beach Bar.

There's a beach bar on the island that sells US$2 beers and plate lunches from US$10 (chicken or fish) to US$20 (lobster).

Places to Stay

The welcoming **Body and Soul** (*☎/fax 497-8364, roots@anguillanet.com*), at the northern end of Sandy Ground, is a great hangout with a relaxed atmosphere. Unfortunately there's only one double room and an apartment, so call ahead to secure your place. The double room, which is US$60 in summer, US$75 in winter, is clean and pleasantly furnished, and has its own bathroom. Breakfast is included in the price. The self-contained apartment can sleep up to six people, and starts at US$90 in summer, US$100 in winter (more for four to six people). There's food available on request (the hangover breakfast for US$8.75 is superb), and a cybercafé and gym on-site.

Syd-An's Apartments (*☎ 497-3180, fax 497-5381, in the USA ☎ 800-553-4939*), on the beach road, has half a dozen very pleasant apartments with separate bedrooms, full kitchens and TV. Rates start at US$75 in summer, US$85 in winter for rooms with fans (more for air-con), US$85 in summer, US$110 in winter for a villa.

If Syd-An's is full, the nearby *Sea View Guest House* (☎ 497-2427) has a couple of fan-cooled apartments at the cheaper rate of US$50 in summer, US$60 in winter.

Sandy Ground's only hotel, *Mariners Cliffside Beach Resort* (☎ 497-2671, fax 497-2901, in the USA ☎ 800-848-7938), is at the quieter south end of the beach. Many of the 67 rooms are in a cluster of attractive West Indian-style cottages with brightly painted shutters and gingerbread trim. Rates begin at US$175 in summer, US$275 in winter.

Places to Eat

One of the most lively and happening places on the island is *Johnno's Beach Bar*, a casual open-air restaurant right on the beach, with picnic tables and a simple menu. A burger with fries costs US$5.50, chicken or ribs US$10 and catch of the day US$12. Happy hour is 5 to 7 pm. It's open noon to midnight daily, and is especially hopping on Saturday night when there's a live band (US$5 cover charge, no cover for diners). There's also live music on Sunday afternoon.

Ripples (☎ 497-3380), on the beach road, is a late-night place with pleasant decor and straightforward food. It has a reputation as one of the better-value restaurants on the island and has a varied menu with the likes of Mexican fare, fish & chips, pasta and local seafood, most priced from US$14 to US$20. It's open noon to at least midnight daily with happy hour from 5 to 7 pm. Saturday's happy hour features three special dinners for US$10.

Overlooking the beach is the *Ship's Galley* (☎ 497-2040), with a relaxed and friendly atmosphere. Home cooking West Indian style makes up most of the menu – conch, whelks, goat – and dinner will set you back US$25 to US$30. At lunch sandwiches can be had for US$4 to US$6, and it's also open for breakfast.

The popular *Barrel Stay* (☎ 497-2831) has a romantic seaside setting and quality fish dishes, such as grilled snapper, swordfish and mahimahi from around US$25 à la carte. The fish soup is regarded as Anguilla's best. It's open for lunch and dinner daily during the winter season. Dinner reservations are recommended.

The Pumphouse, at the north end of Sandy Ground, is operated by a friendly couple, Laurie & Gabi Gumbs, whose family once operated a saltworks in this same building. The Gumbs have turned this little historic site into an atmospheric bar, serving pub food such as kebabs and salads and offering live jazz, blues and acoustic guitar music. It's open 7 pm to 2 am Wednesday to Saturday.

3 C's, a small grocery store in the village, is open 8 am to 4 pm and 5 to 8 pm Monday to Saturday and 8 to 10 am Sunday. For more extensive shopping, drive up to *Vista Food Market*, a well-stocked grocery store a mile away at the roundabout, open 8 am to 6 pm Monday to Saturday.

SANDY GROUND/ROAD BAY

PLACES TO STAY
2   Sea View Guest House
3   Body & Soul
4   Syd-An's Apartments
12 Mariners Cliffside Beach
    Resort

PLACES TO EAT
1   The Pumphouse (Old Salt
    Works)
5   Johnno's Beach Bar
8   Ripples
9   Ship's Galley
10 Barrel Stay
11 3 C's

OTHER
6   Boat Tickets to Sandy
    Island
7   Immigration Office

Road Salt Pond

Road Bay

Dock

0   150   300 m
0   150   300 yards

SOUTH HILL

South Hill, the village that rises above the south end of Road Bay, is essentially a residential area although there are a couple of places to stay. There are no sights in South Hill, but you can take the one-way road that goes west to east above the cliffs for some fine views of Sandy Ground, Road Bay and Sandy Island.

Places to Stay

Easy Corner Villas (☎ 497-6433, fax 497-6410, in the USA ☎ 800-633-7411, PO Box 65), on a hillside just west of Vista Food Market, has a dozen apartments with kitchens, with balconies overlooking Sandy Ground. Rates are US$125/155/195 for one-/two-/three-bedroom apartments in summer, US$160/195/240 in winter. Studio units cost US$90 in summer, US$110 in winter. The office is at Connor's Car Rental, a mile to the west on the same road.

Inter Island Hotel (☎ 497-6259, fax 497-8207, PO Box 194), an older two-story hostelry at the side of the main road, has 14 plain units. Many rooms are on the small side, though some have balconies with distant ocean views. While the hotel is rather oddly located, several beaches are within a 10-minute drive. Rates are the big plus here: For standard rooms, singles/doubles cost US$35/60 in summer, US$40/70 in winter, while one-bedroom apartments cost US$85 in summer, US$95 in winter.

BLOWING POINT

Blowing Point, where the ferry from St Martin docks, is mainly a residential area and not a major tourist center. There is a modest beach west of the immigration office as well as a few reasonably priced apartment-style places to stay, but most visitors arriving for a day visit will want to make their way to better beaches elsewhere around the island.

Places to Stay

Both places listed are within a 10-minute walk from the ferry, on the first road to the left after leaving the terminal.

Ferryboat Inn (☎ 497-6613, fax 497-6713, ferryb@anguillanet.com, PO Box 189) has seven apartments on the beach. The units, with either one or two rooms, are large and modern with rattan furnishings, sliding glass doors to a porch or balcony, air-con and TV. Rates start at US$90 in summer, US$160 in winter.

The Pavillion (☎ 497-6395, fax 497-6234, PO Box 411), directly opposite the Ferryboat Inn, is a modern three-story building with eight one-bedroom apartments for US$85 a night, US$530 a week. Units have full kitchens, balconies and ceiling fans.

Places to Eat

It's slim pickings for a bite to eat at the ferry terminal and in the surrounding area.

On the right side of the road just north of the ferry terminal, there's sometimes a man with a smoke-grill who cooks some of the best grilled ribs and fish on the island.

Ferryboat Inn has a pleasant open-air beachside restaurant. A cheeseburger and fries costs US$10, grilled chicken US$12 and fresh fish a few dollars more. It's open for lunch and dinner.

RENDEZVOUS BAY

Rendezvous Bay is a gorgeous arc of white sand that stretches for more than a mile. There's a hotel at either end and one in the middle, but otherwise it's delightfully free of development. This sheltered bay has protected turquoise waters, a nice sandy bottom and a straight-on view of hilly St Martin to the south. There's good snorkeling to be had near the Rendezvous Bay Hotel end of the beach.

Rendezvous Bay is well known in local history as the site of a 1796 invasion by French forces who hastily plundered the island before British troops from St Kitts came to the rescue.

Beachgoers will find public beach access at the east side of the Anguilla Great House. After turning south off the main road toward the hotel, simply continue along the dirt road that skirts the salt pond until you reach the beach.

Places to Stay

The *Rendezvous Bay Hotel and Villas* (☎ 497-6549, fax 497-6026, in the USA ☎ 800-274-4893, rendezvous@anguillanet.com, PO Box 31) is at the east end of Rendezvous Bay and reached via Blowing Point. The owner, 87-year-old Jeremiah Gumb, started up the hotel in 1962, and still watches the goings-on from his house beside the main office. It has straightforward hotel rooms with twin beds and fan for US$90 in summer, US$120 in winter; newer units with air-con, refrigerators and king beds starting at US$120 in summer, US$235 in winter; and more expensive units with kitchens. There's a quality restaurant and a common room with a mountain of books and a TV.

The Anguilla Great House (☎ 497-6061, fax 497-6019, in the USA ☎ 800-583-9247, flemingw@anguillanet.com, PO Box 157) sits by itself on a quiet stretch of beach at the center of Rendezvous Bay. It's a collection of cottages built in traditional West Indian design and furnished with colonial decor. The 27 rooms have ceiling fans and king or queen beds. There's a restaurant, bar and pool. Rates for up to two people begin at US$137 in summer, US$230 in winter.

Sonesta Beach Resort & Villas (☎ 497-6999, fax 497-6899, in the USA and Canada ☎ 800-766-3782, in Europe ☎ 00800-4000 1000, sonesta@anguillanet.com, PO Box 444) is a 100-room Moroccan-style resort at the west end of Rendezvous Bay. With its pink exterior and exotic arches, it certainly looks quite apropos for the desert if not necessarily an Anguillian one. The whole place exudes a fantasy element, from elaborate tile mosaics in the lobby to the Bogart-reminiscent Casablanca bar, and the spacious rooms have Moorish decor, Italian marble baths and modern amenities such as TV, air-con and minibar. There's a large pool, tennis courts and a fitness room. Rates begin at US$205 in summer, US$370 in winter.

Places to Eat

The Sonesta has a couple of restaurants. With views of the beach and St Martin is *Restaurant Ici*, which serves contemporary cuisine with salads, various side dishes and beef, chicken and fish main courses. It's open 11 am to 3 pm daily and 6 to 10 pm Monday to Saturday. More formal and expensive is *Casablanca*, with Mediterranean and Caribbean-influenced cuisine.

Occupying a great spot right on the beach is *Smokey's* (☎ 497-6582), offering a menu of local creations and typical American fare. It's actually on Cove Bay, not Rendezvous Bay, but is within easy walking distance west of the Sonesta Resort. Pizzas and burgers from US$8 are available for lunch, and dishes like curried goat for US$10 are the mainstay of the dinner menu. It's open 11:30 am to 4 pm and 6 pm till the last person stumbles home.

Cedargrove Café at the Rendezvous Bay Hotel has both an indoor and outdoor eating area with views of the beach. The lunch and dinner menus mix Creole and European flavors, with sandwiches, pizzas and mains between US$10 and US$14 (except for the lobster dishes of course!) Dinner prices are about double that. Breakfast is available from 7:30 to 10:30 am.

MEADS BAY

Meads Bay boasts a lovely mile-long sweep of white sand with calm turquoise waters. It's a good beach for swimming and a great one for strolling.

Although a couple of the island's trendiest hotels and a few small condominium complexes are scattered along the beach, Meads Bay is certainly not crowded – some of the hotels are a good five-minute walk from their nearest neighbor. The bay is backed by a salt pond for most of its length. There are annual boat races from the beach on the first Thursday in August.

Places to Stay

La Sirena (☎ 497-6827, fax 497-6829, in the USA ☎ 800-331-9358, in the UK ☎ 0800-373 742, lasirena@anguillanet.com, PO Box 200) is at the west end of Meads Bay. There are 25 attractive rooms in low-rise whitewashed buildings with red-tile roofs. Rooms have ceiling fans and/or air-con, a room safe and minibar. Even though it's the cheapest of the area's hotels, it's a pleasant place, with singles/doubles for US$110/145 from April to October, US$130/165 November to mid-December and US$200/260 mid-December to March.

Carimar Beach Club (☎ 497-6881, fax 497-6071, in the USA ☎ 800-235-8667, carimar@ anguillanet.com, PO Box 327) is a pleasant, contemporary, two-story beachfront condominium complex on the east side of Meads Bay. The 24 units have ceiling fans, full kitchens, a living/dining room and a balcony or patio. One-bedroom apartments begin at US$140 in summer, US$165 in autumn and spring, and US$320 in winter. Two-bedroom apartments start at US$210, US$245 and US$430, respectively. From May 1 to November 15 there's a special rate for stays of seven nights or more that begins at US$100 per night, as well as dive packages starting at three-nights stay and four dives for US$325.

The *Malliouhana (☎ 497-6111, fax 497-6011, in the USA ☎ 800-835-0796, malliouhana@anguillanet.com, PO Box 173)*, on a low cliff at the east end of Meads Bay, is one of the island's most fashionable luxury hotels. The rooms are air-conditioned and have tile floors, marble baths, rattan furnishings, original artwork and large patios. Of course you pay for the luxury, with rates beginning at US$265 in summer, US$365 in autumn and spring and US$555 in winter. Credit cards are not accepted.

Frangipani Beach Club (☎ 497-6442, fax 497-6440, in the USA ☎ 800-892-4564, frangipani@anguillanet.com, PO Box 1378), on the quiet west side of Meads Bay, is a small condominium complex of Spanish design. Its large suites have air-con, ceiling fans, full kitchens, phones, cable TV, marbled bathrooms, king-size beds and beachfront terraces. Rates for one-bedroom suites start at US$270 in summer, US$550 in winter. There are also some hotel-style rooms available starting at US$185 in summer, US$300 in winter.

Places to Eat
Newly refurbished *Blanchard's (☎ 497-6100)* is an open-air restaurant that's on the beach between the Frangipani and Carimar condo complexes. The food is good and the menu creative, sticking mainly to Asian dishes, but mixing in some American and Jamaican offerings as well. Main dishes range from US$24 to US$48, with grilled lobster being the most expensive. It's open 6:45 pm to 9:15 pm; closed on Sunday (and on Monday in the low season).

There are also restaurants at the hotels. Most affordable is La Sirena's *Top of the Palms*, which has fish, steak and chicken dishes for around US$20 and appetizers for half that. A dinner show, featuring the Mayoumba Folkloric Theatre, who perform Anguillian folk songs and dance, happens every Thursday at 7:30 pm, and Monday night features a steel-band performance.

At the well-regarded *Malliouhana*, which has classic French cuisine and a lovely ocean view, dinner for two will top US$100.

SHOAL BAY WEST
Shoal Bay West is a curving half-moon bay fringed by a pretty white-sand beach. The waters are clear and sheltered. It's rather remote, with just two small resorts, a restaurant and a pink beach estate belonging to actor Chuck Norris. The salt pond that backs the beach was used to harvest salt until just a few decades ago.

There's another glistening white-sand beach, Maunday's Bay, to the east, but it's largely dominated by Cap Juluca, an exclusive resort of Moorish design.

Places to Stay
CoveCastles (☎ 497-6801, fax 497-6051, in the USA ☎ 800-223-1108, covecastles@ anguillanet.com, PO Box 248) is a complex of 14 stark-white villas with a futuristic sculptural design that has won kudos in architectural circles. The island's most upscale retreat, the villas are handsomely decorated with all rooms facing the sea. They have cable TV, VCRs, phones, hammocks on the terraces, full kitchens right down to crystal, and rates that start at US$425 in summer, US$695 in winter. You'd be mad to go at Christmas; rates start at US$1095!

Blue Waters (☎ 497-6292, fax 497-6982, bwaters@anguillanet.com, PO Box 69) is just down the beach from CoveCastles. A bit more conventional in design than its neighbor, it's a modern two-story building with 11 apartments, each with a beachfront balcony or terrace, a kitchen, ceiling fans and TV. Rates are US$125 in summer, US$250 in winter for a one-bedroom unit; US$175 in summer, US$360 in winter for a two-bedroom unit.

Places to Eat
The restaurant at *CoveCastles* (☎ 497-6801) has a talented chef and is the trendiest place to eat on Anguilla. It has a changing menu, but signature dishes include local lobster or crayfish with Creole sauce (US$38), grilled catch-of-the-day with lemon oil (US$28) and homemade ice cream (US$9). It's open to the public for dinner only (closing from late August to mid-October); seating is limited and reservations are required.

East Anguilla

SHOAL BAY EAST
Shoal Bay, often referred to as Shoal Bay East to distinguish it from Shoal Bay West, is considered by beach connoisseurs to be Anguilla's premier strand, if not the Caribbean's. At the northeast side of the island, Shoal Bay East is broad and long with radiant white sands and clear turquoise waters that are ideal for swimming, snorkeling and just plain lazing. To add to its appeal there are a couple of small hotels and restaurants on the beach, but virtually no other development in sight.

A trailer behind Uncle Ernie's beach bar rents snorkel gear (US$8 a day), lounge chairs and umbrellas.

The Fountain
The island's top archaeological site is the Fountain, a huge underground cave along a rocky pathway a few hundred yards southeast of what used to be the Fountain Beach Hotel.

The cave, which draws its name from its former importance as a freshwater spring, contains scores of Amerindian petroglyphs, including a rare stalagmite carving of Jocahu, the Arawak god of creation. The Fountain is

thought to have been a major regional worship site and a place of pilgrimage for Amerindians. A national park, with the Fountain at its centerpiece, has been proposed. In the meantime the Fountain remains the domain of archaeologists only and the ladder leading down into the cave has been fenced off to protect the site from damage.

Places to Stay
Allamanda Beach Club (☎ 497-5217, fax 497-5216, info@allamanda.ai, PO Box 662), just a two-minute walk from the beach, has 16 studio and one-bedroom apartments in a three-story building and is good value for the location. The one-bedroom apartments aren't fancy but they have a small separate kitchen, living room, balcony, TV and ceiling fans. They cost US$129 to US$162 in summer depending largely on their size and whether there's a queen or king bed (government tax and service charges included in summer only), US$165 to US$210 in winter. The couple of studios go for US$85 in summer and US$125 in winter, but sleeping is on a pull-out sofa. There's a pool and restaurant, and you can stay six nights and get the seventh free in summer.

Shoal Bay Villas (☎ 497-2051, fax 497-3631, sbvillas@anguillanet.com, PO Box 81) has a splendid beachfront location and 15 large, comfortable units with tropical decor. For two people, studios cost US$165 in summer, US$270 in winter, one-bedroom apartments cost US$195 in summer, US$295 in winter. Two-bedroom apartments cost US$330 in summer, US$445 in winter for up to four people. All have ceiling fans, a kitchen and a patio or balcony. There's a pool if you're tired of the wonderful, turquoise water and stunning, white-sand beach.

There are two apartment-style places at the east side of Shoal Bay within walking distance of the beach. *Milly's Inn* (☎ 497-2465, fax 497-5591), about five minutes from the beach, is a modern two-story building with just four units, each with a full kitchen, ceiling fans, white tile floors and a large ocean-view balcony. The rate is US$130/140 in summer for downstairs/upstairs units, US$150/160 in winter.

Places to Eat

At *Uncle Ernie's*, a popular local beach bar west of Shoal Bay Villas, you can get barbecued chicken, ribs or a cheeseburger for US$6 and wash it down with a US$2 Heineken or an Ernie's special rum punch. There are also more expensive fish, crayfish and lobster offerings. It's open 9 am to 8 pm daily, and on Sunday afternoon there's live music to be heard.

A bit more upmarket, but still with a casual beachside setting, is *Le Beach Bar* (☎ 497-5598), at Shoal Bay Villas, which has lunchtime sandwiches, salads and burgers from US$8 and dinnertime meat and seafood dishes from around US$20. Every Wednesday night from 6 pm there's a West Indian buffet for US$19 and you can groove to live calypso and reggae music.

Zara's (☎ 497-3229), the restaurant at Allamanda, is the domain of Shamash, a local chef who focuses on Caribbean-influenced dishes such as crusted snapper, Bahamian conch and 'Rasta Pasta.' Most dishes, with the exception of lobster, are priced between US$14 and US$20.

ISLAND HARBOUR

Island Harbour is a working fishing village, not a resort area, and its beach is lined with brightly colored fishing boats rather than chaise lounges. Still it does have a few places to stay and eat and some travelers make their base here.

The area's historic site, albeit sadly neglected, is **Big Spring**, a partially collapsed limestone cave 10 yards west of the Island Pub supermarket. The cave contains 28 Amerindian petroglyphs and an underwater spring that once served as the village water source. The good news is that Big Spring is now under the jurisdiction of the Anguilla National Trust and there are plans to clean it up and make it accessible to visitors.

Just off Island Harbour, in the center of the bay, is the tiny private island of **Scilly Cay**, which has an open-air restaurant and bar and is fringed with a beach of bone-white sands. It has such a reputation as a party destination for an afternoon that people have flown in from St Barts via helicopter just to join in!

Places to Stay

Harbor Lights (☎ 497-4435, in the USA ☎ 800-759-9870, harborlights@anguillanet .com, PO Box 181), a tidy little place right on the ocean at the east side of town, has the area's best-value accommodations. There are four pleasant waterfront studios, all with full kitchens and baths with solar-heated showers. Rates are US$90 to US$110 for the three units that have a queen bed, US$70 for the smaller unit with a double bed. There's a common barbecue area and you can snorkel just a few feet from the deck; diving and other water sports can be arranged, and bicycle rentals are available.

Arawak Beach Inn (☎ 497-4888, fax 497-4889, in the USA and Canada ☎ 877-427-2925, relax@arawakbeach.com, PO Box 284), a small hotel on the west side of Island Harbour, has 17 units in rough two-story buildings that take design influences from the ancient Arawaks, who once occupied this area. The units are comfortable and colorful and have ceiling fans, private baths and refrigerators. Rates for lower-level beachfront rooms range from US$95 in low season to US$175 in high season, from US$105 to US$210 for upper-level rooms.

Places to Eat

Smitty's (☎ 497-4300) is a beachside bar and restaurant opposite the gas station, offering simple barbecue fare served with fries and salad: chicken for US$12, ribs for US$14, fish for US$15 and lobster for US$25. There's a live band on Friday and Saturday evenings.

Hibernia (☎ 497-4290), half a mile east of Island Harbour in the Harbour View residential area, is one of the island's top restaurants and features Caribbean nouvelle cuisine with Asian hints. There's veranda dining and a hillside setting with a spectacular sea view. Starters cost US$8.75 to US$13.50. Main courses range from a US$23 chicken dish to creative seafood dishes such as Thai-style bouillabaisse or grilled crayfish in a lime-soya sauce for US$34.50. In summer it's open for dinner Tuesday to Saturday; in winter it's open for lunch and dinner Tuesday to Sunday.

Scilly Cay (☎ 497-5123) has a casual lunchtime restaurant (open noon to 4 pm) with chicken plates for US$25, fresh lobster for US$40, and a bar that's open 11 am to 5 pm. Guests can pick up a free boat shuttle by going to the Island Harbour pier and waving toward the island. Sunday afternoon is the big event: a reggae band blasting out tunes and the island usually packed with locals and tourists alike. There's also live music on Wednesday and Friday. It's closed on Monday, and all of September and October.

SCRUB ISLAND

Scrub Island is the 2½-mile-long island that lies just off Anguilla's northeastern tip. Befitting its name the island has scrubby vegetation and is inhabited only by goats. It has a beach on its west side, some good snorkeling spots, and a blocked-off airstrip that's rumored to have once been used by cocaine runners. If you don't have your own boat, Smitty's beachside bar (See Island Harbour Places to Eat, earlier) can arrange one to take you to the island for a negotiable price, usually around US$50. There are no facilities; bring your own picnic.

Antigua & Barbuda

Antigua's chief draws are its fine beaches and abundance of colonial-era historic sites. Old stone windmills from long-abandoned sugar plantations are so plentiful that they are the island's main landmarks. The renovated colonial-era naval base of Nelson's Dockyard now attracts yachters from around the world, and the scattered ruins of an extensive hilltop fortress are found at neighboring Shirley Heights.

Antigua's hotels are spread out along its sandy beaches; Dickenson Bay and neighboring Runaway Bay are crowded with places to stay compared to other bays, but remote resorts can be found scattered around the island.

Antigua also makes a good starting point for exploring other islands of the Eastern Caribbean. Many major airlines make regular scheduled flights to the island, and LIAT, one of the area's main airline companies, has its head office at the airport.

Barbuda, 25 miles to the north, is the other half of the dual-island nation. This quiet, single-village island shelters less than 2% of the nation's population. Barbuda gets very few visitors, mainly bird watchers who come to see its frigate-bird colony and a few yachters who enjoy its clear waters and remote beaches. Information on visiting Barbuda is at the end of this chapter.

Highlights

- Exploring colonial-era sights, including a working sugar mill at Betty's Hope and the 18th-century Nelson's Dockyard
- Kicking back at the island's fringing white-sand beaches
- Touring the Caribbean's largest rookery, in Barbuda
- Taking a scenic drive along Fig Tree Drive

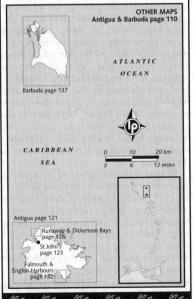

OTHER MAPS
Antigua & Barbuda page 110

Barbuda page 137

ATLANTIC OCEAN

CARIBBEAN SEA

0   10   20 km
0   6   12 miles

Antigua page 121

Runaway & Dickenson Bays page 126

St John's page 123

Falmouth & English Harbours page 132

Facts about Antigua & Barbuda

HISTORY

The first permanent residents in the area are thought to have been migrating Arawaks who established agricultural communities on both Antigua and Barbuda about 2000 years ago. Around AD 1200 the Arawaks were forced out by invading Caribs, who used the islands as bases for their forays in the region but apparently didn't settle them.

Columbus sighted Antigua in 1493 and named it after a church in Seville, Spain. In 1632 the British colonized Antigua, establishing a settlement at Parham, on the east side of the island. The settlers started planting indigo and tobacco, but a glut in the supply for those crops soon drove down prices.

In 1674, Sir Christopher Codrington arrived on Antigua and established the first sugar plantation, Betty's Hope. By the end of the century, a plantation economy had developed, slaves were imported and the central valleys were deforested and planted in cane. To feed the slaves, Codrington leased the island of Barbuda from the British Crown and planted it with food crops.

As Antigua prospered, the British built numerous fortifications around the island, turning it into one of their most secure bases in the Caribbean. The military couldn't secure the economy, however, and in the early 1800s the sugar market began to bottom out. With the abolition of slavery in 1834, the plantations went into a steady decline. Unlike on some other Caribbean islands, as the plantations went under the land was not turned over to former slaves but was instead consolidated under the ownership of a few landowners. Consequently, the lot of most people only worsened. Many former slaves moved off the plantations and into shantytowns, while others crowded onto properties held by the church.

A military-related construction boom during WWII and the development of a tourist industry during the postwar period helped spur economic growth (although the shantytowns that remain along the outskirts of St John's are ample evidence that not everyone has benefited).

After more than 300 years of colonial rule, in 1967 Antigua achieved a measure of self-government as an Associated State of the United Kingdom. On November 1, 1981, it achieved full independence. Vere Cornwall Bird became the nation's first prime minister, and despite leading a government marred by political scandals he held that position through four consecutive terms. He stepped down in 1994 to be succeeded by his son Lester.

Another son, Vere Bird Jr, received international attention in 1991 as the subject of a judicial inquiry into his involvement in smuggling Israeli weapons to the Medellín drug cartel. His signature on documents, required by Israeli authorities to prove that the weapons were bound for a legitimate buyer, allowed the cargo to be shipped to a nonexistent officer of the Antigua Defence Force. After eight hours in port the weapons were transferred to a Colombian boat and shipped to the Medellín cartel without interference by customs. As a consequence of the inquiry, Vere Bird Jr was pressured into resigning his cabinet post but was allowed to keep his parliamentary position; he remains a powerful figure in Antiguan politics.

Despite their stronghold on government, controversy continues to surround the Birds. In 1997, Prime Minister Lester Bird announced that a group of ecologically sensitive nearshore islands, including Guiana Island, which had been proposed for national-park status, were being turned over to Malaysian developers. The deal, which calls for a 1000-room hotel, an 18-hole golf course and a world-class casino, sparked widespread criticism by environmentalists, minority members in parliament and the press. Development

ANTIGUA & BARBUDA

Barbuda

Codrington

CARIBBEAN SEA

0   10   20 km
0   6   12 miles

ATLANTIC OCEAN

Antigua

ST JOHN'S

Falmouth   English Harbour

started in 1998, but protests and debates are still raging over the controversial issue.

GEOGRAPHY

Antigua's land area is 108 sq miles. The island is vaguely rounded in shape, averaging about 11 miles across. The deeply indented coastline is cut by numerous coves and bays, many lined with white-sand beaches. The southwest corner is volcanic in origin and quite hilly, rising to 1319 feet at Boggy Peak, the island's highest point. The rest of the island, which is predominantly of limestone and coral formation, is given to a more gently undulating terrain of open plains and scrubland.

The island of Barbuda, 25 miles north of Antigua, has a land area of 62 sq miles. A low-lying coral island, Barbuda boasts a highest point merely 145 feet above sea level. The west side of Barbuda encompasses the expansive Codrington Lagoon, which is bound by a long, undeveloped barrier beach.

The country's boundaries also include Redonda, an uninhabited rocky islet less than 1 sq mile in size that lies 25 miles southwest of Antigua.

CLIMATE

In January and February, the coolest months, the daily high temperature averages 81°F (27°C), while the nightly low temperature averages 72°F (22°C). In July and August, the hottest months, the high averages 86°F (30°C), the low 77°F (25°C).

Antigua is relatively dry, averaging about 45 inches (1150 mm) of rain annually. The rainiest months are September to November, when measurable precipitation occurs on average eight days each month. February to April is the driest period, with an average of three rainy days each month.

FLORA & FAUNA

As a consequence of colonial-era deforestation, most of Antigua's vegetation is dryland scrub. The island's marshes and salt ponds attract a fair number of stilts, egrets, ducks and pelicans, while hummingbirds are found in garden settings.

Guiana Island, off the northeast coast, has one of Antigua's largest remaining tracts of forest, is the sole habitat for the tropical mockingbird, and supports the largest colony of nesting seabirds on Antigua. These include tropic birds, roseate terns, brown noddies and endangered whistling ducks.

One of the world's rarest snakes, the Antiguan racer, is found on nearby Great Bird Island. The area also supports the fourth-largest mangrove system in the Lesser Antilles. Unfortunately, the government has targeted Guiana Island and eight smaller adjacent islands for intensive resort development.

Barbuda's Codrington Lagoon has the largest frigate-bird colony in the Lesser Antilles. For more information on frigate birds see the Barbuda section.

GOVERNMENT & POLITICS

The nation of Antigua & Barbuda is a member of the Commonwealth and has a parliamentary system of government led by a prime minister and modeled after the British system. There's an elected 17-member House of Representatives and an appointed 17-member Senate. Elections are held at least once every five years.

The British monarchy is represented by a governor-general, who has a role in appointing senators but is otherwise largely an advisory figure.

ECONOMY

Tourism is the island's main industry, accounting for about half of the workforce. Agriculture and fishing employ about 10% of the workforce. There's a bit of small-scale manufacturing, primarily in garment and electronics assembly.

POPULATION & PEOPLE

About 80,000 people live on Antigua. Approximately 90% of them are of African descent. There are also small minority populations of British, Portuguese and Lebanese ancestry. The population of Barbuda is approximately 1200, most of African descent.

SOCIETY & CONDUCT

Away from the resorts, Antigua retains a traditional West Indian character. It's manifested in the gingerbread architecture found around the capital, the popularity of steel-band, calypso and reggae music and in festivities such as Carnival. English traditions also play an important role, as is evident in the national sport of cricket.

Dos & Don'ts

Dress is casual, and simple cotton clothing is suitable attire for most occasions. In a few of the most upscale resort restaurants, jackets and ties are required of men. To avoid offense, restrict swimwear to the beach.

RELIGION

Nearly half of all Antiguans are members of the Anglican Church. Other religious denominations include Roman Catholic, Moravian, Methodist, Seventh Day Adventist, Lutheran and Jehovah's Witness.

LANGUAGE

English is the official language, most often spoken with a distinctive Antiguan lilt, which at times can be hard to understand.

Facts for the Visitor

ORIENTATION

Antigua's airport is at the northeast side of the island, about a 15-minute drive from either St John's or Dickenson Bay.

Finding your way around on Antigua can at times prove difficult. The island is randomly dotted with green road signs pointing you in the right direction but they peter out the further away you get from the main centers. Private signs pointing the way to restaurants, hotels and a few other tourist spots are far more frequent. Beyond that the best landmarks are old stone windmills, which are shown on the Ordnance Survey map of Antigua – a very handy item to have if you intend to do extensive exploring.

Maps

The tourist office distributes free color maps of Antigua & Barbuda, which are sufficient if you're touring by car and sticking to the main roads. The best road map of Antigua is the 1:50,000-scale British Ordnance Survey map, *Tourist Map of Antigua,* reprinted in 1992. It can be bought at the Map Shop in St John's (US$8) and a few other places around the island.

TOURIST OFFICES
Local Tourist Offices

The main tourist office is at the harbor end of Nevis St in St John's. When requesting information by mail, write to Antigua & Barbuda Department of Tourism (☎ 462-0480, fax 462-2483, tourism.antigua@candw.ag), PO Box 363, St John's, Antigua, West Indies. There's a tourist information booth before customs at the airport as well.

Tourist Offices Abroad

Tourist offices abroad include the following:

Canada
Antigua & Barbuda Department of Tourism (☎ 416-961-3085, fax 416-961-7218) 60 St Clair Ave E, Suite 304, Toronto, Ontario M4T 1N5

Germany
Antigua & Barbuda Department of Tourism (☎ 61 72 21 504, fax 61 72 21 513) Thomasstrasse II, D-61328 Bad Homburg

Italy
Antigua & Barbuda Department of Tourism (☎/fax 02-87 79 83) Via Santa Maria Alla Porta No 9, Milan 20123

UK
Antigua & Barbuda Department of Tourism (☎ 020-7486 7073, fax 020-7486 1466, antibar@msn.com) High Commission, Antigua House, 15 Thayer St, London W1M 5LD

USA
Antigua & Barbuda Department of Tourism (☎ 212-541-4117, 888-268-4227 fax 212-757-1607), 610 Fifth Ave, Suite 311, New York, NY 10020
Antigua & Barbuda Department of Tourism (☎ 305-381-6762, fax 305-381-7908) 25 SE 2nd Ave, Suite 200, Miami, Florida 33131

VISAS & DOCUMENTS

Visitors from the USA, Canada and the UK may enter the country for stays of less than six months with either a valid passport or both a birth certificate with a raised seal and a photo ID. Most other visitors, including citizens of Australia, New Zealand and West European countries, must have passports but do not need visas.

Officially all visitors need a roundtrip or onward ticket.

EMBASSIES & CONSULATES
Antiguan & Barbudan Embassies & Consulates

France
(☎ 0153-96 93 96)
43 Ave de Friedland, 75008 Paris

UK
(☎ 020-7486 7073)
15 Thayer St, London W1M5LD

USA
(☎ 202-362-5211)
3216 New Mexico Ave NW, Washington, DC 20016

Foreign Consulates in Antigua & Barbuda

Germany
Honorary Consul (☎ 462-3174)
PO Box 1259, St John's

UK
High Commission (☎ 462-0008/9)
Price Waterhouse Centre, 11 Old Parham Rd, St John's

CUSTOMS

Arriving passengers may bring in a carton of cigarettes, one quart of liquor and six ounces of perfume duty free.

MONEY

The currency of Antigua & Barbuda is the Eastern Caribbean dollar (EC$), and the official exchange rate is EC$2.70 to US$1.

US dollars are widely accepted. However, unless rates are posted in US dollars, as is the norm with accommodations, it usually works out better to pay for things in EC dollars.

MasterCard, Visa and American Express are widely accepted. Credit card charges are made in US dollars, so businesses that quote prices in EC dollars must convert the bill to a US dollar total. Whenever you intend to pay by credit card it's a good idea to ask about the exchange rate first, as some places use EC$2.60 or EC$2.65 to US$1, but others use EC$2.50, a hefty 8% overcharge.

A 10% service charge is added to most restaurant bills, in which case no further tipping is necessary.

POST & COMMUNICATIONS
Post

The main post office is in St John's, and there are branch post offices at Nelson's Dockyard and the airport. The rate to send a postcard to North America or the UK is EC$0.45, to Australia or Europe EC$0.60. An 0.5oz letter costs EC$0.90 and EC$1.20, respectively.

Mail sent to Antigua should have the post office box or street address followed by 'St John's, Antigua, West Indies.'

Telephone

Almost all pay phones have been converted to the Caribbean Phone Card system. Phone cards can be bought from vendors in areas near the phones and from the Cable & Wireless offices in St John's or English Harbour. They're priced from EC$10 to EC$60, depending on the number of time units they have.

Avoid the credit card phones found at the airport and in some hotel lobbies, as they charge a steep US$2 per minute locally, US$4 to other Caribbean islands or the USA and as much as US$8 elsewhere.

When calling Antigua from overseas dial the 268 area code, followed by the seven-digit local phone number.

More information on phone cards and making long-distance calls is under Post & Communications in Facts for the Visitor, in the front of the book.

Email & Internet Access

Parcel Plus (☎ 462-4854), Redcliffe Quay, St John's, has Internet access for US$6 per half-hour. Cable & Wireless in St John's and at the marina in Falmouth Harbour also provides terminals, for EC$20 per half-hour.

INTERNET RESOURCES

Antigua is well set up on the Internet. Two good sites for more information are www .interknowledge.com/antigua-barbuda and www.turq.com/antigua.

BOOKS

Antigua's best-known writer is Jamaica Kincaid, who has authored a number of novels and essays including *A Small Place* (1988), which gives a scathing account of the negative effects of tourism on Antigua. Other internationally recognized works by Kincaid include the novel *Annie John,* which recounts growing up in Antigua, and *At the Bottom of the River,* a collection of short stories.

Author Jamaica Kincaid

Desmond Nicholson, president of the Historical and Archaeological Society of Antigua and Barbuda, has published several works on island history, including *Antigua, Barbuda & Redonda: A Historical Sketch.*

NEWSPAPERS & MAGAZINES

Antigua has two local daily newspapers, the progovernment *Antigua Sun* and the opposition-leaning *Daily Observer.* Both concentrate on local issues.

The best source of tourist information is *The Antiguan,* a free booklet covering everything from history to wedding arrangements. Bigger and glossier is *Living the Life,* a magazine that has a number of feature stories and plenty of ads, and delves into practicalities in a small back section. Both can be picked up at the tourist office, airport tourist-office counter and some hotels.

RADIO & TV

Gem radio, at 93.9 FM, has hourly headline news and marine weather forecasts. Some hotels have cable TV, which is predominantly US network programming.

ELECTRICITY

Most hotels operate on 110V, 60 cycles; however, some places use 220V. Check before plugging anything in.

WEIGHTS & MEASURES

Antigua uses the imperial system of measurement. Car odometers register in miles, speed limits are posted in miles per hour and gas is sold by the gallon.

HEALTH

Antigua's 225-bed Holberton Hospital (☎ 462-0251) is on the eastern outskirts of St John's, just off the Queen Elizabeth Hwy.

DANGERS & ANNOYANCES

Visitors should be careful to not leave their valuables unattended and should be cautious about walking in secluded places after dark. Women traveling alone may find themselves the target of unwanted attention and sexual advances, particularly if they venture into less touristed areas.

EMERGENCIES

The police headquarters (☎ 462-0125) is on American Rd, on the eastern outskirts of St John's. There are substations near Nelson's Dockyard at English Harbour and in central St John's on Newgate St.

BUSINESS HOURS

Typical business hours are 8 am to 5 pm Monday to Saturday; note that shops often close at noon or 3 pm on Thursday and government offices generally close an hour early on Friday.

PUBLIC HOLIDAYS & SPECIAL EVENTS

Public holidays in Antigua & Barbuda include the following:

New Year's Day	January 1
Good Friday	late March/early April
Easter Monday	late March/early April
Labour Day	first Monday in May
Whit Monday	eighth Monday after Easter
Queen's Birthday	second Saturday in June
Carnival Monday & Tuesday	first Monday & Tuesday in August
Antigua & Barbuda Independence Day	November 1
Christmas Day	December 25
Boxing Day	December 26

Carnival, Antigua's big annual festival, is held from the end of July and culminates in a parade on the first Tuesday in August. Calypso music, steel bands, masqueraders, floats and street jump-ups are all part of the celebrations. In May, Barbuda has its own Carnival, the Caribana Festival, but it's by no means the grand affair Antigua's is.

Antigua Sailing Week is a major weeklong yachting event that begins on the last Sunday in April. It's the largest regatta in the Caribbean and generally attracts about 150 boats from a few dozen countries. In addition to a series of five boat races, there are rum parties and a formal ball, with most activities taking place at Nelson's Dockyard and Falmouth Harbour, where the majority of boats are anchored.

ACTIVITIES
Beaches & Swimming

Antigua's tourist office boasts that the island has 365 beaches, 'one for each day of the year.' While the count may be suspect, the island certainly doesn't lack in lovely strands. Most of Antigua's beaches have white or light golden sands, many are protected by coral reefs and all are officially public. You can find nice sandy stretches all around the island, and, generally, wherever there's a resort there's a beach. Prime beaches on the west coast include the adjacent Dickenson and Runaway beaches, Deep Bay and Hawksbill Beach to the west of St John's, and the less populated Darkwood Beach and Johnson's Point Beach to the south. On the east coast, Half Moon Bay and Long Bay are top contenders. Those based in the English Harbour area can make their way to Galleon Beach and the clear waters of secluded Pigeon Beach.

The far ends of some public beaches, including the north side of Dickenson, are favored by topless bathers, and nude bathing is practiced along a section of Hawksbill Beach.

Diving

Antigua has some excellent diving, with coral canyons, wall drops and sea caves hosting a range of marine creatures, including turtles, sharks, barracuda and colorful reef fish. Popular diving sites include the 2-mile-long Cades Reef, whose clear, calm waters have an abundance of fish and numerous soft and hard corals, and Ariadne Shoal, which offers reefs teeming with large fish, lobsters and nurse sharks. A fun spot for both divers and snorkelers is *Jettias*, a 310-foot steamer that sank in 1917 and now provides a habitat for reef fish and coral. The deepest end of the wreck is in about 30 feet of water, while the shallowest part comes up almost to the surface.

Dive Shops The going rate is about US$47 for a one-tank dive, US$70 for a two-tank dive, US$60 for a night dive and US$500 for full certification courses. Nondivers who want to view the underwater world but not overly commit can opt for a half-day resort course that culminates with a reef dive, for around US$90. The rates include rental of tanks and weights, but you'll have to pay an extra US$15 to US$20 for a regulator, BC, snorkel, mask and fins. Most places give a discount for payment by cash or traveler's check.

Dive shops in Antigua include the following:

Deep Bay Divers (☎/fax 463-8000, deepbaydivers@candw.ag), PO Box 2150, at Heritage Quay in St John's

Dive Antigua (☎ 462-3483, fax 462-7787, birkj@candw.ag), PO Box 251, at Rex Halcyon Cove on Dickenson Beach

Dockyard Divers (☎ 460-1178, fax 460-1179), PO Box 184, at Nelson's Dockyard

Jolly Dive (☎/fax 462-8305), PO Box 744, at Jolly Harbour

Octopus Divers (☎ 460-6286, fax 463-8528), PO Box 2105, at Falmouth Harbour

Diving Center Aquarius (☎ 460-9384, rmronan@candw.ag), Long Bay Hotel, Long Bay

Snorkeling

Paradise Reef, which has shallow waters and a variety of fish, is a popular destination for snorkel tours, and some of the dive shops will take visitors there. However, it may be more convenient to go with one of the beach operators, such as Tony's Water Sports (☎ 462-6326), at Dickenson Bay, as they go out a few times a day. The going rate is US$25, snorkel gear included.

For snorkeling from the shore, the wreck of the *Andes*, near the Royal Antiguan Hotel at Deep Bay, and the reef fronting nearby Hawksbill Beach are popular spots. You can rent snorkel sets for US$10 a day from Tony's Water Sports and from some dive shops.

For information on snorkeling with catamaran tours, see Organized Tours in the Getting Around section.

Windsurfing

Antigua's sheltered west coast is best for beginners. The open east coast has conditions more suitable for advanced windsurfers, with onshore winds good for slalom and wave-slalom sailing.

At Dickenson Bay, Rex Halcyon Cove (☎ 462-0256) gives two-hour windsurfing lessons for US$50.

Windsurfing Antigua (☎ 462-9463), a windsurfing school at the Lord Nelson Beach Hotel on Dutchman's Bay, at the northeast side of Antigua, gives two-hour

beginner lessons for US$60. They also deliver to other places on the island.

Rental gear for intermediate and advanced windsurfing costs US$60 a day, US$260 a week, and lessons in waterstart, jibes and advanced windsurfing techniques cost US$30.

Fishing

Game fish caught in Antiguan waters include marlin, tuna and wahoo. Tony's Water Sports (☎ 462-6326), at Dickenson Bay, offers a deep-sea fishing trip for US$440 (half day) or US$780 (full day); prices cover up to four people.

Other Water Activities

Both Tony's Water Sports and Sea Sports (☎ 462-3355), also at Dickenson Bay, offer a range of boating activities, such as waterskiing (US$25), parasailing (US$45) and Jet-skiing (US$35/45 for singles/tandem).

Hiking

The historical society, which operates the Museum of Antigua & Barbuda, sponsors a culturally or environmentally oriented hike once a month. Walks average about 90 minutes and typically visit old estates or interesting landscapes. The walks are free, but donations are welcome. Call the museum (☎ 462-1469) for information on upcoming hikes.

For those who want to move at a quicker pace, the local Hash House Harriers do a morning jog on alternate Saturdays and welcome visitors to come along. Call O'Grady's (☎ 462-5392) for the latest schedule.

Golf

The Cedar Valley Golf Club (☎ 462-0161), a 10-minute drive north of St John's, has an 18-hole course and greens fees of US$35. The 18-hole Jolly Harbour Golf Course (☎ 480-6950), at Jolly Harbour, has greens fees of US$35, half that if you want to play only nine holes. Both have cart and club rentals.

Half Moon Bay Hotel (☎ 460-4300) has a nine-hole course that's been closed since Hurricane Luis but is expected to eventually reopen.

ACCOMMODATIONS

Other than a couple of budget guest houses in St John's and a handful scattered around the island, Antigua is mainly home to resort-type complexes. There are a few good-value, moderate-range places around the island, with prices beginning at about US$70 for a double in summer and closer to US$100 in winter. Still, most of what Antigua has to offer is easily priced at twice that.

Top-end resorts average about US$300 in winter for 'standard' rooms – and many of these rooms really are quite standard, despite the price. If you want better amenities, more space or an ocean view, you often have to step up to a more expensive category.

If you plan on traveling in late summer, keep in mind that many of Antigua's hotels close for September, and some extend that a few weeks in either direction.

In addition to the rates given throughout this chapter, an 8.5% government tax and a 10% service charge are added to all accommodations bills.

FOOD & DRINKS

There's a fairly good range of West Indian, French, Italian, English and North American food around the island. Most restaurants feature fresh seafood, with the catch of the day commonly being one of the better-value options.

For a good, cheap local snack, order a roti, the West Indian version of a burrito, filled with curried potatoes, chicken or beef. Also try one of the locally grown black pineapples, which are quite sweet, rather small and, despite the name, not at all black.

It's best to boil or otherwise treat tap water before drinking it. Bottled water is available in grocery stores.

Cavalier and English Harbour are two locally made rums, and the island brews its own lager under the Wadadli label.

SPECTATOR SPORTS

One of the best things Britain did for the West Indies was introduce the local populace to cricket. It soon became the national passion of Antigua and is played everywhere – on beaches, in backyards or anywhere there's some flat, open ground. National and international games are played at the Antigua Recreation Ground in St John's, and although the West Indies team has fallen from the dizzying heights of the 1970s and early '80s, the game is followed religiously and the atmosphere at a match is electric and enthralling.

Viv Richards (or the 'Master-Blaster,' as he was known in his heyday), who hails from Antigua, is one of the most famous cricketers of the modern game, and it's not uncommon to see him strolling around the streets of St John's.

Soccer and basketball are increasing in popularity, and national and club soccer games, also played in the Antigua Recreation Ground, can produce much the same atmosphere as cricket.

Getting There & Away

DEPARTURE TAX

There's an EC$50 departure tax. Stays of less than 24 hours are exempt from the tax.

AIR
Airports & Airlines

Travelers island-hopping through the Eastern Caribbean can expect to do some transiting through Antigua's VC Bird International Airport. The departure lounge has little or no air-conditioning, a couple of souvenir and duty-free liquor shops, and coin and card phones. The bar sells drinks, sandwiches and slices of pizza, and for long layovers you can order pizza and pasta from the upstairs restaurant via the bar.

Those not in transit will find a tourist information booth between immigration and customs. It's no problem to walk back through customs once you've cleared it, even though the sign over the arrivals exit says 'Strictly no Admittance.' The staff distributes maps and brochures and can help with booking rooms.

Outside the arrivals exit lurk agents for a dozen car rental companies. Nearby is a post office, an exchange bank that's open 9 am to 3 pm weekdays and an affiliated Bureau de Change window that's open 3 to 9:30 pm weekdays and noon to 7 pm weekends. There's also a 24-hour ATM that accepts Visa, MasterCard and Cirrus and Plus cards.

The middle phone of the three that are marked 'card' at the right of the airline ticket counters is a coin phone. A vending machine near the bank sells phone cards.

Following are airlines that operate in or to Antigua & Barbuda:

Air Canada	☎ 462-1147
American Airlines	☎ 462-0950
British Airways	☎ 462-0876
BWIA	☎ 480-2901
Continental Airlines	☎ 462-5353
LIAT	☎ 480-5074
Virgin Atlantic	☎ 800-744-7477

The USA

American Airlines has four daily flights between Antigua and San Juan that connect with direct flights to Boston and New York, and one direct flight daily from Miami. Continental flies from New York to Antigua daily in winter and three times a week in summer. BWIA has daily nonstop flights to Antigua from New York. Fares depend on the season and current promotions, but from the US east coast they generally begin around US$400 for a ticket allowing stays of up to 30 days.

Canada

BWIA flies direct between Toronto and Antigua once a week. Air Canada flies direct between Toronto and Antigua on Saturday. With either airline the cheapest fare is around C$650 and allows a maximum stay of 21 days.

The UK

British Airways has direct flights from London on Tuesday, Thursday and Sunday. Fares vary a bit with the season and are typically between UK£500 and UK£600 for a 21-day advance purchase ticket allowing stays of up to six months.

Virgin Atlantic (☎ 800-744-7477) has a direct flight from London on Wednesday only for about UK£450 roundtrip.

Within the Caribbean

You can get a direct or connecting flight from Antigua to any destination in LIAT's network.

LIAT flights from Antigua to Anguilla cost US$89 one-way, US$169 roundtrip; to St Kitts it's US$66 one-way, US$125 roundtrip; to St Martin they cost US$99 one-way, US$149 for same-day return and US$179 for a 30-day roundtrip; to Martinique it's US$150 one-way, US$246 for a seven-day roundtrip and US$270 for a 30-day roundtrip ticket that allows a stopover in Dominica or Guadeloupe.

The LIAT ticketing and reservation office (☎ 480-5074) is at the airport, behind the American Airlines counter. It's open 5 am to 7 pm daily.

See the Montserrat chapter for information on helicopters to the island.

SEA
Ferry

See the Montserrat chapter on ferries to the island.

Yacht

A favorite place to clear customs is at Nelson's Dockyard in English Harbour (VHF channel 16; for more information, see English Harbour, later in this chapter). Other ports of entry are Falmouth Harbour, Jolly Harbour, St John's Harbour, and Crabbs Marina in Parham Harbour. If you're going on to Barbuda ask for a cruising permit, which will allow you to visit that island without further formalities.

Antigua has many protected harbors and bays, and fine anchorages are found all around the island. Full-service marinas are at English Harbour, Falmouth Harbour, Jolly Harbour and Parham Sound.

Boaters can make reservations at many restaurants around Falmouth Harbour and English Harbour via VHF channel 68.

Yacht charters can be arranged through Sun Yacht Charters (☎ 460-2615), at Nelson's Dockyard.

Cruise Ship

Antigua is a port of call for numerous cruise ships. The island's cruise-ship terminal, at Heritage Quay in St John's Harbour, has a duty-free shopping center and a casino. Heritage Quay is within easy walking distance of St John's main sights: the museum, cathedral and historic Redcliffe Quay.

Cruise ships also anchor near Falmouth Harbor and taxi their passengers into the harbor for the day.

Getting Around

BUS

Antigua's buses are privately owned and are predominantly minivans, although there are a few mid-sized buses. Fares range from EC$1.50 to EC$3.75. Buses from St John's to Falmouth and English Harbour are plentiful, cost around EC$2.50 and take about 30 minutes. They start early and generally run until about 7 pm. Rush hour is particularly bustling, with lots of buses between 4 and 5 pm. There are very few buses on Sunday.

The new main bus station in St John's is opposite the public market. All destinations are allocated a number, and each bus displays a number that indicates where it's heading. Notices are posted about with destination numbers. All you have to do is match your destination number to a bus and you're good to go. Buses line up in the row and don't actually leave until they're full. So just find the bus you need, hop on, and hope it fills up and leaves before you melt.

Buses to the east side of the island leave from the East Bus Station, near the corner of Independence Ave and High St, and go to Piggots and Willikies. The number system doesn't apply here, so you'll need to ask around to find your bus.

There's no bus service to the airport, Dickenson Bay or other resort areas on the northern part of the island.

CAR & MOTORCYCLE
Road Rules

To drive on Antigua you need to buy a temporary 90-day license, which is usually obtainable from car rental agents but can also be picked up at the Inland Revenue Department, on Newgate St in St John's. Simply show your home license and dish out a hefty EC$50.

Driving is on the left. Many rental cars have steering wheels on the left, which can be disorienting.

Antigua's roads have improved over the last few years, but many are still in bad shape. Roads in the west, north and south are quite good, but to the east of the island they are in need of some repair. Fig Tree Drive is more an off-road rally course, with potholes and gravel to contend with. If you plan to get off the beaten track, it's best to hire a jeep.

Be aware of goats darting across the road and of narrow roads in built-up areas, which can be crowded with children after school gets out.

The speed limit is generally 20mph in villages and 40mph in rural areas. Numerous gas stations lie scattered around the island, including one just outside the airport terminal. Gas sells for EC$6.85 per gallon.

Rental

There are more than a dozen car rental agencies on Antigua, most with representatives at the airport. All of the agencies in the following list rent out cars for around US$50

Could Be Dangerous

As is the case on other islands in the Eastern Caribbean, bus drivers on Antigua try to make their vehicles as distinctive as possible by giving them colorful names. Some of the buses, with names like 'Man Standing By' and 'Send Dem Come,' are making an obvious pitch to riders; others, such as 'Could Be Dangerous' or 'Don't Tes' Me,' sound anything but reassuring. Although there's an element of jest to it all, choosing a bus by the name may prove to be a good way of avoiding some of the more reckless drivers.

a day, which can drop as low as US$35 in summer, when things are slow. Discounts are usually offered on longer rentals. Many of the companies also offer jeeps for the same rates, or US$5 to US$10 more.

In part because of the poor road conditions, all but the newest rental cars are generally quite beat. Your best bet (though by no means a sure thing) on getting a roadworthy car is to book with one of the international agencies. Most car rental firms will deliver cars to your hotel free of charge.

Rental companies include the following:

Avis	☎ 462-2840
Capital Rentals	☎ 462-0863
Dollar	☎ 462-0362
Hertz	☎ 462-4114
Lion's	☎ 460-1400
Oakland Rent-A-Car	☎ 462-3021
Stead's Rent-A-Car	☎ 463-9970
Thrifty Rent-A-Car	☎ 462-9532

Paradise Boat Sales (☎ 460-7125), at Jolly Harbour, rents 80cc scooters for US$35 and 125cc motorcycles for US$45. Rates are 20% less on multiple-day rentals.

TAXI

Taxi fares are regulated by the government, but confirm the fare with the driver before riding away. Fares from the airport are US$9 to St John's, US$13 to Runaway or Dickenson Bays, US$20 to Jolly Harbour and US$26 to English Harbour. From Nelson's Dockyard at English Harbour, taxi fares are US$26 to St John's, US$32 to Runaway Bay. Fares are for up to four persons, a fifth person costs another 25%.

In St John's is a taxi stand opposite the public market, and taxi drivers also hang around Heritage Quay. Most hotels have taxis assigned to them; if you don't find one, ask at reception.

BICYCLE

Paradise Boat Sales (☎ 460-7125) at Jolly Harbour rents mountain bikes for US$15 for single-day rentals and US$12 per day if you rent for a minimum of two days.

Putters (☎ 463-4653), at Dickenson Bay, rents bikes for US$15 a day, US$65 a week.

ORGANIZED TOURS
Land Tours

Touring the island by taxi costs about US$80 per car for a half-day tour that takes in Nelson's Dockyard and Shirley Heights, or US$150 for a full-day tour for up to four people.

Boat Tours

Wadadli Cats (☎ 462-4792) offers a number of catamaran trips, including one that features snorkeling time at Cades Reef, and another at Great Bird Island, a small volcanic island a couple of miles off the northeast coast of Antigua. Both trips include lunch, cost US$60 and pick up their guests at Dickenson Bay and other points around the island. Wadadli also does a daylong circumnavigation tour of Antigua for US$75.

Treasure Island Cruises (☎ 461-8675), another large catamaran operator, has a full schedule of similar tours at prices comparable to Wadadli. They also offer a Wednesday and Friday boat-and-land tour that includes a tour of Betty's Hope, Devil's Bridge and the rain forest, a barbecue on the beach with steel-band entertainment, and sailing; it costs US$100.

The *Jolly Roger* 'pirate ship' (☎ 462-2064) is a party boat that offers a day trip of snorkeling, plank-walking, rope swinging and lunch, all for US$75.

Helicopter Tours

Antigua can be seen from above with Caribbean Helicopters (☎ 460-5900). It's not cheap, though; US$69 will get you a 15-minute flight over half the island, US$115 a 30-minute flight taking in the whole island. They also offer a 45-minute tour of Montserrat for US$175.

Antigua

ST JOHN'S

St John's, Antigua's capital and commercial center, has a population of about 36,000,

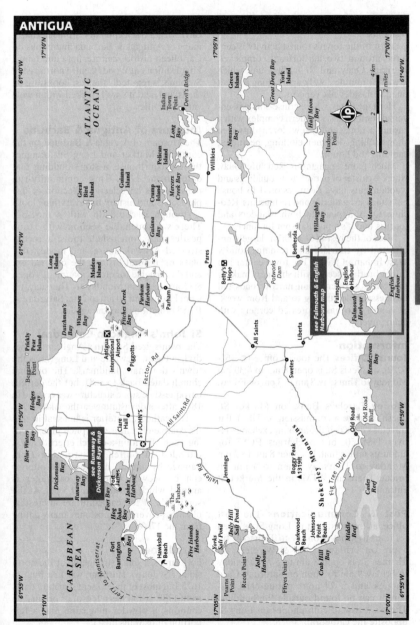

ANTIGUA

making it home to nearly half of the island's residents.

Most of the town's tourist activity is centered around two harborfront complexes, Heritage Quay and Redcliffe Quay, which are a few minutes' walk apart along a street lined with sidewalk vendors.

Heritage Quay, where cruise-ship passengers disembark, is a modern complex with a casino, a hotel and a few dozen duty-free shops selling designer clothing, perfumes, cameras and liquor.

Much more engaging is Redcliffe Quay, where a cluster of period stone buildings and wooden huts have been restored to house gift shops, art galleries and restaurants. Redcliffe Quay appeals to both islanders and tourists, and it's a popular spot for lunch.

Most of the rest of St John's is largely unaffected by tourism and remains solidly West Indian in flavor. The town center is a rather bustling scene, with shoppers making the rounds, taxis crowding narrow roads and businesspeople rushing to and from work. St John's also has depressed corners with deep poverty.

Information

Tourist Offices The tourist office (☎ 462-0029), on Nevis St, is open 8 am to 4:30 pm Monday to Thursday, 8 am to 3 pm on Friday.

Money Barclays Bank, on Market St, doesn't charge a commission on US-dollar traveler's checks if the amount exchanged is over US$150, but it charges EC$5 for amounts under that. It's open 8 am to 2 pm Monday to Thursday, 8 am to 4 pm on Friday. There are ATMs in the Market St entrance.

Post & Communications The post office, at the west end of Long St, is open 8:15 am to 4 pm Monday to Thursday, till 5 pm on Friday. Cable & Wireless, on Thames St, is open 8 am to 5 pm Monday to Friday, 9 am to noon on Saturday. Card phones and a 24-hour phone-card dispenser can be found outside the building. There's a row of coin phones on Long St opposite the cathedral.

Bookstores The Map Shop on St Mary's St carries a good selection of Caribbean charts, maps of Antigua & Barbuda and books on Caribbean history, culture, flora and fauna. First Editions, at Woods Centre northeast of St John's, is reputedly the best bookstore on the island, and it's well stocked with a wide variety of titles.

Museum of Antigua & Barbuda

The Museum of Antigua & Barbuda, on the corner of Market and Long Sts, occupies the old courthouse, a stone building that dates from 1750. This community-run museum has an eclectic collection of displays on island history, but everything looks as though it could do with a dust-off. There's a touchable section with stone pestles and conch-shell tools, a reconstructed Arawak house, and modest displays on natural history, the colonial era and the struggle for emancipation. It's open 8:30 am to 4 pm Monday to Thursday, till 4 pm Friday, and 10 am to 2 pm Saturday. A EC$5 donation is encouraged.

St John's Anglican Cathedral

The twin-spired St John's Anglican Cathedral, between Newgate and Long Sts, is the town's dominant landmark. The original church dated back to 1681, but the current baroque-style stone structure was erected in 1847, after a devastating earthquake.

The cathedral interior is unusual in that it's completely encased in pitch pine, creating a church-within-a-church effect that was intended to buffer the structure from damage by natural disasters. The interior can be viewed when the caretaker is around, which is usually until 5 pm. At the south side of the cathedral are interesting old moss-covered tombstones, many dating from the 1700s.

Fort James

Fort James, a small stronghold at the north side of St John's Harbour, was first built in 1675, but most of the present structure dates from 1739. It still has a few of its original 36 cannons, a powder magazine and a fair portion of its walls intact.

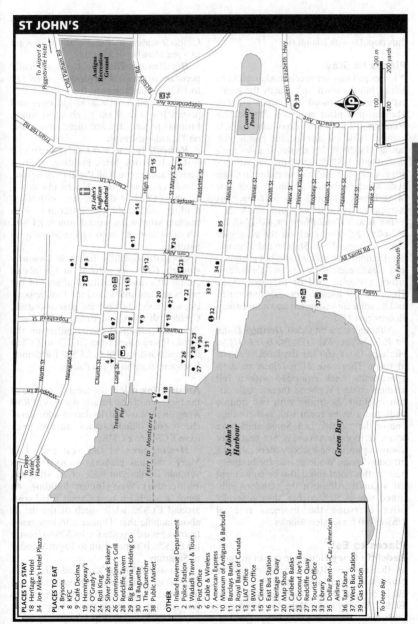

ST JOHN'S

PLACES TO STAY
18 Heritage Hotel
34 Joe Mike's Hotel Plaza

PLACES TO EAT
4 Brysons
8 KFC
9 Café Decima
19 Hemingway's
22 O'Grady's
24 Roti King
25 Silver Streak Bakery
26 Commissioner's Grill
28 Redcliffe Tavern
29 Big Banana Holding Co
30 La Baguette
31 The Quencher
38 Public Market

OTHER
1 Inland Revenue Department
2 Police Station
3 Wadadli Travel & Tours
5 Post Office
6 Cable & Wireless
7 American Express
10 Museum of Antigua & Barbuda
11 Barclays Bank
12 Royal Bank of Canada
13 LIAT Office
14 BWIA Office
15 Cinema
16 East Bus Station
17 Heritage Quay
20 Map Shop
21 Caribelle Batiks
23 Coconut Joe's Bar
27 Redcliffe Quay
32 Tourist Office
33 Library
35 Dollar Rent-A-Car; American Airlines
36 Taxi Stand
37 West Bus Station
39 Gas Station

To Airport &
Piggotsville Hotel

Old Parham Rd

Antigua
Recreation
Ground

Queen Elizabeth Hwy

Factory Rd

Independence Ave

Camacho Ave

Country
Pond

Cross St

25

High St

St Mary's St

Redcliffe St

News St

Tanner St

South St

New St

Prince Klaus St

Rodney St

Nelson St

Hawkins St

Hood St

Drake St

St John's
Anglican
Cathedral

Church St

Temple St

Corn Alley

Market St

All Saints Rd

To Falmouth

Valley Rd

Thames St

Long St

Church St

Newgate St

Popeshead St

North St

Wapping Ln

Treasury Pier

Ferry to Montserrat

St John's Harbour

Green Bay

To Deep Water Harbour

To Deep Bay

0   100   200 m
0   100   200 yards

ANTIGUA & BARBUDA

Fort Bay, which stretches north from the fort, is the closest beach to St John's and is thus popular with islanders.

Places to Stay

It's slim pickings for accommodations in St John's, but the town isn't exactly the greatest place to be based in Antigua anyway. The cheapest place around is *Piggotsville Hotel* (☎ 462-0592, marcellec@candw.ag). It features basic yet comfortable rooms with fan at US$20/35 for singles/doubles with shared bath, US$25/40 with private bath. It's not actually in St John's but rather in Clare Hall, which is about a 30-minute walk east of St John's. Although this isn't the most convenient spot, it is nice, quiet, and local.

Joe Mike's Hotel Plaza (☎ 462-1142, fax 462-6056, PO Box 136), on the corner of Corn Alley and Nevis St, is an older central hotel. Rooms are rather basic, but adequate and clean, each with air-con, phone and either a double bed or two twin beds. There's a TV lounge, free morning coffee and an adjacent restaurant and mini-casino. Rooms cost US$65.

Although it's a bit faded, *Heritage Hotel* (☎ 462-1247, fax 462-1179, PO Box 1532), in Heritage Quay, still has the fanciest rooms in town. There are 21 spacious, modern apartments, each equipped with a full kitchen, cable TV, phone, thermostatic air-con, bathtub, bedroom with two double beds and a living room with two couches, one of them a sofa bed. Some units have scenic harborside verandas, but that's not always a plus, as the harbor waters can get a bit odoriferous. While geared for business-people, this hotel could also be convenient for a family. Although the standard published rate is 50% higher, they generally offer everyone the business rate of US$80/100 for singles/doubles.

Places to Eat

Redcliffe Quay Housed in one of the huts at the rear of Redcliffe Quay is *The Quencher*, which offers sandwiches from EC$5.50 and daily lunch specials from EC$12. Nearby is *La Baguette*, which isn't particularly French but does have a good se-

lection of sandwiches from EC$12 to EC$20 and a few salads for around EC$20. Outdoor seating is available. It's open 8 am to 5 pm Monday to Saturday.

Big Banana Holding Co is a locally popular restaurant, with pizzas from EC$22 to EC$76, depending on the size and toppings, as well as salads, sandwiches and pastas. It's open 9 am to about midnight Monday to Saturday, and there's live music on Thursday evening.

Redcliffe Tavern (☎ 461-4557), in a nicely restored historic brick building, offers a varied lunch menu with the likes of quiche, Creole crab puffs or a chicken platter for around EC$28; at dinner, most dishes, including mahimahi or fettuccine with smoked salmon, are priced around EC$40. It's open from 8 am to 11 pm Monday to Saturday.

Opposite Redcliffe Tavern is *Commissioner's Grill*, specializing in Caribbean cuisine. It's quite a civilized affair, but the prices are reasonable and the food appealing, with dishes like curried goat, swordfish, Creole fish soup, and Creole lobster and *fooungee* (cornmeal mix) regulars on the menu. Prices range from EC$22 to EC$65 for lunch and EC$38 to EC$70 for dinner. It's open 10 am to 11 pm daily.

Around Town Join the locals for some of the biggest and best rotis in Antigua at *Roti King*, on St Mary's St. Its decent selection of cheap, curry-filled pastries range in price from EC$11 to EC$18.

Hemingway's, at the west end of St Mary's St, has pleasant views from its veranda on the 2nd floor of an attractive 19th-century West Indian building. At lunch, a sandwich or a Caesar salad costs around EC$20, while catch of the day is about double that. Dinner offerings range from vegetarian pasta for EC$26 to lobster for EC$70. It's open 9 am to 10 pm Monday to Saturday.

Pub-style *O'Grady's*, on Redcliffe St, is a popular expat hangout with pool, darts and moderately priced English pub grub such as fish & chips or steak-and-kidney pie for around EC$25 to EC$30. It's open 10 am to

10 pm Monday to Saturday, with happy hour from 5 to 7 pm.

Café Declma is a refreshing change to the hustle and bustle of St John's. Tucked away behind a house on busy High St, its garden eating area is a collection of colorful murals and healthy plants. The food, a mixture of Creole and American styles, is excellent, and so is the friendly service and chilled-out tunes. Burgers start at EC$15 and main courses, such as chicken breast, are around EC$45. The highlight, though, is the tender lobster cooked with homemade sauces (EC$65). It's open for breakfast, lunch and dinner.

KFC, on the corner of Thames and High Sts, has the standard two pieces of chicken with fries for EC$10.50 and is open 10:30 am to 11:30 pm daily. *Silver Streak Bakery*, on Cross St, is a good central bakery and a cheap breakfast option.

Brysons supermarket, near the post office, has a deli with inexpensive sandwiches and a decent grocery selection; it's open 8 am to 9 pm Monday to Saturday, till 4 pm on Sunday. The best place for fresh fruits and vegetables is the *public market* at the south end of Market St opposite the bus station, open 6 am to 6 pm Monday to Saturday.

Entertainment & Shopping

The *Ribbit Night Club*, on the road to the Royal Antiguan Hotel in Deep Bay, is where most people head on the weekend. It's from 10:30 pm Friday and Saturday only, but doesn't get going till after midnight. Admission on Friday is EC$10 and Saturday EC$20, including one complimentary drink.

For something closer to town, try *Coconut Joe's Bar*, on Market St. The atmosphere is lively, helped along by the constant loud music that can be heard from its 1st-floor balcony.

There are several casinos near St John's, including one at Heritage Quay and another at the Royal Antiguan Hotel.

Caribelle Batiks in St John's sells quality Caribbean-made wall hangings and clothing. T-shirts, jewelry and other souvenirs are available from vendors along Thames, Mary's and Redcliffe Sts between the two quays.

You can buy 'duty-free' liquor at Heritage Quay or the airport departure lounge, with Johnny Walker Red Label selling for around US$15 and Antiguan rum for US$6. Rum can also be bought in local shops around the island for about the same price.

Getting There & Around

For information on buses and taxis, see Getting Around, earlier. You should have no problem finding a taxi, especially near the harbor.

RUNAWAY BAY

Runaway Bay is a quiet area with an attractive white-sand beach, calm waters and a handful of small, reasonably priced hotels. Note, however, that the north end of the beach has lost virtually all of its sand since Hurricane Luis, and the process of regeneration has been slow. But from Runaway Beach Club south there still is a gorgeous sandy strand and precious few beachgoers to share it with.

Although the area can seem quite sleepy, those staying here who want more action can simply wander over to adjacent Dickenson Bay. A channel dug a few years back for a marina project (which was halted after hitting rock) cuts off shoreline access between Runaway and Dickenson bays, but it's just a short walk along the road between the two areas.

Pelicans dive for food in the inlet created by the new channel and also along Corbison Point, the rocky outcropping at the north end of the bay. The point is the site of an old fort, but there's little left to see there. A large salt pond stretches along the inland side of Runaway Bay, and in the evening egrets come to roost at the pond's southern end.

Places to Stay

Right on the beach, *Lashings* (☎ 462-4438, fax 462-4491, lashings@candw.ag) is a small English-run hotel at the south end of Runaway Bay. Because it's a bit isolated, it's not a perfect choice if you want to explore

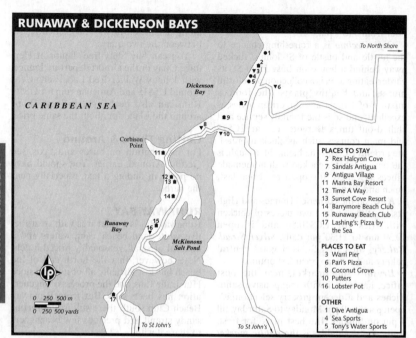

RUNAWAY & DICKENSON BAYS

To North Shore

Dickenson Bay

CARIBBEAN SEA

Corbison Point

Runaway Bay

McKinnons Salt Pond

0   250 500 m
0   250 500 yards

To St John's   To St John's

PLACES TO STAY
2 Rex Halcyon Cove
7 Sandals Antigua
9 Antigua Village
11 Marina Bay Resort
12 Time A Way
13 Sunset Cove Resort
14 Barrymore Beach Club
15 Runaway Beach Club
17 Lashing's; Pizza by the Sea

PLACES TO EAT
3 Warri Pier
6 Pari's Pizza
8 Coconut Grove
10 Putters
16 Lobster Pot

OTHER
1 Dive Antigua
4 Sea Sports
5 Tony's Water Sports

the island; however, it has everything you need for a beach holiday, as there's a small restaurant and bar on-site and the hotel's rates are cheap enough to cover a few taxi fares. Each room has a private bath, ocean-view terrace or balcony, and ceiling fans. Singles/doubles cost US$35/50 in summer, US$65/95 in winter.

Time A Way *(☎ 462-1212, fax 462-2587, PO Box 189)* is a small complex consisting of six good-value one-bedroom apartments. Each has air-con, a kitchenette, a balcony and a living room with a sofa bed. Rates for up to three adults, or for two adults and two children, are US$60 in summer, US$85 in winter. There's no front desk or on-site manager, so reservations should be made in advance.

Barrymore Beach Club *(☎ 462-4101, fax 462-4140, barrymorep@candw.ag, PO Box 1774)* is a 32-room complex. Cheapest are the hotel-style rooms, which are small and ordinary (US$72 in summer, US$115 in

winter). One-/two-bedroom apartments with kitchens cost from US$115/180 in summer, US$180/295 in winter. Units have screened louvered windows and ceiling fans but no air-con. The 2nd-floor units, which have raised wooden ceilings, are the best.

Runaway Beach Club *(☎ 462-1318, fax 462-4172, in the USA ☎ 800-742-4276, sayert@candw.ag, PO Box 874)* has a dozen rooms to choose from. Rates are US$80 in summer US$90 in winter for a standard room with air-con and private bath, and US$130 in summer, US$500 in winter for a studio unit with kitchenette. All rates include breakfast and use of the pool.

Sunset Cove Resort *(☎ 462-3762, fax 462-2684, PO Box 1262)* has 33 modern units in two- and three-story buildings. Hotel rooms, which cost US$100 in summer, US$125 in winter, have rattan furnishings, tiny kitch-enettes, a balcony or porch, TV, air-con and ceiling fans. Ask for one of the top-floor units, which have high ceilings. Studio units, which cost US$230 in summer, US$265 in winter for up to four people, have kitchens and a living room that doubles as the bedroom, with a pull-down double bed and a queen-size sofa bed. If things are slow they sometimes offer a 25% discount. There's a pool here also.

Places to Eat

The *Lobster Pot (☎ 462-2855)*, at Runaway Beach Club, has an appealing beachside setting. At breakfast, from 7:30 to 11 am, you can get a fruit platter or a three-egg omelet with potatoes for less than EC$20. At lunch, from noon to 3 pm, a chicken burger or flying-fish sandwich with fries costs around EC$25, lobster Caesar salad about double that. Seafood is a specialty at dinner, from 6 to 10 pm, with catch of the day for EC$45 and lobster for EC$80, but there are also moderately priced chicken and pasta dishes; call ahead to reserve one of the waterfront tables.

Pizza by the Sea (☎ 462-4438), at Lashings, has waterside dining and a wide range of pizzas. The smallest start at EC$20, and the largest, which two people will struggle to get through, start at EC$60. Happy hour is 5 to 7 pm, and the 24-hour bar has a good party feel to it, particularly on the weekends, when there's live music.

Millers By the Sea, about a two-minute drive south of Lashings at Fort James, has reasonably pricey food but redeems itself with nightly live music that ranges from jazz to calypso, as well as a happy hour from 5 to 7 pm.

DICKENSON BAY

Dickenson Bay, Antigua's main moderate-range resort area, is fronted by a long, lovely white-sand beach with turquoise waters and good swimming conditions.

All of Dickenson Bay's action is centered on the beach, which features its water-sports booths, open-air restaurants and half a dozen hotels and condominiums. It's more touristy than Runaway Bay and can get a little crowded at times. Still, it can be a fun scene, with reggae music, vendors selling T-shirts and jewelry, and women braiding hair.

Places to Stay

The *Marina Bay Resort (☎ 462-3254, fax 462-2151, marinabay@candw.ag)* is a condo complex on Corbison Point, which separates the two bays. The 27 units are sleek and contemporary, with kitchens, air-con, cable TV, phone, and balconies or patios. 'Super studios,' with a double bed in the bedroom and a queen sofa bed in the living room, cost US$105 in summer, US$125 in winter for two people, but can hold up to two more (each an extra US$25). Standard studios cost US$95 in summer, US$115 in winter and hold only two people. One-bedroom units cost US$125 in summer, US$155 in winter, and two-bedroom units US$185 in summer, US$225 in winter.

Antigua Village (☎ 462-2930, fax 462-0375, antiguavillage@candw.ag, PO Box 649) is a well-maintained beachside condominium complex with 100 units spread around landscaped grounds. They're individually owned so the decor varies, but most are quite pleasant and each has cooking facilities, air-con, ceiling fans and a patio or balcony. It's a good value for the area in summer, when roomy studios cost US$110, one-bedroom apartments US$130 and two-bedroom apartments US$260. In winter it's a pricier US$190, US$230 and US$450, respectively. Add another 20% for a beachfront unit. A pool is on the premises.

The *Rex Halcyon Cove (☎ 462-0256, fax 462-0271, in the USA ☎ 800-255-5859, rexhalcyon@candw.ag, PO Box 251)* is a beachfront resort hotel at the north end of Dickenson Bay. The rooms have been renovated and are modern and pleasant enough but pricey. Fan-cooled standard rooms cost US$150 in summer, US$220 in winter, and rooms with air-con begin at US$175 in summer, US$250 in winter. Tennis courts and a pool are available for guest use.

Sandals Antigua (☎ 462-0267, fax 462-4135, in the USA ☎ 800-726-3257, sandals@candw.ag) is a busy couples-only beachside resort with 189 rooms, five pools, four bars, three restaurants, two tennis courts and a variety of water-sports activities. All-inclusive rates per couple start at US$570 in the low season.

ANTIGUA & BARBUDA

ANTIGUA & BARBUDA

Places to Eat

Local hangout *Putters* (☎ 463-4653) is an open-air bar serving filling, tasty food. The service is pleasantly cheeky and the prices reasonable, with breakfasts starting at EC$20 and main courses for lunch and dinner, such as fish & chips, around EC$30. After your meal, head for a round of minigolf in front of the bar.

Pari's Pizza (☎ 462-1501), about 200 yards southeast of Rex Halcyon Cove on the inland road, is popular for takeout pizza. Cheese pizzas cost from EC$24 (small) to EC$43 (extra large), plus a few dollars more for each topping. You can also eat in or have your pizza delivered. Pari's is open 11:30 am to 11:30 pm daily except Monday.

Coconut Grove (☎ 462-1538), on the beach at the south side of Antigua Village, is another casual waterfront restaurant with moderately priced breakfasts and lunchtime sandwiches. At dinner, dishes range from catch of the day, priced at EC$51, to lobster for EC$82.

Warri Pier, at Rex Halcyon Cove, is set above the water on a private pier that juts out from the beach. Consequently, it makes a nice sunset spot for a drink or dinner. Pasta, fresh fish or spareribs cost around EC$40 at lunch or dinner. From noon to 6 pm you can also order sandwiches for EC$28. It's open noon to 2:30 pm for lunch and 6:30 to 10 pm for dinner daily.

There's a very small *grocery store* at Antigua Village that's open from 9 am to 7 pm daily.

NORTH SHORE

The northern part of the island between Dickenson Bay and the airport has the island's most well-to-do residential areas, a golf course, a few exclusive villa developments and small upscale resorts.

Places to Stay

The *Sunsail Club Colonna* (☎ 462-6263, fax 462-4135, in the USA ☎ 800-327-7726, colonnabch@candw.ag, PO Box 591) is a newer complex at Hodges Bay with a Mediterranean atmosphere. Rooms are modern and have air-con, TV, phones, mini-

bars, hair dryers etc. Rates per person start at US$95 in summer, US$135 in late summer and US$145 in winter. Two-bedroom villas that can house up to four people are available for the same price.

The secluded British-run *Blue Waters Beach Hotel* (☎ 462-0290, fax 462-0293, in the USA and Canada ☎ 800-557-6536, in the UK ☎ 020-8350 1000, bluewaters@candw.ag, PO Box 256) is on a little sandy beach at Blue Waters Bay. This all-inclusive hotel has everything you need, with two pools, water sports and a restaurant, bar, gym and tennis court. Surprisingly enough, it's not cheap: Rooms start at US$290/395 for singles/doubles in summer, US$350/480 in winter. Suites begin at US$400/505 in summer, US$475/620 in winter. All rooms have air-con, ceiling fans, cable TV, a phone, a safe and a private patio or balcony.

Places to Eat

Well-regarded *Le Bistro* (☎ 462-3881) serves traditional French food. Snapper, grilled lobster and meat dishes are priced around EC$70, while hors d'oeuvres are about half that. It's open for dinner only, 6:30 to 10:30 pm daily except Monday; reservations are recommended. Le Bistro is about a third of a mile south of Beggars Point and just a bit inland from the main road; a sign marks the turnoff.

Both the Blue Waters Beach Hotel and Colonna Beach Resort have moderately priced restaurants.

AROUND THE AIRPORT

There are no real sights around the airport and it's certainly not a prime tourist destination, but there are two relatively inexpensive places to stay, one just outside the airport and the other on a small beach a mile north of the runway.

Places to Stay & Eat

The *Airport Hotel* (☎ 462-1191, fax 462-0928, PO Box 700) is a concrete motel-style place next to the West Indies gas station, about a 10-minute walk from the airport terminal. The rooms are simple but clean, with TV and a fan, and the hotel provides free transport to and from the airport. Singles/doubles cost US$53/77 year-round, US$70/90 with air-con.

Antigua Beachcomber Hotel (☎ 462-3100, fax 462-4012, beachcom@candw.ag, PO Box 1512), on Winthorpes Bay, is on a nice enough beach, though there's an oil depot nearby. Rooms, which are on par with those of a mid-range motel and feature TVs and private bathrooms, cost US$80 (US$110 with air-con) in summer and US$110 (US$125 with air-con) in winter. There's a pool.

Dining in this area is largely limited to the restaurants in the aforementioned hotels, with the most extensive menu at the Antigua Beachcomber. You can also get sandwiches, salads, pasta and reasonable pizza at moderate prices from *Big Banana Holding Co*, on the 2nd floor of the airport terminal.

DEEP BAY

Deep Bay, west of St John's, is a pleasant little bay with a sandy beach and protected waters. The Royal Antiguan Hotel sits above the beach, and there's a fair amount of resort activity, but it's a good-sized strand and a nice swimming spot.

The coral-encrusted wreck of the *Andes* lies in the middle of Deep Bay with its mast poking up above the water. Nearly 100 years have passed since this bark caught fire and went down, complete with a load of pitch from Trinidad. The waters are shallow enough around the wreck to be snorkeled, but divers tend to bypass it because ooze still kicks up pretty easily from the bottom.

The remains of **Fort Barrington**, which once protected the southern entrance of St John's Harbour, are atop the promontory that juts out at the northern end of the bay. Although the fort was originally constructed in the mid-17th century, most of the present fortifications date to 1779. To hike up to the fort, simply begin walking north along the beach at Deep Bay; the trail takes about 10 minutes.

A salt pond separates Deep Bay from smaller Hog John Bay, where there's another sandy beach and a couple of hotels.

Places to Stay & Eat

The *Yepton Beach Resort* (☎ 462-2520, fax 462-3240, in the USA ☎ 800-361-4621, yepton@candw.ag, PO Box 1427), on Hog John Bay, has 38 modern air-conditioned units with oceanfront balconies or patios. The spacious studios are equipped with full kitchens and cost US$175 in summer, US$250 in winter. Hotel-style rooms cost US$130 in summer, US$200 in winter, and one- and two-bedroom apartments are also available. Rooms can be as low as US$65 and studios US$85 in summer for stays of four nights or more. This pleasant little resort has complimentary windsurfing, sailing, snorkeling and tennis, and doubles as the Austrian consulate if you need it!

Royal Antiguan Hotel (☎ 462-3733, fax 462-3732, in the USA ☎ 800-345-0356, royres@antigua-resorts.com, PO Box 1322), on Deep Bay, is the island's only high-rise resort, with nine stories and 282 rooms. It has a casino, a pool, tennis courts, a fitness center and various water sports. Rooms are comfortable and well appointed, with TV, phone, minibar, bathtub and central air-con. Rates for standard singles/doubles are US$120/150 in summer and US$160/190 in winter; ocean-view rooms with balconies cost US$170/200 in summer, US$220/250 in winter. An all-inclusive rate, covering meals and drinks, is also available. There's a daily shuttle to St John's (US$7 roundtrip). In summer the hotel commonly extends its corporate rate (US$85) to anyone calling from the airport.

Less than 2 miles south of the Royal Antiguan is *Hawksbill Beach Resort* (☎ 462-0301, fax 462-1515, hawksbill@candw.ag, PO Box 108), an exclusive place that encompasses a couple of nice, secluded beaches. The 95 rooms range from pleasant cottages to more traditional two-story buildings. Rates for singles/doubles begin at US$140/165 in summer, US$280/300 in winter. Rooms and breakfast are between US$10 and US$20 extra. The resort has an expensive restaurant, a pool, a tennis court and the usual water sports.

Yepton Beach Resort's *Patio Caribe* has an assorted menu with main courses ranging from US$16 to US$24, a daily special for US$12 and nightly entertainment. The Royal Antiguan has a few dining options: The beach grill is primarily a lunch spot, with US$10 burgers and similar fare; the *Lagoon Cafe* has a typical hotel menu, with prices hovering around the US$15 mark; and there's a fancier dinner restaurant.

JOLLY HARBOUR

Jolly Harbour is a marina and dockside condominium village on Antigua's west coast. Marina facilities include a pharmacy, a supermarket, a bakery, a liquor store, a dive shop, boat rentals and charters, restaurants and handicraft, beachwear and gift shops. There's a helicopter landing pad for airborne tours nearby, as well as a golf course. Free-use showers are in the main complex.

Boaters will find 150 slips, fuel facilities, water, 110/220V power, and a boatyard with a 70-ton lift and repair facilities.

There's a nice albeit busy white-sand beach south of the marina at Club Antigua and a quieter beach fronting Jolly Harbour.

Places to Stay & Eat

The cheapest place to stay in these parts is the 27-room *Jolly Castle Hotel* (☎/fax 463-9001, jollycas@candw.ag). Designed in the form of a castle, it's not the most aesthetically appealing building ever, but the rooms are clean and comfortable and have private bathrooms. Year-round rates range from US$50 for a standard room to US$120 for a family room with three double beds.

The *Jolly Harbour Villas* (☎ 462-7771, fax 462-7772, in the USA ☎ 800-345-0356, jhvillas@candw.ag, PO Box 1793) are a large complex with rows of condos built on artificial breakwaters. Each unit is townhouse-style, featuring a downstairs with a full kitchen, living/dining room and a terrace that looks out onto a private boat mooring. Upstairs are two bedrooms (one with a double bed, the other with two twins), one or two bathrooms and a balcony. Rates are US$120 in summer, US$165 in winter for up to two people (US$30 above the winter rate for the Christmas period), US$20 for each additional person. Add

another US$20 to US$30 if you want air-con. Facilities include a swimming pool, tennis courts and an 18-hole golf course.

The most popular of the marina restaurants is *Al Porto* (☎ 462-7695), which has harborfront dining with good pizza and pasta dishes in the EC$18 to EC$40 range and pricier meat dishes. Lunch is served 11:30 am to 2:30 pm daily, dinner from 6 to 10 pm.

The marina's *Epicurean* market sells sandwiches, liquor and groceries.

JOHNSON'S POINT BEACH

Johnson's Point Beach, at the southwest corner of the island, is a fine stretch of white sand. And it probably has the best views of rumbling Montserrat to boot. Midway between St John's and English Harbour, Johnson's Point might suit people who want to avoid the more touristed parts of the island without being totally secluded. It's not quite as out of the way as it seems, as buses (EC$2) go by about every half-hour (except on Sunday) on the way to St John's.

Places to Stay & Eat

The *Sunset Terrace Guest House* (☎ 460-5979) isn't on the beach, but it has fine views of the strand and Montserrat, and the beach is only about a two-minute walk away. There's one spacious double and a couple of small cottages available, all fan-cooled with private bath. A kitchen and living room are shared. It's quite a bargain, as the double room is US$40 per night and the cottages US$45. Meals are available on request.

Rex Blue Heron (☎ 462-8564, fax 462-8005, in the USA and Canada ☎ 800-255-5859, in the UK ☎ 020-8741 5333, PO Box 1715) is a quiet 40-room all-inclusive package hotel right on the beach. Most of the units face the water; those on the upper floor have balconies, those on the ground level have patios. Rooms are modern but suitably straightforward, with double beds, ceiling fans and showers. Standard singles/doubles with no air-con cost US$200/260 in summer, US$220/280 in winter. The air-conditioned superior rooms start at US$230/290 in summer, US$250/310 in winter. There's a minimum stay of three nights in winter. Water sports, including diving and windsurfing, are available.

The hotel's restaurant serves a Continental breakfast (EC$25) and a full breakfast (EC$30), while at lunch there are burgers, salads and sandwiches, for about EC$20. For dinner the menu features seafood main dishes beginning around EC$65.

FIG TREE DRIVE

After Johnson's Point Beach, the road passes pineapple patches, tall century plants, and pastures with grazing cattle and donkeys. High hills lie on the inland side of the road, topped by the 1319-foot Boggy Peak, the island's highest point.

Old Road, a village with both a fair amount of poverty and the luxury Curtain Bluff Hotel, marks the start of Fig Tree Drive. From there the terrain gets lusher as the road winds up through the hills. The narrow road is lined with bananas (called 'figs' in Antigua), coconut palms and big old mango trees. It's not jungle or rain forest, but it is refreshingly green and makes a pleasant and rewarding rural drive. The road is not great, and a jeep is preferable to a car. A couple of snack bars sell fresh fruit and juices along the way.

Fig Tree Drive ends in the village of Swetes. On the way to Falmouth Harbour you'll pass through the village of Liberta and by the St Barnabus Anglican Chapel, an attractive green-stone-and-brick church built in 1842.

FALMOUTH HARBOUR

Falmouth Harbour is a large, protected horseshoe-shaped bay. There are two main centers of activity: the north side of the harbor, where the small village of Falmouth is located, and the more visitor-oriented east side of the harbor, which has most of the restaurants. The east side is within easy walking distance of Nelson's Dockyard.

St Paul's Anglican Church

St Paul's Anglican Church, on the main road in Falmouth's center, was Antigua's first church. As one of the island's oldest buildings, dating to 1676, the church once doubled as Antigua's courthouse. You can get a sense of its history by poking around the overgrown churchyard, which has some interesting and quite readable colonial-era gravestones. Charles Pitt, the brother of the English prime minister William Pitt, was buried here in 1780, and beside his site is the excessively loquacious memorial to Brigadier General Andrew Dunlop, who died of yellow fever.

Places to Stay

A few houses in the harbor are privately rented and cost around US$80 a night or US$500 a week. Check at the marina complex on the road to Pigeon Beach, or ask at local restaurants.

Marsh Village (☎ 460-1181) is popular with people looking for work on yachts, as it's cheap and within easy walking distance of the harbor. The village consists of one- and two-bedroom apartments, each with kitchen, private bath, double bed and eating area. There's no hot water and only some have ceiling fans, so it's a good idea to have a look at a couple and then choose the one you want. Rates start at US$50 per night but can be as low as US$200 per week.

Falmouth Harbour Beach Apartments (☎ 460-1027, fax 460-1534, admirals@ candw.ag), on the east side of Falmouth Harbour, has 20 straightforward studios in half a dozen two-story buildings. The studios have verandas or patios, full kitchens and ceiling fans, but no air-con. Though the beach fronting the hotel isn't anything special, there's a decent beach about 10 minutes' walk to the east. Singles/doubles start at US$76/94 in summer, US$102/135 in winter. The complex has the same management as the Admiral's Inn in English Harbour.

Catamaran Hotel & Marina (☎ 460-1036, fax 460-1506, in the USA ☎ 800-223-6510, PO Box 958) is on a little beach at the north side of Falmouth Harbour and has its own 30-berth marina. This pleasant 16-room hotel is one of the area's better values. The deluxe rooms on the 2nd floor have bathtubs and four-poster queen-size beds (US$85 in summer, US$120 in winter). The hotel also has four ground-level units with kitchenettes

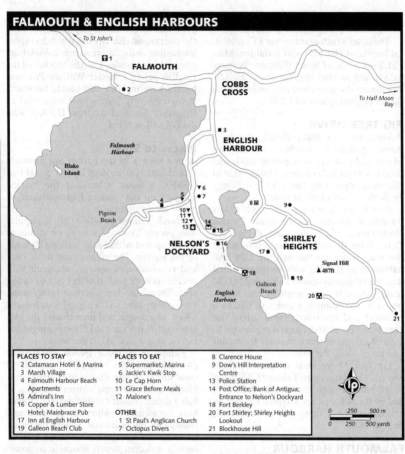

FALMOUTH & ENGLISH HARBOURS

To St John's

FALMOUTH

COBBS CROSS

To Half Moon Bay

Falmouth Harbour

ENGLISH HARBOUR

Blake Island

Pigeon Beach

NELSON'S DOCKYARD

SHIRLEY HEIGHTS

Signal Hill ▲ 487ft

Galleon Beach

English Harbour

Blockhouse Hill

PLACES TO STAY	PLACES TO EAT	8 Clarence House
2 Catamaran Hotel & Marina	5 Supermarket; Marina	9 Dow's Hill Interpretation Centre
3 Marsh Village	6 Jackie's Kwik Stop	13 Police Station
4 Falmouth Harbour Beach Apartments	10 Le Cap Horn	14 Post Office; Bank of Antigua; Entrance to Nelson's Dockyard
15 Admiral's Inn	11 Grace Before Meals	18 Fort Berkley
16 Copper & Lumber Store Hotel; Mainbrace Pub	12 Malone's	20 Fort Shirley; Shirley Heights Lookout
17 Inn at English Harbour	OTHER	21 Blockhouse Hill
19 Galleon Beach Club	1 St Paul's Anglican Church	
	7 Octopus Divers	

0   250   500 m
0   250   500 yards

(US$70 in summer, US$80 in winter) and four simpler standard rooms with standing fans (US$55 in summer, US$65 in winter).

Places to Eat

The following restaurants are all within a few minutes of each other at the east side of Falmouth Harbour. Note that some of them close in the summer as business slacks off.

Malone's, a small grocery store just north of the entrance to Nelson's Dockyard, has a little deli counter that makes sandwiches for around EC$12 to EC$16.

Jackie's Kwik Stop, on the main road, has sandwiches, rotis and omelets for around EC$8 to EC$10 and more substantial meals for about double that. It's open 8 am to 4 pm Monday to Saturday.

Le Cap Horn (☎ 460-1194) has two sides: a pizzeria and a French restaurant. The pizzeria makes brick-oven pizza costing from EC$28 for tomato and cheese to EC$36 for a seafood version, as well as pasta dishes and a meal of the day in the same price range. The French restaurant, open from 6:30 to 11 pm Monday to Saturday, offers up specials such as red snapper in basil sauce for EC$39 and Creole lobster for EC$60.

Just after Le Cap Horn on the road leading to Nelson's Dockyard is the recommended **Grace Before Meals**, which serves pizzas, hot dogs, burgers and fish dishes at very reasonable prices. In the marina-harborside complex on the road leading to Pigeon Beach is a small **supermarket** and liquor store.

ENGLISH HARBOUR

English Harbour has the richest collection of historic sites on the island; collectively, they are the centerpiece of the Antigua & Barbuda National Parks system.

Foremost is Nelson's Dockyard, an 18th-century British naval base named for the English captain Horatio Nelson, who spent the early years of his career here. Today, it's still attracting sailors as the island's most popular yacht haven.

There are also two hilltop forts flanking the entrance to the harbor and a couple of little museums. You could easily spend the better part of a day roaming around the sites. Bus routes from St John's end right at Nelson's Dockyard, but you'd need a car to explore the Shirley Heights area on the opposite side of the harbor.

English Harbour is separated from Falmouth Harbour by a slender neck of land that at its narrowest is just a few hundred yards wide.

Information

The Bank of Antigua, just 100 feet past the entrance to Nelson's Dockyard, is open 9 am to noon and 2 to 4 pm weekdays, and 9 am to 1 pm Saturday. The post office, at the entrance of Nelson's Dockyard, is open 9 am to 3 pm weekdays. There are card and coin phones next to the post office.

The following facilities for boaters are all inside Nelson's Dockyard. The customs office, on the ground level of the old Officer's Quarters building at the south side of the marina, is open 8 am to 4 pm daily. Lord Jim's, south of the customs office, sells nautical charts and cruising guides. Showers (US$2) are open 6 am to 6 pm daily, laundry facilities 8 am to 6 pm daily (US$8 a load).

Nelson's Dockyard

This historic dockyard is Antigua's most popular tourist sight as well as the island's main port of entry for yachts. The dockyard, which dates to 1743, was abandoned in 1899 following a decline in Antigua's economic and strategic importance to the British Crown.

Restoration work began in the 1950s, and this former royal naval base now has a new life closely paralleling its old one – that of an active dockyard. The handsome old brick-and-stone buildings have been converted into yachting and tourist-related facilities. Many duplicate the buildings' original uses. The bakery, for instance, was originally the officers' kitchen and still has the old stone hearth, while some of the hotel rooms that now house travelers were once used as quarters for sailors whose ships were being careened.

The dockyard is English Harbour's main center of activity, with a small market selling T-shirts and souvenirs, a handful of restaurants, two inns, a dive shop, an art center that sells local artwork and inexpensive prints, and numerous boating facilities – all of them occupying old naval buildings. Take time to stop at the interpretive plaques that explain the history of the various buildings.

Upon entering, pick up the free map that shows the dockyard sights and businesses. Admission is EC$13 for adults, free for children under 12. A water-taxi from the dockyard across the harbor to Galleon Beach is US$5 roundtrip.

Museum The dockyard's small museum occupies a former officers' house and features an assorted collection of nautical memorabilia, including clay pipes, rusty swords, muskets, cannonballs and one of Lord Nelson's telescopes. Models of a mid-19th-century schooner and naval brig round off the display. The museum's small gift shop sells books, maps and souvenirs. Admission is free.

Fort Berkley

A pleasant 10-minute stroll starting behind the Copper & Lumber Store Hotel leads to the site of this small fort, which overlooks the western entrance of English Harbour. Dating to 1704, it served as the harbor's first line of defense. You'll find intact walls, a powder magazine, a small guardhouse and a solitary cannon, the last of 25 cannons that once lined the fortress walls. There's also a fine harbor view at the top. The dirt path up is well maintained and passes lots of yucca and succulents, including tall dildo cactus and the stubby Turk's-head cactus, easily identified by its round red head.

Turk's head cactus

Clarence House

Clarence House, on the road to Shirley Heights, was built in 1786 for the Duke of Clarence, who later became King William IV. The aging Georgian-style residence has period furnishings and is now set aside as a rural residence of the governor. In years past, when the governor was not present, visitors could tour the house.

Shirley Heights

Shirley Heights is a fun place to explore, with its scattered 18th-century fort ruins and wonderful hilltop views. A bit over a mile up Shirley Heights Rd you'll reach the **Dow's Hill Interpretation Centre**, which features a view point and an audiovisual presentation on island history and culture; it's open 9 am to 5 pm daily and costs US$4.

For the best views and main concentration of ruins, continue past the museum; the road will fork after about half a mile. The left fork leads shortly to **Blockhouse Hill**, where you'll find remains of the Officers' Quarters dating to 1787 and a clear view of sheltered Mamora Bay to the east. The right fork leads to **Fort Shirley**, which has more ruins, including one that has been turned into a casual restaurant and bar. There's a sweeping view of English Harbour from the rear of the restaurant, while from the top of Signal Hill (487 feet), just a minute's walk from the parking lot, you can see Montserrat 28 miles to the southwest and Guadeloupe 40 miles to the south. It's a perfect spot to catch sight of the wonderful green flash on the horizon as the sun goes down.

Places to Stay

The *Admiral's Inn* (☎ 460-1027, fax 460-1534, in the USA ☎ 800-223-5695, in the UK ☎ 020-8940 3399, admirals@candw.ag, PO Box 713), built as a warehouse in 1788, has 14 rooms above the restaurant in the original brick building and five rooms in a separate modern annex. Rooms vary in size and decor, and some are quite small. Room No 6 is larger and a good choice in the moderate category, while No 3, a quiet corner room with a fine harbor view, is recommended in the superior category; both have hand-hewn open beams. In summer, singles/doubles cost US$70/94 for moderate rooms, US$80/100 for superior rooms. In winter, moderate rooms cost US$108/145, superior rooms US$115/160. Complimentary transport is provided to nearby beaches.

The *Copper & Lumber Store Hotel* (☎ 460-1058, fax 460-1529, in the UK

☎ 014-5383 5801, clhotel@candw.ag) was built in the 1780s to store the copper and lumber needed for ship repairs. It now has 14 studios and suites, all with kitchens and ceiling fans. Rates range from US$195 to US$325 in winter, US$135 to US$275 in summer, with the higher rates for units with antique furnishings. The top-priced Georgian suite is so laden with historic character that you could almost imagine Lord Nelson stepping into the scene.

Galleon Beach Club (☎ 460-1024, fax 460-1450, galleonbeach@candw.ag, PO Box 1003) is a quiet resort on Galleon Beach at the southeast side of English Harbour. Accommodations are in cottages spread along the beach. The units have a kitchen, a deck and a living room with a sofa bed. One-bedroom cottages start at US$140 in summer, US$225 in winter, and two-bedroom cottages are priced from US$185 in summer, US$295 in winter. Each bedroom sleeps two people, and two more can sleep on the sofa bed at no extra cost. An Italian restaurant, a couple of tennis courts and some water-sports activities are available on site.

Inn at English Harbour (☎ 460-1014, fax 460-1603, info@theinn.ag, PO Box 187) is another small beach resort on the southeast side of English Harbour. The rooms, most with beachfront balconies, start at US$190 in summer, US$320 in winter.

Places to Eat
The *Dockyard Bakery*, behind the museum at Nelson's Dockyard, has sandwiches, breads, meat patties, guava Danishes, carrot cake and other tempting pastries at reasonable prices. You can also get takeout coffee (EC$2) and sip it under the 300-year-old sandbox tree that fronts the bakery. It's open 7:30 am to 4 pm weekdays, until 2 pm Saturday.

Admiral's Inn is open for three meals daily. The changing chalkboard menu usually has such things as salads, burgers and curried conch for around EC$30 at lunch, while for dinner there are more elaborate dishes for about double that. There's both indoor dining and outdoor harborfront tables.

Mainbrace Pub, in the Copper & Lumber Store Hotel, serves Continental breakfast, burgers and sandwiches from US$7 and the likes of shepherd's pie and chicken salad for around US$11. The hotel also has a more formal restaurant, *The Wardroom*, which is open in winter only.

Shirley Heights Lookout (☎ 460-1785), in a vintage 1791 guardhouse at Fort Shirley, has a fantastic view of English Harbour and serves lunch and dinner at moderate prices. It's best known for its Sunday barbecues, which are accompanied with steel-band music from 4 to 7 pm and reggae from 7 to 10 pm, with lots of dancing toward the end of the evening. It's so popular that it feels like half the island is attending. There's no admission fee, drinks are reasonably priced and a simple hamburger or chicken plate with salad costs EC$22, a rib plate EC$42. All in all, it's one of the island's nicest scenes.

HALF MOON BAY
Half Moon Bay, on the southeastern side of the island, is a C-shaped bay with a beautiful white-sand beach and turquoise waters. It's largely undeveloped, though there's a hotel at the south side of the bay and a little snack bar on the beach.

Half Moon Bay Hotel (☎ 460-4300, fax 460-4306, halfmoon@candw.ag, PO Box 144) is a 100-room resort on a rise overlooking the beach. Amenities include a pool, tennis courts and a nine-hole golf course. The hotel, which was damaged by Hurricane Luis, was still sorting through some problems, but is expected to reopen with rates starting at US$280 in summer, US$400 in winter, including meals, water sports and golf fees.

An interesting option is *Harmony Hall* (☎ 460-4120, fax 460-4406, VHF channel 68, harmony@candw.ag), on Nonsuch Bay, a 10-minute drive north of Half Moon Bay. It has an atmospheric estate setting and offers rooms with king-size beds, ceiling fans, patios and bathrooms for US$150. The moderately priced restaurant has Caribbean and Italian-influenced food from noon to 4 pm in a secluded setting. Many of the ingredients for the restaurant are flown in from Italy to add that extra bit of authenticity. Harmony Hall also has a fine collection of quality arts and crafts, with changing exhibitions of work by local and regional artists, and a dinghy dock for yachters.

LONG BAY

Long Bay, on the east side of Antigua, has clear blue waters and a quite appealing white-sand beach that's reef-protected and good for snorkeling. Two exclusive resorts lie at the ends of the beach, one housing a dive shop. Other than a few private homes and a couple of beach bars, there's little else in the neighborhood. Unless you're looking for total seclusion or don't mind paying some hefty taxi fares, you'll need a car if you make a base in this area.

Devil's Bridge

A modest little coastal sea arch, Devil's Bridge is at Indian Town Point, an area thought to have been the site of an early Arawak settlement. To get there, turn east onto the paved road a third of a mile before the Long Bay Hotel turnoff. The road ends after a mile at a turnaround; from there the arch is a minute's walk to the east. Be careful when you're walking near the arch, because the Atlantic breakers that have cut the arch out of these limestone cliffs occasionally sweep over the top.

Long Bay Hotel (☎ 463-2005, fax 463-2439, in the USA and Canada ☎ 800-291-2005, info@longbayhotel.com, PO Box 442), on the east end of Long Bay, is an upscale, family-run hotel. The waterfront rooms there start at US$237 in summer, US$355 in winter, including breakfast and dinner, while the six cottages start at US$297 in summer and US$400 in winter, with kitchen facilities but no meals. Tennis, water sports and diving are available. The hotel restaurant offers candlelight dining with an ocean view.

Allegro Resort (☎ 463-2006, fax 463-2452, in the USA ☎ 800-858-2258, PO Box 2000) is a 180-room all-inclusive resort on the west end of Long Bay. Single/double rates, which begin at US$228/350 in summer and US$260/442 in winter, include meals, drinks, water sports activities and airport transfers.

BETTY'S HOPE

Betty's Hope, just southeast of the village of Pares, was the island's first sugar plantation, built by Christopher Codrington in 1674 and named in honor of his daughter Betty. Ruins of two old stone windmills, a still house (distillery) and a few other stone structures remain on the site, which is now under the jurisdiction of the Museum of Antigua & Barbuda. Through a combined local and international effort, one of the mills has been painstakingly restored and returned to working condition. The mill is operated only on special occasions, but the windmill sails remain up all year, with the exception of the hurricane season.

The site's old stable has been converted into a visitors center focusing on Antigua's sugar era, and the amiable caretaker, Lionel George, provides informative tours peppered with insights on the estate's history. The road into Betty's Hope is signposted. It's open 10 am to 4 pm Tuesday to Saturday. A donation of US$2 is appreciated.

Barbuda

Barbuda, 25 miles north of Antigua, remains one of the Eastern Caribbean's least visited places. Other than its frigatebird colony and its beautiful beaches, most of which are best accessed by private boat, there's not much to attract tourists to this low, scrubby island.

The only village, Codrington, is home to most residents and is the site of the island's airport. Barbuda has two small, exclusive resorts at its southern tip, although these clublike places are so removed from the rest of the island that they have their own landing strip and haven't done much to upset Barbuda's isolation.

Most of the 1200 islanders share half a dozen surnames and can trace their lineage to a small group of slaves brought to Barbuda by Sir Codrington, who leased the island in 1685 from the Crown. The slaves raised livestock and grew food crops, turning Barbuda into a breadbasket to feed laborers working the sugar plantations on Antigua.

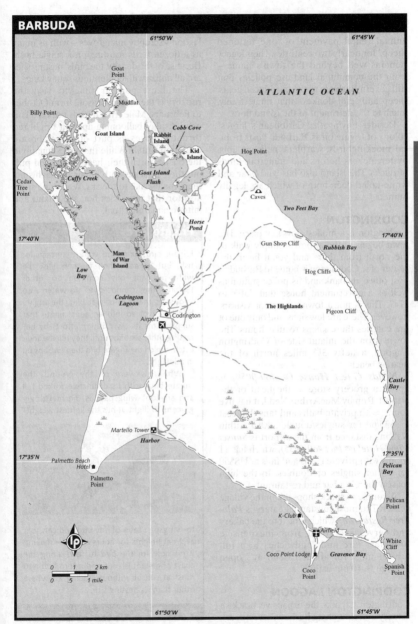

BARBUDA

ATLANTIC OCEAN

Goat
Point
Mudflat
Billy Point
Goat Island
Cobb Cove
Rabbit
Island
Kid Island
Hog Point
Cedar
Tree
Point
Cuffy Creek
Goat Island
Flush
Caves
Two Feet Bay
17°40'N
Horse
Pond
17°40'N
Man
of War
Island
Gun Shop Cliff
Rubbish Bay
Hog Cliffs
Low
Bay
Codrington
Lagoon
The Highlands
Pigeon Cliff
Airport
Codrington
Castle
Bay
Martello Tower
Harbor
17°35'N
17°35'N
Palmetto Beach
Hotel
Pelican
Bay
Palmetto
Point
Pelican
Point
K-Club
Airfield
White
Cliff
Coco Point Lodge
Gravenor Bay
Coco
Point
Spanish
Point

0   1   2 km
0   .5   1 mile

61°50'W
61°45'W

ANTIGUA & BARBUDA

The Codrington family managed to keep their lease, which was negotiated at an annual rental payment of 'one fattened sheep,' for nearly two centuries. Their legacy remains well beyond the town's name – from the communal land-use policies that still govern Barbuda to the introduced goats, sheep and feral donkeys that range freely, much to the detriment of the island flora.

Besides having the Caribbean's largest colony of frigate birds, Barbuda hosts tropical mockingbirds, warblers, pelicans, ibis, oystercatchers, herons and numerous kinds of ducks. The island also has wild boar and white-tailed deer, both of which are legally hunted.

CODRINGTON

Codrington is a modest, low-key place. The town begins at the airport – simply walk to the north from there and you'll be in the center of it. Codrington is home to Barbuda's post office, its bank and its police station as well as a government house that dates to 1743. This is not a town set up for visitors, however: There are few signs, and only one of the eateries there keeps regular hours. The town is on the inland side of Codrington Lagoon, a hefty 3½ miles north of the nearest beach.

Nedds Guest House (☎ 460-0059) is above a grocery store at the head of the airport. Run by MacArthur Nedd, it has five rooms with private baths and fans that cost US$35/60 for singles/doubles. Also within walking distance from the airport is *Sunset View Hotel* (☎ /fax 460-0435), which has 11 rooms with private baths and fans at US$50 for either singles or doubles. In the high season there's a bar and restaurant.

A couple of snack shops are in the village center. The most substantial eatery is *Palm Tree Restaurant*, which is next to the bakery and serves everything from inexpensive breakfast fare and sandwiches to a full lobster meal for about EC$40. It's open 7:30 am to 10 pm daily.

CODRINGTON LAGOON

Codrington Lagoon, the expansive, brackish estuary that runs along Barbuda's west coast, is an intriguing destination for bird watchers. Thousands of frigate birds nest in the lagoon's scrubby mangroves – with as many as a dozen birds roosting on a single bush. Because of the density, the birds' nesting sites are all abuzz with contentious squawking.

The most popular time to visit the rookery is the mating season, from October to February. Male frigate birds put on a colorful display, ballooning up their bright red throat pouches as part of the elaborate courtship rituals. While the males line up in the bushes, arch their heads back and puff out their pouches with an air of machismo, the females take to the sky. When one spots a suitor that impresses her, she'll land and initiate a mating ritual.

Frigate Birds

Frigate birds skim the water's surface for fish, but because their feathers lack the water-resistant oils common to other seabirds, they cannot dive into water. Also known as the man-of-war bird, the frigate bird has evolved into an aerial pirate that supplements its own fishing efforts by harassing other seabirds until they release their catch, which the frigate bird then swoops up in midflight.

While awkward on the ground, the frigate bird, with its distinctive forked tail and six-foot wingspan, is mesmerizingly graceful in flight. It has the lightest weight-

to-wingspan ratio of any bird and can soar at great heights for hours on end – making it possible for the bird to feed along the coast of distant islands and return home to roost at sunset without landing anywhere other than its nesting site.

After mating, a nest is built from twigs that the male gathers. The female lays a single egg that both birds take turns incubating. It takes about seven weeks for the chick to hatch and nearly six months for it to learn to fly and finally leave the nest.

The nesting site is in the upper lagoon area known as Man of War Island and can be reached only by boat. There are a couple of outboards that can take visitors out to the rookery, but arrangements generally need to be made a day in advance. If you're staying over on Barbuda you can arrange it through your guest house – the cost is about US$50 per boat for up to four people, and the trip lasts about 75 minutes. For those going over to Barbuda for the day, there are day tours that include the rookery (see the Organized Tours section, near the end of this chapter).

WEST COAST

The west coast of Barbuda is lined with beautiful white-sand beaches and azure waters. From Palmetto Point northward there's a magnificent pinkish strand that extends 11 miles, most of it lining the narrow barrier of land separating Codrington Lagoon from the ocean. Because of its isolation, however, the beach remains largely the domain of one hotel and a few lone boaters. More accessible beaches are found along the coast south of the harbor, with one of the finest sweeps along the stretch between the two resorts.

The **harbor** has a customs office and a sand-loading operation – Barbuda's sands also glisten on some of Antigua's beaches! To the northwest of the harbor is the 56-foot-high **Martello Tower**, a former lookout station that from a distance looks like an old sugar mill. About half a mile north of Coco Point is a nice white-sand strand with nearshore coral formations that provide good snorkeling.

The pristine waters of **Gravenor Bay**, between Coco Point and Spanish Point, are a favored yacht anchorage with reef formations and excellent snorkeling. Near the center of the bay is an old, deteriorating pier, while the ruins of a small **tower** lie about half a mile away to the east.

Archaeologists believe that the uninhabited peninsula leading to **Spanish Point** was once the site of a major Arawak settlement. A dirt track connects both ends of the bay, and another leads northward from the east side of the salt pond.

Places to Stay

The *Palmetto Beach Hotel* (☎ 460-0442, fax 460-0440, info@palmettohotel.con), at Palmetto Point, is about as isolated as you can get on the island. Its 35 suites are situated right on the pink and white sands of Palmetto Beach. Rates start at US$170 in summer, US$220 in winter and include all meals.

K-Club and *Coco Point Lodge* are two very exclusive resorts at the southern end of Barbuda. Both are incredibly expensive, quite separated from the rest of the island and a bit of a hike to get to.

CAVES

For those who feel like taking a look down under, there are some caves about 5 miles northeast of Codrington, though if it's been raining recently mud holes may well make it impossible to visit them. Dark Cave is an expansive underground cavern with pools of deep water, while another cave near Two Feet Bay contains the faded drawings of Arawaks.

GETTING THERE & AWAY
Air

Since LIAT upgraded its planes, they're now too big to land at Barbuda. Your only option for getting there is with Carib Aviation (☎ 562-2742), which has flights from Antigua to Barbuda at 7:45 am and 4:05 pm daily; flights return from Barbuda to Antigua at 8:50 am and 4:35 pm. The fare is EC$100 one-way, or EC$170 for a roundtrip with reservation, EC$180 without.

Boat

Barbuda's reefs, which extend several miles from shore, are thought to have claimed a good 200 ships since colonial times – a rather impressive number, considering that Barbuda has never been a major port. Some

ANTIGUA & BARBUDA

reefs remain poorly charted, and the challenge of navigating through them is one reason Barbuda remains well off the beaten path. If you're sailing to the island, bring everything you'll need in advance, because there are no yachting facilities on Barbuda.

There's no scheduled passenger-boat service to Barbuda, but if you want to try your luck hitching with a private yacht, check around at the marinas on Antigua.

Organized Tours

Barbuda has a reputation for tours that fail to materialize, drivers that don't show up at the airport or some other missing link. Confirm all reservations.

Some Antiguan travel agents, such as Wadadli Travel & Tours (☎ 462-2227) and Nicholson's Travel Agency (☎ 480-8660), offer day trips to Barbuda that include a visit to the rookery and caves, lobster lunch, and time on one of the lovely beaches. They usually need a minimum of four people, which will cost US$75 per person without airfare, US$150 with. The price rises with less than four people; check with them.

Claudia Richards of The Earl's Barbuda Day Tour (☎/fax 462-5647, visitbarbuda@ hotmail.com) arranges a day trip to Barbuda that includes airfare, the rookery, a short land tour and a lobster lunch for US$150.

The Sunset View Hotel offers a tour to the rookery and beach that includes a lobster lunch, but not the airfare to Barbuda; it costs US$75 per person, with a minimum of two people. Make reservations (☎ 460-0435) in advance.

GETTING AROUND

Barbuda has no public transportation. Distances are too great and the dusty dirt roads too hot to make walking a practical means of exploring. There isn't an established taxi service, but you might be able to arrange to hire someone to drive you around – inquire at your guest house.

Vehicle rental is another option, although the individuals who rent vehicles change from time to time and tracking them down can be tricky. A good place to start is with Claudia Richards (☎ 462-5647) or Beachbums (☎ 460-0146); you should be able to arrange a jeep rental for about US$55 a day.

Barbados

Barbados, the easternmost island in the Caribbean, is one of the most successful at luring visitors to its shores. It has fringing white-sand beaches, a good range of places to stay and eat, and enough organized activities to make for a solid vacation destination.

Highlights

- Relaxing at fine white-sand beaches that fringe the west and south coasts
- Touring grand 17th-century plantation homes and estate gardens
- Reveling in lush tropical plants at Welchman Hall Gully and the Andromeda Botanic Gardens
- Exploring the Barbados Museum and the adjacent history-laden Garrison area
- Joining the crowd at a cricket match or a Saturday horse race

OTHER MAPS
Barbados page 142

ATLANTIC
OCEAN

Holetown &
Around page 178

Bridgetown
page 161

Worthing
page 169

Hastings &
Rockley
page 166

St Lawrence &
Dover Beach
page 171

0   4   8 km
0   2   4 miles

The west and south coasts, which have the lion's share of visitor accommodations, are quite built up with an intermingling of tourist and residential areas. The interior is predominantly rural, with undulating hills of sugarcane, grazing sheep and scattered villages.

Perhaps no other Caribbean island has been as strongly influenced by the British as Barbados. English culture is visible in the national passion for cricket, the old stone Anglican churches found in every parish, the well-tended gardens fronting islanders' homes and the Saturday horse races.

But the 'Little England' analogy goes only so far. Bajans, as islanders call themselves, also draw heavily from West Indian influences. Some of the finest calypso musicians in the Caribbean have hailed from Barbados. The countryside is dotted with rum shops, not pubs, and West Indian cuisine, not kidney pie, is the mainstay of Bajan diets.

Barbados can make for a comfortable mix of the familiar peppered with just enough local flavor to feel exotic. That said, visitors to this island have to make an effort to get beyond the trappings of package tourism. And, facing costs among the highest in the Caribbean, budget travelers may want to seek out other destinations.

Facts about Barbados

HISTORY

The original inhabitants of Barbados were Arawak Indians, who were driven off the island around AD 1200 by invading Carib Indians from Venezuela. The Caribs themselves abandoned Barbados around the time the first Europeans sailed into the region. Although the conditions of the Caribs' departure are unclear, some historians believe the Spanish might have landed on Barbados in the early 1500s and taken some of the Caribs as slaves, prompting the rest of the

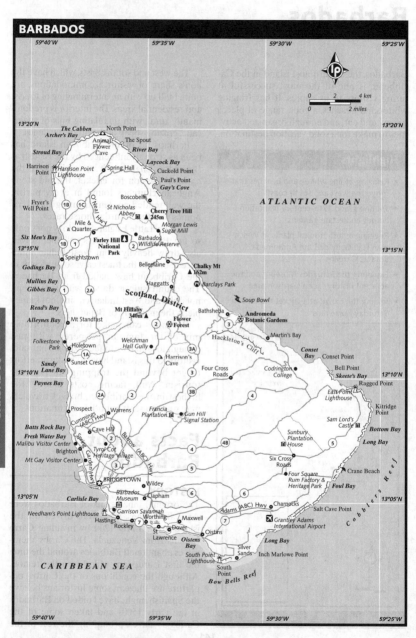

BARBADOS

tribe to flee to the safety of more protected, mountainous islands such as St Lucia.

Portuguese explorer Pedro a Campos stopped on Barbados in 1536 en route to Brazil. Although he had no interest in settling the island, it's thought that he introduced pigs to Barbados with the intention of having them as a food source on return voyages. It was Campos who named the island Los Barbados (Bearded Ones), presumably after the island's fig trees, whose long, hanging aerial roots resemble beards.

In 1625 Captain John Powell landed on Barbados and claimed the uninhabited island for England. Two years later, his brother Captain Henry Powell landed with a party of 80 settlers as well as 10 slaves who had been captured from a trading vessel en route. The group established the island's first European settlement, Jamestown, on the west coast at what is now Holetown. More settlers followed in their wake, and by 1629 the colony's population had grown to 2000.

Within a few years the colonists had cleared much of the native forest and planted tobacco and cotton. In the 1640s they replanted their fields with sugarcane. The new sugar plantations were labor intensive, and the planters, who had previously relied upon indentured servants, began to import large numbers of African slaves. Their estates, the first large sugar plantations in the Caribbean, proved immensely profitable, and by the mid-17th century the islanders – or at least the white planters and merchants – were thriving.

In 1639, island freeholders formed a Legislative Assembly, only the second such parliament established in a British colony (Bermuda was the first). Barbados was loyal to the Crown during Britain's civil wars, and following the beheading of King Charles I in 1649, Oliver Cromwell decided to send a force to establish his authority over the island. The invading fleet arrived in 1651, and by the following year Barbados had surrendered and signed the Articles of Capitulation, which formed the basis for the Charter of Barbados. The charter guaranteed government by an appointed governor and a freely elected assembly, as well as

freedom from taxation without local consent. Upon the restoration of the British Crown in 1660, this charter (with a certain ironic twist) provided Barbados with a greater measure of independence from the English monarchy than that of other British colonies.

The sugar industry continued to boom during the next century, and even after abolition Barbadian planters continued to prosper. In contrast, when the slaves were emancipated in 1834, their difficult living conditions remained largely unchanged. Virtually all of the arable land continued to be owned by large estates, and most black islanders found few options other than staying and working on the plantations. Those who did move off often ended up living in shantytowns in abject poverty.

During the economic depression of the 1930s, unemployment shot upward, living conditions deteriorated and street riots broke out. As a consequence, the British Colonial Welfare and Development Office was established, providing sizable sums of money for Barbados and other Caribbean colonies. To counter growing unrest, the British reluctantly gave black reformers a role in the political process. In the following decade one of those reformers, Grantley Adams, would become the first premier of Barbados and eventually be knighted by the queen.

Barbados was far enough afield to avoid the hostile British-French rivalry that marked the history of the Windward and Leeward Islands. Instead, it experienced an unbroken period of British rule that lasted almost 350 years.

The island gained internal self-government in 1961 and became an independent nation on November 30, 1966, with Errol Barrow as its first prime minister. Since independence, Barbados has remained a stable, growing democracy. It has become an important member of both global organizations, such as the UN and the OAS, and regional alliances, taking a leading role in the formation of the Caribbean Community and Common Market (Caricom).

GEOGRAPHY

Barbados lies 160km east of the Windward Islands. It is somewhat pear-shaped, measuring 34km from north to south and 22km at its widest. The total land area of the island is 430 sq km.

The island is composed largely of coral accumulations built on sedimentary rocks. Water permeates its soft coral cap, creating underground streams, springs and limestone caverns, the most notable of which, Harrison's Cave, is one of the island's leading attractions.

Most of the island's terrain is relatively flat, rising to low, gentle hills in the interior. However, the northeastern part of the island, known as the Scotland District, rises to a relatively lofty 340m at Barbados' highest point, Mt Hillaby.

The west coast has white-sand beaches and calm turquoise waters, while the east side of the island has turbulent Atlantic waters and a coastline punctuated by cliffs. Coral reefs surround most of the island.

CLIMATE

In January the average daily high temperature is 28°C (83°F), while the low averages 21°C (70°F). In July the average daily high is 30°C (86°F), while the low averages 23°C (74°F).

February to May are the driest months, with a mean relative humidity around 68%. The rest of the year the humidity averages between 74% and 79%. In July, the wettest month, there's measurable rainfall for an average of 18 days, while April, the driest month, averages seven days. Annual rainfall averages 1275mm (51 inches). Visitors on the island can get the current weather forecast by calling ☎ 976-2376.

FLORA & FAUNA

As most of Barbados' native forest was leveled by early settlers who cleared the land for farming, the landscape is predominantly one of sugarcane fields, pasture and scrubland. The small sections of native woodlands that still remain are mainly in gullies and cliff lands too steep for cultivation.

One of the island's more notable trees is the bearded fig tree *(Ficus citrofolia)*, for which the island was named (see History, earlier). Other trees common to Barbados are palms, casuarina, locust, white cedar, mahogany and poinciana. There is also a fair number of flowering plants on the island and some attractive cultivated gardens that are open to visitors.

A few introduced mammals are found in the wild, including green monkeys, mongooses, European hares, mice and rats. Found only on Barbados is the nonpoisonous and rarely seen grass snake *(Liophis perfuscus)*. The island also shelters a species of small harmless blind snake, whistling frogs, lizards, red-footed tortoises and eight species of bat.

Hawksbill turtles regularly come ashore to lay their eggs on the island's sandy beaches, and the leatherback turtle is an occasional nester.

More than 180 species of bird have been sighted on Barbados. Most of them are migrating shorebirds and waders that breed in North America and stop over in Barbados en route to winter feeding grounds in South America. Only 28 species nest on Barbados; these include wood doves, blackbirds, bananaquits, guinea fowl, cattle egrets, herons, finches and three kinds of hummingbird.

GOVERNMENT & POLITICS

Barbados is an independent state within the Commonwealth. It has a bicameral parliament consisting of a House of Assembly, with 28 elected members who serve five-year terms, and a Senate, with 21 members appointed by the governor-general. Executive power is vested in the prime minister, who is generally the leader of the majority party in the Assembly. A governor-general representing the queen is the official head of state, but the role is mainly ceremonial in nature.

Universal suffrage dates from 1951. The two main political parties are the Barbados Labour Party (BLP), formed in 1938 by Grantley Adams, and the Democratic Labour Party (DLP), which splintered from the BLP in 1955. Both parties have moderate socialist platforms.

In 1996 a Constitution Review Commission began feasibility studies on changing

Barbados to a republic, similar to Trinidad & Tobago, with a ceremonial president. It's an emotional issue for many people, and discussion continues; a referendum is expected for late 2001.

ECONOMY

Sugar, the mainstay of the Barbadian economy for 300 years, was nudged into second place by tourism in 1970. Presently, the service sector, which includes tourism, accounts for more than 75% of the island's gross domestic product.

Sugar, and its by-products of rum and molasses, are still leading exports. Other crops include yams, sweet potatoes, peanuts, cut flowers and sea-island cotton. However, the amount of land devoted to sugarcane and agriculture in general is rapidly declining as industry and tourism-related uses push up real-estate prices. In 1999, 8000 acres of agricultural land were lost to golf courses.

Barbados has the highest per capita income in the region, at US$9200. In total, agriculture accounts for about 5% of the Barbadian labor force, and industry (including the manufacture of clothing, pharmaceuticals and computer components) for another 15%. Barbados meets nearly half of its energy needs from its domestic oil and natural-gas supplies; there's a refinery in Bridgetown.

However, the largest employer by far is the service sector, providing nearly 80% of Barbadian jobs. Aside from tourism, a major component of this sector is financial services, which Barbados has promoted by signing taxation treaties aimed at attracting insurance firms, foreign sales corporations and offshore banks.

POPULATION & PEOPLE

The population of Barbados is approximately 269,000. More than 90% of Bajans are black, of African descent. The remainder is mostly English and Scottish, along with a small minority of East Indians. Although there are many small villages throughout Barbados, the vast majority of people lives along the leeward side of the island, in an urban sweep running from Speightstown in the northwest to Oistins in the south.

During the height of the tourist season, the actual number of people on the island can increase by another 45,000.

ARTS

Barbadian contributions to West Indian music are renowned in the region, having produced such greats as the calypso artist The Mighty Gabby, whose songs on cultural identity and political protest speak for emerging black pride throughout the Caribbean. Recently, Bajan trends toward faster beats (as reflected in *soca* and *rapso* styles) have influenced Trinidadian artists and Carnival.

One of the Eastern Caribbean's leading contemporary poets is Edward 'Kamau' Brathwaite, who hails from Barbados. Among his writings is *The Arrivants, A New World Trilogy,* which examines the lives of blacks in the Caribbean and the Americas.

The foremost contemporary Barbadian novelist is George Lamming, who has authored six novels and several collections of short fiction. His most acclaimed novel, *The Castle of My Skin,* portrays what it was like growing up black in a colonial Barbados struggling toward independence.

Island architectural styles have their roots in the colonial era, when virtually all land belonged to large sugar estates. The island still has a number of grand plantation homes as well as numerous chattel houses, the latter being a simple wooden home built for easy disassembly and portability.

SOCIETY & CONDUCT

On the surface, Bajan life and culture manifest a strong British influence. Cricket and horse racing are popular pastimes, older women are often seen wearing prim little hats, and special events are carried out with a great deal of pomp and ceremony. However, Afro-Caribbean culture is strongly reflected in family life, food and music. Beliefs and attitudes that have African roots are not always readily visible, but present themselves in music and religious practices. Many local foods are similar

BARBADOS

to those found throughout the world among African cultures.

In politics and social conventions, many look toward English institutions, but a tension between British and Bajan national identity can be seen in art, writing, music and the media. Some Barbadians are concerned about the influence of the images of African-American youth seen on TV and in movies.

Women are the head of the household in many families, and a majority of children are born outside of wedlock. While the fathers are present, it is often the mother or grandmother who raises the children.

Dos & Don'ts

Shorts are not appropriate in nightclubs or in most restaurants at dinnertime. Topless sunbathing is illegal for women. Off the beach, men should always wear a shirt, preferably with sleeves.

RELIGION

The majority of the population is Anglican. Other religious denominations on Barbados include Methodist, Moravian, Roman Catholic, Pentecostal, Baptist, First Church of Christ Scientist, Jehovah's Witnesses and Seventh Day Adventist, as well as Baha'i, Muslim and Jewish. For a current calendar of religious services, see the free tourist publication *Visitor*.

LANGUAGE

The island's language is English, spoken with a distinctive Bajan accent.

Facts for the Visitor

ORIENTATION

Barbados is divided into 11 parishes. The south-coast resorts are in the parish of Christ Church, while most of the west-coast resorts are in St James.

The island's major highways, numbered 1 to 7 from north to south, all begin in Bridgetown. The airport is on the southeast side of the island, 16km from Bridgetown.

Hwy 7 leads from the airport through the south-coast resort area, but if you're heading to Bridgetown or the west coast, the ABC Hwy, a combination of the Adams, Barrow and Cummings Hwys, is much quicker than the coastal road.

Most of the island's rural sights – including plantation houses, gardens and parks – are scattered throughout the interior. With a car you could see the bulk of them in one frenetic day or all of them in a couple of days' leisurely exploring. All are accessible by bus, and many places are clustered together, making convenient day trips to two or three sights a possibility.

Maps

If you intend to explore the island on your own, a good map will certainly come in handy. The best overall map of the island is the Ordnance Survey 1:50,000 map of Barbados, which can be purchased at the Lands and Surveys office on Jemmots Lane off Bay St.

Larger bookstores and Cave Shepherd department stores sell several excellent road maps. Prices vary, but they are all basically the same. A couple of good (though less detailed) free maps are available at tourist-brochure racks in many restaurants and hotels.

TOURIST OFFICES
Local Tourist Offices

The Barbados Tourism Authority has its administrative office (☎ 427-2623, fax 426-4080) on Harbour Rd in Bridgetown, though most visitors will instead be using the convenient and helpful booth (☎ 428-5570) at the airport. When requesting information by mail, write to Barbados Tourism Authority, PO Box 242, Bridgetown, Barbados, West Indies.

The tourism authority sponsors a Web page, www.barbados.org, with links to hotels and guest houses as well as information on most of the activities available in Barbados.

Information on many restaurants, tours, museums and other sights can be found in tourist-brochure racks in most restaurants and hotels, and most all-inclusive hotels have an activities office to help with any plans.

Tourist Offices Abroad

Overseas offices of the Barbados Tourism Authority include:

Australia
(☎ 02-9285-6850, fax 02-9267-4600) 17th floor, 456 Kent St, Sydney 2000

Canada
(☎ 416-214-9880, 800-268-9122, fax 416-214-9882, btapublic@globalserve.net) 105 Adelaide St West, Suite 1010, Toronto, Ontario M5H 1P9
(☎ 514-932-3206, fax 514-932-3775, btasmith@globalserve.net) 4800 de Maisonneuve W, Suite 532, Montreal, Quebec H3Z IM2

France
(☎/fax 01-42 36 51 18/19) 8–10 Rue Saint Marc 75002, Paris

Germany
(☎ 69 23 23 66, fax 69 23 00 77, barbados@ +-online.de) Neue Mainzer Strasse 22, D-60311 Frankfurt

Italy
(☎/fax 02-33 10 58 41/27) 20145 Milano, Via Gheradini 2

Netherlands
(☎/fax 3170 328 0824/38) Breitnerlaan 298, 2596 HG Den Haag

Sweden
(☎/fax 08-411 50 66/67) Skeppsborn 22, SE-111 30 Stockholm

UK
(☎ 020-7636 9448, 051-262 081, fax 020-7637 1496) 263 Tottenham Court Rd, London W1T 7LA

USA
(☎ 212-986-6516, 800-221-9831, fax 212-573-9850, btany@worldnet.att.net) 800 Second Ave, New York, NY 10017
(☎ 213-380-2198, fax 213-384-2763, btala@worldnet.att.net) 3440 Wilshire Blvd, Suite 1215, Los Angeles, CA 90010
(☎ 305-442-7471, fax 305-567-2844) 150 Alhambra Circle, Suite 1270, Coral Gables, FL 33134

VISAS & DOCUMENTS

Citizens of the USA and Canada who are traveling directly from their home countries can enter Barbados without a passport for stays of less than three months, as long as they have an original birth certificate or naturalization certificate along with a photo ID

such as a driver's license. Citizens of all other countries must have a valid passport.

Visas are not required for stays up to six months for citizens of the USA, Canada, Australia, Japan and most Western European countries except Sweden, Switzerland and Portugal, who are limited to stays of 28 days without a visa. Visa requirements and periods of stay vary for other nationalities.

EMBASSIES & CONSULATES
Barbadian Embassies & Consulates

Australia
(☎ 02-93 27 70 09)
4 Warren Rd, Double Bay, NSW 2028

France
(☎ 0142-65 13 04)
64 Rue des Mathurins, 75008 Paris

UK
(☎ 020-7631 4975)
1 Great Russell St, London WC1B3JY

USA
(☎ 202-939-9200)
2144 Wyoming Ave NW, Washington, DC 20008

Foreign Embassies & Consulates in Barbados

Belgium
Consulate (☎ 435-7704)
609 Rockley Resort & Country Club, Christ Church

Brazil
Embassy (☎ 427-1735)
Sunjet House, 3rd floor, Bridgetown

Canada
High Commission (☎ 429-3550)
Bishop's Court Hill, Pine Rd, St Michael

China
Embassy (☎ 435-6607)
17 Golf View Terrace, Golf Club Rd, Rockley, Christ Church

Colombia
Embassy (☎ 429-6821)
Dayrells Rd, Rockley, Christ Church

Costa Rica
Embassy (☎ 431-0250)
Dayrells Court Business Centre, Dayrells Rd, Rockley, Christ Church

Cuba
Embassy (☎ 435-2769)
Erin Court, Collymore Rock, St Michael

BARBADOS

Denmark
Consulate (☎ 436-6300)
c/o Yankee Garments, Grazettes Industrial Park,
St Michael

France
Consulate (☎ 435-6847)
Waverly House, Hastings, Christ Church

Germany
Honorary Consul (☎ 427-1876)

Guatemala
Embassy (☎ 435-2542)
Trident House, Broad St, Bridgetown

Haiti
Honorary Consul (☎ 436-6144)
Salters, St George

Israel
Honorary Consul (☎ 426-4764)
Palmetto St, Bridgetown

Italy
Consulate (☎ 437-1228)
Bannatyne, Christ Church

Netherlands
Consulate (☎ 418-8074)
Balls Plantation, Christ Church

Norway
Honorary Consul (☎ 429-7286)
Nile St, Bridgetown

UK
High Commission (☎ 430-7800)
Lower Collymore Rock, St Michael

USA
Embassy (☎ 436-4950)
Broad St, Bridgetown

Venezuela
Embassy (☎ 435-7619)
Hastings, Christ Church

Other countries with diplomatic representation in Barbados can be located in the yellow pages under 'Consulates Embassies and Foreign Government Representatives.'

CUSTOMS

Visitors may bring in 1L of spirits or wine, 200 cigarettes (or 50 cigars) and a reasonable amount of personal effects.

MONEY

Banks exchange Barbados dollars at the rate of B$1.98 for US$1 in cash, B$1.99 for US$1 in traveler's checks. To exchange Barbados dollars back to US dollars the rate is B$2.04 to US$1. Cash and traveler's checks

in British, Canadian and German currencies can also be readily exchanged at banks, with rates fluctuating daily according to international monetary markets.

Banks charge a stamp fee for each traveler's check cashed – B$0.10 for up to the equivalent of B$50, B$0.50 for larger checks – and generally a commission of B$1 to B$3, depending on the amount of money exchanged. American Express in Bridgetown cashes American Express traveler's checks without charging a commission.

You'll certainly want some Barbados dollars for incidentals, but most larger payments can be made in US dollars or with a credit card. Hotels and guest houses quote rates in US dollars, although you can use either US or Barbadian currency to settle the account; most give an exchange rate of B$2 to US$1 for traveler's checks or cash. When using a credit card, charges are made in Barbados dollars and calculated by the bank at the rate of B$1.97 to US$1.

Most restaurants, hotels and shops accept Visa, MasterCard and American Express.

Banks are easy to find in larger towns and major tourist areas. Credit and debit card holders can obtain cash advances from ATMs at many branches of the Royal Bank of Canada, Scotiabank, Caribbean Commercial Bank, Barclays Bank and Barbados National Bank, most of which are on the Cirrus and Plus networks. There's an ATM at the airport.

Currency

Notes come in B$2 (blue), B$5 (green), B$10 (brown), B$20 (purple), B$50 (orange) and B$100 (gray) denominations.

There are 1-cent copper coins, 5-cent bronze coins and 10-cent, 25-cent and B$1 silver-colored coins.

POST & COMMUNICATIONS
Post

The general post office, on Cheapside, Bridgetown, is open 7:30 am to 5 pm Monday to Friday. There are also district post offices in every parish, as well as one at the airport; most are open 8 am to noon and 1 to 3 pm weekdays.

Airmail postage rates for both postcards and letters up to 10g are B$0.90 to other Caribbean countries, B$1.15 to the USA and Canada and B$1.40 to the UK and Europe.

Mail service is quite efficient, and mail is dispatched daily to both London and New York.

When addressing mail to Barbados from overseas, include both the town and parish name, followed by 'Barbados, West Indies.'

Telephone

The area code for Barbados is 256.

Barbados public phones accept both coins and cards. You'll get three minutes' calling time to anywhere on the island for each B$0.25 cents; 5-, 10- and 25-cent coins are accepted. There are phones at the airport, Bridgetown Harbour and major shopping centers and in other heavily trafficked public places.

Phone cards, available in B$10, B$20, B$40 and B$60 denominations, are sold at the airport, phone company offices, convenience stores and supermarkets. They can also be used in some other parts of the Eastern Caribbean.

Faxes and telegrams can be sent 8 am to 3:30 pm weekdays at the telephone company office on Hincks St in Bridgetown.

More information on phone cards and making long-distance calls is under Post & Communications in the Regional Facts for the Visitor chapter.

Email & Internet Access

There are Internet service centers in Bridgetown, in Holetown and along the south coast. See each area for specific locations.

BOOKS

Numerous books cover Barbadian history and sights. *The Barbados Garrison and its Buildings* by Warren Alleyne & Jill Sheppard is a well-written little volume describing the many historic buildings that comprise the Garrison area.

Other books include *Barbados: Portrait of an Island,* a smart coffee-table book by Dick Scoones; *Treasures of Barbados* (which surveys island architecture), by Henry

Fraser, president of the Barbados National Trust; and books on Barbadian political figures, including *Tom Adams: A Biography* and *Grantley Adams and the Social Revolution,* both by local historian FA Hoyos. Those interested in the natural features of Barbados might enjoy *Geology of Barbados,* by Hans G Machel, or *A Naturalist's Year in Barbados,* by Maurice Batemman Hutt. A variety of Bajan cookbooks can also be found.

NEWSPAPERS & MAGAZINES

Barbados has two daily newspapers, *The Barbados Advocate* and *The Nation.* British and American newspapers are available at convenience stores in the main tourist areas. Two free tourist publications worth picking up are the weekly *Visitor* and the bimonthly *Sunseeker,* both of which have lots of ads and general information.

RADIO & TV

In addition to the government-owned TV station, CBC, which broadcasts on Channel 8, a number of international TV networks, including CNN, ESPN and TNT, are picked up by satellite. Radio listeners will find local news and information on FM 92.9 and 98.1 or AM 790 and 900. For soca music, tune in to FM 95.3, and for gospel, set the dial to FM 102.1.

ELECTRICITY

Electricity in Barbados is 110V, 50 cycles, with a flat two-pronged plug; many hotels have 240V converter outlets in the bathrooms.

WEIGHTS & MEASURES

Despite its British heritage, Barbados has gone metric. Road signs and car odometers are in kilometers, weights are in grams and kilograms. However, many islanders still give directions in feet and miles and sell produce by the pound.

HEALTH

There's a 600-bed government hospital in Bridgetown, the Queen Elizabeth Hospital (☎ 436-6450), on Martindales Rd, and several clinics around the island.

For divers who get the bends, the Barbados Defence Force (☎ 436-6185) maintains a decompression chamber in the Garrison area of Bridgetown.

As a region, the Caribbean has the second-highest level of HIV/AIDS infection in the world; among all nations, Barbados ranks number 20. The vast majority of cases in Barbados are the result of heterosexual contact. Travelers should take this into account, act wisely and take the appropriate precautions.

Outbreaks of dengue fever can occur, especially during the rainy season. The best prevention is to use repellent or mosquito nets.

Leptospirosis, which can be carried by mongooses, can be present in freshwater streams.

DANGERS & ANNOYANCES

Crime, including assaults on tourists, is certainly not unknown on Barbados. Still, crime statistics are not alarming and the usual precautions should suffice.

Sidewalks are not common in Barbados; walking along the narrow roads can be dangerous. Be sure to walk on the right side (facing oncoming traffic).

Portuguese man-of-wars (a type of poisonous jellyfish) are occasionally encountered in Barbadian waters, and poisonous manchineel trees grow along some beaches.

EMERGENCIES

Emergency telephone numbers in Barbados are

Ambulance	☎ 511
Fire	☎ 311
Police	☎ 211

(☎ 436-6600 for routine police matters)

BUSINESS HOURS

Most banks are open 8 am to 3 pm Monday to Thursday, till 5 pm on Friday. A few branches are also open Saturday morning. Most stores are open 8 am to 5 pm Monday to Friday and till noon Saturday. Larger supermarkets stay open until at least 8 pm.

Many restaurants and visitor attractions are closed on public holidays.

PUBLIC HOLIDAYS & SPECIAL EVENTS

Public holidays are

New Year's Day	January 1
Errol Barrow Day	January 21
Good Friday	late March/early April
Easter Monday	late March/early April
Heroes' Day	April 28
Labour Day	May 1
Whit Monday	eighth Monday after Easter
Kadooment Day	first Monday in August
United Nations Day	first Monday in October
Independence Day	November 30
Christmas Day	December 25
Boxing Day	December 26

The island's top event is the Crop-Over Festival, which originated in colonial times as a celebration to mark the end of the sugarcane harvest. Festivities stretch over a three-week period beginning in mid-July with spirited calypso competitions, fairs and other activities around the island. The festival culminates with a Carnival-like costume parade and fireworks on Kadooment Day, a national holiday.

In February, the Holetown Festival celebrates the February 17, 1627, arrival of the first English settlers on Barbados. Holetown's weeklong festivities include street fairs, a music festival at the historic parish church and a road race.

One of the cultural highlights of the year is the Holders Season, a program of opera, music, theater and sporting events throughout the month of March, with international stars such as tenor Luciano Pavarotti taking the stage.

The Oistins Fish Festival, held over Easter weekend, commemorates the signing of the Charter of Barbados and celebrates the skills of local fisherfolk. It's a seaside festivity with events focusing on boat races, fish-boning competitions, local foods, crafts and dancing.

The Congaline Carnival in late April is a big street party with music and arts. The focus of the event is an all-day T-shirt band parade and conga line that wends its way from Bridgetown to St Lawrence Gap.

The Gospel Fest, held each year in late May, celebrates Barbadians' love of gospel music with major performers from the US, UK and Caribbean.

The National Independence Festival of Creative Arts, held throughout November, features talent contests in dance, drama, singing and the like. Performances by the finalists are held on Independence Day, November 30.

There are also a handful of international sporting events, including the Barbados Windsurfing World Cup, held in January; the Caribbean Surfing Championship, in November; Banks Field Hockey Festival, held in late August; and the early December marathon, Run Barbados.

ACTIVITIES

Barbados has a plethora of civic clubs and special-interest groups covering everything from flower arranging and Scottish dance to tae kwon do and transcendental meditation. Many are open to short-term visitors; meeting times and contact numbers are listed in the *Sunseeker* and *Visitor* tourist publications (see Newspapers & Magazines, earlier).

Beaches & Swimming

Some of the island's prettiest beaches and calmest waters are along the west coast. Top spots include Paynes Bay, Alleynes Bay and Mullins Bay – all lovely white-sand beaches that are easily accessible.

The southwest side of the island also has some fine beaches, including Sandy Beach in Worthing, Rockley Beach and Dover Beach. On the southeast side is Crane Beach, a scenic stretch of pink-tinged sand that's popular with bodysurfers but rough for swimming.

Around Bridgetown, the locally popular Pebbles Beach on Carlisle Bay and the area around the Malibu rum distillery are frequented by visitors as well.

The east coast has dangerous water conditions, including rocky nearshore shelves and strong currents, and only the most confident swimmers should take to the waters.

The Bathsheba area, in particular, has been the scene of a number of visitor drownings.

Diving & Snorkeling

The west coast of Barbados has reef dives with soft corals, gorgonians and colorful sponges. There are also about a dozen shipwrecks. The largest and most popular, the 111m freighter *Stavronikita,* was scuttled by the government in 1978 to create an artificial reef. It now sits upright off the central west coast in 42m of water, with the rigging reaching to within 6m of the surface. The coral-encrusted tug *Berwyn,* which sank in 1919 at Carlisle Bay, lies in only 7m of water and makes for good snorkeling as well as diving.

One-tank dives with gear average B$110, two-tank dives B$150. For beginners, most dive companies offer a brief resort course and a shallow dive for B$90 to B$140. Many also offer full certification courses in either PADI or NAUI for B$700 to B$800. Rates often include free transportation from your hotel.

Dive companies include the following:

Dive Blue Reef
(☎ 422-3133, bluereef@sunbeach.net) Mt Standfast, St James

Dive Boat Safari at Grand Barbados Hotel
(☎ 427-4350, fax 436-8946, diveboatsafari@funbarbados.com) Aquatic Gap, St Michael

Dive Shop
(☎ 426-9947, fax 426-2031, hardive@caribnet.net) Pebbles Beach, St Michael

Exploresub Barbados
(☎ 435-6542, x-sub@caribsurf.com) St Lawrence Gap, Christ Church

Underwater Barbados
(☎ 426-0655, diveinfo@underwaterbarbados.com) Carlisle Bay Centre, Bay St, Bridgetown

Snorkeling sets can be rented for about B$20 per day at beach water-sports huts and dive shops around the island. Several companies offer one- to two-hour snorkeling tours that take in the *Berwyn* in Carlisle Bay or swimming with the hawksbill turtles on the west coast.

Windsurfing

Barbados has good windsurfing conditions, with the best winds and waves December to

BARBADOS

June. Maxwell is a popular area for intermediate-level windsurfers, while the Silver Sands area, at the southern tip of the island, has excellent conditions for advanced windsurfing.

Club Mistral rents windsurfing gear year-round at its Windsurfing Club (☎ 428-7277) in Maxwell and from December to June at the Silver Sands Resort (☎ 428-6001, ext 227). At Maxwell, a range of boards and wave and slalom sails rent for B$50/130/500 per hour/day/week. At Silver Sands, Club Mistral rents only short boards (sinkers) and wave sails, by the day/week for B$170/650.

Club Mistral gives lessons to beginners in Maxwell. Group lessons cost B$580 for 10 hours, private lessons B$200 for two hours, including gear.

Windsurfing gear can also be rented from the Silver Rock Hotel (☎ 428-2866, ext 3115), in Silver Sands; Dread or Dead (☎/fax 437-3404), on the main road in Hastings; Charles Watersports (☎ 428-9550), at Dover Beach; and the water-sports hut at Sandy Beach in Worthing.

Surfing

Barbados has some excellent surfing action. The biggest swells hit the east coast, with prime surfing at the Soup Bowl, off Bathsheba. South Point and Rockley Beach on the south coast are sometimes good for surfing, and the west coast can have surfable waves as well.

Though winter sees the highest swells, surfers will find reasonably good conditions on Barbados year-round. The water tends to be flattest in May and June.

In Bathsheba, Bajan Surf Bungalow (☎ 433-9920, bsb@jorgen.com) rents out surfboards for B$80/250 a day/week and boogie boards for B$60/180 a day/week, and gives surfing lessons for B$80 an hour including board. Dread or Dead (☎ 437-3404), on the main road in Hastings, rents out boogie boards for B$20 a day, surfboards for B$40 a day, each requiring a B$100 deposit. Surfboards and boogie boards can also be rented from Charles Watersports (☎ 428-9550), at Dover Beach, and the water-sports hut at Sandy Beach in Worthing.

Deep-Sea Fishing

For those who want to catch their own tuna, barracuda or kingfish for dinner, the Billfisher II (☎ 431-0741) and the Cannon II (☎ 424-6107) have group and private fishing trips. A half day with a group is B$200 per person including hotel pickup. For a whole day, you must charter the boat.

Hiking

Each Sunday at 6 am and 3:30 pm, the Barbados National Trust (☎ 426-2421) leads guided hikes in the countryside. Hike leaders share insights into local history, geology, flora and fauna. Locations vary, but all hikes end where they start, last around three hours and cover about 8km. Once a month, a moonlight hike replaces the afternoon hike. There is no fee. Schedule information can be found in the free tourist publications and is also available by calling the trust.

The Barbados National Trust also manages the new Arbib Nature & Heritage Trail in Speightstown. Hikes of two to 3½ hours take in natural and cultural sites along gullies and down to the sea. You can join a hike at 9 am and 2:30 pm on Wednesday, Thursday and Saturday, by calling ☎ 426-2421 to make a reservation. The fee is B$15 for adults, B$7.50 for children.

Adrian Loveridge at the Peach & Quiet Hotel (☎ 428-5682), near Silver Sands, also leads nature hikes during the busy season.

A nice hike on your own would be along the old railroad bed that runs along the east coast from Belleplaine to St Martins Bay. The whole trip is about 20km, but it can be broken into shorter stretches.

Horseback Riding

The Wilcox Riding Stable (☎ 428-3610) near the airport offers one-hour rides twice daily, on Long Beach on the southeast coast, for B$88 including hotel pickup.

Tennis

There are tennis courts at several resort hotels, including the Casuarina Beach Club at Dover, Southern Palms Beach Club in St Lawrence, Glitter Bay Hotel in Holetown,

Silver Sands Resort on the south coast and Sam Lord's Castle and the Crane Beach Hotel, both on the east coast. There are public tennis courts at Folkestone Park in Holetown and at the Garrison area south of Bridgetown.

Golf

The Barbados Golf Club (☎ 428-8463, bgc@ caribsurf.com), between Oistins and the airport, has an 18-hole championship course. Greens fees are B$158/230 low/high season. They also offer three- and seven-day passes and lessons. Rockley Golf & Country Club (☎ 435-7873), on the south coast, has a nine-hole course, with greens fees of B$110, and B$20 for club and cart rentals.

ACCOMMODATIONS

Though prices for lodging tend to be exorbitant, a handful of relatively inexpensive places can be found. Some of these could use a fresh coat of paint, but most are comfortable and, while not truly budget places, they're good values by Caribbean standards.

Most of the upscale resorts are along the west coast, in the parish of St James, a relatively quiet and subdued area. The south coast, which generally attracts a younger crowd, has most of the low-end accommodations. There's a light scattering of places to stay elsewhere on the island, including a few secluded options on the east and southeast coasts.

Many hotels charge the same rate for single and double occupancy. Some places have three rate schedules: a low rate for summer, a marginally more expensive spring and autumn rate and a high rate for winter.

A list of accommodations, with links to many, can be found on the Barbados Tourism Authority's site, www.barbados .com. Several hotels offer discounts if you book by Internet or directly with them.

If you arrive without a reservation, the tourist office at the airport can book you a room. There's no charge for the service, and they can almost always come up with something in every price range. The tourist office also keeps a short list of families that rent out bedrooms in their homes, from about US$20 per person per night. During the high season, it is best to make arrangements in advance.

Most hotels add a 7.5% government tax plus a 10% service charge. And many have a minimum stay, so be sure to check.

Camping is generally not allowed on Barbados, except for organized outings by designated youth groups.

Reservation Services

The Caribbean Hotel Reservation Association (Charms; in the USA or Canada ☎ 402-398-3217 or 800-742-4276, fax 402-399-9285) books about half of the island's hotels. They don't cover the very cheapest budget hotels or guest houses, but otherwise they book a full spectrum, from small hotels and apartments to luxury resorts. Utell also handles a number of hotels in Barbados and can be reached in Canada and the US by calling ☎ 800-223-6510 or worldwide at www.utell .com. There are no fees to make a reservation with these services (although a credit card guarantee is usually required), and bookings are made at established rates. Keep in mind that island hotels sometimes offer discounted promotional rates that are available only by booking directly with the hotel.

Villas

There are numerous individually owned villas available for rent on Barbados. They are generally quite exclusive; all have maid service, most have a cook and some also have a butler. About half of the villas have private pools.

The West Indies Management Company (Wimco) books 100 such properties, with weekly prices ranging from about US$4000 for a simple two-bedroom place to over US$100,000 for an eight-bedroom great house. Summer prices are 30% to 60% cheaper. For reservations contact Wimco (in the USA and Canada ☎ 401-849-8012, fax 401-847-6290, wimco@well.com, www .wimcovillas.com), PO Box 1461, Newport, RI 02840. Toll-free numbers are ☎ 800-932-3222 in the USA, ☎ 01-30 81 57 30 from Germany and ☎ 0-800-898 318 from the UK.

FOOD

Barbados has a range of international fare from fast-food pizza and fried chicken to fine Continental cuisine. In addition, there's spicier Bajan and Caribbean food to choose from. Some of the more popular local foods, many of which borrow heavily from African and Indian influences, include conkies, coucou, cutters, flying fish, roti, jug-jug and pudding & souse. For descriptions, see the Glossary.

Other common local foods include pigeon peas and rice, pumpkin fritters, fried plantains and coconut pie.

DRINKS

Tap water is safe to drink; it comes from underground reservoirs that are naturally filtered by the island's thick limestone cap as well as from a modern desalination plant.

Barbadian rum is considered some of the finest in the Caribbean, with Mount Gay being the largest and best-known label. A liter of rum costs about B\$16. The island beer, Banks, is a reasonably good brew.

ENTERTAINMENT

The south coast of Barbados has a lively night scene. Most clubs open around 9:30 pm and continue into the wee hours. The music is usually a mix of reggae, calypso, Latin and rock. Several places charge a moderate cover that allows 'free' drinks all evening. Rum shops are common throughout Barbados and can be a good stop for refreshment when touring the island.

Check specific locations throughout this chapter for local activities. Entertainment schedules are in the *Sunseeker* and *Visitor* tourist publications. The Friday inserts in the *Advocate* and *Nation* newspapers also list hot DJ and karaoke spots and special events.

SPECTATOR SPORTS

The national sport, if not the national obsession, is cricket. Barbadians boast more world-class cricket players than any other nation, at least on a per capita basis. One of the world's top all-rounders, Bajan native Garfield Sobers, was knighted by Queen Elizabeth II during her 1975 visit to Barba-

dos, while another cricket hero, Sir Frank Worrell, appears on the face of the B\$5 bill. Cricket matches are played throughout the

Frank Worrell, hero of the cricket green

year at the Kensington Park Oval in Bridgetown. Check the sports section of the newspapers for scheduled games.

Horse races are held at the Garrison Savannah on Saturday afternoons throughout the year except April and September. Admission to the grandstand is B\$20, but for no charge you can also watch the races from benches under the trees around the outside of the track and place a bet at booths on the south or west side. The Barbados Turf Club (☎ 426-3980) offers three packages with reserved seating in the grandstand, a racing program, a betting voucher and either a snack or lunch in the track-view restaurant. Packages start at B\$60 for adults, B\$40 for children.

SHOPPING

You can shop duty free (upon presentation of your passport) at a number of places, including Cave Shepherd, the island's largest department-store chain. It has a branch on Broad St, Bridgetown's main shopping street, and at the West Coast Mall and Sunset Crest Plaza, both in Holetown.

Best of Barbados, a small chain with shops downtown and around the island, has a good selection of crafts, books and other gifts.

There are souvenir shops and art galleries in all the tourist areas and many resort hotels. Watch for signs of artist workshops as you travel around the countryside.

Two lightweight items that make tasty gifts are locally made Cajun hot-pepper sauce and concentrated ginger-beer syrup. For an even more unusual souvenir you might want to pick up a packed box of frozen flying fish at the airport departure lounge.

Getting There & Away

DEPARTURE TAX
Barbados has a departure tax of B$25. This does not apply if you arrive and leave the same day.

AIR
Airports & Airlines
Grantley Adams International Airport is on the island's southeast corner, about 16km from Bridgetown. In season, a steel band greets arriving passengers.

The friendly tourist-office booth can help you book a room and is a good place to pick up tourist brochures; look for the booth before you leave the customs area. A bit hidden, it's to the right of the liquor store and next to Barbados National Bank (open 8 am to 9:30 pm daily); the tourist booth is open 8 am to 10 pm or until the last flight arrives. Near the airline counters there's an ATM that accepts Visa and MasterCard, as well as Cirrus and Plus debit cards.

The airport also has phones that accept both cards and coins, a post office, a sit-down restaurant and a few stalls selling drinks, simple eats and souvenirs. The departure lounge has shops selling duty-free liquor, watches and jewelry as well as a money-exchange window.

Most airlines have offices in Bridgetown: American Airlines is upstairs in the Cave

Shepherd department store on Broad St, British Airways is on Fairchild St, BWIA is on the corner of Fairchild and Probyn Sts, LIAT is on Hincks St west of Prince Alfred St and Virgin Atlantic is on the main road in Hastings. All are open 8 am to 4 pm weekdays. You can also purchase tickets at the airport counters, but it's best to avoid heavy flight times.

The following are airline reservation numbers on Barbados.

Aeropostal	☎ 436-1858
Air Canada	☎ 428-5077
Air Jamaica	☎ 800-523-5585
American Airlines	☎ 428-4170
BWIA	☎ 426-2111
(airport)	☎ 428-1650
British Airways	☎ 436-6413
(airport)	☎ 428-1661
Caribbean Star	☎ 461-7827
LIAT	☎ 434-5428
(airport)	☎ 428-0986
Mustique Airways	☎ 428-1638
Trans Island Air	☎ 418-1654
Virgin Atlantic	☎ 228-4886
(airport)	☎ 418-8505

The USA
Both American Airlines and BWIA fly to Barbados daily from Miami and New York. Air Jamaica has flights daily except Thursday and Sunday. BWIA has daily flights from Washington, DC, and plans to begin flights from Atlanta. Fares fluctuate with the period of travel and current promotions, but during the low season these airlines commonly offer 30-day excursion fares from Miami for as low as US$450 and from New York and Washington for around US$600; in the high season, fares are generally about 50% higher.

Canada
Air Canada flies to/from Toronto daily and to/from Montreal on Saturday. The cheapest excursion fare from either city, with a maximum stay of 21 days, costs C$781.

BWIA flies to/from Toronto on Saturday with a fare of C$837 for an excursion ticket allowing a 21-day stay.

BARBADOS

The UK

British Airways flies to/from London's Gatwick Airport daily. The least expensive regular roundtrip fare is UK£298, with a seven-day minimum stay and a 90-day maximum stay. Virgin Atlantic Air offers a similar fare.

BWIA flies from Heathrow to Barbados on Monday, Thursday and Saturday and charges UK£528 for a 30-day excursion ticket.

Note that these are the standard rates. Travel agents specializing in cheap airfares can often book a ticket for half these prices.

South America

Aeropostal, LIAT and BWIA all fly between Barbados and Caracas. Some flights stop at Porlamar on Venezuela's Isla de Margarita. LIAT and Aeropostal offer an excursion ticket between Caracas and Barbados, with a stopover at Porlamar on Margarita, for US$225 roundtrip; or to and from Porlamar only for US$180.

In addition, LIAT and BWIA have direct flights between Barbados and Guyana's capital of Georgetown, and BWIA offers similar flights via Trinidad. A 30-day excursion ticket is US$174 on LIAT and US$179 on BWIA.

Within the Caribbean

LIAT has direct daily flights to Barbados from Antigua, St Lucia, Grenada, St Vincent, San Juan and Trinidad plus one a week to Tobago. Air Jamaica has daily flights to/from Dominica, Grenada, St Lucia and St Vincent. It also flies four times a week to/from Havana. You can get connecting flights on both airlines to other islands throughout the Eastern Caribbean.

LIAT's fare between Barbados and St Lucia is US$78 one-way, US$119 for a 30-day excursion. Other one-way/excursion fares to Barbados are US$94/141 from Grenada, US$88/134 from St Vincent, US$202/234 from Antigua, US$130/154 from Trinidad or Tobago and US$234/300 from San Juan. When connecting to LIAT on flights from North America, you can add stops at three to six islands to your base fare for US$85 per stop. LIAT also has a Super Explorer fare that

allows 30 days of unlimited visits to all its Caribbean destinations for US$475. Air Jamaica's fares for roundtrip flights are US$160 to/from Dominica, US$87 to/from Grenada, US$246 to/from Jamaica, US$87 to/from St Lucia and US$110 to/from St Vincent. Many flights also allow a free stopover in Jamaica.

Caribbean Star, the newest airline, has flights to many islands in the Caribbean with special incentive prices. Check with the airline for current routes and fares.

Mustique Airways has daily flights to/from St Vincent and the Grenadines. One-way fares from Barbados are US$135 to St Vincent, Canouan or Bequia, US$155 to Mustique and US$130 to Union Island.

Trans Island Air also offers daily flights to/from the Grenadines. A roundtrip flight to Bequia is US$261, to Mustique US$322, to Carricou US$253 and to Union or Canouan US$312.

BWIA has daily flights between Barbados and Trinidad (US$121/138 one-way/roundtrip). Every day except Wednesday and Saturday, BWIA flies between Barbados and Antigua for US$186/190 one-way/roundtrip. These BWIA roundtrip fares allow stays of two to 12 days and require a one-day advance purchase.

Tickets purchased in Barbados for flights originating in Barbados have a 15% tax added on.

SEA

Because of Barbados' easterly position and challenging sailing conditions, it is well off the main track for most sailors and there is no yacht charter industry on the island.

The passenger-cargo ferry M/V Windward runs weekly service between Barbados, St Lucia, St Vincent, Trinidad and Venezuela. Passenger service was temporarily suspended at time of writing, but will resume sometime in 2001. Call ☎ 425-7402 for an update.

Cruise Ship

About 450,000 cruise ship passengers arrive in Barbados each year. Ships dock at Bridgetown Harbour, about a kilometer west of the city center. The port has the usual duty-free shops.

Getting Around

TO/FROM THE AIRPORT

If you're traveling light, it's possible to walk out to the road and wait for a passing bus. Look for buses marked 'Sam Lord's Castle' (or just 'Castle') if you're going east, 'Bridgetown' if you're going to the south coast. For the west coast, occasional buses run to Speightstown, bypassing the capital; alternatively, take a bus to Bridgetown, where you'll have to hike across town to the west-coast terminal. Make sure the bus driver knows your destination.

Otherwise, you'll find a line of taxis outside the arrival lounge. Taxi rates from the airport are about B\$20 to St Lawrence, B\$30 to central Bridgetown, B\$38 to Holetown, B\$48 to Bathsheba and B\$55 to Speightstown.

BUS

It's possible to get to virtually any place on the island by public bus. There are three kinds of buses on Barbados: government-operated public buses, which are blue with a yellow stripe; privately operated minibuses, which are intermediate-size buses painted yellow with a blue stripe; and route taxis, which are white, individually owned minivans that have 'ZR' on their license plates and ply shorter, heavily traveled routes.

Some islanders prefer the minibuses and government buses, which generally don't pack passengers as sardinelike as the route taxis do. The government buses have the advantage of the staff being on salary and not driving hell-bent to collect extra fares. However, the minibuses, on the west coast, and route taxis, in the south, run much more frequently.

All three types of buses charge the same fare: B\$1.50 to any place on the island. You should have exact change when you board the government bus, but minibuses and route taxis will make change.

Most buses transit through Bridgetown, although a few north-south buses bypass the city. Buses to the southeast part of the island generally transit through Oistins. To get to the east coast, you can catch one of the hourly direct buses between Bridgetown and Bathsheba. There's also bus service between Speightstown and Bathsheba; those buses leave Speightstown on odd-numbered hours (9 am, 11 am etc) and return from Bathsheba on the even hour.

Bus stops around the island are marked with red-and-white signs printed with the direction the bus is heading ('To City' or 'Out of City'). Buses usually have their destinations posted on or above the front windshield.

Buses along the main routes, such as Bridgetown to Oistins or Speightstown, are frequent, running from dawn to around midnight. You can get schedule information on any route by calling the Transport Board (☎ 436-6820).

For the locations of terminals in Bridgetown, see that section, later.

CAR & MOTORCYCLE
Road Rules

In Barbados, you drive on the left. At intersections and narrow passages, drivers may flash their lights to indicate that you should proceed. At roundabouts (traffic circles), if taking the first left exit, stay in the left lane. Otherwise, keep right to continue around. Temporary driving permits are required; they cost B\$10 and can be obtained through your car rental agency.

Highways are not very well marked, although key roundabouts and major intersections are usually signposted. The most consistent highway markings are often the low yellow cement posts at the side of the road; they show the highway number and below that the number of kilometers from Bridgetown.

Finding major tourist sights, many of which are on country roads, is not too difficult, as most have signs en route pointing the way. If you get lost, don't hesitate to stop and ask for directions; this is common practice, and Bajans are generally very helpful.

All primary and main secondary roads are paved, although some are a bit narrow. There are lots of gas stations around the island, including one outside the airport.

Some stations in the Bridgetown area are open 24 hours.

Rental

Barbados doesn't have any car rental agents affiliated with major international rental chains. There are, instead, scores of independent car rental companies, some so small that the number rings through to a private home. You simply call to book a car and someone will swing by your hotel to pick you up.

Despite the number of companies, prices don't seem to vary much. The going rate for a small car is about B$150 a day including unlimited mileage and insurance. Most companies rent small convertibles called 'mokes' that are usually cheapest. Rental cars are marked with an 'H' on the license plate.

While most car rental companies don't have booths at the airport, there are a number of nearby agencies that will pick you up there. Inquire at the airport tourist office about the nearest options.

Courtesy Rent-A-Car (☎ 431-4160, fax 429-6387) is one of the island's larger companies and has an airport location (☎ 418-2500). Other car rental companies include the following:

Corbins Car Rentals
(☎ 427-9531, fax 427-7975, rentals@ corbinscars.com) Collymore Rock, St Michael

Direct Rentals
(☎ 420-6372, fax 420-6383, direct@ sunbeach.net) Enterprise, Christ Church

Express Rent-a-Car
(☎ 428-7845 fax 428-1593) St Lawrence Gap, Christ Church

Rayside Car Rental
(☎ 428-0264) Charnocks, Christ Church

Stoutes Car Rental Ltd
(☎ 435-4456)

Sunny Isle Sixt Car Rentals
(☎ 435-7979) Worthing, Christ Church

Sunset Crest Car Rentals
(☎ 432-2222, fax 422-1966) Sunset Crest, St James

Caribbean Scooters (☎ 436-8522, codc@ caribsurf.com) rents out scooters with helmets for B$60/80 per day for one- and two-seaters.

TAXI

Taxis have a 'Z' on the license plate and usually have a 'taxi' sign on the roof. They're easy to find and often wait at the side of the road in popular tourist areas.

Although fares are fixed by the government, taxis are not metered, so you should establish the fare before you start off. The rate per kilometer is about B$1.50, and the flat hourly rate B$35. Some fares from Bridgetown are B$40 to the east coast, B$18 to St Lawrence/Dover, B$20 to Oistins and B$30 to Speightstown.

BICYCLE

Express Rent-a-Car (☎ 428-7845), in St Lawrence Gap, rents mountain bikes for B$23 a day, and Rob's Bike Hire (☎ 437-3404), at the Dread or Dead Surf Shop in Hastings, charges B$20/100 a day/week. Both require a deposit of B$100. Bike aficionados may prefer the attention provided by Gary at Flex Bicycle Rentals (☎ 424-0321, gmgriff@sunbeach.net). One-day rentals are a bit high at B$40 a day, but rates drop to half or less for two days or more, and he'll deliver the bike to you. Gary also leads custom bike tours.

HITCHHIKING

Hitchhiking is tolerated, but the practice is not widespread, in part because buses are cheap and frequent. All the usual safety precautions apply.

ORGANIZED TOURS
Sightseeing Tours

Most tour companies offer a variety of half-day and full-day options that either provide an overview with stops at key sites or emphasize special interests such as nature and gardens. Bajan Tours (☎/fax 437-9389, bajan@caribnet.net) is one of the largest companies and has relatively good prices. Half-/full-day tours cost B$80/112, including entrance fees. Other companies offering island tours include LE Williams Tour Co (☎ 427-1043) and Topaz Tours (☎ 435-8451).

Adventureland 4x4 Tours (☎ 429-3687, fourbyfour@caribsurf.com) and Island Safari (☎ 429-5337) stop at many of the usual sights, but also venture off-road to lesser-known places.

More oriented toward local tourism, the Barbados Transit Authority's Sunday Scenic Rides (☎ 436-6820) depart each Sunday from Independence Square at 2 pm for a five-hour trip, with as many as a dozen public buses caravaning around the island. Each week covers a different area. While not very personalized, it's cheap and almost worth the admission just to see 12 buses snaking through the cane fields. Tickets are available at the Fairchild and Jubilee terminals and cost B$15 for adults, B$10 for children. Entrance fees are additional, but there is usually a discount for tour participants. Bring snacks and drinks. Or get a really different view with Bajan Helicopters (☎ 431-0069, BHL@Caribnet.net). A half-hour tour (B$280 per person) takes you around the periphery of the island, while a 20-minute tour (B$195) focuses on inland landscapes. Flights depart from Needham's Point, south of Bridgetown.

The going rate for custom tours by taxi drivers is B$40 an hour, but you can usually negotiate with individual drivers to work out your own deal.

Open Houses

From mid-January to mid-April, the Barbados National Trust (☎ 436-2421) has an Open House Programme offering visits to some of the island's grander private homes. A different house can be visited 2:30 to 5:30 pm each Wednesday for a price of B$15, which includes a drink. Should you be a member of the National Trust in another Commonwealth country, the fee is only B$6. The tourist office and most Barbados National Trust sites can provide a brochure describing the open houses and directions to them. If you don't have your own transportation, for B$37 you can book a tour that includes hotel pickup and admission; call ☎ 425-1103 for details.

Distillery & Brewery Tours

Tours can be made of three rum distilleries on the island. Rates are about the same at each, with a basic 30- to 45-minute tour explaining the distilling operation and capping off with rum tasting for B$15. The **Mount Gay Rum Visitors' Centre** (☎ 425-9066), about a kilometer north of Bridgetown Harbour, and the **Malibu Beach Club and Visitor Centre** (☎ 425-9393) also offer a tour, with buffet lunch and hotel transfer for B$55. At Malibu, on a wide expanse of beach north of Bridgetown, the lunch tour includes a beach chair and umbrella; alternatively, get a day pass entitling you to lots more drinks and beach time, for B$75. The **Heritage Park & Foursquare Rum Distillery** (☎ 420-1977), although set in an old sugar mill, has some of the most modern equipment. It's as much a theme park as a distillery, and the standard tour (B$15) includes access to the museum and craft shops. It's near Six Cross Roads in

Barbados National Trust

The Barbados National Trust is a nonprofit organization dedicated to the preservation of the island's historic sites and areas of environmental significance. Founded in 1961, the trust is the caretaker of many of the island's leading visitor attractions. In some cases it owns the property outright, but in other cases, as with the great houses, it primarily assists with managing visitor access to the property, which otherwise remains in private hands.

Properties under the Barbados National Trust umbrella include the Gun Hill Signal Station, Tyrol Cot Heritage Village, Welchman Hall Gully, Morgan Lewis Sugar Mill, Andromeda Botanic Gardens, Arbib Nature & Heritage Trail and a handful of other sites.

Each property can be visited by paying a separate admission fee. Annual memberships are also available. Members of the National Trusts of England and Wales; Scotland; Washington, DC; Australia and New Zealand; Fiji; or Zimbabwe, or those of the Heritage Canada Foundation, are admitted for no charge to most Barbados National Trust properties and receive a discount for the Open House Programme.

St Philip; you can take a St Patrick's bus from the Fairchild bus terminal or River Road minibus terminal.

Tours of the **Banks beer brewery** (☎ 228-6486), in Wildey, about 3km east of Bridgetown, are conducted three times a day on weekdays (B$12 for adults, B$10 for children six to 15 years). Call ahead for reservations. The St Patrick's bus also passes the brewery.

Boat & Submarine Cruises

The *Jolly Roger* (☎ 436-6424), a party boat built to replicate a pirate ship, offers a four-hour excursion that includes lunch, an open bar and snorkeling for B$123. It leaves from Bridgetown at 10 am Thursday and Saturday, anchoring off Holetown at lunchtime.

The MV *Harbour Master* (☎ 430-0900), a four-deck vessel with a 70-foot water slide attached, sails every Wednesday and Friday morning for an all-day party. The B$123 includes transfers, snorkeling equipment, lunch and unlimited drinks. Thursday evening, B$130 will get you a moonlight cruise with dinner, a live band and a floor show. When there is enough demand, they bring out their semisubmersible, for underwater viewing.

For a mellower scene, there are a number of small sailboat cruises available. One of the more affordable options is the 60-foot catamaran *El Tigre* (☎ 417-7245, eltigre@sunbeach.net), which offers a three-hour cruise with two snorkeling stops for B$75. Other sailboat operations include Limbo Lady (☎ 420-5418), Secret Love (☎ 432-1972) and Why Not Sailing Cruises (☎ 230-3792).

The *Atlantis* (☎ 436-8929), a 28-seat submarine lined with portholes, takes visitors on underwater tours of the coral reef off the island's west coast. Tours operate on the hour from 9 am to 4 pm weekdays (B$160 for adults, half price for children under 12, who must be at least 107cm tall). The outing lasts 1½ hours, with the underwater segment about 50 minutes. There's a night dive on Tuesday and Thursday for the same price.

The Atlantis operations and most other sailing cruises leave from Bridgetown, but many include transportation from your hotel.

Tours to Other Islands

The most popular interisland day tour from Barbados is to the Grenadines. The day starts with a morning snack, followed by a flight to Union Island and a sail in a catamaran around the spectacular Tobago Cays, Palm Island and Mayreau. The tour includes lunch, complimentary drinks and a bit of beach and snorkeling time, returning to Barbados around 6:30 pm. The price starts at B$590. You can add Mustique for B$200 more.

There are various other day tours to Grenada, St Lucia, Martinique, Dominica, St Vincent and Tobago for about the same price. Two- and three-day tours with accommodations in charming island guest houses are also available.

Three of the largest interisland tour companies are Caribbean Safari Tours (☎ 427-5100, caribsafari@caribsurf.com), Ship Inn Complex, St Lawrence Gap; Grenadine Tours (☎ 435-8451), Dunoun, Dayrells Road, Christ Church; and Chantours (☎ 432-5591, daviddacosta@sunbeach.net), Sunset Crest Plaza No 2, St James.

Bridgetown

Bridgetown, the island capital, is a busy commercial city set on Carlisle Bay, the island's only natural harbor.

Architecturally, the city is a bit of a hodgepodge. Most of the main streets are modern and businesslike in appearance, but there's also a handful of nicely restored colonial buildings, as well as side streets that lead off into residential neighborhoods sprinkled with rum shops and chattel houses.

The Careenage, a fingerlike inlet lined with recreational boats, cuts into the heart of the city. At the south side of the Chamberlain Bridge, which crosses the Careenage to National Heroes Square, is Independence Arch, which commemorates Bajan independence and is adorned by plaques honoring the island's first prime minister, Errol Barrow.

A three-year redevelopment plan, the most elaborate in Bridgetown's history, has begun for the downtown area with the

BRIDGETOWN

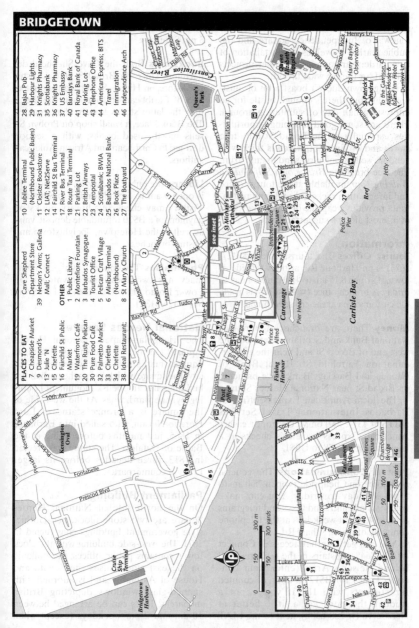

PLACES TO EAT
7 Cheapside Market
9 Desmond's
13 Julie 'N
15 Chefette
16 Fairchild St Public
   Market
19 Waterfront Café
20 The Rusty Pelican
30 Pure Food Café
32 Palmetto Market
33 Chefette
34 Chefette
38 Ideal Restaurant;

Cave Shepherd
Department Store
39 Nelson's Arms; Galleria
   Mall; Connect

OTHER
1 Public Library
3 Montefiore Fountain
3 Barbados Synagogue
4 Tourist Office
5 Pelican Craft Village
6 Minibus Terminal
   (Northbound)
8 St Mary's Church

10 Jubilee Terminal
   (Northbound Public Buses)
11 Cloister Bookstore
12 LIAT; Net2Serve
14 Fairchild St Bus Terminal
17 River Bus Terminal
18 Route Taxi Terminal
21 Parking Lot
22 British Airways
23 Aeropostal
24 Scotiabank; BWIA
25 Barbados National Bank
26 Book Place
27 The Boatyard

28 Bajan Pub
29 Harbour Lights
31 Knights Pharmacy
35 Scotiabank
36 Knights Pharmacy
37 US Embassy
40 Barclays Bank
41 Royal Bank of Canada
42 Parking Lot
43 Telephone Office
44 American Express; BITS
   Travel
45 Immigration
46 Independence Arch

BARBADOS

completion of a waterfront boardwalk and a new craft center on Princess Alice Hwy. The renewal of Independence Square and the public market as well as the installation of new gardens are among the other projects planned for the citywide facelift.

Bridgetown doesn't boast a lot of must-see sights, but there's enough bustle for an interesting half-day of sauntering around. There are some good shopping opportunities, especially at the Broad St duty-free stores and on Swan St, which is thick with vendors selling jewelry, sandals and fruit. The free brochure *Bridgetown Self-Guided Walking Tour,* available at the tourist office and information racks in hotels and restaurants, provides a capsule of several key sites of interest along a suggested route.

Information
Tourist Offices The tourist office (☎ 427-2623) is on Harbour Rd, at the west side of town. It's open 8:15 am to 4:30 pm Monday to Friday. A branch office (☎ 426-1718) is inside the customs area at the cruise terminal.

Money There are branches of Barbados National Bank and Scotiabank at both the west end of Broad St and near the bus terminal on Fairchild St. Royal Bank of Canada and Barclays Bank have branches on Broad St near National Heroes Square.

The local American Express office, at Barbados International Travel Services (BITS; ☎ 431-2400) on McGregor St, cashes American Express traveler's checks at a fixed rate of B$1.78 to US$1.

Post & Communications The general post office, on Cheapside, is open 7:30 am to 5 pm Monday to Friday. You can make overseas calls and send faxes and telegrams 8 am to 4:30 pm weekdays at the telephone company office on Wharf Rd.

You can get Internet access at Connect (☎ 228-8648), upstairs in the Galleria Mall behind Nelson's Arms (enter from Lancaster Lane), for B$12 an hour, discounted for students with ID. If you're not a student, the rates are a little better at Net2Serve (☎ 228-6382), next to the LIAT

office on Hincks St. Both places are open 9 am until at least 5 pm weekdays, till 2 or 3 pm Saturday.

Bookstores Both the Cave Shepherd department store on Broad St and Cloister Bookstore, on Hincks St, carry a wide selection of Caribbean and international literature; the latter stocks Lonely Planet guides. The Book Place, a small shop on Probyn St, sells mostly used books, with a section devoted to Caribbean and African-American authors.

Library The public library, on Coleridge St, is open 9 am to 5 pm Monday to Saturday. Visitors may check out library books on payment of a B$20 refundable deposit, valid as well at the Holetown, Speightstown and Oistins branches.

Pharmacies The modern Knights Pharmacy has two locations downtown: on Lower Broad St (☎ 426-5196) and on Swan St (☎ 426-5135).

National Heroes Square
The triangular-shaped National Heroes Square (formerly known as Trafalgar Square) marks the bustling center of the city. The square, which fronts the parliament buildings, has an obelisk monument honoring bygone war heroes. At the west side of the square is a bronze statue of Lord Horatio Nelson, who sailed into Barbados in 1805, just months before dying at the Battle of Trafalgar. The statue was erected in 1813, three decades before its larger London counterpart.

Parliament Buildings
On the north side of National Heroes Square are two stone-block, neo-Gothic-style government buildings constructed in 1871. The west-side building with the clock tower contains public offices; the building on the east side houses the Senate and House of Assembly and is adorned with stained-glass windows depicting British monarchs. Tours can be arranged between 10 am and 2 pm weekdays (except when

parliament is meeting) with a week's prior notice. Call ☎ 427-2019 for an appointment.

St Michael's Cathedral

St Michael's, the island's Anglican cathedral, is a five-minute walk east of National Heroes Square. The original church, completed in 1665 to accommodate 3000 worshippers, proved to be too much of a windscreen and came tumbling down in a hurricane a century later. The scaled-down, but still substantial, structure that stands today dates from 1789 and seats 1600. At the time of construction it was said to have the widest arched ceiling of its type in the world.

Among the island notables buried in the adjacent churchyard are Sir Grantley Adams, Barbados' first premier and the head of the West Indies Federation from 1958 to 1962, and his son Tom, prime minister of Barbados from 1976 to 1985.

Visitors are welcome to look around (no admission fee).

Barbados Synagogue

This small synagogue, built in 1833 and abandoned in 1929, was restored in 1986 and is now under the jurisdiction of the Barbados National Trust. The pink building is recognizable by its distinctive balustraded roofline and rounded corners. It has a simple but handsome interior with brass chandeliers, a checkerboard marble floor and a women's balcony supported by faux-marble columns.

The island's first synagogue was built on this site in the 1600s, when Barbados had a Jewish population of more than 800. Many were refugees who had fled Portuguese oppression in South America in search of safe havens and became plantation owners in Barbados. The 50 or so remaining Jews descend from more recently arrived Eastern European immigrants.

The synagogue, on Synagogue Lane between James St and Magazine Lane, is a 10-minute walk from National Heroes Square. It's usually open for viewing 9 am to 4 pm Monday to Friday.

Nearby, opposite the public library, is the **Montefiore Fountain**, a decorative little monument that was given to the city in 1864 by John Montefiore, who was a wealthy Jewish resident.

Queen's Park

A green space of grassy lawns, Queen's Park is a popular place for families to picnic and relax on Sunday afternoon. On a knoll at the top of the park is a grand two-story house that was once the residence of the commander of the British forces in the West Indies. Erected in 1786, it was thoroughly restored in 1973 and now houses a theater and a gallery of local art. Nearby are a few cages with green monkeys and exotic birds and a lunchtime restaurant serving inexpensive Bajan fare.

At the edge of the playground stands a huge baobab tree 18m in circumference. A plaque at the site estimates the tree to be 1000 years old, but the claim is somewhat complicated by the fact that the tree is native to Africa, a continent with which Barbados had no known contact until the early 17th century.

Harry Bayley Observatory

The Harry Bayley Observatory (☎ 424-5593), east of central Bridgetown in the Clapham area, off Rendezvous Rd, is the headquarters of the Barbados Astronomical Society. It's open to the public on Friday evening; arrive by 8:30 pm (B$8 for adults, B$5 for children).

The Garrison Area

About 2km south of central Bridgetown, spreading inland from the south side of Carlisle Bay, is the Barbados Garrison, the home base of the British Windward and Leeward Islands Command in the 1800s.

A central focal point is the oval-shaped **Savannah**, which was once large parade grounds and is now used for cricket games, jogging and Saturday horse races. Standing along the west side of the Savannah are some of the Garrison's more ornate colonial buildings, most notably the salmon-colored **Main Guard** with its four-sided clock tower. Fronting the Main Guard you'll find an impressive array of cannons. Barbados, incidentally, claims the world's largest collection of 17th-century iron cannons, including one of only two existing cannons bearing Oliver Cromwell's Republican Arms.

If you're interested in British military history, the entire Garrison area can be fascinating to explore. The first fortifications in the area went up as early as 1650, although many of the current buildings date to the mid-19th century, a consequence of the violent 1831 hurricane that destroyed virtually everything not made of stone or iron.

Barbados Museum The Barbados Museum (☎ 427-0201), on the northeast side of the Savannah, is housed in an early-19th-century military prison. It has engaging displays on all aspects of the island's history, beginning with its early Amerindian inhabitants. Not surprisingly, the most extensive collections cover the colonial era, with exhibits on slavery, emancipation, military history and plantation-house furniture, all accompanied by insightful narratives.

Among the museum's other offerings are an African culture gallery, a children's gallery, natural-history displays, changing exhibits of local contemporary art, and a gift shop. For a quick immersion into island

---

Early Tourists

In 1751, at age 19 – some 38 years before he would become the first US president – George Washington visited Barbados as a companion to his half-brother Lawrence, who suffered from tuberculosis. It was hoped that the tropical climate would prove therapeutic.

The two rented a house in the Garrison area south of Bridgetown (where the Bush Hill House now stands) and stayed on the island for six weeks. Unfortunately, George contracted smallpox while on Barbados, which left his face permanently scarred, and Lawrence died the following year. The Barbados trip was the only overseas journey George Washington ever made.

---

history, you couldn't do better than to spend an hour or two here. The museum is open 9 am to 5 pm Monday to Saturday, 2 to 6 pm on Sunday (B\$11.50 for adults, B\$5.75 for children).

Places to Stay

The *Angle House* (☎ 427-9010), on busy Upper Bay St near the yacht harbor at the southern outskirts of Bridgetown, is an inexpensive guest house with a solidly local flavor. This large old house has nine simple but clean rooms for US\$25 with a double bed, US\$30 with two beds. Guests have use of two kitchens and a common sitting area with TV. Its best quality is its proximity to Carlisle Bay and Pebbles Beach.

Toward the water off Bay St is the *Island Inn Hotel* (☎ 436-6393, fax 437-8035, quaint@caribsurf.com). The popular hotel incorporates a restored 1804 garrison building that was originally a military rum store. There are 23 rooms with a king or queen bed, air-con and phone. Singles/doubles for an all-inclusive package cost US\$150/208 in summer, US\$195/253 in winter.

Places to Eat

The best places to buy fruits and vegetables are at the *Palmetto Market* at the east end of Swan St and the *public markets* on Fairchild St and Cheapside, which are open from 7 am to late afternoon Monday to Saturday. The giant *Julie 'N* supermarket, on Bridge St near the Fairchild bus terminal, stays open till 10 pm.

For a healthy sit-down meal there's *Pure Food Café*, on Chapel St, which has simple inexpensive vegetarian fare and is open weekdays from 8 am to 5 pm, Saturday until 2 pm. *Chefette*, with locations on Broad, Marhill and Fairchild Sts, is a busy local fast-food spot with cheap rotis, burgers and fried chicken.

A lunchtime favorite with office workers is *Ideal Restaurant*, upstairs in the Cave Shepherd department store, with good, inexpensive island-style food. A solid meal of pigeon peas and rice, salad and fish costs B\$14, and there are cheaper specials. It's open 9 am to 3 pm weekdays, till 1:30 pm

Saturday. Similarly hearty fare can be found at **Desmond's Restaurant**, in City Centre Mall near St Mary's Church, from 11 am to 4 pm Monday to Saturday.

Nelson's Arms *(27 Broad Street)*, in the Galleria Mall, is a popular lunch spot with balcony dining and a pleasant pub atmosphere. From 11 am to 4 pm weekdays and 10 am to 3 pm Saturday, you can get hoagies or baguette sandwiches for B$15 and specials such as lasagna or Cajun chicken for around B$22.

Bridgetown's arguably most pleasant lunch location is **The Rusty Pelican** *(☎ 436-7778)*, which has a 2nd-floor waterfront setting overlooking the Careenage near Independence Arch. At lunch you can get flying fish for B$22 or coconut shrimp for B$30; dinners run B$35 to B$50. It's open 10 am until late. Also inviting is **Waterfront Café** *(☎ 427-0093)*, on the ground floor of the same building, with both outdoor waterside tables and indoor seating. Open 10 am to 10 pm Monday to Saturday, the café prepares tasty sandwiches for B$22 and specialty salads or fish of the day for B$30. On Tuesday there's a Caribbean buffet (B$45) with steel pan music.

Brown Sugar *(☎ 426-7684)*, next to the Island Inn at Aquatic Gap in the Garrison area, is a veritable greenhouse of hanging plants, complete with a waterfall and whistling frogs. It has a popular West Indian buffet noon to 2:30 pm daily except Saturday (B$35) and is also open 6 to 10 pm daily for dinner served à la carte, with the likes of shrimp Creole for B$42 and lobster for B$75. Reservations are advised.

Entertainment & Shopping

While visitors are not unwelcome in Bridgetown's many rum shops, a distinct local character prevails. Along Baxters Rd, just north of the center, you'll find a concentration of these watering holes, where alcohol flows freely and fish is fried up on primitive stoves until late in the night. A somewhat tamer option would be **Bajan Pub**, on Bay St, where there's live music on occasion. **Waterfront Café** (see Places to Eat)

has live music 8 to 11 pm Tuesday to Saturday (no cover).

Harbour Lights *(☎ 436-7225)*, an open-air nightclub on Bay St at the south end of Bridgetown, has dancing and live bands most nights. Friday is liveliest, and Monday night there's a beach party. While it's not gay-oriented, it is one of the more gay-friendly places.

Not far away, **The Boatyard** *(☎ 436-2622)* has something special every night, whether it's live bands, DJs, unlimited drinks with a B$25 cover, or their Friday-night fish fry. Sunday afternoon here is popular with local couples.

For art and souvenirs, the Pelican Craft Village, on Princess Alice Hwy between downtown and the cruise-ship terminal, is a growing complex of craft stores and workshops featuring pottery, leather, wood and fabric designs, and you can watch the artists at work.

Getting There & Away

Public buses going south and east leave from the Fairchild St Bus Terminal, on Bridge St, north of Fairchild. Public buses going north up the west coast leave from the Jubilee (Lower Green) Terminal, at the west end of Lower Broad St.

Minibuses use the River Bus Terminal, on the east side of town, for central and eastern routes. Farther east is the route-taxi terminal for Oistins, Silver Sands and other southern points. Minibuses going north up the west coast leave from near the general post office on Cheapside.

Have a Good Day

In Bridgetown center you can expect to have taxi drivers approach and ask if you need a tour or a ride, whether you look like you do or not. This is not a hassle scene, however, and if you politely decline they generally smile and respond with the likes of 'Just stretching legs?' or 'You have a good day, then.'

South Coast

The south coast, from Hastings to Maxwell, has most of the island's budget to mid-range accommodations. Virtually the entire strip is fringed with white-sand beaches and turquoise waters.

Hwy 7 links the south-coast villages; buses and route taxis (No 11) run frequently along this road as they ply between Bridgetown and Oistins.

While the south coast is fairly built up, some areas, such as the coastal roads in St Lawrence and Maxwell, are off the main strip and thus more lightly trafficked. As a rule, the farther you go from Bridgetown the less developed it is.

All the communities described in this section are in the parish of Christ Church, which ends at the airport. For the region east of the airport see the Southeast section.

HASTINGS & ROCKLEY

The Hastings-Rockley area is the first major tourist area east of Bridgetown. The center of activity is Rockley Beach, a roadside white-sand beach with shade trees, snack kiosks and clothing vendors. It's a half-local, half-tourist scene, and, a mere 10-minute bus ride from central Bridgetown, it attracts a crowd, especially on weekends. About halfway between Bridgetown and Rockley is Hastings Rock, a nice spot to enjoy the view. On weekends, community groups set up flea markets and hold activities around the gazebo in this small park above the water.

Information

Boutiques and souvenir shops can be found at several little centers from Hastings to Rockley, including Hastings Plaza and Quayside Center. The Village Supermarket, open 8 am to 6 pm weekdays, is a block west and a block north of the Hastings Rock park. A minimart near Coconut Court and a 99 Convenience Store in Quayside Center are open until 10 pm daily. Three self-service laundries are open daily: Queen's Laundermat, near the

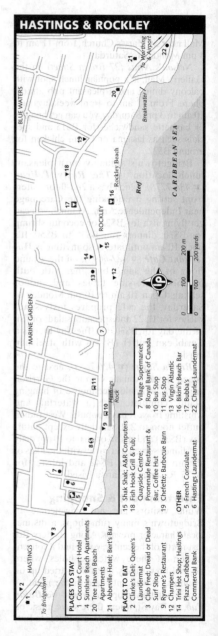

HASTINGS & ROCKLEY

PLACES TO STAY
1 Coconut Court Hotel
4 Sunshine Beach Apartments
20 Tree Haven Beach Apartments
21 Abbeville Hotel; Bert's Bar

PLACES TO EAT
2 Clarke's Deli; Queen's Laundermat
3 Club Fred; Dread or Dead Surf Shop
9 Ryanne's Restaurant
12 Champers
14 Trini Fish Shop; Hastings Plaza; Caribbean Commercial Bank
15 Shak Shak; A&R Computers
18 Fish Hook Grill & Pub; Quayside Centre; Promenade Restaurant & Bar; Coffee Hut
19 Chefette; Barbecue Barn

7 Village Supermarket
8 Royal Bank of Canada
10 Bus Stop
11 Bus Stop
13 Virgin Atlantic
16 Bikini's Beach Bar
17 Bubba's
22 Charles Laundermat

OTHER
5 French Consulate
6 Hastings Laundermat

Coconut Court; Hastings Laundermat, across from the Village Supermarket; and Charles Laundermat, east of the Abbeville Hotel. There's Internet access for B\$15 per hour at A&R Computer Service, across the street from Hastings Plaza, 8:30 am to 5:30 pm weekdays and 9 am to 3 pm Saturday. Royal Bank of Canada, opposite Hastings Rock, and Caribbean Commercial Bank, in Hastings Plaza, have full-service ATM machines.

Places to Stay

The **Abbeville Hotel** (☎ 435-7924, abbeville@sunbeach.net) is on the inland side of Hwy 7, a couple of minutes' walk from Rockley Beach. The former plantation house has 19 straightforward rooms with private baths. Singles/doubles cost US\$45/55, US\$50/60 with air-con. Rates are US\$10 cheaper in summer, and major credit cards are accepted. Bert's Bar, beside the hotel's pool, is a popular local eating and drinking spot.

The five-story beachfront **Coconut Court Hotel** (☎ 427-1655, ccourt@caribsurf.com) is a good-value package resort hotel especially popular with Brits. There are 30 ocean-view rooms with small refrigerators, coffeemakers and toaster-ovens; they run US\$70 in summer, US\$125 in winter. Spacious studio apartments with full kitchens cost US\$65 in summer, US\$120 in winter, while one-bedroom apartments are US\$90 in summer, US\$145 in winter. Additional attractions include a beachside pool, a restaurant, a bar and water-sports rentals.

Cute studio apartments with kitchens, twin beds and patios or balconies are available at two small complexes. In Hastings, about 200m east of the Coconut Court Hotel, **Sunshine Beach Apartments** (☎/fax 427-1234, sunbeach98@hotmail.com) has 15 simple but pretty white-tiled apartments with phones for US\$50 in summer, US\$60 in winter; TV and air-con are extra. Steps lead down to a sundeck and the beach. **Tree Haven Beach Apartments** (☎ 435-6673, arturoolaya@caribsurf.com), just across the road from Rockley Beach, has three spacious units with TV for US\$50, US\$60 with air-con.

Places to Eat

On the inland side of the main road near Coconut Court Hotel is **Clarke's Deli**, open 8 am to 8 pm Monday to Saturday, 10 am to 3 pm Sunday, with filling breakfasts and lunches for B\$7 to B\$15. The Saturday treat, pudding & souse, is B\$7.50. On down the road a bit is **Club Fred**, next door to Dread or Dead surf shop. It's a little pub, run by an Englishman, serving sandwiches and pub pies for B\$5 to B\$15, and there's a pool table.

Farther east, at the edge of Hastings Rock, **Ryanne's Restaurant** serves Bajan breakfasts of saltfish with breadfruit or bakes, and traditional breakfasts of eggs and sausages for B\$17.25. Lunch specials cost about B\$15, soups and salads B\$6 to B\$8 and sandwiches around B\$9. It's open 7:30 am to 10 pm daily and has a small bar. In the center of Hastings Plaza, **Trini Hot Shop** serves inexpensive Trinidadian delicacies 9 am to 3:30 pm Monday to Saturday.

The fast-food combo of **Chefette** and **Barbecue Barn**, opposite Rockley Beach, offers grilled chicken or steak, served with baked potato and garlic bread, for around B\$20; add B\$9 for a simple salad bar. You can also get inexpensive burgers, rotis and fried chicken. Both are open 11 am to 11 pm daily.

At Quayside Plaza, east of Chefette, the best of a variety of options is **Fish Hook Grill & Pub**, with good, reasonably priced seafood. A lunch special with fish, potatoes and salad is big enough for two and costs B\$20. There's also a large selection of tropical juices. It's open 11 am to around midnight daily. Next door is the **Coffee Hut**, with gourmet hot and iced java.

Enjoying a Mediterranean-style setting over the ocean, **Shak Shak** (☎ 435-1234) offers an international menu of fish, chicken and beef, with prices around B\$40, or a bistro and pizzeria menu in the bar for about half that. Friday night there's live music.

Known around the island for its quality food is **Champers** (☎ 455-6644). Its open-air surfside bar and upstairs sea-view restaurant serve lunch and dinner. Seafood salads average B\$35, while dinner specials such as red snapper in ginger-and-coconut sauce go for B\$48.

Entertainment

Whenever there's an important sports event, the place to watch it is on the 10-foot screen at *Bubba's*, on Hwy 7 east of Quayside Centre. The hottest spot in the area is *Bikini's Beach Bar*, set back from the road at the east end of Rockley Beach. The entrance is down a small path across from Bubba's. When the sun shines there's always a beach party, starting at 9 am, with watersports equipment, beach chairs and food and drinks.

Promenade Restaurant & Bar, in Quayside Centre, has karaoke from 8 pm Wednesday and Saturday, when local young people come and show off their talent.

WORTHING

Worthing can make a nice base, particularly if you're on a tight budget but still want to be in the middle of things. It has relatively inexpensive places to eat and a handful of lower-range guest houses that are either on the beach or a stone's throw from it.

Sandy Beach, which fronts Worthing, is a lovely broad strip of powdery white sand. The beach has just enough activity to be interesting, but not so much that it feels crowded.

From Worthing it's only a five-minute stroll to the restaurants and nightlife of St Lawrence. A small movie theater, Vista Cinema, is on Hwy 7 just to the west of Rendezvous Rd.

Information

There's a Scotiabank on Hwy 7 in front of Sandy Beach Hotel and a Barclays Bank on Rendezvous Rd. Both have 24-hour ATMs. North of Barclays is the Worthing post office, which is open 8 am to at least 3 pm weekdays.

Internet access is at Global Learning Methods, on the inland side of the main road a block west of Rendezvous Rd, for B$15 an hour.

The Southshore Laundermat on Hwy 7 charges B$8 to wash and dry a load of clothes. It's usually open 8 am to 4 pm weekdays, until 2 pm Saturday.

Places to Stay

Guest Houses Popular with young German travelers, *House Cleverdale* (☎ 428-3172), set back just a bit from the beach, is a large wooden home. Rooms cost US$25 with mosquito net and fan. Bathrooms and a large kitchen are shared. Nearby is *Maraval Guest House* (☎ 435-7437), which has attractive, simple rooms with shared bath and in-room sinks for US$30 single or double. There's access to a well-equipped kitchen and a pleasant living room with TV and stereo. Beach chairs are available for the use of guests. Heindrun Rice of Karibik Tours (☎ 428-1035, karibik@ sunbeach.net), manager of House Cleverdale, has information about several places with inexpensive rooms on the south coast and other parts of the island; some are nicer than others.

Scandanavian-run *Shell's Guest House* (☎ 435-7253, guest@sunbeach.net), on 1st Ave, is popular with budget travelers and gay visitors. There are seven nonsmoking rooms, each with a ceiling fan, sink, small dresser and lamp. Four rooms have private baths, while three rooms share two baths. Singles/doubles cost a reasonable US$25/38, or US$28/40 with private bath, including Continental breakfast. Credit cards are accepted.

Crystal Waters Guest House (☎ 435-7514, crystalwaters@sunbeach.net), opposite Shell's, is a small beachfront inn with a faded period character. The rooms are clean and have hardwood floors, twin beds with comfortable mattresses, dressers and private baths. Singles share a bath. There's a TV room and a casual beachfront bar. Singles/doubles cost US$31/41 with Continental breakfast.

Hotels & Apartments The little *Chateau Blanc* (☎ 435-7518, chateaublanc@caribsurf .com) is a recommendable apartment building smack on the beach. It has nine air-conditioned units, most with water-view terraces, including a studio for US$50 in summer, US$85 in winter, and a one-bedroom apartment for US$80 in summer, US$115. Credit cards are not accepted.

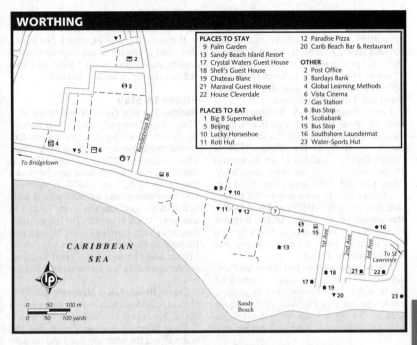

WORTHING

PLACES TO STAY	
9 Palm Garden	12 Paradise Pizza
13 Sandy Beach Island Resort	20 Carib Beach Bar & Restaurant
17 Crystal Waters Guest House	**OTHER**
18 Shell's Guest House	2 Post Office
19 Chateau Blanc	3 Barclays Bank
21 Maraval Guest House	4 Global Learning Methods
22 House Cleverdale	6 Vista Cinema
	7 Gas Station
PLACES TO EAT	8 Bus Stop
1 Big B Supermarket	14 Scotiabank
5 Beijing	15 Bus Stop
10 Lucky Horseshoe	16 Southshore Laundermat
11 Roti Hut	23 Water-Sports Hut

To Bridgetown

CARIBBEAN SEA

To St Lawrence

Sandy Beach

0   50   100 m
0   50   100 yards

The 18-unit *Palm Garden* (☎ 435-6406, ethel@sunbeach.net), on the inland side of Hwy 7, is an older but pleasant family-run place popular with Canadian visitors. Rooms with refrigerators cost US$60 in summer, US$75 in winter, and suites with two bedrooms and full kitchens are US$85 in summer, US$95 in winter. All units have air-con and there's a pool. If you call from the airport and they're not full you can usually get a US$10 walk-in discount.

Sandy Beach Island Resort (☎ 435-8000, sandbar@caribsurf.com) is a modern if rather nondescript four-story beachfront all-inclusive hotel. There are 40 comfortable rooms, each with one queen or two twin beds and refrigerator, for US$91 in summer, US$180 in winter, and 78 one-bedroom suites with kitchenettes for US$138 in summer, US$281 in winter. All units have phones, air-con and cable TV. The hotel has a pool with a coral waterfall and a beachfront bar.

Places to Eat

The *Roti Hut*, on Hwy 7, has cheap rotis ranging in price from B$4 for a potato version to B$9 for a shrimp roti, as well as hearty lunch specials of curried chicken or beef stew for B$8.95. It's open 11 am to 10 pm Monday to Thursday, later on Friday and Saturday.

Paradise Pizza serves breakfast all day. Besides pizza and chicken, there's a filling lunch special for just B$10, including a choice of meat, plus rice, macaroni or salad. Food is available 10 am until 10 pm weekdays, until midnight on weekends, drinks and karaoke until 4 am most nights.

Beijing is a simple but authentic Chinese restaurant near the intersection of Rendezvous Rd and Hwy 7. Lunch specials (B$16) are served 11:30 am to 2 pm and dinner 6 to 10 pm daily.

The cozy little *café* at Shells Guest House (see Places to Stay) offers lunch specials for B$15 and three-course dinners with a

BARBADOS

gourmet touch for B$46. The **Lucky Horse-shoe**, on Hwy 7, has a 24-hour snack menu of cutters (B$16 to B$18) and soups (around B$10). At lunchtime or dinnertime, there are pricier steaks and fish, and from 11 am to 3 pm a barbecue lunch special for B$18.50. Satellite TV and slot machines help keep it lively all the time.

Carib Beach Bar & Restaurant, an open-air eatery right on Sandy Beach, has a fish cutter with fries for B$12 and other fish meals for B$16 at lunchtime, B$24 at dinner. Food is available 11 am to around 10 pm daily, but the bar stays open later. There's a two-for-one happy hour 5 to 6 pm.

The best deal in town may be the beach-side Sunday buffet (B$25) at **Sand Dollar Restaurant** (☎ 435-6956), in the Bagshot House Hotel (see Places to Stay). Served from noon to 3 pm, it's very popular and reservations are a must.

Big B Supermarket, just 100m up Rendezvous Rd, has a wide range of imported foods, a deli with inexpensive local food (stew, chicken legs etc) and a large liquor section. It's open 8 am to at least 8 pm Monday to Saturday, 9 am to 2 pm Sunday.

ST LAWRENCE & DOVER BEACH

St Lawrence has the area's most active night scene as well as numerous mid-range restaurants and places to stay, many of which front the ocean. The western end of St Lawrence is at the junction of Little Bay and Hwy 7, but most of the village lies along the St Lawrence Coast Rd, in the area known as the Gap.

Dover Beach, near the middle of the coastal road, is a nice, broad white-sand beach that attracts swimmers, bodysurfers, windsurfers and board surfers, depending on the water conditions. Equipment can be rented on the beach.

Information

On St Lawrence Coast Rd is a Royal Bank of Canada, beside Ship Inn. Internet access is available 8 am to 5 pm at Happy Days Café (B$15 per hour), in the Chattel House Shopping Village, and Netlink Business Centre (B$18 per hour), downstairs from the Bean 'N Bagel. Netlink also has fax and copy service and is open everyday.

If you need groceries, sundries or liquor, there are a couple of reasonably stocked convenience stores on St Lawrence Coast Rd that stay open until 10 pm daily.

Places to Stay

Budget The **Rio Guest House** (☎/fax 428-1546, riogh@hotmail.com) is a travelers' haunt with seven good, unpretentious fan-cooled rooms. Singles with 'face basin' share a bath and cost US$25 in summer, US$31 in winter; doubles, which have two beds and their own bath, cost US$32 in summer, US$44 in winter; and a studio with double bed and its own kitchen costs US$53 in summer, US$65 in winter. The guest house features a fully equipped guest kitchen and friendly Swiss-Bajan managers who speak French and German. It's a great location, off the main drag but just minutes from the beach.

Dover Woods Guest House (☎ 420-6599, chrismith32@hotmail.com) is popular with a 30s to 50s crowd. It's tucked in the woods halfway between the coast road and the highway, but the whistling frogs and friendly atmosphere make up for the walk to the beach. Doubles with private bath, a shared kitchen and a family room are US$30 in summer, US$50 in winter.

Mid-Range The **Four Aces** (☎ 428-9441) has 11 relatively inexpensive units with phones, private baths and a casual cottage-like setting. They're a bit old, but are gradually being remodeled. Summer rates for large two-bedroom apartments with air-con, full kitchens and living rooms range from US$65 to US$125 for up to four people. Studio and one-bedroom units (some without air-con) cost US$35 to US$58. Rates increase 15% to 25% in winter.

Another reasonably priced place is the nearby **Salt Ash Apartment Hotel** (☎ 428-8753, fax 428-5140), a small, family-run operation that caters to both overseas and Caribbean travelers. The eight spacious units have air-con, private bathrooms with tubs, kitchenettes and balconies, some with

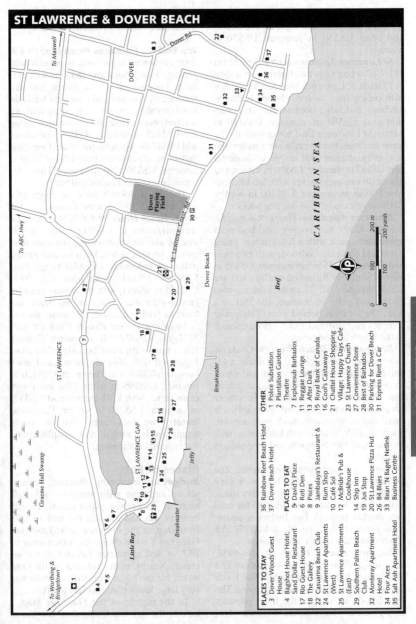

ST LAWRENCE & DOVER BEACH

To Maxwell

Dover Rd

DOVER

To ABC Hwy

Dover Playing Field

St Lawrence Coast Rd

Dover Beach

CARIBBEAN SEA

Ref

Breakwater

ST LAWRENCE

ST LAWRENCE GAP

Breakwater

Jetty

Little Bay

Graeme Hall Swamp

To Worthing & Bridgetown

BARBADOS

0   100   200 m
0   100   200 yards

PLACES TO STAY
- 3   Dover Woods Guest House
- 4   Bagshot House Hotel; Sand Dollar Restaurant
- 17 Rio Guest House
- 18 The Gallery
- 22 Casuarina Beach Club
- 24 St Lawrence Apartments (West)
- 25 St Lawrence Apartments (East)
- 29 Southern Palms Beach Club
- 32 Monteray Apartment Hotel
- 34 Four Aces
- 35 Salt Ash Apartment Hotel

- 36 Rainbow Reef Beach Hotel
- 37 Dover Beach Hotel

PLACES TO EAT
- 5   David's Place
- 6   Roti Den
- 8   Pisces
- 9   Jambalaya's Restaurant & Rum Shop
- 10 Café Sol
- 12 McBride's Pub & Cookhouse
- 14 Ship Inn
- 19 Jus Stop
- 20 St Lawrence Pizza Hut
- 26 B4 Blues
- 33 Bean 'N Bagel; Netlink Business Centre

OTHER
- 1   Police Substation
- 2   Plantation Garden Theatre
- 7   Exploresub Barbados
- 11 Reggae Lounge
- 13 After Dark
- 15 Royal Bank of Canada
- 16 Cool's Castaways
- 21 Chattel House Shopping Village; Happy Days Cafe
- 23 St Lawrence Church
- 27 Convenience Store
- 28 Best of Barbados
- 30 Parking for Dover Beach
- 31 Express Rent a Car

fine ocean views. While certainly not fancy, it's quite adequate and right on the beach, and costs US$50 in summer, US$70 in winter.

St Lawrence Apartments (☎ 435-6950, fax 435-7502) comprises two hotels with a total of 75 units. St Lawrence West has big studios with ceiling fans, air-con, phones, bathtubs, kitchens and large ocean-facing balconies that cost US$68 in summer, US$110 in winter. St Lawrence East has essentially the same facilities, but its units are smaller and less spiffy; studios with simple kitchenettes cost US$63 in summer, US$90 in winter; and one-bedroom apartments with full kitchens cost US$68 in summer, US$100 in winter. Both complexes have swimming pools.

Monteray Apartment Hotel (☎ 428-9152, fax 428-4201) has roomy one-bedroom apartments, each with a full kitchen, living room and separate bedroom with two twin beds. Rates are US$65 in summer, US$95 in winter. Similarly furnished studio units are US$5 cheaper. All 22 units have air-con, phone, and patio or balcony, and there's a pool. The location behind a small shopping complex isn't inspired, but it's close enough to the beach for the price.

Rainbow Reef Beach Hotel (☎ 428-5110, rainbowreef@sunbeach.net) is a modern 43-unit beachfront hotel with a pool and a nice strip of beach. The standard rooms, which cost US$65 in summer, US$90 in winter (single or double, breakfast included), are small but comfortable, each with air-con, phone and TV. Studios with kitchens, as well as one- and two-bedroom apartments, are available.

Formerly a Canadian artist's space, *The Gallery* (☎/fax 435-9756) is now a very pleasant guest house with a woodsy touch to the decor. Studios are US$65/85 for one/ two double beds. A two-bedroom apartment for up to four people is US$150. All rooms have air-con, TV and phones.

Bagshot House Hotel (☎ 246-6956, bagshot@caribsurf.com), at the eastern end of Worthing, is a personable older hotel with the atmosphere of an old-world pension. The little lagoon in front of the hotel provides ideal swimming for children. Singles/doubles

cost US$60/80 in summer and US$80/120 in winter, Continental breakfast included.

Top End The *Casuarina Beach Club* (☎ 428-3600, casbeach@bajan.com) is popular with package-tour groups and families with children. Located on a nice beach and surrounded by coconut and casuarina trees, the hotel contains 129 units with ceiling fans, air-con and phones. Rates for garden-view rooms are US$115 in summer, US$195 in winter; add US$10 for a beachfront studio. One-/two-bedroom apartments cost US$145/220 in summer, US$200/350 in winter. There are tennis courts, a restaurant and bar.

Though it doesn't have as much of a following as the nearby Casuarina, the *Dover Beach Hotel* (☎ 428-8076, resdover@ caribsurf.com) is a better value. The 39 studios and one-bedroom apartments have air-con, phones, radios, kitchens, and private patios or balconies. Doubles range from US$85 to US$115 in summer, US$120 to US$155 in winter, with the lowest rates for garden-view studios. It's on the beach and there's a pool, restaurant, TV lounge and bar.

Southern Palms Beach Club (☎ 428-7171, fax 428-7175) is a modern 92-room resort hotel with a fine beachfront location. Equipped with air-con, phones and mini-bars, smallish rooms begin at US$120 in summer, US$295 in winter; the more spacious suites with kitchenettes cost US$173 in summer, US$280 in winter. The resort features two restaurants, a bar, two pools, tennis courts, minigolf and complimentary water-sports equipment.

Places to Eat

Budget In the evening, streetside vendors set up barbecue grills along the sidewalk near St Lawrence Apartments to sell burgers, fish and chicken for B$5 to B$7. Roti Den, at the entrance to St Lawrence Gap, has a wide choice of rotis averaging B$7, as well as curries, fish dishes and ice cream. Nearby, at the entrance to the Gap, watch for the lunch vans that sell rotis and very large lunch platters ($B6 to $B8).

In the middle of the Gap, *Jus Stop*, a hole-in-the-wall lunch spot near Rio Guest

House, has inexpensive rotis and cutters and lunch specials. On the main road is *St Lawrence Pizza Hut*, which offers New York–style pizza, lasagna and flying fish & chips for B$15 or less.

Bean 'N Bagel, east of Dover Beach, appropriately serves bagels – and muffins, pancakes and sandwiches (around B$10). To go with your bagel and egg (served anytime for B$5), or a rich slice of cheesecake, their other specialty is not beans but coffee. It's open 7 am to 5 pm.

Mid-Range The *Ship Inn* (☎ 435-6961), at the west end of St Lawrence Coast Rd, has a couple of dining spots under one roof. Captain's Carvery, the main restaurant, is pleasant enough, but the food, served buffet-style, is unremarkable. Dinner (6:30 to 10:30 pm) features lamb, roast beef, and ham or turkey accompanied by a simple salad bar for B$45, while a lighter buffet lunch (noon to 3 pm daily) costs B$28. The adjacent Ship Inn Bar has a pub menu, with chicken-and-mushroom pie or steak & chips for around B$25.

A couple of doors to the west is *McBride's Pub & Cookhouse* (☎ 435-6352). The decor is aimed at creating an Irish-pub look, but it's a popular dinner place as well, serving tasty Irish stew, steak-and-Guinness pie, or bangers & mash (B$25 to B$30). Dinner is served from 6 to 11 pm.

At the curve at the west end of the Gap, *Café Sol* (☎ 435-9531) has Mexican dishes from B$12. Next door is *Jambalaya's Restaurant & Rum Shop* (☎ 435-6581), serving creative dishes with clever names. Starters such as Spicy Isle Spinach & Plantain Rounds go for B$19, while curries are B$42 and steak or lamb B$48. Both places become rocking party spots as the evening progresses.

For something a little calmer, except for the waves crashing below, *B4 Blues* (☎ 435-6660) is a well-recommended bistro serving lunch and dinner. There are lots of shrimp options, all for B$46, and fresh fish for B$41. Moussaka or 'shepherdess pie' are B$35 to B$38. Two or three nights a week dinner is accompanied by live guitar or steel pan.

Top-End The top-end places are distinguishable not so much by their price as their preference for reservations and an atmosphere where you may be inclined to spend more by ordering wine and extra courses. While sometimes the prices look similar to the mid-range, they often don't include VAT, which is added on later.

Pisces (☎ 435-6564), at the west end of St Lawrence Coast Rd, is a popular open-air restaurant with candlelight dining to the tune of lapping waves. While the atmosphere is indeed special, the food is unremarkable for the money. Standard fish dishes or seafood fettucini average around B$50, while the menu tops off with lobster for B$76. It's open daily for dinner only, from 5:30pm.

David's Place (☎ 435-9755), on the main road just before you enter the Gap from Worthing, prepares Bajan dishes in an elegant style. Romantic waterfront seating is on a breadfruit fern-hung veranda with the lights of St Lawrence glittering in the near distance. Starters average B$25, while main dishes such as curried lamb or flying fish are about B$50.

Entertainment

There's always something happening in St Lawrence Gap, where several popular venues keep things hopping with live bands and DJs. Most have a cover charge, sometimes partially redeemable in drinks or food. The *Ship Inn* (see Places to Eat) is hottest on Tuesday and Saturday, but there's live music nightly. Nearby *After Dark*, a popular mingling place for locals and tourists, throbs until 6 am and is generally at its best on Friday and Saturday. Check out jazz and blues at *B4 Blues* Tuesday and Friday, or reggae in the earthy open-air setting of *Reggae Lounge*, where Tuesdays are Bajan nights featuring limbo, calypso, fire eating and free hors d'oeuvre. For just casual relaxing with a beer or rum punch, there's *Cool's Castaways*.

The *Plantation Garden Theatre* (☎ 428-5048), on Hwy 7, puts on a flamboyant costumed cabaret show with music, dancing and fire eating at 8 pm Wednesday and Friday.

BARBADOS

The show and drinks cost B$63/50/25 for adults/teens/children; with a buffet dinner at 6 pm and transportation it's B$150/100/50.

MAXWELL

Maxwell has two distinct but adjacent areas. Predominantly residential, Maxwell Rd (Hwy 7) has a few small businesses and a couple of the area's older hotels. Maxwell Coast Rd, which curves south from the highway, is the more touristed area, where resort hotels mingle with abandoned structures.

Maxwell is generally a quieter neighborhood than St Lawrence, but its beaches are equally appealing. There's little nightlife and few dining options, but most of the larger hotels offer meal plans. Depending on where you stay, St Lawrence is a 15- to 30-minute walk away, while the bus to Bridgetown takes roughly 20 minutes.

Places to Stay

The *Fairholme Hotel* (☎ 428-9425), set back 150m from Maxwell Rd, has simple, moderately priced accommodations and a small pool in the courtyard. Studios with cooking facilities, two single beds, private baths and a faded decor cost US$40 in summer, US$65 in winter; optional air-con costs US$3 per eight hours. A better value is the 11 fan-cooled rooms in the main house. These are quite basic but clean and cost US$26/28 for singles/doubles in summer, slightly higher in winter. The Fairholme is about five minutes on foot to the nearest beach or by bus to St Lawrence.

Antoine's Guest House (☎ 420-4463) has four bright studios with private bath and four rooms with shared bath, divided between a large old house and an annex. Singles/doubles are US$30/40 in summer, US$2 more in winter. There's a pleasant atmosphere, and Bajan specialties are served from a large, clean kitchen. It's accessible to beaches at Maxwell, Dover and Oistins.

The *Croton Inn* (☎ 428-7314, crotoninn@ barbadosnow.com), at the corner of the west entrance to Maxwell Coast Rd, has decent though unspectacular rooms and studios with private baths in a split-level house.

Singles/doubles are US$35/45 in summer, and studios are US$55; all are US$10 higher in winter. There's a bar-restaurant and a deck with a fish fry on weekends.

Windsurf Beach Hotel (☎ 420-5862, reservations@butterflybeach.com) is a casual seaside establishment catering to windsurfers. The 24 newly renovated rooms feature private baths and ceiling fans; some have kitchenettes. Rooms for two cost US$50 in summer, US$75 in winter; studios run US$60 in summer, US$85 in winter. Note that it often books solid with windsurfing tours, so availability can be somewhat hit-or-miss.

Sea Breeze Beach Hotel (☎ 428-2825, fax 428-2872, www.sea-breeze.com) is a pleasantly low-key beachfront resort with a couple of pools and restaurants. All 79 rooms have air-con, TV, refrigerators and coffeemakers, and many also have kitchenettes. Request an upper-level unit, as most have small balconies fronting the sea. Rates are US$115 in summer, US$185 in winter, including breakfast; add US$10 for a kitchenette unit.

The *Sand Acres Hotel* (☎ 428-7141, centralres@sunbeach.net) features a restaurant, bar, tennis courts, a pool and a lovely stretch of beachfront. It has 138 spacious contemporary studios with kitchenettes, ocean-view balconies, air-con, TV and phones. Rates are US$95 in May, June, September and October; US$240 from mid-December through March; and US$135 the rest of the year. There are larger one-bedroom apartments for about 25% more.

If you're staying in the area for a while, there are a handful of apartment-for-rent signs along the north end of Maxwell Coast Rd that might be worth checking.

Places to Eat

The *Croton Bar & Deli*, at the Croton Inn, serves a Continental breakfast from 6 am Monday to Saturday and Bajan and Guayanese pudding & souse on Saturday afternoon for B$5.

Mermaid Restaurant (☎ 428-4825), on the east end of Maxwell Coast Rd, has the atmosphere of an upmarket beach house and a splendid waterfront view. From 7 to 10 am there's a simple buffet breakfast of eggs, bacon, pancakes, juice and fruit for B$23. Tuesday night features a Bajan barbecue buffet (B$50), starting at 6:30 pm, with steel-band accompaniment. On other nights there's an à la carte menu with main dishes from B$35.

Gideon's Lobster Restaurant & Bar (☎ 428-5689), the only nonhotel restaurant on the coast road, is near the public beach access on the west curve of the road. It's an unpretentious, open-air place, open evenings only. The simple menu includes steamed shrimp for B$25, crab for B$30 and lobster for B$50, all served with Bajan rice and peas and salad.

The *minimart* about midway along the Maxwell Coast Rd is open 8 am to 8 pm and sells beer, rum and a few grocery and snack items.

OISTINS

The Barbados Charter, the document that provided the island with its first constitutional protections, was signed in Oistins in 1652. Today this decidedly local town, 2km east of Maxwell, is best known as the center of the island's fishing industry. Oistins' heart is the large, bustling seaside fish market, which on Friday and Saturday hosts the island's best party, with soca, reggae, pop and country music, vendors selling barbecued fish, and plenty of rum drinking. It's roughly 80% locals, 20% tourists, and makes a fun scene, whether you're out for partying or just getting a solid local meal at an honest price. The height of the action is between 10 pm and 2 am Friday and Saturday.

SILVER SANDS

At the southernmost tip of the island, between Oistins and the airport, is the breezy Silver Sands area, a mecca for windsurfers. In January and February everything fills up for the Windsurfing Championship. Even if you're not a windsurfer, it's worth coming out for a day to picnic on the tree-shaded dunes of the public beach. Most of the No 11 route taxis continue to Silver Sands from Oistins.

Places to Stay & Eat

In addition to the following listings, there are a number of private places in the Silver Sands area that can be rented by the week. Many windsurfers stay a night or two in a hotel and then through word of mouth find a shared house or apartment nearby.

Round Rock Apartments (☎ 428-7500, roundrck@caribsurf.com), just above the ocean but a two-minute walk from the beach, has seven self-catering units cost US$48 in summer, US$70 in winter for a studio and US$65 in summer, US$112 in winter for a two-bedroom apartment. A pleasant ocean-view restaurant serves a full breakfast for B$10.50 and hamburgers and tasty cutters for around B$5.

A bit farther down the road, *Ocean Bliss Apartments* (☎ 429-6334, kccp@caribsurf .com) has ocean-view studios for up to four people. All apartments have balconies and hammocks, plus there's a storeroom for surfboards and a laundry room, all for US$60 in summer, US$70 in winter.

Although it's not on the main windsurfing beach, a very appealing place is the suitably named *Peach and Quiet Hotel* (☎ 428-5682, fax 428-2467), which has 22 airy rooms with private baths and sea-view patios for US$79 in summer, US$99 in winter. Garden-view rooms are US$10 less. There's an oceanside and a restaurant, which offers a new menu every day and gladly caters to special diets.

The *Silver Sands Resort* (☎ 428-6001, silvsnd@sunbeach.net) is on a sandy beach and surrounded by casuarina trees. All 106 rooms have air-con, phones, radios and balconies; some have kitchenettes. There are two pools, two tennis courts, two restaurants and a Club Mistral windsurf shop. Rates begin at US$70 in summer, US$130 in winter.

The beachside *Silver Rock Hotel* (☎ 428-2866, silver@gemsbarbados.com) has 33 pleasant units, all with air-con, phones, TV and refrigerators, starting at US$95 in summer, US$130 in winter for a studio or US$130 in summer, US$200 in winter for a one-bedroom. There's a pool, a windsurf shop and a restaurant serving three meals a day.

BARBADOS

Southeast

St Philip, the diamond-shaped parish east of the airport, is sparsely populated, with a scattering of small villages. Along the coast are a couple of resort hotels, while inland, just north of Six Cross Roads, is one of the oldest and most interesting plantation houses on the island.

CRANE BEACH

Crane Beach, 7km northeast of the airport, is a broad swath of white sand backed by cliffs and fronted by aqua blue waters. Public access to the beach can be found along the side roads north of the Crane Beach Hotel.

The most spectacular view point is from the hotel, which sits high on a cliff at the south end of the beach. So scenic is the setting that the hotel has managed to turn itself into a bit of a tourist attraction, charging B$5 to tour the grounds. In most cases no one is there to collect before 9:30 am.

Places to Stay & Eat

The **Crane Beach Hotel** (☎ 423-6220, cranebeach@sunbeach.net) occupies an 18th-century mansion and has 18 spacious rooms and suites with mahogany furnishings, hardwood floors and bathrooms with tubs. Though they vary in size and decor, these accommodations are some of the most atmospheric on the island. Rooms cost US$90 in summer, US$160 in winter, and suites begin at US$175 in summer, US$250 in winter. The hotel's dining room has a fine view overlooking the beach. Sunday features a brunch buffet accompanied by a gospel choir for B$40.

SAM LORD'S CASTLE

Sam Lord's Castle, the centerpiece of a resort hotel of the same name, is a limestone mansion with an interesting, albeit much-embellished, history. The mansion was constructed on Long Bay in 1820 by Samuel Lord, who according to legend hung 'wrecker' lanterns off the point here to lure ships onto nearby Cobbler's Reef. After the ships, which thought they were entering a

safe harbor, crashed on the reef, Lord purportedly scurried out to pilfer the cargo. Although there's little doubt that Lord was a scoundrel, most historians discount the lantern story as folklore.

More of a stately residence than a castle, Lord's former home contains the hotel reception and a collection of antique furnishings and paintings. It's interesting enough, but not a major sight worth going out of your way. The hotel charges nonguests a B$15 fee to enter the grounds. If you want drinks or food, you'll need to buy a B$60 pass.

Places to Stay & Eat

A former Marriott affiliate, **Sam Lord's Castle** (☎ 423-7350, fax 423-5918) boasts 248 rooms. A handful of these are on the 2nd floor of the 'castle' and have a colonial decor, but the rest of the accommodations are more typical chain-hotel fare. The hotel beach has a broad stretch of white sand backed by coconut palms (the waters can be dangerous) as well as tennis courts, swimming pools and restaurants. Summer rates begin at US$175, winter rates start at US$245.

Outside the grounds, near the bus stop, **Pot and Barrel** has chicken, beef, lamb-stew or flying-fish lunch specials starting at B$15. It's a simple place, but linen napkins and water goblets give it a touch of elegance. The bus sits quite a while at the turning point, so there's plenty of time to finish your meal and mosey on over.

SUNBURY PLANTATION HOUSE

Sunbury Plantation House (☎ 423-6270) was built between 1660 and 1670 by an early Irish planter, Mathew Chapman. This handsome house changed hands once a century; the 1775 owners who hailed from Sunbury-on-Thames gave it its present name. In 1888 a Scottish planter purchased the property, and after his two unmarried daughters died in 1981, the house was separated from the plantation and sold at an auction. A fire swept through the house in 1995, closing down the property for more than a year and resulting in a major – and painstakingly faithful – restoration.

The house has 2-foot-thick walls built of local coral blocks and ballast stones, the latter from the ships that set sail from England to pick up Barbadian sugar. The interior retains its plantation-era ambience and is furnished in antiques, many made from Barbadian mahogany. In the area behind the house is a collection of horse-drawn carriages.

Tours, given by guides well versed in local history, are conducted 10 am to 4:30 pm daily (B$13.80 adults, B$6.90 children under 12). The plantation house has a pleasant little outdoor café at the rear of the main building. Offerings include English scones or sandwiches and a pot of tea for B$15. An elaborate period-style dinner is held twice weekly inside the house and includes a five-course meal, drinks and a house tour for B$150. Buses from Oistins can drop you at the gate.

West Coast

Barbados' west coast has lovely white-sand beaches and the majority of the island's luxury hotels. Most are in the parish of St James, which in colonial times was a popular holiday area for the upper crust of British society. Over the years their seaside estates have gradually been replaced by resort hotels, many of which continue to cater for the well-to-do.

Hwy 1, the two-lane road that runs north from Bridgetown to Speightstown, is bordered much of the way by a close mix of tourist facilities and residential areas.

PAYNES BAY

Fringed by a fine stretch of white sand, the gently curving Paynes Bay offers good swimming and snorkeling. Beach access walkways are clearly marked by roadside signs. The main public beach site at the southern end of the bay has picnic tables, restrooms and a laid-back local Friday-night fish fry. To locate sites in this section, see the Holetown & Around map.

Places to Stay

On a side road about 200m southeast of the Coconut Creek Hotel, the unpretentious

Angler Apartments (☎/fax 432-0817, gosain@ sunbeach.net) has 13 older but clean apartments facing an asphalt parking lot. One-bedroom units, each including a kitchen, living room, bedroom with either a queen or two twin beds, and a bathroom, cost US$65 in summer, US$87 in winter. Studios in an adjacent old plantation house are similar but lack the living room and cost US$57 in summer, US$82 in winter. Add breakfast for B$15. There's also a small patio bar and restaurant.

Coconut Creek Hotel (☎ 432-0803, fax 432-0272), a kilometer south of Paynes Bay, is a low-key, upscale resort on a private beach. It has 50 air-conditioned rooms in whitewashed Mediterranean-style buildings, as well as a pool and complimentary water sports. Singles/doubles begin at US$270/338 in summer, US$341/426 in winter, including breakfast and dinner.

The *Treasure Beach Hotel* (☎ 432-1346, treasure@caribsurf.com), right on the beach at Paynes Bay, is a personable place that books heavily with repeat guests. Its 30 rooms have typical high-end amenities and cost from US$195 in summer, US$485 in winter for either single or double occupancy. There's a pool and a pricey restaurant. North of Paynes Bay, the exclusive *Sandy Lane Resort and Golf Club* is being completely rebuilt. When it reopens it will feature a 36-hole golf course and some of the world's most expensive hotel rooms.

Places to Eat

For inexpensive local food, *Surfside Bakery*, north of the Esso station, serves a heaping lunch special from 11 am to 3 pm with chicken or fish, rice and salad for B$10. Be sure to sample their coconut turnovers and jam cakes. Next door is *Crocodile's Den* for a casual evening fish cutter to accompany a cold Banks and a game of pool. Some nights there's a live band.

Nico's (☎ 432-6386), on Hwy 1 across from the Coconut Creek Hotel, is a cozy garden-patio restaurant. At lunch, starters such as soup, veggie samosas or seafood salad average B$18, while lasagna, pies, or stuffed potatoes cost B$23. Dinner features fish and meat dishes with creative sauces for around B$40. There are beach access and sunset views at **Bomba's**, where you can also get light meals (about B$20) and drinks 11 am to 11 pm daily.

HOLETOWN

The first English settlers to Barbados landed at Holetown in 1627 aboard the *Olive Blossom*. An obelisk **monument** along the main road in the town center commemorates the event – although the date on the monument, which reads 'July 1605,' is off by two decades.

Despite being the oldest town on the island, Holetown is a rather bustling place that's more modern than traditional in appearance. **St James Church**, on Hwy 1 just north of the town center, stands on the site of the region's oldest church. The initial structure, built in 1628, was replaced by a more substantial version in 1690 and restored in the mid-19th century. A few vestiges of the original church remain, including a bell that was cast in the late seventeenth century and inscribed with the name of King William.

The coastal area north and south of Holetown is designated as the **Barbados Marine Reserve**, with four zones: a scientific zone, two water-sports zones and a recreational zone. These zones don't seem to govern the actual type of activity to be found, but are part of an overall coastal zone-management project.

At the north side of Holetown is **Folkestone Park**, a public park with a narrow beach on the edge of the Marine Reserve's scientific zone. It has reasonable surfing when the waves are up and snorkeling when it's calm. The park has a few picnic tables, a lifeguard, snorkel rentals, a cheap snack shack and usually a couple of clothing vendors. A modest **marine museum** is open 9 am to 5 pm weekdays, with displays on coral, shells, fishing and boat building (B$1.15 adults, B$0.58 children). However, if you're just looking for a nice beach for sunbathing and swimming, there are better ones in the area, including the strip that fronts the Inn on the Beach.

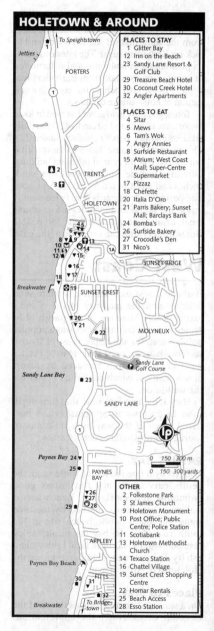

HOLETOWN & AROUND

PLACES TO STAY
1 Glitter Bay
12 Inn on the Beach
23 Sandy Lane Resort & Golf Club
29 Treasure Beach Hotel
30 Coconut Creek Hotel
32 Angler Apartments

PLACES TO EAT
4 Sitar
5 Mews
6 Tam's Wok
7 Angry Annies
8 Surfside Restaurant
15 Atrium; West Coast Mall; Super-Centre Supermarket
17 Pizzaz
18 Chefette
20 Italia D'Oro
21 Parris Bakery; Sunset Mall; Barclays Bank
24 Bomba's
26 Surfside Bakery
27 Crocodile's Den
31 Nico's

OTHER
2 Folkestone Park
3 St James Church
9 Holetown Monument
10 Post Office; Public Centre; Police Station
11 Scotiabank
13 Holetown Methodist Church
14 Texaco Station
16 Chattel Village
19 Sunset Crest Shopping Centre
22 Homar Rentals
25 Beach Access
28 Esso Station

Information

South of Holetown's civic center is a Scotiabank with an ATM that accepts debit cards on the Cirrus and Plus networks. Across the street is the West Coast Mall, with a large supermarket, CBIC bank, a travel agent and a Cave Shepherd. Next door is a Texaco gas station. Just south of the mall is the Chattel Village, a cluster of old-style houses filled with boutiques. The Sunset Crest Shopping Centre at the south side of town has a 99 Convenience store and a fruit stand; there's a Barclays Bank and a Cave Shepherd duty-free shop south of that.

Places to Stay

Homar Rentals (☎ 432-6750, fax 432-7229) in Sunset Crest handles four *apartment properties* on the inland side of the road about 500m from the beach. Each pleasant unit comes with a full kitchen or kitchenette and a separate bedroom with two twin beds. All of these complexes have pools. Rates start at US$65 in summer, US$90 in winter.

Inn on the Beach (☎ 432-0385, fax 432-2440), just south of the Scotiabank, is a quiet beachfront place near the center of Holetown. There are 20 pleasant air-conditioned studios, all with kitchens, dining areas, ocean-view balconies, phones and tubs. It also has a pool. Singles/doubles cost US$65/80 in summer, US$130/150 in winter.

Glitter Bay (☎ 422-4111, fax 422-1367) is a handsome 70-room luxury complex a kilometer north of Holetown. Accommodations are in three- and four-story Mediterranean-style buildings. Rooms have modern amenities and begin at US$259 in summer, US$529 in winter. Also featured are a large free-form pool and an attractive beach. The site, incidentally, was once the home of British tycoon Sir Edward Cunard, a member of the family that founded the Cunard cruise line.

Places to Eat

There's no shortage of places to eat in Holetown. In the parking lot by the 99 Convenience store, you can usually find a few vendors selling fruit and coconuts. Inside the West Coast Mall is the *Atrium* café, where an English breakfast or a lunch plate costs B$17.50. The Super-Centre supermarket, open 8 am to at least 8 pm Monday to Saturday, 9 am to 5 pm Sunday, has a deli selling bakery items, B$5 rotis and cheap barbecued chicken.

For the best deal, watch for vans or small station wagons selling rotis and food-piled plates at midday. They're often around construction sites such as at Sandy Lane, but can also be spotted near the Holetown public beach.

On the beach side of the road is a branch of the Bajan chain eatery *Chefette*, which has long hours and serves up everything from rotis and salads to chicken nuggets, burgers and thick shakes. For pizza, try the nearby *Pizzaz* – prices begin at B$16 for a small pie. They also serve a Bajan, Italian and Indian lunch buffet for B$14. You can pick up bread and inexpensive pastries at *Parris Bakery* and gourmet coffee at *Italia D'Oro*, both in the same complex as Barclays Bank.

For routine food with a memorable beachside view, *Surfside Restaurant* has lunchtime burgers, sandwiches and pastas for B$15 to B$20 and dinners for around $30. Sunday afternoon they host a beachside barbecue with live music.

If you're in the market for something more upscale, try any of several chic multiethnic restaurants along 1st and 2nd Sts in Holetown. Among the most recommendable are Austrian-run *Mews*, the popular *Angry Annies* for ribs, *Tam's Wok* for renowned Chinese food, or *Sitar* for spicy Indian food.

NORTH OF HOLETOWN
Mt Standfast

Mt Standfast is known for the hawksbill turtles that feed on sea grasses just off its shore. Most snorkeling tours make a stop here to offer fish to the turtles and allow customers to swim among them. Without a tour, the beach is accessible by the Blue Reef Dive Shop. The bus stops just beyond at the Lone Star Garage restaurant; you can park on the side street by the Adventist church. The Blue Reef can direct you toward the turtles as well as rent you snorkeling gear. If you come midday, when the tour boats bring lunch to the turtles, you'll be sure to see them. Right on the beach, *Lone Star Garage* opens at 7:30 am to serve classy meals for classy prices. Alternatively, there are three or four decent places up the road toward the village, including *Polly's Vegetarian Restaurant*, which serves good local curry, whole-wheat roti and other meatless treats for B$10 and under.

Mullins Beach

Mullins is a popular roadside beach along Hwy 1 between Holetown and Speightstown. The waters are usually calm and good for swimming and snorkeling. The landmark here is *Mullins Beach Bar & Restaurant*, a bustling watering hole with an open-air veranda right on the sand. Burgers, rotis and fish are served in addition to drinks, but it's not cheap.

SPEIGHTSTOWN

Now a shadow of its former self, Speightstown was a thriving port in the days when sugar was king. A main shipping line ran from Speightstown to Bristol, England, and trade was so extensive between the two areas that Speightstown was once dubbed 'Little Bristol.'

While the construction in 1996 of the luxury marina Port St Charles, just north of town, brought an influx of needed jobs and tourist dollars, Speightstown remains a decidedly Bajan town, its side streets thick with older wooden buildings sporting overhanging galleries. There's more of a genuine town feel here than anywhere else along the west coast, and the waterfront is worth a stroll – not for any particular sights, but to soak up the town's overall character.

Information

In the center of town, opposite the post office, is the Speightstown Mall, which has a fruit stand, a KFC and an ice cream shop, as well as a Barclays Bank. Wish 'N Wash Laundermat is in the complex in front of Jordan's Supermarket. You can wash clothes Monday through Saturday for B$5 and dry them for B$4; full service is B$3 more. There's credit-card-operated Internet access at Fisherman's Pub.

Places to Stay

If you're interested in staying in Speightstown, apartment and house rentals can be arranged at reasonable rates (from around US$40) through the amiable Clement 'Junior' Armstrong, who manages the Fisherman's Pub (☎/fax 422-3146, clemlau@ sunbeach.net).

On the main street north of the town center is the charming *Sunset Sands Apartments (438-1096, fax 438-1881)*, just across from the beach. Each of the four attractive air-conditioned suites costs US$85, but ask about discounts for extended stays. The upstairs apartments have stunning ocean views, and there's a secluded garden.

There are also two top-end resorts: the *Almond Beach Village (☎ 422-4900, vacation@iag.net)*, at the northern outskirts of town; and the exclusive *Cobblers Cove (☎ 422-2291, cobblers@caribsurf.com)*, to the south.

Places to Eat

Vegetable and fruit *vendors* can be found all along the main street. At the southern edge of the central area is Jordan's Supermarket.

Fisherman's Pub, on Queen St down by the waterfront, is a spirited, colorful place with inexpensive local food. Essentially an oversized beach shack, this is the town's most popular eating and drinking spot. You can get a good fish meal for around B$15. Around 7 pm Wednesday night, locals and visitors come for dinner and live steel pan for B$35. As the evening wears on, the scene gets more Bajan.

A fancier dinner option in the town center is *Mango's by the Sea (☎ 422-0704)*. Main dishes include mango chicken, seafood crêpes and fresh fish for around B$55. Shrimp-cocktail or smoked-salmon starters cost about half that.

Central & Eastern Barbados

From Bridgetown a series of highways fans out into the interior. Any one of these can make a nice drive, and scores of secondary roads add still more possibilities for exploration.

The most popular touring route, which takes in some of the finest scenery on Barbados as well as many of its leading attractions, starts along Hwy 2, running northeast from Bridgetown. As you reach the edge of the city you first pass Tyrol Cot Heritage Village. From there the suburbs soon give way to small villages, sugarcane fields and scrubby pastureland with grazing black belly sheep. About 10km out of the city one road leads to Welchman Hall Gully, Harrison's Cave and the Flower Forest. Hwy 2 continues through the hilly Scotland District and then turns westward, leading to a scenic loop drive that takes in the Morgan Lewis Sugar Mill, the vista at Cherry Tree Hill, St Nicholas Abbey, Farley Hill National Park and the Barbados Wildlife Reserve.

From there it's possible to head down the east coast to Bathsheba and return via Gun Hill Signal Station, with a detour to the Francia Plantation.

TYROL COT HERITAGE VILLAGE

Tyrol Cot (☎ 424-2074), on the edge of Bridgetown as you head out on Hwy 2, presents a traditional Bajan village centered on the former home of Sir Grantley Adams, first premier of Barbados, and of his son Tom Adams, second prime minister. The site is complete with chattel houses where artists work on their crafts, a working blacksmith and a slave hut. The stables have been converted into a restaurant, and sandwiches are available in a replica rum shop. Hours are 9 am to 5 pm weekdays. This recent addition to properties managed by the Barbados National Trust charges an admission of B$11.50 for adults, half price for children.

Tyrol Cot is the setting for the popular dinner show *1627 And All That,* a colorful dramatization of the island's history through music and folk dance. The show is held 6:30 to 10 pm Thursday and Sunday. It's all good fun, and the price of B$115 for adults, B$63 for children, includes the show, a Bajan dinner buffet, drinks, a house tour and transportation. For reservations call ☎ 428-1627.

WELCHMAN HALL GULLY

Welchman Hall Gully (☎ 438-6671), along Hwy 2 near the turnoff to Harrison's Cave, is a thickly wooded ravine with a walking track and nearly 200 species of tropical plants. Gullies like this were virtually the only places planters were unable to cultivate crops, and they thus represent an unspoiled slice of forest similar to the one that covered Barbados before the arrival of English settlers.

Geologically, this was once a part of the network of caverns that encompasses the nearby Harrison's Cave, but the caverns here collapsed eons ago, leaving an open gully. It's open 9 am to 5 pm Monday to Saturday (B$11.50 adults, B$5.75 children). Parking for Welchman's Gully is a few hundred meters north of the entrance. By public transport, take a 'Sturdges' minibus from the Cheapside station.

HARRISON'S CAVE

Harrison's Cave, just off Hwy 2, is a fascinating network of limestone caverns, with dripping stalactites, stalagmites and subterranean streams and waterfalls. A tram goes down into the cave, stopping en route to let passengers get out and closely examine some of the more impressive sites, including the Great Hall, a huge domed-shaped cavern, and Cascade Pool, an impressive body of crystal-clear water 50m beneath the cave entrance level. The air temperature inside the cave is 26°C (78°F).

The underground tram tour lasts about 35 minutes, but it's usually preceded by a short video, so the whole thing takes about an hour. At certain times of the day it can get very busy with tour groups; to avoid a wait, call ☎ 438-6640 for reservations. The first tour is at 9 am, the last at 4 pm. The cost is B$25 for adults, half price for children. A snack bar offers drinks and sandwiches.

FLOWER FOREST

Flower Forest, 3km north of Harrison's Cave, at the western edge of the Scotland District, is a 50-acre botanical garden at the site of a former sugar estate. Paths meander through the grounds, which are now planted with virtually every plant found on Barbados, including lots of flowering species. The gardens retain the estate's mature citrus and breadfruit trees, the latter having been introduced to Barbados from the South Pacific as an inexpensive food source for slaves.

Plaques display both the English and Latin names of flowers and trees, making this a particularly nice place to come if you want to identify flora you've seen around the island. The grounds also offer sweeping views of Chalky Mount and the Atlantic Ocean to the east and of Mt Hillaby, the island's highest point, to the west. Some of the paths are wheelchair accessible.

The Flower Forest is open 9 am to 5 pm daily (B$13.80 for adults, half price for children). A snack bar serves moderately priced sandwiches and other simple fare.

A Chalky Mount bus from the Fairchild bus terminal will take you there.

MORGAN LEWIS SUGAR MILL

Morgan Lewis Sugar Mill, at the side of the road 2km southeast of Cherry Tree Hill, claims to be the largest intact sugar windmill surviving in the Caribbean. The recently restored mill interior has a simple display of historic photos, a few artifacts of the plantation era and the original gears, shaft and grinding wheel. A stairway leads up around the works to the top, where you can get a bit of a view of the surrounding area. The mill is open 9 am to 5 pm weekdays (B$10 adults, B$5 children). If you don't mind a walk, you can get there on a St Andrews Church bus, which leaves hourly from the Jubilee terminal, or a Bathsheba bus from Speightstown. Tell the driver where you want to go; then it's about a 2km walk uphill.

CHERRY TREE HILL

Cherry Tree Hill, on the road that turns inland a kilometer north of Morgan Lewis Sugar Mill, offers a fine vista of much of the east coast. The best views are just beneath the summit at the roadside lookout next to the sugarcane fields. There's usually an elderly security guard there who is more than willing to spice up the view with a little local history.

A steep dirt track opposite the lookout leads to the top of the hill, but the view is largely blocked by trees. They are not cherry trees, incidentally; according to local lore, the cherry trees were chopped down long ago because passersby kept taking the fruit. You could continue your walk here from Morgan Lewis Mill, or take a Boscobelle-bound bus from Speightstown.

ST NICHOLAS ABBEY

St Nicholas Abbey, 750m west of Cherry Tree Hill, is one of the oldest plantation houses in the Caribbean. This unique Jacobean-style mansion with curly Dutch gables dates from the 1650s.

One of its early owners, Sir John Yeamans, led a 1663 expedition that colonized Carolina; he went on to become governor of that North American colony. For the last five generations the mansion has been in the family of Colonel Stephen Cave, who resides in the house and manages the surrounding plantation.

Visitors can tour the ground floor of the mansion, which has a fine collection of 19th-century Barbadian and English furnishings. One peculiar feature of the house is the inclusion of fireplaces, apparently the result of strict adherence to an English design that didn't give consideration to Barbados' tropical climate.

Until the 20th century, each plantation on Barbados had its own windmill for crushing cane. The remains of this plantation's mill (and the tower from the former syrup factory) can be seen below the house. These days, the sugarcane is hauled to the Portvale Sugar Factory, near Holetown.

St Nicholas Abbey is open 10 am to 3:30 pm weekdays (B$10). If you time your visit right you can also see a 15-minute film made in 1935 that shows some of the old sugar mills in action; it plays at 11:30 am and 2:30 pm. The same bus that goes to Cherry

Tree Hill will let you off about 15 minutes walking from the Abbey.

FARLEY HILL NATIONAL PARK

Farley Hill, off Hwy 2, is a pleasant hilltop park that would make a fine place to break out a picnic. The centerpiece of the park is the former mansion of Sir Graham Briggs, a wealthy 19th-century sugar baron whose guest list included the Duke of Edinburgh and King George V. In 1957, the stately Georgian-style mansion appeared in the movie *Island in the Sun,* starring Harry Belafonte. Eight years later, a fire swept through the mansion, completely gutting the interior and burning away the roof. Today only the hollow coral block walls still stand – a rather haunting site that nonetheless retains a measure of grandeur. Behind the mansion, a hilltop gazebo offers a fine view clear out to East Point Lighthouse at the eastern tip of the island.

Farley Hill is open 8:30 am to 6 pm daily (B$3 per car). You can get off the Bathsheba/Speightstown bus right at the entrance.

BARBADOS WILDLIFE RESERVE

The Barbados Wildlife Reserve, opposite Farley Hill, is a walk-through zoo with short paths that meander through a mahogany forest of scurrying green monkeys, sluggish red-footed turtles and a caiman pond. Other creatures that might be spotted in the reserve include brocket deer, iguanas and agoutis. There's also a small aviary with macaws and cockatoos, as well as some caged parrots and uncaged peacocks and pelicans. You'll also find an orchid display and an iguana sanctuary.

The free-roaming monkeys are the highlight. They are generally easy to spot, but if you want to stack the odds in your favor come around 3 pm, when feedings take place.

Green monkeys are for the most part brownish gray, with highlights of white fur, but flecks of yellow and olive green give them a greenish cast in some light, hence the name. On average, adult females weigh about 3kg, males about 5kg. There are also caged monkeys on the grounds.

The reserve is a project of the nonprofit Barbados Primate Research Center, which was established in 1985 with assistance from the Canadian International Development Agency. The center supports itself by supplying monkeys to laboratories in the USA and other countries for the production and testing of vaccines.

Adjacent to the reserve is the **Grenade Hall Forest & Signal Station**. Here you'll find a restored signal tower and a short loop

Green Monkeys

The green monkeys that inhabit Barbados were introduced as pets from West Africa some 350 years ago. The monkeys quickly found their way into the wild, where they fared well, free of any predators other than humans.

Today the island's monkey population is estimated at between 5000 and 7000. They are shy of people and live mainly in forested gullies, traveling in groups of about a dozen. Like most other primates, they are active from dawn to dusk and sleep at night.

Green monkeys are not rare or endangered either in Barbados or worldwide. Indeed, because monkeys have many of the same food preferences as humans, they are considered a pest by Barbadian farmers, who can lose as much as a third of their banana, mango and papaya crops to the monkeys.

Consequently, the government has long encouraged the hunting of monkeys. The first bounties were introduced in the late 1600s, with the princely sum of five shillings offered for each monkey head delivered to the parish church. In 1975 the Ministry of Agriculture introduced a new bounty of B$5 for each monkey tail received. After the Barbados Primate Research Center was founded in 1982, it began to offer a more enticing B$50 reward for each monkey captured alive and delivered unharmed to the center. As a result many farmers now trap, rather than shoot, the monkeys.

BARBADOS

trail through a shady forest of native trees, some identified by interpretive plaques.

The properties are jointly managed and open 10 am to 5 pm daily. Admission to both costs B$23 for adults, B$11.50 for children under 12.

Buses between Bathsheba and Speightstown pass by the entrance.

GUN HILL SIGNAL STATION

The 215m Gun Hill, off Hwy 3B in the center of the island, boasts a small hilltop signal tower and a clear view of the surrounding valleys and the southwest coast. The island was once connected by six such signal towers that used flags and lanterns to relay messages. The official function of the towers was to keep watch for approaching enemy ships, but they also served colonial authorities as a mechanism for signaling an alarm in the event of a slave revolt.

The Gun Hill tower, built in 1818, houses a couple of small displays of military artifacts and a pair of old cannons. The grounds are open 9 am to 5 pm Monday to Saturday (B$9.20 for adults, half price for children). Down the slope from the signal station is a British Regiment lion, carved from rock and painted white.

FRANCIA PLANTATION

Francia Plantation, on the side road just south of Gun Hill, is an elegant plantation house with an interior of rich woods, period furnishings and an interesting collection of antique maps and prints. On the grounds are pleasant formal gardens out back, and some surrounding fields of vegetable crops.

The plantation was built in the early 20th century and is still occupied by descendants of the original French owner. The narrow kilometer-long road into the plantation is lined with mahogany trees. Francia Plantation can be visited 10 am to 4 pm weekdays (B$10 for adults, half price for children under 12).

EAST COAST

The east coast has a predominantly rugged shoreline, turbulent seas and an unspoiled rural character. The East Coast Rd, which connects Hwy 2 with Bathsheba, is the only coastal road of any length on this side of the island.

Near the upper end of the East Coast Rd is **Barclays Park**, a public beach and picnic area donated to the government as an independence gift from Barclays Bank. Because of dangerous currents, the beach is best suited for picnicking and strolling about. **Bathsheba**, at the south end of the road, is the island's top surfing locale and has a picturesque coastline of high sea cliffs, untamed beaches and roaring Atlantic waters.

Chalky Mount, the white clay hills that rise inland of the East Coast Rd, are home to a couple of pottery shops. Visitors can view the operations and purchase items direct from the potters at reasonable prices. Access to Chalky Mount is from Hwy 2 near Haggatts.

From 1883 to 1937 a railroad ran from Bridgetown to Belleplaine, a town north of Bathsheba. Today the tracks are gone, but the rail bed remains between Belleplaine and St Martins Bay, making for fine coastal walking or hiking. A sign on the road by the Rail Road café (see Places to Eat), at the Bathsheba Public Beach, tells the history.

Places to Stay

If you're here for surfing, the place to stay is the *Bajan Surf Bungalow* (☎ 433-9920, *bsb@jorgen.com*), right in the center of Bathsheba. It's a laid-back, cozy place with four simple but bright rooms that share separate men's and women's baths. Breakfast is included with the per-person rate of US$25 in summer, US$35 in winter. When not surfing, hang out with the gang to watch videos, play games or work a jigsaw puzzle. Surfing gear is available for rent.

Atlantis Hotel (☎ 433-9445), at the south side of Bathsheba, has eight simple but adequate rooms, an interesting local flavor and agreeable prices. All rooms have private bath, and half have ocean-view balconies. Rates, including breakfast and dinner, are US$45/70 for singles/doubles in summer and US$50/75 in winter. Be sure to request a room with a view.

A nicer choice is the ***Sea-U! Guest House*** (☎ *433-9450, sea-u@caribsurf.com*) – a great place for peace and views. A balcony circles the upper level of the wooden house, affording views of the garden and sea. Studios with queen beds are US$80 in summer, US$110 in winter. Discounts are often available via the Internet. Breakfast and supper can be served in the garden.

Edgewater Inn (☎ *433-9900, reservations@ edgewaterinn.com, www.edgewaterinn.com*) has a fine cliffside setting overlooking the beach at the north side of Bathsheba. The inn has 20 modern and comfortable ocean-facing rooms, each with a sitting area, mahogany furnishings, a tub, a ceiling fan and a phone. Standard rooms cost US$75 in summer, US$95 in winter, while air-conditioned suites cost US$90 in summer, US$110 in winter. Continental breakfast is included in the rates, and there's a pool perched above the ocean plus satellite TV in the lobby.

Places to Eat

A beachside snack bar at Barclays Park serves lunch fare such as burgers and flying-fish sandwiches. At Bathsheba public beach, ***Rail Road Café*** and ***High Tide Café*** also provide inexpensive snacks and light meals. ***Bajan Surf Bungalow & Beach Grill*** has a good view of the surfers and very affordable prices. Cutters and sandwiches, best accompanied by fresh breadfruit chips, are all B$10 and under. Every evening there's a different dinner special (make reservations at ☎ 433-9920).

The most popular spot for food and views is ***Roundhouse Restaurant*** (☎ *433-9678*), in a nineteenth-century house perched high above the surf. Tempting starters such as baked rum nut brie lead into a variety of fish and meat dishes for around B$40. It's open for breakfast at 8 am, lunch from 11:30 am to 3 pm, and dinner from 6:30 pm.

ANDROMEDA BOTANIC GARDENS

Andromeda Botanic Gardens, off Hwy 3 at the top of the southern entrance to Bathsheba, was the private garden of the late Iris Bannochie, one of Barbados' foremost horticulturists. The gardens cover 6 acres and have a wide collection of introduced tropical plants, including orchids, ferns, water lilies, bougainvillea, cacti and palms. The property is managed by the Barbados National Trust and is open 9 am to 5 pm daily ($12 adults, B$6 children). Entry includes booklets that identify the plants on self-guided trails. Buses to and from Bathsheba stop just below the entrance.

BARBADOS

Dominica

Dominica, the 'Nature Island of the Caribbean,' promotes itself in tourist literature as a nontourist destination for divers, hikers and naturalists, and it offers some of the Caribbean's most spectacular scenery, both above and below the water. Despite a

Highlights

- Taking in unsurpassed mountain and rain-forest scenery
- Hiking throughout the isle, ranging from an easy walk to Emerald Pool to an unforgettable trek to Boiling Lake
- Diving at top-notch, unfrequented sites
- Enjoying scenic Roseau, with its colonial architecture and Creole food and culture
- Exploring Cabrits National Park, with fine views from the ruins of Fort Shirley

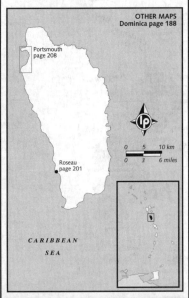

OTHER MAPS
Dominica page 188

Portsmouth
page 208

Roseau
page 201

0   5   10 km
0   3   6 miles

CARIBBEAN
SEA

growing number of cruise-ship visitors, many of the diving spots are still virgin and there's scarcely a soul on most of the trails. Hikes range from short walks to all-day treks and take in rain forests, waterfalls, rivers, lakes, bird sanctuaries, hot springs and other volcanic sites. Dominica's rugged peaks and deep river valleys are the first thing you'll notice when you arrive, but it's hard to really appreciate the scale until you get out in the middle of it all.

Dominica has beaches, but they are not exceptional and they're mostly of black sand. Because of this and the lack of direct flights from Europe or the US, the most popular way to see Dominica is as part of an island-hopping itinerary that also combines more traditional beach destinations.

What Dominica lacks in beaches and luxury resorts it more than makes up for in unspoiled rain forest, unique diving opportunities, vibrant live music and pride in its Creole heritage.

Facts about Dominica

HISTORY
The Caribs, who settled here in the 14th century, called the island Waitikubuli, which means 'tall is her body.' Christopher Columbus, with less poetic flair, named the island after the day of the week that he spotted it – a Sunday ('Doménica' in Italian) – which fell on November 3, 1493.

Daunted by fierce resistance from the Caribs and discouraged by the absence of gold, the Spanish took little interest in Dominica. France laid claim to the island in 1635 and a few years later sent a contingent of missionaries, who were driven off by the unwelcoming Caribs. In 1660 the French and English signed a neutrality treaty in which they agreed to allow the island to remain a possession of the Carib's.

DOMINICA

DOMINICA

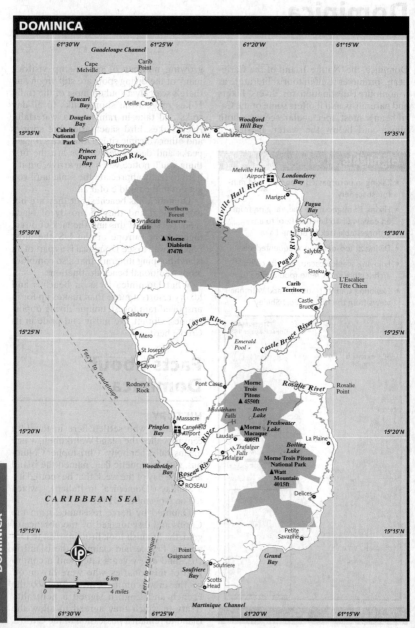

Nevertheless, by the end of the century, French settlers from the neighboring French West Indies began to establish coffee plantations on Dominica. In the 1720s France sent a governor and took formal possession of the island.

For the remainder of the 18th century, Dominica was caught up in the French and British skirmishes that marked the era, with the island changing hands between the two powers several times. In 1763, under the Treaty of Paris, the French reluctantly ceded the island to the British. The French made attempts to recapture Dominica in 1795 and again in 1805, when they burned much of Roseau to the ground.

After 1805 the island remained firmly in the possession of the British, who established sugar plantations on Dominica's more accessible slopes. The British administered the island as part of the Leeward Islands Federation until 1939, when it was transferred to the Windward Islands Federation. In 1967, Dominica gained autonomy in internal affairs as a West Indies Associated State, and on November 3, 1978 (the 485th anniversary of Columbus' 'discovery') Dominica became an independent republic within the Commonwealth.

The initial year of independence was a turbulent one. In June 1979 the island's first prime minister, Patrick John, was forced to resign after a series of corrupt schemes surfaced, including one clandestine land deal that attempted to transfer 15% of the island to US developers. In August 1979, Hurricane David, packing winds of 150mph, struck the island with devastating force, denuding vast tracts of forest, destroying the banana crops and wreaking havoc on much of Roseau. Overall, 42 people were killed and 75% of the islanders' homes were destroyed or severely damaged.

In July 1980 Mary Eugenia Charles was elected prime minister, the first woman in the Caribbean to hold the office. Within a year of her inauguration she survived two unsuccessful coups, including a bizarre attempt orchestrated by Patrick John that involved mercenaries recruited from the US-based Ku Klux Klan. In October 1983,

Massacre

Philip Warner, son of a 17th-century St Kitts governor, was responsible for a ruthless massacre of Carib Indians on Dominica in 1674, as well as for the murder of 'Indian' Warner, his half-brother.

Indian Warner, who had the same father as Philip but whose mother was a Dominican Carib, left his English upbringing on St Kitts to return to Dominica, where he became a Carib chief. Philip, leading a contingent of British troops intent on seeking vengeance for Carib raids on St Kitts, tricked his half-brother into meeting him on the west coast of Dominica in the village now known as Massacre, where Philip then ambushed Indian Warner along with his entire tribe.

as chairperson of the Organization of East Caribbean States, Prime Minister Charles endorsed the US invasion of Grenada and sent a symbolic force of Dominican troops to participate.

Lately, Dominica's politics have been turbulent and fractious, with former PM Edison James facing charges of corruption and embezzlement. But even in these unsettled times, no one was prepared for the news of the sudden death of Prime Minister Roosevelt Douglas on October 1, 2000, after only eight months in office. The passing of 'Rosie,' who was beloved by many in Dominica for his years of fighting for autonomy and working-class issues, has once again put Dominican politics up in the air.

GEOGRAPHY

Dominica is 29 miles long and 16 miles wide, and has a total land mass of 290 sq miles. It has the highest mountains in the Eastern Caribbean; the loftiest peak, Morne Diablotin, is 4747 feet high. The mountains, which act as a magnet for rain, serve as a water source for the hundreds of rivers that run down the lush green mountain valleys. En route to the coast many of the rivers

DOMINICA

Peaks & Valleys

It's said that when Christopher Columbus returned to Spain after his second voyage to the New World, King Ferdinand and Queen Isabella asked him to describe the island of Dominica. Columbus responded by crumpling up a piece of paper and tossing it, with all its sharp edges and folds, onto the table. That, he said, was Dominica.

Of course, Lonely Planet's *Mexico* guide has Cortés doing the same thing. Maybe this was a habit of conquistadores. Perhaps they were all drunk.

cascade over steep cliff faces, giving the island an abundance of waterfalls.

CLIMATE

In January the average high temperature is 85°F (29°C) while the low averages 68°F (20°C). In July the average high temperature is 90°F (32°C) while the low averages 72°F (22°C).

The driest months are February to June, with a mean relative humidity of around 65%. During the rest of the year the humidity is in the low 70s. In August, the wettest month, there's measurable rainfall for an average of 22 days, while April, the driest month, averages 10 days. All these statistics are for Roseau – the mountains are cooler and wetter.

FLORA & FAUNA

More than 160 bird species have been sighted on Dominica, giving it some of the most diverse bird life in the Eastern Caribbean. Of these, 59 species nest on the island, including two endemic and endangered parrot species.

Dominica's national bird, the Sisserou parrot *(Amazona imperialis),* also called the imperial parrot, is about 20 inches long when full grown, the largest of all Amazon parrots. It has a dark purple breast and belly and a green back.

The Jaco parrot *(A. arausiaca)* is somewhat smaller and greener overall, with bright splashes of varied colors. It is also called the red-necked parrot, for the fluff of red feathers commonly found at the throat.

The island has large crapaud frogs, small tree frogs, many lizards, 13 bat species, 55 butterfly species, boa constrictors that grow nearly 10 feet in length and four other types of snakes (none poisonous).

Dominica is well known for its vast rain forests, but the island also has montane thickets, dry scrub woodlands, evergreen forests, fumarole vegetation, cloud forests and elfin woodlands. The most abundant tree on the island is the gommier, a huge gum tree that's traditionally been used to make dugout canoes.

The most colorful of Dominica's endemic plants is its national flower, the bwa kwaib, or Carib tree. A deciduous shrub, it's found on the island's drier west coast. In spring, the bare branches of this shrub suddenly become thick with hundreds of scarlet flowers, adding a bright splash across the countryside.

GOVERNMENT & POLITICS

Dominica, an independent republic within the British Commonwealth, has a unicameral Assembly comprising 21 elected members and nine appointed senators. Members of the Assembly normally sit for five-year terms. The executive branch is headed by a prime minister who represents the majority party in the Assembly.

Tree frogs have it easy in Dominica.

In addition, there's a well-developed system of local government that includes town councils in Roseau and Portsmouth as well as 25 village councils around the island.

Dominica's already unsettled political situation became even more contentious following the sudden death of Prime Minister Douglas in 2000. Decades of political bad blood surfaced as the various parties struggled to fill the power vacuum.

In a bold and unexpected move, Dominica has applied for membership in the European Union, arguing that its position between Guadeloupe and Martinique, two overseas departments of France, entitles the island to the same economic opportunities and protections as its more affluent neighbors.

ECONOMY

Dominica's principal economic earnings are from agriculture. Bananas enjoyed a protected market in England until 1993, when the dismantling of all trade restrictions between Western European nations opened the English market to substantially cheaper Central American bananas. The result has been a steep drop in the export value of the Dominican crop. The government is encouraging farmers to diversify in hopes of reducing Dominica's economic dependency on bananas, which account for 75% of its agricultural production.

Coconuts are the other major agricultural commodity. The largest island employer, Dominica Coconut Products, uses most of the coconut crop to produce body soaps and oils. Spices, coffee and citrus fruits are also grown for export.

New cruise-ship facilities in Roseau and Prince Rupert Bay have resulted in a five-fold increase in cruise-ship arrivals, with some 300 cruise ships now pulling into port annually. Tourism on Dominica is otherwise still small-scale. Only about 90,000 overnight visitors come to the island each year. However, in a move that has some environmentalists worried, the government is making a concerted effort to boost those figures. Plans to expand the Melville Hall Airport runway to accommodate jet aircraft

and to triple the current number of hotel rooms are currently on hold, but they may be revived with the change in Dominica's government.

POPULATION & PEOPLE

Dominica's population is approximately 71,500; about a third live in and around Roseau.

While the majority of islanders are of African descent, about 3000 native Caribs also reside on Dominica, most of them on a 3700-acre reservation on the eastern side of the island.

ARTS

Dominica's most celebrated author, Jean Rhys, was born in Roseau in 1890. Although she moved to England at age 16 and made only one brief return visit to Dominica, much of her work draws upon her childhood experiences in the West Indies. Rhys touches lightly upon her life in Dominica in *Voyage in the Dark* (1934) and her autobiography *Smile Please* (1979). Her most famous work, *Wide Sargasso Sea,* a novel set mostly in Jamaica and an unmentioned Dominica, was made into a film in 1993.

SOCIETY & CONDUCT

Dominica draws on a mix of cultures: There are as many French place names as English; African language, foods and customs mingle with European traditions as part of the island's Creole culture; and the Caribs still carve dugout canoes, build houses on stilts and weave distinctive basketwork. Rastafarian and black pride influences, including dreadlocks and clothing in the Rasta colors of red, gold and green, are common on the island as well. Cricket and soccer are the most popular sports.

While people in Dominica are extremely proud of their island and heritage, they're also aware that they face economic and political challenges not shared with neighboring islands.

Dos & Don'ts

While a laid-back attitude prevails, and tourists will be granted an enormous

DOMINICA

amount of leeway, you should be aware that Dominicans place a lot of emphasis on politeness and appearance. A smile and a bit of respect will make all the difference in social interactions. Bathing suits are appropriate only on the beach, and topless or nude bathing is not acceptable unless you find a place where you're absolutely sure no one can see you.

RELIGION

The French have had a more lasting religious influence on Dominica than the British: Over 50% of the population is Roman Catholic. Other denominations include Anglican, Methodist, Pentecostal, Baptist, Seventh Day Adventist and Baha'i.

LANGUAGE

English is the national language, but a French-based patois is also widely spoken. Dominicans are experts at adjusting the degree of patois in their speech when talking with visitors, depending on whether or not they want their words to be understood.

Facts for the Visitor

ORIENTATION

Most of Dominica's attractions and places to stay are along the west coast or in the mountains just inland from the capital, Roseau.

Dominica has two airports: Canefield, a 10-minute drive from Roseau, and Melville Hall, on the secluded northeast side of the island. If you're planning to base yourself in Roseau, try to avoid Melville Hall Airport, as it's a good 75-minute haul to the capital.

This is a large island, but the primary roads are well paved and getting around is easy. With a reasonably early start, it's possible to drive up the west coast from Roseau to Portsmouth, explore Cabrits National Park, travel down the east coast through the Carib Territory and stop at the Emerald Pool on your way back across the island, all in a full-day outing.

Maps

The best map of the island is the detailed 1:50,000 British Ordnance Survey map, last published in 1991 and not easily available on Dominica. The tourist office in Roseau has a smaller but adequate Dominica Road Map for free.

TOURIST OFFICES
Local Tourist Offices

There are tourist information booths at each airport and at the Old Market in Roseau. When requesting information from overseas, address your mail to Division of Tourism (☎ 448-2045, fax 448-5840), National Development Corp, PO Box 293, Roseau, Commonwealth of Dominica, West Indies.

Tourist Offices Abroad

In Europe, obtain information from the Dominica Tourist Office (☎ 33-0153-42 41 00), 12 Rue de Madrid, Paris 7508, France. In the USA, you should contact the Dominica Tourist Office (☎ 212-949-1711, fax 212-949-1714), 800 Second Ave, Suite 1802, New York, NY 10017.

VISAS & DOCUMENTS

Most visitors to Dominica must have a valid passport, but US and Canadian citizens can enter with just proof of citizenship, such as a photo ID and an official birth certificate. French nationals may visit for up to two weeks with an official Carte d'Indentité. Only citizens of former Eastern Bloc countries require visas. A roundtrip or onward ticket is (in principle) required of all visitors to the island.

EMBASSIES & CONSULATES
Dominican Embassies & Consulates

UK
(☎ 020-7370 5194)1 Collingham Gardens, South Kensington, London SW5 0HW

USA
(☎ 202-332-6280)820 2nd Ave, Suite 900, New York, NY 10017

Shopping for local fabrics is one of the draws of St Lucia.

It's not widely known that lipstick designers try out their new colors on Dominican kayaks.

Spending some quality time, St Martin

It's best not to mess with a spotted cleaner shrimp.

Yellow barrel sponges, Dominica

Gray angelfish...or sullen corporate executive?

Extraterrestrial beings inhabit the Dominican waters.

School's in, Dominica

Foreign Embassies & Consulates in Dominica

Belgium
Consulate (☎ 448-3012)Hanover St 20, Roseau
China
Embassy (☎ 449-1385)PO Box 56, Roseau
UK
Consulate (☎ 448-7655)c/o Courts Dominica Ltd, PO Box 2269, Roseau

CUSTOMS
Visitors may bring in a liter of wine or spirits and 200 cigarettes.

MONEY
Dominica uses the Eastern Caribbean dollar (EC$). The bank exchange rate for US$1 is EC$2.68 for traveler's checks, EC$2.67 for cash. US dollars are widely accepted by shops, restaurants and taxi drivers, usually at an exchange rate of EC$2.60 or EC$2.65.

Most hotels, car rental agencies, dive shops, tour operators and top-end restaurants accept MasterCard, Visa and American Express credit cards.

POST & COMMUNICATIONS
Post
The main post office is in Roseau; there are small post offices in larger villages. All post-office (PO) boxes listed in this chapter are in Roseau; therefore, box numbers should be followed by 'Roseau, Commonwealth of Dominica, West Indies.' When there's no PO box, the address should include the recipient's town. The use of the word 'Commonwealth' on mail is important to prevent mail from being sent to the Dominican Republic by mistake.

Letters sent from Dominica cost EC$0.65 to the Caribbean; EC$0.90 to Europe, the UK or North America; and EC$1.20 to Australia, Africa and the Middle East. It costs EC$0.55 to mail a postcard anywhere in the world.

Telephone
Local numbers have seven digits. When calling from overseas, add the area code ☎ 767. For local directory information dial

☎ 118. For questions with international calls dial ☎ 0.

Dominica has both coin and card phones, commonly side by side. You can buy phone cards at telecommunications offices, the Roseau library and the Canefield Airport gift shop.

NEWSPAPERS & MAGAZINES
Dominica has two weekly newspapers: The *Chronicle,* published Friday, and the *Tropical Star,* published Wednesday.

RADIO & TV
There are four local radio stations, including the government-owned DBS (on 88.1 FM, 595 AM).

Cable TV has a mix of US network fare and local programming, including regional cricket matches. Channel 7 provides general information, exchange rates, a calendar of events and videos on island sightseeing and culture.

ELECTRICITY
Electricity is 220/240V, 50 cycles. Incidentally, 70% of the island's electricity is hydro generated.

WEIGHTS & MEASURES
Dominica follows the imperial system of measurements. Car odometers and speed limits are given in miles.

HEALTH
The Princess Margaret Hospital (☎ 448-2231) is in the Goodwill area at the north side of Roseau, off Federation Dr. See Regional Facts for the Visitor for information on travel health.

DANGERS & ANNOYANCES
While Dominica is generally a safe place, thefts are not unknown and you shouldn't leave any valuables unattended. Around Roseau and Portsmouth you can expect at least a few pestering hustlers to chat you up for change. On days when the cruise ships pull in this can mean polite but *constant* hassling. You'll also have to be firm at places

like Trafalgar Falls, where would-be guides try their utmost to attach themselves to you.

Roads on Dominica are narrow, and you'll need to be quite cautious when walking in trafficked areas. That holds doubly true for Roseau, where cars zip around at a fairly fast pace, with drivers expecting pedestrians always to grant them the right-of-way.

Frequent power outages in Roseau can make these safety concerns more serious, especially at night.

EMERGENCIES

For the police, fire brigade or ambulance, call ☎ 999.

BUSINESS HOURS

Though they vary a bit, typical business hours are 8 am to 1 pm and 2 to 4 pm weekdays. Most government offices stay open an extra hour on Monday, closing at 5 pm.

PUBLIC HOLIDAYS & SPECIAL EVENTS

Public holidays on Dominica include the following:

New Year's Day	January 1
Carnival Monday & Tuesday	two days preceding Ash Wednesday
Good Friday	late March/early April
Easter Monday	late March/early April
May Day	May 1
Whit Monday	eighth Monday after Easter
August Monday	first Monday in August
Independence Day	November 3
Community Service Day	November 4
Christmas Day	December 25
Boxing Day	December 26

Dominica's Carnival celebrations are held during the traditional Mardi Gras period. In the two weeks prior to Lent, there are calypso competitions, a Carnival Queen contest, jump-ups and a costume parade.

The week leading up to Independence Day (November 3) is packed with events.

Creole Day, a vibrant celebration of local heritage, includes parades, schoolkids in traditional outfits, special Creole menus and live music performed in restaurants, banks and grocery stores as well as on sidewalks all around Roseau.

The music continues on through the night at the World Creole Music Festival, usually held on the last weekend of October at Roseau's Festival City. Big-name performers from the Caribbean rock on into the night along with African *soukous* (dance music) Louisiana zydeco and a wide variety of local bands and dance groups.

Roseau is packed solid for Carnival and the week of Independence Day; make hotel reservations in advance or you'll find yourself sleeping well out of town.

ACTIVITIES

In response to the growing numbers of cruise-ship passengers, the government of Dominica instituted user fees for all foreign visitors entering ecotourist sites. These include national parks and other protected areas.

The cost is US$2 per site, US$5 for a day pass or US$10 for a weekly pass, and the proceeds go to conservation efforts and maintenance of the park system. Passes are sold by car rental agencies, tour operators, cruise-ship personnel and the forestry department, as well as at all of the major sites, including Indian River, Boiling Lake, Cabrits National Park and Emerald Pool.

Beaches & Swimming

While Dominica doesn't have the sort of gorgeous strands that make it onto brochure covers, it's not without beaches. On the calmer and more popular west coast, they're predominantly black-sand beaches, with the best of the lot in the Portsmouth area.

The east coast is largely open seas with high surf and turbulent water conditions. There are a few pockets of golden sands just south of Calibishie that are sometimes calm enough for swimming and snorkeling, and a couple of roadside brown-sand beaches a bit farther south.

Diving

Dominica has superb diving. The island's rugged scenery continues under the water, where it forms sheer drop-offs, volcanic arches, pinnacles and caves.

Many of Dominica's top dive sites are in the Soufriere Bay area. Scotts Head Drop-Off is a shallow coral ledge that drops off abruptly more than 150 feet, revealing a wall of huge tube sponges and soft corals. Just west of Scotts Head is The Pinnacle, which starts a few feet below the surface and drops down to a series of walls, arches and caves that are rife with stingrays, snappers, barracudas and parrotfish.

Calmer waters more suitable for snorkelers and amateur divers can be found at another undersea mound, the Soufriere Pinnacle, which rises 160 feet from the floor of the bay to within five feet of the surface and offers a wide range of corals and fish. Also popular for snorkelers and beginners is Champagne, a subaquatic hot spring off Pointe Guignard, where crystal bubbles rise from underwater vents.

The north side of the island still has lots of unexplored territory. Popular sites north of Roseau include Castaways Reef, Grande Savane, Rodney's Rock, Toucari Bay and the wrecks of a barge and tugboat off Canefield.

For much more information, pick up a copy of Lonely Planet's Pisces guide *Diving & Snorkeling Dominica,* with detailed descriptions of 41 top dive sites and advice on when and where to jump in.

Note that by law, all dives (shore and boat) in Dominica must be accompanied by a government-registered, licensed divemaster.

Dive Shops Dive shops on Dominica include the following:

Anchorage Dive Center (☎ 448-2638, fax 448-5680, anchorage@mailtod.dm) PO Box 34, at Anchorage Hotel in Castle Comfort

Dive Castaways (☎ 449-6244, fax 449-6246) PO Box 5, at Castaways Beach Hotel in Mero, on the west coast

Dive Dominica (☎ 448-2188, fax 448-6088, in the USA ☎ 888-262-6611, dive@tod.dm) PO Box 63, at Castle Comfort Lodge, just south of Roseau; it's the island's oldest dive shop

East Carib Dive (☎/fax 449-6575, in the USA ☎ 800-867-4764) PO Box 375, on a black-sand beach 1½ miles north of Castaways Beach Hotel; it's run by a divemaster from Germany

Nature Island Dive (☎ 449-8181, fax 449-8182), based in Soufriere, just minutes from many of the island's best dive spots

The going rate is about US$50 for a one-tank dive or a night dive and US$70 for a two-tank dive. Anchorage offers beginners a resort course with an ocean dive for US$80. A number of the shops offer full PADI certification courses for around US$400.

In addition, Dive Dominica, Nature Island Dive and Anchorage have one-week packages that include accommodations and multiple dives.

Snorkeling

There's good snorkeling in the Soufriere Bay area and at Cabrits National Park. All the dive shops listed in the previous diving section offer snorkeling tours or will take snorkelers out with divers. If you're tagging along with divers, make sure they're doing a shallow dive – staring down at a wreck 50 feet underwater isn't terribly interesting from the surface.

Anchorage Dive Center has a snorkeling trip to Champagne (see the Diving section), and Nature Island Dive offers a snorkeling tour of two sites in Soufriere Bay; both charge US$25, snorkeling gear included.

For those who want to strike out on their own, Anchorage rents snorkeling gear for US$10 a day, Nature Island Dive for US$15.

Kayaking

Nature Island Dive (☎ 449-8181), in Soufriere, rents sea kayaks for US$11 an hour, US$26 a half day or US$42 a day. You can paddle around Soufriere Bay or take an excursion up the coastline, where there are snorkeling sites that can't be reached by land.

Kayak rentals are also available, for EC$20 per hour, just of north of Portsmouth, where you can check out Cabrits National Park and Douglas Bay, with excellent snorkeling spots.

DOMINICA

Whale Watching

Whales and dolphins roam the deep waters off Dominica's sheltered west coast. Sperm whales, which grow to a length of 70 feet and have a blunt, square snout, are the whales most commonly sighted; the main season is October to March. Other resident toothed whales are the orca, pygmy sperm whale, pygmy killer whale, false killer whale and pilot whale. In winter, migrating humpback whales are occasionally spotted as well.

Anchorage Dive Centers (π 448-2638) and Dive Dominica (π 448-2188) run whale-watching boat tours from around 2 pm to sunset a few times a week. Anchorage charges US$40, Dive Dominica, US$50.

Fishing

Deep-sea fishing for marlin, tuna and wahoo aboard a 32-foot sport cruiser is offered by Rainbow Sportfishing (π/fax 448-8650, rollei@tod.dm). The cost per boat, with a maximum of six people, is US$400 for five hours, gear included.

Hiking

Dominica has some excellent hiking. Short walks lead to Emerald Pool and Trafalgar Falls, two of the island's most visited sights. Cabrits National Park has a couple of short hikes. In the Northern Forest Reserve, there's an easy hike through a parrot reserve and a rugged trail to the top of the island's highest mountain. The Morne Trois Pitons National Park offers serious treks into the wilderness, ranging from jaunts through verdant jungles to an all-day trek across a steaming volcanic valley that ends at a boiling lake.

The short hikes to the more popular destinations can generally be done on your own, but most wilderness treks require a guide who's familiar with the route.

Dominica's Forestry Division publishes brochures on many of the trails; each can be purchased for a dollar or so at the forestry headquarters in Roseau's botanical garden.

Individual hikes are described in relevant sections throughout this chapter.

Mountain Biking

Nature Island Dive (π 449-8181), in Soufriere, rents out mountain bikes for US$11 an hour, US$21 a half day, US$32 a full day, helmets and water bottles included. You can explore old estate trails and the nearby sulfur springs; the staff can recommend longer outings for serious bikers. Nature Island also leads guided biking trips, with per-person rates of US$55 (with six people) to US$84 (with two people).

ACCOMMODATIONS

Dominica has only about 750 rooms available for visitors, mainly in small, locally run hotels and guest houses along the west side of the island. There are also three mountain lodges (Papillote, Roxy's and Springfield) just west of Morne Trois Pitons National Park that can make delightful places to stay for those who want to be on the edge of the rain forest.

Budget accommodations are comprised largely of guest houses in the US$25 to US$50 range. The middle range, about US$60 to US$85, also includes some good values, but even the top-end hotels are reasonably priced by Caribbean standards, averaging US$100 to US$125.

The sperm whale – still running from Ahab

Dominica has a 5% room tax, and the more expensive hotels also add a 10% service charge to bills.

FOOD

Dominica's national dish is the mountain chicken, which is not a chicken at all but rather the legs of a giant frog called the crapaud *(Leptodactylus fallax),* which is endemic to Dominica and Montserrat. Found at higher elevations, it's a protected species and can only be caught between autumn and February. Crapaud meat is white and tastes like chicken.

Creole food is quite prevalent on restaurant menus. Be sure to try callaloo soup. Although no two recipes are identical, on Dominica it's invariably a flavorful, creamy concoction.

Roadside stands and small-town restaurants typically serve fried chicken, fish & chips and tasty bakes along with cold drinks.

The island produces numerous fresh fruits, including bananas, coconuts, papayas, guavas, pineapples and mangoes, the latter so plentiful they commonly drop along the roadside.

DRINKS

Rivers flowing down from the mountains provide Dominica with an abundant supply of pure, fresh drinking water. Though tap water is generally safe, most visitors stick with bottled water. Fresh-fruit juices are inexpensive and readily available at most restaurants. You can also find good punch drinks made from fresh fruit and local rum.

Dominica brews its own beer under the Kubuli label; you'll see red-and-white signs all over the island with Kubuli's concise slogan, 'The Beer We Drink.'

SHOPPING

Dominica produces high-quality baskets using native fibers and traditional Carib designs. Prices are surprisingly moderate, and the baskets can be purchased at roadside stands in the Carib Territory or at handicraft shops in Roseau. The handicraft shops also sell woven place mats, hats, pocketbooks and Creole dolls.

Supermarkets around the island carry locally made food items, such as hot pepper sauce, guava jelly and Dominican coffee, as well as island-made coconut-oil soap, shampoo and skin creams, all of which make good, inexpensive souvenirs.

Getting There & Away

DEPARTURE TAX

Visitors ages 12 and older who have stayed more than 24 hours must pay an EC$45 (or a US$17) departure tax when leaving Dominica.

AIR

There are no direct flights available from Europe or the US into Dominica, so overseas visitors must first get to a gateway island. There are direct flights to Dominica from Antigua, Barbados, Guadeloupe, Martinique, Puerto Rico, St Lucia and St Martin.

Airports & Airlines

Dominica has two airports: Canefield Airport, just outside Roseau, and Melville Hall Airport, on the secluded northeast side of the island. On LIAT's printed schedule, the letters C and M after the departure time indicate which airport is being used.

For island hoppers, LIAT has numerous through fares that allow free stopovers on Dominica, including one from Antigua to Martinique for US$133/220 one-way/roundtrip. Otherwise, a regular ticket to Dominica from Antigua costs US$90/170, from Martinique US$82/120 and from St Lucia US$83/150. Roundtrip fares allow stays of up to 30 days. There are flights to both Canefield and Melville Hall Airports. LIAT's ticketing office (☎ 448-2421) is on King George V St in Roseau.

Air Guadeloupe flies to Canefield Airport from Guadeloupe daily. Fares are competitive with LIAT. In Dominica, bookings are handled by Whitchurch Travel (☎ 448-2181), on Old St, Roseau.

DOMINICA

American Eagle (☎ 448-0628) has a daily flight between San Juan, Puerto Rico, and Melville Hall Airport with a US$240 one-way fare and a US$422 regular roundtrip fare, both without any advance purchase required.

Canefield Airport There's a tourist information booth open 7 am to 6 pm daily (closed 11 am to 2 pm weekends), a small gift shop that sells phone cards, a snack bar, restrooms and coin, card and USA Direct phones. Avis has a booth here, and Budget and Valley car rentals have courtesy phones. If you plan on renting a car, it's usually quicker to get your local license at airport immigration even though you may have to wait until incoming passengers are cleared.

Melville Hall Airport Sitting in the midst of the countryside, this airport looks all but abandoned except at flight time. There's a gift shop, a snack bar, a tourist information booth, restrooms and coin and card phones.

SEA
Ferry
L'Express des Iles connects Dominica with both Guadeloupe and Martinique via modern catamarans that seat about 300 passengers. This is a convenient way to arrive in Dominica, as it leaves you right in the center of Roseau, within walking distance of hotels and guest houses.

On its southbound run, a boat leaves Pointe-à-Pitre, Guadeloupe, at 8 am Monday, Wednesday and Saturday, at noon on Friday and at 2 pm on Sunday, arriving in Roseau 1¾ hours later. It then departs Roseau at 10:15 am Monday, Wednesday and Saturday, at 2:15 pm Friday and at 4:15 pm Sunday, arriving in Fort-de-France, Martinique, 1½ hours later.

Northbound, a boat leaves Martinique for Dominica at 2 pm Monday and Wednesday, 3 pm Tuesday and Friday, 9 am Saturday and 3:30 pm Sunday. This boat then continues from Dominica to Guadeloupe at 4 pm Monday and Wednesday, 5 pm Tuesday and Friday, 11 am Saturday and 5:30 pm Sunday.

These schedules change frequently; it's important to confirm departure times a couple days in advance to avoid getting stranded on the island.

The cost in French francs is 305F one-way to Dominica from either Martinique or Guadeloupe, but it's only 10F more to make the one-way trip between Martinique and Guadeloupe with a free stopover on Dominica. From either Martinique or Guadeloupe, the roundtrip fare to Dominica will run you 450F.

From Dominica, the fares are paid in Eastern Caribbean dollars; the one-way fare is EC$104 to Guadeloupe and EC$122 to Martinique.

At 2:15 pm Friday the boat can be taken from Dominica to Castries, St Lucia, and at 7 am Saturday and 1 pm Sunday it can be taken from Castries to Dominica. The St Lucia–Dominica trip takes 3½ hours and costs EC$157 one-way; roundtrip fares are double.

There are discounts of 50% for children ages two to 11 and 10% for passengers under 26 or older than 60. Reservations are made on Dominica through Whitchurch Travel (☎ 448-2181), on Old St, Roseau. For information in Martinique call ☎ 63 12 11, in Guadeloupe ☎ 83 12 45 and in St Lucia ☎ 452-2211.

Yacht
Yachts can clear immigration and customs at Roseau, Portsmouth or Anse Du Mé and get a coastal permit that allows visits at other ports and anchorages along the coast. Mooring in Soufriere Bay, a marine reserve, is not permitted.

Cruise Ship
A growing number of cruise ships call on Dominica, most docking at the new terminal in the center of Roseau.

In hopes of encouraging cruise-ship visitors to spend more time in the northern part of the island, a smaller cruise-ship berth was opened at Cabrits National Park, a scenic setting and the site of historic Fort Shirley (see that section, later in this chapter, for more details on the park).

Getting Around

Dominica is a visitor-friendly island. Road signs mark most towns and villages, and major intersections are clearly signposted.

Primary roads are usually narrow but in good shape – most are well paved and pothole-free. Secondary roads vary; some of the interior mountain roads are steep, narrow and in bad repair. Be careful of deep rain gutters that run along the side of many roads – a slip into one could easily bring any car to a grinding halt.

TO/FROM THE AIRPORT

Avis is the only car rental agency at Canefield Airport, but other agencies will provide customers with free airport pickup. Taxis are readily available, but if you're traveling light you could also walk out to the road and catch a bus into town.

From Melville Hall Airport, there are no car rentals, so visitors must take a shared taxi, even if they intend to rent a car during their stay.

BUS

Buses, which are mostly minivans, run regularly along the coastal routes between Roseau and both Scotts Head and Portsmouth, although the farther north you go past Canefield the less frequent they become.

It's fairly easy to catch a bus in the morning, from around 8 to 10 am, and again from 2 to 3 pm when schools let out and you'll find yourself sandwiched in with uniformed youngsters. Evening buses are few, and there's no Sunday bus service along most routes.

In Roseau you can catch buses heading south for Scotts Head (EC$3) from the Old Market. The same bus will drop you in the Castle Comfort area for EC$1. Buses heading to Canefield (EC$1.50), the Carib Territory (EC$7) and Portsmouth (EC$7.50) leave from the east side of the Roseau River near the public market. Buses to Trafalgar (EC$2.25) and Laudat (EC$3) leave from the north side of the police station.

CAR
Road Rules

Dominicans drive on the left-hand side of the road. Visiting drivers must be between ages 25 and 65 and have a valid driver's license and at least two years' driving experience to drive in Dominica. In addition, a local driver's license (EC$30) is required, which can be picked up from immigration at either airport any day of the week. Licenses can also be obtained at the Traffic Department, High St, Roseau. Hours are 8:30 am to 1 pm and 2 to 3 pm weekdays (to 4 pm Monday). However, when there's a line (and they move slowly!) the office door is commonly shut 10 to 15 minutes before closing time. As a courtesy, car rental agencies will usually pick you up and take you to get your license.

There are gas stations in larger towns around the island, including Canefield, Portsmouth and Marigot.

Rental

Avis (☎ 448-2481) is the only car rental company right at Canefield Airport; it also has an office at 4 High St in Roseau. Daily rates begin at US$48.

Budget (☎ 449-2080), in the village of Canefield, has a courtesy phone at the airport, provides free pickup and has relatively attractive rates, beginning at US$35.

There are many other car rental agencies on the island. Those in Roseau include Courtesy Car Rental (☎ 448-7763), Wide Range Car Rentals (☎ 448-2198) and STL Rent-A-Car (☎ 448-2340). Valley Rent-A-Car conveniently has offices in both Roseau (☎ 448-3233) and Portsmouth (☎ 445-5252).

Note that although most car rentals include unlimited mileage, a few local companies cap the number of free miles before a surcharge is added, so be sure to inquire in advance.

In addition to rental fees, most companies charge US$6 to US$8 a day for an optional collision damage waiver (CDW), though even with the CDW you may still be responsible for the first US$600 or so in damages.

TAXI

From Canefield Airport, the fares for one taxi (up to four people) are EC$20 to Roseau, EC$25 to the Castle Comfort area, EC$65 to Scotts Head, EC$75 to the Layou area and EC$110 to Portsmouth.

At Melville Airport, there's usually an agent who meets arriving passengers and arranges shared taxis. This is a completely legitimate and free service as (per-person) taxi rates are fixed: EC$42 to Roseau, EC$44 to Castle Comfort and EC$30 to Portsmouth.

HITCHHIKING

Hitchhiking is quite popular among islanders. While some travelers just walk out into the street and attempt to wave drivers down, the most acceptable stance is merely to stand at the side of the road and hold out an open hand. The usual safety precautions apply.

ORGANIZED TOURS

There are a number of small companies that provide standard sightseeing tours, wilderness hiking tours or both.

Raffoul Luxury Tours (☎ 448-2895), across from the cruise-ship dock in Roseau, offers a variety of bus tours, including a half-day outing that takes in Trafalgar Falls, Emerald Pool and Roseau's botanical gardens for US$20 and a six-hour round-the-island tour for US$48.

For other vehicle tours you might try Mally's Tour and Taxi Service (☎ 448-3114) or Whitchurch Travel (☎ 448-2181), and for hiking tours, Ken's Hinterland Adventure Tours (☎ 448-4850) or Antours Dominica (☎ 448-2317).

Hiking guides can also be arranged through many hotels and guest houses and in Laudat village, where the hikes begin. Hagan Dorival, who can be contacted at ☎ 448-4861 or through Ma Bass Central Guest House (see Places to Stay in Roseau), has been leading hikes for years and does a great job.

Most taxis can be hired for sightseeing tours at a rate of EC$45 per hour for up to four people.

Roseau

Roseau (pronounced 'rose-oh') is a colorful West Indian capital, its streets lined with old stone-and-wood buildings. Some are strikingly picturesque, with jalousied windows, gingerbread trim and overhanging balconies, while others are little more than weathered shells leaning precariously out over sidewalks. Many of the buildings are two-story structures with shops below and living quarters above. There are a growing number of modern cement structures too, but for the most part walking Roseau's quieter backstreets feels like stepping back a hundred years.

While Roseau is one of the region's poorer capitals, it's not one of the grimmer ones. Shopkeepers wash down the sidewalks every morning, police walk their beats with a rhythmic stride and most people are quite friendly.

Roseau's waterfront, which was severely damaged by Hurricane David, has undergone an ambitious reclamation and now boasts a cruise-ship dock and a promenade with a good view of Scotts Head to the south. A particularly scenic vantage is from the balcony of the new museum.

Information

Tourist Offices The tourist office, at the west side of the Old Market, is open 8 am to 1 pm and 2 to 4 pm weekdays (to 5 pm Monday) and 8 am to noon Saturday.

Money There are several banks in Roseau. Barclays Bank, on Old St, is open 8 am to 3 pm Monday to Thursday, 8 am to 5 pm Friday. The Royal Bank of Canada, on the waterfront near the Old Market, has the same business hours, but also has a 24-hour ATM that accepts credit cards and Cirrus and Plus bank cards.

Post & Communications The post office, on Mary E Charles Blvd, is open 8 am to 4 pm Tuesday to Friday, till 5 pm Monday.

You can buy phone cards, make calls, send faxes and check email at the Dominica

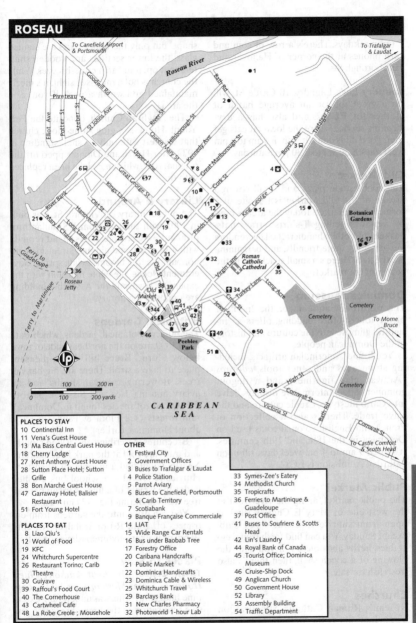

ROSEAU

To Canefield Airport & Portsmouth

To Trafalgar & Laudat

Roseau River

Goodwill Rd

Piveteau St

Elliot Ave

Potter Ave

Streber St

St Johns Ave

Bath Rd

Trafalgar Rd

River St

Hillsborough St

Queen Mary St

Kennedy Ave

Great Marlborough St

Boyd's Ave

Upper Lane

Great George St

Cork St

King George V St

Kings Lane

Old St

Hanover St

Long Lane

Mary E Charles Blvd

River Bank

Fields Lane

Botanical Gardens

Virgin Lane

Roman Catholic Cathedral

Turkey Lane

Long Acre

Ferry to Guadeloupe

Roseau Jetty

Cross St

Jewel St

Cemetery

Old Market

Church St

Castle St

To Morne Bruce

Ferry to Martinique

Peebles Park

High St

Cemetery

To Castle Comfort & Scotts Head

CARIBBEAN SEA

Cornwall St

Victoria St

Bath Rd

Cornwall St

Traffic Department

0   100   200 m
0   100   200 yards

PLACES TO STAY
10 Continental Inn
11 Vena's Guest House
13 Ma Bass Central Guest House
18 Cherry Lodge
27 Kent Anthony Guest House
28 Sutton Place Hotel; Sutton Grille
38 Bon Marché Guest House
47 Garraway Hotel; Balisier Restaurant
51 Fort Young Hotel

PLACES TO EAT
8 Liao Qiu's
12 World of Food
19 KFC
24 Whitchurch Supercentre
26 Restaurant Torino; Carib Theatre
30 Guiyave
39 Raffoul's Food Court
40 The Cornerhouse
43 Cartwheel Cafe
48 La Robe Creole ; Mousehole

OTHER
1 Festival City
2 Government Offices
3 Buses to Trafalgar & Laudat
4 Police Station
5 Parrot Aviary
6 Buses to Canefield, Portsmouth & Carib Territory
7 Scotiabank
9 Banque Française Commerciale
14 LIAT
15 Wide Range Car Rentals
16 Bus under Baobab Tree
17 Forestry Office
20 Caribana Handcrafts
21 Public Market
22 Dominica Handicrafts
23 Dominica Cable & Wireless
25 Whitchurch Travel
29 Barclays Bank
31 New Charles Pharmacy
32 Photoworld 1-hour Lab
33 Symes-Zee's Eatery
34 Methodist Church
35 Tropicrafts
36 Ferries to Martinique & Guadeloupe
37 Post Office
41 Buses to Soufriere & Scotts Head
42 Lin's Laundry
44 Royal Bank of Canada
45 Tourist Office; Dominica Museum
46 Cruise-Ship Dock
49 Anglican Church
50 Government House
52 Library
53 Assembly Building
54 Traffic Department

DOMINICA

Cable & Wireless office on the corner of Hillsborough and Old Sts; it's open 8 am to 7 pm weekdays. There's a row of coin and card phones at the corner of Hanover and Hillsborough Sts.

Laundry Lin's Laundry, 10 Castle St, will do a great job on an average batch of clothes for EC$12, and also has a dry-cleaning service where the local fat cats get their good duds done. It's open 8 am to 6 pm weekdays, 8:30 am to 3:30 pm Saturday.

Old Market
The cobblestone plaza and small covered arcade of the Old Market is the site of a former slave market. Today the area is used by vendors selling T-shirts, straw hats, baskets and other handicrafts. The vendors are generally quite friendly, and bargaining is expected. There's a small snack bar in the center of the market.

Dominica Museum
This worthwhile museum, on the 2nd floor of the tourist-office building, offers an insightful glimpse into the culture and history of the Dominican people.

You'll find Amerindian artifacts, including stone axes and other tools, *adornos* (Arawak clay figurines) and a dugout gommier canoe. Informative displays delve into Carib lifestyles, Creole culture and the slave trade. There's also a collection of French and English colonial coins used on Dominica in the 18th and 19th centuries. It's open 9 am to 4 pm weekdays, till noon Saturday. Admission is EC$2.

Public Market
The public market, along the riverfront at the west end of Mary E Charles Blvd, is open from sunrise to about 4 pm daily except Sunday. You can find fresh fruit, vegetables, herbs and spices – if you hear the blowing of a conch shell, then there's also fresh fish for sale.

Churches
Roseau's Roman Catholic cathedral, on Virgin Lane above the Methodist Church, is an old stone edifice with an expansive interior. The windows are of typical Gothic shape, but only the upper parts are stained glass; the lower sections are wooden shutters that open to catch cross-breezes. While the church is not a must-see sight, it's nicely maintained and worth a peek if you're in the area.

The Anglican Church, opposite the Fort Young Hotel, is a gray stone-block church that was left with only its shell standing in 1979 after Hurricane David ripped off the original roof, which has since been replaced with tin.

Library & Around
The public library, on Victoria St, was built in 1905 with funding from US philanthropist Andrew Carnegie. It has an old veranda with a sea view and a grand streetside cannonball tree that blooms in late spring. **Government House**, the white mansion with the expansive lawn, and the **Assembly building** are opposite the library.

Botanical Gardens
The 40-acre botanical gardens, which date from 1890, are on the northeast side of town below Morne Bruce hill. It's a pleasant place to take a stroll. There are big banyan trees, flowering tropical shrubs and an aviary housing Jaco and Sisserou parrots, the two parrot species found in Dominica's rain forests (see Flora & Fauna in Facts about Dominica, earlier).

Brochures describing the island's parks and trails are sold at the park headquarters. Nearby you'll find a monument of sorts to Hurricane David – a school bus crushed under the weight of a huge African baobab tree that fell during the 1979 hurricane.

You can drive into the gardens from entrances off Bath Rd or Trafalgar Rd until 10 pm or walk in anytime. Admission is free.

Places to Stay
Town Center The *Kent Anthony Guest House* (3 Great Marlborough St), a long-time budget favorite, was undergoing extensive renovation at the time of research and should be worth a look.

Vena's Guest House (☎ 448-3286, 48 Cork St) occupies the site of author Jean Rhys' birthplace and gets a lot of return visitors, but the rooms aren't much. Singles/doubles begin at US$21/27 for a room with bath, and there's a popular restaurant attached.

Bon Marché Guest House (☎ 488-2083, 11 Old St) is a small guest house not far from the waterfront. The four rooms have foam mattresses, portable fans and private baths. There's a shared kitchen and living room with cable TV. Overall, it's a good value for the price range, with singles/doubles costing US$21/37. The office is in the store below the guest house. On Sunday and after 5 pm other days you can reach the owners at ☎ 448-4194.

Ma Bass Central Guest House (☎ 448-2999, 44 Fields Lane) is Roseau's best guest house. The house's friendly owner, Theresa Emanuel (better known as Ma Bass), keeps the place spotlessly clean and goes out of her way to make guests feel at home. There are eight fan-cooled singles/doubles that cost US$25/35 with shared bath, US$45/50 with private bath. This centrally located three-story building rises above its neighbors and has a balcony with a good view of the town.

Cherry Lodge (☎ 448-2366, 20 Kennedy Ave), a small, central place run by a friendly local family, occupies an amazing colonial wooden building, though the rooms are quite simple and can be noisy. Some rooms have balconies and a private shower and toilet. Singles/doubles cost US$25/38 (less in the off-season), and there's a common room with TV and veranda.

Continental Inn (☎ 448-2214, fax 448-7022, 37 Queen Mary St) has a dozen rooms, most quite small and straightforward, but it's clean and ranks as one of the more comfortable of Roseau's budget accommodations. Some rooms have just beds and a fan, others sport TV and air-con as well. Rooms with private bath start at US$50/63. Credit cards are accepted. There's also a small, inexpensive restaurant. Reservations are recommended, as the hotel is often full.

Sutton Place Hotel (☎ 449-8700, fax 448-3045, sutton2@tod.dm, PO Box 2333, 25 Old St) is a classy new boutique-style hotel in the town center. The five standard rooms have ceiling fans, air-con, cable TV, phones and hair dryers and cost US$75 for singles or doubles. The three suites also have antique furnishings, hardwood floors and kitchenettes and cost US$105/135. Continental breakfast is included in the rates.

The modern *Garraway Hotel* (☎ 449-8800, fax 449-8807, in the USA ☎ 800-223-6510, garraway@tod.dm, PO Box 789), a business-style hotel at the east end of the bayfront, has Roseau's cushiest rooms. All 31 rooms are spacious with ocean views and full amenities, including fans, air-con, cable TV, phone, one king or two double beds, and bathrooms with tubs. Choicest are the top-floor units, which have a natural wood decor. Singles or doubles start at US$88. Commodious suites, which have the addition of a pullout couch, range from US$115 to US$155.

Fort Young Hotel (☎ 448-5000, fax 448-5006, in the USA ☎ 800-223-6510, PO Box 519, www.fortyounghotel.com), on Victoria St, is a few minutes south of the town center. This tourist-class hotel incorporates the walls of the 18th-century Fort Young, which once guarded the eastern flank of the capital. While they're not the spiffiest in town, the 33 rooms have hardwood floors, tiled baths, screened louvered windows, ceiling fans, air-con, cable TV and phone. Deluxe rooms, which are on the 2nd floor, also have private ocean-view balconies and cathedral ceilings. Year-round, standard rooms are US$95, superior rooms US$125. Deluxe oceanfront rooms are from US$155 to US$230.

Around Castle Comfort The following hotels are all on a rocky shoreline in the Castle Comfort area, about a mile south of Roseau.

At the *Anchorage Hotel* (☎ 448-2638, fax 448-5680, in the USA ☎ 800-328-5336, anchorage@mailtod.dm, PO Box 34), the 32 pleasant rooms come with air-con, cable TV, phone and private balconies. Standard singles/doubles have one double and one single bed and cost US$60/85 in summer,

US$80/95 in winter. Superior rooms, which are larger, have two double beds and ocean views, cost US$80/95 in summer, US$95/110 in winter. Add US$15 more for a third person. There's a small pool, a squash court, a restaurant and a dive shop.

Evergreen Hotel (☎ 448-3288, fax 448-6800, PO Box 309) is an appealing 16-room hotel with a tropical atmosphere. The buildings incorporate native woods and stonework, and the rooms are comfortable, each with air-con, cable TV, phone and screened windows. The 2nd-floor rooms in the new wing have wonderful oceanfront balconies. Single/double rates, which include breakfast, are US$85/110 for standard rooms and US$95/125 for ocean-view rooms. A third person is US$30 more. There's a big, comfy restaurant with a great view, a bar and a small pool.

Castle Comfort Lodge (☎ 448-2188, fax 448-6088, in the USA ☎ 888-262-6611, dive@tod.dm, PO Box 2253) caters mostly to divers on dive packages. The 15 simple rooms vary in size and amenities, but all have air-con and ceiling fans, and some have TVs. Rates are US$110/125, with breakfast included.

Sea World Guesthouse (☎ 448-5068), a little closer to Roseau, has seven simple rooms in a new bright yellow building. It's a nice, clean place with singles or doubles for US$47 and a cozy restaurant facing the rocky beach.

Places to Eat
Budget & Mid-Range
The ***Mousehole*** (3 Victoria St), downstairs from La Robe Creole (see Places to Eat – Top End), has inexpensive rotis, meat pies, sandwiches and pastries. You can get a nice slab of banana bread for EC$1.25 and a large glass of fresh, creamy papaya or guava juice for EC$3.50. While most people order takeout, there's also a small counter where you can chow down. It's open 8 am to 9 pm Monday to Saturday.

The nicest place to relax and grab a bite in Roseau is ***The Cornerhouse*** (6 King George V St), with a small library, a wrap-around terrace and Internet access for EC$3 per 15 minutes. It draws a mixed crowd of locals and expats chatting over salads, sandwiches (EC$10 to EC$14) and nightly Creole specials. The kitchen stays open late (around midnight) most nights.

Cartwheel Cafe, on Mary E Charles Blvd, is a pleasant little eatery in a historic waterfront building with thick stone walls. The menu, which includes standard breakfast items and lunchtime sandwiches, is priced around EC$5 to EC$10. It's open 8 am to 2:30 pm weekdays.

Guiyave (15 Cork St), has dining on a pleasant 2nd-floor balcony. Breakfast, from 8 to 11:30 am, includes French toast and egg dishes, served with juice or coffee, for EC$12 to EC$21. From noon to 2:30 pm, sandwiches and burgers cost EC$5 to EC$12, goat and chicken meals around EC$20. On Saturday, local dishes such as rotis, goat water and souse are available. If you want value over atmosphere, there's a downstairs bakery/cafeteria with reasonably priced though rather average quiches and pastries, as well as EC$14 plate lunches. It's closed Sunday.

Restaurant Torino, on Old St in the center of town upstairs from the Carib Theatre, serves up fresh salads and Italian dishes, including homemade pastas with a choice of sauce (EC$20), lasagna or eggplant parmigiana (EC$25). It's a the best place in town to carbo-load before or after a big hike, with friendly service, a nice terrace overlooking downtown, and a fancy espresso machine whipping up the island's best cappuccino (EC$5). It's open 8 am to 2:30 pm and 6 to 9:30 pm; no credit cards are accepted.

Liao Qiu's (☎ 448-1921, 72 Queen Mary St), is a small, tidy Chinese restaurant that's open till 11 pm daily. From 11 am to 3 pm there are lunch specials for EC$10 to EC$15. Otherwise, vegetarian dishes cost EC$15 and a range of chicken, pork or seafood dishes are not cheap at EC$20 to EC$38. You can also call ahead for takeout.

World of Food (48 Cork St), an open-air courtyard restaurant connected to Vena's Guest House, is a popular spot for an after-work drink. Sandwiches cost around EC$5, and rabbit or goat meals are EC$20 at both lunch and dinner.

KFC, on Great George St, is open to 11 pm daily, after most places in town are long closed.

Raffoul's Food Court *(13 King George V St)*, is essentially a bread outlet but also sells inexpensive sandwiches 8:30 am to 4 pm weekdays.

There are a number of grocery stores around town, the largest being **Whitchurch Supercentre**, on Old St, which has a deli with cooked chicken, sliced meats and bakery products. It's open 8 am to 7 pm Monday to Thursday, till 8 pm Friday and Saturday. The **public market** is the place to get fruit and vegetables.

Top End The **Sutton Grille** *(25 Old St)*, at the Sutton Place Hotel, has a nice, historic atmosphere. Between 7 and 10 am you can get a breakfast of juice, coffee and a croissant for EC$13. At lunchtime, 11:30 am to 3 pm, a grilled-chicken or tuna filet sandwich costs EC$10; the 'business lunch buffet' of chicken, fish, red meat, salad, rice and local vegetables is EC$25. At dinner the specialty is steak, with prices jumping up to EC$75.

La Robe Creole *(3 Victoria St)* is a cool and cozy stone-walled pub serving breakfasts for EC$15, a lunch buffet for EC$20 and dinner options up to EC$60 for lobster balls (no, *you* ask them). The bar has an extensive wine selection and provides a marvelous spot to catch up on local gossip. It's open from noon to about 10 pm Monday to Saturday.

The restaurant of **Fort Young Hotel** (see Places to Stay) incorporates the stone wall of the fort, though it's a bit too hall-like to make for an intimate dining experience. It has typical breakfast fare for around EC$20, a daily three-course lunch for EC$35 and main courses at dinner for around EC$40. It's also one of the only places on the island where you'll want to dress up for dinner.

Balisier Restaurant, on the 2nd floor of the Garraway Hotel (see Places to Stay), has a great view of Scotts Head. A breakfast of coconut bread, muffin, coffee and juice costs EC$9, full breakfasts about double that. At lunch and dinner, curried goat, ginger pork and seafood main dishes average EC$50. From 12:30 to 2:30 pm Friday there's a special EC$45 buffet lunch.

In the Castle Comfort area, **Evergreen Hotel** has a pleasant seaside terrace dining room. Breakfast and lunch has the usual fare at moderate prices. A full soup-to-dessert dinner costs EC$50 to EC$60, depending on the main course, including fish, chicken and a changing third option. The restaurant at the nearby **Anchorage Hotel** has a vegetarian dinner plate for EC$30 and goat casserole or fresh fish for EC$50.

Entertainment & Shopping

Friday is a big night for entertainment in Roseau: **Fort Young Hotel** has a happy hour 6 to 8 pm and live steel-pan music 7 to 9:30 pm. On Thursday **Symes-Zee's Eatery**, on King George V Street, has a live jazz jam session with talented local musicians.

Carib Theatre, on Old St, has a mixed billing of Hollywood and kung fu flicks. Other entertainment is largely limited to a sunset drink at one of the hotel bars.

At Tropicrafts, at the east end of Queen Mary St in Roseau, you can watch women weaving huge floor mats of *verti-vert*, a native strawlike grass. Tropicrafts sells a wide range of souvenir items, but you can often find cheaper prices at two smaller gift shops in the center of Roseau, Dominica Handicrafts, on Hanover St, and Caribana Handcrafts, on Cork St.

Around Dominica

MORNE BRUCE

Morne Bruce is a rather exclusive hillside suburb that's southeast of Roseau. It has a couple of places to stay, but most people who venture up this way do so for the panoramic hilltop view of Roseau and its surroundings.

One way to get to the view point is to drive up and park below the president's office. You can also hike there from the botanical gardens; the trail begins just east of the parrot aviary and takes about 15 minutes to walk.

Places to Stay

With a view of Roseau and Scotts Head, *Itassi Cottages* (☎ 448-7247, fax 448-3045, PO Box 1333) is in an exclusive hillside neighborhood. These cottages, which have cooking facilities, phone and TV, cost US$60 for one or two people, US$90 for three or four and US$110 for five or six. There's also a studio unit that costs US$40 for one or two people. The manager prefers to rent out the units on a weekly basis (US$380 for one or two people, US$570 for three or four), but accepts daily rentals when they're not full.

Reigate Hall Hotel (☎ 448-4031, fax 448-4034) is in the Reigate area on a hill above Morne Bruce. It has the character of a small mountain inn and a superb view of Roseau a mile below. The 17 rooms are rather simply appointed, but they are modern and have air-con and private balconies. Single rooms, which are quite small, cost US$75, while doubles cost US$95 and larger, more comfortable suites cost US$120 to US$150. There's a small pool, a sauna and a tennis court. The Reigate Hall Hotel is at the very end of a rather tortuous one-lane road.

CANEFIELD AREA

Canefield, a 10-minute drive north of Roseau, is half suburbia, half industrial, and the site of the main interisland airport. While Canefield isn't much of a tourist area, there are a few places to stay, and because it's on a main bus route, getting into Roseau is fairly easy without a car.

Pringles Bay, just south of the airport, is a popular swimming spot for local residents despite being in an industrial setting with a commercial loading dock nearby. There are a couple of wrecks that can be dived in the area: a tugboat in about 65 feet of water near the river mouth and a barge about 10 feet below the surface at the side of a reef.

Half a mile south of the airport, you'll see the **Old Mill Cultural Centre**, an attractive stone building with gears from the old mill rusting on its grounds. Although the center doesn't have regular visitor hours, it occasionally opens for special functions.

Places to Stay & Eat

The *Nello Inn* (☎ 449-1840), on the main road about a five-minute walk south of the airport, has four straightforward singles/doubles with air-con, fans and shared bath for US$35/50. There's a little shop selling simple snacks and drinks downstairs. The owners maintain a strict no-smoking policy.

Springfield Plantation Guest House (☎ 449-1401, fax 449-2160, springfield@ tod.dm, PO Box 456) is a winding 10-minute drive inland from Canefield. This scenic former plantation is now used to house visiting scientists studying tropical ecosystems and as a center for nature tourism. The old plantation house is a bit weathered but quite atmospheric, and it has large rooms with hardwood floors, eclectic furnishings, a smattering of antiques and grand veranda views. Rates begin at US$45 in low season, US$55 in high season. Breakfast and dinner can be included for an additional US$25 per person.

Springfield Plantation also has a few one- and two-bedroom apartments in an adjacent annex. These vary in size and have a mountain cabin decor, but they are quite adequate, have cooking facilities, phone, shower and private veranda, and they cost US$65.

LAYOU RIVER AREA

The Layou River, Dominica's longest, empties into the sea just south of St Joseph, at the center of the west coast. The river basin is a peaceful rural area, with bamboo leaning over the riverbanks and banana and coconut trees at the side of the road. When it's not running strong, the river is a popular place for freshwater swimming.

St Joseph, a simple fishing village of 2600 people, rises up the slope from a small black-sand beach, but the area's best beach is farther north at the Castaways Beach Hotel in Mero. There's good swimming in front of Castaways and fair snorkeling along the rock formations at the southern end of its beach – with a little luck you might even spot stingrays or octopuses.

Just north of Mero, on the inland side of the coastal road, is the **Macoucherie Rum Distillery**. The distillery crushes sugarcane grown in the surrounding fields using an old-fashioned waterwheel. There are no formal tours, but you can view the operation 7 am to 3 pm weekdays. This rum is very popular on Dominica, with some islanders claiming it has aphrodisiac qualities.

The coastal road continues north along the leeward side of Dominica's highest mountain range, an effective rain screen that makes this region one of the driest on the island.

Places to Stay

The *Layou River Hotel* (☎ 449-6281, fax 449-6713, PO Box 8) has a pleasant waterside setting on the north side of the Layou River, 1¼ miles inland from the coastal road. The 34 air-conditioned rooms each have a bath, phone and either a double bed or two twin beds. Singles/doubles/triples cost US$50/60/70.

Sunset Bay Club (☎ 446-6522, fax 446-6523, sunset@cwdom.dm), about a mile north of the town of Salisbury, is a snazzy new hotel with a garden setting on a small, clean stretch of beach. Rooms start at US$93/127/150 for singles/doubles/triples, and there's a pool, sauna and restaurant.

Castaways Beach Hotel (☎ 449-6244, fax 449-6246, castaways@mail-tod-dom.dm, PO Box 5) is an inviting place on a long, attractive gray-sand beach fronted by calm waters. There are 26 rooms in two wings. Those in the south wing have one double bed, while those in the north wing have two single beds and are a bit bigger. All are pleasant enough and have ceiling fans, a shower, a phone and oceanfront balconies. Singles/doubles cost US$82/110. There's a dive operation on-site, a small dock and a tennis court.

Places to Eat

The restaurant at *Castaways Beach Hotel* has a gorgeous open-air setting overlooking the water and makes a nice place to stop for

breakfast on your way north. Haitian, Creole and Continental breakfasts cost EC$18 to EC$24. In the evening the bar fills up with divers swapping stories about the day's adventures.

Four Seasons, at the Sunset Bay Club, catches the sea breezes and has Creole fare at moderate prices along with European cuisine at European prices.

NORTHERN FOREST RESERVE

The Northern Forest Reserve is an extensive area that encompasses 22,000 acres of land in the interior of the island, including 4747-foot Morne Diablotin, the island's highest peak. The main habitat of Dominica's two endangered parrot species is in the eastern section of the reserve.

To get to the reserve, turn east on the signposted road that begins just north of the village of Dublanc and continue to the Syndicate Estate, about 4½ miles inland. There you'll find an easy mile-long loop trail (Syndicate Trail) to a parrot observatory platform, as well as the start of the trail leading up Morne Diablotin, a rugged hike that's best done with a guide (see Organized Tours in Getting Around, earlier in this chapter). The best times for sighting parrots are in the early morning and late afternoon, when the birds are most active; local guides say the parrots like to hang out where oranges grow.

PORTSMOUTH

Dominica's second-largest town (pronounced 'ports-mowth') sits on the banks of Prince Rupert Bay. Columbus entered the bay during his fourth voyage to the New World in 1504, and three decades later the Spanish established a supply station here for their galleons. It was visited by 16th-century buccaneers Sir Francis Drake and his rival John Hawkins, as well as by Prince Rupert of the Rhine.

In 1607, Captain John Smith and his followers stopped for a couple of days before heading north to establish Jamestown, North America's first permanent English settlement. Indeed, the harbor was so important to the British that they intended to

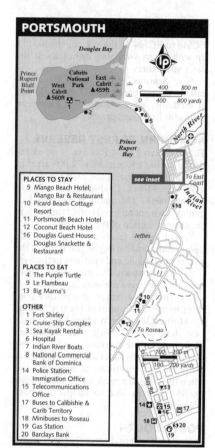

PORTSMOUTH

Douglas Bay

Prince Rupert Bluff Point

Cabrits National Park

East Cabrit ▲459ft

West Cabrit ▲560ft

0   400   800 m
0   400   800 yards

North River

Prince Rupert Bay

see inset

To East Coast

Indian River

Jetties

To Roseau

0   100   200 m
0   100   200 yards

Bay Rd

PLACES TO STAY
5   Mango Beach Hotel;
    Mango Bar & Restaurant
10 Picard Beach Cottage
    Resort
11 Portsmouth Beach Hotel
12 Coconut Beach Hotel
16 Douglas Guest House;
    Douglas Snackette &
    Restaurant

PLACES TO EAT
4   The Purple Turtle
9   Le Flambeau
13 Big Mama's

OTHER
1   Fort Shirley
2   Cruise-Ship Complex
3   Sea Kayak Rentals
6   Hospital
7   Indian River Boats
8   National Commercial
    Bank of Dominica
14 Police Station;
    Immigration Office
15 Telecommunications
    Office
17 Buses to Calibishie &
    Carib Territory
18 Minibuses to Roseau
19 Gas Station
20 Barclays Bank

make Portsmouth the island's capital, until outbreaks of malaria and yellow fever thwarted the plan.

Cabrits National Park, on the north side of town, and Indian River, to the south, are the area's noteworthy attractions. The town center doesn't have any sights per se, but by day it's a pleasant, laid-back Caribbean town. At night, however, Portsmouth shows its seamier side, and visitors can expect some drunken harassment.

Douglas Bay, a couple of miles north of Portsmouth, also has a black-sand beach and decent snorkeling. A good paved road leads to Douglas Bay, but the area remains a bit of a backwater well off the tourist track.

Information

The police and immigration office is on Bay Rd, which is the main road that runs through the center of town. The National Commercial Bank of Dominica is south of the small parking lot where you can pick up the bus to Roseau. You'll find a Barclays Bank on the road to the east coast.

Indian River

Just south of town you can expect to be met by a handful of rowers ready and willing to take you on a boat ride up the Indian River. The boats wind up the shady river through tall swamp bloodwood trees, whose buttressed trunks rise out of the shallows, their roots stretching out laterally along the riverbanks. It can be a fascinating outing, taking you into an otherwise inaccessible habitat and offering a close-up view of the creatures that live at the water's edge.

Though almost everyone you meet in Portsmouth will offer to be your guide, you'll get a lot more from the trip if you go with one of the boaters who work with the Park Service. The rowers, who set up shop along the coastal road at the river mouth, charge EC$25 per person for a tour that takes about 1½ hours, usually with a stop for drinks at the jungle-hut bar.

Cabrits National Park

Cabrits National Park, on a scenic peninsula 1¼ miles north of Portsmouth, is best known as the site of Fort Shirley. In addition to the peninsula, the park encompasses the surrounding coastal area as well as the island's largest swamp. The Cabrits Peninsula, formed by two extinct volcanoes, separates Prince Rupert Bay from Douglas Bay. The coral reefs and waters of the latter are also part of the park.

While the British built a small battery on Cabrits in 1765, it wasn't until 1774 that they began constructing the main elements of Fort Shirley. In 1778 the French captured the island and continued work on the fort. Between the vying powers, a formidable

DOMINICA

garrison was built. France's effort proved to be counterproductive, as Dominica was returned to the British under the 1783 Treaty of Paris and the fort was subsequently used to repel French attacks.

Fort Shirley had more than 50 major structures, including seven gun batteries, quarters for as many as 600 officers and soldiers, numerous storehouses and a hospital. Following the cessation of hostilities between the British and French, the fort gradually slipped into disrepair, and in 1854 it was abandoned.

Today, Cabrits is a fun place to explore. Some of the stone ruins have been cleared and partially reconstructed, while others remain half hidden in the jungle. The powder magazine to the right of the fort entrance has been turned into a small museum with exhibits on the restoration and a display of artifacts unearthed during that work. From the nearby ruins of the Officer's Quarters there's a fine view of Prince Rupert Bay.

The fort is home to scores of hermit crabs, harmless snakes and ground lizards *(Ameiva fuscata)* that scurry about the ruins and along the hiking trails that lead up to the two volcanic peaks. The trail up the 560-foot West Cabrit begins at the back side of Fort Shirley, and the hike takes about 30 minutes. Most of the walk passes through a wooded area, but there's a panoramic view at the top.

There's a parking lot at the end of the road next to the cruise-ship complex, where there's a handicraft center, restrooms and a dock. The path up to the fort begins at the nearby snack shop; it takes about five minutes to reach the main cluster of buildings and the museum.

Places to Stay

In town opposite the bus stop, *Douglas Guest House* (☎ 445-5253) has nine basic but clean singles/doubles with shared bath for US$12/24.

Mango Beach Hotel (☎ 445-3099) is a two-story guest house on the beach at the northern end of town. There are eight straightforward rooms with two beds, a re-frigerator, fan and private bath. The place has seen better days, and some of the rooms are decidedly nicer than others. Have a look first and make sure your room has those little amenities like a seat on the toilet and a shower that turns both on *and* off. Singles/doubles cost US$30/40.

Portsmouth Beach Hotel (☎ 445-5142, PO Box 34) is on a nice black-sand beach half a mile south of town. While there are 96 rooms, most are rented out to foreign students who attend the nearby Ross University medical school. However, the choicest wing, the one nearest the beach, sometimes has rooms available on a daily basis for US$60. Rooms are clean and straightforward with showers, phones, ceiling fans and screened louvered windows. There's a pool and restaurant.

Picard Beach Cottage Resort (☎ 445-5131, fax 445-5599, in the USA ☎ 800-223-6510), which is next to Portsmouth Beach Hotel and shares the same management, has eight pleasantly rustic cottages with big oceanfront porches. Each has a separate bedroom, a small kitchenette and a dining/living room with two single beds. Cottages right on the beach cost US$120 in low season, US$180 in high season, while those a little farther back are US$100 in low season, US$160 in high season.

Coconut Beach Hotel (☎ 445-5393, fax 445-5693, PO Box 37) is on a nice, secluded beach a mile south of town. Good-sized rooms with kitchenettes on the terrace cost US$75, and there are larger bungalows for US$100 double.

Places to Eat

The *Douglas Snackette & Restaurant*, on the ground floor of Douglas Guest House (see Places to Stay), has enormous rotis (EC$6.50), chicken & chips (EC$8.50) and other simple inexpensive dishes.

Le Flambeau, at the Portsmouth Beach Hotel (see Places to Stay), is a pleasant alfresco restaurant on the beach. Simple breakfast items cost EC$10, and sandwiches and burgers are about the same price. There are also vegetarian plates and moderately priced fish and meat dinners.

DOMINICA

Mango Bar & Restaurant, at Mango Beach Hotel (see Places to Stay), has a restaurant serving good Creole chicken (EC$20) and fish (EC$30) meals at lunch and dinner.

Big Mama's, a couple of blocks in from the beach in the town center, serves up traditional tasty Creole dishes like fried chicken or curry shark, with all the fixin's (spaghetti, salad, taro and plantain) for around EC$15.

North of town on the beach toward Cabrits National Park, *The Purple Turtle* attracts a more affluent crowd for lunch and sunset cocktails. The catch of the day runs EC$35, but snacks and sandwiches are around EC$5, and the view can't be beat.

PORTSMOUTH TO THE EAST COAST

The route that cuts across the northern neck of the island from Portsmouth to the east coast is a delightful drive through mountainous jungle. The road is winding and narrow, the terrain is all hills and valleys, and the landscape is lush with tropical greenery. Once you reach the coast there are some fine ocean vistas, a couple of one-lane bridges, and plantations with seemingly endless rows of coconut palms. The road is paved, but be cautious of the deep gutters on the mountainside and steep drops on the cliff side.

CALIBISHIE TO PAGUA BAY

Calibishie, the first sizable village you'll reach on the east coast, consists mostly of a string of beachside houses and the local church. There are a couple nice spots to stop for lunch, particularly *Domcan's Café*, on the north side of town, with outdoor seating, tasty drinks and snacks, a car rental agency and a tourist information counter.

There are a few small villages as you continue south, but the area is made up predominantly of coconut and banana plantations. Occasionally the road winds from the jungle out to the coast. There are brown-sand beaches at **Woodford Hill Bay** and near Melville Hall Airport at **Londonderry Bay**. Both bays have rivers emptying

into them where women gather to wash clothes; at Londonderry the airport fence doubles as the clothesline.

Surrounded by lush, green hills, **Marigot**, the largest town on the east coast, is a pretty village of brightly painted houses, some of them built up on stilts. If you come by during the late afternoon there's a good chance you'll see villagers bringing in their fishing boats and sorting the day's catch.

CARIB TERRITORY

The 3700-acre Carib Territory, which begins around the village of Bataka and continues south for 7½ miles, is home to most of Dominica's 3000 Carib Indians. It's a predominantly rural area with cultivated bananas, breadfruit trees and wild heliconia growing along the roadside. Many of the houses are traditional wooden structures on log stilts, but there are also simple cement homes and, in the poorer areas, shanties made of corrugated tin and tar paper.

The main east-coast road runs right through the Carib Territory. Along the road are several stands where you can stop and buy intricately woven Carib baskets, mostly ranging in price from US$5 to US$30.

Salybia, the main settlement, has a couple of noteworthy buildings. One is the *carbet*, an oval-shaped community center designed in the traditional Carib style with a high-pitched ribbed roof; in pre-Columbian times, these buildings served as collective living quarters. The Catholic church in Salybia, which also has a sharply pitched roof, is decorated with colorful paintings of Carib life and a unique altar made from a dugout canoe.

At Sineku a sign points oceanward to **L'Escalier Tête Chien**, a stairwaylike lava outcrop that seems to climb out of the turbulent ocean. This unique natural formation was thought by the Caribs to be the embodiment of a boa constrictor and is significant in Carib legends.

After leaving the Carib Territory the road offers occasional glimpses of the rugged coastline.

There's an intersection half a mile south of Castle Bruce; take the road marked 'Pont

Casse' to continue to the Emerald Pool and Canefield. This road takes you through a scenic mountain valley with a luxuriant fern forest and lots of rushing rivers.

EMERALD POOL

Emerald Pool, which takes its name from its lush green setting, is at the base of a gentle 40-foot waterfall. The pool, deep enough for a little dip, is reached via a five-minute walk through a rain forest of ferns and tall trees. The path is well defined and easy to follow, although it can get a bit slippery in places. Emerald Pool is generally a serenely quiet area except on cruise-ship days, when one packed minivan after another can pull up to the site.

The pool is on the road that runs between Canefield and Castle Bruce, a nice winding drive with thick jungle vegetation, mountain views and lots of beep-as-you-go hairpin turns. It's about a 30-minute drive from Canefield; the trailhead is marked with a roadside forestry sign.

TRAFALGAR FALLS

Trafalgar Falls, on the eastern edge of Morne Trois Pitons National Park, is both spectacular and easily accessible. The 10-minute walk to the falls begins at Papillote Wilderness Retreat, about a mile east of the village of Trafalgar.

Start the walk at the bottom of the inn's driveway, where you'll find a cement track leading east. Follow the track until you reach a little snack bar; take the footpath that leads downhill from there and in a couple of minutes you'll reach a viewing platform with a clear view of the falls in a verdant jungle setting.

There are two separate waterfalls. Water from the upper falls crosses the Titou Gorge before plunging down the sheer 200-foot rock face that fronts the viewing platform. At the base of the waterfall are hot sulfur springs with a couple of basins in which bathers can sit – look for the yellow streaks on the rocks.

The lower falls flow from the Trois Pitons River, which originates in the Boiling Lake area. This waterfall, which is gentler and broader than the upper falls, has a pool at its base that's deep and wide enough for an invigorating swim.

Young men hang out at the start of the trail and tout their services as guides. Getting to the viewing platform is straightforward and doesn't require a guide, so if you plan to go only that far, save yourself the 'tip' (roughly EC$20), as the guides call their negotiable fee.

Going beyond the platform is trickier, as getting to the base of the falls requires crossing a river. Depending on how sure-footed you are, a guide could be helpful in climbing down the boulders to the lower pool and even more so in clambering over to the hot springs.

Guide or not, be very careful with your footing, as the rocks get moss-covered and can be as slippery as ice. This is a serious river, and during rainy spells it may be too high to cross. Flash floods are also a potential danger, as heavy rains in the upper slopes can bring a sudden torrent – if you're in the river and the waters start to rise, get out immediately.

Places to Stay & Eat

The *Papillote Wilderness Retreat* (☎ 448-2287, fax 448-2285, papillote@tod.dm, PO Box 2287) is a delightful little inn nestled in the mountains above Trafalgar village. American owner and naturalist Anne Baptiste has planted the grounds with nearly 100 types of tropical flowers and trees. The rustic inn has eight simple units with private baths, wooden plank floors and patchwork bed quilts made at the local women's co-op. Singles/doubles cost US$85/90, plus an optional US$30 per person for breakfast and dinner. There's also a two-bedroom, two-bathroom cottage near a waterfall that can be divided into two sections for US$125 each.

Papillote has good food with lunchtime salads for EC$20, a flying-fish plate for EC$25 and a chicken plate for EC$30. Lunch is served from noon to 3 pm. Bring a bathing suit and top it off by relaxing in the inn's hot-springs pool (EC$5). Dinner, a full meal for EC$50, is by reservation.

DOMINICA

The ***D'Auchamps Cottages*** *(☎ 448-3346, honychurchs@tod.dm, PO Box 1889),* on the road to Trafalgar Falls, is set on a 9-acre estate amid a botanical garden. There are two cottages, each with a kitchen, veranda and bath. The smaller one, which has one bedroom, costs US$50. The seventh night is free on weekly stays.

Getting There & Away

To get to Trafalgar from Roseau, take King George V St north from the town center. After crossing the Roseau River, continue up the Roseau Valley road for 2⅓ miles, at which point the road forks; take the right branch. From here it's a 10-minute drive along a narrow potholed road to Papillote, 2 miles away.

Buses go from Roseau to the village of Trafalgar (EC$2.25), from where it's a 15-minute walk to Papillote. Taxis from Canefield Airport to Papillote cost EC$45.

MORNE TROIS PITONS NATIONAL PARK

This national park, in the southern half of the island, encompasses 17,000 acres of Dominica's mountainous volcanic interior.

Most of the park is primordial rain forest, varying from jungles thick with tall, pillar-like gommier trees to the stunted cloud-forest cover on the upper slopes of Morne Trois Pitons (4550 feet), Dominica's second-highest mountain. The park has many of the island's top wilderness sites, including Boiling Lake, Boeri Lake, Freshwater Lake and Middleham Falls. Hikes to all four start at Laudat (elevation 1970 feet), a small hamlet with fine mountain views.

The Emerald Pool, at the northernmost tip of the park, is described earlier in this chapter.

Middleham Falls

The trail to Middleham Falls, one of Dominica's highest waterfalls, is an interesting rain-forest walk. More than 60 species of tree, including the tall buttressed chataignier, form a leafy canopy that inhibits undergrowth and keeps the forest floor relatively clear. The treetops provide a

habitat for light-seeking flora, including climbing vines, bromeliads and various air plants. The forest is also home to numerous bird species and a tiny species of tree frog.

There are usually guides available at the trailhead who charge about EC$50, and the hike takes about 1¼ hours each way. If you don't use a guide, carry a compass and be careful not to stray off the main trail, as it would be easy to lose your bearings in the surrounding wilderness.

Boiling Lake

Dominica's preeminent trek is the rugged daylong hike to Boiling Lake, the world's second-largest actively boiling lake (the largest is in New Zealand). Geologists believe the 207-foot-wide lake is a flooded fumarole, a crack in the earth that allows hot gases to vent from the molten lava below. The eerie-looking lake sits inside a deep basin, its grayish waters veiled in steam, its center emitting bubbly burps.

En route to the lake, the hike passes through the aptly named Valley of Desolation, a former rain forest destroyed by a volcanic eruption in 1880. Today it's an active fumarole area with a barren-looking landscape of crusted lava, steaming sulfur vents and scattered hot springs. The hike follows narrow ridges, snakes up and down mountains and runs along hot streams. Wear sturdy walking shoes and expect to get wet and muddy.

This strenuous 6-mile hike, which begins at Titou Gorge, requires a guide. It's about EC$80 (plus EC$20 for a second person) if you arrange your own guide in Laudat.

Other Trails

The walk to **Freshwater Lake**, Dominica's largest lake, is a straightforward hike that skirts the southern flank of Morne Macaque. As the 2½-mile trail up to the lake is along a well-established 4WD track, this hike doesn't require a guide. It's a relatively gradual walk and takes about 2½ hours roundtrip.

Hikers can continue another 1¼ miles from Freshwater Lake to **Boeri Lake**, a scenic 45-minute walk that passes mountain streams and both hot and cold springs. The 130-foot-deep Boeri Lake occupies a volcanic crater that's nestled between two of the park's highest mountains. En route are ferns, heliconia and various epiphytes, as well as the mossy trees of the elfin woodlands that surround the lake.

For a short walk and a dip there's the trail to **Titou Gorge**, where a deep pool is warmed by a hot spring. Just above the pool the gorge narrows, and when the water's calm it's possible to swim upriver to a small cascading waterfall. If you see any brown water being kicked up, then there's a dangerous current and you should stay out of the pool. To get to the trail, turn at the pay phone in Laudat and follow the short road to the utility station. The trail follows a narrow canal that feeds water to the hydroelectric plant. The walk takes about 15 minutes.

Serious hikers could also hire a guide to tackle **Morne Trois Pitons**, the park's tallest peak, but it's a rough trail that cuts through patches of sharp saw grass and requires scrambling over steep rocks. The trail begins at Pont Casse, at the north side of the park, and takes about five hours roundtrip.

Places to Stay & Eat

In Laudat, *Roxy's Mountain Lodge* (☎ /fax 448-4845, PO Box 265) makes a great base if you're planning to do a lot of hiking. This friendly, family-run place has 17 rooms and an engaging communal atmosphere. There's a TV room, a small bar and a restaurant with inexpensive lunchtime sandwiches and dinner meals for EC$35 to EC$60. Valerie Rock, who runs the guest house with her brother, can arrange reliable trail guides and is a fine source of information about the island. Room rates begin at US$50 for singles, US$75 for doubles with kitchenettes. Rooms with private bath are a few dollars more, and there are also studios that cost US$85.

Getting There & Away

To get to Laudat, take King George V St north from Roseau. After crossing the Roseau River, continue up the Roseau

Valley for 2⅓ miles, at which point the road forks; take the left fork, marked 'Laudat.' The road is narrow and a bit potholed, but passable. The trail to Middleham Falls begins on the left 2½ miles up; the trail to Freshwater and Boeri Lakes begins opposite the shrine, half a mile farther.

There's regular but limited bus service. Buses to Laudat (EC$3) leave from the Roseau police station every other hour from 6:30 am; buses return to Roseau from Laudat about 45 minutes later. Taxis from Roseau to Laudat cost EC$70.

SOUTH OF ROSEAU

The coastal road south of Roseau is a delightful 30-minute drive that takes you through a couple of attractive little seaside villages and ends at Scotts Head. Most of the road skirts the water's edge, although there's a roller-coaster section just before Soufriere that winds up the mountain and gives a bird's-eye coastal view before dropping back down.

Soufriere, population 950, has a picturesque old stone church on the north side of the village. There are steaming sulfur springs in the hills above town, including one about a mile inland on the road that leads east from the village center.

Nature Island Dive Center (☎ 449-8181), in Soufriere, is the place to go for expert advice and rental equipment for a variety of activities, including diving, snorkeling, kayaking and mountain biking.

Scotts Head, population 800, on the southernmost tip of Dominica's west coast, is a picturesque fishing village and a fun place to kick around. It has a gem of a setting along the gently curving shoreline of Soufriere Bay, the rim of a sunken volcanic crater. Mountains form a scenic inland backdrop. At the southern tip of the bay is a promontory, also called Scotts Head, which is connected to the village by a narrow, rocky neck of land. It's a short, easy walk to the top of the promontory, where there's a fine coastal view.

The center of village activity is the waterfront, where brightly painted fishing shacks line the shore and colorful fishing boats are

DOMINICA

hauled up onto the sand. It's a lively, inviting scene, with frequent beach barbecues and dancing in the local bars. The bay offers good swimming and snorkeling conditions, as well as some of the island's best diving.

Places to Stay & Eat

The *Petit Coulibri Guest Cottages* (☎/fax 446-3150, barnardm@tod.dm, PO Box 331), occupy an old sugar estate on the hill slopes a couple of miles inland from Soufriere. Run by an American couple, this pleasant upmarket property consists of three two-bedroom, 1½-bath cottages with kitchens and verandas for US$200, and two smaller studio rooms with private baths for US$90. It's got a pool, splendid views and an engaging atmosphere of seclusion, though the

road in can be rough in an ordinary car. Breakfasts (US$10) and dinners (US$25) are available.

On the main drag in Scotts Head, *Herche's Place* (☎ 448-7749) has modern, clean singles/doubles with TV and fan for US$40/60, US$55/75 with air-con. Across the street, on the beach, *Sundowner Café* serves up tasty snacks and potent drinks in a stylish Caribbean *paillotte* (an open-walled hut).

Next door to Herche's, *Chez Wen Cuisine* (☎ 448-6668) is the place to go for full Creole meals like grilled fish with accras (fritters with saltfish filling), rice, beans and salad for EC$28. Soak up a little local flavor along with fresh-fruit juices and rum punches.

Grenada

Grenada (pronounced 'gren-**ay**-duh') is the smallest independent country in the Western Hemisphere. It's a heady mix of idyllic tropical landscapes – fecund valleys and terraced gardens among mountains, rain forests and rivers that fall away to white-sand beaches, bays and craggy cliffs. St George's, the busy, beautiful capital, gives Grenada a small-town urban character that is sophisticated, dynamic and yet intimate. The Carenage, in the capital, is the most beautiful harbor in the Caribbean, lined with 19th-century buildings that rise up the steep hillsides and into the surrounding greenery.

The tourism juggernaut is smaller and quieter in Grenada than in the more famous Caribbean holiday destinations. There are large hotels and plush resorts, but most places to stay are smaller, offering comfort at a reasonable price. Tourist facilities and matters of business are confined to Grenada's busy southern tip, but the rest of the main island remains true to traditional West Indian culture. Most Grenadians live simple lives tilling gardens, fishing, working aboard local ships and sitting around limin'.

Grenada has 90% of the land and people, but several Grenadine islands also make up the tiny nation. The biggest of these are Carriacou and Petit Martinique. Carriacou gets a handful of visitors, but Petit Martinique gets few, yet both are just a short boat ride away from Grenada and offer comfortable lodgings, beaches and a laid-back tempo.

Highlights

- Riding the buses around St George's, Grenada's busy capital, with its sparkling harbor
- Eating barbecued corncobs from street vendors
- Swimming at famous Grand Anse beach
- Driving through the Grand Etang National Park
- Enjoying lazy Carriacou and the ferry ride out there
- Walking around tiny Petit Martinique

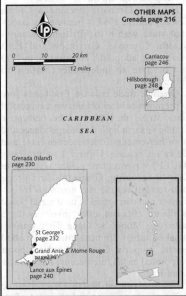

OTHER MAPS
Grenada page 216

0   10   20 km
0   6   12 miles

Carriacou
page 246

Hillsborough
page 248

CARIBBEAN
SEA

Grenada (Island)
page 230

St George's
page 232

Grand Anse & Morne Rouge
page 236

Lance aux Épines
page 240

Facts about Grenada

HISTORY

In 1498, Christopher Columbus became the first European to sight Grenada, during his third voyage to the New World. He did not land, and other Europeans bypassed the island for the next century. The first European settlement was established in 1609 by 208 English tobacco planters, but within a year most had fallen victim to

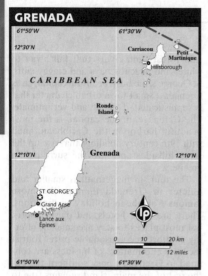

GRENADA

CARIBBEAN SEA

raiding Caribs and the settlement was abandoned.

In 1650, Governor Du Parquet of Martinique 'purchased' the island of Grenada from the Caribs for a few hatchets, some glass beads and two bottles of brandy. He moved in 200 French settlers and a pre-fabricated fort, and established a trading station, Port Louis, on a narrow strip of land separating the Lagoon from St George's harbor. The land sank over time, and today the site of Port Louis is submerged near the Lagoon mouth.

In 1651 the French, weary of ongoing skirmishes with the Caribs, sent soldiers to drive the natives off the island. French troops routed the last of the Caribs to Sauteurs Bay at the north end of Grenada, where, rather than submitting to the colonists, the remaining Caribs – men, women and children – jumped to their deaths off the rugged coastal cliffs.

French planters established stands of indigo, tobacco, coffee, cocoa and sugar, tended by African slaves. Grenada remained under French control until 1762, when Admiral George Rodney captured the island for Britain. Over the next two

decades, colonial control of Grenada shifted back and forth between Britain and France – until 1783, when the French ceded Grenada to the British under the Treaty of Paris. Britain continued to rule Grenada until independence.

Animosity between the new British colonists and the remaining French settlers persisted. In 1795 a group of French Catholics, encouraged by the French Revolution and supported by comrades in Martinique, armed themselves for rebellion. Led by Julien Fedon, an African-French planter from Grenada's central mountains, they attacked the British at Grenville in early March. They captured the British governor and executed him along with a bunch of hostages. Fedon's guerrillas, who controlled much of the island for more than a year, were finally overcome by the British navy. Fedon was never captured – he likely escaped to Martinique or drowned attempting to get there, though some islanders believe he lived out his days hiding in Grenada's mountainous jungles.

In 1877, Grenada became a Crown Colony, and in 1967 it became an associated state within the British Commonwealth. Grenada, Carriacou and Petit Martinique adopted a constitution in 1973 and became an independent nation on February 7, 1974.

Onetime trade unionist Eric Gairy rose to prominence after organizing a successful labor strike in 1950, and he became a leading voice in both the independence and labor movements. Independence came, and Gairy's Grenada United Labour Party (GULP) was swept to power, resulting in Gairy's becoming Grenada's first prime minister. His regime was notorious for patronage and corruption. It used secret police to silence criticism, often involving thugs called the Mongoose Gang. They brutally attacked antigovernment critics and robbed private property. Gairy's popular support evaporated as his rule became increasingly dictatorial.

Before dawn on March 13, 1979, while Gairy was overseas, a band of armed rebels supported by the opposition party, the New

Jewel Movement (NJM), led a bloodless coup. Maurice Bishop, head of the NJM, became prime minister of the new People's Revolutionary Government (PRG) regime. Charismatic Bishop was a 34-year-old London-educated lawyer. He reinstated basic human rights and promised resolution of the country's economic problems. Although he had widespread public support, his socialist leanings didn't sit well with the USA and some of Grenada's more conservative Caribbean neighbors, such as Barbados.

Bishop built schools and medical clinics and created credit unions and farmers' cooperatives. Ostracized by the West, Bishop turned to Cuba for aid. The Cubans built Grenada's Point Salines International Airport, enabling jet-aircraft access to the rest of the world. But divisions were developing in the PRG between Bishop and other more authoritarian leaders. In October 1983 the struggle between Bishop and military hard-liners resulted in his overthrow. On October 19, after Bishop's house arrest, 30,000 supporters – the largest spontaneous crowd ever gathered in Grenada – forced his release. Together they marched to Fort George. At the fort the military opened fire on the crowd, killing an estimated 40 protesters. Bishop and several of his followers were taken prisoner and summarily executed in the courtyard.

In the following turmoil US President Reagan's government convinced some Caribbean nations to pledge support for a US invasion. American troops landed on October 25 along with a few soldiers from half a dozen Caribbean states. Seventy Cubans, 42 Americans and 170 Grenadians were killed in the fighting, and 18 died when the US forces mistakenly bombed the island's mental hospital. Most US forces withdrew in December 1983, although a joint Caribbean force and 300 US support troops remained on the island for two more years. This was the beginning of the end of the Cold War.

Elections were held again in December 1985, and Herbert Blaize and his New National Party won in a landslide. In July 1991,

Gren-AY-duh

The Carib Indians called the island 'Camerhogne,' and Columbus, in passing, named it 'Concepción.' However, Spanish explorers soon began calling the island 'Granada,' after the city in Spain. When the French moved in they renamed the island 'Grenade,' which the British later changed to 'Grenada.' Be sure to pronounce it 'gren-**ay**-duh,' not 'gren-**ah**-da'!

death sentences for 14 people condemned to hang for the murder of Maurice Bishop and his supporters were commuted to life in prison.

The current Grenadian prime minister is Dr Keith Mitchell. At the time of writing he was under siege by the United States' Federal Bureau of Investigation (FBI) over a controversial offshore bank, the First International Bank of Grenada (FIBG). Mitchell was reported to have obstructed FBI efforts to properly investigate FIBG dealings.

GEOGRAPHY

Grenada, Carriacou and Petit Martinique have a total land area of 133 sq miles. Grenada, at 121 sq miles, measures 12 miles wide by 21 miles long. The island is volcanic, though part of the northern end is coral limestone. Grenada's rainy interior is rugged, thickly forested and cut by valleys and streams. The island rises to 2757 feet at Mt St Catherine, an extinct volcano in the northern interior.

Grenada's indented southern coastline has jutting peninsulas, deep bays and small nearshore islands, making it a favorite haunt for yachters.

Carriacou, just under 5 sq miles, is the largest of the Grenadine islands that lie between Grenada and St Vincent.

CLIMATE

While the tropical climate is hot it's tempered by northeast trade winds. In St

George's the average daily high temperature in January is 84°F (29°C) and the average low is 75°F (24°C). In July the average daily high temperature is 86°F (30°C) and the low is 77°F (25°C).

During the rainy season, June to November, rain falls an average of 22 days a month in St George's, and the mean relative humidity is 78%. In the driest months, January to April, there's measurable rainfall 12 days a month and the humidity averages 71%.

Annual rainfall is about 60 inches (1520mm) in St George's and about 160 inches (4060mm) in the Grand Etang rain forest. Carriacou is substantially drier, averaging 40 to 60 inches of rain a year.

FLORA & FAUNA

Grenada has a varied ecosystem of rain forests, montane thickets, elfin woodlands and lowland dry forests. Breadfruit, immortelle, flamboyant and palms are some of the more prominent trees.

A dozen troops of Mona monkeys, introduced from West Africa centuries ago, live in Grenada's wooded areas. Other mammals include the nine-banded armadillo (tatou), opossum (manicou) and mongoose. Bird life features hummingbirds, pelicans, brown boobies, osprey hawks, endangered hook-billed kites and hooded tanagers.

There are no poisonous snakes, but Grenada does have tree boas. These nocturnal serpents spend the day wound around branches high above the ground, and human contact is quite unusual.

Sea turtles nest along some of Grenada's sandy beaches. Although all sea turtles are endangered, their shells are still used to make many of the souvenirs that tourists buy, and they also appear on the menus of a few island restaurants.

GOVERNMENT & POLITICS

Grenada, a member of the British Commonwealth, has a parliamentary government headed by a prime minister. The governor-general, who represents the British queen, has a largely advisory role but is responsible, on the advice of majority

and opposition party leaders, for appointing the 13-member Senate. The 15-member House of Representatives is elected by universal suffrage.

The prime minister since 1995 has been Dr Keith Mitchell, a member of the New National Party, which has been criticized for bringing Grenada into closer ties with the USA. At the time of writing Mitchell was implicated in the machinations of a controversial offshore bank (see History, earlier).

ECONOMY

Grenada is the world's second-largest producer of nutmeg, and it also exports mace, cloves, cinnamon, cocoa and bananas.

Agriculture remains the most important sector of the economy, but the government has been trying to boost tourism since the 1980s, and it's now the leading foreign-exchange earner. In the last 15 years overnight visitors to Grenada have more than doubled, and visitors from cruise ships have increased many times over. Of the 400,000 visitors who arrive annually, more than 70% disembark from a cruise ship. The government has been seeking foreign investment for resort projects on Grenada, and both Carriacou and Petit Martinique

Nutmeg

The nutmeg tree *(Myristica frangrans)*, originally from India, was commercially introduced by the Dutch in the mid-19th century. It thrived so well that Grenada now produces a third of the world's nutmeg.

A fragrant evergreen with glossy leaves and small yellow flowers, the nutmeg tree produces two spices: nutmeg and mace. The tree's yellow fruit, the pericarp, splits open when ripe to reveal a brown nut, the nutmeg, which is covered with a lacy, orange-red webbing of mace.

Nutmeg is used to flavor baked goods, drinks, sauces and preserves. Mace is used as a seasoning and in cosmetics. The pericarp is used in nutmeg syrup.

may yet get their first large-scale resort developments.

The unemployment rate, while still substantial (around 16%), has been falling over the last decade.

POPULATION & PEOPLE
Of Grenada's 100,700 people, nearly a third live in St George's. Another 6000 people live on Carriacou and 1000 on Petit Martinique. Around 82% of Grenadians are black, of African descent, and 13% have mixed origins. The other 5% is comprised of people of East Indian and European descent. Few island residents can claim more than a trace of Arawak or Carib heritage.

SOCIETY & CONDUCT
Grenadian culture is a mix of British, French, African and West Indian influences. African names are often given to Grenadian children, and reggae and Rastafarian culture is vibrant and visible. But just below the surface is a nation of fairly conservative people who attend church on Sundays and don't approve of topless bathing at the beach or skimpy clothing in town. Grenadians are politically savvy because of their nation's turbulent history, but don't assume that the open imbibing of *ganja* on the beaches is indicative of a progressive society – cannabis is still illegal (possession can get you thrown in jail and/or deported) and attitudes towards gays and lesbians are old-fashioned.

Grenadians' love of music and sport binds them together. Pan (steel-band) and calypso music are popular, as is reggae in all its forms.

Cricket and soccer are the most popular sports; formal matches are held in St George's at Queen's Park and the Tanteen.

Dos & Don'ts
Dress is casual on Grenada, and simple cotton clothing is suitable for all occasions. To avoid offense and unwanted attention, swimwear should be restricted to the beach. Topless or nude bathing is not a normal part of Grenadian beach etiquette, although there may be resorts where they are tolerated.

Beach Cricket

All-day spontaneous beach-cricket events are played on the water's edge with a wet tennis ball, a bat and three stick wickets in the sand. It's a Sunday afternoon tradition; families bring food and drinks in coolers down to the beach, and there's an easy carnival atmosphere as people relax and swim and enjoy their day of rest. There are kids' and family games, as well as the 'seniors,' who play hard. The orthodox high-paced crook-arm chuck, tacitly adjudged legal by all, is the preferred method of 'bowling.'

Haki (soccer-style 'juggling') is played too, with a soccer ball, and the skills and speed are astonishing.

RELIGION
Almost 60% of all Grenadians are Roman Catholic. There are also churches for Anglicans, Seventh Day Adventists, Methodists, Christian Scientists, Presbyterians, Scots Kirk, Baptists and Jehovah's Witnesses, as well as Baha'i temples.

LANGUAGE
The official language is English. A French-African patois is spoken only by elderly people.

Facts for the Visitor

ORIENTATION
Point Salines International Airport is at the southwestern tip of the island, 5½ miles from St George's. Midway between the two lies Grande Anse beach, Grenada's main tourist area.

You can see most of the island's main sights on a day trip. The most common sightseeing route is up the scenic Grand Etang Rd and north to Sauteurs via Grenville, Pearls and Bathways Beach, returning to St George's via the west-coast road.

Grenada is divided into six parishes that serve as island regions or neighborhoods. From north to south, they are St Patrick, St Mark, St Andrew, St John, St George and St David.

Maps

The best road map of Grenada is the Ordnance Survey's 1:50,000 map, which can be bought for EC$15 at bookstores in St George's.

TOURIST OFFICES
Local Tourist Offices

The postal address of the Grenada Board of Tourism (☎ 440-2279, fax 440-6637, www.grenada.org) is the Carenage, St George's, Grenada, West Indies.

There's a tourist office booth at Point Salines International Airport, just before immigration, where you can pick up tourist brochures; the staff can also help you book a room. There are also tourist offices at the cruise-ship dock in St George's and in Hillsborough, on Carriacou.

Tourist Offices Abroad

Tourist offices abroad include the following:

Canada
Grenada Board of Tourism (☎ 416-595-1339, fax 416-595-8278) 439 University Ave, Suite 820, Toronto, Ontario M5G 1Y8

Germany
Marketing Services International (☎ 069-61 11 78, fax 069-62 92 64) Johanna-Melber-Weg 12, D-60599 Frankfurt

UK
Grenada Board of Tourism (☎ 020-7370 5164, fax 020-7244 0177) 1 Collingham Gardens, Earls Court, London SW5 0HW

USA
Grenada Board of Tourism (☎ 212-687-9554, 800-927-9554, fax 212-573-9731) 800 Second Ave, Suite 400K, New York, NY 10017

VISAS & DOCUMENTS

Passports are not required of citizens of the USA, Canada or the UK, as long as they have both proof of citizenship, such as an official birth certificate or naturalization papers, and a photo ID, such as a driver's license. Citizens of other countries must have a valid passport. Visas are not required.

As immigration officials generally stamp in the exact number of days you tell them you intend to stay, be sure to include any time you plan to spend in Carriacou in your calculations. They will also ask where you intend to stay.

Driver's License

To drive a vehicle you need to purchase a Grenadian driving license from a police station (EC$30).

EMBASSIES & CONSULATES
Grenadian Embassies & Consulates

Belgium
(☎ 02-514 1242/2513)
24 Ave de la Toison d'Or, 1050 Brussels

UK
(☎ 020-7373 7809)
1 Collingham Gardens, London SW50HW

USA
(☎ 202-265-2561)
1701 New Hampshire Ave NW, Washington, DC 20009

Foreign Embassies & Consulates in Grenada

Guyana
Consulate (☎ 440-2189)
Gore St, St George's

Netherlands
Consulate (☎ 440-2031)
Huggins Building, Grand Etang Rd, St George's

UK
High Commission (☎ 440-3536)
14 Church St, St George's

USA
Embassy (☎ 444-1173)
Point Salines

Venezuela
Embassy (☎ 440-1721)
Archibald Ave, St George's

CUSTOMS

Visitors can bring in 200 cigarettes and a quart of spirits duty-free.

MONEY

The official currency is the Eastern Caribbean dollar (EC$2.67 equals US$1). Most hotels, shops and restaurants will accept US dollars, but you'll get a better exchange rate by changing to EC dollars at a bank and using local currency. Major credit cards are accepted by most hotels, top-end restaurants and car rental agencies. Be clear about whether prices are being quoted in EC or US dollars, particularly with taxi drivers.

Barclays Bank exchanges traveler's checks free of commission for amounts more than EC$500; it charges EC$5 for lesser amounts. Scotiabank charges a 1% commission to exchange all traveler's checks, while the National Commercial Bank charges EC$5 per transaction. Grenada has ATMs in St George's and at Grande Anse. There are no banks at the airport.

An 8% tax and 10% service charge is added to most hotel and restaurant bills. If no service charge is added, a 10% tip is generally expected. Prices quoted in this book do not include the 18% tax and charge.

POST & COMMUNICATIONS
Post

Grenada's general post office is in St George's, and there are smaller post offices in many villages.

The cost to mail an aerogram to America and Canada is EC$0.50, to Europe EC$0.75 and to Australia EC$0.80. To mail an airmail letter under 20g costs EC$0.75 to the USA, Canada or the UK, EC$1.00 to Europe, and EC$1.60 to Australia or the Far East.

When addressing a letter, include the street name or box number, the village and 'Grenada (or Carriacou), West Indies.'

Telephone

Local phone numbers have seven digits; when calling from outside the Caribbean, add the area code 473.

Grenada has coin-operated and card phones. Coin phones take 25-cent coins (either EC or US) or EC$1 coins; each 25 cents allows three minutes on a call within the country. Card phones accept the same

Caribbean Phonecard used on other Eastern Caribbean islands; cards are sold at the airport, harbors and numerous shops.

International phone calls can be made, and faxes and telexes sent, from the Cable & Wireless office at the Carenage in St George's 7:30 am to 6 pm weekdays, till 1 pm Saturday and 10 am to noon Sunday. Expect lines.

More information on phone cards and making international phone calls is in the Post & Communications section in the Regional Facts for the Visitor chapter.

Email & Internet Access

St George's has a couple of Internet cafés, and there is also one on Carriacou. Rates usually start around EC$10 per hour.

INTERNET RESOURCES

There is some good information on the Internet about traveling in Grenada. Some of the best sites include the following:

www.grenada.org
This is the official site of the Grenada Board of Tourism, and features links to masses of excellent information.

www.grenadaexplorer.com
This is an online tourist guide with information in English and German.

www.grenadaguide.com
This is another site with tourist information. It has a good search engine.

www.travelgrenada.com
This site is similar to grenadaguide.com.

www.spiceisle.com
Spiceisle.com hosts many of Grenada's commercial Web pages. It also maintains a good links page.

www.grenadahotelsinfo.com
The Grenada Hotel Association maintains this site, from which you can book accommodations online.

BOOKS

A good book about geology, flora and fauna is *A Natural History of the Island of Grenada,* by John R Groome, a past president of the Grenada National Trust. *The Mermaid Wakes: Paintings of a Caribbean Isle* is a hardcover book featuring paintings by Carriacou artist Canute Caliste; the text, by Lora Berg, is about island life.

Grenada 1983 (Men in Arms, 159), by Lee Russell and others, is a good book on events that surrounded US President Ronald Reagan's invasion of Grenada in 1983. The book is rather pro-US, but it does not demonize Bishop and does explain that Cuba was reluctantly embroiled in a war that it did not want.

Revolution in Reverse, by James Ferguson, presents a critical account of Grenada's development since the US invasion.

Lorna McDaniel's *The Big Drum Ritual of Carriacou: Praisesongs for Rememory of Flight* explores the Big Drum rituals, as practiced in Carriacou, that call ancestors as part of an Afro-Caribbean religious experience. Performed since the early 1700s, it is the only ceremony of its type that has survived in the Caribbean.

NEWSPAPERS & MAGAZINES

The handful of local newspapers includes the monthly *Barnacle,* distributed free. The weekly *Grenada Today* sells for EC$1.25 from street vendors. It's an interesting read and includes lots of opinion pieces. The *Grenadian Voice* is another weekly. International newspapers, including *USA Today,* can be found in large grocery stores.

The tourist office issues *Discover Grenada,* a glossy magazine with general information on Grenada, Carriacou and Petit Martinique. The 100-page magazine *The Greeting* is similar. Both publications are free.

RADIO & TV

Grenada has three local TV stations and four radio stations. Most hotels also have satellite or cable TV, which pick up major US network broadcasts.

ELECTRICITY

The electrical current is 220V, 50 cycles. British-style three-pin plugs are used.

WEIGHTS & MEASURES

Grenada uses the imperial system of feet, miles, pounds and gallons.

HEALTH

St George's General Hospital (☎ 440-2051), the island's main medical facility, is in St George's near Fort George. There's a small hospital on Carriacou, the Princess Royal Hospital (☎ 443-7400). The quality of medical care on Grenada is not highly regarded, and for serious health issues evacuation to Miami (Florida) or Barbados is common.

WOMEN TRAVELERS

It's unusual for women to travel alone at night, and such travelers are likely to attract attention, but taking care if you're out after dark is prudent for both sexes. Otherwise, women needn't expect too many unwanted hassles.

GAY & LESBIAN TRAVELERS

Attitudes to same-sex couples in Grenada (and the Caribbean generally) are not modern or tolerant. Gay and lesbian couples should be discreet in public to avoid hassles.

DANGERS & ANNOYANCES

It's wise to be careful after dark around St George's. Tourists have been mugged in the Grand Anse area on the beach at night, and in the Lagoon area on the south side of St George's. Paranoia is not warranted, but be security conscious if you're on foot after dark.

Yachters should have everything as secure as possible, and belongings should not be left unattended, especially in St George's.

EMERGENCIES

To contact the police or fire department, dial ☎ 911.

BUSINESS HOURS

Shops are generally open 8 am to noon and 1 to 4 pm weekdays and 8 am to noon Saturday, although some larger shops stay open through the lunch hour.

Banking hours are generally 8 am to 3 pm (some close earlier) Monday to Thursday and 8 am to 5 pm Friday.

PUBLIC HOLIDAYS & SPECIAL EVENTS

Public holidays include the following:

New Year's Day	January 1
Independence Day	February 7
Good Friday	late March/early April
Easter Monday	late March/early April
Labour Day	May 1
Whit Monday	eighth Monday after Easter
Corpus Christi	ninth Thursday after Easter
Emancipation Days	first Monday & Tuesday in August
Thanksgiving Day	October 25
Christmas Day	December 25
Boxing Day	December 26

Grenada's Carnival, held on the second weekend in August, is the big annual event. The celebration is spirited and includes calypso and steel-band competitions, costumed revelers, pageants and a big grand-finale jump-up on Tuesday. Many events occur in Queen's Park, at the north side of St George's.

Carriacou's Carnival usually takes place in early March. The island also has a major sailing event, the Carriacou Regatta, held in late July or early August. The regatta features races to Grenada, Union Island and Bequia; various sporting events, from volleyball to donkey races; and plenty of music, including Big Drum performances.

The annual Carriacou Maroon Jazz Festival is held in mid-June.

Petit Martinique holds a regatta over Easter that includes a swimming relay, rowboat races, kite flying, music and a beer-drinking competition.

ACTIVITIES
Beaches & Swimming

Grenada's most popular beach, Grand Anse, is justifiably famous – it's broad and long, a beautiful sweep of fine white sands. Grande Anse is also thronged with bodies (and beach chairs, jewelry sellers, Jet-ski renters and parasailing operators). Morne

Rouge Bay, on the other side of Quarantine Point, also has a lovely secluded beach that's much more quiet. The calm Caribbean water is warm and clear, and a delight to be immersed in.

There are also nice beaches on either side of the airport runway and along the Lance aux Épines peninsula.

Calivigny Island, east of Lance aux Épines, has a couple of pretty beaches, some walking tracks and the remains of an old hotel. The Moorings (☎ 444-4439), at Secret Harbour in Lance aux Épines, can shuttle people over for US$15 per person.

Diving

The waters around Grenada have extensive reefs and a wide variety of corals, fish, turtles and other marine life. There are shallow reef dives, wall dives, drift dives and shipwrecks.

One popular dive is the wreck of the *Bianca C* ocean liner, off Grenada's southwest coast (see 'The *Bianca C*,' later in this chapter). Strong currents and a depth of more than 100 feet make it strictly for experienced divers.

Other Grenada dive sites include Bose Reef, an extensive reef off Grand Anse that supports manta rays and barracuda; Dragon Bay, a wall dive rich in marine life including moray eels and black coral; and Grand Mal Point, a reef and wall dive with varied soft and hard corals.

The islands between Grenada and Carriacou are also popular dive spots. These

Don't be freaked out by sea anemones.

include Kick 'em Jenny and The Sisters, where there's a challenging wall dive with gorgonians and barracuda.

Dive Shops Dive shops on Grenada and Carriacou include the following:

Aquanauts Grenada (☎ 444-1126, fax 444-1127, aquanauts@caribsurf.com, www.spicedivers.com) PO Box 11, St George's, at Lance aux Epines. These folks offer resort courses for US$65, single dives for US$40 and PADI certification for US$350.

Carriacou Silver Diving (☎/fax 443-7882, scubamax@ caribsurf.com, www.scubamax.com) Hillsborough, Carriacou. This dive shop offers one-tank dives for US$50, two-tank dives for US$90 and resort courses for US$75.

Dive Grenada (☎ 444-1092, fax 444-5875, diveg'da@ caribsurf.com) PO Box 771, St George's, at Cot Bam on Grand Anse Beach. Dive Grenada offers dives to the *Bianca C* and night dives for US$45, a resort course with a reef dive that runs US$75 and open-water PADI certification for US$375 (US$325 if there are two or more people). It offers a 10% discount for Internet bookings.

EcoDive (☎ 444-7777, fax 444-4808, davidcoe@ caribsurf.com, www.scubadivegrenada.com) PO Box 336, St George's, at the Coyaba Beach Resort. This operation has dives to the *Bianca C* and night dives for US$55, other one-tank dives as low as US$45, resort courses for US$60 and also open-water PADI certification for US$375 (US$300 if more than one person).

Scuba Express (☎ 444-2133, fax 444-0516, trueblue@ caribsurf.com) PO Box 302, St George's, at True Blue Bay. This small operation offers dives from US$40 and Discover Scuba courses for US$75, as well as open-water PADI certification courses for US$375.

Tanki's Watersport Paradise (☎ 443-8406, fax 443-8391, paradise@cacounet.com) Carriacou, at the Paradise Inn. This operation offers single dives for US$45, Discover Scuba courses for US$70 and open-water PADI certification for US$400.

Snorkeling

Molinière Point, north of St George's, has some of the best snorkeling on Grenada, though land access is difficult. Grand Anse Aquatics offers daily two-hour snorkeling trips to Molinière Point for US$20, as does Dive Grenada.

You can find coral and colorful fish at the south side of Morne Rouge Bay. Dive shops rent out snorkeling gear.

Windsurfing

Grenada is not known for windsurfing, but you can rent sailboards at The Moorings, at Secret Harbour, for US$15 an hour. Lessons are available too.

On Carriacou you can rent sailboards from Carriacou Silver Diving (☎/fax 443-7882), on Main St in Hillsborough, for US$50 a day.

Sailing

The Moorings, at Secret Harbour, rents Sunfish for US$15 an hour, 14-foot Catalinas for US$20 an hour and 21-foot Impulses for US$25 an hour or US$100 a day. You must have appropriate sailing skills.

For information on day sails, see Organized Tours in the Getting Around section, later in this chapter.

Fishing

Grenada offers good game fishing for blue marlin, white marlin, sailfish and yellowfin tuna. Winter is the best season. Tropix Sport Fishing (☎ 440-4961), Evans Chartering Services (☎ 444-4422) and Bezo Charters (☎ 443-5021) are three fishing charterers. Expect a boat to cost about US$500 a day.

The Spice Island Billfish Tournament, held yearly in January, attracts anglers from North America and around the Caribbean. Information is available from the Grenada Billfish Association, PO Box 14, St George's.

Hiking

Grenada's most popular hiking area is the Grand Etang rain forest, where trails wind through a forest of mahogany and ferns, leading to a crater lake, waterfalls and mountain ridges. For details on specific trails, see the Grand Etang National Park, La Sagesse Nature Centre and Concord Falls sections.

The Hash House Harriers sponsor a 'hash' (a fun-run or brisk walk, popular with older people) on alternate Saturdays.

The idyllic Emerald Pond, Dominica

Exploring Annandale Falls, Grenada

The long, peaceful sweep of Anse de Colombier, St Barts

Gazing at the Pitons, St Lucia

Don't you need a spear to spearfish?

Representing the style industry in Grenada

Dominica's version of a traffic jam

You can boat with flair in St Lucia.

Colorful buildings are well protected in Dominica.

A place to buy souse on Anguilla

A place to get soused on St Lucia

Visitors are welcome to join; schedules are posted at Rudolf's restaurant, on Wharf Rd in St George's.

Tennis
Several hotels have tennis courts for guests' use. The Coyaba Beach Resort in Grand Anse allows nonguests access for EC$25 an hour, including use of rackets and balls.

Golf
The Grenada Golf Club (☎ 444-4128), near Grand Anse, has a nine-hole course open to visitors 8 am to 6 pm daily (till 1 pm Sunday). Greens fees are US$15 for nine holes, US$22 for 18 holes, and clubs can be rented.

ACCOMMODATIONS
The main tourist precincts are Grand Anse and Lance aux Épines, and both have some moderate and top-end places to stay. Because of the hilly topography, almost all rooms, whether beachfront or not, come with a million-dollar view.

It is worth noting that budget guest houses in Grenada, catering mostly to locals, rarely charge the 8% tax or the 10% service charge, which results in considerable savings on the cost of a room. Also, some of the best rooms in the established guest houses are well appointed with comforts – TV, air-con, fridge and the like. The better guest-house rooms are often more comfortable than mid-range rooms in the resorts and hotels. Grenada's guest houses are concentrated in St George's away from the beach.

In the Point Salines area are some moderately priced hotels and a few pricey beachside resorts. Beyond that, there are only a few scattered inns around the rest of Grenada.

Carriacou, which gets few overnight visitors, has a range of good-value accommodations options.

Some hotels can be booked through the Grenada Hotel Association (☎ 444-1353, fax 444-4847, in the USA ☎ 800-322-1753, www.grenadahotelsinfo.com), PO Box 440, St George's.

Camping
Camping is allowed in Grand Etang National Park, but there are no established facilities and the park is in one of the rainiest parts of the island. Arrangements can be made through the park visitors center (☎ 440-6160). There is a modest fee.

FOOD
Italian and French food as well as seafood make the basis of most upmarket cuisine served at Grenadian restaurants and resorts. The fine-dining options are many and various, but you can also take advantage of inexpensive local eateries, which serve fish stews, curried *lambi* (conch) and rotis that make a delicious alternative to Western fare. Pigeon peas and rice, plantains, yams and callaloo soup are common local side dishes. The pervasive mealtime aroma of West Indian cooking is a highlight of traveling in the Caribbean.

Many restaurants enjoy panoramic harbor and ocean views.

DRINKS
The official word is that tap water is safe to drink, but many expatriates boil their drinking water nonetheless. Bottled water is available in grocery stores.

Carib beer is a fine brew that's made on Grenada. Rum is also made locally using imported sugar; Westerhall sells for about EC$15 a bottle. Local nutmeg and spices are incorporated into some very drinkable cocktails that pack quite a punch. Grenada Breweries Ltd also bottles nonalcoholic fruit juices, mauby (a bittersweet drink made from the bark of the rhamnaceous tree) and ginger beer.

ENTERTAINMENT & SHOPPING
Live entertainment is limited on Grenada, although there are steel bands or other dinner entertainment at Grand Anse hotels a few nights a week. The main venues are the Renaissance Hotel, Spice Island Inn, Flamboyant Hotel and Coyaba Beach Resort.

The quality of materials and workmanship in Caribbean wood carvings is rather disappointing. Travelers who have been to Africa and the South Pacific might be underwhelmed by the artifacts offered locally.

There are vendors selling jewelry, batiks and carvings who walk up and down the main beach strips (this activity is often a front for selling cannabis to tourists).

Getting There & Away

DEPARTURE TAX

There's an EC$50 departure tax for stays of longer than 24 hours (half price for children ages five to 10). Children under five are exempt.

AIR
Airports & Airlines

Point Salines International Airport has car rental offices, an ATM, pay phones and a restaurant. A tourist office booth is in the arrivals section *before* you reach immigration. Between immigration and customs is a courtesy phone that connects you with car rental agencies, hotels and guest houses. There's no bank or exchange office – so if you're not already carrying EC currency it'll be very useful to have US currency in small denominations, as taxis routinely accept either.

The departure lounge has a duty-free liquor store and gift shop.

Airline reservation numbers in Grenada include the following:

Air Jamaica	☎ 440-5428
Airlines of Carriacou (SVG)	☎ 444-3549
American Airlines	☎ 444-2222
British Airways	☎ 440-8280
toll-free	☎ 1-800-744-2997
BWIA	☎ 444-1221
LIAT	
reservations	☎ 440-2796
at Point Salines Airport	☎ 444-4121
on Carriacou	☎ 443-7362

The USA

From New York, Air Jamaica offers two direct flights per week to Grenada.

Roundtrip fares start from around US$550. American Airlines has daily flights from New York to Grenada via San Juan, Puerto Rico, for around US$450. BWIA also flies daily from New York and Miami via Port of Spain, Trinidad. From Miami expect to pay around US$550 roundtrip.

The UK

British Airways has two flights per week from London to Grenada, via Tobago, for UK£600 roundtrip. BWIA has a daily flight from London to Grenada, via Port of Spain, for a bargain UK£340 roundtrip.

Within the Caribbean

LIAT, BWIA and Air Jamaica offer regular flights from Grenada to other destinations within the Caribbean. Other, smaller carriers also operate flights, and fares are generally the same on all airlines. There are some good-value fares for day trips from Grenada. In the case of Tobago and St Lucia, a roundtrip flight is cheaper than one-way.

Both LIAT and Air Jamaica fly from Grenada to Barbados (55 minutes). LIAT has four flights a day and Air Jamaica two, and the fares are US$94 one-way, US$108 roundtrip.

From Grenada to St Lucia (40 minutes), LIAT, Air Jamaica and BWIA all operate several flights a day for US$111 one-way, US$100 roundtrip.

LIAT flies twice a day to St Vincent (30 minutes), Air Jamaica once and Caribbean Star Airlines twice. The fare is US$30 for each way.

To Port of Spain (35 minutes) LIAT, Air Jamaica, Caribbean Star Airlines and Air Caribbean all operate daily flights for US$89 one-way, US$95 roundtrip.

To Tobago (30 minutes) LIAT's daily service costs US$80/75.

SEA

For boats between Carriacou and Union Island, see Getting There & Away in the Union Island section of the St Vincent & the Grenadines chapter. For boats between Grenada and Carriacou, see Getting There

& Away in the Carriacou section of this chapter.

Yacht

Customs and immigration can be cleared in Grenada at St George's or at Spice Island Marine Services (☎ 444-4342), on Prickly Bay; in Carriacou, clearance can be made at Hillsborough.

In St George's, customs is at Grenada Yacht Services (GYS; ☎ 440-2508), and most yachts anchor between GYS and the Grenada Yacht Club. Customs and immigration are open 8 am to 3:45 pm weekdays.

The most frequented anchorages are along the southwest side of Grenada, including Prickly Bay, Mt Hartman Bay, Hog Island and True Blue Bay.

The Moorings (☎ 444-4439) bases its yacht charter operation at Secret Harbour, and Sea Breeze Yacht Charters (☎ 444-4924) is at Spice Island Marine Services, both at Lance aux Épines.

Cruise Ship

Grenada is a port of call for numerous cruise ships, which dock at the southeast side of St George's harbor, the Carenage. At the dock are a tourist office, waiting taxis and a line of souvenir shops. It's an easy walk around the harbor to where most of St George's sights and shops are situated. When a cruise ship docks, St George's goes into overdrive with locals keen to sell trinkets, jewelry and souvenirs, or to offer their services as guides on a walk about town. St George's is easy to explore on your own; alternatively, you can arrange an island tour with a taxi driver.

Getting Around

This section describes options for getting around Grenada. For information on getting around Carriacou, see the end of the Carriacou section.

BUS

Buses on Grenada are privately operated minivans. Catching the buses is a good way to rub shoulders with locals and experience the rhythms of daily life on Grenada.

A local bus ride is a spirited event, as the driver steers his van around the skinny, hilly streets, in and around the traffic, dropping and collecting passengers on the roadside, punching out Morse code on the horn, all at breakneck speed.

For locations of bus terminals in St George's, see that section, later. Fares in the greater St George's area and to Grande Anse are EC$1.50. From St George's, fares are EC$3 to La Sagesse, EC$3.50 to

---

Doof Doof Bus

Ragga is the music that blasts from the buses that ply the hilly sounds of St George's. It's an electronic form of reggae recorded on computers in studios in Jamaica, London and the USA, and it is characterized by the scuba sub-bass lines that verge at the edge of human hearing and the high-pitched sibilance of electronic high hats that sound like insects. It's an unusual form of music because there are no middle frequencies in it, just the high insect noises and bass...and more bass below that. And it is *very* groovy.

All the new flashy buses are fitted out with audio systems tailor-made for this kind of music – two tiny tweeter speakers, and under the rear seat a massive subwoofer that makes the chassis vibrate. The best subwoofer is called 'Bazooka.' You can hear these 'rigged' buses coming from far away in the hills, with a 'doof doof' sound, and when they get near enough, a clipped 'cling cling,' like a pair of tiny finger cymbals.

Gouyave or Grand Etang, and EC$5 to Grenville or Sauteurs. Depending on passengers, it takes about 45 minutes from St George's to Grenville and 1½ hours to Sauteurs.

Buses run frequently all day from around 7 am. They start getting hard to catch after 6 pm, so head back early enough so as not to get stuck. A few buses run on Sunday, though they are much more infrequent.

To get let off the bus, rap your knuckle on the metal interior a few times, or yell 'drop one!'

CAR & MOTORCYCLE
Road Rules
Drive on the left-hand side of the road. The roads are very narrow and curving and the bus drivers are pretty crazy. For safety, slow down when approaching blind curves and toot your horn liberally. There are few road signs on the island, so a road map and a measure of caution are useful when driving.

You'll need to buy a local driver's license (EC$30) to drive in Grenada. You can get it from most car rental companies, police stations or the Traffic Department booth (☎ 440-2267) at the fire station on the east side of the Carenage in St George's.

Grenada's larger towns, including Grenville, Sauteurs and Victoria, have gas stations; expect a gallon of unleaded to cost around EC$8.

There are a lot of hilly one-way streets in St George's, but some of them are not marked, so be careful and watch the traffic flow. Better yet, avoid driving around the town center, especially on the north side of the Carenage.

Rental
Car There are a number of local car rental agencies, but many of them have very small fleets. You're better off dealing with international companies because you're more likely to be adequately insured in the rental agreement.

Dollar (☎ 444-4786) has an office at the airport, while Budget has offices at both the airport (☎ 444-2877) and Le Marquis Complex (☎ 444-2277), in Grand Anse. Avis

(☎ 440-3936) is in St George's at the Shell station on the corner of Paddock and Lagoon Rds but will pick up renters at the airport or their hotel at no charge.

Cars cost from around US$65 a day, jeeps US$80. Optional CDW insurance, which limits your liability in the event of an accident, starts at an additional US$8 per day, but you still have to pay at least a US$2000 excess.

Scooter Step-through scooters are rented from Eze Rentals (☎ 444-3263) within 'D' Green Grocer at the Grande Anse traffic circle for US$21 daily, US$120 weekly, plus deposit. You need to purchase a Grenadian license from a police station for US$30 despite the size of little 90 horsepower scooters.

TAXI
Taxi fares are regulated by the government. From the airport to Grand Anse or Lance aux Épines costs EC$25, to St George's it's EC$30. From central St George's it costs EC$8 to other parts of the city, EC$25 to Grand Anse or Morne Rouge and EC$35 to Lance aux Épines.

Elsewhere, taxis charge EC$4 per mile up to 10 miles and EC$3 per mile after that. The waiting charge is EC$15 per hour. Taxis can be hired for a flat EC$40-per-hour rate for sightseeing. A EC$10 surcharge is added to fares between 6 pm and 6 am.

ORGANIZED TOURS
Land Tours
Several Grenadian-owned companies provide local land tours. Prices are all about the same and depend on numbers.

Mandoo Tours (☎ 440-1428, madoo@ caribsurf.com, www.grenadatours.com) offers full- and half-day tours of the island from US$40. They typically take in Concord Falls, the Dougaldston Estate, the Gouyave nutmeg station, Carib's Leap and lunch at the Morne Fendue Plantation House, and return via Grenville and Grand Etang National Park, but there's a choice of routes across the island. Treks to the Seven Sisters Falls cost US$40, and to Concord Falls it's US$90.

Caribbean Horizons (☎ 444-1555, fax 444-2899, macford@caribsurf.com) is part of the McIntyre Bros car rental business. It offers a range of excursions and self-drive options that can include hiking, sailing and fishing, and 'moonlight delite' tours of the rain forest at Grand Etang starting from around US$40 for a half day. The options are many, and full-day outings are accompanied by lunch.

Sunsation Tours (☎ 444-1594, fax 444-1103, www.grenadasunsation.com), at Le Marquis complex, Grand Anse, offers a variety of land tours. English-, German-, French- and Spanish-speaking guides are available.

Various treks into the interior are offered by Henry's Safari Tours (☎ 444-5313, fax 444-4460, safari@travelgrenada.com, www.travelgrenada.com/safari.htm), which specializes in hiking tours. Lunch and drinks are included. There's a five-hour tour that includes a hike to the Seven Sisters Falls for US$40 per person for three or more.

Another reputable operator is Adventure Tours (☎ 444-5337, adventure@caribsurf.com, www.grenadajeeptours.com). A full-day tour that takes in Government House, Annandale Waterfall, Grand Etang Crater Lake, a walk and swim at Clabony Sulphur Pond, lunch at Rosemount Plantation House and swimming at Dragon Bay costs US$65. Lunch and admission prices are included.

All companies listed in this section offer a half-day triangle tour that takes in Concord Falls, the nutmeg station in Gouyave and Dougaldston Estate before turning inland to cut down through Grand Etang National Park on the way back. The cost starts at US$30. These companies also arrange interisland trips by boat and/or plane within the region.

Boat Tours
Several boats in Grenada offer trips to nearshore islands as well as through the Grenadines, often including snorkeling time. Tour frequency depends on demand, and most require a minimum of four to six passengers.

If you want to plan your own itinerary, contact The Moorings (☎ 444-4439, www.moorings.com), at Secret Harbour, which will arrange yacht charters, with a skipper, for half- (US$35) and full-day (US$60) sails. Rates are per person, with a minimum of four people.

The *Rhum Runner* (☎ 440-4386) is Grenada's party boat, with rum punch, steel-band music and limbo dancing. The cruise (US$25) includes snorkeling and beach swimming.

Grenada

ST GEORGE'S
St George's is a very attractive hillside town that lines the curve of a deep horseshoe-shaped harbor called the Carenage. There's a small museum, the remains of two old forts with commanding views, lots of old churches and colonial buildings, a bright public market and a busy waterfront. The maze of skinny, hilly streets gives St George's real character, and the small cluster of harborside restaurants and boutiques creates a sophisticated air.

Two catastrophic fires in the late 18th century destroyed the old timber houses, which were subsequently banned. Now there's a predominance of 19th-century structures of brick and stone, many of them roofed with orange fish-scale tiles brought over as ship ballast from Europe.

Opposite the LIAT office in the Carenage is *Christ of the Deep,* a life-size bronze statue put up by Costa Cruise Line in honor of its ship, the *Bianca C,* which went up in flames inside the harbor in 1961. Boats that sail between Grenada and Carriacou are loaded nearby, on the west side of the Carenage. Farther along Wharf Rd are some 19th-century warehouses, including one restored building housing the National Library.

Orientation
The picturesque little town is divided into two parts – first, the Carenage, and second, the city blocks that surround the market

GRENADA (ISLAND)

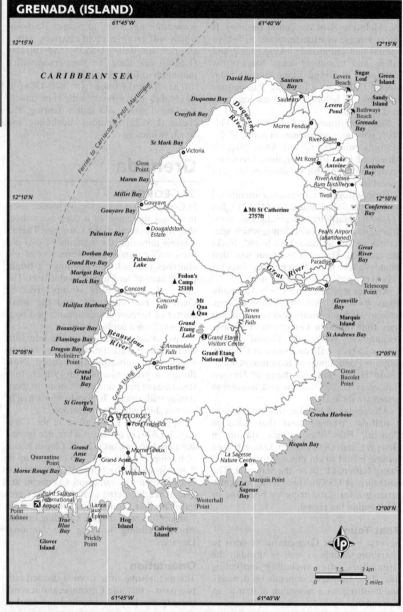

CARIBBEAN SEA

Ferries to Carriacou & Petit Martinique

12°15'N

61°45'W · 61°40'W

David Bay
Sauteurs Bay
Levera Beach
Sugar Loaf
Green Island
Duquesne Bay
Sauteurs
Sandy Island
Duquesne River
Crayfish Bay
Levera Pond
Bathways Beach
Grenada Bay
Morne Fendue
St Mark Bay
River Sallee
Victoria
Gros Point
Mt Rose
Lake Antoine
Antoine Bay
Maran Bay
River Antoine Rum Distillery
Millet Bay
Tivoli
Gouyave
▲ Mt St Catherine 2757ft
12°10'N
Gouyave Bay
Conference Bay
Palmiste Bay
Dougaldston Estate
Pearls Airport (abandoned)
Dothan Bay
Palmiste Lake
Great River Bay
Grand Roy Bay
Marigot Bay
▲ Fedon's Camp 2510ft
Black Bay
Concord
Mt Qua ▲ Qua
Paradise
Concord Falls
Great River
Halifax Harbour
Grenville
Seven Sisters Falls
Telescope Point
Beauséjour Bay
Grand Etang Lake
Grenville Bay
Flamingo Bay
Beauséjour River
ⓘ Grand Etang Visitors Center
Marquis Island
Dragon Bay
Molinière Point
Annandale Falls
St Andrews Bay
12°05'N
Grand Mal Bay
Grand Etang National Park
Constantine
Great Bacolet Point
St George's Bay
Grand Etang Rd
ST GEORGE'S
ⓘ Fort Frederick
Crochu Harbour
Grand Anse Bay
Morne Jaloux
Requin Bay
Quarantine Point
Grand Anse
La Sagesse Nature Centre
Morne Rouge Bay
Woburn
La Sagesse Bay
Marquis Point
Point Salines International Airport
Lance aux Epines
Westerhall Point
12°00'N
Point Salines
True Blue Bay
Hog Island
Calivigny Island
Glover Island
Prickly Point

0 · 1.5 · 3 km
0 · 1 · 2 miles

61°45'W · 61°40'W

area over the hill to the west of the harbor. Most tourist amenities are located around the Carenage (the prestigious address), while the local shops and services tend to be in the market area. Farther south from the Carenage, the road sweeps around another deep inlet called the Lagoon on its way to the long resort precinct at Grand Anse.

The maze of streets on the west side of the Carenage is fun to wander through. At Scott and Lucas Sts a smartly uniformed police officer (locally dubbed 'cop in a box') directs traffic at a busy blind corner. On congested Young St are some interesting craft shops and art galleries. There's a neglected botanical garden at the southeast side of town, a 10-minute walk from the post office.

At the cruise-ship dock you'll find a line of stalls where island women sell fragrant spice baskets, cloth dolls and other souvenir items. On cruise-ship days water taxis shuttle from the cruise-ship dock to the Renaissance Hotel at Grand Anse Beach.

Information

Tourist Offices The Grenada Tourist Board (☎ 440-6637, www.grenada.org), at the cruise-ship dock, is open 8 am to 4 pm weekdays.

Money Barclays Bank and Scotiabank are both on Halifax St and open 8 am to 3 pm Monday to Thursday, 8 am to 5 pm Friday. Both banks have 24-hour ATMs. There are more banks with ATMs at Grande Anse.

Post & Communications The general post office (☎ 440-2526), on the south side of the harbor, is open from 8 am to 3:30 pm weekdays.

You can make phone calls and send faxes from the Cable & Wireless office at the Carenage 7:30 am to 6 pm weekdays, 7:30 am to 1 pm Saturday and 10 am to noon Sunday.

Email & Internet Access Hankey's Computer Services (☎ 443-050, fax 443-0506), upstairs in the One Stop Building on Grenville St at the rear of the market, has a

---

The *Bianca C*

At over 600 feet in length, the Italian liner *Bianca C* is the largest shipwreck in the Eastern Caribbean. In 1939 construction began in France. While the boat was still incomplete, she was sunk by the Germans during their retreat in August 1944. She was raised and refitted, and changed hands (and names) several times before an Italian magnate purchased her for a Naples to Guaira (Venezuela) run. For such voyages, Grenada was a regular port of call.

In the early morning of October 22, 1961, the ship was anchored in St George's outer harbor preparing to sail when an explosion ripped through the engine room, setting off a fire that quickly engulfed the vessel.

A flotilla of yachts, fishing boats and interisland schooners came to assist in the rescue, and 672 of 673 people aboard were saved. Twelve crewmen were badly burned and taken to hospital; one, Rodizza Napale, subsequently died.

A few days later, a British frigate *Londonderry* arrived from Puerto Rico and towed the smoldering vessel out of the harbor and toward the shallows around Point Saline. But the towrope broke, and the *Bianca C* foundered and sank in 167 feet of water. Now the region's best-known dive wreck, she lies upright on a sand bed with her upper decks 100 feet below the surface.

The cause of the explosion remains a mystery.

---

dozen or so terminals and charges EC$10 per hour for Internet access. Carenage Cafe has access for EC$20 per hour. There are just two terminals, and often a wait.

Bookstores St George's Bookshop (☎ 440-2309), on Halifax St, has a fairly good collection of Caribbean books. Sea Change Bookshop (☎ 440-3402) is below The Nutmeg restaurant and sells local and US newspapers. Both sell maps of Grenada.

GRENADA

ST GEORGE'S

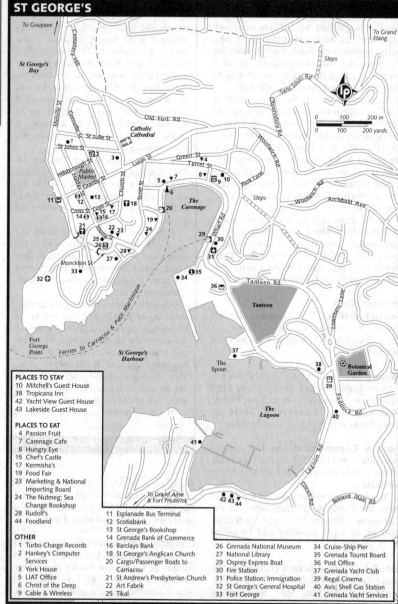

To Gouyave
To Grand Etang

St George's Bay

Cemetery Hill

Melville St
Grenville St

St Julie St
St Johns St
Hillsborough St
Granby St
Church St
Cross St
Young St
Scott St
Monckton St

Old Fort Rd
Catholic Cathedral
Lucas St
Green St
Tyrrel St
Park Lane
Observatory Rd
Sans Souci Rd
Woolwich Rd
Archibald Ave
Steps

Public Market

The Carenage

Wharf Rd

Fort George Point
Ferries to Carriacou & Petit Martinique

St George's Harbour

The Spout

The Lagoon

Tanteen Rd
Tanteen
Lowther's Lane

Botanical Garden
Paddock Rd
Regal Cinema

Lagoon Rd
Green Rd
Belmont Main Rd

To Grand Anse & Fort Frederick

0   100   200 m
0   100   200 yards

PLACES TO STAY
10 Mitchell's Guest House
38 Tropicana Inn
42 Yacht View Guest House
43 Lakeside Guest House

PLACES TO EAT
4 Passion Fruit
7 Carenage Cafe
8 Hungry Eye
15 Chef's Castle
17 Kermisha's
19 Food Fair
23 Marketing & National Importing Board
24 The Nutmeg; Sea Change Bookshop
28 Rudolf's
44 Foodland

OTHER
1 Turbo Charge Records
2 Hankey's Computer Services
5 LIAT Office
6 Christ of the Deep
9 Cable & Wireless
11 Esplanade Bus Terminal
12 Scotiabank
13 St George's Bookshop
14 Grenada Bank of Commerce
16 Barclays Bank
18 St George's Anglican Church
20 Cargo/Passenger Boats to Carriacou
21 St Andrew's Presbyterian Church
22 Art Fabrik
25 Tikal
26 Grenada National Museum
27 National Library
29 Osprey Express Boat
30 Fire Station
31 Police Station; Immigration
32 St George's General Hospital
33 Fort George
34 Cruise-Ship Pier
35 Grenada Tourist Board
36 Post Office
37 Grenada Yacht Club
39 Regal Cinema
40 Avis; Shell Gas Station
41 Grenada Yacht Services

Grenada National Museum

The Grenada National Museum, on the corner of Young and Monckton Sts, incorporates old French barracks dating from 1704. The building served as a prison from 1766 to 1880 and as the island's first hotel, in the 1900s.

The collection of exhibits includes Amerindian pottery fragments, an old rum still and a grubby marble bathtub that once belonged to Empress Josephine. There's also a display on the events leading to the assassination of Maurice Bishop and the US invasion that followed.

The museum is open 9 am to 4:30 pm weekdays, 10 am to 1:30 pm Saturday. Admission is EC$5 for adults and EC$1 for children.

Fort George

Fort George, on the hilltop promontory at the west side of the Carenage, is Grenada's oldest fort, established by the French in 1705. The site provides stunning views of the harbor, the Lagoon and down toward Grande Anse. The national police occupy many of the fort buildings, but the grounds are open to the public and it's well worth the steep climb up from town. The church spires, red-tile roofs and colonial façades, the green mountains behind, and the docks and tethered ships make a glorious picture.

In the inner fort, just below the row of cannons, is the courtyard where Maurice Bishop was executed. You can see the bullet holes in the basketball pole made by the firing squad, and the spot is marked by a fading graffito that reads 'No Pain No Gain Brother.'

The entrance to the fort is at the end of Church St. Admission is free.

Churches

St George's has a number of 19th-century churches. They are not themselves extraordinary, but they combine nicely with the architecture and the skyline.

The most interesting is St George's Anglican Church, on Church St. Built in 1825, it has a four-sided clock tower that serves as the town timepiece. A marble tablet commemorates the English colonists killed in the 1795 French-inspired Fedon uprising.

The Catholic cathedral, the largest, has a brightly painted interior. It's opposite York House, a building of early Georgian architecture that holds the Supreme Court, House of Representatives and Senate.

The yellow brick church immediately north of Fort George is St Andrew's Presbyterian Church, which dates from 1833 and has a spired four-sided clock tower.

Fort Frederick

Fort Frederick, atop Richmond Hill 1¼ miles east of St George's, was constructed by the French in 1779 after they had wrested control of the island from the British. After 1783, when the French were forced by treaty to return Grenada to the British, the fort served to guard against the threat of French attacks. Cessation of hostilities between the two powers led to the fort's abandonment in the 1850s. It now provides a fine panoramic view that includes Quarantine Point, Point Salines and Grover Island (Grover Island, incidentally, was used until 1927 as a Norwegian whaling station).

Fort Frederick remains intact due to a targeting blunder made by the US during the 1983 invasion. US forces intended to hit Fort Frederick, then used by the Grenadian military, but instead bombed Fort Matthew, just a few hundred yards to the north, which was then a mental hospital. You can walk the grounds of the fort free.

Places to Stay

Most visitors stay in the resort areas of Grande Anse and Morne Rouge, but St George's has a good collection of budget rooms. Prices quoted here do not include the 18% tax and service charge.

Bailey's Inn (☎ 440-2912, fax 440-0532), just outside St George's on a hillside in Springs, has simple accommodations for US$20 per person.

Yacht View Guest House (☎ 440-3607), on Lagoon Rd, is near the Foodland supermarket. It's straightforward and clean, with five rooms that share two baths. There's a common kitchen and a little balcony that overlooks the yacht harbor. Singles/doubles cost just US$23/26, but it's often booked solid in winter.

A few doors away on Lagoon Rd is *Lakeside Guest House* (☎ 440-2365), where clean singles/doubles with sink can be had for a reasonable US$15/30.

St Ann's Guest House (☎ 440-2717, 16 Paddock Rd), is on the southeast side of town. It's a characterless modern building, 20 minutes' walk from the center on a main bus route. There are a dozen clean, simple rooms, each with sink. Singles/doubles with private bath cost US$25/50.

Mitchell's Guest House (☎ 440-2803), on Tyrrel St, is an older place in town. Simple singles/doubles with shared bath cost US$23/36. It can be noisy.

Tropicana Inn (☎ 440-1586, fax 440-9797, tropicana@caribsurf.com), on Lagoon Rd, is a terrific place fronting the Lagoon on the south side of town. The rooms have air-con, TV and phone, and the year-round rates are US$55/65/75 for singles/doubles/triples, some with balconies. There's a pleasant restaurant and a bar downstairs.

Mount Helicon Great House (☎ 440-2444, fax 440-7168, mthelicon@caribsurf .com), Upper Lucas St, on the hillside above St George's, occupies a restored estate house. The seven rooms are simple but pleasant, with phones, fans and private baths, and some with air-con. Singles/doubles cost US$40/65. The guest house is 100 yards east of St George's northernmost traffic circle and can be reached via the St Paul's bus (EC$1.50).

Places to Eat

Budget On the inner Carenage, *Hungry Eye* has good, cheap eats, with chicken rotis for EC$6 and plate lunches for EC$11. It's open 7 am until late Monday to Saturday, 10 am to 10 pm Sunday.

Chef's Castle (☎ 440-7494), at Halifax and Gore Sts, is a modern fast-food restaurant with ice cream, hot burgers and rotis for around EC$10; open 9 am to 10 pm Monday to Saturday.

Excellent local food is served nearby at *Kermisha's* (☎ 440-1146), which is located on the upper floor of the Singer building on Gore St. It's neat and friendly, with rotis and sandwiches from EC$7 and a meal of the day for EC$12. There are good views from its windows. It's open 9 am to 5 pm weekdays.

Passion Fruit (☎ 440-5910), on Tyrrel St, is popular. Inexpensive fish sandwiches, rotis and juices are served. It's open 9 am to 4:30 pm weekdays.

The Italian *Carenage Cafe* (☎ 440-8701), next to the LIAT office at the Carenage, has homemade ice cream for EC$1.80 a scoop and Italian coffee, juice, sandwiches, pizza and other light fare. It's central and in a scenic location, and it's a good place to rest from the midday heat. It's open 8 am to 11 pm Monday to Saturday.

Foodland (☎ 440-1991), on Lagoon Rd, is Grenada's largest supermarket and the best place to find imported Western foods; it's open 9 am to 7:30 pm Monday to Saturday. On the west side of the Carenage, *Food Fair* (☎ 440-2588) also sells groceries for those who went to prepare their own food.

Fruit and vegetables are sold at the *public market* and at the *Marketing & National Importing Board*, a farmers' cooperative on Young St.

Mid-Range The harbor-view tables upstairs at *The Nutmeg* (☎ 440-2539), on the west side of the Carenage, make it very popular. At lunch and dinner, there are sandwiches and rotis for EC$12, fish & chips for EC$20 and curried conch for EC$30. Specialties include spicy callaloo soup, seafood and potent nutmeg rum punch. The local Carib beer is on tap. It's open 9 am to around 10:30 pm Monday to Saturday, from 5 pm Sunday.

Rudolf's (☎ 440-2241), on Wharf Rd in the Carenage, is a relaxed pub-style restaurant that's often frequented by expats. Sandwiches start at EC$8, and flying fish, mahimahi or chicken with french fries costs EC$25. Lambi is a few more dollars. It's open 10 am to midnight Monday to Saturday.

Mount Helicon Restaurant (☎ 440-2444), on Upper Lucas St, serves upmarket West Indian food in a atmospheric dining room decorated in colonial-estate-house style. Traditional Grenadian breakfasts of fish cakes and saltfish souse, or light lunch fare, costs around EC$17. At lunch and dinner you can get main courses like flying fish for EC$30 and lobster for EC$65.

Entertainment & Shopping

The *Regal Cinema* (☎ 440-2403), on Paddock Rd, shows Hollywood films each evening for EC$6.50.

A good place to pick up quality spices at good prices is the Marketing & National Importing Board (☎ 440-1791), on Young St, which also sells local hot sauces, sorrel, nutmeg syrups, and nutmeg and guava jams.

Art Fabrik (☎ 440-0568), next door at 9 Young St, sells batik wall hangings and clothing that are made on site. Tikal (☎ 440-2310), also on Young St, has a collection of local handicrafts, batiks and wood carvings.

Turbo Charge Records (☎ 440-0586), on St John St, is a good music store.

Getting There & Around

Buses leave St George's from the Esplanade bus terminal at the west end of Granby St. Signs mark some routes; ask someone if you're not sure who's going where or which bus you need. From the terminal it's better to jump aboard a bus when's it's nearly full, because they don't leave until they are. There are stops along all the major routes, and you can flag down a bus pretty much anywhere.

Taxis within the city cost EC$8.

GRAND ANSE

Grenada's main resort area is along Grand Anse Beach, a long, broad sweep of white sand fronted by aqua blue Caribbean water. Grande Anse is very beautiful. It does have vendors selling T-shirts and spice baskets, and others offering to braid hair, but overall the activity is low-key and hassle-free. Grande Anse is the essence and focus of experience for so many visitors to Grenada – staying in a beachside room and shuffling down to the beach for the day with a book and a beach chair, eating, drinking and relaxing. The beach offers everything for the tourist with the American dollar – parasailing, Jet-ski rental, water taxis, snorkeling, sailing. There's an atmosphere of glamorous indulgence in physical pleasures, and a letting-go of tensions and anxieties that is the Caribbean way – 'walk slowly, speak easy.'

There are numerous places to eat and stay around Grand Anse. The most expensive hotels front the beach, and rates drop as you get farther away. Many hotels are built on the hillsides that front Grand Anse Beach, and thus many hotel rooms have spectacular views.

Information

The Grand Anse Shopping Centre, opposite Renaissance Hotel, has a Scotiabank, a gift shop and a Food Fair supermarket (☎ 444-4573) open 9 am to 5:30 pm Monday to Thursday, till 7 pm Friday and Saturday.

Another cluster of shops a few hundred yards to the west, at the roundabout, features a drugstore, two banks with ATMs and a 'D' Green Grocer, a small general store. Le Marquis Complex is on the southern corner of the roundabout and has some good places to eat, a record shop and a travel agent.

Places to Stay

Budget About a 10-minute walk from the beach is *Palm Grove Guest House* (☎ 444-4578, fax 444-0943, palmgro@caribsurf.com, PO Box 568, St George's), 200 yards uphill from the Grand Anse Shopping Centre. The dozen cheerless rooms have private baths and there's a communal kitchen. Singles/doubles cost US$30/40.

The Village Hotel (☎ 444-4097, fax 444-4098, kbboy@caribsurf.com, PO Box 602, St George's) is in the same area but closer to the beach. The dozen simple self-catering singles/doubles (US$40/60) feature private baths. It's comfortable and a good value.

Camerhogne Park Hotel (☎ 444-4110, fax 444-3111, camhotel@caribsurf.com), a block from the beach, has 25 rooms in a few two-story buildings. The rooms are worn but have air-con, TV and phone. Singles/doubles cost US$45/55 year-round. There are also

GRENADA

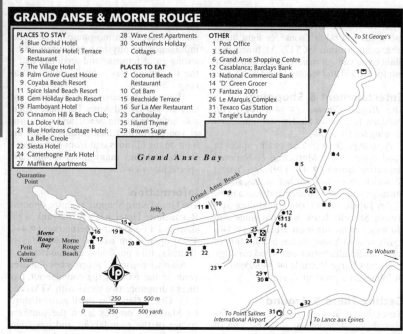

GRAND ANSE & MORNE ROUGE

PLACES TO STAY
4 Blue Orchid Hotel
5 Renaissance Hotel; Terrace Restaurant
7 The Village Hotel
8 Palm Grove Guest House
9 Coyaba Beach Resort
11 Spice Island Beach Resort
18 Gem Holiday Beach Resort
19 Flamboyant Hotel
20 Cinnamon Hill & Beach Club; La Dolce Vita
21 Blue Horizons Cottage Hotel; La Belle Creole
22 Siesta Hotel
24 Camerhogne Park Hotel
27 Maffiken Apartments
28 Wave Crest Apartments
30 Southwinds Holiday Cottages

PLACES TO EAT
2 Coconut Beach Restaurant
10 Cot Bam
15 Beachside Terrace
16 Sur La Mer Restaurant
23 Canboulay
25 Island Thyme
29 Brown Sugar

OTHER
1 Post Office
3 School
6 Grand Anse Shopping Centre
12 Casablanca; Barclays Bank
13 National Commercial Bank
14 'D' Green Grocer
17 Fantazia 2001
26 Le Marquis Complex
31 Texaco Gas Station
32 Tangie's Laundry

To St George's

Grand Anse Bay

Quarantine Point

Grand Anse Beach

Jetty

Morne Rouge Bay

Morne Rouge Beach

Petit Cabrits Point

0   250   500 m
0   250   500 yards

To Point Salines International Airport

To Woburn

To Lance aux Épines

self-contained apartments that accommodate six people and cost from US$90 to US$130.

Southwinds Holiday Cottages (☎ 444-4310, fax 444-4404, PO Box 118, St George's) has 19 apartments in boxy two-story buildings about a 10-minute walk from the beach. The simple units have kitchens, phones and TV. Fan-cooled one-bedroom apartments cost US$50, and air-conditioned singles are US$60. Two-bedroom air-conditioned apartments cost US$90 for up to four people. Rates are US$10 less during the summer.

Wave Crest Apartments (☎/fax 444-4116, wavecrest@grenadaexplorer.com, PO Box 278, St George's) is close by and offers attractive one-bedroom singles/doubles with air-con, TV, phone, kitchen/dining area and balcony with great views for US$55/80 in summer and US$65/95 in winter. Two-bedroom apartments cost US$80 in summer, US$100 in winter for up to four

people. Wave Crest is a five-minute walk from the Grande Anse beach.

Maffiken Apartments (☎ 444-4255, fax 444-2832, PO Box 534, St George's) offers good-value apartments with kitchen, air-con, phone, TV and veranda. One-bedroom singles/doubles cost US$70 a day, US$380 a week in summer; US$80 a day, US$430 a week in winter. Two-bedroom units cost US$80 a day, US$410 a week in summer; US$90 a day, US$480 a week in winter.

Blue Orchid Hotel (☎ 444-0999, fax 444-1846, dovetail@caribsurf.com, PO Box 857, St George's) is a 15-room hotel a few minutes' walk from the beach. The singles/doubles, with air-con, TV, fridge, private bath and balcony, cost from US$60/70 in summer, US$60/80 in winter. Rooms with kitchenettes are US$10 more.

Mid-Range The ***Siesta Hotel*** (☎ 444-4645, fax 444-4647, siesta@caribsurf.com, www.cpscaribnet.com/ads/siesta, PO Box 27, St

George's) has 37 rooms and is popular with Europeans. The rooms are very comfortable, with balconies, TV, air-con, bathtubs and tile floors. There's also a pool that is shaped like a piano. Singles/doubles cost from US$85/115 upward, with breakfast included. You can also get a kitchenette unit without breakfast for the same rate or a spacious one-bedroom apartment which costs US$109/140.

Coyaba Beach Resort (☎ 444-4129, fax 444-4808, coyaba@caribsurf.com, www .coyaba.com, PO Box 336, St George's) is a 70-room beachfront resort on Grand Anse. Rooms are comfortable, with satellite TV, air-con, phones, hair dryers and terraces, and most have at least a partial ocean view. Singles/doubles cost US$95/120 in summer, US$155/210 in winter. There's a swimming pool and tennis court, too.

Top End A good top-end option is *Flamboyant Hotel* (☎ 444-4247, fax 444-1234, flambo@caribsurf.com, www.flamboyant .com, PO Box 214, St George's), an attractive hillside complex at the west end of Grand Anse Beach. There's a variety of accommodations, mostly in buildings of two to four units. All have ocean-facing terraces, phones, TV, air-con and bathtubs; some have hardwood floors. There's a pool, fine wines and steps leading down to the beach. Singles/doubles start at US$85/95 in summer, US$125/145 in winter. Better-value one-bedroom suites have full kitchens and cost US$10 to US$20 more. The Flamboyant has deluxe rooms also; a two-bedroom suite costs US$400 for four people.

The *Cinnamon Hill & Beach Club* (☎ 444-4301, fax 444-2874, cinnamonhill@ grenadaexplorer.com, www.cpscaribnet.com /ads/cinnhill, PO Box 292, St George's) has 26 units in a two-story Spanish-style villa. The units are large, with kitchens, big balconies and at least four beds and two bathrooms. The 2nd-floor apartments have beam ceilings and water views. Rates for one or two people are US$85 in summer, US$130 in winter for a one-bedroom apartment, or US$115 in summer, US$194 in winter for four in the two-bedroom apartments.

There's a pool and an Italian restaurant on the premises.

Blue Horizons Cottage Hotel (☎ 444-4316, fax 444-2815, blue@caribsurf.com, www.bluegrenada.com, PO Box 41, St George's) is a very nice place a just few minutes from Grand Anse Beach. The Mediterranean-style buildings house 32 spacious suites with kitchens, tile floors, ceiling fans, air-con, TV and phones. Single/ doubles cost from US$115/120 in summer and US$165/170 in winter. There's a pool, restaurant and bar.

Renaissance Hotel (☎ 444-4371, fax 444-4800, higda@caribsurf.com, PO Box 441, St George's) is Grenada's largest hotel, with 186 rooms in a sprawling, low-rise complex of beachside buildings. The Renaissance is typical of a large resort and the rooms lack any Caribbean flavor, but they are very comfortable, with air-con, TV and phones. The hotel boasts a beachfront pool and tennis courts. Singles/doubles begin at US$149/170 in summer, US$210/240 in winter.

Grenada's most plush place to stay is the *Spice Island Beach Resort* (☎ 444-4258, fax 444-4807, spiceisl@caribsurf.com, www .spicebeachresort.com, PO Box 6, St George's). It's an all-inclusive beachfront-resort-lifestyle experience. Some of the 56 suites have private pools, and all are fitted with luxuries. Rates start at US$346/429 in summer and US$411/515 in winter. You can't afford to stay here.

Places to Eat
Budget In the Grand Anse Shopping Centre, *Rick's Cafe* (☎ 444-4597) sells ice cream for EC$4 a cone, as well as sandwiches, burgers and pizza. It's open 11 am to 9:30 pm Monday to Saturday, from 4 pm Sunday.

Three good spots are in Le Marquis Complex. *La Boulangerie* (☎ 444-1131) is a French bakery and coffee shop. Excellent breads are sold here along with raisin rolls, apple turnovers, pastries and Italian ice cream – each for around EC$5. Sandwiches, generous pizza slices (EC$5) and pizzas to order (from EC$20) are also on offer. It's open 8 am to 8 pm Monday to Saturday, 9 am to 2 pm Sunday. *Nick's Donut World* (☎ 444-2460) is not quite as classy, but does do good sandwiches and rolls (EC$6 to EC$10). Nick's sells fresh muffins and donuts also. *Le Chateau* (☎ 444-2552) is a simple bar that serves light meals as well. It's open 10 am to midnight weekdays, 6 pm to midnight Sunday.

Island Thyme (☎ 444-5205), located next to the Camerhogne Park Hotel, serves simple West Indian food for lunch and dinner.

Cot Bam, a large open-air bar and restaurant on Grand Anse Beach, has rotis, sandwiches, chicken or fish & chips for EC$16 and fish dishes for EC$35. It's open 9:30 am to 11 pm.

Mid-Range The *veranda restaurant* at the Siesta Hotel (see Places to Stay – Mid-Range) has a relaxed feel. Full breakfasts cost EC$30, and a nice mix of local and Mediterranean evening dishes costs from EC$35. It's open from 7:30 to 11 am and 6 to 9:30 pm.

Flamboyant Hotel's *Beachside Terrace* (☎ 444-4247) is an open-air restaurant with a fine sea view. Breakfasts are served for EC$25; fish & chips, rotis or fresh tuna salad are available through the day. At dinner, main dishes cost from EC$40 for fish dishes to EC$65 for lobster. It's open 7:30 am to 10:30 pm daily.

Fine Italian food is prepared at *La Dolce Vita* (☎ 444-3456), at the Cinnamon Hill & Beach Club. Tables and chairs are set up on a pleasant veranda cooled by evening breezes. The Italian chef makes his own pasta and combines traditional Italian dishes with the abundant local seafood. A small plate of antipasto is EC$16, and main dishes range from EC$30 to EC$60. It's open for dinner 7 to 11 pm daily except Monday.

The Renaissance's open-air *Terrace Restaurant* (☎ 444-4371) has a good breakfast buffet of juices, fresh fruit, yogurt, pastries and omelets to order. It's served from 7 to 10 am and costs EC$20 Continental style or EC$35 for the full selection. The evening

table d'hôte menu is reasonable, if a little unimaginative.

Brown Sugar (☎ 444-2374, fax 444-5777) is a bit special. The decor resembles that of an old plantation house and the food is an upmarket blend of traditional West Indian cuisine and international influences. Entrees begin at EC$20 and include callaloo soup with dumplings and saltfish souse. Main dishes start at around EC$35 and feature local seafood and spices with a fine touch of elegance. It's open from 6 to 11 pm daily, and there's live pan music every Friday night.

La Belle Creole (☎ 444-4316, fax 444-2815) is on the grounds of the Blue Horizons Cottage Hotel. Here too the food is a creative blend of West Indian and contemporary influences – fish fondue, spiced ginger pork chops and callaloo chicken casserole. Main dishes start at EC$40, and reservations are recommended. Meals are served from 7:30 to 10 am, 11 am to 2 pm and 7 to 9 pm

Top End The *Coconut Beach Restaurant* (☎ 444-4644) is a casual place on the water at the east side of Grand Anse Beach that specializes in French Creole cuisine with a touch of Grenadian spices. At lunch you can get a sandwich, a cheese-and-tomato crêpe or quiche lorraine for under EC$20. At dinner, à la carte main courses, such as curried lambi or fresh fish, average EC$50. You can dine indoors, but fine dining on the Grande Anse beach sand under a thatched umbrella is a memorable experience. It's open 12:30 to 10 pm daily except Tuesday.

The much-lauded *Canboulay* (☎ 444-4401) sits on a hillside with a panoramic view. This is Grenada's finest restaurant and regarded among the best in the entire Caribbean region, with creative cuisine that combines West Indian, African and European influences. You won't get too much change from EC$100 per person, but the food and the setting are nothing short of spectacular. It's open for dinner from 6:30 pm nightly except Sunday, and reservations are recommended.

Entertainment & Shopping

A popular nightspot, *Casablanca* (☎ 444-1631), above Barclays Bank in Grand Anse, features jazz and live music a few nights a week, and a DJ on other nights. It's open nightly until at least 1 am. There's no cover charge. Fantazia 2001 (see Morne Rouge) has dancing on Wednesday, Friday and Saturday evenings with a modest cover charge.

Roots Record Shop (☎ 440-8423) is a small specialist reggae and Jamaican music store in Le Marquis Complex. The staff are friendly and can help with your selection if you're not sure what you want. You can listen to CDs before you buy.

The House of Tobacco (☎ 440-8369) is also in Le Marquis Complex. Come here for a large range of Cuban and Dominican cigars and smokers' paraphernalia.

MORNE ROUGE

Morne Rouge is an affluent little neighborhood that fronts a lovely beach-lined bay, just over the little peninsula that leads out to Quarantine Point, 10 minutes' walk from the end of Grande Anse Beach. It has a quieter, more exclusive air. The walk from Grande Anse is a pleasant climb over the hill past the site of a former leper colony. From the point there are views to Point Salines to the south and to Molinière Point to the north.

The swimming at Morne Rouge Beach is delicious – sparkling water, white sands and green hills all around. Tethered yachts move imperceptibly just offshore, and water taxis idle between the pleasure craft and beach looking for fares.

A few trees are in the sand for those who prefer their beach in the shade, and there's good snorkeling, with sea fans and coral, around Petit Carib Point at the south end of the bay.

Places to Stay & Eat

The *Gem Holiday Beach Resort* (☎ 444-3737, fax 444-1189, gem@caribsurf.com, PO Box 58, St George's) has a fantastic location on the beachfront at the north side of Morne Rouge Bay. This is a pleasant place, but it's looking a little worn. The 18 units, all

have terraces, TV, phone and kitchenettes. One-bedroom singles/doubles cost from US$65/75, depending on the view and season. Quads start at US$135. There are sometimes discount walk-in rates, but it can be hard to get a room in winter, when it's heavily booked.

Sur La Mer Restaurant (☎ 444-2288) is on the beach and has a nice water view. It serves three meals a day, with an emphasis on seafood and West Indian dishes. There's often live music, and even fire eating and limbo dancing sometimes.

Nightclubbers go to the adjacent *Fantazia 2001* (☎ 444-3737), where there's dancing until 2 am Wednesday to Saturday.

POINT SALINES

The Point Salines area, around the airport, is dry and scrubby. St George's Medical School, a private school serving foreign students, is at the eastern tip of the airport runway. Ronald Reagan used the safety of the students at this small American-run facility as an excuse to justify his invading Grenada after the 1983 military coup.

There are good, less crowded beaches on either side of the airport runway, but otherwise there's not much to do around Point Salines. Some reasonably priced places to stay line the airport road, and a few resorts are north of the airport. Passing taxis are plentiful, but bus traffic is much lighter out here.

Places to Stay & Eat

The *No Problem Apartments* (☎ 444-4634, fax 444-2803, noprob@mail.idt.net, PO Box 280, St George's) are on the main road between the airport and Grand Anse. The 20 spacious apartments each have a kitchen, living room, separate bedroom with two twin beds, air-con, TV and phone. There's a pool, free airport transfer, shuttles to Grand Anse Beach and a small, moderately priced restaurant. Singles/doubles cost US$55/65 in summer, US$75/85 in winter.

Fox Inn (☎ 444-4123, fax 444-4177, PO Box 205, St George's) is a mile east of the terminal. Its 16 motel-style singles/doubles cost US$65/70 in summer and US$75/80 in winter. Also available are single apartments that cost US$80 in summer, US$95 in winter. Rooms have TV and phones, and there's a pool and restaurant.

The grand 212-room **Rex Grenadian Hotel** (☎ 444-3333, fax 444-1111, genrex@ caribsurf.com), on Magazin Beach, cost US$15 million to build in 1992. The Rex package includes all meals and certain activities. Hillside doubles start at US$270 in summer, US$300 in winter, and beachfront rooms are US$390 in summer, US$420 in winter.

With plush 102 rooms fronting Pingouin Beach, **La Source** (☎ 444-2556, fax 444-2561, info@lasourcegrenada.com, www .lasourcegrenada.com) is an upmarket resort that offers all-inclusive packages (from US$325 per person).

LANCE AUX ÉPINES

Lance aux Épines (pronounced 'lance-a-peen') is the peninsula that forms the southernmost point of Grenada. It's an affluent and quiet area with fine coastal views, some good places to stay and pretty little beaches. Most activity is centered on the west side, which fronts Prickly Bay, the island's most popular yachting anchorage.

Information

Spice Island Marine Services (☎ 444-4342/4257, fax 444-2816, VHF channel 16) is a full-service marina on Prickly Bay. There's a customs and immigration office (☎ 444-4509), stern-to berths for 30 boats, fuel, water, electricity and public showers.

Places to Stay

The pleasant **Coral Cove** (☎ 444-4422, fax 444-4718, in the USA ☎ 800-322-1753, coralcv@caribsurf.com, PO Box 487, St George's) is a pleasant place on a knoll at the east side of Lance aux Épines. There's a view across Mt Hartman Bay to a run of peninsulas and islets. Apartments and cottages are fitted with modern kitchens, high ceilings, screened louvered windows and phones. Two-bedroom apartments have huge dining areas and balconies; views from the 2nd floor are better. One-/two-bedroom

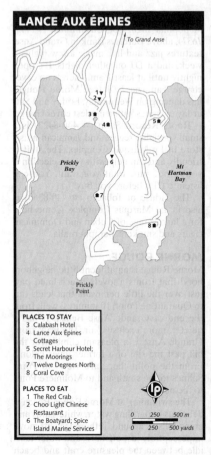

LANCE AUX ÉPINES

To Grand Anse

Prickly Bay

Mt Hartman Bay

Prickly Point

PLACES TO STAY
3 Calabash Hotel
4 Lance Aux Épines Cottages
5 Secret Harbour Hotel; The Moorings
7 Twelve Degrees North
8 Coral Cove

PLACES TO EAT
1 The Red Crab
2 Choo Light Chinese Restaurant
6 The Boatyard; Spice Island Marine Services

0   250   500 m
0   250   500 yards

apartments cost US$75/95 in summer and US$120/170 in winter. There's a swimming pool, tennis court and small beach, and snorkeling over the reef off the jetty.

Lance Aux Épines Cottages (☎ 444-4565, fax 444-2802, cottages@caribsurf.com, www.laecottages.com, PO Box 187, St George's) has 14 large apartments in duplex cottages, with full kitchens, screened windows, ceiling fans and TV. The cottages front a lovely tree-shaded beach. It's a good value and popular with return visitors. Rates are US$85 in summer, US$120 in winter for two people in a one-bedroom unit. Various other rooms are available, including a three-bedroom, two-bathroom apartment that sleeps six people for US$195 in summer, US$270 in winter. There are discounts for extended stays.

The small, exclusive beachside *Twelve Degrees North* (☎ /fax 444-4580, 12degrsn@caribsurf.com, www.twelvedegreesnorth.com, PO Box 241, St George's) is a resort on the west side of Lance aux Épines. The eight elegant apartments each come with a maid and have ocean-view balconies, and there's a pool, tennis court and small beach. One-bedroom apartments cost US$150 in summer, US$225 in winter for two people. Two-bedroom apartments cost US$265 in summer, US$350 in winter. Children under 12 are not allowed.

Owned by The Moorings, *Secret Harbour Hotel* (☎ 444-4548, fax 444-4819, in the USA ☎ 800-437-7880, secret@caribsurf.com, www.caribbeanhighlights.com/secretharbour, PO Box 11, St George's) is perched above Mt Hartman Bay. It has a pool, a restaurant and cool Mediterranean decor. There are 20 suites with balconies, two four-poster double beds, refrigerators and air-con. Rates are US$140 in summer, US$260 in winter for one or two people.

The *Calabash Hotel* (☎ 444-4334, fax 444-5050, calabash@caribsurf.com, www .calabashhotel.com, PO Box 382, St George's) is an upmarket beachside resort. The 28 suites have fans, air-con, sitting areas, terraces and tropical decor. Eight suites have private pools. Doubles with breakfast begin at US$250 in summer, US$415 in winter.

Places to Eat

The *Boatyard* (☎ 444-4662, fax 444-3636, boatyard@caribsurf.com), at Spice Island Marine Services, is open 8 am to 11 pm every day but Sunday. Burgers with fries cost EC$20, and fish or chicken dishes cost from EC$35. A Friday-evening steel band makes for an enjoyable atmosphere.

Choo Light Chinese Restaurant (☎ 444-2196), near the Calabash Hotel, has regular Cantonese food with main dishes from EC$30. It's open 11 am to 2:30 pm and 6 to 11 pm daily. Sunday it's closed for lunch.

The Red Crab (☎ 444-4424, redcrab@grenadaexplorer.com), next door, is a serious restaurant and has a following among locals and visitors. The steaks are excellent and the varied seasonal cuisine is imaginative. Seafood dishes are a good value from EC$30. There are salads, hamburgers, omelets and crêpes, all under EC$35. Dinner is à la carte, and a 'light bites' menu is offered from EC$35 along with other mains from EC$50. It's open 11 am to 2 pm and 6 to 11 pm Monday to Saturday.

LA SAGESSE NATURE CENTRE

La Sagesse Nature Centre fronts a deep, coconut-lined bay with protected swimming and a network of hiking trails. The center occupies the former estate of the late Lord Brownlow, a cousin of Queen Elizabeth II. His beachside estate house, built in 1968, has been turned into a small inn, and the agricultural property is now a government-operated banana plantation. The beach has a sandy bottom and calm waters. Just outside the gate is a water faucet where bathers can rinse off.

La Sagesse is about a 25-minute drive from St George's on the Eastern Main Rd.

Brownlow's Gate

Lord Brownlow gained infamy in the early 1970s when he built a gate at the entrance to his estate house of La Sagesse, blocking public access to the area's best beach. The Joint Endeavor for Welfare, Education and Liberation (Jewel) Movement, the opposition party, targeted 'Brownlow's Gate' as a symbol of lingering colonialism and incited islanders to tear the gate down. Brownlow fled the country.

When the People's Revolutionary Government gained control of the island in 1979, the estate was taken over and turned into a public agricultural campus. After the military coup of 1983 the property was abandoned until 1986, when it was restored as La Sagesse Nature Centre.

The great blue heron, stuck in reverse

The entrance is opposite an old abandoned rum distillery mill. From there it's half a mile through banana fields to La Sagesse Bay. St David–bound buses (EC$2.50) can drop you at the old distillery.

La Sagesse Trails

A trail to the northeast begins opposite the water faucet, outside Brownlow's Gate, and leads 20 minutes through scrubby terrain to Marquis Point, where there are good coastal views, including that of a sea arch. Don't get too close to the edge of the point, which is eroded and crumbly.

Another trail leads west from the center to a mangrove swamp and salt-pond habitat for herons, egrets and other shorebirds. It takes less than 10 minutes to reach the swamp.

La Sagesse Nature Centre (☎/fax 444-6458, in the USA ☎ 800-322-1753, isnature@caribsurf.com), PO Box 44, St George's, offers a tour that includes an hour-long guided nature walk through the nature center, some time on the beach, lunch and roundtrip transportation from your hotel for US$32.

Places to Stay & Eat

The handful of airy rooms at *La Sagesse Nature Centre* feature private baths, ceiling fans and double beds. A room with a kitchenette starts at US$80 in summer, US$110 in winter, while a budget room with fridge costs US$50 in summer, US$60 in winter.

The beachside restaurant, open daily for lunch and dinner, has fish sandwiches and burgers for EC$18 and fish or chicken dishes.

GRAND ETANG ROAD

The Grand Etang Rd cuts across the mountainous center of the island through the Grand Etang National Park. A waterfall and a number of forest trails are easily accessible. Take River Rd or Sans Souci Rd out of St George's, and when you reach the Mt Gay traffic circle, take the road north.

The road is in dreadful condition and is tortuously narrow and twisting, but otherwise it's a lovely drive through the rain forest. The area is thick with ferns, bamboo groves, heliconia and buttressed kapok trees, as well as roadside plantations of nutmeg, cocoa and bananas.

Annandale Falls

Annandale Falls is an idyllic waterfall with a 30-foot drop, surrounded by a grotto of lush vegetation. There's a pool beneath the falls where you can take a refreshing swim. Avoid the falls on days when a cruise ship arrives, because it's jam-packed with tourists and young men hustling for tips.

In the village of Constantine, 4 miles northeast of St George's, turn left on the road that leads downhill immediately past the yellow Methodist church. After three-quarters of a mile you'll reach the Annandale Falls visitors center. The falls are just a two-minute walk along a begonia-lined path that begins at the side of the center.

The visitors center is open 8 am to 4 pm weekdays, but the falls can be visited at any time. There's no entrance fee.

Grand Etang National Park

Two and a half miles north of Constantine, after the road winds steeply up to an elevation of 1900 feet, a roadside sign welcomes visitors to Grand Etang National Park.

Half a mile after entering the park you reach the visitors center, which overlooks Grand Etang Lake, a crater lake that forms the park's centerpiece. The visitors center (☎ 440-6160), open 8:30 am to 4 pm weekdays (and weekends if cruise ships are in), has displays on flora and fauna. Near the parking lot are a couple of stalls selling soft drinks and souvenirs.

Heading north from the park, the road hairpins down, offering views into valleys thickly forested with immortelle trees, which bloom bright red-orange in winter.

Park Trails The visitors center is the starting point for several trails that lead into the forest. Easiest is the **Morne La Baye Trail**, an interpretive walk that starts behind the visitors center, takes in a few view points and passes native vegetation, including the Grand Etang fern, whose sole habitat is in this area. The walk takes about 30 minutes roundtrip.

The **Grand Etang Shoreline Trail** is a 1½-hour loop walk around Grand Etang Lake. This is gentle but it can get muddy, and it doesn't offer the same sort of views as the higher trails.

The **Mt Qua Qua Trail** is a moderately difficult three-hour roundtrip hike that leads to the top of a ridge, offering some fine views of the interior forest.

Serious hikers branch off shortly before the end of the Mt Qua Qua Trail to pick up the **Concord Falls Trail** for a long trek to Concord Falls. This takes five hours one-way from the visitors center. From Concord Falls, you can walk another 1½ miles to the village of Concord on the west coast, where you can pick up a bus back to St George's.

A long, arduous hike leads deep into the forested interior to **Fedon's Camp**, the site where Julien Fedon, a rebel French plantation owner, hid out after a 1795 uprising in which he and his followers massacred the British governor and 47 other people (see History, earlier).

One of the nicest hikes is to the **Seven Sisters Falls**, a series of seven waterfalls in the forested interior east of the Grand Etang Rd. The main track is from the tin shed used by the banana association, 1¼ miles north of the visitors center on the right side of the Grand Etang Rd. The hike

from the shed takes about two hours roundtrip; there's a charge of EC$5 per person.

If you prefer a guide on the longer hikes the visitors center can arrange one.

GRENVILLE

Grenville is the main port on the east coast and a regional center for collecting cocoa, nutmeg and other crops. Grenada's second-largest town, known as La Baye by the French, it was established in 1763.

The town center consists of a couple of blocks along the waterfront. There's a Barclays Bank, police station, post office, supermarket and public market. Near the public market is the island's largest nutmeg processing station.

While the town doesn't hold a lot of interest for most visitors, there are a few older buildings of some note, including the Grenville Court House (c. 1886) near the market, the old police station and a couple of churches.

Grenville is fairly easy to get to by bus, and the ride (EC$5) from St George's, along Grand Etang Rd, is the island's most scenic.

Pearls Airport

The Grenville area's best-known site is Pearls Airport, 2 miles north of town, which served as the island's airport until the Cubans built Point Salines International Airport in 1983. The runway at Pearls still has a Russian biplane and a rusting Cubana aircraft, abandoned during the US invasion in October 1983. The Grenada Defense Force has barracks at the airstrip, but there's no problem driving into the site. The runway is overrun with weeds and goats and cows, and it looks a little forlorn.

Grenada was one of the first islands settled by migrating Amerindians from South America, and the airport area was a major settlement and burial ground. Thousands of pottery shards and grinding stones have been collected over the years. Although the construction of the airport in the 1940s damaged much of the site, the area north of the runway still has significant Amerindian remains; these are all protected by restrictions prohibiting souvenir hunting.

NORTH OF GRENVILLE

As the road continues north from Grenville, it passes through a run of small towns, occasional stone churches and abandoned mills, and lots of old wooden homes, some on stilts. At the large church in Tivoli village, turn right to continue north to the distillery and Lake Antoine.

The **River Antoine Rum Distillery** (☎ 442-7109) has been producing rum since 1785 and claims to have the oldest working water mill in the Caribbean. It's incredible that it works at all, considering how run-down the distillery is. For EC$5 one of the workers will provide a tour; it's open 8 am to 4 pm weekdays. The distillery is south of the lake and most easily accessed from the Tivoli direction. **Lake Antoine**, a crater lake in an extinct volcano, is a mile south of River Sallee.

BATHWAYS BEACH & AROUND

From River Sallee, a road leads to Bathways Beach, where's there's a beach of speckled coral sands. At the north end a rock shelf parallels the shoreline, creating a very long, 30-foot-wide pool that's great for swimming in. The pool is protected from the strong currents and Atlantic seas outside the shelf.

There's a small visitor facility opposite the beach housing simple displays on shells, coral and ecology, as well as restrooms.

Three islands lie off Bathways Beach. From west to east they are Sugar Loaf, a privately owned island with a cottage on its south shore; Green Island, which has a few abandoned buildings but no beach; and **Sandy Island**, an uninhabited island with a freshwater cistern. Sandy Island also shelters an abandoned hotel, crystal-clear waters and a beautiful beach on its leeward side that offers fine swimming and snorkeling. It's possible to arrange for a boat in Sauteurs to take you to Sandy Island; make inquiries with the fishers on Sauteurs Beach – expect to pay about EC$150 per boat roundtrip.

LEVERA BEACH

Levera Beach is a wild, beautiful sweep of sand backed by eroded sea cliffs. Just offshore is the high, pointed Sugar Loaf Island (also called Levera Island), while the Grenadine Islands dot the horizon to the north. The beach, the mangrove swamp and the nearby pond have been incorporated into Grenada's national-park system and are an important waterfowl habitat and sea-turtle nesting site.

The road north from Bathways Beach to Levera Beach is usually passable in a vehicle, but it can be rough, so most visitors end up hiking in. The walk from Bathways Beach takes about 30 minutes; stick to the road, as sea cliffs and rough surf make it impossible to walk along the coast between the two beaches.

SAUTEURS

Sauteurs is the largest town on the north side of Grenada, taking its name from the French word for 'jump' and its place in history as the site where, in 1651, Carib families jumped to their deaths in their final retreat from approaching French soldiers. Today these 130-foot-high coastal cliffs are called Caribs' Leap. They are the town's main tourist site.

The cliffs are on the north side of the cemetery, behind St Patrick's Church – from the ledge you can look down on the fishing boats along the village beach and get a view of the offshore islands. The largest is Isle de Ronde, home to a few families. The small islets to the left are called The Sisters; to the right, and closer to shore, is London Bridge, an arch-shaped rock.

Places to Stay & Eat

Most people touring the island dine at *Morne Fendue Plantation House* (☎ 442-9330), 1½ miles south of Sauteurs. The house was built in 1908 with river stones and a mortar of lime and molasses. Simple guest rooms upstairs have creaky floors and lots of character, and cost US$35 per person, US$40 with a private bathroom.

A West Indian buffet is served up nightly on the veranda; dishes include pepperpot, chicken fricassee, callaloo soup, pigeon peas and rice, christophene and plantain – many of the items grown in the gardens. Lunch, available from 12:30 to 3 pm Monday to Saturday, costs EC$40. Reservations are advised.

The house, marked by a small sign, is in the village of Morne Fendue.

VICTORIA

The west-coast road can be a bit hair-raising – sections of it are along eroded cliffs that occasionally release falling rocks. One of the larger of the fishing villages that dot the west coast is Victoria, which has churches, schools, a post office, a market, a police station and a health clinic. Grass Roots, by the Victoria Bridge at the south end of town, sells quality crafts. Buses to St George's cost EC$3.50 and take about 30 minutes.

Places to Stay & Eat

The *Victoria Hotel* (☎ 444-9367, fax 444-4116), on Queen St, is a 10-room hotel on the waterfront in the village center. The rooms, above a restaurant and bar, have high ceilings, fans, satellite TV and either a double bed or two single beds. Singles/doubles cost US$30/45. The hotel restaurant has reasonably priced West Indian fare at lunch and dinner.

GOUYAVE

Gouyave, between Victoria and Concord, has a market, a bank and a couple of snack shops in the town center. On the town's main road is a large **nutmeg processing station**. One of the workers will take visitors on a tour through fragrant vats of curing nuts and various sorting operations. Tickets are sold at the office for US$1, and a tip to the guide of about the same amount is the norm. It's open 8 am to 4 pm weekdays.

Just south of the bridge, on the south side of Gouyave, a road leads inland half a mile along the river to the **Dougaldston Estate**, where cocoa and spices are processed.

CONCORD FALLS

There are a couple of scenic waterfalls along the Concord River. The lowest, a pic-turesque 100-foot cascade, can be viewed by driving to the end of Concord Mountain Rd, a side road leading 1½ miles inland from the village of Concord. These falls, which have a swimming pool, are on private property and the owner charges US$1 to visit them.

The trail to the upper falls begins at the end of the road and takes about 30 minutes to hike each way. Because of a history of muggings, the tourist office now provides a uniformed security guard, who will on request accompany visitors on the walk to the upper falls. Concord Falls are also accessible by a five-hour hiking trail from the Grand Etang National Park; see that section for details.

Back on the main road, just south of the turnoff to Concord Mountain Rd, there's a small roadside monument dedicated to the nine people killed when a dislodged boulder crushed the minibus they were traveling in.

Carriacou

Carriacou, 17 miles northeast of Grenada, is a rural island with small villages and good beaches. After the razzmatazz of St George's and Grenada, you'll find sleepy Carriacou ('carry-coo'), a laid-back delight and nice place to spend a day or three.

It's a hilly island, about 7 miles long and a third as wide. The dry, scrubby landscape is dotted with cacti and acacia, with bougainvillea adding color. Carriacou shelters 6000 people and a few more goats and sheep. It gets a few day-trippers who have bought roundtrip ferry tickets from St George's, and the island's low-key character and natural harbor attract yachters, but few other people have Carriacou on their itinerary. So you can swing your cat on the beach without hitting someone. The locals are friendly, and there are some nice places to eat and relax.

Carriacou has fantastic views of the neighboring Grenadines. You can spend a few hours on one of Carriacou's own nearshore islets picnicking, snorkeling and diving.

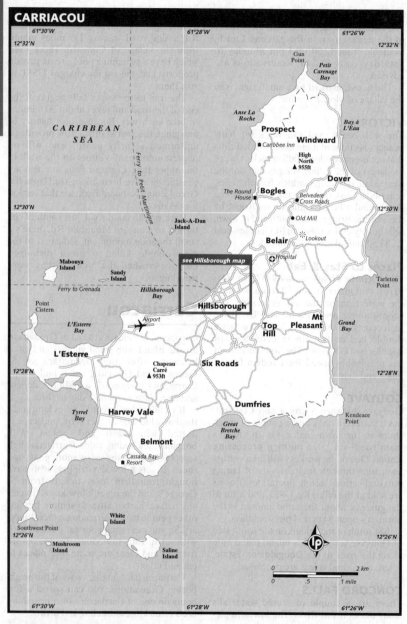

CARRIACOU

Prospect

Windward

Gun Point

Petit Carenage Bay

Anse La Roche

Bay á L'Eau

Dover

■ Caribbee Inn

High North
▲ 955ft

CARIBBEAN SEA

The Round House ■

Bogles

Belvedere
Cross Roads

● Old Mill

Jack-A-Dan Island

Belair

☼ *Lookout*

✚ *Hospital*

see Hillsborough map

Mabouya Island

Sandy Island

Ferry to Grenada

Hillsborough Bay

Hillsborough

Tarleton Point

Point Cistern

L'Esterre Bay

✈ *Airport*

Top Hill

Mt Pleasant

Grand Bay

L'Esterre

Chapeau Carré
▲ 953ft

Six Roads

Dumfries

Kendeace Point

Tyrrel Bay

Harvey Vale

Belmont

Great Bretche Bay

Cassada Bay
Resort ■

○ Mushroom Island

White Island

Southwest Point

Saline Island

0   1   2 km
0   .5   1 mile

Big Drum Dance

The Big Drum Dance is traditionally performed at weddings and ceremonies, and a tourist version is performed in Caribbean islands far away from Carriacou, but it's here that the tradition is authentic. The drums are just rum kegs with goatskin stretched over them, struck like congas and played in ensembles. The dancing is spectacular, as are the costumes.

Carriacou's people came from West Africa – Nigeria, Ghana, Sierra Leone and Guinea. Marriages between these peoples traditionally involved a lot of cultural interaction, and drums were used to assert tribal identity in the ceremonies. The Big Drum Dance is also involved in pre-Christian ancestor worship that goes back to West Africa and the tribal lands. The British were so unnerved by the practice that drumming was banned on Carriacou until independence – the colonists feared that the drums would lead an uprising against them.

The tradition has survived in Carriacou for 350 years despite repression, and it's the only surviving ceremony of its type in the Caribbean.

The island has a unique musical troupe that performs the Big Drum Dance, which is a quasi-religious rite with a lineage back to Africa (see 'Big Drum Dance').

There's also a strong history of boat building in Carriacou, and because of this, a prominent Scottish element in the local bloodline and family names – Scottish boat builders were imported during the British colonial period. Some might find it weird to be served by a white European bank teller with a thick West Indian accent, but this person may be as native to Carriacou as many of the black locals.

HILLSBOROUGH

Hillsborough, the administrative and commercial center of Carriacou, is an unspoiled and unhurried place – a mix of colorful wooden shops, cement buildings and ramshackle tin structures. It's almost completely undeveloped and has an easygoing tumbledown feel about it. Main St parallels the beach and has some interesting 19th-century buildings with stone ground floors and upper floors of shingle wood. These small buildings served as seaside warehouses.

Town activity is centered around the pier, where the ferries dock. The customs and immigration offices, public market, tourist office, post office, museum and bakery are all within an easy two-minute walk of the pier.

The pier's end offers a nice view out to Union Island and Hillsborough Bay and back at the little town – to the north is the beach at the Silver Beach Resort and to the south is the beach that fronts the rather imposing Catholic church. The grounds of the hospital, on a hilltop just north of town, offer a commanding view of the bay, the town and the nearby islands.

After the long manicured sweeps of beach at Grand Anse and Morne Rouge, Hillsborough's beach seems a little plain, narrow, white (flecked with black volcanic sand) and littered.

Information

Tourist Offices The tourist office (☎ 443-7948), on Patterson St, is open 8 am to noon and 1 to 4 pm weekdays.

Money Barclays Bank (☎ 443-7232) is on Main St toward the town's south side. National Commercial Bank (☎ 443-7289) is next to the pier; both are open normal banking hours on weekdays. There are no ATMs on Carriacou.

Post & Communications The post office (☎ 443-6014), in front of the pier, is open 8 to noon and 1 to 4 pm weekdays.

At Cable & Wireless (☎ 443-7000), on Patterson St, you can buy phone cards, send faxes and make international phone calls. It's open 7:30 am to 6 pm weekdays, till 1 pm Saturday. There are pay phones outside.

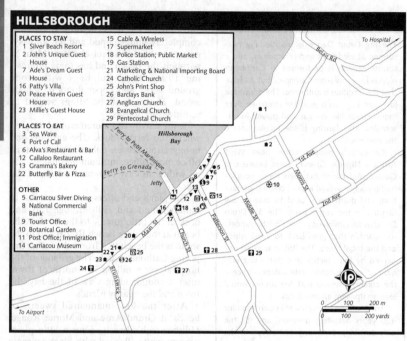

HILLSBOROUGH

PLACES TO STAY
1 Silver Beach Resort
2 John's Unique Guest
  House
7 Ade's Dream Guest
  House
16 Patty's Villa
20 Peace Haven Guest
  House
23 Millie's Guest House

PLACES TO EAT
3 Sea Wave
4 Port of Call
6 Alva's Restaurant & Bar
12 Callaloo Restaurant
13 Gramma's Bakery
22 Butterfly Bar & Pizza

OTHER
5 Carriacou Silver Diving
8 National Commercial
  Bank
9 Tourist Office
10 Botanical Garden
11 Post Office; Immigration
14 Carriacou Museum

15 Cable & Wireless
17 Supermarket
18 Police Station; Public Market
19 Gas Station
21 Marketing & National Importing Board
24 Catholic Church
25 John's Print Shop
26 Barclays Bank
27 Anglican Church
28 Evangelical Church
29 Pentecostal Church

To Hospital

Beaujir Rd

Hillsborough
Bay

Ferry to Petit Martinique

Ferry to Grenada

Jetty

Main St

Church St

Patterson St

Middle St

Morris St

1st Ave

2nd Ave

Brunswick St

To Airport

0   100   200 m
0   100   200 yards

Near Barclays Bank is John's Print Shop (☎ 443-8207, webmaster@grenadines.net), upstairs above the Grenada General Insurance office on Main St. Internet access costs EC$10 per half-hour with a complimentary cool drink.

Carriacou Museum

When the gin distillery (c. 1825) closed in 1979 to be refitted as the Carriacou Museum (☎ 443-8288), it was the second-oldest working distillery in the world. The little community-run museum displays an interesting collection of Amerindian grinding stones and shards of sophisticated glazed pottery. There is also an odd collection of colonial-era objects, including clay pipes, tools, chinaware and an old urinal. Also featured are a small African display and paintings by local artists.

It's open 9:30 am to 3:45 pm weekdays. Admission is EC$5 for adults, EC$2.50 for children.

Places to Stay

In the center of Hillsborough, *Ade's Dream Guest House* (☎ 443-7317, fax 443-8435, adesdea@caribsurf.com), on Main St, is a great place to stay. It has 16 rooms in a three-story building and seven rooms in an older wing. The older rooms, which cost US$21, are small and simple with shared baths, but they have fans and there's a large group kitchen. The new rooms, which have kitchenettes, private baths, little balconies and air-con, cost US$52. These are easily as comfortable as mid-range rooms in St George's, and the 18% tax and service charge are not levied. There's a grocery store on the ground floor of the hotel.

Millie's Guest House (☎ 443-7310, fax 443-7475), on Main St, has a variety of rooms in three-bedroom apartments – you rent one bedroom and share the kitchen and bathroom with other guests, if there are any. Fan-cooled singles/doubles cost

US$25/30. Rooms with air-con and one with a private bathroom are also available.

Peace Haven Guest House (☎ 443-7475, jhingram@grenadines.net), on Main St, is another good central guest house with comfortable rooms. Summer rates begin at US$25/30 for singles/doubles in a simple room with shared bath, to US$55 for a comfortable apartment with full kitchen, two double beds and a balcony perched over the beach. Room Nos 1 and 2 have oceanfront balconies and views of Sandy Island.

Patty's Villa (☎ 443-8412), on Main St, has two apartments with kitchens and separate bedrooms on the beachfront. The cost is US$45.

Silver Beach Resort (☎ 443-7337, fax 443-7165, silverbeach@grenadines.net) fronts a nice gray-sand beach at the north side of Hillsborough. There are 18 units and a few worn cottages. Some rooms in the main building have balconies with pleasant ocean views, but they're rather unremarkable. Singles/doubles begin at US$80/95.

John's Unique Guest House (☎ 443-8345, fax 443-8348, johnresort@grenadines.net) is a new guest house with a bar and restaurant attached. Accommodations cost from US$20 to US$55 per person.

The five-room *Green Roof Inn* (☎ /fax 443-6399, greenroof@caribsurf.com, www .greenroofinn.com) has singles/doubles from US$35/60 in summer and US$40/70 in winter.

Places to Eat

Next to Ade's Dream Guest House, *Alva's Restaurant & Bar* serves local food and cold drinks in a pleasant and simple atmosphere.

Gramma's Bakery (☎ 443-7256), in the town center, has good pastries and bread baked fresh every morning. You can also get cheese sandwiches, rotis and drinks throughout the day. There are a few café-style street tables. Gramma's is open 7 am to 7 pm Monday to Saturday.

Callaloo Restaurant (☎ 443-8004, callaloo@grenadines.net) serves excellent West Indian dishes at reasonable prices. At lunch sandwiches cost from EC$10 to

EC$13.50, and fish or chicken & chips run EC$15.50. At dinner, grilled fish or garlic shrimp, with fried plantains, rice and peas, costs EC$35, and lobster dishes start at EC$60. For another EC$10 you can add soup or salad and dessert. It's open 10 am to 2 pm and 6 to 10 pm Monday to Saturday.

Sea Wave, operated by Ade's Dream Guest House, is just over the road on the beachfront. Snacks, drinks and full meals are available, including baked chicken or steamed fish from EC$17. It's open 7 am to 10 pm daily. It also doubles as the town's ice cream parlor.

Silver Beach Resort (see Places to Stay) has a seafront alfresco *restaurant* serving three meals a day. At lunch, rotis, burgers and sandwiches are priced from EC$12. Dinner main dishes include fine Creole fish (EC$40), grilled lamb chops with mushroom sauce (EC$45) and also broiled lobster (EC$65).

At the west end of town, *Butterfly Bar & Pizza* is a pleasant place for snacks, drinks and light meals. Pizzas cost from EC$22.

Talk of the Town, on Main St, has rotis and other inexpensive local food at lunch. *Hillsborough Bar*, at the opposite end of Main St, has pizza and other simple food and drinks.

Port of Call, opposite Ade's, is a popular watering hole that's often full of day-trippers awaiting the ferry to arrive at the pier.

NORTH OF HILLSBOROUGH

The northern region of Carriacou has some of the island's finest scenery, a couple of secluded beaches and agricultural areas that were formerly sugarcane plantations.

The hilltop **hospital**, just north of Hillsborough, has a magnificent view of the bay and offshore islands. Take Belair Rd, about a third of a mile north of Silver Beach Resort, and follow it uphill for half a mile, then bear right on the side road that leads to the hospital. The hospital grounds have a couple of cannons and relics of a colonial-era British fort.

Continuing north from the hospital, the road traverses the crest of **Belvedere Hill**, providing fine views of the east coast and the islands of Petit St Vincent and Petit Martinique. There are the remains of an **old stone sugar mill** just before the Belvedere Crossroads. From there, the route northeast (called the High Rd) leads down to **Windward**, a small, windy village backed by gentle hills that's home to many of the Scottish descendants of shipwrights brought to Carriacou to build interisland boats for the planters.

The road from Windward leads another mile to **Petit Carenage Bay**, at Carriacou's northeastern tip. There's a good beach and views of the northern Grenadines.

If instead you go west from the Belvedere Crossroads, you'll soon come upon the village of **Bogles**. There's a lovely, secluded beach just to the north at **Anse La Roche**. Buses can drop you at Bogles (EC$2.50); it's about half an hour's walk to the beach.

Places to Stay & Eat

In Bogles, *The Round House* (☎/fax 443-7841, roundhouse@grenadines.net) has a few cottages on a seaside hilltop, and it's a terrific place to stay. The cottages have mosquito nets, fans, refrigerators and hot plates, and double-occupancy starts at US$50 in summer, US$65 in winter. Prices include the tax and service charge, and are sometimes negotiable; there are discounts for groups and extended stays. The Round House itself is an attractive stone building housing a fine intimate restaurant that seats just 18 diners. A three-course dinner costs EC$50 per person.

In Prospect, *Caribbee Inn* (☎ 443-7380, fax 443-8142, caribbeeinn@caribsurf.com, www.caribbeeinn.com) is between Bogles and Anse La Roche. It's a small, plush resort with a rural setting, bordering a national park. The eight suites are furnished with four-poster beds, ceiling fans, mosquito nets and private baths. Large louvered windows open to the trade winds and expansive views. Doubles begin at US$130 in summer, US$170 in winter; breakfast and dinner can be included for an extra US$40 per person.

In Windward is *Bayaleau Point Cottages* (☎/fax 443-7984, goldhill@caribsurf.com), ideal for couples or families on weekly stays. Each cottage is different, but all are comfortable, private and stylish. The 'Little Yellow Cottage' is the smallest and features a queen-size bed, fridge and sun shower; the weekly rate is US$245 in summer, US$345 in winter for two adults.

L'ESTERRE

L'Esterre is a small village southwest of the airport that retains a bit of French influence, which is manifested most noticeably in the French patois that some of village elders still speak.

The village's main sight is the home of Carriacou artist Canute Caliste, who paints naïve visions of mermaids and sailing vessels. After many decades, his art has gained some international following and is the subject of the book *The Mermaid Wakes: Paintings of a Caribbean Isle* (see Books in Facts about Grenada, earlier). To get to his shop, follow the road west at the main village T-junction rather than turning south towards Tyrrel Bay.

Places to Stay & Eat

A basic guest house, *Hope's Inn* (☎ 443-7457), is on a sandy beach at the north side

Boat Building

Carriacou islanders have traditionally made their living from the sea as fisherfolk, mariners and boat builders. It is still possible to see a few wooden schooners being built along the beach in Windward, with the boat builders using the same handcrafting techniques that the early Scottish settlers brought with them in colonial times. However, modern steel hulls have undermined traditional boat building, and now there is much less boat building going on in Carriacou.

The situation is similar on the more northerly Grenadine island of Bequia, which also has a sizable settlement of Scottish descendants.

of L'Esterre on the airport road. There are seven rooms with fans, shared baths, two shared kitchens and a small communal sitting area. Singles/doubles cost US$35/45. There's also a self-contained apartment that costs US$50.

Also near the beach is *Paradise Inn* (☎ 443-8406, fax 443-8391, paradiseinn@ caribsurf.com, www.cacounet.com/paradise). The six large bedrooms have ceiling fans, rattan furnishings and private baths. Single/double rooms start at US$60/75 in summer and US$70/85 in winter. Moderately priced meals are served at the beachside bar.

TYRREL BAY

Tyrrel Bay is a deep, protected bay with a sandy beach that fronts the village and green undulating paddocks of rural Harvey Vale. The bay is a popular anchorage for visiting yachters. The deep, narrow lagoon at the north side of the bay is known as Hurricane Bay, because it's a safe harbor for yachters during severe storms. Locals know the bay as Oyster Bed – oysters grow on the mangrove roots.

Opposite the beach are a couple of places to stay and eat, including a popular restaurant run by a young French couple. A relatively frequent bus route operates from Hillsborough to Belmont via Tyrrel Bay.

Places to Stay

The *Constant Spring* (☎ 443-7396), a small guest house at the south side of Tyrrel Bay, has three simple rooms with shared baths and a shared kitchen. Singles/doubles are priced at US$17/33.

Scraper's Cottages (☎/fax 443-7403), adjacent to the restaurant of the same name, consists of eight apartments in duplex cottages. Most are nice, with kitchen, private bath and bedroom with two double beds. Singles/doubles cost US$45/50 in summer and US$50/55 in winter.

Alexis Luxury Apartments (☎/fax 443-7179) has 13 simple, clean rooms with private baths, opposite the beach at the center of Tyrrel Bay. Singles/doubles cost US$65/85 with kitchenettes, US$45/55

without. Basic single/doubles cost US$25/45, and there are discounts on weekly stays.

Carriacou Yacht & Beach Club (☎/fax 443-6292, cyc@grenadines.net, VHF channel 16), on the south side of Tyrrel Bay, is about a 15-minute walk from Harvey Vale and geared primarily to visiting yachties. It has five simple, neat rooms with refrigerators, coffeemakers, ceiling fans and private baths that cost from US$45. The club features a dinghy dock, a small store and an open-air restaurant.

Cassada Bay Resort (☎ 443-7494, fax 443-7672, cassada@grenadines.net), between Tyrrel Bay and Belmont, about a 20-minute walk from either, has 16 hillside rooms and splendid views. The wooden cottages have a weathered character and were once part of a marine biology school, 'Camp Carriacou,' which catered to wealthy American children. The pleasant, roomy cottages are simple, with ocean-view decks, screened louvered windows, a table and couch. Singles/doubles start at US$45/50 in summer, US$65/75 in winter.

Places to Eat

Lively *Poivre et Sel* (☎ 443-8390, VHF channel 16), above Alexis Supermarket, serves fine French food. Lunchtime pastas, omelets and salads range from EC$12 to EC$30. At dinner, starters range from onion soup (EC$12) to shrimp Provençale (EC$30), and main courses include fresh fish preparations or lobster crêpes from EC$40. It's open 10 am to 2 pm and 5:30 pm to midnight.

Scraper's Restaurant, opposite the beach, has a varied menu that includes fish, sandwiches or hamburgers for EC$10, and main dishes, including pasta, from EC$18 and lobster for EC$55. It is open 9 am to 11 pm Monday to Saturday and 11 am to 11 pm Sunday.

Le Petit Conch Shell (☎ 443-6174) is on the road leading back towards Harvey Vale. It's a low-key bar-restaurant serving inexpensive meals, including fish, seafood and chicken dishes from EC$30.

Al's is one of a few inexpensive bars and eateries opposite the beach that serve

GRENADA

simple West Indian food. You can pick up groceries and liquor at *Alexis Supermarket*, near the center of the beach, and *Barba's Supermarket*, closer to the dockyard.

Cassada Bay Resort (☎ 443-7494) has an open-air veranda restaurant and bar with a fine view and good food. At lunch, fish or meat burgers cost EC$15, while at dinnertime, chicken, catch of the day or curried lambi costs around EC$40.

NEARSHORE ISLANDS

Little **Sandy Island**, off the west side of Hillsborough Bay, is a favorite daytime destination for snorkelers and yachters. It's a tiny postcard-perfect reef island – glistening sands dotted with coconut palms, surrounded by turquoise waters. Snorkelers take to the shallow waters fronting Sandy Island, while the deeper waters on the far side are popular for diving. Unfortunately, the island's easy accessibility has caused its surrounding coral gardens to be badly damaged by dropped and dragging anchors.

A speedboat for up to two people costs EC$70 (EC$10 more for additional passengers) through the tourist office. Alternatively, call Israel James (☎ 443-7544) or Kenroy Noel (☎ 443-6214), who run water taxis. Be clear about when you want to be picked up – as the island takes only a couple of minutes to walk around, a whole afternoon ticks by very slowly.

White Island makes for a nice day trip. It has a good, sandy beach and a pristine reef for snorkeling. White Island is about a mile off the southern tip of Carriacou, and is also easy to get to. Cassada Bay Resort will shuttle day-trippers over to White Island, just a five-minute ride from the resort's pier, at EC$50 for up to five passengers. You can also make boat arrangements through the tourist office.

GETTING THERE & AWAY
Air

Airlines of Carriacou was bought out by St Vincent & the Grenadines Airways (SVG) in September 1999. The combined airline (☎ 444-3549) has two or three daily flights (depending on the day) between Grenada

and Carriacou. The first flight leaves Grenada at 7:50 am, and the latest return from Carriacou is 5 pm. Fares are US$34 each way. There are also daily flights from Grenada to Union Island for US$80 oneway, US$150 roundtrip, and daily flights from Carriacou to Union Island for US$32 each way.

Airport Information Carriacou's airport, just over a mile west of Hillsborough, is such a modest facility that the island's main road cuts clear across the center of the runway, with traffic yielding to planes!

The terminal has a tiny souvenir shop, a bar, public phones and a single check-in counter for LIAT, Airlines of Carriacou and Region Air Caribbean.

Boat

There are two types of boats plying between Grenada and Carriacou. You can either hop on an old-fashioned cargo boat that takes three to four hours, or ride on a modern express catamaran that takes half as long and costs twice as much.

Cargo/Passenger Boats The *Adelaide,* an older wooden boat that still uses its sail, departs from Grenada at 9:30 am Wednesday and Saturday and leaves Carriacou at 9:30 am Monday and Thursday. The *Alexia IV,* a steel-hulled ship that's a little more modern, has the same schedule as the *Adelaide.*

A sister ship, the *Alexia III,* departs Grenada at 9:30 am Tuesday, 11 am Friday and 7 am Sunday, and leaves Carriacou at 9:30 am Wednesday and Saturday and 5 pm Sunday.

The fare on any of the three boats is EC$20 one-way; buy your ticket on the boat. On Grenada the boats dock at the north side of the Carenage in St George's and on Carriacou, at Hillsborough's town pier.

Catamaran The *Osprey* is a 144-seat motorized catamaran that connects Grenada's three populated islands. For reservations call ☎ 407-0470, although it's simpler to show up dockside 10 minutes before sailing time.

The following schedule covers the *Osprey's* sailings Monday to Saturday; Sunday's schedule is slightly different. The boat leaves Petit Martinique for Carriacou at 5:30 am and 3 pm (3:30 pm on Saturday), leaves Carriacou for Grenada at 6 am and 3:30 pm (4 pm on Saturday), leaves Grenada for Carriacou at 9 am and 5:30 pm (only at 9 am on Saturday) and leaves Carriacou for Petit Martinique at 11 am and 7 pm weekdays.

The one-way fares are EC$10 between Petit Martinique and Carriacou and EC$40 between Grenada and either Carriacou or Petit Martinique. Roundtrip fares from Grenada are EC$75.

GETTING AROUND
Bus & Taxi

Buses, privately owned minivans, charge EC$2.50 to go anywhere on the island (EC$1 if the distance is less than a mile). The two main routes run from Hillsborough, one south to Tyrrel Bay, the other north to Windward. Minibuses start around 7 am and stop around 4:30 pm – they're easiest to catch in the early morning, when people are going to school and work.

You can get a cheap island tour by hopping on a minibus departing from Hillsborough and either breaking en route or staying on the bus for the return ride. The Windward-bound buses usually take the High Rd going one-way and the Low Rd going the other, making for a good loop tour.

Some minibuses double as taxis, and usually you can count on a couple of them swinging by the airport when a flight comes in. Taxis from the airport charge EC$10 to Hillsborough and EC$20 to Tyrrel Bay, Cassada Bay or Bogles.

Car

The island's only gas station, on Patterson St in Hillsborough, is open 8 am to 6 pm daily.

There are a couple of places to rent vehicles on Carriacou, with rates typically around US$50 a day. Barba Gabriel (☎ 443-7454), at Barba's Supermarket in Tyrrel Bay, rents out both 4WD Suzukis and Geo Trackers, while Bullen Car Rental (☎ 443-7221), at the gas station, rents out jeeps.

Organized Tours

You can hire a taxi for a 2½-hour island tour that costs EC$150 for up to five people, or you could tour just the northern half of the island, which only takes half as long and costs EC$75.

Petit Martinique

Near-circular Petit Martinique is 3 miles northeast of Carriacou. It's about a mile wide and has a volcanic cone rising to 738 feet.

Most of the 900 islanders make their living from the sea, either as fishers or mariners working the region's ships. The islanders have a close-knit community, sharing a half-dozen surnames. Renowned as smugglers, the people are also devoutly Catholic. This makes for very quiet Sundays, as people are attending church. There are a couple of schools, a restaurant and a few stores.

There's a road along the west coast; otherwise, people get about on foot, and it's a nice place to walk around.

Places to Stay

The simple *Miracle Mart Guesthouse* (☎ 443-9065, fax 443-9022) has three singles/doubles for US$21/24. *Melodies Guest House* (☎ 473-9052, melodies@grenadines .net) has simple rooms with prices starting at US$20/30.

Seaside View Holiday Cottages (☎ 443-9210, fax 443-9113, logan@grenadines.net) has three self-contained air-conditioned cottages overlooking the harbor. Singles/doubles cost US$25/35. Seaside View can arrange transfers to/from Carriacou.

Getting There & Away

The *Osprey* catamaran ferries passengers between Grenada, Carriacou and Petit Martinique daily. Adult one-way fares are

EC$40 for Grenada to Petit Martinique and US$10 for Carriacou to Petit Martinique. For scheduling and contact information, see Getting There & Away in the Carriacou section.

The Carriacou tourist office in Hillsborough can arrange for a speedboat to zip you over to Petit Martinique from Windward in Carriacou's north. The roundtrip will cost around EC$120.

Guadeloupe

Guadeloupe, the center of the Caribbean's Creole culture, boasts a spirited blend of French and African influences. The island archipelago is largely provincial in nature and remains as well known for its sugar and rum as for its beaches and resorts.

Highlights

- Enjoying authentic Creole culture, which permeates the islands
- Exploring the extensive national park, with verdant rain forest, magnificent waterfalls and a steaming volcano
- Kicking back in charming Terre-de-Haut and checking out its grand French fort
- Getting acquainted with the timeless rural character of the sleepy isles of La Désirade and Marie-Galante

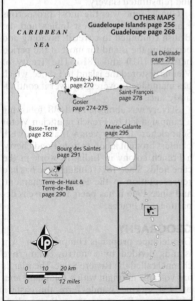

OTHER MAPS
Guadeloupe Islands page 256
Guadeloupe page 268

CARIBBEAN SEA

La Désirade page 298

Pointe-à-Pitre page 270

Saint-François page 278

Gosier page 274-275

Basse-Terre page 282

Marie-Galante page 295

Bourg des Saintes page 291

Terre-de-Haut & Terre-de-Bas page 290

0   10   20 km
0   6   12 miles

Guadeloupe's shape inevitably invites comparison to a butterfly, as it has two abutting wing-shaped islands. The outline of the two islands is somewhat symmetrical, but the topography is anything but. Grande-Terre, the eastern wing, has a terrain of gently rolling hills and level plains, much of which is cultivated in sugarcane. Basse-Terre, the western wing, is dominated by rugged hills and mountains that are wrapped in a dense rain forest of tall trees and lush ferns. Much of the interior of Basse-Terre has been set aside as a national park, which includes trails through the rain forest, the Eastern Caribbean's highest waterfalls and the island's highest peak, La Soufrière, a smoldering volcano.

The center of the island and its principal city is the bustling Pointe-à-Pitre, while the sleepy capital of Basse-Terre is on the remote southwestern side. Virtually all of the resort hotels, as well as the larger marinas, are along the southern shore of Grande-Terre.

Guadeloupe's surrounding offshore islands make interesting side excursions. The most visited, Terre-de-Haut, is a delightful place with a quaint central village and harbor, good beaches and restaurants and some reasonably priced places to stay. The other populated islands – Terre-de-Bas, Marie-Galante and La Désirade – have very little tourism development and offer visitors a glimpse of a rural French West Indies that has changed little in recent times.

Facts about Guadeloupe

HISTORY

When sighted by Columbus on November 14, 1493, Guadeloupe was inhabited by Carib Indians, who called it Karukera (Island of Beautiful Waters). The Spanish made two attempts to settle Guadeloupe in the early 1500s but were repelled both times by fierce Carib resistance, and finally in 1604 they abandoned their claim to the island.

Three decades later, French colonists sponsored by the Compagnie des Îles d'Amérique, an association of French entrepreneurs, set sail to establish the first European settlement on Guadeloupe. On June 28, 1635, the party, led by Charles Liénard de l'Olive and Jean Duplessis d'Ossonville, landed on the southeastern shore of Basse-Terre and claimed Guadeloupe for France. They drove the Caribs off the island, planted crops and within a decade had built the first sugar mill. By the time France officially annexed the island in 1674, a slavery-based plantation system had been well established.

The English invaded Guadeloupe several times and occupied it from 1759 to 1763. During this time they developed Pointe-à-Pitre into a major harbor, opened profitable English and North American markets to Guadeloupean sugar and allowed the planters to import cheap American lumber and food. Many French colonists actually grew wealthier under the British occupation, and the economy expanded rapidly. In 1763, British occupation ended with the signing of the Treaty of Paris, provisions of which relinquished French claims in Canada in exchange for the return of Guadeloupe.

Amid the chaos of the French Revolution, the British invaded Guadeloupe again in 1794. In response to that invasion, the French sent a contingent of soldiers led by Victor Hugues, a black nationalist. Hugues freed and armed Guadeloupean slaves. On the day the British withdrew from Guadeloupe, Hugues went on a rampage and killed 300 royalists, many of them plantation owners. It marked the start of a reign of terror. In all, Hugues was responsible for the deaths of more than 1000 colonists, and as a consequence of his attacks on US ships, the USA declared war on France.

In 1802, Napoleon Bonaparte, anxious to get the situation under control, sent General Antoine Richepance to Guadeloupe. Richepance put down the uprising, restored the prerevolutionary government and reinstituted slavery.

Guadeloupe was the most prosperous island in the French West Indies, and the British continued to covet it, invading and occupying the island for most of the period between 1810 and 1816. The Treaty of Vienna restored the island to France, which has maintained sovereignty over it continuously since 1816.

Slavery was abolished in 1848, following a campaign led by French politician Victor Schoelcher. In the years that followed, planters brought laborers from Pondicherry, a French colony in India, to work in the cane fields. Since 1871, Guadeloupe has had representation in the French parliament, and since 1946 it has been an overseas department of France.

GEOGRAPHY

Guadeloupe proper is comprised of twin islands divided by a narrow mangrove channel called the Rivière Salée. The islands are volcanic in origin with a total land area of 1434 sq km. Grande-Terre, the eastern island, has a limestone cover, the result of being submerged during earlier geologic

GUADELOUPE ISLANDS

61°50'W   61°30'W   61°10'W

CARIBBEAN SEA

0   10   20 km
0   6   12 miles

16°30'N

Guadeloupe   La Désirade

Pointe-à-Pitre   Grande
Gosier   Saint-   Anse
            François

16°10'N

Îles de la
Petite-Terre

BASSE-TERRE   Marie-Galante

St-Louis

Les Saintes   Capesterre
Terre-de-Haut
Terre-   Bourg   Grand-
de-Bas   des Saintes Bourg   15°50'N

61°50'W   61°30'W   61°10'W

Big Land, Flat Land

At first glance, the names given to the twin islands that make up Guadeloupe proper are perplexing. The eastern island, which is smaller and flatter, is named Grande-Terre, which means 'big land,' while the larger, more mountainous western side is named Basse-Terre, meaning 'flat land.'

The names were not meant to describe the terrain, however, but the winds that blow over them. The trade winds, which come from the northeast, blow *grande* over the flat plains of Grande-Terre but are stopped by the mountains to the west, ending up flat *(basse)* on Basse-Terre.

periods. Basse-Terre, the larger, western island, is rugged and mountainous. Guadeloupe's highest point is La Soufrière, a 1467m active volcano.

Of the nearby offshore islands, Les Saintes (14 sq km) are high and rugged, Marie-Galante (158 sq km) is round and flat and La Désirade (22 sq km) has an intermediate topography with hills that rise up to an elevation of 273m.

CLIMATE
Pointe-à-Pitre's average daily high temperature in January is 28°C (83°F) while the low averages 19°C (67°F). In July the average daily high temperature is 31°C (88°F) while the low averages 23°C (74°F).

The annual rainfall in Pointe-à-Pitre is 1814mm (71 inches). February to April is the driest period, when measurable rain falls an average of seven days a month and the average humidity is around 77%. The wettest months are July to November, when rain falls about 14 days a month and the average humidity reaches 85%.

Because of its height, the Basse-Terre side is both cooler and rainier than Grande-Terre. Its highest point, La Soufrière, averages 9900mm (390 inches) of rain a year.

The trade winds, called *alizés,* often temper the climate.

FLORA & FAUNA
Guadeloupe's diverse vegetation ranges from mangrove swamps to mountainous rain forest. Basse-Terre has an abundance of tropical hardwood trees, including lofty gommiers and large buttressed chataigniers, and thick fern forests punctuated with flowering heliconia and ginger plants.

Birds found on Guadeloupe include various members of the heron family, pelicans, hummingbirds and the endangered Guadeloupe wren. A common sighting is the bright yellow-bellied bananaquit, a small nectar-feeding bird that's a frequent visitor at open-air restaurants, where it raids unattended sugar bowls.

The raccoon, whose main habitat is in the forests of Basse-Terre, is the official symbol of the Parc National de la Guadeloupe. You can expect to see drawings of raccoons on park brochures and in Guadeloupean advertising as a means of projecting a 'natural' image.

Guadeloupe has mongooses aplenty, introduced long ago in a futile attempt to control rats in the sugarcane fields. Agoutis – short-haired, short-eared rabbit-like rodents that look a bit like guinea pigs – are found on La Désirade. There are iguanas on Les Saintes and La Désirade.

GOVERNMENT & POLITICS
Guadeloupe is an overseas department of France and has a status on par with the 96 *départements* on the French mainland. The department of Guadeloupe, which also encompasses St Barts and the French side of St Martin, is represented in the French parliament by four elected deputies and two senators.

A prefect, who is appointed by the French Minister of the Interior and assisted by two general secretaries and two *sous-préfets* (sub-prefects), represents the central government and oversees island authorities. There are two locally elected legislative bodies, the Conseil Général and the Conseil Régional, each with about 40 members. Guadeloupe is further divided into three districts and 34 communes. Each commune has a municipal council elected by popular vote and a mayor elected from the council.

ECONOMY

Guadeloupe's economy is heavily dependent upon subsidies from the French government and upon its economic ties with mainland France, which absorbs the majority of Guadeloupe's exports and provides 75% of its imports. Guadeloupe has a sizable trade imbalance; total exports are valued at an estimated US$130 million, while imports are valued at US$1.4 billion.

Agriculture remains a cornerstone of Guadeloupe's economy. The leading export crop is bananas, the bulk of which grow along the southern flanks of La Soufrière. About two-thirds of all bananas eaten in France are from Guadeloupe. Although the importance of sugar is diminishing, a third of Guadeloupe's cultivable land is still planted in cane. Much of the sugar is used in the production of rum, which is second only to bananas in export value.

In the industrial sector, Guadeloupe has about 150 small-scale enterprises, including food processing, cement, plastics and furniture. Tourism is the fastest-growing sector of the economy. Of the island's 165,000 annual overnight visitors, about 70% come from France, 13% from other parts of Europe and a little over 10% from the USA. In addition, about 75,000 cruise-ship passengers call on Guadeloupe each year.

POPULATION & PEOPLE

The population of Guadeloupe (Basse-Terre and Grande-Terre) is about 350,000. In addition, about 3000 people live on Les Saintes, 1600 on La Désirade and 13,000 on Marie-Galante.

About three-quarters of the population is of mixed ethnicity, a combination of African, European and East Indian descent. There's also a sizable population of white islanders who trace their ancestry to the early French settlers, as well as a number of more recently arrived French from the mainland.

ARTS

Guadeloupe's most renowned native son is Saint-John Perse, the pseudonym of Alexis Léger, who was born in Guadeloupe in 1887 and won the Nobel Prize for literature in 1960 for the evocative imagery of his poetry. One of his many noted works is *Anabase* (1925), which was translated into English by TS Eliot.

SOCIETY & CONDUCT

Guadeloupean culture draws on French, African, East Indian and West Indian influences. The mix is visible in the architecture, which ranges from French colonial buildings to Hindu temples; in the food, which merges influences from all the cultures into a unique Creole cuisine; and in the local Creole language that predominates in the home.

Guadeloupe is one place where you're apt to see women wearing traditional Creole dress, especially at festivals and cultural events. The typical costume consists of a full, brightly colored skirt, commonly a madras-type plaid of oranges and yellows, with a matching headdress, a white lace-trimmed blouse and petticoat, and a scarf draped over the shoulder.

Dos & Don'ts

Except for fine dining, dress is casual but generally stylish. Topless bathing is common on the island, particularly at resort beaches. Swimwear is not appropriate away from the beach.

RELIGION

The predominant religion is Roman Catholicism. There are also Methodist, Seventh Day Adventist, Jehovah's Witness and Evangelical denominations, as well as a sizable Hindu community.

LANGUAGE

French is the official language, but islanders commonly speak a local Creole dialect among themselves.

While English is not widely spoken, most desk clerks in larger hotels are quite fluent, and a fair number of other people in tourist-related areas are willing to communicate in a combination of slow French and broken English. If you don't speak French, refer to the Language chapter. You may also consider bringing a French-English dictionary and phrasebook.

If you do speak French, you may be surprised by how readily people on the island *tutoyer* you. Though it's always best to start with the formal *vous,* you'll find that islanders of all ages and ethnic backgrounds switch quickly to *tu.* It's just island life, nothing to get upset about.

Facts for the Visitor

ORIENTATION
The airport is north of Pointe-à-Pitre, just a 10-minute drive from the city center and 20 minutes from Gosier, the largest tourist area. Roads are good, and the island can readily be explored in a series of day trips, with a day given to circling Grande-Terre, another day to northern Basse-Terre and the Route de la Traversée and a third day to southern Basse-Terre.

Ferries link Guadeloupe to the islands of Terre-de-Haut, Marie-Galante and La Désirade, with schedules that allow daytrippers to sail over to any of these islands in the morning and return to Guadeloupe in the late afternoon.

Maps
The best map of Guadeloupe is the No 510 (1:100,000) map published by the Institut Géographique National (IGN), which is sold at bookstores around the island for 55F. Although the paper quality is inferior, you can get the same detailed IGN map in a glossy version, free of charge, from island car rental agencies.

TOURIST OFFICES
Local Tourist Offices
The mailing address for the central tourist office on Guadeloupe is Office Départemental du Tourisme de la Guadeloupe (☎ 82 09 30, fax 83 89 22), 5 Square de la Banque, BP 422, 97100 Pointe-à-Pitre, Guadeloupe, French West Indies.

There are also regional tourist offices in the towns of Basse-Terre (☎ 81 24 83) and Saint-François (☎ 88 48 74) and local information bureaus *(syndicats d'initiative)* in some smaller towns.

Tourist Offices Abroad
Overseas tourism representatives include the following:

France
Office du Tourisme de Guadeloupe (☎ 0146-04 00 08, fax 0146-04 74 03) 43 Rue des Tilleuls, 92100 Boulogne-Billancourt

Germany
Maison de la France (☎ 069-74 22 79 32, fax 069-75 21 87) Westendstrasse 47, 60325 Frankfurt an Main

Italy
Ente Nazionale Francese per il Turismo (☎ 02-58 31 64 71, fax 02-58 31 65 79) 5 Via Sant Andrea, 20121 Milan

UK
French Government Tourist Office (☎ 44 020-7493 6694, fax 020-7493 6594) 178 Piccadilly, London W1V OAL

USA
French Government Tourist Office (☎ 212-838-7800, fax 212-838-7855) 444 Madison Ave, 16th floor, New York, NY 10022

VISAS & DOCUMENTS
US and Canadian citizens can stay up to three months by showing proof of citizenship in the form of either a valid or expired (up to five years) passport, or an official birth certificate accompanied by either a driver's license or other government-authorized photo ID.

Citizens of the European Union (EU) need an official identity card, passport or valid French *carte de séjour* (visitor card). Citizens of most other foreign countries, including Australia, need a valid passport and a visa for France. Visitors officially require a return or onward ticket.

CUSTOMS
Citizens of EU countries are allowed to bring in 300 cigarettes, 1.5L of spirits and 4L of wine duty-free. Non-EU citizens are allowed to bring in 200 cigarettes, a bottle of spirits and 2L of wine duty-free. All visitors are allowed to bring in 'large allowances of rum' as well.

GUADELOUPE

MONEY

The French franc is the island currency; the Euro is due to replace the franc, but is not yet commonly used. Hotels, larger restaurants and car rental agencies accept Visa (Carte Bleue), American Express and MasterCard (Eurocard). For most other situations, you'll need to use francs.

Avoid changing money at hotel lobbies, where the rates are worse than at exchange offices or banks. Currency exchange offices, called *bureaux de change,* are scattered along the waterfront of Pointe-à-Pitre, and ATMs *(distributeurs des billets* or *distributeurs automatiques)* will usually give good rates.

As this guide went to press, the exchange rate was 7.76F to US$1.

POST & COMMUNICATIONS
Post

There are post offices in Pointe-à-Pitre, Basse-Terre, Gosier, Saint-François and other major towns. It costs 3F to send a postcard to France, 3.80F to the Caribbean or the USA, 4.40F to other parts of the Americas and 5.20F to the rest of the world. This rate also covers letters up to 20g.

Postage stamps can be purchased at *tabacs* (tobacco shops) and some hotels in addition to post offices.

Mail addressed to Guadeloupe should end with the postal code, town name and 'Guadeloupe, French West Indies.'

Telephone

Public phones in Guadeloupe accept French *télécartes* (phonecards), not coins. The cards cost 37F or 89F, depending on the calling time, and are sold at post offices and at shops marked *télécarte en vente ici.* Public phones can be found at most post offices, the airport, city parks and other public places. For directory assistance, dial ☎ 12.

When making a local call, dial just the six-digit local number. When calling from outside Guadeloupe, add the 590 area code to the six-digit local number. To call direct from the USA, dial ☎ 011 + 590 + the number.

More information on phone cards and making long-distance calls is under Post & Communications in the Regional Facts for the Visitor chapter.

Email & Internet Access

Internet access on Guadeloupe is limited but growing. Tourist towns such as St Anne and Saint-François have cybercafés, and the some of the larger hotels have facilities for guests. In Pointe-à-Pitre your best bet is Rapido, in the Centre Saint-John Perse.

BOOKS

There are many books about Guadeloupe and its flora and fauna in French, but books in English are harder to find. In Pointe-à-Pitre, try Espace St-John Perse, on Rue de Nozières, or the Boutique de la Presse in the Centre Saint-John Perse.

The leading contemporary novelist in the French West Indies is Guadeloupe native Maryse Condé. Two of her best-selling novels have been translated into English. The epic *Tree of Life* centers on the life of a Guadeloupean family, their roots and the identity of Guadeloupean society itself. *Crossing the Mangrove* (Anchor Books, 1995) is a very enjoyable yarn that gently reveals nuances of rural Guadeloupean relationships as it unravels the life, and untimely death, of a controversial villager.

The bilingual French/English *A Cruising Guide to Guadeloupe,* part of the Guide Trois Rivières series (Edition Caripress, 30 Rue Montesquieu, 97200 Fort-de-France, Martinique), is a comprehensive sailing manual for cruising Guadeloupe and the offshore islands.

NEWSPAPERS & MAGAZINES

The island's local daily is the *France-Antilles.* Other French-language newspapers, such as *Le Monde,* are flown in daily from the mainland. Larger newsstands in Pointe-à-Pitre and major tourist areas sell the *International Herald-Tribune* and a few other English-language newspapers.

For tourist information, these free and bilingual publications are useful: *Ti Gourmet,* a pocket-sized restaurant guide offering a complimentary drink at many island restaurants, and *Le Guide Créole,* a more general publication with everything from historical background to entertainment listings.

RADIO & TV
Radio France Outre-Mer (RFO) provides public radio and TV broadcasting. Guadeloupe also has two private TV stations and a number of independent FM radio stations.

ELECTRICITY
Electricity is 220V, 50 cycles, as in France. Some hotels have adapted outlets in bathrooms that allow for the use of 110V electric razors.

WEIGHTS & MEASURES
Guadeloupe uses the metric system and the 24-hour clock.

HEALTH
The main hospital is the Centre Hospitalier (☎ 89 10 10), on Rue Victor Hugo in Pointe-à-Pitre, at the east end of Faubourg. There's also a hospital (☎ 80 54 54) in Basse-Terre and a number of smaller medical facilities around Guadeloupe.

Bilharzia (schistosomiasis) is found throughout Grande-Terre and in much of Basse-Terre, including Grand Étang lake. The main method of prevention is to avoid swimming or wading in freshwater. More information is in the Health section in Regional Facts for the Visitor.

DANGERS & ANNOYANCES
Guadeloupe's crime rate is relatively low compared to other large islands in the Eastern Caribbean, though a recent story in the *France-Antilles* newspaper reported an alarming increase in car thefts, with rental cars the favorite target.

There are poisonous manchineel trees on some of the beaches, usually marked with a warning sign.

EMERGENCIES
In an emergency, dial ☎ 17 for police and ☎ 18 for the fire department. For more routine police assistance, dial ☎ 89 77 17 in Pointe-à-Pitre, ☎ 81 11 55 in Basse-Terre.

BUSINESS HOURS
Although they vary, typical shop hours are 9 am to 1 pm and 3 to 6 pm weekdays. Many shops are also open Saturday morning.

Bank hours are commonly 8 am to noon and 2 to 4 pm weekdays. During the summer, many banks change their hours to 8 am to 3 pm. Banks close at noon on the day before a public holiday.

PUBLIC HOLIDAYS & SPECIAL EVENTS
Public holidays in Guadeloupe include the following:

New Year's Day	January 1
Easter Sunday	late March/early April
Easter Monday	late March/early April
Labor Day	May 1
Victory Day	May 8
Ascension Thursday	40th day after Easter
Pentecost Monday	eighth Monday after Easter
Slavery Abolition Day	May 27
Bastille Day	July 14
Schoelcher Day	July 21
Assumption Day	August 15
All Saints Day	November 1
Armistice Day	November 11
Christmas Day	December 25

Carnival celebrations, which are held during the traditional weeklong Mardi Gras period that ends on Ash Wednesday, features costume parades, dancing, music and other festivities.

The Fête des Cuisinières (Festival of Women Cooks) is a colorful event held in Pointe-à-Pitre in early August. Women in Creole dress, carrying baskets of traditional foods, parade through the streets to the cathedral, where they are blessed by the bishop. It is followed by a banquet and dancing.

The Tour Cycliste de la Guadeloupe, a 10-day international cycling race, is also held in early August.

GUADELOUPE

ACTIVITIES
Beaches & Swimming

White-sand beaches fringe Gosier, Sainte-Anne and Saint-François. At the north side of the peninsula leading to Pointe des Châteaux lie two remote beaches: Anse à la Gourde, a gorgeous sweep of white coral sands, and Anse Tarare, the adjacent nudist beach. While most of Grande-Terre's east coast has rough surf, there is a swimmable beach at Le Moule and a little protected cove at Porte d'Enfer. On the west side of Grande-Terre, Port-Louis is the most popular swimming spot, especially on weekends.

The beaches along Basse-Terre's rugged northwest coast are wilder and less crowded, with long, empty stretches of golden sands and views of Montserrat smoldering in the distance. There are also a handful of black-sand beaches along Basse-Terre's southern shore.

Diving

Guadeloupe's top diving site is the Réserve Cousteau, at Pigeon Island off the west coast of Basse-Terre. Spearfishing has long been banned in this underwater reserve, and consequently the waters surrounding Pigeon Island, which is just a kilometer offshore, are teeming with colorful tropical fish, sponges, sea fans and corals.

Dive Shops There are numerous dive shops in Guadeloupe, including the following three in the Réserve Cousteau area; each goes out daily at 10 am and 12:30 and 3 pm. Single-dive rates average 200F, with discounts given on multiple-dive packages.

Aux Aquanautes Antillais, Plage de Malendure (☎ 98 87 30, fax 90 11 85) 97125 Bouillante. This is a friendly local operation right on Malendure Beach.

Chez Guy et Christian, Plage de Malendure (☎ 98 82 43, fax 98 82 84) 97132 Pigeon. Another beachside operator, Chezy Guy offers night dives in addition to day outings.

Les Heures Saines, Rocher Malendure (☎ 98 86 63, fax 98 77 76) 97132 Pigeon. Popular with English speakers, this well-regarded operation has modern equipment, a large catamaran, and both NAUI and CMAS programs.

Snorkeling

Guadeloupe's most popular snorkeling spot is Pigeon Island. The company Nautilus (☎ 98 89 08) offers glass-bottom boat trips from Malendure Beach that include about 20 minutes of snorkeling time.

On Grande-Terre, there's reasonable snorkeling off Îlet du Gosier, which can be reached by boat from Gosier. Snorkeling equipment can be rented at many beachside tourist resorts.

Most of the dive shops mentioned above will provide snorkel equipment and boat transportation to the reserve for around 100F for a one-hour tour.

Surfing

Le Moule, Port-Louis and Anse Bertrand commonly have good surfing conditions from around October to May. In summer, Sainte-Anne, Saint-François and Petit-Havre can have good wave action.

Windsurfing

Windsurfing is quite popular on Guadeloupe. Much of the activity is centered near the resorts on the south side of Grande-Terre and on the island of Terre-de-Haut. Windsurfing gear can be rented from beach huts for about 75F an hour. For those new to the sport, a number of reputable places offer courses, including Nathalie Simon Sport Away (☎ 88 72 04), at the south side of the marina in Saint-François, which has a 90-minute beginner course for 280F. The shop also rents out surfboards and body boards for 70F a half day.

The Union des Centres de Plein Air (UCPA; ☎ 88 64 80), 97118 Saint-François, has weeklong windsurfing/hotel packages in both Saint-François and Terre-de-Haut.

Fishing

Deep-sea fishing can be arranged with Caraïbe Pêche (☎ 90 97 51), Evasion Exotic (☎ 90 94 17) and other boats at the Bas du Fort Marina.

Hiking

Guadeloupe has wonderful trails that take in waterfalls, primordial rain forest and botanical gardens. A number of them are simple 10- to 30-minute walks that can be enjoyed as part of a tour around the island.

Serious hikers will find many longer, more rigorous trails in the national park. The most popular are those leading to the volcanic summit of La Soufrière, the island's highest point, and to the base of Chutes du Carbet, the Eastern Caribbean's highest waterfalls. Both make for scenic half-day treks. Keep in mind that this is serious rainforest hiking, so be prepared for wet conditions and wear good hiking shoes. More information is found under individual sites in this chapter.

Horseback Riding
La Manade (☎ 81 52 21), a stable in Saint-Claude in the foothills of La Soufrière, offers half-day rain-forest outings for 200F as well as shorter outings for 150F.

Golf
Guadeloupe's only golf course is the 18-hole, par 71 Golf de St François (☎ 88 41 87), designed by Robert Trent Jones, in Saint-François.

Tennis
Many resort hotels have tennis courts for their guests. In addition, municipal courts open to the general public can be found in many of the large towns.

ACCOMMODATIONS
Camping
The only established campground on Guadeloupe is Camping Traversée (☎ 98 21 23), which has a pleasant seaside setting south of Pointe-Noire on the northwest side of Basse-Terre.

Hotels
There are nearly 8000 hotel rooms in Guadeloupe, most in small to mid-size hotels. The bulk of the accommodations are along the south coast of Grande-Terre, between Pointe-à-Pitre and Saint-François. Rooms on the outlying islands of Les Saintes, Marie-Galante and La Desirade are limited, but if you ask around you can easily

find a place, sometimes in a private house with a local family.

Some hotels have a three-night minimum stay in winter, and as that's a busy season, advance reservations are a good idea.

By Caribbean standards rates are reasonable, with good low-end doubles available for around 320F, mid-range for around 600F and top-end around 1000F. As in France, taxes and service charges are included in the quoted rate; many hotels also include breakfast.

Gîtes
Some of the best-value places to stay are not hotels but small family-run facilities known as *gîtes*. Gîtes de France Guadeloupe (☎ 82 09 30), BP 759, 97171 Pointe-à-Pitre, is an association of homeowners who rent private rooms and apartments. Most of the gîtes are quite comfortable; all are rated on a scale of one to three by the association – the higher the number, the higher the standard. The gîtes are spread around Guadeloupe, with the largest collection in the Gosier, Sainte-Anne and Saint-François areas. Generally they're booked by the week, and arrangements can be made in advance through the association. Although rates vary, on average you can find a nice place for around 1600F a week for two people. Most hosts do not speak English, so a working knowledge of French is often essential. A full list of gîtes can be obtained from the association or at the tourist office.

FOOD
Island cuisine draws upon a wide range of seafood, including crayfish *(ouassous)*, octopus *(chatrou)*, conch *(lambi)* and more traditional fishes such as red snapper *(vivanneau)*. Some typical Guadeloupean dishes include *accras* (cod fritters), *crabes farci* (spicy stuffed land crabs), *colombo cabri* (curried goat), rice and beans, and breadfruit gratin. Another popular Creole dish is *blaff*, a seafood preparation poached in a spicy broth.

Breakfasts are typically French-style social affairs, usually at patisseries serving up espresso, pastries, sandwiches and fresh fruit juices. It's just the thing to go with the first swim of the day.

DRINKS

Tap water is safe to drink. There are lots of excellent local rums, and some distilleries have tasting rooms. Homemade flavored rums made by adding fruit are also popular; in bars and restaurants you'll commonly see these in large glass jars behind the counter. A common restaurant drink (and the locals' beverage of choice) is 'ti-punch,' where you're brought white rum, cane sugar and a fresh lime to mix to your own proportions. Locally brewed Corsaire beer goes well with Creole food and lazy days on the beach.

Excellent French wines are served at nicer restaurants, and can also be picked up (for very reasonable prices) at the supermarkets in the larger towns.

Getting There & Away

AIR
Airports & Airlines

Guadeloupe Pole Caraïbes Airport is north of Pointe-à-Pitre, 6km from the city center on N5.

The terminal has a tourist information booth, car rental booths, a couple of restaurants, a pharmacy and gift shops. The two Tabac Presse newsstands sell phone cards and the IGN map of Guadeloupe. There are car rentals and a taxi stand for transportation, but no airport bus.

During banking hours you can exchange money and traveler's checks at the Crédit Agricole bank in the arrival lounge. You can also exchange US and other major foreign currency bills using the 24-hour currency-exchange ATM next to the bank. Another franc-dispensing ATM that accepts credit and bank cards can be found on the upper level next to the self-service restaurant.

Intra-Caribbean airlines that service Guadeloupe include the following:

Air Caraïbes	☎ 21 13 34
Air Guadeloupe	☎ 82 47 40
Air Martinique	☎ 21 13 42
Air St Martin	☎ 21 12 88
LIAT	☎ 82 12 26

The major international carriers servicing the region are as follows:

Air Canada	☎ 83 62 49
Air France	☎ 82 61 61
Air Liberté/Minerve	☎ 90 00 08
American Airlines	☎ 21 13 66
Nouvelles Frontières	☎ 82 35 30

Within the Caribbean

Air Martinique has numerous daily flights between Pointe-à-Pitre and Fort-de-France, Martinique; fares are 539F one-way and 836F roundtrip. Air Guadeloupe also has frequent flights from Pointe-à-Pitre and Fort-de-France at similar fares.

Air Guadeloupe and two smaller commuter airlines offer daily flights between Guadeloupe and St Martin with 614F one-way fares; Air Caraïbes has the cheapest roundtrip deal with its 788F 'superpromo' fare, while Air St Martin offers an 856F excursion fare.

LIAT connects Guadeloupe with the English-speaking Caribbean. There are daily flights running from Dominica to Guadeloupe for US$88/147 one-way/roundtrip, from St Lucia for US$113/174 and from Antigua for US$73/115.

The USA

American Airlines (☎ 21 13 66) has twice-daily flights to Guadeloupe from San Juan, Puerto Rico, that connect with mainland USA flights. Fares vary, but in the low season a ticket allowing a stay of up to 30 days generally begins around US$500 from east-coast cities such as Miami, New York and Boston. In the high season prices average about US$100 more.

Air France (☎ 82 61 61) has a flight from Miami to Guadeloupe on Tuesday and Saturday. The fare for a 21-day excursion ticket hovers around US$500.

Canada

Air Canada (☎ 83 62 49) has a Saturday flight from Montreal; fares depend on the season, beginning at C$750 roundtrip.

UK

British Airways (☎ 26 61 31) offers connecting flights from London. Prices hover around UK£650. American Airlines also offers service from London.

Continental Europe

Air France (☎ 82 61 61) flies to Guadeloupe from Paris at least once daily, with connections throughout Europe.

Air Liberté/Minerve (☎ 90 00 08) and Nouvelles Frontières (☎ 82 35 30) also have flights from Paris, with the frequency depending on the season.

It's a competitive market, with the cheapest roundtrip fares from Paris to Pointe-à-Pitre generally beginning around 2600F or so.

South America

Air France has scheduled flights from Pointe-à-Pitre to Cayenne, in French Guiana, and Caracas, Venezuela. An excursion ticket that's good for a stay of two to 17 days costs around 2000F from either South American port.

SEA
Passenger/Cargo Boat

Compagnie Générale Maritime (☎ 83 04 43) operates weekly 'banana boats' that carry passengers between the French West Indies and mainland France. Information is in the Getting There & Away chapter in the front of the book.

Ferry

There are two companies providing regular boat service between Guadeloupe and Martinique; the larger of the two also has service to Dominica and St Lucia.

L'Express des Îles L'Express des Îles operates modern 300-seat catamarans between Guadeloupe and Martinique, some of which stop en route in Dominica. The boats have both air-conditioned and open-air decks and a snack bar.

Southbound, the boats leave Pointe-à-Pitre at 8 am Monday to Saturday and also at noon Friday and 2 pm Sunday. The Tuesday- and Thursday-morning boats travel nonstop to Fort-de-France, Martinique, arriving there at 11 am. Most other boats make an en route stop at Roseau, Dominica (a 1¾-hour ride), before arriving at Martinique 3¾ hours after leaving Guadeloupe.

In the opposite direction, boats depart Martinique for Guadeloupe at 2 pm Monday and Wednesday, 1 and 3 pm Tuesday, 1 pm Thursday, 3 pm Friday, 9 am Saturday and 3:30 pm Sunday. All boats except those that depart from Martinique on Thursday afternoon stop in Dominica. In addition, the Tuesday and Thursday boats from Martinique stop en route in Les Saintes.

Once a week in the off-season, two or three days a week in the summer and winter peak seasons, there's also a boat between Guadeloupe and Castries, St Lucia.

Departure days and times for these services change frequently and often bear no relation to the printed schedule. The only way to be sure is to call L'Express des Îles or check with a local travel agent.

The Guadeloupe-Martinique fare (in either direction) costs 355F one-way, with a free stopover allowed in Dominica or Les Saintes. An excursion fare allowing a stay of up to seven days but no en route stopover costs 540F. The Guadeloupe–St Lucia fare is 500F one-way (Dominica or Martinique stopover allowed), or 750F for the excursion fare. Buying two one-way tickets with stopovers can make island-hopping in the region very affordable.

There are discounts of 50% for children ages two to 11 and 10% for passengers under 26 or age 60 and older. For reservations in Martinique, call ☎ 63 12 11, in Guadeloupe ☎ 83 12 45, in Dominica ☎ 44 82 181, in Saint Lucia ☎ 452-2211; alternatively, check with any travel agent.

Brudey Frères Brudey Frères has a 350-passenger catamaran with service between Pointe-à-Pitre and Fort-de-France. The boat departs from Guadeloupe at 8:10 am Monday, Wednesday, Friday, Saturday and Sunday, and from Martinique at 1 pm the same days. The fare is 304F one-way, 513F roundtrip. Brudey offers discounts similar to the competition for youths and elders.

Reservation numbers are ☎ 90 04 48 in Guadeloupe, ☎ 70 08 50 in Martinique.

Yacht

Guadeloupe has three marinas. Marina de Bas du Fort (☎ 90 84 85), between Pointe-à-Pitre and Gosier, has 700 berths, 55 of which are available for visiting boats. It can handle craft up to 39m in length and has full facilities including fuel, water, electricity, sanitation, ice, chandlery and a maintenance area.

Marina de Saint-François (☎ 88 47 28), in the center of Saint-François, has about 250 moorings, as well as fuel, water, ice and electricity.

Marina de Rivière-Sens (☎ 90 00 01), on the southern outskirts of the town of Basse-Terre, has 220 moorings, as well as fuel, water and ice.

There are customs and immigration offices in Pointe-à-Pitre, Basse-Terre and Deshaies.

The yacht charter companies The Moorings (☎ 90 81 81), Stardust Marine (☎ 90 92 02) and Star Voyage (☎ 90 86 26) are based at the Bas du Fort Marina.

Cruise Ship

Cruise ships dock right in the city at Centre Saint-John Perse, Pointe-à-Pitre's port complex, which has shops, restaurants and a hotel.

Getting Around

AIR

Air Guadeloupe has daily flights between Pointe-à-Pitre and Marie-Galante, La Désirade and Terre-de-Haut. See those island sections, later, for details.

BUS

Guadeloupe has a good public bus system that operates from about 5:30 am to 6:30 pm, with fairly frequent service on main routes. On Saturday afternoon service is much lighter, and there are almost no buses on Sunday.

Many bus routes start and end in Pointe-à-Pitre. Buses to Basse-Terre leave from the bus stop northwest of the center of town on Blvd Chanzy. Buses to Gosier, St Anne and the east coast leave from a smaller terminal east of the town center on Rue Dubouchage. Schedules are a bit loose and buses generally don't depart Pointe-à-Pitre until they're near capacity. Jump seats fold down and block the aisle as the bus fills, so try to get a seat near the front if you're not going far.

The bus from Pointe-à-Pitre to Gosier costs 7F and takes about 15 minutes. If you're going to the Bas du Fort Marina, you can take this bus and get off just past the university. Other fares from Pointe-à-Pitre are 10F to Sainte-Anne, 15F to Saint-François, 20F to Pointe-Noire (via Route de la Traversée) and 30F to Basse-Terre.

Pay the driver (or sometimes his assistant at the rear door) as you get off the bus. Having the correct fare is not essential, although larger-denomination notes could be problematic.

Destinations are written on the buses. Bus stops have blue signs picturing a bus; in less developed areas you can wave buses down along their routes.

CAR & MOTORCYCLE
Road Rules

In Guadeloupe drive on the right; your home driver's license is valid.

Roads are excellent by Caribbean standards and almost invariably hard-surfaced, although secondary and mountain roads are often narrow. Around Pointe-à-Pitre there are multilane highways, with traffic zipping along at 110km/h. Outside the Pointe-à-Pitre area, most highways have a single lane in each direction and an 80km/h speed limit.

Traffic regulations and road signs are of European standards. Exits and intersections are clearly marked, and speed limits are posted.

Rental

Car Several car rental companies have offices at the airport and in major resort areas. Some agents will let you rent a car near your hotel and drop it off free of charge at the airport, which can save a hefty taxi fare.

Companies generally drop their rates the longer you keep the car, with the weekly rate working out to be about 15% cheaper than the daily rate. Note that many companies have both an unlimited-kilometers rate and a cheaper rate with a per-kilometer charge; as the island is big, fees on the latter can rack up quite quickly.

Rates for small cars with unlimited kilometers are advertised from around 200F a day, although the rates offered on a walk-in basis can vary greatly with the season. It's a competitive market, and when business is slow it's generally possible to find something for as low as 150F. At the height of the season you might not find anything available for less than 300F, and sometimes all categories of automobiles are sold out completely. Certainly if you're traveling in winter it's not a bad idea at all to book in advance.

Car rental companies include the following organizations:

Avis	☎ 21 13 54 at the airport
	☎ 84 22 27 in Gosier
	☎ 85 00 11 in Saint-François
Budget	☎ 82 95 58 at the airport
	☎ 84 24 24 in Gosier
Citer	☎ 82 10 94 at the airport
Europcar	☎ 21 13 52 at the airport
	☎ 84 45 84 in Gosier
	☎ 88 69 77 in Saint-François
Hertz	☎ 93 89 45 at the airport
	☎ 84 23 23 in Gosier
Thrifty	☎ 91 42 17 at the airport
	☎ 90 86 32 in Bas du Fort
	☎ 84 51 26 in Gosier

Motorcycle CFM, on D119 in Gosier (☎ 84 41 81) and at Le Méridien in Saint-François (☎ 88 51 00), rents out scooters for 220F a day and has bigger bikes, up to 600cc, for 470F a day. Dom Location (☎ 88 84 81),

on Rue Saint-Aude Ferly in Saint-François, has attractive rates, with scooters for 170F a day, 125cc motorcycles for 290F and 600cc motorcycles for 390F.

TAXI

Taxis are plentiful but expensive. There are taxi stands at the airport, in Pointe-à-Pitre and in Basse-Terre. The larger hotels commonly have taxis assigned to them, with the drivers waiting in the lobby.

The fare from the airport is about 80F to Pointe-à-Pitre, 100F to Gosier, 200F to Sainte-Anne and 300F to Saint-François. Fares are 40% higher from 9 pm to 7 am nightly, as well as all day on Sunday and holidays. You can call for a taxi by dialing ☎ 82 00 00 or 83 99 99 in the Pointe-à-Pitre area, ☎ 81 79 70 in Basse-Terre.

BICYCLE

Dom Location (☎ 88 84 81), on Rue Saint-Aude Ferly in Saint-François, has mountain bikes for 80F a day or 25% less on a three-day rental. CFM (see Car & Motorcycle, earlier) rents out mountain bikes for 90F a day.

HITCHHIKING

Hitchhiking is fairly common on Guadeloupe, particularly when the bus drivers decide to go on strike. The proper stance is to hold out an open palm at a slightly downward angle. All the usual safety precautions apply.

BOAT

Ferries to Les Saintes leave from Pointe-à-Pitre, Saint-François and Trois-Rivières. Ferries to Marie-Galante leave from Pointe-à-Pitre and Saint-François. Ferries to La Désirade leave from Saint-François.

Schedule and fare information is given later in this chapter under the individual island sections.

ORGANIZED TOURS

Emeraude Guadeloupe (☎ 81 98 28) organizes 'green tourism' sightseeing outings. These trips offer an emphasis on nature and hiking.

GUADELOUPE

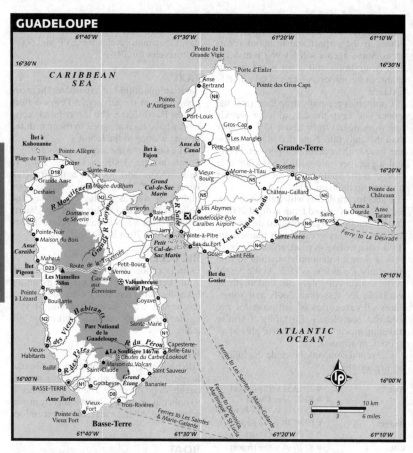

GUADELOUPE

Pointe-à-Pitre

In 1654 a merchant named Peter, a Dutch Jew who settled in Guadeloupe after being exiled from Brazil, began a fish market on an undeveloped harborside jut of land. The area became known as Peter's Point and eventually grew into the settlement of Pointe-à-Pitre.

Guadeloupe's largest municipality, Pointe-à-Pitre is a conglomerate of old and new and is largely commercial in appearance. There are a couple of small

museums, but other than that the most interesting sight is the bustling harborside market.

The town hub is Place de la Victoire, an open space punctuated with tall royal palms that extends north a few blocks from the inner harbor. There are sidewalk cafés opposite its west side, a line of big old mango trees to the north and some older buildings along with the sous-préfecture office at the park's east side.

While it's not a major tourist destination, all visitors can expect to at least pass through Pointe-à-Pitre, as it's the main port for ferries to Guadeloupe's outer islands and shelters the central bus terminal.

Central Pointe-à-Pitre is quite compact, and nothing there is more than a five- or 10-minute walk from Place de la Victoire.

Information

Tourist Offices The tourist office (☎ 82 09 30), 5 Square de la Banque, opposite the northwest end of the harbor, is open 8 am to 5 pm weekdays, 8 am to noon Saturday. A second office in the Centre Saint-John Perse, next to the police booth, is open when cruise ships are in port.

Money The BDAF bank next to the tourist office is open 8 am to noon and 2 to 4 pm weekdays; there are a few more banks nearby on Rue Boisneuf.

Post & Communications The post office, a block north of the cathedral on Boulevard Hanne, is open 8 am to 6 pm weekdays, till noon Saturday; expect long, slow-moving lines. In addition to utilizing normal mail services, you can also send faxes and telegrams from the post office.

Rapido, in the Centre Saint-John Perse, has Internet access for 20F for 15 minutes, 35F per half-hour.

Bookstores The largest and best-stocked bookstore in town is the Espace St-John Perse, 11 Rue de Nozières, with a decent English-language section. The Boutique de la Presse in the Centre Saint-John Perse sells English- and French-language newspapers and Institut Géographique National maps of Guadeloupe and other French West Indies islands. Le Presse Papier, the tobacco shop next to Délifrance, also sells international newspapers and maps of Guadeloupe.

Public Markets

There's a lively, colorful open-air market running along La Darse, the inner harbor. Women wearing madras cloth turbans sell island fruit, vegetables, flowers, pungent spices, handicrafts and clothing, while a few fishing boats docked at the edge of the harbor sell fresh fish.

Another large public market, the Marché Couvert, is just a few blocks to the west at Rue Peynier and Rue Schoelcher and has a good collection of handicrafts and spices. To get there from the waterfront, take the pedestrian Rue St-John Perse.

Centre Saint-John Perse

This large port complex is on the west side of the harbor, less than a five-minute walk from Place de la Victoire. It has the cruise-ship dock, port authority offices, a tourist booth, boutiques, shops and restaurants.

Musée Schoelcher

This museum, which occupies an interesting period building at 24 Rue Peynier, is dedicated to abolitionist Victor Schoelcher. The main exhibits are personal objects belonging to Schoelcher and artifacts relating to slavery. The museum is open 8:30 am to 12:30 pm Monday to Saturday, as well as 2 to 5:30 pm Monday and Tuesday and 2 to 6 pm Thursday and Friday. Admission will cost you 10F.

Musée Saint-John Perse

This municipal museum, 9 Rue de Noziéres, occupies an attractive 19th-century colonial building with ornate wrought-iron balconies. The museum is dedicated to the renowned poet and Nobel laureate Alexis Léger (1887–1975), better known as Saint-John Perse. The house offers both a glimpse of a period Creole home and displays on Perse's life and work. Perse grew up a bit farther down the same street, at No 54. The museum is open 9 am to 5 pm weekdays, 8:30 am to 12:30 pm Saturday. Admission is priced at 10F.

Cathédrale de St Pierre et St Paul

Rather than the traditional arches, this weathered sand-colored church, nicknamed the 'Iron Cathedral,' is supported by iron girders intended to brace it against earthquakes and hurricanes. The church, which is a couple of minutes' walk northwest of Place de la Victoire, is worth a look, particularly on Sunday.

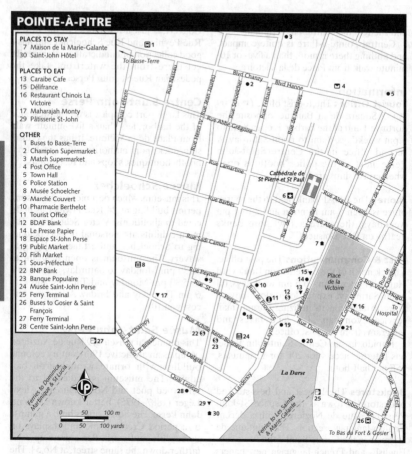

POINTE-À-PITRE

PLACES TO STAY
7 Maison de la Marie-Galante
30 Saint-John Hôtel

PLACES TO EAT
13 Caraibe Cafe
15 Délifrance
16 Restaurant Chinois La
   Victoire
17 Maharajah Monty
29 Pâtisserie St-John

OTHER
1 Buses to Basse-Terre
2 Champion Supermarket
3 Match Supermarket
4 Post Office
5 Town Hall
6 Police Station
8 Musée Schoelcher
9 Marché Couvert
10 Pharmacie Berthelot
11 Tourist Office
12 BDAF Bank
14 Le Presse Papier
18 Espace St-John Perse
19 Public Market
20 Fish Market
21 Sous-Préfecture
22 BNP Bank
23 Banque Populaire
24 Musée Saint-John Perse
25 Ferry Terminal
26 Buses to Gosier & Saint
   François
27 Ferry Terminal
28 Centre Saint-John Perse

Places to Stay

Pointe-à-Pitre has few places to stay and
even fewer reasons to spend the night.
Shops close early, and the streets are almost
empty after dark. If you're looking for
island culture or a cozy beachside getaway
you might as well keep moving.

Maison de la Marie-Galante (☎ 90 10
41, 12 Place de la Victoire) is centrally
located but run-down, with sporadic electricity problems. Basic singles/doubles with
twin beds and private baths cost 300/350F.

A significant step up is *Saint-John Hôtel*
(☎ 82 51 57, fax 82 52 61), in the Centre

Saint-John Perse. A member of the Anchorage chain, it's centrally located and extremely convenient if you're catching an
early-morning boat. It has 44 compact but
otherwise comfortable rooms with air-con,
room safes, cable TV, phones and small
shared balconies overlooking the harbor.
Singles/doubles cost 385/490F in summer,
435/535F in winter, breakfast included.

Places to Eat

A great place for a cheap breakfast is
Délifrance, on the west side of Place de la
Victoire. It has good croissants, pastries and

mini-quiches for 6F to 13F, as well as inexpensive salads and sandwiches. This popular spot has sidewalk café tables and is open from 6:30 am every day but Sunday.

A few doors down, *Café Caraibe* has outdoor tables and a French café feel, with salads and crêpes (12F to 35F) as well as French wine and draft beer.

Restaurant Chinois la Victoire, on the other side of the square, rates an absolute zero on the ambience scale but comes through with tasty Chinese food at low prices.

At the other end of the spectrum, *Maharaja Monty (47 Rue Achille Rene-Boisneuf)* has delicious Indian food in an opulent, low-lit second-story pleasure palace. It's open noon to 3 pm and 7:30 to 11 pm, offering main dishes like tandoori chicken for around 50F.

Pâtisserie St-John, at the side of the Saint-John Hôtel in Centre Saint-John Perse, has good inexpensive sandwiches, quiches and pastries.

There's a *Match* supermarket north of town; the food stalls outside are a great place to get street food like christophene gratin and accras. The well-stocked *Champion* supermarket, on Boulevard Chanzy, is one of the few places open Sunday and holidays (until 12:30 pm only).

Shopping
The harborfront market in Pointe-à-Pitre is a good place to buy island handicrafts, including straw dolls, straw hats and primitive African-style wood carvings. It's also a good spot to pick up locally grown coffee and a wide array of fragrant spices.

One of the most popular island souvenirs is *bois bandé*, the allegedly aphrodisiac bark of a local tree, usually sold soaked in rum. The nice ladies at the market will gladly explain its dosage and effects.

Getting There & Around
Buses to Gosier, Sainte-Anne and Saint-François leave from Rue Dubouchage at the east side of the harbor. Buses to places in Basse-Terre leave from the northwest side of town near Bergevin Stadium, a 10-minute walk from the center along Boulevard Chanzy.

On weekdays, traffic in the center is congested and parking can be tight. There are parking meters (5F an hour) along the east side of Place de la Victoire and on many of the smaller side streets throughout the city.

Grande-Terre

The southern coast of Grande-Terre, with its reef-protected waters, is Guadeloupe's main resort area. The eastern side of the island is largely open Atlantic, with crashing surf and a decidedly rural character. In the interior there's a mix of rolling hills and flat plains, the latter still largely given over to sugarcane.

BAS DU FORT
Bas du Fort, on the southern outskirts of Pointe-à-Pitre, has Guadeloupe's largest marina, a university and some new condo and hotel developments. The main hotel area is a couple of kilometers by road south of the marina. Bas du Fort takes its name from its location at the base *(bas)* of Fort Fleur-d'Épée.

Marina Bas du Fort
This expansive marina has full yachting facilities, a pharmacy, coin laundries, shops and eateries.

Crédit Agricole has a 24-hour change machine near Restaurant Shangai that will change US and Canadian dollars, British pounds and other major currencies to French francs.

Aquarium de la Guadeloupe
This harborside aquarium (☎ 90 92 38), rated as France's fourth best, has 60 species of tropical fish as well as turtles and sharks. Television monitors scattered around the rooms run videos with a strong conservation message. To get there, turn off the N4 east of the roundabout, between the Elf and Esso gas stations. The aquarium is open 9 am to 7 pm daily and costs 38F for adults, 20F for children.

GUADELOUPE

Fort Fleur-d'Épée

This small 18th-century hilltop garrison offers views of Gosier and the island of Marie-Galante. Much of the coral block walls and a few of the buildings stand intact, and there are rusting cannons and flowering flamboyant trees on the grounds. To get there, turn off the N4 at the 'Bas du Fort' sign and head south for about a kilometer; an inconspicuous sign on the left marks the side road that leads 800m up to the fort.

Places to Stay

A good-value place is *Village Viva* (☎ 90 98 98, fax 90 96 16, Bas du Fort, 97190 Gosier), on a point near the mouth of the marina. The 76 units, in contemporary four-story buildings, have air-con, TV, phone, balconies and kitchenettes. The shoreline is rocky, but there's a large pool. Rates for one or two people are 305F in summer, 430F in winter; optional breakfast is an additional 50F per person.

Fleur d'Épée Novotel (☎ 90 40 00, fax 90 99 07, Bas du Fort, 97190 Gosier) is an older but popular top-end resort. The 190 rooms are in three-story buildings and have all the standard amenities, including room safes and balconies. There's a pool, tennis courts, a white-sand beach and a couple of restaurants and bars. Singles/doubles start at 700/940F in summer and run about 50% more in winter.

Places to Eat

You'll find a cluster of cafés and restaurants all within a few minutes' walk of each other at the marina. The bakery, next to the Thrifty car rental, has good pastries, crispy bread and filling baguette sandwiches for 12F to 18F.

For Chinese food, the nearby *Restaurant Shangai* has a soup-to-dessert plat du jour for 90F, vegetarian main dishes for 45F and pork and chicken dishes for 55F. There's also a cheaper takeout stand at the side of the restaurant.

Arizona Grill, at the marina, is a French-run Americana café with strangely authentic diner decor. Try such exotic treats as a cheeseburger (17F) or chili con carne (48F).

Le Fregate is a nice harborside place with fresh fish dishes and daily chalkboard specials for around 70F. A popular place on the north side of the marina is *La Route du Rhum*, which has an open-air setting, salads from 50F, brochettes for 60F and fish dishes from 75F. Across the street, *Caraibe Pizza* draws students from the nearby university with tasty pizzas from 37F to 75F.

North of the parking area is a supermarket, and across the road a couple of vendors sell fruit and flowers.

GOSIER

Guadeloupe's most popular tourist resort is Gosier, 8km southeast of Pointe-à-Pitre. It's really two towns, neatly divided: a cluster of high-rise hotels full of French families on one side and a growing Caribbean village next door.

On the west side of Gosier is a tourist strip with a run of resort hotels, a casino, car rental agents and restaurants. The beach forms a series of scalloped sandy coves, with a hotel backing each cove. The water is generally calm, and all kinds of water sports are vigorously practiced.

Gosier's village center, about a 15-minute walk away, lacks the fine beaches found in the main hotel area, but it is more local in character. On the west side of the village center you'll find a park planted with flamboyant, white cedar and tropical almond trees. There's also a small but swimmable beach and a good view across the water to Îlet du Gosier. The village's Catholic church is modernistic, with a cement steeple, and there's a cemetery with aboveground vaults and tombs opposite the post office.

Many of Guadeloupe's most popular nightspots, attracting a young and fashionable French crowd until early morning, are clustered together on the outskirts of Gosier on the road to Pointe-à-Pitre.

Information

Post The post office in the Gosier village center is open 8 am to 5 pm Monday, Tuesday, Thursday and Friday, and 8 am to noon Wednesday and Saturday.

Laundry Laverie du Gosier, a laundry near the post office, is open 7:30 am to 7:30 pm Monday to Saturday. It costs 53F to wash and dry a load of clothes.

Bookstores La Gazette, in the village center, sells the IGN map of Guadeloupe, local newspapers, international newspapers including *USA Today* and *The International Herald-Tribune* and a wide variety of French magazines.

Îlet du Gosier

Just 600m off Gosier village is lovely Îlet du Gosier, a little undeveloped island surrounded by calm turquoise waters. This relaxed place has an old lighthouse and attractive white-sand beaches, making it popular with swimmers, sunbathers and families out for a picnic. A small restaurant serves cold drinks throughout the day and simple fish dishes in the afternoon.

There's decent snorkeling on the northwest side of the island; if you go out about 20m from the dilapidated green shed, you'll come to a sunken boat hull harboring big-eyed fish, and a bit beyond you'll find a few coral heads.

Motorboats shuttle beachgoers between Gosier and the island (15F roundtrip, three minutes each way), departing from the little dock at the end of Rue Félix Éboué.

Water Sports

Beach huts in front of the resort hotels rent snorkeling gear for 40F a day, windsurfing equipment for 50F an hour, Sunfish sailboats for 80F an hour, larger Hobie Cat boats for 200F an hour. Also available there are fun boards, pedal boats and other water-activities gear.

Places to Stay

Budget Offering *hotellerie à la carte*, *La Formule Économique* (☎ 84 54 91, fax 84 29 42, 112/120 Lot Gisors, 97190 Gosier) calculates rates based on the amenities you select. A very comfortable basic room with a double bed begins at 199F, studios at 250F. Add another 50F if you want air-con, 30F for TV. There's a terrace bar and a down-stairs restaurant. You'll see signs in town directing you to the hotel, about 200m up a side road that passes the Jehovah's Witness temple.

Les Flamboyants (☎ 84 14 11, fax 84 53 56, Chemin des Phares et Blaises, 97190 Gosier) has a quiet hilltop location about a kilometer east of the village and a five-minute walk from the nearest bus stop. This cozy hostelry has a view of Îlet du Gosier, a small pool and personable management. The 14 compact rooms are spotlessly clean and suitably simple, with comfortable beds, air-con and private baths. Singles/doubles cost 260/300F in summer, 320/360F in winter; add 60F to 80F more if you want a kitchenette. A simple breakfast is included in the rates. Popular with budget travelers, it commonly books up in advance during the high season; phone reservations generally require a command of French.

Mid-Range In town, *Hotel Pergola Plage* (☎ 84 44 44, 97190 Gosier) has pleasant rooms overlooking a small beach near the center of town. Rooms go for as little as 300F in the off-season, and the bar-restaurant down the hill is a popular local watering hole.

Canella Beach Residence (☎ 90 44 00, fax 90 44 44, in the USA ☎ 800-223-9815, Pointe de la Verdure, BP 73, 97190 Gosier) has 146 air-con units in two three-story buildings. The studios have rattan furniture, a queen or two twin beds, a little sitting area with a sofa bed, TV, phone, a balcony and a kitchenette. Some studios on the ground level are wheelchair-accessible. Singles/doubles cost 462/583F in summer, 650/840F in winter. There are also suites and duplex apartments. Rates include use of the pool, tennis courts, paddleboats and canoes.

Top End The *Callinago Hotel & Village* (☎ 84 25 25, fax 84 24 90, BP 1, 97190 Gosier) has two separate wings: the 'hotel,' with 40 rooms, and the 'village,' with 93 studios. The village units have kitchenettes, while the hotel units have no cooking facilities but include breakfast in the rate. Both wings have air-con and phones, and there's a

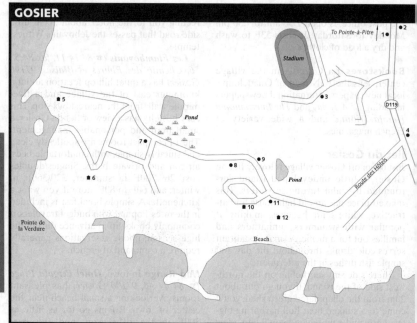

GOSIER

To Pointe-à-Pitre

Stadium

Pond

Pond

Pointe de
la Verdure

Beach

GUADELOUPE

beachside pool. The Callinago was recently remodeled from top to bottom and is no longer one of the cheaper options; expect rates around 740/900F for singles/doubles.

The following are modern beachside resorts with standard 1st-class amenities, including swimming pools, activity centers, restaurants and well-appointed rooms with balconies.

La Créole Beach Hôtel (☎ 90 46 46, fax 90 46 66, BP 19, 97190 Gosier) is a 156-room complex with contemporary singles/doubles costing 590/800F in summer, 870/1100F in winter.

The eight-story *Hôtel Arawak* (☎ 84 24 24, fax 84 38 45, BP 396, 97162 Pointe-à-Pitre) has 200 singles/doubles that cost 700/750F in summer, 750/1000F in winter.

The lobby of the 160-room *Auberge de la Vieille Tour* (☎ 84 23 23, fax 84 33 43, Montauban, 97190 Gosier), incorporates an 18th-century windmill, but most of the rooms are in more ordinary buildings. Stan-

dard singles/doubles cost 750/900F in summer, 890/1010F in winter.

Places to Eat
The center of Gosier has a number of inexpensive eating options. There are two bakeries right opposite each other at the main intersection. One of them, *Brioche Passion*, has a few sidewalk tables where you can have coffee and croissants, good inexpensive sandwiches and crêpes. For mouthwatering French pastries, cakes and fruit tarts, the bakery across the street is in a class by itself. A few steps up the hill, *Glacier du Centre* serves up delicious fresh ice cream, with island flavors like coconut or mango, at 6F a scoop.

A stone's throw from the bakeries is *Chez Titi*, where a sidewalk barbecue stand cooks up inexpensive grilled chicken in the evenings. A plate of chicken with fries costs 32F; it's closed Monday. Down the hill toward the beach you'll find an *Ecomax*

GOSIER

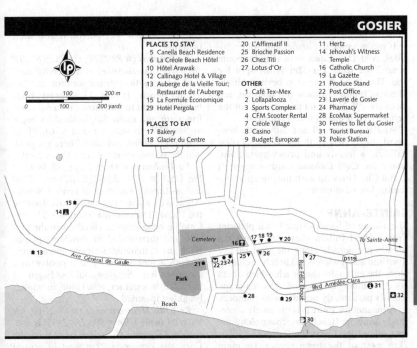

PLACES TO STAY
5 Canella Beach Residence
6 La Créole Beach Hôtel
10 Hôtel Arawak
12 Callinago Hotel & Village
13 Auberge de la Vieille Tour;
   Restaurant de l'Auberge
15 La Formule Économique
29 Hotel Pergola

PLACES TO EAT
17 Bakery
18 Glacier du Centre

20 L'Affirmatif II
25 Brioche Passion
26 Chez Titi
27 Lotus d'Or

OTHER
1 Café Tex-Mex
2 Lollapalooza
3 Sports Complex
4 CFM Scooter Rental
7 Créole Village
8 Casino
9 Budget; Europcar

11 Hertz
14 Jehovah's Witness
   Temple
16 Catholic Church
19 La Gazette
21 Produce Stand
22 Post Office
23 Laverie de Gosier
24 Pharmacy
28 EcoMax Supermarket
30 Ferries to Îlet du Gosier
31 Tourist Bureau
32 Police Station

GUADELOUPE

supermarket, and there's a daytime produce stand next to the post office.

L'Affirmatif II is an inviting little place with delicious Creole food at reasonable prices. The 65F menu du jour includes salad with accras, christophene gratin, dessert and the seafood dish of the day. They also make good wood-fired pizza from 50F. It's open for dinner only, 6 pm to midnight daily.

On a hill with great ocean views, ***Le Lotus d'Or*** (☎ 84 35 73, 38 Blvd Gen de Gaulle) has Guadeloupe's best Vietnamese cuisine. You can get a full meal of spring rolls or salad, main course, dessert and coffee for 110F.

Restaurant de l'Auberge, at the Auberge de la Vieille Tour (see Places to Stay) has Gosier's most upmarket fine-dining restaurant, serving traditional French and Creole cuisine. Everything's à la carte; expect dinner to run around 300F per person, without wine.

In the main beach hotel area, the Créole Village shopping center has half a dozen places to eat, including a pizzeria, a small patisserie selling pastries and baguette sandwiches, and an ice cream and crêpe shop. All the big hotels have fancy but unexciting French restaurants, most with weekend lunch buffets.

Entertainment

Gosier is easily the most hopping nightlife spot on the island. In town the local rum shops get feisty until late, while cooler heads prevail at the air-conditioned ***pool hall***. Most of the fancy hotels have live music and poolside barbecues on a regular basis. The local ***casino***, on the road into town, is a small yet high-stakes joint without any real character; proper dress is *exigée* (mandatory).

The outskirts of Gosier, north on the D119 toward Pointe-à-Pitre, host a string of late-night restaurants, bars and discos, a long walk or a quick but pricey taxi ride from the hotels.

If you've come to Guadeloupe for enchiladas, cold Dos Equis or a tequila 'boum boum,' the *Café Tex-Mex* is the spot for you. The decor is one step beyond kitsch, Mexican bullfight videos run nonstop, and tacos are 79F. You can't miss it; look for the neon-covered wagon wheel out front.

And if you're still not sufficiently confused, head across the street to Lollapalooza, a trendy and pricey restaurant, where the *Café Cubana* features waitstaff in full Ché Guevara garb mixing up an assembly line of *mojitos*.

SAINTE-ANNE

The village of Sainte-Anne has a pleasant French West Indian character. There's a seaside promenade along the west side of town and a fine white-sand beach stretching along the east side. The beach, which offers good swimming and is shaded by sea-grape trees, is particularly popular with islanders.

A magnet for tourists is the lovely white-sand Caravelle Beach, stretching along the east side of the Caravelle Peninsula, about 2km west of the town center. Its main tenant is Club Med, but the entire beach is public, though of course Club Med won't let you play with their toys unless you're staying there. The unmarked road to Caravelle Beach is off N4, opposite Motel l'Accra Sainte-Anne.

Places to Stay

In Town The *Auberge le Grand Large* (☎ 85 48 28, fax 88 16 69, Route de la Plage, 97180 Sainte-Anne) is opposite Sainte-Anne Beach on the corner of the beach access road. It has 13 suitably casual bungalows with air-con and phones for 350F to 600F, with the rate based on whether you opt to use the kitchenette and on how long you stay.

Motel l'Accra Sainte-Anne (☎ 88 22 40, fax 88 28 29, Durivage, 97180 Sainte-Anne) is on the N4 at the west side of town, across from the road to Caravelle Beach. This two-story motel has 10 good-sized air-conditioned rooms, some with kitchenettes. Rates begin at

a reasonable 250F in summer, 370F in winter; add another 35F per person if you want breakfast.

Le Rotabas (☎ 88 25 60, fax 88 26 87, BP 30, 97180 Sainte-Anne) is a friendly, laid-back place with a prime location at Caravelle Beach. It has 43 unpretentious bungalows and rooms, most with air-con, refrigerator and radio. Singles/doubles begin at 389/437F in summer and 631/679F in winter, breakfast included. There's a pool, and the ocean is just a stone's throw away.

La Toubana (☎ 88 25 78, fax 88 38 90, in the USA ☎ 800-223-9815, BP 63, 97180 Sainte-Anne), 2km west of central Sainte-Anne, is on a quiet coastal cliff overlooking the Caravelle Peninsula. There are 32 comfortable bungalows terraced down the hillside and surrounded by flowering plants. Each has a kitchenette, air-con and a porch. There's a tennis court and a pool with a swim-up bar. Singles/doubles begin at 567/722F in summer, 896/1140F in winter, breakfast included.

Le Club Méditerrannée (☎ 88 21 00, fax 88 06 06, in the USA ☎ 800-258-2633) is a secluded 322-room all-inclusive hotel on the Caravelle Peninsula, 2km west of central Sainte-Anne. It has an attractive white-sand beach, its own dock and all the standard Club Med amenities. Weekly rates, which include meals and an array of water-sports activities, are 6000/10,000F in summer, 7800/13,000F in winter; prorated daily stays are accepted when they're not fully booked.

Around Sainte-Anne If you have a car, an interesting option is the rural gîte *Les Hesperides* (☎ 88 96 50, c/o Annie Henry-Coûannier, 16 lot Eugénie, Montmain, 97180 Sainte-Anne), located in the hills between Gosier and Sainte-Anne, 9km from both. This attractive country home is in a tropical setting with lots of flowering bushes, and the helpful proprietor speaks English and welcomes foreign visitors. Double rooms, which have private baths and cooking facilities, begin at 1485F a week; two of the rooms can be combined to accommodate up to four people for 2440F. There's also a second property 2km from the beach at Sainte-Anne that has two new studios with kitchenettes on the veranda, each renting for 1800/2200F a week double/triple.

Relais du Moulin (☎ 88 23 96, fax 88 03 92, Chateaubrun, 97180 Sainte-Anne) has a picturesque old sugar mill used as a reception area and nicely planted grounds. Accommodations are in 40 rather rustic freestanding one-bedroom bungalows with phones, porches and refrigerators. The hotel has a country setting on the south side of the N4, 6km east of Sainte-Anne. There's a pool, tennis court, children's playground and upscale Creole restaurant. Singles/doubles begin at 440/490F in summer, 650/700F in winter.

Places to Eat

Opposite Sainte-Anne Beach is a row of simple open-air restaurants with tables in the sand and barbecue grills at the side. Recommended is *Le Coquillage*, which has meal specials that include crab farci for 38F, *blaff* (spicy fish stew) for 65F, lambi fricassee for 150F and crayfish for 115F; it doubles as a dance club at night, with a zouk soiree on Wednesday. Two other popular spots are *Chez Monique*, which has Creole decor and big servings of straightforward food (chicken for 40F, grilled fish for 70F), and *Chez Jose*, which has sandwiches for around 15F as well as reasonably priced fish, chicken and beef dishes like grilled shark for 55F. The sandwich shop next door has great filling treats for 10F to go, 13F if you want to eat them there.

At Caravelle Beach, near La Rotabas, there are snack shops selling crêpes, hot dogs, sandwiches and other simple eats as well as a couple of beachside spots offering plate meals from around 60F. *La Rotabas* has a restaurant serving more substantial Creole food at moderate prices.

On the opposite side of the Caravelle Peninsula, near La Toubana, the *Sicilienne Pizzeria* has pastas and a wide variety of good pizzas from 40F to 55F; it opens at 6:30 pm. The restaurant at *La Toubana* has a gorgeous ocean view and specializes in lobster, with prices beginning at 165F.

SAINT-FRANÇOIS

Saint-François is a former fishing village that has boomed into Guadeloupe's second-largest tourist area. The west side of town is a sleepy provincial backwater, while the east side has been given over to tourism development and feels a lot like a small city in south Florida. The center of the action is the deep U-shaped harbor, which is lined with restaurants, hotels, car rental offices, boutiques and marina facilities. Just north of the marina there's a golf course.

A small beach fronts Le Méridien hotel, and an undistinguished strand runs along the south side of the town center, but the best beaches in the area are just a 10-minute drive east of town in the direction of Pointe des Châteaux.

Saint-François is a major jumping-off point for trips to Guadeloupe's smaller islands. The dock for boats to La Désirade, Marie-Galante and Les Saintes is at the south side of the marina, as is free parking. Full information on these destinations can be found later in this chapter.

Information

Tourist Offices The tourist office, on Avenue de l'Europe, is open 8 am to noon Monday to Saturday and also 2 to 5 pm most weekdays; it closes Wednesday at 12:30 pm.

Money Banque Populaire has an exchange office on the north side of the marina. It doesn't charge commissions and is open 7:45 am to noon and 2 to 4:45 pm weekdays and 7:45 am to 12:30 pm Saturday. If you need a full-service bank, try the BNP (with ATM) next to the post office.

Post & Communications The post office, a block west of the harbor, is open from 8 am to noon Monday to Saturday and also from 2 to 4 pm Monday, Tuesday, Thursday and Friday. Phone cards can be purchased at the Match supermarket.

Laundry There's a small laundromat on Rue Junon in town; a 15kg load costs 70F.

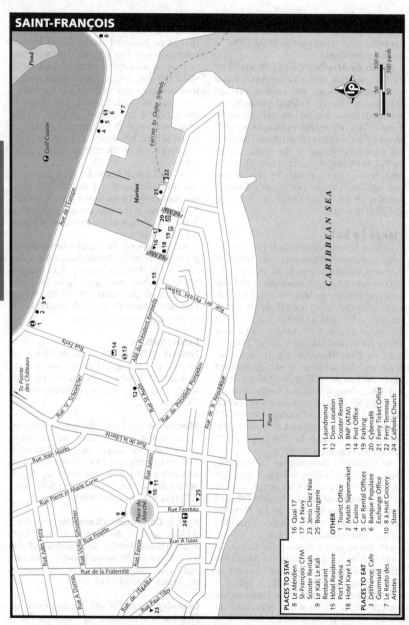

SAINT-FRANÇOIS

Pond

Golf Course

Ave de l'Europe

Marina

Ferries to Outer Islands

CARIBBEAN SEA

To Pointe des Châteaux

Rue V Schoelcher
Rue St Aude
Rue Ferry
Rue du Président Pompidou
Rue de la République
Allée du Président Kennedy
Rue des Petites Salines
Piers

Rue Jean Jaurès
Rue de la Liberté
Rue Pierre et Marie Curie
Rue Junon
Rue Favreau

Place du Marché

Rue Jules Ferry
Rue Victor Schoelcher
Rue Finette
Rue Fanon
Rue A Isaac
Rue de la Fratemité
Rue A Dumas
Rue de l'Égalité
Rue Paul-Tilby

0   50   100 m
0   50   100 yards

PLACES TO STAY
8 Le Méridien
   St-François; CFM
   Scooter Rentals
9 Le Kali; Le Kali
   Restaurant
15 Hôtel Residence
   Port Marina
18 Hotel Kayé La

PLACES TO EAT
3 Délifrance; Café
   Gourmand
7 Le Resto des
   Artistes

16 Quai 17
17 Le Navy
23 Jerco Chez Nise
25 Boulangerie

OTHER
1 Tourist Office
2 Match Supermarket
4 Casino
5 Car Rental Offices
6 Banque Populaire
   Exchange Office
10 à Huit Grocery
   Store

11 Laundromat
12 Dom Location
   Scooter Rental
13 BNP (ATM)
14 Post Office
19 Parking
20 Cybercafé
21 Ferry Ticket Office
22 Ferry Terminal
24 Catholic Church

Places to Stay

In the center of town opposite the market, *Le Kali (☎ 88 40 10, Place du Marché, 97118 Saint-François)* is a laid-back, old-time restaurant with upstairs accommodations. It has a handful of simple rooms, each with a bed, sink and fan. Bathrooms are shared. The cost is a reasonable 200F for a room with a fan and shared bath, 300F with air-conditioning and private bath and breakfast included.

Hotel Kayé La (☎ 88 10 10, fax 88 74 67, BP 204, 97118 Saint-François), at the marina, has 75 pleasant contemporary rooms with waterfront balconies, phones, TVs, air-con and bathtubs. Singles/doubles start at 400/610F in summer, 650/800F in winter, breakfast included. Request an upper-floor room for a water view.

Kayé La also books the adjacent *Hotel Residence Port Marina,* a modern three-story apartment building with 33 air-conditioned (and generic) studios that cost 500F in summer, 650F in winter.

Le Méridien St-François (☎ 88 51 00, fax 88 40 71, BP 37, 97118 Saint-François) is a five-story hotel with a little white-sand beach. The 265 rooms are 1st-class, though not posh. Each has a TV, phone, air-con and a small balcony. There's a pool and tennis courts as well. Singles or doubles with breakfast start at 1000F in summer, 1400 to 2450F in winter. It can be booked through Forte Hotels worldwide (in the USA and Canada ☎ 800-543-4300).

Places to Eat

Also a restaurant, *Le Kali* (see Places to Stay) offers multicourse dinners, with fish for 65F, steak au poivre for 95F and lobster priced by weight. South of the market, on Rue de la République, there's a local *boulangerie* with good croissants and breads.

A recommendable local favorite is *Jerco Chez Nise,* a pleasant neighborhood restaurant on Rue Paul-Tilby. For groups of two or more it offers set Creole meals ranging from chicken colombo, accras and dessert for 55F to a nine-dish seafood meal for 95F. It's open for lunch Tuesday to

Sunday and for dinner from 6 pm Tuesday to Saturday.

On the southwest corner of the marina, there's a line of inexpensive harborside eateries that sell pastries, sandwiches, ice cream and grilled foods. *Le Navy* has chicken with fries, as well as various salads, for around 40F and seafood dishes for 60F. *Quai 17*, at the end of the row, specializes in fresh seafood. Main dishes are priced in the 60F to 100F range.

On the north side of the marina, near the car rental booths, *Le Resto des Artistes* has a great waterfront setting and simple Italian fare. Pizza starts at 50F, while pasta is priced from 50F to 65F. It's open for lunch and dinner daily except Monday.

Clustered at the northwest side of the marina are *Délifrance* and *Café Gourmand,* serving salads and tasty panini for around 20F. There's also a large *Match* supermarket that's open 8:30 am to 8 pm daily (till 1 pm Sunday).

POINTE DES CHÂTEAUX

It's just a 10-minute drive from Saint-François to **Pointe des Châteaux**, the easternmost point of Grande-Terre. This intriguing coastal area has white-sand beaches, limestone cliffs and fine views of the jagged nearshore islets and the island of La Desirade.

From the end of the road you can make a couple of short hikes, though the walk to the cross on the hilltop is currently closed. The beach at the end of the point has rough surf and a steep shoreline, but there are more protected white-sand beaches farther to the northwest.

Anse Tarare is a popular nudist beach on a sheltered cove a couple of kilometers west of the road's end. The dirt road north of the main road is marked by a sign reading 'Plage Tarare.'

A few minutes drive to the west, a side road (follow the 'Chez Honoré' signs) leads a kilometer north to **Anse à la Gourde**, a gorgeous sweep of white coral sands. The waters are good for swimming and snorkeling, but be careful of nearshore coral shelves.

Places to Stay & Eat

A beach restaurant at the end of the road at Pointe des Châteaux, *La Paillotte* sells sandwiches and fresh tropical juices as well as a variety of Creole meals ranging from 60F for chicken to 150F for lobster.

Chez Honoré, an open-air restaurant facing the beach at Anse à la Gourde, specializes in seafood. A complete dinner that includes crab farci, grilled fish and dessert costs 100F; the same dinner with grilled lobster instead of fish costs 150F.

Chez Honoré also operates the adjacent *Village Bungalows* (☎ 85 03 93, fax 85 03 92), which consists of a row of pleasant one-room bungalows just a minute's walk from the beach. Each has air-con, a private bath and kitchenette; the rate is 2800F for a week.

LE MOULE

Le Moule served as an early French capital of Guadeloupe and was an important Amerindian settlement in precolonial times. Consequently, major archaeological excavations have taken place in the area and Guadeloupe's archaeological museum is located on the outskirts of town.

Although the town itself is not a must-see sight, the center is worth a stroll if you've come this way. The town square has a few historic buildings, including the town hall and a neoclassical Catholic church. Along the river are some discernible waterfront ruins from an old customs building and a fortress dating back to the original French settlement.

There's a tranquil beach with reef-protected waters at l'Autre Bord, about a kilometer east of town, while Baie du Moule, on the west side of town, is popular with surfers and has its own surf school.

Edgar Clerc Archaeological Museum

This modern museum (☎ 23 57 57), on a coastal cliff in the Rosette area, has Amerindian petroglyphs, pottery shards, tools made of shells and stone and an exhibition on local excavations. It's open 9 am to 5 pm daily except Monday from September

to March, 10 am to 6 pm daily except Monday from April to August. Admission is 10F for adults, 5F for children under 12. The museum is about a kilometer north on La Rosette Rd (D123), on the western outskirts of Le Moule.

Places to Stay & Eat

Asking around town is the best way to find a cheap place to stay; local guest houses charge as little as 100F a night…*if* there's an empty room.

Tropical Club Hotel (☎ 93 97 97, fax 93 97 00, BP 121, 97160 Le Moule), is a 72-room hotel on a nice white-sand beach about a kilometer east of Le Moule. Rooms have balcony kitchenettes, TV, air-con and phones. There's a pool and a moderately priced French/Creole restaurant. Rooms begin at 550F in summer, 650F in winter.

There are reasonably priced restaurants in town, including *Point Pizza Express*, right off the square, and *La Tortue*, at the end of Rue St Jean.

NORTHERN GRANDE-TERRE

The northern half of Grande-Terre is a rural area of grazing cattle, cane fields and abandoned roadside sugar mills. The main sights are the beach at Anse Maurice, east of Gros Cap, and Porte d'Enfer and Pointe de la Grande Vigie, about a 40-minute drive north of Le Moule. The road can be a bit narrow, but it's in good condition and paved all the way.

From Le Moule, drive up past the museum in Rosette, then turn right on the D120 and follow that road north. As you get closer to Porte d'Enfer the route will be signposted.

Anse Maurice

East of Gros Cap, off the D120, the beach at Anse Maurice is scenic, clean and nearly empty. The trade winds keep things cool, but watch out for sunburn.

To get there, take the road across from the post office in Gros Cap, and take a right turn after the water tower. Keep going straight until you get to a parking lot. There's a bar-restaurant open every day.

Porte d'Enfer

Despite its name, Porte d'Enfer (Gate of Hell) is a lovely sheltered cove surrounded by cliffs and backed by a small beach. Inside the cove the water is shallow but deep enough for swimming, while the entire coastline outside of the cove is tumultuous, with pounding surf and strong currents. There are picnic tables and sea cotton trees near the beach – it would make a fine spot to break for a picnic lunch.

As you continue north there's a view point about a kilometer beyond Porte d'Enfer that looks back at the beach and the area's craggy coastal cliffs. About a kilometer farther along, if you look to the east you'll see a series of seven coastal points, the second of which has a blowhole.

Pointe de la Grande Vigie

Pointe de la Grande Vigie, the island's northernmost point, offers scenic views from its high sea cliffs. On a clear day you can see Antigua to the north and Montserrat to the northwest, both about 75km away. There's a good view of Grande-Terre's east side from the parking lot, and you can take a short walk out to the farthest point for a view of the west side of the island.

Anse Bertrand

Anse Bertrand is a modest coastal town, a mix of concrete homes and simple wooden structures. The coastal section still shows signs of damage from Hurricane Hugo, which hit in 1989.

At Anse Laborde, about a kilometer north of town, there's an attractive little beach, but it often has gusty winds and dangerous waves.

Port-Louis

Port-Louis is a sleepy fishing village full of character, from its aging wooden houses splashed in bright colors to the main street lined with late-19th-century iron lampposts.

At the north side of town is La Plage de Souffleur, a nice, long bathing beach that's especially popular on weekends. The beach is backed by white cedar trees *(poui)* that drop delicate pink flowers twice a year.

South to Morne-à-l'Eau

South of Port-Louis the road passes inland through a couple of agricultural towns. The coast, however, is largely mangrove swamp.

The main tourist attraction in Morne-à-l'Eau, the largest town in central Grande-Terre, is its cemetery, at the intersection of the N5 and N6. Guadeloupe's most elaborate burial ground, it looks like a miniature city, terraced with raised vaults and tombs, many decorated in checkered black and white tiles. Locals are getting a little fed up with tour buses full of strangers gawking and taking photos of their relatives' resting places; a little courtesy and discretion are strongly advised.

Grands Fonds

The central part of Grande-Terre, known as the Grands Fonds (Great Valleys), is an undulating landscape of mounded hills and deeply creviced valleys. It's a pretty rural area that's given over to small farms and lush green pastures and crossed by narrow winding roads.

The northern section of Grands Fonds is home to the Blancs Matignons, descendants of white colonists who settled these hills at the beginning of the 19th century and who have maintained strict isolation ever since.

Grands Fonds is a fun place to drive – expect to get lost in the crisscross of roads, but as long as you head in a southerly direction, you'll eventually come out to the coast.

To get into the heart of Grands Fonds, simply take the N5 east 1km from Morne-à-l'Eau and then turn south on the D109.

Basse-Terre

Shortly after entering the island of Basse-Terre from Pointe-à-Pitre, you have a choice of three main routes: north along the coast, south along the coast, or across the interior along the Route de la Traversée, through the national park.

ROUTE DE LA TRAVERSÉE

The road that heads across the center of the island, the Route de la Traversée (D23),

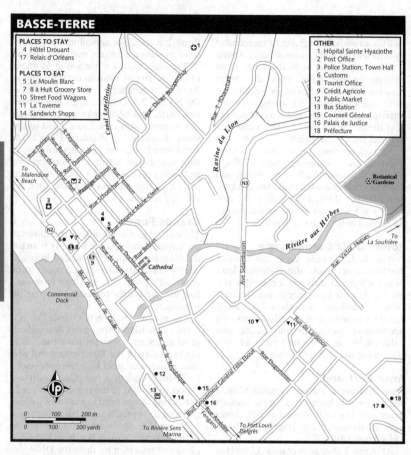

BASSE-TERRE

PLACES TO STAY
4   Hôtel Drouant
17 Relais d'Orléans

PLACES TO EAT
5   Le Moulin Blanc
7   à Huit Grocery Store
10 Street Food Wagons
11 La Taverne
14 Sandwich Shops

OTHER
1   Hôpital Sainte Hyacinthe
2   Post Office
3   Police Station; Town Hall
6   Customs
8   Tourist Office
9   Crédit Agricole
12 Public Market
13 Bus Station
15 Counseil Général
16 Palais de Justice
18 Préfecture

Map labels: Canal Lepelletier, Rue Dugommier, Rue T-Louverture, Ravine du Lion, Rue Delney, Rue Peynier, Rue du Docteur Pitat, Rue Dumanoir, Rue Perrinon, Rue Schoelcher, Rue Maurice Marie-Claire, Passage Giceron, Rue du Docteur Cabre, Rue Bebian, Rue du Cours Nolivos, Cathedral, N3, Rivière aux Herbes, Ave Sidambarom, Rue Victor Hugues, Botanical Gardens, To La Soufrière, To Malendure Beach, N2, Blvd du Général de Gaulle, Commercial Dock, Rue de la République, Rue de Lardenoy, Rue Dugommier, Blvd Gouverneur Général Félix Eboué, Rue Amédée Fengarol, To Rivière Sens Marina, To Fort Louis Delgrès

0   100   200 m
0   100   200 yards

(side tab: GUADELOUPE)

slices through the Parc National de la Guadeloupe, the 17,300-hectare forest reserve that occupies the interior of Basse-Terre. It's a lovely mountain drive that passes fern-covered hillsides, thick bamboo stands and enormous mahogany and gum trees. Other rain-forest vegetation en route includes orchids, heliconia and ginger.

The Route de la Traversée begins off the N1 about 15 minutes west of Pointe-à-Pitre and is well signposted. There are a few switchbacks, but driving is not tricky if you don't rush, and it's a good two-lane road all the way. Although the road could easily be

driven in an hour, give yourself double that to stop and enjoy the scenery – more if you want to do any hiking or break for lunch.

Don't miss the **Cascade aux Ecrevisses**, an idyllic little jungle waterfall that drops into a broad pool. From the parking area the waterfall is just a three-minute walk on a well-beaten but lushly green trail. The roadside pull-off is clearly marked on the D23, 2km after you enter the park's eastern boundary. Try to go early; in late afternoon busloads of tourists arrive.

At **Maison de la Forêt**, 2km farther west, there's a staffed roadside exhibit center with a few simple displays on the forest (in French only), open 9:30 am to 4:30 pm daily. A map board and the beginning of an enjoyable 20-minute **loop trail** is at the back of the center. The trail crosses a swing bridge over the Bas-David River and then proceeds through a verdant jungle of gommier trees, tall ferns and squawking tropical birds.

Picnic tables have been placed near the riverside and at roadside spots throughout the park.

Continuing west, if the weather's clear you'll find a view of Pointe-à-Pitre from the rear of **Gîte de Mamelles**, a hilltop restaurant on the north side of the road. The restaurant takes its name from the smooth double-mounded hills to the south.

Before winding down to the coast, there's a very modest zoo, the **parc des mamelles**, on the north side of the road. It features caged raccoons, birds and a few other creatures along a pleasant jungle walk; admission (35F) includes a drink at the snack bar. On the same side of the road, a few minutes before the zoo, a signposted road leads up to **Morne à Louis**, which offers a nice hilltop view on a clear day.

Places to Stay
The **Auberge de la Distillerie** (☎ 94 25 91, fax 94 11 91, Sommet Route de Versailles, 97170 Petit-Bourg), on the north side of the D23 about 6km west of the N1, is an unpretentious and inviting 15-room hostelry. Rooms have air-con, TV, a phone, a small refrigerator and a patio strung with a hammock. There's a pool and lots of flowering plants on the grounds. Singles/doubles cost from 350/450F in summer, 450/650F in winter, breakfast included. It's a 15-minute drive from Pointe-à-Pitre and just a few minutes east of the national park.

Mr and Mrs Tiburce Accipe (☎ 94 23 92, fax 94 12 08), Barbotteau, 97170 Petit-Bourg, have two quite classy three-star gîtes in Vernou on the eastern perimeter of the national park. One, **Le Mont Fleuri**, has five rooms, each with air-con and private bathroom, plus a shared kitchen and pool, which cost 1750F per week for two people. At the

other, **Les Alpinias**, there are eight air-conditioned apartments with kitchenettes, balconies and TV that rent for 3500F a week for up to four people.

Places to Eat
For those who want to grab something to eat on the way into the national park, **Auberge de la Distillerie** has a small bakery with crispy baguettes and croissants. The hotel also has a restaurant with a full breakfast for 50F as well as a lunchtime plat du jour for a reasonable 65F.

A popular lunch break for people touring the island is **Gîte de Mamelles**, which has a hilltop location on the N11, a five-minute drive west of Maison de la Forêt. The menu includes crab farci for 40F, grilled chicken for 50F and fish for 80F.

NORTHERN BASSE-TERRE
The northern half of Basse-Terre offers interesting contrasts. High hills and mountains rise above the west coast providing a lush green setting for the handful of small villages along the shoreline. Although much of the west coast is rocky, there are a couple of attractive swimming beaches, the most popular of which is Grande Anse.

Once you reach the northern tip of the island the terrain becomes gentler and the vegetation dry and scrubby. Continuing down the east coast, the countryside gradually gives over to sugarcane and the towns become larger and more suburban as you approach Pointe-à-Pitre.

Pointe-Noire
Pointe-Noire (Black Point) is a good-sized town that gets its name from being in the shadow of the mountains that loom to the east. Some residents make their living from fishing, others from working the coffee plantations in the hills above town.

The area is best known for its furniture- and cabinet-making industries. Just off the N2, at the south side of town, is **Maison du Bois**, a small museum of traditional woodworking tools and products (admission 5F). There's also a showroom selling furniture made of mahogany and other native woods that are harvested from the surrounding forests.

Places to Stay A few kilometers south of Pointe-Noire lies *Camping Traversée (☎ 98 21 23)*, a campground at Anse de la Grande Plaine. Setting up a tent costs 60F per day for one person, 40F for each additional person; there are also some rustic cabins with little verandas that rent for 180F double. Breakfast is available for 30F.

Deshaies

Deshaies is an appealing little harborside village surrounded by green hills. It has a deep sheltered bay and is a popular stop with yachters; there's a customs office at the southernmost end of town. The local seafaring traditions have carried on into the tourist trade, with several dive shops and deep-sea fishing boats operating from the town pier.

Grande Anse, a mere 2km north of Deshaies, is an absolutely beautiful beach with no development in sight. There are scenic hills at both ends of the beach and mounds of glistening sand along the shore. While it's arguably the finest beach in Basse-Terre, with the exception of weekends it's usually not crowded, and the weekend crowds are a fun mix, with picnicking local families, pick-

up soccer games and extremely bronze French sun worshippers.

A more secluded spot, **Plage de Tillet** is a lovely beach on a quiet cove; look for the roadside pull-off along the N2, 1km northeast of the Fort Royal Touring Club. Park along the edge of the pavement and continue on foot along the main path heading downhill to the north; you'll reach the beach in a couple of minutes.

Places to Stay There are a handful of gîtes on the road that leads inland from the Grande Anse beach toward Caféière. One of the larger and better-priced ones is *Jacky Location (☎ 28 43 53, fax 28 50 95, Plage de la Grande Anse, 97126 Deshaies)*, which has studios and apartments for 1260F to 2900F per week, with the most expensive accommodating six people. It's about a five-minute walk from the beach and has a swimming pool.

North of Deshaies, *Fleurs des Iles (☎ 28 54 44, fax 28 54 45, 97126 Deshaies)* has clean and comfy bungalows in a garden setting with a pool just off the Grande Anse beach. They're usually rented by the week, but you might get one for 400F a night if there's a vacancy. Weekly rates start at 2800F for doubles in May to early July and again from late August to late October, climbing to 5960F around the Christmas holidays.

Fort Royal Touring Club (☎ 25 50 00, fax 25 50 01, Pointe du Petit Bas-Vent, 97126 Deshaies) is on a sandy stretch a couple of kilometers north of Grande Anse. The hotel, which was formerly a Club Med, has 198 rooms and bungalows with TVs and phones. It has tennis courts, complimentary windsurfing equipment and two beaches, one of which is clothing-optional. Singles/doubles are pretty steep, at 750/1200F in winter and from 560/760F in summer.

Places to Eat In the village of Deshaies there's a line of harborside restaurants that cater mostly to beachgoers, sailors and weekend visitors. *Le Madras* is a quaint, moderately priced Creole restaurant that's opposite the waterfront on the north side of town, which serves local specialties like christophene farci for 35F. If you want to be right on the water there's **Le Mouillage**, a popular dockside restaurant specializing in seafood and Creole dishes with main courses averaging 75F. At the south end of town, **La Note Bleue** has a stylish bar popular with visiting yachties and a French restaurant with indoor and outdoor seating. A three course *menu Creole* is 150F, a little more with lobster.

In the parking area fronting the Grande Anse beach you'll find a couple of food stalls selling inexpensive crêpes and sandwiches. **Le Fromager 2000**, opposite the parking lot, has excellent Creole fare and a 60F menu du jour. A tasty lambi fricassee or grilled fish, served with rice and beans, costs just 45F. If you have a big appetite, head for **Edmonds**, at the south end of the parking lot, a loud local hangout on weekends. It features a 65F *menu complet* that includes accras, Creole crayfish, banana flambé and a ti-punch.

More upscale is **Le Karacoli** (☎ 28 41 17), a traditional Creole restaurant with a garden setting right on the Grande Anse beach. A tasty starter is the crab farci, while main courses include lobster, spicy colombo dishes and red snapper with cloves. Main courses are priced from 70F to 150F, while starters are half that. There's also a simpler menu du jour for 80F.

Sainte-Rose

In days past Sainte-Rose was a major agricultural town. While sugar production has declined on Guadeloupe and a number of the mills have closed, sugarcane is still an important crop in this area. There are vast undulating fields of cane and a couple of rum-related tourist sights on the outskirts of town.

Musée du Rhum Dedicated to the history of sugar and rum production (and also with an inexplicable but fascinating collection of giant insects from around the world), the Rum Museum is at the site of the former Reimonenq Distillery, about 500m inland

from the N2 in the village of Bellevue, just southeast of Sainte-Rose. Exhibits include an old distillery, cane-extraction gears and a vapor machine dating from 1707. It's open 9 am to 5pm Monday to Saturday. Admission (including a small tasting) is 40F for adults, 20F for children.

Domaine de Séverin A fun place to stop is Domaine de Séverin, a working mill and distillery that doesn't charge an entrance fee and has exhibits in English explaining the distillation process. Visitors are free to walk out back and get a close-up look of the distillery works, the antique waterwheel and cane crushers and the foaming vats of rum. In the tasting room are samples of the final products, including a nice light citron-flavored rum.

Domaine de Séverin is near the village of Cadet, which is off the N2 midway between Sainte-Rose and Lamentin. The turnoff from the N2, as well as the five-minute drive up to the site, is well signposted. It's open from 8 am to 12:30 pm and 2 to 5 pm weekdays, and from 8 am to 12:30 pm Saturday.

SOUTH TO CAPESTERRE-BELLE-EAU

The N1, the road that runs along the east coast of Basse-Terre, is for the most part pleasantly rural, a mix of sugarcane fields, cattle pastures, banana plantations and small towns.

Valombreuse Floral Parc, nestled in the hills west of Petit-Bourg, is a pleasant 14-hectare botanical garden. Trails wind through thick growths of flowering heliconia and ginger, and there are lots of orchids, anthuriums and other tropical plants. The park is open 9 am to 6 pm daily. Admission is 38F for adults, 20F for children. The road leading off the N1 to the park, 5km inland, is well signposted.

In the center of the village of **Sainte-Marie** a bust of Columbus and two huge anchors comprise a modest roadside monument honoring the explorer who landed on this shore in 1493. If you're up for a dip, try the brown-sand beach, **Plage de Roseau**, over on the south side of town.

The road is lined with flamboyant trees on the north side of **Capesterre-Belle-Eau**, a good-size town that has a supermarket, some local eateries and a gas station.

On the south side of Capesterre-Belle-Eau is the **Allée Dumanoir**, a stretch of the N1 that's bordered on both sides by majestic century-old royal palms.

CHUTES DU CARBET

Unless it's overcast, the drive up to the Chutes du Carbet lookout will reward you with a view of two magnificent waterfalls plunging down a sheer mountain face.

Starting from Saint Sauveur on the N1, the road runs 8.5km inland, making for a beautiful 15-minute drive up through a lush green rain forest. It's a good hard-surfaced road all the way, although it's a bit narrow and twisting. Three kilometers before the end of the road is a marked stop at the trailhead to **Grand Étang**, a placid lake circled by a loop trail. It's just a five-minute walk from the roadside parking area down to the edge of the lake, and it takes about an hour more to stroll the lake's perimeter. (Due to the danger of bilharzia infection, this is not a place for a swim.)

The road ends at the **Chutes du Carbet lookout**. You can see the two highest waterfalls from the upper parking lot, where a signboard marks the trailhead to the base of the falls. The well-trodden walk to the second-highest waterfall (110m) takes 30 minutes; it's about a two-hour hike to the highest waterfall (115m). It's also possible to hike from the lookout to the summit of La Soufrière, a hardy three-hour walk with some wonderfully varied scenery.

There are picnic facilities at the lookout along with a few food stalls selling plate lunches of simple barbecue fare. This is a very popular spot for outings and can get quite crowded on weekends and holidays.

A nice stop on the way back is the flower nursery **Les Jardins de Saint-Eloi**, where there's a short path through a garden of ginger, heliconia and anthuriums. It's at the side of the road about 1.5km south of Grand Étang; there's no admission charge.

TROIS-RIVIÈRES

Most often visited as a jumping-off point to Les Saintes, Trois-Rivières has a sleepy town center of old, leaning buildings with delicate gingerbread trims and rusting tin roofs. The town is surrounded by lush vegetation and has fine views of Les Saintes, just 10km offshore to the south.

Signs at the west side of the town center point the way from the N1 to the dock, 1km away, where the ferry leaves for Terre-de-Haut. La Roche Gravée restaurant, a few minutes' walk from the dock, provides parking for ferry passengers for 12F a day.

There's a black-sand beach that's good for swimming at Grande Anse, a few kilometers west of Trois-Rivières.

Parc Archéologique des Roches Gravées

If you're killing time in Trois-Riviéres, don't miss the archeological park, featuring rocks carved with petroglyphs of human, animal and abstract forms. Some of the rocks were found on the site; others were brought from around Basse-Terre. The visitors center at the entrance has informative displays and pamphlets on island history.

Almost as interesting as the petroglyphs, the trail through the park requires some scrambling through boulder fields, around tree trunks and through a garden of native plants. It's nicest in the afternoon, when shadows play through the trees and lizards scatter away from your footsteps.

The park is on the road to the ferry dock, 200m north of the waterfront. It's open 9 am to 4:30 pm daily; admission (10F) is a bargain.

Places to Stay & Eat

A pleasant little place is *Le Joyeux* (☎ 92 74 78, Faubourg, 97114 Trois-Rivières), in the village of Le Faubourg, about a kilometer west of Trois-Rivières. It has doubles with air-con, cooking facilities and sea-view terraces for 260F and smaller rooms without views for 200F.

A few snack bars and restaurants are on the waterfront near the ferry dock. *La Terrasse du Park*, in the center near the town hall, serves moderately priced Creole food.

LA SOUFRIÈRE

From Trois-Rivières there are a couple of ways to get to La Soufrière, the active volcano that looms above the southern half of the island.

If you have extra time you could take the D6 coastal road through Vieux-Fort, a town known for its eyelet embroidery, and then turn north to La Soufrière when you reach Basse-Terre.

However, the most direct route to La Soufrière is to follow the D7 northwest from Trois-Rivières, turn west on the N1 for a few kilometers and then follow the signs north to Saint-Claude. This is a nice jungly drive into the mountains; you'll cross some small streams and pass banana plantations before reaching the village of Saint-Claude, just south of the national-park boundaries. There's no food available in the park, but Saint-Claude has a few local restaurants and small grocers.

From Saint-Claude, signs point to La Soufrière, 6km to the northeast on the D11. The steep road up into the park has a few beep-as-you-go hairpin turns, and it narrows in places to almost one lane, but it's a good solid road all the way. If it's fogged in, proceed slowly, as visibility can drop to just a few meters.

Maison du Volcan, on the right about 2km after entering the park, has a small exhibit center (free admission) with displays on vulcanology and La Soufrière's last eruption, in July 1976. The center is also the

trailhead for a couple of hour-long walks, including one to Chute de Galleon, a scenic 40m waterfall on the Galleon River.

There are a couple of view points and picnic areas as the road continues up the mountain for the 15-minute drive to **La Savane à Mulet**, a parking area at an elevation of 1142m. From here, there's a clear view straight up La Soufrière (when it's not covered in clouds or mist), and you can see and smell vapors rising from nearby fumaroles.

For an adventurous 1½-hour hike to La Soufrière's sulfurous, moonscape summit, a well-beaten trail starts at the end of the parking lot along a gravel bed and continues steeply up the mountain through a cover of low shrubs and thick ferns. In addition to a close-up view of the steaming volcano, the hike offers some fine vistas of the island. It's also possible to make a four-hour trek from La Savane à Mulet to the Chutes du Carbet lookout.

The road continues east another 1.75km, taking in a lookout and views of sulfur vents before it dead-ends at a relay station.

BASSE-TERRE

Basse-Terre, the administrative capital of Guadeloupe, is home to a population of 14,000. As the capital, it's somewhat active on weekdays during work hours, but almost deserted after dark and on weekends, with most shops and restaurants closed.

The south side of town, along the Boulevard Gouverneur Général Félix Eboué, has a couple of rather imposing government buildings, including the Palais de Justice and the sprawling Conseil Général, the latter flanked by fountains.

At the north side of town, opposite the commercial dock, is the old town square. It's bordered by the aging Hôtel de Ville (Town Hall), the tourist office, customs and some older two- and three-story buildings that overall are more run-down than quaint. There's also a pharmacy on the square, a Crédit Agricole and a central parking area.

There's an unadorned cathedral near the river about five minutes' walk south of the

Precautions at La Soufrière

The higher you go into La Soufrière's rain forest, the cooler it gets and the more likely you are to encounter rain. Even when it's sunny below, it's a good idea to bring along rain gear if you plan to do any hiking. Hikers should also bring along a light jacket or sweater and a full canteen.

Young children and people with heart conditions or respiratory ailments should be cautious when hiking near the sulfur vents.

square, as well as a modest little botanical garden on the west side of town.

The bus station is on the shoreline at the western end of Boulevard Gouverneur Général Félix Eboué. Opposite the north end of the station is the public market.

Fort Louis Delgrès, which dates from 1643, is at the south side of town, as is the Rivière Sens Marina.

Places to Stay

A cheap option is **Hôtel Drouant** (*☎ 81 28 90, 26 Rue Docteur Cabre, 97100 Basse-Terre),* which has small rooms that are equipped with an old bed, a sink and a bidet. Singles/doubles cost 110/160F, 220/225F with air-conditioning.

Relais d'Orléans, on Rue de Lardenoy across from the prefecture, has friendly management and small, clean rooms with private bathrooms from 160F, or 260F with air-conditioning.

Places to Eat

Both **Hotel Drouant** and **Relais d'Orléans** have simple restaurants with authentic Creole food at very affordable prices.

Opposite the bus terminal are a handful of cheap, if somewhat scruffy, snack shops serving sandwiches from around 8F; in the evenings, food wagons set up shop on the town's central park, selling sandwiches, crêpes and other quickies.

Le Moulin Blanc, in the town center on the corner of Rues Marie Claire and Docteur Cabre, is a jumping local lunch spot with counter seats, fresh-fruit juices and grilled-meat sandwiches (10F).

Later at night the French crowd files in to **La Taverne**, a funky over-air-conditioned stone hideout on Blvd Félix Eboué. Whole-wheat pizzas go for 40 to 65F, and a shocking amount of French wine gets consumed. It's open noon to 2:30 pm weekdays and also 6:30 to 10:30 pm Monday to Saturday.

MALENDURE BEACH & PIGEON ISLAND

The road up the west coast from Basse-Terre (N2) follows the shoreline much of the way, passing fishing villages, small towns and a few black-sand beaches. The landscape gets drier as you continue north into the lee of the mountains. There's not much of interest for visitors until Malendure Beach, a rather popular dark-sand beach that's the departure point for snorkeling and diving tours to nearby Pigeon Island.

Jacques Cousteau brought Pigeon Island to international attention a couple of decades ago by declaring it to be one of the world's top dive sites. The waters surrounding the island are now protected as the Reserve Cousteau, an underwater park.

There are a few dive shops (see Diving in Facts for the Visitor, earlier in this chapter) and a tourist information booth on Malendure Beach.

Nautilus (*☎ 98 89 08) has a glass-bottom-boat tour from Malendure Beach at 10:30 am, noon, 2:30 and 4 pm daily. It takes 1¼ hours and costs 80F; snorkeling gear is provided for those who want to jump in for a closer look.

It's a 4km drive from Malendure Beach to the beginning of Route de la Traversée (D23) for the scenic 45-minute drive back to Pointe-à-Pitre. See the Route de la Traversée section, earlier.

Jacques Cousteau

Places to Stay

In the center of the village of Pigeon, just south of Malendure Beach, there are several private room-for-rent and gîte signs. One is for *Gîte de Guy Yoko* (☎ *98 71 42, la Grange Bel'O, Chemin Poirier, Pigeon, 97125 Bouillante)*, a member of the Gîte de France network. Guy has a handful of units for weekly rental, ranging from 2300F for a double to 5200F for an apartment that can accommodate eight people.

Le Rocher de Malendure (☎ 98 70 84, fax 98 89 92, Malendure, 97125 Bouillante) has a scenic cliff-side setting just south of Malendure Beach with its own dive shop and deep-sea-fishing operation. Singles and doubles cost 280F in low season, 360 in high.

Places to Eat

There are huts on Malendure Beach selling cheap sandwiches and snacks, and a couple of simple open-air beachside restaurants with more substantial meals.

For something more upmarket, most people head south to the village of Pigeon. Le Rocher de Malendure (see Places to Stay) has a seaside setting and good French/Creole food featuring fresh-caught marlin, tuna etc for less than 100F.

Terre-de-Haut

Lying 10km off Guadeloupe is Terre-de-Haut, the largest of the eight small islands that make up Les Saintes. Since the island was too hilly and dry for sugar plantations, slavery never took hold here. Consequently, the older islanders still trace their roots to the early seafaring Norman and Breton colonists. The younger generation is more mixed group, sporting a look best described as 'Rasta pirate.'

Terre-de-Haut is quaint and unhurried, quite French in nature and almost Mediterranean in appearance. Although it's a tiny package, it's got a lot to offer, including a strikingly beautiful landscape of volcanic hills and deep bays. The island has fine protected beaches with good swimming and

windsurfing, a fort with a botanical garden, good restaurants and a range of places to stay at reasonable prices. In all, it's one of the most appealing little islands in the Eastern Caribbean, though it can get overrun with tourists on weekends and in the height of the high season.

Although tourism is growing, many islanders still rely on fishing as a mainstay. You can often find the fishers mending their nets along the waterfront and see their colorful locally made boats, called *saintoises*, lined along the shore.

Terre-de-Haut is only 5km long and about half as wide. If you don't mind uphill walks you can get around on foot, although many people opt to rent motorbikes. Ferries to Guadeloupe and Terre-de-Bas dock right in the center of Bourg des Saintes, the island's only village. The airstrip is to the east, a 10-minute walk from the village center.

BOURG DES SAINTES

Home to most of the island's residents, Bourg des Saintes is a picturesque village with a decidedly Norman accent. Its narrow streets are lined with whitewashed red-roofed houses with shuttered windows and yards of flowering hibiscus.

The ferry is met by young girls peddling *tourment d'amour* (agony of love) cakes with a sweet coconut filling – an almost painfully delicious island treat that makes for a tasty light breakfast.

At the end of the pier is a small courtyard with a gilded column commemorating the French Revolution; it's a bustling place at ferry times, quiet at others. Turn right and in a minute you'll be at the central town square, flanked by the *mairie* (town hall) and an old stone church.

It's a fun town to kick around. There are small restaurants, ice cream shops, scooter rentals, art galleries and gift shops clustered along the main road, which is pedestrian-only during the day. Most shops close around 1 pm; some reopen in the evening, but in the off-season many places stay closed.

TERRE-DE-HAUT & TERRE-DE-BAS

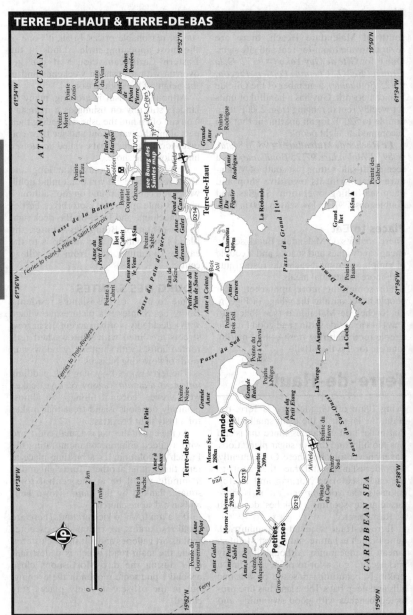

GUADELOUPE

ATLANTIC OCEAN

Pointe du Vent
Baie de Pointe Pierre
Roches Percées
Pointe Zozio
Pointe Morel
Pointe de l'Eau
Baie de Marigot
UCPA
Tête des Crêtes
Grande Anse
Pointe Rodrigue
Fort Napoléon
Anse Du Figuier
Anse Rodrigue
Pointe Coquelet
Kanaoa
see Bourg des Saintes map
Airfield
Terre-de-Haut
Passe de la Baleine
Pointe à l'Eau
Fond du Curé
Anse du Galet
D214
La Redonde
Îlet à Cabrit
85m
Anse Levrau
Anse du Petit Étang
Pointe Sable
Le Chameau 309m
Grand Îlet
165m
Pointe des Colibris
Pointe à Cabrit
Anse sous le Vent
Pain de Sucre
Bois Joli
Passe du Grand Îlet
Grand Îlet
Ferries to Point-à-Pitre & Saint François
Passe du Pain de Sucre
Petite Anse du Pain de Sucre
Anse à Cointe
Anse Craven
Pointe Basse
Passe des Dames
Pointe Bois Joli
La Coche
Ferries to Trois-Rivières
Passe du Sud
Pointe du Fer à Cheval
Les Augustins
Pointe à Nègre
La Vierge
Pointe Noire
Grande Anse
Grande Baie
Anse du Petit Étang
Passe du Sud-Ouest
Pointe du Havre
Le Pâté
Terre-de-Bas
Morne Sec 288m
Grande Anse
D213
Morne Paquette 209m
Airfield
Anse à Chaux
trail
Morne Abymes 293m
D213
Pointe Sud
Pointe du Gouvernail
Anse Pujot
Anse Galet
Anse Petit Sable
Petites-Anses
Pointe du Cap
Pointe à Vache
Anse à Dos
Pointe Miquelon
Gros-Cap
Ferry
CARIBBEAN SEA

2 km
1 mile

15°52'N
15°50'N
61°34'W
61°36'W
61°38'W
15°52'N
15°50'N

Information

Money It's best to bring along sufficient francs to cover your stay, as the island's sole bank, Crédit Agricole, is open only 9 am to 2:30 pm Tuesday, Thursday and Friday. There's an ATM on Rue de la Grande Anse, next to the tourist office.

Credit cards are accepted at hotels (but not budget guest houses) and by the motorbike rental companies.

Post & Communications There are card phones at the pier. The post office is on the main road a few minutes' walk south of the town hall.

Places to Stay

Town Center There are room-for-rent signs around the island, but keep in mind that if you're traveling during the high season the competition for rooms can be overwhelming, so it's wise to try to book ahead.

On Rue Charles Foy, just up the street from Bar Chris-Bo, *Chez Cassin Victor* (☎ 99 54 65, fax 99 58 70) has comfortable, fan-cooled rooms for 200F with shared bath. The proprietors are friendly, the neighborhood is quiet and it's a nice short walk to the restaurants and shops.

La Saintoise (☎ 99 52 50, 97137 Les Saintes), a 10-room hotel on the square opposite the town hall, has rooms with private bath, air-conditioning and phone for 360F year-round.

Jeanne d'Arc (☎ 99 50 41), on the south side of town, has recently undergone a total renovation and raised its rates to 650F for double rooms.

Town Outskirts The *Résidence Iguann'la* (☎ /fax 99 57 69, Route de Grande Anse, 97137 Les Saintes), between town and the airport, has four cozy units within walking distance of Grande Anse. All have air-con,

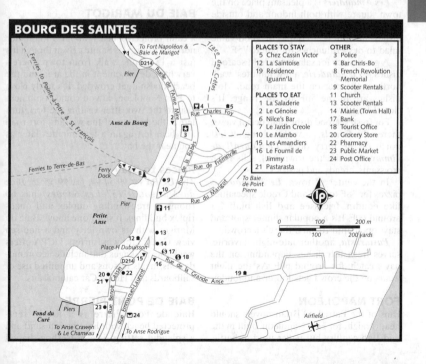

BOURG DES SAINTES

To Fort Napoléon &
Baie de Marigot

Pier

Ferries to Pointe-à-pitre & St François

Anse du Bourg

Rue Charles Foy

Trace des Crêtes

Rue de l'Anse Mire

Ferries to Terre-de-Bas

Ferry Dock

Rue de la Balbès

Rue de Tréminville

Rue du Marigot

To Baie de Point Pierre

Pier

Petite Anse

Place H Dubuisson

Rue de la Grande Anse

Rue Emmanuel Laurent

Rue Benoît Cassin

Piers

Fond du Curé

To Anse Crawen & Le Chameau

To Anse Rodrigue

Airfield

PLACES TO STAY	OTHER
5 Chez Cassin Victor	3 Police
12 La Saintoise	4 Bar Chris-Bo
19 Résidence Iguann'la	8 French Revolution Memorial
	9 Scooter Rentals
PLACES TO EAT	11 Church
1 La Saladerie	13 Scooter Rentals
2 Le Génoise	14 Mairie (Town Hall)
6 Nilce's Bar	17 Bank
7 Le Jardin Creole	18 Tourist Office
10 Le Mambo	20 Grocery Store
15 Les Amandiers	22 Pharmacy
16 Le Fournil de Jimmy	23 Public Market
21 Pastarasta	24 Post Office

0   100   200 m
0   100   200 yards

TV, a kitchen and terrace. The three studios cost 400F for one or two people, the apartment 650F for up to four people. Each of the units can accommodate an additional two people, at a cost of 60F per person.

Kanaoa (☎ 99 51 36, fax 99 55 04, 97137 Les Saintes), adjacent to Village Creole, has 19 simple seaside rooms and bungalows. Rooms start at 290F, bungalows at 400F, breakfast included.

Places to Eat
There are lots of casual restaurants around town that cater to day-trippers and offer a meal of the day in the 60F to 90F range.

Right at the ferry dock, *Nilce's Bar* has cheap sandwiches at lunchtime and pricier seafood in the evening, with tables hanging over the water. Next door, *Le Jardin Creole* has snacks, drinks and fresh-fruit juices, with an African decor and a cool balcony for people-watching.

Les Amandiers is a pleasant place on the town square with both indoor and outside dining. It specializes in Creole seafood dishes and offers a couple of good-value salad-to-dessert lunches for 60F to 75F.

A good place for salads and light seafood dishes is *La Saladerie*, a few minutes' walk north of the pier on the main road. Most dishes are in the 50F to 75F range. It's closed Tuesday.

For fresh seafood dishes and ocean views, there's *Le Génoise*, a yachtie hangout just north of the ferry dock. *Le Fournil de Jimmy*, opposite the town hall, sells fresh croissants, breads and pastries.

In the center of town, *Le Mambo* has pizzas for 38F to 55F and Creole specialties like boudin, fricassee and fish blaff for around 60F. It's a popular dinner spot and stays open until 10 pm if there's a crowd.

Pastarasta, another late-night favorite, serves fresh fish dishes, depending on the day's catch, for around 60F. As the night wears on the crowd gets looser and louder.

FORT NAPOLÉON
Fans of the Patrick O'Brian novels should head straight for Fort Napoléon, built in the mid-19th century but never used in battle, now dedicated to a museum of naval history. There's a fine hilltop view of Bourg des Saintes, and you can look across the channel to Fort Josephine, a small fortification on Îlet à Cabrit. On a clear day you can also see Marie-Galante and La Désirade.

The grounds surrounding the fort are planted in cactus gardens, home to some sizable iguanas that are completely unfazed by humans. The fort's barracks contain a museum focusing on maritime history, including local fishing methods and the historic naval battles between the French and British. You can walk through on your own or join an informative 30-minute guided tour conducted in French; English-language audiocassette tours are available for 5F. The fort is open only 9 am to 12:30 pm daily; admission is 20F. Fort Napoléon is 1.5km north of the center of Bourg des Saintes; simply turn left as you come off the pier and follow the road uphill.

BAIE DU MARIGOT
Baie du Marigot is a pleasant little bay with a calm protected beach about a kilometer north of Bourg des Saintes. Even though it's just a 15-minute walk from town, there's very little development in the area and the beach doesn't get crowded. It's fairly close to Fort Napoléon, so you could combine a visit to the two; after visiting the fort, turn left at the bottom of the winding fort road and bear left again a few minutes later as you near the bay.

Places to Stay
The *UCPA (☎ 99 54 94, fax 99 55 28, Baie du Marigot, 97137 Les Saintes)* has 60 rooms in freestanding duplex and quadriplex buildings. It sits alone above Baie du Marigot with its own jetty and a fine sea view. Geared for windsurfers, UCPA offers weeklong packages that include accommodations, meals, lessons and unlimited use of sailboards and Hobie Cat catamarans.

BAIE DE PONT PIERRE
Baie de Pont Pierre is a lovely reef-protected beach with light brown sand and a splendid setting. The horseshoe-shaped

bay is backed by sea-grape trees and flanked on both sides by high cliffs, while an offshore islet at its mouth gives the illusion of closing the bay off as a complete circle. It's a very gentle spot, with a nice mix of tourists and locals; there are even tame goats that mosey onto the beach and lie down next to sunbathers. The beach is an easy 1.5km walk northeast of Bourg des Saintes.

EAST-COAST BEACHES

The long, sandy **Grande Anse**, immediately east of the airport runway, has rough seas and water conditions, and swimming is not allowed. The north side of this windy beach is backed by clay cliffs.

South of Grande Anse and about 2km from town is **Anse Rodrique**, a nice beach on a protected cove that usually has good swimming conditions.

SOUTHWEST BEACHES

Two kilometers southwest of Bourg des Saintes, **Anse à Cointe** is a good beach for combining swimming and snorkeling. The snorkeling is best at the north side. There's also good snorkeling and a sandy beach at **Pain de Sucre** (Sugarloaf), the basalt peninsula that's about 700m to the north.

Anse Crawen, 500m south of Bois Joli, is a secluded, clothing-optional beach just a couple of minutes' walk down a dirt path that starts where the coastal road ends. It's a perfect spot for **naked snorkeling**; bring plenty of water and sunscreen.

Places to Stay & Eat

Fronting a golden-sand each, *Bois Joli* (☎ 99 50 38, fax 99 55 05, Anse à Cointe, 97137 Les Saintes) has 31 rooms. Most are bungalow-style with small porches, air-con, showers, toilets and bidets; the cost is 1450F double. There are also some small straightforward singles/doubles with good views that cost 825/1100F. Rates include breakfast and dinner. The hotel's poolside restaurant has a fine sea view and is a great spot for a splurge, with steak and seafood dishes priced around 100F, about twice that if you add a starter and dessert.

LE CHAMEAU

A winding cement road leads to the summit of Le Chameau, which at 309m is the island's highest point. There are picture-perfect views of Bourg des Saintes and Îlet à Cabrit on the way up and sweeping views of the other Les Saintes islands, Marie-Galante, Basse-Terre and Dominica from the top of the hill. The summit is capped by an old stone sentry tower that has deteriorated but still has metal steps leading to the top, where there's an unobstructed view as far as the eye can see.

To get to Le Chameau, turn south from the Bourg des Saintes pier and continue 1km on the coastal road. At Restaurant Plongée turn inland on the D214; 500m later, turn left on the cement road and follow it up 1.75km to where it ends at the tower. From town it's a moderately difficult hour-long walk to the top. A more fun alternative is to ride a motorbike, which takes five minutes.

GETTING THERE & AWAY

Air

Air Guadeloupe (☎ 99 51 23) flies to Terre-de-Haut from Pointe-à-Pitre at 8 am and 1:30 pm (the latter via Marie-Galante) Monday to Saturday and at 4:45 pm daily, returning 15 minutes later. The fare is 180F one-way (135F for students), 270F for a one-day excursion.

Sea

L'Express des Îles (☎ 83 12 45) leaves for Terre-de-Haut from the east side of the Pointe-à-Pitre harbor at 8 am daily, returning from Terre-de-Haut at 4 pm. The crossing takes 50 minutes.

L'Express des Îles also has a seasonal boat service from the Saint-François marina (☎ 88 48 63). From mid-December to mid-May and from mid-July to the end of August, the boat leaves Saint-François at 8 am Tuesday and Thursday and returns from Terre-de-Haut at 4 pm. (Note that between mid-May and mid-July, there's usually a weekly service on Wednesday.) The crossing takes 80 minutes, as the boat stops at Marie-Galante en route.

GUADELOUPE

Brudey Frères (☎ 90 04 48) leaves Pointe-à-Pitre at 8 am daily for Terre-de-Haut, departing Terre-de-Haut at 3:45 pm. In the high season, there's also a Monday and Friday boat from Saint-François, with the same departure times.

The roundtrip fare with either company, from either Guadeloupean port, is 170F for adults, 90F for children.

GETTING AROUND

With advance reservations, most hotels will pick up guests free of charge at the airport or pier.

Motorcycle

Motorbikes are a great way to tour the island. Although roads are narrow, there are only a few dozen cars (and no car rentals) on Terre-de-Haut, so you won't encounter much traffic. With a motorbike you can zip up to the top of Le Chameau and Fort Napoléon, get out to the beaches and explore the island pretty thoroughly in a day. The motorbikes are capable of carrying two people, but because the roads are so winding, unless you're an accomplished driver it's not advisable to carry a passenger.

There are lots of rental locations on the main road leading south from the pier, but the ones that set up dockside seem as good as any. If you arrive on a busy day it's wise to grab a bike as soon as possible, as they sometimes sell out. Most charge 180F for day visitors (200F on a 24-hour basis) and require a 2000F deposit or an imprint of a major credit card. Motorbikes come with gas but not damage insurance, so if you get in an accident or spill the bike, the repairs will be charged to your credit card.

Motorbike riding is prohibited in the center of Bourg des Saintes from 9 am to noon and 2 to 4 pm. Although you'll see people ignoring the law, if you run into a gendarme expect to get stopped.

Organized Tours

Air-conditioned minivans provide two-hour tours of the island for 50F per person, if there are enough people, or 350F for the whole van. Look for them parked along the street between the pier and the town hall right after the ferry arrives.

Terre-de-Bas

Terre-de-Bas, lying just a kilometer to the west of Terre-de-Haut, is the only other inhabited island in Les Saintes. A bit less craggy than Terre-de-Haut, Terre-de-Bas once had small sugar and coffee plantations and is populated largely by the descendants of African slaves. It's a quiet rural island, and tourism has yet to take root, but there is regular ferry service between the islands, making it possible for visitors to go over and poke around on a day excursion.

The main village, Petites-Anses, is on the west coast. It has hilly streets lined with trim houses, a small fishing harbor and a quaint church with a graveyard of tombs decorated with conch shells and plastic flowers. Grande Anse, diagonally across the island on the east coast, is a small village with a little 17th-century church and a nice beach.

One-lane roads link the island's two villages; one of the roads cuts across the center of the island, passing between the two highest peaks – Morne Abymes and Morne Paquette – and the other goes along the south coast. If you enjoy long country walks it's possible to make a loop walk between the two villages (about 9km roundtrip) by going out on one road and returning on the other. Otherwise, there's sometimes an inexpensive jitney bus that runs between the villages.

Petite-Anses has a good bakery and pastry shop, and both villages have a couple of reasonably priced local restaurants.

The boat L'Inter shuttles between Terre-de-Haut and Terre-de-Bas (30F) five times a day between 8 am and 4 pm.

Marie-Galante

Marie-Galante, 25km southeast of Guadeloupe proper, is the largest of Guadeloupe's outer islands. Compared with the archipelago's other islands, Marie-Galante is relatively flat, its dual limestone plateaus rising only 150m. It is roughly round in shape with a total land area of 158 sq km, much of which is planted in sugarcane.

The island is rural in character; it's pretty much sugarcane and cows, totally untouched by mass tourism. It offers visitors lovely, uncrowded beaches and some pleasant country scenery. Very few English-speaking tourists come this way, and few islanders speak any English at all.

Marie-Galante has a population of about 13,000, half of whom live in Grand-Bourg, on the southwest coast. Most of the rest are evenly divided between its two smaller towns, Saint-Louis and Capesterre.

In the early 1800s the island of Marie-Galante boasted nearly 100 sugar mills, and the countryside is still dotted with their scattered ruins. Today sugar production is concentrated at one mill, while cane is distilled into rum at three distilleries. Most of the cane is still cut by hand and hauled from the fields using oxcarts.

The distilleries are among the island's main 'sights.' The Distillerie Poisson, midway between Saint-Louis and Grand-Bourg, bottles the island's best-known rum under

MARIE-GALANTE

the Père Labat label. Distillerie Bielle, between Grand-Bourg and Capesterre, offers tours of its age-old distillery operation. Both places have tasting rooms and sell rum.

GRAND-BOURG

Grand-Bourg is the commercial and administrative center of the island. The town was leveled by fire in 1901, and its architecture is a mix of early-20th-century buildings and more recent, drab concrete structures.

The ferry dock is at the center of town. The post office, customs office and town hall are all within a couple of blocks of the waterfront. There's a pharmacy and a couple of banks with ATMs on the square in front of the church.

Château Murat, about 2km from Grand-Bourg on the north side of the road to Capesterre, is an 18th-century sugar estate that's undergone extensive restorations. The grounds are open to the public all the time, and there's a visitors center that is open sporadically.

Places to Stay & Eat

A member of the Gîtes de France network, **Philippe Bavarday** (☎ 97 83 94, fax 97 81 90, 97112 Grand-Bourg) has an attractive home with four air-conditioned rooms that cost 240F per night or 1650F per week for two people. It's near the coast, a few kilometers east of town in the section of Les Basses, between the airport and the center of Grand-Bourg.

If you want to be in the center of town, try **Auberge de l'Arbre à Pain** (☎ 97 73 69, Rue Docteur Etzol, 97112 Grand-Bourg), a few minutes' walk from the dock. Its seven small, straightforward singles/doubles have private baths and cost 250/300F. There's a small Creole restaurant on-site. Across the street, **La Mirabelle** is without question the most authentic little bistro in town for grabbing a drink and a snack.

Opposite the dock you'll find a handful of local cafés and restaurants, most specializing in seafood. There's a bakery and a supermarket about two blocks inland.

The heart of Grand-Bourg's action, such as it is, **La Galante des Îles**, on your left as

you walk off the ferry dock, is a loud and smoky bar with cheap snacks. The real draw here is off-track betting – legal gambling on televised horse races from France. You'll need a solid command of French to play the ponies.

SAINT-LOUIS

Saint-Louis, a fishing village of about 4000 residents, is the island's main anchorage for yachters as well as a secondary port for ferries from Guadeloupe. There's a little market at the end of the dock, and a couple of restaurants and the post office are just east of that.

Although there are beaches along the outskirts of Saint-Louis, some of the island's most beautiful strands lie a few kilometers to the north. The golden sands of Plage de Moustique, Anse Canot and Anse du Vieux-Fort unfold one after the other once you round the point that marks the north end of Saint-Louis Bay.

Places to Stay & Eat

The island's largest hotel, in-town **Le Salut** (☎ 97 02 67, 97134 Saint-Louis) has 15 simple rooms with sinks and showers for 200F with fan and 250F with air-con.

Next to the Royal Café, **Residence Desmarais** (☎ 97 07 40) rents out large, clean rooms with air-con for 250F.

A good gîte is **Le Refuge** (☎/fax 97 02 95, Section Saint-Charles, 97134 Saint-Louis), about 2km southeast of central Saint-Louis. It offers air-conditioned doubles for 300F and a good multicourse dinner of traditional island fare for 80F.

Chez Henri, just south of the dock, is quite popular for seafront dining and has good local food at moderate prices.

CAPESTERRE

Capesterre (population 4100), on the southeast coast, is a seaside town backed by hills. You can explore sea cliffs and hiking trails to the north of the village.

On the south side of town is a beautiful beach, Plage de la Feuillère, and a second attractive beach, Petite Anse, is about a kilometer to the southwest.

Places to Stay & Eat

The *Hôtel Hajo* (☎ 97 32 76, 97140 *Capesterre)*, which has an unusual Mediterranean decor and six ocean-view rooms, is about 2km southwest of Capesterre on a rocky strand of Plage Ferriere. Singles/doubles, which have fans and private bathrooms, cost 300F, and there's a reasonably priced French/Creole restaurant on-site.

Le Soleil Levant, in the center of town, has a peaceful setting with a view of the bay, as well as a downstairs bar-restaurant where locals gather to play dominoes. Doubles start at 300F; larger and more expensive apartments are also available.

GETTING THERE & AWAY
Air

Air Guadeloupe (☎ 82 28 35) flies to Marie-Galante from Pointe-à-Pitre at 6:30 am and 1:30 and 6:15 pm Monday to Saturday and 6:15 pm Sunday. Flights return from Marie-Galante half an hour later. The fare is 180F one-way (135F for students) and 290F for a one-day excursion. The airport is midway between Grand-Bourg and Capesterre, about 5km from either.

Sea

The interisland crossing to Marie-Galante can be a bit rough, so if you're not used to bouncy seas it's best to travel on a light stomach and sit on deck.

There are two boat companies that make the run to Marie-Galante. On both, the roundtrip fare is 170F for adults, 90F for children.

L'Express des Îles L'Express des Îles (☎ 83 12 45) leaves from the east side of the Pointe-à-Pitre harbor at 8 am and 12:30 and 5 pm Monday to Saturday and 8 am and 5 and 7 pm Sunday. The 12:30 pm boat goes via Saint-Louis, but all other sailings are to Grand-Bourg only. The boat leaves Grand-Bourg at 6 and 9 am and 3:45 pm Monday to Saturday and 6 am and 3:45 and 6 pm Sunday. The crossing takes about 45 minutes.

In winter, L'Express des Îles has boat service to Saint-Louis from the Saint-François marina (☎ 88 48 63), leaving at 8 am Tuesday and Thursday and returning from Marie-Galante at 4:45 pm. The trip takes 45 minutes. In summer the schedule is more flexible, so you should call in advance.

Brudey Frères Brudey Frères (☎ 90 04 48) sails to Grand-Bourg, leaving Pointe-à-Pitre at 8 am and 3 pm weekdays, 8 am and 1 pm Saturday and 8 am and 4:45 pm Sunday. The ferry departs Grand-Bourg at 1 and 4:30 pm weekdays, 9:30 am and 4:30 pm Saturday, and 3:30 and 6 pm Sunday. Some boats go via Saint-Louis.

GETTING AROUND
Bus

During the day, except for Sunday, inexpensive minibuses make regular runs between the three villages.

Car, Motorcycle & Bicycle

Cars, motorbikes and bicycles can be rented from Caneval (☎ 97 97 76), at the Shell station in Grand-Bourg. Other agents include Magauto (☎ 97 98 75), near the docks in both Grand-Bourg and Saint-Louis, and Location 2000 (☎ 97 12 83), south of the dockside town hall in Saint-Louis.

Bicycles can also be rented from the Bureau Touristique de Marie-Galante (☎ 97 77 48), 51 Rue du Presbytère, Grand-Bourg. Roads are generally flat, well paved and free of cars, making Marie-Galante an excellent destination for bike touring. The downside is the condition of most rental bikes, which are more suited for pedaling around town than for distance riding.

Cars generally start at 200F to 300F a day, motorbikes at 150F and bicycles at about 70F.

La Désirade

La Désirade, about 10km off the eastern tip of Grande-Terre, is the archipelago's least-developed and least-visited island. Looking somewhat like an overturned boat when viewed from Guadeloupe, La Désirade is 11km long and 2km wide, with a central

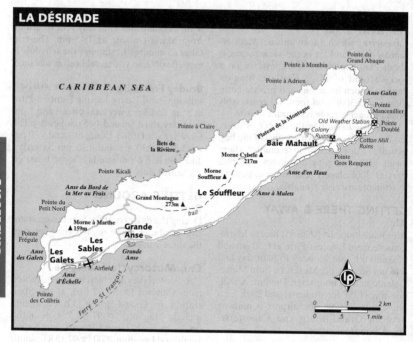

LA DÉSIRADE

CARIBBEAN SEA

Pointe du
Grand Abaque

Pointe à Mombin

Pointe à Adrien

Anse Galets

Pointe
Mancenillier

Pointe à Claire

Plateau de la Montagne

Old Weather Station

Pointe
Doublé

Leper Colony
Ruins

Cotton Mill
Ruins

Baie Mahault

Îlets de
la Rivière

Morne Cybèle ▲
217m

Pointe
Gros Rempart

Pointe Kicali

Morne
Souffleur ▲

Anse d'en Haut

Anse du Bord de
la Mer au Frais

Grand Montagne
273m ▲

Le Souffleur

Anse à Mulets

Pointe du
Petit Nord

trail

Pointe
Frégule

Morne à Marthe
▲ 159m

Grande
Anse

Anse
des Galets

Les
Sables

Les
Galets

Grande
Anse

Airfield

Anse
d'Échelle

Pointe
des Colibris

Ferry to St François

0   1   2 km
0   .5   1 mile

plateau that rises 273m at its highest point, Grand Montagne.

The terrain is desertlike, with coconut and sea-grape trees along the coast and scrub and cactus on the hillsides. It's too dry and arid for extensive agriculture and though some people raise sheep, most of La Désirade's 1600 inhabitants make their living from fishing and boat building.

The uninhabited north side of the island has a rocky coastline with rough open seas, while the south side has sandy beaches and reef-protected waters.

La Désirade's harbor and airport are on the southwest side of the island in **Grande Anse** (also called Le Bourg), the main village. The island's town hall, post office and library are also in Grande Anse. There are smaller settlements at **Le Souffleur** and **Baie Mahault**. La Désirade's main road runs along the south coast, joining the villages.

In 1725 Guadeloupe established a leper colony on La Désirade, and for more than two centuries victims of the dreaded disease were forced to make a one-way trip to the island. The **leprosarium**, which was run by the Catholic Sisters of Charity, closed in the mid-1950s. Its remains, a chapel and a cemetery, are just east of Baie Mahault.

Places to Stay & Eat

The hotel-restaurant *L'Oasis du Désert* (☎ 20 02 12) and *Hôtel Le Mirage* (☎ 20 01 08) are both small hostelries in the Desert Saline quarter of Grand Anse with simple singles/doubles at 200/220F. There are also a few rooms in private homes around Grande Anse for around 200F; help with bookings is available from Location 2000 (☎ 20 03 74).

Grande Anse and Baie Mahault both have a handful of moderately priced seafood restaurants and cheaper snack bars.

Two restaurants on the Petite Riviere beach, east of Baie Mahault, are worth the trip. The aptly named *Restaurant de la Plage* (☎ 20 01 89, fax 20 01 48) is pricey but worth it for the beachfront setting and refreshing pool. Creole dishes like lambi and chatrou curry go for 90F; lobster with all the trimmings is 180F. Next door, *Chez Nounoune* is a simpler and cheaper option on the same protected beach.

GETTING THERE & AWAY
Air
Air Guadeloupe flies to La Désirade from Pointe-à-Pitre at 7 am daily except Sunday and at 4 pm daily except Saturday; return flights depart from La Désirade 25 minutes later. The fare is 180F one-way (135F for students).

Sea
There are two ferries to La Désirade. *Sotramade* (☎ 20 02 30) leaves from the Saint-François marina at 8 am and 5 pm daily, with an extra departure at 11 am Saturday. It returns at 6:15 am and 4 pm daily, as well as at 2 pm Saturday. The roundtrip fare is 130F, and the ride takes about 45 minutes.

Imperiale (☎ 88 58 06) departs from Saint-François at 8 am and 5 pm daily, with an extra sailing at 2 pm Saturday. On the return, the boat leaves La Désirade at 6:15 am and 4 pm daily. The roundtrip fare is 150F for adults, 80F for children.

GETTING AROUND
Bicycle and scooter rentals are available at the ferry dock for 70F to 150F a day. The coastal road is a lot more hilly than it appears from the boat, making bicycling a sweaty workout. Most locals and visitors prefer the scooters.

Martinique

Martinique, a little slice of France set down in the tropics, has shops full of Paris fashions, corner pâtisseries selling freshly baked baguettes and croissants, and resorts crowded with vacationers from mainland France. It's also home to a fascinating and dynamic Caribbean society, with a distinct culture and a long history of resistance to French authority.

The capital, Fort-de-France, is a bustling city of 100,000, the largest in the French West Indies. Most of the island's other large towns are modern and suburban, linked to the capital by multilane highways and fast-moving traffic.

Nevertheless, nearly a third of Martinique is forested, and other parts of the island are given over to pineapples, bananas and sugarcane fields. You can still find sleepy fishing villages untouched by development, remote beaches and lots of hiking trails into the mountains.

Martinique is volcanic in origin, topped by the 1397m Mont Pelée, an active volcano. Pelée last erupted in 1902, gaining an infamous place in history by wiping out the then-capital city of Saint-Pierre, along with its entire population. Today the ruins of Saint-Pierre are Martinique's foremost tourist sight.

Highlights

- Enjoying the Eastern Caribbean's most cosmopolitan society, with a blended French/Creole culture
- Exploring Saint-Pierre's ruins from the 1902 volcanic eruption
- Soaking in the sun at Les Salines, with vast stretches of beaches full of vacationers and islanders
- Cruising the Route de la Trace, a scenic rain-forest drive across the mountainous interior
- Admiring Fort-de-France, with its French colonial architecture

OTHER MAPS
Martinique page 302

Saint-Pierre
page 319

ATLANTIC OCEAN

Fort-de-France
page 314

Pointe du Bout
& Anse Mitan
page 325

Sainte-Anne
page 330

CARIBBEAN SEA

0   5   10 km
0   3   6 miles

Facts about Martinique

HISTORY

When Columbus sighted Martinique it was inhabited by Carib Indians who called the island Madinina, which means 'Island of Flowers.' Three decades passed before the first party of French settlers, who were led by Pierre Belain d'Esnambuc, landed on the northwest side of the island. There they built a small fort and established a settlement that would become the capital city, Saint-Pierre. The next year, on October 31, 1636, King Louis XIII signed a decree authorizing the use of slaves in the French West Indies.

The settlers quickly went about colonizing the land and by 1640 had extended their grip south to Fort-de-France, where they constructed a fort on the rise above the harbor. As forests were cleared to make room for sugar plantations, conflicts with the native Caribs escalated into warfare, and in 1660 those Caribs who had survived the fighting were finally forced off the island.

The British took a keen interest in Martinique as well, invading and holding the island for most of the period from 1794 to 1815. The island prospered under British occupation; the planters simply sold their sugar in British markets rather than French. Perhaps more importantly, the occupation allowed Martinique to avoid the turmoil and bloodshed of the French Revolution.

By the time the British returned the island to France in 1815, the Napoleonic Wars had ended and the French empire was again entering a period of stability.

Not long after the French administration was reestablished on Martinique, the golden era of sugarcane began to wane, as glutted markets and the introduction of sugar beets on mainland France eroded prices. With their wealth diminished, the aristocratic plantation owners lost much of their political influence, and the abolitionist movement, led by Victor Schoelcher, gained momentum.

It was Schoelcher, the French cabinet minister responsible for overseas possessions, who convinced the provisional government to sign the 1848 Emancipation Proclamation, which brought an end to

The Empress Josephine

Martinique's most famous colonial daughter was the Empress Josephine. Born in Trois-Îlets in June 1763 and baptized Marie Joseph Rose Tascher de la Pagerie, the child, it's rumored, was pronounced by a soothsayer to be a future queen. Her route to royalty wouldn't be a very direct one, however.

In 1779 she married a wealthy army officer, Alexandre de Beauharnais, and moved to France. A decade later, de Beauharnais got caught up in the turmoil of the French Revolution and lost his head to a guillotine. Shortly after, Josephine met a young, and still largely unknown, military officer named Napoleon Bonaparte.

A passionate love affair began and in 1796, at the age of 33, she married Napoleon. In the years that followed, Napoleon's victories in battle gained him world attention and in 1804, in a ceremony officiated by the pope and held at the Notre Dame cathedral, Napoleon was proclaimed Emperor of France and Josephine was crowned empress.

When Josephine married Napoleon she was six years older than he, a fact that she went to great lengths to conceal. Although she had two children by her first marriage, she was unable to bear Napoleon an heir. In 1809 Napoleon divorced Josephine and shortly after he married the Archduchess Marie Louise of Austria. Josephine retired to a château at Malmaison, outside Paris, and despite the divorce, Napoleon continued to call on her.

Curiously, Josephine's daughter from her first marriage, Hortense de Beauharnais, married Napoleon's brother and gave birth to a son, Louis, who would take the French throne as Napoleon III in 1852.

MARTINIQUE

MARTINIQUE

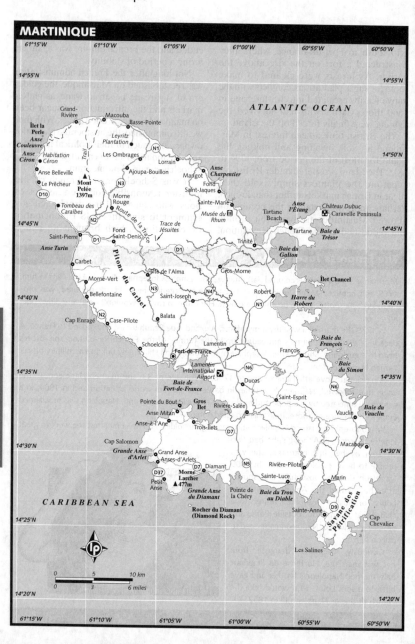

ATLANTIC OCEAN

Grand-Rivière
Macouba
Basse-Pointe
Îlet la Perle
Anse Couleuvre
Leyritz Plantation
Anse Céron
Habitation Céron
Les Ombrages
Anse Belleville
Lorrain
Ajoupa-Bouillon
Margot
Anse Charpentier
Le Prêcheur
Mont Pelée 1397m
N3
Fond Saint-Jacques
Morne Rouge
Sainte-Marie
Tombeau des Caraïbes
N2
Musée du Rhum
Anse l'Étang
Château Dubuc
Caravelle Peninsula
Saint-Pierre
D1
Fond Saint-Denis
Trace de Jésuites
Tartane Beach
Tartane
Baie du Trésor
Anse Turin
Route de la Trace
Trinité
Baie du Galion
Carbet
Pitons du Carbet
Site de l'Alma
Îlet Chancel
Morne-Vert
Gros-Morne
Bellefontaine
N3
Saint-Joseph
N4
Robert
Havre du Robert
Cap Enragé
N2
Case-Pilote
Balata
N1
Schoelcher
Fort-de-France
Lamentin
François
Baie du François
Lamentin International Airport
N6
Baie du Simon
Baie de Fort-de-France
Ducos
N6
Pointe du Bout
Gros Îlet
Rivière-Salée
Saint-Esprit
Vauclin
Baie du Vauclin
Anse Mitan
Anse-à-l'Ane
Trois-Îlets
D7
Cap Salomon
Grande Anse d'Arlet
Grand Anse
Anses-d'Arlets
D7
Macabou
Cap Salomon
D37
Morne Larcher 477m
Diamant
N5
Rivière-Pilote
Petit Anse
Grande Anse du Diamant
Pointe de la Chéry
Sainte-Luce
Marin
CARIBBEAN SEA
Rocher du Diamant (Diamond Rock)
Baie du Trou au Diable
Sainte-Anne
Savane des Pétrifications
Cap Chevalier
Les Salines

0 5 10 km
0 3 6 miles

61°15'W 61°10'W 61°05'W 61°00'W 60°55'W 60°50'W
14°55'N 14°50'N 14°45'N 14°40'N 14°35'N 14°30'N 14°25'N 14°20'N

slavery in the French West Indies. Widely reviled by the white aristocracy of the time, Schoelcher is now regarded as one of Martinique's heroes.

On March 8, 1902, in the most devastating natural disaster in Caribbean history, the Mont Pelée volcano erupted violently, destroying the city of Saint-Pierre and claiming the lives of its 30,000 inhabitants. Shortly thereafter, the capital was moved permanently to Fort-de-France. Saint-Pierre, which had been regarded as the most cultured city in the French West Indies, was eventually rebuilt, but it has never been more than a shadow of its former self.

In 1946 Martinique became an overseas department of France, with a status similar to those of metropolitan departments, and in 1974 it was further assimilated into the political fold as a department of France.

GEOGRAPHY

At 1080 sq km, Martinique is the second-largest island in the French West Indies. Roughly 65km long and 20km wide, it has a terrain punctuated by hills, plateaus and mountains.

The highest point is the 1397m Mont Pelée, an active volcano at the northern end of the island. The center of the island is dominated by the Pitons du Carbet, a scenic mountain range reaching 1207m.

Martinique's irregular coastline is cut by deep bays and coves while the mountainous rain forest in the interior feeds numerous rivers.

CLIMATE

Fort-de-France's average daily high temperature in January is 28°C (83°F) while the low averages 21°C (70°F). In July the average daily high temperature is 30°C (86°F) while the low averages 23°C (74°F).

The annual rainfall in Fort-de-France is 1840mm (72 inches). Measurable rain falls an average of 13 days a month in April, the driest month, and about twice as often in September, the rainiest month. Martinique's average humidity is high, ranging from 80% in March and April to 87% in October and November.

The mountainous northern interior is both cooler and rainier than the coast.

FLORA & FAUNA

Martinique has lots of colorful flowering plants, with the type of vegetation varying with altitude and rainfall. Rain forests cover the slopes of the mountains in the northern interior, which are luxuriant with tree ferns, bamboo groves, climbing vines and hardwood trees like mahogany, rosewood, locust and gommier.

The drier southern part of the island has brushy savanna vegetation such as cacti, frangipani trees, balsam, logwood and acacia shrubs. Common landscape plantings include splashy bougainvillea, red hibiscus and yellow-flowered allamanda trees.

Martinique has *Anolis* lizards, manicous (opossums), mongooses and venomous fer-de-lance snakes. The mongoose, which was introduced from India in the late 19th century, preys on eggs and has been responsible for the demise of many bird species. Some native birds, such as parrots, are no longer found on the island at all, while others have seen significant declines in their numbers. Endangered birds include the Martinique trembler, white-breasted trembler and white-breasted thrasher.

GOVERNMENT & POLITICS

Martinique, an overseas department of France, is represented in the French parliament by four elected deputies and two senators.

A prefect, who is appointed by the French minister of the interior, represents the central government and oversees the execution of French law by island authorities. There are two islandwide legislative bodies, the *conseil général* (general council) and the *conseil régional* (regional council), each with about 40 members who are elected by universal suffrage.

Martinique is further divided into 34 *communes* (parishes); each has an elected municipal council, which in turn appoints a mayor. Quite a bit of political diversity and power rests at the municipal level.

MARTINIQUE

ECONOMY

The economy of Martinique is heavily dependent upon outlays from the French government, whose expenditures account for more than 50% of the island's gross national product (GNP). Although by Caribbean standards Martinique has a high per-capita GNP, at US$10,500, it's less than half of what prevails on the French mainland. Unemployment is a major problem, running as high as 24%.

Agriculture accounts for many of the jobs in Martinique; sugarcane, bananas and pineapples are the leading crops. The cane is used by Martinique's 14 distilleries to produce rum, the island's best-known export item. Other export items include cut flowers and processed foods.

Tourism is the leading growth sector of the economy and has increased as the government, in a drive to encourage more investment, has subsidized the construction of new hotels. About 375,000 overnight tourists visit the island annually; approximately 80% of them come from France and 10% from the USA and Canada. In addition, about 400,000 cruise-ship visitors, 85% of them from the USA and Canada, make a stop on Martinique each year.

POPULATION & PEOPLE

The population of Martinique is about 415,000, of which more than a quarter live in the Fort-de-France area. The majority of residents are of mixed ethnic origin. The earliest settlers were from Normandy, Brittany, Paris and other parts of France; shortly afterward, African slaves were brought to the island; later, smaller numbers of immigrants came from India, Syria and Lebanon. These days Martinique is also home to thousands of aliens, some of them staying illegally, from poorer Caribbean islands such as Dominica, St Lucia and Haiti.

ARTS

French and Creole influences are dominant in Martinique's cuisine, language, music and customs.

The Black Pride movement known as *négritude* emerged as a philosophical and literary movement in the 1930s largely through the writings of Martinican native Aimé Césaire, a poet who was eventually elected mayor of Fort-de-France. The movement advanced black social and cultural values and reestablished bonds with African traditions, which had been suppressed by French colonialism.

The *biguine* (or beguine), an Afro-French dance music with a bolero rhythm, originated in Martinique in the 1930s. A more contemporary French West Indies creation, *zouk,* draws on the biguine and other French-Caribbean folk forms. With its Carnival-like rhythm and hot dance beat, zouk has become as popular in Europe as it is in the French Caribbean. The Martinican zouk band Kassav' has made a number of top-selling recordings including the English-language album *Shades of Black*. For more information on music, see the Music of the Eastern Caribbean section near the beginning of this book.

SOCIETY & CONDUCT

Martinique's society combines French traditions with Caribbean Creole culture. Always be respectful, and take your cue from the islanders. Politeness is highly valued on Martinique, so brush up on your manners.

Dos & Don'ts

Many of the hotel restaurants enforce a dress code; look for signs that read *tenue correcte est exigée*. Elsewhere, dress is casual but generally stylish. Topless bathing is common on the island, particularly at resort beaches.

RELIGION

An estimated 90% of all islanders are Roman Catholic. There are also Seventh Day Adventist, Baptist and Evangelical Christian denominations as well as Hindus, Baha'is and a small Jewish community.

LANGUAGE

French is the official language, but islanders commonly speak Creole when chatting among themselves. English is spoken at larger hotels but is understood rather sporadically elsewhere, so if you don't have a fair command of French, a dictionary and phrasebook will prove quite useful. For some common phrases and an introduction to French grammar and pronunciation, see the Language chapter at the end of this book.

Facts for the Visitor

ORIENTATION
Martinique's only commercial airport is in Lamentin, 9km east of Fort-de-France. The main resort areas are on Martinique's southwest coast, from Pointe du Bout to Sainte-Anne. Roads on Martinique are good, and despite the island's large size, no place is more than a two-hour drive from Fort-de-France.

Maps
The best road map of Martinique is the Institut Géographique National's No 511 map, which is sold around the island for 57F. However, this same map (on glossy paper, dotted with ads and labeled 'Carte Routière') is distributed by car rental agencies at the airport at no charge.

TOURIST OFFICES
Local Tourist Offices
Martinique's main tourist office is the Office Départemental du Tourisme (☎ 63 79 60, fax 73 66 93), 2 Rue Ernest Deproge, 97206 Fort-de-France, Martinique, French West Indies.

There is also a tourist information booth at the airport that usually stays open until the last flight comes in.

There are local syndicats d'initiative (information bureaus) in several towns including Sainte-Anne (☎ 76 73 45), Diamant (☎ 76 40 11), Saint-Pierre (☎ 78 15 41), Le Prêcheur (☎ 52 91 43) and Grand-Rivière (☎ 55 72 74). Most information distributed by the syndicats d'initiative is in French only.

Tourist Offices Abroad
Martinique has the following overseas tourist office representatives:

Canada
Martinique Tourist Office (☎ 514-844-8566, fax 514-844-8901) 2159 Rue Mackay, 1st floor, Montreal, Quebec H3G 2J2

France
Office du Tourisme de la Martinique (☎ 0144-77 86 00, fax 0149-26 03 63) 2 Rue des Moulins, 75001 Paris

Germany
Fremdenverkehrsamt Martinique (☎ 069-97 59 04 97, fax 069-97 59 04 99) Westendstrasse 47, Postfach 100128, D60325 Frankfurt am Main

Italy
Ente Nationale Francese per il Turismo (☎ 02-58 31 64 71, fax 02-58 31 65 79) 7 Via Larga, 20122 Milan

UK
French Government Tourist Office (☎ 020-7493 6694, fax 020-7493 6594) 178 Piccadilly, London W1V OAL

USA
Martinique Promotion Bureau (☎ 212-838-7800, 800-391-4909, fax 212-838-7855) 444 Madison Ave, 16th floor, New York, NY 10022

VISAS & DOCUMENTS
US and Canadian citizens can stay up to three months by showing proof of citizenship in the form of a current passport, an expired (up to five years) passport, or an official birth certificate that's accompanied by a driver's license or other government-authorized photo ID. Citizens of the European Union (EU) need an official identity card, valid passport or French carte de séjour (visitor permit). Citizens of most other countries, including Australia, need a valid passport and a visa for France.

A roundtrip or onward ticket is officially required of visitors. This may be checked at customs upon arrival or, if you're coming from within the Caribbean, before you depart for Martinique.

EMBASSIES & CONSULATES
Martinique is represented in your home country by the embassy or consulate of France.

Foreign Consulates in Martinique

Germany
Consulate (☎ 50 38 39)
Acajou, 97232 Le Lamentin

Netherlands
Consulate (☎ 73 31 61) 44/46 Ave Maurice
Bishop, 97200 Fort-de-France

UK
Consulate (☎ 61 56 30)
Route du Phare, 97200 Fort-de-France

CUSTOMS

Citizens of EU countries are allowed to bring in 300 cigarettes, 1.5L of spirits and 4L of wine duty free. Non-EU citizens are allowed to bring in 200 cigarettes, a bottle of spirits and 2L of wine duty free. All visitors are allowed to bring in 'large allowances of rum' as well.

MONEY

The French franc is the island currency, with the euro slowly being phased in. Hotels, larger restaurants and car rental agencies accept Visa (Carte Bleue) and MasterCard (Eurocard). Most shops and restaurants in Fort-de-France and other tourist areas accept US dollars, but at criminally poor exchange rates – 5F to the dollar. Avoid changing money at hotel lobbies, where the rates are worse than at exchange offices or banks. More information is under Money in the Regional Facts for the Visitor chapter.

POST & COMMUNICATIONS
Post

There are post offices in all major towns. It costs 3F to send a postcard to France, 5.20F to other destinations in Europe, 3.80F to any place in the Caribbean or the USA and 4.40F to other parts of the Americas. This rate also covers letters up to 20g. You can buy postage stamps at some tobacco shops (*tabacs*), hotels and souvenir shops in addition to post offices.

Mailing addresses given in this chapter should be followed by 'Martinique, French West Indies.'

Telephone

When making a local call, dial just the six-digit local number. When calling Martinique from outside the island, add the 596 area code in front of the six digits.

Public phones in Martinique accept French phone cards (*télécartes*), not coins. The cards cost 37F or 89F, depending on the amount of calling time on them, and are sold at post offices and at shops marked *télécarte en vente ici*. Card phones can be found at post offices, the airport, city parks and other public places.

For directory assistance, dial ☎ 12.

More information on phone cards and making long-distance calls is under Post & Communications in the Regional Facts for the Visitor chapter.

INTERNET RESOURCES

The best Internet resource for information about Martinique is the Martinique Promotion Bureau's Web site, which is located at www.martinique.org. Here you'll find travel planning tips, news of upcoming events and contact information for travel agencies and accommodations – along with extremely annoying computer-generated 'Caribbean music' sound effects.

BOOKS

Texaco, a novel by Patrick Chamoiseau that won the prestigious Prix Goncourt, tells the story of the growth and modernization of Fort-de-France through the eyes of some of its poorer inhabitants, and also recounts the riotous heyday and sudden destruction of Saint-Pierre.

Le Quatrième Siècle (1962) and *Malemort* (1975), by Martinican native Édouard Glissant, examine contemporary West Indian life against the backdrop of slavery and colonial rule.

NEWSPAPERS & MAGAZINES

The daily *France-Antilles* focuses on events occurring in the French West Indies. Other French-language newspapers, such as *Le Monde*, are flown in from the mainland. Larger newsstands in Fort-de-France and in other major tourist areas also sell a few

English-language newspapers including the *International Herald Tribune.*

For tourist information the following free bilingual publications are useful: *Ti Gourmet,* a pocket-size restaurant guide offering a complimentary drink at many island restaurants; and the 100-page *Choubouloute,* with detailed listings of events, entertainment, ferry schedules and other current information.

RADIO & TV

Radio France Outre-Mer (RFO) has FM radio frequencies at 92MHz and 94.5MHz. The TV networks RFO 1 and RFO 2 carry local programming, while other stations air standard programming from mainland France. CNN is available at some hotels, but that's usually the extent of English-language coverage.

ELECTRICITY

Electricity is 220V, 50 cycles, and plugs have two round prongs. Hotel bathrooms commonly have an adapted shaver outlet that accepts both 110V and 220V plugs.

WEIGHTS & MEASURES

Martinique uses the metric system, with elevations noted in meters, speed-limit signs in kilometers and weights in grams. Time is given using the 24-hour clock.

HEALTH

Medical care is of high quality by Caribbean standards. There are a number of general hospitals on the island, including Hôpital de la Meynard (☎ 55 20 00), on the D13 at the northeast side of Fort-de-France, and Hôpital du Lamentin (☎ 57 11 11), on Blvd Fernand Guilon in Lamentin.

There is a risk of bilharzia (schistosomiasis) infection throughout the island; the main precaution is to avoid wading or swimming in freshwater. More information on this disease is under Health in the Regional Facts for the Visitor chapter.

DANGERS & ANNOYANCES

The fer-de-lance, a large, aggressive pit viper, can be found on Martinique, particularly in overgrown and brushy fields. The snake's bite is highly toxic and sometimes fatal; it's essential for victims to get an antivenin injection as soon as possible. Hikers should be alert for the snakes and stick to established trails.

Beware of manchineel trees on some beaches, particularly on the south coast, as rainwater dripping off them can cause skin rashes and blistering. They're usually marked with a band of red paint.

After dark the center of Fort-de-France, particularly around La Savane, is a not a safe place to walk alone; robbery is the main concern. Islanders will be quick to tell you to watch your back.

EMERGENCIES

The following are Martinique's emergency telephone numbers:

Medical	☎ 75 15 15
Fire	☎ 18
Police	☎ 17
Sea rescue	☎ 71 92 92

BUSINESS HOURS

Although hours vary, many shops are open 8:30 am to 6 pm weekdays, until 1 pm Saturday. Banks, and many other offices, are typically open 7:30 am to 4:30 pm, with a two-hour lunch siesta beginning at noon. Note that banks close at noon on the day before a public holiday.

PUBLIC HOLIDAYS & SPECIAL EVENTS

Public holidays on Martinique are as follows:

New Year's Day	January 1
Good Friday	late March/early April
Easter Sunday	late March/early April
Easter Monday	late March/early April
Ascension Thursday	40th day after Easter
Pentecost Monday	eighth Monday after Easter
Labor Day	May 1
Victory Day	May 8

Slavery Abolition Day	May 22
Bastille Day	July 14
Schoelcher Day	July 21
Assumption Day	August 15
All Saints Day	November 1
Fête des Morts	November 2
Armistice Day	November 11
Christmas Day	December 25

Martinique has a spirited Mardi Gras Carnival during the five-day period leading up to Ash Wednesday. The streets spill over with revelers, rum-fueled partying, costume parades, music and dancing. Much of the carnival activity is centered around La Savane in Fort-de-France.

On a smaller scale, every village in Martinique has festivities to celebrate its patron saint's day. Saint-Pierre commemorates the May 8, 1902, eruption of Mont Pelée with live jazz and a candlelight procession from the cathedral.

The Tour de la Martinique, a weeklong bicycle race, is held in mid-July. The Tour des Yoles Rondes, a weeklong race of traditional sailboats, is held in early August. A 22km semi-marathon around Fort-de-France is held in November. The biennial weeklong Martinique Jazz Festival is held in December on odd-numbered years, while a guitar festival is held on even-numbered years.

On All Saints Day (Toussaint), November 2, the graves of the dead are whitewashed and decorated with fresh flowers; in the evening there are church ceremonies and lovely candlelight processions to the cemeteries.

ACTIVITIES
Beaches & Swimming
The beaches in the southern half of the island have white or tan sands while those in the northern half have gray or black sands. Many of Martinique's nicest beaches are scattered along the southwest coast from Grand Anse to Les Salines. In the Trois-Îlets area, Anse-à-l'Ane and Anse Mitan both have sandy beaches that attract a crowd. Popular east-coast beaches include Cap Chevalier and Macabou to the south

and the Caravelle Peninsula beaches of Anse l'Étang and Tartane. However, beaches along the northeast side of the island can have very dangerous water conditions and have been the site of a number of visitor drownings.

Diving
Saint-Pierre is one of the island's top dive sites with wrecks, coral reefs and plenty of marine life. More than a dozen ships that were anchored in the harbor when the 1902 volcanic eruption hit now lie on the sea bed, most in 10m to 50m of water; they include a 50m sailing ship, cargo ships and a tug.

Grand Anse, with its calm waters and good coral, is a popular diving spot for beginners. Cap Enragé, north of Case-Pilote, has underwater caves harboring lots of sea life. Rocher du Diamant (Diamond Rock) also has interesting cave formations but trickier water conditions. Îlet la Perle, a rock off the northwest coast, is a good place to see groupers, eels and lobsters when water conditions aren't too rough.

The going rate is 200F to 250F for single dives, with the higher prices for night dives and more distant dive sites. There are discounts for packages of three or more dives.

Dive Shops Dive shops on Martinique include the following:

Corail Club Caraïbes (☎ 68 42 99, fax 68 37 65), at the Frantour hotel in Anse à-l'Ane, with a small pool for beginner lessons

Espace Plongée (☎/fax 66 01 79), at the Méridien hotel in Pointe du Bout

Planète Bleue (☎ 66 06 22), a dive boat that docks at the marina at Pointe du Bout

Sub Diamond Rock (☎/fax 76 25 80), at the Novotel hotel in Diamant

Tropicasub (☎ 78 38 03, fax 52 46 82), in Saint-Pierre, which specializes in wreck dives

Snorkeling
Snorkeling is good around Grand Anse and also around Sainte-Anne and along the coast from Saint-Pierre to Anse Céron. Most larger hotels rent snorkeling gear and many provide it complimentary to their

guests. Some of the dive shops offer snorkeling trips, others let snorkelers tag along with divers.

Windsurfing

Most beachfront hotels have beach huts and rent windsurfing gear. Rentals generally cost 70F to 80F an hour for nonguests, but are often complimentary to hotel guests.

Hiking

Martinique has numerous hiking trails. From Route de la Trace a number of signposted trails lead into the rain forest and up and around the Pitons du Carbet. Also popular is the hike to the ruins of Château Dubuc on the Caravelle Peninsula.

There are strenuous trails leading up both the northern and southern flanks of Mont Pelée. The shortest and steepest begins in Morne Rouge and takes about four hours roundtrip. The hike up the northern flank is 8km long and takes about 4½ hours one-way; two trails begin just east of Grand-Rivière and converge halfway up the mountain.

A bit less strenuous but still moderately difficult is the 20km hike around the undeveloped northern tip of the island between Grand-Rivière and Anse Couleuvre. An easy way to do this trail is to join one of the guided hikes organized by the syndicat d'initiative (☎ 55 72 74) in Grand-Rivière, which conducts outings on Thursdays and Sundays. Hikers leave from Grand-Rivière's town hall, arriving in Anse Couleuvre about five hours later and then return to Grand-Rivière by boat. The outing costs 180F; make reservations in advance.

Other syndicats d'initiative organize hikes in other parts of the island, and the Parc Naturel Regional (☎ 73 19 30), 9 Blvd du Général de Gaulle, Fort-de-France, leads guided hikes several times a week.

Horseback Riding

A number of stables offer horseback riding. The cost of guided outings varies with the destination and length, but is generally around 150F to 200F. Stables include Ranch Black Horse (☎ 66 00 04), in Trois-Îlets;

Ranch Jack (☎ 68 37 69), near Anse d'Arlet; and La Cavale (☎ 76 22 94), in Diamant.

Mountain Biking

Mountain-bike tours can be arranged with VT Tilt (☎ 66 01 01) in Anse Mitan. Half-day outings start at 150F, full-day outings are 300F.

Golf

Martinique has one golf course, the 18-hole Golf de la Martinique (☎ 68 32 81) in Trois-Îlets. It costs 145F to play nine holes, 270F for 18 holes. There's a pro shop; cart and club rentals are available.

Tennis

Most of the larger resort hotels have tennis courts that are free to their guests and some let nonguests use the courts at reasonable fees. There are also three lighted tennis courts at the golf course in Trois-Îlets that are open to the public at 70F per person.

ACCOMMODATIONS

Martinique has about 120 hotels. While the French shun the mega-resorts found elsewhere in the Caribbean, Martinique has about a dozen mid-size resorts with 100 rooms or more. Most of the island's other hotels range from 12 to 40 rooms. By Caribbean standards rates are moderate, with upper-end hotels averaging US$250, mid-range US$125 and the budget end about US$65.

As in France, taxes and service charges are included in the quoted rates.

Camping

There are established campgrounds with facilities at Vivre et Camper in Sainte-Anne and Le Nid Tropical in Anse à-l'Ane; for details see those sections, later.

Camping is also allowed along the beach at Les Salines and in a few other areas on weekends and during school holidays.

Private Rooms & Apartments

Gîtes de France (☎ 73 74 74, fax 63 55 92, in Paris 0149-70 75 75, www2.gites-de-france .fr), BP 1122, 97209 Fort-de-France, offers rooms and apartments in private homes, with weekly rates beginning around 1100F for two people.

Centrale de Réservation (☎ 63 79 60, fax 63 11 64, in Paris ☎ 0144-77 86 11), BP 823, 97208 Fort-de-France, opposite the tourist office, books studios, apartments and houses, with weekly rates from 1500F.

FOOD

Most restaurants serve either Creole or French food with an emphasis on local seafood. Red snapper, conch, crayfish and lobster are popular, although the latter is pricey at about 40F per 100g. The best value at many restaurants is the fixed-price menu, which is sometimes labeled *menu touristique* – a three- or four-course meal that usually runs from 90F to 160F, depending on the main course. Remember that this is France, so bring a good book or someone to talk to; it can take a couple of hours for all the courses to be served.

For more moderately priced meals there are a number of Italian restaurants and pizzerias on the island. Bakeries make good budget places to grab a quick meal, because most of them make sandwiches to go and some have a few café tables out front.

The island of Martinique grows much of its own produce, including some very sweet pineapples.

DRINKS

Water is safe to drink from the tap. In restaurants, if you ask for water you'll usually get served bottled water; if you don't want to pay extra for that, ask for *l'eau du robinet* to get tap water.

The legal drinking age is 18. Lorraine is the tasty local beer, but island rums are far more popular. Martinique's de rigueur apéritif is *ti-punch,* a mixture of white rum, sugarcane juice and a squeeze of lemon. It's a fiesty little drink that could cause you problems. Also popular is planteur punch, a mix of rum and fruit juice.

ENTERTAINMENT

The larger hotels in southern Martinique offer a good range of entertainment, including steel-band music, dancing and various shows.

The most popular tourist show on the island is the performance by the 30-member folk troupe Ballet Martiniquais, which does a dinner show at a different hotel each night, including Thursday at Le Méridien Trois-Îlets and Friday at the Bakoua, both in Pointe du Bout.

There are a number of lively dance clubs in Fort-de-France, including Manhattan at 18 Rue François-Arago and New Hippo at 24 Blvd Allègre.

The casino at Le Méridien Trois-Îlets in Pointe du Bout offers slot machines, roulette and blackjack.

Getting There & Away

AIR
Airports & Airlines

Lamentin International Airport has a friendly tourist information booth where you can get maps and brochures in English, car rental booths, a Délifrance snack bar, restaurants, souvenir shops, a newsstand and a pharmacy. The public phones take phone cards. You can buy phone cards and exchange money at the Change Caraïbes office, which occasionally changes its hours but is generally open from at least 8am to 7 pm daily.

The following are airline reservation numbers on Martinique:

Air France	☎ 55 33 33
Air Guadeloupe	☎ 42 16 72
Air Liberté	☎ 42 18 34
LIAT	☎ 42 16 03
Nouvelles Frontières	☎ 42 16 40

Within the Caribbean

LIAT flies between Martinique and the English-speaking Caribbean. A roundtrip ticket from Martinique allowing a 30-day stay costs US$308 to Barbados, US$320 to Grenada and US$160 to St Lucia.

The USA

Travelers from the USA can take American Airlines or TWA to San Juan, Puerto Rico, and connect with LIAT or BWIA there. Fares vary but in the low season a ticket allowing a stay of up to 30 days generally begins at around US$550 from east-coast cities such as Miami, New York and Boston. In the high season prices average about US$100 more.

Air France has a daily flight to Martinique from Miami. The lowest fare of US$480 allows a stay of up to 21 days.

France

Air France, Air Liberté and Nouvelles Frontières have daily flights between Paris and Martinique. Fares are competitive, beginning at around 2700F roundtrip.

SEA
Passenger/Cargo Boat

Compagnie Générale Maritime (☎ 71 34 23), 8 Blvd du Général de Gaulle, Fort-de-France, has a weekly passenger/cargo boat between the French West Indies and mainland France. Information is in the Getting There & Away chapter in the front of the book.

Ferry

L'Express des Îles (☎ 63 12 11) operates modern catamaran ferries daily between Martinique, Guadeloupe and Dominica, with additional weekly service to St Lucia. The smaller Brudey Frères (☎ 70 08 50) offers express catamarans between Martinique and Guadeloupe. Detailed information on both of these boats is in the Getting There & Away section of the Guadeloupe chapter.

Yacht

The main port of entry is in Fort-de-France but yachts may also clear at Saint-Pierre or Marin.

Yachting is very popular in Martinique and there are numerous yacht charter companies operating on the island. The Moorings (☎ 74 75 39), Stardust (☎ 74 98 17) and Sunsail (☎ 74 77 61) are based at the marina

in Marin. Star Voyage (☎ 66 00 72) is based at the Pointe du Bout marina.

Cruise Ship

Cruise ships land at Pointe Simon in Fort-de-France, at the west side of the harbor and within easy walking distance of the city center and main sights. The arrival facilities have phones, restrooms, a taxi stand and a tourist information booth that opens on cruise-ship days.

Getting Around

TO/FROM THE AIRPORT

The airport is just a 10-minute ride from Fort-de-France, traffic permitting, and about 20 minutes from the Pointe du Bout resort area. Taxis are readily available at the airport but are expensive (about 100F to Fort-de-France), so if you plan to rent a car during your stay consider picking it up at the airport upon arrival. If you need to refuel a rental car, head for one of the 24-hour gas stations on the N5 near the airport.

Because of the taxi union, there's no direct bus service from the airport. However, on the return it's possible, if not terribly practical, to take a bus from Pointe Simon in Fort-de-France heading to Ducos (8.70F) and ask to be dropped off on the highway outside the airport.

BUS

Although there are some larger public buses, most buses are minivans, marked 'TC' (for *taxis collectifs*) on top. Destinations are marked on the vans, sometimes on the side doors and sometimes on a small sign stuck in the front window. Bus stops are marked *arrêt autobus* or with signs showing a picture of a bus.

Fort-de-France's busy main taxi collectifs terminal is at Pointe Simon, on the west side of the harbor. Buses to Saint-Pierre leave frequently on weekdays, less frequently on Sunday, take 45 minutes and cost 17F. Other bus fares from Fort-de-France are 17F to Trois-Îlets, 19F to Diamant, 31F to Sainte-Anne and 40F to

MARTINIQUE

Grand-Rivière. You can pick up buses to the Balata Gardens and Morne Rouge alongside the cemetery south of the Parc Floral; they leave about every 30 minutes during the day, Sunday excepted.

CAR & MOTORCYCLE
Road Rules
In Martinique, drive on the right. Your home driver's license is valid. Traffic regulations and road signs are the same as in Europe, speed limits are posted, and exits and intersections are clearly marked.

Roads are excellent by Caribbean standards and there are multilane freeways (and rush-hour traffic) in the Fort-de-France area. Be sure to give yourself extra time if you're driving to the airport during rush hour, as the N5 carries lots of commuters.

Rental
Car There are numerous car rental agencies at the airport. The daily rate for an economy car with unlimited kilometers ranges from 195F with the local company Euradom to 280F with Avis. During the sluggish summer season many agencies will discount an additional 20% (and sometimes even throw in a free collision damage waiver – CDW), while at the height of winter you might not find anything available at the lower range without advance reservations.

Be aware that many companies also offer a rate that adds on an extra charge for every kilometer you drive; for example, an economy car from Euradom could be as cheap as 107F per day if you're willing to add an additional 1.1F per kilometer, or with Avis 160F a day plus 1.6F per kilometer. Be sure you know which deal you're getting; if you want to really tour the island thoroughly, your best bet will likely be a car with unlimited kilometers.

Optional CDW insurance that covers collision damage to the car, after a 2000F excess (a fixed payment in the event of an accident), costs 45F a day with Eurodom to 70F a day with most other companies. The minimum age to rent a car is 21 and some companies add an extra 100F surcharge for drivers under the age of 25.

Car rental companies on the island include the following:

Avis	☎ 42 16 92 at the airport
	☎ 66 04 27 in Pointe du Bout
Budget	☎ 51 36 48 at the airport
	☎ 63 69 00 in Fort-de-France
	☎ 66 00 45 in Pointe du Bout
Citer	☎ 42 16 82 at the airport
	☎ 72 66 48 in Fort-de-France
	☎ 76 85 57 in Sainte-Anne
Euradom	☎ 42 17 05 at the airport
	☎ 60 43 62 in Fort-de-France
Europcar	☎ 42 16 88 at the airport
	☎ 73 33 13 in Fort-de-France
	☎ 66 04 29 in Pointe du Bout
Hertz	☎ 51 01 01 at the airport
Thrifty	☎ 42 16 99 at the airport
	☎ 66 09 59 in Pointe du Bout

Motorcycle Motorcycles can be rented from Funny (☎ 63 33 05), 80 Rue Ernest Deproge, Fort-de-France. The cost for a 50cc bike is 126F per day, helmet included. The cost for a 80cc bike that can hold both a passenger and driver is 155F per day. Optional insurance costs 44F a day; without it, you'll have to pay a 5000F deposit.

TAXI
The taxi fare from the airport is 90F to 100F to Fort-de-France, 300F to Sainte-Anne and 180F to Pointe du Bout or Anse Mitan. A 40% surcharge is added onto all fares between 8 pm and 6 am and also all day on Sundays and holidays. To call a taxi, dial ☎ 63 63 62 or 63 10 10; both dispatch on a 24-hour basis.

HITCHHIKING
Hitchhiking is fairly common on Martinique, although of course the usual precautions apply.

BOAT
There are a couple of regular *vedettes* (ferries) between main resort areas and Fort-de-France that provide a nice alternative to dealing with heavy bus and car traffic, allow you to avoid the hassles of city parking and are quicker to boot. In

Fort-de-France the ferries dock at the quay fronting La Savane. Schedules are posted at the docks; the ferries leave promptly and occasionally even a few minutes early.

Fort-de-France to Pointe du Bout

Somatours Vedettes (☎ 73 05 53) runs a ferry between Fort-de-France and the Pointe du Bout marina. It's quite a pleasant way to cross and takes only 20 minutes. The boat runs daily from early morning to around midnight, with 22 crossings on the weekdays, 14 on the weekends. The fare is 19/32F one-way/roundtrip for adults, 10/15F for children ages two to 10.

Fort-de-France to Anse Mitan & Anse-à-l'Ane

Madinina Vedettes (☎ 63 06 46) follows a triangular route between Fort-de-France, Anse Mitan and Anse-à-l'Ane. The boats run daily, every 30 to 60 minutes, from about 6 am Monday to Saturday (8:30 am on Sunday) to about 6pm.

The fare between Fort-de-France and Anse Mitan is 30F roundtrip (13F for children). The fare between Anse Mitan and Anse-à-l'Ane is 5F.

Fort-de-France to Trois-Îlets

Martinik Cruise Line (☎ 68 39 19, 68 42 13) runs a ferry about every 75 minutes between Fort-de-France and the town dock in the village of Trois-Îlets. The first boat departs from Trois-Îlets at 6:10 am and the last boat returns from Fort-de-France at 5:45 pm. There are no boats on Sunday. The fare is 15F each way.

ORGANIZED TOURS

Taxi tours cost about 250F an hour, or about 600F for a half-day tour that typically includes a drive up the Route de la Trace, a visit to Saint-Pierre and a return to Fort-de-France down the west coast.

There are various catamaran tours and boat charters operating around the island. For the latest information check with the tourist office, ask at your hotel desk or leaf through the tourist magazines.

Fort-de-France

Fort-de-France, the island capital, is the largest and most cosmopolitan city in the French West Indies. It has a pretty harborfront setting with the Pitons du Carbet rising up beyond, a view best appreciated when approaching the city by ferry.

The narrow, bustling streets opposite La Savane (the harborfront central park) are lined with a mixture of ordinary offices and interesting turn-of-the-century buildings housing French cafés and designer boutiques. It has as much of the flavor of the side streets of Paris as it does of the Caribbean.

Give yourself a few hours to wander around and take in the handful of historic sites and museums the city has to offer, longer if you want to shop or enjoy a meal.

Information

Tourist Offices The tourist office (☎ 63 79 60), 2 Rue Ernest Deproge, is open 8 am to 1 pm and 2 to 5 pm weekdays and 8 am to noon Saturday.

Money Change Caraïbes, 4 Rue Ernest Deproge, is open 7:30 am to 6 pm weekdays and 8 am to 12:30 pm Saturday. Change Point, a block away, is open 8 am to 5:30 pm weekdays, until 12:30 pm Saturday. Both exchange major currencies and neither charges commissions for most transactions.

Full-service banks can be found next door to Change Caraïbes on Rue Ernest Deproge and along Rue de la Liberté, opposite La Savane.

Post & Communications You can send faxes, buy phone cards, use a card phone or pick up mail sent poste restante at the central post office on the corner of Rue Antoine Siger and Rue de la Liberté. It's open 7 am to 6 pm weekdays, to noon Saturday; expect long lines.

Other public card phones can be found in La Savane, opposite the post office, and around the city.

You can check your email or surf the Internet at Le Web Cyber Café, 4 Rue Blénac, a smoky bar with expensive drinks, open

FORT-DE-FRANCE

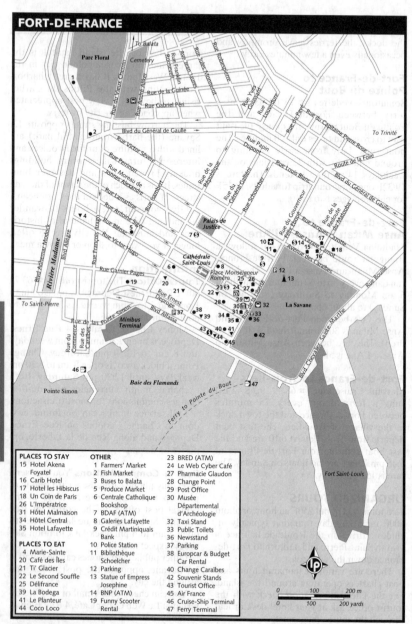

To Balata

Parc Floral

Cemetery

Rue du Vieux Chemin
Rue André Aliker
Rue de la Guinée
Rue Gabriel Péri
Rue Franklin Roosevelt
Rue Jean Jaurès
Rue Jules Monnerot
Rue Redouté
Rue Rochepelle
Rue Yves Coussard
Rue du Loupgarou
Rue du Pont
Rue du Capitaine Pierre Rose

To Trinité

Blvd du Général de Gaulle

Rue Victor Sévère
Rue Perrinon
Rue Moreau de Jonnes Alexandre
Rue Lamartine
Rue Antoine Siger
Rue Blénac
Rue Victor Hugo
Rue Garnier Pagès
Rue Gambetta
Rue François Arago
Rue Papin Dupont
Rue de la République
Rue du Général-Galliéni
Rue Schoelcher
Rue Louis Blanc
Route de la Folie
Blvd du Général de Gaulle

Blvd Achterman-Modrick
Blvd Allègre

Rivière Madame

To Saint-Pierre

Rue de las Poinre Simon
Rue du Commerce
Rue des Caraïbes

Minibus Terminal

Rue Ernest Deproge
Blvd Allassa

Palais de Justice 7

Cathédrale Saint-Louis

Place Monseigneur Roméro

Rue du Gouverneur Ponty-Rope
Rue de la Liberté
Rue Lazare Carnot
Rue Jacques Cazotte
Avenue des Caraïbes
Rue de la Redoute du Matouba
Rue Bouillé

La Savane

Pointe Simon

Baie des Flamands

Ferry to Pointe du Bout

Blvd Chevalier Sainte-Marthe

Fort Saint-Louis

0   100   200 m
0   100   200 yards

MARTINIQUE

11 am to 2 am weekdays, 6 pm to 2 am Saturday. The cost is 25F for 15 minutes.

Bookstores The newsstand at the west corner of La Savane sells the *International Herald-Tribune* and numerous French-language newspapers and magazines.

Centrale Catholique, 57 Rue Blénac, sells books in French about Martinique (history, flora and fauna and other topics) and the Institut Géographique National's map of Martinique.

Pharmacies There are several pharmacies around town, including Pharmacie Glaudon on the corner of Rue de la Liberté and Rue Antoine Siger.

Parking Parking is not a problem on weekends and holidays, but is quite a challenge on weekdays. There's a parking lot along the north side of La Savane that's entered at the intersection of Ave des Caraïbes and Rue de la Liberté; it costs 8F an hour or 70F for 12 hours Monday to Saturday, 2F per hour Sunday.

Streetside parking is free in the evenings and on Sunday and holidays.

La Savane

This large central park sports grassy lawns, tall trees, clumps of bamboo and lots of benches. The harbor side of La Savane has souvenir stalls, a newsstand and statues dedicated to early settlers and fallen soldiers.

At the park's north side, near bustling Rue de la Liberté, is a statue of the Empress Josephine holding a locket with a portrait of Napoleon. You can't miss it – years ago the statue's head was lopped off and red paint splashed over it. No real efforts have been made to repair the damage. Evidently the empress is not highly regarded by islanders, who believe she was directly responsible for convincing Napoleon to continue slavery in the French West Indies so that her family plantation in Trois-Îlets would not suffer.

Fort Saint-Louis

Opposite the south side of La Savane is Fort Saint-Louis. The original fort, built in the Vauban style, dates from 1640, although most of the extensive fort that stands today is the result of subsequent additions. The fort is still an active military base and can be visited only as part of a 45-minute tour (25F), escorted by a guide and sailor; tours begin on the hour 10 am to 3 pm.

Musée Départemental d'Archéologie

This archaeological museum, 9 Rue de la Liberté, displays Amerindian artifacts, including stone tools, ritual objects and pottery. Most engaging are the 100 or so clay *adornos*, the decorative figurines that Arawaks used to adorn vases and bowls. There are also illustrations of the Caribs and a diorama of thatched huts. Overall, the presentation is simple and a bit dry, and you can walk through it all in about 20 minutes. Most signs are in French only. It's open 8 am to 5 pm weekdays, 9 am to noon Saturday. Admission is 15F for adults, 5F for children under 12.

Bibliothèque Schoelcher

The Bibliothèque Schoelcher (Schoelcher Library), on Rue de la Liberté, is Fort-de-France's most visible landmark, an elaborate, colorful building with a Byzantine dome. The work of architect Henri Pick, a contemporary of Gustave Eiffel, the library was built in Paris and displayed at the 1889 World Exposition. It was then dismantled, shipped in pieces to Fort-de-France and reassembled on this site. The ornate interior is also interesting; the front section contains antique books and period furnishing, while the back is still a functioning lending library. It's open 1 to 5:30 pm Monday, 8:30 am to 5:30 pm other weekdays (till 5 pm Friday) and 8:30 am to noon Saturday.

Cathèdral Saint-Louis

With its neo-Byzantine style and 57m-high steeple, the Saint-Louis Cathèdral on Rue Schoelcher, a block northwest of La Savane, is one of the city's most distinguished landmarks. Built in 1895 by Henri Pick, the church fronts a small square and is picturesquely framed by two royal palms. The

MARTINIQUE

spacious, ornate interior is well worth a look.

Palais de Justice

The Palais de Justice, a neoclassical courthouse built in 1906, is two blocks northeast of the cathedral. The design resembles a French railroad station, as the plaque out front unabashedly points out. The square fronting the courthouse has a statue of French abolitionist Victor Schoelcher.

Parc Floral & Public Markets

The Parc Floral, a public park at the north side of the city, is worth a stroll if you're already in the area.

A farmers market runs along the west side of Parc Floral and spills over into the street along the Rivière Madame. In addition to island-grown fruits and vegetables, the market sells drinking coconuts and cut flowers. The fish market is a block to the south, while a second and larger public produce market is on the north side of Rue Isambert. The busiest day for these markets is Saturday, and they're closed Sunday.

Places to Stay

City Center The *Hotel les Hibiscus* (☎ 60 29 59, 1 Rue de la Redoute Matouba, 97200 Fort-de-France) has Spartan rooms for 175/200F single/double with shared bath; a double room with private bath costs 250F.

Un Coin de Paris (☎ 70 08 52, fax 63 69 51, 54 Rue Lazare Carnot, 97200 Fort-de-France Cédex) is a well-maintained place that's geared toward budget travelers rather than local boarders. There are 14 clean, straightforward singles/doubles with private baths and air-con for 210/250F.

The *Hotel Malmaison* (☎ 63 90 85, fax 60 03 93, 7 Rue de la Liberté, 97200 Fort-de-France) has 20 rooms that vary in size and amenities. All have private baths and most have a TV. Although a few of the rooms have saggy mattresses and at least one has no windows, the rooms are clean and the desk clerk will usually let you look around and pick one to your liking. Singles/doubles cost 305/335F for fan-cooled rooms, 335/360F for rooms with air-con.

Hotel Central (☎ 70 02 12, fax 63 80 00, 3 Rue Victor Hugo, 97200 Fort-de-France) is a small hotel with 18 rooms, most on the compact side but clean and adequate. Each has TV, air-con and private bath; the rates are 270/290F for singles/doubles and they are commonly discounted 10% in summer.

L'Impératrice (☎ 63 06 82, fax 72 66 30, 15 Rue de la Liberté, 97200 Fort-de-France) is getting a little run-down, though all 24 rooms have air-con, private baths and phones; some have four-poster beds and balconies facing La Savane. In summer, singles/doubles begin at 300/350F, in winter at 340/400F. Breakfast is included in the rates.

Hotel Lafayette (☎ 73 80 50, fax 60 97 75, 5 Rue de la Liberté, 97200 Fort-de-France) is a three-story hotel with 24 rooms that have air-con, phones, TV, minibars and private baths. They're clean, adequate and centrally located, and not a bad deal at 280/330F for singles/doubles.

Carib Hotel (☎ 60 19 85, fax 60 19 88, 9 Rue de la Redoute-du-Matouba) is an excellent budget choice with a French feel. Comfortable rooms with bathroom, telephone and air-conditioning go for 250F single/double, and there's a cozy downstairs bar.

The fanciest in-town option, *Hotel Akena Foyatel* (☎ 72 46 46, fax 73 28 23, 68 Avenue des Caraibes) is part of a worldwide chain of French business hotels. Considering what you'd pay at the run-down places nearby, it might be worth it to cough up 449/499F single/double to stay in an immaculately clean room with air-conditioning, hot shower, telephone and cable TV. Breakfast in the bright, plant-filled first floor is included.

Around Fort-de-France The *Squash Hotel* (☎ 72 80 80, fax 63 00 74, 3 Blvd de la Marne, 97200 Fort-de-France) is 1km west of the town center. This modern, mid-priced hotel has 108 comfortable rooms with air-con, TV, phones and minibars. There's also a pool, restaurant, fitness center and three squash courts. Singles cost from 480F to 575F, doubles from 590F to 790F, breakfast included.

La Batelière (☎ 61 49 49, fax 61 70 57, 97233 Schoelcher), a couple of kilometers west of central Fort-de-France, is a modern luxury hotel that caters in part to business-people. The hotel has a beach, a pool, a gym, a dive shop, tennis courts and restaurants. The 190 rooms and suites have heavy curtains, four-poster beds, marble baths and other top-end amenities. Doubles range from 845F for a standard room to 3515F for a suite in summer, from 1300F to 3515F in winter.

Places to Eat

There are a number of cafés and restaurants opposite La Savane on Rue de la Liberté. If you want to eat cheaply you can easily find takeout food and freshly baked bread for a picnic in the park. Bakeries selling pastries and inexpensive sandwiches are scattered throughout the city. In the evenings food vans selling crêpes, barbecued chicken and other cheap local food park along the Blvd Chevalier Sainte Marthe at the south side of La Savane.

Délifrance, on Rue Antoine Siger, has good baguette sandwiches from 18F.

Café des Îles (59 Rue Victor Hugo) is a small owner-run café with freshly squeezed orange juice (13F), salads (40F) and reasonably priced sandwiches. Nearby on the same street is *Ti' Glacier*, a stand with inexpensive ice cream and fruit juice mixes like orange–passion fruit.

Le Second Souffle, diagonally opposite the cathedral at 27 Rue Blénac, is a good vegetarian restaurant. Salads are priced from 15F to 38F and there's a plat du jour for 50F. It's open 10 am to 4 pm weekdays.

La Bodega (28 Rue Ernest Deproge) is a pub-style restaurant with a variety of salads, pizzas and pasta dishes from 45F to 60F, brochettes for 70F and a three-course menu du jour for 75F. It's open 10 am to 11:30 pm daily.

Near the river, *Marie-Sainte (160 Rue Victor Hugo)* is a popular little hole-in-the-wall serving moderately priced Creole food such as accras, lambi, fricassee and banana fritters. It's open for breakfast and lunch 8 am to 3 pm Monday to Saturday.

More upscale is *Le Planteur (1 Rue de la Liberté)*, overlooking La Savane, with good Creole and French food. Three-course set lunches range from 80F for chicken to 150F for lobster. Otherwise, most à la carte main dishes cost 75F to 130F. It's open weekdays for lunch and nightly for dinner.

Coco Loco (☎ 63 63 77, Rue Ernest Deproge) looks strangely like a misplaced Chevy's, but don't be fooled; it's actually one of the nicest and most popular places in town for French food. The daily special menu is a very affordable 48F, while dinner courses like *magret du canard* (filet of duck) will run you 95F.

Shopping

Fort-de-France is a shopper's paradise, where air-conditioned shops sell the latest Paris fashions, French perfumes, leather handbags, crystal, silk scarves etc. The main boutique area is along Rue Victor Hugo, particularly from Rue de la République to Rue de la Liberté. The department store Galeries LaFayette, near the cathedral, has a little of everything. Foreigners who pay with traveler's checks or a credit card get 20% off the posted price at Galeries LaFayette and at many of the fancier shops.

Local handicrafts such as wicker baskets, dolls in madras costumes, wooden carvings and T-shirts are sold by vendors at the northwest corner of La Savane and at craft shops around the island.

Local rum makes a popular souvenir and sells from about 35F to 200F a liter, depending on the quality.

Northern Martinique

Several roads head north from Fort-de-France. The most interesting sightseeing routes are the coastal road (N2) to Saint-Pierre and the Route de la Trace (N3), which crosses the lush mountainous interior before ending in Morne Rouge. The two routes can be combined to make a nice loop drive; the highlights can be seen in a half day or the trip could be stretched into a leisurely full-day outing.

FORT-DE-FRANCE TO SAINT-PIERRE

The N2, the coastal road north to Saint-Pierre, passes along dry, scrubby terrain and goes through a line of small towns, a merging of modern suburbia and old fishing villages. If you were to drive without stopping, it would take about 45 minutes to reach Saint-Pierre from Fort-de-France.

It's worth swinging off the highway at **Case-Pilote** to take a peek at the old village center. Turn west off the N2 at the Total gas station and you'll immediately come to a quaint stone church, one of Martinique's oldest. Just 75m south is a pleasant town square with a water fountain, a historic town hall, a tourist office and a moderately priced café. In Case-Pilote, as well as in the next village, **Bellefontaine**, you can find brightly painted wooden fishing boats called *gommiers* (after the trees they're constructed from) lined up along the shore. At Bellefontaine, look inland at the hillside to spot one of Martinique's more unusual buildings, a blue-and-white house designed in the shape of a boat.

The town of **Carbet**, where Christopher Columbus briefly came ashore in 1502, fronts a long sandy beach and has a few tourist amenities, including a bunch of restaurants and a scenic garden.

Anse Turin, a long gray-sand beach that attracts a crowd on weekends, is along the highway 1.5km north of Carbet. Opposite the beach is the **Musée Paul Gauguin**, marked by a few inconspicuous signs. This interesting museum contains Gauguin memorabilia, letters from the artist to his wife and reproductions of Gauguin's paintings, including *Bord de Mer I* and *L'Anse Turin avec les raisiniers,* which were both painted on the nearby beach during Gauguin's five-month stay on Martinique in 1887. There's also a collection of works by local artists, more or less in the style of Gauguin, and a basement full of extremely creepy mannequins in period costumes. The museum is open 9am to 5:30 pm daily. Admission is 20F.

Just north of the Gauguin museum is the driveway up to **La Vallée des Papillons** (☎ 78 18 07), where the scattered stone ruins of one of the island's earliest plantations have been enhanced with gardens and a butterfly farm. It's open 9:30 am to 4:15 pm daily. Admission is 38F for adults, 28F for children, and there's a restaurant on-site.

SAINT-PIERRE

Saint-Pierre is on the coast 7km south of Mont Pelée, the still-active volcano that laid the town to waste at the beginning of the 20th century. It's a fascinating town to wander around. There are ruins throughout Saint-Pierre, some of which are little more than foundations, others partially intact. Many of the surviving stone walls have been incorporated into the town's reconstruction, forming the base for the buildings that replaced them. Even these 'newer' buildings have a period character, with shuttered doors and wrought-iron balconies.

The center of town is long and narrow, with two parallel one-way streets running its length. All of the major sights have signs in both French and English, and you can explore the area thoroughly in a few hours.

These days Saint-Pierre has 6000 residents, which is just one-fifth of the pre-eruption population. The central gathering spot is the waterfront town park, next to the market. A beach of soft black sand fronts the town and extends to the south.

Musée Vulcanologique

This small but very interesting museum, founded in 1932 by American vulcanologist Franck Perret, gives a glimpse of the devastating 1902 eruption of Mont Pelée. On display are items plucked from the rubble, including petrified rice, a box of nails melted into a sculpturelike mass, glass cups fused together by heat and the cast-iron bell from the cathedral tower squashed like a saucer. There are also historic photos of the town before and immediately after the eruption. The displays are in both English and French.

There's free parking adjacent to the museum, which occupies the site of an old hillside gun battery. From the old stone walls along the parking lot you can get a good perspective of the harbor and city, and look down upon a line of ruins on the street below. The museum, on Rue Victor Hugo, is open 9 am to 5 pm daily. Admission is 10F.

Ruins

Saint-Pierre's most impressive ruins are those of the old **theater**, just 100m north of the museum. While most of the theater was destroyed, enough remains to give a sense of the former grandeur of this building, which once seated 800 and hosted theater troupes from mainland France. A double set of stairs still leads up to the partial walls of the lower story.

On the northeast side of the theater you can look over the wall to the tiny, thick-walled **jail cell** that housed Cyparis, the town's sole survivor.

Another area rich in ruins is the **Quartier du Figuier**, along Rue Bouillé, directly below the vulcanology museum. Two sets of steps, one just north of the theater and the other just south of the museum, connect Rue Victor Hugo with the bayfront Rue Bouillé.

Places to Stay & Eat

The only in-town hotel is the aging *Nouvelle Vague* (☎ 78 14 34, 97250 Saint-Pierre), which has five very simple rooms for 250F and a comfortable waterfront restaurant.

There's a *8 à Huit* grocery store in the center of town; *Patisserie Pomme Cannelle*, a bakery south of the cathedral; a wood-fired pizza place, *Pizzaria Marina*, south of the museum; and another pizzeria, *La Paillote*, on the waterfront.

Habitation Josephine, a courtyard restaurant opposite the waterfront park, is a friendly family-run operation serving excellent Creole food, including a complete menu du jour for 60F and a *menu pecheur* (fisherman's special) for 95F; it's open 11:30 am to 5 pm daily.

SAINT-PIERRE TO ANSE CÉRON

From Saint-Pierre, the N2 turns inland but the D10 continues north for 13km along the

SAINT-PIERRE

PLACES TO STAY & EAT
7 Pizzaria Marina
9 La Paillote
15 Habitation Josephine
18 Nouvelle Vague
19 Pâtisserie Pomme Cannelle

OTHER
1 Old Fort Church Ruins
2 Belain d'Esnambuc Monument
3 Cyparis' Jail Cell
4 Theater Ruins
5 Syndicat d'Initiative
6 Musée Vulcanologique
8 Crédit Agricole Bank
10 Pharmacy
11 Waterfront Park
12 Crédit Martiniquais
13 Mairie (Town Hall)
14 Public Market
16 Post Office
17 8 à Huit Grocery Store
20 Esso Gas Station

Quartier du Fort
To Anse Céron
Rivière Roxelane
Rue Isambert
To Morne Rouge
Le Centre
To Fond Saint-Denis
Rade de Saint-Pierre
Rue Bouillé
Rue Victor Hugo
Rue de la barque
Cathedral
Cemetery
To Fort-de-France

0   200   400 m
0   200   400 yards

MARTINIQUE

The Eruption of Mont Pelée

At the end of the 19th century Saint-Pierre, then the capital of Martinique, was a flourishing port city, so cosmopolitan it was dubbed the 'Little Paris of the West Indies.' Mont Pelée, the island's highest mountain, provided a scenic backdrop to the city.

In the spring of 1902, sulfurous steam vents on Mont Pelée began emitting gases, and a crater lake started to fill with boiling water. Authorities dismissed it all as the normal cycle of the volcano, which had experienced periods of activity in the past without dire consequences.

But in late spring the lake broke and spilled down the mountainside in Rivière Blanche, just north of the city, burying a plantation and its workers in hot mud. On April 25 the volcano spewed a shower of ash onto Saint-Pierre. Up until this point the volcanic activity had largely been seen as a curiosity, but now people became apprehensive, and some sent their children to stay with relatives on other parts of the island. The governor of Martinique, hoping to convince residents that there was no need to evacuate the city, brought his family to Saint-Pierre.

At 8 am on Sunday, May 8, 1902, Mont Pelée exploded into a glowing burst of superheated gas and burning ash, with a force 40 times stronger than the nuclear blast over Hiroshima. Between the suffocating gases and the fiery inferno, Saint-Pierre was laid to waste within minutes.

When rescuers from the French navy landed ashore that afternoon, they found only three survivors among the city's 30,000 inhabitants. Two of them had received fatal injuries, but the third, a prisoner named Cyparis, survived with only minor burns – ironically, he owed his life to having been locked in a tomblike solitary-confinement cell at the local jail. Following the commutation of his prison sentence by the new governor, Cyparis joined the PT Barnum circus where he toured as a sideshow act.

Pelée continued to smolder for months, but by 1904 people began to resettle the town, building among the crumbled ruins.

coast and makes a scenic side drive, ending in 20 minutes at a remote beach. The shoreline is rocky for much of the way and the landscape is lush, with roadside clumps of bamboo.

The limestone cliffs 4km north of Saint-Pierre, called **Tombeau des Caraïbes**, are said to be the place where the last Caribs jumped to their deaths rather than succumb to capture by the French.

The road goes through the town of **Le Prêcheur**, where green and orange fishing boats dot the shoreline, and **Anse Belleville**, a village so narrow that there's only room for a single row of houses between the cliffs and the sea.

Half a kilometer before the end of the road you will find the **Habitation Céron** (☎ 52 94 53), a former sugar plantation that is open to visitors 9:30 am to 5 pm daily. Admission is 35F for adults, 15F for children ages five to 12.

The road ends at **Anse Céron**, a beautiful black-sand beach in a wild, junglelike setting. Anse Céron is backed by coconut palms and faces Îlet la Perle, a rounded offshore rock that's a popular dive site. Despite the remote location, the beach has a shower, toilets, picnic tables and a snack shop.

A very steep one-lane route continues for 1600m beyond the beach. This is the start of a six-hour, 20km hike to Grand-Rivière.

ROUTE DE LA TRACE

The Route de la Trace (N3) winds up into the mountains north from Fort-de-France. It's a beautiful drive through a lush rain forest of tall tree ferns, anthurium-covered hillsides and thick clumps of roadside bamboo. The road passes along the eastern flanks of the pointed volcanic mountain peaks of the Pitons du Carbet. Several well-marked hiking trails lead from the Route de la Trace into the rain forest and up to the peaks.

The road follows a route cut by the Jesuits in the 17th century; islanders like to say that the Jesuits' fondness for rum accounts for the twisting nature of the road.

Less than a 10-minute drive north of Fort-de-France, you'll reach the **Sacré-Coeur de Balata**, a scaled-down replica of the Sacré-Coeur Basilica in Paris. This interesting domed church, in the Roman-Byzantine style, has a stunning hilltop setting – the Pitons du Carbet rise up as a backdrop and there's a view across Fort-de-France to Pointe du Bout below.

The **Jardin de Balata**, on the west side of the road a 10-minute drive north of the Balata Church, is a mature botanical garden in a rain-forest setting. Walkways wind past tropical trees and flowers including lots of ginger, heliconia, anthuriums and bromeliads. Many of the plants are numbered; you can pick up a free corresponding handout listing 200 of the specimens with their Latin and common French names. This pleasant garden takes about 30 to 45 minutes to stroll through and is a great place to photograph flowers and hummingbirds. It's open 9 am to 5 pm daily. Admission is 35F for adults, 15F for children.

After the garden, the N3 winds up into the mountains and reaches an elevation of 600m before dropping back down to **Site de l'Alma**, where a river runs through a lush green gorge. There are riverside picnic tables, trinket sellers and a couple of short trails into the rain forest.

Four kilometers later the N3 is intersected by the D1, a winding scenic drive that leads west 14km via Fond Saint-Denis to Saint-Pierre. Just beyond this intersection, N3 leads through a cobblestone tunnel, and a kilometer beyond that, on the east side of the road, is the signposted trailhead for **Trace des Jésuites**. This popular hike is 5km long and takes about three hours one-way. It winds up and down through a variety of terrain, ranging in elevation from 310m at the Lorrain River crossing to 670m at its termination on the D1.

Continuing north on the N3, the Route de la Trace passes banana plantations and flower nurseries before reaching a T-junction at Morne Rouge, on the southern slopes of Mont Pelée. From here, the N2 winds west 8km down to Saint-Pierre, while the N3 heads east to Ajoupa-Bouillon.

Morne Rouge was partially destroyed by Mont Pelée in August 1902, several months after the eruption that wiped out Saint-Pierre. At 450m it has the highest elevation of any town on Martinique, and it enjoys some nice mountain scenery.

About 2km north of the T-junction, a road (D39) signposted to Aileron leads 3km up the slopes of Mont Pelée, from where there's a rugged trail (four hours roundtrip) up to the volcano's summit.

LES OMBRAGES

Les Ombrages (☎ 53 31 90) is a botanical garden at the site of a former rum distillery. A trail passes by stands of bamboo, tall trees with buttressed roots, torch gingers and the ruins of the old mill. It's a nice jungle walk.

The garden is open 9 am to 5 pm daily. Tour guides lead 45-minute walks, in French only. Admission is 20F for adults and 10F for children. Les Ombrages is 250m east of the N3, immediately north of the town of Ajoupa-Bouillon.

BASSE-POINTE

As the N3 nears the Atlantic it meets the N1, which runs along the coast both north and south. The northern segment of the road edges the eastern slopes of Mont Pelée and passes through banana and pineapple plantations before reaching the coastal town of Basse-Pointe.

Leyritz Plantation

Leyritz Plantation, dating from the early 18th century, is a former sugar plantation that now houses a hotel and restaurant.

It's an interesting place with a parklike setting. You can stroll around the grounds at your leisure and explore some of the old buildings. Most intriguing is the former plantation house, a weathered two-story building with period furnishings.

Inside the gift shop near the entrance is a 'museum' that's essentially a small collection of Victorian-style dolls made of dried plants and fibers.

If you're not eating at the plantation it costs 15F (children 5F) to explore the grounds and visit the museum. It's open 9 am to 5 pm daily. The plantation is on the D21, 2km southeast of Basse-Pointe.

Places to Stay & Eat

The *Leyritz Plantation (☎ 78 53 92, fax 78 92 44, 97218 Basse-Pointe)* has 67 guest rooms spread across its grounds, many in the old plantation quarters. Rooms vary, but most are comfortable and full of atmosphere. Some of the nicer ones are in the renovated stone cottages that once served as dwellings for married slaves. All rooms have air-con, TV and phones, some have minibars, and there's a pool and a tennis court. It's a popular place with returning retirees from mainland France, but its secluded country setting may prove too remote for first-time visitors intent on exploring the entire island. Rooms start at 470F in summer, 630F in winter, breakfast included.

The Leyritz Plantation dining room, within the old stone walls of the refinery, has an engaging setting despite the rush of tour buses that arrive at lunchtime. A set lunch of various Creole foods costs 120F; otherwise salads and main dishes begin around 60F. It's open from noon to 2:30 pm and from 7 to 9 pm.

In the center of Basse-Pointe, along the main road, *Chez Mally (☎ 78 51 18)* is a pleasant little family restaurant serving home-cooked food at honest prices. Chicken colombo is 70F; you can get a daily set meal that includes dessert for the same price. If you're heading toward Grand-Rivière it's on the right, just before the cultural center, at Ruelle Saint-Jean.

GRAND-RIVIÈRE

From Basse-Pointe it's a pleasant 20-minute drive to Grand-Rivière along a winding, but good, paved road. En route you'll go through the coastal village of Macouba,

where there's a rum distillery, pass two trails leading up the northern flank of Mont Pelée, cross a couple of one-lane bridges and finally wind down into Grand-Rivière.

Grand-Rivière is an unspoiled fishing village scenically tucked beneath coastal cliffs at the northern tip of Martinique. Mont Pelée forms a rugged backdrop to the south while there's a fine view of neighboring Dominica to the north.

The road dead-ends at the sea where there's a fish market and rows of bright fishing boats lined up on a little black-sand beach. The waters are sometimes good for surfing at the west side of town. The syndicat d'initiative, in the town center, has local tourist information and organizes guided hikes in the region.

While there's no road around the tip of the island there is a 20km hiking trail leading to Anse Couleuvre, on the northwest coast. The trailhead begins on the road opposite the quaint two-story *mairie* (town hall), just up from the beach. For more information see the Hiking section, earlier in this chapter.

Places to Stay & Eat

The *Chanteur Vacances (☎ 55 73 73, 97218 Grand-Rivière)* is a restaurant and hotel with friendly management. There are seven straightforward rooms on the 3rd floor that cost 160/230F for singles/doubles, breakfast included. The 2nd-floor restaurant has fixed-price meals with soup or salad, Creole rice and ice cream or fruit. The cost depends on the main dish, ranging from 76F for fish blaff to 123F for lobster, the house specialty. Lunch is from noon to 4:30 pm.

Chez Tante Arlette (☎ 55 75 75), about 50m from the syndicat d'initiative, is another Creole restaurant with three-course meals (from 80F for chicken to 150F for lobster) and a handful of simple rooms (doubles 200F, 300F with air-con, breakfast included) on the floor above. Meals are served from noon to 9 pm.

Yva Chez Vava, on the outskirts of town near the river, is slightly more upmarket and has fine Creole fare with an emphasis on seafood. A full meal will cost from 100F to 170F. It's open from noon to 5 pm.

BASSE-POINTE TO LAMENTIN

The highway (N1) from Basse-Pointe to Lamentin runs along relatively tame terrain and is not one of the island's most interesting drives, although there are a few worthwhile sights. The communities along the way are largely modern towns that become increasingly more suburban as you continue south.

Fond Saint-Jacques (☎ 69 10 12), 2km north of Sainte-Marie, is the site of an old Dominican monastery and sugar plantation dating from 1660. One of the early plantation managers, Father Jean-Baptiste Labat, created a type of boiler (the *père labat*) that modernized the distilling of rum. During the French Revolution, the plantation was confiscated by the state and it's now under the domain of the local government, which is developing it as a cultural center. The chapel and most of the living quarters are still intact and there are many ruins on the grounds including those of the mill, distillery basins, boiling house and sugar factory. This site, 150m inland from the N1, is open 8:30 am to 5 pm weekdays and by appointment weekends.

The **Museé du Rhum** (☎ 69 30 02), at the site of Saint-James Plantation's working distillery, is a fun place to stop. The plantation is on the D24, 200m west of the N1, on the northern outskirts of Sainte-Marie. There are both indoor and outside displays of old sugar-making equipment including steam engines, rum stills and cane-crushing gears. There's also a tasting room where you can sample different rums, and if you don't get too heady you might want to go out back to check out the sugar mill and distillery. Admission is free for poking about on your own, or you can join a guided tour for 20F. It's open 9 am to 5 pm weekdays, to 1 pm weekends.

The road continues south through cane fields and passes the **Presqu'île de Caravelle** (Caravelle Peninsula), which can make an interesting side trip if you have extra time. On the north side of the peninsula there are

a couple of nice protected beaches, Tartane and Anse l'Étang. Tartane, the larger of the two, has lots of fishing shacks and colorful gommier boats; both places have plenty of beachside restaurants selling everything from crêpes and ice cream to pizza and Creole food. Out at the tip of the peninsula are the deteriorated ruins of Château Dubuc, an old 17th-century estate whose master gained notoriety by using a lantern to lure ships into wrecking off the coast and then gathering the loot. The site has trails and a small museum (10F).

Southern Martinique

The southern part of Martinique has many of the island's best beaches and most of its hotels. The largest concentration of places to stay is in the greater Trois-Îlets area, which encompasses Pointe du Bout, Anse Mitan and Anse-à-l'Ane. Other important resort areas are Diamant and Sainte-Anne.

The interior of the southern half of the island is largely a mix of agricultural land and residential areas. Lamentin, the site of the international airport, is Martinique's second-largest city but like other interior towns has little that is targeted for tourists.

TROIS-ÎLETS

Trois-Îlets is a pretty little village with a central square that's bordered by a small market, a quaint town hall and the church where Empress Josephine was baptized in 1763. Despite its proximity to the island's busiest resort area, the village retains a delightful rural charm that's unaltered by tourism.

Pointe du Bout and Anse Mitan (both of which use Trois-Îlets as their postal address) are a few kilometers west of the village center, as are the island's golf course, the birthplace of Josephine and a small botanical park.

The area's other chief attractions, a sugar museum and a pottery village, are both east of central Trois-Îlets.

Musée de la Pagerie

This former sugar estate was the birthplace of Marie Joseph Rose Tascher de la Pagerie, the future Empress Josephine. A picturesque stone building, formerly the family kitchen, has been turned into a museum containing Josephine's childhood bed and other memorabilia. Multilingual interpreters relate anecdotal tidbits about Josephine's life, such as the doctoring of the marriage certificate to make Josephine, six years Napoleon's elder, appear to be the same age as her spouse.

A couple of other buildings on the museum grounds contain such things as the Bonaparte family chart, old sugarcane equipment, and love letters to Josephine from Napoleon.

The road leading up to the museum, 1km inland, begins opposite the golf course entrance. The museum is open 9 am to 5:30 pm daily except Monday, and admission is 20F.

You can poke around in the ruins of the old mill directly opposite the museum for free.

Parc des Floralies

Parc des Floralies, halfway up the road to the Musée de la Pagerie, is a modest botanical park with a pond, picnic tables, a few birds in cages and identified plants and trees. It's open 8:30 am to 5 pm weekdays, 9:30 am to 1 pm weekends. Admission is 10F for adults, 5F for children.

Maison de la Canne

This worthwhile sugarcane museum occupies the site of an old sugar refinery and distillery. Artifacts include an old locomotive once used to carry cane from the fields to the distillery, some antique cane crushers and period photos. Displays are in both French and English. It's open 9 am to 5 pm daily except Monday. Admission is 15F for adults, 5F for children ages five to 12. The museum is on the D7, 1.5km east of Trois-Îlets' center.

Pottery Village

There's an interesting brick kiln and pottery village on the north side of the D7 1km east of Maison de la Canne. A sign ('Village de la Poterie') marks the red clay road that leads 750m to the site.

The main workshop is International Atelier Caraïbe, but there are a few other potters in the village as well, all working out of old brick buildings. You can watch them at work making cups, vases, figurines and jewelry. The wares are quite nice and the prices are reasonable.

POINTE DU BOUT

Pointe du Bout has Martinique's most frequented yachting marina and three of its largest resort hotels. The point is a Y-shaped peninsula, with the hotels fringing the coast and the marina in the middle. All roads intersect south of the marina, and traffic can get congested.

The three resorts (Bakoua, Le Méridien and Novotel Carayou) each have their own little sandy beaches. There's also a lengthy public beach, Plage de l'Anse Mitan, which runs along the western side of the neck of the peninsula between Pointe du Bout and Anse Mitan.

Information

Ferries to and from Fort-de-France leave from the west side of the marina, where a money-changing office, a laundry, the port bureau and marine supply shops are all clustered together.

Also at the marina is a newsstand, souvenir shops, boutiques and a Crédit Agricole, open 7:30 am to 12:30 pm Tuesday to Saturday and also 2:15 to 4 pm Tuesday to Friday.

Thrifty, Budget and Avis car rental agencies have offices near the peninsula's main intersection.

Places to Stay

The *Davidiana* (☎ 66 00 54, fax 66 00 70, 97229 Trois-Îlets) is a good-value 14-room hotel above the harborfront Restaurant Chez Choucroun. The rooms are modern and comfortable with private bath, air-con and one or two beds; some have balconies. Nightly rates, which are the same for one or two people, start at 195F.

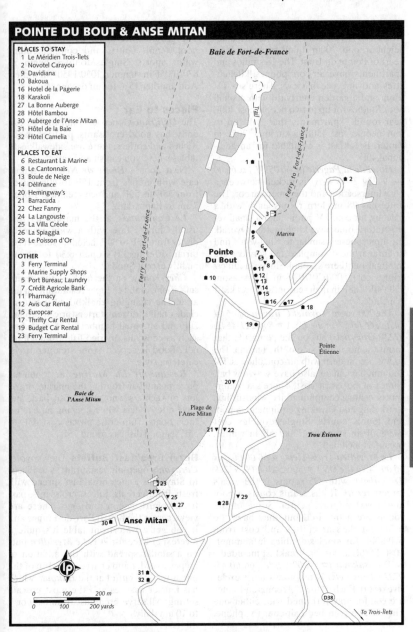

POINTE DU BOUT & ANSE MITAN

PLACES TO STAY
1 Le Méridien Trois-Îlets
2 Novotel Carayou
9 Davidiana
10 Bakoua
16 Hotel de la Pagerie
18 Karakoli
27 La Bonne Auberge
28 Hôtel Bambou
30 Auberge de l'Anse Mitan
31 Hôtel de la Baie
32 Hôtel Camelia

PLACES TO EAT
6 Restaurant La Marine
8 Le Cantonnais
13 Boule de Neige
14 Délifrance
20 Hemingway's
21 Barracuda
22 Chez Fanny
24 La Langouste
25 La Villa Créole
26 La Spiaggia
29 Le Poisson d'Or

OTHER
3 Ferry Terminal
4 Marine Supply Shops
5 Port Bureau; Laundry
7 Crédit Agricole Bank
11 Pharmacy
12 Avis Car Rental
15 Europcar
17 Thrifty Car Rental
19 Budget Car Rental
23 Ferry Terminal

Baie de Fort-de-France

Ferry to Fort-de-France

Ferry to Fort-de-France

Marina

Pointe Du Bout

Baie de l'Anse Mitan

Plage de l'Anse Mitan

Pointe Étienne

Trou Étienne

Anse Mitan

0   100   200 m
0   100   200 yards

To Trois-Îlets

D38

MARTINIQUE

Karakoli (☎ 66 02 67, fax 66 02 41, 97229 *Trois-Îlets*) is a pleasant little hotel in a quiet neighborhood, 100m uphill from the busy heart of Pointe du Bout. The 18 studios and apartments have air-con, phones, kitchenettes and fine ocean views. There's a TV room and a garden courtyard with a small pool. Studios for up to two people cost 400F year-round. Apartments that hold up to four people cost 450F in summer, 705F in winter. Breakfast is available for an additional 40F.

Hotel de la Pagerie (☎ 66 05 30, fax 66 00 99, 97229 *Trois-Îlets*) is tucked between a busy intersection and the inner harbor. The hotel has 98 modern rooms, each with a balcony, air-con, TV, phone and a small refrigerator; some have kitchenettes. Overall, the atmosphere is similar to what you'd find in an apartment complex and services are minimal, but there's a pool. Singles/doubles/triples cost 500/620/792F in low season, 760/940/1188F in high season, and breakfast is included.

The 200-room *Novotel Carayou* (☎ 66 04 04, fax 66 00 57, in the USA ☎ 800-221-4542, 97229 *Trois-Îlets*) sits on the peninsula that forms the northeast side of the marina. The rooms are modern with air-con, phones, TV and minibars; many also have sea-view balconies at no extra cost. There's a water-sports center, complimentary windsurfing, snorkeling and kayaking equipment, a pool and tennis courts. Singles/doubles cost 645/830F in summer, 700/935F in winter, breakfast included.

Le Méridien Trois-Îlets (☎ 66 00 00, fax 66 00 74, in the USA ☎ 800-543-4300, 97229 *Trois-Îlets*), with 295 rooms, is the area's largest resort. It has tennis courts, a pool and a water-sports center. Some of the rooms are a bit tired but they have the usual 1st-class amenities and cost from 670/800F for singles/doubles in summer, 1080/1480F in winter, breakfast included.

The *Bakoua* (☎ 66 02 02, fax 66 00 41, 97229 *Trois-Îlets*) is the area's most exclusive resort. Each of the 139 rooms and suites are comfortably furnished with either one king or two twin beds, air-con, TV, phone,

minibar, room safe and a terrace or balcony. The grounds are spacious and there's a pool, tennis courts and complimentary water sports. Singles/doubles begin at 830/1005F in summer, 1030/1950F in winter. Add another 15% for an ocean view.

Places to Eat

The *Délifrance*, open 6:30 am to 7:30 pm daily, has good croissants, pastries, sandwiches and coffees; there are sidewalk café tables where you can sit and eat.

Next door is *Boule de Neige*, a simple café with crêpes from 15F to 40F, salads from 35F to 50F and ice cream. It's open 7 am to 10 pm daily.

Le Cantonnais, at the marina, has the usual Chinese fare with a wide range of dishes from 55F to 60F, including some vegetarian offerings. It's open 6:30 to 11 pm nightly except Sunday.

Chez Fanny, on the neck of the peninsula, is one of the cheaper restaurants in the area. The changing chalkboard menu includes half a dozen starters priced around 20F and an equal number of main dishes, such as couscous or fried fish, from 40F to 60F. Food is served from steamer trays, cafeteria-style.

Restaurant La Marine, an open-air pizzeria and bar fronting the marina, draws lots of yachters who want to sit back and have a few beers while keeping an eye on their boats. Thin-crust pizzas cost 45F to 55F, seafood dishes around 75F.

Hotel Breakfast Buffets The *Novotel Carayou*'s open-air restaurant (see Places to Stay) has a nice breakfast spread with fresh fruit, cereals, juices, croissants, pastries, yogurt, bacon and eggs. There are views across the bay to Fort-de-France and if you get a waterfront table it's quite a nice experience for 70F. *Le Méridien* puts on a similar spread with the addition of crêpes to order and charges 60F. Top of the line is the 75F buffet at the *Bakoua*, which has fancier pastries and the most upscale setting. All serve breakfast from 6:30 or 7 to 10 am daily.

ANSE MITAN

Overall, the small seaside tourist area of Anse Mitan is cheaper and more casual than neighboring Pointe du Bout, a kilometer to the north. There are no large resorts, but rather a number of smaller moderately priced hotels and guest houses strung along the beach. The village, which has a cluster of restaurants, is also a popular dinner spot.

Anse Mitan has a pleasant view across the bay to Fort-de-France, to which it's connected by ferry. The sandy Plage de l'Anse Mitan extends north from the village.

Places to Stay

La Bonne Auberge (☎ 66 01 55, fax 66 04 50, 97229 Trois-Îlets) is a three-story hotel on the main road in the village center. The 32 rooms, which open onto a small garden courtyard, are simple with private baths, phones and either air-con or a ceiling fan. Singles/doubles cost 330/450F in summer, 420/610F in winter, breakfast included.

The *Auberge de l'Anse Mitan* (☎ 66 01 12, fax 66 01 05) is across from the beach in a quieter neighborhood south of town. Air-conditioned rooms go for 280/330F in low season, 330/420F in high season. There are also some larger studios available.

A good value is *Hotel de la Baie* (☎ 66 06 66, fax 63 00 70, 97229 Trois-Îlets), on a hillside a few minutes' walk from the main road, which has a dozen comfortable rooms with air-con, private bath, kitchenette and phone. Summer rates are 250F for a standard room, 320F for a room with a balcony, some of which have views of Fort-de-France. Winter rates range from 320F to 380F.

Hotel Camelia (☎ 66 05 85, fax 66 11 12, 97229 Trois-Îlets), a member of the Best Western chain, is a modern, reasonably priced hotel about a five-minute uphill walk from the village center, with panoramic views and a pool. Each of the 49 rooms is compact but pleasant, with air-con, TV, refrigerator, phone and private bath. About half of the units also have balcony kitchenettes for the same rate: 340F in summer, 563F in winter. Ask for a 2nd- or 3rd-floor room as they have views of Fort-de-France.

Hotel Bambou (☎ 66 01 39, fax 66 05 05, 97229 Trois-Îlets), at the south end of the road between Anse Mitan and Pointe du Bout, is a sprawling complex with 118 cabin-like duplex bungalows that often fill with package tourists. The simple units have rustic pine interiors, air-con and private baths. The complex is set back from the beach and there's a pool and restaurant. Singles/doubles start at 476/550F in summer, 700/810F in winter, breakfast included.

Places to Eat

There are a number of restaurants on the beach at Anse Mitan, serving tasty Creole seafood indoors and out on the sand. *Barracuda*, across the street from Chez Fanny, is great place to soak up some sun while enjoying a three-course menu for 50F to 70F.

Farther north, *Hemingway's* has similar fare (Creole menu for 70F) in a shady wooden beachside hideout, popular for evening drinks.

La Spiaggia, in the village center, attracts a crowd with a menu that includes good pizzas and pasta from 39F to 70F and a handful of meat dishes, heavy on the veal, for around 85F. It's open for lunch and dinner.

Le Poisson d'Or, on the road between Pointe du Bout and Anse Mitan, has a friendly Creole atmosphere, good food, generous portions and reasonable prices. Best value is the menu du jour for 80F, which includes accras or salad, Creole fish and dessert, but you can also order à la carte, with main dishes from 70F to 85F, or splurge on a three-course lobster meal for 200F. It's open for lunch and dinner daily except Monday in high season, dinner only in low season.

La Langouste, next to the Anse Mitan pier, is a popular bar and restaurant and the only place right on the water. There's a three-course meal for 100F that usually features grilled fish or chicken colombo. Otherwise, most beef or chicken main dishes average 65F, seafood dishes 80F, and lobster

MARTINIQUE

is available at market prices. It's open daily for lunch and dinner.

La Villa Créole, a top-end French/Creole restaurant, features two fixed menus at 160F and 250F. The cheaper includes a starter, grilled fish and dessert, while the more expensive pairs salmon pâté with half a lobster. There's also an à la carte menu with main dishes averaging 90F and a fixed children's menu for 55F. It's open for dinner daily except Sunday.

ANSE-À-L'ANE

Anse-à-l'Ane is a modern seaside village with a nice beach of light gray sand. The north side of the village is largely residential, while the south side is developed for tourism; it's quite compact and nothing is more than a few minutes' walk from anywhere else. The bay, which is generally calm, is a rather popular anchorage for yachts. At night you can see the lights of Fort-de-France twinkling across the water.

Anse-à-l'Ane is connected to Fort-de-France by ferry, and on weekends the beach attracts a crowd. The ferry dock is in the center of the beach, near Le Nid Tropical.

Places to Stay

Le Nid Tropical (☎ 68 31 30, 97229 Trois-Îlets) has simple bungalows along the beach for 200F; add another 50F if you want air-con. If you have your own gear, it's also possible to camp on the beach. It costs 60F for one person, 100F for two people, to pitch a tent.

Le Tulipier (☎ 68 41 21, fax 68 41 54, 7 Rue des Oursins, 97229 Trois-Îlets), family-run and a good value, consists of a dozen simple units with air-con and kitchenettes in a quiet residential area, a five-minute walk from the beach. Though weekly rentals are preferred, they'll rent out by the day if space is available: Studios cost 300F for two people, one-bedroom apartments cost 400F for up to four people. Rates drop about 10% in summer. Not much English is spoken, but the managers are patient with non-French-speakers.

The *Frantour* (☎ 68 31 67, fax 68 37 65, 97229 Trois-Îlets) is a fancy contemporary resort hotel conveniently located in the center of the beach. The 77 rooms have air-con, ceiling fans, TV, minibars, room safes and small balconies or terraces. There's a pool and a water-sports center with kayaks, sailboats and sailboards along with a popular dive shop. Singles/doubles begin at 450/550F in summer, 790/1200F in winter.

Places to Eat

In addition to the restaurants at the hotels there are a number of places to eat on or near the waterfront. *La Case a Glace*, next to Le Nid Tropical, has ice cream, beer, sandwiches and Creole snacks. *Chez Jojo*, a popular local bar and eatery near the Texaco gas station, has Creole seafood dishes and meat or fish brochettes for 40F; the daily menu is 70F. In the town center there's a *8 à Huit* supermarket where you can easily stock up on groceries and picnic supplies.

GRAND ANSE

Grand Anse, on Grand Anse d'Arlet Bay, is lined with brightly painted fishing boats and beachside restaurants. On weekends the area is packed with urbanites from Fort-de-France, yachters and other tourists.

Grand Anse has lots of boat traffic, but good snorkeling can be found along the south end of the bay just off Morne Champagne, the volcanic peninsula that separates Grand Anse from Anse d'Arlet. A trail at the south end of the beach leads up to the top of Morne Champagne.

Places to Eat

The beachfront road has a few restaurants with reasonably priced meals, and it's easy to stroll along the beach and compare menus. A number of places offer a three-course menu du jour for 65F to 90F. *Chez Gaby*, a simple, pleasant beachfront restaurant directly across from the pier at the south end of the bay, has spicy Creole specialties like fish soup (38F) and *feroce d'avocat* (40F).

GRAND ANSE TO DIAMANT

The coastal road south of Grand Anse passes through **Anse d'Arlet** and **Petit**

Anse, two quiet seaside villages with a handful of restaurants and bars, and then winds around the south side of **Morne Larcher** (477m). As you come around a curve, the offshore islet Rocher du Diamant (Diamond Rock) pops into view before the road drops down to the town of Diamant. Beware of the rough road and high speed bumps near the beach on the western outskirts of Diamant.

A great place to stop for lunch, dinner or drinks, *Le Bois Lélé*, west of Diamant, has an excellent view of the ocean, friendly service and an elegant French flavor. The Creole menu is a very reasonable 79F; a complete lobster dinner, 160F.

DIAMANT

Diamant is a small seaside town facing Diamond Rock. The center of Diamant is far more local than touristy in character, and even though a number of hotels list Diamant as their address, most are on the outskirts of town, with the biggest resorts a couple of kilometers to the east.

A long and narrow gray-sand beach extends nearly 2km along the west side of Diamant. Despite being less than 100m from the D37, the beach has a delightfully natural setting with a wooded strip of sea grape, coconut and tropical almond trees providing a buffer between the waterfront and the road. The whole beach is quite popular; several pull-offs along the main road provide beach access.

Places to Stay

The *Diamant les Bains* (☎ 76 40 14, fax 76 27 00, 97223 Diamant) is a small in-town hotel with a pleasant West Indian character. It has a pool, a landscape of flowering plants and a nice beachfront view, although the beach itself is narrow and not terribly appealing. The rooms are small and straightforward, but not uncomfortable, and have air-con, twin beds and phones, while the bungalows also have refrigerators. In summer, rooms cost 310/380F for singles/doubles; bungalows cost 380/450F. In winter, rooms cost 380/500F, bungalows 480/600F. Rates include breakfast.

The beachside *Village du Diamant* (☎ 76 28 93, La Dizac, 97223 Diamant) is a three-story hotel 2.5km west of Diamant's center. The 59 modern studio-style rooms have air-con, balconies, kitchenettes and phones. There's a pool and a TV lounge. Singles/doubles cost 700F in winter, 400F in summer.

The *Marine Hôtel* (☎ 76 46 00, fax 76 25 99, Pointe de la Chéry, 97223 Diamant) is a modern 150-room resort hotel situated on a predominantly rocky shoreline. It lies about 2km east of Diamant's center and on the same peninsula as the Novotel. The rooms have air-conditioning, both a king bed and a sofa bed, room safes, kitchenettes on the balconies and nice ocean views. There's a restaurant, a large pool, tennis courts and water sports. Single/double rooms are priced at 550/730F in summer and 800/1080F in winter.

Diamond Rock

The 176m-high Rocher du Diamant, or Diamond Rock, is a gumdrop-shaped volcanic islet 3km off the southwestern tip of Martinique. It is a haven for seabirds and favored by scuba divers, but most intriguing of all is its history.

In 1804 the British landed 120 sailors on Diamond Rock who quickly established barracks and warehouses within the rock's caves and cliffs, reinforcing it all with cannons. In one of the more unusual moments of British military history, the Royal Navy then registered the rock as a fighting ship, the unsinkable HMS *Diamond Rock*, and for the next 17 months used it to harass French vessels trying to navigate the passage. French attacks proved unsuccessful until French Admiral Villaret de Joyeuse devised a plan to catch the enemy off balance. According to the French account, the admiral cut loose a skiff loaded with rum in the direction of Diamond Rock, the isolated British sailors chugged down the hooch and the French forces retook the island.

MARTINIQUE

The ***Novotel Diamant*** (☎ 76 42 42, fax 76 22 87, Pointe de la Chéry, 97223 Diamant) has a secluded location at the end of the peninsula that forms the eastern edge of Diamant Bay. This is the area's largest and most exclusive resort. The 180 rooms feature air-con, TV, phones and room safes. There are a couple of restaurants, a car rental agency, a pool, a white-sand beach and complimentary water sports. Singles/doubles cost 680/910F in summer, 1070/1430F in winter.

Places to Eat

For cheap eats in the town center, there's the ***Restaurant Snack 82***, with sandwiches, burgers and fried chicken, on the waterfront opposite the church. For pizza there's ***Pizza Pépé***, a couple of minutes' walk southeast of the town hall, by the Esso station.

There are half a dozen cozy little restaurants on either side of the town hall. ***Chez Lucie*** has a waterfront location with a great view of Diamond Rock and very tasty local Creole food at reasonable prices. At lunch and dinner you can get a three-course meal with goat colombo or lambi fricassee for 95F, with lobster for 125F.

MARIN

Marin, at the head of a deep protected bay, is one of the island's two sub-prefectures and the region's commercial center. A large marina on the west side of town offers full yachting services and is home port to Martinique's yacht charter industry.

In the center of town, opposite the tourist office, there's a handsome stone church that dates from 1766. To get there turn south off the main road at Rue Schoelcher; the church is on the plaza just 200m down.

SAINTE-ANNE

Sainte-Anne, the southernmost village on Martinique, has an attractive seaside setting. Its most popular swimming beach is the long, lovely strand that stretches along the peninsula to Club Med, a kilometer north of the town center. Despite the number of visitors that flock to the town on weekends and during the winter season, Sainte-Anne remains a casual, low-key place.

The area waters have abundant nearshore reef formations that make for good snorkeling. If you want to see the underwater world without getting your feet wet, Aquascope, a semi-submerged vessel with viewing windows, operates daily at 9:30 and 11 am, 2 and 3:30 pm and charges 120F for adults, 60F for children.

Places to Stay

There's camping available at ***Vivre & Camper*** (☎ 76 72 79, fax 76 97 82, BP 8, Pointe Marin, 97227 Sainte-Anne), opposite the beach near Club Med Buccaneer's

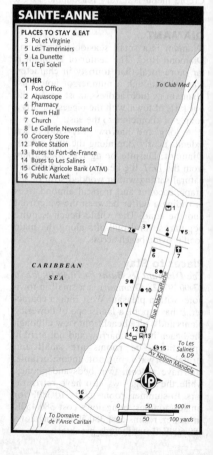

SAINTE-ANNE

PLACES TO STAY & EAT
3 Poi et Virginie
5 Les Tameriniers
9 La Dunette
11 L'Epi Soleil

OTHER
1 Post Office
2 Aquascope
4 Pharmacy
6 Town Hall
7 Church
8 Le Gallerie Newsstand
10 Grocery Store
12 Police Station
13 Buses to Fort-de-France
14 Buses to Les Salines
15 Crédit Agricole Bank (ATM)
16 Public Market

To Club Med

CARIBBEAN SEA

Rue Abbé Saffache

To Les Salines & D9

Av. Nelson Mandela

To Domaine de l'Anse Caritan

0   50   100 m
0   50   100 yards

Creek. At this well-organized campground, you can rent an equipped tent for 160F a day (minimum three nights) or set up your own tent and pay just 50F. The campground is very popular and often fills during the summer and on holiday weekends.

In town, *La Dunette* (☎ 76 73 90, fax 76 76 05, 97227 Sainte-Anne) has 18 modern rooms with air-con, hair dryers and phones. Some of the rooms have balconies looking out over the water, and there's a small beach fronting the hotel and a nice little restaurant. Singles/doubles cost 300/400F in summer, 500/600F in winter, breakfast included.

Hameau de Beauregard (☎ 76 75 75, fax 76 97 13, 97227 Sainte-Anne) is a modern condolike hotel on the D9, about 500m southeast of the village center. A family-oriented hotel, it has 90 studio and one-bedroom units with kitchenettes, air-con, TV, phones and balconies. Rates start at 490F in summer, 690F in winter. There's a pool.

Domaine de l'Anse Caritan (☎ 76 74 12, fax 76 72 59, 97227 Sainte-Anne) has a secluded location 1km south of the village center. This modern hotel has 96 contemporary rooms with kitchenettes, air-con, phones and terraces or balconies. There's a restaurant, dive center, a pool and a white-sand beach. Singles/doubles cost 675/775F in summer, 897/1077F in winter; add 120F for an ocean view.

Club Med's Buccaneer's Creek (☎ 76 72 72, fax 76 72 02, 97227 Sainte-Anne) is at the end of the Pointe Marin peninsula that juts out north of Sainte-Anne. It's fronted by a lovely white-sand beach and is virtually a little village unto itself. There are 300 rooms with air-conditioning, queen or twin beds, and the usual Club Med amenities. Weekly rates for singles/doubles, including meals, begin at 4200/8400F in summer and 6300/10500F in winter, but they'll also rent rooms for 740F per person per day if there's a vacancy.

Places to Eat

There are numerous reasonably priced eateries on the beach near the campground

north of Sainte-Anne's center, serving up everything from sandwiches, pizzas and crêpes to three-course meals du jour (60F to 90F).

In the town center, there's a snack bar on the coastal road in front of the public market and a grocery store a minute's walk to the north. In the same area, *L'Epi Soleil* sells pastries, bread and sandwiches and has a small dining area.

Also in the village is the upscale *Poi et Virginie*, which has a cozy waterfront setting. Starters and desserts are priced from 35F (75F for a dozen local oysters), while main courses range from goat colombo for 67F to grilled lobster for 190F.

If you're looking for a splurge in St Anne, head straight to *Les Tameriniers* (☎ 76 75 62, 97227 St Anne), north of the church, and do not hesitate to get in on such treats as avocado with lobster (70F) and whole grilled fish stuffed with crab (75F), washed down with good French wines or the biggest Lorraines ever. The atmosphere is chic, the staff is friendly and the food is worth every franc.

LES SALINES

Les Salines, at the undeveloped southern tip of the island, is widely regarded as Martinique's finest beach. The long stretch of golden sands attracts hundreds of visitors, scantily clad French tourists and local families alike, on weekends and holidays, but it's big enough to accommodate everyone without feeling crowded.

Les Salines is 5km south of Sainte-Anne at the end of the D9. There are showers and food vans near the center of the beach, and about 500m farther south you'll find snack shops selling reasonably priced sandwiches, burgers and chicken. Camping is allowed at the west side of the beach on weekends and during school holidays.

Les Salines gets its name from Étang des Salines, the large salt pond that backs it. Beware of poisonous manchineel trees (most marked with red paint) on the beach, particularly at the southeast end. There's some nice snorkeling at the west end of the beach.

Savane des Pétrifications

From the end of the D9 highway at Les Salines, the road continues southeast along the beach for another 2km to the site of a petrified forest that unfortunately has been heavily scavenged by decades of souvenir hunters. A blazed trail makes it way through the former forest; the trail begins at the end of the road. It is also possible to continue walking up along the coast; the track continues all the way to Macabou, about 25km away.

Montserrat

Montserrat, a small island that has long prided itself on its unspoiled rural character, has had its serenity shattered by an awakening volcano.

Ever since July 18, 1995, when the Soufrière Hills Volcano ended 400 years of dormancy, the island has had to come to grips with living with an active volcano as a neighbor. Plymouth, the island's capital and

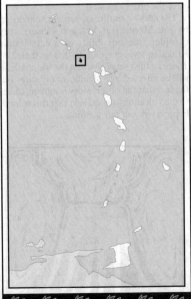

only significant town, had the misfortune of being just a couple of miles from the volcano and was abandoned soon after the initial eruptions, as drifting ash settled over it.

With the evacuation of Plymouth and nearby villages, more than half of the island's 11,000 residents suddenly became homeless. Some went overseas; others resettled elsewhere on the island, particularly in the Salem area, which became a makeshift boomtown.

Shortly after the eruptions began, a cadre of vulcanologists and other scientists from the UK, Trinidad and the USA rushed to Montserrat to study the Soufrière Hills Volcano and advise the government on its status. Based on the data they provided, the island was divided into seven 'volcanic risk zones,' rated from A for high risk to G for low risk. Every place riskier than the mid-range – essentially all parts of the island south and east of Plymouth – was declared off-limits.

Nonetheless, since much of the island's food was grown on small farms in an exclusion zone that ran from the hazardous northeast slopes of the volcano up to just south of the airport, farmers continued to tend livestock and work many of the off-limit fields.

On June 25, 1997, the volcano erupted violently with avalanches of fiery debris and ash that raced down its northeastern slope, engulfing a half-dozen villages in the off-limits zone between Soufrière Hills and the airport. Helicopters searched the charred villages for survivors and airlifted five burn victims to hospitals on Guadeloupe and Martinique. In all, more than 50 people were rescued by the helicopters, which had to lower harnesses because the earth was too hot for landings. Nineteen people, most of them farmers, were killed.

In the wake of the eruption, the safety zone was redrawn, cutting the still-habitable area of the island by half. Salem, which had become the island's temporary capital after the evacuation of Plymouth, was now on the wrong side of the exclusion zone, which for many meant an unwelcome second evacuation.

In August 1997, a superheated pyroclastic flow (see 'Don't Try This at Home') entered the abandoned town of Plymouth, setting it on fire. One of the Caribbean's most appealing West Indian capitals, lined as it was with period wood-and-stone houses, was lost as the blaze destroyed an estimated 80% of the buildings.

The volcano has cooled somewhat over the last few years, but it still lets off steam on a regular basis. Though recent events are fresh in the minds of all Montserratians, those who have stayed are making a go of it. Life has regained some semblance of normalcy in the wake of the devastation, and the safety lines have been redrawn and pushed south to include Salem again. Tourism is a low-key affair but doors are opening once again to visitors.

Even though only a third of the island can be visited, there's still enough to keep you busy for a few days. Montserrat's main attraction (apart form the volcano of course) is relaxation, and the slow, rural pace of the island will suit some holidaymakers perfectly.

Soufrière Hills Volcano

No one knows why the Soufrière Hills Volcano, which had been dormant since before the island was colonized in 1632, came to life when it did.

The first indications that an eruption could be in the making occurred in 1992, when seismographs began to record a growing number of minor earthquakes. The earthquakes led to the onset of the current eruption, beginning with a relatively small phreatic explosion that released steam and ash on July 18, 1995.

Since spring 1996, the volcano has been periodically producing superheated fast-moving pyroclastic flows that travel from the crater toward the ocean, destroying everything in their paths. These flows, along with noxious clouds of hot ash that can reach more than 15,000 feet high, have

provided the main hazards to life on the island.

The nature of the buildups and subsequent collapses of the lava dome within the volcano allows flows to move down the mountainside in different directions. Areas that have been hit by pyroclastic flows include the White River, south of the volcano; Plymouth, on the volcano's western slope; and the airport and nearby villages northeast of Soufrière Hills.

While scientists cannot predict exactly how the volcano will play out, many feel that volcanic activity on Montserrat will probably continue for at least a few more years. So far, following each eruption, material has continued to build up within the volcanic dome. The volcano's proximity to the capital – a mere 2½ miles – casts doubts that Plymouth will ever be deemed safe for rebuilding. The lava flows cannot be explored until 10 years after the volcano dies down, and the general consensus is that the entire southern part of the island may not be considered habitable for at least 20 years after the eruptions stop.

The latest scientific assessment announced by the Montserrat Volcano Observatory considers the possibility of a cataclysmic Krakatau-style eruption to be less than 2%. There is still a small risk that the whole island will be affected by a significant eruption, but the fact that the observatory is moving closer to the volcano is a good sign that this will not happen without fair warning.

Don't Try This at Home

Pyroclastic flows, which are common to Caribbean volcanoes, are comprised of hot rocks, ash, pumice and gases that can move at speeds of more than 100mph and reach temperatures in excess of 1000°F. They usually result from an explosive eruption or the collapse of a lava dome.

The lava domes themselves are made up of thick walls of extruded lava that build up in a cone shape atop an active volcano. These domes often have steep sides and become increasingly unstable as they grow. Under building pressure, entire sections of a lava dome can simply break away and tumble down the mountainside, filling the valleys below with volcanic debris.

Facts about Montserrat

HISTORY

Amerindians called the island Alliouagana, meaning 'Land of the Prickly Bush.' When Columbus sighted the island in 1493, he named it Montserrat, as its craggy landscape reminded him of the serrated mountains above the Monastery of Montserrat near Barcelona, Spain.

The first settlers from Europe were Catholics, mainly Irish, who moved to Montserrat in 1632 to escape persecution from Protestant rule on neighboring St Kitts. In the years that followed, Montserrat continued to attract Catholics from other New World colonies as well as new immigrants from Ireland. Many came as indentured servants who paid off their passage by toiling in the fields of the early plantations.

By the mid-17th century Montserrat was thick with sugarcane fields and the need for labor had outstripped the supply of Irish field hands. Over the next century thousands of African slaves were brought to Montserrat as the island developed the same slavery-based plantation economy found throughout the rest of the British West Indies.

For two centuries sugar production flourished and in its heyday in the 1760s more than 100 sugar plantations dotted the island. By the early 1800s the sugar market had deteriorated and with the abolition of slavery in 1834 many of the plantations slipped into decline. Some were divided among small farmers and planted with lime trees, a crop that attained a certain measure of success, but other estates were simply abandoned.

Montserrat has been under British control almost continuously since 1632. There were, of course, the usual skirmishes with the French, who held the island briefly in 1665 and 1712, thanks in part to assistance from Irish-born islanders who distrusted the English. The French moved in again in 1782, but the Treaty of Paris, signed in 1783, returned Montserrat permanently to the British.

With the breakup of the Federation of the West Indies in 1962, Britain offered self-government to all its Caribbean dependencies. Montserrat, too small to stand alone, balked at being lumped into a coalition government with either Antigua or St Kitts and successfully petitioned the British to remain a Crown Colony.

GEOGRAPHY

Montserrat is shaped like a teardrop, about 11 miles in length and 6 miles at its widest point. The total land area is 39 sq miles.

Three distinct mountains run down the center of the island. In the north, Silver Hill reaches a height of 1323 feet. In the middle are the Centre Hills, topped by the 2429-foot Katy Hill. The south is home to the Soufrière Hills, whose highest point before the volcano was the 3000-foot Chances Peak. Since the volcano has begun erupting, an active lava dome to the east of Chances Peak has grown to heights of 3180 feet.

CLIMATE

The coolest months are December, January and February, when average temperatures range from a low of 70°F (21°C) in the

MONTSERRAT

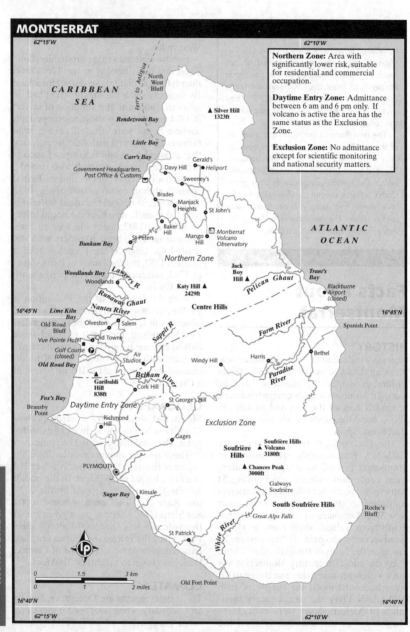

MONTSERRAT

Northern Zone: Area with significantly lower risk, suitable for residential and commercial occupation.

Daytime Entry Zone: Admittance between 6 am and 6 pm only. If volcano is active the area has the same status as the Exclusion Zone.

Exclusion Zone: No admittance except for scientific monitoring and national security matters.

CARIBBEAN SEA

Rendezvous Bay

North West Bluff

▲ Silver Hill 1323ft

Little Bay

Carr's Bay

Government Headquarters, Post Office & Customs

Gerald's

Davy Hill ● Heliport

Sweeney's

Brades

Manjack Heights

St John's

Baker Hill

St Peters

Mango Hill

Montserrat Volcano Observatory

Bunkum Bay

Northern Zone

ATLANTIC OCEAN

Woodlands Bay

Woodlands

Lawyers R

Katy Hill ▲ 2429ft

Jack Boy Hill ▲

Pelican Ghaut

Trant's Bay

Blackburne Airport (closed)

Runaway Ghaut

Nantes River

Centre Hills

Lime Kiln Bay

Olveston

Salem

Old Road Bluff

Old Towne

Vue Pointe Hotel

Golf Course (closed)

Old Road Bay

Air Studios

Sappit R

Windy Hill

Harris

Bethel

Spanish Point

Farm River

▲ Garibaldi Hill 838ft

Belham River

Cork Hill

St George's Hill

Paradise River

Fox's Bay

Bransby Point

Daytime Entry Zone

Richmond Hill

Gages

Exclusion Zone

Soufrière Hills

Soufrière Hills ▲ Volcano 3180ft

▲ Chances Peak 3000ft

Galways Soufrière

South Soufrière Hills

PLYMOUTH

Sugar Bay

Kinsale

White River

Great Alps Falls

Roche's Bluff

St Patrick's

Old Fort Point

Ferry to Antigua

0   1.5   3 km
0   1   2 miles

62°15'W   62°10'W
16°45'N
16°40'N

evening to a high of 83°F (28°C) in the day. From May to October, the average low is 74°F (23°C) and the average high is 88°F (31°C). The annual rainfall is about 59 inches (1500mm). Although there's no clearly defined rainy season, the driest time is generally between February and May.

FLORA & FAUNA
Montserrat has rain forests, tree fern forests, montane thickets and elfin woodland. The island is home to iguanas, agouti, large crapaud frogs, seven bat species and numerous bird species.

The long-term impact of the volcano on native flora and fauna remains unknown, but it certainly will be profound. For example, the national bird, the endemic Montserrat oriole, survives solely in the island's mountains. Prior to the volcanic eruptions, fewer than 500 pairs existed. A bamboo forest on the slopes of the Soufrière Hills contained the largest known oriole colony, but that forest was literally turned into an ash heap by the volcano.

Concerns about environmental damage reach beyond the land to Montserrat's surrounding coral reefs, some of which have been severely damaged by volcanic ash and flows.

GOVERNMENT & POLITICS
Montserrat remains, by its own volition, a British Overseas Territory. A governor, who represents the Queen, presides over both the executive council and the legislative council. Seven members of Montserrat's legislature are elected in general elections while four others are appointed.

Many Montserratians feel that the British were less than forthcoming in responding to the current crisis. There was confusion as to just what relocation aid would be provided to those who fled the island and to the level of commitment the British would make to rebuild Montserrat for those who stayed. Indeed, the British minister in London responsible for aid to Montserrat issued a dire warning of a possible cataclysmic eruption that could threaten the entire island, even while scientists on Montserrat were discounting the possibility of such an apocalyptic event.

In August 1997 a British offer to evacuate all remaining Montserratians was met with street protests by islanders who felt that the British, faced with the high costs of resettlement projects in the northern part of the island, were more concerned with keeping a lid on expenditures than they were in the well-being of Montserratians. The lack of clarity in government policy so frustrated islanders who were trying to decide whether to leave or stay that Montserrat's chief minister, perceived as being weak in his dealings with the British, was forced to resign.

Feelings have calmed over the last few years as the volcano has become part of everyone's daily life. The British Government has tentatively come to the party by agreeing to supply UK£60 to UK£65 million more in funding over the next three years to help Montserratians continue to rebuild.

ECONOMY
Before Soufrière Hills began erupting, Montserrat was self-sufficient in fruit and vegetable production, and even exported some small-scale crops such as herbal teas. Although only about 30,000 tourists visited Montserrat annually, tourism accounted for roughly 25% of the island's GNP. Tourist numbers dropped away to almost nothing after the eruption, but have picked up in recent years. In the year 2000, almost 15,000 tourists took advantage of Montserrat's hospitality.

Britain has been much criticized for failing to live up to its underlying obligations to Montserrat, and for keeping the hardships of the colony at arm's length. Partly to blame is the fact that Britain funds its few remaining dependent territories from the same overseas aid pool that it uses to fund development projects in unrelated Third World countries – meaning that Montserrat's claim has to be measured against those of some of the world's poorest nations. When perceived simply as aid to an overseas people, Britain's contributions to Montserrat could seem generous, but when viewed as disaster relief to colonial subjects by their own government, they appear tight-fisted.

Relocation aid from Britain also fell well short of what most people needed to adequately relocate (a measly US$3850 per adult, US$1000 per child) but about 1000 islanders moved to Britain, where most qualified for public housing. About 1000 more evacuees made their way to US territories and were offered work permits and temporary asylum. Most Montserratians, however, haven chosen to remain close to home. An estimated 3000 have relocated in nearby Antigua, some moving in with relatives, others living as refugees.

Stung by criticism in the press, the British government upped its funding to US$112 million in aid to redevelop the northern third of Montserrat.

POPULATION & PEOPLE
The pre-volcano population was about 11,000. Between 4000 and 5000 people remain on Montserrat, and there is a slow trickle of Montserratians returning to the island. Most inhabitants are of African descent, although there is an admixture of Irish blood.

ARTS
Every cloud has a silver lining, and one of the volcano's silver linings is its affect on the art of Montserrat. Many islands have felt the urge to express their feelings over the volcano, and have done so through dance, music, song, painting, poetry and photography. There's even a street theater company, appropriately named Ash, which performs regularly. Be sure to look out for craft shops scattered throughout the island selling local creations.

SOCIETY & CONDUCT
Although the island's African heritage remains strong, it blends uniquely with Irish influences. For instance, island folk dances incorporate Irish steps enlivened with an African beat.

Montserrat plays up its Irish connection (only two nations in the world have made St

Patrick's Day a public holiday, Montserrat and Ireland). Green shamrocks show up in business logos and are stamped into visitors' passports. There are nearly 100 Montserratian families with the surname Ryan and dozens of O'Briens, Galloways and Sweeneys; village names include the likes of St Patrick's, Kinsale and Cork Hill.

These days, the Montserratian most recognized throughout the Caribbean is Alphonsus Cassell, otherwise known as Arrow, whose tune *Hot! Hot! Hot!* is a soca classic.

RELIGION
Most Montserratians are Anglican, but Methodist, Pentecostal, Roman Catholic and Seventh Day Adventist denominations are also represented.

LANGUAGE
English is the main language on Montserrat, usually spoken with an island patois. Some islanders have a noticeable Irish brogue as well.

Facts for the Visitor

ORIENTATION
In general, Montserrat is very easy to navigate as there's one main road running around the edge of the island, from Salem in the west to Trant's Bay in the east passing through all the main villages. Helicopters land at Gerald's in the north, and ferries dock at Little Bay.

The only area on the island where things can get a bit confusing is around Salem and Old Towne, where roads head off in all directions and there's not one road sign in sight. In fact, there aren't any road signs anywhere on the island, so if you need to find somewhere, you'll have to ask for directions. The area around the old golf course near the daytime entry zone can also be puzzling as it's been covered in continuous mudslides. Locals have made their own tracks across the barren area and it's advisable to follow their lead.

It's pretty damn hard to accidentally enter the exclusion zone; steel gates don't allow cars to pass that easily.

Maps

It's a very good idea to pick up an up-to-date map, as the exclusion zones can change without notice. On arrival, the immigration office should provide you with a map, but if they have none check with the tourist office.

TOURIST OFFICES
Local Tourist Offices

Salem is home to the Montserrat Department of Tourism (☎ 491-2230, fax 491-7430, mrattouristboard@candw.ag). You can call, email or write PO Box 7, Montserrat, West Indies to request information. In addition, up-to-date information is available on the Montserrat tourism Web site found at www.visitmontserrat.com.

Tourist Offices Abroad

Overseas tourism representatives include:

Germany

Montserrat Tourist Board (☎ 40-695 8846, fax 40-380 0051) The West India Committee, Lomer Strasse 28, 22047 Hamburg

UK

Caribbean Tourism Organisation (☎ 020-7222 4335, fax 020-7222 4325) 42 Westminster Palace Gardens, Artillery Row, London SW1P 1RR

USA

Caribbean Tourism Organisation (☎ 212-635-9530, fax 212-635-9511) 80 Broad St, 32nd Floor, New York, NY 10004

VISAS & DOCUMENTS

All visitors must have a valid passport, with the exception of US, Canadian and British citizens who may instead present an official ID, such as a birth certificate, as proof of citizenship. Some countries may require visas; check with a British embassy or consulate.

An onward ticket is officially requested.

MONEY

The Eastern Caribbean dollar (EC$) is the official currency, but US dollars are also widely accepted. If you are staying any length of time, though, it's best to operate in EC dollars. Expect an exchange rate of around EC$2.70 to US$1.

POST & COMMUNICATIONS
Post

Montserrat's main post office is located in the Government Headquarters building near Carr's Bay. When writing, follow the business name with 'Montserrat, West Indies.'

It costs EC$1.15 to send either a postcard or 10g letter to almost anywhere in the world.

Telephone

When calling from overseas add the area code 664 to the local seven-digit number.

Card phones and coin phones are scattered throughout the northern zone. Cable & Wireless in Sweeney's sells phone cards.

Email & Internet Access

The public library, next to Erindell Villa in Woodlands, lets you check your email for free if you're quick. Grant Enterprises, in Davy Hill, is open 9 am to 5 pm Monday to Friday and provides Internet access for EC$15 a half hour.

INTERNET RESOURCES

A good source of information on the tourist aspects of Montserrat is the Web site www.visitmontserrat.com, run by the tourist office.

For in-depth knowledge on the history, activity and current consensus of the volcano, log on to www.mvomrat.com. It's quite comprehensive and information on the volcano is updated regularly. To listen to Radio Montserrat live online go to www.mratgov.com/zjb.htm.

NEWSPAPERS & MAGAZINES

The *Montserrat Reporter* is the local rag, and the monthly *Montserrat Newsletter* has stories and comments on daily life in Montserrat. *Holiday Montserrat,* a small but

MONTSERRAT

informative magazine produced by the tourist board, has lots of practical information and listings of the coming attractions and festivities.

RADIO & TV

Local radio station Radio Montserrat broadcasts on 91.9 and 95.5 FM (see also Internet Resources, earlier). Cable TV generally picks up US television.

ELECTRICITY

The electric current is 220V, 60 cycles.

WEIGHTS & MEASURES

Montserrat uses the imperial system.

HEALTH

The main hospital (☎ 491-2836) is located in St John's.

DANGERS & ANNOYANCES

Even though the volcano has calmed down slightly, it's still an active volcano that could blow its top at any moment. It's advisable to tune into the local radio station (91.9 or 95.5 FM) when driving around as it broadcasts warnings of any rumblings and/or eruptions and instructions on what to do should the island's warning sirens sound.

It's also a good idea to carry dust masks with you to be on the safe side. The prevailing winds seldom blow in a northerly direction, so the northern part of Montserrat does not receive much volcanic ash fallout. Nevertheless, on high-ash days, residents do commonly don dust masks as a health precaution. Your hotel or guest house will be able to provide you one.

Be aware that mudslides are quite common during and after rain in the Belham River valley area. If you're on the southern side of the old golf course, admiring the view from Garibaldi Hill or in the daytime entry zone, it's highly advisable to head back to the north side as soon as possible if rain looks imminent. The area is very susceptible to slides, which happen in an instant. The risks are high, and at the very least you could be stranded for a few days.

EMERGENCIES

For medical emergencies dial ☎ 491-2802. The main police station (☎ 491-2555) is in Salem.

BUSINESS HOURS

Offices and shops are generally open from 8:30 am to 4 pm Monday to Friday, while some shops also operate from 9 am to noon Saturday.

PUBLIC HOLIDAYS & SPECIAL EVENTS

Public holidays on Montserrat are:

New Year's Day	January 1
St Patrick's Day	March 17
Good Friday	late March/early April
Easter Monday	late March/early April
Labour Day	first Monday in May
Whit Monday	eighth Monday after Easter
Queen's Birthday	second Saturday in June
August Monday	first Monday in August
Christmas Day	December 25
Boxing Day	December 26
Festival Day	December 31

Montserrat observes March 17 not only for its Irish connection but also to commemorate a rebellion by island slaves in 1768. Montserrat's main festival begins on Christmas Eve and culminates with a jump-up on New Year's Day.

ACTIVITIES
Volcano Watching

Although Soufrière Hills is out of bounds, it can still be viewed from a couple of places on the island. The best vantage point is Garibaldi Hill, which is in the northern zone and is the only viewing point for Plymouth. To get there follow the main road south from Salem toward the daytime entry zone, and after crossing the mudslide turn right and follow the road around the base of the hill toward the sea. Take your next left, and another left, and follow the winding road up the hill, which stops about a 10-minute walk from the top. The views of smothered Plymouth and the smoking volcano are stupendous. There's talk of building a viewing platform with telescopes on top of the hill, but finding out when it'll happen is like asking how long a piece of string is.

Another viewing point is Jack Boy Hill on the east coast, but it's a fair hike from the road and the views aren't as spectacular.

At the time of writing the daytime entry zone was closed due to build-up in the dome, but normally it's open 6 am to 6 pm daily. The zone, encompassing an area west of the volcano, includes the deserted villages of Richmond Hill and Cork Hill and should prove to be an eerie place to visit. There's no charge for entering this zone.

Entering the exclusion zone is completely out of the question. Not only is it extremely dangerous, but you'll receive a heavy fine and be instantly deported.

Hiking
Over the last few years the National Trust (☎ 491-3086, mnatrust@candw.ag) and Forestry Rangers have marked out a total of 23 trails in the northern zone. The trails are mainly in the Centre Hills and around Silver Hill, and vary in intensity from short 15-minute walks to leg-numbing six-hour treks. For a map of the top trails, check with the National Trust, which is next door to the tourist office.

At the time of writing the Trust was in the process of creating the Oriole Trail, which will run through the Centre Hills and provide grand views of the volcano and the northern zone. Plans are afoot to build a campground with four or five sites along the way, making it easier on the legs.

It's possible to do the hikes by yourself, but the National Trust can arrange forest-ranger guides, which costs between EC$20 and EC$30 for a full day. Horse treks are also an option; the Trust can also organize these for you for EC$120 a day.

Diving & Snorkeling
The volcano has limited Montserrat's dive sites, and the majority are now found between Old Road Bluff and North West Bluff. The island's only dive shop, Sea Wolf (☎ 491-7807, fax 491-3599, krebs@candw.ag), in Woodlands, offers one-tank dives starting at US$40, two-tank dives for US$70, and kayak dives for US$50. They rent snorkel gear for US$10 a day.

Little Bay has an underwater snorkel trail 75 yards west of the jetty.

Beaches & Swimming
Montserrat is not the place to come if you're looking for a beach holiday. The eastern side is dangerous and rocky and a definite no-go. On the west coast, beaches generally have black sand, and are small but good enough for a dip.

Rendezvous Bay, Montserrat's only white-sand beach, is long and secluded and the island's best. There's no road to it, so you'll either have to rent a boat to take you there (around US$20) or make the 1½-hour trek from Little Bay.

Although the island's jetty is at Little Bay, the southern end of the bay is still good for swimming. Woodlands Bay and Bunkum Bay are possible destinations, but much of the sand has been washed away by the latest hurricanes.

ACCOMMODATIONS
The bulk of places to stay on Montserrat consist of small, friendly and accommodating guest houses or apartments. Prices are moderate for Caribbean standards and hover around the US$50 to US$70 mark. The island also has two hotels, one that is due to reopen and the other newly built. At the time of writing camping was not allowed, but the National Trust, in association with the Forestry Rangers, was in the process of building a campground in the Centre Hills.

You'll need to add between 7% and 10% government tax to the rates mentioned. Many places also add 10% service charge.

FOOD
You'll find a mixture of Creole and Continental dishes on most menus on Montserrat. Two local concoctions are worth testing on your taste buds – 'mountain chicken,'

which is actually a frog native to the island, and 'goat water,' a thick stew made from goat meat.

DRINKS

Water from the tap is safe to drink, but if you want bottled water it's available from the island's supermarkets.

Getting There & Away

DEPARTURE TAX

The departure tax is EC$35.

AIR

Landing at Blackburne Airport would be a very bumpy ride – it's been closed since June 1997 due to a volcanic flow across its runway. In its place a helicopter service has been set up to run between Antigua and Montserrat, and it proves to be quite a thrilling ride. Helicopters, operated by Carib Aviation (☎ 491-2533 in Montserrat, ☎ 268-462-3147 in Antigua), land at Gerald's where you can catch a taxi to other parts of the island. Seats are very limited (there are only eight in fact) so it's essential that you call and reserve your seat a few days before your departure date.

The service runs daily except Wednesday and helicopters leave from the airport in Antigua at 7:30 am, 10 am (except weekends), 3 pm (Sunday only) and 4:30 pm. From Montserrat trips are made at 8 am, 3:30 pm (except Saturday) and 5 pm. The fare is EC$89 roundtrip, half that for a one-way ticket.

SEA
Ferry

The 300-seat ferry *Opale Express* operates between Montserrat and Antigua daily except Sunday. The ferry departs from Heritage Quay in St John's, Antigua, at 6:30 am and 4 pm and arrives at Montserrat's jetty at Little Bay at 7:30 am and 5 pm. Return trips are made about 30 minutes after arrival on

Montserrat. You should check in one hour before departure to secure your seat. On weekends the fare is as low as EC$75 roundtrip, during the week it rises to EC$150.

For tickets contact Montserrat Aviation Services (☎ 491-2533) or Carib World Travel (☎ 268-460-6101), at Heritage Quay.

Yacht

Landing on the exclusion zone is strictly prohibited and will result in a hefty fine and deportation. Little Bay is the point of entry for yachts, and immigration can be cleared through the Montserrat Port Authority (☎ 491-3816, VHF channel 16).

Getting Around

BUS

Minivans provide the bus service around the island, and the fare is fixed at EC$2 no matter how far you intend to go. Buses are easy to spot as they all have 'H' license plates. The only problem is that taxis also have 'H' license plates, so check with the driver before hopping in or you may get a nasty surprise at the end of the journey. It's easy to hail a bus – just stand on the side of the road and wave.

CAR & MOTORCYCLE

If you want to explore the island in any detail it's best to rent some form of transport. The roads are generally in good condition, but they can get a little bumpy in places. Be prepared to do a lot of upper-body exercise – much of the island is hilly and the roads have a tendency to twist and turn as they go up and down.

Locals don't seem to need directions or signposts as they're aren't any on the island. The only way to find most places is to ask for directions.

Road Rules

Driving is on the left, and you'll need to purchase a Montserrat temporary license. The police headquarters in Salem or immigration issue them for EC$30.

Rental

None of the major car rental companies operate on the island, but the local populace has jumped on the business opportunity in enough numbers to satisfy all visitors' requirements. Expect to pay between US$30 and US$45 for either a car or jeep. The vehicles aren't in pristine condition, but they do the job well. The tourist office has a list of rental agencies, or check at your guest house for referals.

Tropical Mansions (☎ 491-8767) in Sweeney's rents 50cc scooters for EC$53 per day, 125cc motorcycles for EC$75 per day.

TAXI

It's not hard to find a taxi as they are on hand to meet ferry and helicopter arrivals. From Little Bay to Woodlands is EC$25, and from Gerald's it's EC$40. Your hotel or guest house should be able to arrange one for your departure.

ORGANIZED TOURS

For EC$120 you can enjoy an eight-hour tour of the island by taxi for up to four people.

A couple of tour operators in Antigua arrange full-day excursions to the Emerald Isle that include a tour of the island and its sights, breakfast and lunch, and a return trip on the ferry. Prices range between US$130 and US$150; contact Jenny's Tours (☎ 268-461-9361) or D&J Tours (☎ 268-773-9766) for more information.

Around Montserrat

Currently the only inhabited part of Montserrat is the northern third (albeit a large third) of the island. Consequently, northern villages that were once tiny and rural, such as Davy Hill and St John's, are now the island's main population centers. Only lightly settled before the volcano's eruption, the north is an attractive area with green landscapes, low mountains and a couple of Montserrat's better beaches.

Carr's Bay, a fishing village on the west coast, is thought to have been the landing site of the first Irish settlers. It has a roadside black-sand beach with a view of uninhabited Redonda Island to the northwest, and on a clear day you can also see Nevis beyond.

North of Carr's Bay is **Little Bay**, where there's a black-sand beach backed by hilly pastures. Little Bay serves as the island's main port. About a half-mile beyond Little Bay is appealing **Rendezvous Bay**, which has broad golden sands.

From Carr's Bay the main road cuts east across the island between **Silver Hill** and the **Centre Hills**. Midway is the village of **St John's**, where many island services are centered. **Gerald's**, north of St John's, has the island's heliport. East of St John's are a couple of newly constructed villages but largely it's uninhabited valleys. The road, which continues south, passes through rugged, untouched country and abruptly ends just north of the old airport, where lava crosses the runway and the villages become ghost towns.

Centre Hills, which act as a natural barrier between the volcano and the northern zone, are lush and green and offer some good hiking trails. Silver Hill, at the very north of the island, is not as forested as the Centre Hills, but still has a number of inviting hikes. The National Trust is in the process of creating a hiking-trail map of the island, so check when you're there.

Farther south along the west coast, **Woodlands** and **Salem** are starting to compete with the more northern villages for the largest population density. The area also has a couple of decent beaches, a few restaurants and bars, accommodations, the governor's office, the tourist office and the main police station. As the name suggests, Woodlands has just that, lots of lush, tropical woodlands.

Information

The tourist office (☎ 491-2230), on your right heading into Salem from the north by the main road, is open 8 am to 4 pm Monday to Friday.

The Bank of Montserrat, in St Peter's, is open 8 am to 2 pm Monday, Tuesday and

Thursday, to 1 pm Wednesday and 3 pm Friday. Royal Bank of Canada, at Olveston, has a 24-hour ATM and, with the exception of American Express and Royal Bank checks, charges EC$2 for cashing traveler's checks under EC$5000. It's open 9 am to 2 pm Monday to Thursday, to 3 pm Friday.

The main post office, in the Government Headquarters overlooking Carr's Bay, is open 8:15 am to 3:55 pm Monday to Friday.

National Trust

Occupying the same building as the tourist office is the National Trust, an organization set up to promote and protect the natural heritage and wildlife of Montserrat. Apart from helping to maintain and create hiking trails, the Trust has forged ahead with its plans to build a history center and botanical gardens next to its office. The center focuses on the history of the island, its flora, fauna and marine life and the effect the volcano has had on all aspects of island life. It also houses the Montserrat museum, which features artifacts dating back to the Amerindians and Arawaks.

The gardens are made up of the vegetation found on Montserrat.

At the time of writing the complex was not open to the public. Check with the tourist office for hours and admission prices.

Garibaldi Hill & Daytime Entry Zone

Garibaldi Hill and the daytime entry zone, near Plymouth, are the best places to view the volcano puffing away. For more details see the Activities section, earlier in this chapter.

Montserrat Volcano Observatory

The MVO, as it's been shortened to, has, in one shape or form, been observing the volcano since it first started acting up. A 30-minute tour of the office encompasses a rundown on the history of the volcano, a short video of the biggest and best eruptions and a look at the operations room, which has a wonderful machine that records

seismic activity (lots of squiggly lines), a monitor showing live pictures of the volcano, and a few people transfixed to computer screens.

For some reason they're based at Mango Hill and have absolutely no view of the volcano. But plans are afoot to move to Salem to get a bit closer, so check with the tourist office before making the steep drive up Mango Hill. The tour is at 3:30 pm Monday to Saturday, and is free of charge, but will cost EC$5 once the move has been made.

Runaway Ghaut

Runaway Ghaut is a short walk into the hills in the Woodlands area. The walk, which starts at a picnic area on the main road, isn't overly interesting but the natural spring close by is. Legend has it that once you've drunk from the natural spring you'll be drawn to Montserrat again and again during your lifetime.

Places to Stay

Accommodation options are few in number and visitors should make sure they have a room squared away before heading off to the island.

There are a couple of cottages within walking distance of Woodlands Bay, which makes for a nice base.

Egret House (☎ 491-5316) is a 400-sq-foot apartment at the Woodlands home of Salo and Gloria Boekbinder Mulder, an Anglo-Dutch couple. The unit, which has a queen bed, sitting area, kitchen and stunning views of Woodlands Bay and the ocean, costs US$50. There's also use of a pool.

Also in Woodlands, *Erindell Villa* (☎ 491-3655, erindell@candw.ag, PO Box 36) is one of the nicest and friendliest places you'll find in the Caribbean. Shirley and Lou Spycalla are wonderful hosts and make you feel quite at home. The rooms have two comfortable twin beds, limited cooking facilities, refrigerator, cable TV, phone, ceiling fan and private bathroom. Singles/doubles cost US$55/65, which includes Continental breakfast, email and laundry service, and use of their pool and snorkeling gear. The

Spycallas also offer lunch and dinner meals at reasonable prices.

Farther north, in Baker Hill, you'll find the *Grand View Bed & Breakfast* (☎ 491-2284, fax 491-6876, grand@candw.ag, PO Box 350), which has great views in all directions. The rooms vary in price, depending on the facilities. Singles/doubles are US$50/60 with shared bath, US$55/65 with private bath, and US$65/75 with private bath and kitchen.

Montserrat Moments Inn (☎ 491-7707, fax 491-3599, flogriff@candw.ag, PO Box 196), in Manjack Heights, has accommodating rooms with cable TV, refrigerator and air-con. There are email and laundry services, both US$5, and free mangoes when they're in season. Rooms are US$48/78, including Continental breakfast.

David Lea (☎ 491-5812, lead@candw.ag), in St Peter's, rents out two rooms in his home. The rooms have private patio and cable TV, and rates are US$45/55 including breakfast.

Vue Pointe Hotel (☎ 491-5210, fax 491-4813, PO Box 65), on the beach at Old Road Bay, which closed down after the volcano erupted, is finally due to reopen in the not-too-distant future. It's a pleasant family-run place with 36 cottages and hotel rooms with expansive views of Old Road Bay. Prior to closing costs ranged from US$90 to US$160.

Montserrat's newest hotel, *Tropical Mansion Suites* (☎ 491-8767, fax 491-8275, hotel@candw.ag), in Sweeney's, has a commanding view of Carr's Bay. Rooms have all the normal luxuries of a hotel, and cost US$90/120. Rooms with kitchenette are US$130/140, and there's a small pool.

It's possible to rent villas by the week around the island. Friendly *Tradewinds Real Estate* (☎ 491-2004, fax 491-6229, tradewinds@candw.ag, PO Box 365), in Olveston, has a number of fine choices on their books; contact them to get the going rate.

Places to Eat

The selection of places to eat isn't particularly large but is growing. The choices are evenly spread throughout the island, and there's usually something close by. If you're going out for a meal at night make sure to call ahead to check whether the restaurant is actually serving dinner. This means calling in the morning or in some cases the day before! Most places won't open unless there's enough customers to make it worthwhile, and often don't serve food after 7 pm.

Salem's *Attic Restaurant* (☎ 491-2008) is a good spot for lunch. The chicken roti (EC$9) is particularly tasty, and you have the choice of burgers, sandwiches and fish & chips for around EC$8 to EC$15. It's open 8 am to 4 pm Monday to Friday.

Danny and Margaret make the best tuna sandwich (EC$10) on the island at their beach bar *Jumping Jacks* (☎ 491-5645), on Old Road Bay. This is because Danny heads out fishing on Monday and Tuesday to keep the customers happy with fresh fish. Sunday lunchtime the bar is at its best, with crowds of people queuing up for the barbecue special (grilled fish, chicken, ribs) for EC$20. Choose from the tree- or veranda-shaded seating. It's open from 10 am to at least 7 pm Wednesday to Sunday.

Tina's Restaurant (☎ 491-3538), off the main road in Brades, is popular for both lunch and dinner. The menu is a mixture of all sorts, ranging from pizzas to filling chicken fried rice (EC$18). They also do great burgers (from EC$10 to EC$12) and sandwiches (from EC$8 to EC$15).

The Bitter End Beach Bar (☎ 491-3146), near the ferry terminal at Little Bay, is an open-air restaurant with a good reputation. It has a casual setting, and fresh lobster on hand for EC$65. Bring some insect repellent: Mosquitoes as big as small dogs turn up after sunset.

St John's is home to *Morgan's Place* (☎ 491-5419), where the colorful Mrs Morgan still cooks up – as she has for decades – the island's best goat-water stew.

It's reservations-only for dinner at *Ziggy's* (491-8282), one of the better, if not the best restaurant on the island. The menu will depend on what the chef has on hand and how he's feeling, but you'll invariably have choices such as butterfly shrimp, tenderloin steak and jerk pork, and it's sure to be good. Expect to pay around EC$100 for a full-course menu and drinks.

Economy Bakery, in Brades, has inexpensive sandwiches and freshly baked bread.

In Salem you'll find *Ram's Supermarket*, the island's biggest. It's open 8:30 am to 1 pm and 2:30 to 7 pm Monday to Saturday, and 9 am to noon and 5:30 to 7:30 pm Sunday.

Saba

Dubbed the 'Unspoiled Queen,' Saba (pronounced '**say**-bah') is both the smallest and loftiest of the islands that comprise the Netherlands Antilles. This ruggedly steep island has beautiful scenery, good hiking, pristine diving and strikingly little tourism.

Highlights

- Taking in Saba's crisp mountain air and bucolic scenery
- Diving the pristine waters of Saba Marine Park
- Making a hardy sunrise walk to the top of Mt Scenery
- Strolling Windwardside, with its lace makers and art galleries
- Enjoying the tranquil and friendly atmosphere of the island

OTHER MAPS
Saba page 348

Windwardside
page 358

CARIBBEAN
SEA

0   .5   1 km
0   .25   .5 mile

At first glance, Saba appears more like a misplaced Alpine community than part of the West Indies. As the tip of an immense underwater mountain, the island looms out of the sea, with no pause for lowlands or beaches. Saba's central volcanic peak, Mt Scenery, is cloaked in clouds. Its slopes are dotted with quaint white houses with green shutters, red roofs and gingerbread trim, while tiny vegetable plots sprout between rock-strewn hillsides.

The island has four villages, all spotlessly neat. Although The Bottom is the island's capital, Windwardside is the largest village and the most popular base for visitors. The villages of St John's and Hell's Gate are largely residential areas.

With only 1500 inhabitants on the isle, everyone on Saba knows everyone else. It's certainly one of the gentlest and friendliest places in the Caribbean.

Facts about Saba

HISTORY

Because of the island's rugged terrain, Saba was probably not heavily settled in pre-Columbian times. However, artifacts uncovered in the Spring Bay area indicate the existence of a small Arawak settlement at that site about 1300 years ago.

During his second trip to the New World, on November 13, 1493, Christopher Columbus became the first European to sight Saba. The Dutch laid claim to the island in 1632 and sent a party of colonists from St Eustatius in 1640 to form a permanent settlement. These early colonists originally lived at Middle Island and Mary's Point, where bits of a few cisterns and stone walls can still be found, but soon moved to The Bottom, which remains the administrative center of the island.

Because the steep topography of the island precluded large-scale plantations, colonial-era slavery was quite limited on

Saba. Those colonists who did own slaves generally had only a few and often worked side by side with them in the fields, resulting in a more integrated society than on larger Dutch islands.

GEOGRAPHY

Saba's land area is just 13 sq km, but because of its topography of folding mountains, Saba is far more substantial than any mere area measurement would indicate. The island is the emerged peak of an extinct volcano that rises to 887m at Mt Scenery, Saba's highest point and also the

highest point in the entire kingdom of the Netherlands.

There are no rivers or streams on the island. The leeward (western side) is dry with cacti and scrub, the windward (eastern) side has thicker vegetation, and the mountainous interior is given over to lush jungle growth.

CLIMATE

Saba's rainfall averages 1070mm (42 inches) a year. The mean monthly temperature is 27°C (80°F), with about a 2°C (4°F) variance from summer to winter. Because of the difference in elevation, temperatures are a bit cooler in Windwardside than in The Bottom. In winter, evening temperatures often dip to around 17°C (63°F), and while summers are generally a little more comfortable than on neighboring islands, hot and sticky summer nights are not unknown.

FLORA & FAUNA
Saba has a wide variety of flowering plants, ranging from the prolific oleander and hibiscus that decorate yards to the wildflowers and orchids that thrive in the rain forest. The elephant ear plant, found along the trails, has large leaves that make perfect umbrellas during the odd rain shower. Bird life is also abundant and varied, with more than 60 species sighted on Saba. Bridled terns, sooty terns and brown noddies breed on the island, tropic birds nest on the cliffs and frigate birds soar near the coast. Redtailed hawks can be spotted on the lower slopes, while thrashers and hummingbirds are found at higher elevations.

Saba has a harmless racer snake that's quite common to spot as it suns itself along trails and roadsides, although it generally darts off as people approach. Expect to see the friendly little *Anolis sabanus* lizard that's endemic to the island and to hear the tiny tree frogs whose wonderful symphony can be almost deafening at night. Mosquitoes are thankfully few on Saba.

GOVERNMENT & POLITICS
Saba is part of the Dutch kingdom, one of five islands in the Netherlands Antilles whose central administration is in Curaçao. As with the other four islands, Saba is treated as a municipality and has its own lieutenant governor who, along with two elected commissioners, is responsible for running the island's daily affairs.

ECONOMY
Although the scale of tourism is quite moderate, it is a major source of revenue for the island, second only to government employment. The largest growth of visitors has been among divers, who are attracted in ever-increasing numbers by Saba's pro-environmental stance and its superb diving conditions.

Until a few years ago Saba was a popular destination for young Dutch, who flew there to obtain their driver's licenses and escape strict and costly regulations in Holland. It was a thriving business for a handful of driving schools and for guest houses that catered to them, but new regulations put an end to the practice. One of the old driving schools in The Bottom has been converted into a small medical school for overseas students.

Sabans grow much of their own food, from Irish potatoes and taro to hydroponically grown lettuce. Locally caught fish and lobster are exported to neighboring islands. There's also a small quarry that exports crushed stone and gravel.

POPULATION & PEOPLE
Saba's permanent population is about 1500. It's fairly evenly divided between descendants of African slaves and descendants of the early Scottish, Irish and Scandinavian settlers. Most people can trace their lineage

---

The Impossible Road

Until a few decades ago, Saba's villages were connected solely by footpaths. For years engineers from low-lying Holland had declared that the island's steep terrain made road construction impossible.

One skeptical islander, Josephus Lambert Hassell, decided to take matters into his own hands. He enrolled in an engineering correspondence course and then organized a local construction team.

In the 1940s, Hassell's 20-man crew constructed the first section of the concrete road from Fort Bay to The Bottom, and over the next 20 years they gradually extended the road to Hell's Gate. They built the entire road by hand, and though it may be narrow and twisting, it is free of the patchwork potholes that characterize so many roads elsewhere in the Caribbean.

to one of half a dozen families, and just two names, Hassell and Johnson, account for almost a third of the phone-book listings. Incidentally, despite its Dutch government, Saba is home to very few people of Dutch descent.

SOCIETY & CONDUCT

Saba's culture is almost unique in the islands, with its mixture of Scottish, Irish and African heritages. It's a relatively conservative society: Nude bathing is not allowed on the island, and wearing a bathing suit within the villages is frowned upon.

RELIGION

Catholicism is the predominant religion on Saba, but the island's eight churches also include Anglican, Wesleyan Holiness and Seventh Day Adventist denominations.

LANGUAGE

Although Dutch is the 'official' language, English is the primary language of the island and the language most commonly spoken in the home. To accommodate this reality the Dutch government recently allowed the Saban school system to switch from Dutch to English as the principal classroom language. Schoolchildren now study Dutch as a second language. The local accent can sometimes be hard to understand, even to native English speakers, and comes across as a motley mix of Dutch/Irish/Caribbean just to make things more confusing.

Facts for the Visitor

ORIENTATION

It's virtually impossible to get lost on Saba. There is only one main road, which runs from the airport at the northeast side of the island, through the villages of Hell's Gate, Windwardside, St John's and The Bottom, and continues down to Fort Bay, the island's main port. A second road connects The Bottom with Well's Bay, on the island's northwest side.

Maps

The tourist office has free island maps that show the roads and hiking trails.

TOURIST OFFICES
Local Tourist Offices

The very helpful Saba Tourist Bureau (☎ 416-2231, fax 416-2350, iluvsaba@ unspoiledqueen.com) has its office in Windwardside. When requesting information by mail, write to Saba Tourist Bureau, PO Box 527, Windwardside, Saba, Netherlands Antilles.

Tourist Offices Abroad

Overseas tourism representatives include the following:

Germany
Dutch Caribbean Travel Center (☎ 069-24 00 18 30, fax 069-24 27 15 21) Karlstrasse 12, 60329 Frankfurt/Main

Netherlands
Antillen Huis (Kabinet van de Gevolmachtigde Minister van de Nederlandse Antillen; ☎ 070-306-6111, fax 070-306-6110) Badhuisweg 173–175, 2597 JP 'S-Gravenhage

VISAS & DOCUMENTS

Valid passports are required of all visitors except US and Canadian citizens, who need only proof of citizenship, such as an official birth certificate plus a driver's license. A roundtrip or onward ticket is officially required.

CUSTOMS

Saba is a free port, and there are no customs regulations.

MONEY

The official currency is the Netherlands Antilles guilder or florin, but US dollars are accepted everywhere. Islander-geared businesses such as grocers and shops post prices in guilders, while visitor-related businesses such as hotels, restaurants and dive shops post prices in US dollars. The exchange rate is 1.80 guilders to US$1. Generally, there's no advantage in changing your money to guilders unless you're planning a lengthy stay. For more information, see Money in the Regional Facts for the Visitor chapter.

The island's two banks, Barclays and the Antilles Banking Corporation Bank, are both in Windwardside. Credit cards are accepted at most hotels and some restaurants.

POST & COMMUNICATIONS
Post
Saba's two post offices are in Windwardside and The Bottom. When writing to Saba from abroad, just address mail with the individual or business name, followed by the town and 'Saba, Netherlands Antilles.'

It costs Fls 1.10 to mail a postcard and Fls 2.25 to mail a letter to the USA, Canada, UK or Europe; and Fls 1.30 for a postcard and Fls 3.25 for a letter to Australia, Asia or Africa.

Telephone
Local phone numbers have seven digits. The area code, which must be added when calling Saba from overseas, is 599.

Card phones are scattered throughout the island, and each has a list of places to buy phone cards plastered to its side. There are also two coin phones – at Fort Bay and the airport. For more information, see Post & Communications in the Regional Facts for the Visitor chapter.

Fax
Faxes can be sent and received from the Antelecom office, in The Bottom.

Email & Internet Access
Check up on the goings-on at home at Breadline Internet Services, opposite Barclays Bank in Windwardside. Ten minutes will cost you US$3.

INTERNET RESOURCES
The Web site www.sabatourism.com provides some excellent pre-trip information online.

BOOKS
The *Guide to the Saba Marine Park* (Saba Conservation Foundation, 1991), by marine biologist Tom van't Hof is an authoritative guide to underwater Saba. Van't Hof, who spearheaded the development of the Saba Marine Park, gives detailed descriptions of each of Saba's 26 dive sites, accompanied by color photos illustrating coral and marine life.

Saban Cottages, a hardcover book by artist Heleen Cornet, contains lovely watercolor drawings of scores of the island's picturesque buildings.

Both books can be purchased in shops and art galleries on the island.

NEWSPAPERS & MAGAZINES
As Saba has no newspaper, local news and announcements are posted on bulletin boards in the villages. St Martin's *The Daily Herald,* which includes Saba news, can be purchased at the Big Rock Market in Windwardside.

RADIO & TV
Radio PJF-1, 'The Voice of Saba,' is at 94.7 FM. The island has cable TV with US network programming.

ELECTRICITY
Electricity is 110V, 60 cycles, and a flat two-pronged plug is used.

WEIGHTS & MEASURES
Saba uses the metric system. Distances are given in meters and kilometers.

HEALTH
In The Bottom, the AM Edwards Medical Center (☎ 416-3289) is the island's medical facility.

There's a decompression chamber for the use of divers at Fort Bay, which also serves divers who get the bends on neighboring islands.

EMERGENCIES
In case of emergency, call the police at ☎ 416-3237.

BUSINESS HOURS
Shops and offices are commonly open from 8 or 9 am to noon and 2 to 6 pm Monday to Saturday.

PUBLIC HOLIDAYS & SPECIAL EVENTS

Public holidays on Saba include the following days:

New Year's Day	January 1
Good Friday	Friday before Easter
Easter Sunday	late March/early April
Easter Monday	late March/early April
Queen's Day	April 30
Labor Day	May 1
Ascension Thursday	40th day after Easter
Christmas Day	December 25
Boxing Day	December 26

The Saba Summer Festival, held in late July, is the island's Carnival. The weeklong event includes jump-ups, a queen contest, a calypso-king competition and a costumed parade around The Bottom, and a grandfinale fireworks display.

Saba Days, held on the first week of December, features sporting events, steel bands, dancing, donkey races and barbecues.

ACTIVITIES
Beaches & Swimming

Saba is definitely not the place to go if you want to lie out on sandy strands. The main swimming spot is Well's Bay, at the northwestern side of the island, which has a small, rocky beach. Ladder Bay is another choice for swimmers, but it's better for snorkeling. All the island hotels have swimming pools.

Diving & Snorkeling

Saba's stunning scenery extends beneath the surface, with steep wall drops just offshore and nearshore reef dives. It has a reputation as one of the best diving destinations in the Caribbean due to the abundance and diversity of marine life and variety of diving options so close at hand. Most of the island's 26 dive spots are along the calmer leeward side, between Tent Bay and Diamond Rock.

Some of the more exciting dives include Tent Reef Wall, which has colorful tube sponges and corals and lots of fish activity;

Third Encounter and Twilight Zone, adjacent sponge- and coral-encrusted pinnacles that rise about 30m from the ocean floor; and Diamond Rock, which has a great variety of marine life, including stingrays, black-tip sharks and bull sharks.

The waters surrounding Saba are protected under the auspices of Saba Marine Park, which has undertaken a number of conservation efforts, including installing permanent mooring buoys at dive sites. To help cover the park's operating expenses, a US$3 marine-park fee is added onto each dive and snorkel trip.

For snorkelers, Well's Bay and the adjacent Torrens Point are popular spots, and there's even a marked underwater trail. Ladders Bay is also popular, but it's a good 30-minute hike down to the shore from the road and double that back up.

Dive Shops The island boasts three dive shops. Sea Saba (☎ 416-2246, fax 416-2362, divemaster@seasaba.com), based in Windwardside, generally does a 10 am and a noon dive daily and night dives on request. Single-tank dives cost US$50, double-tank dives US$90 and night dives US$60. Masks and fins can be rented for US$8. Sea Saba also does a resort course for beginners for US$80 and a five-day certification course for US$350. There is a three-person minimum for courses. Snorkelers can go out with the dive boat for US$25.

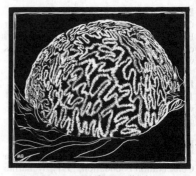

Be smart: Go diving off Saba.

Saba Marine Park

Established in 1987, Saba Marine Park encompasses all the waters surrounding the island from the high-water mark to a depth of 71m. The park has established zones for different marine uses. For example, it limits anchoring to the Fort Bay and Ladder Bay areas and sets aside the waters between the two bays exclusively for diving. Fishing is permitted in most other Saba waters, but some restrictions will apply, and there are quotas for at-risk creatures like conch.

The park was established with funding from the World Wildlife Fund and from the Saban and Dutch governments. It is administered by the Saba Conservation Foundation, a nonprofit group. For more information, you can check out the official Web site: www.sabapark.com.

Saba's original dive shop, Saba Deep (☎ 416-3347, fax 416-3397, in the USA ☎ 888-348-3722, diving@sabadeep.com), at Fort Bay and Windwardside, goes out at 9 and 11 am and 1 pm, taking no more than eight divers per boat. The first dive of the day is a deep dive, the second intermediate, and the last a shallow dive. Rates, which include all gear, are US$50/90/125 for single-/double-/triple-tank dives and US$65 for a night dive. Snorkel trips are US$30.

Saba Divers (☎ 416-2740, fax 416-2741, sabadivers@unspoiledqueen.com), the isle's newest operation, operates out of Scout's Place (see Places to Stay in Windwardside, later). It goes out four times a day and charges US$41/92/124 for single-/double-/triple-tank dives, US$55 for a night dive. Rates include gear. PADI open-water certification and advanced open-water courses are available. Dedicated snorkeling tours are offered for US$20, including snorkel gear.

All three dive shops offer discount dive packages, which include a certain number of dives and nights at one of the accommodations on the island. Check with the individual shops to find out the rates.

Live-Aboard Boats The live-aboard dive boat M/V *Caribbean Explorer* generally starts and ends its weeklong trips in St Martin, but spends much of its time around Saba. For more information, see Organized Tours in the Getting There & Away chapter.

Hiking

Saba has some excellent and varied hiking opportunities. There are nine signposted and maintained hikes, ranging from a 15-minute walk to tide pools just beyond the airport to a steep climb through a cloud forest up Mt Scenery, Saba's highest point. Interpretive plaques describing natural history and trailside bird and plant life have been erected along the trails by the Saba Conservation Foundation.

The Trail Shop (☎ 416-2630), in Windwardside, set up as a nonprofit organization by the Saba Conservation Foundation, is an excellent source of information and advice on hiking around the island, and doubles as a souvenir shop. It's open 10 am to 4 pm Monday to Saturday.

Although all the hikes can be done on your own, it's worth hiring a guide if you want the lowdown on native flora and fauna. The local 'hardman' of the bush, James 'Crocodile' Johnson, closely resembles Rambo, but he makes an exceptionally good guide and has a huge depth of knowledge on Saba. The Trail Shop can organize a guide, which costs US$40 for up to four persons.

As the trails cross private property, hikers should stick to established paths. There are no poisonous creatures on Saba, and it's one of the safest places in the Caribbean, so this is one island where you can feel free to concentrate all your attention on the environment.

Some of the trails, such as the Crispeen Track between The Bottom and Windwardside, follow the old footpaths that linked the villages before the first vehicle roads were built. After completing even the easiest hike, you have to feel sorry for the poor donkeys that had to lug all the equipment around before the coming of the road. A simple trail brochure and map are available free at the trail shop and the tourist office.

The tourist office also produces handy leaflets for walking tours of Windwardside and The Bottom.

ACCOMMODATIONS

Most of Saba's accommodations fall in the moderate price range, with rates averaging around US$100. If you're on a budget, there is one delightful low-end option, El Momo Cottages in Booby Hill, at just US$30 in summer. There are also a couple of pampering top-end hotels with rooms from US$150 to US$400.

In addition to the hotels listed in this chapter, there are a handful of cottages and apartments for rent on Saba, with prices ranging from US$50 to US$125 nightly, US$300 to US$900 weekly. The Saba Tourist Bureau will send out an annually updated list with rates and contact numbers. While you can book these cottages on your own, it's also possible to do it through the tourist office, and generally that's an easier route to take, as the office staff know which cottages are available at any given time.

To rates given in this chapter add a 5% government room tax. Many hotels also add a 10% service charge, no matter the standard of service.

FOOD

Food in Saba has Continental and Creole influences, with an emphasis on fish and seafood, though popular local dishes also include goat meat, johnnycakes and barbecued ribs. A variety of fruit is grown on the island, including bananas, papayas, mangoes, avocados and soursop.

DRINKS

Water is by catchment, but generally OK to drink from the tap – although you should inquire first.

Be sure to try Saba Spice, a rum-based liqueur spiced with a 'secret concoction' that varies depending on whose liquor you buy. It can be purchased in bars for US$1 a shot or US$10 for a 750mL bottle. Some shops also stock the spicy substance.

SHOPPING

Saba lace handwork in the form of handkerchiefs, table runners, place mats, bun warmers and similar items are available at reasonable prices from local craftswomen. In Windwardside, the women have small shops in their homes, while in The Bottom, lace makers will commonly stroll around with boxes of their work. A good islandwide selection can be found at the community center in Hell's Gate.

The women at the Hell's Gate community center also sell homemade Saba Spice liqueur. Most varieties have a licorice-like flavor, as one of the common ingredients is the fennel that's planted at the side of some Saban homes.

Saba has attracted a number of good contemporary artists whose paintings and drawings are inspired by the island's natural scenery. Original oils and watercolors, glass jewelry, cards and prints can be found at several island shops, the best of which is the Breadfruit Gallery in Windwardside.

The Saba Artisans Foundation, in The Bottom, makes silkscreen cotton bags and clothing on-site; it also sells T-shirts, Saba Spice liqueur and pareus. The Trail Shop in Windwardside stocks similar goods.

Getting There & Away

DEPARTURE TAX

The departure tax, for people aged two and older, is US$5 for those going to a Netherlands Antilles island and US$20 for those going to a non-Dutch island.

Passengers connecting with an international flight from St Martin pay US$20; be sure to pick up a transit pass at your airline check-in counter in St Martin, which exempts you from paying an additional departure tax there.

AIR

Saba's seaside airstrip is a mere 400m long, the region's shortest. It's similarly narrow, with the plane touching down just meters

Saba Lace

The craft most associated with the island is Spanish work, or Saba lace, a drawn thread work first introduced to Saba in the 1870s by a woman who learned the stitching technique in a Venezuelan convent. While this lacelike embroidery work is high quality, the market for it is so limited that the craft is not being practiced by the younger generation and is a dying art.

away from a sheer cliff. If you're looking for a joyride to match most roller coasters in the world, make sure you jump on a plane heading for Saba.

The small airport has a Winair booth, restrooms, a coin telephone and a stall selling beer and soda.

The only scheduled flight service to Saba is with Winair (☎ 416-2212, 416-2255), which has five flights a day from St Martin, a 15-minute hop. Winair also has a daily flight from St Eustatius.

The one-way fare to Saba is US$47 from St Martin, US$25 from St Eustatius. Roundtrip fares are double. A roundtrip to St Barts via St Martin is US$161.

SEA
Ferry

Two motorized catamarans run between Dutch Sint Maarten, French St Martin and Saba.

The Edge (☎ 545-2640) leaves Pelican Marina in Simpson Bay at 9 am Wednesday, Friday and Sunday.

The Voyager (☎ 525-4096) departs from Marigot Marina in Marigot at 8:45 am Tuesday and Bobby's Marina in Philipsburg at 8:30 am Thursday.

Both boats arrive at Saba's Fort Bay around 10 am, departing from Saba around 4pm. *The Edge* charges US$60 for the roundtrip journey, while *The Voyager* is slightly cheaper, at US$57.

If you're planning on visiting Saba and St Barts, *The Voyager* offers a nice way of saving a little money. You can purchase

roundtrip tickets to both destinations from St Martin for US$90, which is a bit of a bargain for Caribbean standards.

Yacht

Saba has two designated anchorages: the harbor at Fort Bay and the area from Well's Bay to Ladder Bay. Under normal conditions, Well's Bay is the best anchorage and offers excellent holding in sand. Ladder Bay also has good holding but has some tricky downdrafts, as well as boulders in the shallower waters. Yellow buoys in Ladder Bay and Well's Bay can be used by visiting yachts; however, the white and orange buoys are reserved for dive boats.

People arriving by boat should clear immigration at the harbor office at Fort Bay. The office monitors VHF channels 16 and 11. If there's no one at the harbor office, check in at the adjacent Saba Marine Park office.

To help support Saba Marine Park, there is a yacht visitor fee of US$3 per person.

Cruise Ship

Saba does not have a deepwater port that is capable of handling large cruise ships. However, Windjammer Barefoot Cruises and a few other small ships stop at Saba by anchoring in Fort Bay and bringing passengers ashore by dinghy.

ORGANIZED TOURS

Dive packages that include accommodations and airport transfers can be arranged from all three dive shops, or in the USA through Dive Saba Travel (☎ 360-871-7332, 800-883-7222, fax 360-871-7335, divesaba@ aol.com). Rates vary according to the accommodations you select, but average about US$500 in summer, US$575 in winter for a five-night, six-dive package, based on double occupancy.

Getting Around

There are no public buses and no scooters or bicycles for rent on Saba. Hitchhiking is the easiest and preferred method of getting around.

CAR

Saba has very narrow and steep roads that are pretty hairy and may intimidate some drivers. Even Sabans are challenged by tight corners in Windwardside – you'd be hard pressed to find a car that doesn't bear scrape marks from kissing at least one stone wall! Unfortunately, this doesn't necessarily mean locals drive any slower than the rest of the world.

Road Rules

Drive on the right side of the road. Your home driver's license is valid for driving on Saba. The island's sole gas station is in Fort Bay; it's open 8 am to 3 pm Monday to Saturday.

Rental

There aren't many rental cars on the island, so if you're dead set on hiring a car you may need to book in advance. The going rate for a small car is around US$50 a day. The main rental agent is Johnson's Rent a Car (☎ 416-2269), which is at Juliana's. Scout's Place (☎ 416-2205) may or may not be renting out cars; phone and check before turning up. For both these places, see Places to Stay in Windwardside. And remember – when you're behind the wheel, you'll be concentrating so hard you'll miss the wonderful scenery and drop-off cliffs!

TAXI

Taxi fares are set by the government. Taxis meet flights at the airport; from there, the fare is US$8 to Windwardside and US$12.50 to The Bottom for up to four people, plus an additional US$0.50 for each piece of luggage.

From Windwardside it costs US$6.50 to The Bottom, US$9.50 to Fort Bay. A sightseeing tour, which lasts 1½ to two hours and covers most of the island, costs US$40 per taxi for up to four persons.

As there are only a dozen full-time taxis, they can get tied up at busy times; if you're unable to find one, the tourist office (☎ 416-2231) or your hotel will try to hunt one down for you.

HITCHHIKING

Hitchhiking is a common means of transportation, and eight out of 10 cars will stop for you. In Windwardside, the main hitching spot is near the wall by the Big Rock Market, and in The Bottom it's by the Department of Public Works. But anywhere on the island just stick your thumb out and someone will stop. The usual safety precautions apply.

Around Saba

COVE BAY

Although the waters off Saba's east coast are often turbulent, Cove Bay, near the airport, has a little boulder-protected pool that provides a safe spot for cooling off on a hot day. The bay is reached after a five-minute walk along the side road that begins just outside the terminal.

Along the road into Cove Bay there's a signposted trail that begins at an old leather factory (it's now a classroom for medical students) and goes out along coastal bluffs to some nice tidal pools at **Flat Point**, behind the airport. The hike takes about 15 minutes one-way.

To the south of Cove Bay is **Spring Bay**, which was named after a freshwater spring and was the site of an Arawak settlement.

HELL'S GATE

When you stand at the airport and look up the mountain, you see the village of Hell's Gate, whose houses seem to cling precariously to the side of the mountain slopes. The road from the airport to Windwardside passes directly through the village. The origin of the town's moniker is unclear; however, according to one local it was so named due to its being 'one hell of a walk from the airport.'

The main landmark in Hell's Gate is the Holy Rosary Church, a seemingly old stone church that was built just three decades ago. Behind the church is the Hell's Gate community center, which sells the best collection of Saba lace on the island, as well as bottles of homemade Saba Spice liqueur. The community center is usually open 9 to 11 am daily.

The ride from Hell's Gate to Windwardside is steep and winding. It passes through a variety of terrains, offering some fine, scenic views of Saba itself and glimpses of the neighboring islands of St Eustatius, St Kitts, Nevis and St Barts.

Places to Stay & Eat

The six cheery rooms at *The Gate House* (☎ 416-2416, fax 416-2550, in the USA ☎ 708-354-9641, sabagate@aol.com) have private baths, tile floors and either one king or two single beds. Two rooms also have kitchenettes. All have a stylish decor with works by American artist Jim Siegel, who runs the place along with his Dutch partner Manuella. There are a pool and wraparound balconies with fine views. Singles/doubles cost US$75/95 in summer, US$85/110 in winter, Continental breakfast included. In the evening a set dinner with salad, dessert and a main dish, such as jerk pork or coconut shrimp, is available for US$25. Free pick-up for dinner is offered from Windwardside, Hell's Gate and Booby Hill. The restaurant is closed Wednesday.

WINDWARDSIDE

The island's largest hamlet, Windwardside has curving alleyways lined with picturesque cottages and flower-filled gardens. Being, appropriately enough, on the windward side of the island, just below Mt Scenery, this hillside village is pleasantly green and a tad cooler than other parts of the island. It's a delightfully unhurried and friendly place.

Windwardside makes the best base for visitors, as it has the most hotels, restaurants and shops, as well as the tourist office, the museum, the trail shop, a good art gallery and the trailhead for the island's most popular hike. While you are walking around you'll probably notice that many homes have Dutch doors. The top halves of these doors are commonly kept open in the evening, allowing people to chat from their living rooms with neighbors strolling by.

Information

Tourist Office The Saba Tourist Bureau (☎ 416-2231, fax 416-2350, iluvsaba @unspoiledqueen.com) is at the northwest side of town and is open 8 am to 5 pm weekdays.

Money Barclays Bank, near the crossroads, is open 8:30 am to 3:30 pm weekdays. Barclays cashes Visa traveler's checks free of charge and others for a 1% fee. The island's only other bank, the Antilles Banking Corporation Bank, is opposite the post office and open 8:30 am to 3 pm weekdays (till 4 pm Thursday and Friday). Neither has ATMs.

Post & Communications The Windwardside post office is open 8 am to noon and 1 to 5 pm weekdays, 8 am to noon Saturday. Breadline Internet Services, opposite Barclays Bank, offers Internet access for US$3 per 10 minutes.

Libraries The library, which is next to the post office, is open 8 am to noon Monday, 2 to 5 pm Tuesday and Thursday, 7 to 9 pm Saturday.

Harry L Johnson Museum

The museum is in a gardenlike setting surrounded by wildflowers, including blackeyed susans, the official island flower. The collection is housed in a typical Saban home, whitewashed with green-shuttered windows, and the interior recreates the living quarters of a 19th-century Dutch sea captain. Exhibits include a four-poster bed with period decor, a collection of pottery fragments, Amerindian hand tools and lots of memorabilia, including maritime documents, sextants and a compass. Curiously, there's also a bust of the South American revolutionary Simón Bolívar on the grounds, which was presented to Saba by the Venezuelan government. The museum is open 10 am to noon and 2 to 4 pm weekdays. Admission is US$2.

Maskehorne Hill Trail

For a quick sense of what Saban wilderness is like, take this 45-minute roundtrip hike

SABA

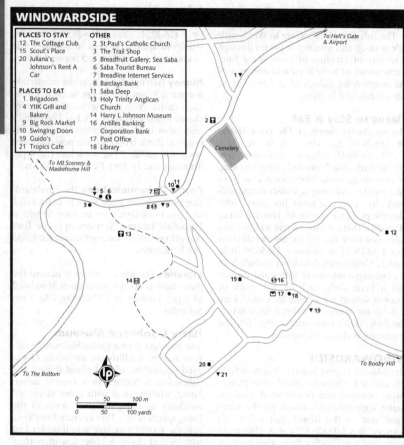

WINDWARDSIDE

PLACES TO STAY
12 The Cottage Club
15 Scout's Place
20 Juliana's;
    Johnson's Rent A
    Car

PLACES TO EAT
1   Brigadoon
4   YIIK Grill and
    Bakery
9   Big Rock Market
10 Swinging Doors
19 Guido's
21 Tropics Cafe

OTHER
2   St Paul's Catholic Church
3   The Trail Shop
5   Breadfruit Gallery; Sea Saba
6   Saba Tourist Bureau
7   Breadline Internet Services
8   Barclays Bank
11 Saba Deep
13 Holy Trinity Anglican
    Church
14 Harry L Johnson Museum
16 Antilles Banking
    Corporation Bank
17 Post Office
18 Library

To Hell's Gate
& Airport

To Mt Scenery &
Maskehorne Hill

Cemetery

To The Bottom

To Booby Hill

0   50   100 m
0   50   100 yards

that starts on the Mt Scenery Trail out of
Windwardside. After about 10 minutes of
climbing old stone steps through a forest
thick with tall elephant ears and birdsong,
you'll reach a small dasheen farm. At the
farmer's hut, turn left off the Mt Scenery
Trail onto the Maskehorne Hill Trail, a dirt
path through the forest that continues to
nearby Maskehorne Hill and a view of
Windwardside.

Mt Scenery Trail

The island's premier hike is to the top of Mt
Scenery, a strenuous climb up a virtual

nonstop run of stairs (1064 in all!) that ends
at the highest point in all of the Netherlands. The trail, which is clearly marked and
easy to follow, begins at the side of the road
a couple of minutes' walk west of the tourist
office. Hiking time is about 2½ hours
roundtrip.

As ample reward for a good workout,
you'll get a close-up view of an elfin forest
with a lush growth of ferns, tropical flowers
and epiphyte-covered mahogany trees. If
the clouds decide to part, the summit provides panoramic views of Saba and neighboring islands. There are interpretive signs

along the trail that describe some of the prolific flora and fauna, and a couple of shelters erected by Cable & Wireless, which maintains the trail.

If you get an early start the two maintenance men who hike to work at the summit antenna tower may pass you on the way up. After reaching the summit be sure to continue along the left side of the radio tower to reach a scenic lookout 100m beyond.

The trail can be very slippery in places; wear shoes with good traction, watch your footing and be especially careful where there are fallen leaves. This hike is only partially shaded and can get very hot at midday. Bring water; most hotels will provide guests with canteens.

Places to Stay

Windwardside Center With a cliff-side location, *Scout's Place* (☎ 416-2205, fax 416-2388, sabadivers@unspoiledqueen.com) is a very pleasant 14-room inn in the village center. The rooms are attractively decked out and painted in warm colors, with private baths and TV, and many enjoy distant ocean views. Breakfast is included in the rates, which start at US$60/77 for singles/doubles in summer, US$66/85 in winter. There's a pool, bar and restaurant. The German owners also run Saba Divers, located on the premises.

Friendly *Juliana's* (☎ 416-2269, fax 416-2389, in the USA ☎ 800-883-7222, julianas@unspoiledqueen.com) is a family-run operation with nine pleasant rooms. Each has a private bath, terrace, coffeemaker, ceiling fan, and screened windows to keep the occasional mosquito out. There's a common room with TV, a pool, a reasonably priced restaurant and a prize collection of flowering hibiscus on the grounds. Single/double rates are from US$70/90 in summer, US$90/115 in winter. Juliana's also has a couple of two-bedroom cottages (US$145 in summer, US$165 in winter) and an apartment (US$125 in summer, US$150 in winter), all with kitchens.

If you're planning on preparing your own meals, you should consider *The Cottage Club*

(☎ 416-2386, fax 416-2476, cottageclub@unspoiledqueen.com), which has five duplex cottages with fine hillside views. The 10 roomy studio-style units each have a full kitchen, a dining table, a queen bed and cable TV. There's a pool available. The Cottage Club enjoys a rural setting at the eastern edge of the village, but it is still within easy walking distance of the center. The units cost US$105 in summer, US$145 in winter.

Booby Hill Booby Hill, a rural area about a kilometer south of the Windwardside town center, has two interesting new hotels – one the island's cheapest, the other its priciest.

El Momo Cottages (☎/fax 416-2265, info@elmomo.com, PO Box 519), on the edge of the rain forest, is a delightful travelers' haunt with Robinson Crusoe charm. An absolute gem of a place, it's lovingly run by a friendly German/Italian couple and their daughter, dog and cat, all of whom treat their grounds like a nature sanctuary. The cottages, which are linked by flower-lined paths that are used by sunning lizards, are comfortable, clean and simple and have gables with gingerbread trim, a porch and two twin beds. Showers are out in the open air (with a privacy screen), utilizing solar-heated water bottles. Guests share a pool and a lounge with a fantastic view and two very inviting hammocks. Full breakfast is available for US$6, sandwiches for half that. Rates are US$30/40 for singles/doubles in summer, US$40/50 in winter. As there are only six cottages, advance reservations are essential.

Willard's of Saba (☎ 416-2498, fax 416-2482, willard@sintmaarten.net) is a small American-run luxury hotel with a scenic cliffside location and seven attractive rooms. There's a hot tub, a large heated lap pool, a tennis court and an upmarket restaurant. The least expensive room, which lacks a balcony, begins in summer at US$250/300 for singles/doubles, while the top-priced 'Room in the Sky,' a honeymoon suite with splendid 180° views, is way out of most peoples' price range! Winter rates are US$50 to US$100 higher, but at least breakfast is included.

Places to Eat

The *YIIK Grill and Bakery* (☎ 416-2539), opposite the trail shop, has views of the distant coast and is a great value. There's a large selection of salads, sandwiches and burgers at lunch from US$3.50, and international cuisine is the order of the day for dinner. Pastas start at US$9 and other main courses at US$11. It's closed Sunday.

Another good-value spot is *Tropics Cafe* (☎ 416-2469), next to the pool at Juliana's. Tasty tropical-flavored muffins cost a mere US$1.50. Breakfasts such as French toast or an omelet with coffee, as well as lunchtime burgers with fries, go for US$5 to US$10. They'll also prepare sandwich-and-fruit box lunches for US$5. Dinner is a mix of Italian and Chinese cuisine ranging from US$15 to US$25. It's open 7 to 9 am Tuesday to Sunday, and noon to 3 pm and 6 to 10 pm daily.

Swinging Doors (☎ 416-2506) is a good option in the center of Windwardside. Lunch, served from 11 am to 2 pm, consists of filling burgers for around US$4.25. Dinner takes place from 5 to 8 pm, and Tuesday and Friday nights – barbecue time – are not to be missed: You'll be stuffed full for only US$10. Get there early, as it's popular with the locals and the food has been known to run out way before 8 pm. Swinging Doors is also a pleasant spot for a drink and chat with friendly Sabans.

Guido's (☎ 416-2230) is the Windwardside party place, serving as the island's pool hall during the week and a disco on weekends. Guido's has burgers with fries for US$5.50 and pizzas from US$8. It's open 11:30 am to 2:30 pm for lunch and 6:30 to 9:30 pm Monday to Saturday for dinner. The party starts once the restaurant closes Friday and Saturday nights.

Scout's Place (see Places to Stay, earlier) has nice views and a combination of Caribbean and European-style food. At lunch, sandwiches cost US$5.50, while hot dishes, including fresh fish or goat stew, are around US$13. Dinner is more expensive, with main dishes ranging from US$12 to US$20. It's open 7:30 to 10:30 am for breakfast, noon to 2:30 pm for lunch and 5:30 pm to 10:30 pm for dinner.

Brigadoon (☎ 416-2380) is one of the best restaurants on the island, with pleasant alfresco dining and excellent food with tasty homemade sauces. The style is Creole and Caribbean with some Continental dishes thrown in. Main courses start at US$10, and the fresh daily special, usually fish, is a little more, at $US15 to US$17, but worth the extra money. You can also take your pick of the live lobsters as you walk in the door. If you sweet-talk Tricia, the owner, you may wrangle a ride home, or at least get some entertaining stories. It's open for dinner from 6:30 pm Wednesday to Monday.

Big Rock Market, Saba's largest grocery store, has beer, wine, local gossip and a wide selection of food items. It's open 8 am to noon and 2 to 6 pm Monday to Saturday.

Entertainment & Shopping

From 9:30 pm to 2 am Friday to Saturday, *Guido's* (see Places to Eat) pushes the pool tables aside and turns into a disco; there's no cover charge.

Every three weeks, on a Monday, the resident medical students sit for an exam, and needless to say there's just a little drinking going on afterward. So expect to find the bars to be livelier every third Monday, nicknamed 'Black Monday.'

Otherwise, the island is generally quiet at night, so don't expect too much during the week.

The Breadfruit Gallery, near the tourist office, is the best place to pick up island handicrafts and artwork.

ST JOHN'S

The road from Windwardside to The Bottom passes by the village of St John's. The most notable site along the way is the roadside plaque to Josephus Lambert Hassell, the man responsible for constructing the island's road (see 'The Impossible Road,' earlier), a nearby section of which bears a striking resemblance to China's Great Wall.

St John's has Saba's only school, which provides all island children with primary and secondary education. The area also boasts **Lollipop's**, a popular after-dark weekend haunt.

There is a lovely view of The Bottom as you drive down from St John's. The trailhead for the Crispeen Track begins at the side of the main road 500m before reaching The Bottom. This rural track leads to Windwardside, connecting with the Mt Scenery trail after about an hour.

THE BOTTOM

The Bottom, on a 250m plateau surrounded by hills, is the island's lowest town. It's also Saba's administrative center.

As you first enter The Bottom you'll come upon the Department of Public Works, a quaint former schoolhouse flanked by 3m-high night-blooming cacti that give off a wonderful fragrance in the evening. On the next corner is the Anglican church, a picturesque stone structure more than 200 years old. The church is followed by the police and fire station, in front of which you'll find a bell that was rung every hour on the hour until just a few years ago.

The Bottom also has a couple of cobblestone streets lined with old stone walls, as well as a public library and the island's government offices.

The attractive 'governor's house' (actually home to the lieutenant governor) is on the left as you leave The Bottom for Well's Bay. The gate is marked with orange balls, for the House of Orange, which rules the Netherlands.

Information

The post office and the phone company (Antelecom) are at the government center; both are open 8 am to noon and 1 to 5 pm weekdays. Saba's small rural hospital is at the northwest end of the village.

Places to Stay

Old-fashioned and slightly neglected, **Cranston's Antique Inn** (☎ 416-3203, fax 416-3469) is in the center of town. It has five

rooms, hardwood floors, a smattering of antiques and a pool. A couple of rooms have private baths; the others share a bath. In the summer rooms will cost US$99; in the winter they'll run US$129.

Queen's Gardens Resort (☎ 416-3494, fax 416-3495, in the USA ☎ 800-599-9407, info@ queensaba.com, PO Box 2), is a 12-unit luxury condo resort in a verdant setting 800m east of town. The units are pleasant, with cable TV, a phone, four-poster beds, a fully equipped kitchen and a separate living room. In addition, the one- and two-bedroom units have veranda Jacuzzis with a view. The facility has a fitness center, a tennis court and a well-regarded restaurant. In summer, studios are US$150, with one-bedroom apartments and two-bedroom units costing more. In winter, accommodations start at US$200. Rates include breakfast for two.

Places to Eat

The Bottom has a few eateries serving local food in simple surroundings. **My Store**, immediately south of the government center, is a well-stocked grocery store that sells fresh pastries from Windwardside's bakery. It's open 8 am to noon and 2 to 6:30 pm Monday to Saturday.

The appropriately named **Lime Time Bar & Restaurant** (☎ 416-3351) is a popular local hangout for food or just a drink and a chat. This is reflected in the prices, which are quoted in Antilles guilders, but the mighty dollar is also accepted. The dishes have a definite local feel to their concoction, and sandwiches and burgers start at US$3.50 at lunchtime. The dinner special, barbecue platter (US$14), is a meat lover's delight, as are the baby back ribs (US$10). It's open 8 am to midnight.

Mango Royale, at Queen's Gardens Resort, has a romantic setting and is the trendiest restaurant in Saba. Lunch is reasonably priced, with chicken and Caesar salads or barbecue chicken for under US$12. At dinner, main dishes such as duck breast in pineapple sauce or seafood *timbale* (assorted platter) average US$19. It's open for lunch

11:30 am to 3:30 pm and for dinner from 6:30 pm. Reservations are recommended.

FORT BAY

The main road continues south from The Bottom to Fort Bay, the island's commercial port. This winding section of road, which is 1.2km long, leads down through dry terrain punctuated by Turk's-head cacti. Fort Bay shelters dive shops, the marine-park office, the island's power station, a water desalination plant and Saba's only gas station.

The Saba Marine Park office has a few brochures to give away and sells marine-park-logo T-shirts and books on diving. The office is usually open 8 am to noon and 1 to 5 pm weekdays, and Saturday morning. The region's only hyperbaric facility is also at Fort Bay.

While there's no beach at Fort Bay, it's possible to join the local kids swimming at the pier – there's even a shower.

Places to Eat

Above the Saba Deep dive shop, *In Two Deep* (416-3438), a cozy little restaurant and bar, has reasonably priced breakfasts and lunchtime sandwiches and salads for US$10 to US$12, including a drink. It's open 8 am to 4 pm daily.

There's also a snack shop, *Pop's Place* (Pop's motto: 'cold beer and warm conversation'), which sells hot dogs, soda and ice-cold beer.

LADDER BAY

Before Fort Bay was enlarged as a port, Saba's supplies were commonly unloaded at Ladder Bay. They were then hauled up to The Bottom via the Ladder, a series of hundreds of steps hewn into the rock. Everything from building materials and schoolbooks to a Steinway piano entered the island via the Ladder.

These days there's not much at Ladder Bay other than an abandoned customs house and the coastal views, but the curious can still walk the route, which takes about half an hour down and a bit longer back up. The road to the bay leads steeply downhill to the left after the last house in The Bottom, not far from Nicholson's store.

WELL'S BAY

Saba's newest stretch of road runs from The Bottom to Well's Bay, where it terminates at the island's only beach. Just before the road itself nose-dives for Well's Bay there's a fine view of the coast that invites you to pull over for a snapshot.

The beach at Well's Bay has a small patch of chocolate-colored sand, though the amount of sand varies with the season, with the best conditions in summer. The shoreline is generally quite rocky. Those thinking of sunbathing might pause to look up at the cliffs towering above the beach – an eroding conglomerate of sand and boulders with many rocks hanging precariously directly overhead.

The bay, which is part of the Saba Marine Park, offers good swimming and snorkeling. You can find some coral-encrusted rocks in shallow waters along the north side of the bay, but the best snorkeling is near **Torrens Point**, at the northeast end of the bay, about a 15-minute swim from the beach. About 50m short of the point, a partially emerged sea tunnel cuts through the rock leading to deeper waters, where there's good coral, schools of larger fish and an occasional sea turtle and nurse shark.

Off Torrens Point is glistening **Diamond Rock**, the tip of an underwater pinnacle and a bird nesting site. All that glitters, in this case, is simply guano.

There are no facilities at Well's Bay, and you should bring water.

St Barthélemy (St Barts)

St Barts, officially called St Barthélemy and often spelled 'St Barth,' is the smallest of the French West Indies, a mere 10km long and at its widest just 4km across.

The island's attractions include lovely beaches and a relaxed pace. St Barts is hilly and dry, with a landscape that includes rock-strewn pastures, deeply indented bays, and villages of trim white houses with red-tiled roofs. There's such a quintessential French flavor to the place that it's easy to forget you're in the Caribbean and instead to imagine little St Barts as some Mediterranean isle off the coast of France. The architecture, lifestyle, culture and food are all solidly French.

St Barts' low-key character has long appealed to wealthy escapists. Decades ago, the Rockefellers and Rothschilds built estates here, and in more recent times the island has become a chic destination for the well heeled, attracting royalty, rock stars and Hollywood celebrities.

Although the island has a reputation as an expensive destination and is getting more expensive by the season, it's possible to get by in reasonable comfort on a moderate budget. St Barts can also be visited inexpensively as a day trip aboard one of several catamaran shuttles from St Martin. Keep in mind that many of the island's amenities close in September and October, so it's advisable to call beforehand to make sure you can arrange a place to stay and can find a place to eat.

Facts about St Barthélemy

HISTORY
In pre-Columbian times, Carib Indians made fishing expeditions to St Barts, but the absence of a reliable freshwater source on the island hindered the establishment of permanent Amerindian settlements. During his second New World voyage in 1493, Christopher Columbus sighted the island and named it after his older brother Bartholomew.

The first European attempt to settle the island was not until 1648, when a party of French colonists arrived from St Kitts. After Caribs raided in 1656 and massacred the

> ### Highlights
>
> - Reveling in the classy French ambience, fine restaurants and upscale hotels
> - Day-tripping in quaint Gustavia
> - Forgetting your troubles at the lovely, secluded Anse de Colombier and the scenic coastal hike leading to it
> - Windsurfing at Grand Cul-de-Sac and St Jean

OTHER MAPS
St Barthélemy (St Barts)
page 364

St Jean
page 376

Gustavia
page 372

CARIBBEAN
SEA

0   1.5   3 km
0   1   2 miles

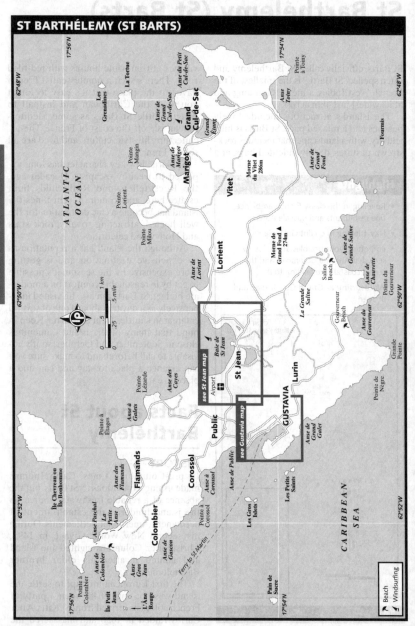

ST BARTHÉLEMY (ST BARTS)

La Tortue

Les Grenadines

La Grande Saline

17°56'N

17°54'N

62°48'W

62°50'W

62°52'W

ATLANTIC OCEAN

CARIBBEAN SEA

Anse de Grand Cul-de-Sac

Anse du Petit Cul-de-Sac

Pointe à Toiny

Anse Toiny

Fourmis

Grand Cul-de-Sac

Grand Fond

Anse de Marigot

Marigot

Vitet

Morne du Vitet 286m

Anse de Grand Fond

Pointe Mangin

Pointe Lorient

Lorient

Morne de Grand Fond 274m

Anse de Grande Saline

Pointe Milou

Anse de Lorient

Saline Beach

Anse de Chauvette

Pointe du Gouverneur

Baie de St Jean

see St Jean map

St Jean

Gouverneur Beach

Anse du Gouverneur

Pointe Lézarde

Anse des Caves

Airport

Lurin

Grande Pointe

Pointe à Galets

Anse à Galets

GUSTAVIA

see Gustavia map

Pointe de Nègre

Public

Anse de Grand Galet

Pointe à Étages

Flamands

Corossol

Anse des Flamands

Anse à Corossol

Anse de Public

Les Petits Saints

La Petite Anse

Pointe à Corossol

Les Gros Islets

Anse Paschal

Colombier

Anse de Gascon

Ferry to St-Martin

Anse de Colombier

Île Chevreau ou Île Bonhomme

Anse Gros Jean

Pain de Sucre

Pointe à Colombier

Île Petit Jean

L'Âne Rouge

0   .25   .5   1 km
0   .25   .5   1 mile

🏖 Beach
🏄 Windsurfing

entire colony, St Barts was abandoned. In 1673 Huguenots from Normandy and Brittany established the first permanent settlement. The island's prosperity didn't come from fishing and farming, however, but rather from the booty captured by French buccaneers who used St Barts as a base for their raids on Spanish galleons.

Conditions on arid St Barts didn't favor the development of sugar plantations, so unlike other Caribbean islands where large numbers of slaves were brought in, the population remained predominantly European.

In 1784, King Louis XVI ceded the island to his friend King Gustaf III of Sweden in exchange for trading rights in the Swedish port of Gothenburg. The Swedes changed the name of St Barts' port from Carenage to Gustavia, built a town hall and constructed three small forts, named Gustaf, Octave and Karl. Hoping to make money on their new outpost, the Swedes turned St Barts into a duty-free port, and by 1800 the population had swelled to 6000.

In 1852 a catastrophic fire swept across much of Gustavia. By this time a change in European-American trade routes had led to a decline in both trade and population, and most of the city was not rebuilt. In 1878 the Swedes, anxious to cut their losses on St Barts, sold the island back to France for the sum of 320,000F (about US$44,000 today). Although today St Barts is decidedly French, traces of the Swedish era still remain in the form of a few period buildings and Swedish street names, as well as in the island's duty-free status.

GEOGRAPHY & CLIMATE
St Barts' total land area is a mere 21 sq km, although its elongated shape and hilly terrain make it seem larger. The island lies 25km southeast of St Martin.

St Barts has numerous dry and rocky offshore islets. The largest, Île Fourchue, is a half-sunken volcanic crater whose large bay is a popular yacht anchorage and a destination for divers and snorkelers.

The island is dry; the temperature averages 26°C (79°F) in the winter, 28°C (82°F) in the summer. The water temperature averages about one degree warmer than the air temperature.

FLORA & FAUNA
St Barts' arid climate sustains dryland flora such as cacti and bougainvillea. Local reptiles include lizards, iguanas and harmless grass snakes. From April to August, sea turtles lay eggs along the beaches on the northwest side of the island. The numerous islets off St Barts support seabird colonies, including those of frigate birds.

Iguanas don't need sunscreen – you do.

GOVERNMENT & POLITICS
St Barts, together with St Martin, is a subprefecture of Guadeloupe, which in turn is an overseas department of France. While the subprefect resides in St Martin, St Barts has its own mayor, who is responsible for administering local affairs.

ECONOMY
Some islanders still make a living from fishing, but tourism is the mainstay of the economy these days. St Barts gets about 150,000 visitors annually; more than half of them come by boat, mostly on day trips from St Martin. In winter the majority of visitors come from the USA; in the summer, from France.

POPULATION & PEOPLE
St Barts has a population of nearly 7000. While most native islanders trace their roots to the 17th-century Norman and Breton settlers, the island is also home to the descendants of latter-day Swedish merchants and

more recent arrivals from mainland France. Unlike on most of the Eastern Caribbean islands, people of African descent are rare on St Barts.

SOCIETY & CONDUCT

The island's culture is very French, with a rural character that's manifested in the local dialect, the architecture and the slow-paced lifestyle of the islanders.

Although topless bathing is de rigueur, nudity is officially banned on St Barts. Still, on some of the more secluded beaches, such as Saline and Gouverneur, the restriction is not strictly adhered to.

While the island has some very exclusive restaurants, jackets and ties are not required for dining.

RELIGION

Catholicism is the dominant religion. There are Roman Catholic churches in Gustavia and Lorient, and an Anglican church in Gustavia.

LANGUAGE

French is the official language, although the type spoken by many islanders is heavily influenced by the old Norman dialect of their ancestors.

Many people speak some English, particularly those in hotels and restaurants. A French-English dictionary and phrasebook will come in handy, but a working knowledge of French is not essential.

Facts for the Visitor

ORIENTATION

The airport is at the western end of St Jean, just a kilometer from Gustavia. As there aren't many roads on the island and most destinations are signposted, it isn't difficult to find your way around.

Maps

There are free tourist maps of the island that are suitable for most purposes. If you want something more detailed, obtain the Institut Géographique National's Serie Bleue map 4608-G (1:25,000), which includes St Martin and St Barts, showing both roads and topography.

TOURIST OFFICES

The extremely helpful St Barts Tourist Office (☎ 27 87 27, fax 27 74 47, odtsb@ wanadoo.fr) is on the harborfront in Gustavia at Quai du Général de Gaulle. When requesting information by mail, write to Office Municipal du Tourisme, Quai du Général de Gaulle, Gustavia, 97133 St Barthélemy, French West Indies. If you're online, check out their Web site at www .st-barths.com for more information.

Tourist representatives abroad are listed in the Facts for the Visitor section of the Guadeloupe chapter.

VISAS & DOCUMENTS

US and Canadian citizens can stay up to two weeks by showing proof of citizenship in the form of a current passport. Citizens of the EU need an official identity card, valid passport or French carte de séjour (visitor card). Citizens of most other foreign countries need both a valid passport and a visa for France.

A roundtrip or onward ticket is officially required of visitors.

CUSTOMS

St Barthélemy is a duty-free port, and there are no restrictions on items brought in for personal use.

MONEY

The French franc (F) is the official currency, and most transactions on St Barts are calculated in francs. US dollars are readily accepted everywhere, though each shop sets its own exchange rate, so if you're going to be on the island any length of time you'll probably be better off paying in francs. Be aware that as of July 2002, the French franc will be replaced by the Euro throughout the French territories (unless the French tire of the new currency's crashing through the floor and decide have no part of it). It is anyone's guess how this will affect St Barts and other French Caribbean islands, but it will probably depend on which currency, the US dollar or Euro, is the stronger at the time.

At the time of publishing, 100F was equivalent to US$13.10, while €1 was equivalent to US$0.86.

Major credit cards are widely accepted in shops and at most hotels and restaurants. More information can be found under Money in the Regional Facts for the Visitor chapter.

POST & COMMUNICATIONS
Post
There are post offices in Gustavia, St Jean and Lorient. It costs 3F to send a postcard (or lightweight letter) to France, 3.80F to the USA and the Caribbean, 4.40F to other places in the Americas and 5.20F to the rest of the world.

To address mail to the island, follow the business name (and the post-office box number – BP – when there is one) with the town or beach name and '97133 St Barthélemy, French West Indies.'

Telephone
Almost all pay phones are card phones. *Télécartes* (phone cards) are sold at post offices and some shops.

If you're calling within St Barts or from Guadeloupe or French St Martin, dial the six-digit local number. If you're calling from outside these areas, add the area code 590 in front of the six-digit local number.

More information can be found under Post & Communications in the introductory Facts for the Visitor chapter.

Email & Internet Access
Centre Alizes (☎ 29 89 89), on Rue de la République in Gustavia, provides Internet access for 1F per minute. It is open from 8:30 am to 1 pm and 2:30 to 6 pm weekdays, 9:30 am to 12:30 pm Saturday.

NEWSPAPERS & MAGAZINES
The free monthly *St-Barth Magazine* newspaper has local news in French and tourist information in both French and English. *Le Journal de St Barth* is a free weekly newspaper in French that's published on Wednesday. The free daily *News* (in French) has popped up, offering a brief lowdown on the island's activities; it's available all over St Barts.

Discover Saint Barthélemy and *Tropical St Barth* are substantial, glossy magazines with history and destination articles, as well as ads for shops, restaurants and hotels. Both are published annually and distributed free by the tourist office.

Ti Gourmet, a small booklet with a good listing of restaurants and a smattering of other information in French and English, is well worth picking up at the tourist office on arrival. Some of the listed establishments offer discounts or free drinks on presentation of the booklet.

RADIO & TV
There are two radio stations: Radio St-Barth, at 98.7 FM, and Radio Transat, at 100.3 FM. As there's currently no cable network, TV on St Barts is limited to a couple of channels from Guadeloupe, except for places with satellite dishes.

ELECTRICITY
The electric current is 220V, 50/60 cycles. Many hotels have dual-voltage (110/220V) shaver adapters.

WEIGHTS & MEASURES
St Barts uses the metric system and the 24-hour clock.

HEALTH
There's a small medical facility, Bruyn Hospital (☎ 27 60 35), in Gustavia, as well as pharmacies in Gustavia and St Jean. An after-hours doctor can be contacted at ☎ 27 76 03.

DANGERS & ANNOYANCES
St Barts has very little crime, and no unusual safety precautions are necessary.

EMERGENCIES
For police emergencies, dial ☎ 27 60 12.

ST BARTS

BUSINESS HOURS

While business hours vary, offices and shops are generally open from about 8 am to 7 pm Monday to Saturday, with most taking a lunchtime siesta. Note that many places shut down for the day on Wednesday afternoon.

Banking hours are 8 am to noon and 2 to 3:30 pm weekdays.

PUBLIC HOLIDAYS & SPECIAL EVENTS

Public holidays on St Barts include the following:

New Year's Day	January 1
Easter Sunday	late March/early April
Easter Monday	late March/early April
Labor Day	May 1
Ascension Thursday	40th day after Easter
Pentecost Monday	seventh Monday after Easter
Bastille Day	July 14
Assumption Day	August 15
All Saints Day	November 1
All Souls Day	November 2
Armistice Day	November 11
Christmas Day	December 25

A number of festivals are celebrated on St Barts throughout the year. The St Barth Music Festival, in mid-January, features two weeks of jazz, chamber music and dance performances. The St Barth Festival of Caribbean Cinema, on the last weekend in April, screens films from Caribbean and European filmmakers.

Carnival is held for five days before Lent and includes a pageant, costumes and street dancing, ending with the burning of a King Carnival figure at Shell Beach, Gustavia. Many businesses close during Carnival.

The Festival of St Barts, the feast day of the island's patron saint, is celebrated on August 24 and includes fireworks, a public ball, boat races and other competitions.

St Barts is the setting for several regattas, including St Barth's Cup, a three-day yachting race sponsored by the St Barth's Yacht Club, held in late January; the St Barth Regatta, a colorful four-day regatta in mid-February; and the International Regatta of St Barthélemy, held for three days in mid-May. There's also a biennial transatlantic race, the Transat AG2R, that leaves Lorient, France, in mid-April in even-numbered years.

ACTIVITIES
Beaches & Swimming

St Barts, with its numerous bays and coves, boasts nearly two dozen beaches. Those looking for 'in-town' beaches will find that, St Jean, Flamands, Lorient and Shell Beach all have beautiful, sandy strands. For more secluded spots, Colombier, Saline and Gouverneur are all fine choices.

Diving

The most popular diving spots are off the islets surrounding St Barts, which are rich in marine life and coral. Almost all of the dive sites and surrounding islands are managed by the St Barts Natural Marine Reserve (☎ 27 88 18). For more information on the reserve, head for the town hall.

Two of the largest dive shops are West Indies Dive (☎ 27 70 34, fax 27 70 36, marine.service.stbarth@wanadoo.fr), at the Marine Service, and La Bulle (☎ 27 62 25, fax 27 95 17, oceanmust@wanadoo.fr), at the Océan Must Marina, both at La Pointe in Gustavia. Single dives average 300F; for beginners, there are four-day open-water certification courses for 2960F, and single beginner dives for 400F. Night dives average 400F.

Snorkeling

Popular snorkeling spots include Anse de Colombier, La Petite Anse and Lorient. For snorkel/sail day trips, see Organized Tours in the Getting Around section.

Snorkeling gear can be rented for around 60F a day from Marine Service (☎ 27 70 34), in Gustavia, or at Sub One (☎/fax 27 79 85), in St Jean.

Windsurfing

Grand Cul-de-Sac, the main windsurfing center, has a large protected bay that's ideal for beginners and some nice wave action beyond the reef good for advanced windsurfers. Wind Wave Power (☎ 27 82 57), at St Barts Beach Hotel in Grand Cul-de-Sac, gives 1½-hour windsurfing lessons for 380F and rents out equipment for 150F an hour.

There's also good windsurfing at St Jean, where the St Barth Wind School (☎ 27 71 22) rents out equipment for roughly the same price.

Surfing

The main surfing spots are at Lorient, Anse des Cayes and Anse Toiny. Hookipa Surf Shop (☎ 27 71 31), in St Jean, rents out surfboards for 100F a day, 170F for two days, and boogie boards for 80F a day. Totem Surf (☎ 27 83 72), in Gustavia, rents surfboards for 120F per day and boogie boards for half that. The per-day price gets cheaper the more days you rent them.

Fishing

Tuna, dorado, marlin and wahoo are caught in the waters off St Barts. Marine Service (☎ 27 70 34), a member of the Big Game Fishing Club of France, can arrange charter boats for deep-sea fishing. The cost is 5100F for a full day with drinks and lunch, 3200F for a half day.

Marine Service's main rival, Océan Must (☎ 27 62 25), offers full-day deep-sea fishing trips for 5500F and half-day trips for 3000F.

Horseback Riding

Ranch de Flamands (☎ 27 11 01) offers 1½-hour excursions for beginning and experienced riders for 390F, or 250F per person with a minimum of five persons. Rides depart most days at 3:30 pm.

ACCOMMODATIONS

Accommodations on St Barts are all small-scale. The island has about 40 hotels, with a combined capacity of only 650 rooms. Virtually all are in the moderate to high range; there are none of the local-style guest houses that shore up the bottom range on many other Caribbean islands.

Some hotels set prices in US dollars; others set them in French francs. As the ex-change rate between the two currencies can fluctuate rather substantially, rates in this chapter are listed in the currency quoted by each hotel.

Most hotels include the tax and service charge in their quoted rates, although a few places add 5% to 10% onto the bill.

Villas

In addition to hotels, St Barts has numerous villas for rent. The biggest agent is Sibarth (☎ 29 88 90, fax 27 60 52, villas@ sibarth.com), BP 55, on Rue de Centenaire in Gustavia, which handles around 200 villas and apartments. Weekly rates start at US$920 (6350F) in summer, US$1315 (9070F) in winter for a one-bedroom apartment and rise to US$7000 (48,300F) in summer, US$11,500 (79,350F) in winter for a five-bedroom five-bath villa with a pool.

Sibarth's representative in the USA is the West Indies Management Company (Wimco; ☎ 401-849-8012, 800-932-3222, fax 401-847-6290, info@wimco.com). Outside the USA and St Barts, Sibarth can be reached toll free at ☎ 800-555-5555, or log on to the Web site, www.wimcovillas.com.

FOOD & DRINKS

St Barts has many fine French restaurants, and if money is no object you can eat very well indeed. There are also moderately priced places to eat, but as most of the island's food is imported the only inexpensive options are pretty much limited to grocery stores and bakeries.

St Barts lacks a freshwater source. The island has a desalination plant, but water prices are so high that many places maintain their own rainwater-catching systems. If your tap water is from this source, the best policy is to boil it before drinking. You can buy bottled water at grocery stores.

Wine is the drink of choice on St Barts, and French wines and champagnes can be purchased from grocery stores around the island at duty-free prices, which make them one of the best buys on St Barts. Restaurants generally have extensive wine lists, although their prices are much higher.

ENTERTAINMENT & SHOPPING

An evening out on St Barts is most commonly a dinner affair. However, there are a few places where you can find dancing; for the latest in entertainment information, pick up a copy of *St-Barth Magazine*.

Gustavia is the place for duty-free shopping, with plenty of shops selling perfumes, French and Italian designer clothing, Swiss watches and jewelry. L'Carré d'Or, a shopping complex on Rue de la République, has the largest collection of quality shops. The popular clothes label *Pati de St Barth* can be found in many of the clothing boutiques on the island.

The most traditional island crafts are the straw products from the lantana palm made and sold in the village of Corossol.

Getting There & Away

DEPARTURE TAX

St Barts has a US$7 (50F) passenger tax that's generally added onto the air or boat fare when you purchase your ticket.

AIR
Airports & Airlines

St Barts' modest airport terminal has a liquor store, a small gift shop, an ATM and a magazine stand that sells a few English-language newspapers. Three airlines serve the island: Aircaraïbes (☎ 27 61 90), Winair (☎ 27 61 01) and Tyden Air (see the Anguilla chapter).

Within the Caribbean

The landing strip at St Barts can't handle anything larger than 20-seater STOL aircraft, and it's not equipped for night landings. While there are no long-distance direct flights to St Barts, there are frequent flights from the neighboring islands of St Martin and Guadeloupe.

Air Caraïbes flies to St Barts twice daily from Guadeloupe, with normal fares of 580F one-way, 1100F roundtrip. There are a few flights a day between French St Martin

and St Barts that cost 275F one-way, 550F roundtrip.

Winair flies to St Barts up to 15 times a day from Dutch Sint Maarten, targeting day-trippers. The flight costs US$58 (400F) one-way in the winter or US$76 (524F) on a same-day excursion (there are no day excursions over Christmas and Easter).

Check the Getting There & Away section in the Anguilla chapter for connections to Anguilla with Tyden Air.

SEA
Ferry

There's regular boat service between St Martin and St Barts. As the seas can be a bit choppy, all of the companies use stable catamaran-type boats.

The main company is Voyager (☎ 27 54 10, in Marigot ☎ 87 10 68, in Philipsburg ☎ 599-542-4096), which has two modern high-speed boats. One leaves daily from Marigot at 9 am and 6:15 pm for the 1½-hour journey; it departs from Gustavia at 7:15 am and 4:30 pm. The second boat leaves from Bobby's Marina in Philipsburg at 8:30 am and returns from Gustavia in the late afternoon daily except Thursday and Saturday. The cost is US$57 (393F) roundtrip, US$34 (235F) one-way.

A couple of other boats ply between Dutch Sint Maarten and Gustavia a few times a week. *The Edge* (☎ 599-544-2640), a high-speed catamaran that departs from Pelican Marina on Simpson Bay and takes just 45 minutes, charges US$50 (345F).

If you're planning on visiting St Barts and Saba, Voyager offers a nice way of saving a little money. You can purchase roundtrip tickets to both destinations from St Martin for US$90 (621F); it's possible to make the connection from one island to the other via St Martin in one day.

Yacht

Those arriving by yacht can clear immigration at the port office (☎ 27 99 52, VHF channel 16 or 10) on the east side of Gustavia Harbor. In the winter, it's open 7 am to 6 pm Monday to Saturday, 9 am to noon Sunday. In the summer, it's open 7:30 am to

12:30 pm and 2:30 to 5:30 pm Monday to Saturday only.

Gustavia Harbor has mooring and docking facilities for about 40 yachts. Popular anchorages can be found up the coast at Public, Corossol and Colombier.

Getting Around

St Barts has no public bus system, so renting a vehicle is essential to thoroughly explore the island.

TO/FROM THE AIRPORT
Many hotels will provide free transportation from the airport with advance notice. There are usually taxis parked in front of the airport, though occasionally it's necessary to wait a few minutes for one to show. A taxi to Gustavia or St Jean costs about US$8 (55F).

CAR & MOTORCYCLE
The most popular rental vehicle on the island is the open-air Mini Moke, although small cars can be rented for about the same price. Scooters and motorcycles are also available; however, the motorcycle option is best suited to experienced riders, as the island's roads have a cement surface that can get slippery when wet, and many roads are narrow, winding and steep. Many of Gustavia's roads are one-way. There are two gas stations on St Barts: one opposite the airport and the other in Lorient.

Road Rules
Drive on the right. Your home driver's license is valid in St Barts. The speed limit is 45km/h unless otherwise posted.

Rental
About ten car rental companies have booths at the airport, including Hertz, Avis, Thrifty, Budget and Europcar. Cars can also be rented from most hotels and in Gustavia. There's a lot of competition, and prices fluctuate, but in summer you can generally get a Mini Moke or a small car for about US$35 (240F) per day, in winter

for about US$50 (345F). Jeeps are a little more expensive.

Chez Beranger (☎ 27 89 00), on Rue du Général de Gaulle in Gustavia, rents out motor scooters for US$25), motorcycles (125cc and 175cc) for US$35 and cars for US$50 per day.

TAXI
In addition to the taxi terminal at the airport, there's one in Gustavia near the tourist office. To call for a taxi, dial ☎ 27 66 31 for the Gustavia stand or ☎ 27 75 81 for the airport stand.

A taxi from the airport to either St Jean or Gustavia costs about US$8 (55F). For US$40 (276F) day trippers can get a one-hour tour of the island, be dropped off at a beach or in town and be picked up at a pre-arranged time and driven back to the airport.

HITCHHIKING
Hitchhiking is both legal and common on St Barts. The usual safety precautions apply, of course.

ORGANIZED TOURS
Sightseeing Tours
The tourist office has leaflets of suggested circuits of the island, but you'll need to contact the taxi drivers directly to organize a tour. There's a 45-minute tour (150F) of the western side of St Barts, taking in Gustavia, Flamands, Colombier, Corossol and Public, an hour tour (200F) of the eastern side, covering Gustavia, St Jean, Salines, Grand Fond, Cul de Sac, Marigot and Lorient, and a 90-minute tour (250F) of the whole island. The price covers up to three people; add 50F per person for more than three.

Sailing/Snorkeling Tours
Marine Service (☎ 27 70 34) offers a half-day snorkel sail aboard the catamaran Ne Me Quitte Pas that takes in Île Fourchue and Anse de Colombier for 350 F, or 500F with lunch. Snorkel gear is included, as is an open bar. Marine Service also has a 1½-hour sunset sail for 270F.

Océan Must Marina (☎ 27 62 25), in Gustavia, also offers sailing and snorkeling cruises. A half-day snorkeling or sailing trip on the *Ttoko-Ttoko* catamaran is 320F, a full day 530F.

Gustavia

Gustavia, the island's capital and main port, is an appealing horseshoe-shaped town built up around a deep harbor. It shelters streetside cafés where day visitors linger the

afternoon away, a couple of historic sites worth a stroll and a nice beach within walking distance. As Gustavia is a duty-free port, there are also numerous jewelry shops and exclusive boutiques, with the highest concentration lying along the Rue de la République.

The new *mairie* (town hall), replacing the old hall at the end of Rue Couturier, is between the Musée de St-Barth and Fort Oscar on the western side of the harbor. There's a small fruit and vegetable market 100m east of the old mairie, and adjacent to

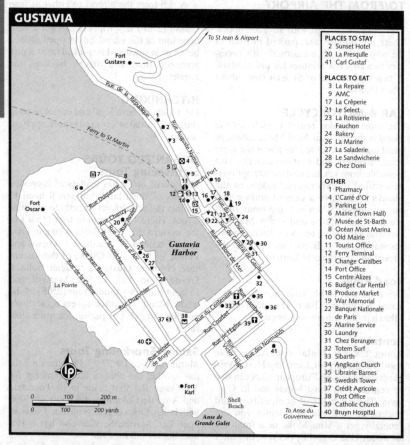

GUSTAVIA

To St Jean & Airport

Fort Gustave ●

Rue de la République

Ferry to St Martin

Fort Oscar ●

Fort Gustave ●

Rue Auguste Nyman

Rue du Port

Rue Duquesne

Rue Chanzy

Rue Oscar II

Rue Schœlcher

Rue de la Colline

La Pointe

Rue Jeanne d'Arc

Rue Jean Bart

Gustavia Harbor

Rue du Général de Gaulle

Rue du Bord de Mer

Rue Dugommier

Rue du Centenaire

Rue Courbet

Rue de l'Église

Rue Gambetta

Rue Victor Hugo

Rue des Normands

Rue Irénée de Bruyn

Fort Karl

Shell Beach

Anse de Grande Galet

To Anse du Gouverneur

| 0 | 100 | 200 m |
| 0 | 100 | 200 yards |

PLACES TO STAY
2 Sunset Hotel
20 La Presqu'île
41 Carl Gustaf

PLACES TO EAT
3 La Repaire
9 AMC
17 La Crêperie
21 Le Select
23 La Rotisserie Fauchon
24 Bakery
26 La Marine
27 La Saladerie
28 Le Sandwicherie
29 Chez Domi

OTHER
1 Pharmacy
4 L'Carré d'Or
5 Parking Lot
6 Mairie (Town Hall)
7 Musée de St-Barth
8 Océan Must Marina
10 Old Mairie
11 Tourist Office
12 Ferry Terminal
13 Change Caraïbes
14 Port Office
15 Centre Alizes
16 Budget Car Rental
18 Produce Market
19 War Memorial
22 Banque Nationale de Paris
25 Marine Service
30 Laundry
31 Chez Beranger
32 Totem Surf
33 Sibarth
34 Anglican Church
35 Librairie Barnes
36 Swedish Tower
37 Crédit Agricole
38 Post Office
39 Catholic Church
40 Bruyn Hospital

that is a little war memorial. As you walk around, you'll notice that some of the street signs in this neighborhood still bear Swedish names, ending in the suffix '-gaten.'

At the inner harbor, in the area around Rue du Centenaire, you'll find a stone Anglican church dating from 1855 and the town's landmark Swedish tower, which houses an antique clock that is still hand-wound daily.

Information

Tourist Offices The helpful tourist office (☎ 27 87 27) is on the east side of the harbor, at Quai du Général de Gaulle. The office is open 8 am to 6:50 pm Monday, Tuesday, Thursday and Friday, 8 am to 12:50 pm Wednesday, 8 am to 4:50 pm Saturday.

Money You can change money at Change Caraïbes, on Rue de la République, or Crédit Agricole, on Rue Jeanne d'Arc. The post office has a 24-hour ATM. For those who need a full-service bank, there's a branch of the Banque Nationale de Paris on Rue du Bord de Mer.

Post The Gustavia post office, on the corner of Rue Jeanne d'Arc and Rue du Centenaire, is open from 8 am to 3 pm Monday, Tuesday, Thursday and Friday, 8 am to noon Wednesday and Saturday.

Bookstores Librairie Barnes, on Rue Courbet, has French-language books and newspapers as well as the English-language *International Herald-Tribune* and *USA Today*. It's open 7:30 am to 5:30 pm Monday to Saturday.

Musée de St-Barth

The Municipal Museum of St Barts (☎ 29 71 55), at the northwest side of La Pointe, is a modest but developing museum established in 1989. On the ground floor of an atmospheric stone warehouse, it has period photo exhibits, engravings and some simple displays that give a glimpse into the island's history. It's open 8:30 am to 12:30 pm and 2:30 to 6 pm weekdays (from 3 pm Friday), 8:30 to 11 am Saturday. Admission is 10F.

Anse de Grand Galet (Shell Beach)

Shell Beach, the common name for the beach at Anse de Grand Galet, is a nice sandy beach with a shoreline packed high with tiny shells. Only a 10-minute walk from the harbor, the beach makes a fine swimming spot. To get there, go south on Rue Gambetta, turn right, go past the Catholic church and continue on that road until you reach the beach.

Fort Gustave

The site of old Fort Gustave has a couple of cannons and a mildly bottle-shaped lighthouse, but most people come here for the fine view of Gustavia and the harbor. An interpretive plaque points out local sights and landmarks. Across the harbor to the south is Fort Oscar, which is still used as a military installation, and on a clear day you can see the islands of St Kitts and Statia.

To get there, take the Gustavia road 700m from the airport crossroads, and then, as the road curves left down to Gustavia, pull off to the right where there's space for a couple of cars. The fort isn't marked, but you'll see a 'Meteo France' sign here. It's just a minute's walk up the hill to the fort.

Places to Stay

The 10 good-value rooms at *La Presqu'île* (☎ 27 64 60, fax 27 72 30), on Rue Avaler in La Pointe, aren't fancy, but all are clean and have refrigerators, air-con and private baths. Some also sport balconies, which provide pleasant day and night views of the harbor. The manager is friendly, and singles/doubles are about the cheapest you'll find on St Barts, at 220/330F.

Sunset Hotel (☎ 27 77 21, fax 27 81 59, sunset-hotel@wanadoo.fr, BP 661), on Rue de la République, is an unpretentious hotel with eight pleasant rooms, each with air-con, TV, phone, minibar and private bath. From its 3rd-floor balcony there are fine views of the harbor and Gustavia. Singles/doubles/triples cost 380/440/620F in summer, 510/560/740F in winter; add another 40F in summer, 110F in winter for one of the two larger 'superior' rooms with harbor views. From mid-December to mid-January the prices rise even higher: 580/630F for a standard room, 680/730F for a superior one.

Carl Gustaf (☎ 27 82 83, fax 27 82 37), Rue des Normands, on a hillside overlooking the harbor, is a modern luxury hotel with 14 suites, each with a VCR, fax, a couple of phones and a private 'plunge' pool. Rates begin at US$470 (3243F) in summer, US$570 (3933F) in winter.

Places to Eat

Moderately priced *La Rotisserie Fauchon*, on Rue du Roi Oscar II, has excellent French pastries, deli items, mini-quiches and rotisserie chicken. It's open daily 7am to 7 pm. The nearby *bakery*, also on Rue du Roi Oscar II, is good for morning croissants and buns; a croissant and two raisin/cream circle buns cost 15F. It's open 5:30 am to 1 pm daily.

The outdoor patio of *Le Select*, on the corner of Rue de France and Rue du Général de Gaulle, is an excellent spot to hang out, down a few drinks, and watch the human and vehicle traffic pass by. Famed as the place where Jimmy Buffett, who once was a part owner of the bar, wrote *Cheeseburger in Paradise,* it specializes – not surprisingly – in cheeseburgers (US$5), which are available 10:30 am to 2:30 pm and 6 to 10 pm Monday to Saturday.

Little *La Crêperie*, on Rue du Roi Oscar II, attracts a crowd with a variety of main-course crêpes and sandwiches from about 50F and dessert crêpes for around 25F. You can also get a Continental breakfast with coffee for 35F. It's open 7 am to 10 pm Monday to Saturday.

On the western side of the harbor you'll find an excellent, cheap sandwich shop, *Le Sandwicherie.* A range of filling, tasty sandwiches is offered for between 15F and 25F, along with some nice chilled-out tunes and beer (but no harbor view). It's open 7:30 am to midnight Monday to Saturday.

Chez Domi, an inviting café on Rue du Général de Gaulle, blends French and West Indian cuisines. Main dishes such as conch stew, octopus with dumplings or fish in Creole sauce average 90F, while salads and appetizers start at 55F. There's also a daily special for around 50F. It's open daily noon to 3 pm and 6:30 to 10 pm.

Le Repaire, a streetside restaurant opposite the harbor, is open for lunch and dinner, serving meat dishes from 85F, grilled fish for 95F and a range of salads and burgers from 60F upward. It's closed on Sunday.

La Saladerie (☎ 27 52 48), a waterfront café on the west side of the harbor, specializes in salads, from simple green for 25F to seafood salad for 70F. Pizzas and a few grilled dishes are also available at moderate prices. It's open from noon to 2:30 pm and 7 to 10:30 pm.

Nearby family-run *La Marine* (☎ 27 68 91), also on the harborfront, is open for lunch and dinner Monday to Saturday. Burgers and omelets cost 35F to 70F, fish and meat dishes start at around 100F. The restaurant is packed on Thursday night (reserve early), when they serve mussels with french fries (95F), flown in from France and prepared in a garlic-wine broth.

Carl Gustaf (see Places to Stay) has an exclusive French restaurant where dinner for two can easily top 1000F. *AMC*, a large grocery store on Rue de la République, sells everything from pastries and wine to deli foods. It's open 8 am to at least 5 pm Monday to Saturday, except for Wednesday, when it closes at 1pm.

Around St Barts

COROSSOL

About 2km northwest of Gustavia sprawls Corossol, one of the island's most traditional fishing villages. The brown-sand beach is lined with blue and orange fishing boats and stacks of lobster traps. Women here still weave the leaves of the lantana palm into straw hats, baskets and place mats, which they line up on the walls in front of their homes to attract buyers.

On the southeast end of the beach, just 50m down a dirt road, is the **Inter Oceans Museum**, a collection of 9000 seashells in the home of Ingénu Magras, who started the museum half a century ago. It's open 9 am to 12:30 pm and 2 to 5 pm Tuesday to Sunday; admission is 20F.

FLAMANDS

Flamands, a small village on the northwestern side of the island, retains a pleasantly rural character. The village stretches along a curving bay whose long, broad white-sand beach and clear waters are very popular with beachgoers. There's easy beach access with streetside parking at the westernmost end of Flamands Bay.

The peninsula on the west side of the beach separates Flamands from nearby La Petite Anse, where rocky waters afford good snorkeling. To get there, continue west past Flamands for about 200m and take the short spur that curves down to the right before the main road reaches a dead end.

Places to Stay & Eat

The *Auberge de La Petite Anse* (☎ 27 64 89, fax 27 83 09, BP 153) has 16 condolike units above a rocky coastline. It's within walking distance of Flamands Beach and right at the trailhead to Anse de Colombier. Each unit has a bedroom with two beds, a kitchenette, an ocean-facing terrace and air-con. Singles/doubles are a reasonable 300/400F in summer, 500/700F in winter.

St-Barth Isle de France (☎ 27 61 81, fax 27 86 83, BP 612), a luxury hotel at the east end of the bay, has 31 spacious rooms and suites that start at US$360 (2484F) in summer, US$490 (3381F) in winter, breakfast included.

Restaurant options are limited. For something quick and cheap, there's *Epicerie Sainte Helen*, a small bakery on the village's main road about 50m before the beach.

ANSE DE COLOMBIER

Colombier Beach is a beautiful, secluded white-sand beach fronted by turquoise waters and backed by undulating hills. It's reached by boat or via a scenic 20-minute walk that begins at the end of the road in La Petite Anse, just beyond Flamands.

The well-trodden trail leads through a fascinating desertlike terrain punctuated by organ-pipe cacti and wildflowers. En route it provides some wonderful coastal views of La Petite Anse and the rugged shoreline of Anse Paschal before crossing a ridge and ending at the north side of Colombier Bay. Steps lead down to the beach.

The sandy bottom at the beach is ideal for swimming, and there's fairly good snorkeling at the north side. Take drinking water, as the trail is unshaded and there are no facilities.

ST JEAN

St Jean, the island's most touristed area, is spread along a large, curving bay lined with a white-sand beach. The town has no real center, and from the road it can seem like a nondescript strip of small shopping complexes, hotels and restaurants. But it's quite a bustling little stretch and makes for a good place to have coffee and a meal and watch the world go by. It's also quite appealing once you're on the beach, where reef-protected turquoise waters provide good conditions for swimming, snorkeling and windsurfing. The beach is divided into two separate sections by a quartzite hill topped by the picturesque Eden Rock Hotel. The airport is at the west end of St Jean.

Places to Stay

The *Tropical Hotel* (☎ 27 64 87, fax 27 81 74, BP 147), on a hillside a couple of minutes' walk from the beach, has 20 rooms with air-con, refrigerators, TV and balconies. Singles/doubles start at 570/730F in summer, 990/1250F in winter, for garden-view rooms with breakfast. It's closed from early September to mid-October.

Emeraude Plage (☎ 27 64 78, fax 27 83 08, emeraudeplage@wanadoo.fr) is a pleasant beachfront hotel landscaped with oleander and hibiscus. It has 24 bungalow-style units, each with a kitchenette that opens onto a terrace, and contains a TV, phone, air-con and ceiling fan. There are also three suites and one villa. Rates, which vary depending on the size of the bungalow and its proximity to the beach, begin at 750F in summer, 1200F in winter for one-bedroom bungalows. Studios are 800F in summer,

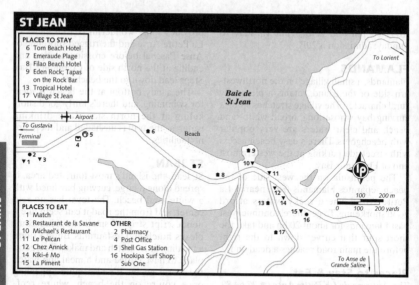

ST JEAN

PLACES TO STAY
6 Tom Beach Hotel
7 Emeraude Plage
8 Filao Beach Hotel
9 Eden Rock; Tapas
   on the Rock Bar
13 Tropical Hotel
17 Village St Jean

PLACES TO EAT
1 Match
3 Restaurant de la Savane
10 Michael's Restaurant
11 Le Pelican
12 Chez Annick
14 Kiki-é Mo
15 La Piment

OTHER
2 Pharmacy
4 Post Office
5 Shell Gas Station
16 Hookipa Surf Shop;
   Sub One

Baie de
St Jean

To Lorient

Airport

To Gustavia
Terminal

Beach

To Anse de
Grande Saline

0   100   200 m
0   100   200 yards

1200F in winter, and the villa can be rented for 2100F in summer, 3300F in winter.

Village St Jean (☎ 27 61 39, fax 27 77 96, in the USA ☎ 800-651-8366, vsjhotel@wanadoo.fr, BP 623) is a pleasant family-run hotel a five-minute walk uphill from the beach. The 20 modern cottages have kitchens, air-con, ceiling fans and private terraces. The hotel features a pool with a view of the bay, a Jacuzzi and a small 'honor store' with soft drinks and snacks. Two-bedroom deluxe cottages are US$295 (2035F) in summer, US$490 (3381F) in winter, but there are cheaper, standard cottages. There are also four hotel rooms with air-con, without kitchens but including breakfast, for US$95 (656F) in summer, US$160 (1104F) in winter.

At the airport-end of St Jean is ***Tom Beach Hotel*** (☎ 27 53 13, fax 27 53 15, tombeach@wanadoo.fr), a bustling, colorful 12-room hotel right on the beach. It's livelier than the other options in and around St Jean, and it has a restaurant open to the beach. Rooms get more expensive the closer you are to the beach, starting at US$192 (1325F) in summer and US$268

(1849F) in winter (double that over the Christmas period). The rooms can accommodate up to four people, which makes it a bit lighter on the pocket if you're traveling in a group.

Filao Beach Hotel (☎ 27 64 84, fax 27 62 24, BP 667) has 30 rooms in a number of buildings. This upmarket hotel has attractive grounds, an amiable staff and a nice beachfront location. Rooms are comfortably furnished with a TV, ceiling fan, air-con and a queen- or king-size bed. Rates, which include breakfast, are 1000F to 2500F in summer, 2000F to 3300F in winter.

Eden Rock (☎ 29 79 89, fax 27 88 37, info@edenrockhotel.com), St Barts' first hotel, sits on the rocky promontory that separates the two sandy strands of St Jean Beach. Although the property has been modernized, many of the 14 rooms still have antique furnishings and a pleasant old-fashioned decor. You can even sleep in the same four-poster bed that Greta Garbo slept in. The only drawback is the price, which ranges from US$275 (1898F) to US$1550 (10,695F), depending on the room and the season (breakfast is included).

Places to Eat

Town Center In a colorful little roadside hut, *Kiki-é Mo* has deli-style Italian sandwiches, pastas, antipasto salads, tiramisu, espresso and cappuccino, all at moderate prices (pastas and sandwiches around US$7). There are a couple of café tables outside where you can sit and eat. Right next door is another reasonably priced sandwich shop, *Chez Annick*, which seems to be the flavor of the month with the young crowd. Again, sandwiches are around US$7 (50F), even for smoked salmon.

La Piment, on the corner of the road leading to Saline Beach, is a good choice for Continental breakfast (55F), with outdoor seating and a bubbly atmosphere. Sandwiches and burgers make up the bulk of the choice for lunch, which average around 80F.

Right on the beach opposite Chez Annick is *Le Pelican*, which is popular for lunch. Main dishes, a collection of French and American cuisine, start at 75F, with the most expensive being the T-bone steak, which runs 150F.

Eden Rock's *Michael's Restaurant*, with its alfresco waterside dining, is another popular lunch spot. Salads and light fare cost around 80F, while meat, duck and fish main dishes average 100F to 160F. The *Eden Rock* restaurant is a fine-dining dinner restaurant with a pleasant balcony setting and expensive Continental fare. The complex's other choice for dinner is *Tapas on the Rock Bar*, serving up a selection of tapas-like lobster minestrone, mussels and all flavors of *fajita*. Prices range from 45F up to 70F.

Around the Airport Opposite the airport terminal is *Restaurant de la Savane*, with 30F sandwiches and French/American main dishes from 45F. A small courtyard area has tables at the rear. In the same center is a large *Match* supermarket with a good deli section and French wines from 30F a bottle. It's open 8 am to 8 pm Monday to Saturday (closed 1 to 3 pm Monday to Thursday), 9 am to 1 pm and 4 to 7 pm Sunday.

LORIENT

Lorient, the site of St Barts' first French settlement (1648), is a small village fronted by a nice white-sand beach. When it's calm, snorkelers take to the water, but when the surf's up, this is one of the island's best surfing spots.

To get to the beach, turn left at the cemetery on the east side of the village. Be sure you don't confuse this with the cemetery at the intersection that fronts an attractive old church.

Lorient is a quiet spot, but it has a good selection of amenities, with a postage-stamp-size post office, a gas station, and Jojo's grocery store with an attached burger shop, all on the main road.

Places to Stay

The village has two recommendable accommodation options on the inland road within easy walking distance of the beach. The more conventional is *La Normandie Hôtel* (☎ 27 61 66, fax 27 98 83, studiooceane@ wanadoo.fr), which has eight pleasant rooms with refrigerators, ceiling fans and air-con from 250F in summer and 280/330F for singles/doubles in winter. There's also a pool.

Delightful *Le Manoir* (☎ 27 79 27, fax 27 65 75) features accommodations in 17th-century-style cottages surrounding a manor house that was built in Normandy in 1610 and reconstructed here in 1984. The brainchild of Jeanne Audy-Roland, creator of the 'M' natural-cosmetic line, Le Manoir was designed for visiting artists and other like-minded travelers. The cottages are rustic, with mosquito nets over the beds, small kitchens and private gardens. Rooms range from 300F to 500F.

LORIENT TO GRAND CUL-DE-SAC

On the eastern outskirts of Lorient the road climbs up into the hills, offering some fine coastal views. The area encompasses the coastal headland of **Pointe Milou**; the hamlet of **Vitet**, at the foothills of 286m Morne du Vitet; and **Marigot**, a little seaside village on a small bay.

Hubert Delamotte, a New Age astrologer and chef, operates ***Hostellerie des 3 Forces*** (☎ *27 61 25, fax 27 81 38, 3-forces@ st-barths.com*) in Vitet. The site, which has a fantastic view over Marigot, consists of a dozen simple rooms, each named for a sign of the zodiac; all of them have private bathrooms and balconies, mosquito nets and mini-refrigerators. Fan-cooled singles/ doubles cost US$150/200 (1035/1380F) in summer, US$200/300 (1380/2070F) in winter. Air-conditioned rooms are about 20% more. The restaurant serves French and Creole food. Lunch offerings range from omelets (45F) to beef brochette (105F), while dinner features a 270F three-course meal with a choice of seafood, vegetarian or red-meat main dishes.

Christopher Hotel (☎ *27 63 63, fax 27 92 92, in the USA* ☎ *800-221-4542, BP 571, Pointe Milou*) is an upscale resort with 40 luxurious rooms. Each has an ocean-view patio, separate bathtub and shower, silent air-con, ceiling fan, minibar, room safe, TV and phone. While the beach is rocky, the hotel has a large, free-form swimming pool and a fitness center. Rates start at 1500F in summer, 2600F in winter, full breakfast included. Guests staying more than a couple of nights should take advantage of some good-value package deals, which cut the rates by a third. The hotel's seaside restaurant, ***L'Orchidée***, offers a three-course dinner of the day for 250F. The restaurant is closed mid-September to mid-October.

GRAND CUL-DE-SAC

Grand Cul-de-Sac has a sandy beach and a reef-protected bay with good water-sports conditions. The area attracts an active crowd that includes lots of windsurfers. The beach is along a narrow strip of land that separates the bay from a large salt pond (sand fleas can be a nuisance). Fronting the bay are a couple of hotels and restaurants, along with a windsurfing and water-sports center.

Places to Stay

The ***St Barths Beach Hotel*** (☎ *27 60 70, fax 27 75 57, sbbh@st-barths.com, BP 580*) is in fact right on the beach, with 36 rooms in two-story buildings, each with air-con, a balcony, phone, TV and minibar. There's also a gym on-site. Rates are pricey, US$140/190 (966/1311F) for singles/doubles in summer, US$230/330 (1587/2277F) in winter.

At the beach's north end is ***El Sereno*** (☎ *27 64 80, fax 27 75 47, serenohotel@ wanadoo.fr, BP 19*), which has 34 rooms surrounding a central courtyard garden. While each has a TV, small refrigerator, air-con and room safe, the rates are steep, beginning at 1000 in summer, 1400F in winter. You can hit the pool if you're not keen on the salty sea.

Places to Eat

Popular ***Le Rivage*** (☎ *27 82 42*), at St Barths Beach Hotel, offers a fine beachfront setting. Sandwiches start at 45F, and main dishes such as mahimahi and grilled lamb chops begin around 90F. It's open noon to 3 pm and 7 to 10 pm daily.

Bobou's, at El Sereno, offers a mix of North African and Creole food, including a Moroccan salad assortment and fish fillet in Creole sauce for 95F to 140F. It's open noon to 4:30 pm and 6:30 to 11 pm daily, with happy hour in between the two.

BEYOND GRAND CUL-DE-SAC

From Grand Cul-de-Sac the road makes a curving sweep around the base of the 286m Morne du Vitet and the 274m Morne de Grand Fond, the island's highest mountains. It's a nice country drive that passes grassy green slopes, handsome stone walls, grazing cows and the occasional farmer, creating a scene that's often compared to rural Normandy.

ANSE DE GRANDE SALINE

Saline Beach is a long, lovely beach, broad and secluded, named after the large salt pond that backs it. Stilts and other waterbirds flock to the pond, but so do biting gnats, which sometimes can be an obstacle to enjoying the beach. Saline Beach is off the main tourist track but is considered a special place by islanders and return visitors.

The cement road into Saline Beach ends about half a kilometer before the beach, but you can often continue to drive along the south side of the salt pond on a rutted dirt road that will take you within a two-minute walk of the beach.

For an enjoyable lunch, *Le Tamarin*, on the way to the beach, has a pleasant setting and offers a melange of good Creole and French food at moderate prices. It's also the closest place to the beach for food.

ANSE DU GOUVERNEUR

Gouverneur Beach is a gorgeous, sandy beach lining a U-shaped bay that's embraced by high cliffs at both ends. It's one of the more broad and secluded spots in the entire region, and it makes a splendid spot for sunbathing and picnics. There are no facilities, however. To get there from Gustavia, head southeast past the Carl Gustaf hotel. The road becomes increasingly steep until you reach the mountain crest in Lurin, where you turn right and wind down a narrow cement road that will test your brakes (use low gear). You'll catch some spectacular glimpses of the coast en route, as well as a sign stating that it's a private road, and that you are proceeding at your own risk!

ST BARTS

St Eustatius (Statia)

St Eustatius – spelled 'Sint Eustatius' in Dutch, and more commonly known as Statia – is a tranquil little outpost with an intriguing colonial history. Part of the Netherlands Antilles, the island has interesting historical sites (the local car number-plate signature – 'The Historic Gem' – definitely holds true) and some good hiking and diving opportunities.

Highlights

- Hiking up to The Quill, Statia's extinct volcano
- Ambling around Oranjestad's colonial sites and historic fort
- Visiting the 18th-century Simon Doncker House, now a superb museum
- Diving at Hangover Reef

OTHER MAPS
St Eustatius (Statia)
page 382

Oranjestad
page 389

CARIBBEAN
SEA

| 0 | 1.5 | 3 km |
| 0 | 1 | 2 miles |

Just a few kilometers wide, Statia is essentially a one-town island. The capital of Oranjestad is surrounded by the airport and a few residential neighborhoods, which lie on its outskirts.

Although it's only a 20-minute flight from St Martin, Statia is one of the most overlooked destinations in the Leeward Islands, partly because it has none of the tourist-luring beaches that St Martin's closer neighbors boast. Of course, the lack of crowds is part of the appeal for travelers who do come this way. In many ways, landing in Statia is a bit like stepping back into a niche of the Caribbean from the 1950s – islanders enjoy striking up conversations, stray chickens and goats mosey in the streets and the pace is delightfully slow. Statia offers a nice, quiet break for those looking to get away from the more touristed islands.

Facts about St Eustatius

HISTORY
The Caribs called the island Alo, which means 'cashew tree,' while Columbus named the island after St Anastasia. Although the French began construction of a fort in 1629, the Dutch established the first permanent settlement, in 1636, after they routed the small French contingent off the island. Statia subsequently changed hands 22 times among the squabbling Dutch, French and British.

In the 18th century, as the British and French buried their colonies in taxes and duties, the Dutch turned Statia into a duty-free port. As a result, West Indian and North American colonies were able to circumvent duties by shipping goods via Statia, which boomed into a thriving entrepôt and a major trade center between the Old and New Worlds.

ST EUSTATIUS (STATIA)

During the island's heyday in the 1770s, as many as 300 trading ships pulled into port each month, and the population swelled to 20,000. The resulting prosperity earned Statia the nickname 'Golden Rock of the Caribbean.'

Many of the goods destined for the rebellious North American colonies passed through Statia. Along with 'legal' cargoes of molasses and slaves, the merchant ships sailing from Statia also smuggled in arms and gunpowder to New England, much to the ire of British officials, whose protests to the mercantile Dutch drew little response.

One event that particularly irritated the British took place on November 16, 1776, when Statia, rather inadvertently, became the first foreign land to recognize the American colonies' Declaration of Independence by returning a cannon salute to the passing American war brig *Andrew Doria*. Unfortunately for Statia, another American vessel went on to capture a British ship in nearby waters, adding an element of significance to the gesture.

In 1781, British admiral George Rodney settled the score by launching a naval attack on Statia, ransacking the warehouses, exiling the island's merchants and auctioning off their goods. The Dutch regained possession of the island a few years later, but the British invasion marked the end of Statia's predominance as a trade center.

Ironically, US independence, and the signing of a peace treaty between the USA and Britain in 1783, allowed the former American colonies to establish more direct trade routes and bypass Statia altogether. To this day, Statia remains well off the beaten path.

GEOGRAPHY

Statia is 8km long and 3km wide, with about 21 sq km of land. The island is 61km south of St Martin and 27km southeast of Saba.

The Quill (whose name is derived from the Dutch word *kwil,* meaning 'volcano') looms above the southern half of the island. This extinct volcano, which reaches 600m at Mazinga, the highest point on the rim, is responsible for the high, conical appearance Statia has when viewed from neighboring islands.

Cliffs drop straight to the sea along much of the shoreline, and the island has precious few beaches. At the north side of Statia there are a few low mountains, while the island's central plain contains the airport and town.

CLIMATE

In January the average daily high temperature is 29°C (85°F), while the low averages 22°C (72°F). In July the average daily high is 32°C (90°F) and the average low hovers around 24°C (76°F).

The annual rainfall in Statia averages 1145mm (45 inches) and is fairly evenly dispersed throughout the year. Relative humidity is in the low 70s from March to December and in the mid-70s in January and February.

FLORA & FAUNA

Most of the island is dry with scrubby vegetation, although oleander, bougainvillea, hibiscus and chain-of-love flowers add a splash of color here and there. The greatest variety of flora is in The Quill, which collects enough cloud cover for its central crater to harbor a rain forest with ferns, elephant ears, bromeliads, bananas and tall trees. The island also has 18 varieties of orchids, all but three of which are found within The Quill.

There are 25 resident species of birds on Statia, including white-tailed tropic birds that nest on the cliffs along the beach north of Lower Town. There are also harmless racer snakes, iguanas, lizards and tree frogs. Other than that, most animal life is limited to goats, chickens, cows and donkeys.

GOVERNMENT & POLITICS

Statia is part of the Dutch kingdom, one of five islands in the Netherlands Antilles whose central administration is in Curaçao. As with the other four islands, Statia is treated as a municipality and has its own lieutenant governor, appointed by Queen Beatrix of the Netherlands. The lieutenant governor and two elected commissioners are responsible for running Statia's daily affairs.

ECONOMY

A large proportion of Statia's work force is employed in government administration. The rest of the island's economy is dependent upon a mix of fishing, small retail businesses and a bit of tourism. There are large, unsightly oil tanks on the northwest side of the island where oil is offloaded and stored for transshipment to other islands.

POPULATION & PEOPLE

The population of Statia is about 2800. The majority of the people are black, largely the descendants of African slaves brought to Statia to work in the warehouses in Lower Town and on a handful of long-vanished plantations.

SOCIETY & CONDUCT

The culture is a mix of African and Dutch heritages, similar to that found on other Dutch islands. The lifestyle is casual, but a bit more conservative than on neighboring islands – bathing suits should certainly be limited to beach areas and hotel pools. Nude bathing is not acceptable.

ST EUSTATIUS

RELIGION
There are Methodist, Roman Catholic, Seventh Day Adventist, Anglican, Baptist, Apostolic and Baha'i churches on Statia.

LANGUAGE
While Dutch is the official language, English is most commonly spoken.

Facts for the Visitor

ORIENTATION
Statia has few roads and is easy to get around. Oranjestad, the island's town, is 1.5km south of the airport. It is divided by a cliff into Upper Town and Lower Town, and the two sections are connected by both a footpath and a vehicle road.

The tourist office has free island maps that show the roads and hiking trails.

TOURIST OFFICES
Local Tourist Offices
The main tourist office is in Fort Oranje, Upper Town, Oranjestad, and there's a tourist information booth at the airport.

When requesting information by mail, write to the St Eustatius Tourism Development Foundation (☎/fax 3-182433, euxtour@ goldenrock.net), Fort Oranjestaat, Oranjestad, St Eustatius, Netherlands Antilles.

Tourist Offices Abroad
Overseas tourism representatives include the following:

Netherlands
Antillen Huis (Kabinet van de Gevolmachtigde Minister van de Nederlandse Antillen; ☎ 070-306-6111, fax 070-306-6110) Badhuisweg 173–175, 2597 JP 'S-Gravenhage

USA
Statia Tourist Office (☎ 561-394-8580, fax 561-488-4294) PO Box 6322, Boca Raton, FL 33427

VISAS & DOCUMENTS
Valid passports are required of all visitors except for US and Canadian citizens, who need only proof of citizenship, such as an official birth certificate accompanied by a driver's license. A roundtrip or onward ticket is officially required.

CUSTOMS
Statia is a free port and there are no customs regulations.

MONEY
The Netherlands Antilles guilder or florin is the official currency, but US dollars are accepted everywhere. Hotel, car rental and dive-shop prices are given in dollars, while islander-geared businesses post prices in guilders. The exchange rate is officially 1.80 guilders to US$1. For more information, see Money in the Regional Facts for the Visitor chapter.

Credit cards are accepted by car rental agencies, larger hotels and a few shops.

POST & COMMUNICATIONS
Post
Statia's only post office is on Cattageweg in Oranjestad. When writing to Statia from abroad, if a post-office box number is not listed simply address mail with the individual or business name, followed by 'St Eustatius, Netherlands Antilles.'

It costs Fls 1.10 to mail a postcard and Fls 2.25 to mail a letter to the USA, Canada, UK or Europe; and Fls 1.30 for a postcard and Fls 3.25 for a letter to Australia, Asia or Africa.

Telephone
There are card phones at the airport, the port and in a number of places around town. Phone cards are sold at the Antelecom telephone office, the airport and several stores.

To call Statia from overseas, add the area code 599 in front of the seven-digit local number.

For more information, see Post & Communications in Regional Facts for the Visitor.

INTERNET RESOURCES
Statia's official Web site, www.turq.com/ statia, is a comprehensive source of general information online.

NEWSPAPERS & MAGAZINES

There currently is no island newspaper or magazine published on Statia, but St Martin's *Daily Herald* has a bit of Statia news and is sold around the island.

RADIO & TV

Statia has its own radio station at 92.3 FM. Cable TV delivers two dozen channels, heavy on US programming.

ELECTRICITY

Electricity is 110V, 60 cycles, and a flat two-pronged plug is used, the same type as in the United States.

WEIGHTS & MEASURES

Statia uses the metric system.

HEALTH

Statia's hospital, the Queen Beatrix Medical Center (☎ 3-182211), is at Prinsesweg 25 on the east side of Oranjestad.

DANGERS & ANNOYANCES

There is little crime on Statia, and most locals don't even lock their doors. However, it's best not to leave things unattended on the beach – snorkeling gear is one item that sometimes seems to wander off.

EMERGENCIES

If you need to get in touch with the police, call ☎ 3-182333.

BUSINESS HOURS

Shops and offices are commonly open 8 or 9 am to 6 or 7 pm Monday to Saturday. Supermarkets are often open 9 am to 1 pm Sunday as well.

PUBLIC HOLIDAYS & SPECIAL EVENTS

Public holidays on Statia are as follows:

New Year's Day	January 1
Good Friday	Friday before Easter
Easter Sunday	late March/early April
Easter Monday	late March/early April
Queen's Day	April 30
Labor Day	May 1
Ascension Thursday	40th day after Easter
Christmas Day	December 25
Boxing Day	December 26

The Statia Carnival, 10 days of revelry kicking off at the end of July, is the island's biggest festival, culminating on a Monday. Music, jump-ups (including early-morning pajama ones), competitions and local food are the highlights.

Fort Oranje is the site of ceremonies held on Statia-America Day, November 16, which commemorates the date in 1776 when Statia became the first foreign land to salute the US flag.

ACTIVITIES

Beaches & Swimming

No one visits Statia for its beaches, which can't compare with other islands' and are few in number. The island's best beach for swimming is the usually calm Oranje Beach in Lower Town. Zeelandia Bay, on the east coast, has rough surf and undertows and is not recommended for swimming; nonetheless, it rates as Statia's second beach.

Diving & Snorkeling

Statia has a score of dive sites, the majority of which are coral formations on old lava flows. There are also a few wrecks of colonial trading ships, although the remains are basically piles of ballast stones, as the ships themselves have disintegrated. To protect the island's historical remains from souvenir hunters, much of the water surrounding Statia became a marine park in January 1998. Along with the standing rule that all divers must be accompanied by a local guide, you also cannot anchor within the Marine Park, use spearguns, remove animals or plants (dead or alive) or touch or feed the marine life. To help keep the Marine Park afloat, so to speak, a fee of US$3 per dive or snorkeling trip is payable to Marine Park office, or to your dive operator. For more information on the park, contact the Statia Marine Park office (☎ 3-182884, fax 3-182913), in Oranjestad.

ST EUSTATIUS

The *Stingray* wreck (1768), in 15m of water a few minutes from Lower Town, is near a ledge with a rich concentration of marine life, including stingrays, spotted eels and octopuses.

Hangover Reef, at the southwest side of the island, is a popular reef dive with a wide variety of sponges, corals and sea fans. It also has many ledges and crevices harboring lobsters, sea turtles and numerous species of fish.

For a deep dive, Doobie Crack, a large cleft in a reef at the northwest side of the island, has black-tip sharks and schools of large fish.

Snorkeling tours of some of the shallower reefs are available from the dive shops for around US$25.

Dive Shops Despite Statia's light tourism, there are three dive shops offering competitive rates. One-tank dives average US$45, two-tank dives US$80. Night dives, certification courses and multidive packages are also available. Dive shop choices comprise the following:

Dive Statia (☎ 3-182435, fax 3-182539, in the USA ☎ 405-843-7846, info@divestatia.com)

Golden Rock Dive Center (☎/fax 3-182964, in the USA ☎ 800-311-6658, grdivers@goldenrock.net)

Scubaqua Dive Center (☎/fax 3-182160, dive@scubaqua.com)

Hiking

The tourist office has a free hiking brochure with descriptions of 12 trails, and it can provide information on current trail conditions. Most of the trails are signposted, and some of them are marked with orange ribbons.

The most popular hike is to The Quill, Statia's extinct volcano. The Quill, and its surrounding slopes, was designated a national park in May 1998. The trail leading up the mountain begins at the end of Rosemary Laan in Oranjestad and takes about 50 minutes to reach the edge of the crater. From there you can continue in either direction along the rim. The trail to the right

(southeast) takes about 45 minutes and ends atop the 600m Mazinga, Statia's highest point. The shorter Panorama Track to the left offers spectacular views and takes only about 15 minutes. A third option is the steep track leading down into the crater, where there's a thick rain forest of tall trees, some with huge buttressed trunks. This track, which takes about 30 minutes each way, can be very slippery, so sturdy shoes are essential.

Guided tours are a good idea if you want to find out more about the native flora and fauna; they can be organized through the tourist office or the St Eustatius National Parks Foundation (Stenapa; ☎ 3-182884), the organization that oversees the national park.

ACCOMMODATIONS

Most accommodations are in Oranjestad or near the airport. All places are quite modest in scale, and prices are moderate by Caribbean standards.

There's a 7% government tax on accommodations in Statia, and hotels tack on a 10% to 15% service charge.

FOOD & DRINKS

Considering its size, Statia has a reasonable number and variety of restaurants, including a couple of Chinese places; most are moderately priced. There are several small grocery stores in Oranjestad, with the Windward Islands Supermarket on Heilligerweg being one of the better stocked.

Most tap water comes from individual rainwater catchment systems and should be boiled before drinking. Bottled water is available at grocery stores.

Getting There & Away

DEPARTURE TAX

For stays of more than 24 hours, there's a departure tax of US$5.65 for travel within the Netherlands Antilles, US$12 to other destinations.

AIR

Statia's Franklin Delano Roosevelt Airport has a staffed tourist information booth, a card phone, a refreshment stand and a Winair counter.

The largeness of the airport runway unfortunately doesn't equate to the amount of air traffic entering Statia. The only scheduled flights to Statia are with Winair (☎ 3-182735), which has five flights a day from St Martin.

Statia can be easily visited as a day trip. The first flight from St Martin leaves at 7 am, and the last flight returns at 6 pm weekdays and 9 pm weekends. The fare is US$49 one-way, and from US$98 roundtrip.

Winair also makes the 10-minute hop from Saba to Statia every afternoon, as well as a couple of mornings a week, for US$25 each way.

SEA

Statia has a 210m L-shaped breakwater at the south end of Lower Town. The harbor includes an anchorage for fishing boats and space for visiting yachts. Yachters should check in with the harbormaster upon arrival.

Cruise Ship

Statia does not have a deepwater port capable of handling large cruise ships, but the island is visited by Windjammer Barefoot Cruises' schooners and a few other small cruise ships.

Getting Around

Statia has no buses, so renting a car is useful if you want to explore the island properly, which could be done in a day. If you're staying in Oranjestad, you probably won't need a car for most of your stay, but expect to do some serious walking, as the town is spread out.

TO/FROM THE AIRPORT

There are usually one or two taxis on hand to meet flights. If you miss the taxis, look for Rosie, the cheery ex–St Martiner who owns Rainbow Car Rental, as she'll drop you off in town for the same rate. Otherwise, the person at the tourist information booth can call a taxi for you.

CAR & MOTORCYCLE
Road Rules

Drive on the right-hand side of the road. Your home driver's license is valid for driving on Statia.

By Caribbean standards Statia's roads are good, albeit sometimes narrow, and you need to watch out for stray animals on the road. Surprisingly, Oranjestad has quite a few one-way streets.

Statia's only gas station is in Lower Town opposite the pier. It's usually open 7:30 am to 7 pm Monday to Saturday.

Rental

Rainbow Car Rental (☎ 3-182811) rents out cars for US$35, plus US$5 for CWD insurance; although there's no booth, Rosie, who manages Rainbow, is often at the airport to meet flights.

Other rental companies include ARC Car Rental (☎ 3-182595), Brown's Car Rental (☎ 3-182266) and Lady Ama's Services (☎ 3-182712). Try Richarson Jeep Rental (☎ 3-182149), which has jeeps for US$40 a day.

Mansion Scooter & Car Rental (☎ 3-182764), half a kilometer south of the airport on LE Saddlerweg, rents motor scooters for US$25 per day.

TAXI

Taxis rates are set, and drivers will charge exactly US$5 between the airport and Upper Town, US$3 from Upper Town to Lower Town, US$5 from the airport to the jetty, and US$3 from town to the Quill trailhead; add US$1 after sunset.

HITCHHIKING

Hitchhiking is practiced on Statia, but traffic is light to the more distant parts of the island, and, of course, the usual precautions apply.

ST EUSTATIUS

ORGANIZED TOURS
A two-hour taxi tour of the island costs US$40 for up to five people.

Oranjestad

Oranjestad, the island's capital and its only town, has a pleasant rural feeling with a fine sense of history. It consists of Lower Town, which is the area down along the waterfront, and Upper Town, which is on the bluff above.

Lower Town was the location of the original port town and still has some ruins from the colonial era, as well as the island's best beach and Statia's harbor.

Upper Town is Oranjestad's main commercial and residential area. That said, you'll still come across donkeys, chickens and dogs roaming around freely. It has numerous historical sites, all of which can easily be explored on foot in a few leisurely hours. Bay Rd, a steep cobbled lane that was once used to march Africans from the slave ships, provides a pedestrian route up the coastal cliff to link the two parts of town.

You can pick up a useful historical walking-tour book and map of Oranjestad for US$7 at the museum.

Information
Tourist Offices The very helpful St Eustatius Tourist Bureau (☎ 3-182433) is located in Fort Oranje in an old stone building overlooking the inner fort. It's open 8 am to noon and 1 to 5 pm Monday to Thursday, till 4:30 pm Friday. Local artists often exhibit their work at the office.

Money There are two banks in the town center: Barclays Bank, between the library and museum, and Windward Islands Bank, on Fort Oranje Straat. Barclays Bank is open 8:30 am to 3:30 pm weekdays. Windward Islands Bank has similar hours, but closes at noon for an hour. Neither bank has an ATM.

Post & Communications The post office, on Cottageweg, is open 7:30 am to noon and 1 to 5 pm Monday to Thursday, till 4:30 pm Friday. Antelecom, the telephone office, is to the south.

Internet access is available at the public library for around US$5 per half-hour. It's open noon to 5 pm Monday and 8 am to 5 pm Tuesday to Friday.

Fort Oranje
Right in the center of town, Fort Oranje is an intact fort complete with cannons, triple bastions and a cobblestone courtyard. It's perched on the cliffside directly above Lower Town and offers a broad view of the waterfront below. The first rampart here was erected by the French in 1629, but most of the fort was built after the Dutch took the island from the French in 1636. They added to the fort a number of times over the years, enlarging it into the largest fortress on Statia.

The courtyard has a couple of memorials, including a plaque presented by US President Franklin Roosevelt to commemorate the fort's fateful 1776 salute of the American war vessel *Andrew Doria*. At the time, the British on neighboring Antigua didn't take too kindly to Statia being the first foreign power to officially recognize the new American nation. The British navy later sailed for Oranjestad, mercilessly bombed the crap out of it, and then took possession of the island and all its wealth. The fort is always open, and there's no admission fee.

Sint Eustatius Museum
This museum (☎ 3-182288), operated by the Sint Eustatius Historical Foundation, gives visitors a glimpse of upper-class colonial life on Statia and is one of the Eastern Caribbean's finest historical museums.

It occupies the Simon Doncker House, a restored 18th-century Dutch merchant's home that's decorated with period furnishings and holds collections of nautical artifacts, china and hand-blown bottles. The basement, formerly a wine cellar, houses the museum's pre-Columbian collection.

The house's history includes a stint as the headquarters of Admiral George Rodney following the British invasion of the island

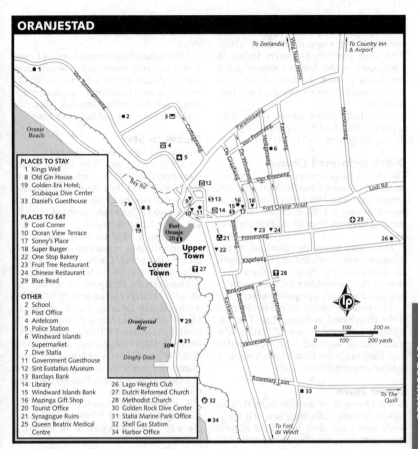

ORANJESTAD

To Zeelandia

To Country Inn & Airport

Oranje Beach

Oranjestad Bay

Dinghy Dock

Fort Oranje

Upper Town

Lower Town

To The Quill

To Fort de Windt

PLACES TO STAY
1 Kings Well
8 Old Gin House
19 Golden Era Hotel;
   Scubaqua Dive Center
33 Daniel's Guesthouse

PLACES TO EAT
9 Cool Corner
10 Ocean View Terrace
17 Sonny's Place
18 Super Burger
22 One Stop Bakery
23 Fruit Tree Restaurant
24 Chinese Restaurant
29 Blue Bead

OTHER
2 School
3 Post Office
4 Antelcom
5 Police Station
6 Windward Islands
   Supermarket
7 Dive Statia
11 Government Guesthouse
12 Sint Eustatius Museum
13 Barclays Bank
14 Library
15 Windward Islands Bank
16 Mazinga Gift Shop
20 Tourist Office
21 Synagogue Ruins
25 Queen Beatrix Medical
   Centre
26 Lago Heights Club
27 Dutch Reformed Church
28 Methodist Church
30 Golden Rock Dive Center
31 Statia Marine Park Office
32 Shell Gas Station
34 Harbor Office

0   100   200 m
0   100   200 yards

ST EUSTATIUS

in 1781. The museum is open 9 am to 5 pm weekdays, till noon Saturday. Admission is US$2/1 for adults/children.

Government Guesthouse

The Government Guesthouse is the handsome 18th-century stone-and-wood building opposite Barclays Bank. It was thoroughly renovated in 1992 with funding from the EU and is now the government headquarters, with the offices of the lieutenant governor and commissioners on the ground floor and the courtroom on the upper floor.

The building, which once served as the Dutch naval commander's quarters, derived its name from its 1920s spell as a guest house.

Synagogue Ruins

Those with a particular interest in Jewish history or old buildings can explore the roofless and slowly decaying yellow-brick walls of the Honen Dalim, an abandoned synagogue that dates from 1739. It's 30m down the alleyway opposite the south side of the library. The synagogue is the second oldest in the Western Hemisphere.

Statia's rising influence as a trade center was accompanied by a large influx of Jewish merchants beginning in the early 1700s. With their livelihoods closely linked to trade, most of the Jewish community left the island around the turn of the 19th century, when Statia's importance as a port declined.

About half a kilometer east of the synagogue ruins is a Jewish cemetery with gravestones dating from 1742 to 1843.

Dutch Reformed Church

The thick (600mm) stone walls of the old Dutch Reformed Church, built in 1755, remain perfectly intact, but the roof collapsed during a 1792 hurricane and the building has been open to the heavens ever since.

The church tower, also damaged by the hurricane, was renovated in 1981, and you can now climb the steep steps for a good view of the surrounding area. Entrance is free, and it's usually open until sunset.

Also noteworthy are the old tombstones in the churchyard, including that of Jan de Windt, a former governor of Statia, Saba and St Martin, who died in 1775. The church is on Kerkweg, a few minutes' walk south of the Government Guesthouse.

Lower Town

Lower Town is a narrow coastal area backed by steep cliffs. High seas and hurricanes have taken their toll on the historic waterfront; however, the remains of the old foundations from some of the 18th-century warehouses that once lined the coast can still be seen jutting into the water along the shore. Submerged sections of the old seawall that once protected the harborfront can be explored by donning a mask and snorkel.

On both sides of the coastal road you'll see a handful of brick warehouses from the period, a few still in use. The building opposite Dive Statia was once used to house slaves, while the dive shop itself occupies a former lighthouse.

With a little imagination, the fading ruins can help conjure up an image of the past,

when the area was bustling with traders and merchants and the bay was chock full of ships.

Oranje Beach, at the north end of Lower Town, has gray sands and generally calm waters. Modest as it may be, it's the island's best all-around beach and a popular swimming spot for Statian families. There's a harbor at the south end of Lower Town.

Places to Stay

Accommodations have become fairly scarce on Statia after a new School of Medicine was opened in 1999. A number of places to stay have closed their doors to the public and rented out their rooms to the students, so it's a good idea to phone ahead to make sure something is available.

Camping is legal on Statia, but at the time of writing there were no camping facilities on the island. Check with the tourist office for suitable places to pitch a tent.

Oranjestad's cheapest rooms can be found at *Daniel's Guesthouse* (☎ 3-182358), on Rosemary Laan at the south side of Upper Town, about five to 10 minutes' walk from the town center. There are a couple of singles/doubles available on a daily basis for US$35/40, with air-con and cable TV. Jacob Daniel, the owner, is a walking encyclopedia of local information and offers excellent historical tours of Statia.

For something closer to the planes, *Country Inn* (☎/fax 3-182484) is in Concordia, a 10-minute walk east of the airport. It has six pleasant rooms, simple but clean and each with air-con, cable TV and radio alarm clock. Rooms cost US$40/55, including the government tax. Breakfast is an extra US$4.50. The friendly owner, Iris Pompier, is a fine cook, and lunch and dinner are available on request.

Golden Era Hotel (☎ 3-182345, fax 3-182445, in the USA ☎ 800-223-9815, in Canada ☎ 800-344-0023), in the center of Lower Town on a rocky shoreline, is a two-story hotel with 20 adequate but ordinary rooms, each with a TV, phone and air-con, and most with refrigerators. There's an oceanfront pool. Singles/doubles/triples are US$70/88/104, not including government tax.

Kings Well (☎/fax 3-182538), on Van Ton-ningenweg, the road winding down to Lower Town, has eleven straightforward rooms with cable TV and refrigerators. Best are the upstairs rooms, which have ocean-view balconies and start at US$102/114 for singles/doubles, taxes included. Ground-floor rooms go for US$78/84. The place is very casual, and the owners have a couple of large dogs that some people may find a bit intimidating.

Across from Dive Statia in Lower Town is the *Old Gin House (☎ 3-182319, fax 3-182135, info@oldginhouse.com),* a lovely stone construction that originally housed cotton and sugar. The 14 rooms are quite plush and airy. Each of them includes a king-size bed, cable TV and air-con. There's also a restaurant and bar on-site, so it's not too far to stumble to bed. Rooms cost US$80/980 in summer, US$125/135 in winter, including breakfast but not govern-ment tax.

Places to Eat

The *One Stop Bakery,* near the Dutch Re-formed Church in Upper Town, has inex-pensive breads, fruit pies, saltfish and meat patties, cheese rolls and sandwiches. It's open 6 am to 7:30 pm weekdays, till 1 pm Saturday.

Super Burger, a friendly spot at the south end of De Graafweg, has ice cream, milk shakes and good, inexpensive sandwiches. For a treat, try the johnnycake and sword-fish. Nothing costs more than US$6. It's open 8 am to 11:30 pm daily.

Fruit Tree Restaurant, on Prinsesweg, is an inviting little place with tables under a fruit tree. It has a variety of fresh tropical fruit juices for US$1.50 and home-cooked Caribbean fish, goat and chicken meals for around US$8. It's open weekdays for lunch and dinner and Sundays for brunch.

The small Chinese community on Statia has led to a smattering of decent Chinese restaurants. *Cool Corner,* a bar and restau-rant in the center of town, offers Chinese-Caribbean-style food with curries, chop suey and similar dishes from about US$10. It's open 10 am to midnight daily.

For more conventional Chinese food, there's the *Chinese Restaurant* on Prins-esweg or *Sonny's Place,* on Fort Oranje Straat between Super Burger and the Wind-ward Islands Bank. Both serve large por-tions for around the same price as Cool Corner, and Sonny's throws in loud music along with your meal.

Ocean View Terrace, in the courtyard next to the Government Guesthouse, has a quiet open-air setting. A breakfast of eggs, ham and home fries or a lunch of a burger with fries costs around US$7, while dinner dishes are double that. It's open 7:30 am to 2 pm and 6 to 9 pm daily.

Blue Bead, a bar and restaurant at Oran-jestad Bay, offers pleasant water-view dining and reasonable prices. At lunch everything is under US$10, including salads, burgers, chicken satay, calamari or fish & chips. At dinner a main dish with salad av-erages US$17 to US$20, and there are daily specials. It's open 11:30 am to 2:30 pm and 6 to 10 pm daily.

The restaurant at *Golden Era Hotel* (see Places to Stay) has an attractive oceanfront setting. At lunch you can get sandwiches for US$5, while standard West Indian–style chicken, meat and seafood dishes are US$12 to US$20 at dinner.

Entertainment

The entertainment hot spot is *Lago Heights Club,* in Upper Town, which has dancing on weekends to live music and DJs.

Around the heart of Upper Town are a couple of loud and lively drinking holes. Airy *Sonny's Place* is the loudest and liveli-est of them all, and is popular on Friday night. *Cool Corner* is a tad more conven-tional, with a nice bar to plunk yourself at. *Blue Bead,* in Lower Town, is a nice place to sit and sip a tropical drink while taking in Oranjestad Bay. For details on these three spots, see Places to Stay, earlier.

Shopping

Mazinga Gift Shop, on Fort Oranje Straat in Upper Town, sells a little bit of everything, including T-shirts, jewelry and various other souvenirs.

ST EUSTATIUS

Around Statia

FORT DE WINDT
The road south from Oranjestad ends abruptly at Fort de Windt, where a couple of rusty cannons sit atop a cliff-side stone wall. While there's not much else to this small 18th-century fort, you'll be rewarded with a fine view of St Kitts to the southeast. The most interesting geological feature in the area is the white cliffs to the east of Fort de Windt, a landmark readily visible from neighboring islands.

To get there, take the road that runs past the old Dutch Reformed Church and follow it south, through a dry terrain of cacti and stray goats, to its end 3km away.

ZEELANDIA
Zeelandia, 3km northeast of Oranjestad, takes its name from Statia's first Dutch settlers, who were from Zeeland province in the Netherlands.

The dark-sand beach at Zeelandia Bay collects a fair share of flotsam and is not a good beach for swimming; the Atlantic side of the island is turbulent, and there are dangerous currents and undertows. It is a reasonable strolling beach, however, and you can find private niches by walking south along the beach toward the cliffs.

For those who are up for a longer walk, a track from the main road leads north to the partially secluded Venus Bay. There's no beach, but it makes for a nice hike, taking about 45 minutes one-way.

Places to Stay & Eat
Functioning as a health resort, **Thallaso Resort** (☎ 3-182173, fax 3-182831), the only development at Zeelandia Bay, has rooms in five duplex cottages, each with a private bath and TV. There's also a pool, a Jacuzzi, and a plethora of health treatments. The resort was undergoing some renovation and refurbishment at the time of writing, and the prices were yet to be set. Call ahead to check the rates. As this is an isolated area, you'll need a car.

Thallaso has a great restaurant on the premises, serving traditional French, Italian and Belgian cuisine for lunch and dinner. It has an open-air setting above the beach with a view of The Quill. It's relatively expensive, and reservations are recommended.

St Kitts & Nevis

The islands of St Kitts and Nevis constitute a fairly low-key destination, and can make for a nice, quiet holiday. Some people find the islands' relaxed nature ideal, while others get restless after a few days, as there's not a great deal of activity on either. St Kitts is by far the livelier of the two, with its share of resorts, fine beaches, and a harbor able to deal with cruise ships. Nevis plays second fiddle to its bigger brother in terms of its ability to attract tourists, but this is by no means a bad thing, especially if you want to escape the crowds and find a little rural peacefulness.

A ferry links the islands, making it easy to visit both halves of this two-island nation on a single trip. Most visitors to the islands fly into St Kitts, which on a clear day provides a wonderful introduction to that island. You'll get a glimpse of the mountainous interior, the patchwork of cane fields that carpets the lowlands and the curving southeast peninsula with its rugged hills, salt ponds and deeply indented bays.

While St Kitts has about 75% of the population, both islands are small, rural and invitingly lightly populated. Basseterre and Charlestown, the main towns on St Kitts and Nevis respectively, are quite accommodating and provide you with everything you need. On both St Kitts and Nevis the colonial past is evident in the numerous old sugar mills and plantation estates found throughout the countryside. Many of the grander plantation houses have been converted into atmospheric inns (with prices to match the atmosphere).

The island known today as St Kitts was called Liamuiga (Fertile Island) by its Amerindian inhabitants. When Columbus sighted the island on his second voyage to the New World, in 1493, he named it St Christopher after his patron saint. 'St Kitts,' the shortened name that came later, is today used by virtually everyone, including government offices.

Columbus used the Spanish word for 'snow,' *nieves,* to name Nevis, presumably because the clouds shrouding its mountain reminded him of a snowcapped peak. Native Caribs knew the island as Oualie (Land of Beautiful Waters).

Highlights

- Exploring Brimstone Hill Fortress National Park, with its historic significance and coastal views
- Enjoying St Kitts' southeast peninsula, with its fine scenery and beaches
- Taking the ferry between Basseterre and Charlestown for an inexpensive day tour
- Strolling the expansive coconut-lined Pinney's Beach on Nevis
- Staying in cozy plantation inns on both islands

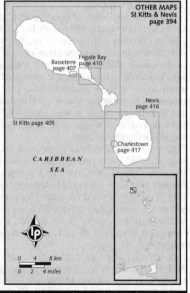

OTHER MAPS
St Kitts & Nevis page 394

Basseterre page 407
Frigate Bay page 410

Nevis page 416

St Kitts page 405

Charlestown page 417

CARIBBEAN SEA

0   4   8 km
0   2   4 miles

Facts about St Kitts & Nevis

HISTORY

St Kitts, settled by Sir Thomas Warner in 1623, was the site of the first British colony in the West Indies. The following year the French also settled part of St Kitts, a situation Warner tolerated in part to gain an upper hand against the native Caribs living on the island.

After they massacred the Caribs in a series of battles, the British and French turned on each other, and St Kitts changed hands between the two colonial powers several times before the 1783 Treaty of Paris brought the island firmly under British control. During this era, sugar plantations thrived on St Kitts.

Nevis had a similar colonial history. In 1628, Sir Warner sent a party of about 100 colonists to establish a British settlement on the west coast of Nevis. Although their original settlement, near Cotton Ground, fell to an earthquake in 1680, Nevis went on to prosper, developing one of the most affluent plantation societies in the Eastern Caribbean. As on St Kitts, most of the island's wealth was built upon the labor of African slaves who toiled in the island's sugarcane fields.

By the late 18th century, Nevis, buoyed by the attraction of its thermal baths, had become a major retreat for Britain's rich and famous.

In 1816 the British linked St Kitts and Nevis with Anguilla and the Virgin Islands as a single colony. In 1958 these islands became part of the West Indies Federation, a grand but ultimately unsuccessful attempt to combine all of Britain's Caribbean colonies into a united political entity. When the federation dissolved in 1962, the British opted to lump St Kitts, Nevis and Anguilla together as a new state.

In February 1967 the three islands were given independence from the Crown as an Associated State, with its capital in Basseterre. Within months, Anguilla, fearful of

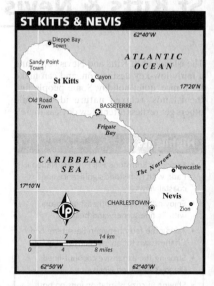

domination by a larger St Kitts, rebelled and eventually found its way back into the British fold as a colony.

Nevis was also wary of bonding with St Kitts and threatened to follow suit, but after a period of unrest it agreed to the union with the stipulation that it be given a heightened measure of internal autonomy and the right to secede in the future if it so desired. It was only after these conditions were guaranteed to Nevis under a new constitution that St Kitts and Nevis, in September 1983, were linked as a single federated state within the Commonwealth.

Kennedy Simmons, head of the predominant political party, the People's Action Movement (PAM), held the nation's prime-minister post from the eve of independence in 1980 to 1995. Toward the end of his rule, however, Simmons found himself leading an increasingly unpopular party marred by corruption issues and alleged links to drug smuggling.

In national elections held in November 1993, PAM failed to win a majority, leaving it with only four of the 11 parliamentary seats. PAM captured just 41% of the popular vote, versus the 54% cast for the opposition Labour Party, which also carried four seats. Protests and street violence erupted after PAM made a deal with a minority splinter party that excluded the Labour Party from the ruling coalition.

In the fall of 1994, a son of the deputy prime minister was found murdered, and two other sons were arrested on drug and firearms charges. In December of that year, when the two jailed brothers were abruptly released from prison, their fellow inmates rioted and all 150 of them broke out of the Basseterre prison. The situation got so out of hand that a regional security force from Barbados and Trinidad was brought in to assist local police.

The riots, corruption and civil unrest guaranteed the end of Simmons' 15-year rule. In parliamentary elections called in 1995, PAM won just a single seat and was overwhelmingly ousted by the Labour Party. The latest elections, held in 2000, saw the Labour Party win all the parliamentary seats.

While St Kitts sorted out its dirty laundry, a secessionist movement simmered on Nevis. In 1997 the pro-independence Concerned Citizens Movement, lead by Nevis premier Vance Armory, won three of Nevis' five parliamentary seats – just one seat short of the four seats required to call a plebiscite on independence from St Kitts. When election time comes around again, the pro-independence party will be making another strong bid to win separate statehood for Nevis.

GEOGRAPHY

St Kitts is 23 miles long and 6½ miles wide, with a land area of 68 sq miles. It has a central mountain range dominated by Mt Liamuiga, a dormant 3792-foot volcano. The higher mountain slopes are covered by rain forest, while the drier foothills and lowlands are largely planted with sugarcane.

Nevis, a couple of miles south of St Kitts, is a nearly round island of 36 sq miles that's dominated by a central volcanic peak, the 3232-foot Nevis Peak. Rain forests form Nevis' hilly interior, while dry scrub lowlands predominate near the coast.

CLIMATE

In January the average daily high temperature is 81°F (27°C) while the low averages 72°F (22°C). In July the average daily high is 86°F (30°C), the average low 76°F (24°C).

Annual rainfall averages 55 inches (1400mm) and is fairly consistent throughout the year. The driest months are February to June, when there's an average of 11 days of measurable rain a month and a mean relative humidity around 70%. The rest of the year the humidity averages 73%, with measurable rain falling an average of 16 days each month.

FLORA & FAUNA

Vegetation on both islands ranges from grassy coastal areas to a rain-forested interior of ferns and tall trees. Flowering plumeria, hibiscus and chains of love are common along roadsides and in garden landscaping. St Kitts' uninhabited southeast peninsula has a sparse, desertlike cover of dryland grasses dotted with cacti, yucca and century plants.

Salt ponds on the southeast peninsula provide feeding grounds for a variety of shorebirds, such as plovers, stilts and oyster-catchers. Pelicans and frigate birds are common along the coast, and you can spot Antillean crested hummingbirds and nectar-feeding bananaquits wherever there are flowering plants. The country's only endemic bird, the St Kitts bullfinch, was recently spotted after having been considered extinct for decades.

The most commonly spotted wild mammal is the mongoose, introduced to the islands by plantation owners for the purpose of controlling rats in the cane fields; these slender ferretlike creatures hunt during the day, when the nocturnal rats sleep, so the two seldom meet. Another exotic creature, the green vervet monkey, is mainly found in the interior of both islands, but has recently made the move into inhabited areas to take advantage of abundant food scraps.

ST KITTS & NEVIS

GOVERNMENT & POLITICS

St Kitts & Nevis is a federation officially headed by the British monarch, who is represented by a governor-general. Legislative power is vested in a unicameral 11-member National Assembly – eight of whose members are elected from St Kitts and three from Nevis – and in the prime minister, who is the leader of the majority party.

Nevis has internal home rule and a separate legislature, as well as an island administration that mirrors that of the federation on a smaller scale.

Incidentally, the federation of St Kitts & Nevis forms the smallest nation in the Western Hemisphere. As it's part of the British Commonwealth, however, it's not considered the smallest independent country – Grenada has that title.

ECONOMY

Although sugar production is declining, St Kitts remains heavily planted in sugarcane, and agriculture still accounts for nearly 25% of the work force. Small-scale garment manufacturing, electronic assembly and a brewery and bottling plant account for 15% of St Kitts' labor force, while tourism, which is being actively promoted by the government, accounts for 12%.

On Nevis, where the economy is more sluggish, sugar has long been abandoned, but honey and some vegetables are produced, and attempts are being made to revive one traditional crop, sea-island cotton. Tourism is Nevis' largest employer; the Four Seasons Resort employs more than 600 people – roughly a quarter of the island's labor force.

POPULATION & PEOPLE

The population is approximately 42,000, with 32,000 on St Kitts and 10,000 on Nevis. More than 90% are of African descent. The rest of the population is predominantly of European, or mixed European and African, descent.

People on St Kitts are called Kittitians (kit-**tee**-shuns), while on Nevis they are called Nevisians (nee-**vee**-shuns).

SOCIETY & CONDUCT

Culturally, the islands draw upon a mix of European, African and West Indian traditions. Architecture is predominantly British in style and cricket is the national sport.

The cultural mix is evident in island dance and entertainment. Masquerades, St Kitts' popular folk troupe, performs dances ranging from traditional French quadrilles to spirited African war dances. The troupe wears colorful costumes of a unique West Indian design.

Dos & Don'ts

Dress is very casual on both St Kitts and Nevis. Cotton clothing is suitable attire for any occasion; however, swimwear should be restricted to the beach.

RELIGION

Just over one-third of all islanders are Anglican. The rest are Methodists, Roman Catholics, Baptists, Adventists, Moravians and Jehovah's Witnesses.

LANGUAGE

The language of the islands is English.

Facts for the Visitor

ORIENTATION

St Kitts' shape resembles a large chicken drumstick, with an oval road running around the perimeter of its main body and another extending down the spine of its southern arm. It takes about 1½ hours to make a nonstop loop around the northern road and about 30 minutes to drive from Basseterre, the capital, to the end of the southeast peninsula.

St Kitts' airport is on the northern outskirts of Basseterre, just a five-minute drive from the center.

On Nevis the airport is in Newcastle at the north side of the island, about a 20-minute drive from Charlestown, the main town. A loop road circles the island, making exploring quite straightforward.

Maps

The simple maps handed out by the tourist office will be suitable for most visitors planning to hire transportation.

The best map is the Ordnance Survey's 1:50,000 map of St Kitts & Nevis, which includes inset maps of Basseterre, Brimstone Hill Fortress and Charlestown. It can be purchased for EC$25 at Wall's Deluxe Record & Bookshop in Basseterre and at the gift shop at Brimstone Hill Fortress National Park.

TOURIST OFFICES
Local Tourist Offices

St Kitts' main tourist office is in the Pelican Mall in Basseterre, and there's also an information booth at the airport. The Nevis tourist office is on Main St in Charlestown.

When requesting information by mail, write to the St Kitts & Nevis Department of Tourism (☎ 465-4040, fax 465-8794, mintc&e@stkitts-nevis.com), PO Box 132, Basseterre, St Kitts, West Indies; or the Nevis Bureau of Tourism (☎ 469-1042, fax 469-1066, nevtour@caribsurf.com), Main St, Charlestown, Nevis.

Tourist Offices Abroad

Overseas St Kitts & Nevis tourist offices include the following:

Canada
(☎ 416-368-6707, fax 416-368-3934) 365 Bay St, Suite 806, Toronto, Ontario M5H 2V1

Germany
(☎ 06031-73 76 30, fax 6031-72 50 81) Leonhardstrasse 22, D-61169 Friedberg

UK
(☎ 020-7376 0881, fax 020-7937 3611) 10 Kensington Court, London W8 5DL

USA
(☎ 212-535-1234, 800-582-6208, fax 212-734-6511) 414 East 75th St, New York, NY 10021

VISAS & DOCUMENTS

Passports are required of all visitors except US and Canadian citizens, who may enter with proof of citizenship such as both an official birth certificate and a photo ID.

Visas are not required of most visitors, including citizens of the UK, Western Europe and Commonwealth countries, for stays of up to six months. All visitors are required to be in possession of a roundtrip or onward ticket.

EMBASSIES & CONSULATES
Kittian & Nevisian Embassies & Consulates

UK
(☎ 020-7937 9522)
10 Kensington Court, 2nd floor, London W85DL

USA
(☎ 202-686-2636)
3216 New Mexico Ave NW, Washington, DC 20016

CUSTOMS

One bottle of wine or spirits and 200 cigarettes can be brought in duty free.

MONEY

The Eastern Caribbean Dollar (EC$) is the official currency. The exchange rate is fixed at EC$2.70 to US$1.

Larger tourist-related charges, such as car rental and hotel bills, are generally quoted in US dollars, although you can pay in either US or EC dollars. Most hotels, car rental agencies and restaurants accept major credit cards. Note that many businesses will use an exchange rate of EC$2.65 to US$1 when converting a bill from EC to US dollars, a slight disadvantage if you're paying in US dollars.

Hotels and restaurants add a 7% tax and usually a 10% service charge as well. When a restaurant doesn't add a service charge, a 10% tip is appropriate.

POST & COMMUNICATIONS
Post

The main post offices are in Basseterre and Charlestown.

Airmail postage to most Caribbean countries is EC$0.50 for a postcard and EC$0.60 for a 10g letter. To the USA and Canada it's EC$0.80 and EC$0.90, respectively. Postcards to the UK and Europe cost

EC$1, letters EC$1.20; to Australia and other far-flung countries it costs EC$1.20 for a postcard and EC$1.60 for a letter.

When mailing a letter to the islands, follow the addressee's name with the town and then 'St Kitts, West Indies' or 'Nevis, West Indies.'

Telephone

St Kitts phone numbers start with 465 or 466, Nevis numbers with 469. To make a local call, dial all seven digits. When calling the islands from overseas, add the area code 869 to the local number.

The islands have both coin and card phones. To use a coin phone, insert a minimum of EC$0.25 and dial the number. If you want to make another call, push the 'follow-on call' button on the left under the hook, rather than hanging up the receiver.

Card phones, common in busier public places, take Caribbean Phonecards, which can be purchased at the airports, Cable & Wireless (telephone) offices and numerous shops.

For directory assistance, phone ☎ 411; for international inquiries, call ☎ 412. More details can be found under Post & Communications in the Regional Facts for the Visitor chapter.

Email & Internet Access

Leyton's Internet Café (☎ 466-7873), in the cellar of the TDC Mall on Fort St, Basseterre, charges a whopping US$7.50 per half-hour to surf the net. It's open 9 am to 8 pm Monday to Saturday. Unfortunately, the public library has no access.

On Nevis, Internet access is available at the library in Charlestown.

INTERNET RESOURCES

The Web site www.interknowledge.com/stkitts-nevis has general information about the islands. For something a little more in-depth on Nevis, check out www.nevisisland.com.

NEWSPAPERS & MAGAZINES

There are three local newspapers: The Democrat and The Obser er, both published on Saturday, and the semiweekly Labour

Spokesman, published on Wednesday and Saturday.

The St Kitts & Ne is Visitor magazine, published annually, is a good source of general tourist information and can be picked up free at tourist offices and hotels.

RADIO & TV

The government radio station, ZIZ, can be heard on 555 AM and 96 FM. The Voice of Nevis is on 895 AM, and there's a gospel station at 825 AM. There's a government-operated TV station as well as US network TV via cable.

ELECTRICITY

Most electric current is 220V, 60 cycles; some hotels supply electricity at 110V.

WEIGHTS & MEASURES

St Kitts uses the imperial system of measurement. Speed-limit signs are in miles, as are rental car odometers.

HEALTH

The main hospital on St Kitts, JNF General (☎ 465-2551), is at the west end of Cayon St in Basseterre. On Nevis, the small Alexandra Hospital (☎ 469-5473) is on Government Rd in Charlestown.

DANGERS & ANNOYANCES

Manchineel trees, whose sap can cause a skin rash, grow along the coast, particularly on the leeward side of the islands.

Even though the monkeys look cuddly, it's better to be overly cautious than overly friendly.

Common sense should prevail while walking around Basseterre at night.

EMERGENCIES

For police and ambulance dial ☎ 911.

BUSINESS HOURS

Business hours for offices and shops are generally 8 am to noon and 1 to 4 or 4:30 pm weekdays; however, on Thursday some shops close for the afternoon. Most banks are open 8 am to 3pm Monday to Thursday, till 5 pm Friday.

PUBLIC HOLIDAYS & SPECIAL EVENTS

Public holidays on St Kitts & Nevis include the following:

New Year's Day	January 1
Good Friday	late March/early April
Easter Monday	late March/early April
Labour Day	first Monday in May
Whit Monday	eighth Monday after Easter
Queen's Birthday	second Saturday in June
August Monday	first Monday in August
Independence Day	September 19
Christmas Day	December 25
Boxing Day	December 26

On St Kitts, the biggest yearly event is the 10-day Carnival held from December 24 to January 3, with calypso competitions, costumed street dances and steel band music. Many businesses are closed during this period.

In the last week in June, the four-day St Kitts Music Festival brings together top-name calypso, soca, reggae, salsa, jazz and gospel performers from throughout the Caribbean.

Nevis has a weeklong 'Culturama' from early to mid-August featuring music, crafts and beauty and talent pageants, culminating with a parade on Culturama Tuesday. Late August sees the start of another cultural event, Carifesta, a 10-day celebration drawing artists and craftspeople from throughout the Caribbean.

ACTIVITIES
Beaches & Swimming

The islands' beaches have a hard time competing with the white stretches found on Anguilla and Antigua, but there are reasonable strands on St Kitts and a couple of attractive options on Nevis.

St Kitts' best beaches are on the south end of the island at Frigate Bay and in the sheltered bays along the southeast peninsula. Beaches along the main body of the island are mostly thin strands of black and gray sands.

On Nevis, Pinney's Beach, which runs north from Charlestown, has a Robinson Crusoe look and feel. It's long and lovely, backed by coconut palms. There's also a nice white-sand beach fronting the Nisbet Plantation Beach Club on the north shore in Newcastle and a pleasant little beach at Oualie Bay.

Diving & Snorkeling

St Kitts has healthy, expansive reefs and varied marine life that includes rays, barracuda, garden eels, nurse sharks, sea turtles, sea fans, giant barrel sponges and black coral.

One popular dive spot is Sandy Point Bay, below Brimstone Hill, with an array of corals, sponges and reef fish as well as some coral-encrusted anchors from the colonial era. Among a handful of wreck dives is the 148-foot freighter *River Taw,* which sank in 50 feet of water in 1985 and now harbors soft corals and reef fish. Nevis has good diving off its west side, including some colorful caves at a depth of about 40 feet.

On St Kitts, Pro-Divers (☎/fax 465-3223, prodiver@caribsurf.com), at Turtle Beach, offers single-tank dives for US$45, two-tank dives for US$70, night dives for US$50, an introductory three-hour resort course for US$80, a three-day PADI certification course for US$300 and a half-day snorkeling trip for US$35.

There are two other dive operations on St Kitts that both offer similar services at

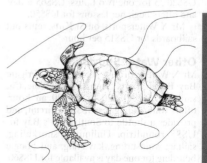
Swimming is the key to long life.

comparable rates: St Kitts Scuba (☎ 465-1189, fax 465-1675, in the USA ☎ 800-621-1270, bebh@caribsurf.com), at Bird Rock Beach Hotel; and Kenneth's Dive Centre (☎/fax 465-2670, in the USA ☎ 732-787-8130) on Bay Road at the east side of Basseterre.

Nevis' diving scene is a low-key affair, with an emphasis on untouched coral reefs that are seldom visited by divers. Two popular sites are Monkey Shoals, a densely covered reef close to Oualie Beach, and Devil's Caves, on the western side of Nevis, with coral grottoes and underwater lava tubes in 40 feet of water.

Scuba Safaris (☎ 469-9518, fax 469-9619, scubanevis@caribsurf.com), at Oualie Beach in Nevis, offers single-tank dives for US$45, two-tank dives for US$80, night dives for US$70 and also a half-day snorkeling trip for US$35.

A favorite place for snorkeling is White House Bay on St Kitts' southeast peninsula. All of the dive companies rent snorkel gear for around US$10 a day, as does Mr X Watersports (☎ 465-4995), at Frigate Bay Beach, which also offers a snorkeling tour for US$20 to US$25.

Windsurfing

Oualie Bay, at the northwest side of Nevis, catches the trade winds and offers a sandy launch in shallow waters that's good for beginners. There are also opportunities for wave jumping and other advanced techniques.

Windsurfing Nevis (☎ 469-9682, fax 469-9176), at Oualie Beach, rents out boards for US$20/35 for one/two hours, US$65 a day, and offers beginner lessons for US$50.

Mr X Watersports, on St Kitts, rents out sailboards for US$15 per hour.

Other Water Sports

Mr X Watersports (☎ 465-4995), on Frigate Bay Beach, rents Sunfish and Hobie Cat sailboats for US$20 to US$30 an hour, offers water skiing for US$15 a circuit, and provides a shuttle to South Friar's Bay for US$5 roundtrip. Unlimited snorkeling, sailing, windsurfing, kayaking, and boogie boarding for one day is available for US$60, or four days for US$150.

Hiking

Both St Kitts and Nevis have an abundance of untouched native vegetation, a good selection of easy and tough treks, and great views from the mountainous interiors. Tracks on St Kitts and Nevis are not well defined, but there are moves to improve the tracks, and it's advisable to do any major trekking with a guide.

Greg's Safaris (☎ 465-4121, fax 465-0707, g-safari@caribsurf.com) has a half-day hike into the rain forest of St Kitts for US$40. The guide moves at a comfortable pace suitable for all ages, identifies flora and fauna, and stops to sample fruits along the way. Greg's also offers a full-day volcano tour for US$80, including lunch.

The amiable Kriss Berry of Kriss Tours (☎ 465-4042) also offers a full-day trek that goes through the St Kitts rain forest to the volcano. It costs a reasonable US$50, lunch included.

On Nevis, Top to Bottom (☎ 469-9080, walknevis@caribsurf.com) offers a choice of well over a dozen hikes, ranging from walks to estate ruins, monkey-spotting hikes in the jungle and the more strenuous hikes to the top of Nevis Peak. Each outing costs US$20, except for the mud-sliding and leg-aching treks to Nevis Peak, which cost from US$30 to US$40.

Mountain Biking

Mountain-bike rentals are available on Nevis for US$20 a day from Windsurfing Nevis (☎ 469-9682), at Oualie Beach Hotel.

Horseback Riding

You can choose from beach or trail rides, or a combination of the two, on both St Kitts and Nevis. Rides start at around US$25 for one hour.

Horseback riding is available on St Kitts from Trinity Stables (☎ 465-3226). On Nevis it's offered by Nevis Equestrian Centre (☎ 469-8118) and The Hermitage (☎ 469-3477); the latter also has carriage rides.

Golf

The Four Seasons Resort on Nevis has a championship 18-hole golf course designed by Robert Trent Jones II. Greens fees are US$125 for 18 holes, including cart rental.

On St Kitts, the 18-hole Royal St Kitts Golf Club (☎ 465-8339), at Frigate Bay, has greens fees of US$40. The greens fees are waived for guests at some of Frigate Bay's hotels and condominiums, so golfers might want to inquire when booking a place to stay. Clubs can be rented for US$25 and carts for another US$50.

Both courses offer club rentals and have lower rates for nine-hole play.

ACCOMMODATIONS

There are only two large resorts, the Jack Tar Village Beach Resort & Casino on St Kitts and the Four Seasons Resort on Nevis, each with about 200 rooms.

Other than that, accommodations are mostly in small-scale hotels and condominiums. There are also some fine upscale inns in converted plantation estate homes.

Places in St Kitts can book up pretty solidly in winter, so early reservations are a good idea, particularly if you want to stay in one of the better-value options. Hotels add a 7% tax and a 10% service charge on top of their rates.

Camping is legal on both St Kitts and Nevis, but there are no camping facilities provided. It's a good idea to register at the police station before heading off to set up camp.

FOOD

Reasonably priced local fresh fish and other seafood are plentiful on the islands and are generally the best bet. Beef and many other items are imported and tend to be expensive, particularly on Nevis. In Basseterre and Charlestown there are a few good, inexpensive local restaurants, while the plantation inns on both islands offer some fine upscale opportunities for romantic dining.

DRINKS

Tap water is safe to drink on both islands. Cane Spirit Rothschild, more commonly known as CSR, is a clear sugarcane spirit distilled on St Kitts. CSR is often served on the rocks with Ting, a popular grapefruit soft drink. Ting, Ginseng Up and Carib beer are bottled on St Kitts.

Getting There & Away

See the Getting Around section for information on traveling between St Kitts and Nevis by air and boat.

DEPARTURE TAX

The departure tax is EC$44 (US$16.50) if you leave by air. For stays less than 24 hours the tax is EC$4 (US$1.50). The departure tax for cruise ships and yachts is US$5.

AIR
Airports & Airlines

St Kitts' newly expanded Robert Llewellyn Bradshaw Airport (☎ 465-8121), on the outskirts of Basseterre, is modern, spacious and underutilized. The few duty-free shops and snack bars in the airport do little to fill the interior. There's a tourist office stand with the usual tourist handouts, and a taxi area right outside customs clearance.

Nevis' airport, in Newcastle, is a small operation with Winair, LIAT, Nevis Express, Carib Aviation, an ATM and a couple of charter desks. Construction is currently under way to build a bigger, better, brighter terminal beside the runway.

American Airlines (☎ 465-2273) is one of the few international carriers with service to St Kitts & Nevis. Most travel to the area is via other Caribbean islands with the following airlines:

Carib Aviation	(☎ 465-3055, on Nevis ☎ 469-9295)
LIAT	(☎ 465-2286, on Nevis 469-9333)
WinAir	(☎ 465-2186)

Within the Caribbean

LIAT LIAT has daily nonstop flights to St Kitts from Antigua, St Martin and Anguilla, and connecting flights from those hubs to the rest of its Caribbean network.

The fare from St Martin to St Kitts is US$70 one-way, US$86 for a one-day excursion and US$102 for a 30-day excursion.

LIAT flights from Antigua to St Kitts or Nevis cost US$66 one-way, US$103 for a two-day excursion and US$125 for a 30-day excursion ticket.

Anguilla to St Kitts or Nevis costs US$69 one-way, US$116 for a seven-day excursion and US$131 for a 30-day excursion.

Winair Winair has daily flights from St Martin to St Kitts and Nevis. Fares to either island are US$74 one-way, US$101 for a one-day excursion, US$80 for a seven-day excursion and US$142 for a roundtrip open for a year.

Carib Aviation Carib Aviation is primarily a charter airline, but it currently offers scheduled service between Antigua and St Kitts and Nevis, starting at around EC$179 one-way.

The USA

American Airlines (☎ 465-2273) flies from the USA to St Kitts daily via San Juan, Puerto Rico. The regular fare for a 30-day excursion ticket is about US$420 from Miami and around US$420 from New York or Boston.

There's currently no scheduled service to St Kitts from the UK, Europe or Canada; travel from those areas is via other Caribbean islands, most commonly Antigua, St Martin or San Juan.

SEA
Yacht

The two ports of entry are Basseterre and Charlestown. On both islands, customs is near the ferry dock and is open 8 am to noon and 1 to 4 pm weekdays. Yachters will need cruising permits to visit other anchorages and a special pass to go between the two islands.

White House Bay, Ballast Bay and Major's Bay on St Kitts' southeast peninsula make good anchorages. On Nevis, Pinney's Beach is the most popular anchorage.

Cruise Ship

Numerous cruise ships visit St Kitts; they dock at Basseterre's deep-water harbor. Charlestown has undertaken an expansion of its pier, which is taking some considerable time, so sleepy Nevis will eventually be added to the itinerary of a few smaller cruise lines.

Getting Around

AIR

LIAT (☎ 465-2286, 469-9333) has three flights a day between St Kitts and Nevis, with an early-morning, midday and late-afternoon flight in each direction. Departure times from St Kitts are 6:40 am, noon and 2:05 pm. The fare is US$25 one-way, US$45 roundtrip.

The Nevis Express company (☎ 469-9755, reservations@nevisexpress.com) operates a small prop-plane shuttle between St Kitts and Nevis about seven times a day. The fare is US$25 one-way, US$45 for a same-day roundtrip, and US$50 for an open roundtrip ticket. See the Getting Around section at the beginning of this chapter.

BUS

The buses are privately owned minivans and are hard to miss. They're usually careening around corners at breakneck speeds, blasting out hip-hop and reggae beats, and have some bizarre name plastered across the top of the front window. In Basseterre, most leave from the bus stop on Bay Road. From Basseterre it's EC$2 to Sandy Point Town, EC$2.50 to St Paul's and EC$3 to Dieppe Bay Town.

Bus service is fairly sporadic and there's no schedule, although buses are generally most plentiful in the early morning and late afternoon. The last bus is usually around 6 or 7 pm. Frigate Bay is outside regular bus routes.

On Nevis, buses going up the west coast leave from the square in front of the tourist office on Charlestown's Main St. Some west-coast buses go only as far as Cotton Ground;

others go to Newcastle, and a few continue on to Butlers. Buses going east to the towns of Gingerland and Zion leave from Charlestown's courthouse square. There's rarely a bus between Butlers and Zion, and thus no circle-island bus route. Also, service is sketchy and it's risky relying on buses if you're trying to see Nevis on a day tour.

Generally, buses don't leave Charlestown until they are full, which might be as often as every 15 minutes in the morning and late afternoon, or as infrequently as every hour in the middle part of the day. On Sunday there's virtually no service. The one-way fare to the farthest point is EC$3.

CAR & MOTORCYCLE
Road Rules
Drive on the left side of the road. Speed limits are posted in miles per hour, and are generally between 20mph and 40mph. Gas costs about EC$6 a gallon.

Basseterre has quite a few one-way streets, some of which are not clearly marked. Keep an eye out for road signs, and when in doubt, simply follow the rest of the traffic.

On Nevis, there are no gas stations on the east side between Market Shop and Newcastle, so make certain you have enough gas before heading off to explore the island.

Driver's License
Foreign visitors must purchase a visitor driver's license, which costs EC$50 (or US$20) and is valid for 90 days. The easiest place to get them is at the fire station on Pond Rd at the east side of Basseterre, which is open 24 hours and has a separate window designated for issuing visitor licenses. If you're flying into St Kitts and renting a car, the rental agency will usually pick you up at the airport and then stop at the fire station on the way to their office.

During weekday business hours, driver's licenses can also be obtained at the Inland Revenue Office, above the post office on Bay Rd.

In Nevis, visitor driver's licenses can be obtained at police stations.

Rental
St Kitts There are numerous car rental agencies on St Kitts. Rates begin at about US$30/180 a day/week with unlimited mileage for a small car such as a Nissan March or Suzuki Swift. In addition, optional collision damage waivers (CDW) cost about US$10 a day plus a 5% government levy. With some companies you're still responsible for the first few hundred dollars worth of damage, while with others the CDW waives all liability.

In Basseterre, two of the largest agents are Avis (☎ 465-6507, in the USA ☎ 800-228-0668), on South Independence Square and TDC Auto Rentals (☎ 465-2991), on West Independence Square. Both provide free airport or hotel pick-up.

Other car rental agents include Delisle Walwyn Car Rental (☎ 465-8449), Liverpool Row, Basseterre, and Caines Rent a Car (☎ 465-2366), Princes St, Basseterre.

The cheapest scooter rental company is Islandwide Scooter Rentals (☎ 466-7841), Caunt St, Newtown, Basseterre. Rates start at US$25 a day or US$150 a week including insurance and tax. It's possible to take a scooter across on the ferry to Nevis; check with the ferry ticketing office for the current price.

Nevis Parry's Car Rental (☎ 469-5917) is a friendly, locally owned operation. If you're arriving by ferry, call Parry in advance and he'll meet you at the harbor (give him a few minutes). When returning the car, you simply park it near the dock with the keys in the ignition. Rates begin around US$30.

TDC Auto Rentals (☎ 469-5690, on St Kitts 465-2991) has an office opposite the Charlestown ferry dock. Rates are US$30 for a small car. If you rent a car for a minimum of three days their exchange program allows you to use vehicles on both St Kitts and Nevis at no extra cost, but this option is based on availability, so be sure to confirm both islands when you make a reservation. The office is closed Sunday, so call the Four Seasons Resort (☎ 469-1111) for service.

Other companies are Nevis Car Rental (☎ 469-9837), in Newcastle; Striker's Car Rental (☎ 469-2654), opposite the Hermitage Inn; and Teach Tours (☎ 469-1140), in Charlestown. All three rent out cars for about US$35.

Most places charge US$10 a day more for a collision damage waiver (CDW).

TAXI

Taxis meet scheduled flights. On St Kitts, a taxi from the airport costs EC$18 to Basseterre, EC$29 to Frigate Bay, EC$47 to St Paul's.

From the Circus in Basseterre, the main taxi stand, it costs EC$10 to points within town, EC$20 to Frigate Bay and EC$85 to Brimstone Hill roundtrip. Rates are 25% higher between 11 pm and 6 am. There's an EC$3 charge for each 15 minutes of waiting. To call a taxi, dial ☎ 465-4253.

On Nevis, taxis congregate by the Charlestown pier and charge about EC$130 for a three-hour sightseeing tour. One-way taxi rates from the center of Charlestown are EC$10 to Bath or Pinney's Beach, EC$25 to Oualie Beach and EC$37 to Newcastle. Taxis also meet scheduled flights at Newcastle Airport. Between 10 pm and 6 am add another 50% to the fare.

BOAT

The government-run passenger ferry *Caribe Queen* and privately owned *Sea Hustler* ply the waters between St Kitts and Nevis. The ferry docks are in central Basseterre and Charlestown, which for most people makes the ferry more practical than flying between the two islands.

From Basseterre the *Caribe Queen* departs for Charlestown at 8 am and 4 pm on Monday, at 1 pm Tuesday, at 7 am and 4 and 7 pm Wednesday, and at 8:30 am and 4 pm Friday and Saturday.

From Charlestown the ferry departs for Basseterre at 7 am and 3 pm Monday, at 7:30 am and 6 pm Tuesday, at 8 am and 6 pm Wednesday, at 7:30 am and 3 pm Friday and Saturday.

The *Sea Hustler* basically runs by the same schedule, but heads in the opposite di-

rection; it departs from Basseterre for Charlestown at 7 am and 3 pm Monday, at 7:30 am and 6 pm Tuesday, at 8 am and 6 pm Wednesday etc.

The *Sea Hustler* also runs on Thursday and Sunday; from Basseterre it departs for Charlestown at 12:30 pm Thursday and at 8 am and 4 pm Sunday; from Charlestown it departs for Basseterre at 7:30 am and 5 pm Thursday and at 9 am and 5 pm Sunday.

The ferries strictly enforce their 150-passenger limit and sell tickets on the day of travel only (if you're going over for a day trip you can, and should, buy a return ticket in the morning). Dockside booths begin selling tickets about an hour before the scheduled departure time. As sailings occasionally reach capacity, it's wise to arrive early. Also note that if a boat does reach capacity it sometimes sails a few minutes before its scheduled departure time – so don't stroll too far away after you've bought your ticket!

The fare is EC$15 each way, EC$20 for air-con. The ride, which takes between 45 minutes and an hour, is usually a smooth trip and offers good views of both islands, best from the small outdoor deck at either the front or back of the boat.

ORGANIZED TOURS

On St Kitts, Tropical Tours (☎ 465-4039) and Kantours (☎ 465-2098) have half-day circle-island tours for around US$50. The same companies also offer catamaran cruises and deep-sea fishing.

Blue Water Safaris (☎ 466-4933), Princes St, Basseterre, have full-day catamaran cruises for US$65, with snorkeling, lunch on Pinney's Beach, and an open bar thrown in. Sunset and moonlight cruises are US$40 per person, and half-day fishing trips for a maximum of six persons cost US$350.

Taxis charge about US$60 (for one to four people) for a half-day island tour.

St Kitts

BASSETERRE

Founded and named by the French in the 17th century, Basseterre is not one of the

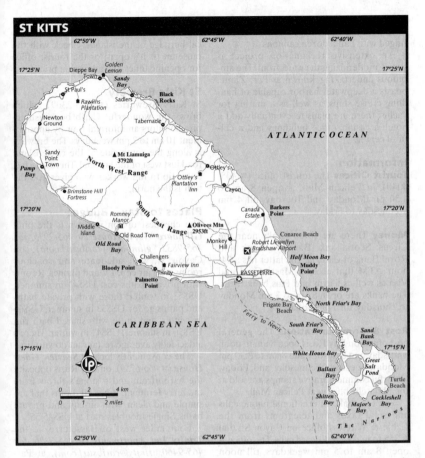

ST KITTS

ATLANTIC OCEAN

CARIBBEAN SEA

Dieppe Bay
Golden
Town
Lemon
*Sandy
Bay*
St Paul's
*Rawlins
Plantation*
Sadlers
**Black
Rocks**
Newton
Ground
Tabernacle
▲Mt Liamuiga
3792ft
North West Range
Ottley's
*Ottley's
Plantation
Inn*
Cayon
Sandy
Point Town
*Pump
Bay*
●Brimstone Hill
Fortress
South East Range
Canada
Estate
**Barkers
Point**
Romney
Manor
▲Olivees Mtn
2953ft
Middle
Island
Old Road Town
*Old Road
Bay*
Monkey
Hill
Conaree Beach
*Robert Llewellyn
Bradshaw Airport*
Challengers
Fairview Inn
Trinity
Bloody Point
*Palmetto
Point*
BASSETERRE
Half Moon Bay
**Muddy
Point**
North Frigate Bay
North Friar's Bay
Frigate Bay
Beach
Dr Kennedy Simmonds Hwy
Ferry to Nevis
*South Friar's
Bay*
**Sand
Bank
Bay**
White House Bay
*Great
Salt
Pond*
*Ballast
Bay*
Turtle
Beach
*Shitten
Bay*
*Cockleshell
Bay*
*Major's
Bay*
The Narrows

0   2   4 km
0   1   2 miles

grander Caribbean capitals, in part because of a fire that swept through the town in 1867, destroying most of its early colonial buildings.

Nonetheless, Basseterre has a fair number of appealing Victorian-era stone-block structures topped by wooden second stories and decorated with fancy latticework and gingerbread trim. The town center is the **Circus**, a roundabout featuring a four-sided clock tower. It's supposedly modeled on London's Piccadilly Circus, but the most noticeable similarity lies in its people and traffic congestion. Most of the island's

banks, airline offices and travel agents are in the streets radiating out from the Circus, while taxis, clothing and souvenir shops cluster at the roundabout.

The nearby **Independence Square**, once the site of slave auctions, is now a small public park with a central fountain. The square is flanked by some of Basseterre's more substantial buildings, including a few Georgian-style houses and the twin-towered Immaculate Conception Cathedral that dates from 1927.

On the west side of town, Fort Thomas Hotel sits at the site of the old **Fort Thomas**.

Though it's not a major sight, just below the hotel pool you can find a bit of the fort walls ringed with half a dozen cannons.

An extensive reclamation project is slowly modernizing the waterfront. The ambitious undertaking, known as Port Zante, boasts a deepwater harbor capable of handling cruise ships, as well as a marina for yachts; there are plans to eventually add a hotel, a casino, office buildings and a cultural center.

Information

Tourist Offices The tourist office (☎ 465-4040), in Pelican Mall, is open 8 am to 4:30 pm Monday and Tuesday, till 4 pm Wednesday to Friday.

Money There are three banks near the Circus: Scotiabank, Barclays Bank and Royal Bank of Canada. The latter has a 24-hour ATM that accepts MasterCard and Visa as well as Cirrus and Plus bank cards. The banks are open 8 am to 3 pm Monday to Thursday, till 5 pm Friday.

Post & Communications The general post office, on Bay Rd, is open 8 am to noon Thursday and Saturday, 8 am to 3:30 pm Monday, Tuesday, Wednesday and Friday. Colorful commemorative stamps are sold at the philatelic bureau at Pelican Mall.

You can make international phone calls and send faxes and telegrams from the Cable & Wireless office on Cayon St; dial ☎ 355 to make credit-card calls. The office is open 8 am to 5 pm weekdays, till noon Saturday.

Bookstores Wall's Deluxe Record & Bookshop, on Fort St, sells maps, a fairly good selection of books on the Caribbean and a range of music from Caribbean artists.

National Museum

The St Christopher Heritage Society is in the process of establishing a substantial national museum in the waterfront Treasury Building. It seems to be a long process, mainly due to serious hurricane damage to the building and the time expended sorting through the museum collection. The displays will focus on the cultural and historical heritage of the islands. Check with the museum (if it's open) or the tourist office for opening times and admission prices.

St Kitts Brewery

St Kitts Breweries (☎ 465-2309), which brews the wonderful Carib beer, usually offers visitors an informal tour by appointment 10 am to 2 pm weekdays. The brewery is along the south side of the circle-island road just west of the hospital. There's no fee, but a tip to the worker who gives you the tour is the norm.

Places to Stay – Budget

The cheapest option in town is the pink *Glimbaro Guest House* (☎ 465-2935, fax 465-9832, glimbaro@caribsurf.com), on Cayon St, with adequate and spacious rooms with air-con, TV and phones. Rooms with private baths cost US$41 in summer, US$53 in winter; those with private baths and patios go for US$53 in summer, US$65 in winter; and those with shared bath run US$30 in summer, US$41 in winter. There's a decidedly average restaurant downstairs.

The conveniently located *Seaview Guest House* (☎ 466-6759), on Bay Rd, is opposite the harborfront and a stone's throw from the ferry terminal. It has 10 rooms that are simple and clean, with air-con and private baths. Singles/doubles start at US$45/55.

Four miles west of Basseterre lie the *Trinity Inn Apartments* (☎ 465-3226, fax 465-9460, trinity@caribsurf.com), at Palmetto Point. Housed in a small apartment building on the coastal road are 10 one-bedroom units with kitchens that rent for US$60 in summer, US$70 in winter. There's also a pool.

Places to Stay – Mid-Range & Top End

Town Center The *Palms Hotel* (☎ 465-0800, fax 465-5889, palmshotel@caribsurf .com, PO Box 64), overlooking the Circus, is a modern business hotel with 12 spiffy units. Roomy junior suites, which each have two double beds, TV, air-con, phones,

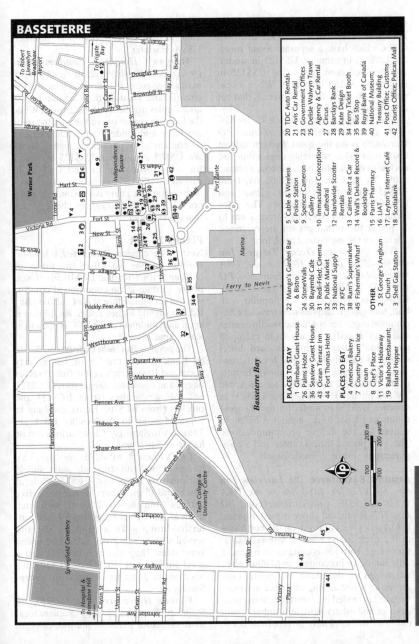

BASSETERRE

PLACES TO STAY
1 Glimbaro Guest House
26 Palms Hotel
36 Seaview Guest House
43 Ocean Terrace Inn
44 Fort Thomas Hotel

PLACES TO EAT
4 American Bakery
7 Country Churn Ice Cream
8 Chef's Place
11 Victor's Hideaway
19 Ballahoo Restaurant; Island Hopper
22 Mango's Garden Bar & Bistro
24 StoneWalls
30 Bayembi Cafe
31 Redi-Fried; Cinema
32 Public Market
33 National Supply
37 KFC
38 Ram's Supermarket
45 Fisherman's Wharf

OTHER
2 St George's Anglican Church
3 Shell Gas Station
5 Cable & Wireless
6 Police Station
9 Spencer Cameron Gallery
10 Immaculate Conception Cathedral
12 Islandwide Scooter Rentals
13 Caines Rent a Car
14 Wall's Deluxe Record & Bookshop
15 Parris Pharmacy
16 LIAT
17 Leyton's Internet Café
18 Scotiabank
20 TDC Auto Rentals
21 Avis Car Rental
25 Government Offices
   Delisle Walwyn Travel Agency & Car Rental
27 Circus
28 Barclays Bank
29 Kate Design
34 Ferry Ticket Booth
35 Bus Stop
39 Royal Bank of Canada
40 National Museum; Treasury Building
41 Post Office; Customs
42 Tourist Office; Pelican Mall

ST KITTS & NEVIS

refrigerators and coffeemakers, cost US$85 in summer, US$95 in winter. One-bedroom suites, which have a separate living room, are US$105 in summer, US$125 in winter, and two-bedroom suites cost US$135 in summer, US$180 in winter. When occupancy is low they often run specials that cut rates by about US$20.

Fort Thomas Hotel (☎ 465-2695, fax 465-7518, f_thomashotel@caribsurf.com, PO Box 1628) is on the quiet western side of town. It has 64 comfortable singles/doubles, each with two double beds, air-con, a phone, cable TV, a bath and a balcony, from US$95/140 with mountain views and US$105/150 with ocean views. The rates include food and beverages from 7 am to 11 pm at the restaurant on the premises. There's an Olympic-sized pool, too.

With 78 rooms, *Ocean Terrace Inn* (☎ 465-2754, fax 465-1057, in the USA ☎ 800-524-0512, otiskitts@caribsurf.com, PO Box 65) is Basseterre's biggest hotel. Known locally as OTI, it's popular with both tour groups and business travelers. Accommodations are spread across three sites and vary greatly, ranging from cramped streetside cottages and standard hotel rooms to commodious split-level ocean-view apartments perched above Fisherman's Wharf. All rooms have air-con, cable TV and phones. Rooms begin at US$135 in summer, US$150 in winter for the cheapest rooms and US$240 in summer, US$280 in winter for the deluxe accommodations. There's a pool, a fitness center and a complimentary shuttle to Turtle Beach.

Around Basseterre The *Fairview Inn* (☎ 465-2472, fax 465-1056, in the USA ☎ 800-223-9815, wall@caribsurf.com, PO Box 212) is situated above a working cane field 4 miles west of town, on the north side of the circle-island road. A former plantation estate, Fairview is quite ordinary and a little run-down in comparison to other plantation inns on the island. The main house serves as a restaurant, while accommodations are provided in 30 cottages, some nondescript and others more atmospheric, with old stone walls. All have private bathrooms,

and some have TV and a separate dining area. Rooms start at US$70 in summer, US$90 in winter.

Morgan Heights Condominiums (☎ 465-8633, fax 465-9272, morganheights@mail.skbee.com, PO Box 536) is on the circle-island road in the Canada Estate area 2 miles northeast of the airport. While the location is a bit out of the way, the units are large and modern with full kitchens, air-con, cable TV, phones and patios. Rates are US$85 in summer, US$125 in winter for one-bedroom suites, and US$125 in summer, US$185 in winter for two-bedroom suites. There is a restaurant and a pool. It's for sale, so call to check to see that it's still operating.

Places to Eat

Next to the cinema, *Redi-Fried*, a hole-in-the-wall on Bay Rd, offers two pieces of chicken with fries for EC$10.50. If you prefer to dine in air-conditioned comfort you can get similar fare at *KFC*, also on Bay Rd, for slightly higher prices. Redi-Fried is open until midnight daily; KFC is open to at least 11 pm.

The popular *Bayembi Cafe* (☎ 466-5280), on Bank St near the Circus, has an arty decor and Basseterre's best coffee. It serves bagels and croissants, veggie rotis (EC$12), hot sub sandwiches (from EC$13) and omelets (from EC$16). Hours are 7 am to 9 pm Monday to Wednesday, till 1 am Thursday to Saturday. Cheap drinks can be had from 5 to 6 pm.

Chef's Place (☎ 465-6176), on Church St, has good food and streetside patio dining. Various breakfasts cost EC$15, while at lunch and dinner there are four or five choices from the chalkboard, with such items as garlic chicken, grilled fish and butterfly shrimp – all around EC$20 and served with rice, a green salad and island vegetables. They also sell burgers and a good chicken roti (EC$10 to EC$12). It's open about 8 am to 11 pm daily except Sunday.

Victor's Hideaway (☎ 465-2518), on Stainforth St, serves up some excellent local food. Generous plates of mutton, chicken, conch or pork, with vegetables, salad and rice, cost around EC$25. It's open 11:30 am to 3 pm and 6 to 10 pm Monday to Saturday.

The popular *Ballahoo Restaurant* (☎ 465-4197) has a cheery 2nd-floor balcony overlooking the Circus. Full breakfasts, including Creole saltfish or pancakes with bacon, cost EC$20. At lunch, rotis, burgers and sandwiches start at EC$10, while the meal of the day is EC$22 or more, depending on the day. Dinner offerings, which include vegetarian stuffed peppers, chicken kebabs, parrotfish fillet and lobster, range from EC$35 to EC$70. A tasty treat is the tangy fresh-squeezed ginger beer. It's open 8 am to 10 pm daily except Sunday.

Fisherman's Wharf is a good-value, fun place to eat with dining at picnic tables on a waterfront dock below Ocean Terrace Inn. Dinners, cooked to order over an open grill, are accompanied by a self-service buffet of salad, Creole rice, sautéed potatoes, local vegetables and garlic bread. The price depends on the main dish you select: Grilled lobster is top dog at US$24; freshly caught fillet snapper is US$18.50. It's open 6:30 to 11 pm nightly.

StoneWalls (☎ 465-5248) is easy to spot – just look for the stone walls! *Newsweek* listed it as one of top bars in the world, which is saying something. This trendy pub on Princes St is run by a Canadian-English couple, has a pleasant courtyard setting and offers Creole, Cajun and Caribbean cuisine. Dinner without drinks averages EC$50. It's open 5 to 11 pm Monday to Saturday; reservations are suggested.

Mango's Garden Bar & Bistro (☎ 465-4049) has a nice outdoor eating area on Independence Square. Its big nights are the barbecue buffet nights, which range from EC$35 to EC$58. It's open for breakfast, lunch and dinner daily. It's also the island's party center Friday and Saturday nights.

For an excellent, cheap and stomach-expanding meal, head for the area around the bus stand and ferry terminal on Bay Rd Friday and Saturday nights. The place comes alive with jump-ups, rum bars and grill stands. EC$20 will buy you more spareribs than you can shake a stick at! A particularly good stand is at the western end, near the road.

American Bakery, on Victoria Rd, specializes in fresh bread and pastries and is open 6 am to 7 pm daily. *Country Churn Ice Cream*, on Cayon St, serves homemade ice cream, including a rich chocolate flavor.

The green-walled, tin-roofed *public market* on Bay Rd is the best place to pick up fruits and vegetables. There are a couple of grocery stores between the public market and the post office – *National Supply* and *Ram's Supermarket* – but the best food selection hands down is at the new *Valu Mart*, an American-style supermarket on Wellington St, a third of a mile northeast of the Cayon St traffic circle on the way to the airport.

Entertainment

The place to be Friday and Saturday nights is *Mango's Garden Bar & Bistro*, which transforms into a nightclub at 11 pm. It doesn't get going until 1 am, when up to 300 people try to fit onto a dance floor big enough for 50. It makes for a hot, sweaty affair!

StoneWalls, on Princes St, plays some great reggae and jazz, and is a pleasant place to meet chatty expats and locals alike. It's not the cheapest bar around, though.

Shopping

Caribelle Batik makes high-quality batik clothing, including shirts, pareus and skirts. A good selection of Caribelle batiks is available at Island Hopper, on the corner of Bank and Fort Sts.

Spencer Cameron Gallery, on the north side of Independence Square, has island artwork and prints at reasonable prices. Kate Design, on Bank St, features attractive watercolors, prints, cards and silks by island artist Kate Spencer. There are duty-free shops selling jewelry, watches and liquor at Pelican Mall.

FRIGATE BAY

Frigate Bay, 3 miles southeast of Basseterre, is the main beach resort area for St Kitts. It has two beaches, North Frigate Bay (also called Atlantic Beach) and Frigate Bay Beach (also known as Caribbean Beach or Timothy Beach). It's a 15-minute walk between the two bays.

The calmer Frigate Bay Beach, on the south side of the peninsula, is the island's most popular bathing spot. The facilities at this gray-sand beach include water-sports huts and an open-air drinking spot, the Monkey Bar, which attracts a crowd on weekends. The beach is backed by a salt pond, while the nearshore waters are a feeding ground for pelicans and frigate birds.

North Frigate Bay has rough waters and a long stretch of golden sand. Most of the area's development is along North Frigate Bay, with condominiums and shops lined up along the beach, opposite the golf course and Jack Tar Village. Despite the fact that Jack Tar has a casino, Frigate Bay is nonetheless a pretty low-key, uneventful area.

Buses generally don't run to Frigate Bay, so if you don't have your own rental car you'll have to plan on doing some hefty walking or rely on taxis.

Places to Stay

Cheapest in the area is the **Gateway Inn** (☎ 465-7155, fax 465-9322, gateway@ caribsurf.com, PO Box 1253), off by itself at the side of the main road between Basseterre and Frigate Bay. This unpretentious one-story apartment complex has 10 furnished units, each with a full kitchen, living room, separate bedroom, air-con, phone and cable TV. Rates are US$60 in summer, US$80 in winter.

Timothy Beach Resort (☎ 465-8597, fax 466-7085, in the USA and Canada ☎ 800-288-7991, tbr-stkitts@usa.net, PO Box 1198) is a small condo-style hotel affiliated with the Colony resort chain. The resort has a good beachside location on the east side of Frigate Bay Beach. Mountain-view rooms

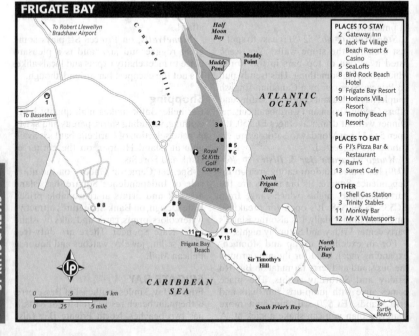

FRIGATE BAY

To Robert Llewellyn
Bradshaw Airport

Conaree Hills

Half
Moon
Bay

Muddy
Pond

Muddy
Point

To Basseterre

*ATLANTIC
OCEAN*

Royal
St Kitts
Golf
Course

North
Frigate
Bay

Frigate Bay
Beach

Sir Timothy's
Hill

North
Friar's
Bay

To
Turtle
Beach

*CARIBBEAN
SEA*

South Friar's Bay

0   .5   1 km
0   .25   .5 mile

PLACES TO STAY
2   Gateway Inn
4   Jack Tar Village
     Beach Resort &
     Casino
5   SeaLofts
8   Bird Rock Beach
     Hotel
9   Frigate Bay Resort
10 Horizons Villa
     Resort
14 Timothy Beach
     Resort

PLACES TO EAT
6   PJ's Pizza Bar &
     Restaurant
7   Ram's
13 Sunset Cafe

OTHER
1   Shell Gas Station
3   Trinity Stables
11 Monkey Bar
12 Mr X Watersports

are the cheapest; they have a tiny balcony, mini-refrigerator, air-con and phone and cost US$80 in summer, US$100 in winter. Studios with a kitchen cost US$105 in summer, US$150 in winter; one-bedroom apartments run US$130 in summer, US$175 in winter. Cheaper rates are sometimes offered in summer if the season is slow.

Frigate Bay Resort (☎ 465-8935, fax 465-7050, in the USA ☎ 800-266-2185, frigbay@caribsurf.com, PO Box 137) is a contemporary 64-room hotel on a hillside above Frigate Bay. Rooms are pleasant, with tiled floors, ceiling fans, air-con, TV, bathtubs and phones. The cheapest rooms, which have hillside views, cost US$105 in summer, US$160 in winter, while suites with kitchenettes start at US$230 in summer, US$295 in winter. Rates rise another US$10 or so over Christmas. There's a restaurant and a large pool accessible to the public, and it's possible to walk down to Frigate Bay Beach via a path behind the hotel.

If you need a lot of space, then *SeaLofts* (☎ 465-1075, fax 466-5034, sealofts@caribsurf.com, PO Box 813) is the place for you. The two-bedroom town-house-style units each have a living room with sofa bed, wicker and rattan furnishings, dining area, full kitchen, large balcony, cable TV and a washing machine and dryer. It's on the beach, and there are two tennis courts and a pool. Rates are US$177 to US$225 in winter, depending on the view, US$142 to US$167 in summer. There's no housekeeping service and thus no service charge.

Horizons Villa Resort (☎ 465-0584, fax 465-0785, in the USA ☎ 800-830-9069, trafalga@caribsurf.com, PO Box 1143) is a large development with spacious contemporary units spread along an oceanside knoll. Hotel units, which have a sea-view balcony, king bed, TV, thermostatic air-con and phone, cost US$112 in summer, US$200 in winter. Split-level one-bedroom units that feature an additional separate living room and full kitchen cost US$160 in summer, US$250 in winter; there are also two-, three- and four-bedroom units. Prices skyrocket over the Christmas period, usually doubling the winter rate.

The resort has two pools, a tennis court and a restaurant.

Jack Tar Village Beach Resort & Casino (☎ 465-8651, fax 465-1033, in the USA and Canada ☎ 800-858-2258, PO Box 406) is a 267-room all-inclusive casino/resort. Single/double rates, which include meals, drinks and activities, are from US$160/214.

Bird Rock Beach Hotel (☎ 465-8914, fax 465-1675, in the USA ☎ 800-621-1270, brbh@caribsurf.com, PO Box 227) is in the suburbs 2 miles east of central Basseterre. All the rooms are well appointed, with cable TV, air-con, fans, phones, tubs and cliff-side ocean-view balconies. The studios and suites have simple kitchenettes as well. There's a moderately priced restaurant, tennis courts, a pool and a small black-sand beach. The units are spread across six contemporary two-story buildings; the farthest two are the newest and have the best views. Rates are US$75 in summer, US$150 in winter for a room; US$90 in summer, US$175 in winter for a studio; and US$125 in summer, US$295 in winter for a two-bedroom suite.

Places to Eat

Run by two Canadian women, *PJ's Pizza Bar & Restaurant* (☎ 465-8373) is a popular place with both eat-in and takeout service. Small pizzas cost from EC$16 for plain cheese to EC$26 for Mexican; large pizzas are double that price. PJ's also has sandwiches, salads, chili and lasagna and sometimes sells loaves of freshly baked whole-wheat and French bread. Happy hour is 6 to 7 pm, with the last Thursday of every month a tequila happy hour. It's open 5:30 to 11 pm daily except Monday.

Part of Timothy Beach resort is *Sunset Cafe*, an open-air restaurant right on Frigate Bay Beach. The menu covers a lot of ground, with burgers, curries and Creole food available. A light breakfast costs EC$9, a breakfast with everything EC$21. At lunch, burgers start at EC$23, while tasty dishes like chicken-seasoned rice and catch of the day average EC$29. The dinner menu concentrates on West Indian seafood dishes priced between EC$34 and EC$48. It's open 7 am to 11 pm daily.

The restaurant at *Frigate Bay Resort* has a good array of breakfasts, starting at US$10.50. Lunchtime sandwiches and salads range from US$6 to US$12, and the specials, usually fish and seafood, from US$12 to US$17. Main courses in the evening average are around US$22. It's open 7 am to 9:30 pm daily.

Near PJ's Pizza Bar is a minimart, *Ram's*, open 9 am to 6 pm daily except Sunday.

SOUTHEAST PENINSULA

St Kitts' southeast peninsula is wild, unspoiled and dotted with white-sand beaches. The scenery has a certain stark beauty, with barren salt ponds, grass-covered hills and scrubby vegetation. The main inhabitants are green vervet monkeys, which you may see bounding across the road, and a few wild deer.

Until the early 1990s, when the 6½-mile Dr Kennedy Simmonds Hwy was constructed along its twisting spine, most visitors to this rugged peninsula arrived by boat. The highway signals grand plans to develop the peninsula for tourism, and a couple of new resorts are still in the planning stages.

The highway is the island's best road, but be cautious of occasional deep V-shaped rain gutters at the edge, particularly if you're tempted to pull off quickly to enjoy the view. Also, it's not uncommon to encounter small landslides along the road.

The neck at the beginning of the peninsula has sandy beaches on both sides: **North Friar's Bay** and **South Friar's Bay**. South Friar's Bay, which has calmer waters and better swimming conditions, is reached via a dirt road that's on the right a mile south of the start of the highway.

About 2¼ miles from the start of the highway, you'll reach the crest of the peninsula, where there's an unmarked lookout that offers a good view of the salt ponds and coastline. There's another viewpoint about 1½ miles farther south. Soon after that, a dirt road to the right leads to **White House Bay**, which has an old jetty and a couple of minor wrecks that provide reasonable snorkeling.

The highway then passes the **Great Salt Pond**, which is rimmed with salt crystals and attracts plovers, oystercatchers, stilts, whimbrels and other shorebirds. A dirt track runs off to the left of the pond to **Sand Bank Bay**, a quiet, sheltered white-sand beach, which on a weekday in summer you'll have to yourself. After that the road forks. The right fork leads to **Major's Bay**, which has a predominantly rocky shoreline, though if you walk west a few minutes from road's end you'll discover a quiet little sandy strand. The left fork leads to **Cockleshell Bay**, which has a pleasant gray-sand beach and a wonderful view of Nevis.

On the road to Cockleshell Bay, just past an old sugar mill, a sign points to **Turtle Beach**, which also has a sandy beach and a Nevis view. Turtle Beach has a restaurant with accommodations on the first floor, as well as a dive shop. When cruise ships are in, many of the day-trippers are taxied to the beach.

Places to Stay & Eat

The only place of substance on the southeast peninsula is *Turtle Beach Bar & Grill* (☎ 465-9086, gary@caribsurf.com), at Turtle Beach. There's a superb apartment available for rent above the restaurant, with a full kitchen, large living room, huge deck with great views of Nevis and the bay, and a big comfy double bed for US$120 in summer, US$150 in winter. There's also a double room with private bath adjacent to the apartment, for US$60. The restaurant is open 9 am to 6 pm daily (longer in winter), with decent offerings such as barbecued ribs and chicken roti for around US$15. It's a regular destination for cruise-ship day-trippers as well as monkeys, who hang around in packs and will steal the food from your plate if you're not watching. On Sunday there's a steel band.

On Sand Bank Bay is a small bar, *Gong on the Beach*, which opens at irregular hours and has a small selection of food and drink.

CIRCLE-ISLAND ROAD

The major sightseeing spot on St Kitts is Brimstone Hill Fortress National Park, but the circle-island road passes a few other points of interest as well, including petroglyphs, a batik factory and the crumbling stacks of numerous abandoned sugar mills.

It's a pleasant rural drive with scenery dominated by fields of sugarcane, broken up here and there by scattered villages. The narrow-gauge tracks of the sugarcane train run alongside the road, and odds are good that you'll see these vintage trains hauling loads of freshly cut cane from the fields to the mill.

The villages themselves, with their weathered stone churches and old wooden houses with rusty tin roofs, offer a closer glimpse of island life. All have small stores or rum shacks that sell sodas, liquor and a few basic provisions.

The road is paved and in fairly good condition, though you'll have to slow down for potholes, rain gutters and the occasional stray goat. The circle-island tour can easily be done in half a day; however, giving yourself a few more hours would allow for a more leisurely exploration.

Bloody Point

A little over 4 miles west of Basseterre, at the north end of the village of Challengers, a faded sign marks Bloody Point, the site where more than 2000 native Caribs were massacred by joint British and French forces in 1626.

Shortly after that sign is a curve in the road and a small place to pull off – stop here for a scenic view of the coast and Brimstone Hill.

Old Road Town

After Bloody Point the road swings down to the seaside village of Old Road Town, the landing site of the first British settlers in 1623. Amerindians left an earlier mark in the form of petroglyphs, and a 17th-century sugar estate has been turned into a well-regarded batik factory.

In the center of the village a sign pointing to Caribelle Batik marks Wingfield Rd. Immediately after turning inland on Wingfield, there's a yellow nursery school on the left. At the side of the road just past the school

you'll find three large black stones with **petroglyphs**; the middle one has two distinct human-like figures carved by Caribs. There are no fees to visit the site.

The road continues another half-mile through corn and cane fields and up past the ruins of the mill, chimney and stone arches of the Wingfield Estate before reaching Romney Manor, the old estate grounds that now contain **Caribelle Batik**.

The estate is located at the edge of a rain forest and this drive makes a nice diversion from the more arid lowlands that edge the coast. Although the manor house itself burned down a few years ago, Romney Manor still has interesting landscaping, with lush vegetation and grand flowering trees.

Batiks are made and sold on-site and you can watch wax being painted on cloth in a small demonstration area. It's open from 8:30 am to 4 pm weekdays.

Middle Island

The village of Middle Island is the site of the tomb of Sir Thomas Warner, the leader of the first British landing party on St Kitts, who died in March 1648. His marble-topped tomb with its verbose epitaph is under a white wooden shelter fronting the aging St Thomas church, which sits on a rise in the middle of town.

Brimstone Hill Fortress National Park

This rambling 18th-century compound, which in its day was nicknamed the 'Gibraltar of the West Indies,' is one of the largest forts in the Caribbean. As a major British garrison, Brimstone Hill played a key role in battles with the French, who seized the fort in 1782 but returned it the next year under the terms of the Treaty of Paris. The treaty ushered in a more peaceful era, and by the 1850s the fort was abandoned.

After the 1867 fire swept through Basseterre, some of the fort structures were partially dismantled and the stones used to rebuild the capital. In the 1960s major restoration was undertaken, and much of the fortress has been returned to its earlier grandeur. Queen Elizabeth II inaugurated

JOHN CASTELLANO

The might of the Citadel wasn't enough to prevent the French from taking Brimstone Hill.

the fort as a national park during her visit to St Kitts in October 1985.

The main hilltop compound, the Citadel, is lined with 24 cannons and provides excellent views of St Eustatius and Sandy Point Town. Inside the Citadel's old barrack rooms are museum displays on colonial history that feature cannonballs, swords and other period odds and ends. There's also a small collection of Amerindian adzes, a few pottery fragments and a rubbing of the Carib petroglyphs in Old Road Town. Another room contains a display on the American Revolution and the West Indian role in that revolt.

Also worthwhile is the short stroll above the cookhouse to the top of Monkey Hill, which provides excellent coastal views. A small theater next to the gift shop plays a brief video on the fort's history; a nearby canteen sells drinks and sandwiches.

Brimstone Hill, upon which the fortress stands, is an 800-foot volcanic cone named for the odoriferous sulfur vents you will undoubtedly detect as you drive past the hill along the coastal road.

Buses from Basseterre to Sandy Point Town can drop you off at the signposted road leading up to the fortress, from where it's a 1¼-mile uphill walk on a narrow, winding road. If you're driving up, be sure to beep your horn as you approach blind curves.

The fortress is open 9:30 am to 5:30 pm daily. Admission for foreign visitors costs US$5 for adults, US$2.50 for children.

Northeast Coast

As you continue from Brimstone Hill Fortress, you'll pass through lowlands of cane while circling **Mt Liamuiga**, the 3792-foot volcano that dominates the island interior. The north side of St Kitts has two exclusive resorts: Rawlins Plantation, in the hills east of St Paul's, and the Golden Lemon, down on the coast at Dieppe Bay. **Dieppe Bay Town** is a seaside fishing village with the requisite stone mill but not much else of note.

At the south end of Sadlers, you'll spot an old stone church down in the cane fields; shortly beyond that a sign points to **Black Rocks**. A short drive down that side road ends at coastal cliffs and a view of some seaside lava rock formations. For when the road proves too rough to drive on, the cliffs are only a five-minute walk from the circle-island road.

As the circle-island road continues south along the east coast, it passes more small towns, old sugar mills peeking above the cane fields and some stone churches, though there are no particular sights to stop for along the way. One of the villages on this side of the island, **Ottley's**, is the site of another exclusive plantation estate.

Places to Stay A mile inland from St Paul's, *Rawlins Plantation* (☎ 465-6221, fax 465-4954, rawplant@caribsurf.com, PO Box 340) is the most gracious of St Kitts' plantation inns. A former sugar estate that's still bordered by cane fields, it nicely incorporates its historic buildings. A period stone mill has been turned into a romantic honeymoon suite, while other accommodations are in comfortable cottages with wooden floors, four-poster beds and separate sitting rooms or verandas. There's also a pool. Single/double rates for the 10 rooms, which include breakfast, afternoon tea and dinner, are US$200/295 in summer, US$320/430 in winter.

Golden Lemon (☎ 465-7260, fax 465-4019, info@goldenlemon.com) is on a stony black-sand beach right in Dieppe Bay Town. A 17th-century plantation house is the centerpiece of the complex; however, most units are housed in a modern condolike facility next door. Single/double rooms begin at US$160/245 in summer and increase to US$200/300 in winter, breakfast included.

Ottley's Plantation Inn (☎ 465-7234, fax 465-4760, in the USA ☎ 800-772-3039, ottleys@caribsurf.com, PO Box 345) is a handsome 18th-century plantation house inland from the village of Ottley's. There are 24 air-conditioned rooms in the main building and surrounding cottages. All are comfortably furnished, each with a ceiling fan and a queen or king bed, some with antiques. Rates, including breakfast, range from US$225 in summer, US$295 in winter for a room in the 'great house' to US$510 in summer, US$725 in winter for the two-room English cottage with plunge pool and Jacuzzi, where Princess Margaret once stayed. It's US$25 less for single occupancy. There's a spring-fed pool and a daily shuttle to the beach and town.

Places to Eat The *Rawlins Plantation* (see Places to Stay), with its splendid view across cane fields to St Eustatius, is the choice place to have lunch on a circle-island tour. The West Indian lunch buffet, served daily on the patio from 12:30 to 2 pm, includes numerous dishes, such as chicken and breadfruit curry, beef brochettes, flying-fish fritters and fresh-fruit sorbet. The cost is EC$65. Dinner, a set four-course meal costing EC$120, is available at 8 pm by reservation only. The plantation is a mile up a signposted cane road that begins half a mile east of St Paul's.

Golden Lemon (see Places to Stay) serves lunch from noon to 2:30 pm, offering salads, sandwiches and fish & chips for around EC$30 to EC$45. Dinner, by reservation only, changes daily but commonly includes a seafood main dish complete with an appetizer, a soup and a dessert for around EC$120.

Royal Palm Restaurant, at Ottley's Plantation Inn (see Places to Stay), has pleasant alfresco dining within the partial stone walls of a former sugar warehouse. Try the Palm's famous banana pancakes (US$10.95) for breakfast or the Continental compilation (US$11.95). At lunch, the menu features sandwiches and simple dishes such as cheeseburgers for around US$13, and a selection of salads for US$19.95. At dinner a four-course meal is offered for US$65.

Nevis

Despite the opening of its first resort hotel, Nevis is still a pleasantly quiet, sleepy little backwater. It's a friendly island with a delightfully rural character and some reasonably good beaches.

Sightseeing on Nevis is limited mainly to poking around the old stone churches and sugar-plantation ruins scattered about the countryside. A paved road circles the island, and car rentals are inexpensive, making it easy to explore Nevis on a day trip. The island has a forested interior rising to scenic Nevis Peak, which is often cloaked in

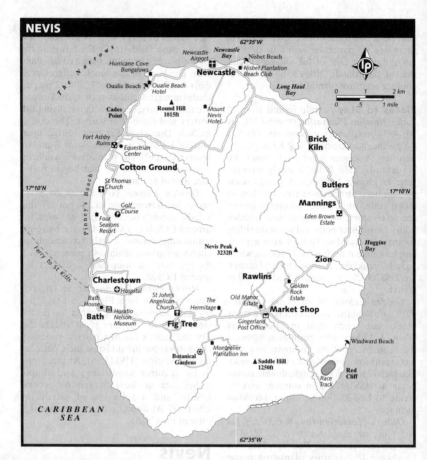

NEVIS

Newcastle Airport
Newcastle Bay
Nisbet Beach
The Narrows
Hurricane Cove Bungalows
Newcastle
Nisbet Plantation Beach Club
Oualie Beach
Oualie Beach Hotel
Long Haul Bay
Cades Point
Round Hill 1015ft
Mount Nevis Hotel
Brick Kiln
Fort Ashby Ruins
Equestrian Center
17°10'N
Cotton Ground
St Thomas Church
Butlers
Mannings
Eden Brown Estate
Golf Course
Pinney's Beach
Four Seasons Resort
Nevis Peak 3232ft
Huggins Bay
Zion
Ferry to St Kitts
Rawlins
Charlestown
Hospital
Golden Rock Estate
Bath House
St John's Anglican Church
The Hermitage
Old Manor Estate
Market Shop
Bath
Horatio Nelson Museum
Fig Tree
Gingerland Post Office
Windward Beach
Botanical Gardens
Montpelier Plantation Inn
Saddle Hill 1250ft
Race Track
Red Cliff
CARIBBEAN SEA
62°35'W
0   1   2 km
0   .5   1 mile

clouds. The coastal lowlands, where the larger villages are located, are much drier and support bougainvillea, hibiscus and other flowering bushes that attract numerous hummingbirds.

While most visitors arrive on the St Kitts ferry for just a one-day outing, Nevis has some interesting accommodations options for travelers seeking a quiet West Indian getaway.

CHARLESTOWN

The ferry from St Kitts docks in Charlestown, the island's largest town and

commercial center. The town has a few buildings with gingerbread trim, some old stone structures and a center that's marked by two tiny squares. Flanking one square is the tourist office and taxi stand, while the second square, a block to the south, fronts the courthouse and library.

The greater Charlestown area can be readily explored on foot – the museums and the bathhouse are within walking distance. Just a 15-minute jaunt north of the center will put you on a lovely stretch of Pinney's Beach that's lined with coconut trees and invites long strolls.

Information

Tourist Offices The Nevis Tourist Office (☎ 469-1042), a two-minute walk east of the pier, is open 8 am to 4 pm weekdays and 9 am to 1 pm Saturday. There's also a smaller tourist information booth at the ferry ticket office, but it's generally busier because it's managed by the ticket agent.

Money The St Kitts and Nevis National Bank will cash traveler's checks in any amount free of commission, while Barclays Bank charges an EC$2 commission for amounts under US$100. Banking hours are 8 am to 3 pm Monday to Wednesday, 8 am to 2 pm Thursday, 8 am to 5 pm Friday. Both the National Bank and Scotiabank have 24-hour ATMs.

Post & Communications The post office, on Main St, is open 8 to noon Thursday and Saturday, 8 am to 3:30 pm other weekdays. Commemorative stamps are sold at the Nevis Philatelic Bureau, which is near the public market and open from 8 am to 4 pm weekdays.

You can make international phone calls and send faxes and telegrams from the

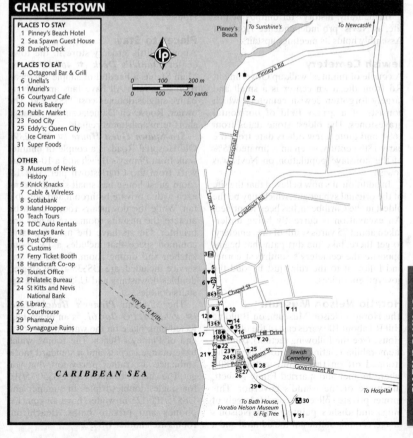

CHARLESTOWN

PLACES TO STAY
1 Pinney's Beach Hotel
2 Sea Spawn Guest House
28 Daniel's Deck

PLACES TO EAT
4 Octagonal Bar & Grill
6 Unella's
11 Muriel's
16 Courtyard Cafe
20 Nevis Bakery
21 Public Market
23 Food City
25 Eddy's; Queen City Ice Cream
31 Super Foods

OTHER
3 Museum of Nevis History
5 Knick Knacks
7 Cable & Wireless
8 Scotiabank
9 Island Hopper
10 Teach Tours
12 TDC Auto Rentals
13 Barclays Bank
14 Post Office
15 Customs
17 Ferry Ticket Booth
18 Handicraft Co-op
19 Tourist Office
22 Philatelic Bureau
24 St Kitts and Nevis National Bank
26 Library
27 Courthouse
29 Pharmacy
30 Synagogue Ruins

Pinney's Beach   To Sunshine's   To Newcastle

Pinney's Rd

Old Hospital Rd

Craddock Rd

Low St

Chapel St

Ferry to St Kitts

Happy Hill Drive

Jewish Cemetery

Government Rd

William St

Prince

Market

Sq

To Bath House, Horatio Nelson Museum & Fig Tree

To Hospital

CARIBBEAN SEA

ST KITTS & NEVIS

Cable & Wireless office on Main St, which is open 8 am to 5 pm weekdays, till noon Saturday.

Museum of Nevis History

The Museum of Nevis History occupies a Georgian-style building at the site where American statesman Alexander Hamilton was born in 1757 (the original home was toppled by an earthquake in the mid-1800s). In addition to portraits of Hamilton, this pleasant little museum has period photos with interpretive captions and other bits and pieces of Nevis culture and history. It's open 8 am to 4 pm weekdays and 9 am to noon Saturday. Admission is US$2.

Incidentally, history still unfolds at this site, as Nevis' pro-independence House of Assembly holds its meetings upstairs.

Jewish Cemetery

A couple of minutes' walk up Government Rd from the town center is a small and largely forgotten Jewish cemetery, which consists of a grassy field of horizontal gravestones. The oldest stone dates from 1684, and quite a few others date from the early 18th century, when an estimated 25% of the nonslave population on Nevis was Jewish.

In addition, it's now believed that the site of the original synagogue, which may be the oldest in the Caribbean, has been identified. An excavation is currently being undertaken about 75 yards south of the cemetery; to get there, take the dirt path that begins opposite the cemetery's southwest corner and follow it to the ruins just beyond the government offices.

Horatio Nelson Museum

The Horatio Nelson Museum, on Building Hill Rd about 100 yards east of the old Bath House (see the following section), contains memorabilia relating to Lord Nelson, who stopped off on this island in the 1780s, where he met and married Fanny Nisbett, the niece of the island's governor. This former private collection consists largely of mugs and dishes painted with Nelson's image, ceramic statues of the admiral and a few everyday items once used by Nelson. The museum is open 9 am to 4 pm weekdays, 10 am to 1 pm Saturday. Admission is US$2.

Bath House

The Bath House, a 15-minute walk south of the center of Charlestown, is a defunct hotel dating from 1778 that sits above thermal springs. Its mineral-laden waters, thought to have regenerative qualities, were the island's main attraction in colonial days, when wealthy visitors flocked here to soak in the warm baths. The springhouse is now closed, but you can join the locals and bathe in the stream that runs below the Bath House.

Places to Stay

Above a little grocery store in the town center, *Daniel's Deck* (☎ 469-5265), on Main St, has a handful of simple but clean rooms for rent. All have fans and private baths; singles/doubles cost US$25/50. The owner, Roosevelt Daniel, can also arrange short-term apartment rentals.

Sea Spawn Guest House (☎ 469-5239), Old Hospital Road, is a couple of minutes walk from Pinney's Beach and a 10-minute walk from the Charlestown pier. This 18-room guest house has small simple rooms, each with a private bathroom and portable fan. While the downstairs rooms are a bit austere, the upstairs rooms are bigger and brighter. Guests have the use of a large common space that includes a TV room, kitchen and dining room. Rates, tax and service included, are US$35/41 for singles/doubles downstairs and US$47 for the upstairs doubles.

The 55-room *Pinney's Beach Hotel* (☎ 469-5207, PO Box 61) is an older, neglected pink place on the water at the south end of Pinney's Beach. The rooms, which have orange carpets and a standard motel ambiance, are rather pricey for what you get. The cheapest, which cost US$50/75/100 for singles/doubles/triples in summer and US$75/100/125 in winter, have air-con, TV, phones and private baths. Beachfront rooms are another US$35.

Places to Eat

Eating options are a tad scarce in Charlestown. *Courtyard Cafe* serves local fare in a quiet garden courtyard shaded by banana trees. Breakfast pancakes and lunchtime sandwiches or burgers cost around EC$12. It's open 7:30 am to 3:30 pm Monday to Saturday.

Eddy's, run by a Canadian–West Indian couple, has a pleasant 2nd-floor veranda dining area that overlooks Main St. There's homemade soup and bread for EC$12, salads and burgers for EC$20 and chicken stir-fry for EC$25. It's open for lunch noon to 3 pm daily except Thursday and Sunday. Wednesday night is party night, from around 7:30 pm till the last person leaves.

There are a few restaurants just north of the dock. *Octagonal Bar & Grill* offers barbecued chicken (EC$15) and fish (EC$25) meals in a casual seaside setting, complete with reggae music and ice-cold beer. It's closed Sunday.

Nearby *Unella's* (☎ 469-5574), a 2nd-floor open-air restaurant, has a good views of St Kitts and a fine selection of seafood dishes, such as fish of the day for EC$41, snapper for EC$42 and lobster over EC$60.

For local food without a view, there's *Muriel's* (☎ 469-5920), an unpretentious little spot just beyond Happy Hill Drive, at the back of the Lime Tree store. The dinner menu includes chicken or fish for EC$35 and lobster for EC$45, served with rice and peas, christophene and fried plantain. Lighter and cheaper lunches are available from noon to 3 pm. It's open daily except Sunday.

Ten minutes' walk north on Pinney's Beach is the party-central beach bar, *Sunshine's*. It's stumbling distance to the ocean and a fun place to hang out (the photos on the walls are comment enough), and many expats and locals do just that. The food – a selection of fish, chicken and lobster dishes ranging from EC$14 to EC$20 – is quite good, but is overshadowed by the legendary drink served here: the Killer Bee. It's a secret concoction of the bar owner Sunshine, tasting like a nice fruit punch but with a kick like a very large mule. A visit to Nevis

would be incomplete without sampling the wonderful nectar. Be daring and have two!

Nevis Bakery, on Happy Hill Drive, has breads, tasty pineapple-cinnamon rolls and inexpensive rotis. For ice cream, head to *Queen City Ice Cream*, below Eddy's.

The best place to go for produce is the *public market*, which is open from around 7 am to 4:30 pm daily except Sunday. *Food City*, in the center of town, is a well-stocked supermarket open 6:30 am to 9:30 pm daily. *Super Foods*, at the south side of Main St, is the island's biggest supermarket; it's open 8 am to 8 pm Monday to Saturday.

Shopping

There's a handicraft co-op next to the tourist office on Main St in Charlestown. Knick Knacks, near the Cable & Wireless office, has a good selection of local arts and crafts.

SOUTH NEVIS

The circle-island road crosses the southern part of Nevis between cloud-shrouded Nevis Peak and Saddle Hill, passing through the districts of Fig Tree and Gingerland. This area was the center of Nevis' sugar industry in colonial days, and there are many crumbling sugar-mill stacks that evoke that era. A few of the former plantation estates have been converted into atmospheric inns.

St John's Anglican Church

St John's, on the main road in the village of Fig Tree, is a stone church that dates from 1680. A copy of the church register, dated March 11, 1787, which records the marriage of Lord Horatio Nelson and Francis Nisbett, can be found in a glass case at the rear of the church. If you peek beneath the red carpet in the center aisle you'll find a continuous row of tombstones of island notables who died in the 1700s.

Botanical Gardens

Covering 8 acres of land only a few minutes' drive southwest of Montpelier Inn, the Botanical Gardens make for a nice detour, especially if you don't manage to make the trek into the island's rain-forest interior.

The glasshouse conservatory provides a good taste of the flora found in a typical rain forest, and there's a selection of other plant life, ranging from thorny roses and cacti to perfumed orchids. It's open 9 am to 4:30 pm Monday to Saturday; admission costs US$9, US$4 for children.

Windward Beach

Windward Beach, also known as Indian Castle Beach, is the only easily accessible beach on the southern part of the island. Backed by beach morning glory and low scrubby trees, the beach has fine gray sand and fairly active surf. Unless it's a weekend, the odds are good that, with the exception of a few rummaging goats, you'll have the beach to yourself.

To get there, turn south at the Gingerland Post Office in Market Shop and continue straight ahead for 2 miles. (Be aware of bumps and dips in the road; just south of the church there's an especially sharp dip that's not visible until you're on top of it.) Then turn left and follow the road for another three-quarters of a mile. After passing the racetrack (where horse races are held on holidays), the road turns to dirt and becomes somewhat rough, but it should be passable unless it's been raining heavily. There are no facilities at the beach.

Places to Stay

The following four plantation inns are all on the grounds of former sugar estates. All are within 3 miles of each other, and none is more than a few minutes' drive from the circle-island road.

The Hermitage (☎ 469-3477, fax 469-2481, in the USA ☎ 800-682-4025, nevherm@caribsurf.com), in St John's Parish, about a mile northeast of Fig Tree, is a quiet 15-room inn run by an American couple. The main plantation house, which is 260 years old and furnished with antiques, serves as a parlor and evening gathering spot. Accommodations are in one- and two-story cottages spread around the grounds. The cottages are pleasantly rustic, with four-poster beds, hardwood floors, sitting rooms, ceiling fans, mini-refrigerators and lattice-shuttered windows. There's a pool, tennis court and horse treks. Prices range from US$170 to US$265 in summer, US$325 to US$450 in winter, breakfast included.

Montpelier Plantation Inn (☎ 469-3462, fax 469-2932, montpinn@caribsurf.com, PO Box 474), 1½ miles southeast of Fig Tree, is an exclusive 17-room cottage-style English inn. The estate was the site of Horatio Nelson's marriage in 1787, and in more recent times it hosted the late Princess Diana. Despite a regal guest list, the inn has a relaxed and personable appeal that has won it numerous accolades, including top place in *Condé Nast* reader polls. It has flower gardens, a beach shuttle and a swimming pool scenically set beside the ruins of an old sugar mill. All cottages have sea-view balconies, a pleasant subdued décor, and a king or two double beds. Singles/doubles cost US$185/210 in summer, US$215/240 in autumn, US$320/350 in winter, breakfast included.

The *Old Manor Estate* (☎ 469-3445, fax 469-3388, in the USA ☎ 800-892-7093, oldmanor@caribsurf.com, PO Box 70), at the north side of Market Shop, has an engaging setting. The grounds are scattered with the remains of an 18th-century sugar plantation, including a mill stack, a nearly intact boiler and the huge steel rollers that until 1936 were used to crush the plantation's cane. The inn's 13 atmospheric rooms, which occupy some of the estate's renovated buildings, are very large, cooled by ceiling fans and furnished with either king or queen beds; some also have separate sitting rooms. The cheapest rooms cost from US$150 in summer, US$185 in spring and autumn and US$230 in winter, breakfast for two included. There's a complimentary beach and town shuttle.

Golden Rock Estate (☎ 469-3346, fax 469-2113, goldenrockhotel@caribsurf.com, PO Box 493) is a casual, family-run inn with 14 rooms, set in the countryside between Market Shop and Zion. The main stone-block plantation house (c. 1815) has a bar, library and sitting room. Most accommodations are in cottages with four-poster beds, and there's also a stone sugar mill that's been converted into a two-bedroom, two-bathroom suite. There's a pool, tennis court, nature trails and a complimentary beach and town shuttle. Singles/doubles cost US$120/140 in summer, US$195/210 in winter.

Places to Eat

The restaurant at *The Hermitage* (see Places to Stay) has pleasant open-air dining. The dinner menu changes regularly but usually offers a choice of meat and seafood selections, such as salmon and lamb for around US$30. Lunch is a more simple affair, with sandwiches, rotis and salads for around half that. A good night for dinner is Wednesday during the winter season, when there's a string band and a hearty West Indian buffet for the fixed dinner price.

Montpelier Plantation Inn (☎ 469-3462) has a casual terrace where lunch is served from 12:30 to 2:30 pm; sandwiches, chef salads and simple pastas average US$11.50. Dinner, a more pampering affair that's served on the main veranda overlooking spotlighted gardens, is prepared by the inn's Welsh chef and features a changing four-course menu for either US$49 or US$59; advance dinner reservations are required.

Cooperage Restaurant (☎ 469-3445), at the Old Manor Estate, occupies an old cooperage and offers alfresco dining with a distant ocean view. A full breakfast or light lunch costs around US$14. At dinner, there's a range of main dishes, including flying fish, grilled fresh fish or filet mignon for US$15 to US$25; soup or salad costs around US$5 to US$9, and excellent rum punch is mixed at the bar. Reservations are suggested.

Golden Rock Estate (☎ 469-3346) has outdoor dining on a cobblestone patio. At lunch, noon to 2:30 pm, lobster salad (US$20.50) is a specialty, and there are sandwiches from US$6.50. Dinner features a changing four-course meal and requires advance reservations.

EAST NEVIS

As you continue around the circle-island road up the east coast, the villages become smaller and houses fewer. The area's main sight is the **Eden Brown Estate**, on the inland side of the main road just south of Mannings. The estate house, built around 1740, is most interesting for its macabre history.

Shortly after Julia Huggins inherited this estate from her father, she got engaged. However, the plans were shattered when, on the eve of the wedding in 1822, her celebrating groom and his best man got into a drunken duel and killed each other. After the jolting event, Julia became a recluse in this house and was seldom seen by Nevisians. Following her death the house was abandoned, and to this day some islanders still believe it to be haunted by Julia's ghost.

There are extensive stone ruins of the old plantation, including the remains of a mill behind the house. The estate, now owned by the government, is marked by a sign and free to explore.

NEWCASTLE

Newcastle, at the north end of the island, has Nevis' airport, a small selection of places to stay and eat and a roadside pottery shop where traditional coal pots are made and sold.

Newcastle's biggest attractions are its beaches. The fine strand of white sand fronting the Nisbet Plantation Beach Club is Nevis' best. To get there, follow the road that runs along the side of the hotel down to the shore, where there's beachside parking. There's also a little beach along Newcastle Bay, where there's a restaurant and a seasonal water-sports shop.

Places to Stay

The *Mount Nevis Hotel* (☎ 469-9373, fax 469-9375, in the USA and Canada ☎ 800-756-3847, mountnevis@aol.com, PO Box 494) is an upmarket family-run hotel with a peaceful setting on the slopes of Mt Nevis. The 32 rooms, which are in four contemporary two-story buildings, have full amenities, including cable TV, VCRs, phones, ceiling fans, air-con, refrigerators and terraces. There's a fine view of St Kitts from the pool and from many of the rooms. The hotel has a complimentary beach shuttle. Double rooms cost US$165 in summer, US$235 in winter, while suites with cooking facilities cost US$210 in summer, US$300 in winter. Rates include Continental breakfast.

Nisbet Plantation Beach Club (☎ 469-9325, fax 469-9864, in the USA ☎ 800-742-6008, nisbetbc@caribsurf.com) is a contemporary beach resort on the site of a former plantation. It's a pleasant place with cottages spread across an expansive lawn that fronts a beautiful picture-postcard white-sand beach. There are tennis courts, a beachside pool, a restaurant and a beach bar. The cheapest rooms, which cost US$290 for doubles in summer, US$320 in autumn, US$475 in winter (US$500 over the Christmas period), have wicker furnishings, tiled floors, screened porches, ceiling fans and minibars. Larger rooms are US$80 to US$100 more. Rates include breakfast and dinner.

Places to Eat

A good value is *Pizza Beach*, run by Mount Nevis Hotel on the beach at Newcastle Bay. There's a good pizza selection available, ranging from EC$22 for the smallest to EC$56 for the largest. It's open 6 to 10 pm Thursday to Tuesday.

The restaurant at *Mount Nevis Hotel* (see Places to Stay) is a classier affair, with great views and some of the best food on the island. The changing menu features creative Caribbean and Continental cuisine. At dinner, à la carte seafood and meat main dishes range from US$18 to US$36, while at breakfast and lunch there are simpler, moderately priced offerings such as Creole chicken sandwiches for US$10.

Nisbet Plantation Beach Club (see Places to Stay) has a beachside café serving burgers, rotis and sandwiches for around EC$25, Caesar salad for a couple of dollars more.

OUALIE BEACH

Oualie Beach is a long, thin strip of light gray sand fronted by waters that are shallow and generally calm. It's a quiet, laid-back area with a couple of places to stay. The

Oualie Beach Hotel has a dive and watersports shop.

Places to Stay

The *Oualie Beach Hotel* (☎ 469-9735, fax 469-9176, in the USA ☎ 800-682-5431, oualie@caribsurf.com) is a pleasant place right on the beach. Most of the rooms are in duplex waterfront cottages. The rooms are comfortable, with a four-poster queen bed or two double beds, tiled floor, ceiling fan, refrigerator and screened ocean-view patio. Prices change from month to month, with the cheapest ranging from US$105 to US$165 in summer, US$195 to US$245 in winter. Singles are 10% less, and a studio with air-con and a kitchen costs US$60 more.

Hurricane Cove Bungalows (☎/fax 469-9462, hcove@caribsurf.com) has a cliff-top location at the north end of Oualie Beach. Accommodations are in pleasantly rustic wooden cottages, each with a kitchen, porch and ceiling fan. The one-bedroom cottages start at US$95 in summer, US$125 in spring and late autumn, US$175 in winter. Two-bedroom cottages are available from US$155 in summer, US$200 in spring and late autumn, US$275 in winter. In winter a minimum one-week stay is required; at other times, a minimum three-night stay is mandatory.

Places to Eat

The *Oualie Beach Hotel* has an open-air beachside restaurant with standard breakfast offerings and lunchtime salads and sandwiches at moderate prices. At dinner there's a three-course meal that includes conch chowder or salad, a choice of six main dishes and dessert.

PINNEY'S BEACH

Pinney's Beach is a long stretch of soft white sand that runs along the west coast down to the north side of Charlestown. The beach, which is backed almost its entire length by tall coconut palms, has lovely views of St Kitts across the channel.

The site of **Fort Ashby**, which was built around 1702, is on the beach just north of

Cotton Ground. It's the last of eight small fortifications that once extended along the coast north of Charlestown, but not much remains other than a few cannons and some partially reconstructed walls. This area was also the site of Jamestown, the island's original settlement, which was washed into the sea by the combination of an earthquake and tidal wave in 1680.

Places to Stay & Eat

The **Four Seasons Resort** (☎ 469-1111, fax 469-1112, in the USA ☎ 800-332-3442, in Canada ☎ 800-268-6282, PO Box 565) is an upscale resort on a quiet stretch of Pinney's Beach. It was hit hard by Hurricane Lenny and has recently been revamped. There's an 18-hole golf course, 10 tennis courts, a pool and a health club. The 196 posh rooms each have tiled floors, marble baths, terraces, ceiling fans, air-con, phones, TV and VCRs. Rates are US$325 in summer and US$675 in winter for a golf-course view, and US$75 more for an oceanfront room.

There are a couple of expensive dinner restaurants at Four Seasons and a few small local restaurants scattered along the coast. See Places to Eat in Charlestown, earlier, for **Sunshine's**, one of better options along the beach.

St Lucia

St Lucia is a high, green island with a mountainous interior and a coastline pocketed with secluded coves and beaches. Its most dramatic scenery is in the south, where the twin peaks of the Pitons rise sharply from the Soufrière shoreline to form one of the Eastern Caribbean's most distinctive landmarks.

Highlights

- Strolling around downtown Castries, from its grand cathedral to colorful rum shops
- Exploring Pigeon Island, which offers fort ruins, hiking, snorkeling and a white-sand beach
- Taking in the Soufrière area for its fine scenery, great diving, rainfalls and steaming sulfur vents
- Participating in the colorful Friday-night jump-ups at Gros Islet and Anse La Raye

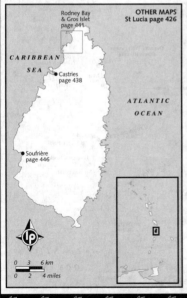

In recent years, St Lucia has rapidly become a trendy packaged-tourism destination for cruise-ship passengers and well-heeled honeymooners. Fortunately, there has also been a rise in the number of small family-run hotels and guest houses geared towards individual travelers. Most hotels and visitor facilities are on the northwest coast, along the road that runs north from the capital city of Castries.

Once you go south beyond Castries, St Lucia is markedly rural in nature, a mix of small fishing villages, sprawling banana plantations and untamed jungle. The interior rain forest is home to tall hardwood trees, climbing vines, tree ferns and one of the last remaining species of parrot in the Eastern Caribbean.

Facts about St Lucia

HISTORY

Archaeological finds on the island indicate that St Lucia was settled by Arawaks between 1000 and 500 BC. Around AD 800 migrating Caribs conquered the Arawaks and established permanent settlements on the island.

St Lucia was outside the routes taken by Columbus during his four visits to the New World and was probably first sighted by Spanish explorers during the early 1500s. The first attempt at European colonization wasn't made until 1605, when a party of English settlers was quickly routed off the island by unreceptive Caribs. A second attempt by about 400 British colonists from St Kitts was made in 1638, but the settlement was abandoned within two years after most of the settlers were killed in Carib attacks.

After the British left, the French laid claim to the island and attempted to reach an agreement with the Caribs. The French established the island's first lasting European settlement, Soufrière, in 1746 and

ST LUCIA

425

ST LUCIA

Pointe du Cap
Pointe Hardy
Pigeon Island National Park
Cap Estate
Cas-en-Bas
Anse Lavoutte
Fous Island
Pigeon Point
Cap Islet
Gros Islet
Rodney Bay
Lapins Island
Labrellotte Point
Monchy
Cape Marquis
Choc Bay
Rat Island
Marquis River
Cassimi Point
D'Estrées Point
Vigie Airport
Monier
Marquis
CARIBBEAN SEA
La Toc Bay
CASTRIES
Babonneau
Grande Anse
Coubaril Point
Morne Fortune
Tortue Point
Cul de Sac River
Castries Waterworks Forest Reserve
Forestière
Louvet Point
Marigot Point
Piton Flore 1871 ft
L'Islet à Ramier
Roseau Bay
Marigot Bay
Roseau River
Rouche Island
Fond d'Or River
Anse La Raye
Grand Rivière
Povert Point
Pointe la Ville
Fond d'Or Bay
Anse Cochon
Morne la Cambe 1446 ft
Dennery
La Croix Point
Jambette Point
Anse des Canaries
Canaries
Dennery Island
Mandelé Point
Grand Bois Forest
Dennery Waterworks Forest Reserve
Blanche Point
Nature Reserve
Praslin
Frigate Islands Nature Reserve
Anse Chastanet
Mt Gimie 3118 ft
Quilesse Forest Reserve
Mon Repos
Trou Gras Point
Soufrière
Diamond Botanical Gardens
Soufrière Bay
Sulphur Springs
Edmond Forest Reserve
Malgretoute
Fond St Jacques
Petit Piton 2460 ft
Mount Grand Magazin 2022 ft
Troumassée R
Micoud
Anse des Pitons
Etangs
Vierge Point
Gros Piton Point
Gros Piton 2617 ft
Saltibus
Liverpool Rocks
Caraibe Point
Canelles River
Micoud Point
Banse
Grace
Anse l'Islet
Choiseul Bay
Choiseul
Scorpion Island
Piaye
Laborie
Laborie Bay
Hewanorra International Airport
ATLANTIC OCEAN
Black Bay
Vieux Fort
Maria Islands Nature Reserve
Vieux Fort Bay
Cape Moule à Chique
Caesar Point

Ferry to Fort-de-France

Gros Islet Rd

0   3   6 km
0   2   4 miles

14°05'N
14°00'N
13°55'N
13°50'N
13°45'N

61°05'W   61°00'W   60°55'W   60°50'W

went about developing plantations. St Lucia's colonial history was marred by warfare, however, as the British still maintained their claim to the island.

In 1778 the British successfully invaded St Lucia and established naval bases at Gros Islet and Pigeon Island, which they used as staging grounds for attacks on the French islands to the north. For the next few decades, St Lucia seesawed between the British and the French. In 1814 the Treaty of Paris finally ceded the island to the British, ending 150 years of conflict during which St Lucia changed flags 14 times.

Culturally, the British were slow in replacing French customs, and it wasn't until 1842 that English nudged out French as St Lucia's official language. Other customs linger, and to this day the majority of people speak a French-based patois among themselves, attend Catholic services and live in villages with French names.

St Lucia gained internal autonomy in 1967 and full independence, as a member of the Commonwealth, on February 22, 1979.

GEOGRAPHY

St Lucia is teardrop-shaped, roughly 27 miles in length and 14 miles in width, with a land area of 238 sq miles. The isle's interior is largely mountainous, reaching its highest point at the 3118-foot Mt Gimie in the southwest. Deep valleys, many of which are planted with bananas and coconuts, reach down from the mountains.

The Soufrière area has the island's best-known geological features: the twin volcanic cones of the Pitons, which rise up some 2500 feet from the shoreline, and the hot, bubbling Sulphur Springs, just inland from the town. Despite this little show of geological activity, there hasn't been a volcanic eruption on St Lucia since 1766.

CLIMATE

In January the average daily high temperature in Castries is 81°F (27°C), while the low temperature averages 68°F (20°C). In July the average daily high is 85°F (29°C), while the low averages 72°F (22°C).

Annual rainfall ranges from 59 inches (1500 mm) on the coast to 136 inches (3450 mm) in the mountains. In Castries, measurable rain falls an average of 11 days a month from January to March, the driest months. The rainiest months, June to December, have an average of 18 days of rain. Humidity ranges from 76% in February to 83% in November.

FLORA & FAUNA

St Lucia's vegetation ranges from dry and scrubby areas of cacti and hibiscus to lush jungly valleys with wild orchids, bromeliads, heliconia and lianas.

Under the British colonial administration, much of St Lucia's rain forest was targeted for timber harvesting. In many ways the independent St Lucian government has proved a far more effective environmental force, and while only about 10% of the island remains covered in rain forest, most of that has now been set aside as nature reserve. The largest indigenous trees in the rain forest are the gommier, a towering gum tree, and the chatagnier, a huge buttress-trunked tree.

Island fauna includes St Lucia parrots, St Lucian orioles, purple-throated Carib hummingbirds, bats, lizards, iguana, tree frogs, introduced mongooses, rabbitlike agoutis and several snake species, including the venomous fer-de-lance and the boa constrictor.

It's illegal to damage, collect, buy or sell any type of coral on St Lucia, and nothing should be removed from any of the island's many marine reserves.

GOVERNMENT & POLITICS

St Lucia is an independent state within the Commonwealth, with the British monarchy being represented by an appointed governor-general. The bicameral parliament has an 11-member Senate that's appointed by the governor-general and a more powerful 17-member House elected by universal suffrage for five-year terms. The prime minister, a member of the majority party of the House, is the effective head of state.

ECONOMY

Agriculture still accounts for nearly one-third of St Lucia's employment and gross national product. The leading export crop is bananas, followed by coconuts and cocoa. Tourism, which has been booming in recent years with the construction of new hotels and resorts, represents the fastest-growing segment of the economy, and either directly or indirectly it accounts for about 15% of the labor force.

POPULATION & PEOPLE

The population is about 150,000, one-third of whom live in Castries. Approximately 85% of all islanders are of pure African ancestry. Another 10% are an admixture of African, British, French and East Indian ancestry, while about 4% are of pure East Indian or European descent.

SOCIETY & CONDUCT

St Lucia has a mix of English, French, African and Caribbean cultural influences, which are manifested in many ways. For instance, if you walk into the Catholic cathedral in Castries, you'll find a building of French design, an interior richly painted in bright African-inspired colors, portraits of a black Madonna and child, and church services delivered in English.

Derek Walcott, the renowned Caribbean poet and playwright and winner of the 1992 Nobel Prize for literature, is a native of St Lucia. Walcott, who teaches at Boston University, still maintains his connections with the island and is spearheading a movement to renovate the buildings on Rat Island, a former quarantine station off Choc Beach, and turn it into a retreat for writers and artists.

Another Nobel laureate with island connections is former Princeton University professor Sir Arthur Lewis (1915–91), who was born in Castries but as a teenager moved to England, where he was educated in the field of political economy. Lewis, who eventually returned to the Caribbean to teach at the University of the West Indies (1959–63), was a founder of the Caribbean Development Bank (1970) and the creator of the 'Lewis Model,' which explores the transition developing countries experience as they move from an agrarian to an industrial economy. Lewis received the Nobel Prize for economics in 1979.

St Lucia's scenic landscape has been the backdrop for several foreign films, including the British movies *Water* (1985), starring Michael Caine, and *Firepower* (1979), with Sophia Loren, as well as Hollywood's *Doctor Dolittle* (1967) and *Superman II* (1980).

Dos & Don'ts

Dress is casual, and simple cotton clothing is suitable attire for any occasion. To avoid offense, swimwear should be restricted solely to the beach. Topless or nude bathing is not acceptable on public beaches.

RELIGION

About 85% of St Lucians are Roman Catholics. Anglican, Baptist, Christian Science, Methodist, Pentecostal and Seventh Day Adventist denominations are also represented on the island.

LANGUAGE

The official language is English. When chatting among themselves, islanders commonly speak a French-based patois that's spiced with West African and English words.

Facts for the Visitor

ORIENTATION

St Lucia has two airports: International flights land at Hewanorra International Airport, near Vieux Fort at the southern end of the island, while most interisland flights land at the more conveniently located Vigie Airport, near Castries, the capital.

Maps

The best map is the 1:50,000 Ordnance Survey map of St Lucia, which is difficult to find on the island. A reduced black-and-white print of the map can be found on the centerfold of *Tropical Traveller*, the free tourist newspaper. Less detailed road maps are available at the local tourist offices.

TOURIST OFFICES
Local Tourist Offices

The St Lucia Tourist Board has an office opposite the port-police office on Jeremie St in Castries and booths at the two airports and the cruise-ship dock in Pointe Seraphine.

When requesting information by mail, write to the St Lucia Tourist Board (☎ 452-4094, fax 453-1121), PO Box 221, Castries, St Lucia, West Indies.

Tourist Offices Abroad

The St Lucia Tourist Board has the following overseas offices:

Canada
(☎ 416-362-4242, fax 416-362-7832)
8 King St, Toronto, Ontario M5C 1B5

France
(☎ 0147-20 39 66, fax 0147-23 09 65)
53 Rue François 1er, 7th floor, Paris 75008

Germany
(☎ 06172-77 80 13, fax 06172-77 80 33)
PO Box 1525, 61366 Friedrichsdorf

UK
(☎/fax 020-7431 3675, fax 020-7431 7920)
421a Finchley Rd, London NW3 6HJ

USA
(☎ 212-867-2950, 800-456-3984, fax 212-867-2795)
820 2nd Ave, 9th floor, New York, NY 10017

VISAS & DOCUMENTS

Citizens of the USA and Canada can enter St Lucia with proof of citizenship, such as an official birth certificate, and a photo ID, such as a driver's license. French citizens can enter with a national identity card. Citizens of the UK, Australia and most other countries must be in possession of a valid passport. For all foreign visitors, stays of over 28 days generally require a visa.

An onward or roundtrip ticket or proof of sufficient funds is officially required.

EMBASSIES & CONSULATES
St Lucian Embassies & Consulates

Germany
(☎ 06172-30 23 24)
Postfach 2304, 61293 Bad Homburg

UK
(☎ 020-7937 9522)
10 Kensington Court, London W85DL

USA
(☎ 202-364-6792)
3216 New Mexico Ave NW, Washington, DC 20016

Foreign Consulates in St Lucia

Germany
Honorary Consul (☎ 450-8050)
Care Service Building, Massade Industrial Estate, Gros Islet

UK
High Commission (☎ 452-2484/5)
NIS Waterfront building, 2nd floor, PO Box 227, Castries

CUSTOMS

Visitors are allowed to bring in 200 cigarettes and one bottle of spirits.

MONEY

The Eastern Caribbean dollar (EC$) is the island currency. One US dollar equals EC$2.70. US-dollar traveler's checks are the most convenient, but Canadian-dollar and UK-sterling checks can also be changed without difficulty. Other currencies are more problematic – many banks, including Barclays, commonly tag on an EC$80 fee per transaction to exchange French francs and EC$54 to exchange Dutch guilders or German marks.

Barclays, which has branches in Castries, Soufrière, Rodney Bay Marina and Vieux Fort, will cash traveler's checks in US, Canadian and UK currencies free of charge for transactions of EC$500 or more, and with an EC$2 charge for lesser amounts. (The fee is waived for Barclays/Visa traveler's checks.) In addition, all banks charge a EC$0.30 government stamp fee per check.

You can get cash advances using Visa or MasterCard, or make withdrawals from your bank account using a Cirrus or Plus bank card, from ATMs at the Royal Bank of Canada branches in Castries and Rodney Bay.

Visa, MasterCard and American Express are the most widely accepted credit cards and can be used for car rentals and at most mid-range and top-end restaurants and hotels.

An 8% tax and a 10% service charge are added onto the bill at all but the cheapest hotels and restaurants; there's no need for additional tipping.

POST & COMMUNICATIONS
Post
There are post offices in major towns and villages around St Lucia. When addressing mail to the island, the town name should be followed by 'St Lucia, West Indies.'

Telephone
There are both card and coin phones around the island. Phone cards are sold at tourist office booths, Cable & Wireless offices and the Rodney Bay Marina office.

You can send international faxes and make phone calls from the Cable & Wireless office on Bridge St in Castries.

For local calls, dial all seven numbers. When calling St Lucia from overseas, add the area code 758. More information on phone cards and on making long-distance calls is in Post & Communications in the Regional Facts for the Visitor chapter.

Email & Internet Access
Internet access is limited but expanding all the time. In downtown Castries email and Internet access are available at the Cable & Wireless office on Bridge St; another office is at the Gablewoods Mall. In Marigot Bay there's one computer with Internet access at the office of the Marigot Beach Club. In Rodney Bay, check out Fishnet, just down the beach road from the Rodney Bay Mall, where you can get email access along with helpful travel advice.

NEWSPAPERS & MAGAZINES
St Lucia's main newspaper is the *Voice*, published three times a week, and there are a handful of weeklies that hit the newsstand on Saturday. You can buy local, US and UK newspapers in Sunshine Bookstore at the Gablewoods Mall and at Pieces of Eight at Rodney Bay Marina.

In addition there's *Tropical Traveller*, a useful monthly tourist newspaper loaded with promotional articles, ads and visitor information, and *Visions of St Lucia*, a glossy magazine with detailed hotel listings; both of these free publications can be picked up at tourist offices or hotel lobbies.

RADIO & TV
Several radio stations can be received on St Lucia. Most hotels have cable TV, which has about 40 channels and provides an eclectic combination of programming from the US (particularly south Florida), South America, the Caribbean and Europe.

ELECTRICITY
Electricity is 220V, 50 cycles. Many hotels have adapter outlets in the bathrooms that allow 110V shavers to be used.

WEIGHTS & MEASURES
St Lucia follows the imperial system: Distances and car odometers are measured in miles, and maps note elevations in feet.

HEALTH
The island's two largest hospitals, Victoria Hospital (☎ 452-2421), in Castries, and St Jude's Hospital (☎ 454-6684), in Vieux Fort, both have 24-hour emergency service. For more serious medical conditions people often obtain medical evacuation to Barbados, Martinique or Miami.

Bilharzia (schistosomiasis) is endemic to St Lucia; the general precaution is to avoid wading or swimming in freshwater. St Lucia also has the fer-de-lance, a poisonous pit viper. More information on both the fer-de-lance and bilharzia is under Health in Regional Facts for the Visitor.

DANGERS & ANNOYANCES
Though St Lucia is generally safe, crime is a growing problem, and Lucians are increasingly concerned. A vicious attack in Castries' Cathedral of the Immaculate Conception

during New Year's Mass on December 30, 2000, left an Irish nun dead and several people injured, tarnishing St Lucia's image as a peaceful holiday resort. But the fact is that visitors to the island are unlikely to be affected, though sensible precautions – such as keeping an eye on your valuables while at the beach and avoiding the backstreets of Castries at night – are definitely advised.

Hikers should keep in mind that the poisonous fer-de-lance favors brushy undergrowth, so stick to well-trodden trails.

EMERGENCIES

For medical, fire and police emergencies dial ☎ 999.

BUSINESS HOURS

Government and business hours are generally 8:30 am to 12:30 pm and 1:30 to 4:30 pm weekdays. Many stores are also open 8 am to noon Saturday. Bank hours are usually 8:30 am to 3 pm Monday to Thursday, till 5 pm Friday. A few bank branches, particularly in resort areas, are open Saturday morning as well.

PUBLIC HOLIDAYS & SPECIAL EVENTS

St Lucia has the following public holidays:

New Year's Day	January 1
New Year's Holiday	January 2
Independence Day	February 22
Good Friday	late March/early April
Easter Monday	late March/early April
Labour Day	May 1
Whit Monday	eighth Monday after Easter
Corpus Christi	ninth Thursday after Easter
Emancipation Day	August 3
Thanksgiving Day	October 5
National Day	December 13
Christmas Day	December 25
Boxing Day	December 26

Note that when some holidays fall on Sunday, they're celebrated on the following Monday.

St Lucia's Carnival takes place the two days before Ash Wednesday, with calypso tents, costume parades, music contests and the like.

The biggest music event of the year is the four-day St Lucian Jazz Festival, which takes place in mid-May and has featured musicians such as Herbie Hancock, Chaka Khan and Chuck Mangione.

The Atlantic Rally for Cruisers (ARC), one of the largest transatlantic yacht races, is held in December, starting in the Canary Islands and ending at Rodney Bay Marina, St Lucia's largest yacht port. About 150 boats cross the finish line.

ACTIVITIES
Beaches & Swimming

All of St Lucia's beaches are public. On the touristed northwest side of the island there's a fine white-sand beach along the causeway linking Gros Islet and Pigeon Point, and another at Reduit Beach, the resort strip south of Rodney Bay. There are also nice golden strands at Choc Beach, which stretches north from Sandals Halcyon

Along the southwest coast are numerous coves and bays, many accessible by boat only, that offer good swimming and snorkeling.

The east side of the island is less protected, with rougher water conditions, some off-limits to swimmers.

Diving & Snorkeling

St Lucia's rugged mountain terrain continues beneath the sea as underwater mounts, caves and drop-offs. Most of the diving takes place on the western side of the island, with some of the top sites in the south-central area.

Anse Chastanet, near Soufrière, has been designated a marine park and boasts spectacular nearshore reefs with a wide variety of corals, sponges and reef fish; it's excellent for both diving and snorkeling.

A popular dive just a bit farther south is Key Hole Pinnacles, consisting of coral-encrusted underwater mounts that rise to within a few feet of the surface.

There are a couple of wreck dives, including *Lesleen,* a 165-foot freighter that was deliberately sunk in 1986 to create an artificial reef. It now sits upright in 65 feet of water near Anse Cochon, another popular dive area. Anse Cochon is also a favored snorkeling stop on day sails to Soufrière.

In addition, there's good snorkeling and diving beneath both Petit Piton and Gros Piton, the coastal mountains that loom to the south of Soufrière. In the main resort area north of Castries, Pigeon Island offers fair snorkeling.

Dive Shops There are a number of dive shops on St Lucia:

Buddies Scuba
(☎/fax 452-5288, buddies@candw.lc) PO Box 565, Castries. Another PADI facility, this is based at the Vigie Marina in Castries and has dives to Anse Chastanet and Anse Cochon, charging US$60 for a two-tank dive. Also offered is an introductory scuba course (US$60).

Dolphin Divers
(☎ 452-9485) PO Box 1538, Castries, at Rodney Bay Marina

Frog's Diving
(℅ 452-0913, fax 452-1494) PO Box 3049, Castries, at Windjammer Landing (see Places to Stay in the North of Castries section, later)

Rosemond's Trench Divers
(☎ 451-4761, fax 453-7605) PO Box 1809, Castries. The island's other PADI facility, this operates out of Marigot Bay, offering two-tank dives for US$70, night dives for US$65 and an introductory scuba course for US$75.

Scuba St Lucia
(℅ 459-7000, fax 459-7700, ansechastanet@candw.lc) Anse Chastanet Hotel, PO Box 7000, Soufrière. A well-regarded PADI facility, it offers one-tank dives for US$30, an introductory scuba course for US$75, open-water certification courses for US$425 and referral courses for US$220. Boat transport from Castries is available.

Windsurfing

Some of the large beachfront hotels, including the Royal St Lucian, at Reduit Beach, and the Windjammer Landing, between Castries and Gros Islet, rent out windsurfing equipment. The going rate is US$10 an hour for rentals, US$30 for a three-hour lesson.

The Vieux Fort area, at the southern tip of the island, gets strong winds and rough seas, making it a favorite with experienced windsurfers looking for a challenge.

Hiking

There are three main trails into the mountainous interior on public lands administered by the Department of Forest & Lands. To help maintain the trails, the department has initiated an EC$25 per-person park fee for hikers.

The Barre de L'isle Trail is a good choice if you're on a budget, as you can get to the trailhead from Castries for EC$2.50 by hopping a Vieux Fort bus (about 30 minutes). This lush rain forest hike, which is in the center of the island along the ridge that divides the eastern and western halves of St Lucia, leads to the top of the 1446-foot Morne la Cambe. It provides some fine views along the way and takes about three hours roundtrip. The trailhead, which begins at the south side of the highway, is clearly marked; on weekdays Department of Forest & Lands personnel wait at the trailhead to collect the park fee and are available as guides.

St Lucia Parrot

The rain forest is home to the St Lucia parrot (*Amazona versicolor*), locally called the jacquot, the island's colorful endemic parrot. Despite the jacquot's status as the national bird and its appearance on everything from T-shirts to St Lucian passports, it has teetered on the brink of extinction.

However, a successful effort to educate islanders on the plight of the parrot and new environmental laws seem to be working to save the parrots, which occasionally made it onto island dinner tables in times past. Fines for shooting or capturing parrots have been increased a hundredfold while much of the parrots' habitat has been set aside for protection. So far the protection measures have been a success; the 2000 parrot census found 800 birds, up from less than 100 in the mid-1970s. Most of the parrots nest in the Edmond and Quilesse Forest Reserves, east of Soufrière.

Because trailhead access for the other two forest-reserve hikes are inland from major roads and bus routes, these hikes are usually undertaken as part of an organized tour. The Des Cartiers Rainforest Trail at the Quilesse Forest Reserve begins 6 miles inland from Micoud and passes through the habitat of the rare St Lucia parrot. The Edmond Forest Reserve Trail begins about 7 miles east of Soufrière, crosses a rain forest of tall trees interlaced with orchids and bromeliads and offers a fine view of St Lucia's highest peak, the 3118-foot Mt Gimie.

Although the latter two forest-reserve hikes take only a few hours to walk, the travel time to either trailhead is about 90 minutes each way from Castries, so the hikes are full-day outings. The Department of Forest & Lands (☎ 450-2231) and the island's main tour agencies arrange outings several days a week.

Horseback Riding
Trim's National Riding (☎ 450-8273) offers a US$30 hour-long ride along the beach in Cas-en-Bas and a US$45 two-hour ride that also includes crossing the interior to Gros Islet.

Fox Grove Inn (☎ 455-3271) offers horseback trail rides along the central Atlantic coast at Mon Repos, charging US$20 for a ride that last about 75 minutes.

Tennis & Squash
Most of the larger hotels have tennis courts. The St Lucia Yacht Club (☎ 452-8350), at Reduit Beach, has squash courts open to visitors for a fee.

Golf
The St Lucia Golf & Country Club (☎ 450-8523), on the northern tip of the island, has a nine-hole course. When played as 18 holes, greens fees are US$27; golf clubs can be rented for US$10 and carts cost US$25.

ACCOMMODATIONS
St Lucia has a number of good-value, moderately priced guest houses, with the lion's share in the Rodney Bay area.

The island's main resort area, at nearby Reduit Beach, has reasonably priced mid-

range hotels, as do other places scattered around the island.

St Lucia also has some good, albeit pricey, upper-end offerings and a growing number of all-inclusive resorts targeted at honeymooning North Americans.

FOOD
Standard Western fare predominates at most hotels. In contrast, local restaurants generally feature West Indian and Creole dishes – even those booked into an all-inclusive hotel will find it's worth slipping away for at least one good local meal. St Lucia has numerous restaurants in all price ranges, with the better ones invariably featuring fresh seafood.

Street food is excellent, especially in the morning when it's hot and fresh. Roadside stands around the island serve up treats like stuffed bakes, fried chicken and fish & chips.

DRINKS
Water is generally safe to drink from the tap. The island's local beer, Piton, is a tasty light lager brewed in Vieux Fort, perfect for a day on the beach.

ENTERTAINMENT
Most of the entertainment options on St Lucia are in the Rodney Bay area, where the tourists are. Downtown Castries is a ghost town after dark, except for the somewhat seedy rum shops around the bus depots.

On Friday nights Gros Islet holds its jump-up, a long-standing tourist favorite, with loud music, greasy grilled street food and dancing in the streets.

South of Castries, Anse La Raye has Seafood Fridays, drawing a mostly local crowd from all over the island for a carnival of fresh food and dancing until dawn.

Getting There & Away

AIR
Airports & Airlines
St Lucia has two airports: Hewanorra International Airport, in Vieux Fort at the remote

southern tip of the island, and Vigie Airport, in Castries near the main tourist area.

International jet flights land at Hewanorra, which has a longer runway, while flights from within the Caribbean generally land at Vigie. Most visitors will find it significantly more convenient to book a flight that lands at Vigie.

Both Vigie and Hewanorra Airports have tourist information booths, taxi stands, card and coin phones and booths for Avis, Hertz, National and a few small local car rental agencies. The tourist information booths book rooms, sell phone cards and will exchange US cash into EC dollars at slightly disadvantaged rates.

Offices for the main airlines serving St Lucia are in central Castries. The LIAT office, on Derek Walcott Square, also takes care of bookings for BWIA and is open 8 am to 4 pm weekdays, till noon Saturday.

British Airways is above Scotiabank on William Peter Blvd, and American Airlines is on the corner of Micoud and Mongiraud Sts.

The following are the airline reservation numbers on St Lucia:

Air Canada	☎ 452-6406
Air Jamaica	☎ 454-6263
Air Martinique	☎ 452-2463
American Airlines	☎ 454-6777
British Airways	☎ 452-7444
BWIA	☎ 452-3778
LIAT	☎ 452-3051
	☎ 452-2348 after hours

Departure Tax
Air passengers leaving St Lucia must pay an EC$27 departure tax.

Within the Caribbean
LIAT has daily nonstop flights to Vigie Airport from Antigua, Barbados, Dominica, Martinique, St Vincent and Trinidad, and connecting flights from the rest of LIAT's network.

LIAT's one-way fares to St Lucia are US$142 from Trinidad, US$78 from Barbados, US$64 from Martinique, US$90 from Dominica, US$142 from Antigua and US$51 from St Vincent.

LIAT also has roundtrip excursion fares, which are good for 30 days, between St Lucia and Trinidad (US$177), Martinique (US$101), Dominica (US$161), Antigua (US$265) and Barbados (US$124).

Air Martinique has flights from Martinique to St Lucia for US$108 roundtrip with a 21-day maximum stay.

The USA
American Airlines has flights to each of St Lucia's airports at least once daily from San Juan, Puerto Rico, with connections to its USA flights. Fares vary with the season and current promotions but generally start at around US$500 for midweek travel from the US east coast.

BWIA flies to St Lucia twice weekly from both Miami and New York, while Air Jamaica flies four times weekly from New York. Their rates are comparable to those charged by American Airlines.

Canada
Air Canada flies to St Lucia from Toronto on Saturday. A roundtrip ticket with a minimum stay of seven days and a maximum stay of 14 days costs C$634.

The UK
British Airways has flights from London's Gatwick Airport to St Lucia on Wednesday, Friday and Sunday, and BWIA flies from Heathrow Airport on Tuesday, Saturday and Sunday. The roundtrip fare with either airline is UK£762 with a minimum stay of seven days and a maximum stay of six months.

South America
LIAT has flights between St Lucia and Caracas on Tuesday and Friday. The one-way fare costs US$198, and a 21-day excursion ticket is US$297.

SEA
Ferry
L'Express des Iles operates an express catamaran between Castries and Fort-de-France, Martinique. The boat, which takes 80 minutes, leaves Castries once or twice a

week depending on the season. Departure days and times change frequently; check in advance with any local travel agent. The one-way/roundtrip fare is EC$104/175 from Castries, 305/450F from Fort-de-France. On St Lucia, tickets can be purchased from Cox & Co (☎ 452-2211), a block southwest of the tourist office in Castries. More information on this boat – which also connects with Dominica and Guadeloupe – is in the Getting There & Away section of the Guadeloupe chapter.

Yacht

Customs and immigration can be cleared at Rodney Bay, Castries, Marigot Bay or Vieux Fort. Most yachties pull in at Rodney Bay, where there's a full-service marina and a couple of marked customs slips opposite the customs office.

It's also easy to clear in at Marigot Bay, where you can anchor in the inner harbor and dinghy over to the customs office. Castries is a more congested scene, and yachts entering the harbor are required to go directly to the customs dock. If there's no room, you should head for the anchorage spot east of the customs buoy. At Vieux Fort, you can anchor off the big ship dock, where customs is located.

Popular anchorages around the island include Reduit Beach, the area southeast of Pigeon Island, Rodney Bay Lagoon, Marigot Bay, Anse Chastanet, Anse Cochon and Soufrière Bay.

Yacht charters are available from Sunsail (☎ 452-8648) and DSL Yachting (☎ 452-8531), both at Rodney Bay Marina, and from The Moorings (☎ 451-4357), at Marigot Bay. For addresses and booking information, see the Yacht Charters section in the Getting Around the Region chapter at the beginning of the book.

Cruise Ship

Cruise ships dock in Castries. There are a number of berths, some on the east side of the harbor near the town center and others at Pointe Seraphine on the north side of the harbor, where there's a duty-free shopping complex.

Getting Around

TO/FROM THE AIRPORT
Hewanorra Airport

A taxi from Vieux Fort costs about EC$120 to Castries, EC$135 to Reduit Beach; travel time is about 1½ hours. If you're traveling light and are in no hurry, take an inexpensive local bus from Vieux Fort to Castries (EC$6); however, they're not terribly frequent after about early afternoon and may charge more for baggage.

Vigie Airport

Taxi fares from Vigie Airport are EC$12 to Modern Inn or Halcyon Beach Club, EC$30 to Reduit Beach, EC$35 to Rodney Bay Marina, EC$12 to the Castries town center and EC$60 to Marigot.

In part because of the pressure from the taxi union, minibuses avoid Vigie Airport; the nearest bus stop is about a mile away, at the northern end of the runway.

BUS

Bus service is via privately owned minivans. They're a cheap way to get around and the means by which most islanders get to town, school and work. Buses are frequent on main routes (such as Castries to Gros Islet) during the workday but drop off quickly after the evening rush hour, so that getting a bus after about 7 pm can be challenging. Very few buses run on Sunday.

If there's no bus stop nearby, you can wave buses down en route as long as there's space for the bus to pull over. Pay the fare directly to the driver.

If you're trying to circle the island by bus, note that afternoon service between Soufrière and Castries is unreliable, so it's best to travel in a counterclockwise direction, catching a morning bus from Castries to Soufrière and returning via Vieux Fort (up the east coast) in the afternoon.

If you're traveling in the southwest of the island, be aware that southbound buses are often completely full, and it's sometimes more convenient to backtrack north to Castries, where you can be sure of getting a seat.

Sample fares from Castries are EC$2 to Gros Islet (Route 1A) or Marigot (Route 3C), EC$6 to Vieux Fort (Route 2H) and EC$7 to Soufrière (Route 3D). Route numbers are displayed on the buses.

In Castries, buses going south to Soufrière can be picked up at the east side of the public market, while buses to Gros Islet and Vieux Fort can be found nearby on Darling Rd.

CAR & MOTORCYCLE
Road Rules
On St Lucia, drive on the left. Unless you have an International Driving Permit, you'll need to purchase a local license, which can be picked up from immigration at either airport and costs EC$30. If you don't get it upon arrival, most car rental companies will either issue you a license or take you to a nearby police station to get one.

Roads vary greatly around the island, with some sections being newly surfaced and others deeply potholed. Make sure you have a workable jack and spare tire. Be cautious when driving around Castries, where many of the roads are very narrow and lined with deep rain gutters. Many of the interior and southern roads are also very winding and narrow. Speed limits are generally 15mph in towns and 30mph on major roads. Gas stations are distributed around the island.

Rental
Car Avis, Hertz and National operate out of both airports. All three companies allow 100 free miles per day on their standard rentals and charge US$0.40 for each additional mile.

The cheapest cars, usually little Daihatsu Cuores or Suzuki Altos, rent for US$49 a day from National (☎ 450-8500); from Avis (☎ 452-2046) they're US$63 and from Hertz (☎ 452-0680) they're US$55. Renters can sometimes get better deals with the international companies by booking in advance from their home country.

Car rental companies offer optional collision damage waiver (CDW) for about US$16 a day, which covers theft and collision damages to the car, but the renter is still responsible for the first US$300 to US$500 in damages. If the CDW is not taken, the renter is usually responsible for the first US$1200 to US$2000 in damages.

One local company offering good prices with unlimited mileage is CTL Rent A Car (☎ 452-0732, fax 452-0401), which operates out of Rodney Bay Marina. Rates begin at US$45 a day for a Coure and CTL provides free hotel pick-up.

Motorcycle Wayne's Motorcycle Center (☎ 452-2059), on the main road between Castries and Rodney Bay, rents out 500cc Honda motorcycles for EC$80 a day, helmet included.

TAXI
Taxis are plentiful at the airports, in Castries and in the main resort areas. Always establish the fare with the driver before you get in, doubly so if you want to do anything 'unusual,' like stopping to see a view.

From your guest house or hotel you can ask the receptionist to call a taxi; the rates are the same as waving one down, and the odds of having to squabble over the fare are lower. To call a taxi yourself, phone ☎ 452-1599 in Castries, ☎ 454-6136 in Vieux Fort.

ORGANIZED TOURS
Sightseeing tours by taxi cost about US$15 to US$20 an hour. A taxi tour of the Soufrière area and back to Castries generally costs around US$120 with up to four passengers.

Local tour companies offer a range of land tours of the island, boat tours around St Lucia and air tours of neighboring islands. Most land tours average US$50, including a hiking outing to the Des Cartiers rain forest in the Quilesse Forest Reserve or an around-the-island van tour that stops at Marigot, Soufrière and the sulfur springs. Other tours take in estate homes and plantations that are otherwise inaccessible to individual travelers.

Two of the main tour companies are Sunlink Tours (☎ 452-8232), at Reduit Beach, and Pitons Travel Agency (☎ 450-1486), in Castries. Most hotels can book tours as well.

The St Lucia National Trust (☎ 452-5005, natrust@isis.org.lc) can arrange tours to the island's coastal nature reserves: the Maria

Island Nature Reserve, off the southeast coast, and the Frigate Islands Nature Reserve, off the east coast; both are popular with bird watchers.

Boat Tours

Daylong sails down the coast from Rodney Bay to Soufrière are very popular. They stop at Marigot Bay, include a minivan tour of Sulphur Springs and Diamond Botanical Gardens, and take you snorkeling at Anse Cochon or Anse Chastanet on the return trip.

The sailing time between Rodney Bay and Soufrière is about two hours each way, and the tours tend to last from about 9 am to 5 pm.

Several companies offer these sails, which can be booked directly or through tour agencies or hotels. The cost is about US$75 including hotel pick-up and lunch.

From Rodney Bay you can make the trip on the 56-foot *Endless Summer* (☎ 450-8651) catamaran, or, if you want to go in style, on the *Brig Unicorn* (☎ 452-8232), a 140-foot-long tall ship that replicates a 19th-century brigantine.

Castries

Castries, the island's commercial center and capital, is a bustling port city set on a large natural harbor. The liveliest part of the city is just southeast of the port, at Jeremie and Peynier Sts, where the colorful Castries Market houses scores of produce, handicraft and souvenir stands.

The city, which was founded by the French in the 18th century, was ravaged by fire three times between 1785 and 1812 and again in 1948. Consequently, most of the city's historic buildings have been lost.

One area that survived the last fire was Derek Walcott Square, a quiet central square surrounded by a handful of 19th-century wooden buildings with gingerbread-trim balconies, an attractive Victorian-style library and the imposing Cathedral of the Immaculate Conception. Opposite the cathedral at the east side of the square is a lofty saman (monkey pod) tree that's estimated to be 400 years old.

Information

The tourist office (☎ 452-2479), on Jeremie St opposite the port police station, is open 8 am to 12:30 pm and 1:30 to 4 pm weekdays, 9 am to 12:30 pm Saturday.

The Royal Bank of Canada, on William Peter Blvd, is open 8 am to 3pm Monday to Thursday, till 5 pm Friday. There's a Scotiabank a block to the west and a Barclays Bank farther west, on Bridge St.

The GPO (general post office), on Bridge St a block south of the port, is open 8:15 am to 4 pm weekdays. Stamp collectors can buy commemorative stamps at the philatelic bureau inside the GPO.

Phone calls can be made and faxes sent from the Cable & Wireless office on Bridge St, open 7:30 am to 6:30 pm weekdays, 8 am to 12:30 pm Saturday.

The public library is open 9 am to 6 pm weekdays, till 12:30 pm Saturday. Visitors can check out books for a refundable deposit of EC$50. The Book Salon, on the corner of Laborie and Jeremie Sts, sells books about the Caribbean.

Cathedral of the Immaculate Conception

The city's Catholic cathedral, built in 1897, is a grand stone structure with a splendidly painted interior of trompe l'oeil columns and colorfully detailed biblical scenes. The island's patron saint, St Lucia, is portrayed directly above the altar. The church richly incorporates both Caribbean and African influences, including images of a black Jesus and Mary and the liberal use of bright tones of red, green and yellow.

Morne Fortune

Sitting atop the 2795-foot Morne Fortune, about 3 miles south of Castries center, is **Fort Charlotte**, whose construction began under the French and was continued by the British. Because of its strategic hilltop vantage overlooking Castries, the fort was a source of fierce fighting between the French and British in colonial times. The fort buildings have been renovated and given a new life as the Sir Arthur Lewis Community College.

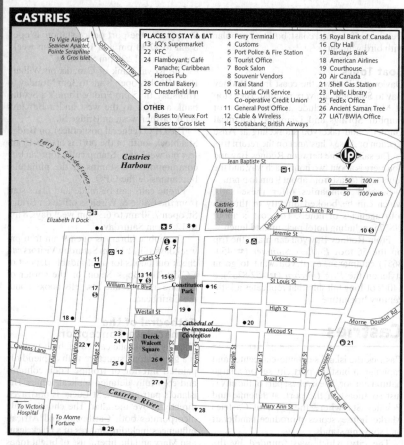

CASTRIES

To Vigie Airport,
Seaview Apartel,
Pointe Seraphine
& Gros Islet

John Compton Hwy

PLACES TO STAY & EAT
13 JQ's Supermarket
22 KFC
24 Flamboyant; Café
   Panache; Caribbean
   Heroes Pub
28 Central Bakery
29 Chesterfield Inn

OTHER
1 Buses to Vieux Fort
2 Buses to Gros Islet

3 Ferry Terminal
4 Customs
5 Port Police & Fire Station
6 Tourist Office
7 Book Salon
8 Souvenir Vendors
9 Taxi Stand
10 St Lucia Civil Service
   Co-operative Credit Union
11 General Post Office
12 Cable & Wireless
14 Scotiabank; British Airways

15 Royal Bank of Canada
16 City Hall
17 Barclays Bank
18 American Airlines
19 Courthouse
20 Air Canada
21 Shell Gas Station
23 Public Library
25 FedEx Office
26 Ancient Saman Tree
27 LIAT/BWIA Office

Ferry to Fort-de-France

Castries
Harbour

Elizabeth II Dock

Castries
Market

Jean Baptiste St

Trinity Church Rd

Darling Rd

0   50   100 m
0   50   100 yards

Jeremie St

Victoria St

St Louis St

High St

Micoud St

Morne Doudon Rd

Cadet St

William Peter Blvd

Constitution
Park

Westall St

Cathedral of
the Immaculate
Conception

Queens Lane

Manoel St

Mongiraud St

Bridge St

Bourbon St

Laborie St

Peynier St

Broglie St

Coral St

Chisel St

Chausee St

Leslie Land Rd

Derek
Walcott
Square

Brazil St

Castries River

Mary Ann St

To Victoria
Hospital

To Morne
Fortune

At the rear of the college a small obelisk monument commemorates the 27th Inniskilling Regiment's retaking of the hill from French forces in 1796. Near the monument you'll also find a couple of cannons and a fairly good view of the coast north to Pigeon Point.

If you just want a good view of the city, there's no need to venture as far as the college. The scenic lookout opposite Government House, about a half-mile south of Castries, has a fine view of the port and capital and also gives a glimpse of the attractive crown-topped Victorian mansion

that serves as the residence of the governor-general.

Places to Stay

The *Chesterfield Inn* (☎ 452-1295, PO Box 415) is on Bridge St, in a quiet neighborhood about a five-minute uphill walk from central Castries. The inn has a dozen comfy singles/doubles with air-con, TV and private baths for US$35/50; there's a commodious common area with colonial antiques, but otherwise the place is quite straightforward.

Seaview Apartel (☎ 452-4359, PO Box 527) has 10 big units, each with TV, air-con, phones, refrigerators, bathtubs and balconies. Although the 'sea view' is but a distant glimpse, it's still a good value at US$53 (US$59 for a unit with an oven). The main drawback is the odd location, on the east side of the airport runway, but it does lie on the Castries–Gros Islet bus route. Reception is at the Shell gas station next door.

Bon Appetit (☎ 452-2757, PO Box 884), at the south side of town near the top of Morne Fortune, has a lovely ocean view with Martinique on the horizon. It's run by an Italian couple, Renato and Cheryl Venturi, who operate a small restaurant at the same site. There are four spotlessly clean rooms, each with a double bed, fan, private bath and cable TV. Singles/doubles cost US$37/42, including tax and breakfast.

Green Parrot (☎ 452-3399, fax 453-2272, PO Box 648) has 50 nice, large rooms with air-con, cable TV, private baths, comfortable furnishings and balconies with fine views. There's a pool and a good restaurant. The main disadvantage is that, like Bon Appetit, Green Parrot is a bit out of the way, on the hillside of Morne Fortune, about 3 miles from central Castries. Singles/doubles cost US$60/80 year-round.

Places to Eat

Town Center There's row of bars, restaurants and bakeries along Mary Ann St, perfect for grabbing a sandwich and a beer and chatting with locals. For good, cheap rotis and local dishes, try the food stalls at the south side of Castries Market; the stalls are open 11 am to around 2:30 pm Monday to Saturday. You can get drinking coconuts for EC$1 at the market and at the Darling Rd bus stand.

If you're looking for the perfect picnic, you could pick up some fruit at the market and then walk over to **Central Bakery**, at the south end of Peynier St for fresh-baked bread and inexpensive coconut pies. For conventional fast food, there's a **KFC** on Bridge St that's open 9:30 am to at least midnight daily.

JQ's Supermarket, on William Peter Blvd, is a large, well-stocked grocery store that's open 8 am to at least 5 pm weekdays, till 4 pm Saturday.

Flamboyant (3 Bourbon St) is downtown Castries' fine-dining hot spot, overlooking Derek Walcott Square. Expect traditional island dishes done with an upscale flair; jerk chicken is EC$41, cajun fish EC$29. It's open noon to 2:30 pm for lunch weekdays, 7 to 9 pm for dinner Tuesday to Saturday.

Downstairs from Flamboyant, **Café Panache** has nice, cafeteria-style island food, popular with workers on their lunch break. Step past the lunch line, through the doors in the back of the room, to **Caribbean Heroes Pub**, where expats and the local wheelers and dealers spend the day enjoying overpriced cocktails and cable TV.

Morne Fortune For a French-inspired treat, head up to **Green Parrot Restaurant** (☎ 452-3399), which serves a weekday business lunch from noon to 3 pm for EC$25 or sandwiches and salads for EC$10 to EC$20. Dinner is a more expensive proposal, with a four-course meal, selected from a full menu, priced at EC$90. Be sure to get one of the window tables to enjoy the restaurant's fine hilltop view of Castries and the northwest coast. The restaurant is in Morne Fortune, 3 miles from the town center (EC$10 by taxi).

Bon Appetit (☎ 452-2757), also in Morne Fortune, is an intimate little restaurant with home-cooked food and a wonderful view. It's open noon to 2 pm weekdays and 7 to 11 pm nightly. Main dishes range from EC$40 for fish to EC$90 for freshwater crayfish, the house specialty. As there are only five tables, reservations are recommended.

Shopping

On Jeremie St in Castries, on the west side of the public market, you'll find vendors selling T-shirts, dolls, wood carvings and other handicrafts and souvenirs.

Pointe Seraphine, the main cruise-ship dock, has a duty-free shopping complex with about 25 shops selling jewelry, watches, liquor, crystal, china and other imported goods. There are also a couple of clothing shops, including Bagshaws, which sells island-made silk-screened clothing. Although its business hours fluctuate a bit with the season, the complex is generally open 9 am to 5 pm weekdays, 9 am to 2 pm Saturday, and Sunday if cruise ships are in port.

Northern St Lucia

NORTH OF CASTRIES

Gros Islet Rd runs up the coast connecting northern Castries to Rodney Bay. This area has a number of beachside resort hotels, as well as some moderately priced guest houses. Most of the guest houses are on the inland side of the road but within walking distance of the beach.

Gablewoods Mall, just south of the Halcyon, has a supermarket, eateries, a bank, a pharmacy, clothing shops, a bookstore and Internet access.

Places to Stay

The following are on Gros Islet Rd, a couple of miles north of the airport and a 10-minute walk from Gablewoods Mall.

Modern Inn (☎ 452-4001, fax 453-7313, PO Box 457, Vide Bouteille, Castries) is a good-value family-run hostelry with five guest rooms and a small common sitting area with cable TV and a refrigerator. The rooms are straightforward but clean and have comfortable mattresses and air-con. Rates are US$25 for singles, which share a bathroom, and US$30 for doubles, which have private baths. There are also three adjacent apartments with kitchens, cable TV, air-con and phones for US$40.

The roadside *Friendship Inn* (☎ 452-4201, fax 453-2635) is a small concrete two-story building with a line of simple motel-style rooms. Each has cable TV, a phone, a small kitchenette, air-con and a private bathroom. Singles/doubles cost US$55/65. There's also a small pool.

The *Windjammer Landing* (☎ 452-0913, fax 452-0907, in the USA ☎ 800-743-9609, in the UK ☎ 800-373-742, PO Box 1504, Castries), on a quiet beach at Labrelotte Bay, is a sprawling villa-style complex with an upscale Mediterranean appearance. Units are contemporary, with beam ceilings, rattan furnishings, kitchenettes, living rooms, terraces and air-conditioned bedrooms. There are two tennis courts, three restaurants and four pools. Rates vary throughout the year, with one-bedroom villas costing US$225 to US$385, two-bedroom villas from US$375 to US$590.

Sandals Halcyon (☎ 452-3081, fax 452-1012, in the UK 020-7581 9895, PO Box 399, Castries) is a 178-room all-inclusive resort on a nice sandy beach a couple of miles north of the airport. Per-person rates for a seven-night stay start around US$1800, including meals, water sports and other activities.

Wyndham Morgan Bay Resort (☎ 450-2511, fax 450-1050, in the USA ☎ 800-327-8321) is a modern, all-inclusive hotel with 238 rooms at the north side of Choc Bay. The rooms have full amenities, and there's a fitness center, tennis courts, a pool and a water-sports center. Singles/doubles begin at US$265/360 in summer, US$300/430 in winter.

Places to Eat

Gablewoods Mall has a few fast-food stalls around a central dining court. One of the best cheap options is *Sub-Station*, with made-to-order sandwiches for around EC$7. In addition, the mall has a good *deli* that sells bagels, luncheon meats and cheeses.

RODNEY BAY & GROS ISLET
Rodney Bay

Rodney Bay is a large protected bay that encompasses the resort area of Reduit Beach and the village of Gros Islet. An artificial channel cuts between Reduit Beach and Gros Islet, opening to a large lagoon that's the site of Rodney Bay Marina, the island's largest yachting port.

Rodney Bay Marina is a modern facility with a car rental agency, dive shops, a launderette, a bookshop, a travel agency, marine supply shops, a grocery store and some good eating spots – many of which are run by expatriates. There are also two banks, the Royal Bank of Canada and Barclays Bank, open 8:30 am to 3 pm Monday to

Thursday, till 5 pm Friday and till noon Saturday. The marina is a bustling yachters' scene and a good place to make contact with sailors if you're looking to hitch a ride or find a crew job.

In contrast, Reduit Beach, just southwest of the marina, is a more typical tourist resort, with a fine sandy beach, clear blue waters, fancy ethnic restaurants and a range of places to stay. It's a 30-minute round-about walk by road between the marina and the beach, but there's a small ferry that crosses the lagoon between the two areas several times a day for US$4 roundtrip.

Places to Stay The *Genmar Apartments* (☎ *452-0834, fax 452-0165, PO Box 213, Reduit)* comprise a recommendable little apartment cluster off Gros Islet Rd, near the bus route and about a 10-minute walk from Reduit Beach. The dozen units are straightforward but have private bathrooms, refrigerators, stoves and fans. Single/double rates for a studio are US$35/45 in summer, US$45/60 in winter. For a one-bedroom unit, the rates are US$40/50 in summer, US$50/65 in winter. To get there, turn left on the first dirt road after the Texaco gas station and then take the first right and look for the 'Gene' sign.

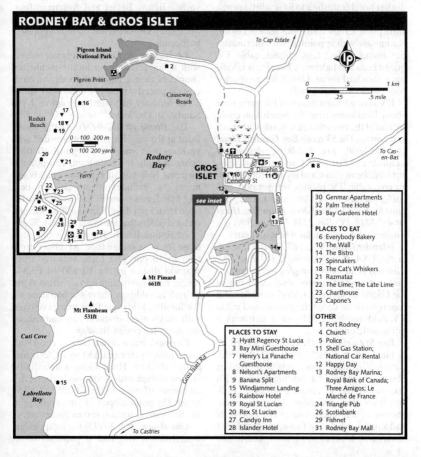

RODNEY BAY & GROS ISLET

To Cap Estate

Pigeon Island National Park

Pigeon Point

Causeway Beach

0   .5   1 km
0   .25   .5 mile

Reduit Beach

0 100 200 m
0 100 200 yards

Rodney Bay

Ferry

GROS ISLET

Church St
Dauphin St
Cemetery St

see inset

To Cas-en-Bas

Mt Pimard 661ft

Mt Flambeau 531ft

Cuti Cove

Labrellotte Bay

Gros Islet Rd

To Castries

PLACES TO STAY
2 Hyatt Regency St Lucia
3 Bay Mini Guesthouse
7 Henry's La Panache Guesthouse
8 Nelson's Apartments
9 Banana Split
15 Windjammer Landing
16 Rainbow Hotel
19 Royal St Lucian
20 Rex St Lucian
27 Candyo Inn
28 Islander Hotel
30 Genmar Apartments
32 Palm Tree Hotel
33 Bay Gardens Hotel

PLACES TO EAT
6 Everybody Bakery
10 The Wall
14 The Bistro
17 Spinnakers
18 The Cat's Whiskers
21 Razmataz
22 The Lime; The Late Lime
23 Charthouse
25 Capone's

OTHER
1 Fort Rodney
4 Church
5 Police
11 Shell Gas Station; National Car Rental
12 Happy Day
13 Rodney Bay Marina; Royal Bank of Canada; Three Amigos; Le Marché de France
24 Triangle Pub
26 Scotiabank
29 Fishnet
31 Rodney Bay Mall

Candyo Inn *(☎ 452-0712, fax 452-0774, PO Box 386, Rodney Bay)*, a five-minute walk from Reduit Beach, is a pleasantly upscale inn with four rooms at US$75 and eight roomy suites with full kitchens, living rooms and separate bedrooms for US$90. All are neat and comfortable with air-con, phones and cable TV. Rates are US$15 cheaper in summer. There's a pool, flower-laden landscaping and a friendly staff.

Rainbow Hotel *(☎ 452-0148, fax 452-0158, PO Box 3050, Castries)* is just a minute's walk from the water but half the price of its beachfront neighbors. This three-decker hotel is starting to look a little rough around the edges, but it has a large court-yard pool, tennis court and fitness center. Rooms are well appointed, with thermostatic air-con, ceiling fans, phones, cable TV, queen beds and balconies. The rate is US$60 for a standard room, US$75 for a superior room with two queen beds.

If you don't mind being on the main road about 10 minutes from the beach, you could try one of the two other new hotels with moderate prices. The 53-room *Bay Gardens Hotel* *(☎ 452-8060, fax 452-8059, destangd@candw.lc, PO Box 1892, Castries)* has a pleasant Caribbean decor and inviting rooms with air-con, cable TV, phones, refrigerators and coffeemakers for US$90 and kitchenette units for US$110. Next door, *Palm Tree Hotel* *(☎ 452-8718, PO Box 2233, Rodney Bay)* is a smaller hotel with similar rooms and rates.

Islander Hotel *(☎ 452-8757, fax 452-0958, in the USA ☎ 800-223-9815, PO Box 907, Castries)* is an older complex with a restaurant, a pool and comfortable, clean rooms for US$60 in summer, US$85 in winter. All rooms have air-con, refrigerators and cable TV. Add another US$10 for a unit with a kitchenette on the deck.

Rex St Lucian *(☎ 452-8351, fax 452-8331, in the USA ☎ 800-255-5859, PO Box 512, Castries)* fronts a fine section of Reduit Beach. The hotel is a rambling place, with 260 rooms spread across a series of two- and three-story buildings. All rooms have phones, a room safe, a king or two twin beds and a patio or balcony. Fan-cooled standard rooms cost US$115 in summer, US$135 in

winter; air-conditioned superior rooms cost US$140 in summer, US$175 in winter.

Royal St Lucian *(☎ 452-9999, fax 452-9639, PO Box 977, Castries)* is a modern three-story complex on Reduit Beach. It has 98 upmarket suites, each with a separate sitting area, private patio, TV, room safe, and minibar; rates begin at US$310 in summer, US$385 in winter.

Places to Eat The center of the action in Rodney Bay is *Three Amigos*, which claims to be St Lucia's only Mexican restaurant. It's usually filled with gringos talking about yachts, Jimmy Buffet and American football, but the food and the margaritas are quite tasty. On weekends there are poolside barbecues.

Le Marché de France is a small market with a fair selection, including meal-sized chunks of cheese, imported foods and moderately priced wines. It's open 8:30 am to 7 pm Monday to Saturday, 9 am to 1 pm Sunday and holidays.

The *Bistro* *(☎ 452-9494)*, on the waterfront at Rodney Bay, is often crowded with yachters who can literally jump off their boats and into the restaurant. This popular watering hole has an extensive chalkboard menu that includes various chicken, beef and fish dishes from EC$35 to EC$60. It's open from 5 pm daily. There's a 20% discount on food orders that are made before 6:30 pm.

At Reduit Beach, *The Lime* is the place to go for West Indian food. At dinner, from 6:30 to 10 pm, The Lime features fresh seafood dishes in the EC$30 to EC$45 range; reasonably appropriate dress is required. In addition, there's a barbecue on Wednesday, Friday and Saturday evenings, with inexpensive chicken, ribs and fish by the piece. It's closed Tuesday.

Capone's has a casual patio section with inexpensive pizza (EC$30 to EC$50) and grilled chicken. There's also a fine dining indoor section with Italian-style pasta, fish and meat offerings in the EC$35 to EC$50 range. The patio is open 11 am to midnight; the fine-dining section serves dinner only.

Charthouse *(☎ 452-8115)* has an appealing waterfront setting and is popular for its grilled steaks and baby back ribs; it also has chicken and fish dishes. Prices average EC$50 to EC$70; add another EC$8 for a green salad. It's open from 6 pm daily except Sunday.

Farther down the beach, **Razmataz** stands out among the local ethnic restaurants for its excellent Indian cuisine and elegant decor, with live music on weekend evenings. Check out the variety of vegetarian options, or spring for the EC$55 tandoori plates. It's open for dinner only, 4 to 11 pm daily except Thursday.

If you want to dine right on Reduit Beach, try **Spinnakers**, a thatch-roofed eatery and beach bar that draws quite a crowd when the cruise ships are in town. The chalkboard menu includes lunchtime burgers for EC$12 and fish dishes for EC$30; dinner adds on pricier seafoods such as a cold lobster plate (EC$85). It's open 9 am to 11 pm daily.

Between Spinnaker's and the Royal St Lucian hotel you'll find **The Cat's Whiskers**, the local British pub, authentic right down to the cranky couple who run the place. The Piton comes in pints (EC$8), and there's real pub food such as fish & chips with mushy peas (EC$35). One side of the building is open, allowing a very un-publike breeze of fresh air and a view of the beach.

The coffee shop at **Rex St Lucian** (see Places to Stay) has a tempting variety of tropical ice creams (EC$2.50 a cone) and is open 7 am to 10 pm daily.

There are a couple of small stores selling groceries and spirits, and there's a well-stocked grocery store at the Rodney Bay Mall.

Entertainment Above The Lime (see Places to Eat), **The Late Lime** has music and dancing on Wednesday, Friday and Saturday nights. The cover of EC$15 is waived if you have dinner at the restaurant. Across the street, **Triangle Pub** rocks out on weekends, with DJs and occasional live music.

Nearby, right on Reduit Beach, **Spinnakers** has calypso and other music several nights a week.

In the early evening, don't be surprised if you're served two drinks for each one you order; many of the local bars and restaurants are in competition to see who can put on the longest and most generous happy hour. The clear winner is **Happy Day**, an open-air beach hut at the end of the Reduit Beach road, where it's *always* two-for-one. There's an interesting mix of well-oiled tourists and sociable St Lucians. Or something like that…details on Happy Day remain blurry.

Gros Islet

Gros Islet is a small fishing village of simple wooden houses with rusting tin roofs, lots of rum shops and a shore dotted with gaily painted wooden boats. If you hear a conch shell being blown, it's the signal that fishing boats have arrived with a catch to sell.

Though the town doesn't have any sights per se, there's a small market near the shore where you can often find fishermen and women mending nets. The bars along the beach are the habitual hangouts of the local Rastafarian community. Gros Islet is also famous for its spirited Friday night jump-up, where islanders and visitors alike grub up on grilled chicken, swill rum punch and dance in the streets as best they can.

From Gros Islet, walk a couple of minutes north along the shore and you'll come to an expansive stretch of white-sand beach that curves around to Pigeon Island. The beach is quite beautiful and the calm turquoise waters are inviting, but it's unfortunately become an ongoing construction site as the garish Hyatt Regency St Lucia continues to expand.

Most buses making the coastal drive north from Castries terminate in the center of Gros Islet.

Places to Stay For a nice cheap place to stay right on the beach, head to **Banana Split** (☎ 450-8125), where the friendly proprietor rents nine small but comfortable singles/doubles with fan and private bath, some with ocean views, for US$20/40.

Farther north, **Bay Mini Guesthouse** (☎ 450-8956), painted a unique shade of orange, is popular with budget travelers for its comfortable air-conditioned rooms at US$25/30. Larger doubles with kitchenettes are a very reasonable US$40.

Henry's La Panache Guesthouse (☎ 450-0765, fax 450-0453, Cas-en-Bas Rd, Gros Islet) is a relaxed and friendly place about a five-minute walk west of the highway. The rooms are straightforward but have refrigerators, fans and private bathrooms, and the setting is pleasantly natural. Singles/doubles cost US$30/40. There's an outdoor dining area where meals can be arranged at reasonable prices. Henry also books self-catering apartments in his neighbor's contemporary house for US$50.

Nelson's Apartments (☎ 450-8275, PO Box 1174, Castries) is 75 yards west of Henry's. It has six good-value apartments with full kitchens, cable TV, portable fans and mosquito netting above the beds. Singles/doubles cost US$30/45.

On the causeway beach to Pigeon Island, *Hyatt Regency St Lucia* (☎ 451-1234, in the USA ☎ 800-633-7313) is a new luxury hotel with all the amenities. Low-season singles or doubles start at US$230.

Places to Eat For delicious home-style Creole food, check out *The Wall*, in the center of town. Simple fare like grilled fish or fried chicken is around EC$12, served up with a filling array of side dishes including salad, plantain, spaghetti and whatever else is available that day.

You can find simple breads and fresh coconut buns at *Everybody Bakery*, a little hole-in-the-wall on the inland side of the highway opposite the Shell gas station.

PIGEON ISLAND NATIONAL PARK

Pigeon Island has a spicy history dating back to the 1550s, when St Lucia's first French settler, Jambe de Bois (Wooden Leg), used the island as a base for raiding passing Spanish ships. Two centuries later, British admiral George Rodney fortified Pigeon Island, using it to monitor the French fleet on Martinique. Rodney's fleet set sail from Pigeon Island in 1782 for his most decisive military engagement, the Battle of the Saintes.

With the end of hostilities between the two European rivals, the fort slipped into disuse in the 19th century, although the USA established a small signal station here during WWII.

In the 1970s a sandy causeway was constructed between Gros Islet and Pigeon Island, turning the island into a peninsula, and in 1979 Pigeon 'Island' was established as a national park.

It's a fun place to explore, with walking paths winding around the scattered remains of Fort Rodney, whose partially intact stone buildings create a certain ghost-town effect. The grounds are well endowed with lofty trees, including a few big banyans, and fine coastal views.

As soon as you go through the entrance gate, you'll see the remains of an 1824 kitchen and officers' mess. While some people make a beeline from here to the main fortress at Fort Rodney Hill on the outer point, a walk which takes about 15 minutes, it's enjoyable just to mosey through the ruins and gradually work your way in that direction. A good route is to continue northwest from the officers' mess past the soldiers' barracks (1782) and then loop down toward the bay, where you can pick up the main path.

At the top of Fort Rodney Hill, you'll find a small but well-preserved fortress, a few rusting cannons and a spectacular view. You can see south across Rodney Bay to the gumdrop-shaped hills dotting the coast, and north past Pointe du Cap to Martinique. For more views, continue north past the stone foundations of the ridge battery to the top of the 359-foot Signal Peak, about a 20-minute walk.

Pigeon Island, administered by the St Lucia National Trust, is open 9 am to 5 pm daily. Admission, which includes entry to an interpretation center with multimedia historic displays, costs EC$10 for foreign visitors. There's a pub and restaurant selling sandwiches at moderate prices.

Most of the coastline around Pigeon Island is rocky, though there's a nice little sandy beach just east of the jetty.

The walk along the causeway from Gros Islet to Pigeon Point takes about 20 minutes.

Southern St Lucia

The main road in the southern part of the island makes a loop that can be done as a full day trip.

The road to Soufrière is a scenic drive, winding in and out of lush jungle valleys and up into the mountains. It goes through banana plantations, passes the fishing villages of Anse La Raye and Canaries, and offers fine coastal and mountain vistas, including some lovely views of the Pitons as you approach Soufrière.

Choiseul, a little village south of Soufrière, has an active handicraft industry, and its roadside arts-and-crafts center is a good place to pick up locally made dolls, baskets, pottery and wood carvings.

MARIGOT BAY

Marigot Bay is a lovely sheltered bay that's backed by green hillsides and sports a little palm-fringed beach. The inner harbor is so long and deep that an entire British fleet is said to have once escaped French warships by ducking inside and covering their masts with coconut fronds. The bay was the setting for the 1967 musical *Doctor Dolittle,* starring Rex Harrison.

Doctor Dolittle would hardly recognize the place today, with its string of hotels and beach bars, but it's still a tranquil spot, perfect for wasting the day in a beach chair.

Marigot Bay is a popular anchorage for yachters and the site of a marina with a customs office, a small market, water, ice and fuel. The Moorings (☎ 451-4357) bases its bareboat charters here and runs the marina facilities.

A little pontoon boat shuttles back and forth on request (EC$2 roundtrip), connecting the two sides of the inner harbor.

Places to Stay & Eat

The *Moorings' Marigot Bay Hotel* (☎ 451-4357, fax 451-4353, in the USA and Canada ☎ 800-437-7880, PO Box 101, Castries) is on the south side of the bay. It has 16 pleasant stone cottages, each with tasteful tropical decor, rattan furniture, a refrigerator, coffeemaker, ceiling fan and lots of open-air screened windows; singles/doubles cost US$70/85 in summer, US$120/135 in winter.

Marigot Beach Club (☎ 451-4974, fax 451-4973, in the USA and Canada ☎ 800-278-5842, PO Box 101, Castries) is a similar property on the north side of the bay. There are fan-cooled studios with kitchenettes for US$75 standard, US$85 superior, and one-bedroom hillside villas priced from US$110 to US$205 in summer, US$155 to US$232 in winter. It's an older place, but it has character and many units have patios with idyllic water views.

Dolittle's Restaurant & Beach Bar, a pleasant waterside spot at the Marigot Beach Club, has lunchtime sandwiches and salads for around EC$20 and chicken and fish dishes for EC$30.

The Rusty Anchor, a poolside restaurant and bar at the Marigot Bay Hotel, has sandwiches, burgers, rotis and omelets for about EC$20 at lunch, as well as fresh seafood dinners from around EC$50.

A popular local eatery is *JJ's Restaurant & Bar* (☎ 451-4076), in the village, a 10-minute walk up the hill from the harbor. The fish Creole and chicken curry are both tasty dinner dishes that cost EC$37 and include rice, salad, vegetables and dessert. From noon to 3 pm JJ's has a lighter lunch menu that includes inexpensive rotis and chicken & chips. On Wednesday and Friday nights there's live music.

ANSE LA RAYE

South of Marigot Bay the winding coast road continues to Anse La Raye, a sleepy fishing village that's become the island's Friday-night hot spot. Seafood Friday has eclipsed Gros Islet's jump-up as *the* place to be on Friday for street food (everything from bakes for EC$1 to grilled lobster for EC$40), loud music and dancing (both in the street and in at least two nightclubs and numerous bars). The crowd is mostly local, and the party goes on all night.

The rest of the week Anse La Raye is a typical island town, with colorful houses and an attractive beach, though swimming is apparently discouraged.

There are a couple of guest houses in town; ask around at the local rum shops and restaurants. If you arrive early on Friday you may be able to rent an entire house for around EC$60, but don't expect peace and quiet.

SOUFRIÈRE

Founded by the French in 1746 and named after the nearby sulfur springs, the town of Soufrière has a lovely bay setting. The coastal Pitons provide a scenic backdrop to the south, and the island's highest peaks rise above the rain forest just a few miles inland.

Like other fishing communities along the coast, Soufrière has lots of old weathered buildings, some still adorned with delicate gingerbread trim, others more ramshackle. There is an interesting stone Catholic church in the town center. At the north side of the dock is the Soufrière Market, where you can buy baskets, straw hats, T-shirts and spices.

The main sights, the Sulphur Springs, Morne Coubaril Estate and Diamond Botanical Gardens, are on the outskirts of town and can be visited in a couple of hours.

Although most visitors are day-trippers on one of the many boat or land tours that

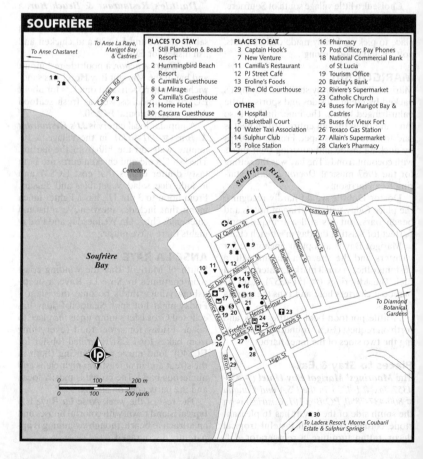

SOUFRIÈRE

To Anse La Raye, Marigot Bay & Castries

To Anse Chastanet

PLACES TO STAY
1 Still Plantation & Beach Resort
2 Hummingbird Beach Resort
6 Camilla's Guesthouse
8 La Mirage
9 Camilla's Guesthouse
21 Home Hotel
30 Cascara Guesthouse

PLACES TO EAT
3 Captain Hook's
7 New Venture
11 Camilla's Restaurant
12 PJ Street Café
13 Eroline's Foods
29 The Old Courthouse

OTHER
4 Hospital
5 Basketball Court
10 Water Taxi Association
14 Sulphur Club
15 Police Station

16 Pharmacy
17 Post Office; Pay Phones
18 National Commercial Bank of St Lucia
19 Tourism Office
20 Barclay's Bank
22 Riviere's Supermarket
23 Catholic Church
24 Buses for Marigot Bay & Castries
25 Buses for Vieux Fort
26 Texaco Gas Station
27 Allain's Supermarket
28 Clarke's Pharmacy

Cemetery

Soufrière River

Soufrière Bay

Desmond Ave

W Quinlan St

Sir Darnley Alexander St

Maurice Mason St

Bridge St

Church St

Victoria St

Boulevard St

Etienne St

Delieu St

Smiths St

Henry Belmar St

Frederick St

Clarke St

Sir Arthur Lewis St

Baron Drive

High St

To Diamond Botanical Gardens

To Ladera Resort, Morne Coubaril Estate & Sulphur Springs

0   100   200 m
0   100   200 yards

take in Soufrière, much of what Soufrière has to offer, including its relaxed provincial character, is best appreciated by those who stay on. There are some interesting places to stay, ranging from affordable guest houses to secluded top-end retreats. Nightlife centers on the hotel bars and the downtown Sulphur Club, with pool tables and televised sports.

Anse Chastanet

Soufrière's picturesque scenery is equally impressive beneath the water's surface. Anse Chastanet, a lovely sheltered bay a little over a mile north of Soufrière, has some of the finest nearshore snorkeling and diving on St Lucia. (*Really* nearshore: Most dive trips don't get out of sight of the hotel.) It also makes a fine choice if you're simply up for a swim.

At the beach is a hotel, a dive shop that rents out snorkeling equipment (EC$12 an hour), a bar and a restaurant that serves both simple snacks and full meals. On foot, Anse Chastanet is about a 35-minute walk from Soufrière along the hilly coastal road that skirts the north side of Soufrière Bay. If you're not up for a walk, you can easily arrange a water taxi from the village.

Sulphur Springs

Sulphur Springs is a barren and somewhat moonscapish terrain pocked with pools of boiling mud and steaming vents. The vents release great quantities of sulfuric gases, which are responsible for the yellow mineral deposits blanketing the area. The putrid smell, resembling rotten eggs, is hydrogen sulfide.

Visitors used to walk up close to the vents and peer directly into the mud ponds until a local guide leading a group of German tourists stepped through the soft earth and plunged waist-deep into the boiling mud. He lived to tell the story, but everything is now viewed from the safety of overlooks.

Despite the fact that this area is promoted as a 'drive-in volcano,' those expecting to peer down into a volcanic crater will be disappointed. The crater walls eroded away eons ago, and now the volcanic activity is along the side of a hill.

Sulphur Springs is open 9 am to 5pm daily; admission is EC$3. Having a guide walk through with you is compulsory; although the price of the guide is theoretically included in the entrance fee, a tip will be expected.

To get there from Soufrière, go south on the Vieux Fort road, which winds uphill as it leaves town. About a five-minute drive out of Soufrière, take the downhill fork to the left at the Sulphur Springs sign, from where it's a half-mile farther to the park entrance. En route be sure not to miss the small pull-off, just south of Soufrière, which offers a picturesque view of the town.

Morne Coubaril Estate

Morne Coubaril Estate, on the Vieux Fort road about a half-mile north of Sulphur Springs, is a working cocoa and coconut plantation that has been set up to give visitors a sense of life on the farm. There are displays on the processing of copra, cocoa and manioc; traditional buildings; and the ruins of a water and sugar mill. The EC$15 admission price includes an informative 35-minute guided tour. It's open 9 am to 5 pm daily.

Diamond Botanical Gardens

The Diamond Estate's botanical gardens, waterfall and mineral baths are all at the same site and have an entrance fee of EC$7 for adults, EC$3.50 for children under 12.

Paths wind through the gardens, which are planted with tropical flowers and trees, including numerous heliconia and ginger specimens. At the back of the gardens a small waterfall drops down a rock face that is stained a rich orange from the warm mineral waters. The waterfall featured briefly in the movie *Superman II* as the site from which Superman plucked an orchid for Lois Lane.

The mineral baths date from 1784, when they were built atop hot springs so that the troops of King Louis XVI of France could take advantage of their therapeutic effects. The baths were largely destroyed during the French Revolution, but in recent times a few have been restored and are open to visitors for an additional EC$6.50 (communal use) or EC$10 (private bath).

The Diamond Estate is a mile east of the Soufrière town center, via Sir Arthur Lewis St, and the way is signposted. The grounds are open 10 am to 5 pm Monday to Saturday and 10 am to 3 pm Sunday and holidays. There's an inexpensive snack bar.

Malgretout

A 20-minute walk along the dirt coastal road south of town leads to a quiet, undeveloped beach and to a mineral waterfall at Malgretout. Not only does this most unfrequented waterfall have a beautiful Eden-like setting, but visitors are allowed to shower in its warm volcanic waters – a situation that is not allowed at the more touristed waterfall at Diamond Botanical Gardens. To get to the falls, continue along the coastal dirt road until you reach the pensioners' home, then follow the steep road uphill for about 200 yards – a sign marks the way. Admission is EC$2.50.

Places to Stay

The *Home Hotel* (☎ 459-7318), on Bridge St in the town center, next to the bus stop, has a friendly manager and seven simple but inviting singles/doubles with fans and shared baths costing US$20/30. Guests have use of a kitchen and a common sitting area – whittle the day away watching the action on the central square from the veranda.

Mrs Camilla at Camilla's Restaurant (☎ 459-5379, 7 Bridge St) rents out a variety of comfortable rooms in a couple of houses in town, both called *Camilla's Guesthouse*. The rates, which vary a bit with the season and how long you stay, are around US$30/55.

The hotel-restaurant *La Mirage* (☎ 459-7010), on Church St, has four simple and pleasant rooms with bath. Singles/doubles start at US$25/40.

On the road heading south out of town, *Cascara Guesthouse* rises up on a hill overlooking town. The rooms are very simple, starting at US$10, US$20 with bath and kitchenette, but the view is impressive.

Hummingbird Beach Resort (☎ 459-7232, PO Box 280, Soufrière), on the north side of the harbor, has 10 rooms, a pool and a terrific view across the bay to the Pitons.

Rooms are pleasantly rustic with lots of wood, but have handy conveniences like mosquito nets and cable TV. From April to mid-December standard singles/doubles with shared baths cost US$30/40, while fancier rooms with private baths start at US$70/80; in winter there's a mandatory breakfast and dinner plan that adds about US$50 per person to the rates.

Still Plantation and Beach Resort (☎ 459-5179, fax 459-7301), a few steps up the hill from the Hummingbird, has eight rooms with private bath, TV and ocean views starting at US$50, US$75 with air-con and kitchenette. There's also a two-room double apartment for US$100.

Anse Chastanet Hotel (☎ 459-7000, fax 459-7700, in the USA ☎ 800-223-1108, PO Box 7000, Soufrière), on the beach at Anse Chastanet, is an appealing hideaway hotel with 48 rooms, some on the beach and others terraced up the hillside. All of them have a refrigerator, coffeemaker, ceiling fan and hardwood floors; many also have open-beam ceilings and fine views of the Pitons. There's a scuba facility, a tennis court and various water sports. Most guests book weeklong dive and accommodation packages, but rooms are also available starting at for US$420 in winter, including breakfast and dinner; in summer the rates are US$200 without meals.

Ladera Resort (☎ 459-7323, fax 459-5156, in the USA and Canada ☎ 800-841-4145, PO Box 225, Soufrière) is an exclusive resort with a stunning hillside setting. There are 19 suites and villas; most have private plunge pools and all have canopy beds with mosquito nets. The west side of every unit is wall-less, open to direct views of the nearby Pitons. Rates begin at US$215 in summer, US$395 in winter, including breakfast and airport transfer. The resort is on the Vieux Fort road south of Soufrière.

Places to Eat

There are a handful of local restaurants offering good food at reasonable prices near the central square that borders Church, Sir Arthur Lewis and Bridge Sts. At *New Venture*, on Church St, you can get a decent

Creole meal for EC$15. *Camilla's Restaurant*, on Bridge St, has good rotis and sandwiches at reasonable prices, as well as a variety of Creole seafood and meat dishes from EC$25 to EC$70. *PJ Street Café*, on Bridge St, is known for its fried chicken. *Eroline's Foods*, in the center of town on Church St, is the local supermarket.

The Old Courthouse, on the dock at the south end of downtown, is a fancier alternative, built in 1898. It's fairly pricey but has a nice seaside terrace, perfect for people-watching at lunch.

Captain Hook's, at the north end of town, is a popular spot for full Creole dinners and drinks. There's a friendly atmosphere and lively conversation at the bar. A filling Creole menu goes for around EC$40, and usually features the catch of the day.

Most tourists on a day visit pack in at *Hummingbird*, a waterfront restaurant with a fine view of the Pitons. It features French and Creole dishes such as freshwater crayfish, shrimp coquilles St Jacques and Châteaubriand. Main courses range from EC$30 to EC$90, but there are also cheaper sandwiches and salads.

For those continuing south, an interesting option is *The Barbican*, on the Vieux Fort road between Soufrière and Etangs. Run by a friendly St Lucian couple with British ties, it serves up homegrown organic produce and juices. The menu includes pumpkin or callaloo soup (EC$6), saltfish rotis (EC$11) and lambi (EC$25); it's closed on Monday.

VIEUX FORT

Vieux Fort, St Lucia's southernmost town, would be beyond the itinerary of most visitors if it weren't the site of the island's international airport, which is just north of the town center. The town has a mix of older wooden buildings and newer structures, as well as the island's second-largest port. If you're overnighting here before a flight, check out the white-sand beaches at the east side of town.

There's a lighthouse atop a 730-foot hill on Moule à Chique, the island's southernmost point, which offers a view of the Maria Islands, St Lucia's interior mountains and, if the weather's clear, the island of St Vincent to the south.

Vieux Fort catches strong ocean breezes that can make it feel unpleasantly chilly in the daytime. The good news is that the island's best windsurfing is on the beaches east of town.

Places to Stay

In the town center, *St Martin's Guesthouse* (*☎/fax 454-6674*), on Clarke St, has small, simple rooms with shared bath. The elderly woman who runs the guest house, Mrs Romain, keeps the place tidy and clean; the cost is US$20.

Juliette's Lodge (*☎ 454-5300, fax 454-5305, PO Box 482, Beanefield, Vieux Fort*) is currently adding on two new buildings and has comfortable singles/doubles with air-con, TV, bathtubs and balconies for US$60/65 in summer, US$75/95 in winter. It's a long walk northeast of the airport; taxis will take you for a reasonable EC$15. There's a pool and a moderately priced restaurant.

Slightly closer to the airport is *Skyway Inn* (*☎ 454-6670, fax 454-7116, PO Box 353, Vieux Fort*), popular with the jet-set business crowd and American medical students. It has 39 air-conditioned singles/doubles starting at US$75/85; rates are US$10 cheaper in summer.

Places to Eat

Clarke St, Vieux Fort's main road, has grocery stores, a bakery and some inexpensive eateries. Across the street from the *KFC* at the airport road rotary, *Schernell's Pizza* serves up tasty pizzas from EC$9 to EC$28. *Chak Chak*, not far from the airport, has an unbeatable beachside setting, inexpensive sandwiches, fish & chips and reasonably priced Creole-style seafood dishes.

EAST COAST

The road up the east coast from Vieux Fort is relatively straight and uneventful, passing through a few local villages and numerous banana plantations before turning inland at the town of Dennery and making a scenic, winding cut across the mountainous rain forest to Castries.

There are two nature sanctuaries off the east coast. The Maria Islands Nature Reserve, east of Vieux Fort, is the only habitat of the *kouwes* snake, one of the world's rarest grass snakes, and the Maria Islands ground lizard. Because it's a sanctuary for terns, noddies and other seabirds, this two-island reserve is not accessible during the summer nesting season, but it can be visited at other times of the year on tours arranged by the St Lucia National Trust (☎ 452-5005).

The Frigate Islands Nature Reserve encompasses two small, rocky nearshore islands that are a summer nesting site for frigate birds. The area is also a habitat for several types of herons, a couple of the island's indigenous rare birds (the Ramier pigeon and the St Lucian oriole), boa constrictors and the more dangerous fer-de-lance. There's a small interpretation center

on the north side of Praslin Bay, and tours of the area can be arranged through local tour agencies or the St Lucia National Trust.

Places to Stay

For those who want to be near the jungle interior, *Fox Grove Inn* (☎ /fax 455-3271), in Mon Repos, is a pleasant off-the-beaten-path option. This European-managed inn offers nature trails, horseback riding and a hike to a secluded beach. The 11 rooms, which have ceiling fans and private baths, cost US$45/55 for singles/doubles, US$55/65 for superior rooms with balconies, breakfast included. There's a pool, restaurant, bar and pool table. French and German are spoken. The inn is about a mile inland off the highway. The Vieux Fort bus (EC$4.50 from Castries) can drop you at the highway; call ahead and the manager will pick you up from there.

St Martin/Sint Maarten

St Martin, as it's known on the French side, or Sint Maarten, as it's called on the Dutch side, is the world's smallest land area to be shared by two countries. Despite the island's dual nationality, the border crossings are marked only with inconspicuous signs and

Highlights

- Fine dining at Grand Case, St Martin's 'gourmet capital'
- Snorkeling the offshore islands of Îlet Pinel and Green Cay
- Experiencing Marigot, with its French-designer clothing boutiques and French flair
- Exploring Philipsburg's Frontstreet, with its duty-free jewelry and electronic shops
- Sunbathing at clothing-optional Orient Beach

OTHER MAPS
St Martin/Sint Maarten
page 452

Grand Case
page 469

French Cul-de-Sac
& Orient Beach
page 472

Marigot
page 464

Philipsburg
page 476

CARIBBEAN
SEA

0   2   4 km
0   1   2 miles

there are no stops or other formalities when passing between the two sides.

The isle is also one of the Eastern Caribbean's most touristed islands. Almost 540,000 holidaymakers shop, lounge and sun-worship on St Martin every year. It boasts lovely white-sand beaches, a wide range of places to stay, good restaurants and two quite distinct cultures.

The French side is developed on a smaller scale and has a decidedly Gallic influence in language, food and culture. The Dutch side is more commercial, with large resorts, casinos and fast-food chains – and precious little that's solidly Dutch. Both sides are duty-free, and the two island capitals, Philipsburg and Marigot, are chock-full of fashionable shops.

The island is rather small and quite overdeveloped in many places, and it can be hard to escape the crowds and find some peace and quiet. There are, however, still a few quiet niches to explore, and the beaches are surprisingly diverse, ranging from secluded coves and naturist retreats to busy resort-front strands.

St Martin is a prime jumping-off point for trips to neighboring islands – it's inexpensive and easy to get to Anguilla, Saba and Statia, some of the Eastern Caribbean's most rural and least developed destinations. St Barts, another well-developed French Antilles island, is also an easy day trip from St Martin.

The Dutch side of the island is spelled 'Sint Maarten' and the French side is spelled 'St Martin'; this practice is followed in the chapter when referring to the different sides. When referring to the island as a whole, 'St Martin' is used.

Facts about St Martin

HISTORY

Because of its many salt ponds, Amerindians called this island Soualiga (Land of Salt).

According to popular belief, Columbus 'discovered' the island on November 11, 1493, and named it in honor of Bishop St Martin of Tours. However, some historians now believe that the island Columbus chanced upon that day was the more southerly Nevis, and that he never actually sighted St Martin. At any rate, it wasn't until 1631 that the first attempts at colonization were made, with the Dutch settling at Little Bay and the French in the Orleans area.

In 1633, the Spanish (who had claimed but not colonized the island) invaded St Martin, deporting all 128 inhabitants. The

Spanish reinforced a fort that the Dutch had started and then built a second fort. In 1644 an attempt to retake the island was led by the renowned Dutch colonizer Peter Stuyvesant, who lost a leg to a cannonball in the fighting. Although the Dutch assault was unsuccessful, four years later the Spanish reassessed their interests in the Eastern Caribbean and simply left on their own.

Both the Dutch and French hastily moved back and agreed to share the island, signing a partition agreement in 1648 that was to be repeatedly violated. During the period from 1670 to 1702 the French controlled the entire

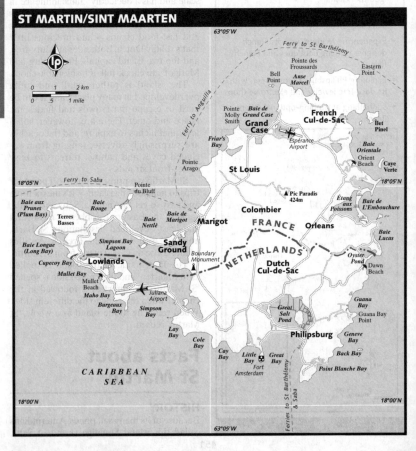

ST MARTIN/SINT MAARTEN

ST MARTIN / SINT MAARTEN

Ferry to St Barthélemy

Ferry to Anguilla

Pointe des Froussards

Eastern Point

Bell Point

Anse Marcel

Pointe Molly Smith

Baie de Grand Case

Grand Case

French Cul-de-Sac

Îlet Pinel

Espérance Airport

Friar's Bay

Baie Orientale

Orient Beach

Caye Verte

Pointe Arago

St Louis

Ferry to Saba

Pointe du Bluff

Pic Paradis 424m

Étang aux Poissons

Baie de L'Embouchure

Baie aux Prunes (Plum Bay)

Baie Rouge

Terres Basses

Baie Nettlé

Baie de Marigot

Marigot

Colombier

FRANCE

Orleans

Baie Lucas

Baie Longue (Long Bay)

Simpson Bay Lagoon

Sandy Ground

Boundary Monument

NETHERLANDS

Oyster Pond

Dawn Beach

Cupecoy Bay

Lowlands

Mullet Bay

Mullet Beach

Dutch Cul-de-Sac

Maho Bay

Juliana Airport

Burgeaux Bay

Simpson Bay

Guana Bay

Guana Bay Point

Great Salt Pond

Lay Bay

Cole Bay

Philipsburg

Geneve Bay

Back Bay

Cay Bay

Little Bay

Fort Amsterdam

Great Bay

Point Blanche Bay

CARIBBEAN SEA

Ferries to St Barthélemy & Saba

0 1 2 km
0 .5 1 mile

18°05'N

18°05'N

18°00'N

18°00'N

63°05'W

63°05'W

island. In 1703 the Dutch invaded from St Eustatius and then deported any French settlers who refused to leave the island.

On April 11, 1713, the Treaty of Utrecht returned half of the island to France. Nevertheless, St Martin continued to be batted back and forth, with the Dutch and the French each having complete control of the island for years at a time. The English also got involved, taking control in 1784 for 10 years and in 1810 for six years. In 1817 the current boundary was established and a peaceful resolution found.

In the meantime, a plantation economy was established, slaves were imported from Africa and trade flourished. The first crops were tobacco and indigo, followed by cotton, cocoa, coffee and, most importantly, sugarcane. The Dutch also harvested huge amounts of salt, which was shipped to Holland for use in the herring industry. After slavery was abolished (in 1848 on the French side, 1863 on the Dutch side), the plantations declined and the island slipped into a subsistence economy.

When the Netherlands fell to the Nazis in 1940, the French took 'protective control' of the Dutch side of the island, but within two weeks France itself was under German control. An Allied occupation of the island followed, and in 1943 the USA built a military airfield, now Juliana Airport. After the war, the new airport, the region's largest, spurred the island's growth as a regional hub and brought on an early advent of tourism.

On September 4, 1995, St Martin took a direct hit from mighty Hurricane Luis, which swept the island with 210km/h (130mph) winds, killed six people and caused US$1 billion in damage. Hundreds of boats were shattered onto piers, thousands of homes and businesses had their roofs blown off and scores of beachside places were pulverized by high surf, some simply disappearing at the foundations. In the wake of the storm, tourism – the island's largest employer – ground to a halt. It has taken a number of years to recover from the blow, and even now scars pop up around the island in the shape of abandoned hotels and homes.

GEOGRAPHY

The island is 15km across at its widest and 13km at its longest. The French side of the island has 54 sq km of land; the Dutch side has 34 sq km.

St Martin has an interesting topography. Its shoreline is indented with bays and coves, and its coastal flats are pocketed with salt ponds. The interior is hilly, with the highest point, Pic Paradis, rising 424m from the center of French St Martin.

The west side of the island is more water than land, dominated by the expansive Simpson Bay Lagoon, which is one of the largest landlocked bodies of water in the Caribbean and has moorings for a large array of boats.

Divvying Up St Martin

Local lore has it that the contentious Dutch and French colonists decided to settle their ongoing land disputes by having a Dutchman and a Frenchman stand back to back at one end of the island and then walk in opposite directions around the coastline. The island's boundary line would be established at the end of the day at whatever spot they finally met. As it turned out, the Frenchman walked much faster than the Dutchman, and consequently the French side of St Martin ended up larger than the Dutch side.

It's said that the Frenchman quenched his thirst along the way with French wine, while the Dutchman quenched his with more potent Dutch gin, thus accounting for the latter's slower pace.

CLIMATE

In January the average daily high temperature is 28°C (83°F), while the low averages 22°C (72°F). In July the average daily high is 30°C (86°F), while the low averages 24°C (76°F).

The average annual rainfall is around 1060 mm (45 inches). The heaviest rainfall is from August to November, the lightest from February to April.

FLORA & FAUNA

The terrain is largely green but dry, with more palms, hibiscus and cacti than ferns or forests, although there are a few thickly vegetated areas in the interior.

Herons, egrets, stilts, pelicans, laughing gulls and other shorebirds are plentiful in the island's brackish ponds. Frigate birds can be spotted along the coast, hummingbirds and bright yellow-bellied bananaquits are common in gardens, and there are colorful woodland birds in the hills. Lizards are abundant and can be seen scurrying about on walkways and other sunny areas.

GOVERNMENT & POLITICS

The northern part of St Martin is a subprefecture of Guadeloupe, which is an overseas department of France. Local control is in the hands of a subprefect appointed by the French government, as well as a locally elected mayor and town council.

The southern section of the island belongs to the Netherlands Antilles, which is part of the Kingdom of the Netherlands. Regional control of the Netherlands Antilles is based in the southern Caribbean island of Curaçao, but Sint Maarten has its own lieutenant governor elected every six years who, in conjunction with an elected island council and an appointed executive council, is responsible for local affairs.

ECONOMY

The island's economy has long been fueled by tourism, which has turned St Martin into one of the most heavily developed islands in the region. In part because of a glut in room inventory, some resorts on the Dutch side of the island never reopened after Hurricane Luis wreaked havoc.

The whole island is one big duty-free shop, and while many of the goods are geared for vacationing tourists, islanders from throughout the Caribbean also come here to buy electronics and other high-priced items, and sometimes to stock up on expensive food items.

POPULATION & PEOPLE

The official population is approximately 35,000 on the French side, 39,000 on the Dutch side, although it's estimated that up to 20,000 illegal aliens also reside on the island, many from Haiti and the Dominican Republic.

The tourist boom of the past few decades has resulted in such a large influx of job-seekers from elsewhere in the Caribbean that only about 20% of all residents were born on the island. Many of the people who run small hotels, restaurants and shops on the French side are from mainland France.

SOCIETY & CONDUCT

The island culture has its roots largely in African, French and Dutch influences, though scores of more recent immigrants have added their own elements to this multicultural society.

Dos & Don'ts

Topless sunbathing is customary on both sides of the island, and nude bathing is sanctioned at Orient Beach on the northeast side of French St Martin.

RELIGION

The French side of the island is predominantly Catholic, while the Dutch side is more varied, with Anglican, Baptist, Jehovah's Witness, Methodist and Seventh Day Adventist churches.

LANGUAGE

French is the official language of French St Martin, but English is also widely understood.

Dutch is the official language of Dutch Sint Maarten, although in practice English is the first language spoken, Dutch the second.

On both sides, most island-born people are multilingual and can speak English, French and Creole. There's also a sizable Spanish-speaking immigrant community, mainly from the Dominican Republic.

Facts for the Visitor

ORIENTATION
Marigot and Philipsburg are each about a 15-minute drive from Juliana Airport, although if you happen to hit heavy traffic you could be stuck in a jam for much longer. Because of the way traffic funnels into the capitals, both Marigot and Philipsburg can get heavily congested, with the worst traffic jams typically occurring in late afternoon.

Driving around the island is fairly simple, because essentially one road loops around the western side of the island and another around the main eastern part of the island. Side roads leading to beaches and resorts are generally marked.

Maps
There are a number of simple island maps that can be picked up at tourist offices and hotels; these will probably suffice for most exploration. The Institut Géographique National's 4608-G Série Bleue (1:25,000) map that covers both St Martin and St Barts is a detailed topographical map and the best road map of the island; it can be picked up at bookstores or newspaper stands around the island for about 50F.

TOURIST OFFICES
Local Tourist Offices
Several free tourist publications with information on sights, activities, restaurants and shopping are available at tourist offices.

On the Dutch side, the tourist office is in the Vineyard Park Complex, Philipsburg. There are also information booths at Juliana Airport and at Wathey Square, Philipsburg.

You can contact the office at Sint Maarten Tourist Bureau (☎ 542-2337, fax 542-2734, info@st-maarten.com), Vineyard Park Complex, 33 WG Buncamper Rd, Philipsburg, Sint Maarten, Netherlands Antilles.

On the French side, the tourist office is at the western end of town, next to the archaeological museum. There's also an unstaffed booth near the ferry terminal. The contact information is as follows: St Martin Tourist Office (☎ 87 57 21, fax 87 56 43, sxmto@wanadoo.fr), Port de Marigot, 97150 Marigot, St Martin, French West Indies.

Avoid the numerous information booths that line the streets of Philipsburg – they're generally a cover for time-share sales.

Tourist Offices Abroad
Overseas tourist offices for the French West Indies are listed under Tourist Offices in the Facts for the Visitor section of the Guadeloupe chapter. The following are overseas tourist offices for Dutch Sint Maarten:

Canada
Sint Maarten Information Center (☎ 416-622-4300, fax 416-622-3431) 703 Evans Ave, Suite 106, Toronto, M9C 5E9

Germany
Sint Maarten Tourist Office (☎ 69-240 01 83, fax 69-242 71 52 1) Karlsstrasse 12, 60329 Frankfurt

Netherlands
Minister Plenipotentiary of the Netherlands Antilles (☎ 070-306 6111, fax 070-306 6110) Badhuisweg 173–175, 2597 JP, 'S-Gravenhage

USA
(☎ 212-953-2084, 800-786-2278, fax 212-953-2145) 675 Third Ave, Suite 1806, New York, NY 10017

VISAS & DOCUMENTS
US and Canadian citizens arriving at Juliana Airport on the Dutch side can stay up to three months with proof of citizenship. Acceptable ID includes either a birth certificate with a raised seal, plus a government-approved photo ID such as a driver's license, or a passport that is not more than five years past its expiration date. Citizens of other countries entering the island on the Dutch side require a valid passport.

If entering the island on the French side, US and Canadian citizens are allowed entry

ST MARTIN / SINT MAARTEN

for stays of up to two weeks (maximum three months, on request) without a passport if they have the same type of documentation listed above for the Dutch side. Citizens of the EU need an official identity card, valid passport or French *carte de séjour* (visitor card). Citizens of most other foreign countries need both a valid passport and a visa for France if entering the island on the French side.

A roundtrip or onward ticket is officially required of all visitors to St Martin, regardless of whether entry is made on the French or Dutch side.

While documents are checked upon arrival, beyond that immigration controls are quite lax, a situation that is partially the result of unrestricted movement between the two sides of the island.

CUSTOMS

Although the police make occasional spot checks when suspicious, there are otherwise no customs checks coming into Juliana Airport – there's not even a counter for inspecting luggage.

MONEY

The French franc (F) is the official legal tender on the French side and the Netherlands Antilles guilder (Fls) on the Dutch side, but on both sides US dollars are widely used as well. This makes the US dollar the most convenient currency to carry, as it's the only one readily accepted on both sides of the island. See Money in the St Barts chapter for information on the Euro, which should be introduced by mid-2002.

On the French side, restaurants and hotels are split between posting prices in French francs or US dollars, while on the Dutch side they're virtually always posted in US dollars.

On both sides, grocery stores mark goods in the local currency but generally have cash registers equipped with a key that can automatically convert the total to US dollars. Larger grocery stores, such as Match in Marigot and Food Center on the Dutch side, accept US-dollar traveler's checks like cash and generally offer the full market rate – so you'll do better cashing your traveler's checks on food purchases than you would exchanging at a bank.

It's useful to carry some francs for those times when a French business gives a bad exchange rate, but most places calculate at a fair rate, and it generally works out fine to simply pay in dollars.

MasterCard and Visa are widely, though not universally, accepted around the island. ATMs that accept major credit cards and Cirrus and Plus bank cards can be found at some banks.

For details on the two island currencies, including exchange rates, see Money in the Regional Facts for the Visitor chapter.

POST & COMMUNICATIONS
Post

The main post offices are in Philipsburg and Marigot. When writing to the French side, end the address with '97150 St Martin, French West Indies.' When writing to the Dutch side, end the address with 'Sint Maarten, Netherlands Antilles.'

From the Dutch side, it costs Fls 0.90 to mail a postcard and Fls 1.75 to mail a 10g letter within the Caribbean; Fls 1.10 for a postcard and Fls 2.25 for a letter to the USA, Canada, UK or Europe; and Fls 1.30 for a postcard and Fls 3.25 for a letter to Australia, Asia or Africa.

From the French side, it costs 3F to send a postcard to France, 3.80F to the Caribbean or the USA, 4.40F to other parts of the Americas and 5.20F to the rest of the world. This rate also covers letters up to 20g.

Telephone

Local numbers have seven digits on the Dutch side, six digits on the French side. Calls between the two sides are charged as long-distance.

To phone the Dutch side from the French side, dial 00599 before the local number. To call the French side from the Dutch side, dial 00590 before the local number.

When calling the island from overseas, you must prefix local numbers with area code 590 for the French side, 599 for the Dutch side.

On the French side virtually all pay phones are the card-phone type, while on the Dutch side card phones predominate, but there are some coin phones that take US quarters as well as Netherlands Antilles guilders.

For more details on phone cards, see Post & Communications in the Regional Facts for the Visitor chapter.

Email & Internet Access

The public library in Philipsburg has the cheapest Internet access on the island, at US$4 for half an hour. It's popular so you may have to book ahead to get on a computer. Check the Philipsburg section for the library's hours.

INTERNET RESOURCES

The official Dutch and French Web sites are decidedly average and hard to navigate, but give you a taste of the island before you go. Check out the Dutch site at www .st-maarten.com and the French site at www.st-martin.org.

NEWSPAPERS & MAGAZINES

The Dutch side's two daily newspapers, *The Daily Herald* and *Today,* are printed in English. The French side has two weekly papers, *l'Hebdo* and *St Martin's Week,* both in French. Two useful free visitor magazines available at hotels and tourist offices are *Discover Saint Martin/Sint Maarten* and *Sint Maarten Events.* Look out for the free *Ti Gourmet,* a small booklet listing restaurants and hotels. Many of the places within its pages offer discounts upon presentation of the booklet.

The *International Herald-Tribune, New York Times, USA Today, Le Monde, Die Welt* and other foreign publications are available at larger grocery stores and newsstands around the island.

RADIO & TV

The handful of radio stations includes The Voice of Sint Maarten at 102.7 FM and 1300 AM, which broadcasts news at 1 and 6 pm and has talk shows in English. For European news in French, there's RFO at 88.9 FM.

Cable TV on the Dutch side carries a full range of North American network programs

and movie channels. The English-language Leeward Broadcasting Corporation, on channel 7, has island news as well as CNN broadcasts.

On the French side, TV is usually limited to three French-language channels, CNN news and a couple of US movie channels.

ELECTRICITY

On the French side the voltage is 220V, 60 cycles, and plugs have two round prongs. On the Dutch side it's 110V, 50 cycles, and plugs have two flat prongs. Many hotels provide dual-voltage plugs for electric shavers.

WEIGHTS & MEASURES

Islanders use the metric system. Elevation is in meters, and road signs are in kilometers.

HEALTH

There are hospitals in Marigot (☎ 29 57 57) near Fort Louis and east of Philipsburg (☎ 543-1111), in the Cay Hill area.

DANGERS & ANNOYANCES

St Martin has a well-founded reputation as being a little unsafe for the careless tourist. Be a bit cautious when carrying around cameras and other expensive items, and don't stray down darkened alleys late at night. Women should be cautious walking alone on deserted beaches and if hitchhiking. Don't leave valuables in your car, as break-ins, especially in remote spots, can be a problem.

EMERGENCIES

On the Dutch side, dial ☎ 542-2222 for police emergencies, ☎ 542-2111 for an ambulance. On the French side, dial ☎ 87 50 10 for the police, ☎ 87 86 25 for an ambulance.

BUSINESS HOURS

Shop hours in Philipsburg are generally 8 am to noon and 2 to 6 pm Monday to Saturday. In Marigot, business hours vary but are typically from about 9 am to 12:30 pm and 3 to 7 pm Monday to Saturday. In Philipsburg, some shops open on Sunday if cruise ships are in port.

ST MARTIN / SINT MAARTEN

PUBLIC HOLIDAYS & SPECIAL EVENTS

Public holidays on the island include the following:

New Year's Day	January 1
Good Friday	late March/early April
Easter Sunday	late March/early April
Easter Monday	late March/early April
Queen's Day	April 30; Dutch side
Labor Day	May 1
Government Holiday	the day after the last Carnival parade, about a month after Easter; Dutch side
Ascension Thursday	40th day after Easter
Pentecost Monday	eighth Monday after Easter; French side
Bastille Day	July 14; French side
Assumption Day	August 15; French side
Sint Maarten Day/ Concordia Day	November 11
Christmas Day	December 25
Boxing Day	December 26; Dutch side

On the French side, Carnival celebrations are held during the traditional five-day Mardi Gras period that ends on Ash Wednesday. It features the selection of a Carnival Queen, costume parades, dancing and music.

On the Dutch side, which has the larger Carnival, activities usually begin the second week after Easter and last for two weeks, with steel-band competitions, jump-ups, calypso concerts, beauty contests and costume parades. Events are centered at Carnival Village on the north side of Philipsburg.

Bastille Day, France's national holiday, is celebrated with a parade, sporting events and fireworks.

The November 11 holiday, called Sint Maarten Day by the Dutch and Concordia Day by the French, is marked by a ceremony at the Boundary Monument obelisk that notes the amicable coexistence of the two countries.

For sailors, the annual Heineken Regatta, held the first weekend in March,

features competitions for racing yachts, large sailboats and small multihulls. For fishers, there's the Marlin Open de St Martin invitational tournament held in June.

ACTIVITIES
Beaches & Swimming

The island has beautiful white-sand beaches (although they don't compare with Anguilla's), ranging from crowded resort strands to long, secluded sweeps. Most of the best and least-developed beaches are on the French side. The clothing-optional Orient Beach is lovely, though it attracts a crowd. Long Beach is great for seclusion, while Baie Rouge, Dawn Beach and the islets off the northeast coast are good places for both snorkeling and swimming. All beaches are public, although some of the Dutch resorts make access difficult and mark their beaches with the tiniest of signs.

Diving

The most popular diving is at Proselyte Reef, a few kilometers south of Philipsburg, where in 1802 the British frigate HMS *Proselyte* sank in 15m of water. In addition to the remains of the ship, there are 10 dive sites in that area, including coral reefs with caverns.

Dive Shops The following dive shops are full-service facilities. Prices are competitive. On average, single dives cost around US$45, while multidive packages lower the price to around US$40 per dive. Night dives are around US$60. Most of the shops also conduct open-water certification courses for around US$350 and accept referred students for about US$55 per dive. Some also offer half-day Discover Scuba resort courses for beginners, including a little beach dive, for US$45 to US$60. Some shops offer shark dives for US$60, if you're keen!

Aquamania Watersports (☎ 544-2640, fax 544-2476) Pelican Marina, Simpson Bay

Blue Ocean Dive Center (☎ 87 89 73, fax 87 26 36) Royal Food Store center, Baie Nettlé

Dive Safaris (☎ 542-9001, fax 542-8983) Bobby's Marina, Philipsburg

(☎ 545-3213, fax 545-3209) La Palapa Marina, Simpson Bay

Octoplus Dive Center (☎ 87 20 62, fax 87 20 63) Grand Case

Scuba Fun Caraibes (☎ 87 36 13, fax 87 36 52) Marina, Anse Marcel

Sea Dolphin Dive Center (☎ 87 60 72, fax 87 60 73) Le Flamboyant hotel, Baie Nettlé

Sea Horse Diving (☎/fax 87 84 15) Mercure Hotel, Baie Nettlé

Snorkeling

There's decent snorkeling at a number of places, including Baie Rouge, Dawn Beach and the islands of Green Cay and Îlet Pinel off the northeast coast.

You can rent snorkeling gear at most dive shops and hotel beach huts; the going rate is about US$10 a day or US$35 a week. Many of the dive shops offer half-day snorkeling tours for around US$35.

A few boats offer day trips to offshore islands and to the more pristine waters around Anguilla, with the greatest frequency of cruises in the winter season. Scoobidoo (☎ 87 20 28, fax 87 20 78) has trips to Prickly Pear on Wednesday and Friday for US$82 and Anguilla on Thursday and Sunday for US$87, including lunch and all you can drink.

Windsurfing

Two of the island's top windsurfing spots are at Orient Bay and at the north end of Baie de l'Embouchure.

At Orient Beach, the Windsurfing Club (☎ 29 41 57), run by French windsurfing champion Nathalie Simon, rents boards from US$20 an hour, US$50 a day and US$220 a week. There's a beginner's course for US$140 (three 1½-hour sessions) and one-hour private lessons for US$55. The shop also rents surfboards and boogie boards for US$12 to US$15 per half day.

At quieter Baie de l'Embouchure, Tropical Wave (☎ 87 37 25) and Windy Reef (☎ 87 08 37) have good spots and rent out windsurfing equipment, surfboards and snorkeling gear at comparable rates.

The St Martin Windsurfing Association (☎ 87 93 24) has information on races and tournaments.

Other Water Activites

Sint Maarten 12 Metre Challenge (☎ 542-0045), at Bobby's Marina in Philipsburg, has three-hour excursions on America's Cup racing yachts, which are large, fast and sleek. Their fleet includes *Stars & Stripes*, the very yacht Dennis Conner used in the 1987 challenge for the America's Cup in Australia. The trips cost US$70 per person.

For lovers of motors, speed and the smell of gasoline, Jet-skis can be hired (if you're 18 or over) for around US$45 per half-hour from Bikini Watersport (☎ 27 07 48), at Orient Beach, and Beach Boy Watersports (☎ 547-1731), on the beach in Philipsburg. Beach Boy also offers waterskiing if the conditions are right for US$20 for 2 miles.

Sunfish sailboats can be rented at some resort-area beaches and sailing cruise concessions; deep-sea fishing and yacht charters can be arranged through the marinas. When the swell picks up, Mullet Bay and Orient Bay can be good for boogie boarding.

Hiking

The island's most popular hike is up to Pic Paradis, St Martin's highest point. Not only will this hike reward you with great views, but Pic Paradis also serves as a takeoff point for a few longer hikes that reach down to the coast. For details, see Pic Paradis, later in this chapter.

For those who don't want to trek off on their own, guided hikes are offered by St

Martin Action Nature (☎ 87 97 87), an organization that helps keep the island trails clear, and Sint Maarten's Heritage Foundation (☎ 542-4917), which is affiliated with the Sint Maarten Museum in Philipsburg.

Horseback Riding

Horseback riding is available from Bayside Riding Club (on the French side ☎ 87 36 64, on the Dutch side ☎ 547-6822), near Orient Beach; the OK Corral (☎ 87 40 72), at Baie Lucas; Caïd & Isa (☎ 87 45 70), at Anse Marcel; and Lucky Stables (☎ 544-5255), on Cape Bay Rd. The cost for a one-hour beach ride is typically US$35, a two-hour ride is between US$45 and US$55.

Golf

The island's golf course, the 18-hole Mullet Bay Golf (☎ 545-2801) has greens fees of US$109, cart included.

ACCOMMODATIONS

Almost all of the Dutch-side accommodations are between Philipsburg and Mullet Bay, with the majority of rooms being in large resorts. On the French side there's a resort cluster at Baie Nettlé, but beyond that things are fairly widely dispersed, with the majority of rooms in small-scale hotels and villa-style places. Accordingly, the places on the French side tend to be more personal and friendly.

At first glance rates may appear cheaper on the Dutch side. However, the Dutch add on to their quoted rates a 5% room tax and usually a 10% to 15% service charge – and a few of them pad the bill with an additional 5% 'energy charge'! On the French side some hotels have begun charging the 5% room tax on top of the bill, but service charges are usually included in the quoted room rates.

FOOD

There are numerous quality French restaurants on the island with prices that are quite moderate by Caribbean standards. Many people, regardless of where they're staying, drive to Grand Case for dinner, because it has one of the best concentrations of good eating spots anywhere on the island.

Marigot also has a number of good dining options, with the largest selection at the Port La Royale Marina.

On the Dutch side, Philipsburg has an abundance of restaurants and cheap fast-food joints. There are plenty of fast-food eateries around the airport as well.

As for grocery stores, the ones on the French side are predominately stocked with European foods, while the ones on the Dutch side are heavily stocked with American foods. The biggest grocery stores in St Martin, if not the entire Eastern Caribbean, are the two Food Centers, one on Bush Rd west of Philipsburg and the other on Union Rd just south of the boundary monument.

Note that some restaurants include a 15% service charge in their prices and at others you are expected to tip an equivalent amount.

DRINKS

There are water desalination plants on the island, but because of the high water prices many places still use catchments. The desalinated water is fine to drink from the tap, but catchment water varies in quality and should generally be treated first. Reasonably priced bottled water is readily available at grocery stores.

Inexpensive Caribbean rums and French wines are plentiful and can be purchased at any grocery store. You might want to sample the local guavaberry liqueur, a sweet rum-based drink flavored with a small cranberry-like berry, *Eugenia floribunda*, which grows on the island's hills. The Guavaberry World Headquarters, which stocks all things guavaberry-oriented, can be found on Frontstreet in Philipsburg.

SHOPPING

St Martin is the Eastern Caribbean's top duty-free shopping spot. Philipsburg's Frontstreet is the island's most commercial strip and has the largest selection of camera and electronics shops. In both Philipsburg and Marigot, shoppers will find chic boutiques, jewelers and perfume stores carrying top-name European products. In Marigot there's a concentration of shops at the north side of Port La Royale Marina and along the adjacent Rue du Général de Gaulle. For something more local, Marigot's harborfront market has handicrafts, T-shirts, pareus and the like.

If you're interested in art, you can help support the St Martin Archeological Museum by buying from its gallery, which sells watercolors, oils and prints of island scenes at reasonable prices.

Duty-free alcohol is a bargain. You can buy bottles of rum at shops around the island for around US$5.

Getting There & Away

DEPARTURE TAX
From Juliana Airport, there's a departure tax of US$20 for international departures and US$6 for flights to destinations in the Netherlands Antilles. There's no departure tax for children aged two and under, or for anyone who has been on St Martin for less than 24 hours. There are no departure taxes at all from Espérance Airport. Boat departure taxes are the same as for Juliana Airport.

AIR
Airports & Airlines
All international flights arrive at Juliana Airport, on the Dutch side. The tourist information booth, near the arrivals exit, is not terribly helpful with hands-on information, but nearby is a rack of useful tourist publications and a direct-line courtesy phone to a couple of hotels. There's a taxi stand just outside the arrivals exit and a line of car rental booths nearby.

Outside the departure lounge is a bank, a newsstand with international newspapers and magazines, and duty-free shops selling liquor, jewelry, perfume etc. There's a 2nd-floor restaurant open noon to midnight and a more reasonably priced ground-level booth with pastries, sandwiches and drinks.

Both card phones and phones that accept US quarters are spread around the airport. Netherlands Antilles phone cards are sold

at the airport post office. There's an ATM in the departure lounge.

Note that Juliana is a sluggish and ill-planned airport, so don't cut anything close. Lines can be astoundingly long. Certainly give yourself extra time if you're flying out with LIAT, as tickets are sold at the check-in counter and at times lines can move tediously slowly.

Tiny Espérance Airport, in Grand Case in French St Martin, handles prop-plane flights to St Barts, Guadeloupe and Martinique. The airport has card phones, car rentals and a snack bar.

The following are the local reservation numbers for airlines that have scheduled flights to Juliana Airport:

Air Caraïbes	☎ 545-4212
Air France	☎ 545-4212
ALM	☎ 545-4240
American Airlines	☎ 545-2040
AOM	☎ 545-3444
BWIA	☎ 545-4646
Continental Airlines	☎ 545-3444
Corsair	☎ 545-4344
KLM	☎ 545-4344
LIAT	☎ 545-4203
Winair	☎ 545-4237

Within the Caribbean
American Airlines has four flights daily to St Martin from Puerto Rico; the one-way fare is US$128, the roundtrip excursion fare US$239.

You can fly to St Martin from any of LIAT's Caribbean destinations, in most cases with same-day connections via Antigua. LIAT flights from Antigua to St Martin cost US$99 one-way, US$149 for a same-day roundtrip and US$179 for a 30-day excursion.

Winair has its head office at St Martin and can get you to most of the neighboring islands. Check the various island chapters for Winair prices and schedules.

Air Caraïbes offers daily flights between Guadeloupe and St Martin from around US$110 one-way and has a low-priced excursion, a 'superpromo' fare of US$150, but the other airlines also have attractive discount schemes on roundtrip tickets.

The USA & Canada

Continental and American Airlines have daily nonstop flights to St Martin from New York. American also has direct flights from Miami and connecting flights to numerous US cities via San Juan, Puerto Rico. There are occasional discounted fares as cheap as US$300 roundtrip, but expect to pay at least double that for the more typical excursion fare from the east coast.

Europe

There are a few flights offered weekly from Paris to St Martin by Air France and from Amsterdam to St Martin by KLM. Full-fare excursion tickets cost about US$1200, but travel agents can discount these fares substantially.

SEA
Ferry

From St Martin, there are numerous daily ferries to and from Anguilla, daily catamarans to and from St Barts, and a ferry several times a week to and from Saba. Full details are in the Getting There & Away sections of the Anguilla, St Barts and Saba chapters.

Yacht

Yachts can clear immigration at Philipsburg and Marigot. There are marinas at Philipsburg, Marigot, Simpson Bay Lagoon, Oyster Pond and Anse Marcel.

Landlocked Simpson Bay Lagoon is one of the most protected anchorages in the Eastern Caribbean. There are two drawbridge entrances to it that open on set schedules: 9 and 11 am and 5:30 pm daily at Simpson Bay on the Dutch side, and 9 am and 2 and 5:30 pm daily (no 2 pm opening on weekends) at Sandy Ground on the French side.

Cruise Ship

St Martin is a popular cruise-ship destination, largely because of the duty-free shopping there. Cruise ships land passengers in Philipsburg and Marigot. Philipsburg's harbor facilities have recently been expanded to handle up to four ships at a time, so expect the town to be swamped with day-trippers when the harbor is full.

Getting Around

TO/FROM THE AIRPORTS

From Juliana Airport taxis charge US$12 to either Marigot or Philipsburg, US$20 to Grand Case and US$25 to Orient Bay.

A couple of taxis meet each flight arriving at Espérance Airport; if you miss them, security can call one for you. From Espérance Airport, taxis cost US$10 to Marigot and US$15 Orient Beach.

BUS

Buses are a good, cheap way of getting to and from the major destinations on the island. There are two kinds of buses: larger public buses, which make Philipsburg-Marigot and Marigot–Grand Case runs and charge US$1.50, and more frequent private minivans that charge according to distance, from US$1 to US$3.

Buses have their starting and ending points marked on them, usually on the front window. The Marigot-Philipsburg buses have the longest operating hours, generally 6 am to midnight; on most other routes buses are hard to get after 8 pm. In addition to the main Philipsburg-Marigot-Grand Case routes, there are less frequent buses to Mullet Bay, Simpson Bay and Orleans. Beyond that bus service is sketchy, so touring the whole island by bus is not practical.

Although there are no airport buses per se, if you're traveling light you can try catching one of the Philipsburg–Mullet Bay buses, which pass right by the airport.

In the capitals you have to stand at bus stops, which are found along Backstreet in Philipsburg and on Rue de Hollande in Marigot. In rural areas you can flag down buses anywhere along the route.

CAR & MOTORCYCLE
Road Rules

Driving is on the right side of the road on both sides of the island, and your home driver's license is valid. Road signs and most car odometers are in kilometers. The speed limit in built-up areas varies from 20km/h to

40km/h, while outside residential areas it's 60km/h unless otherwise posted.

Rental

Car There are scores of car rental companies on the island, with the greatest abundance at Juliana Airport. If you don't have a reservation you can stroll the row of booths just outside the airport arrival lounge and compare prices. It's a competitive market, and when things are slow, as is common in the off-season, you can often find someone willing to drop rates to around US$25 a day. At busier times the going rate is closer to US$45. Rates include unlimited kilometers; an optional collision damage waiver (CDW) costs about US$10 a day extra.

TDC Rental (☎ 29 24 24) and Vacation Car Rental (☎ 87 95 25) have offices at Espérance Airport in Grand Case.

The following companies have offices at or near Juliana Airport:

Avis	☎ 545-2316
Budget	☎ 545-4030
Hertz	☎ 545-4440
National	☎ 544-2168
Paradise Island	☎ 545-2361
Sunshine	☎ 545-2685

Warning: Be careful not to leave any valuables in your rented car. A local pastime is to rent a car, copy the keys and then wait for an unsuspecting tourist to leave bags, money and valuables supposedly safely locked in the trunk or glove compartment.

Motorcycle Getting around the island on two wheels is easy and enjoyable. Motorcycles are available from Rent A Scoot (☎ 87 20 59), opposite the Hotel Laguna Beach in Baie Nettlé, and Eugene Moto Scooter Rental (☎ 87 13 97), next to the museum in Marigot. Daily rates, including helmet and lock, are around US$23 for a 50cc scooter (no license required), US$28 for an 80cc scooter (driver's license required) and US$65 for a 650cc motorcycle (motorcycle license required).

Rumor has it that scooters have about a six-day life on the island before being stolen.

They are popular and easy to steal if not locked up properly, so it's advisable to take extra precautions. If your scooter is stolen you'll lose your deposit.

TAXI

Taxi fares are set by the government. The minimum fare is US$6. From Marigot it costs US$12 to Philipsburg, Grand Case or the airports. Taxis from Philipsburg charge US$12 to Juliana Airport and US$16 to Mullet Bay. Add US$4 for each additional passenger beyond two. There's a surcharge of 25% on fares between 10 pm and midnight and 50% from midnight to 6 am. There are taxi stands at the airports, Wathey Square in Philipsburg and the public market in Marigot.

BICYCLE

Frogs Legs Cyclery (☎ 87 05 11), next to the Match supermarket in Marigot, rents out mountain bikes from US$15 a day and organizes island cycling tours for US$20. BN Food Store (☎ 87 97 47), at the side of the Marine Hotel in Baie Nettlé, has a few mountain bikes for US$10 a day.

HITCHHIKING

It's possible to hitch rides on the island – indeed, many islanders do so. All of the usual safety precautions apply.

ORGANIZED TOURS

Taxi tours of the island that last about 2½ hours cost US$50 for one or two people. There's an additional fee of US$18 for each extra passenger.

St Martin Archaeological Museum, in Marigot, offers a morning bus tour of St Martin with an emphasis on island history. It lasts two hours and costs US$30; for reservations call ☎ 29 22 84.

French St Martin

MARIGOT

Marigot is the capital of French St Martin, and most of it has a distinct French, rather than Caribbean, feel. It has some good restaurants and a couple of worthy sights.

ST MARTIN / SINT MAARTEN

Although it is not a large town, Marigot has two commercial centers. One of them, the area around the harborfront, has the public market, with food vendors and souvenir stalls. The dock for boats to Anguilla and St Barts is also there. The other center encompasses the Port La Royale Marina, which is surrounded by a cluster of restaurants and boutiques that spill out onto bustling Rue du Général de Gaulle. The tourist office is close to the marina, on the road to Sandy Ground. The farther away from the harbor you get, the less French and the more Caribbean Marigot becomes.

Marigot is a historic town making an attempt to modernize itself. There are still a number of older West Indian-style buildings with fancy fretwork and 2nd-floor balconies, but many other such buildings have made way for newer structures. The land reclamation project along the harborfront has modified that section of town and turned much of it into a parking lot. Construction in some parts is still under way.

Information

Tourist Offices The tourist office, southwest of the marina, is open 8:30 am to 1 pm

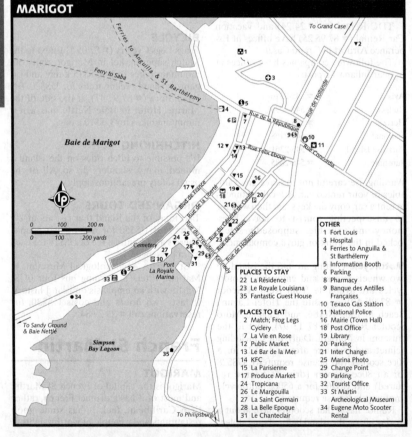

MARIGOT

Baie de Marigot

To Grand Case

Ferries to Anguilla & St Barthélemy

Ferry to Saba

Rue de Hollande

Rue de la République

Rue Félix Eboué

Rue Concordia

Rue de France

Rue de la Liberté

Rue du Président Kennedy

Rue du Général de Gaulle

Rue St James

Rue de Hollande

Port La Royale Marina

Cemetery

To Sandy Ground & Baie Nettlé

Simpson Bay Lagoon

To Philipsburg

0   100   200 m
0   100   200 yards

OTHER
1 Fort Louis
3 Hospital
4 Ferries to Anguilla & St Barthélemy
5 Information Booth
6 Parking
8 Pharmacy
9 Banque des Antilles Françaises
10 Texaco Gas Station
11 National Police
16 Mairie (Town Hall)
18 Post Office
19 Library
20 Parking
21 Inter Change
25 Marina Photo
29 Change Point
30 Parking
32 Tourist Office
33 St Martin Archeological Museum
34 Eugene Moto Scooter Rental

PLACES TO STAY
22 La Résidence
23 Le Royale Louisiana
35 Fantastic Guest House

PLACES TO EAT
2 Match; Frog Legs Cyclery
7 La Vie en Rose
12 Public Market
13 Le Bar de la Mer
14 KFC
15 La Parisienne
17 Produce Market
24 Tropicana
26 Le Margouilla
27 La Saint Germain
28 La Belle Epoque
31 Le Chanteclair

and 2:30 to 5:30 pm weekdays, 8 am to noon Saturday. There's also an information booth on Rue de la République near the ferry terminal.

Money You can avoid transaction fees and long waits by bypassing the banks and instead changing money at the storefront currency exchange booths. Inter Change, on Rue du Général de Gaulle, is open 8 am to 6:30 pm. Change Point, near the marina, is open 7:30 am to 7 pm. Both are closed Sunday.

Post & Communications The post office, on Rue de la Liberté, is open 7:45 to 4:45 pm weekdays, till 11:30 am Saturday. There are card phones outside the post office. Phone cards are sold in the various souvenir shops around town.

Film There's one-hour film processing (24 prints for 97F) at Marina Photo, at the Port La Royale Marina.

Fort Louis

Fort Louis (also called Fort de Marigot) was built in 1789 to protect Marigot's warehouses from the frequent raids being staged by British privateers based on nearby Anguilla. After French and English hostilities ended in the 19th century, the fort was abandoned and slipped into decay. Today not much remains of Fort Louis other than some partially intact stone walls and a couple of cannons, but the hilltop locale offers a fine view of Marigot and Simpson Bay Lagoon.

To get there, drive up past the hospital and park at the large cross, where you'll find steps leading up to the fort – just two minutes away. If you walk up from the harbor it takes about 15 minutes.

St Martin Archaeological Museum

This worthwhile little museum, on the road to Sandy Ground, is nicely presented, with a focus on the Arawak Period. Shell amulets, bone artifacts, arrow points and bits of pottery help illustrate the culture of the island's early Amerindian inhabitants. There are also presentations on flora and fauna, period photos of Marigot and historical displays on the French-Dutch divide and St Martin's plantation era of sugar and salt production. There are detailed interpretive plaques in both French and English.

Hours are 9 am to 1 pm and 3 to 6 pm Monday to Saturday. Admission is US$5 for adults, US$2 for children under 12.

Places to Stay

The *Fantastic Guest House* (☎ 87 71 09, fax 87 73 51) has 20 rooms above an auto-parts shop, a few minutes' walk south of the marina. The standard rooms are US$50, and there are larger rooms with well-equipped kitchenettes for US$70; both types have private baths, TV, air-con and refrigerators. It's a good value, especially in winter, as the rates are the same year-round.

Le Royale Louisiana (☎ 87 86 51, fax 87 96 49, louisiana@top-saint-martin.com), on Rue du Général de Gaulle, is one of the older in-town hotels, but many of its 58 rooms have recently been given a new lease on life. The rooms include air-con, TV, phones and refrigerators, and cost a reasonable US$50/69 for singles/doubles in summer, US$65/82 in winter, breakfast included. If you're sensitive to noise, ask for a room away from the street.

The 21-room *La Résidence* (☎ 87 70 37, fax 87 90 44), also on Rue du Général de Gaulle, has large, adequate rooms with TV, air-con, room safes, balconies and minibars. Singles/doubles cost US$64/82 in summer, US$74/92 in winter, breakfast included.

Places to Eat

Marina Port La Royale Marina has a waterfront lined with restaurants offering everything from pizza and burgers to seafood and nouvelle cuisine. There's fierce competition, with some of the island's lowest menu prices and lots of chalkboard specials. The best bet is to just wander around and see what catches your fancy.

Head to *La Saint Germain* (☎ 87 92 87), where you'll find a good selection of crêpes from 25F to 50F. It has a pleasant spot on the marina and is open 7 am to 11 pm daily.

Popular with young, hip French folks is *Le Margouilla*, near the marina facing away from the water. There isn't a view, but it does have good burgers (30F) and a relaxing, laid-back atmosphere. It's not a bad spot to prop up the bar, either.

Harborside *La Belle Epoque* (☎ 87 87 70) is large and popular, serving standard fare that includes seafood, pasta and pizza, beginning around 47F. Continental breakfast is available from 7:30 am for 35F.

A top choice for fine dining is little family-run *Le Chanteclair* (☎ 87 94 60), where a full-course dinner costs around 150F, with a wide range of standard French starters and main dishes.

Another good intimate dinner option is *Tropicana* (☎ 87 79 07), which has classic French fare but isn't cheap; expect dinner for two with wine to run closer to US$100.

Downtown   There's a complex at the *public market* with a dozen bars and *lolos* (barbecue stands) selling burgers, hot dogs and barbecued meals. Their chalkboard menus list lots of chicken and fish dishes served with plantain, peas and rice for around 40F, and island favorites like bullfoot and pigtail soups. For ordinary fast food, there's a *KFC* with air-con on the opposite side of the street.

La Parisienne is a very popular bakery café with sidewalk tables, fresh salads, generous baguette sandwiches, quiche and lasagna, all at reasonable prices (from around US$6). It's open 6 am to 8 pm Monday to Saturday, till 12:30 pm Sunday.

Le Bar de la Mer (☎ 29 03 82), near the harbor, draws a predominantly French-speaking crowd and is a popular spot to have a drink. It also has pizzas and salads from about 60F as well as fish and meat dishes for around 90F. Opening hours are 8 am to 2 am daily.

La Vie en Rose (☎ 87 54 42) is a fashionable French restaurant with a choice location opposite the harbor. At lunch there's a sidewalk café with fish and meat dishes in the 80F to 120F range. Dinner is served in a more formal upstairs dining room. The à la carte menu features a dozen main courses, including the likes of lobster medallions and duck in raspberry sauce, all priced from 170F to 195F. It's open for lunch and dinner daily.

Match, on the north side of Marigot, is a large, modern supermarket at the back of a shopping complex with pretty good deli and wine selections. It's open 9 am to 1 pm Sunday, till 8 pm other days.

The *produce market* on Marigot's waterfront has tropical fruit such as passion fruit and bananas as well as local root vegetables, but the prices – especially for tourists – can be nearly as high as at grocery stores. There's usually someone selling drinking coconuts for US$2. It's open from sunrise to around 2 pm Wednesday to Saturday.

SANDY GROUND & BAIE NETTLÉ

Sandy Ground is the long, narrow, curving strip of land that extends west from Marigot, with Baie Nettlé (Nettle Bay) on one side of the road and Simpson Bay Lagoon on the other. The first hotel went up just a decade ago, but these days there's a strip with hotels, restaurants and small shopping centers one after the other.

In itself, Sandy Ground is not a place of any great interest – the ocean beach is marginal, with a rocky shoreline shelf, and the lagoon side is a bit mucky for swimming – but it can be a convenient base if you get a good hotel deal, and some of St Martin's finest beaches are just down the road.

The Royal Food Store shopping center, within walking distance of the Baie Nettlé hotels, has scooter and car rentals, a dive shop, a pharmacy, a newsstand and a post office. There's a coin laundry at Laguna Beach Hotel.

Places to Stay

The *Hotel Royal Beach* (☎ 29 12 12, fax 29 12 04) is an older 113-room hotel on the bay side. Although it's not as spiffy as its more upmarket neighbors and looks run-down, the rooms are suitable for the price and have a two-burner hot plate, refrigerator, air-con, phone and TV. There's also a pool.

Singles/doubles start at US$60/76, including breakfast and tax, and are usually the same price year-round.

Marine Hôtel (☎ 87 54 54, fax 87 92 11) is a relatively large package-tour hotel with modern if nondescript rooms. Each has a ceiling fan, air-con, TV, phone, kitchenette and large balcony, some with a view across Simpson Bay Lagoon. There's a pool, tennis courts and a dive shop. Rates include a buffet breakfast. Standard singles/doubles cost US$110/122 in summer, US$160/172 in winter.

Nettlé Bay Beach Club (☎ 87 68 68, fax 87 21 51) has some 40 triplex villas spread out along the edge of the bay. Hotel-style 2nd-story loft rooms with a queen-size bed, sundeck, and in some cases a kitchenette, cost US$115 in summer, US$165 in winter. One-bedroom apartments, which have a separate living room and kitchen, as well as an ocean-facing terrace, cost US$150 in summer, US$260 in winter. All units have ceiling fans, thermostatic air-con, TV, phones and pleasant decor. The complex has four large pools, two restaurants and a water-sports center.

Places to Eat
The *Royal Food Store*, open 7:30 am to 8:30 pm daily, is a small grocery with deli items, Häagen-Dazs bars, fresh baguettes and a good wine selection. In the same center is *Chez Swann*, where you can get Continental breakfast or lunchtime sandwiches for 40F, dinner salads or pasta dishes from 40F to 55F.

There are a couple of relaxing beach bars at either end of the bay. *Layla's Beach*, at the Marigot end of the beach next to Hotel Royal, is open and breezy, serving standard American fare at moderate prices.

Ma Ti Beach (☎ 87 01 30), occupying the western end of the beach, is a more solid affair, in looks and menu. There are plenty of fish dishes, ranging from 80F to 110F, as well as pastas from 60F and meat and poultry from 85F. It's open for lunch and dinner daily.

BAIE ROUGE
Baie Rouge, 3km west of Sandy Ground, is a long, beautiful sandy strand with good

swimming, though if you have children be aware that it drops off quickly to overhead depths. Although this golden-sand beach is just 150m from the main road it retains an inviting natural setting. For the best snorkeling, swim to the right toward the rocky outcrop and arch.

The dirt drive leading to the beach is at a 90° turn on the road from Sandy Ground to Mullet Bay – as you have to virtually stop to negotiate the turn, it's easy to find. A couple of beach shacks sell drinks and barbecued foods and rent umbrellas, lounge chairs and snorkel gear, but the beach is delightfully free of Jet-skis and other motorized toys.

BAIE AUX PRUNES (PLUM BAY)
The remote and unspoiled Baie aux Prunes is a gently curving bay with polished shell-like grains of golden sand. The beach is popular for swimming and sunbathing, and it's backed by a little grove of white cedar trees with pink blossoms that attract hummingbirds.

The bay can be reached by turning right 1.3km south of Baie Rouge and immediately taking the signposted left fork. After 2km you'll come to a junction; veer right and continue for another 300m, where there's a parking area and a short walkway to the beach.

BAIE LONGUE (LONG BAY)
Long Beach, at Baie Longue, embraces two splendid kilometers of seemingly endless white sand. The only commercial development along the shoreline is La Samanna hotel, down at the very southern tip. The beach is very big and well off the beaten path – a great place for long strolls and quiet sunsets.

You can get to Long Beach by continuing south from Baie aux Prunes or by taking the La Samanna turnoff from the main road and continuing past the hotel for 800m. There's a parking area in front of a chain-link fence and a short footpath leading to the beach.

Places to Stay
A favorite of the rich and famous is *La Samanna* (☎ 87 64 00, fax 87 87 86, in the

USA ☎ *800-854-2252),* a low-profile, exclusive beachside hotel with 80 rooms, each with air-con, a ceiling fan, minibar and ocean-fronting balcony. There's a pool, tennis courts and complimentary water sports. Rates start at US$325 in summer, US$575 in winter and go up to US$1900 for a multiterraced three-bedroom suite.

FRIAR'S BAY

Friar's Bay, 2km north of Marigot's center, is a pretty cove with a broad sandy beach. This popular local swimming spot is just beyond the residential neighborhood of St Louis, and the road leading in is signposted. There are a couple of beach huts selling burgers, beer and grilled chicken.

COLOMBIER

For St Martin's version of a country drive, take the road that leads 2km inland to the hamlet of Colombier. This short, pleasant side trip offers a glimpse of a rural lifestyle that has long disappeared elsewhere on the island. The scenery along the way is bucolic, with stone fences, big mango trees, an old coconut-palm plantation and hillside pastures with grazing cattle.

The road to Colombier begins 350m north of the turnoff to Friar's Bay.

PIC PARADIS (PARADISE PEAK)

The 424m Pic Paradis, the highest point on the island, offers fine vistas and good hiking opportunities. The peak is topped with a communications tower and is accessible by a rough maintenance road that doubles as a hiking trail. You can drive as far as the last house and then walk the final kilometer to the top.

The mountain gets more rain than the rest of the island, and the woods are thick with vine-covered trees and colorful forest birds. Ten minutes up, just before the tower, a sign to the left points the way to the best view point. Take this trail for about 75m, then veer to the right where the path branches and you'll come to a cliff with a broad view of the island's east side. You can see Orient Salt Pond and the expansive Etang aux Poissons

to the east, the village of Orleans at your feet and Philipsburg to the south.

For a good view of the west side of the island, go back to the main trail and walk up past the communications tower. From the rocks directly beyond you can see Marigot, Simpson Bay Lagoon and Baie Nettlé.

For those who want to do more serious hiking, a network of trails leads from the Pic Paradis area to Orient Bay, Orleans and the Dutch side of the island. Flash Media's St Martin map, available free at the tourist office, shows the trails.

The road to Pic Paradis is 500m north of the road to Colombier. Take the road inland for 2km, turn left at the fork (signed 'Sentier des Crêtes NE, Pic Paradis') and continue 500m farther to the last house, where there's space to pull over and park. Taxis charge an extra US$10 to take you right to the end of the road.

GRAND CASE

The small beachside town of Grand Case has been dubbed 'the gourmet capital of St Martin.' The beachfront road is lined with an appealing range of places to eat, from local lolos to top-notch French restaurants. Some of the places are open for lunch, but Grand Case is at its liveliest in the evening.

For a town that attracts its fair share of tourists, it still retains a nice local feel. While there are a few colorful buildings, dining is the premier attraction. Espérance Airport, which is bordered by salt ponds that attract waterbirds, is at the east side of town.

As for the beach, Grand Case's long curving strand is fine if you're staying there, but it's not a destination for day-trippers, who generally opt for less-developed north-side beaches.

Places to Stay

Air-conditioned *Hévéa* (☎ *87 56 85, fax 87 83 88),* at the restaurant of the same name, has half a dozen good-value colonial-style rooms. In summer, singles/doubles cost from US$34/45 for standard rooms, US$78/88 for units with kitchenettes. Winter rates are about 50% higher.

***Grand Case Beach Motel** (☎ 87 87 75, fax 87 26 55)* is an older hotel with a dated decor, but it's got a pleasant beachside location, and the seven large units have fans, air-con, kitchenettes and small seaside patios. Rates are US$55 in summer, US$80 in winter, plus a 10% service charge and an additional US$10 charge to use the air-con.

***Les Alizés Motel** (☎ 87 95 38, fax 29 31 71)* has seen better days, but its 10 small studios are right on the beach and each has cooking facilities and TVs. The cost is US$50 in summer, US$75 in winter for regular units, US$60 in summer, US$100 in winter for ocean views.

***Chez Martine** (☎ 87 51 59, fax 87 87 30, chezmartine@powerantilles.com)* has five air-conditioned rooms with private baths at the side of its restaurant. The rates, which include breakfast for two, are US$85 in summer, US$110 in winter.

***Hôtel** Atlantide (☎ 87 09 80, fax 87 12 36, atlantide@bigfoot.com)* is a modern beachside complex with 10 commodious apartments. The units are well equipped, each with a full kitchen, living room, a big oceanfront balcony that serves as a dining room, TV, phone, air-con, bathtub and marble floors. Rates begin at US$118 in summer, US$208 in winter for one-bedroom units, while the fanciest two-bedroom units top off at US$252 in summer, US$373 in winter. If they're not full you can often negotiate a discount of about 25%.

***Grand Case Beach Club** (☎ 87 51 87, fax 87 59 93, in the USA ☎ 800-447-7462, info@gcbc.com)*, on the quiet northeast end of the beach, has 73 pleasant condo-like units with air-con, full kitchen and balcony. Studios have two double beds and a small dining table, and the roomy one-bedroom units have a separate living room. Garden-view studios cost US$115 in summer, US$145 in autumn and US$240 in winter. The one-bedroom units are US$130 in summer, US$190 in spring and autumn, and US$295 in winter. There are also two-bedroom, two-bath units. Children aged 12 and under stay free in all rooms other than the studios. There's a restaurant, pool and

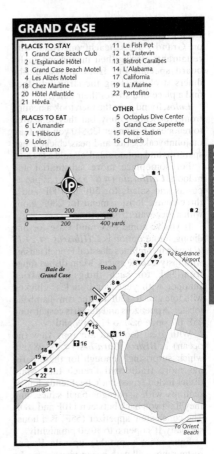

GRAND CASE

PLACES TO STAY	
1	Grand Case Beach Club
2	L'Esplanade Hôtel
3	Grand Case Beach Motel
4	Les Alizés Motel
18	Chez Martine
20	Hôtel Atlantide
21	Hévéa
11	Le Fish Pot
12	Le Tastevin
13	Bistrot Caraïbes
14	L'Alabama
17	California
19	La Marine
22	Portofino

PLACES TO EAT	
6	L'Amandier
7	L'Hibiscus
9	Lolos
10	Il Nettuno

OTHER	
5	Octoplus Dive Center
8	Grand Case Superette
15	Police Station
16	Church

tennis court, and rates include Continental breakfast.

***L'Esplanade Hôtel** (☎ 87 06 55, fax 87 29 15, info@esplanade-caraibes.com)* is a newer hillside hotel on the northeast edge of town. There are 24 studios and one-bedroom suites, each with a kitchen, ceiling fan, air-con, TV, phone and ocean-view terrace. The one-bedroom units, which have a king bed and a living room with a sofa bed, cost US$170/230 in summer for singles/doubles, US$280/360 in winter. Studios cost US$120/170 in summer, US$180/270 in winter.

Places to Eat

Each evening, a ritual of sorts takes place on Grand Case's beachfront road, with restaurants placing their menus and chalkboard specials out front and would-be diners strolling along the strip until they find a place that strikes their fancy.

Lolos, found near the pier, took a beating from Hurricane Lenny, but they've started to reappear. For under US$10 you can feast on johnnycakes, rice and peas, chicken legs, spareribs and potato salad, all sold à la carte.

For someplace more substantial and indoors, *California* (☎ 87 55 57) has pizzas, pastas and salads for 50F to 100F and a three-course lobster menu for 280F, along with a nice waterfront setting.

If you've come to Grand Case for fine dining, a fine option is *L'Hibiscus* (☎ 29 17 91), which combines classical French cuisine with tasty Creole spices. Main dishes range from 99F for such things as panfried snapper with yucca or boneless chicken with foie gras to 130F for the rum-flambéed lobster. Appetizers and desserts cost around 45F. It's open 6:30 to 11 pm nightly.

With great food but a crappy view (no ocean) is *Bistrot Caraïbes* (☎ 29 08 29), which, surprisingly enough for these parts, has more traditional French fare. Main dishes include roast duck, beef tenderloin or scallops with asparagus-basil sauce, and they'll set you back between 110F and 180F. The conch-stew appetizer (55F) is a house specialty. It's open 6 to 10:30 pm nightly.

Four other reputable upscale French restaurants – all with ocean views – are *La Marine* (☎ 87 02 31), *Chez Martine* (see Places to Stay), *Le Fish Pot* (☎ 87 50 88), *L'Amandier* (☎ 87 24 33) and *Le Tastevin* (☎ 87 55 45), the last three among only a handful of top-end places open daily for lunch as well as dinner.

Other restaurants worth a look are *Il Nettuno* (☎ 87 77 38), with an Italian/Creole slant; *Portofino* (☎ 29 08 28), good for reasonably priced pizza and Italian food, as well as live country & western music on Wednesdays; and *L'Alabama* (☎ 87 81 66), with moderately priced French/Continental fare.

ANSE MARCEL

Secluded Anse Marcel is a deeply indented bay with calm protected waters and a long, sandy beach that's backed by French St Martin's largest resort hotel.

Anse Marcel has a very plush marina that looks like a small playground for the rich and famous. It's home base to a couple of yacht charter companies, including Stardust and Nautor's Swan Charters. The marina itself has a few fashionable boutiques, a small convenience store that sells liquor and foreign newspapers, a dive shop, a laundry, Hertz and Sanaco car rentals, and a store that sells charts and basic yachting supplies. The port office will hold mail for boaters.

Places to Stay

Beachfront *Le Méridien* (☎ 87 67 00, fax 87 30 38, in the USA and Canada ☎ 800-543-4300, resasxm@powerantilles.com) is an impressive 400-room hotel with full resort amenities, including two pools, tennis and squash courts, a fitness center, snorkeling gear and standard 1st-class rooms. Rates are pretty steep, beginning at US$200 in summer, US$340 in winter (US$540 over the Christmas period).

Nearby *Hôtel* Privilège (☎ 87 37 37, fax 87 33 75, hotel.privilege@wanadoo.fr) has friendly management and 16 roomy units located above the marina shops. Each has a pleasant wood interior, TV, bathtub, queen or king bed, air-con and a large balcony with a hammock. There's no pool, but guests can use the beach fronting Le Méridien. Studios cost US$110/145 for singles/doubles in summer and US$320 in winter regardless of occupancy. Suites, which have a sofa bed in the living room, cost US$195 for two in summer and US$365 in winter. A two-bedroom suite with a kitchenette costs US$210/305 for two/four people in summer, US$385/510 in winter. From mid-June to mid-August and November to mid-December, rates are around US$60 more than the above summer rates.

Places to Eat

There are four fairly expensive restaurants in Le Méridien, but the best affordable place to eat in Anse Marcel is harborside *La Louisiane*, which is open 7 am to about 10 pm daily. In addition to reasonably priced sandwiches, there are salads, omelets and pasta dishes from about 60F and meat and fish dishes around 70F to 90F.

FRENCH CUL-DE-SAC

French Cul-de-Sac is a small but spread-out seaside community just north of Orient Bay. While there's no beach of note, local fishers run boats back and forth all day to the white sands of nearby Îlet Pinel.

Îlet Pinel

The most visited of the area's offshore islands, Pinel is just a kilometer from French Cul-de-Sac. Totally undeveloped, it's the domain of day-trippers, who are deposited on the islet's calm west-facing beach, where there's good swimming, a water-sports hut (snorkel gear US$10) and a couple of lolos (barbecued chicken meals around US$10).

The island is under the auspices of the national forest system, and two-minutes' walk south of the swimming beach is a little roped-off area set aside for snorkelers. For the best coral and fish, head for the single white buoy in the center.

It's easy to get to Pinel – simply go to the dock at the road's end in French Cul-de-Sac, where you can catch a small boat. The five-minute ride costs US$5 roundtrip. Boats also go to Pinel from Orient Beach.

Places to Stay

All of the following, except for Sunrise, which is in the village, are on the south side of French Cul-de-Sac and within walking distance of Orient Beach.

Jardins de Chevrise (☎ 87 31 10, fax 87 37 66) is not the newest or spiffiest of places, but the price is fair and it's about a 10-minute walk to the beach. This two-story complex, which is partly residential, has 29 apartment units and a pool. Rates start at US$95 in summer, US$135 in winter.

Sunrise Hotel (☎ 29 57 00, fax 87 39 28, sunrisesxm@wanadoo.fr) is a cozy 20-room hotel managed by a friendly young French couple. The rooms are modern and com-

fortable, each with fully equipped kitchen, air-con, TV, phone, room safe and private terrace. There's a small pool, an ice machine, a collection of French and English books and a storage room where you can leave gear between stays. The rates begin at US$74 in summer, US$110 in winter. Children under 12 stay free, and the owners throw in a free trip to Îlet Pinel.

Orient Bay Hotel (☎ 87 31 10, fax 87 37 66, in the USA ☎ 800-818-5992, orientbay@ powerantilles.com) is a pleasant 31-unit place with a tropical decor in a quiet location just outside the Blue Bay Mont Vernon. Units each have a kitchen, living room, air-con, phone and at least one terrace or balcony. Rates are US$115 in summer, US$160 in winter for two people in one-bedroom units, US$155 in summer, US$205 in winter for up to four people in two-bedroom units. There's a pool.

Blue Bay Mont Vernon (☎ 87 62 00, fax 87 37 27, sto@bluebayresorts.com) is a rambling hotel perched on a rise overlooking the northernmost end of Orient Bay. Catering to package tours, it has standard resort rooms, each with a balcony. All-inclusive singles/doubles begin at US$170/280 in summer, US$215/370 in winter (service charge included). You can usually get significantly cheaper rates if you book the hotel as part of a package tour. There's a large pool, tennis courts, a water-sports center and a couple of restaurants.

Places to Eat

The following places are on the village's main road.

For a cheap bite to eat, head to *Le Jocker*, where the road forks to Anse Marcel and the bay. Sandwiches and burgers range from 16F to 27F.

Excellent music and food in a chilled-out atmosphere are the attractions of *Les 13 Travaux* (☎ 87 43 32). Good-value meat dishes, such as ribs, range from 45F to 85F, and a variety of seafood main courses like red snapper and mahimahi start at 45F.

Le Piccolo Café (☎ 87 32 47) is an unpretentious place serving gourmet-quality food at café prices. This brightly painted

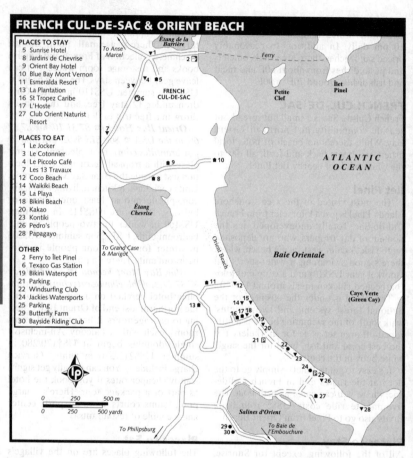

FRENCH CUL-DE-SAC & ORIENT BEACH

PLACES TO STAY
5 Sunrise Hotel
8 Jardins de Chevrise
9 Orient Bay Hotel
10 Blue Bay Mont Vernon
11 Esmeralda Resort
13 La Plantation
16 St Tropez Caribe
17 L'Hoste
27 Club Orient Naturist Resort

PLACES TO EAT
1 Le Jocker
3 Le Cotonnier
4 Le Piccolo Café
7 Les 13 Travaux
12 Coco Beach
14 Waikiki Beach
15 La Playa
18 Bikini Beach
20 Kakao
23 Kontiki
26 Pedro's
28 Papagayo

OTHER
2 Ferry to Îlet Pinel
6 Texaco Gas Station
19 Bikini Watersport
21 Parking
22 Windsurfing Club
24 Jackies Watersports
25 Parking
29 Butterfly Farm
30 Bayside Riding Club

little eatery is so popular that reservations are usually necessary. Piccolo is run by a classically trained French chef with a penchant for Creole spices. Instead of the clichéd red-snapper-with-lemon-butter, the snapper preparation here is enlivened with peanuts, cream and a little hot pepper. Most dishes cost just 55F to 80F. It's open 6:30 to 10:30 pm nightly except Tuesday.

Also good, but pricier, is the nearby *Le Cotonnier* (☎ 87 44 56), where fish and meat main courses, including atypical options such as king prawns and roast lamb, range

from 85F to 125F. It's open for dinner nightly except Sunday in summer.

ORIENT BEACH

Orient Beach is a splendid, gently curving sweep of white sand and bright turquoise waters. Clothing is optional along the entire 2km beach, although nudity is de rigueur only at the southern end, where there's a naturist resort, Club Orient. A decade ago the club was the only development in the area. In recent years a handful of villa-type places have been built near the center of the stretch, but fortunately none is right on the beach and all are relatively small-scale.

The bay is an underwater nature reserve, and the waters are usually calm and good for swimming. The bay is also an active spot for water sports, including windsurfing, Hobie Cat sailing and Jet-skiing. The latter in particular warrants caution, as amateur Jet-skiers zip through the same waters swimmers use.

The easiest public beach access is adjacent to Pedro's beachside bar. Here you'll find a touristy scene with lines of lounge chairs and beached Jet-skis, and vendors selling T-shirts and batik pareus. During the height of the day this strip can take on a certain carnival atmosphere, attracting a few voyeurs with cameras, but for the most part it's just a mixed bag of people enjoying the beach.

If you're into nude sunbathing, walk south to the Club Orient beach, where there are like-minded souls. If you just want to avoid the crowds that pack the center of Orient Beach, especially on weekends, head for the quiet north end of Orient Bay.

Information

There are numerous water-sports centers along Orient Beach, with the largest concentration at the north side of Club Orient. Jackie's Watersports, next to Pedro's, rents snorkel sets for US$10 a day and beach chairs or umbrellas for US$5, and makes speedboat runs to Green Cay (US$10 per person roundtrip) and Îlet Pinel (US$15).

Other water-sports centers front each of the beachside restaurants. Papagayo Watersports, Bikini Watersport and Kontiki Watersports all rent snorkel sets and provide boat taxis to the offshore islands for the same price as Jackie's.

Behind Pedro's are showers (US$1) and restrooms (US$0.50). Taxis can usually be found nearby, charging around US$20 (per taxi) to either Marigot or Philipsburg.

Caye Verte (Green Cay)

Green Cay is a small islet 500m off Orient Beach with a nice sandy spit at its southern end and reasonably good snorkeling in the surrounding waters. The water-sports centers

can shuttle you over by speedboat and pick you up at a prearranged time. There's no shade or facilities, so consider bringing along a beach umbrella and something to drink.

Don't try to grab shade or rain cover from the trees at the rocky end of the beach, as they're poisonous manchineel trees. The rocks are a habitat for numerous small *Anolis* lizards; the males put on an interesting show, puffing up orange sacs under their necks as a territorial warning.

Butterfly Farm

You can walk amid 45 varieties of colorful butterflies imported mainly from the rain forests of Brazil and Indonesia at the Butterfly Farm, on the road south of Orient Beach. Admission includes an informative guided tour with a close-up view of butterflies in all stages, from foraging caterpillars and emerging pupae to adults on the wing. Although tickets may seem a bit steep at US$10 (US$5 for children), they allow multiple entries for the length of your vacation. It's open 9 am to 4:30 pm daily.

Places to Stay

One good-value option in the area is *La Plantation* (☎ 29 58 00, fax 29 58 08, hotel@la-plantation.com). It features 17 villas of plantation-house design, each with a one-bedroom suite and two studios. All units are large and pleasant, with high-pitched ceilings, air-con, ceiling fans, TV, room safes, kitchens and private verandas facing the ocean. In summer, studios cost US$109/133 for singles/doubles. Suites, which have a separate living room, cost US$184 for doubles; add US$13 for each additional person. Winter rates are a bit complicated, varying by the month, with a studio for two people, for example, costing US$115 in January and March and US$127 in February. Rates include a breakfast of fruit, yogurt and bread. There's a restaurant and pool; it's about a five-minute walk to the beach.

St Tropez Caribe (☎ 87 42 01, fax 87 41 69, in the USA ☎ 800-622-7836, info@sttropez-caraibes.com) is an 84-unit complex just inland from the beach. The rooms are in Mediterranean-style three-story buildings and have a sitting area, terrace or balcony, central air-con, TV, small refrigerator, room safe and phone. All have either a king bed or two twins. Rates are US$90 to US$130 in summer, US$113 to US$160 in winter, with the lower rates for ground-floor rooms. Add around US$8 to the winter rates for the period over Christmas.

A bit closer to the beach – and therefore more expensive – is *L'Hoste* (☎ 87 42 08, fax 87 39 96, in the USA ☎ 800-843-4779, contact@hostehotel.com) with 28 units identical to those in the adjacent St Tropez Caribe. Rates are US$165 to US$215 in summer, US$215 to US$265 in winter (US$265 to US$340 during the Christmas break).

Club Orient Naturist Resort (☎ 87 33 85, fax 87 33 76, clubo@cluborient.com) is the Eastern Caribbean's only clothing-optional resort. All activities, including dining, water sports, tennis and sailing cruises, are au naturel. The accommodations, which were leveled by Hurricane Luis, have been completely rebuilt. The 136 units are generally red-pine chalets with a queen bed, sofa, desk and chair, air-con, bathroom, kitchen and an outdoor dining area with a picnic table. Studios, which are in duplex chalets, start at US$135 in summer, US$205 in winter for doubles. One-bedroom units occupy a whole chalet and cost from US$180 in summer, US$305 in winter. Single rates are between US$20 and US$40 cheaper.

The upscale *Esmeralda Resort* (☎ 87 36 36, fax 87 35 18, esmeral@wanadoo.fr) has 65 rooms and suites in 18 villa-style buildings. Rooms have cooking facilities, TV, phones, air-con, ceiling fans and room safes and start at US$200 in summer, US$300 in winter. Suites, which have a separate living room and kitchen area, start at US$320 in summer, US$550 in winter. Christmastime adds another 40% to 50% onto winter prices. Each villa has its own pool.

Places to Eat

Near the parking lot at the southern end of the beach you'll find a couple of stalls selling cheap hot dogs and burgers, as well as *Pedro's*, a popular beachside bar with barbecued chicken for US$9 and fish for

US$12, open 9 am to 5 pm daily. There are a handful of other beach bars nearby offering a similar menu.

In addition, there are five simple open-air restaurants spread along the center of the beach that are primarily lunch spots, although a couple of them stay open late enough for an early dinner. You can get a meal at any of them for US$10 to US$25. From south to north they are *Kontiki*, which specializes in seafood; *Kakao*, with pizza and pastas; *Bikini Beach*, with a tapas-style menu; *Waikiki Beach*, which has a tank full of lobsters; and *Coco Beach*, with French and Creole dishes.

At the southern end of the beach is *Papagayo*, the restaurant at Club Orient. It offers omelets, salads, sandwiches and burgers from US$10 and fish and meat dishes for around US$25. It's open daily for breakfast, lunch and dinner.

The beachside bar *La Playa* is popular mingling spot and good for liming.

Farther south on Baie de l'Embouchure, *Tropical Wave*, which rents out windsurfing gear, has filling sandwiches and burgers for around US$6.

OYSTER POND

The Dutch-French border slices straight across Oyster Pond, a largely rural area with a number of small condominiums and other vacation rentals. A marina and most of the accommodations fall on the French side, while the area's finest beach, Dawn Beach, is on the Dutch side (see the end of this chapter).

Oyster Pond is not a pond, but rather a protected bay whose shape resembles an oyster. For a good vantage of Oyster Pond, take the short path leading up the cactus-studded hill on the northeast side of the bay.

Captain Oliver's Marina has 100 slips, the standard marina services, a couple of places to eat, scuba gear rentals and a few shops and offices, including those of The Moorings and Sun Yacht Charters companies.

Places to Stay

A few minutes' walk from the marina is *Columbus Hotel* (☎ 87 42 52, fax 87 39 85, colombus@wanadoo.fr), a newer-style complex with condo-type units. Each has a separate bedroom, TV, phone, kitchenette and a terrace or balcony. Summer rates begin at US$68/108 for singles/doubles, while in winter rates are US$100/157, Continental breakfast included.

Captain Oliver's (☎ 87 40 26, fax 87 40 84, captoli@wanadoo.fr), at the marina, has 42 standard hotel rooms with air-con, kitchenettes, phones, TV, room safes and balconies. There's a pool. Singles/doubles with marina views start at US$90/120 in summer, US$130/175 in winter, buffet breakfast included. Ocean-view rooms cost another US$30.

The nearby *Blue Beach Hotel* (☎ 87 33 44, fax 87 42 13) has 42 small, modern rooms with kitchenettes, air-con, phones, TV and terraces. Some rooms have ocean views at no extra charge. In summer, singles/doubles cost US$150/170 and are US$200/220 in winter. There's a pool and restaurant.

Places to Eat

The *Dinghy Dock Bar*, a snack bar with picnic tables on the marina dock, serves up sandwiches, chili dogs and full meals from US$5 and has Foster's on tap for some strange reason. Happy hour is 5 to 7 pm. Next door is a small convenience store with groceries, alcohol and sundries.

Captain Oliver's, an open-air restaurant at the marina dock, has a daily US$10 breakfast buffet, burgers with fries for about the same price, and seafood and meat dishes at lunch for US$13 to US$15, about double that for dinner. Saturday night is lobster-buffet night, with all you can eat for US$33. It's open 7 to 10 am and noon to 10 pm daily.

Dutch Sint Maarten

PHILIPSBURG

Philipsburg, Dutch Sint Maarten's main town, is centered on a long, narrow stretch of land that separates Great Salt Pond from Great Bay. There are some older buildings mixed among the new, but overall the town is far more commercial than quaint. Most of the action is along Frontstreet, the bayfront road, which is lined with boutiques, jewelry shops, restaurants, casinos and duty-free shops selling everything from Danish porcelain to Japanese cameras and electronics.

Wathey Square, the town center of sorts, has a tourist information booth, a wharf where cruise-ship tenders dock and an old courthouse that dates from 1793. On cruise-ship days, vendors on the square sell drinking coconuts and souvenirs; more street vendors, selling T-shirts and wood carvings, can be found at the north side of the courthouse. Cruise-ship tenders also dock at Bobby's Marina, at the eastern end of town, and many vendors set up shop around the museum and along Frontstreet to catch the day-trippers.

Great Bay Beach borders the entire town of Philipsburg, but the buildings lining Frontstreet face inland and it's easy to walk along the street without noticing the beach at all. Although Great Bay is not one of Sint Maarten's more pristine beaches, the water is calm and some people do opt to swim there.

Orientation

Four streets run east to west, and numerous narrow lanes (called *steegjes*) connect them north to south. Frontstreet has one-way traffic that moves in an easterly direction, and Backstreet has one-way traffic heading west. Public buses can be picked up along Backstreet. The north side of Philipsburg is sometimes referred to as Pondfill, as much of this area is reclaimed land.

Information

Tourist Offices The tourist office, at the east end of town in the Vineyard Park Complex on WG Buncamper Rd, is open 8 am to 5 pm weekdays.

Money There are a number of banks around Philipsburg, including Barclays Bank, Frontstreet 19, open 8:30 am to 3 pm weekdays, and Windward Islands Bank, on CA Cannegiefer St, open 8:30 am to

ST MARTIN / SINT MAARTEN

PHILIPSBURG

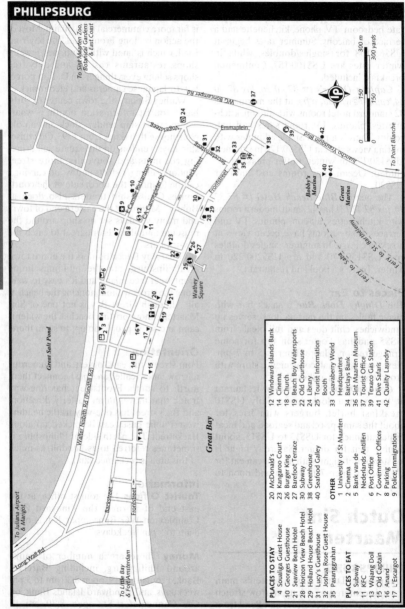

To Sint Maarten Zoo,
Botanical Gardens
& East Coast

To Juliana Airport
& Marigot

To Little Bay
& Fort Amsterdam

To Point Blanche

Ferry to St Barthélemy

Ferry to Saba

Great Salt Pond

Great Bay

Bobby's
Marina

Great
Marina

WC Boncamper Rd

Walter Nisbeth Rd (Pondfill Rd)

Emmaplein

Juancho Yrausquin Blvd

Walthey
Square

0   150   300 m
0   150   300 yards

PLACES TO STAY
4 Soualiga Guest House
10 Georges Guesthouse
21 Seaview Beach Hotel
28 Horizon View Beach Hotel
29 Holland House Beach Hotel
31 Lucy's Guesthouse
32 Joshua Rose Guest House
35 Pasanggrahan

PLACES TO EAT
3 Subway
11 KFC
13 Wajang Doll
15 Old Captain
16 Anand
17 L'Escargot

20 McDonald's
23 Kangaroo Court
26 Burger King
27 Barefoot Terrace
30 Subway
38 Greenhouse
40 Seafood Galley

OTHER
1 University of St Maarten
2 Cinema
5 Bank van de
   Nederlands Antillen
6 Post Office
7 Government Offices
8 Parking
9 Police; Immigration

12 Windward Islands Bank
14 Cinema
18 Church
19 Beach Boy Watersports
22 Old Courthouse
24 Library
25 Tourist Information
   Booth
33 Guavaberry World
   Headquarters
34 Barclays Bank
36 Sint Maarten Museum
37 Tourist Office
39 Texaco Gas Station
41 Dive Safaris
42 Quality Laundry

3:30 pm weekdays. Both have 24-hour ATMs that accept Cirrus, Plus, MasterCard and Visa, but the Barclays ATM dishes out only US dollars.

Post The post office, at the west end of E Camille Richardson St, is open 7:30 am to 5 pm Monday to Thursday, till 4:30 pm Friday.

Libraries The public library, on Vogesssteeg, carries the *New York Times,* has a good collection of English-language Caribbean books and provides Internet access for US$4 per half-hour. It's open 10 am to 1 pm Saturday, 9 am to 12:30 pm Tuesday, Wednesday and Friday, and also 4 to at least 6:30 pm weekdays.

Laundry Quality Laundry, opposite Bobby's Marina, has coin-operated machines costing US$4 per wash. It's open 7:30 am to 6 pm Monday to Saturday.

Sint Maarten Museum
This little but growing museum, in an alley at Frontstreet 7, has displays on island history, including Arawak pottery shards, plantation-era artifacts, period photos and a few items from HMS *Proselyte,* the frigate that sank off Fort Amsterdam in 1801. If you're interested in hurricanes and the damage they can cause, there's a good exhibit on the havoc wreaked by Hurricane Luis and the more recent Hurricane Lenny. The little shop downstairs sells an assortment of Caribbean arts and crafts. It's open 10 am to 4 pm weekdays, 10 am to 2 pm Saturday. Admission is US$1.

Fort Amsterdam
In 1631 the Dutch built their first Caribbean fort, Fort Amsterdam, on the peninsula separating Great Bay and Little Bay. It didn't withstand an invasion by the Spanish, who captured the fort two years later, expanding it and adding a small church.

Despite its historic significance, the fort site is neglected, with little remaining other than crumbling walls and a few rusting cannons. It does, however, offer a reasonably nice view across the bay to Philipsburg.

To get there, drive to Little Bay and park near the Little Bay Beach Resort tennis courts. The fort is a 10-minute walk up the hill to the south.

Sint Maarten Zoo & Botanical Garden
This very small zoo, with some 35 reptile, bird and mammal species, is located beneath the hillside TV satellite dishes on Arch Rd, on the north side of Great Salt Pond. Admission is US$5 (US$2 for kids). It's open 10 am to 6 pm daily.

Marina Area
Great Bay Marina and adjoining Bobby's Marina, on the southeast side of Philipsburg, have a couple of restaurants, a small grocery store, car rental agencies, a dive shop, and several stores with marine supplies. For information on crews wanted, boats for sale etc, check the bulletin board next to the Island Water World marine store (which also sells charts).

Boats going to St Barts leave from Great Bay Marina, and boats to Saba from Bobby's Marina.

Places to Stay
Philipsburg's best budget option is *Soualiga Guest House* (☎ 542-0077, Walter Nisbeth Rd 29A), which has 11 clean rooms with cable TV, air-con, refrigerators, and private baths. Singles/doubles cost US$40/50 in summer, US$50/60 in winter, but it gets cheaper the longer you stay. Suites are also available for US$65 in summer, US$75 in winter. As it's on a busy road, ask for a room as far back as possible if you're sensitive to traffic noise.

George's Guesthouse (☎ 542-2126), on E Camilie Richardson St, is a cheaper option but the rooms are more basic and there's no TV. Singles/doubles/triples are US$40/60/75. They have another *guest house* (☎ /fax 544-5363) on Union Rd in Cole Bay.

Lucy's Guesthouse (☎ 542-2995, Backstreet 10) is quite rudimentary, with small, bare rooms, and overpriced at US$48/58 for singles/doubles in summer, US$53/63 in winter.

ST MARTIN / SINT MAARTEN

Joshua Rose Guest House *(☎ 542-4317, fax 543-0080, in the USA ☎ 800-223-9815, joshrose@sintmaarten.net, Backstreet 7)* has 14 straightforward rooms with private baths, air-con, phones, TV and mini-refrigerators. Standard rooms, which have one double and one twin bed, cost US$50/60 for singles/doubles in summer, US$70/80 in winter. A third person is an additional US$15.

A step up is the family-run ***Seaview Beach Hotel*** *(☎ 542-2323, fax 542-4356, in the USA ☎ 800-223-9815, PO Box 965),* a two-story hotel on the beach above a casino. Most rooms are on the small side, but they're adequate and have air-con, TV and private baths. Singles/doubles start at US$58/69 in summer, US$78/122 in winter. Refrigerators are an extra US$5.

The recently renovated ***Pasanggrahan*** *(☎ 542-3588, fax 542-2885, in the USA ☎ 800-223-9815, tini@megatropic.com, PO Box 151)* is a 28-room beachfront inn on Frontstreet. The restaurant and lobby are in a former governor's residence, but most rooms are in less distinguished side buildings. The standard rooms, which cost US$78 in summer, US$128 in winter, are simple and small, with a shared seaside balcony. The deluxe rooms are larger and fancier, with private balconies; they cost US$100 in summer, US$168 in winter. All rooms have ceiling fans, air-con and private baths.

Holland House Beach Hotel *(☎ 542-2572, fax 542-4673, in the USA ☎ 800-223-9815, hollandhousehotel@megatropic.com, PO Box 393)* has a central beachfront location in the heart of Philipsburg and 54 spacious rooms. Overall, they're Philipsburg's nicest, featuring hardwood floors, balconies, cable TV, phones, air-con and in most cases a kitchenette. Singles/doubles begin at US$84/99 in summer, US$140/155 in winter.

Just down FrontStreet is ***Horizon View Beach Hotel*** *(☎ 543-2120, fax 542-0705, horizon@sintmaarten.net, PO Box 1054),* a condo complex with 30 units. Studios, some with balcony, have a double bed and kitchenette for US$90 in summer, US$123 in winter. The beachfront suites each have a separate bedroom, kitchen and large living room with plate-glass windows that provide

a fine bay view and start at US$139 in summer, US$185 in winter. All units have air-con, cable TV and phones.

Places to Eat

Budget With an attractive view, ***Barefoot Terrace***, right on the waterfront at Wathey Square, has alfresco dining with breakfast omelets and lunchtime sandwiches or burgers costing around US$6, Creole specials from US$6 to US$10 and a full menu of local dishes, like goat stew, at reasonable prices. The restaurant is open 7:30 am to 6:30 pm daily.

Follow the kangaroo murals to ***Kangaroo Court***, at the east side of the courthouse, a pleasant deli cafe with courtyard dining and a distinctive Australian slant. The emphasis is on light, healthy food, and in addition to fresh-brewed espresso and cappuccino, there's homemade zucchini bread and carrot cake, fresh-fruit plates, US$7 sandwiches and various pastas and salads from US$8. It's open 7 am to 7 pm Monday to Saturday.

For a diet change, try ***Anand*** *(Hotelsteeg 5),* a popular little place serving good, cheap East Indian fare. A range of vegetable and chicken dishes cost around US$6, goat and beef dishes a tad more. It's open 11:30 am to 3 pm Monday to Saturday and 6 to 10 pm nightly.

Chain fast-food eateries include ***Burger King***, at Wathey Square, ***McDonald's***, on Frontstreet, ***KFC***, on CA Cannegieter St and ***Subway***, on Walter Nisbeth Rd and Frontstreet.

Mid-Range & Top End The ***Greenhouse*** *(☎ 542-2941),* at the north end of the marina, is a lively spot that pulls in the punters during its happy hour from 4:30 to 7 pm, which has two-for-one drinks and half-price snacks. It's open for food 11 am to 10 pm daily. At lunch there are burgers and sandwiches for around US$9, barbecued ribs or chicken for twice that. At dinner, meat and seafood dishes cost US$13 to US$24.

Seafood Galley *(☎ 542-3253),* at Bobby's Marina, has nautical decor and a raw bar with oysters and clams on the half-shell. From 11:30 am to 3 pm, you can get a

Spanish omelet, fish burger or teriyaki chicken sandwich with fries for around US$8, salads and seafood dishes for a few dollars more. Dinner, from 5:30 to 10 pm, ranges from local catch of the day for US$17 to lobster at market prices. While you're there, take a look at the giant mullet that swarm below the pier.

Pasanggrahan, at the Frontstreet inn of the same name, is an atmospheric place with a quiet garden courtyard. Pancakes (US$6) are a nice option for breakfast, and from noon to 3 pm there's a range of lunch specials, including pasta and salads, for around US$9. Dinners are priced from US$17. Happy hour, from 5 to 7 pm, has two drinks for the price of one.

L'Escargot (☎ 542-2483), a French restaurant in a colorful 19th-century house, has light lunches such as seafood crêpes or quiche with salad for around US$8.50. Dinner features various escargot appetizers for under US$10 and main courses, such as crisp duck in pineapple-and-banana sauce, for around US$23.

Wajang Doll (☎ 542-2687, Frontstreet 237) is well known for its rijsttafel, a traditional Indonesian buffet. It costs US$20 for 14 dishes, US$26 for 19 dishes. It's open 6:45 to 10 pm Monday to Saturday.

Recommended *Old Captain* (☎ 542-6988) serves excellent Indonesian, Japanese and Chinese cuisine in a beachfront setting. Most dishes range from US$8 to US$20, with main dishes such as Peking duck a little more, at US$30. There's a good vegetarian menu as well.

Entertainment

The *Greenhouse* is a popular drinking hole, due mainly to its happy hour, from 4:30 pm to 7 pm. *Holland House*, in the hotel of the same name, is 'the bomb' or 'swinging' on Friday night and the place to be seen. Most people dress up for the occasion, and the dance floor jumps till the wee hours of the morning.

SIMPSON BAY

The Simpson Bay area is a narrow strip of land separating Simpson Bay from Simpson Bay Lagoon. A channel between the two bodies of water is spanned by a drawbridge that is raised three times a day to allow boats to pass.

West of the drawbridge is a sandy beach with some moderately priced guest houses, but it's an odd destination, as the airport runway stretches the entire length, just a few hundred meters away. Despite the proximity to the airport, staying in this area is not a convenient way to avoid taxi fares or car rentals, as you'd have to walk clear around the runway to get to the guest houses, a good 20-minute haul along a busy road. On the other hand, airport noise shouldn't disturb early risers, as there are no scheduled flights between 9 pm and 7 am.

East of the drawbridge is quite a lively spot, with a couple of marinas, a clutter of bars and restaurants, and a few complexes with casinos and condos.

Places to Stay

The first three places can be reached by turning south on Houtman Rd at the east end of the airport runway. Just 100m down Houtman Rd is *Calypso Guest House* (☎ 545-4233, fax 545-2881), the cheapest and closest place to the airport. Rooms, which are on the 2nd floor above a Mexican restaurant, are not fancy, but they're large and have a kitchenette, table and chairs, aircon and TV. Summer rates for singles/doubles begin at US$58/69, winter rates at US$69/92. It's a few minutes' walk to the beach.

About 700m beyond is beachfront *Mary's Boon* (☎ 545-4235, fax 545-3403, info@marysboon.com, PO Box 2078), which has 16 large, spiffy studios with kitchenettes and balconies. The studios also have four-poster king beds, cable TV and air-con. Rates are from US$90 in summer, US$125 in spring and autumn and US$175 in winter.

If you like the color pink you'll love *La Chatelaine* (☎ 545-4269, fax 545-3195, PO Box 2065). It's a modern pink complex just before Mary's Boon with a pool, a beachside location and 17 units with kitchenettes and patios. Rates begin at US$85 in summer, US$120 in winter for studios; US$116 in summer, US$166 in winter for one-bedroom apartments; and US$173 in summer, US$243 in winter for two-bedroom apartments.

On a beach at the east side of Simpson Bay is the *Pelican Resort Club* (☎ 544-2503, fax 544-2133, in the USA ☎ 800-550-7088, info@pelicanresort.com, PO Box 431). This time-share complex has rooms ranging from studios to two-bedroom suites, all with kitchenettes, queen or king beds and the standard amenities. Studios cost US$110 in summer, US$160 in winter, while one-bedroom units begin at US$150 in summer, US$220 in winter. There are pools, tennis courts, water sports, restaurants and a shopping arcade.

Places to Eat
A number of eateries line the airport road. A good place for a cheap bite is *Bagel Factory*, next to Burger King, which has good New York-style bagels and makes its own frozen yogurt.

Don Carlos, a moderately priced Mexican restaurant beneath Calypso Guest House, has tostadas or an enchilada with rice and beans for US$13 and standard breakfast fare for US$6 to US$9. There's live music 7 to 10 pm Tuesday night and happy hour 4 to 7 pm daily.

Boulevard, a 24-hour North American-style diner at the east end of Simpson Bay, is right on a busy road but the atmosphere is lively and the food is good. Creole dishes like mahimahi (US$14.75) are mixed in with a mainly Italian menu of pizzas (US$6 to US$9) and main dishes ranging from US$10 to US$22. Burgers are also available, for around US$8.

Indiana Beach Bar & Restaurant (544-2797), next to Lightning Casino on the east side of Simpson Bay, looks like something out of an Indiana Jones movie. The food is standard fare, with burgers from US$6 and salads and sandwiches from US$8. Happy hour is 5 to 7 pm, and Wednesday night is all-you-can-eat barbecue. The big night, though, is Thursday, where Indiana transforms itself into party central. The place is packed with revelers taking advantage of a DJ spinning tunes, but more importantly, two-for-one drinks all night.

Directly opposite the airport terminal is a *Stop & Shop* grocery store with a deli inside and a lagoon-view café out back. You can get salads, a cheeseburger or a boneless chicken roti for US$5 to US$7 and breakfast standards for about half that price. It's open 7:30 am to 8:30 pm daily.

MAHO BAY & MULLET BAY
Maho and Mullet Bays are adjacent resort areas along the southwest shore. Driving into the Maho Bay area is a bit like suddenly finding yourself on the central strip in Las Vegas. While little more than a block long, it's dense with multistory buildings housing exclusive jewelers, boutiques, art galleries, restaurants and a huge resort and casino. Parking streetside is nearly impossible; it's best to pull into the Maho Beach complex, where there's inexpensive indoor parking.

Maho Bay has a nice enough beach – except that it's at the very end of the runway, literally. The area is even marked with a sign warning beachgoers that 'low flying and departing aircraft blast can cause physical injury'!

Mullet Bay, dominated by a single resort that seems constantly under construction (due to hurricane damage or simply expansion) has an operational golf course that fronts a fine white-sand beach. Although access to the north end of the beach is restricted by the resort, there's public parking at the south side of the golf course.

The island's main south-coast road runs straight across the golf course, and consequently some killer speed bumps have been installed that are apt to bottom out many low-slung cars.

Places to Stay
The *Maho Beach Hotel* (☎ 545-2115, fax 545-3180, in the USA ☎ 800-223-0757, seasun@worldnet.att.net) was hit hard by Hurricane Lenny in 1999 and is still undergoing some repair work. It has 600 air-conditioned rooms with private balconies, and once it's open again, rates will start at US$165/175 for singles/doubles in summer, US$225/245 in winter. One hotel wing faces Maho Beach, while another fronts Maho

Bay's commercial strip. The hotel has pools, tennis courts and a casino.

Places to Eat

One of the island's liveliest eat-and-meet spots, **Cheri's Cafe** is a large open-air restaurant and bar beside the Casino Royale in Mullet Bay. The varied menu includes salads, sandwiches and burgers around US$7, grilled seafood dishes for about double that, and kids' dishes for US$5. It's open 11 am to midnight Wednesday to Monday, with live music beginning at 8 pm. Credit cards are not accepted. The **West Indies Yogurt Co**, next to Cheri's, has Häagen-Dazs ice cream and Colombo frozen yogurt.

Trattoria Pizzeria, a small, unpretentious eatery in the alley behind Cheri's, has pasta and pizzas for US$9 to US$15 as well as cheaper sandwiches. Also in this area is **Fountain of Health Natural Foods**, which has packaged natural-food items, dried fruits and vitamins.

Sunset Beach Bar has a perfect spot for viewing the big 747s coming in to land. Squeezed between the end of the runway and the beach at Maho Bay, it lets you sip your beer and get as close to the big birds as you will almost anywhere else in the world. There are burgers and sandwiches on offer, and live entertainment 6:30 to 9:30 pm Wednesday, Friday and Sunday.

CUPECOY BAY

If you're looking for a beach that's quiet but not totally secluded, Cupecoy is a good choice. This pleasant white-sand beach is backed by low sandstone cliffs which are eroded in such a way that they provide a run of small semiprivate coves. There's beach parking down an unmarked drive at the north side of the Ocean Club in Cupecoy.

DAWN BEACH

Dawn Beach, on the east coast near the French-Dutch border, is a lovely white-sand beach with clear turquoise waters. Swimming and snorkeling are good when the seas are calm. Although it's a bit silted, snorkelers can expect to find waving sea fans, soft corals and small tropical fish.

To get to Dawn Beach from French St Martin, follow the road around the south side of Oyster Pond (see that section, earlier). There's parking, a shower and snorkel-gear rentals near Mr Busby's, at the north end of the beach.

Places to Eat

A likable open-air eatery right on the beach, **Mr Busby's** has salads, sandwiches and burgers from US$6 and good grilled-fish plates for US$15 upward. It's open 10 am to 11 pm daily. There's a happy hour with half-price drinks 4 to 6 pm weekdays.

St Vincent & the Grenadines

St Vincent & the Grenadines (often abbreviated to SVG) is a multiisland nation well known to wintering yachters but off the beaten path for most other visitors. With no airstrips capable of landing jet aircraft, travelers must enter St Vincent & the Grenadines by propeller plane from elsewhere in the Caribbean. For this reason, the islands get relatively few international tourists.

St Vincent, the northernmost island, is the nation's commercial and political center, accounting for 90% of both the land area and population. The island is lush and green, with deep valleys cultivated with bananas, coconuts and arrowroot, and a mountainous interior that peaks at spectacular 4048-foot La Soufrière, an active volcano.

The island of St Vincent has no major resort hotels, and its beaches are plain and somewhat generic compared to those of the Grenadines in the south. While St Vincent disappoints some visitors, others find its raw edge and rugged natural qualities refreshing. St Vincent is also a good place to learn about and appreciate traditional black West Indian culture away from the glitz and hurly-burly that accompanies most mass-tourism destinations.

The Grenadines, on the other hand, are one of the most popular yachting and cruising areas in the Caribbean. These small islands, which reach like stepping-stones between St Vincent and Grenada, are surrounded by coral reefs and clear blue waters that prove ideal spots for activities such as diving, snorkeling and boating. The Tobago Cays in particular constitute perhaps the most beautiful part of the whole Caribbean.

All of the Grenadine islands are lightly populated and mostly undeveloped. Rock stars and royalty spend time in their holiday mansions on Mustique and Palm Island, which both feature an array of exclusive resorts that cater to well-heeled vacationers. Other islands of the Grenadines, such as Bequia and Union Island, are yachting havens that attract an international crowd and offer reasonable places to stay and eat.

Hightlights

- Doing nothing in Bequia
- Drinking with Mick Jagger in Mustique
- Climbing St Vincent's La Soufrière
- Enjoying the pristine beaches and reefs of the Tobago Cays
- Seeing Bligh's sucker at St Vincent's Botanic Gardens
- Climbing Fort Duvernette with the lizards and birds
- Relaxing on black-sand surf beaches on St Vincent's Atlantic coast

OTHER MAPS
St Vincent &
the Grenadines
page 483

St Vincent
page 495

Kingstown
page 496

CARIBBEAN
SEA

Bequia
page 506

Villa Beach
& Indian Bay
page 499

Port Elizabeth
page 507

0   5   10 km
0   3   6 miles

Union Island
page 516

Clifton
page 517

Facts about St Vincent & the Grenadines

HISTORY

St Vincent was inhabited at least 7000 years ago by Ciboney Indians from South America. Arawaks displaced the Ciboney around the time of Christ. Carib Indians in turn overran Arawak settlers a few thousand years later, and when Spanish explorers first sighted St Vincent, the island was densely populated with Carib Indians. Fierce Carib resistance kept European colonists at bay long after most other Caribbean islands sheltered well-established European settlements. This was in part because many Caribs from other islands fled to St Vincent after their home islands fell to European control.

The islands felt the earliest major impact of foreign influence in 1675, when a Dutch slave ship sank between St Vincent and neighboring Bequia. None of the European crew survived, but numerous Africans made it to shore. The shipwrecked slaves were accepted by the Caribs and took Carib wives. Their progeny became known as Black Caribs, distinct from native Yellow Caribs. Tensions developed after the Black Caribs began to increase in number, and separate communities were established.

The Caribs were hostile to all Europeans, but they found the British, who claimed their land by royal grants, more objectionable than the French. The Caribs allowed the French to establish the first European settlement on the island in the early 1700s.

In 1783, after a century of competing claims between the British and French, the Treaty of Paris placed St Vincent under British domain, and rebellions followed. In 1795, under French instigation, Black and Yellow Caribs simultaneously swept the island, torching plantations and massacring English settlers. They joined forces on Dorsetshire Hill, where Chief Chattawae of the Black Caribs, buoyed by the success of his raids, challenged British commander Alexander Leith to a sword duel. Leith was an accomplished swordsman, and within moments Chattawae was dead. Leith himself died shortly after the duel, reportedly of 'great fatigue,' but it's likely that he too was mortally wounded in the sword fight.

The following year British troops were dispatched to St Vincent to round up the insurgents, who, except for a few hiding in the hills, were shipped to Roatan, an island off the Honduran coast. More than 5000 Caribs were forcibly repatriated. A small

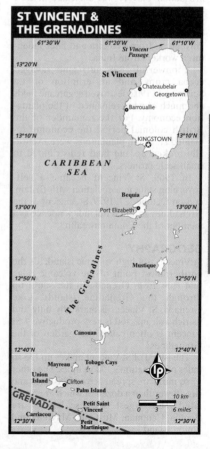

ST VINCENT & THE GRENADINES

number of Yellow Caribs not involved in the uprising were relocated at Sandy Bay, on the remote northeastern side of the island.

With the native opposition gone, the planters quickly achieved the success that had eluded them. In 1812, however, a major eruption of La Soufrière spewed suffocating ash over northern St Vincent, destroying most of the coffee and cocoa trees. The eruption also took a heavy toll on the Carib reservation at Sandy Bay.

Around the same time the British abolitionist movement was gaining momentum in London. Slavery was abolished in 1834 and the plantation owners were forced to free more than 18,000 slaves. The planters began bringing in foreign laborers – first Portuguese from Madeira and later indentured workers from India.

A powerful 1898 hurricane ravaged cocoa crops, and an eruption of La Soufrière in 1902 destroyed sugarcane fields and much of what remained of the plantation economy. For the remainder of the British colonial period the economy remained stagnant; plantations were eventually broken up and land redistributed to small-scale farmers.

In 1969, St Vincent became a self-governing state in association with Britain, and on October 27, 1979, St Vincent & the Grenadines acquired full independence as a member of the Commonwealth.

GEOGRAPHY

St Vincent is a high volcanic island; it's the northernmost point of the volcanic ridge that runs from Grenada in the south up through the Grenadine islands. Like Grenada, St Vincent is markedly hilly and its rich volcanic soil is very productive – St Vincent is often called the 'garden of the Grenadines.'

The island of St Vincent makes up 133 sq miles of the nation's 150 sq miles. The other 17 sq miles are spread across 32 islands and cays, fewer than a dozen of which are populated. The largest of these islands are Bequia, Canouan, Mustique, Mayreau and Union Island.

The highest peak on St Vincent is La Soufrière, an active volcano that reaches to 4048 feet. On May 7, 1902, the volcano erupted violently, wreaking havoc on the island's northern region and causing an estimated 2000 deaths. Again on April 13, 1979, La Soufrière erupted, spewing ash over much of the island and forcing 20,000 people to evacuate the northern villages. Crop damage was substantial, but no lives were lost.

The larger of the Grenadine islands are hilly, but relatively low-lying, and most have no source of freshwater other than rainfall. All have beautiful white-sand beaches.

CLIMATE

In January the average daily high temperature is 85°F (29°C), while the low averages 72°F (22°C). In July the average daily high is 86°F (30°C), while the low averages 76°F (24°C).

January to May are the driest months, with a mean relative humidity around 76%. During the rest of the year the humidity averages about 80%. In July, the wettest month, there's measurable rainfall for an average of 26 days, while April, the driest month, averages six days' measurable rainfall. All these statistics are for Kingstown; the Grenadine islands to the south are drier and marginally warmer.

FLORA & FAUNA

St Vincent has a rugged interior of tropical rain forest and lowlands thick with coconut trees and banana estates. The Mesopotamia Valley, northeast of Kingstown, has some of the most fertile farmland and luxuriant landscapes.

The national bird is the endangered St Vincent parrot, a beautiful multihued Amazon parrot about 18 inches in length. The parrot lives in St Vincent's interior rain forest, as do numerous other tropical birds. The forest also provides a habitat for opossum (locally called *manicou*) and agouti, a short-haired rabbitlike rodent. Agouti roam freely on Young Island, where they are easy to spot.

St Vincent has three snake species: the Congo snake, which coils itself around tree branches, and two terrestrial species, the black snake and the white snake. All three are harmless.

GOVERNMENT & POLITICS

St Vincent & the Grenadines is an independent nation within the Commonwealth. The British monarchy is represented by a governor-general, but executive power is in the hands of the prime minister and cabinet. The unicameral legislature consists of 13 members, each elected for a five-year term.

On Independence Day, October 27, 2000, Sir James Mitchell, leader and founder of the majority New Democratic Party (NDP), stepped down as prime minister, passing the mantle to his successor, former finance minister Arnhim Eustace. Sir James, only the nation's second prime minister, had served as the country's leader for 16 years and as a minister of parliament for 34 years. He is regarded as the father of the nation and one of the Caribbean's greatest political leaders.

The new prime minister, Arnhim Eustace, intends to further develop tourism and offshore banking, as well as to fight crime, joblessness and drugs.

ECONOMY

On St Vincent, agriculture and fishing are mainstays of the economy, accounting for more than half of all employment. Bananas are the leading export crop, followed by arrowroot, coconuts, cocoa and spices. Until recently, St Vincent supplied Britain with more than 50% of its bananas, but global moves towards free trade have undermined this market, and Vincentian bananas are struggling to compete against the cheaper South American fruit. The government is encouraging crop diversification.

Attempts to revive the sugar industry in 1981, to provide a source for domestic rum production, were unsuccessful and abandoned a few years later. A budding cut-flower industry and small-scale vegetable farming are meeting with more success – government land reforms have turned idle plantation lands into small family farms.

On the outer islands, tourism and fishing provide most of the income. The government has been slow to recognize the importance of tourism, but over the last couple of years it has actively sought to develop the tourism sector in conjunction with private investors.

Unemployment remains at 22%.

POPULATION & PEOPLE

St Vincent & the Grenadines has just over 115,000 people. More than 90% live on St Vincent, with 30,000 of those in the Kingstown area. About 75% of all islanders are of pure African descent, while 15% are of mixed descent, including nearly a thousand Black Caribs, most of whom live on the lower slopes of La Soufrière. On Bequia and St Vincent are sizable populations of Scottish descendants – encountering white Anglo-Saxon types with broad West Indian accents can be slightly disorienting. Many local blacks also have traces of Scottish blood in their lineage. There are small populations of English, Irish, French and Asians also.

SOCIETY & CONDUCT

Local culture in St Vincent is less sullied with the crass commercialism of tourism than is evident elsewhere in the Caribbean. It's a place where travelers can get a little closer to traditional black West Indian culture without getting harangued too much by touts and peddlers (although there are some of both). Most people live simple lives, much as they have for generations, working gardens, fishing and crewing regional ships.

As elsewhere in the Caribbean, music and sports are central elements of local culture, and they both take informal forms – locals often break into improvised song as they make their way down the footpaths or along the beach, and spontaneous games of beach cricket or soccer embroiling passersby are regular events, especially on the weekends.

Reggae, calypso and steel-band music are popular. Boat building, both full-scale and models, is an island art form in some of the Grenadine islands, particularly in Bequia.

Dos & Don'ts

Casual cotton clothing is suitable for almost any occasion, including dining at the more

ST VINCENT & THE GRENADINES

exclusive Grenadine resorts. Skimpy clothing and beachwear should confined to the beach. Topless bathing is not practiced in St Vincent & the Grenadines (except perhaps at remote and exclusive resorts).

RELIGION

The majority of islanders are Protestant, with Anglicans representing the largest denomination. Other religions include Methodist, Seventh Day Adventist, Baptist, Streams of Power and Baha'i. About 20% of Vincentians are Roman Catholic. Most people take their religion seriously and regularly attend church on a Sunday.

The trappings of Rastafarianism are popular expressions of fashion and West Indian identity, but locals do not participate in its religious elements as do some devotees in Jamaica.

LANGUAGE

English is the official language. The oldest island generations also speak a French patois, but this language is rapidly dying out.

Facts for the Visitor

ORIENTATION

St Vincent's ET Joshua Airport is midway between Kingstown and the island's main resort area at Villa, about 1½ miles from both. The Windward Hwy runs up the east coast to Fancy at the island's northernmost tip, but the Leeward Hwy goes only three-quarters of the way up the west coast. If you want to tour both coasts, you have to backtrack through Kingstown.

The main Grenadine islands, with the exception of Mustique, are all served by ferries from Kingstown. Bequia, Union Island, Canouan and Mustique each have airports.

Maps

The Ordnance Survey's 1:50,000-scale map of St Vincent is the most detailed map available. It can be purchased at the Wayfarer Book Store, on Upper Bay St, Kingstown, or at the airport sundry shop.

TOURIST OFFICES
Local Tourist Offices

The main Department of Tourism office for St Vincent & the Grenadines (☎ 457-1502, fax 456-2610) is at PO Box 834, Kingstown, St Vincent, West Indies. Their Web site is at www.svgtourism.com.

In addition, there's a tourist information desk at St Vincent's ET Joshua Airport and branch tourist offices in Bequia and Union Island.

Tourist Offices Abroad

Overseas offices of the St Vincent & the Grenadines Department of Tourism include the following:

Canada
(☎ 416-924-5796, fax 416-924-5844) 32 Park Rd, Toronto, Ontario N4W 2N4

Germany
(☎ 7031-80 10 33, fax 7031-80 50 12) Karibik Pur, Wurmberg Str 26, D-7032 Sindelfinger

UK
(☎ 020-7937 6570, fax 020-7937 3611) 10 Kensington Court, London W8 5DL, England

USA
(☎ 212-687-4981, fax 800-949-5946) 801 Second Ave, 21st floor, New York, NY 10017
(☎ 972-239-6451, 800-235-3029) 6505 Cove Creek Place, Dallas, TX 75240

VISAS & DOCUMENTS

Citizens of the USA, Canada and the UK can visit St Vincent & the Grenadines with proof of citizenship in the form of a birth certificate or voter registration card, accompanied by an official photo ID, such as a driver's license. Citizens of other countries must be in possession of a valid passport. A roundtrip or onward ticket is officially required of all visitors.

EMBASSIES & CONSULATES
Vincentian & Grenadine Embassies & Consulates

Belgium
(☎ 02-513 8724) 24 Ave de la Toison d'Or, 1050 Brussels

UK
(☎ 020-7565 2874) 10 Kensington Court,
London W85DL

USA
(☎ 202-364-6730) 3216 New Mexico Ave NW,
Washington, DC 20016

Embassies in St Vincent & the Grenadines

UK
High Commission (☎ 457-1701) Granby St, PO
Box 132, Kingstown, St Vincent

CUSTOMS

Up to a quart of wine or spirits and 200 cigarettes may be brought into the country duty-free.

MONEY

The Eastern Caribbean dollar (EC$) is the local currency. The exchange rate is EC$2.67 to US$1.

Major credit cards, while not as widely used as on other Caribbean islands, are accepted at most hotels, car rental agencies and dive shops.

A 7% government tax and a 10% service charge is added onto most hotel and restaurant bills, in which case no further tipping is necessary.

POST & COMMUNICATIONS
Post

The general post office (☎ 456-1111) is on Halifax St in Kingstown, and there are branch post offices in larger towns and villages.

It costs EC$0.65 to mail postcards within the Caribbean and the Americas, EC$0.70 to Europe and EC$0.75 to Australia or Asia. A letter weighing up to half an ounce costs EC$0.70 within the Caribbean, EC$0.90 to the USA and Canada, EC$1.10 to the UK and Europe, and EC$1.40 to Australia or Asia.

International mail is routed through other Caribbean nations, so mail sent to the UK takes about a week, while mail sent to other international destinations, including the USA, can easily take double that.

To write to hotels or other businesses listed in this chapter, follow the business name with the village and/or island name.

Telephone

St Vincent phone numbers have seven digits. When calling from overseas add the area code 784.

Both coin and card phones can be found on the major islands. Phone cards can be purchased at Cable & Wireless offices or from vendors near the phones. It costs EC$0.25 to make a local call. For more information on card phones and making international calls, see Post & Communications in the Regional Facts for the Visitor chapter.

Email & Internet Access

Kingstown has a few Internet cafés, as do larger towns and communities where tourists and yachters frequent.

INTERNET RESOURCES

The Internet has some good information about St Vincent & the Grenadines. Some of the better sites are the following:

www.svgtourism.com
This is the official Web site for the Department of Tourism for St Vincent & the Grenadines.

www.vincy.com
This is a leading Vincentian Internet service provider, and it has links from its home page to the Web sites of many of its important clients.

www.scubasvg.com
Primarily a site for diving and water-sports information, this also has some good historical and cultural information.

www.hwcn.org/~aa462/svgref.html
This site is maintained by hobbyist Russ Filman, and it is an excellent source of information and links of a noncommercial nature.

www.caribbeansupersite.com
This has regional Caribbean information, but also contains some good information on St Vincent & the Grenadines.

www.caribbeanchoice.com
This site is similar to www.caribbeansupersite.com.

www.kingstown.com
This is another good resource on St Vincent & the Grenadines.

www.bequiasweet.com
This excellent site is maintained by the Bequia Tourism Association.

NEWSPAPERS & MAGAZINES

There are two local weekly newspapers, *The Vincentian* and *The News*, that focus on local issues and hit the streets on Friday or Saturday. Both cost EC$1 and are lively, offering strong editorials and opinion pieces. *Cross Country* is a midweek paper that comes out on Wednesday and costs EC$1. *The Herald* is a daily paper that covers international news and has a Web site at www.heraldsvg.com.

You can buy *Time* and *Newsweek* at the airport sundry shop.

There are two useful publications available at no cost through the tourist office and hotels. The *Escape Tourist Guide* is a 100-page glossy magazine with general tourist information, lists of places to stay and eat, ads and a few feature articles. *Discover St Vincent & the Grenadines* is pocket-sized, with similar content.

RADIO & TV

St Vincent has one broadcast TV station, SVGBC, on channel 9, and two local cable TV broadcasters. Additionally, most hotels pick up US cable-TV feeds.

The one local AM radio station, NBCSVG, broadcasts at 705 kHz. Three stations broadcast on the FM band: NICE FM 96.3, HITZ FM 107.3, and WE FM 99.9.

ELECTRICITY

The electric current is 220–240V, 50 cycles. British-style three-pin plugs are used.

WEIGHTS & MEASURES

St Vincent & the Grenadines uses the imperial system of feet, miles and pounds.

HEALTH

The main hospital (☎ 456-1185), a 200-bed facility, is in Kingstown. There's also a hospital in Port Elizabeth on Bequia (☎ 458-3294), clinics throughout the islands, and pharmacies in Kingstown and Port Elizabeth.

WOMEN TRAVELERS

Women traveling in St Vincent & the Grenadines needn't expect any hassles unique to this country. Normal precautions are sensible, especially after dark, but Vincentians are generally very friendly and hospitable, and good manners are important to the local culture. The jewelry peddlers and touts are certainly not shy about approaching travelers, nor are the beggars, but they are usually good-natured, amiable and nonthreatening.

GAY & LESBIAN TRAVELERS

Caribbean attitudes to same-sex couples are a few decades behind the rest of the developed world. In the former British colonies, such as St Vincent & the Grenadines, the orthodox values are like Britain's in the 1950s or '60s – very conservative. For this reason, same-sex couples should exercise discretion in public.

DANGERS & ANNOYANCES

Kingstown has a few beggars and young men who want to carry your bags from the ferry or to act as a tour guide. If you're not interested in their services, turn them down politely but firmly.

On the Grenadines, which are far more laid-back, hassles are rare.

EMERGENCIES

Dial ☎ 999 for fire, police and coast-guard emergencies.

BUSINESS HOURS

Shops are generally open 8 am to 4 pm weekdays, till noon Saturday, although supermarkets often have extended hours. Most government offices are open 8 am to noon and 1 to 4:15 pm weekdays. Banks are generally open 8 am to 1 pm Monday to Thursday, 8 am to 1 pm and 3 to 5 pm Friday.

PUBLIC HOLIDAYS
& SPECIAL EVENTS

Public holidays are as follows:

New Year's Day	January 1
St Vincent & the Grenadines Day	January 22
Good Friday	late March/early April
Easter Monday	late March/early April
Labour Day	first Monday in May
Whit Monday	eighth Monday after Easter

Caricom Day	second Monday in July
Carnival Tuesday	usually second Tuesday in mid-July
August Monday	first Monday in August
Independence Day	October 27
Christmas Day	December 25
Boxing Day	December 26

St Vincent's Carnival, called Vincy Mas, is the main cultural event of the year. It usually takes place around the first two weeks of July, with a 12-day run of calypso and steel-band music, colorful costume parades and lots of dancing and activities. Most of the action is centered on Kingstown.

On Bequia, there's a major regatta held over the Easter weekend, and on Canouan there's another major sailing event held in mid-May.

ACTIVITIES
Beaches & Swimming
There are exceptional white-sand beaches on virtually all of the Grenadine islands and some tan- and black-sand beaches on St Vincent. For details on specific beaches, see the individual island sections.

Diving
World-class dive sites lie off virtually all the islands, with excellent visibility and extensive coral reefs. Divers will find colorful sponges, soft corals, great stands of elkhorn coral, branching gorgonian, black coral and a few sunken wrecks. There's a range of dives suitable for any level of experience, from calm, shallow dives to wall dives and drift dives. Spearfishing is prohibited.

Dive shops on four islands – Dive St Vincent, Dive Bequia, Dive Canouan and Grenadines Dive (on Union Island) – offer a 'pick-and-mix' 10-dive package for US$450 that allows divers to take their dives as they please from any of the four shops. Otherwise, the going rates are around US$50 for a single dive, US$90 for a two-tank dive and US$60 for a night dive. A 'resort course' for beginners that includes a couple of hours of instruction and a shallow dive is available, the price is around US$70.

Many dive shops also offer complete certification courses. Dive St Vincent, one of the islands' best-regarded shops, charges US$435 and offers PADI, NAUI or CMAS accreditation.

Dive Shops Dive shops in St Vincent & the Grenadines include the following:

Bequia Dive Adventures
(☎ 458-3826, fax 665-7088, adventures@ caribsurf.com, www.bequiadiveadventures .com) PO Box 129, Bequia

Dive Bequia
(☎ 458-3504, fax 458-3886, bobsax@ caribsurf.com, www.dive-bequia.com) PO Box 16, Bequia

Dive Canouan
(☎ 458-8044, fax 458-8875) Tamarind Beach Hotel, Canouan

Dive St Vincent
(☎ 457-4714, fax 457-4948, bill2s@caribsurf.com, www.divestvincent.com) PO Box 864, Young Island Dock, St Vincent

Grenadines Dive
(☎ 458-8138, fax 458-8122, gdive@caribsurf.com) Sunny Grenadines Hotel, Union Island

Sunsports
(☎ 458-3577, fax 457-3031, sunsport@ caribsurf.com) PO Box 1, Bequia

Other Water Sports
Trade winds blow unimpeded across the Grenadines, creating some fine windsurfing conditions. Many resorts offer guests free use of windsurfing gear, and there are water-sports huts on many of the more developed tourist beaches that rent windsurfing equipment.

On Bequia, there's good windsurfing at Admiralty Bay, Friendship Bay and Paget Farm and Industry Bay. Most hotels offer sailboard rental, and at some the gear is free for guests. Sunsports (see Dive Shops), at Gingerbread, Port Elizabeth, offers a 1½-hour snorkeling trip for US$25.

Some of the huts also rent out snorkeling gear, Hobie Cats and Sunfish boats.

Hiking
Hiking trails are not well developed on St Vincent, and access to them can be difficult.

The most popular walking area is the Vermont Nature Trails, a series of short walking tracks 3½ miles inland from the Leeward Hwy. See Leeward Highway, later in this chapter, for details.

The most challenging hike on St Vincent is to La Soufrière. The route passes through banana estates and rain forest, up past the tree line to the volcano's barren summit, where, weather permitting, hikers are rewarded with views down into the crater and out over St Vincent. The easiest access is from the island's east side, but even that is a strenuous 7-mile roundtrip hike. As the trailhead is 1½ miles west of the Windward Hwy and the nearest bus drop, the easiest way to do the hike is to join a tour. See Organized Tours in the Getting Around section of this chapter.

ACCOMMODATIONS

There are a handful of exclusive resorts in St Vincent & the Grenadines, and they're all of the 'barefoot' variety, situated on remote beaches. Hotels of all categories are small-scale operations – few have more than a couple of dozen rooms. Many hotels have the same rates year-round. The rates listed in this chapter do not include the 7% hotel tax or the 10% service charge.

There are no campgrounds on St Vincent & the Grenadines, and camping is not encouraged.

FOOD

St Vincent's rich volcanic soil is very fertile and produces most of the fruits and vegetables sold throughout the Grenadines. The sweet, juicy St Vincent orange is ripe while still green, and sells for about EC$0.50 each. Avocados, tomatoes and bell peppers (capsicums) are common and very good, as is a vast array of tropical fruit. Produce markets are found in larger towns and are the best places to pick up fruits and vegetables. Seafood is abundant, with conch, fish, shrimp and lobster making an appearance on most menus.

Common West Indian foods include callaloo soup, pumpkin soup, saltfish, pigfoot souse and various breadfruit preparations. A popular St Vincent dish is *bul jol,* which is made of roasted breadfruit and saltfish with tomatoes and onions.

DRINKS

St Vincent's tap water comes from mountain reserves and is chlorinated and safe to drink. On the Grenadines water comes from individual rain-catchment systems and should be boiled or treated before drinking. Bottled water is available on all the islands.

St Vincent Brewery, in Kingstown, makes the local lager, Hairoun, which is quite a nice drop. 'Hairoun' is the original Carib name for St Vincent. St Vincent Brewery also produces the region's Guinness stout.

ENTERTAINMENT

The larger hotels often have live entertainment in the evenings – local bands play jazz, calypso, reggae and soca. There are a couple of nightclubs in Kingstown and another at Villa Beach.

SHOPPING

T-shirts and souvenirs are plentiful and inexpensive, and various shops in Kingstown sell locally made straw bags, place mats, pottery, banana-leaf art and West Indian dolls. Bequia, Mustique and Union Island all have good boutiques and gift shops, and their wares are generally more attractive than those in Kingstown.

Getting There & Away

DEPARTURE TAX

The departure tax is EC$30 for stays longer than 24 hours.

AIR

There are no direct flights to St Vincent & the Grenadines from outside the Caribbean, as the runway is too small to land jet aircraft. International passengers first fly into a neighboring island and then switch to a prop plane for the final leg of their journey. There are various same-day connecting flights from Antigua, Barbados, Trinidad and Puerto Rico.

From the US, American Airlines flies daily from New York to St Vincent, via San Juan, Puerto Rico. Other flights from New York are offered by Delta Airlines and Air Jamaica/BWIA, all via Barbados. Expect to pay around US$684 for a roundtrip flight from New York. One-way fares can be expensive and are generally not discounted; expect to pay US$750.

From the UK, BWIA (www.bwia.com) flies via Antigua to St Vincent, with roundtrip fares from around £485. Other options for travel from the UK include BWIA/Caribbean Star Airlines via Trinidad and Air Jamaica/Virgin Atlantic flights via Barbados.

LIAT, Air Jamaica (www.airjamaica.com) and BWIA offer direct scheduled flights between St Vincent and Barbados. Expect to pay US$110/134 one-way/roundtrip on any of nine daily flights. LIAT and Air Jamaica offer three daily flights St Lucia to St Vincent for US$51/96 one-way/roundtrip.

From Grenada there are five flights per day to St Vincent. LIAT, Caribbean Star Airlines and Air Jamaica have flights for around for US$69/138 one-way/roundtrip.

One of a couple of small Grenadine carriers, Airlines of Carriacou, was taken over by St Vincent & the Grenadines Air (SVG Air) in September 1999. SVG Air was maintaining the schedule of Airlines of Carriacou to the end of 2001. SVG Air, Mustique Airways and Eastern Caribbean Express have a number of island connections.

SVG Air (☎ 457-5124, www.svgair.com) has connections between Grenada and St Vincent: daily flights between Grenada and Union Island are US$80/150 one-way/roundtrip, and Grenada to Bequia or St Vincent costs US$100 each way; daily flights between Carriacou and Union Island cost US$32 each way.

SVG Air also has two daily flights from Barbados to St Vincent and Bequia for US$120 each way, to Mustique for US$140 each way and to Canouan and Union Island for US$135 each way. You can fly daily from Bequia to St Lucia for US$90 each way and

from Union Island to St Lucia for US$85 each way.

Mustique Airways (☎ 458-4380, www.mustique.com) has daily scheduled flights from Barbados to St Vincent (US$120), Mustique (US$140), Bequia (US$120), Canouan and Union Island (US$135). Roundtrip fares are double.

Eastern Caribbean Express (☎ 457-5124) has daily flights from St Vincent to Barbados for US$110, to Dominica for US$218 and Grenada and St Lucia for US$96.

For information on flights between islands in the Grenadines, see the Getting Around section of this chapter.

Airports

St Vincent's ET Joshua Airport, in Arnos Vale, is a modest facility with an exchange bureau open 8 am to noon and 3 to 5 pm weekdays, a small bar, two gift shops, a duty-free liquor shop, and coin and card phones.

If your luggage is very light, it's possible to get a minibus to Kingstown or Villa Beach from the main road in front of the terminal. Otherwise, taxis meet the flights. Taxis into town cost EC$25.

SEA

The passenger/cargo boat M/V *Windward* links St Vincent with Barbados, St Lucia, Trinidad and Venezuela. For details, see Boat in the Getting Around the Region chapter.

Information on boats between Carriacou (Grenada) and Union Island is in Getting There & Away in the Union Island section.

Yacht

On the island of St Vincent, yachts can clear immigration and customs at either Kingstown or Wallilabou Bay.

Wallilabou has a customs officer on duty 4 to 6 pm daily, and outside these hours you can clear customs at the police station in the village of Barrouallie, immediately south of Wallilabou Bay. Many yachters prefer to clear customs here and avoid the hassles and long lines sometimes encountered in Kingstown. Moorings, water, ice and showers are available at Wallilabou Anchorage (☎ 458-7270, VHF channel 68).

Other popular anchorages on St Vincent include remote Petit Byahaut to the north of Kingstown and the more frequented Young Island Cut and Blue Lagoon to the south. Blue Lagoon (☎ 458-4308) has a 20-berth marina with fuel, water, electricity, laundry and showers.

On the outer islands, there are customs and immigration offices at Bequia, Mustique and Union Island.

Cruise Ship

Cruise ships dock at the deepwater wharf in Kingstown Harbour, at the south side of the town center. Cruise ships also make stops at some of the Grenadine islands, with Bequia, Mayreau and Union Island being the most popular destinations.

Getting Around

AIR

Mustique Airways (☎ 458-4380) has inter-island flights connecting various Grenadine islands with St Vincent. The one-way fare runs US$21 between St Vincent and Bequia, US$25 between St Vincent and Canouan and US$29 between Bequia and Canouan. Fares between Union Island and either St Vincent, Bequia or Canouan are US$28. There's a discount of about 20% on roundtrip fares.

SVG Air (☎ 457-5124) also flies between Union Island and Bequia or St Vincent for US$32 one-way.

BUS

Buses on St Vincent are privately owned minivans that can cram in a good 20 people (more if necessary!). Destinations are usually posted on the front windshield. There's a 'conductor' on board who collects fares; you pay as you get off. Many buses have sound systems, and the (loud) music is all part of the experience. Buses are a good, reliable and cheap way to travel, and a nice way to meet locals.

Kingstown's central bus station, next to the Little Tokyo fish market, is a busy and colorful place, and the buses line up in clearly marked lanes – Leeward, Windward

or Kingstown. Getting on the right bus is pretty simple, but you can always ask someone if you're unsure.

Fares around Kingstown are EC$1. Fares from Kingstown are EC$1.50 to Villa, EC$2 to Layou, EC$3 to Barrouallie, EC$4 to Georgetown and EC$5 to Sandy Bay or Chateaubelair. The buses are most frequent in the morning and from mid- to late afternoon, when they load up with students and Kingstown commuters. But getting a bus on a main route, such as between Villa and Kingstown, is easy all day.

There are also buses on Bequia and Union Island; see those island sections for details.

CAR
Road Rules

Driving is on the left. In order to drive within St Vincent & the Grenadines you must purchase a EC$40 local license. In Kingstown, licenses can be obtained at the Traffic & Transport office, inside the main police station, 24 hours a day.

St Vincent's roads are narrow and pot-holed, but generally the main roads are in reasonable condition – the farther north you go the worse they become. Be cautious, however, because local drivers usually switch to whichever side of the road has the least potholes, and there are many blind turns. Always toot your horn when approaching blind corners.

The northernmost gas stations on St Vincent are at Georgetown on the Windward Hwy and Chateaubelair on the Leeward Hwy.

Rental

Rentals typically begin at around US$50 a day for a car and from US$65 for a 4WD vehicle. Around 75 free miles are commonly allowed, and a fee of EC$1 is charged for each additional mile driven. Note that collision damage insurance is not a common concept, and if you get into an accident you're likely to be liable for damages.

Avis (☎ 457-2847, fax 456-2777), on Paul's Ave, is the only internationally affiliated car rental agency, but there are several local companies, including Ben's Auto Rental (☎/ fax 456-2907) and Unico Auto Rentals (☎ 456-5744, fax 456-5745), which are both at the airport. Other hirers include Star Garage (☎ 456-1743) and Kim's Rentals (☎ 456-1884), both on Grenville St in Kingstown. Most will deliver cars to your hotel.

Most Grenadine islands have no car rentals at all. On some there are no roads.

TAXI
On St Vincent, taxis line up at the airport, and there are a couple of stands in central Kingstown. Your hotel can arrange a booking or flag one along the street.

From the airport it costs EC$25 to either Kingstown or Villa Beach. From Kingstown, it's about EC$10 to Fort Charlotte, EC$25 to Villa Beach, EC$40 to Layou and EC$80 to Georgetown.

BICYCLE
Sailor's Cycle Centre (☎ 457-1274, modernp@ caribsurf.com), on Middle St in Kingstown, rents road bikes and mountain bikes from EC$25 per day.

BOAT
For information on the main ferry service that operates between Bequia and Kingstown, see Getting There & Away in the Bequia section.

The mail boat M/V *Barracuda* carries passengers and cargo five times weekly between St Vincent, Bequia, Canouan, Mayreau and Union Island. The boat leaves St Vincent at 10:30 am Monday and Thursday and 10 am Saturday, arriving in Union Island around 4 pm. En route it stops at Bequia (bypassed on Saturday), Canouan and Mayreau. On Tuesday and Friday the boat departs from Union Island at 6:30, making the same stopovers on the north-bound route back to St Vincent. On Saturday the boat leaves Union Island at 5:30 pm and makes the return nonstop, arriving in St Vincent at 10:30 pm.

Fares from St Vincent are EC$15 to Bequia, EC$15 to Canouan, EC$20 to Mayreau and EC$25 to Union Island.

Although en route departure times vary depending on how long it takes to unload

cargo, the sailing time between islands is one hour from St Vincent to Bequia, two hours from Bequia to Canouan, one hour from Canouan to Mayreau and 20 minutes from Mayreau to Union Island.

ORGANIZED TOURS
All tour operators can customize tours around clients' specific interests.

Sam's Taxi Tours (☎ 458-4338, fax 456-4233, sams-taxi-tours@caribsurf.com) offers day tours that take in the sights of either St Vincent's west coast or east coast for around US$100 for up to two people. Hiking trips to La Soufrière cost US$100 for up to six people.

HazEco Tours (☎/fax 457-8634) concentrates on St Vincent's natural scenery, with a half-day outing to the Vermont Nature Trails for US$30 per person, or a hiking trip to the summit of La Soufrière for US$100 for up to two people. It also arranges sightseeing trips to either the west or east coast of St Vincent from US$35 per person.

For an interesting high-energy alternative, Sailor's Cycle Centre (☎ 457-1274, modernp@caribsurf.com), on Middle St in Kingstown, offers various mountain-bike outings from US$18 per person for a four-person minimum. Well-organized excursions take in most of St Vincent's sights, and include a ride/hike to La Soufrière's summit for US$60 per person.

SVG Tours (☎ 458-4534, fax 456-4721, svgtours@caribsurf.com) runs a series of land-based tours of St Vincent with an emphasis on agronomy. Tour leader Dominique speaks French and has an intimate understanding of agricultural land usage as well as the island's wildlife and wilderness areas.

Fantasea Tours (☎ 457-4477, fax 457-5577, fantasea@caribsurf.com) arranges sailing day tours from St Vincent to the Grenadine islands. One goes to Mustique and Bequia for US$70 and another takes in Canouan, Mayreau and the Tobago Cays for US$90.

For information on tours to the Falls of Baleine, see that section under Leeward Highway, later in this chapter.

ST VINCENT & THE GRENADINES

St Vincent

KINGSTOWN

Kingstown is the capital and commercial center of St Vincent & the Grenadines. It's a bustling city of about 30,000 people that makes few concessions to tourists. Most businesses are geared to the local population, and although Kingstown has everything that travelers need – banks, shops, restaurants, Internet cafés, a tourist office – it has no tourist precinct. You may feel a little peripheral walking the busy streets as people go about their daily lives. Nor is Kingstown a particularly attractive city. It is colorful and lively, but built on flatlands fronting Kingstown Bay. For all of this it has an authentic, uncontrived feeling about it.

Orientation

The city center consists of 12 small blocks that can be explored in a few hours. There are some appealing old cobblestone streets, brick archways and stone-block colonial buildings scattered around the center; worth a look are the buildings lining Melville St and the churches, the courthouse (with goats grazing on the grounds) and the police station. Still, none of these buildings are grand, and overall Kingstown is more interesting for its local character than any particular sights. It's the locals selling wares along Bay and Bedford Sts and produce in the new market, the crowds at the fish market and the rum shops at the bus terminal that give the town its color.

Ferries from the Grenadines arrive at the jetty just south of the city center. On days when the banana boats are being loaded, the port is abuzz with activity as trucks packed with stalks of bananas line the streets to the dock.

Note that Upper and Lower Middle St is more properly called Upper and Lower Long Lane, although people use these names interchangeably.

Information

Tourist Offices The tourist office (☎ 457-1502) is on the ground floor of the government complex on Upper Bay St. It's open 8 am to noon and 1 to 4:15 pm weekdays.

Money There's a Barclays Bank (☎ 456-1706) on Halifax St, opposite the LIAT office, and a Scotiabank (☎ 457-1601) a block west on Halifax St. National Commercial Bank (☎ 457-1844) is on the corner of Bedford and Grenville Sts, and Caribbean Banking Corporation (☎ 456-1501) is at 81 South River Rd. All are open 8 am to 3 pm Monday to Thursday, till 5 pm Friday, and all have 24-hour ATMs.

Post & Communications The general post office (☎ 456-1111), on Halifax St, is open 8:30 am to 3 pm weekdays, till 11:30 am Saturday.

You can make phone calls and send faxes, telexes and telegrams at the Cable & Wireless office (☎ 457-1901) on Halifax St. It's open 7 am to 7 pm Monday to Saturday, 8 to 10 am and 6 to 8 pm Sunday.

Beachcombers Hotel (☎ 458-4283) has a business center that can get you on the Internet for EC$8 per hour.

Office Essentials (☎ 457 2235), Bonadie Plaza, Middle St, has more than 20 terminals and charges EC$6 per hour for Internet access. MSA Internet Cafe (☎/fax 457-1131, internetcafe@vincysurf.com) is on Upper Middle St at the east end of town. Open 9 am to 10 pm daily, it too charges EC$6 per hour.

Laundry For laundry and dry cleaning, there's MagiKleen (☎ 457-1514), on Lower Bay St, open 7:30 am to 5 pm weekdays, till 2 pm Saturday. Drop off your laundry early and you can pick it up later the same day. It costs EC$2.50 a pound to wash and dry.

Botanic Gardens

The St Vincent Botanic Gardens are the oldest botanical gardens in the West Indies, and they are lovingly tended – an oasis of calm amid the frenetic buzz of Kingstown. Originally established in 1763 to propagate spices and medicinal plants, the gardens now comprise a neatly landscaped 20-acre park with lots of flowering bushes and tall trees.

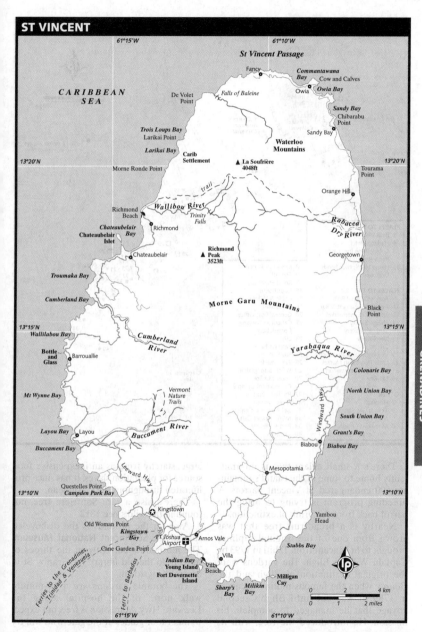

ST VINCENT

61°15'W 61°10'W

St Vincent Passage

Fancy

Commantawana Bay

Cow and Calves

CARIBBEAN SEA

De Volet Point

Falls of Baleine

Owia

Owia Bay

Sandy Bay

Chibarabu Point

Sandy Bay

Trois Loups Bay

Larikai Point

Larikai Bay

Carib Settlement

Waterloo Mountains

13°20'N 13°20'N

Morne Ronde Point

▲ La Soufrière 4048ft

Tourama Point

Orange Hill

Richmond Beach

Wallibou River

trail

Trinity Falls

Rabacca Dry River

Chateaubelair Bay

Richmond

Chateaubelair Islet

Chateaubelair

Richmond Peak ▲ 3523ft

Georgetown

Troumaka Bay

Cumberland Bay

Morne Garu Mountains

Black Point

13°15'N 13°15'N

Wallilabou Bay

Bottle and Glass

Barrouallie

Cumberland River

Yarabaqua River

Colonarie Bay

North Union Bay

Vermont Nature Trails

South Union Bay

Mt Wynne Bay

Grant's Bay

Layou Bay

Layou

Buccament River

Biabou

Biabou Bay

Buccament Bay

Mesopotamia

Leeward Hwy

Windward Hwy

Questelles Point

Campden Park Bay

13°10'N 13°10'N

Kingstown

Yambou Head

Old Woman Point

Kingstown Bay

ET Joshua Airport

Arnos Vale

Cane Garden Point

Stubbs Bay

Villa

Indian Bay
Young Island
Fort Duvernette Island

Villa Beach

Milligan Cay

Ferries to the Grenadines, Trinidad & Venezuela

Ferry to Barbados

Sharp's Bay

Milikin Bay

0 2 4 km
0 1 2 miles

61°15'W 61°10'W

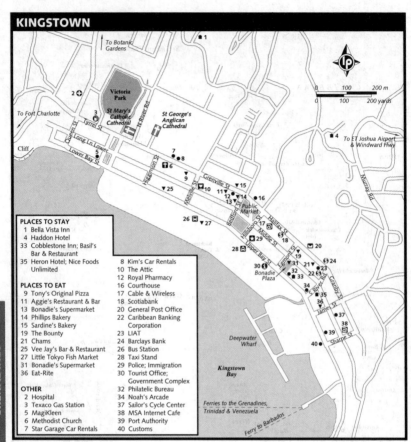

KINGSTOWN

To Botanic Gardens
To Fort Charlotte
Cliff

Victoria Park
St Mary's Catholic Cathedral
St George's Anglican Cathedral

To ET Joshua Airport & Windward Hwy

Tyrrel St
Grenville St
Halifax St
Middle St
Melville St
Higginson St
Bedford St
Hillsboro St
Upper Bay St
N River Rd
Que Long Ln Lower Bay St
Murray Rd
Granby St
River Rd
James St
Sharpe St

Public Market
Bonadie Plaza

Deepwater Wharf

Kingstown Bay

Ferries to the Grenadines, Trinidad & Venezuela
Ferry to Barbados

0   100   200 m
0   100   200 yards

PLACES TO STAY
1 Bella Vista Inn
4 Haddon Hotel
33 Cobblestone Inn; Basil's Bar & Restaurant
35 Heron Hotel; Nice Foods Unlimited

PLACES TO EAT
9 Tony's Original Pizza
11 Aggie's Restaurant & Bar
13 Bonadie's Supermarket
14 Phillips Bakery
15 Sardine's Bakery
19 The Bounty
21 Chams
25 Vee Jay's Bar & Restaurant
27 Little Tokyo Fish Market
31 Bonadie's Supermarket
36 Eat-Rite

OTHER
2 Hospital
3 Texaco Gas Station
5 MagiKleen
6 Methodist Church
7 Star Garage Car Rentals

8 Kim's Car Rentals
10 The Attic
12 Royal Pharmacy
16 Courthouse
17 Cable & Wireless
18 Scotiabank
20 General Post Office
22 Caribbean Banking Corporation
23 LIAT
24 Barclays Bank
26 Bus Station
28 Taxi Stand
29 Police; Immigration
30 Tourist Office; Government Complex
32 Philatelic Bureau
34 Noah's Arcade
37 Sailor's Cycle Center
38 MSA Internet Cafe
39 Port Authority
40 Customs

There's a small **aviary** that is intermittently home to some of the island's remaining 500 endangered St Vincent parrots. A breeding program is trying to bring the parrot back from the brink of extinction.

Nearby is a breadfruit tree that was grown from one of the original saplings brought to St Vincent from Tahiti in 1793 by Captain William Bligh. The gardens were the original destination of Bligh and the *Bounty* when the famous mutiny occurred in 1789. It was not until Bligh's second voyage that he managed to complete his mission. He introduced the tree, with its large, starchy fruit, as an inexpensive food source for plantation slaves. It has since proliferated throughout the Caribbean.

There's also a rare Soufrière tree, not found in the wild since 1812.

Also on the grounds is the disheveled ruin of the **St Vincent National Museum**. The museum is currently in the throes of moving to the old library on Granby St in central Kingstown.

The botanic gardens are a 10-minute walk north of the hospital along the Leeward Hwy. Admission is free, but expect to meet tour guides at the gate who will try to convince you to accept their services for US$3 per person. Some of the guides are very knowledgeable, but the gardens are pleasant enough to stroll through quietly on your own.

Churches

There are three interesting churches along Grenville St. **St Mary's Catholic Cathedral** is an unusual edifice, rather eclectic in design. The original church dates from 1823, but most of the present structure was built in the 1930s by Flemish monk Dom Charles Verbeke. The cathedral, fashioned in dark volcanic sand bricks, incorporates a remarkable mixture of architectural styles – Romanesque arches and columns, Gothic spires and elements of Georgian and Moorish ornamentation.

St George's Anglican Cathedral (c. 1820) is late Georgian in style. The interior has the typically Anglican altar and stained-glass windows, but the walls are painted bright yellow and turquoise. One of the stained-glass windows depicts an angel in red robes that overlooks the street; this was commissioned by Queen Victoria in honor of her first grandson, the Duke of Clarence, and was made for St Paul's Cathedral in London. The queen, it seems, objected to the scarlet-clad angel because the Bible makes it plain that all angels wear white. The window made its way to St Vincent and was installed in the cathedral.

There are also many interesting inscribed marble plaques. One in the center aisle beneath the chandelier venerates the British colonel Alexander Leith (1771–98), who took the life of Carib chief Chattawae in a sword duel (see History, earlier). In recent times a carpet was laid over the plaque, and it may not be visible.

From the outside, the **Methodist Church**, on the other side of the street, is an unremarkable structure. The interior, however, is aqua blue, bright and colorful, and bears remarkably little resemblance to the exterior. The church has a huge and ornate pipe organ in the choir balcony opposite the altar.

Fort Charlotte

Fort Charlotte, on a 660-foot ridge north of the city, provides a panoramic view of Kingstown and the Grenadines to the south. You can walk through the old officers' quarters, whose walls are lined with paintings depicting Black Carib history. Most of the rest of this 18th-century fort is off-limits, and one area is used as a women's prison. The fort, named after King George III's wife, was built in 1806 to fend off the French navy, and in its prime it housed 600 troops and 34 cannons.

The fort is an hour's walk from the center of town, but buses can drop you off nearby on the main road, from where it's a 10-minute uphill walk – ask at the bus terminal.

Places to Stay

The **Bella Vista Inn** (☎ 457-2757, fax 457-1894), on a hill above the west side of town, offers seven simple rooms in a private residence. Most have two single beds and standing fans, and some have private bathrooms. The cost is US$20/35 for singles/doubles. Bella Vista is a 10-minute walk from the city center; take the steep footpath leading uphill opposite St Martin's School.

Haddon Hotel (☎ 456-1897, fax 456-2726, PO Box 144) is a few minutes' walk from the city center. The hotel has 17 simple rooms that vary in size, but all have private baths. Rates are US$38/52 for singles/doubles, US$45/61 with air-con. There's also a new tower wing with eight large, modern units, with kitchens, pleasant rattan furnishings, air-con and TV, starting at US$75/130.

Cobblestone Inn (☎ 456-1937, fax 456-1938, PO Box 867), on Upper Bay St, is an atmospheric hotel in a renovated 1813 Georgian-style cobblestone warehouse that is one of Kingstown's most famous buildings. The 19 rooms have an old-world character, wooden floors, bathtub, air-con and cobblestone walls. The hotel is popular with business travelers and is the most comfortable place to stay in the city center. Singles/doubles cost US$65/76. There's a rooftop bar, a restaurant and a shopping arcade below.

Heron Hotel (☎ 457-1631, fax 457-1189, PO Box 226), on Upper Bay St, a block south of Cobblestone Inn, has 15 basic rooms with private baths, air-con and phones. The streetside rooms can get a bit noisy. It's well located but a bit grungy. Singles/doubles cost US$46/60 year-round.

Adams Apartments (☎ 458-4656, fax 456-4728, PO Box 120, abel@caribsurf.com) is in Arnos Vale next to the airport, two minutes' walk from the terminal. It's cheap and convenient, with 14 run-down singles/doubles from US$25/30. Some rooms have cooking facilities while others lack fans and have broken windows, so check out the room before you check in.

Places to Eat

A friendly 2nd-floor place run by a Canadian couple, *The Bounty* (☎ 456-1776), on Egmont St, boasts a balcony view overlooking the street. Rotis, omelets or macaroni & cheese pie costs around EC$6, fish or chicken & chips EC$14. It's open 7:30 am to 5 pm weekdays, till 1:30 pm Saturday.

Chams (☎ 457-2430, fax 457-2292) is in a quiet courtyard off Halifax St. It's a good lunch spot that's popular with local office workers. Good rotis sell for EC$8 and full meals cost from EC$15. It also serves up breakfast – bacon and eggs with coffee costs EC$12. It's open 8 am to 5 pm weekdays, till 2 pm Saturday.

Aggie's Restaurant & Bar (☎ 456-2110, PO Box 457) is a 2nd-floor place that's popular with expats. It's well regarded and has good local and seafood dishes at reasonable prices. Rotis cost EC$7, and fish with rice is EC$20. It's open from 9 am (noon on Sunday) until late at night.

Basil's Bar & Restaurant (☎ 457-2713, fax 456-2597, PO Box 1245), on Upper Bay St, is beneath Cobblestone Inn. It has a pleasant colonial character and is patronized by foreign businesspeople who discuss joint ventures with local politicians – serious business happens at Basil's. The weekday lunch buffet (noon to 2 pm) is popular and features hot West Indian main dishes, pumpkin fritters, salad and desserts for EC$35. The evening à la carte menu is good and offers a mix of international and West Indian dishes, with main courses starting at EC$38.

Cobblestone Inn (☎ 456-1937) has a breezy rooftop restaurant serving mostly light fare – cooked breakfasts, sandwiches and fish & chips in the EC$7 to EC$20 range. It's open 7:30 am to 3 pm daily.

Tony's Original Pizza (☎ 457-1506, fax 456-2141) has all the trappings of an American-style pizza diner. Pizza slices go for EC$6 and whole pizzas cost around EC$20. Burgers, fries and beers are available too. Tony's is open 10:30 am to 11 pm Monday through Thursday, till midnight Friday and Saturday, and 6 pm to midnight Sunday.

Eat-Rite (☎ 456-2449, PO Box 1283), on James St, is a simple fast-food place serving local dishes. It's open 7:30 am to 5 pm weekdays. *Lady J* (☎ 456-1900, PO Box 788), on Halifax St, is another cafeteria-style place a few doors south from Cham's.

Vee Jay's Bar & Restaurant (☎ /fax 457-2845), on Lower Bay St, is a good place for West Indian food and cold drinks. Locals eat at Vee Jay's, and the atmosphere is simple and unpretentious.

Nice Foods Unlimited (☎ 456-1391), on Upper Middle St, is directly below the Herron Hotel in a 19th-century building. Simple cafeteria-style meals are available 7 am to 11 pm daily except Sunday.

Self-caterers can stock up on food at *Phillips Bakery* (☎ 457-2869), on Lower Middle St, or *Sardine's Bakery* (☎ 456-1272), on Grenville St, within a block of each other. Both are open 6 am to 5 pm weekdays, till 1 pm Saturday. There are several grocery stores in town; perhaps the best stocked is *Bonadie's Supermarket* (☎ 456-1616), on Upper Middle St.

Fresh fish and seafood is available from *Little Tokyo Fish Market*, next to the bus terminal on Lower Bay St. It's open from 7 am Monday to Saturday. Fresh fruit and vegetables are cheap and abundant at the nearby public market. At the bus terminal you'll also find rows of rum shops, popcorn stands and sidewalk vendors selling roasted corn on the cob and drinking coconuts for EC$1.

Entertainment & Shopping

The Attic (☎ 457-2559, PO Box 1436, Grenville St) is a pleasant 2nd-floor club in an old stone building on Melville St. It has live jazz a few nights a week and sometimes soca bands on Saturday. There's a cover charge between EC$10 to EC$15.

Noah's Arcade (☎ 456-1513), on Upper Bay St, is an excellent little arts-and-crafts shop that sells all sorts of things, from cheap souvenirs to local art, books, maps, oil-drum art, gourmet coffee and spices, and West Indian dolls. It's well worth a browse. Artisans Art & Craft Shop (☎ 456-2306) is similar but not as well or carefully stocked. It's upstairs in Bonadie Plaza.

Voyager 1 & 2 (☎ 456-1686), on Upper Bay St and on Halifax St, respectively, are modern duty-free stores that stock the standard range of cosmetics and jewelry, as well as a vast range of trashy souvenirs. If you want fridge magnets, miniature flags, coffee mugs or T-shirts, this the place.

You can buy colorful commemorative stamps at the Philatelic Bureau, also on Upper Bay St.

VILLA BEACH & INDIAN BAY

St Vincent's main 'resort' district is Villa, a couple of miles southeast of Kingstown on the other side of the airport. It begins at Villa Point and runs along Indian Bay and Villa Beach, and past Young Island Cut, a narrow channel that separates Young Island from the St Vincent mainland.

The Villa area is a well-to-do seaside suburb with a dozen small hotels and inns, but it's not really the type of place most people would imagine when thinking of a Caribbean vacation. It's fairly well populated and the beaches are not pristine. Indian Bay Beach has grainy golden sand and is clean, but Villa Beach has a couple of storm-water drains emptying across it, and it gets a bit messed up after heavy rains. Some 'Happy New Year 2000' graffiti, rendered with a fat brush in white paint on the craggy rocks at the northwestern end of Villa Beach, are a blight on an otherwise attractive scene.

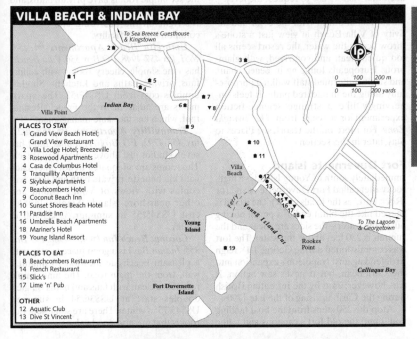

VILLA BEACH & INDIAN BAY

To Sea Breeze Guesthouse & Kingstown

Villa Point

Indian Bay

0   100   200 m
0   100   200 yards

Villa Beach

Young Island

Young Island Cut

Fort Duvernette Island

Rookes Point

To The Lagoon & Georgetown

Calliaqua Bay

PLACES TO STAY
1   Grand View Beach Hotel; Grand View Restaurant
2   Villa Lodge Hotel; Breezeville
3   Rosewood Apartments
4   Casa de Columbus Hotel
5   Tranquillity Apartments
6   Skyblue Apartments
7   Beachcombers Hotel
9   Coconut Beach Inn
10 Sunset Shores Beach Hotel
11 Paradise Inn
16 Umbrella Beach Apartments
18 Mariner's Hotel
19 Young Island Resort

PLACES TO EAT
8   Beachcombers Restaurant
14 French Restaurant
15 Slick's
17 Lime 'n' Pub

OTHER
12 Aquatic Club
13 Dive St Vincent

ST VINCENT & THE GRENADINES

There's decent snorkeling around the rocky islet with the cross on top, but beware of spiny black sea urchins. There's also snorkeling closer to shore at the south side of Indian Bay.

Most services, including water taxis, land taxis and the largest concentration of places to eat, are near Young Island Cut.

Young Island

Young Island is a small private island 200 yards off Villa Beach, and it's an exclusive resort. It's said that Young Island was once the home of a Carib chief who traded it for a black stallion. Access is via a small blue-and-white African Queen–era ferry that shuttles guests, restaurant diners and staff between Young Island and the Villa Beach dock.

You are supposed get permission to visit the island, so call ahead (☎ 458-4826). 'What is the purpose of your visit?' you'll be asked, and usually 'sightseeing' is good enough. There's a courtesy phone at Villa Beach dock that visitors use to request the ferry.

Young Island Resort has something of an unreal feel about it. With the color and activity of Villa Beach in view just a stone's throw across the water, the resort seems all too quiet, clean and contrived, with glamorous Europeans lounging in beach chairs and stiffly uniformed staff walking purposefully along the manicured paths. It feels unnervingly like a strange science-fiction experiment or a scene from *The Twilight Zone*. For more on the resort, see Places to Stay, later in this section.

Fort Duvernette Island

Immediately south of Young Island is a high, rocky islet called Fort Duvernette Island (or 'Rock Fort,' as the locals call it). The island is shaped like the blunt end of a pencil poking out of the water – the sides are sheer and the summit is 250 feet above the water. The fort was commissioned during George III's reign to defend against Napoleon's expansion into the Caribbean, but it never saw action. It was, however, used by the retreating British during the Carib uprising of the late 1790s.

Atop the 250 steps from the boat landing you'll find the old fort's cannons and a fine view of the Grenadines. You can hire a water taxi for a roundtrip ride (EC$20) from the jetty where the Young Island ferry pulls up – just let the water-taxi driver know what time you want to be collected. An hour on Fort Duvernette will give you enough time to climb up to the summit, poke around the cannons and crumbling brick walls, and sit and admire the view for a while. The top is thick with lizards, nesting birds and spooky noises in the overgrowth, and there are wonderful views of sea hawks and ospreys that circle and glide in the air currents that rise off the cliffs.

Take extreme care on the crumbling lower reaches of the climb – Fort Duvernette is considered unsafe by government engineers.

Places to Stay

Budget The *Sea Breeze Guesthouse* (☎ 458-4969), in Arnos Vale, is a mile east of the airport at a busy corner between the airport and Villa Beach. The location isn't great, but the six simple rooms have private baths, and the single/double rates are just US$20/30. It's right on the bus route and there's a common kitchen facility.

Umbrella Beach Apartments (☎ 458-4651, fax 457-4948, PO Box 530, Villa Beach) has nine simple, cheery rooms with ceiling fans, private baths and kitchens. Singles/doubles cost from US$42/52. The apartments are adjacent to the French Restaurant, which has the same management.

Tranquillity Apartments (☎ 458-4021, fax 457-4792, PO Box 71, Indian Bay) has seven studios just above Indian Bay Beach. The rooms are adequate but not fancy, each with kitchenette, private bath and little balconies with views of Young Island and other nearshore islands. Singles/doubles cost US$45/55 in summer, US$50/60 in winter.

Coconut Beach Inn (☎ 457-4900, PO Box 355, Indian Bay) is a good place to stay with a pleasant beachside location 10 minutes' walk from the main road. The nine simple rooms are clean with fans and baths. Singles/doubles start at US$36/54 in summer, US$45/75 in winter. There are some superior rooms that are also good values.

Skyblue Apartments (☎ 457-4394, fax 457-5232, skyblue@caribsurf.com, PO Box 87, Indian Bay) is a good value, with eight large single/double apartments, each with kitchen and TV, for US$45/55.

Paradise Inn (☎ 457-4795, fax 457-4221, paradinn@caribsurf.com, PO Box 1286, Villa Beach) is yet another good value right on the beach. The eight rooms have fans, air-con, TV, phone and bath. Winter rates are US$60 to US$70 for singles and US$80 to US$95 for doubles; the higher-priced rooms have refrigerators and lovely sea-view balconies. Rates are US$10 cheaper in summer.

Mid-Range The **Rosewood Apartments** (☎ 457-5051, fax 457-5141, rosewood@caribsurf.com, www.rosewoodsvg.com, PO Box 687, Villa) is a new place on a hill above the main road to Villa, about a five-minute walk to the beach. All singles/doubles have air-con, phone, TV, kitchenette and balcony and cost from US$64/74 in summer and US$68/78 in winter.

Beachcombers Hotel (☎ 458-4283, fax 458-4385, beachcombers@cariaccess.com, www.beachcombershotel.com, PO Box 126, Villa), on the west side of Villa Beach, is a friendly family-run operation with a dozen rooms. The rooms vary in size and decor but have private baths, ceiling fans and patios, and the hotel has a fine beachside location, swimming pool, bar-restaurant and business center with Internet access. Singles/doubles cost US$65/90, Continental breakfast included, and air-conditioned or kitchenette rooms cost a further US$13 per day each.

Casa de Columbus Hotel (☎ 458-4001, fax 458-4777, indianbay@casadecolumbus.com, PO Box 993, Indian Bay) was formerly the Indian Bay Beach Hotel. It has been refurbished and is now a very comfortable place to stay. Rates are US$95 single and US$45 for each additional person, meals included. Rooms have air-con, TV, phone and private bath.

Ten minutes' walk east of Villa is The Lagoon, which is the site of **The Lagoon Marina & Hotel** (☎ 458-4308, sunsailsvg@caribsurf.com, www.lagoonmarina.com, PO Box 133, Ratho Mill). This is essentially a service marina for touring yachts, but it's also a good place to stay. Rooms have private bath, phone, TV and balcony, and there's also an Internet café, pool, supermarket and restaurant. Singles cost US$70 in summer (US$80 in winter) with ceiling fans, US$80 (US$95) with air-con, and doubles are US$85 (US$100) with fan, US$95 (US$120) with air-con. These rates are *inclusive* of the 7% tax.

Top End The **Mariner's Hotel** (☎/fax 457-2561, mariners-hotel@caribsurf.com) is on the Villa waterfront, with its own little jetty. Rooms have air-con, TV, en suite bathrooms and balconies, and the hotel has a restaurant, bar, swimming pool and Internet access. Single/double rates begin at US$95/125 in summer and US$115/145 in winter.

Sunset Shores Beach Hotel (☎ 458-4411, fax 457-4800, in the USA ☎ 800-424-6510, sunshore@caribsurf, www.sunsetshores.com, PO Box 849, Villa Beach) has 32 smallish rooms with air-con, TV and phones. There's a pool, restaurant and bar. Sunset Shores is comfortable but overpriced, with singles/doubles beginning at US$95/120 in summer, US$140/170 in winter.

Villa Lodge Hotel (☎ 458-4641, fax 457-4468, villodge@caribsurf.com, PO Box 1191, Indian Bay) is popular with visiting Caribbean politicians and business travelers. There are 10 attractive rooms with TV, air-con, small fridges, phones and bathrooms with tubs; rooms 7 through 10 have splendid views. Singles/doubles cost US$95/105 in summer, US$120/130 in winter. Children aged two to 12 are charged US$10 per night. Attractive self-contained apartments with full amenities cost US$140 for one-bedroom units, US$170 for two-bedroom, two-bath units. There's a pool, a breezy sitting room and a small, moderately priced restaurant.

On Villa Point, **Grand View Beach Hotel** (☎ 458-4811, fax 457-4174, in the USA ☎ 800-223-6510, grandview@caribsurf.com, www.grandviewhotel.com, PO Box 173, Villa Point) is an old hilltop plantation house with commanding views. The 19 rooms are large and plush, and many have fine ocean views. Doubles begin at US$210 for older rooms and US$270 for refurbished rooms with modern amenities. There's a gym, tennis courts and a pool.

Exclusive **Young Island Resort** (☎ 458-4826, fax 457-4567, in the USA ☎ 800-223-1108, y-island@caribsurf.com, www.youngisland.com, PO Box 211) occupies the whole of Young Island. Pleasant stone cottages open to surrounding gardens, and some have private pools. The cottages have simple amenities, louvered windows, patios, alfresco showers, ceiling fans and refrigerators, and they're stocked daily with fresh fruit and flowers. Rates include breakfast and dinner, beginning at US$325 in summer, US$450 in winter for doubles. Singles are US$90 cheaper. Various packages offer sailing and diving, and there are 'Lover's Packages' available too. You can even get married on Young Island.

Places to Eat

Budget & Mid-Range The oceanfront restaurant at **Coconut Beach Inn** (see Places to Stay) is casual and friendly, with good, inexpensive food. Cooked breakfasts cost EC$18. At lunch, rotis or sandwiches are priced at EC$10, and hearty evening meals cost from EC$30.

Lime 'n' Pub (☎ 458-4227), fronting Young Island Cut in Villa, is an unusual place with an easygoing bar that serves inexpensive pub food – bangers & chips for EC$24, flying fish and salad for EC$35 – as well as a more upmarket restaurant with an à la carte menu that specializes in fresh seafood with a West Indian twist. Main courses start at EC$45, and there's an extensive wine list.

The breezy open-air **Beachcombers Restaurant** (☎ 457-4954), above Villa Beach, has sandwiches and burgers for EC$15 and pizzas from EC$22. Evening main courses start at around EC$40 and include international and West Indian chicken and fish dishes.

Breezeville (☎ 458-4641), at the Villa Lodge Hotel, has good food at reasonable prices and is open for three meals a day. Creole chicken, catch of the day or Cajun fish all cost around EC$35 and come with salad, rice and rolls.

Casa de Columbus Hotel (see Places to Stay) has waterfront dining at its restaurant. At lunch, there are burgers or rotis for EC$10 and fish & chips for EC$25. Evening meals begin at EC$45.

Slick's (☎ 457-5783) is perhaps the pick of the bunch. This bar-restaurant has a very pleasant atmosphere and offers a range of Italian and French dishes as well as traditional West Indian fare, but the overall temperament is seafood and Creole. Main courses start at EC$40 and include lobster, shrimp and steak dishes. There's a small play area for children, a wine list and terrific service.

Top End The **French Restaurant** (☎ 458-4972, frenchella@caribsurf, PO Box 530), at Villa Beach, serves French food and seafood with a West Indian accent, and it's regarded as the best restaurant in St Vincent. It's open for lunch and dinner, and lunchtime sandwiches start at a very reasonable EC$15; simple fish or chicken dishes cost from EC$30. In the evening, starters such as the superb onion soup begin around EC$30, while main seafood and beef dishes cost from EC$55. It's closed Sunday.

Grand View Restaurant (☎ 458-4811), at the Grand View Beach Hotel at Villa Point, offers Continental breakfasts for EC$20 and full breakfasts from EC$35. At lunch there are sandwiches, salads and omelets, most in the EC$18 to EC$35 range. Dinner is a fixed-price meal, by reservation, with a choice of two main dishes (usually meat and fish), soup, dessert and coffee, all for EC$75.

The fancy **Young Island Resort** (☎ 458-4826) serves an EC$120 five-course dinner from 7:30 to 9:30 pm. Lunches are served too and generally cost around EC$60. Reservations are required for all meals.

Entertainment

The **Aquatic Club** (☎ 458-4205, PO Box 831, Kingstown), at Young Island Cut, has local bands playing every Saturday and alternate Fridays, usually a variation of calypso, soca or reggae. There's often a cover charge between EC$15 and EC$25. The Aquatic Club also offers lunch and dinner daily.

WINDWARD HIGHWAY

St Vincent's windward east coast is raw and rugged, with Atlantic surf lashing its shoreline and a densely jungled interior. The Windward Hwy winds up and down the east coast, passing black-sand beaches, banana plantations and deep valleys thickly planted in coconut trees. Small villages of old wooden shanties and simple cement homes intermittently appear along the roadside.

The road is potholed and narrow in places, but by St Vincent standards it's in reasonably good condition. The final leg between Owia and Fancy is part cement and part dirt. It takes at least an hour to drive from Kingstown to Georgetown, and the 35 miles from Kingstown to the end of the road at Fancy take a good two hours each way, not including time to stop and explore.

Buses from Kingstown to Georgetown are fairly regular (except on Sunday) and cost EC$5. Buses driving north from Georgetown are irregular, so get information from the Kingstown bus terminal before heading off.

Georgetown

Georgetown is a poor town that was once the center of the island's sugar industry. Now just a relic of its former glory, its main street is lined with cobblestone sidewalks and two-story buildings with overhanging balconies. Most of the once-stylish buildings are now in disrepair, and many lie fallen apart and abandoned.

Few tourists come this way, and there's not much to see. Two churches, one Methodist and one Anglican, sit side by side on the main street and are open to visitors.

The 2nd-story *Footsteps Restaurant & Bar* (☎ 458-6433), above the grocery store on the main road in the center of town, serves simple but hearty West Indian food – breakfast costs about EC$12 and lunch or dinner cost about EC$20. There are a couple of rooms for rent as well.

North of Georgetown

The farther north you go, the wilder the landscape gets; the valleys are deeper and the villages fewer and less developed. The active volcano of La Soufrière looms inland as you continue along the road, adding a malevolent and primeval feeling to the surrounds.

A mile north of Georgetown the road goes over the Rabacca Dry River, a hardened lava flow that was a stream which filled with lava during La Soufrière's violent 1902 eruption. The river now flows beneath the lava, but during heavy rains the river can flow above it, causing flash floods and making the road crossing hazardous or impossible.

North of the dry river, a 4WD road heads inland through coconut and banana plantations toward **La Soufrière** and the beginning of a 3¼-mile hiking trail that leads to the rim of the crater.

Continuing north, the Windward Hwy passes through **Orange Hill**, where a 3160-acre coconut estate, once the world's largest, has been divided up and parceled out to small farmers as part of a government land-reform project. Orange Hill also produces bananas, limes, spices and vegetables.

A couple of miles farther is **Sandy Bay**, a sizable village that has the island's largest concentration of Black Caribs. They are physically distinguished from other Vincentians by their short, stocky builds and high cheekbones.

North of Sandy Bay is Owia Bay and the village of **Owia**. Turn east on the main village road at the police station to reach the coastal Owia Salt Pond. Here you'll find tidal pools protected from the crashing Atlantic by a massive stone shield. This is a popular swimming hole with crystal-clear waters; there are thatched shelters, picnic tables, restrooms and a view of St Lucia to the north. Use caution during high tide or if the waves are breaking over the rocks, and watch out for yellow sea anemones, which can sting. Owia also has an arrowroot mill and a couple of churches that can be visited.

True diehards can go to **Fancy**, where the road ends at St Vincent's most remote village, a rather rudimentary settlement with no electricity or phones. An old arrowroot mill with a rusting mill wheel now serves as the medical clinic; nearby are a school and a couple of simple shops selling groceries and provisions.

LEEWARD HIGHWAY

The Leeward Hwy runs north from Kingstown along St Vincent's west coast for 25 miles, ending at Richmond Beach. The west coast offers some lovely scenery. The road climbs into the mountains as it leaves Kingstown and then winds through the hillside and back down to deeply cut coastal valleys that open to coconut plantations, fishing villages and bays lined with black-sand beaches.

The drive from Kingstown to Richmond Beach takes about 1½ hours. Just north of Kingstown are a few narrow sections where the shoulderless road is crumbly – take care or tumble over the cliff. Otherwise, the road as far as Barrouallie is in good condition, albeit narrow and winding.

There are fairly frequent weekday buses from Kingstown to Barrouallie (EC$4, 45 minutes). Buses don't run in the evening, so catch your return bus to Kingstown by 5 pm. It's a 15-minute walk from the last Barrouallie bus stop to Wallilabou Bay. Generally, only four buses a day (two in the morning, two in the afternoon) continue north from Barrouallie to Richmond.

Vermont Nature Trails

About a 15-minute drive north of Kingstown is a sign along the Leeward Hwy pointing east to the Vermont Nature Trails, 3½ miles inland. Here you'll find the Parrot Lookout Trail, a 1¾-mile loop trail that passes through the southwestern tip of the St Vincent Parrot Reserve. The island forestry department, with assistance from the Worldwide Fund for Nature, established the reserve in 1987 to protect the endangered St Vincent parrot, which numbers only about 500 in the wild.

The Parrot Lookout Trail climbs 500 feet in elevation into a mixed tropical rain forest of towering native hardwood trees, lush ferns, bromeliads, heliconia, abandoned cocoa trees and introduced groves of eucalyptus. The hike takes about two hours and can get slippery; solid footwear is recom-

mended. Be prepared for wet conditions, as the forest averages 200 inches of annual rainfall, and bring insect repellent. Hikers should wear long sleeves and pants for protection against chiggers.

Near the trailhead you'll find a welcome-board with background information and a map. Twenty interpretive signs posted along the trail give brief descriptions of the flora and fauna encountered along the way.

The best times to sight a parrot are early morning and late afternoon. Other birds seen along the trail include the rare whistling warbler, brightly colored hooded tanagers, hummingbirds, broad-winged hawks and common black hawks.

Layou & Barrouallie

The Leeward Hwy comes out to the coast for the first time at the black sands of Buccament Bay. Shortly after that the road curves around the coastal mountains before descending to Layou Bay. There are petroglyphs on St Vincent's west coast. The best known are in Layou, a short walk from the river near the Bible Camp on the main road at the north end of town. They're on private property, and you need to make arrangements to see them with the owner, Victor Hendrickson (☎ 458-7243), who charges visitors EC$5.

After Layou the road goes inland before coming back out to the coast at the north side of Mt Wynne Bay, a lovely black-sand beach backed by a broad sweep of coconut trees.

The villagers of Barrouallie, about 5km north of Layou, are perhaps best known for their hunting of pilot whales, which are referred to as 'blackfish' on the island.

The village has some interesting older architecture with gingerbread trim, and there are petroglyphs in the yard of the Barrouallie secondary school.

Wallilabou Bay & Falls

Wallilabou is a quiet little bay lined with a black-sand beach surrounded by high cliffs and a little rock arch at its northern end. The waters are usually calm, and there's snorkeling at the bay's southern end.

Wallilabou is a port of entry to the island. A small flotilla of young men often rows out to the yachts as they pull into the bay to sell provisions and run errands.

Wallilabou Falls are near the inland side of the main road about a mile north of Wallilabou Bay. They're about 13 feet high and drop into a waist-deep bathing pool.

Wallilabou Anchorage (☎ 458-7270, *VHF channel 68, wallanch@caribsurf.com, PO Box 851, Wallilabou)* runs the mooring facilities and has a pleasant bayside restaurant and bar. Adjacent to the restaurant is a small hotel with seafront rooms from US$50 up.

North of Wallilabou

North of Wallilabou, the next beach you come to is **Cumberland Bay**, an anchorage backed by coconut palms and lush green hills.

The road passes a few settlements, including the town of **Chateaubelair**, before ending at **Richmond Beach**. This long black-sand beach has stands of tropical almond trees and is a popular swimming spot.

East of Richmond is the trailhead to **Trinity Falls**, a remote triple cascade with a 40-foot drop. The falls are about 3 miles inland on the road beginning at the old Richmond Vale Academy. The road is bad, but with a 4WD vehicle it's usually possible to drive about half the distance through the rain forest and continue to the falls on foot. The pool beneath the falls is deep enough for a swim, but there can be strong currents, and loose rocks overhead sometimes fall into the pool.

Also from Richmond, it's possible to hike up to the crater rim of La Soufrière. However, this trail is rougher and less defined than the one on the windward side of the island, and a local guide is necessary. The hike takes about five hours roundtrip.

FALLS OF BALEINE

The 60-foot Falls of Baleine, at the isolated northwestern tip of the island, are accessible only by boat. The scenic falls, which cascade down a fern-draped rock face into a wide pool, are a few minutes' walk from the beach where the boats anchor.

Hotels, guest houses and dive shops do tours to Baleine, most stopping en route for snorkeling. Some tours use speedboats, which reach the falls in about an hour from Kingstown. Sailboats offer less noise and a more leisurely pace, usually taking a couple of hours each way.

Most tour operators charge around US$50 for the day tour and require at least three people to make the trip. Sea Breeze Boat Service (☎ 458-4969) uses a 36-foot sloop and charges US$40.

Bequia

Bequia (pronounced 'beck-way') is the northernmost of St Vincent's Grenadine islands. It's also the largest (7 sq miles) and, with 5000 people, it's the most populated too. It has a well-developed tourist infrastructure – the lodgings are comfortable and the restaurants are excellent – yet it's small and intimate. It's an essential stop on any local itinerary.

Bequia is a delightful place, neat, hilly and green, with lots of flowering bushes and some fine golden-sand beaches. It's popular with yachters and returning visitors, and there's a rather glamorous international air about the place. As you shuffle lazily between the beaches and boutiques you get the feeling that you're in on one of the best-kept secrets of the Caribbean.

The island was once the region's most important whaling station, and there's also a strong boat-building tradition. Modern vessels are usually steel-hulled, so today local boat-building manifests mostly in scale models. More than 90% of the boats pulling into beautiful Admiralty Bay are visiting yachts, and in the height of the season the harbor is packed with yachts of all shapes and sizes.

PORT ELIZABETH

Port Elizabeth, built along the curve of Admiralty Bay, is an appealing seaside community and the island's commercial center. The town has an international flavor, and many restaurants and shops are operated

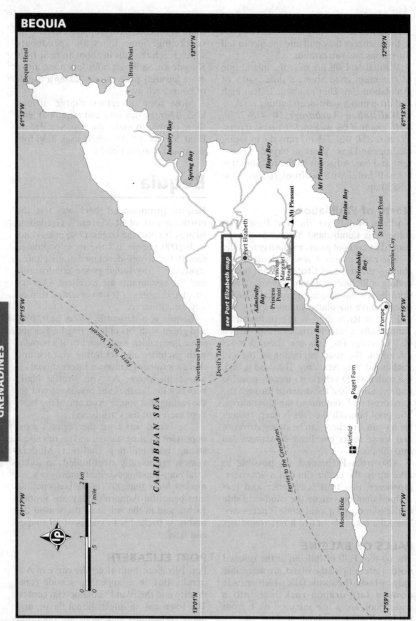

BEQUIA

13°01'N

12°59'N

61°13'W

61°15'W

61°17'W

Bequia Head

Brute Point

Industry Bay

Spring Bay

Hope Bay

Mt Pleasant Bay

▲ Mt Pleasant

Ravine Bay

St Hilaire Point

Port Elizabeth ●

see Port Elizabeth map

Princess
Margaret Beach

Admiralty Bay

Princess
Point

Friendship Bay

Semples Cay

ferry to St Vincent

CARIBBEAN SEA

Northwest Point

Devil's Table

Lower Bay

La Pompe ●

Ferries to the Grenadines

● Paget Farm

Moon Hole

✈ Airfield

2 km

1 mile

.5   1

0

0   1

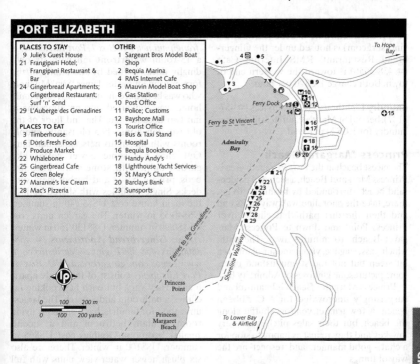

PORT ELIZABETH

PLACES TO STAY	OTHER
9 Julie's Guest House	1 Sargeant Bros Model Boat
21 Frangipani Hotel;	Shop
Frangipani Restaurant &	2 Bequia Marina
Bar	4 RMS Internet Cafe
24 Gingerbread Apartments;	5 Mauvin Model Boat Shop
Gingerbread Restaurant;	8 Gas Station
Surf 'n' Send	10 Post Office
29 L'Auberge des Grenadines	11 Police; Customs
	12 Bayshore Mall
PLACES TO EAT	13 Tourist Office
3 Timberhouse	14 Bus & Taxi Stand
6 Doris Fresh Food	15 Hospital
7 Produce Market	16 Bequia Bookshop
22 Whaleboner	17 Handy Andy's
25 Gingerbread Cafe	18 Lighthouse Yacht Services
26 Green Boley	19 St Mary's Church
27 Maranne's Ice Cream	20 Barclays Bank
28 Mac's Pizzeria	23 Sunsports

To Hope Bay

Ferry Dock

Ferry to St Vincent

Admiralty Bay

Ferries to the Grenadines

Princess Point

Shoreline Walkway

0   100   200 m
0   100   200 yards

Princess Margaret Beach

To Lower Bay & Airfield

by expatriates – mostly yachters who came to visit and stayed on. Many of the waterfront businesses cater to visiting boaters and offer several services – you can pick up ice and drop off laundry, and there are good bars and dining spots.

The town has lots of trendy boutiques that sell batik and silk-screen clothing, frond baskets and crafts.

Orientation

A narrow shoreline walkway at the south side of Port Elizabeth provides the main access to many of the town's restaurants and places to stay. Gentle waves engulf the little walkway at high tide, making the route rather a wet one. This causes much mirth as people try to negotiate the path without getting their shoes wet – timing is everything.

Although there's barely a beach here, this southerly section of Port Elizabeth is sometimes called Belmont Beach.

Information

Tourist Offices The Bequia Tourism Association's tourist office (☎ 458-3286) at the ferry dock is open 9 am to noon and 1:30 to 4 pm weekdays, mornings only Saturday. The association maintains a good Web site at www.bequiasweet.com.

Money Barclays Bank is at the north end of the shoreline walkway, and the Caribbean Banking Corporation (☎ 458-3846) is at Bayshore Mall opposite the ferry dock. Both are open 8 am to 1 pm Monday to Thursday, 8 am to 1 pm and 3 to 5 pm Friday. Each has a 24-hour ATM.

Post & Communications The Port Elizabeth post office (☎ 458-3350), opposite the ferry dock, is open 9 am to noon and 1 to 3 pm weekdays, 9 to 11:30 am Saturday.

There are card and coin phones outside the tourist office.

There are a couple of small Internet cafés in Port Elizabeth. Surf 'n' Send (surfnsend@vincysurf.com) is housed under the Gingerbread Restaurant. RMS Internet Cafe (☎ 458-3556) is toward the western end of town. Both charge EC$20 per hour.

Laundry Lighthouse Yacht Services (☎ 457-3187), behind St Mary's Church, will do your laundry for EC$20 per load.

Princess Margaret Beach

The nicest beach in the Port Elizabeth area is Princess Margaret Beach, a secluded golden-sand beach surrounded by bushland. To get there, take the shoreline walkway to its end and then the dirt path that climbs over Princess Point and down to Princess Margaret Beach, 10 minutes away. The path, which passes agave, yucca and air plants, is a bit steep but not too strenuous and offers some picturesque glimpses of Admiralty Bay.

Princess Margaret Beach is beautiful and surprisingly uncrowded for a Caribbean beach. A few trinket vendors shuffle along the beach, but their sales pitches are very low-key and they're just as happy to stop for a chat – good manners and 'respect' are the way of things.

Places to Stay

On the waterfront, *L'Auberge des Grenadines* (☎ 458-3201) has six simple rooms above the restaurant of the same name. The guest house has a 200-year-old fig tree on its grounds. Rates are US$30/40 single/double with shared bath, US$48 for a double with private bath.

Julie's Guesthouse (☎ 458-3304, fax 458-3812, julies@caribsurf.com) is an old wooden boardinghouse. The 1st floor has a bar and restaurant, while the 2nd floor has simple, clean rooms with (cold) showers and toilets separated by a curtain. The thin wooden walls are poor sound barriers. The rooms have louvered windows and no screens, but there are mosquito nets over the beds. For those who prefer comfort (hot showers) to character, Julie's also has rooms in a new cement building. Singles/doubles cost US$39/65.

The *Frangipani Hotel* (☎ 458-3255, fax 458-3824, frangi@caribsurf.com, www.frangipani.net, PO Box 1, Port Elizabeth) is a 15-room waterfront inn with its own dinghy dock. Owned by the family of the former prime minister James 'Son' Mitchell, who was born here in room No 1, this family home was converted into an atmospheric inn two decades ago. The 2nd floor of the old wooden house has pleasantly simple rooms with mosquito nets, sinks and fans. Out back are some newer cottagelike garden units, with stone walls, king-size beds, private baths and harbor-view sundecks. Singles/doubles with shared bath in the main house cost US$30/40 in summer, US$40/55 in winter. The garden units cost US$80/90 in summer, US$130/150 in winter.

The *Gingerbread Apartments* (☎ 458-3800, fax 458-3907, ginger@caribsurf.com, www.begos.com/gingerbread, PO Box 1, Port Elizabeth) consist of three tidy apartments. They vary, but each has cooking facilities, a bathroom and a porch. The largest unit, good for families, has a spacious living room, a main bedroom and a second smaller bedroom. Doubles cost US$65 in summer, US$100 in winter. There are also six plush newer water-view units with full kitchens and porches that begin at US$110 in summer, US$150 in winter.

Village Apartments (☎ fax 458-3883, in the USA ☎ 800-265-3447, tvabqsvg@caribsurf.com, PO Box 1621, Kingstown) offers weekly rentals in seven units on the Paget Farm road in Belmont, a 10-minute uphill walk from the center of Port Elizabeth. These modern apartments have kitchenettes, fans, porches and red-tile floors; some have air-con. There's a studio apartment for US$350 a week in summer, US$450 in winter; one-bedroom apartments from US$400 in summer, US$500 in winter; and two-bedroom cottages for US$500 in summer, US$580 in winter.

Places to Eat

A little kiosk just north of Mac's Pizzeria, *Maranne's Ice Cream* (☎ 458-3041) has good homemade ice cream, sorbet and frozen yogurt (EC$2.80 a cone) and is open 11 am to 6 pm daily. The *Green Boley*

(☎ 457-3625), in a shack north of Maranne's, serves inexpensive rotis and callaloo soup.

Mac's Pizzeria (☎ 458-3474) has porch-side dining overlooking Admiralty Bay. It has pizzas from EC$24 to a 15-inch lobster pizza for EC$80. There are also whole-wheat or pita-bread sandwiches from EC$12, as well as quiches and pasta dishes. It's open 11 am to 10 pm daily.

The waterfront *Frangipani Restaurant & Bar* (☎ 458-3255) is on the lower level of the old Mitchell house, which once stored the 130-foot *Gloria Colita*, the largest schooner ever built on Bequia. (The boat disappeared in 1940 and was found drifting in the Bermuda Triangle, with no trace of its crew.) Today it's a seaside bar-restaurant and Bequia's favorite watering hole. Until 5 pm there are sandwiches, burgers, salads and omelets from EC$12 or a fresh fish dish for EC$30. Seafood and West Indian fare are served up at dinner; main dishes cost from EC$35. It's open 7:30 am to 9 pm daily.

The 2nd-floor *Gingerbread Restaurant* (☎ 458-3800) is a popular dining spot with high ceilings, gingerbread trim and a fine harbor view. At lunch there are sand-wiches, omelets and pasta dishes from EC$12 to EC$25. Dinner features inter-national and West Indian food with a seafood slant, and main courses start at EC$35. There's live music on Sunday evening. The Gingerbread Restaurant is open 8 am to 9:30 pm daily. *Gingerbread Cafe*, at the south side of the restaurant, has cakes, ice cream, coffee and cappuc-cino. It's open 7:30 am to 6:30 pm daily.

Vestiges of Bequia's whaling history can be found at *Whaleboner* (☎ 458-3233), where the bar is made from a huge piece of whalebone and the bar stools from verte-brae. The cuisine is inexpensive West Indian.

Timberhouse (☎ 457-3495), at Bequia Marina on the north side of the bay, is a large open-air bar-restaurant. At lunch there are burgers, sandwiches and smoked-fish salads for EC$12 to EC$30; at dinner, rum chicken or catch of the day costs EC$35.

Vendors sell drinking coconuts (EC$1.50) near the ferry dock. The *produce market*, just west of the dock, sells fresh fruit and vegetables. Simple pastries can be bought at *Bread Basket*, in the Bayshore Mall. For groceries, you'll find a handful of super-markets on the waterfront road.

Doris Fresh Food (☎ 458-3625), opposite the market, sells wine, cheese and fresh crois-sants, baguettes and whole-wheat bread.

Shopping

The Bequia Bookshop (☎ 458-3905, fax 458-3874), in Port Elizabeth, is an excellent book-store that stocks everything from charts and survey maps to yachting books, guides on flora and fauna, and a selection of West Indian literature. There's also a fine selection of scrimshaw pieces for sale in display cabi-nets (see 'Sam the Scrimhander').

Several artisans sell model boats, and there are a couple of shops devoted to the craft. Mauvin is on the western end of town, while the famous Sargeant Brothers (☎ 458-3344) have a workshop and store just a little farther west. There are also a couple of wannabe makers who have stalls at the market. They sell boats from US$50. See 'Model Boats.'

At the market vendors sell T-shirts, hand-made dolls, jewelry and other islands crafts. Consider avoiding purchasing jewelry made from coral and turtle shell – the production of these artifacts is unsustainable and detri-mental to the environment.

LOWER BAY

Lower Bay is a quiet little beachside com-munity at the southern end of Admiralty Bay. It's fronted by a delightful golden-sand beach and clear turquoise waters. Lower Bay is one of Bequia's nicest beaches. There are a few guest houses, but it's off the main tourist track, perfect for dropping out and playing beach bum.

It's a 10-minute walk to Lower Bay from the Port Elizabeth–Paget Farm road, the nearest bus stop. There's also a footpath leading from Princess Margaret Beach to Lower Bay. Beware of manchineel trees that grow around Lower Bay Beach – these large, shady trees look inviting, but oils from their leaves can cause a serious rash.

ST VINCENT & THE GRENADINES

Places to Stay

Right across from Lower Bay Beach, **Keegan's Guesthouse** (☎ 458-3530, fax 457-3313) has 11 rooms. Two nice ones are Nos 8

Model Boats

Bequia's shipbuilding heritage lives on through local artisans who build wooden scale models of traditional schooners and Bequian whaling boats. The boats are crafted to exact proportions, painted in traditional colors and outfitted with sails and rigging.

There are a couple of workshops opposite the waterfront on the north side of Port Elizabeth. The best known is the Sargeant Brothers Model Boat Shop, near the Bequia Marina. Laconic Timothy Sargeant is the youngest of the current generation, and he mans the tiny shop. He'll show you through the workshop, where no power tools are used. The Sargeant Brothers have been making model boats since 1966, and a true Sargeant model boat will cost you upward of US$400. There are others who work out of the workshop, some apprentices, some now masters themselves, and the shop sells small boats from US$100.

Most of the models are made for custom orders, replicas of visiting yachts made for their owners. One of their best-known works was a model of the royal yacht, HMS *Britannia*, which was presented to Queen Elizabeth II during her 1985 visit. Many of the models are shipped off the island and sold to collectors.

---

and 9, which are big and well appointed and share a balcony with an ocean view. All rooms have private baths, fans and comfortable beds with mosquito nets. Rooms in the older wing are smaller, but even they are good values compared to most places at Port Elizabeth. Rates, which include breakfast and dinner, start at US$45/70 for singles/doubles.

Lower Bay Guesthouse (☎ 458-3675, fax 456-2344), a minute's walk up from the beach, has eight small, basic rooms with sink, louvered windows and shared bath. Singles/doubles cost US$28/42.

De Reef Apartments (☎ 458-3484, fax 457-3103) features five self-contained apartments, just inland of the beachside De Reef restaurant, that start at US$250/415 weekly in summer and US$330/480 in winter.

Places to Eat

The restaurant at **Keegan's** (see Places to Stay) serves breakfast, lunch and dinner daily. Dinner is by reservation only and usually features fresh seafood. There's a small bar.

Fernando's Hideaway (☎ 458-3758), in the village center, serves local West Indian food and is open for dinner.

At the east end of the beach is **Theresa's** (☎ 458-3802), a simple little concrete hut with a handful of tables that offers moderately priced West Indian dinners, lunchtime sandwiches and burgers, and a good selection of vegetarian dishes. Sunday afternoon features a jam session.

Coco's Place (☎ 458-3463), on a hill at the south end of Lower Bay, is a very popular lunch and dinner spot with good, moderately priced seafood dishes. The bar is lively, and there's live music on Tuesday and Friday nights.

FRIENDSHIP BAY

Friendship Bay is a deep, beautiful bay with a long golden-sand beach. The area is quiet and caters to tourists, mostly European, more than sailors. The waterfront is a few minutes' walk from the Port Elizabeth–Paget Farm road, where buses run past.

The uninhabited island of Petit Nevis lies about a mile south of Friendship Bay, and it's the site of a deserted whaling station. Piles of whalebone lie about, and there are a few rusting iron try-pots that were used for boiling down blubber. The island is a popular day anchorage with good snorkeling.

Places to Stay & Eat

The *Blue Tropic Hotel* (☎ 458-3573, fax 457-3074, bluetropic@caribsurf.com), on the main road just above Friendship Bay, has 10 basic rooms with kitchenettes, showers, ceiling fans and balconies with partial views of the bay. Singles/doubles cost US$55/75 year-round.

Bequia Beach Club (☎ 458-3248, fax 458-3689, bequiabeachclub@caribsurf.com), on Friendship Bay, has eight attractive beach-side apartments with ceiling fans, kitchens and one king or two double beds. It's rather pricey: Singles/doubles cost US$100/150.

Friendship Bay Hotel (☎ 458-3222, fax 458-3840, labambas@caribsurf.com, www.friendshipbay.com, PO Box 9, Friendship Bay) is a pleasant Swedish-run beachfront hotel with 27 rooms. Doubles begin at US$150 in summer, US$165 in winter. The hotel has a tennis court, a dive shop and a jetty. There's a beach hut and bar selling sandwiches from EC$16, and restaurant with a splendid water view.

GETTING THERE & AWAY
Air

Bequia's airport is near Paget Farm, at the southwest end of the island. Daily flights connect Bequia with St Vincent and the other Grenadine islands. For details, see the Getting Around section at the beginning of this chapter.

Sea

Ferry The scheduled ferry between Bequia and St Vincent is cheaper than flying and more convenient. The docks are located in the center of Kingstown and Port Elizabeth, the ferries are generally punctual and the crossing takes only one hour. Tickets are sold on board; the fare is EC$15 one-way, EC$28 roundtrip.

Boats leave Bequia at 6:30, 7:30 am, 2 and 5 pm weekdays; at 6:30 am and 5 pm Satur-

day; and at 7:30 am and 5 pm Sunday. Departures from St Vincent are at 9, 10:30 am, 12:30, 4:30 and 7 pm weekdays; 11:30 am, 12:30 and 7 pm Saturday; and 9 am and 7 pm Sunday.

For details on the cargo/passenger ferry *Barracuda*, which plies between St Vincent and Union Island, see the Getting Around section at the beginning of this chapter.

Yacht Port Elizabeth is a port of entry for St Vincent & the Grenadines. Customs and immigration, opposite the ferry dock, are open 9 am to 3 pm. There are a couple of well-stocked supply stores in Port Elizabeth, and water, fuel, bottled gas, ice and nautical charts are readily available.

Sam the Scrimhander

Sam McDowell, a one-time Californian and Princeton art professor, lives on Bequia, and he's regarded as the world's best scrimhander. A scrimhander makes scrimshaw, and scrimshaw is the old seaman's art, dating back to the early 1800s, of etching seafaring scenes into whale's teeth and bones. Because of Sam's influence and because of Bequia's history as a whaling center, scrimshaw has really taken off on the island.

Scrimshaw is fine, painstaking work, and Indian ink is worked into the etching to bring out the design. Sam supports efforts to protect whales and works exclusively in camel bone and micarta, a high-tech plastic. He's also keen to pass on his skills to local artists, and employs apprentices at his studio.

Mostly Sam works pocketknife handles, but he also does money clips, cuff links and corkscrews, among other things. The prices vary depending on the detail and size of the piece; the smallest pocketknives (about 2½ inches long) start at US$100, and some of the bigger ones can cost US$600 or more. Fine pieces from famous 19th-century whaling ships can fetch US$90,000 at antique auctions.

Sam's Paget Farm studio is open by appointment – call ☎ 458-3865.

If you don't have a boat you might be able to find someone willing to take you on for shared expenses or for crew work. The Bequia Marina and the bar at Frangipani Hotel can be good spots to touch base with sailors, and Mac's Pizzeria has a yachties notice board that's worth checking out.

GETTING AROUND

The island is small, and from Port Elizabeth a lot of places are accessible on foot. Three of the island's best beaches – Lower Bay, Friendship Bay and Hope Bay – are within 45 minutes' walk.

Bus

Local transportation is a system of private 'dollar cabs,' which are shared taxis that will take you on short trips for EC$1 and longer trips for EC$2. The busiest route is from Port Elizabeth to Paget Sound.

Car, Motorcycle & Bicycle

Handy Andy's (☎ 458-3722), opposite the waterfront in Port Elizabeth, rents out mountain bikes (US$18), motor scooters (US$25), Honda 250cc motorcycles (US$55) and Jeep Wranglers (US$75).

Taxi

Taxis are commonly open-air pickup trucks with bench-type seats in the back. Taxis charge set fees and are generally distinguished from dollar cabs by a 'taxi service' sign. From Port Elizabeth it costs EC$18 to Lower Bay or Friendship Bay and EC$30 to the airport. Taxis meet flights at the airport.

Organized Tours

A handful of boats offer cruises through the Grenadines. You can usually find a few options posted on the notice board at Mac's Pizzeria or at the tourist office. Sailing schedules are usually a bit pliable, and boats generally don't sail if there aren't enough passengers to make it worthwhile.

The 80-foot *Friendship Rose* (☎ 458-3202) is a Bequian-built wooden schooner that once served as the mail boat between Bequia and St Vincent. The schedule varies,

but each week there are typically day trips from Bequia to Mustique for US$70 and others to Canouan or the Tobago Cays for US$90. Onboard lunch is included. Tours vary in length from 8½ to 11 hours.

The 60-foot catamaran *Passion* (☎ 458-3884) offers day trips Tuesday and Thursday to Mustique via Moonhole and Petit Nevis, stopping for snorkeling and lunch at Basil's. The cost is US$70, not including lunch. On Wednesday and Sunday the boat usually makes an 11-hour trip to the Tobago Cays for US$85.

The S/Y *Pelangi* (☎ 458-3255), a 44-foot cutter with two double guest cabins, is available for private charter. Day trips cost US$60 per person, with a minimum of four people. A three-day, two-night charter costs US$800 for two people, US$1200 for four people, including meals and drinks.

Mustique

Mustique, lying 7 miles southeast of Bequia, is a privately owned island that has been developed into an exclusive haven for the rich and famous. Like the other Grenadines, this 5-mile-long island is dry and hilly. It has a population of about 800, most of whom work either directly or indirectly for those who vacation here.

Colin Tennant, an eccentric Scotsman, purchased the island in 1958 to turn it into a retreat that would appeal to his aristocratic friends. Tennant brought the island's free-roaming sheep and cattle under control and planted coconut palms and citrus trees. In 1960 he presented Princess Margaret with a wedding gift of a 10-acre house lot perched between Gelliceaux Bay and Deep Bay. Today there are 72 privately owned villas on the island belonging to people of wealth, including such celebrities as Mick Jagger and David Bowie.

The island is now under the management of the Mustique Company, which is responsible for everything from operating the medical clinic and desalination plant to providing accommodations for the Britannia Bay fishers who still live on Mustique.

The top of Trinidad's Waterloo Temple

Typically Dutch architecture on Sint Maarten

A divinely illuminated Catholic church, Dominica

Plantation ruins on St Kitts, with St Eustatius lurking in the background

St George's bustling northern waterfront, Grenada

A dangling cocoa pod, Barbados

Doing the shuffle dance on drying cocoa pods, Grenada

The makings of a spicy meal, Grenada

'Prepackaged' foods, St Lucia

Marigot's market, St Lucia

Ways to spice up your stew, St Lucia

The island has an irregular coastline richly indented with bays and coves, most of which harbor fine, sandy beaches.

There are no towns on the island. Britannia Bay has Mustique's dock, a general store and a handful of boutiques, and the airport is about a mile northeast of the dock. The post office, telephone exchange and Mustique Company office are opposite the airport terminal.

There's good swimming and snorkeling along the west coast, including at Britannia Bay, although sea urchins are particularly thick on the reef running south of the dock. The Mustique Company can arrange diving and horseback riding.

Places to Stay

Set on a cliffside, *Firefly Hotel* (☎ 458-4621, fax 456-4499, fireflymus@caribsurf.com, www.mustiquefirefly.com, PO Box 349, Mustique) overlooks Britannia Bay. Each of the four rooms has a private bath and ocean view. Once the only moderately priced guest house on the island, Firefly has been upgraded and now it's just as expensive as everywhere else: Rooms start at US$480 a night, breakfast included. Firefly is a five-minute walk from Basil's Bar & Restaurant.

Cotton House (☎ 456-4777, fax 456-5887, in the USA ☎ 800-826-2809, caribisles@aol.com, www.cottonhouseresort.com, PO Box 349, Mustique) the island's only sizable hotel, is built around a renovated 18th-century stone-and-coral warehouse once used to store cotton. There's also an old stone sugar mill on the grounds and a collection of cottages. The hotel's 20 rooms have ceiling fans, verandas and understated plantation decor. There are tennis courts and a pool, and a sandy beach at Endeavour Bay is a few minutes' walk away. Doubles, which include breakfast, afternoon tea and dinner, begin at US$590 in summer and US$900 in winter.

The Mustique Company (☎ 458-4621, in the USA ☎ 800-225-4255, in the UK ☎ 0628-755 44), PO Box 349, Mustique, rents out 50 of Mustique's exclusive *homes*. As the houses are privately owned, the decor and amenities vary, but each house comes with a cook/housekeeper and most with a swimming pool. In winter, weekly rates range from US$5000 for a 'simple' two-bedroom villa that can accommodate four people to US$18,000 for a lavish five-bedroom villa. In summer the prices drop by an average of 20%. Rates include the use of a jeep or similar vehicle.

Places to Eat

A delightful open-air thatch-and-bamboo restaurant that extends out into Britannia Bay, *Basil's Bar & Restaurant* (☎ 458-4621, fax 456-5887, VHF channel 68) is *the* place to eat, drink and be seen on Mustique. Breakfast and lunch are moderately priced, while at dinner grilled fish costs EC$70 and lobster costs EC$95. On Wednesday night, Basil's has a lively jump-up with a steel band and barbecue buffet for EC$75.

You can pick up groceries at the general store near Basil's.

Getting There & Away

Britannia Bay is the port of entry and the only suitable anchorage for visiting yachts; immigration and customs can be cleared at the airport.

There is no scheduled passenger boat service to Mustique. There are scheduled flights from Barbados and other Grenadine islands; see Getting There & Away and Getting Around at the beginning of this chapter. For day tours to Mustique, see the Bequia section and the Barbados chapter.

Canouan

Canouan, midway in the Grenadine chain, has dry scrubby hills and near-deserted beaches. It extends 3½ miles in length, but in places this anchor-shaped island is so narrow that it can be walked across in a few minutes. There are about 700 people and lots of goats. A large resort with an 18-hole golf course and luxury villas has recently been finished at the north side of the island, and now Canouan is well and truly on the upmarket tourist map.

Canouan's main attraction is its exceptional long, sandy beaches, several of which are reef-protected, and good for swimming and snorkeling. Other than that, you can take long walks, including one to the old stone Anglican church that sits at the site of an abandoned village which was destroyed by a hurricane in 1921.

The main anchorage is in Grand Bay, where the jetty is located, while the airport is about a mile to the west. Diving can be arranged with Dive Canouan, which is based at the Tamarind Beach Hotel.

Places to Stay

The *Anchor Inn Guesthouse* (☎ 458-8568), at Grand Bay, has three straightforward rooms in a two-story home. Singles/doubles cost US$65/100, breakfast and dinner included. It's only a few minutes' walk to the beach.

The 43-room French-owned *Canouan Beach Hotel* (☎ 458-8888, fax 458-8875, cbh@grenadines.net, PO Box 530, Canouan) is on a nice sandy beach in South Glossy Bay. Single/double rates, which include all meals and some water sports, are US$190/292 in summer, US$275/366 in winter. Rooms are cottage-style, with air-con and patios.

The deluxe *Tamarind Beach Hotel* (☎ 458-8044, fax 458-8851, cantbh@caribsurf.com) is currently closed for refurbishment.

Carenage Bay Beach & Golf Club (☎ 459-8000, fax 458-8885, in the USA ☎ 800-336-4571, in the UK ☎ 020-8580 5627, info@canouan.com, www.canouan.com) is set on 800 acres of beach and bushland. Its 178 suites offer all the luxuries you can imagine. There's an 18-hole golf course, a pool that ranks among the Caribbean's biggest, and a Town Square village replete with boutiques, restaurants, a gym, beauty salon, nightclub and casino. Doubles cost from US$260 in summer, US$440 in winter.

Places to Eat

The *Anchor Inn Guesthouse* (see Places to Stay) offers a West Indian dinner for EC$50, but you need to book ahead. *Canouan Beach Hotel* offers breakfast from 7:30 to 9 am, lunch from 12:30 to 2 pm and dinner from 7:30 to 10 pm. The French chef serves up Continental and West Indian dishes with an emphasis on seafood. There are barbecues a few times a week, and a band plays on Saturday. At dinner, most meals, including lobster, are priced around EC$75, appetizer included.

Getting There & Away

A mail boat from St Vincent connects Canouan with the other Grenadine islands, and there are also prop-plane flights to Canouan. For information, see the Getting There & Away and the Getting Around sections at the beginning of this chapter.

Mayreau

Mayreau is a small island, 1½ miles in length, with a population of 200. There's no airport and just one short road, which runs from the dock at Saline Bay, on the central west coast, up to the island's sole village.

Lying just west of the Tobago Cays, Mayreau is most commonly visited on sailing cruises that trawl through the cays and then sail into the deep U-shaped Saltwhistle Bay, at the island's northern tip.

Saltwhistle Bay is protected by a long, narrow arm, which at its narrowest is just a few yards wide. The bay is stunning, with clear waters, beautiful white sands, calm water and a protected anchorage for visiting yachts. The Saltwhistle Bay Club, tucked back from the beach just beyond the palms, operates a beachside restaurant and bar.

There are no roads from Saltwhistle Bay, but a track leads south to the village, a 20-minute walk away. The footpath begins through the gate at the beach's southern end. The track passes cacti and offers nice views near the crest. For a particularly good view, check out the hilltop stone church at the northern side of the village.

Saline Bay is where the mail boat, the M/V *Barracuda*, pulls in a few times a week. Cruise ships occasionally come into Saline Bay as well, discharging hundreds of passengers to picnic on the beach.

It's about a five-minute uphill walk from the dock to the village center. There's a sandy beach along Saline Bay and deserted beaches within easy walking distance on the east side of the island.

Places to Stay

In Saline Bay, *Dennis' Hideaway* (☎/fax *458-8594, VHF channel 68*) has five rooms with private baths and ocean-view balconies above a grocery store in the village center. Singles/doubles cost US$50/70 in winter and US$40/50 in summer, breakfast included.

Saltwhistle Bay Club (☎ *458-8444, fax 458-8944, VHF channel 16/68, saltwhistle@ grenadines.net*) is a minimalist-style beach-side resort with simple but spacious stone bungalows. The rooms vary, but all have ceiling fans, patios and king-size beds. Guests get picked up at the airport in Union Island and shuttled by boat to Mayreau, a 30-minute ride. Singles/doubles begin at US$230/320 in summer, US$360/480 in winter, including breakfast and dinner.

Places to Eat

The Rastafarian-run *Robert Righteous & De Youths* (☎ *458-8203*), uphill in the village, is a good snack bar with pizza, rotis and West Indian food such as breadfruit and saltfish. You can eat well for around EC$20.

Dennis' Hideaway (see Places to Stay) is open from 7 am for inexpensive breakfasts and lunchtime sandwiches from EC$10. Dinners served with soup cost EC$45 for conch or fish and EC$70 for lobster.

Island Paradise (☎ *458-8941*) is a popular bar and eatery with good views and Creole food at reasonable prices: Evening main dishes cost around EC$40. Nearby is *J&C Bar, Restaurant & Supermarket* (☎ *458-8558*), serving three meals a day.

On the other side of the island, the open-air restaurant at *Saltwhistle Bay Club* (☎ *458-8444*) offers cooked breakfasts from 8:30 to 10:30 am for EC$35. At lunch, noon to 2:30 pm, sandwiches and salads are EC$18 to EC$35. At dinner, 7 to 8:30 pm, a three-course meal with a choice of fish or meat main courses costs EC$75.

Getting There & Away

For information on the M/V *Barracuda*, the mail boat that connects Mayreau with the other Grenadine islands, see the Getting Around section at the beginning of this chapter.

The Captain Yannis catamaran tours from Union Island can drop passengers off at Mayreau one day and pick them up the next day at no charge other than the usual cost of the day tour. More information is under Union Island.

Union Island

Union Island, the southernmost port of entry in St Vincent & the Grenadines, is high, rocky and dry. About 3 miles in length and half that in width, the land is largely covered in thorny scrub, and dotted with cacti and free-ranging goats. Its population is 1900.

The island's west side reaches 1000 feet at Mt Tabor, but otherwise the island's most substantial landmark is The Pinnacle, a 738-foot plug-shaped rock face that rises abruptly in the interior of the island between Clifton and Ashton, the two main villages.

There are a few nice beaches, but most visitors use Union as a jumping-off point for cruising the uninhabited Tobago Cays and other nearby islands.

CLIFTON

Clifton is the commercial center of the island and has a marina, airport, shops and restaurants; it's the center of Union Island's thriving tour industry.

Every morning, tour groups are flown in from Barbados, Martinique and other Caribbean islands, taken by bus to the dock in the center of town and then by catamaran to the Tobago Cays. In the late afternoon they sail back into the bay and are taken back to their chartered planes. While they see little of Clifton, these transiting passengers make up about half of the island's visitors. Most of the rest are yachters who use Clifton as a base for exploring the region.

Information

The Union Island Tourist Bureau has a tourist office (☎ 458-8350) just south of the

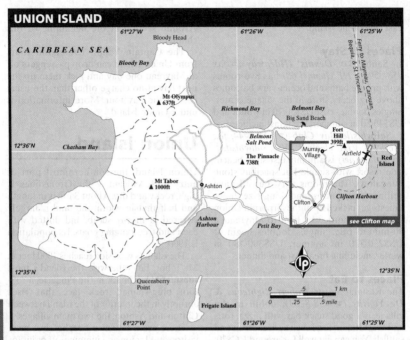

UNION ISLAND

ST VINCENT & THE GRENADINES

post office, open 9 am to noon and 1 to 4 pm daily.

The National Commercial Bank is open 8 am to 1 pm Monday to Thursday, 8 am to 1 pm and 3 to 5 pm Friday.

There are a several gift shops around town, including Chic Unique, which has a selection of books, T-shirts and other souvenirs.

Places to Stay

The ***Clifton Beach Hotel*** (*☎/fax 458-8235*) has 17 simple rooms in a friendly hostelry, most of them in two buildings opposite each other in the center of Clifton but with a few rooms above the nearby Grand Union Supermarket. A few of the rooms in the main building have ocean views, as do the units above the supermarket. Fan-cooled singles/doubles begin at US$32/60 in summer, US$37/70 in winter. If you want air-con, add US$15. The hotel can also arrange cottage rentals for US$350 a week.

Lambi's Guesthouse (*☎/fax 458-8395*), above Lambi's Restaurant and grocery store, has a dozen island-style rooms – it's essentially just a place to sleep and shower. Singles/doubles cost US$19/28 year-round.

Sunny Grenadines Hotel (*☎ 458-8327, fax 458-8398, kingmitchell@caribsurf.com*), in the center of Clifton, has 18 rooms. Doubles cost US$85.

Anchorage Yacht Club Hotel (*☎ 458-8221, fax 458-8365*), on the waterfront and close to the airport, is Union Island's most upmarket option, and it's popular with French tourists and visiting sailors. Rooms are comfortable with ocean-facing balconies, air-con and phones; rates begin at US$110 in summer, US$120 in winter.

Places to Eat

There's a bakery at the back of the ***Grand Union Supermarket*** (*☎ 458-8178*). Every third building in Clifton is a grocery store, painted in bright colors and posted with

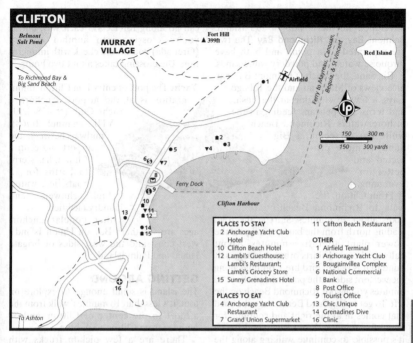

CLIFTON

Belmont
Salt Pond

MURRAY
VILLAGE

Fort Hill
▲ 399ft

To Richmond Bay &
Big Sand Beach

Airfield

Red Island

Ferry to Mayreau, Canouan, Bequia & St Vincent

0   150   300 m
0   150   300 yards

Ferry Dock

Clifton Harbour

To Ashton

PLACES TO STAY
2   Anchorage Yacht Club
    Hotel
10 Clifton Beach Hotel
12 Lambi's Guesthouse;
    Lambi's Restaurant;
    Lambi's Grocery Store
15 Sunny Grenadines Hotel

PLACES TO EAT
4   Anchorage Yacht Club
    Restaurant
7   Grand Union Supermarket

11 Clifton Beach Restaurant

OTHER
1   Airfield Terminal
3   Anchorage Yacht Club
5   Bougainvillea Complex
6   National Commercial
    Bank
8   Post Office
9   Tourist Office
13 Chic Unique
14 Grenadines Dive
16 Clinic

names like Kash & Karry, Pay & Take and
Determination Bar & Grocery. Grand
Union Supermarket and *Lambi's Grocery
Store* are two of the biggest supermarkets.
Grenadines Vine Shop, in the Bougainvillea complex, carries a good selection of
imported wines, as well as other liquor and
fruit juices. Virtually all produce is imported from other islands, so prices are
high.

*Clifton Beach Restaurant (☎/fax 458-
8235)* makes lunchtime sandwiches from
EC$12 and serves good fresh fish and conch
meals for EC$35 in an open-air setting
behind the Clifton Beach Hotel, at the edge
of the water.

Lambi's Restaurant (☎ /fax 458-8395), a
large waterfront restaurant in the village
center, is named after its friendly owner,
Lambert Baptiste, as well as for the conch
(lambi) shells that deck the walls. At lunch
and dinner there are chicken, fresh-fish and
conch dishes from around EC$32.

Anchorage Yacht Club (see Places to
Stay) operates the pleasant open-air *Anchorage Yacht Club Restaurant* and bar on
the waterfront. Appetizers cost from EC$12
for callaloo soup, while main courses range
from grilled chicken for EC$38 to lobster
for EC$80. During the afternoon the bar
serves baguette sandwiches, pastries and
croissants at reasonable prices and pizza to
order.

AROUND UNION ISLAND

A quiet place, **Ashton** is backed by high hills
and untouched by tourism. There are a few
older homes with weathered gingerbread
trim and many brightly painted houses and
shops, but no real sights. There are a few
grocery stores in town.

For those who want to do some exploring, a few hiking tracks lead into the hills
above Ashton, with one of the smoother
tracks beginning at the upper road on the
northwest side of the village.

There are two remote beaches on the undeveloped northern side of the island: **Belmont Bay** and **Richmond Bay**. The two are separated by a point, and both have turquoise waters and powdery white sands.

Big Sand, the beach at Belmont Bay, has nice views of Mayreau and the Tobago Cays, a few cows lazing in the bush, and terns and pelicans feeding in the inshore waters. Richmond Beach, while not as scenic as Big Sand, is more protected and better for swimming.

From Clifton, the walk to Richmond Beach takes about 25 minutes. Start at the road leading north from the bank; you'll pass the power plant after five minutes. About halfway the road skirts around a large salt pond that is rich in bird life. Continue along the western side of the pond and in about 10 minutes you'll spot Richmond Beach on the left. To get to Big Sand Beach, take the road that comes in at the right and continue for about five minutes. From Richmond Beach it's possible to continue walking along the coastal road southwest to Ashton, a walk of about 35 minutes.

GETTING THERE & AWAY

Air

Airlines of Carriacou, Grenadine Express, Region Air Caribbean and Mustique Airways have flights to Union Island. Details are in the Getting There & Away and Getting Around sections at the beginning of this chapter.

Sea

Details on the M/V *Barracuda,* which connects Union Island with St Vincent's other main islands, are in the Getting Around section at the beginning of this chapter.

Two very small wooden sailing boats, *Wisdom* and *Jasper,* run between Ashton and Hillsborough (Carriacou) Monday and Thursday. The boats leave from the pier near Waterfront Trading in Ashton around 7:30 am, unload their cargo in Carriacou

and then return around noon. Passengers can go along for EC$15 each way, but as you're crossing into another country (Grenada) you should check with immigration. The crossing takes about two hours.

Yacht The port of entry is in Clifton. Immigration is at the airport. Anchorage Yacht Club (☎ 458-8221, VHF channel 16/68), midway between the airport and central Clifton, has stern-to berths for 15 boats, ice, water, fuel, showers and laundry facilities.

Other popular anchorages are Chatham Bay on Union Island's west coast and the west sides of Frigate Island and Palm Island.

GETTING AROUND

The island is small enough to explore on foot. It's less than 10 minutes' walk from the airport to the center of Clifton, and 30 minutes from Clifton to Ashton.

There are a few pickup trucks with double rows of benches that serve as buses, making runs between Clifton and Ashton for EC$2.50. Hotels will often pick you up at the airport if you have a reservation; otherwise, it costs EC$12 for a taxi from the airport to central Clifton.

Organized Tours

Captain Yannis (☎ 458-8513) operates three 60-foot sailboats – the catamarans *Cyclone, Typhoon* and *Tornado* – which account for most of the daytime sailing business from Union Island. There's a good buffet lunch and an open bar of rum punch and beer. The cruise includes a stop on Palm Island, a few hours in the Tobago Cays for lunch and snorkeling and an hour on Mayreau, before returning to Union in the late afternoon. The boats leave Clifton around 9 am, but the exact time depends on when the charter flights come in, as most passengers fly into Union Island to pick up the tour. The price is a bargain at EC$140.

Other Islands

TOBAGO CAYS

Many consider the Tobago Cays to be the crown jewels of the Grenadines. They comprise a number of small, deserted islands surrounded by coral reefs and splendidly clear turquoise waters. The islands, which are rocky and cactus-studded, have tiny coves and beaches of powdery white sand.

The Tobago Cays have been set aside as a national park. Several measures have been taken to protect the area, including the installation of moorings and prohibitions against the taking of marine life. Perhaps the biggest danger to the cays is their popularity, as the waters often get fairly crowded with visiting yachts.

The Tobago Cays offer great snorkeling and windsurfing. See Union Island, earlier, for information on day trips to the Cays.

PALM ISLAND

Palm Island, a 10-minute boat ride southeast of Union Island, is a small whale-shaped island that's the domain of a private resort. The beach has long been a popular anchorage with yachters and is a stopover on many day tours between Union Island and the Tobago Cays.

Spread along the sandy fringe of this 130-acre island are two dozen cottages operated by Texan John Caldwell, who took out a 99-year lease from the government back in the mid-1960s. Swamps were filled, palm trees were added to the shady casuarina trees that grow along the beach, and the island name was changed from Prune Island to the more alluring Palm Island.

At the western side of the island, where boats dock, is the picture-perfect Casuarina Beach, with sands composed of small bits of white shells and pink coral.

Places to Stay & Eat

The very plush *Palm Island Beach Club* (☎ 458-8824, fax 458-8804, in the USA ☎ 800-345-0271, res@palmislandresorts.com, www.plamislandresorts.com) has 40 rooms in bungalows of wood and stone on a 135-acre property, each furnished with either two twin beds or one king bed, a private bath and a refrigerator. Rooms are airy, with screened, louvered windows, a ceiling fan and sliding glass doors that open to a patio. Doubles start at US$680 in summer, US$720 in winter, and rates include meals and use of windsurfing gear and Sunfish boats. The resort also books a handful of villas and apartments. A convivial beachside bar and restaurant welcomes day-trippers.

PETIT ST VINCENT

Petit St Vincent (PSV) is the southernmost and smallest of the inhabited islands that make up St Vincent & the Grenadines. Its 113 acres are fringed by white-sand beaches, coral reefs and clear waters.

The island has been developed into a single-resort 'hideaway' destination. As with Palm Island, guests must first get to Union Island. At the Union airport they're met by resort staff and taken over to PSV by motorboat, a 30-minute crossing.

While a few yachters anchor off PSV, day sails generally bypass the island, and it sees less traffic than its neighbors to the north. Visiting yachts can anchor off the southwestern side of the island; there's a dinghy dock just below the restaurant.

Places to Stay

The *Petit St Vincent Resort* (☎ 458-8801, fax 458-8428, in the USA ☎ 800-654-9326, psv@fuse.net, www.psvresort.com, PO Box 12506, Cincinnati, Ohio 45212) has 22 suites in stone bungalows spread around the island to offer maximum privacy. The bungalows have a bedroom with two queen beds, fans, a living room with tropical decor and pleasant sundecks. There are no TVs, air-con or other conveniences; each cottage has a bamboo flagpole used to 'call' for room service. A creation of US expatriate Haze Richardson, the resort is considered the ultimate retreat among the Grenadine getaway islands, and it has rates to match. Singles/doubles cost US$430/680 in summer, US$550/860 in winter, including meals and use of a tennis court, sailboards, glass-bottom kayaks, Hobie Cats and Sunfish sailboats.

Trinidad & Tobago

Trinidad and Tobago are the southernmost islands in the Caribbean, just 11km off the coast of Venezuela. Surprisingly, there's little South American cultural influence – instead, the country draws strongly from its British, African and East Indian heritage.

Trinidad, the dominant partner in the twin-island nation, is the Eastern Caribbean's largest and most heavily populated island. It has a mix of urban sprawl, rainforested mountains and small farming communities.

Despite its size, Trinidad is one of the least touristed islands in the Caribbean – it doesn't have the sort of resorts that attracts crowds of vacationers, and the capital city, Port of Spain, certainly has more bustle than charm. What makes Trinidad such a worthwhile destination is its ethnic diversity. You'll find Anglican and Spanish churches beside Hindu temples and Moslem mosques, while festivals throughout the year reflect the mix of cultures past and present. And Trinidad has the Caribbean's most festive Carnival, when Port of Spain turns into one huge street party, attracting thousands of revelers from around the world. The island also offers some of the Caribbean's finest bird watching, from flocks of scarlet ibis roosting in mangrove swamps to jungle interiors teeming with colorful forest birds.

The 'little sister' island of Tobago, with just 4% of the country's population and 6% of its land area, stands in sharp contrast to Trinidad. Some claim that Daniel Defoe had Tobago in mind when he wrote *Robinson Crusoe*. Indeed, some visitors who happen upon Tobago these days think of it as the last undiscovered gem in the Caribbean. It's pleasantly relaxed, with good beaches, reef-protected waters and casual oceanside hotels. It too boasts rain forests with good bird-watching opportunities, and in addition has excellent diving and snorkeling.

'Trinidad & Tobago' is often abbreviated 'T&T,' and 'Port of Spain' is written 'POS' for short – expect to see the latter on highway signs. 'Trini' is the common nickname for a native of Trinidad.

Highlights

- Enjoying a vibrant blend of African, East Indian and Spanish cultures expressed through music, food and festivals
- Partying at Port of Spain's spectacular Carnival festival
- Relaxing at Tobago's lovely white-sand beaches and affordable hotels
- Delighting in excellent birding, including brilliant flocks of scarlet ibis at Trinidad's Caroni Swamp
- Diving and snorkeling at Tobago's top-notch sites

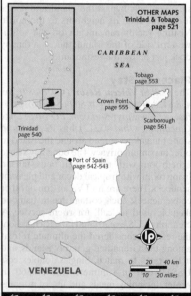

Facts about Trinidad & Tobago

HISTORY

Although Trinidad and Tobago share geological origins, their more recent histories are quite distinct. Both islands were discovered by the Spanish, but Trinidad was colonized first, leaving Tobago for later settlers.

Trinidad

Known to Amerindians as Iere (Land of the Hummingbirds), Trinidad was sighted in 1498 by Columbus, who christened it 'La Isla de la Trinidad,' for the Holy Trinity. The Spanish who followed in Columbus' wake enslaved many of Trinidad's Amerindian inhabitants, taking them to toil in the new South American colonies. Spain, in its rush for gold, gave only scant attention to Trinidad, which lacked precious minerals. Finally, in 1592, the Spanish established their first settlement, San Josef, just east of the present-day capital of Port of Spain. Over the next two centuries unsuccessful attempts were made by Spanish colonizers to establish tobacco and cacao plantations, but crop failures and a general lack of support from Spain left the island only lightly settled.

In 1783 the Spanish government, concerned that the British might take the island if it remained undeveloped, enacted the Cedula, a decree offering generous land grants and other incentives to encourage Roman Catholic settlers to move to Trinidad from other Caribbean islands. As a consequence, scores of settlers came to Trinidad, mostly from the French islands.

The new settlers imported slaves from Africa and established sugar and cotton plantations. The island took on many French influences, but the influx of settlers did nothing to keep the British from snatching the islands from the Spanish in 1797.

The British banned the slave trade in 1807, and in 1834 slavery was abolished outright. From the 1830s to the early 20th century, thousands of indentured workers, most from India, were brought to Trinidad to work the cane fields.

Tobago

Tobago's early history stands separate from neighboring Trinidad's. Also sighted by Columbus, Tobago was claimed by the Spanish, but they didn't attempt to colonize it. In 1628, Charles I of England decided to charter the island to the Earl of Pembroke. In response, a handful of nations took an immediate interest in colonizing Tobago. English, Dutch, French and Courlanders (present-day Latvians) wrestled for control, encountering resistance from both the native Amerindians and the Spanish on neighboring Trinidad. During the 17th century, Tobago changed hands numerous times between the competing colonizers, with entire settlements sometimes being burned to the ground in the process.

In 1704, in an attempt to quell the fighting, Tobago was declared a neutral territory. As a result pirates began to frequent the island and use it as a base from which to raid ships in the Eastern Caribbean. In 1763, following the Treaty of Paris, the British finally established a colonial administration on Tobago. Within two decades 10,000 African slaves were brought to the island and plantations of sugar, cotton and

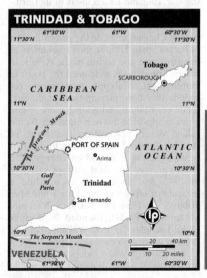

TRINIDAD & TOBAGO

indigo were established. The French gained control of the island a couple of times in the following decades, but by the early 1800s Tobago was firmly under British control.

Tobago's plantation economy slid into decline after the abolition of slavery, but sugar and rum production continued until 1884, when the London firm that controlled finances for the island's plantations went bankrupt. The plantation owners, unable to sell their sugar and rum, quickly sold or abandoned most of their land. While this left Tobago's economy in shambles, it also left most of the islanders with a plot of land – those who had no money to buy it simply squatted. In 1889 the British made Tobago, which previously had its own independent legislature, a ward of neighboring Trinidad.

Birth of a Nation

The economic depression of the 1930s led to a series of strikes and riots and the growth of a labor movement on the islands. However, the government tolerated only so much unrest, and by the time WWII broke out, it had imprisoned Uriah Butler, the firebrand founder of the oil workers' union, and prohibited Carnival festivities. During the war, England leased areas of its Caribbean colonies to the United States for military operations, and the US set up a major base at Chaguaramas, on the peninsula east of Port of Spain. Despite their resentment at the arrogance and racism of the American troops, Trinidadians welcomed the boost in employment. Calypso performers responded by downplaying their traditional social orientation and adding more risqué lyrics to appeal to this new audience. At the Allied victory celebration, the strains of steel bands were heard in public for the first time, signaling a period of change. The British granted universal suffrage, effective in 1946, and took steps to institute a measure of self-government for Trinidad & Tobago. In 1956 the People's National Movement (PNM), founded by former Oxford scholar Dr Eric Williams, became the first party with enough support to form its own cabinet. When independence came on August 31, 1962, Williams became the

nation's first prime minister, a position he held until his death in 1981.

Growing Pains

An oil boom in the late 1970s brought prosperity to the nation and helped buoy the PNM's grip on power, despite the party's growing reputation for corruption and its failure to appeal to the interests of the East Indian community. But in 1986, with the economy suffering, the PNM was defeated resoundingly by a coalition party, the National Alliance for Reconstruction (NAR).

On July 27, 1990, members of the Jamaat al Muslimeen, a minority Muslim group, attempted a coup. They stormed the parliament and took 45 hostages, including Prime Minister ANR Robinson, and seized the TV station and police headquarters. The rebels surrendered five days later, after the president of the senate, in his capacity as acting head of state, offered an amnesty to end the crisis. All in all, 30 people died and another 500 were injured in the coup attempt and during concurrent street riots that broke out in the capital. The PNM regained the leadership in 1991 but was again defeated in November 1995 when it called a snap general election a year ahead of schedule. The PNM and United National Congress (UNC) each took 17 of the 36 parliamentary seats, but the latter party had the edge after forming a coalition with the NAR, which won the two seats represented by its traditional stronghold Tobago. UNC leader Basdeo Panday became the country's first prime minister of East Indian descent. The UNC consolidated its dominance in the elections of December 2000, grabbing 19 parliamentary seats, while the NAR held on to only one, eastern Tobago. The rest of the seats were taken by the PNM.

GEOGRAPHY

Trinidad's land area is 4828 sq km, and Tobago's is 300 sq km. Geographically, boot-shaped Trinidad was once part of the South American mainland. Over time a channel developed, separating Trinidad from present-day Venezuela. The connection to South America is readily visible in Trinidad's lofty Northern Range, a continuation of the Andes, and in its abundant oil and gas reserves, which are concentrated on the southwestern side of the island, facing oil-rich Venezuela.

The Northern Range spreads east to west, forming a scenic backdrop to Port of Spain. In the center of the range, above Arima, lies the 941m Cerro del Aripo, the country's highest peak. Much of the rest of the island is given to plains, undulating hills and mangrove swamps. Trinidad's numerous rivers include the Ortoire River, which runs 50km on its way to the southeast coast, and the 40km Caroni River, which empties into the Caroni Swamp.

The island of Tobago, 20km northeast of Trinidad, has a central mountain range that reaches 620m at its highest point. Deep, fertile valleys run from the ridge down toward the coast, which is indented with bays and sandy beaches.

CLIMATE

Because of Trinidad's southerly location, temperatures are equable year-round. The average daily high temperature in Port of Spain is 31°C (88°F) in both January and July, while the low averages 22°C (72°F) in July and is only one degree cooler in January.

February to May are the driest months, with a mean relative humidity of 74%. The rest of the year the humidity ranges from 78% to 83%. June to August, the wettest months, average 260mm (10 inches) of rain and 23 rainy days each month. In contrast, March sees only 34mm (1½ inches) of rain, with measurable precipitation on an average of nine days. These measurements are for Piarco International Airport, near Port of Spain; the rain forests get significantly higher amounts of rainfall.

Trinidad and Tobago are outside the central hurricane belt and as a consequence generally don't experience the severe storms that hit the more northerly Caribbean islands.

FLORA & FAUNA

Because of its proximity to the South American continent, Trinidad & Tobago has the widest variety of plant and animal life in the Eastern Caribbean. There are more than 430 species of bird, 600 species of butterfly, 70 kinds of reptiles and 100 types of mammals, including red howler monkeys, anteaters, agouti and armadillos.

Tobago has fewer species than Trinidad, but parrots and other bright tropical birds are nonetheless abundant in the mountainous interior. You can commonly spot pelicans, osprey and frigate birds along Tobago's coast.

Plant life is equally diverse, with more than 700 orchid species and 1600 other types of flowering plants. Both islands have luxuriant rain forests, and Trinidad also features elfin forests, savannas and both freshwater and brackish mangrove swamps.

GOVERNMENT & POLITICS

Trinidad & Tobago is an independent republic within the British Commonwealth. The nation is headed by a president, although political power is concentrated in the office of the prime minister. The legislature is comprised of a House of Representatives, whose 36 members are elected every five years by popular vote, and a Senate, whose 31 members are appointed by the president upon the advice of the prime minister and minority party leader.

Political parties are largely divided along ethnic lines, with the PNM being the predominant party of Afro-Trinidadians and the UNC representing the interests of the East Indian community. UNC leader Basdeo Panday began a second term in late 2000, when his party narrowly defeated the PNM in elections.

Local government is divided into three municipalities, eight counties and the island of Tobago. Tobago has its own legislative assembly and since 1987 has exercised an extended measure of internal self-government in an effort to protect itself from becoming co-opted by more dominant political forces on Trinidad.

ECONOMY

Trinidad has sizable oil and gas reserves. Petroleum exports are the mainstay of the economy, accounting for nearly 50% of government revenue. Reliance upon world oil prices has led to uneven economic growth, however, and the government is attempting to diversify the economy. Although the country is far less reliant on tourism than other Caribbean nations, the industry is growing, with particularly strong growth in the pleasure-boat sector. Concerted efforts are being made to develop Tobago into a resort destination, and tourism is one of the island's main sources of employment, along with fishing and government-related work.

Trinidad has deposits of asphalt, coal, iron ore and limestone. Industry includes the production of petroleum, processed foods, beverages, chemicals, cement and cotton textiles. The main agricultural products are sugar, rice, cocoa, citrus, coffee, vegetables and poultry.

Nationwide unemployment in Trinidad has declined in recent years to an estimated 14%, with 64% of Trinidadians working in services, 14% in manufacturing and mining, 12% in construction and utilities, and 9.5% in agriculture.

POPULATION & PEOPLE

Of the country's 1.3 million inhabitants, just 50,000 live on Tobago. Trinidad has one of the most ethnically diverse populations in the Caribbean, a legacy of its checkered colonial history. The majority are of African (39.5%) and East Indian (40.3%) descent. Most other islanders are of mixed ancestry, but there are also notable minorities of European, Chinese, Syrian and Lebanese people. In addition, a community of a few hundred native Caribs lives in the Arima area.

ARTS

Music is a focal point of island life. Calypso, a medium for political and social satire, hearkens back to the days when slaves would sing in patois mocking their colonial masters. Mighty Sparrow, long acknowledged the king of calypso, has voiced the popular concerns of the day since the 1950s, though like many other performers in the genre, he has lately embraced *soca,* which favors danceable rhythms and risqué lyrics over pointed social commentary and verbal wordplay. Besides calypso, other vital styles on the Trinidadian soundscape include *chutney, rapso* and *parang* – Christmas music of Venezuelan origin and sung in Spanish. See Facts about the Eastern Caribbean for more on the music of Trinidad.

Trinidad boasts a number of acclaimed writers, among them Samuel Selvon, Earl Lovelace, CLR James and, most notably, the Naipaul brothers – VS and Shiva (see 'VS Naipaul'). Both VS' *A House for Mr Biswas* and Shiva's *The Chip Chip Gatherers* create a vivid portrait of East Indian life in Trinidad. St Lucian native Derek Walcott, the 1992 Nobel Prize winner in literature, has lived in Trinidad for much of his adult life.

SOCIETY & CONDUCT

Carnival reaches its heights in Trinidad, which has the most elaborate costumes and festivities in all the Caribbean. Integral to Carnival is the music of the steel drum (pan), which uses the hammered-out ends of discarded oil drums. Steel-pan music originated in Trinidad half a century ago and has grown from its working-class origins to become a cultural icon of the twin-island nation.

Cricket is the most popular sport. Cricket fields can be found in most every town, large or small, and children spend many hours practicing. The west end of Independence Square has been renamed Brian Lara Promenade in honor of the famous Trinidadian player.

Dos & Don'ts

Dress is casual on both Tobago and Trinidad, but skimpy clothing should be

VS Naipaul

Sir Vidiadhar Surajprasad (VS) Naipaul is Trinidad's foremost literary figure. His writing has been both widely praised for its artistic merit and harshly criticized for its unflattering view of postcolonial societies. Despite his international stature, Naipaul's controversial views have been coolly received in his native Trinidad, a country he has not inhabited for many years.

VS Naipaul was born in Chaguanas, Trinidad, in 1932, the son of Seepersad Naipaul, a prominent Trinidadian journalist. The young Naipaul had his primary education in Port of Spain, graduating from Queen's Royal College in 1950. He left Trinidad at 17 to attend Oxford on an Island scholarship. His debut novel, *The Mystic Masseur,* was published in 1957. It is a satirical story set amid the chaos of Trinidad's first parliamentary elections.

Other novels followed. *Miguel Street* (1959) anecdotally depicts the rough-and-tumble streets and colorful inhabitants of 1940s Port of Spain. *A House for Mr Biswas* (1960), Naipaul's most acclaimed novel, takes as its setting his childhood home in Chaguanas, Trinidad's center of East Indian life. (The house of the book's title, now called the House of Lions, still stands, though it is currently unoccupied.) The author received the Booker Prize in 1971 for *In a Free State*.

Naipaul's prodigious literary output – he has written over 20 books – takes multiple forms, from fiction to straightforward history to richly nuanced travel writing. *The Middle Passage* (1962), his first nonfiction effort, unravels the sordid history of the Caribbean. His extensive travels have provided the material for books such as *An Area of Darkness* (on India), *Beyond Belief* (the Islamic world) and *A Turn in the South* (the United States). His more recent travel writing makes use of mosaics of interviews with local characters.

The author's writings generally take a critical view of the effects of colonial rule on the societies that once came under its sway. He sees cultural alienation as its unfortunate legacy. An early work, *The Mimic Men,* deals with the inability of postcolonial societies to rise above the tendency to ape their former oppressors, making it impossible for them to achieve anything of worth.

Naipaul has earned disapproval for his barbed observations on Third World societies, in which critics detect racist overtones. And he emerges as an intolerant – and rather cranky – figure from *Sir Vidia's Shadow,* Paul Theroux's account of the two authors' decades-long but ultimately aborted friendship. Although nurtured as a writer by Naipaul, Theroux depicts his Trinidadian mentor as a difficult companion who made unreasonable demands on his friends and held his peers in disdain.

As a product of the very societies he has denounced – one more colonial castoff cut off from his own heritage – Naipaul has lamented his own difficulties in defining himself. *The Enigma of Arrival* (1987), an autobiographical work that some consider his most cryptic, deals with the author's ambivalence toward the land of his colonial masters, England, which he eventually adopted as his homeland. Theroux and others savored the irony of Naipaul's being knighted (in 1989) by the country he had once so forcefully condemned.

Whatever his inconsistencies as a human being, VS Naipaul remains an articulate voice of the dispossessed, an extraordinarily knowledgeable interpreter of the colonial experience and an author of undeniable depth and power.

The novels of Shiva Naipaul, VS Naipaul's younger brother, also deserve to be read for their sharply drawn depictions of Indian family life in Trinidad, among them *The Chip Chip Gatherers*. Like VS, Shiva traveled widely, setting down his observations in travel books such as *North And South: An African Journey* (1978) and *A Hot Country* (1983). The troubled author died in England at the age of 40.

restricted to the beach. When visiting communities with strong ethnic identities, be sensitive to local traditions and customs.

RELIGION

Roughly a third of all islanders are Roman Catholic. Another 25% are Hindu, 11% are Anglican, 13% various other Protestant denominations and 6% Muslim. Traditional African beliefs also remain strong in some areas, and Rastafarianism has a strong following as well.

LANGUAGE

The official language is English. Also spoken in ethnic enclaves are Hindi, Creole and Spanish.

Facts for the Visitor

ORIENTATION

Most of Trinidad's better-known attractions, such as Maracas Bay and the Caroni Bird Sanctuary, are within an hour's drive of Port of Spain. West of the capital, a peninsula points toward Venezuela, ending at Chaguaramas, one of the Caribbean's chief yachting centers, and a group of offshore isles. East of Port of Spain is Piarco International Airport, with the key northern towns of Arima and Sangre Grande beyond. Along the east coast lie endless palm-fringed beaches. To the north is the remote Northern Range and the turtle nesting area of Grande Rivière, to the south of Port of Spain are Chaguanas, the heart of East Indian Trinidad, and San Fernando, the industrial center of the country.

Tobago's airport is in the midst of the central resort area at the southwest tip of the island. The ferry comes and goes from the boat terminal in lower Scarborough (Tobago's capital). Lovely, quiet beaches, tranquil villages and excellent hiking can be found on the northern part of the island, along with a variety of small guest houses.

Maps

The tourist office distributes free, reasonably good maps of both Trinidad and Tobago. Still, if you're going to be doing a lot of exploring, the best resources are the government Lands & Surveys Division maps of Tobago, Trinidad and Port of Spain (TT$23 each), sold at the Lands & Surveys office on Frederick St and at Trinidad Book World in Port of Spain. They're also available at the airport tourist office in Tobago.

TOURIST OFFICES
Local Tourist Offices

The Tourism and Industrial Development Company of Trinidad & Tobago (Tidco) has offices at the airports on Trinidad and Tobago, on Philipps St in Port of Spain, and in Scarborough. When requesting information by mail, write to TIDCO, 10-14 Philipps St, Port of Spain, Trinidad & Tobago, West Indies; or email totourism-info@tidco.co.tt. From the USA call ☎ 888-595-4868, from Canada ☎ 888-535-5617, from the UK ☎ 0800-960-057, from Germany ☎ 06-13 17 33 37 and from Italy ☎ 1-67 87 75 30. Tidco's Web site (www.visitTNT.com) is worth a visit, too. The Tobago House of Assembly Dept of Tourism office can be contacted directly by from the USA and Canada by calling ☎ 888-689-1884 or writing tourbago@tstt.net.tt.

Tourist Offices Abroad

Overseas offices of Tidco include the following:

Canada
(☎ 416-485-8724, fax 416-485-8256) Taurus House, 512 Duplex Ave, Toronto M4R 2E3, Ontario

Germany
(☎ 06-13 17 33 37, fax 06-13 17 33 07) Ges Fur Tourismus und Dienstleistung mbH, Am Schleifweg 16, D-55128 Mainz

UK
(☎ 020-8350 1015, fax 020-8350 1011) Morris Kevan International, Mitre House, 66 Abbey Rd, Bush Hill Park, EN1 2QE, England

USA
(☎ 305-444-4033, fax 305-447-0415) 331 Almeria Ave, Coral Gables, FL 33134

VISAS & DOCUMENTS
All visitors must be in possession of a valid passport. Visas are not necessary for citizens of the USA, Canada, the UK or most European countries for stays of under three months.

Visas are required by citizens of Australia, New Zealand and India but not of most other Commonwealth countries. In most countries, visas are obtained through the British embassy.

EMBASSIES & CONSULATES
Trinidadian & Tobagonian Embassies & Consulates

Belgium
(☎ 32-2-762-9400)
14 Ave de la Faisanderie, 1150 Brussels

UK
(☎ 020-72 45 93 51)
42 Belgrave Square, London SW1 X8NT

USA
(☎ 202-467-1340)
1708 Massachusetts Ave NW, Washington, DC 20036

Foreign Embassies & Consulates in Trinidad & Tobago

Canada
High Commission (☎ 622-6232)
3-3A Sweet Briar Rd, St Clair, Port of Spain

France
Embassy (☎ 622-7446)
Tatil Building, 11 Maraval Rd, Port of Spain

UK
High Commission (☎ 622-2748)
19 St Clair Ave, Port of Spain

USA
Embassy (☎ 622-6371)
15 Queen's Park W, Port of Spain

Venezuela
Honorary Consul (☎ 627-9773)
16 Victoria Ave, Port of Spain

Embassies or consulates for Austria, Barbados, Belgium, Denmark, Germany, Guyana, India, Italy, Jamaica, Japan, the Netherlands, Norway, Sweden and Switzerland are listed in the yellow pages of the phone book under the heading 'Diplomatic Missions.'

CUSTOMS
Visitors can bring in one quart (about 1L) of liquor, 200 cigarettes or 50 cigars, or gifts valued up to US$200 without paying duty.

MONEY
The Trinidad & Tobago dollar (TT$) is the official currency. Banks will exchange a number of foreign currencies, including British pounds sterling, Canadian dollars, Australian dollars, German marks and French francs, but you'll generally get better rates for US dollars.

Both MasterCard and Visa credit cards can be used at most moderately priced restaurants, hotels and guest houses. Such establishments generally add a 10% service charge; for those that don't, a tip of 10% is standard.

Currency
The Trinidad & Tobago dollar is divided into 100 cents. Coins are in 1-, 5-, 10-, and 25-cent denominations. Notes, which are colorfully adorned with birds, pan drums and oil rigs, come in denominations of TT$1 (red), TT$5 (green), TT$10 (gray), TT$20 (purple) and TT$100 (blue).

Exchange Rates
The current exchange rate can be found on page 4 of the newspaper *Trinidad Express*. As this book went to press, the current rates of exchange for the TT$ were the following:

country	unit		T&T dollar
Australia	A$1	=	TT$3.19
Canada	C$1	=	TT$4.05
France	FF1	=	TT$0.80
Germany	DM1	=	TT$2.68
UK	UK£1	=	TT$8.60
US	US$1	=	TT$6.18

POST & COMMUNICATIONS
Post
Postcards and letters up to 20g cost TT$2 to other Caribbean countries, TT$3.75 to the USA or Canada, TT$4.50 to the UK or Europe and TT$5.25 to Australia.

When addressing mail from overseas, follow the street or box number with the town and 'Trinidad & Tobago, West Indies.'

Telephone

The country's area code is 868, which is added in front of the seven-digit local number when calling from overseas.

Public phones in Trinidad and Tobago are numerous, but few are functional. Those that do work are either coin- or card-operated. Coin phones accept 5¢, 10¢ or 25¢ coins. Phone cards are of two types. One can be inserted and is good only for calls within T&T; these are sold in denominations of TT$10, TT$20, TT$60 and TT$100 and can be purchased at airports, shopping malls and other public places. Another type of card, usable on any touch-tone phone, has an access code that must be dialed before the number you are calling. It's good for both local and international calls. More information on phone cards and making long-distance calls is under Post & Communications in Regional Facts for the Visitor.

Email & Internet Access

Internet service can be found at or near the airport in both Trinidad and Tobago, as well as in several shopping malls in downtown Port of Spain. Some smaller towns also have internet cafés. The rate ranges from as much as TT$50 per hour (at the airports) to TT$10 per hour (at the ferry terminal and downtown Port of Spain).

BOOKS

Lonely Planet's *Diving and Snorkeling Trinidad & Tobago* details the country's 49 best dive sites, from popular Tobago spots to Trinidad's less explored Bocas Islands.

For bird watchers, in addition to James Bond's well-regarded *Field Guide to Birds of the West Indies,* there's Richard ffrench's comprehensive *A Guide to the Birds of Trinidad and Tobago* and William L Murphy's 125-page *A Birder's Guide to Trinidad and Tobago.*

The Trinidad and Tobago Field Naturalists Club Trail Guide describes hiking trails on the islands, complete with sketch maps.

For more details on Carnival and the music associated with it, look at Peter Mason's *Bacchanal.* And for those interested in food, *Callaloo, Calypso & Carnival,* by Dave deWitt and Mary Jane Wilan, has recipes and tidbits on the exotic flavors of Trinidad & Tobago.

NEWSPAPERS & MAGAZINES

The *Trinidad Express, Newsday* and the *Trinidad Guardian* are the main daily newspapers, all published in the morning. *Discover Trinidad & Tobago,* a handy full-color 100-plus-page magazine chock full of general tourist information and ads, can be picked up free at airport tourist offices and many hotels.

RADIO & TV

The country boasts a dozen independent radio stations. Radio Trinidad (730 AM) broadcasts Voice of America from midnight to 5 am.

The state-sponsored TV network, TTT (channels 2 and 13), carries a variety of programming, TIC (channel 4) is the educational channel and TV-6 (channels 6 and 18) features CNN newscasts. All have a pretty heavy dose of US programming. Cable also carries movie channels such as HBO.

ELECTRICITY

Trinidad & Tobago has electric current of both 110V and 220V, 60 cycles. Check the voltage before plugging in anything.

WEIGHTS & MEASURES

Officially, Trinidad & Tobago uses the metric system. Highway signs and car odometers are in kilometers, but the small highway markers at the sides of some roads still measure miles, and many people give directions in miles.

HEALTH

In Trinidad & Tobago, the laboratory-reported rate of people infected with HIV for the population was 5.3% in the early 1990s and has been growing at a rate of about 1% annually since then. Fifty-two percent of AIDS cases are contracted through heterosexual contact, and 72% of HIV/AIDS deaths occur among males age 20 to 35 years. Travelers should keep this in mind, act wisely, and take the appropriate precautions. If you would like more information, contact the Trinidad National AIDS Hotline at ☎ 625-2437 or aidsline@tstt.net.tt.

Children in Trinidad are routinely vaccinated for yellow fever. Although there have been no reported occurrences of the illness in humans, yellow-fever vaccines are recommended for travel outside urban areas, especially in the southeast. Leptospirosis can be present in freshwater streams. Outbreaks of dengue fever occur, especially during the rainy season. The best prevention is mosquito repellant, screens and mosquito nets.

On Trinidad, the general hospital (☎ 623-2951) is at 56–57 Charlotte St in Port of Spain, but most expatriates prefer to use the St Clair Medical Centre (☎ 628-1451), 18 Elizabeth St. There are smaller hospitals in San Fernando and Mt Hope, the latter near Tunapuna.

On Tobago, there is a 98-bed general hospital (☎ 639-2551) at Fort King George in Scarborough.

DANGERS & ANNOYANCES

Tobagonians warn of rampant lawlessness in Trinidad, and Trinidadians say crime has reached epidemic proportions in Tobago. While such claims indicate a real concern over rising levels of crime, they tend to exaggerate the dangers of travel on the islands. At night it is best to avoid walking around dark areas, particularly in Port of Spain. Theft can be a problem, particularly in touristed parts of Tobago, so be sure to keep an eye on your valuables.

Poisonous manchineel trees inhabit some beaches on Tobago and the isle of Gasparee near Chaguaramas. Trinidad has venomous bushmaster, fer-de-lance and coral snakes; however, snake bites are rare. There are no poisonous snakes on Tobago.

EMERGENCIES

Dial ☎ 999 for police, ☎ 990 for fire or ambulance emergencies, ☎ 634-4440 for the Coast Guard.

BUSINESS HOURS

Government offices are usually open 8 am to noon and 1 to 4:30 pm weekdays. Business hours are generally 8 am to 4:30 pm weekdays, 8 am to noon Saturday; however, most malls are open later and all day Saturday. Most banks are open 8 am to 2 pm Monday to Thursday, 8 am to noon and 3 to 5 pm Friday.

PUBLIC HOLIDAYS & SPECIAL EVENTS

Trinidad & Tobago has the following public holidays:

New Year's Day	January 1
Eid Ul Fitr	late December/January
Good Friday	late March/early April
Easter Monday	late March/early April
Spiritual/Shouter Baptist Liberation Day	March 30
Indian Arrival Day	May 30
Corpus Christi	ninth Thursday after Easter
Labour Day	June 19
Emancipation Day	August 1
Independence Day	August 31
Christmas Day	December 25
Boxing Day	December 26

Carnival Monday and Tuesday, and some religious festival days, are also holidays in practice, with banks and most businesses closed.

Trinidad's main annual event is of course Carnival, which formally begins two days before Ash Wednesday (see 'Carnival'). There are a number of smaller music festivals as well, including the following:

The World Steelband Festival – October.

Pan Ramajay – May. A competition of small steel bands.

Caribbean Latin Jazz Festival – September.

National Pan Chutney Competition – November.

National Parang Competition – December. A legacy of Venezuelan immigrants, parang is traditional Christmas music sung in Spanish and accompanied by Latin instruments such as the *cuatro*, maracas and box-bass. Finalists compete in Arima and Paramin.

East Indian festivals, whose dates vary with the lunar calendar, draw large crowds of locals and visitors. They provide a good opportunity to experience South Asian culture.

Divali – November. This is the Hindu festival of lights, when elaborate towers are constructed of thousands of tiny earthenware lamps called *deyas*. Festivities take place in and around Chaguanas.

Carnival

The king of all Caribbean Carnivals is unmistakably Trinidad's. Many Trinidadians prepare for Carnival with a near-consuming devotion. From New Year's Day, activities swing into full gear. The *mas* (short for 'masquerade') camps work late into the evenings creating costumes, the panyards are full of steel-band performers tuning up their rhythms, and calypso music blasts through the night at pre-Carnival jams. A week before Carnival, competitions for the king and queen get under way.

Carnival festivities begin on Monday morning, two days before Ash Wednesday, with the predawn J'Ouvert, or 'dirty mas,' when revelers take to the streets smeared in mud and grease and dressed in scary costumes, while iron bands beat their simple instruments of hubcaps, metal lids and bottles. As the day proceeds, masquerade bands hit the streets for 'pretty mas,' with members of each troupe wearing identical costumes. Tens of thousands parade and dance throughout the night, accompanied by steel bands, brass bands, and soca trucks with DJs, and the event takes on the character of a massive street party. On Tuesday, the activities culminate with competitions for the Band of the Year and by midnight Carnival is officially over.

Most of the larger events take place at the Queen's Park Savannah in the center of Port of Spain, including the major steel-band and calypso competitions.

Information on upcoming Carnivals is available from the National Carnival Commission (☎ 627-1350, nccmac@tstt.net.tt), Grandstand, Queen's Park Savannah, Port of Spain. The Web site, www.carnivalncc.com, includes a list of events for the current year's Carnival, links to mas camps and the location of panyards, calypso tents and fetes. It also includes a list of associated events and a link for online purchase of Carnival tickets.

CARNIVAL CALENDAR

Saturday two weeks prior to Carnival	National Panorama preliminaries
Saturday prior	Red Cross children's parade of the bands; Calypso Monarch semifinals
Carnival Friday	National Single Pan Bands Final; International Soca Monarch Finals; Carnival King and Queen semifinals
Carnival Saturday	National Panorama finals (at Queen's Park Savannah); Junior parade of bands
Carnival Sunday	Dimanche Gras: Crowning of Carnival King and Queen; Calypso Monarch finals (at Queen's Park Savannah)
Monday morning	J'Ouvert
Monday-Tuesday	Parade of the bands; crowning of King of de Road
Tuesday	Last lap
Saturday after	Carnival champs in concert (at Queen's Park Savannah)

Phagwa – March. The arrival of spring is celebrated with the lighting of a big bonfire and singing of Hindi folk songs, and it all culminates by spraying everyone with lavender-colored water called *abeer*. The main events take place in Chaguanas.

Hosay – March or April. The three-night Muslim celebration commemorates the martyrdom of the prophet's grandsons. Key events include the parading of brightly decorated replicas of the martyrs' tomb, and the Moon Dance, in which a dancing duo cavorts through the streets twirling a pair of giant red and green moons symbolizing the martyred brothers to the driving rhythms of *tassa* drums. Key locations are in St James, Curepe and Cedros.

Festival of Santa Rosa de Lima – August. The Carib community in Arima hosts processions, dancing and parang music.

Tobago has its own lively Carnival, which runs simultaneously with the much larger festivities in Port of Spain. Tobago also has a Heritage Festival – two weeks of traditional-style festivities that begin in late July. For something quintessentially local, you can watch goat and crab racing in Tobago's Buccoo village on the Tuesday after Easter.

Information about other festivals and sporting events can be found in the free Tidco publication *Discover Trinidad & Tobago*.

ACTIVITIES
Beaches & Swimming
Tobago has some fine strands of beach on par with many of the Caribbean's better-known destinations. There are attractive white-sand beaches at Store Bay and Pigeon Point and numerous protected bays around the island, some fronting small villages, others more secluded.

Though not as well known for its beaches, Trinidad, too, has some exceptionally fine coastline. Most popular is Maracas Bay, in a scenic setting north of Port of Spain. The northeast coast around Toco and Grande Rivière consists of pleasant, quiet beaches where leatherback turtles nest. Along Trinidad's east coast are spectacular, undeveloped beaches shaded by coconut palm forests. The shoreline is unprotected and water conditions can be hazardous; however, around Mayaro lifeguards keep watch, and flags note the safer areas.

Diving
Tobago offers extensive coral reefs, a great diversity of marine life and some top-notch diving. The largest concentration of dive sites is around the islets off Tobago's north coast. There are drift dives off the east side of Goat Island, rocky pinnacles and an underwater canyon off St Giles Island and a manta-ray feeding ground off Little Tobago. Elsewhere around Tobago, diving is good at Arnos Vale, which has eels and rays, and at the Mt Irvine Wall, popular for night dives.

Dive Shops Tobago is a competitive market, and you can usually find cut rates with start-up companies. Otherwise, the going rate for single dives averages TT$210 if you bring your own gear, TT$300 with equipment included. Multidive packages can lower the cost. PADI open-water certification courses are available from a number of dive shops for around TT$2250

Dive companies include the following:

AquaMarine Dive (☎ 660-4341, amdtobago@ trinidad.net, www.bluewatersinn.com), at Blue Waters Inn in Speyside

Dive Tobago (☎ 639-0202, cohel@tstt.net.tt), at the gate to Club Pigeon Point

Man Friday Diving (☎/fax 660-4676, bjarne@ manfridaydiving.com), a Danish-run operation in Charlotteville

Scuba Adventure Safari (☎ 660-7333, info@ divetobago.com), at Pigeon Point

Sunsplash Scuba (☎ 639-7743), near Conrado Beach Hotel at Pigeon Point

Tobago Dive Experience (☎ 639-7034, in the USA ☎ 800-544-7631, Info@TobagoDiveExperience.com, www .tobagodiveexperience.com), at Manta Lodge, Speyside and Turtle Beach

Wild Turtle Dive (☎ 639-7936, fax 639-7232), at Pigeon Point

Snorkeling
In addition to the standard Buccoo Reef tour (see the Buccoo section), you can find very good snorkeling in Tobago at Pirate's Bay on

the north side of Charlotteville; at Angel Reef, off Goat Island; and in Arnos Vale Bay. Snorkel sets can be rented at various dive shops and at Pigeon Point for TT$60 a day.

Windsurfing

There are spots around the southwestern end of Tobago with decent windsurfing conditions, including Pigeon Point. At the very tip of the point is a shelter where you can rent standard windsurfing boards for TT$90 an hour, TT$240 a day, or high-performance boards for TT$120 an hour, TT$300 a day. Windsurfing lessons can be arranged for TT$150 an hour.

Kayaking

Paddling through wetland areas along the east and west coasts of Trinidad is an ideal way to observe the diverse wildlife of the swamp. Wildways (☎/fax 623-7332, info@ wildways.org) conducts sunrise kayaking tours of the Nariva and Caroni wetland areas, as well as sea-kayaking expeditions among the islands off Chaguaramas Bay and along the northern coast, with snorkeling and turtle-viewing opportunities.

Hiking

There are several excellent hikes on Trinidad, including trails to waterfalls. Robberies and attacks on hikers are not unknown, but most hikes can be done safely with local guides or through ecotourism operators. Some top trails include the Paria Falls from Blanchisseuse and the 8km hike along the coastal cliff from Grande Rivière to Sans Souci. There's good hiking in the Nariva Swamp area on the east coast and in the Trinity Hills, with possible sightings of howler and capuchin monkeys, agoutis and a variety of bird life. Keith Rodriguez at South East Eco Tours (☎ 644-1072, secotour@tstt.net.tt) leads hikes in the Nariva Swamp and into the Trinity Hills for US$40 per person. Hikes depart from Mayaro. The Asa Wright Nature Centre has a network of trails within its confines; another fine place to hike is behind Pax Guest House, at Mt St Benedict in Tunapuna.

In Tobago, the Tobago Forest Reserve, in the north-central part of the island, has some short trails that you can do on your own and longer treks more suitable for walking with a guide. Other good hikes can be made to the Argyle waterfall or the Hillsborough Dam. Three well-versed Tobagonian guides who lead nature walks are forestry ranger Renson Jack (☎ 660-5175), Jerry Kahloo (☎ 639-5381) and ornithologist David Rooks (☎ 639-4276). Be cautious when striking out on your own in Tobago, especially in areas frequented by tourists.

Bird Watching

Both Trinidad and Tobago have an abundance of bird life and superb bird-watching opportunities. On Trinidad, Caroni Bird Sanctuary, Pointe-à-Pierre Wildfowl Trust and the Asa Wright Nature Centre are the principal birding destinations. All are detailed in the Around Trinidad section of this chapter.

In Tobago, bird-watching activities are concentrated in the northern part of the island, where there are a couple of small resorts geared for bird watchers. Little Tobago, the island off Speyside, is the most visited bird sanctuary.

Golf

There are 18-hole par 72 courses at St Andrew's Golf Club (☎ 629-2314), in Maraval on Trinidad, and Mt Irvine Bay Golf Club (☎ 639-8871) and Tobago Hilton (☎ 660-8500), on Tobago. Also on Trinidad is the nine-hole Chaguaramas Public Golf Club (☎ 634-4349), in Chaguaramas, and courses in Pointe-à-Pierre and La Brea.

ACCOMMODATIONS

Both islands have good-value guest houses and small hotels. If you arrive without reservations, the airport tourist offices can assist in booking rooms. Finding a room in Tobago is seldom a problem, but during Carnival season reservations in Trinidad should be made far in advance, and rates increase dramatically. The Trinidad & Tobago Bed & Breakfast Co-Operative Society (☎/fax 663-4413, maredwards@hotmail.com) can help you find accommodations in northwestern Trinidad and on Tobago. Low-season rates average US$25/40 for singles/doubles in private guest houses. Some have private baths, kitchenettes and TV.

A 15% value-added tax (VAT) and a 10% service charge are tacked onto hotel rates, though rates are often quoted before the additional charges are made. Many, but not all, hotels allow children under 12 to stay for free; if you're traveling with children, inquire when booking.

FOOD

Trinidad and Tobago have West Indian, Creole, Chinese and Continental restaurants. East Indian influence prevails in the roti, a Trinidadian creation found throughout the Caribbean, and a similar fast food called 'doubles,' a sandwich of curried chickpeas wrapped in a soft, flat bread. Curried meats and seafood are common local main dishes, often served with a side of *pelau* (rice mixed with peas, meat and coconut).

Another popular Trinidadian fast food is shark & bake. This sandwich, made with a slab of fresh shark and deep-fried bread, is the standard at informal beachside eateries. Fried flying fish & chips is another inexpensive local favorite.

Because of the large East Indian population and a sizable number of Seventh Day Adventists, vegetarian food is easy to come by on both Trinidad and Tobago.

DRINKS

Tap water is safe to drink on Trinidad and Tobago. The Eastern Caribbean's premium beer, Carib, hails from Trinidad. The local beer, Stag, is promoted as 'a man's beer' because of its slightly higher alcohol level. The island also produces a number of rums, including Vat 19 and Royal Oak. Fresh-fruit juices and drinks are common, especially sorrel, mauby and ginger beer. Sorrel is made from the blossoms of a type of hibiscus and mixed with cinnamon and other spices. Its bright red color makes it very popular at Christmastime. Mauby is made from the bark of the carob tree, also known as the mauby tree; its bitter taste takes getting used

to. Ginger beer, made with lots of ginger root, is another potent (though nonalcoholic) drink.

ENTERTAINMENT

Throughout Trinidad, you can find 'panyards' – warehouses or covered lots where steel bands store their instruments – where during the weeks before Carnival you're welcome to stop by and listen to them practice. Somewhat tamer in style, steel bands play at several Port of Spain or Tobago hotels on weekends.

Nightclubs have a quintessential local flavor; most play a combination of soca,

Panyards & Mas Camps

Panyards and mas camps are vital features of Trinidad's urban landscape. Little more than vacant lots where instruments are stored for much of the year, panyards become lively rehearsal spaces for steel bands in the weeks leading up to Carnival. For those who want to pay close attention to the elaborate arrangements of the steel bands, they may be a better venue than the frantic Carnival streets. The Amoco Renegades, 138 Charlotte Street in Port of Spain, sometimes have rehearsals and activities throughout the year. Another very accessible panyard is that of the Woodbrook Playboyz, on Tragarete Rd. More adventurous listeners may want to seek out the panyard of the seminal Desperadoes ensemble, located in the working-class Laventille district.

Mas camps are workshops where designers put together Carnival costumes; they're busy for months before the main event. You can usually drop by and watch the costume designers at work, or, like other Trinidadians, shop for an outfit and sign up to join a band. If you'd like to visit a mas camp or perhaps join a mas band for Carnival, try Masquerade (www.masquerade.co.tt), on Cipriani Boulevard. Another good one is Legends (☎ 622-7466, www.legendscarnival.com), 88 Robert Street in Woodbrook.

TRINIDAD & TOBAGO

calypso, reggae, American chart hits and a bit of Euro-techno. While the mix may be a strange one, locals find it ideal for 'wining,' a favored dance in which men and women grind their bodies together in time to the music. Wednesday and Friday nights are the most active, when everyone comes out for an 'after-work lime.' Saturdays, however, are noticeably quieter.

There are five cinemas in Port of Spain and one in Scarborough. Hollywood movies are most popular, though Hong Kong kung fu and movies from India are also shown.

SPECTATOR SPORTS
Cricket
The main venue for cricket is the Queen's Park Oval, a few blocks west of the Queen's Park Savannah on Tragarete Rd, Port of Spain. The Oval, originally built in 1896, is the site of both regional and international matches. The current pavilion, with the northern hills providing a spectacular backdrop, can hold 25,000 spectators. For information on matches, phone the Queen's Park Cricket Club (☎ 622-2295).

Horse Racing
In Trinidad, the Arima Race Club (☎ 646-2450) has horse racing 40 days a year, mostly on Saturdays and holidays, at Santa Rosa Park in Arima. Admission to the ground floor of the stands is free; Level 1 is TT$5.

SHOPPING
Some interesting locally made products that could make good souvenirs include hot pepper sauce, Trinidadian rum, and Angostura bitters, an herbal concoction used as a drink flavoring and made from a secret recipe. A recording of steel-band or calypso music makes a lightweight souvenir. South of Chaguanas, in the village of Edinburg near Chase Village, potters make *deya* lamps (used in the festival of Divali; see Public Holidays & Special Events, earlier) and other ceramic items using traditional styles and methods. Several large pottery workshops are on the main road. Some especially nice work is done by Michael Dobson; to find him, turn west at Toco's Restaurant in Edinburg, then ask.

Getting There & Away

DEPARTURE TAX
A TT$75 departure tax and a TT$25 security fee must be paid in local currency. There's no departure tax when flying between Trinidad and Tobago. At the Trinidad airport, the fee can be paid via a special ATM machine. Show the ATM receipt, or pay the tax, as you enter the departure security area.

AIR
Airports & Airlines
Trinidad's only airport, Piarco International Airport, is 23km east of Port of Spain. There's a tourist office, duty-free shops, car rental booths and fast-food restaurants near the international ticketing area. Three ATMs are just outside the terminal, all connected to the Cirrus and Plus networks. A currency exchange office inside the terminal is open 6 am to 10 pm daily.

The established fare for a taxi from the airport to Port of Spain is TT$120. Alternatively, take an Arouca route taxi (to the left just outside the terminal) and get off at the Eastern Main Rd (TT$2); from there catch a red-striped maxi-taxi to the capital (TT$4). From Port of Spain, take an Arima maxi, then pick up a local taxi at the Piarco junction.

Tobago's Crown Point International Airport dominates the island's southwest corner. Across the road from the terminal is a small complex with a snack bar, a Royal Castle restaurant, a tourist information office, a newsstand and a Republic Bank with ATM.

Many airlines have offices near Independence Square in Port of Spain. The LIAT and BWIA offices are on Edward St, two blocks west of Woodford Square.

Airline reservation numbers in Trinidad & Tobago include the following:

Aeropostal	☎ 623-4174
Air Canada	☎ 669-4065
ALM	☎ 623-8243
American Airlines	☎ 669-4661
British Airways	☎ 800-744-2997

BWIA	☎ 627-2942 (Trinidad)
	☎ 660-2942 (Tobago)
Caledonian Airways	☎ 639-2285
Guyana Airways	☎ 627-2753
LIAT	☎ 627-6274 (Trinidad)
	☎ 639-0484 (Tobago)
Surinam Airways	☎ 627-0102

The USA

American Airlines has daily flights to Trinidad direct from Miami and via San Juan or Miami from New York; Washington, DC; and Dallas. The typical midweek excursion fare to Trinidad is around US$600 from Miami, US$960 from New York, US$850 from Dallas and US$680 from Washington, DC, in the off-season; fares are about US$150 more in winter.

BWIA flies direct daily to Trinidad from Miami; Washington, DC; and New York, with fares comparable to American Airlines'. ALM offers a twice weekly service between Miami and Trinidad, via Curaçao, for US$365 in the low season and around US$430 in winter.

All these fares allow stays of up to 60 days.

Canada

Air Canada flies from Toronto to Trinidad Monday through Friday. The midweek fare is C$850 in the low season for a 21-day midweek excursion ticket. A 60-day ticket is C$1070.

BWIA flies from Toronto to Trinidad three times a week with fares that are comparable to Air Canada's.

The UK

British Airways flies directly to Tobago from London on Wednesday and Sunday. Daily flights to Tobago can be made via Barbados. An excursion ticket, allowing a stay of 90 days, costs UK£560. BWIA has daily flights between London and Trinidad for UK£710. Caledonian Airways, which has a reputation as a price cutter, flies twice weekly to Port of Spain from London and commonly offers discounted fares of around UK£775 in the winter and UK£415 in summer.

South America

BWIA flies daily from Georgetown, Guyana, to Trinidad for US$173 one-way, US$219 for a 30-day excursion ticket. Daily flights from Caracas are US$146 one-way, US$213 roundtrip. Aeropostal has similar fares for daily flights, many of which stop on the Isla de Margarita en route. Surinam Airways has flights once a week between Georgetown (Guyana) and Port of Spain at US$145 for a seven-day ticket; a 30-day excursion ticket to Suriname is US$340. ALM also has flights via Curaçao to Caracas, Maracaibo and Valencia in Venezuela and to Paramaribo, Suriname.

Within the Caribbean

LIAT LIAT has nonstop flights between Port of Spain and St Lucia, Grenada and St Croix. In addition, the airline has connecting flights via Grenada and Barbados to the rest of its Caribbean network. The fare from Grenada to either Port of Spain or Tobago is US$89 one-way, US$116 for a 30-day excursion fare. Between Trinidad and Barbados it's US$130 one-way and US$154 roundtrip.

LIAT also offers good-value fares between Trinidad and some of the more distant Caribbean islands. For example, you can fly roundtrip between Trinidad and St Martin on an excursion ticket allowing a seven-day stay for just US$321, about 30% under the cost of the regular 30-day roundtrip ticket.

BWIA BWIA has direct flights daily between Barbados and Trinidad with a one-way fare of US$153 and a roundtrip fare of US$206 that allows a stay of 30 days. There are daily flights from Antigua to Trinidad for US$303 one-way and US$289 for a 21-day excursion, flights daily except Thursday from St Lucia to Trinidad for US$155 one-way and US$217 for a 30-day excursion, and flights three times a week from St Martin to Trinidad for US$336 one-way and US$456 for a 30-day excursion. BWIA sometimes offers discounted seven-day roundtrip tickets for less than the one-way fare.

ALM Connections can be made on ALM via Curaçao to Aruba for US$306 roundtrip. Connections can also be made to Bonair,

Kingston, Santo Domingo, San Juan, Port au Prince and St Martin.

SEA
Passenger/Cargo Boat

Windward Lines Limited has a passenger/cargo boat that connects Trinidad with St Lucia, Barbados, St Vincent and Venezuela. For more information, you can call Global Steamship Agencies (☎ 624-2279, globalship @carib-link.net), in the Mariners Club Building on Wrightson Rd, Port of Spain.

If you have some sailing experience, you may be able to arrange transport to other islands and beyond by signing on as crew on a yacht. For information, ask at one of the marina offices in Chaguaramas (see Yacht). The Web site www.crewseekers.co.uk connects prospective crew with yacht owners.

There are a couple of boatmen at the Island Homeowners' jetty on the west side of Chaguaramas who are able to transport people to Venezuela. Prices must be negotiated directly with them.

Yacht

Trinidad & Tobago is beyond the main sweep of most hurricanes, making it a safe haven for yachters. Chaguaramas Bay has the primary mooring and marina facilities as well as immigration and the customs office for yachters. The Trinidad & Tobago Yacht Club (☎ 637-4260, fax 633-6388, ttyc@tstt.net.tt), in Bayshore, has 50 berths, water, electricity, showers, Internet hookups, laundry and a restaurant. At Carenage, Chaguaramas Bay, Power Boat Mutual Facilities (☎ 634-4303, fax 634-4327, pbmfl@powerboats.co.tt) has laundry, a grocery store, apartments and an outhaul and storage facility.

The tourism department, Tidco, publishes a *Boater's Directory,* with an array of information for yacht travelers.

Cruise Ship

Cruise ships dock at the south side of Port of Spain. The large cruise-ship complex contains a customs hall, souvenir and clothing shops, car rental agencies, taxis and a couple of local eateries. There's a smaller cruise-ship facility in central Scarborough on Tobago.

Getting Around

AIR

Since the closure of Air Caribbean, BWIA (in Trinidad ☎ 627-2942, in Tobago ☎ 660-2942) is the main carrier between Tobago and Trinidad, with up to nine daily flights making the 15-minute jaunt between the islands. The cost is US$25 each way. In Port of Spain, reservations can be made by phone and tickets purchased at the airport two hours before departure. It is possible to buy an open return ticket good for one year.

BUS
Trinidad

The main departure point for buses in Port of Spain is the City Gate terminal on South Quay. Purchase tickets from the booth at the west end of the terminal.

Three types of bus service link Trinidad's largest towns. Red, white and black ECS buses are fast, reliable and air-conditioned. Blue Transit and Super Express buses are cheaper, less frequent and (despite the name) slower. ECS service to San Fernando (TT$6, 1 hour) and Arima (TT$4, 45 minutes) departs every 15 minutes from 6 am to 9 pm weekdays, every 30 minutes from 7 am to 7 pm Saturday. Transit buses to the same destinations depart hourly every day. There are eight departures Monday to Saturday for Maracas Bay (TT$4, 45 minutes) and Blanchisseuse (TT$8, 1½ hours), four on Sunday.

Other destinations from City Gate terminal are as follows:

destination	fare	duration
Chaguanas	TT$2 (ECS TT$4)	30 minutes
Chaguaramas	TT$2	1 hour
Sangre Grande	TT$4.50	1½ hours
Tunapuna	TT$2	30 minutes

The City Gate terminal contains several fast-food restaurants, ATMs, a post office and Internet service. The bus company maintains an information booth (☎ 623-7872) on the west side of the bus platform. It's manned 7 am to 7 pm weekdays, till noon Saturday.

Tobago

There's regular bus service from Scarborough to Crown Point, Plymouth (via Buccoo and Mt Irvine) and most villages on the island. Buses to/from Crown Point (TT$2, 20 minutes) and Plymouth (TT$2, 20 minutes) run from dawn to 8 pm, with departures every half-hour at peak periods, hourly at other times of day. Service decreases on weekends.

Other departures from Scarborough include the following:

Charlotteville via Speyside (TT$8, 1½ hours, seven departures 5 am to 6 pm)

Parlatuvier via Castara (TT$6, 45 minutes, departures at 6 am and 2:30, 4, and 6 pm)

Roxborough (TT$5, 30 minutes, six departures 6:30 am to 4 pm)

Tickets are purchased in advance at the bus terminal in Scarborough. In Crown Point, get them at the minimart in front of Jimmy's Holiday Resort, or near the airport from Donut Boys (unless they're out).

CAR & MOTORCYCLE
Road Rules

Driving is on the left. A home driver's license from the USA, Canada, UK, France or Germany or an International Driving Permit is valid on Trinidad & Tobago for stays of up to three months.

All gas stations are National (NP), a state-owned network. Gas is at a fixed price of TT$2.45 a liter for regular and TT$2.85 for super throughout Trinidad & Tobago.

Rental

Trinidad A number of small car rental companies operate on Trinidad. Prices average about TT$300 a day with insurance and unlimited mileage. Discounts are usually offered for weekly rentals.

The best deals are offered by Econo-Car Rentals, with offices in Port of Spain (☎ 622-8074, econocar@trinidad.net) and at the airport (☎ 669-2342), charging under TT$200 a day, TT$1200 per week, for a Mitsubishi Lancer. Other reasonably priced rental outfits include Reesal's Auto Rentals (☎/fax 669-

3330), at the airport; Discounts Auto Rentals (☎ 622-6596, brettpillac@hotmail.com), in St James; and Singh's Auto Rentals, in Port of Spain (☎ 623-0150, singhs1@tstt.net.tt) and at the airport (☎ 669-5417).

Tobago You must be over 25 to rent a car in Tobago. Daily rates for a compact such as a Nissan Sentra average US$40 a day, US$210 a week, including unlimited mileage and insurance; jeep rentals are about US$45 a day, US$245 a week. Car rental companies at Crown Point International Airport include AR Auto Rentals (☎ 639-0644, fax 639-0305) and Thrifty Car Rental (☎ 639-8507, eontab@tstt.net.tt). In Crown Point itself, most hotels and guest houses can make arrangements.

Gas stations are sparsely scattered around the island, so it's wisest to fill up before doing extensive touring, as hours can be random and stations occasionally run out of gas.

TAXI
Regular Taxi

Regular taxis, locally called 'tourist taxis,' are readily available at the airport, the cruise-ship complex and hotels. These large, often left-hand-drive vehicles are unmetered, but rates are established by the government; hotel desks and the airport tourist office have a list of fares. Make sure you have established the rate before riding off. From the airport to Port of Spain the fare is TT$120, to Maraval TT$144 and to San Fernando TT$186. There's a 50% surcharge between 10 pm and 6 am. To call for a taxi, dial ☎ 669-1689 (airport), or ☎ 625-3032 (Independence Square taxi stand) in Port of Spain. Kalloo's Taxi Service (☎ 622-9073), open 24 hours, has an office at 31 French St in Port of Spain, just a block north of Ariapita Ave and very convenient after an evening of liming at the Mas Camp pub.

In Tobago, taxis are available at Crown Point International Airport and charge about TT$25 to hotels around Crown Point, TT$30 to Pigeon Point, TT$50 to Scarborough, TT$60 to Mt Irvine or Buccoo and TT$260 to Charlotteville. There's another taxi stand at Club Pigeon Point. It's also possible to hire a taxi for an island tour for around TT$120.

Route Taxi

The predominant mode of public transport within Port of Spain is the route taxi, a shared car that travels along a prescribed route and charges TT$2 to drop you anywhere along the way. They are recognizable by the letter 'H' on their license plates. Route taxis also serve as inexpensive interurban transport.

Route taxis to Maraval can be picked up on Charlotte St just south of Oxford St; those to St Ann's and St James leave from the south side of Woodford Square. St Ann's taxis circle Queen's Park Savannah, and St James taxis go via Tragarete Rd. Route taxis to Chaguanas leave from the middle of Broadway, just south of Independence Square; San Fernando–bound taxis, from the corner of South Quay and Broadway.

Outside the city center, route taxis be hailed along the route. Occasionally, drivers of private vehicles (with 'P' on the license plate) also offer route-taxi service, though these cannot be recommended.

In lower Scarborough, Tobago, taxis to Plymouth depart from opposite the market (TT$4), and to Crown Point from in front of the ferry terminal (TT$5). In upper Scarborough, taxis to Speyside leave from Republic Bank (TT$10), and to Charlotteville from James Park (TT$11).

Maxi-Taxi

Sort of a hybrid bus and route taxi, maxitaxis are minibuses that ply a regular route within a specific zone. They're color-coded by route and run 24 hours. In Port of Spain, the main maxi-taxi terminal (☎ 624-3505) for southbound and eastbound buses is on South Quay, adjacent to City Gate. Other routes depart from stops elsewhere in town. If you're going to a location that's a little off the main road, maxi-taxis can usually drop you off at the door if you pay an additional fare.

Maxi-taxis to Arima and Sangre Grande (TT$4 and TT$6, respectively), with connections to the east and northeast coasts, have a red stripe and depart from City Gate. Those to Chaguanas and San Fernando (TT$4 and TT$6) have green stripes and also leave from City Gate (from San Fernando, maxitaxis connecting to outlying areas have black or brown stripes). Maxis for Chaguaramas via St James (TT$4) have a yellow stripe and leave from South Quay at St Vincent St. Finally, maxis to Maracas and Blanchisseuse via Maraval (TT$8 and TT$15) also have a yellow stripe, but leave from George St and Prince St.

BICYCLE

In Tobago, Glorious Ride Cycle (☎ 639-7124), at the Milford Rd curve in Crown Point, rents all-terrain bikes for TT$40 per 24 hours, no deposit required. Child seats are available. They're open 9 am to 3 pm daily. First Class Bicycle Rentals, on a corner lot a block north of the airport in Crown Point, charges TT$60, with discounts for longer periods, and they can arrange guided cycle tours.

HITCHHIKING

Hitchhiking is common among islanders, especially with children, who hitch to and from school, and with workers trying to get home at night. However, it is not necessarily a safe mode of transport for foreign visitors. Lonely Planet does not recommend hitchhiking.

BOAT

Ferries run daily between Port of Spain in Trinidad and Scarborough in Tobago. The journey takes about five hours and costs TT$25 each way for economy-class tickets. Tourist class (TT$30) supposedly assures you a reclining seat in the passenger lounge, but in reality seating is minimally controlled. Cabins are available for TT$80.

The boat departs from Port of Spain at 2 pm weekdays and at 11 am Sunday; from Scarborough at 11 pm Sunday to Friday. There are generally no passenger ferries on Saturday, except in August, around Carnival and at Christmas and Easter. Schedules may vary some at holiday periods. Tickets are sold at the ferry terminal 7 am to 3 pm weekdays. Be sure to arrive at least two hours before sailing or your ticket can be resold. If your travel date is near the weekend or a holiday, it's wise to book as far in advance as possible.

For more information, call the Port Authority (in Trinidad ☎ 625-3055 or 625-4906, in Tobago ☎ 639-2417 or 639-2668).

ORGANIZED TOURS

You can arrange island tours with individual taxi drivers. For an all-day round-the-island tour, drivers will generally ask about TT$1000, though you should be able to negotiate that down by about 25%.

Trinidad & Tobago Sightseeing Tours (☎ 628-1051, www.trintours.com), 12 Western Main Rd in St James, offers a variety of full-day tours, most for TT$390 to TT$450. One skirts the perimeter of Trinidad; a second combines Asa Wright Nature Centre and the north coast, taking in a couple of hours of bird watching and some of Trinidad's most dramatic scenery; and a third tour heads south, visiting Pitch Lake and the pottery shops near Chaguanas. Less ambitious itineraries cover Maracas Bay (TT$240); the Caroni Bird Sanctuary, including a boat tour to see scarlet ibis (TT$205); and Port of Spain (TT$150), a three-hour ramble through the capital.

Ecotourism

Those wanting to piece together an organized 'ecotour,' whether it be bird watching, rain-forest tours or just general environmental and cultural appreciation outings, will find a number of excellent tour guides on Trinidad and Tobago.

Perhaps the most renowned is David Rooks Nature Tours (☎/fax 639-4276, rookstobago@trinidad.net). Rooks is president of the Trinidad & Tobago Field Naturalist Club (www.wow.net/ttfnc) and has worked on BBC and PBS nature programs. Other well-regarded ecotourism operators on Tobago include Jerry Kahloo (☎ 639-5381), Pat Turpin (☎ 660-4327, fax 660-4328) and Hubert 'Renson' Jack (☎ 660-5175). On Trinidad, David Rooks' son, Courtenay Rooks (☎ 622-8826, fax 628-1525, rooks@pariasprings.com), 44 La Seiva Rd, Maraval, Trinidad, specializes in birding and natural-history hikes. Wildways (☎ 623-7332, info@wildways.com) leads nature-oriented camping, cycling, hiking and kayaking tours, and participants can choose from a range of skill levels. Island Experiences (☎ 625-2410, gunda@wow.net) embarks on a variety of half- and full-day 'eco-cultural tours.'

The Foundation for Sustainable Community Tourism (Foscom; ☎/fax 628-4146, foscomtnt@wow.net), a nonprofit organization affiliated with Tidco, works with rural and urban communities throughout Trinidad to develop tours around local cultures and environments. Brasso Seco village, in the center of the Northern Range; the East Indian community of Carapichaima; Toco; and the villages of the northeast coast are some of the participating communities. Foscom arranges all transport, meals, guides and optional homestays. Tour prices are set by the individual communities; phone for details.

From March through midsummer, most ecotour operators offer an overnight turtle observation expedition that involves a stroll along the beach at Grand Rivière on Trinidad's north coast to search for nesting leatherbacks.

Trinidad

PORT OF SPAIN

Port of Spain, the country's capital and commercial center, is a bustling metropolitan hub of some 350,000 people. It's not a tourist city. All the same, it's a lively place with a variety of good restaurants and clubs, and it makes a vibrant base from which to visit other parts of the island.

The center has a mingling of modern office buildings, old corrugated tin stalls and 19th-century colonial buildings – some are worth a look, but few rate as must-see sights. The south end of Frederick St is the central shopping area, bustling and congested, with both air-conditioned indoor malls and labyrinthine pedestrian arcades. Don't miss the quirky People's Mall, filled with Rasta businesses, snack bars and mini rum shops. Along the street, vendors hawk fruit and jewelry.

The heart of the city is Independence Square – not really a square, but rather two

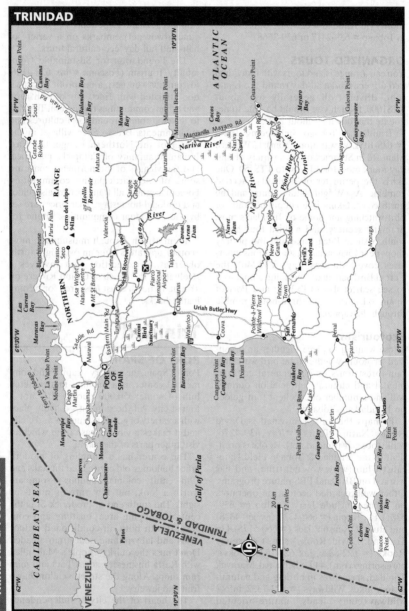

TRINIDAD

long streets bordering a narrow pedestrian strip. Here you can pick up a taxi and find travel agents, banks and cheap eats. Strolling around this part of town in daytime you're apt to be approached by panhandlers, and at night it feels unsafe.

Outside central Port of Spain are the neighborhoods, or suburbs, of Laventille (home of steel pan), Belmont, Cascade, St Ann's, Maraval, St Clair, Woodbrook, New Town and St James. Those looking for lively nightlife will often end up in the western suburb of St James, entered through an arch at the west end of Tragarete Road. A predominately Indian district, it is also a center of activities during the Muslim festival of Hosay.

Port of Spain is at its best and brightest during Carnival. If you happen to be in the city in the weeks preceding Carnival, be sure to take a look into some of the many *mas* camps, where artists create colorful costumes, and visit the panyards, where local steel bands diligently practice their rhythms for the upcoming festivities.

Information

Tourist Offices
The Tidco office (☎ 623-6022), 10–14 Philipps St, is open 8 am to 4 pm weekdays.

Money
The major banks – Republic Bank, ScotiaBank, Royal Bank and First Citizens Bank – have branches on Park St east of Frederick St and on Independence Square. Most are open 8 am to 2 pm Monday to Thursday, 8 am to 1 pm and 3 to 5 pm Friday, and have 24-hour ATMs.

Post & Communications
The post office on Wrightson Rd near French St is open 8 am to 4 pm weekdays. Another branch in the City Gate bus terminal (open 7 am to 7 pm weekdays, 8 am to 1 pm Saturday) has a collectors' section. Other branches are in the Excellent City Centre mall and on Tragarete Rd near the Roxy Pizza Hut at the entrance to St James.

One Stop Compu-Shop, in a small shopping corridor on Independence Square, offers the cheapest Internet access, at

TT$10 per hour. Tech, at the corner of Frederick and Queen Sts, is also reasonable, at TT$15 per hour, and has an iMac cluster. It's open 8:30 am to 5 pm weekdays, till 12:30 pm Saturday.

Travel Agencies
Constellation Tours (☎ 623-9269), on the corner of Duke and Edward Sts, offers packages to Barbados and other neighboring isles. The Travel Centre (☎ 625-1636), in the Uptown Mall on Edward St, is the American Express representative.

Bookstores
You can get maps and books on the region at Trinidad Book World, on Queen St opposite the cathedral. Metropolitan Book Suppliers, upstairs in the Colsort Mall on Frederick St, has an even wider selection of Caribbeana.

Pharmacies
Bhagan's Drugs (☎ 627-5541), on Broadway south of Independence Square, and Express Drugs (☎ 628-1527), 102 Western Main Rd, St James, are both open until 11 pm Monday to Saturday, till 9 pm Sunday.

National Museum & Art Gallery

Housed in a classic colonial building at the corner of Frederick and Keate Sts, the museum contains simple displays on rocks, shells, colonial agriculture and oil exploration. One room is devoted to Carnival, with a nice exhibit on the evolution of steel-pan instruments, a photo gallery of calypso greats and videos of mas bands in action, as well as a room full of dusty costumes. The upper-level galleries feature paintings by Trinidadian artists and an ambitious new natural-history section with informative exhibits on leatherbacks, coral-reef creatures and other T&T flora and fauna.

The museum is open 10 am to 6 pm Tuesday to Saturday, 2 to 6 pm Sunday (free).

Woodford Square

Sometimes referred to as the University of Woodford Square for its occasional use as a forum for soapbox speakers and gospel preachers, this public park marks the symbolic

PORT OF SPAIN

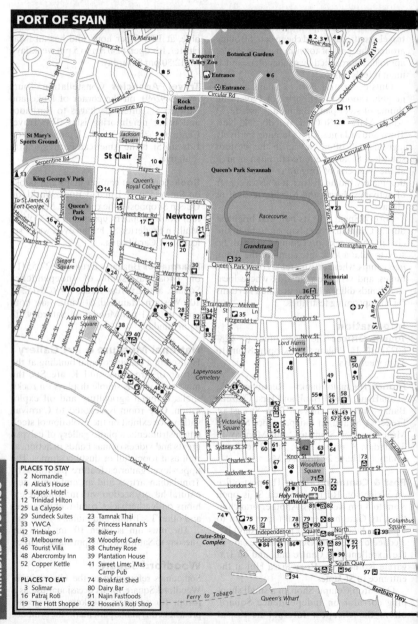

center of downtown Port of Spain. Surrounding the park are some interesting edifices, including **Red House**, the imposing red parliament building constructed in 1906 in Renaissance style; the contemporary steel-and-concrete **Hall of Justice**; and the Anglican Holy Trinity Cathedral. Behind Red House is the shell of the **police station** burned in the 1990 coup attempt. Opposite the square's southwest corner, the new **National Library** will consolidate the contents of several Port of Spain libraries when completed sometime in 2001.

Holy Trinity Cathedral
This majestic Anglican church at the south side of Woodford Square dates from 1818, seats 1200 and has a Gothic design. Its impressive ceiling is supported by an elaborate system of mahogany beams, whose design is said to have been modeled on London's Westminster Hall. Stained-glass windows open to the breeze, and there's a marble monument to Sir Ralph Woodford, the British governor responsible for the church's construction.

Queen's Park Savannah
The city is crowned by Queen's Park Savannah, once part of a sugar plantation and now a public park. It's the center of activity during Carnival, and throughout the year residents play soccer and cricket and fly kites in the expansive grassy field. In the park's northwest corner there's a small **rock garden** with a lily pond and benches. The road circling the park has one-way traffic flowing in a clockwise direction; locals call it the world's largest roundabout.

Magnificent Seven
Along the west side of the Queen's Park Savannah are the Magnificent Seven, a line of seven fancy colonial buildings constructed in the late 19th and early 20th centuries. From south to north, they are the Queen's Royal College, of German Renaissance design; Hayes Court, the Anglican bishop's residence; two private homes; the Catholic archbishop's residence; stately White Hall, the prime minis-

ter's office; and Stollmeyer's Castle, built to resemble a Scottish castle complete with turrets.

Emperor Valley Zoo & Botanical Gardens

Just north of Queen's Park Savannah is the zoo, which has some local creatures, including colorful tropic birds, ocelots, monkeys, scarlet ibis, red brocket deer, agoutis and various snakes, as well as a few large felines. The park is open 9:30 am to 6 pm daily (TT$4, TT$2 for children ages three to 12).

East of the zoo are the botanical gardens, dating from 1818, with grand trees and attractive strolling paths, plus pavilions containing orchids and sensual anthuriums. The gardens are open 6 am to 6 pm daily (free). The **President's House**, a mansion originally built as the governor's residence in 1875, is adjacent to the gardens, as is the **prime minister's residence**.

City Views

The Hilton offers a good view of the city. If you want a higher perch you could drive up to **Fort George**, site of a former British signal station, 4km northwest of the city at the end of Fort George Rd. Another excellent lookout is **Fort Picton**, in the suburb of Laventille. This fort dates back to 1800 and was named after Thomas Picton, Trinidad's first British governor. Laventille has a reputation as a rough area, so it is best to go with a guide or hire a taxi.

Lord Kitchener Monument

Port of Spain honors Aldwyn Roberts, better known as Lord Kitchener, with this statue of the calypso legend that welcomes visitors on their way into St James. Captured here in midperformance and wearing his trademark hat and suit, Kitchener is considered the greatest of the postwar calypsonians. The singer/composer achieved fame in London during the 1950s before a triumphant return to his newly independent homeland, where his songs ruled the Carnival Road March for 10 of the next 13 years.

Places to Stay

Many visitors to the capital stay at the quiet north end, where several hotels are located, or in Maraval, a rather cushy suburb a couple of kilometers farther north, but there are plenty of reasonable options in the heart of the city that allow for good access to restaurants, shopping and nightlife.

Budget The *YWCA* (☎ 627-6388, 8 Cipriani Blvd), a couple of blocks south of Queen's Park Savannah, is central and has simple doubles for women at US$15 per person.

Copper Kettle (☎ 625-4381, 66 Edward St) has clean, no-frills rooms with private bath, ceiling fans and wood floors for US$20 single or double, US$25 with air-con. The attached restaurant does fresh-cooked daily specials including soup, salad and meat for TT$20, and there's a cozy cocktail lounge.

Located on a heavily trafficked street, *Trinbago* (☎ 627-7114, tourist@tstt.net.tt, 37 Ariapita Ave) is a small guest house containing six simple rooms with TV and fan. Singles/doubles cost US$20/30 with shared bath, while a double with a private bath costs US$35. Guests can use the pool at the nearby Tourist Villa.

Tourist Villa (☎ 627-5423, tourist@ tstt.net.tt, 7 Methuen St), on a quieter street, is a pleasant place with lots of balconies and patios and a small pool. Singles/doubles/ triples with shared bath and ceiling fans are US$25/35/40; two double beds with private bath and air-con start at US$35.

La Calypso (☎ 622-4077, fax 628-6895, 46 French St) is a recommendable guest house for those on a budget. It has 18 compact rooms with fan or air-con, plus a Jacuzzi. Singles/doubles cost US$20/30 with shared bath, US$30/36 with a private bath. Good restaurants and nightclubs are within walking distance.

The homey *Melbourne Inn* (☎ /fax 623-4006, melbourn@caribsurf.com, 7 French St) is a place offering 16 basic but clean rooms with TV. Doubles with fan cost US$25, US$35 with private bath. Rooms with air-con or kitchen are higher. Breakfast is served for TT$20. An upper patio has workout equipment.

French St Martin: a tropical Paris

The many ways to hydrate on St Martin

Sint Maarten's tipple of choice

You gotta wonder why they bother with the prices.

Les Plats Du Jour. Francs
Ragout De Cabri 52.00
Colombo de Poulet 52.00
Ragout queue de Boeuf 52.00
Crevettes A l'ail 52.00
Crevettes Creole 52.00
Filet de Vivaneau creole 52.00
Poisson Pint creole 52.00
Poisson Court-bouillon 52.00
Entrecote 52.00

Anguilla's answer to New Orleans' crayfish

Dinnertime on St Martin

AARON MCCOY

Looking west toward Maracas Bay, Trinidad

BILL BACHMANN

The sunset dance of the palms, Nevis

MICHAEL LAWRENCE

The sun never sets on the tall ships of Dominica – except here.

If you have a very early flight, you might consider *Airport View Guesthouse* (☎ 669-4186, rossi@tstt.net.tt), in a nondescript building over a supermarket that's just two minutes from the airport. Large, very clean but uninspiring singles/doubles with air-con and TV cost US$29/34. The helpful management offers courtesy airport transfers.

Mid-Range The *Abercromby Inn* (☎ 623-5259, aberinn@carib-link.net, 101 Abercromby St) is a high-quality but inexpensive place in the heart of the city. Singles or doubles including private bath, central air-con, TV and breakfast start at US$45. Several basic single rooms with fans and exterior bath are US$22. Seven-night Carnival packages start at US$840.

Modern *Alicia's House* (☎ 623-2802, 2getaway@tstt.net.tt, 7 Coblentz Gardens), in an upmarket neighborhood north of Queen's Park Savannah, offers simple singles/doubles with fans and shared bath from US$35/45. Deluxe rooms with refrigerator, private bath, air-con and TV start at US$38/48; some overlook the pool/Jacuzzi area. Breakfast is served (TT$36).

Sundeck Suites (☎ 622-9560, sundeck@carib-link.net, 42–44 Picton St) offers city and mountain views from atop its broad rooftop deck. The suites each have two or three beds, a kitchenette, air-con, TV, a phone and a small veranda. Singles/doubles/triples are US$49/68/84. Ten-night Carnival packages start at US$1200.

In Maraval, *Monique's Guest House* (☎ 628-3334, moniques@carib-link.net, 114 Saddle Rd), 3km north of Queen's Park Savannah, has 10 pleasant rooms with two single or double beds, private bath, air-con and TV for US$60/66/72 single/double/triple. A hillside annex has 10 large studios with cooking facilities and balconies from which you can sometimes spot parrots in the treetops; these cost US$72/78/90. At Carnival time, all units have a five-night rate of US$900.

Carnetta's House (☎ 628-2732, Carnetta@trinidad.net, 28 Scotland Terrace), also in Maravel, is comprised of two separate buildings. Five rooms are at the home of Winston and Carnetta Borrell, in a quiet neighborhood alongside the Maraval River. Six newer units, most with kitchenettes, are on Saddle Rd, opposite Monique's Guest House. Rates in either building begin at US$60 for two people; add US$6 for a kitchenette. All rooms include air-con, cable TV, phones and private bath. Carnetta's riverside bar serves Creole-style meals. Winston, a former tourist-board director, enjoys helping guests plan their daily outings.

Top End The *Kapok Hotel* (☎ 622-5765, stay@kapok.co.tt, 16–18 Cotton Hill), a popular business hotel at the south end of Saddle Rd, has 94 rooms with rattan furnishings, TV, phones and air-con. Singles/doubles cost US$98/113; add US$7 if you want a kitchenette. There's a pool, restaurant, gym and computer room.

The 54-room *Normandie* (☎ 624-1181, normandie@wow.net, 10 Nook Ave) has a relaxed, old-fashioned style. The rooms are pleasant if pricey, and most face a central courtyard and pool. Standard singles/doubles with air-con, phone and double bed cost US$62/72, while more spacious superior rooms with two double beds are US$77/87.

The 394-room *Trinidad Hilton* (☎ 624-3211, hiltonpos@wow.net), on Lady Young Rd, is Trinidad's largest and most upscale hotel. Its hillside setting affords a sweeping city view across Queen's Park Savannah. Large, modern singles/doubles, most with balconies, begin at US$215/245. There are also a couple of restaurants and a very large pool.

Places to Eat
Budget Pickup trucks piled high with chilled drinking coconuts (TT$2) can be found along the road that circles Queen's Park Savannah; after sunset they're joined by vendors selling raw oysters and other snacks. Supermarkets are on French St a block south of Tragarete Rd, on Charlotte St near Independence Square and in Maraval.

The food courts in the malls along Frederick St are handy spots for a quick, TT$15 sit-down lunch. Most have a choice of Creole, Chinese, Indian or fried chicken.

They're usually open 10 am to 5 pm weekdays, until 2 pm Saturday.

A number of local and international fast-food places are around Independence Square. *Hossein's Roti Shop*, on the south side, is a hugely popular carryout for mini-rotis at TT$5 to TT$8 and *dhal puri* (a type of roti stuffed with split peas) for TT$6 to TT$12. *Najin Fastfoods*, around the corner on Henry St, serves good, cheap Chinese food. An excellent filling wonton-and-bok choy soup or a plate of vegetables and rice is just TT$13.

On the other side of the square, *Princess Hannah's Bakery* sells take-out rotis, meat pies and various pastries (another branch is at French St and Tragarete Rd). *Dairy Bar* has TT$5 ice cream cones as well as peanut and seamoss (kelp) punches.

Some of the best rotis are a little out of the center. On Maraval Rd, *The Hott Shoppe* is bright and clean and offers a wide choice of fillings. Vegetarian minis cost TT$3.50; regulars are TT$9.50. Fresh orange and grapefruit juice are available. *Patraj Roti*, on Tragarete Rd catercorner from the Queen's Park Oval, is another roti institution, popular as well for its *buss-up-shut* (torn rotis).

Breakfast Shed, literally a tin shed in front of the cruise-ship complex, is a good place to rub shoulders with locals and try local delicacies. Everything is made from scratch by island women in stalls around the perimeter of the shed. A big meal of Trinidadian fare, including fish, dasheen, plantains and rice, costs TT$15. Weekend specials feature cow-heel soup, curried crab & dumplings, and breadfruit oildown. Service is from 7 am to about 4 pm – try to arrive before 2 pm, as the food sometimes runs out early.

Mid-Range For a good-value meal, *Woodford Cafe* (☎ 622-2233, 62 Tragarete Rd) has tasty Caribbean food that's served from steamer trays but kept fresh. Both the food and atmosphere are pleasant. It's open 11 am to 10 pm Wednesday to Saturday, until 3:30 Monday and Tuesday.

Sweet Lime, attached to Mas Camp Pub on Ariapita Ave, is a casual sidewalk restaurant/bar with an open-air kitchen. The menu includes salads (TT$35), grilled meats and fish (TT$35 to TT$65), vegetarian options and a few exotic specialties, such as Viagra Broth (a spicy fish soup) or *lambie souse* (conch in lemon marinade).

Chutney Rose (☎ 628-8541), on Ariapita Ave at the corner of Fitt St, provides elegant dining for a reasonable price. The specialties are northern Indian cuisine and kind, helpful service. There's a wide choice of vegetable, lamb, chicken and fish dishes. Dinner for two can be had for as little as TT$175 including beer. An attached take-out operation offers dhal puri and buss-up-shut from 11 am to 8 pm.

Top End For an atmospheric treat, *Plantation House* (☎ 628-5551, 38 Ariapita Ave) serves quality Cajun-Creole cuisine in a charming gingerbread-trimmed colonial house. Bayou country favorites go for around TT$80, while Caribbean Creole specialties are slightly more. Lunch is served from 11:30 am to 2:30 pm, dinner from 6:30 to 10:30 pm daily. Bring a sweater: The aircon is overzealous.

Tamnak Thai (☎ 625-0647, 13 Queen's Park East) is a sensual experience, from the latticed, tropical-wood tables to the lily-pad pond to the exotic spices of Thai curries. Dishes include lemongrass-seasoned soups (TT$30 to TT$40); seafood salad (TT$60); vegetable, lamb and shrimp curries; and spicy tofu with vegetables (TT$80 to TT$100).

Solimar (☎ 624-6267, 6 Nook Ave), near the Normandie, is an innovative restaurant run by an Englishman, Joe Brown, a well-traveled former chef for the Hilton chain. On any given night the menu might include Asian, Indian and Italian food. Prices are in the TT$95 to TT$300 range. It's open from 6:30 pm Tuesday to Saturday.

Entertainment

You can find steel-pan music year-round at the various panyards in Port of Spain and St James. The Amoco Renegades panyard on Charlotte St often holds practices on the weekends, particularly on Friday nights.

For a variety of live music and DJs, *Mas Camp Pub* (☎ 627-8449), at the corner of French St and Ariapita Ave, has something going most evenings. Odds are you'll catch calypso, Latin or soca, and, at Christmas, a parang party. An adjoining sports room has pool tables and slot machines. Pick up a weekly program at the door. North of the Hilton, on Coblentz Ave, is *Pelican Inn* (☎ 624-7486), popular with expats. Wednesday night it's one of the liveliest places in town, with bands or DJs, and Friday night it's popular for after-work liming. A more mature crowd limes around the mahogany bar of *The Cellar* (☎ 625-1807), at Jenny's on Cipriani Blvd. Across the way is *Martin's* (☎ 623-7632), where occasionally there's jazz in the rear garden. Nearby, on the corner of Warner and Woodford Sts, *Rafters* (☎ 628-9258) is a quiet place for a chat over a rum.

The suburb of St James, just west of central Port of Spain, is a hub of activity almost any evening. Most places are along the main road. The hot spot to start the evening and rub shoulders with politicians, cricket stars or just about anyone is *Smokey & Bunty's*. The casual *Cheers 2 Pub* (☎ 622-6669) is also popular. The original *Cheers*, a couple blocks north, is smaller, with a more neighborhood atmosphere, and occasionally hosts some excellent local bands. Between drinks, grab a roti, some corn soup or tasty vegetarian food from one of the many street food stalls; Chinky's Nite Bite is best for vegetarian snacks.

If you'd like someone to accompany you for your first night on the town, contact Gunda Harewood (☎ 625-2410, gunda@ wow.net) for an Evening Entertainment Tour. She'll plan activities around your interests and what is happening at the moment. An evening out might include visits to a couple of panyards, a local live band, and guidance in choosing the best street snacks. About four hours of fun and transport costs TT$120 per person.

Shopping

The central area of Port of Spain, especially around Independence Square, Queen St and Frederick St, is filled with malls and arcades, selling everything from spices to fabric by the yard. You can pick up the latest tunes at Crosby's Records, in St James; Cleve's One Stop Music Shop, in a small shopping center east of Woodford Square on Frederick St; or Rhyner's Record Shop, 54 Prince St, Port of Spain; and at Piarco International Airport.

CHAGUARAMAS

The site of a major US military installation during WWII, Chaguaramas now hosts American and other yacht owners at its formidable pleasure-craft facilities. Besides its status as a safe haven for boaters, Chaguaramas is also known as a nightclub district. In addition, the whole area has been designated as a national park and is the launching point for tours to a chain of offshore islands. Other attractions include a military-history museum and a small golf course. Chaguaramas is about a 25-minute drive west of the capital.

A popular destination is the isle of **Gasparee Grande**, at the south side of Chaguaramas Bay, where stalactite caves can be toured by appointment (☎ 634-2052) 9 am to 2:30 pm daily (TT$20). The most distant island, **Chacachacare**, was once a leper colony; camping is permitted on the now-deserted isle. **Scotland Bay**, on the western edge of the peninsula, has a pleasant beach that's accessible only by boat.

Hiking, swimming and history tours to the islands and around the peninsula can be arranged through the Chaguaramas Development Authority (☎ 634-2052/4048, fax 634-4311). The tours include transport from the Chaguaramas Hotel and Convention Centre, boats and entry fees. Most tour prices are based on a minimum of 10 people; contact the CDA about individualized tours. For descriptions of CDA's tours, see their Web site: www.chagdev.com/Eng/2/09.html.

Trips out to the islands can otherwise be arranged with boatmen at the Island Homeowners' jetty, on the west side of Chaguaramas. Joseph Richards (☎ 624-6080) is a reliable mariner. Expect to pay about TT$120 per person for Gasparee Grande or Scotland Bay. A boat to drop you off and pick you up at Chacachacare will run about TT$400 for up to six people.

TRINIDAD & TOBAGO

Places to Eat

A fine waterfront location to enjoy a drink or a reasonably priced seafood meal is *Anchorage* (☎ 634-4334), on Point Gorde Rd. Most of the marina facilities include hotels and restaurants.

Entertainment

Chaguaramas has gained a reputation as a party center. Designed to evoke the atmosphere of a 1940s military-base club, *The Base* (☎ 634-4004) is open 9 pm to 4 am Friday and Saturday only. DJs at The Base aim to please a young, affluent crowd; it's a no-T-shirts-or-sneakers kind of a place. Somewhat more open-minded, *Anchorage* often has live bands, especially during Carnival season. *MOBS II* (☎ 634-2255) features a large amphitheater and hosts Carnival launches for mas bands. Another popular spot is *Pier One* (☎ 634-4472), open 9 pm to 3 am Thursday (Latin Night) and Friday (Thank God It's Free Drinks Night). For those returning to Port of Spain, maxi-taxis often wait on the Western Main Rd near the entrance to the clubs.

MT ST BENEDICT

A Benedictine monastery sits on the hillside north of Tunapuna. Though not a major sight in itself, the monastery attracts people who want to stay or eat at its secluded guest house or walk in the rain forest.

A hikers' haven, the thickly wooded hills behind the monastery are habitat for hawks, owls and myriad colorful forest birds, as well as the occasional monkey. A favorite track is the Donkey Trail, which offers good birding and takes just a couple of hours to walk roundtrip from the guest house.

To get there from Tunapuna, take St John's Rd north 3.3km from Eastern Main Rd. During the day there's bus service roughly every 30 minutes from the turnoff at the Eastern Main Rd.

Places to Stay & Eat

The *Pax Guest House* (☎ /fax 662-4084, info@mtplaisir.com) is a restored colonial house owned by the monastery. This pleasantly relaxed place has long been a favored destination for bird watchers, but it's a fine choice for anyone seeking a peaceful retreat. The 18 rooms feature teak floorboards, washbasins and fine views. Some have two twin beds, others antique four-poster queen-size beds. Bathrooms are shared. Singles/doubles cost US$55/93, including breakfast and a multicourse dinner. The helpful management treats guests like family.

Nonguests can have a full breakfast for TT$22 or lunch for TT$44, or just come up for a delightful afternoon tea with scones or Trinidadian sweet bread (dessert cakes or rolls) for TT$15. Reservations are appreciated for the meals but are not necessary for tea (served from 3:30 to 6 pm.)

ASA WRIGHT NATURE CENTRE

The Asa Wright Nature Centre is a former cocoa and coffee plantation that has been turned into an 80-hectare nature reserve. Located amid the rain forest of the Northern Range, the center has attracted naturalists from around the world since its founding in 1967. There's a lodge catering to birding tour groups, a research station for biologists and a series of hiking trails on the property.

A wide range of bird species inhabits the area, including blue-crowned motmots, chestnut woodpeckers, palm tanagers, channel-billed toucans, blue-headed parrots, 10 species of hummingbird and numerous raptors. The sanctuary encompasses Dunston Cave, which is home to a breeding colony of the elusive nocturnal guacharo, or oilbird.

The trail network starts at the main house and branches out through the property. The Bellbird Trail is a lightly trodden path with rewarding sightings that might include the bearded bellbird. Day visitors can join guided walks along the center's trails for US$6; reservations should be made at least 24 hours in advance. A variety of seminars and field trips is also offered, most geared for people staying at the center's lodge.

Asa Wright Nature Centre is about a 1½-hour drive from Port of Spain. At Arima, head north on Blanchisseuse Rd for 12km, turning left into the center after the 7½ mile marker. Mt Pleasant maxi-taxis from Arima pass the entrance.

Places to Stay & Eat

The *Asa Wright Nature Centre and Lodge* (☎ 667-4655, in the USA ☎ 800-426-7781, asawright@caligo.com) has 24 rooms, some in the weathered main house and others in nearby cottages, all quite simple but with private baths. Singles/doubles cost US$120/180 in summer, US$155/240 in winter, including three ample meals a day, afternoon tea, a rum punch each evening, tax and service charge. A minimum stay of three days includes a guided tour of the grounds and the oilbird cave. Airport transfers can be arranged for US$40 per person roundtrip. You can find more information about Asa Wright at www.asawright.org/index.html.

Nonguests can eat at the lodge, but reservations need to be made 48 hours in advance.

MARACAS BAY & AROUND

Just 40 minutes from Port of Spain, Maracas Bay is Trinidad's most popular beach. Not only is the beach quite lovely, but the views along the way make for a very scenic drive. The North Coast Rd, which begins north of Maraval, climbs up over the mountains through a lush tropical forest of tall trees, ferns and bamboo.

Maracas Bay has a broad, sandy beach thick with palm trees, a small fishing hamlet at one side and a backdrop of verdant mountains. The waters can be flat in the summer, but at other times the bay usually has good waves for bodysurfing. There's a lifeguard, changing rooms, showers, picnic shelters and huts selling inexpensive shark & bake sandwiches. On weekends the beach gets pretty crowded, but the rest of the week it can feel almost deserted.

Tyrico Bay, just to the east of Maracas Bay, is quieter and less commercial. **Las Cuevas Bay**, 8km east of Maracas Bay, is a pretty U-shaped bay with a nice brown-sand beach; there's surfing at its west end and calmer conditions at the center.

BLANCHISSEUSE

The road narrows farther east, crossing several small wooden bridges, ending up at the village of Blanchisseuse, where some of Port of Spain's wealthy own weekend homes. The beaches aren't the best for swimming, but the surfing is usually good and the scenery is lovely.

Blanchisseuse makes a good base for hiking. A day hike can be made to the Paria Falls. Parts of the trail aren't well marked and there are warnings of assaults, so it's best to go with a local guide; see Ecotourism, earlier in this chapter, or ask at one of the guest houses. Eric Blackman has a good reputation. More ambitiously, a two- to three-day trek can be done to Matelot, on the northeast coast.

Places to Stay & Eat

Despite the name, *Marianne's Beach Resort* (☎ 669-4683) is little more than a parking lot at the west end of the longest beach in Blanchisseuse. For US$13 you can camp just above the beach and use the kitchen and showers at the adjacent funky house. Rooms for rugged souls can be rented in the house for the same price.

More comfortable, *Almond Brook* (☎ 678-0822) has three pleasant, clean rooms – two with queen-size beds – and a view on the inland side to the center of the village. There's a large shared kitchen and sitting area. Singles/doubles cost US$30/50.

The most upscale place in the area, *Laguna Mar* (☎ 669-2963) comprises a pair of two-story buildings on the hillside at the end of the road. Singles/doubles, some with carpets or mosquito nets, are US$45/65 in low season, US$10 more in high season. Upstairs rooms have balconies.

Meals are available at *Los Cocos*, a small, cozy place at the end of the road under the same ownership as Laguna Mar. Double-decker sandwiches with a heaping side of potato salad run around TT$30; a fresh fish or chicken platter is TT$60 to $80. If you plan to cook, bring food from Port of Spain, as local supplies are limited.

CARONI BIRD SANCTUARY

Caroni Bird Sanctuary is the roosting site for thousands of scarlet ibis, the national bird of Trinidad & Tobago. At sunset the birds fly in to roost in the swamp's mangroves, giving the trees the appearance of being abloom with brilliant scarlet blossoms. Even if you're not an avid bird watcher, the sight of the ibis flying over the swamp, glowing almost fluorescent red in the final rays of the evening sun, is not to be missed.

Long, flat-bottomed motorboats, holding up to 30 passengers, pass slowly through the swamp's channels. They stop deep in the midst of the swamp for a good vantage point under the flight path of the ibis.

To avoid disturbing the birds, the boats keep a fair distance from the roosting sites, so a pair of binoculars is recommended. You can also expect to see lots of herons and egrets, predominant among the swamp's 150 bird species. Note that during the summer months very few ibis are sighted.

The main swamp tour companies are David Ramsahai (☎ 663-4767), Nanan Tours (☎ 645-1305, nantour@tstt.net.tt) and James Madoo Tours (☎ 662-7356). All offer tours 4 to 6:30 pm daily. Reservations are recommended, but if you just show up you'll probably be able to find space on one of the boats. Ramsahai charges TT$40, the others TT$60. If your main interest is photography, the light is more favorable in the morning. Morning tours, which leave at 4:30 am, can be arranged through David Ramsahai.

The sanctuary is off the Uriah Butler Hwy, 14km south of Port of Spain; the turnoff is marked. Park near the old LPG gas plant opposite the boat dock. If you don't have your own vehicle, Nanan Tours will combine transport from Port of Spain with the tour for TT$210 per person. Although it's possible to get dropped off by a southbound maxi-taxi, it would be problematic on the return, as you'd have to walk out to the highway and try to wave down a fast-moving vehicle in the dark – you'd certainly be better off arranging in advance for a taxi.

WATERLOO TEMPLE

This tranquil, almost surreal Hindu temple sits at the end of a causeway jutting 90m off the central west coast. Its formal name is the Siewdass Sadhu Shiv Mandir, after its spiritual creator. Construction was begun in 1947 by Siewdass Sadhu, who, grateful for his safe return from India through the

WWI-embattled waters of the Pacific, committed himself to building a temple here. Initially he built on land owned by the state, which subsequently had it demolished. Undaunted, Sadhu then began to build out in the sea, carrying each foundation stone on his bicycle to the water's edge. When he died in 1970, his work was still incomplete. In 1994 the temple was completed by the community to coincide with celebrations of Indian Arrival Day. It is reached through the Waterloo Bay Recreation Park, where prayer flags and seabirds add to the sense of serenity.

To get to Waterloo, travel south on the Uriah Butler Hwy to Chaguanas, then 8.5km on the Southern Main Rd to St Mary's. Turn west on the Waterloo Rd until you reach the temple. Alternatively, take a maxi-taxi to Chaguanas, then another to St Mary's (TT$1), from where you can get a route taxi (TT$2) to the temple.

NORTHEAST COAST

The northeast coast is an extension of the rugged Maracas-Blanchisseuse coastline, but you may see more sea turtles than tourists. Inaccessible by road from Blanchisseuse, the region is most easily approached via the towns of Arima or Sangre Grande at the end of the Eastern Main Rd. This joins the Toco Main Rd, which extends northeast along the coast, skirting some wild beaches and pleasant bays ideal for picnicking. At **Galera Point** are a lighthouse and views of the dramatic coastline. Rounding the northeast corner is the village of **Toco**, with a small folk museum. Farther west at **Grande Rivière**, giant leatherback turtles nest on the beach of an enchanting bay between March and August. The road ends at Matelot, which is the eastern end of the north-coast trail to Blanchisseuse.

Maxi-taxis depart from both Arima and Sangre Grande for Toco and beyond to Matelot.

Places to Stay

Some small guest houses are available in Grande Rivière. Henderson Guy occasionally has a basic room upstairs from Guys'

Recreation Center bar. He can also put you in touch with Matthew Charles, who rents a simple house on the beach. The impressive *Mt Plaisir Estate Hotel & Spa* (☎ 670-8381, info@mtplaisir.com), in Grande Rivière, is an ecotourist resort offering guided activities and classy accommodations on the beach. Suites for up to four start at US$73 per person, while beach lofts for up to six are US$90 per person. Meals are included.

EAST COAST

Trinidad's east coast is wild and rural, a mix of lonely beaches with rough Atlantic waters, mangrove swamps and coconut plantations, comprising some of the most dramatic scenery in the country. Deserted most of the year, the area sees big crowds after Carnival, when it becomes *the* post-festivities chill-out destination.

To get to the east coast from Port of Spain, take the Eastern Main Rd or the Churchill Roosevelt Hwy (to avoid traffic). At Waller Field, where the two highways merge, signs will guide you through Sangre Grande and south to Manzanilla. By public transport, take a Sangre Grande maxi-taxi from the City Gate terminal, about an hour's journey (TT$6). In Sangre Grande, route taxis and maxi-taxis go south to Manzanilla (TT$3, 20 minutes) and Mayaro (TT$4, 40 minutes).

The Manzanilla-Mayaro Rd, along the east coast, is narrow but traffic is light. Cows and water buffalo roam freely, you can easily spot vultures, egrets and herons along the way. In places, coconut palms and orange heliconia line the roadside.

The main east-coast beach, **Manzanilla Beach**, has brown sand, palm trees and white beach morning glory. The winds are often strong and the waters tempestuous. At the northern end is a public beach facility with changing rooms and lifeguards.

The road continues south, skirting the freshwater Nariva Swamp much of the way, and crosses the meandering **Nariva River** a couple of times.

After crossing the **Ortoire River**, Trinidad's longest, you'll encounter a couple of small settlements with simple wooden houses on stilts before reaching the town of **Mayaro** (shown as 'Pierreville' on some maps), where a sign points west to San Fernando, 56km away. At Mayaro is a small, minimally maintained beach facility, open only at Easter, but lifeguards patrol most weekends and holidays. Flags are posted to alert swimmers of safety conditions.

Places to Stay & Eat

In Manzanilla village, *Dougie's Guesthouse & Bar* (☎ 668-1504) is a couple of kilometers from the beach; however, the rooms are clean and spacious if spartan, with hot water for US$17 per bedroom with a bath that is sometimes shared. There's a snack shop open during the day and a rum shop.

Just north of the public beach facilities, *Calypso Beach Hotel* (☎ 668-5113, fax 668-5116) is a modern two-level building on the north end of the beach. All rooms have private bath and fan for US$35 single or double. Next door is *Amelia's on the Beach* (☎ 668-5308), with several good-value studio apartments including private bath, hot water and TV for about US$25. Right on the Mayaro beach and farther south are several places. Most of the guest houses are aimed primarily at local families, who bring their own bedding, food and cleaning supplies. If you're traveling with friends and stock up in the city, these can be quite a good deal for a peaceful stay. Be sure to make arrangements in advance, as owners may live elsewhere on the island. Check the classified section of the newspapers for phone numbers of houses for rent.

BBS Beach Resort (☎ 653-3158) has two large new buildings near the beach at the end of a palm- and banana-lined lane. Each house has five bedrooms, one bathroom and a large kitchen for US$35. Bring all your own linens, food etc. *West Side Beach House* (☎ 652-8276) is just steps from the beach, about 1km south of Mayaro. Next door is *Sea Breeze Restaurant & Bar*, open most days.

About 5km south of Mayaro on the Guayaguare Rd, *Azee's* (☎ 630-4619, williafi@bp.com) caters primarily to oil workers, with straightforward rooms for US$46 and a restaurant that serves *bul jol* (roasted plantains with salt fish, tomatoes and onions) and coconut bake breakfasts for TT$30.

SOUTH-CENTRAL TRINIDAD

The south-central part of Trinidad is heavily populated, largely by the descendants of East Indians brought to the island to work the plantations after the abolition of slavery. In time they came to own much of the land. The towns now have a decidedly East Indian appearance, from the style of the homes to the roadside temples and mosques.

The countryside is tame, with undulating hills planted with citrus, coffee, cocoa and bananas. In **Rio Claro** is a Muslim mosque, a couple of bakeries, a central produce market and a Hindu temple along the main road.

If you're curious you can check out **Devil's Woodyard**, one of the island's dozen 'mud volcano' sites, where small mounds of mud have built up as a result of gases released from the earth. Hindustan Rd, a narrow cane road, leads 3.5km south from the highway to Devil's Woodyard; the turnoff is signposted about 1.5km west of New Grant.

SAN FERNANDO

San Fernando, Trinidad's second-largest city, is the center of the island's gas and oil industries. The center of town is dominated by San Fernando Hill, a spot once sacred to Amerindians. The hill is oddly shaped, a consequence of earlier excavations that have now been halted.

San Fernando is the transport hub for the region. Maxi-taxis and route taxis run regularly from here to outlying areas. There's service between here and Mayaro on the east coast even on major holidays.

PITCH LAKE

Pitch Lake is perhaps Trinidad's greatest oddity. This 40-hectare expanse of tar is 90m deep at its center, where hot bitumen is continuously replenished from a subterranean fault. The lake is the world's single largest supply of natural bitumen, and as much as 300 tons (about 275 metric tons) are extracted daily. The surface of Pitch Lake has a wrinkled elephantlike skin that is hard to walk across in many places.

Pitch Lake is on the west side of the highway, just south of La Brea. It's possible to get an express bus or maxi-taxi from Port of Spain to San Fernando, and from there another maxi onward to the lake.

Pitch Lake is open 9 am to 5 pm daily. Tour guides at the lake will show you around for TT$15 to TT$20; call ahead to make arrangements (☎ 648-7426). There's a small museum (TT$30 adults, TT$12 children).

POINTE-À-PIERRE WILDFOWL TRUST

The Pointe-à-Pierre Wildfowl Trust (☎ 658-4200, ext 2512) is a special place. Despite being in the midst of the island's sprawling oil refinery, a few kilometers north of San Fernando, this wetland sanctuary has a rich abundance of bird life in a highly concentrated (26-hectare) area. There are about 90 species of bird, both wild and in cages, including endangered waterfowl, colorful songbirds, ibis, herons and other wading birds. Trails edge a lake and lead into the woods. In a 20-minute stroll around the grounds you can easily spot a few dozen bird species.

A nonprofit organization, the trust is a center for breeding endangered species and has programs in environmental education. The visitors center has small exhibits and a gift shop.

Reservations should be made a few days in advance. Several entrances lead into the surrounding PetroTrin oil refinery, and gate access to the sanctuary occasionally changes, so get directions when you make reservations. Hours are 8 am to 5 pm weekdays, with shorter weekend hours (TT$5/3/2 adults/teens/children).

Tobago

Tobago is a delightfully relaxed island with much to offer travelers. There are good beaches, pristine snorkeling and diving spots, excellent bird-watching opportunities and just enough tourism to make visiting Tobago easy, yet not so much that the island feels overrun. Although it's no longer the sleeper it was just a few years ago, Tobago is

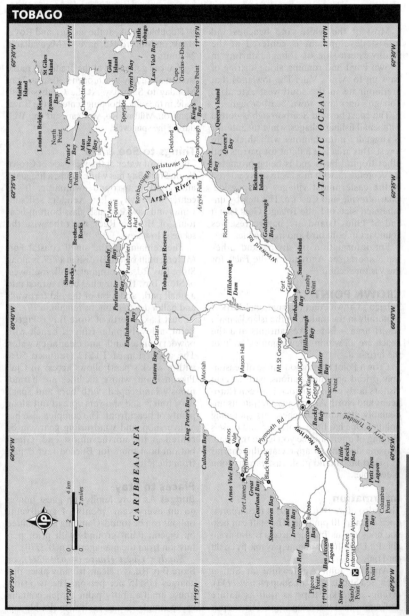

TOBAGO

Marble Island
St Giles Island
London Bridge Rock
Iguana Bay
Giant Island
Tyrrel's Bay
Little Tobago
Charlotteville
North Point
Lucy Vale Bay
Cape Gracias-a-Dios
Pirate's Bay
Man of War Bay
Speyside
Pedro Point
Queen's Island
Corvo Point
Roxborough
Delaford
Parlatuvier Rd
Prince's Bay
Queen's Bay
L'anse Fourmi
Lookout Hut
Argyle River
Argyle Falls
Richmond Island
Brothers Rocks
Bloody Bay
Parlatuvier
Parlatuvier Bay
Tobago Forest Reserve
Richmond
Goldsborough Bay
Sisters Rocks
Englishman's Bay
Castara
Castara Bay
Hillsborough Dam
Smith's Island
Granby
Fort Granby
Granby Point
Barbados Bay
King Peter's Bay
Moriah
Mason Hall
Mt St George
Hillsborough Bay
Minister Bay
SCARBOROUGH
Bacolet Point
Culloden Bay
Amos Vale
Amos Vale Bay
Plymouth
Black Rock
Plymouth Rd
Fort King George
Rocky Bay
Little Rocky Bay
Fort James
Great Courland Bay
Stone Haven Bay
Mount Irvine Bay
Buccoo
Buccoo Bay
Petit Trou Lagoon
Buccoo Reef
Bon Accord Lagoon
Crown Point International Airport
Canoe Bay
Columbus Point
Pigeon Point
Store Bay
Sandy Point
Crown Point

CARIBBEAN SEA

ATLANTIC OCEAN

Ferry to Trinidad

Claude Noel Hwy

Mingueel Rd

0   2   4 km
0   1   2 miles

11°20'N
11°15'N
11°10'N

60°50'W
60°45'W
60°40'W
60°35'W
60°30'W

still one of the most overlooked and best-value destinations in the Caribbean.

Most of the white-sand beaches and tourist development is centered at the southwestern side of Tobago, starting in Crown Point and running along a string of bays up to Arnos Vale. The lowlands that predominate in the southwest extend to Tobago's only large town, Scarborough.

The coast beyond Scarborough is dotted with small fishing villages, while the interior is ruggedly mountainous with thick rain forest. This area is a habitat for parrots and other tropical birds and is being promoted for ecotourism, with most activities centered in the easternmost villages of Speyside, Charlotteville and Castara. The nearby uninhabited islets of Little Tobago, Goat Island and St Giles Island are nature reserves abundant in both bird and marine life.

For information on diving and other water sports, see Activities in the Facts for the Visitor section.

CROWN POINT

Tobago's Crown Point International Airport is literally in the middle of the island's main resort area – hotels, restaurants and the beach are all within a few minutes' walk of the terminal.

Crown Point has a good range of reasonably priced accommodations, with foreign visitors fairly evenly divided between Europeans and North Americans. Despite its undeniably attractive beaches, this sprawling holiday zone has little character, and there's nothing of interest once you leave the sand. Anyone desiring to appreciate the charms of island life should push eastward as soon as feasible.

Information

The Tidco office (☎ 639-0509) at the airport is open 8 am to 10 pm daily. The staff can help you book rooms. Internet access is also available for US$0.16 per minute, payable by credit card only.

Amiable John Applewhite, at Sunset View Sea Sports & Craft Shop (☎ 639-7743), arranges snorkel trips as well as nature walks and bird-watching tours. His shop is just beyond the Conrado Beach Hotel, on the way out to Pigeon Point.

Republic Bank, at the airport, and Royal Bank, on Milford Rd, have ATMs available 24 hours.

You can get online at the Traditions music store at Store Bay beach, open 9:30 am to 7 pm Monday to Saturday. At the Clothes Wash Café, in the same shopping center as the Royal Bank on Milford Rd, you can surf the Web during the spin cycle.

Things to See & Do

The body of water at the west side of Crown Point, **Store Bay** has white sands, a lifeguard and good year-round swimming. It's a center of activity where vendors sell souvenirs and hawkers push glass-bottom-boat tours of Buccoo Reef, but otherwise the scene is low-key.

The remains of the small coastal **Fort Milford**, built by the British in 1777, is along Store Bay Rd, a five-minute walk southwest of Store Bay. The area has been turned into a small park, and a bit of the old fort walls and half a dozen cannons remain.

Just 1.5km north of Store Bay is **Pigeon Point**, a lovely palm-fringed beach with powdery white sands and clear aqua water. The admission of TT$12 (reduced 50% with a week's pass) allows access to Club Pigeon Point, whose facilities are harmoniously landscaped, with bars and snack bars, toilets and showers spread out along plenty of beachfront. The complex also has a dive shop, and windsurfing gear can be rented at the northernmost end. Glass-bottom-boat tours for Buccoo reef depart from the jetty.

Places to Stay

Budget As more family-run guest houses go up every year, plenty of good-value options can be found. Camping is permitted on Pigeon Point grounds with prior permission from the manager (☎ 660-8770).

Sandy's Guest House (☎ 639-9221), on Store Bay Rd, is a clean, friendly place that charges US$15 per person. The two-story house amid a pretty palm garden contains seven simple rooms, each with double and

CROWN POINT

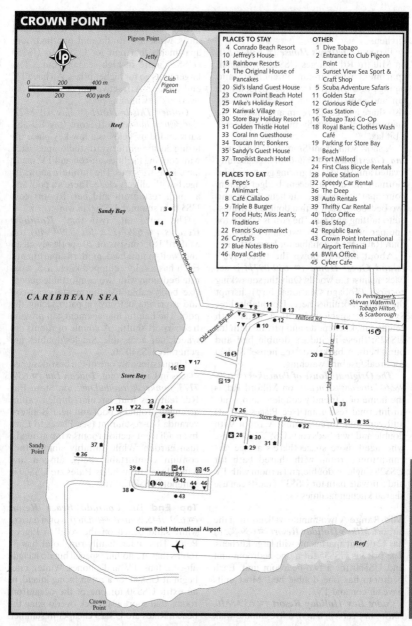

PLACES TO STAY
4   Conrado Beach Resort
10 Jeffrey's House
13 Rainbow Resorts
14 The Original House of
    Pancakes
20 Sid's Island Guest House
23 Crown Point Beach Hotel
25 Mike's Holiday Resort
29 Kariwak Village
30 Store Bay Holiday Resort
31 Golden Thistle Hotel
33 Coral Inn Guesthouse
34 Toucan Inn; Bonkers
35 Sandy's Guest House
37 Tropikist Beach Hotel

PLACES TO EAT
6   Pepe's
7   Minimart
8   Café Callaloo
9   Triple B Burger
17 Food Huts; Miss Jean's;
    Traditions
22 Francis Supermarket
26 Crystal's
27 Blue Notes Bistro
46 Royal Castle

OTHER
1   Dive Tobago
2   Entrance to Club Pigeon
    Point
3   Sunset View Sea Sport &
    Craft Shop
5   Scuba Adventure Safaris
11 Golden Star
12 Glorious Ride Cycle
15 Gas Station
16 Tobago Taxi Co-Op
18 Royal Bank; Clothes Wash
    Café
19 Parking for Store Bay
    Beach
21 Fort Milford
24 First Class Bicycle Rentals
28 Police Station
32 Speedy Car Rental
36 The Deep
38 Auto Rentals
39 Thrifty Car Rental
40 Tidco Office
41 Bus Stop
42 Republic Bank
43 Crown Point International
    Airport Terminal
44 BWIA Office
45 Cyber Cafe

Pigeon Point

Jetty

Club
Pigeon
Point

Reef

Sandy Bay

Pigeon Point Rd

CARIBBEAN SEA

Store Bay

Sandy
Point

To Pennysaver's,
Shirvan Watermill,
Tobago Hilton,
& Scarborough

Old Store Bay Rd

Milford Rd

Tidco Gourmet Trace

Store Bay Rd

Milford Rd

Crown Point International Airport

Reef

Crown
Point

TRINIDAD & TOBAGO

twin bed, portable fan and a bathroom behind a curtain. Guests have access to a kitchen.

Two-story *Jeffrey's House* (☎ 639-0617), on Milford Rd, charges US$25 for a small apartment with air-con, kitchenette and piping hot shower, or US$9 per person with fan and shared bath and kitchen. Guests also share a large TV room and videos. The management is friendly, but security seems a bit lax.

A short walk from Store Bay Rd, *Coral Inn Guesthouse* (☎ 639-0967), peacefully located amid fields and grazing goats on John Gorman Trace, is a decent budget option. Four apartments have kitchens, baths and two bedrooms each with a double bed, mosquito netting and fan. The cost is US$18 for one person, US$30 for two, and US$60 for four. Rates are negotiable for longer stays.

About midway down the trace, *Syd's Island Guest House* (☎ 639-0971) is set back against the woods. Only the squawking *cocricos* (Tobago's national bird) disrupt the silent mornings here. Hospitable host Syd offers spacious, spotless units with ceiling fan, kitchenette and private bath for US$25; these include a double bed and bunk beds. A backyard 'tree house' is ideal for breakfast bird watching.

The Original House of Pancakes (☎ 639-9866, kittycat@tstt.net.tt), on Milford Rd, is the home of a friendly couple who operate an informal restaurant (see Places to Eat) and rent out three rooms. A room with double and twin beds costs US$27. For those who need more space there's a nice air-conditioned room with shared bath for US$25 single or double, and a room with TV and a private bath for US$37. Guests can use shared kitchen facilities.

Mid-Range A two-minute walk north of the airport, *Mike's Holiday Resort* (☎ 639-8050) has 12 decent apartments with large kitchens. The price is US$35 for a one-bedroom unit and US$60 for a two-bedroom unit. Each bedroom has one double bed. Most units have air-con and TV.

Store Bay Holiday Resort (☎ 639-8810, sbaymair@cablenett.net), a five-minute walk

east of the airport, is a recommendable family-run place with 20 self-contained units. Most are studio and one-bedroom apartments that rent for US$39 to US$50 (US$20 more in high season), but a few larger units go for higher prices. All have TV and air-con. Attractive upper-level decks overlook a swimming pool.

Golden Thistle Hotel (☎/fax 639-8521, clyde@trinidad.net), off Store Bay Rd and surrounded by fields, is a low-key place offering 36 straightforward studio units, each with cooking facilities, air-con and TV; many have king-size beds. The furniture shows its age, but it's all very clean. There's a pool and a small restaurant and bar. Rooms cost US$45 in summer, US$60 in winter.

The pleasant two-story *Rainbow Resorts* (☎ 639-8271, fax 639-9940), on Milford Rd, consists of 20 spotlessly clean and well-maintained modern apartments. Each has a fully equipped kitchen, a separate bedroom with two comfortable queen-size beds, cable TV, thermostatic air-con and a private balcony or patio facing the pool. The helpful management can provide free airport shuttle. A couple of rooms are wheelchair accessible. Singles/doubles are generally US$40/50.

Unquestionably one of the best-designed places in Crown Point, *Toucan Inn* (☎ 639-7173, bonkers@trinidad.net), on Store Bay Rd, features four circular duplex cabins arranged around a pool and near Bonkers' veranda bar-restaurant (see Places to Eat). In an adjacent section rooms wrap around a lush garden. While suitably simple, they contain comfortable beds, air-con and natural teak furnishings. Rates are US$60 in summer, US$80 in winter.

Top End The *Conrado Beach Resort* (☎ 639-0145, conrado@tstt.net) is on a narrow white-sand beach on the road to Pigeon Point. This older, family-run hotel has 31 rooms that are nothing special but do include air-con, fans, TV and phones. Winter rates begin at US$90 for a room facing inland, or an extra US$30 for one of the oceanfront rooms that sport a sundeck overlooking the beach. Rates are US$25 cheaper in summer.

Kariwak Village (☎ 639-8442, *karwak@ tstt.net.tt*), off Store Bay Rd, has a pleasant atmosphere and two dozen air-conditioned rooms in duplex cabanas nestled among tropical gardens. There's an herb garden, two pools (one with waterfall) and activities such as yoga and tai chi. Rates are US$113 in summer, US$156 in winter.

Tropikist Beach Hotel (☎ 639-8512, *tropikist@wow.net*), about a 10-minute walk west of the airport, is a modern seaside hotel with 33 comfortable rooms, each equipped with air-con, a phone and a small refrigerator. Rates for standard rooms, most with sea-view balconies, are US$96 in summer, US$120 in winter.

Although it's seen better days, *Crown Point Beach Hotel* (☎ 639-8781, *crownpoint@ trinidad.net*) has a good location next to Fort Milford. There are 77 self-catering rooms, a pool and tennis courts. Summer and winter rates for two people are US$90 and US$96, respectively, in a small studio, US$102 and US$108 in a cabana, and US$120 and US$132 in a one-bedroom apartment.

Inaugurated in December 2000, the *Tobago Hilton* (☎ 660-8500, *tobhilt@ tstt.net.tt*) occupies 20 acres of the previously undeveloped Lowlands area east of Crown Point, including its own protected mangrove forest. You'll find an 18-hole golf course, a seaside pool, several restaurants and bars and a dive shop. The hotel's 200 luxurious rooms/suites start at US$310/400.

Places to Eat

Budget & Mid-Range A row of *food huts* opposite the beach at Store Bay offers rotis, shark & bake, crab & dumplings and simple plate lunches for TT$8 to TT$25. *Miss Jean's* stall is a favorite. Wash it all down with a drinking coconut (TT$2), which you can pick up from beachside vendors.

A popular place for an evening beer or cheap local food is *Crystal's*, on the corner of Store Bay and Milford Rds. It has fruit juices, shark & bake, flying fish and heaping supper plates; hours are 7:30 am to 10 pm.

Another restaurant with good reasonably priced food is *Pepe's*, where Old Store Bay Rd turns off Milford, with a varied menu,

large servings and friendly service. Outdoors under the palms, they serve everything from pizza and burgers to hearty TT$80 seafood meals. It's open for dinner 6 to 10:30 pm nightly.

At *The Original House of Pancakes* (see Places to Stay), breakfast is served on a pleasant wooden deck, often shared by aggressively hungry grackles. A plate of buttermilk cakes, eggs and fresh fruit is TT$36; a home-cooked Creole dinner or vegetarian meal is about double that. *Triple B Burger*, where Milford Rd curves east, is a good, busy roadside stand. Beef, chicken and fish burgers (TT$14) are cleanly prepared on the grill. It may be the only place in Tobago where you can find a T-bone steak for TT$35, served with some fine potato wedges. Though it's primarily a carryout operation, there are a few indoor and outdoor picnic tables.

A favorite liming spot is *Bonkers* (☎ 639-7173), on Store Bay Rd. Run by a pair of English expatriates, this open-air restaurant and bar serves breakfast, sandwiches, salads and fish & chips for around TT$30. Dinner main courses are in the TT$70 to TT$100 range. Food is available from 7:30 am to 10 pm, and the bar stays open to around midnight. There's a 'lime table' Monday, Wednesday, Thursday and Saturday from 8 pm, with live steel pan or African dancing.

A small but well-stocked *minimart* is at Jimmy's Holiday Resort, open 7 am to 11 pm daily. More convenient to Store Bay Rd accommodations is *Francis Supermarket*, at the side of the Crown Point Beach Hotel. Though a bit remote from most accommodations, *Pennysaver's*, on Milford Rd near Canaan, has the largest selection.

If you're waiting for a flight and you're not too choosy, grab some fried chicken or a burger at the *Royal Castle* just across from the airport terminal.

Top End The *Blue Notes Bistro* (☎ 639-8492), on Store Bay Rd across from Crystal's, is a stylishly casual hangout with a good music collection and occasional live jazz. Entrees like blackened swordfish and lamb tajine (a spicy Middle Eastern stew) average TT$100. It's open from 7 pm nightly.

For excellent Creole cuisine with a serious East Indian influence, check out *Café Callaloo* (☎ 639-9020), at the junction of Old Store Bay and Milford. At TT$49, lunch specials offer an economical way to sample things like curried lobster, served with salad and *chokas* (a saucelike dish made with tomatoes). Live music adds some spice from 8 pm Thursday and Sunday evenings.

Shirvan Watermill (☎ 639-0000), on Shirvan Rd between Crown Point and Buccoo Bay, is located beside the mill of a former sugar estate. This dinner restaurant has pleasant gazebo dining and some of the island's best food. Gazpacho, salads and appetizers begin around TT$20, while entrées range from chicken Creole for TT$75 to lobster for TT$180.

Entertainment
The *Golden Star* (☎ 639-0873) is a locally popular club with a sizable dance floor, open nightly. Wednesday night there are live steel bands; Friday features an Afterwork Lime with DJs, dancing, and, occasionally, local bands (cover averages TT$30). Next door is Golden Star's restaurant and beer garden. Another dance destination is *The Deep*, at Sandy Point Village out beyond Fort Milford, where DJs spin soca, salsa and merengue. The usually packed disco is open from around 9 pm to dawn Friday and Saturday nights only.

BUCCOO
The narrow brown-sand beach at Buccoo Bay doesn't compete with the generous white sands of Store Bay, and swimming here isn't recommended because of pollution from new developments inland. But lightly touristed Buccoo is a more atmospheric place to stay than Crown Point, offering glimpses of village life and breathtaking sunsets over the bay. Besides, it boasts some pretty good accommodations and a high-spirited weekly fiesta.

Buccoo Reef Tours
A handful of glass-bottom boats provide tours of the extensive fringing reef between Buccoo and Pigeon Point. The boats pass over the reef, much of which is just a meter or two beneath the surface, stop for snorkeling and end with a swim in the **Nylon Pool**, a calm, shallow area with a sandy bottom and clear turquoise waters.

Johnson & Sons (☎ 639-8519) does a nice tour. Unlike most boats, which go out at 11 am every day, Johnson goes out when the tide is low (and the snorkeling best), leaving between 9 am and 2 pm. Meet at the end of the pier at Buccoo Beach. If you're an avid snorkeler, let Johnson know beforehand and he can stop at some deeper spots with pristine coral, otherwise the tours generally stick to shallower waters. Tours last about 2½ hours and cost TT$90 per person, including snorkel gear.

Other boats to Buccoo Reef leave from Store Bay and the jetty at Club Pigeon Point for around the same price.

Special Events
Lacking any religious affiliation, **Sunday School** is the sly title for a weekly street party held in Buccoo every Sunday night. Live steel-pan music kicks off the festivities at around 9 pm, to the delight of foreign visitors. Later on, DJs and soca suit local tastes. Snack on corn soup, souse and pricey plates of meat salad and rice sold from various stalls; there's plenty of rum and beer as well. Goat and crab races are the unlikely highlights at Eastertime, heartily celebrated here.

Places to Stay
Casual *Miller's Guest House* (☎ 639-9591, themillers1@hotmail.com) has eight comfortable rooms with private bath, brass beds and good, thick mattresses in cottages sloping up from the glass-bottom-boat jetty. Singles/doubles are US$14/18. The waterfront bar affords great sunset views; expect late-night partying.

For a quieter scene, there's *Casa Blanca* (☎ 639-0081, peiser@tstt.net.tt, 10 Battery St), a few minutes inland from the beach, which is run by a Trini–South African couple. Basic studios, some with kitchenettes and private baths, cost US$11 per person for up to three occupants. A new dormitory section has 10 bunk beds at about US$6.50 per person.

The Sea-Side Garden (☎ /fax 639-0682) is one of the nicest small guest houses in Tobago. Rooms that sleep three cost US$25 inside the house, or US$35 with outside access; a larger apartment costs US$75. All rooms have mosquito nets, fans and private baths. A tastefully decorated sitting room with a bay window enhances the serenity of the place. A fruit-filled breakfast is available for TT$40 and dinner for TT$65; alternatively, you can use the kitchen.

Places to Eat

There are a few food huts near the beach serving cheap, simple fare. Good pizza comes with seven toppings at *Teaside Pizza House*, on Battery St 200m north of the beach. Prices start at TT$30 for a small pizza; you can order meat or vegetarian, whole-wheat or white crust. Teaside also has fruit juices and desserts. It's open 3 to 10 pm daily except Tuesday.

For something fancier, *La Tartaruga* (☎ 639-0940), opposite the beach, has authentic Italian food. It's open nightly except Sunday.

MT IRVINE TO GREAT COURLAND BAY

The stretch of coastline from Mt Irvine to Great Courland Bay is a rather exclusive area replete with a golf course, elegant guest houses and several resort hotels, each hugging its own bay.

A roadside public recreation facility at **Mt Irvine Beach**, 200m north of Mt Irvine Bay Hotel, has sheltered picnic tables and a beach bar selling rotis, fish & bake and sandwiches. This beach attracts surfers December to March.

On a rocky hill at the north side of Stone Haven Bay is **Fort Bennett**, about 500m west of a marked turnoff on the main road. The fort was built by the British in 1778 to defend against US enemy ships. Little remains of it other than a couple of cannons, but there's a good view of the coast from this site.

Places to Stay

At the Buccoo Junction, less than a kilometer east of Buccoo, is *Golf View Apartments*

(☎ 639-0979, PO Box 354, Scarborough). Though the setting is as nondescript as its name implies, the Golf View does have a pool and a dozen good-value apartments, starting at US$45 in summer, US$56 in winter for studios with cable TV and air-con. Kitchen units are US$60 in summer, US$76 in winter. Much nicer is the adjacent *Old Grange Inn* (☎ /fax 639-9395), an 18-unit lodge that's a bit off the road and beyond the sound of traffic. Spacious rooms with high wooden ceilings, cable TV, private bath and small fridge cost US$50 in summer, US$70 in winter; some smaller units without TV are US$40 in summer, US$55 in winter. A broad balcony overlooks an inviting pool that's secluded by woods. Both places are within a short walk of the public beach at Grange Bay.

Three resorts sit along the smaller bays in this area, each with standard resort amenities. *Mount Irvine Bay Hotel* (☎ 639-8871, in the USA ☎ 800-448-8355, mtirvine@tstt.net.tt) has its own 18-hole golf course. Rates are US$240 in summer, US$290 in winter.

Grafton Beach Resort (☎ 639-0191, fax 639-0030, in the USA ☎ 800-223-6510, grafton@trinidad.net) has handicapped-accessible facilities. Standard rates are from US$162 in summer, US$225 in winter.

Rex Turtle Beach Hotel (☎ 639-2851, fax 639-1495, in the USA ☎ 800-448-8355, turtle@tstt.net.tt) is the area's largest. The rooms, which are not as upmarket as the other resorts', start at US$200 in summer, US$250 in the height of winter.

Contrasting with these sprawling resorts, *Seahorse Inn* (☎ 639-0686, seahorse@trinidad.net), just below the Grafton Beach Resort, is a low-key establishment. Four spacious rooms with teak floors and broad balconies facing Stone Haven Bay are US$75 in summer, US$120 in winter, including breakfast.

Places to Eat

The *Papillon Restaurant*, at the Old Grange Inn is owned and operated by Swiss chef Jakob Straessle and has food that's both better and cheaper than at neighboring resort restaurants. A complete set dinner of the day, from soup to dessert, can range from TT$60 for chicken to TT$110 for lobster.

The recommended **Seahorse Inn Restaurant & Bar**, open noon to 3 pm for lunch and 6:30 to 10 pm for dinner, specializes in gourmet Creole cuisine, with main courses averaging TT$90 to TT$120. Alfresco dining on a beachside patio is an option.

PLYMOUTH

Plymouth, the largest town on the west coast (though home to just a few thousand inhabitants), is not a major destination, but its proximity to fine beaches and affordable lodging makes it an appealing if quiet place to stay. In addition, it has a few attractions clustered along its west side. At the end of Shelbourne St is the **Mystery Tombstone** of Betty Stiven, who died in 1783, presumably during childbirth. Her tombstone reads, rather cryptically, 'She was a mother without knowing it, and a wife without letting her husband know it, except by her kind indulgences to him.'

Plymouth was the first British capital of Tobago, and it was here that the British built **Fort James** in 1811, the remains of which stand 200m west of the tombstone. Affording extraordinary views of Great Courland Bay, this small hilltop fortification remains largely intact, with four of its cannons still mounted.

Coming back from Fort James, turn right after the bus stop and continue 150m to reach the **Great Courland Bay Monument**, an odd concrete creation honoring the early Courlander colonists who settled the area in the 17th century.

Places to Stay & Eat

Signless and inconspicuous, **Bailey's Guest House** (☎ 639-2797), on the corner of Great and Shelbourne Sts, contains seven basic but clean rooms sharing one bathroom for just US$6 per person. It's casual and friendly, and guests may use the large kitchen downstairs.

King Solomon's Mine (☎ 639-2545) is at the end of George St. It's a few steps from the cliffs leading down to Back Bay, a cove that's fine for swimming. The congenial owner, Leroy Solomon, has six originally de-

signed units, all with private baths, at bargain prices. Standard rooms with shared kitchen access are US$10 per person, while 'family' apartments with their own kitchens are US$20 to US$40 for four to six people, and a very nice upstairs 'executive suite' is US$60.

Named after Tobago's noisy national bird, **Cocrico Inn** (☎ 639-2961, in the USA ☎ 800-223-9815, cocrico@tstt.net.tt), on Commissioner St a block west of King Solomon's Mine, is a rather ordinary L-shaped block enclosing a swimming pool. Its 16 tidy, carpeted rooms include private baths, refrigerators and balconies overlooking other houses. Singles/doubles cost US$42/54 in summer, US$60/72 in winter, US$10 to US$20 more with air-conditioning.

Plymouth's dining options are limited. Cocrico Inn has a reasonably priced restaurant open for three meals a day. A full breakfast, or a lunch of flying fish & chips or crab & dumplings is under TT$40. At dinner, fresh fish of the day, served with rice and callaloo, costs TT$65.

SCARBOROUGH

Scarborough, the island's administrative center, is a bustling port with one-way streets and congested traffic. Largely commercial in character, it's Tobago's only real town to speak of. Those arriving by ferry after dark will likely want to spend at least a night, and affordable accommodations are easily found.

The area was originally settled as the port of Lampinsburg in 1654 by the Dutch, who built a church, warehouses and an imposing star-shaped fort. French invaders stormed the fort and destroyed it, aided by a stray cannonball that landed right on a cache of gunpowder, but after sacking the town they withdrew. Following a period of neutrality, colonists from Barbados established the settlement of Georgetown, the first British capital of Tobago, east of Lampinsberg. The next year the Tobago House of Assembly was moved to Lampinsberg, whose name was changed to Scarborough.

The French conquered Scarborough a decade later and changed its name to Port Louis, enjoying a brief reign before the British regained it in 1793; the colony

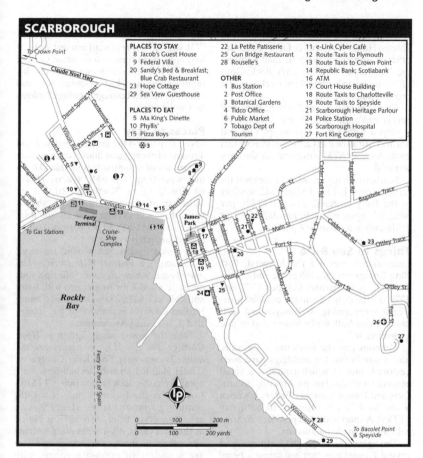

SCARBOROUGH

PLACES TO STAY
8 Jacob's Guest House
9 Federal Villa
20 Sandy's Bed & Breakfast;
Blue Crab Restaurant
23 Hope Cottage
29 Sea View Guesthouse

PLACES TO EAT
5 Ma King's Dinette
10 Phyllis'
15 Pizza Boys

22 La Petite Patisserie
25 Gun Bridge Restaurant
28 Rouselle's

OTHER
1 Bus Station
2 Post Office
3 Botanical Gardens
4 Tidco Office
6 Public Market
7 Tobago Dept of
Tourism

11 e-Link Cyber Café
12 Route Taxis to Plymouth
13 Route Taxis to Crown Point
14 Republic Bank; Scotiabank
16 ATM
17 Court House Building
18 Route Taxis to Charlotteville
19 Route Taxis to Speyside
21 Scarborough Heritage Parlour
24 Police Station
26 Scarborough Hospital
27 Fort King George

changed hands once again before the British retook it in 1803, retaining control until independence.

Orientation

The town is divided between lower and upper sections. Docks for cruise ships, the Trinidad ferries and visiting yachts are in a row, along with the customs office, in the Lower Scarborough area, from which it's a short walk up Wilson Rd to the public market and bus terminal.

A steep climb up Castries St, immediately east of the cruise-ship complex, brings you

to Main St and the center of Upper Scarborough. A block north is James Park, the central plaza, surrounded by businesses and the Court House building, the current site of the Tobago House of Assembly. Climbing farther up Main, you reach a quieter residential area, as Rockly Bay spreads out below. Still higher stand the hospital and Fort King George.

Information

Tobago's central post office is north of the market, on Post Office St. The Tidco office (☎ 639-4333, dtrim@tidco.co.tt) is in a small

TRINIDAD & TOBAGO

shopping center off Sangster Hill Rd, about 200m west of the cruise-ship complex. The Tobago House of Assembly Dept of Tourism office is upstairs in the NIB mall between the bus station and the ferry dock. Both offices are open 8 am to 4 pm weekdays and provide similar services.

There are branches of Republic Bank and Scotiabank just east of the docks, both equipped with ATMs that accept Visa and MasterCard as well as Cirrus and Plus system cards. Another ATM is right outside the ferry terminal.

Scarborough has the island's cheapest Internet access: E-Link Cyber Café, upstairs in the ferry terminal, charges TT$10 per hour. It's open till 11:30 pm daily (except Friday, when it closes at 4 pm).

Things to See & Do

Immediately beyond the hospital, **Fort King George** sits on a hill at the end of Fort St. Built by the British between 1777 and 1779, it's the only substantial colonial fortification remaining in Tobago, and well worth a visit both for its history and its fine coastal view.

Cannons line the fort's old stone walls, and a number of the buildings have been restored, one of which contains a small museum with displays on Amerindian artifacts and Tobago's colonial history. It's open 9 am to 4:30 pm Monday to Saturday (TT$5). A shop in the old powder magazine sells locally made handicrafts.

The lighthouse at the fort features a lead crystal Fresnel lens that can throw a beam 50km out to sea using just a 3000-watt light.

The fort is well worth a visit, too, for its parklike grounds, where benches under enormous trees allow you to both gape at the harbor and observe exotic birds darting about. At the edge of the grounds, a small Tobago-shaped hedge is cleverly labeled to indicate the locations of the island's other forts.

The **Botanical Gardens**, in Lower Scarborough with an entrance east of the bus terminal, occupy the 18 acres of a former sugar estate. A variety of flowering trees and shrubs is on display, including flamboy-ants, African tulips and *poui,* and there's an orchid house.

If you have a profound interest in local lore and lots of time, octogenarian George Leacock will proudly show you around his family home and history-laden personal effects in his **Scarborough Heritage Parlour**, on Cuyler St.

Places to Stay

Those arriving on the evening ferry will find a couple of cheap guest houses conveniently located about a 10-minute walk inland from the waterfront. *Jacob's Guest House* (☎ 639-2271), on Northside Rd, has six rather musty rooms, three with shared baths, three with private baths, all with floor fans and all at US$8.50 per person. A small shared kitchen is available.

A cozier option, just around the bend from Jacob's, is *Federal Villa* (☎ 639-3926, maredwards@hotmail.com), offering four pleasant wood-floor rooms, two with toilet and sink, at US$15/25 single/double. Owner Miriam Edwards is director of the Tobago Bed & Breakfast Association.

Still, the best budget option is *Hope Cottage* (☎ 639-2179, hopecottage100@ hotmail.com), near Fort King George on Calder Hall Rd, an arduous half-hour walk uphill from the dock (a taxi ride is TT$10). Located in the former home of a 19th-century governor (James Henry Keens, acting governor from 1856–1857, is buried in the backyard), it's a great place to hang out awhile or meet other travelers. There are a variety of good-size rooms, with private baths for US$20 single or double, and others with shared bath for US$17. A group of up to seven can negotiate a reasonable price on an adjacent three-room cottage with shared bath. Guests can order breakfast (TT$20 to TT$40) or whip up their own meals in the big group kitchen. Palm-frond sheds strung with hammocks edge the peaceful, shady grounds.

Sandy's Bed & Breakfast (☎ 639-2737), at the back of the Blue Crab Restaurant on Robinson St, consists of two rooms in the home of Ken and Alison Sardinha. Set off a bit for privacy, the air-conditioned rooms are pleasantly simple, with pine floors, ceiling fans and private baths. Singles/doubles cost US$25/50, breakfast included.

A few more reasonably priced options hug the coast along the Windward Rd on its way out to Bacolet Bay. The best is the aptly named *Sea View Guesthouse* (☎ 639-6243, *verleen@tstt.net.tt*), whose compact units make the most of their cliffside perch. Equipped with private bath, kitchen and cable TV, double rooms are US$40, with discounts available for longer stays. A steep path leads down to a swimming hole.

Places to Eat

Opposite the post office, *Ma King's Dinette* is a locally popular snack shed, with an emphasis on natural foods, offering stick-to-your-ribs breakfasts like bake & smoked herring, with fresh-squeezed orange juice and the best coffee around. It's open 9 am to 8 pm daily except Sunday. Another first-rate Caribbean kitchen is *Phyllis'*, an island of calm in the hectic market area, where a large lunch platter of steamed fish and all the 'provisions' goes for TT$21.

East Indian–influenced fare can be found at *Gun Bridge Restaurant*, down Bacolet St, serving *phulourie* and *saheena* (fried breads made from split-pea flour), buss-up-shut and so on. *Pizza Boys*, opposite the dock, stays open late. A medium pizza starts at TT$35; add TT$8 for toppings. They also do burgers, bagels and breakfasts.

In Upper Scarborough, on Cuyler just north of Main St, *La Petite Patisserie* serves fresh pastries and cappuccino on a delightful palm-garden patio. It opens at 7 am daily except Sunday. *Blue Crab Restaurant* (☎ 639-2737), on the corner of Main and Robinson Sts, is a family-run restaurant with a pleasant alfresco setting and good West Indian food. At lunch, 11 am to 3 pm weekdays, there's a choice of main dishes such as Creole chicken or flying fish served with rice and vegetables for TT$45. Dinner is pricier and by reservation.

At *Rouselle's* (☎ 639-4738), down on Old Windward Rd south of town, dinner is served from 7 pm on a sea-view terrace with African print tablecloths. Their nouveau Creole dinners are a fair value, from TT$95 for a four-course meal.

WINDWARD ROAD

Just east of Scarborough, the landscape turns mountainous and rural. The Windward Rd, which connects Scarborough with Speyside, winds in and out from the coast, passing scattered villages, jungly valleys and the occasional brown-sand beach. The farther east you go, the more ruggedly beautiful the scenery becomes. Although much of the road is quite narrow and curving, it's easily drivable in a standard vehicle. If you were to drive straight through from Scarborough to Speyside, it would take about 1½ hours.

Eight kilometers east of Scarborough is Granby Point, a jut of land separating Barbados Bay from Pinfold Bay. In 1764 the British established a temporary capital on the east side of Barbados Bay and built **Fort Granby** at the tip of the point. It's only a couple of minutes' walk from the parking lot to the old fort site, but little remains other than a solitary soldier's gravestone. Day-trippers will find a couple of hilltop picnic tables, a nice view of nearby Smith's Island, a brown-sand beach and changing rooms.

The triple-tiered **Argyle Falls** are on the Argyle River, just west of Roxborough; the entrance to the site, open 7 am to 5:30 pm daily, is 600m north of the Windward Rd. In addition to the TT$20 admission fee, you must pay an authorized guide TT$15 to lead you on the 20-minute hike up to the falls. Along the way you can cool off in a series of natural pools. **Roxborough** itself is a sizable village with a post office, a gas station and a few stores where you can pick up snacks.

Five kilometers east of Roxborough is the lovely **King's Bay**, at the foot of a lush green hillside, site of an old plantation. The bay is fringed by a dark-sand beach; facilities include changing rooms, toilets and a small bar. After King's Bay the road winds and twists its way over the mountains to Speyside.

Places to Stay & Eat

The *Richmond Great House* (☎ /fax 660-4467), Belle Garden, is a small inn which was once a plantation house at the edge of the rain forest. The inn has antique-furnished singles/doubles with private baths for US$84/102 in summer, US$96/114 in winter, breakfast included. There are tennis courts, a pool and hilltop views. The owner, Hollis Lynch, is a former African-history professor at New York's Columbia University. Nonguests can come up for a tour of the house and the African and Asian crafts within (TT$15), as well as for a full-course lunch (TT$75) or dinner (TT$150). Reservations are required. The inn is 150m north of the main road, 750m after entering the village of Richmond; the turnoff is marked.

King's Bay Riverside Guest House (☎ 660-4383, jitt_celestine@excite.com), just up the road from King's Bay, is a sturdy old wood home. With a pair of simple, tidy bedrooms sharing a bathroom, as well a large kitchen, the house rents for US$40 for up to four people.

For no-frills accommodations on the beach, *Sea Gardens Guest House* (☎ 660-4220), at Delaford, offers cheap, decent rooms for US$10 per person for up to four, including kitchenette and private bath, but you'll need a mosquito net. Get fresh fish when the catch comes in. The front porch faces magnificent King's Bay.

SPEYSIDE

Speyside is a small fishing village fronting Tyrrel's Bay and is the jumping-off point for excursions to the uninhabited island of Little Tobago, a bird sanctuary 2km offshore. There are facilities at the south end of the beach, where the Windward Rd makes its first contact with the bay.

Tyrrel's Bay has protected inshore waters, where high visibility, abundant coral and extraordinarily diverse marine life make for choice diving and snorkeling. However, for the best snorkeling consider taking one of the glass-bottom boats (see Little Tobago, later) or arranging with a fisherman to take you out to the reefs; either way, the cost is around TT$70. Be particularly careful if swimming around the offshore islands, as there is a ferocious current between Goat Island and Little Tobago.

Information

Speyside has a tourist information office (☎ 660-6012) at the point where the Windward Rd meets the waterfront, open 9 am to 5 pm daily. Nimroy K Yeates (☎ 660-6157) offers Internet access; he's up on Top Hill St but has plans to move closer to the waterfront.

Places to Stay

Perched atop a hill as you approach Speyside are a pair of recommendable small inns. *Country Haven Guest House* (☎ 660-5901), run by helpful Merla & Earl Braithwaite, charges US$25 for small, well-kept rooms with fan, private bath and mosquito nets, US$5 more with kitchen facilities. Several decks are good for sunning and stargazing. Reached via a series of steps from Top Hill Rd is *Top Ranking Hill View Guest House* (☎ 660-4904), with plusher accommodations in several stone-and-wood buildings. Handsomely furnished rooms with one/two double beds cost US$35/40. Wraparound balconies provide excellent views of both ocean and rain forest. Top Ranking also runs a minimart at the bottom of the steps.

Turn right at the coast for *Seacrest Guesthouse* (☎ 660-6642), which is across from a waterfront hut that's a hangout for the downstairs bar patrons. Rates are US$30 for four pleasant rooms with bath and attractive murals of tropical birds. Donna Yawching, a journalist from Canada, operates the six-room *Speyside Inn* (☎ 660-4852, speysideinn@trinidad.net, 189–193 Windward Rd), opposite Jemma's restaurant. The four upstairs rooms are particularly pleasant, with high ceilings, red-tile floors and private baths; French doors lead to small balconies with nice breezes and a good sea view across Goat Island to Little Tobago. Singles/doubles with breakfast cost from US$60/75 in summer and US$80/95 in winter.

Geared toward divers, *Manta Lodge* (☎ 660-5268, in the USA ☎ 800-544-7631, dive-manta@trinidad.net, PO Box 433, Scarborough) is a modern plantation-style house fronting the beach. Its 22 airy rooms feature wicker furniture, private baths and ocean-view balconies. Singles/doubles with ceiling fan cost US$75/95 in summer and US$95/115 in winter; add US$20 for air-con. A ground-level bar-restaurant opens onto the pool. There's also a dive shop on-site.

Places to Eat

A trio of seaside restaurants along the coast road serves three meals a day. **Bird Watchers Restaurant & Bar** has a candlelit deck and very good food with a gourmet touch. A fish-steak dinner loaded with tasty veggie sides costs TT$70. Next is **Jemma's** (☎ 660-4066), a simple seaside restaurant with an interesting tree-house setting and good local food. Fish, chicken and shrimp dishes are priced from around TT$60. **Redman's**, another raised-deck affair, is a bit cheaper and less refined than the others, charging TT$50 for a barracuda platter.

LITTLE TOBAGO

Little Tobago, also known as Bird of Paradise Island, was a cotton plantation during the late 1800s. In 1909, Englishman Sir William Ingram imported 50 greater birds of paradise from the Aru Islands, off New Guinea, and established a sanctuary on Little Tobago to protect the endangered bird. In 1963, Hurricane Flora devastated the habitat and decimated the flock; the bird of paradise hasn't been sighted on Little Tobago since 1981.

Now managed by the government, Little Tobago remains an important seabird sanctuary nonetheless. Red-billed tropic birds, magnificent frigate birds, brown boobies, Audubon's shearwaters, laughing gulls, brown noddies and sooty terns are some of the species found here. For those who want to hike, the hilly, arid island, which averages just 1.5km in width, has a couple of short trails. Be sure to bring something to drink.

Glass-bottom boats run by Frank's (☎ 660-5438) and Top Ranking (☎ 660-4904) cruise daily to Little Tobago Island, a 15-minute crossing. Both depart from the jetty at Blue Waters Inn, about a kilometer north of Speyside, at around 10 am and again at 2 pm. Both charge TT$100 for a tour that in-

cludes bird watching at Little Tobago and snorkeling at Angel Reef. Mask and fins are provided. You can also take the boats solely for snorkeling, in which case the charge is TT$70. Another operator, Fear Not (☎ 660-4654), leaves from the beach at Jemma's, in Speyside (ask for Mr Roberts).

Serious birders can get a more in-depth tour by making advance arrangements with one of three naturalist guides who are very knowledgeable about island ecology: Renson Jack (☎ 660-5175), Pat Turpin (☎ 660-4327) and David Rooks (☎ 639-4276).

CHARLOTTEVILLE

It's four scenic, winding kilometers over the mountains from Speyside to Charlotteville. At the summit, before the road snakes down to Charlotteville, a marked gravel road leads north to Flagstaff Hill.

Charlotteville is a delightful little fishing village. Sleepy, secluded and with an earthy simplicity, it has the appearance of some long-forgotten outpost. In the winter, the hillsides behind the village are bright with the orange blossoms of immortelle trees, which were introduced from Martinique in colonial times to shade cocoa plantations.

Man of War Bay, the large, horseshoe-shaped harbor that fronts the village, is edged by a palm-studded brown-sand beach

that's good for swimming. When it's calm, there's excellent snorkeling at Pirate's Bay, a 15-minute walk across the point at the north side of Charlotteville, and good snorkeling around Booby Island, just south of the village.

If you're up for more exploring, take a walk to the site of the old Fort Campbelton, on the west side of the bay, which offers a good coastal view; or take a more substantial hike up Flagstaff Hill, a popular spot for sunset picnics, and a good place to watch the birds circling St Giles' Islands.

Places to Stay

There are a number of small, unofficial guest houses in Charlotteville, most found by word of mouth, and there's seldom a problem getting a room. A reasonably priced alternative is *Belle Aire Inn (☎ /fax 660-5984)*, an attractive wooden home reached by climbing a steep street at the north end of the village. Affable owner Gifford Neptune offers straightforward singles/doubles with sunken bathroom and minibar at US$20/35. Guests are welcome to use the kitchen or relax in the gazebo.

There are also some self-catering flats, including *Cholson Chalets (☎ 639-8553)*, a clean, friendly place right on the beach. It has nine units of varying size, some in the main house and others in a newer annex. The cost for one or two people ranges from US$25 for a studio to US$60 for a large two-bedroom apartment with kitchen and private bath. Add US$11 for each additional person.

Man-O-War Bay Cottages (☎ 660-4327, fax 660-4328) is on the beach about a five-minute walk south of the village. The grounds are like a little botanical garden, with lots of tropical trees, ferns and flowering plants. Nine simple cottages with private baths, kitchens and screened louvered windows open to the breeze and the sound of the surf. Rates range from US$65 for two people in a one-bedroom cottage to US$135 for up to eight people in a four-bedroom cottage. The cottages are owned by Pat Turpin, who leads nature tours around Tobago.

Places to Eat

There are a couple of minimarts in town and another with basic supplies at Man-O-War Bay Cottages. Along the waterfront are several small huts selling rotis, baked goods and even meals. Recommended *Jane's Quality Kitchen* offers seating in the shade of an almond tree.

A handful of family-run restaurants in Charlotteville offers good food at honest prices. *Eastman's*, an open-air eatery by the waterfront, does fish dinners served with rice, steamed veggies and salad (TT$40). At the north end is *Gail's*, whose forte is rice, greens and fish. It's open from 8:30 am for breakfast, from 7 pm for dinner. *Charlotteville Beach Bar & Restaurant*, at the beach facility, dishes up all the local favorites, as well as cocktails, daily. Wednesday there's a beach barbecue with live music.

TOBAGO FOREST RESERVE

The Roxborough Parlatuvier Rd, which crosses the island from Roxborough to Bloody Bay, is a bit narrow and curving, but it's paved and rates as one of the best roads on the island. It's a nice 30-minute jungle drive, completely undeveloped, with pretty valley and mountain views.

The road passes through the Tobago Forest Reserve, which was established in 1765, making it the oldest forest reserve in the Caribbean. A number of trailheads lead off the main road into the rain forest. There's excellent bird watching in this area, and it's not uncommon to hear squawking parrots and see hummingbirds, cocricos, woodpeckers, hawks and blue-crowned motmots.

Three-quarters of the way across is the head of the **Gilpin Trail**, which branches northeast to Bloody Bay, a 5km walk through the rain forest. Authorized guides at the trailhead charge TT$100 per person to take you down to a waterfall, or TT$180 for a two-hour hike through the forest to the Main Ridge lookout hut, a bit farther down the road. Rubber boots are provided for handling the muddy trails. The lookout hut affords scenic views of Bloody Bay and the offshore Sisters Rocks. On a clear day you can see Grenada, 120km away. Local women sell homemade cakes and natural fruit drinks here, and other guides offer their services.

From the lookout hut, it's just a five-minute drive down to Bloody Bay, which takes its name from a fierce battle that occurred here between the Dutch, French and British in the 1600s.

CASTARA & AROUND

Once you reach Bloody Bay, it's an hour's drive south to Plymouth, a stretch of coast punctuated along the way by pretty beaches and villages, unhurried places with kids playing cricket in the road. Just west of Bloody Bay is **Parlatuvier**, a tiny fishing village on a strikingly beautiful circular bay. Continuing down the coast is **Englishman's Bay**, a superb, undeveloped beach shaded by stands of bamboos and coconut palms. Its gentle waters are recommended for snorkeling – a coral reef lies 20m offshore. A snack bar and latrine serve the handful of visitors who make it up here.

Castara, farther south, is a pleasant fishing village that has become popular with independent-minded travelers, attracted by its wide, sandy beach, relaxed atmosphere and picturesque setting. A few bars face the harbor, where a fleet of modest fishing boats are moored. Snorkeling is good in the calm inlet to the right of the main beach.

Places to Stay & Eat

In Castara, you'll find three charming guest houses on the way down to the beach. Near the top, *Blue Mango Cottages* (☎ 639-2060, *bluemang@tstt.net.tt*) has seven rustic but comfortable cabins of varying size scattered around the heights, starting at US$55 in summer, US$60 in winter for two people. All include private bath with cold water, kitchens and mosquito nets. The most spectacular cabin, at US$150, takes maximum advantage of its cliff setting.

Down the road, *Sea Level Guesthouse* (☎ 660-7311) lacks an ocean view but sits peacefully amid woods. Seven spacious doubles/quads (US$35/45) have balconies or patios; all come with kitchenettes, bathrooms, fans and handcrafted beds.

At beach level is *The Naturalist Beach Resort* (☎ 639-5901, *natural@trinidad.net*), a cheerful, family-run place. Its cozy apartments include kitchens, TVs, fans and reading lamps but no views. Rates range from US$28 to US$44; some have air-con. Airport transfer can be arranged for US$25.

The obvious gathering place is the beachfront *CasCreole Bar*, with simple wood tables under a palm-frond roof, and an adjoining sunset deck on the sand. It serves a hearty kingfish platter with tasty potato salad and other provisions. It's lively most nights, but there's live music Friday night.

Although English is the primary language of the Eastern Caribbean, several languages and dialects are spoken throughout the islands. French is the primary language in Guadeloupe, Martinique, St Barts and the French side of St Martin, and it is to that language that this chapter is dedicated. For some common colloquial expressions heard in the English-speaking portion of the Eastern Caribbean, see the boxed text in the Facts about the Eastern Caribbean chapter.

Travelers should note that there's a vast difference between the Creole-influenced French spoken by longtime islanders and the smooth dialects of visitors from mainland France. However, simple, standard French as presented in this chapter is understood by all.

FRENCH IN THE EASTERN CARIBBEAN

The French used in the Eastern Caribbean reflects hundreds of years of intermingling with English as well as West African languages. In addition to borrowing words freely from these other tongues, it's flatter in intonation, with less of the traditional French lilting cadence. Also, speakers of Creole pay less attention to gender; anything or anyone can be *il*.

In general, you'll find that francophones in the Caribbean are a lot more forgiving of your efforts to speak French, no matter how egregious those efforts may be, than anyone you'd meet in Paris.

PHRASEBOOKS & DICTIONARIES

A good resource to facilitate your hopping around the French-speaking islands is Lonely Planet's *French phrasebook*. Lightweight and compact, it won't burden anyone's backpack or suitcase, and it'll provide you with all the basics you need to get around and make new friends. In addition, there are a number of good French-English/English-French pocket dictionaries, including ones produced by Langenscheidt's, Larousse and Oxford Hachette.

PRONUNCIATION

French is certainly not the easiest language to pronounce, and its convolutions can prove frustrating for the impatient. Listen carefully to how others around you speak and don't be afraid to try saying new words. With a little practice, you'll get the hang of it.

Vowels

The pronunciation of vowels is not entirely consistent, but here are some basic rules to get you started:

a	as the *u* in 'cup'
e	sometimes as the *e* in 'open,' sometimes as the *e* in 'merry'; often barely pronounced
é	as the *ay* in 'may'
è	as the *e* in 'merry,' but slightly longer
i	as the *ee* in 'sweet'
o	as the *o* in the British pronunciation of 'lot,' but sometimes as the *o* in 'spoke'
u	with the lips rounded, as for the *oo* in 'moose,' but sounding the *ee* in 'meet'
ai	as the *e* in 'bet'
au	as the *o* in 'or'
eau	as the *ow* in 'show'
eu	as if you don't know what to say: 'uhhh…'
oi	as the *wa* in 'water'
ou	as the *oo* in 'book'

When a syllable ends in a single *m, n* or *nt,* the consonant is not pronounced; instead, the preceding vowel is nasalized. Don't worry about the circumflex that sometimes appears atop some vowels (as in *île* – island); it merely marks the spot where an *s* appeared historically.

Consonants

Most consonants in French are pronounced more or less the same as their English equivalents. Following are a few that may cause confusion:

c	before *e* and *i,* as the *s* in 'sit'; before *a, o* and *u,* as the *k* in 'kitten'
ç	as the *s* in 'sit'
g	before *e* and *i,* as the French *j;* before *a, o* and *u,* as the *g* in 'get'
h	silent
j	as the *s* in 'leisure'
q	as the *k* in 'kitten'
r	as…like…sort of…we'll let you figure this out on your own
s	usually as the *s* in 'sit'; between two vowels as the *z* in 'zebra'

Liaisons In French, consonants at the ends of words are silent. The exception is when the following word begins with a vowel or a silent *h,* in which case the consonant is fully pronounced and referred to as a *liaison.*

Stress

Stress in French is much weaker than in English, usually amounting to merely a lengthening of a word's final syllable. Try to give every syllable almost equal stress.

BASIC GRAMMAR

As a Romance language, French exhibits the same word order and basic grammatical structure of other tongues derived from Latin, such as Spanish and Italian. The basic word order is subject-verb-object, as in *Je mange le gâteau* (I eat the cake). When the object is turned into a pronoun, however, the word order becomes subject-object-verb: *Je le mange* (I eat it).

Nouns & Pronouns

All French nouns are either masculine or feminine. The gender of a noun is indicated by the preceding article (see Articles, Adjectives & Adverbs, later) and sometimes by the spelling, and some nouns have both masculine and feminine forms. If a noun ends in *-acle, -age, -eau, -ème, -isme, -ment, -ier* or *ien,* it's likely to be masculine; if it ends in *-aison, -nce, -nse, -ée, -ion, -ude, -ure, -elle* or *-ille,* chances are that it's feminine.

However, there are tons of exceptions to these rules.

The general rules for making a noun plural is to add *s.* As the *s* is not pronounced, often the only way you can tell whether the noun is singular or plural is by the preceding article. Words ending in *-al, -eau* and *-eu* are pluralized by adding *x* to the end.

Following are the subject pronouns in French:

je	I
tu	you (singular informal)
il	he/it
elle	she/it
nous	we
vous	you (plural informal, singular or plural formal)
ils	they (at least one male)
elles	they (all female)

Although many folks in the Eastern Caribbean will switch to the *tu* form quickly, it's safer for visitors just to stick with *vous* to mean 'you,' to avoid offending anyone.

Like adjectives, possessive pronouns must agree in number and gender with the object they refer to, *not* the possessor. Following are the possessive pronouns, given in the order masculine singular/feminine singular/plural:

mon/ma/mes	my
ton/ta/tes	your (singular informal)
son/sa/ses	his/her/its
notre/notre/nos	our
votre/votre/vos	your (plural informal, singular or plural formal)
leur/leur/leurs	their

Examples: *mon chien* (my dog), *ta jupe* (your skirt), *nos livres* (our books)

Articles, Adjectives & Adverbs

Articles and adverbs in French always reflect the gender (masculine or feminine) and number (single or plural) of nouns they modify. To form the feminine of most adjectives, just add an *e* to the end: *Un grand arbre* means 'a big tree,' while *une grande maison* means 'a big house.' In general, to make an adjective plural, you add an *s* or *x: Le chat laid* means 'the ugly cat,' while *les chats laids* means 'the ugly cats.' As a rule, adjectives are placed after the nouns they modify.

Like English, French has both definite and indefinite articles; however, it features three of each type. As with other adjectives, which article you use depends on the noun being modified. The indefinite article, 'the' in English, is represented in the masculine singular, feminine singular and plural, respectively, by *le, la* and *les*. Thus you have *le garçon* (the boy), *la fille* (the girl) and *les enfants* (the children).

The corresponding indefinite articles are *un, une* and *des*. Examples include *un pays* (a country), *une région* (a region) and *des arbres* (some trees). Note that both *le* and *la* change to *l'* before a noun beginning with a vowel or silent *h*, as in *l'oreille* (the ear) or *l'hôtel* (the hotel).

In general, adverbs are formed by adding *-ment* to the feminine form of the adjective. Hence *heureux* (happy) becomes *heureusement* (happily). However, if the adjective ends in a vowel, simply add *-ment* to the masculine form; eg, *vrai* (true) becomes *vraiment* (truly). As usual, there are heaps of exceptions to these rules.

Verbs

As with most Romance languages, verbs are the hardest part of French. All verbs must be conjugated according to the subject, and furthermore their endings change according to tense and mood. For more information on conjugating French verbs, see Lonely Planet's *French phrasebook*.

There are three types of verbs in French – those ending in *-ir* (such as *finir* – to finish), those ending in *-er* (such as *parler* – to speak) and those ending in *-re* (such as *vendre* – to sell). The stems of the verbs are discovered by dropping these endings (thus, the stems of the examples given would be *fin-, parl-* and *vend-*).

To form the negatives of sentences, place *ne...pas* around the verb. Thus, *Elle joue* ('She plays') becomes *Elle ne joue pas* ('She doesn't play').

Key verbs in French include the following:

aimer	to like/love
aller	to go
avoir	to have
dire	to say/tell
donner	to give
être	to be
faire	to do/make
pouvoir	to be able
savoir	to know
venir	to come
voir	to see
vouloir	to want/wish

VOCABULARY

Sure, getting your tongue around those combinations is difficult, but keep a careful ear out and feel free to experiment with different combinations of words. French-speaking inhabitants of the Eastern Caribbean will usually appreciate and reward sincere efforts at communication.

Basics

Yes.	*Oui.*
No.	*Non.*
Maybe.	*Peut-être.*
Please.	*S'il vous plaît.*
Thank you.	*Merci.*
You're welcome.	*Je vous en prie.*
Excuse me.	*Excusez-moi.*
Sorry/Forgive me.	*Pardon.*

Emergencies

Help!	*Au secours!*
Go away!	*Allez-vous-en!*
Careful/Look out!	*Attention!*
Fire!	*Au feu!*
Thief!	*Au voleur!*
It's an emergency!	*C'est urgent!*
Call...	*Appelez...*
a doctor	*un médecin*
an ambulance	*une ambulance*
the police	*la police*
I'm ill.	*Je suis malade.*
I've been robbed.	*J'ai été volé/volée.*
I've been raped.	*J'ai été violé/violée.*
I'm lost.	*Je me suis perdu/ perdue/*

Questions

Who?	*Qui?*	When?	*Quand?*
What?	*Quoi?*	How?	*Comment?*
Which?	*Quel/Quelle?*	Why?	*Pourquoi?*
Where?	*Où?*		

Greetings

Hello/Good morning.	*Bonjour.*	Goodbye.	*Au revoir.*
Good evening.	*Bonsoir.*	See you soon.	*À bientôt.*
Good night.	*Bonne nuit.*	See you tomorrow.	*À demain.*

Small Talk

How are you?	*Comment allez-vous?* (polite)
	Comment ça va? (informal)
Fine, thanks.	*Bien, merci.*
What's your name?	*Comment vous appelez-vous?*
My name is…	*Je m'appele…*
Pleased to meet you.	*Enchanté(e).*
How old are you?	*Quel âge avez-vous?*
I'm…years old.	*J'ai…ans.*
Where are you from?	*De quel pays êtes-vous?*

I come…	*Je viens…*		
from Australia	*d'Australie*	from New Zealand	*de Nouvelle Zélande*
from Canada	*du Canada*	from Scotland	*d'Écosse*
from England	*d'Angleterre*	from Wales	*du Pays de Galle*
from Germany	*d'Allemagne*	from the USA	*des États-Unis*
from Ireland	*d'Irlande*		

Language Difficulties

I understand.	Speak slowly, please.
Je comprends.	*Lentement, s'il vous plaît.*
I don't understand.	Could you repeat that?
Je ne comprends pas.	*Vous pouvez le répéter?*
Do you speak English?	Could you please write it down?
Parlez-vous anglais?	*Est-ce que vous pouvez l'ecrire?*

Getting Around

I want to go to…	*Je voudrais aller à…*
I'd like to book a seat for…	*Je voudrais réserver une place pour…*
What time does the…leave/arrive?	*À quelle heure part/arrive…?*
airplane	*l'avion*
flight	*le vol*
bus	*le bus*
boat	*le bateau*
I'd like a…ticket.	*Je voudrais un billet…*
one-way	*aller-simple*
roundtrip	*aller-retour*

The flight is…
  late
  on time
  early
I'd like to rent…
  a car
  a bicycle
  a mountain bike

  a motorcycle
  a motorscooter
I'm looking for…
  a bank
  an exchange office
  the hospital
  the market
  the police
  the post office
  a public phone
  a public toilet
  the tourist office
Where is…?
  the beach
  the church
  the main square
Go straight ahead.
Turn left.
Turn right.

Le vol est…
  en retard
  à l'heure
  en avance
Je voudrais louer…
  une voiture
  un vélo
  un VTT (pronounced 'vay-teh-teh,'
    for *vélo tout terrain*)
  une moto
  un scooter
Je cherche…
  une banque
  un bureau de change
  l'hôpital
  le marché
  la police
  la poste
  une cabine téléphonique
  les toilettes
  l'office de tourisme
Où est…?
  la plage
  l'église
  la place central
Continuez tout droit.
Tournez à gauche.
Tournez à droite.

Accommodations

I'm looking for…
  the youth hostel
  the campground
  a hotel
Do you have any rooms available?
I'd like to book…
  a bed
  a single room
  a double room
  a room with a shower and toilet
  an air-conditioned room
  a room with a fan
How much is it…?
  per night
  per person
Can I see the room?
Is breakfast included?
I'm going to stay…
  one day
  two days
  one week

Je cherche…
  l'auberge de jeunesse
  le camping
  un hôtel
Est-ce que vous avez des chambres libres?
Je voudrais réserver…
  un lit
  une chambre pour une personne
  une chambre double
  une chambre avec douche et WC
  une chambre climatisée
  une chambre avec ventilateur
Quel est le prix…?
  par nuit
  par personne
Est-ce que je peux voir la chambre?
Est-ce que le petit déjeuner est compris?
Je resterai…
  un jour
  deux jours
  une semaine

Shopping

How much is it?	*C'est combien?*
It's too expensive for me.	*C'est trop cher pour moi.*
It's too big/small.	*C'est trop grand/petit.*
Can I look at it?	*Est-ce que je peux le/la voir?*
I'm just looking.	*Je ne fais que regarder.*
Can I pay with a credit card?	*Est-ce que je peux payer avec une carte de crédit?*
Can I pay with traveler's checks?	*Est-ce que je peux payer avec des chèques de voyage?*

more	*plus*	cheap	*bon marché*
less	*moins*	less expensive	*moins cher*

Times & Dates

What time is it?	*Quelle heure est-il?*
It's (two) o'clock.	*Il est (deux) heures.*
When?	*Quand?*
today	*aujourd'hui*
tonight	*ce soir*
tomorrow	*demain*
yesterday	*hier*
Monday	*lundi*
Tuesday	*mardi*
Wednesday	*mercredi*
Thursday	*jeudi*
Friday	*vendredi*
Saturday	*samedi*

Sunday	*dimanche*
January	*janvier*
February	*février*
March	*mars*
April	*avril*
May	*mai*
June	*juin*
July	*juillet*
August	*août*
September	*septembre*
October	*octobre*
November	*novembre*
December	*décembre*

Cardinal Numbers

1	*un*	12	*douze*
2	*deux*	13	*treize*
3	*trois*	14	*quatorze*
4	*quatre*	15	*quinze*
5	*cinq*	16	*seize*
6	*six*	17	*dix-sept*
7	*sept*	18	*dix-huit*
8	*huit*	19	*dix-neuf*
9	*neuf*	20	*vingt*
10	*dix*	100	*cent*
11	*onze*	1000	*mille*

Ordinal Numbers

first	*premier/première*	eighth	*huitième*
second	*second/deuxième*	ninth	*neuvième*
third	*troisième*	tenth	*dixième*
fourth	*quatrième*	twentieth	*vingtième*
fifth	*cinquième*	hundredth	*centième*
sixth	*sixième*	thousandth	*millième*
seventh	*septième*		

Glossary

For descriptions of what's on the table or at the bar, see the Food & Drink Glossary, later.

agouti – a short-haired rabbitlike rodent that resembles a guinea pig with short ears and long legs, and which has a fondness for sugarcane

biguine – also spelled 'beguine,' an Afro-French dance music with a bolero rhythm that originated in Martinique in the 1930s

calypso – a popular Caribbean music that's essential to Carnival
Carnival – the major Caribbean festival that originated as a pre-Lenten festivity but is now observed at various times throughout the year on different islands
chattel house – a type of simple wooden dwelling placed upon cement or stone blocks so it can be easily moved; often erected on rented land
Creole – in terms of people, a person of mixed black and European ancestry; in terms of language, local pidgin that's predominantly a combination of French and African; in terms of food, a cuisine characterized by spicy, full-flavored sauces and a heavy use of green peppers and onions

frangipani – a low tree with fragrant pink or white flowers; also known as 'plumeria'

gommier – a large native gum tree found in Caribbean rain forests

jump-up – a nighttime street party that usually involves dancing and plenty of rum

lime or **limin'** – to hang out, relax
lolo – a sidewalk barbecue stand where meat is grilled and sold

mairie – the name for town hall in the French West Indies
manchineel – a common tree on Eastern Caribbean beaches whose poisonous sap can cause a skin rash
manicou – opossum, a small marsupial
mas camps – short for 'masquerade camps,' workshops where artists create Carnival costumes

obeah – one of a group of Afro-Caribbean belief systems combining shamanism and witchcraft

panyards – the places where steel-pan bands practice their music in the months leading up to Carnival
pareu – a type of wrap skirt that's commonly sold on beaches in the Caribbean
pitt – in the French West Indies, an arena where cockfights take place

steel pan – also called 'steel drum,' an instrument made from oil drums or the music it produces

zouk – popular French West Indies music that draws from the biguine, cadence and other French Caribbean folk forms

Food & Drink Glossary

accras – Creole-style fritters made with cod or vegetables

bake – a sandwich made with fried bread and usually filled with shark or fish

blaff – a seafood preparation poached in a spicy broth

breadfruit – a large, round, green fruit; a Caribbean staple comparable to potatoes in its carbohydrate content and prepared in much the same way

bul jol – roasted breadfruit and saltfish made with tomatoes and onions

callaloo soup – the quintessential Eastern Caribbean soup, resembling a creamy spinach soup, made with dasheen leaves and often with coconut milk

christophene – also known as 'chayote,' a common Caribbean vegetable shaped like a large pear; eaten raw in salads, used in soup or cooked like a squash

colombo – a spicy, East Indian–influenced dish that resembles curry

conch – also called *lambi,* the chewy meat of a large gastropod.; common throughout the Caribbean and often prepared in a spicy Creole sauce

conkies – a mixture of cornmeal, coconut, pumpkin, sweet potatoes, raisins and spice, steamed in a plantain leaf

cou-cou – a creamy cornmeal and okra mash, commonly served with saltfish

crabes farcis – spicy stuffed land crabs

Creole – when referring to food, a cuisine characterized by spicy, full-flavored sauces and heavy use of green peppers and onions

cutter – a salt-bread roll used to make meat and fish sandwiches, or the sandwich itself

dasheen – a type of taro; the leaves, known as 'callaloo,' are cooked like spinach leaves and the starchy root is boiled like a potato

dolphin – a common type of white-meat fish, also called 'mahimahi'; no relation to the marine mammal of the same name

feroce d'avocat – mashed avocado mixed with salted fish, manioc flour, spices and hot pepper oil, served cold

flying fish – a gray-meat fish named for its ability to skim above the water, particularly plentiful in Barbados

goat water – a spicy goat-meat stew often flavored with cloves and rum

guava – a round, yellow fruit about 2½ inches in diameter, with a moist, pink, seedy flesh, all of which is edible; often a little tart but tend to sweeten as they ripen; a good source of vitamin C and niacin

Ital – a natural style of vegetarian cooking practiced by Rastafarians

jambalaya – a Creole dish usually consisting of rice cooked with ham, chicken or shellfish, spices, tomatoes, onions and peppers

johnnycake – a corn-flour griddle cake

jug-jug – a mixture of Guinea cornmeal, green peas and salted meat

lambi – Caribbean name for conch; see 'conch'

mahimahi – see 'dolphin'

mango – a fruit abundant in the Caribbean. The juicy oblong fruits are about 3 inches in diameter and 5 inches long; they ripen to a red-gold color. Mango is sweet and a good source of vitamins A and C; mainly a summer fruit

mauby – a bittersweet drink made from the bark of the mauby tree, sweetened with sugar and spices

mountain chicken – the legs of the *crapaud,* a type of frog

oil down – a mix of breadfruit, pork, callaloo and coconut milk

papaya – usually called 'paw paw' in the Eastern Caribbean, a sweet orange fruit, harvested year-round, which is a good source of calcium and vitamins A and C

passionfruit – a vine with beautiful flowers that bears small, round fruits whose skin is generally purple or yellow; the pulp is juicy, seedy and slightly tart

paw paw – common Caribbean name for papaya; see 'papaya'

pepperpot – a spicy stew made with various meats, accompanied by peppers and cassareep (extract of cassava)

pigeon peas – the brown, pealike seeds of a tropical shrub that are cooked like peas and served mixed with rice

pineapple – a tropical fruit. There are many kinds in the Caribbean; the small ones known as 'black pineapples' are among the sweetest

plantain – a starchy fruit of the banana family, usually fried or grilled like a vegetable

Planters punch – also known as Planteur, a punch mixing rum and fruit juice

roti – a curry filling, commonly potatoes and chicken, rolled inside a tortilla-like flat bread

soursop – a large green fruit with a pulpy texture that's slightly acidic, often made into a vitamin-rich drink

sorrel juice – a lightly tart, bright-red drink rich in vitamin C made from the flowers of the sorrel plant

souse – a dish made out of a pickled pig's head and belly, spices and a few vegetables, commonly served with a pig-blood sausage called 'pudding'

starfruit – also called carambola, this translucent yellow-green fruit has five ribs like the points of a star and its crisp, juicy pulp can be eaten without being peeled

tamarind – the pod of a large tropical tree of the legume family; with a juicy, acidic pulp that is used in beverages

Thanks

A heartfelt thank-you goes out to the following readers, whose suggestions helped in developing this third edition of *Eastern Caribbean*. We're so sorry if we misspelled your name.

David Abbott, Steve Addison, Johan Anderson, Larry Axelrod, Marion Bevington, Roger Bohl, Lia Tonnini Cardinali, Tracey Cooper, Janet De Heerdt, Barbara Elias, Tony Goff, Stephane Guegan, Kate Hare, Glenn Havelock, Amanda Hepburn, Patrick Holian, Peter Holmes, So Yin Hui, Ian Hunter, Jeremy Hutt, Paul Erik Jensen, Katherine Kelly, Christoph Kessel, Owen Kimber, Rachael Lazenby, King Leong, Mervyn Lewis, David Louvel, Louis Mann, Peter Marshall, Clara Marullo, Joe McPhee, Axel Niemeyer, Christine Norwood, Margery Nzerem, Tom Ohlert, W & Bruno Ozman, Louis Palmer, Sara Partington, Cory & Evelyn Perez, Henning Pytterud, Derek Rosen, Matt Saunders, Dirk & Kirsten Schumacher, A Tom, John Tooth, Maria R Vacarisas, Nicholas Yu, Ondrej Zapletal, Andrew Zimet

Thanks

I hereby thank you once more the following acknowledgements, most helped to developing this third edition of the work, and we're so sorry if we misspelled your name.

LONELY PLANET

You already know that Lonely Planet produces more than this one guidebook, but you might not be aware of the other products we have on this region. Here is a selection of titles which you may want to check out as well:

Miami
ISBN 0 86442 653 4
US$15.95 • UK£9.99

Virgin Islands
ISBN 0 86442 735 2
US$15.99 • UK£9.99

World Food Caribbean
ISBN 1 86450 348 3
US$13.99 • UK£8.99

Diving & Snorkeling Dominica
ISBN 0 86442 764 6
US$15.95 • UK£9.99

Diving & Snorkeling Trinidad & Tobago
ISBN 0 86442 777 8
US$15.95 • UK£9.99

French phrasebook
ISBN 1 86442 450 7
US$5.95 • UK£3.99

Available wherever books are sold.

Lonely Planet Guides by Region

Lonely Planet is known worldwide for publishing practical, reliable and no-nonsense travel information in our guides and on our Web site. The Lonely Planet list covers just about every accessible part of the world. Currently there are 16 series: Travel guides, Shoestring guides, Condensed guides, Phrasebooks, Read This First, Healthy Travel, Walking guides, Cycling guides, Watching Wildlife guides, Pisces Diving & Snorkeling guides, City Maps, Road Atlases, Out to Eat, World Food, Journeys travel literature and Pictorials.

AFRICA Africa on a shoestring • Botswana • Cairo • Cairo City Map • Cape Town • Cape Town City Map • East Africa • Egypt • Egyptian Arabic phrasebook • Ethiopia, Eritrea & Djibouti • Ethiopian Amharic phrasebook • The Gambia & Senegal • Healthy Travel Africa • Kenya • Malawi • Morocco • Moroccan Arabic phrasebook • Mozambique • Namibia • Read This First: Africa • South Africa, Lesotho & Swaziland • Southern Africa • Southern Africa Road Atlas • Swahili phrasebook • Tanzania, Zanzibar & Pemba • Trekking in East Africa • Tunisia • Watching Wildlife East Africa • Watching Wildlife Southern Africa • West Africa • World Food Morocco • Zambia • Zimbabwe, Botswana & Namibia
Travel Literature: Mali Blues: Traveling to an African Beat • The Rainbird: A Central African Journey • Songs to an African Sunset: A Zimbabwean Story

AUSTRALIA & THE PACIFIC Aboriginal Australia & the Torres Strait Islands • Auckland • Australia • Australian phrasebook • Australia Road Atlas • Cycling Australia • Cycling New Zealand • Fiji • Fijian phrasebook • Healthy Travel Australia, NZ and the Pacific • Islands of Australia's Great Barrier Reef • Melbourne • Melbourne City Map • Micronesia • New Caledonia • New South Wales • New Zealand • Northern Territory • Outback Australia • Out to Eat – Melbourne • Out to Eat – Sydney • Papua New Guinea • Pidgin phrasebook • Queensland • Rarotonga & the Cook Islands • Samoa • Solomon Islands • South Australia • South Pacific • South Pacific phrasebook • Sydney • Sydney City Map • Sydney Condensed • Tahiti & French Polynesia • Tasmania • Tonga • Tramping in New Zealand • Vanuatu • Victoria • Walking in Australia • Watching Wildlife Australia • Western Australia
Travel Literature: Islands in the Clouds: Travel in the Highlands of New Guinea • Kiwi Tracks: A New Zealand Journey • Sean & David's Long Drive

CENTRAL AMERICA & THE CARIBBEAN Bahamas, Turks & Caicos • Baja California • Belize, Guatemala & Yucatán • Bermuda • Central America on a shoestring • Costa Rica • Costa Rica Spanish phrasebook • Cuba • Cycling Cuba • Dominican Republic & Haiti • Eastern Caribbean • Guatemala • Havana • Healthy Travel Central & South America • Jamaica • Mexico • Mexico City • Panama • Puerto Rico • Read This First: Central & South America • Virgin Islands • World Food Caribbean • World Food Mexico • Yucatán
Travel Literature: Green Dreams: Travels in Central America

EUROPE Amsterdam • Amsterdam City Map • Amsterdam Condensed • Andalucía • Athens • Austria • Baltic States phrasebook • Barcelona • Barcelona City Map • Belgium & Luxembourg • Berlin • Berlin City Map • Britain • British phrasebook • Brussels, Bruges & Antwerp • Brussels City Map • Budapest • Budapest City Map • Canary Islands • Catalunya & the Costa Brava • Central Europe • Central Europe phrasebook • Copenhagen • Corfu & the Ionians • Corsica • Crete • Crete Condensed • Croatia • Cycling Britain • Cycling France • Cyprus • Czech & Slovak Republics • Czech phrasebook • Denmark • Dublin • Dublin City Map • Dublin Condensed • Eastern Europe • Eastern Europe phrasebook • Edinburgh • Edinburgh City Map • England • Estonia, Latvia & Lithuania • Europe on a shoestring • Europe phrasebook • Finland • Florence • Florence City Map • France • Frankfurt City Map • Frankfurt Condensed • French phrasebook • Georgia, Armenia & Azerbaijan • Germany • German phrasebook • Greece • Greek Islands • Greek phrasebook • Hungary • Iceland, Greenland & the Faroe Islands • Ireland • Italian phrasebook • Italy • Kraków • Lisbon • The Loire • London • London City Map • London Condensed • Madrid • Madrid City Map • Malta • Mediterranean Europe • Milan, Turin & Genoa • Moscow • Munich • Netherlands • Normandy • Norway • Out to Eat – London • Out to Eat – Paris • Paris • Paris City Map • Paris Condensed • Poland • Polish phrasebook • Portugal • Portuguese phrasebook • Prague • Prague City Map • Provence & the Côte d'Azur • Read This First: Europe • Rhodes & the Dodecanese • Romania & Moldova • Rome • Rome City Map • Rome Condensed • Russia, Ukraine & Belarus • Russian phrasebook • Scandinavian & Baltic Europe • Scandinavian phrasebook • Scotland • Sicily • Slovenia • South-West France • Spain • Spanish phrasebook • Stockholm • St Petersburg • St Petersburg City Map • Sweden • Switzerland • Tuscany • Ukrainian phrasebook • Venice • Vienna • Wales • Walking in Britain • Walking in France • Walking in Ireland • Walking in Italy • Walking in Scotland • Walking in Spain • Walking in Switzerland • Western Europe • World Food France • World Food Greece • World Food Ireland • World Food Italy • World Food Spain **Travel Literature:** After Yugoslavia • Love and War in the Apennines • The Olive Grove: Travels in Greece • On the Shores of the Mediterranean • Round Ireland in Low Gear • A Small Place in Italy

Mail Order

Lonely Planet products are distributed worldwide. They are also available by mail order from Lonely Planet, so if you have difficulty finding a title please write to us. North and South American residents should write to 150 Linden St, Oakland, CA 94607, USA; European and African residents should write to 10a Spring Place, London NW5 3BH, UK; and residents of other countries to Locked Bag 1, Footscray, Victoria 3011, Australia.

INDIAN SUBCONTINENT & THE INDIAN OCEAN Bangladesh • Bengali phrasebook • Bhutan • Delhi • Goa • Healthy Travel Asia & India • Hindi & Urdu phrasebook • India • India & Bangladesh City Map • Indian Himalaya • Karakoram Highway • Kathmandu City Map • Kerala • Madagascar • Maldives • Mauritius, Réunion & Seychelles • Mumbai (Bombay) • Nepal • Nepali phrasebook • North India • Pakistan • Rajasthan • Read This First: Asia & India • South India • Sri Lanka • Sri Lanka phrasebook • Tibet • Tibetan phrasebook • Trekking in the Indian Himalaya • Trekking in the Karakoram & Hindukush • Trekking in the Nepal Himalaya • World Food India **Travel Literature:** The Age of Kali: Indian Travels and Encounters • Hello Goodnight: A Life of Goa • In Rajasthan • Maverick in Madagascar • A Season in Heaven: True Tales from the Road to Kathmandu • Shopping for Buddhas • A Short Walk in the Hindu Kush • Slowly Down the Ganges

MIDDLE EAST & CENTRAL ASIA Bahrain, Kuwait & Qatar • Central Asia • Central Asia phrasebook • Dubai • Farsi (Persian) phrasebook • Hebrew phrasebook • Iran • Israel & the Palestinian Territories • Istanbul • Istanbul City Map • Istanbul to Cairo • Istanbul to Kathmandu • Jerusalem • Jerusalem City Map • Jordan • Lebanon • Middle East • Oman & the United Arab Emirates • Syria • Turkey • Turkish phrasebook • World Food Turkey • Yemen **Travel Literature**: Black on Black: Iran Revisited • Breaking Ranks: Turbulent Travels in the Promised Land • The Gates of Damascus • Kingdom of the Film Stars: Journey into Jordan

NORTH AMERICA Alaska • Boston • Boston City Map • Boston Condensed • British Columbia • California & Nevada • California Condensed • Canada • Chicago • Chicago City Map • Chicago Condensed • Florida • Georgia & the Carolinas • Great Lakes • Hawaii • Hiking in Alaska • Hiking in the USA • Honolulu & Oahu City Map • Las Vegas • Los Angeles • Los Angeles City Map • Louisiana & the Deep South • Miami • Miami City Map • Montréal • New England • New Orleans • New Orleans City Map • New York City • New York City City Map • New York City Condensed • New York, New Jersey & Pennsylvania • Oahu • Out to Eat – San Francisco • Pacific Northwest • Rocky Mountains • San Diego & Tijuana • San Francisco • San Francisco City Map • Seattle • Seattle City Map • Southwest • Texas • Toronto • USA • USA phrasebook • Vancouver • Vancouver City Map • Virginia & the Capital Region • Washington, DC • Washington, DC City Map • World Food New Orleans **Travel Literature**: Caught Inside: A Surfer's Year on the California Coast • Drive Thru America

NORTH-EAST ASIA Beijing • Beijing City Map • Cantonese phrasebook • China • Hiking in Japan • Hong Kong & Macau • Hong Kong City Map • Hong Kong Condensed • Japan • Japanese phrasebook • Korea • Korean phrasebook • Kyoto • Mandarin phrasebook • Mongolia • Mongolian phrasebook • Seoul • Shanghai • South-West China • Taiwan • Tokyo • World Food Hong Kong • World Food Japan
Travel Literature: In Xanadu: A Quest • Lost Japan

SOUTH AMERICA Argentina, Uruguay & Paraguay • Bolivia • Brazil • Brazilian phrasebook • Buenos Aires • Buenos Aires City Map • Chile & Easter Island • Colombia • Ecuador & the Galápagos Islands • Healthy Travel Central & South America • Latin American Spanish phrasebook • Peru • Quechua phrasebook • Read This First: Central & South America • Rio de Janeiro • Rio de Janeiro City Map • Santiago de Chile • South America on a shoestring • Trekking in the Patagonian Andes • Venezuela **Travel Literature:** Full Circle: A South American Journey

SOUTH-EAST ASIA Bali & Lombok • Bangkok • Bangkok City Map • Burmese phrasebook • Cambodia • Cycling Vietnam, Laos & Cambodia • East Timor phrasebook • Hanoi • Healthy Travel Asia & India • Hill Tribes phrasebook • Ho Chi Minh City (Saigon) • Indonesia • Indonesian phrasebook • Indonesia's Eastern Islands • Java • Lao phrasebook • Laos • Malay phrasebook • Malaysia, Singapore & Brunei • Myanmar (Burma) • Philippines • Pilipino (Tagalog) phrasebook • Read This First: Asia & India • Singapore • Singapore City Map • South-East Asia on a shoestring • South-East Asia phrasebook • Thailand • Thailand's Islands & Beaches • Thailand, Vietnam, Laos & Cambodia Road Atlas • Thai phrasebook • Vietnam • Vietnamese phrasebook • World Food Indonesia • World Food Thailand • World Food Vietnam

ALSO AVAILABLE: Antarctica • The Arctic • The Blue Man: Tales of Travel, Love and Coffee • Brief Encounters: Stories of Love, Sex & Travel • Buddhist Stupas in Asia: The Shape of Perfection • Chasing Rickshaws • The Last Grain Race • Lonely Planet…On the Edge: Adventurous Escapades from Around the World • Lonely Planet Unpacked • Lonely Planet Unpacked Again • Not the Only Planet: Science Fiction Travel Stories • Ports of Call: A Journey by Sea • Sacred India • Travel Photography: A Guide to Taking Better Pictures • Travel with Children • Tuvalu: Portrait of an Island Nation

Index

Abbreviations

Text

A

Bold indicates maps.

Bold indicates maps.